Maudsley and Burn's

Trusts and Trustees
Cases and Materials

Fifth Edition

E H Burn BCL, MA
Barrister and Honorary Bencher of Lincoln's Inn;
Professor of Law in the City University;
Emeritus Student of Christ Church, Oxford

R.T.C. LIBRARY, LETTERKENNY

346
.059

Butterworths
London, Dublin, Edinburgh
1996

United Kingdom	Butterworths a Division of Reed Elsevier (UK) Ltd, Halsbury House, 35 Chancery Lane, LONDON WC2A 1EL and 4 Hill Street, EDINBURGH EH2 3JZ
Australia	Butterworths, SYDNEY, MELBOURNE, BRISBANE, ADELAIDE, PERTH, CANBERRA and HOBART
Canada	Butterworths Canada Ltd, TORONTO and VANCOUVER
Ireland	Butterworth (Ireland) Ltd, DUBLIN
Malaysia	Malayan Law Journal Sdn Bhd, KUALA LUMPUR
New Zealand	Butterworths of New Zealand Ltd, WELLINGTON and AUCKLAND
Singapore	Reed Elsevier (Singapore) Pte Ltd, SINGAPORE
South Africa	Butterworths Publishers (Pty) Ltd, DURBAN
USA	Michie, Charlottesville, VIRGINIA

All rights reserved. No part of this publication may be reproduced in any material form (including photocopying or storing it in any medium by electronic means and whether or not transiently or incidentally to some other use of this publication) without the written permission of the copyright owner except in accordance with the provisions of the Copyright, Designs and Patents Act 1988 or under the terms of a licence issued by the Copyright Licensing Agency Ltd, 90 Tottenham Court Road, London, England W1P 9HE. Applications for the copyright owner's written permission to reproduce any part of this publication should be addressed to the publisher.

Warning: The doing of an unauthorised act in relation to a copyright work may result in both a civil claim for damages and criminal prosecution.

Any Crown copyright material is reproduced with the permission of the Controller of Her Majesty's Stationery Office.

© Reed Elsevier (UK) Ltd 1996

A CIP Catalogue record for this book is available from the British Library.

ISBN 0 406 01445 0

Typeset by York House Typographic, London
Printed by Mackays of Chatham plc, Chatham, Kent

Preface

Many important changes have taken place in the law of trusts and trustees since the last edition appeared in 1990. There has been widespread judicial activity, especially in the House of Lords. Some twenty-five new cases have been added to the text.

The House of Lords has restricted the acquisition of a beneficial interest by implied common intention; refused to adopt a flexible approach where a transfer of property is made for an illegal purpose; decided that dishonesty is not a necessary ingredient of accessory liability; adopted a liberal construction of section 1 of the Recreational Charities Act 1958; provided a further example of the rule that a fiduciary cannot make a profit where his duty and interest conflict; redrawn the measure of liability where a trustee has paid trust money to the wrong person; reiterated the rules of tracing both at common law and in equity; and accepted the defence of change of position (in the context of gaming chips at a casino).

The Privy Council has rejected the distinction hitherto drawn between bribes and other secret profits received by a fiduciary.

The Court of Appeal has twice examined assistance in a breach of trust and knowing receipt (once in the context of international money laundering on a large scale); has thrice decided that, where both parties acquire joint beneficial interests in family property, shares in it are not necessarily proportionate to their direct contributions; and reviewed the duties of trustees in the selection of investments, and of charitable trustees in relation to the ethical considerations in their so doing.

Important decisions at first instance include those on certainty of subject-matter; the intervention of the court where pension trustees are in breach of their duties; their entitlement to the surplus funds on the winding-up of a pension scheme; the meaning of under-value in the Insolvency Act 1986; mutual wills so that benefit to the survivor is not necessary; tax avoidance; the appointment of foreign trustees of an English trust; limitation and laches; and the application of the Rule in Clayton's case.

Pre-eminent among the new statutes are the Charities Act 1993, which is based on the 1989 White Paper on Charities: A Framework for the Future. It consolidates most but not all of the Charities Act 1992. There are also extracts from the Annual Reports, Decisions (now published separately and more fully since 1993) and the valuable Leaflets of the Charity Commissioners for England and Wales. The Taxation of Chargeable Gains Act 1994 consolidates the law on capital gains tax; and the Pensions Act 1995 makes important new provisions on the functions of pension trustees. The concepts and principles which underlie the Act could with advantage be replicated for trustees in general. Peripherally the Transfer of Land and Appointments of Trustees Bill 1995 is also mentioned in so far as it is relevant to the holding of charitable land and the appointment of trustees.

Impetus has been given to reform of the law of trusts and trustees by the setting up in 1995 of the Trusts Law Committee under Sir John Vinelott. It has already started work on collective delegation, investment and the balance of apportionment between capital and income. The Committee is working in conjunction with the Law Commission and hopes to publish consultation papers in 1996 with the hope of legislation not before late 1997.

This new material, and much else besides, has been incorporated into the fifth edition. I am most grateful to all those friends and critics who have given me their help and advice.

I would particularly like to thank Jill Martin, Barrister of Lincoln's Inn and Professor of Law, King's College, London; Marilyn Kennedy-McGregor, Barrister of Lincoln's Inn and Gray's Inn; John Cartwright, Student of Christ Church, Oxford; Geraint Thomas, Barrister of Lincoln's Inn and Senior Lecturer in Law at Queen Mary and Westfield College, London, who revised Part III on Trusts and Taxes; and Jonathan Herring, Lecturer in Law at Christ Church, Oxford, who revised the index. For their many valuable suggestions of form and substance I am most grateful.

Finally, I wish to thank the publishers for undertaking the compilation of the Tables of Cases, Statutes and Statutory Instruments, and for their ready and expert help at all times.

This edition purports to state the law as it was on 1 January 1996, but more recent developments have been incorporated where space permitted.

E.H.B.
St Hugh's College
Oxford
20 May 1996

Contents

Acknowledgements

The permissions which were granted to reproduce extracts from the following publications are gratefully acknowledged:

Law Reports and Statutes:

All England Law Reports
Incorporated Council of Law Reporting for England and Wales
Commonwealth Law Reports
New Zealand Law Reports
Property and Compensation Reports
Rating and Valuation Reporter
Simon's Tax Cases
Taxation Reports
Times Law Reports

Textbooks and Treatises

Chapman: *Inheritance Tax* (8th edn 1989, TLPC)
Cretney and Masson: *Principles of Family Law* (5th edn 1990, Sweet & Maxwell)
Goff & Jones: *Law of Restitution* (4th edn 1993, Sweet & Maxwell)
Hackney: *Understanding Equity and Trusts* (1987, Fontana Press)
Hallett's *Conveyancing Precedents* (1965, Sweet & Maxwell)
Hanbury and Martin: *Modern Equity* (14th edn 1993, Sweet & Maxwell)
Harris: *Variation of Trusts* (1975, Sweet & Maxwell)
Jarman on Wills (8th edn 1951, Sweet & Maxwell)
Josling: *Apportionments for Executors and Trustees* (4th edn, 1976, Oyez)
Key & Elphinstone: *Conveyancing Precedents* (15th edn 1953: Sweet & Maxwell)
Lewin on Trusts (16th edn 1964, Sweet & Maxwell)
Maitland: *Lectures on Equity* (1969, Cambridge University Press)
McKendrick: ed. *Commercial Aspects of Trusts and Obligations* (1992, Oxford University Press)
Miller: *Machinery of Succession* (2nd edn 1996, Dartmouth Publishing Co Ltd)
Morris and Leach: *Rule Against Perpetuities* (2nd edn 1962, Sweet & Maxwell)
Parker & Mellows: *Modern Law of Trusts* (6th edn 1994, Sweet & Maxwell)
Perspectives of Law: *Essays for Austin Wakeman Scott* (1964, Little, Brown & Co)
Pettit: *Equity and the Law of Trusts* (7th edn 1993, Butterworths)
Scott: *Trusts* (3rd edn 1967, Little, Brown and Co)
Snell: *Principles of Equity* (29th edn 1990, Sweet & Maxwell)
Thomas: *Taxation and Trusts* (1981, Sweet & Maxwell)

xiv   *Acknowledgements*

Tudor on Charities (8th edn 1995, Sweet & Maxwell)
Underhill and Hayton: *Law Relating to Trusts and Trustees* (15th edn 1995, Butterworths)

Restatement of Law:

Restitution (1936, American Law Institute)
Trusts (2nd edn 1959, American Law Institute)

Journals:

Conveyancer and Property Lawyer
Law Quarterly Review
Modern Law Review
New Law Journal
Solicitors' Journal

Reports:

Charity Commissioners for England and Wales: Annual Reports; Decisions and Leaflets
Goode Report on Pensions Law Reform
Goodman Committee Report on Charity Law and Voluntary Organisations
House of Commons Expenditure Committee: Tenth Report
Law Commission Reports
Law Reform Committee: 24th Report on Powers and Duties of Trustees
Public Trust Office: Annual Reports

Cross-References

The following books have been cross-referenced, and abbreviated as follows:

H & M	Hanbury and Martin, *Modern Equity* (14th edn 1993)
K & S	Keeton and Sheridan: *Law of Trusts* (12th edn 1993)
P & M	Parker and Mellows: *Modern Law of Trusts* (6th edn 1994)
Pettit	*Equity and the Law of Trusts* (7th edn 1993)
Riddall	*Law of Trusts* (4th edn 1992)
S & K	Sheridan and Keeton: *Modern Law of Charities* (4th edn 1992)
Snell	*Principles of Equity* (29th edn 1990)
Underhill	Underhill and Hayton: *Law Ruling to Trusts and Trustees* (15th edn 1995)

Table of Statutes

References in this Table to *Statutes* are to Halsbury's Statutes of England (Fourth Edition) showing the volume and page at which the annotated text of the Act will be found. Page references in **bold** indicate where the section is set out in part or in full.

TABLE OF OTHER STATUTES

Table of Statutory Instruments

Table of Cases

Page numbers printed in bold type indicate where a case is set out.

A

B

E

F

G

H

l *Table of Cases*

J

K

M

N

O

P

S

W

Part One. Trusts

1. The Nature of a Trust

R.T.C. LIBRARY, LETTERKENNY

I. Introduction

For many reasons, it may be better to avoid having the whole of the capital of a family owned by one person. In some circumstances it will be preferable to provide for successive enjoyment; in others for the enjoyment to be shared; or to provide protection against creditors; or to provide for interests to arise in the future. These situations, and others, can be effected by means of a trust. When property is held in a way other than in the absolute ownership of one person, it is usually held under some form of trust. In the case of land, for example, it has been achieved by the use of a strict settlement or a trust for sale.

The beneficiaries under a trust are the owners in equity of the beneficial interests given to them. The trustees are the legal owners. Trustees' ownership is wholly burdensome. The trusteeship obligates them to manage the property in the exclusive interest of the beneficiaries, and imposes onerous duties and liabilities upon them. All the advantage is with the beneficiaries.

Trusts may be created inter vivos or by will. On death, the owner of property has to do something with it. He cannot take it with him. He may give it to a devisee or legatee absolutely, or may create successive interests; for example, a man may leave property to his wife for her life and after her death to the children. Within limits, a testator can do as he wishes with his property and will usually decide after consulting his family, his friends and his solicitor; in any event he should make a will as soon as he has property, even an insurance policy, to leave.

Inter vivos trusts are usually created for tax-saving purposes. There is no point in keeping more property than one reasonably can need. A taxpayer may

3

wish to transfer property to a member of his family who might then pay a lower rate of tax on the income. Transfer of property between spouses is always tax-free, but the majority of gifts by will other than to spouses is subject to inheritance tax even on quite modest estates.[1] Where tax is payable on an inter vivos gift, however, it never exceeds half the rate payable on death. If a property owner wishes to protect both the property and his family or friends, a trust is the most effective way of doing so. Some trusts enjoy especially favourable tax treatment, but the situation changes frequently and good legal and financial advice is essential.

The sphere of trusts is not confined to the family. Their commercial use has become increasingly widespread, for example, in private occupational pension schemes, where the pension fund is held by trustees for the benefit of employees; and in unit trusts, where trustees hold investments in a large range of stock exchange securities in trust for members of the public who have purchased units or shares in the trust fund.[2] The pension trust is said to "lie at the interface between trust and employment law."[3]

Trusts may be intentionally created by the settlor or the testator. Their existence depends upon a manifestation of his intention to create a trust. A trust can also arise however without any such intention being manifested. In some circumstances, discussed in Chapter 7, a trust results in favour of the settlor, and this is usually, but not necessarily, consistent with the settlor's intention. Constructive trusts are imposed by equity independently of any indication of intention. They arise in a wide variety of circumstances, as explained in Chapter 8, the most significant of which is the prevention of fraud.

Trusts may be created for public (i.e. charitable) purposes as well as for private individuals. Charitable trusts form a large and important area of the law of trusts. They are specially favoured by the law, being in effect free from liability to tax, and being permitted to continue in perpetuity. Many English charities are ancient; and, until the Charities Act 1960 provided that charities (with exceptions) should be registered, no-one had any idea how many existed. The total number of charities registered with the Charity Commissioners at the end of 1994 was 178,609.[4]

Law reform is under way in the law of trusts. The Law Commission intends to examine the rule against perpetuities and excessive accumulations; the formal requirements for the creation of trusts and interests in land and for the disposition of equitable interests; and also the personal and proprietary

---

1 Inheritance tax is payable on estates of over £200,000: p. 572, post.
2 Financial Services Act 1986, chap. 8 (unit trusts authorised by the Securities and Investments Board under the Act). See Linklaters and Paines: *Unit Trusts, The Law and Practice.*
3 (1994) Trust Law International 35 (Sir John VINELOTT). In 1991 10.7 million employees were members of occupational pension schemes: Goode Report: Pension Law Reform 1993 (Cm. 2343): and in 1995 about £500 billion was invested in pensions: *Simon's Weekly Tax Intelligence* (1995), p.7. In spite of criticism of the trust basis of the schemes, the Report recommended its retention, p. 7 post, and the Pensions Act 1995 has kept it.
    See generally Ellison, *Private Pension Schemes; Pensions Law and Practice;* Moffatt and Chesterman, *Trusts Law* (1994), chap. 13; (1992) 6 Trust Law International 119 (Lord BROWNE-WILKINSON); (1993) 56 MLR 471 (G. Moffatt); [1994] 14 LS 345 (R. Nobles); (1996) 59 MLR 241 (R. Nobles).
4 See the Report of the Charity Commissioners for England and Wales 1994, p. 6.

remedies available for the recovery of property transferred in breach of trust.[5] In 1995 a Trusts Law Committee was set up under Sir John Vinelott to examine various aspects of trust law in co-operation with the Law Commission. It has begun with the collective delegation of trustees' powers and duties, to be followed by their duties and powers of investment, and the balance and apportionment between capital and income.[6]

Maitland: *Selected Essays*, p. 129
"If we were asked what is the greatest and most distinctive achievement performed by Englishmen in the field of jurisprudence I cannot think that we should have any better answer to give than this, namely, the development from century to century of the trust idea."[7]

II. Definition[8]

Maitland: *Lectures on Equity* (2nd edn) p. 44

"Where judges and text-writers fear to tread professors of law have to rush in. I should define a trust in some such way as the following — When a person has rights which he is bound to exercise upon behalf of another or for the accomplishment of some particular purpose he is said to have those rights in trust for that other or for that purpose and he is called a trustee.

It is a wide vague definition, but the best that I can make. I shall comment on it by distinguishing cases of trust from some other cases."

Underhill and Hayton: *Law Relating to Trusts and Trustees* (15th edn) p. 3
"A trust is an equitable obligation, binding a person (who is called a trustee) to deal with property over which he has control (which is called the trust property), for the benefit of persons (who are called the beneficiaries or cestuis que trust), of whom he may himself be one, and any one of whom may enforce the obligation. Any act or neglect on the part of a trustee which is not *authorised or excused by the terms of the trust instrument, or by law, is called a breach of trust.*

5 Law Commission Sixth Programme of Law Reform 1995 (Law Com No. 234); Law Commission Thirtieth Annual Report 1995 (Law Com No. 239), paras 5.15–5.21.
6 (1995) 8 Trust Law International 42. See pp. 667, 717, 745. Consultation papers are to be issued.
7 Of Maitland SCRUTTON LJ said in *Holmes – Laski Letters* (1913), vol 2, at p. 1142: "Most historians throw light on dark places; he threw a searchlight into the unknown". And MACNAGHTEN J said, at p. 1412: "Maitland was not a lawyer at all, but a poet". Both are cited by Sir Robert MEGARRY in *Inns Ancient and Modern* (Selden Society 1977), p. 3.
8 H & M, pp. 46–47; K & S, pp. 3–5; P & M, pp. 7–11; Pettit, pp. 23–24; Snell pp. 89–90; Underhill, pp. 3–5.

authorised or excused by the terms of the trust instrument, or by law, is called a breach of trust.''[9]

Scott: *Trusts* (4th edn) §2.3

"Even if it were possible to frame an exact definition of a legal concept, the definition would not be of great practical value. A definition cannot properly be used as though it were a major premise so that rules governing conduct can be deduced from it. Our law, at least, has not grown in that way. When the rules have been arrived at from other sources, it may be possible to attempt to frame a definition. But the definition results from the rules, and not the rules from the definition.

All that one can properly attempt to do is to give such a description of a legal concept that others will know in a general way what one is talking about. It is possible to state the principal distinguishing characteristics of the concept so that others will have a general idea of what the writer means. With this in mind, those responsible for the Restatement of Trusts proposed the following definition or description of an express trust. It is 'a fiduciary relationship with respect to property, subjecting the person by whom the title to property is held to equitable duties to deal with the property for the benefit of another person, which arises as a result of a manifestation of an intention to create it.' In this definition or description the following characteristics are to be noticed: (1) a trust is a relationship; (2) it is a relationship of a fiduciary character; (3) it is a relationship with respect to property, not one involving merely personal duties; (4) it involves the existence of equitable duties imposed upon the holder of the title to the property to deal with it for the benefit of another; and (5) it arises as a result of a manifestation of an intention to create the relationship. The combination of these things characterizes the notion of the trust as that notion has been developed in the Anglo-American law.''

Hanbury & Martin: *Modern Equity* (14th edn) p. 46

"Many attempts have been made to define a trust;[10] but none of them has been wholly successful. It is not thought that a dissection and criticism of earlier definitions are very rewarding; rather it is better to describe than to define a trust, and then to distinguish it from related but distinguishable concepts.''[11]

---

9 Approved by Cohen J in *Re Marshall's Will Trusts* [1945] Ch 217 at 219, [1945] 1 All ER 550 at 551; and by Romer LJ in *Green v Russell* [1959] 2 QB 226 at 241, [1959] 2 All ER 525 at 531. *Cestuis que trust* is the correct plural: (1910) 26 LQR 196 (C. Sweet).

10 Co Litt 272b; Underhill and Hayton: *Law Relating to Trusts and Trustees* (15th edn), p. 3; used by Cohen J in *Re Marshall's Will Trusts* [1945] Ch 217 at 219, [1945] 1 All ER 550 at 551, and by Romer LJ in *Green v Russell* [1959] 2 QB 226 at 241, [1959] 2 All ER 525 at 531; *Lewin on Trusts* (16th edn), p. 1; Snell, p. 89; *Halsbury's Laws of England* (4th edn), vol. 48, para. 32; *Restatement of Trusts* (U.S.A.), §2; Scott, *Law of Trusts*, §2; (1955) 71 LQR 39 (A. W. Scott).

11 See also Recognition of Trusts Act 1987, s. 1, Sched., p. 50, post.

III. Trusts and Occupational Pensions

Goode Report: Pensions Law Reform 1993 (Cm 2342), paras. 4.1.5, 4.1.8–4.1.14 and 4.2.3.

"THE FRAMEWORK AND POLICIES OF OCCUPATIONAL PENSIONS LAW

4.1.5 The root of the problem is that there is no comprehensive legal framework governing occupational pensions. Numerous reports have drawn attention to this over the years, including the Wilson Report,[12] the Gower Review,[13] the 1982 report of the OPB,[14] and, more recently a report of the House of Commons Select Committee on Social Security.[15] Pensions law is an amalgam of equity and trust law, contract and labour law, heavily overlaid with complex legislation governing the occupational pensions aspects of social security, taxation and financial services. One can search in vain for a code in which the essential rights and obligations flowing from the establishment of pension schemes are clearly laid out. Much of the law is to be found only in reports of court decisions about the interpretation of scheme documents and the duties of trustees and employers at common law. Legislation is at present spread over more than thirty statutes and well over a hundred statutory instruments. The planned consolidation Act for occupational pensions will certainly improve matters. But it will do nothing to resolve the much greater problem of complex subordinate legislation, not to mention the profusion of memoranda, guidance notes, practice notes and other documents produced by the various government departments and professional bodies. Nor will it deal with the fundamental weakness of the present system, the lack of a properly structured framework of rights and obligations.

THE ROLE AND ADEQUACY OF TRUST LAW

4.1.8 The weaknesses to which we have drawn attention have led to suggestions that trust law should be abandoned for occupational pensions, and that pension rights should be defined by contract and/or legislation. Following on the Maxwell affair some commentators have derided trust law as medieval and archaic and as having failed its purpose in the pensions field.

4.1.9 Trust law is indeed of considerable antiquity, but it has shown a remarkable ability to adapt itself to modern commercial requirements. Indeed, the full range and power of the modern trust are to be found not in the family trust, with which the pension trust is customarily contrasted, but with the trust used in commerce and finance. The trust is not only a means of segregating assets for the protection of the beneficiaries, thus insulating them from the consequences of the settlor's bankruptcy; its equally important function is to provide a mechanism for the collective representation and

---

12 *Report of the Committee to Review the Functioning of Financial Institutions* (Chairman: The Rt Hon Harold Wilson), Cmnd 7937, 1980.
13 *Review of Investor Protection* (Professor LCB Gower), Cmnd 9125, 1982.
14 Cmnd 8649.
15 Second Report, *The Operation of Pension Funds* (Chairman: Mr Frank Field). HC 61-11, 1991–92.

protection of members of a group of people linked by a common interest. Good examples of such a mechanism are the unit trust and the bond or debenture trust deed. Under these, the individual interests of substantial numbers of holders of units, bonds and debenture stock are channelled into the trust and held and protected by the trustees for the benefit of all holders, so providing the collective mechanism without which efficient administration would be impossible. This mechanism is valuable even where there is no trust property in the normal sense, merely an aggregation of personal rights.[16]

4.1.10 In our consultation document we directly posed the question whether the use of the trust should be abandoned. Whilst there were those who continued to advocate the movement from trust to contract, there was a widespread recognition of the need to retain trust law as the basis of pension scheme regulation. It was felt that trust law embodies highly developed concepts of fiduciary responsibility which it is important to preserve (see para. 4.2.2).

4.1.11 Though contract law has a role to play in the field of pensions it is not in itself adequate to take over the functions performed by the trust. Individual employment contracts on their own provide neither the security resulting from a segregation of assets nor the collective mechanism that is so important for the administration of pension schemes. If the employer operating an unfunded scheme becomes insolvent the scheme members are merely unsecured creditors. Moreover, under English law contract rights cannot in general be enforced by or against those who are strangers to the contract, so that a contract between employer and employee would not of itself be enough to give the employee a right to take proceedings against third parties (for example, fund managers) for failing in their duty.

4.1.12 The dissatisfaction expressed with the trust as an institution, understandable though this may be in the light of pension fund losses resulting from improper conduct, is largely misplaced, for it demands more of trust law than this can reasonably be expected to perform. The deliberate misappropriation of trust funds is both a civil wrong and a criminal offence. Trust law cannot in itself prevent breaches of trust any more than criminal law can prevent the commission of crimes.

4.1.13 The rules of trust law are not, for the most part, statutory. They have been developed by the courts over a long period and are based on the assumption that every settlor is free to write his or her own trust rules. That approach is inevitable, for to override the provisions of a lawful trust would be tantamount to legislation, and it is the function of Parliament, not the courts, to legislate. Trust law plays little part in the normal employer-employee contract, though the flexibility of trust law has enabled the courts to distinguish the pension trust from the family trust and to emphasise the significance of the contract of employment for the exercise of powers conferred by the scheme documents. Trust law itself cannot prescribe rules to

---

16 For example, where unsecured bonds are issued, so that there are no assets securing repayment, there will still be a trust deed providing for the appointment of trustees for the bondholders and conferring powers on the trustees to take action for the protection of all bondholders if, for example, the issuer of the bond defaults in payment.

secure the solvency of schemes, or the monitoring of pension funds. That too is the function of Parliament.

4.1.14 We therefore endorse the view expressed in the great weight of evidence submitted to us that trust law in itself is broadly satisfactory and should continue to provide the foundation for interests, rights and duties arising in relation to pension schemes. But some of the principles of trust law require modification in their application to pensions. In particular, some curbs need to be placed on the permissible content of scheme rules, especially in relation to certain of the powers that can be reserved to the employer and the trustees and the scope of exemptions given to trustees from liability for breach of duty. Trust law also requires statutory reinforcement in other ways. This is reflected in the growing volume of legislation enacted in recent times to strengthen the rights of scheme members and the duties of employers, trustees, auditors and actuaries. The question is whether this legislation is adequate or has always moved in the right direction. We have already made clear our view that what is now needed is comprehensive legislation to regulate occupational pension schemes.

The family trust and the pension trust
4.2.3 In the early days of occupational pension schemes there was a much closer affinity than at present between the pension trust and the traditional family trust. Pensions were in many cases seen as acts of bounty, tangible expressions of gratitude by the employer for long and faithful service. In those cases, as with the family trust it was for the settlor, the employer, to decide upon what terms his or her bounty were to be provided. The employees were not seen as having any interest in the constitution or administration of the scheme; it was not for them to look a gift horse in the mouth. That approach has long since changed. Pension benefits are now seen as an integral part of a total remuneration package earned by service and contributed to by the employee. Hence for certain purposes the perception of pensions as deferred pay, a concept endorsed both by courts in this country[17] and, for the purposes of Article 119 of the Treaty of Rome, by the European Court of Justice. (See para. 3.2.41)".[18]

The Goode Committee recommended that the rights of pension beneficiaries should be enhanced and safeguarded by the enactment of special rules which go beyond the protection given to beneficiaries under general trust law.[18a] The Pensions Act 1995 implemented most of these recommendations, some in modified form. In particular, the Act introduced a new Occupational Pensions Regulatory Body (replacing the Occupational Pensions Board) to supervise pension trusts (ss. 1–15); reforms related to the appointment, removal and

---

17 See para. 3.2.6 text and note 4. The concept is not new, see para. 2.1.38.
18 For examples of the role of trust law in pensions, see *Cowan v Scargill* [1985] Ch 270, [1984] 2 All ER 750, p. 679 post; *Re Courage Group's Pension Schemes* [1987] 1 WLR 495, [1987] 1 All ER 528; *Davis v Richards and Wallington Industries Ltd* [1990] 1 WLR 1511, [1991] 2 All ER 563, p. 208 post; *Imperial Group Pension Trust Ltd v Imperial Tobacco Ltd* [1991] 1 WLR 589, [1991] 2 All ER 597; *Mettoy Pension Trustees Ltd* v *Evans* [1990] 1 WLR 1587, [1991] 2 All ER 513, p.45 post.
18aSee (1993) 7 Trust Law International 91 (D. Chatterton); [1993] Conv 283 (D. Hayton).

disqualification of trustees (ss. 16–31); a minimum funding requirement to prevent a shortfall of funds in the case of funded schemes (ss. 56–61); restrictions on employers' rights to surplus funds (ss. 37, 73–77); and a compensation scheme administered by a new Pensions Compensation Board, to diminish hardships such as those suffered by the victims of the Maxwell fraud (ss. 78–86 and Sched 2).

Important new provisions were made for the functions of pension trustees in section 33 (Investments powers: duty of care); 34 (Power of investment and delegation); 35 (Investment principles); and 36 (Choosing investments). See pp. 706–708, post. The concepts and principles which underlie these sections of the Act could with advantage be replicated for trusts in general.

IV. Distinctions[19]

A. Bailment[20]

Maitland: *Lectures on Equity* (2nd edn) p. 45

"We must distinguish the trust from the bailment. This is not very easy to do, for in some of our classical text-books perplexing language is used about this matter. For example, Blackstone defines a bailment thus: 'Bailment, from the French *bailler*, is a delivery of goods in trust, upon a contract expressed or implied, that the trust shall be faithfully executed on the part of the bailee' (*Comm.* II, 451).

Here a bailment seems to be made a kind of trust. Now of course in one way it is easy enough to distinguish a bailment from those trusts enforced by equity, and only by equity, of which we are speaking. We say that the rights of a bailor against his bailee are legal, are common law rights, while those of a *cestui que trust* against his trustee are never common law rights. But then this seems to be a putting of the cart before the horse; we do not explain why certain rights are enforced at law while other rights are left to equity.

Let us look at the matter a little more closely. On the one hand we will have a bailment — A lends B a quantity of books — A lets to B a quantity of books in return for a periodical payment — A deposits a lot of books with B for safe custody. In each of these cases B receives rights from A, and in each of these cases B is under an obligation to A; he is bound with more or less rigour to keep the books safely and to return them to A. Still we do not I think conceive that B is bound to use on A's behalf the rights that he, B, has in the books. Such rights as B has in them he has on his own behalf, and those rights he may enjoy as seems best to him. On the other hand, S is making a marriage settlement and the property that he is settling includes a library of books; he vests the whole ownership of these books in T and T' who are to permit S to enjoy them during his life and then to permit his firstborn son to enjoy them and so forth. Not unfrequently valuable chattels are thus settled so that whoever dwells in a certain mansion during the continuance of the settlement shall have the use of

19 H & M, pp. 46–67; K & S, pp. 6–18; P & M, pp. 7–25; Pettit, pp. 23–37; Snell, pp. 91–100; Underhill, pp. 5–28.
20 H & M, pp. 47–48; K & S, p. 13; Pettit, p. 24; Snell, pp. 91–92; Underhill, p. 12; Bell, *Modern Law of Personal Property in England and Ireland* (1989), chap. 5; Crossley Vaines, *Personal Property* (5th edn 1973), chap. 6; *Aluminium Industrie Vaassen BV v Romalpa Aluminium Ltd* [1976] 1 WLR 676, [1976] 2 All ER 552, p. 896, post.

the pictures, books, plate, and so forth. Now here T and T' are full owners of the chattels. S and the other *cestui que trusts* have no rights in the chattels, but T and T' are bound to use their rights according to the words of the settlement, words which compel them to allow S and the other *cestui que trusts* to enjoy those things.

You may say the distinction is a fine one, almost a metaphysical one — and very likely I am not stating it well — but there are two tests which will bring out the distinction. The one is afforded by the law of sale, ...

(*a*) A is the bailor, B is the bailee of goods; B sells the goods to X, the sale not being authorised by the terms of the bailment and not being made in market overt or within the Factors' Acts.[1] X, though he purchases in good faith, and though he has no notice of A's rights, does not get a good title to the goods. A can recover them from him; if he converts them to his use he wrongs A. Why? Because he bought them from one who was not owner of them. Turn to the other case. T is holding goods as trustee of S's marriage settlement. In breach of trust he sells them to X; X buys in good faith and has no notice of the trust. X gets a good title to the goods. T was the owner of the goods; he passed his rights to X; X became the owner of the goods and S has no right against X — for it is an elementary rule, to which I must often refer hereafter, that trust rights can not be enforced against one who has acquired legal (i.e. common law) ownership bona fide, for value, and without notice of the existence of those trust rights. Here you see one difference between the bailee and the trustee ...

Cases can be conceived where it would be difficult to say whether there was a bailment by deposit or a trust. For instance, I go abroad in a hurry and do not know whether I shall return. I send a piano to a friend, and I say to him, 'Take care of my piano and if I don't return give it to my daughter.' This may be construed both ways, as a bailment or as a trust. Perhaps the age of my daughter — a thing strictly irrelevant — would decide which way it would go."

B. Agency[2]

The relationship between trustee and beneficiary, and that between principal and agent, is *fiduciary*. For that reason there are many similarities between them. The crucial distinction is that the agency relationship is *personal*, the trust relationship *proprietary*.

Hanbury & Martin: *Modern Equity* (14th edn), pp. 48–49.
"In many ways the relationship of principal and agent resembles that of beneficiary and trustee.[3] Agents, like trustees, must act personally in the business of the agency, and are accountable to their principals, as are trustees to beneficiaries, for any profits made out of the property or business entrusted to them. The relationship of beneficiary and trustee is a fiduciary relationship,

---

1 See Factors Act 1889, ss. 2, 8, 9; Sale of Goods Act 1979, ss. 21–26; Consumer Credit Act 1974, Sch. 4, para. 22.
2 H & M, pp. 48–49; K & S, pp. 17–18; P & M, p. 22; Pettit, pp. 25–26; Snell, p. 92; Underhill, pp. 5–6; (1892) 8 LQR 220 (C. Sweet); Hanbury, *Principles of Agency* (2nd edn), pp. 3–10; *Bowstead on Agency* (15th edn, 1985), pp. 16–17.
3 See Bowstead, *Agency* (15th ed.), pp. 16–17.

while that of principal and agent may or may not be.[4] But the vital difference is that a trust is *proprietary*. The beneficiary is equitable and beneficial owner of the property. Where money is due on an account between principal and agent, it is recoverable on the basis of a personal claim.

A right to claim £100 against a defendant may be just as good as beneficial ownership of £100 in the hands of the defendant as trustee; so long as the defendant can pay. But if the defendant is insolvent, the distinction becomes clear. The personal claim is one against the general assets of the defendant; and will abate with the claims of other creditors if the defendant cannot pay in full. However, if the claim is a proprietary one, the property held by the defendant as trustee is not available for the trustee's debts. It may be claimed by the beneficiary as his own if it is identifiable; and, for the purposes of identification, a 'tracing remedy'[5] is available where the assets have been mixed with the trustee's own funds. 'Equity,' as Maitland said, 'has been always striving to prevent the *cestui que trust* from falling to the level of an unsecured creditor.'[6] On the other hand, property for which the agent is liable to account to his principal is subject only to a personal claim; the principal is not owner at law or in equity of the money due, and the tracing remedy is not available.[7] Further, there is usually a contractual relationship between a principal and agent, but not between a trustee and beneficiary. And many of the rules governing principal and agent are based on the common law; the trust relationship is exclusively equitable.''

C. Contract[8]

Trust and contract are very different concepts. Contract is a common law concept based upon agreement, requiring either a deed or consideration, and creates a personal right against the other party. Trust is equitable, dependent essentially upon the intention of the settlor, and creating a proprietary interest in the beneficiary. Nevertheless, there are situations in which the dividing line is not clear. Difficulties most commonly arise in distinguishing trust from debt, and this situation will be considered here. The other situations will merely be mentioned now, and discussed in other sections of the book.

i. DEBT[9]

(a) Loan and Trust

A debt is a personal obligation. A trust is proprietary.

---

4 P. 836 post.
5 *Re Hallett's Estate* (1880) 13 ChD 696, p. 898, post.
6 Maitland, *Lectures on Equity* (2nd edn), p. 220.
7 *Lister & Co v Stubbs* (1890) 45 ChD 1. The case itself was not followed by PC in *A-G for Hong Kong v Reid* [1994] 1 AC 324, [1994], 1 All ER 1, p. 854 post.
8 H & M, pp. 49–50; K & S, pp. 6–13; P & M, pp. 12–16; Pettit, p. 25; Snell, pp. 92–96, Underhill, pp. 7–8.
9 H & M, pp. 50–53; P & M, pp. 16–19; Pettit, p. 150–151; Riddall, pp. 49–50; Snell, p. 92; Underhill, pp. 8–12. See generally *Space Investments Ltd v Canadian Imperial Bank of Commerce Trust Co (Bahamas) Ltd* [1986] 1 WLR 1072, [1986] 3 All ER 75; (1987) 103 LQR 433 (R. M. Goode); *Ross v Lord Advocate* [1986] 1 WLR 1077, [1986] 3 All ER 79; (1987) 50 MLR 231 (M. Percival). For an example of a debt which is the subject matter of a trust, see *Barclays Bank plc v Willowbrook International Ltd* [1987] 1 FTLR 386 (when A charges to B a debt owed to A by C, any money paid by C to A is held by A as constructive trustee for B).

MORLEY v MORLEY
(1678) 2 Cas in Ch 2 (Lord NOTTINGHAM LC)

The Defendant was Trustee for the Plaintiff an Infant, and received for him 40*l.* in Gold; a Servant of the Defendant living in the House with him robbed his Master of 200*l.* and the 40*l.* out of his House. The Robbery, *viz.* That the Defendant was robbed of Money, was proved; the Sum of 40*l.* was proved by only the Defendant's Oath.

LORD CHANCELLOR: He was to keep it but as his own, and allowed it on Account; so in Case of a Factor; so in Case of a Person robbed, for he cannot possibly have other Proof.

A line of cases suggests that where a lender is sufficiently well-advised to make his loan in specific legal language, he may convert what on the face of it is a debt into a resulting trust, thereby avoiding the consequence of being an unsecured creditor, if the borrower becomes insolvent.

BARCLAYS BANK LTD v QUISTCLOSE INVESTMENTS LTD
[1970] AC 567, [1968] 3 All ER 651 (HL, Lords REID, MORRIS OF BORTH-Y-GEST, GUEST, PEARCE and WILBERFORCE)

Rolls Razor Ltd. had declared a dividend upon their ordinary shares. They were in serious financial difficulties and were unable to pay the dividend without a loan of £209,719 8s. 6d., which the respondents Quistclose Investments Ltd. agreed to make on the condition "that it is used to pay the forthcoming dividend due on July 24 next."

The cheque for £209,719 8s. 6d. was paid into a separate account at Barclays Bank Ltd. with whom it was agreed that the account would "only be used to meet the dividend due on July 24, 1964". Before the dividend was paid, Rolls Razor Ltd. went into liquidation. The question was whether Barclays Bank Ltd. could set that sum against Rolls Razor's overdraft;[10] or whether they held it on trust for Quistclose.

Held. Barclays Bank held the money on trust for Quistclose. The fact that the transaction was a loan did not prevent there being also a trust.

LORD WILBERFORCE: Two questions arise, both of which must be answered favourably to the respondents if they are to recover the money from the bank. The first is whether as between the respondents and Rolls Razor Ltd. the terms upon which the loan was made were such as to impress upon the sum of £209,719 8s. 6d. a trust in their favour in the event of the dividend not being paid. The second is whether, in that event, the bank had such notice of the trust or of the circumstances giving rise to it as to make the trust binding upon them.

It is not difficult to establish precisely upon what terms the money was advanced by the respondents to Rolls Razor Ltd. There is no doubt that the loan was made specifically in order to enable Rolls Razor Ltd. to pay the dividend. There is equally, in my opinion, no doubt that the loan was made only so as to enable Rolls Razor Ltd. to pay the dividend and for no other

---

10 Insolvency Act 1986, s. 323; *Rolls Razor Ltd v Cox* [1967] 1 QB 552, [1967] 1 All ER 397; *National Westminster Bank Ltd v Halesowen Presswork and Assemblies Ltd* [1972] AC 785, [1972] 1 All ER 641.

purpose. This follows quite clearly from the terms of the letter of Rolls Razor Ltd. to the bank of July 15, 1964, which letter, before transmission to the bank, was sent to the respondents under open cover in order that the cheque might be (as it was) enclosed in it. The mutual intention of the respondents and of Rolls Razor Ltd., and the essence of the bargain, was that the sum advanced should not become part of the assets of Rolls Razor Ltd., but should be used exclusively for payment of a particular class of its creditors, namely, those entitled to the dividend. A necessary consequence from this, by process simply of interpretation, must be that if, for any reason, the dividend could not be paid, the money was to be returned to the respondents: the word "only" or "exclusively" can have no other meaning or effect.

That arrangements of this character for the payment of a person's creditors by a third person, give rise to a relationship of a fiduciary character or trust, in favour, as a primary trust, of the creditors, and secondarily, if the primary trust fails, of the third person, has been recognised in a series of cases over some 150 years.

In *Toovey v Milne* (1819) 2 B & Ald 683 part of the money advanced was, on the failure of the purpose for which it was lent (viz., to pay certain debts), repaid by the bankrupt to the person who had advanced it. On action being brought by the assignee of the bankrupt to recover it, the plaintiff was nonsuited and the nonsuit was upheld on a motion for a retrial. In his judgment Abbot CJ said, at 684:

> "I thought at the trial, and still think, that the fair inference from the facts proved was that this money was advanced for a special purpose, and that being so clothed with a specific trust, no property in it passed to the assignee of the bankrupt. Then the purpose having failed, there is an implied stipulation that the money shall be repaid. That has been done in the present case; and I am of opinion that the repayment was lawful, and that the nonsuit was right."

The basis for the decision was thus clearly stated, viz., that the money advanced for the specific purpose did not become part of the bankrupt's estate. This case has been repeatedly followed and applied: see *Edwards v Glyn* (1859) 2 E & E 29; *Re Rogers, ex p Holland and Hannen* (1891) 8 Morr 243; *Re Drucker* [1902] 2 KB 237; *Re Hooley, ex p Trustee* [1915] HBR 181. *Re Rogers* (1891) 8 Morr 243 was a decision of a strong Court of Appeal. In that case, the money provided by the third party had been paid to the creditors before the bankruptcy. Afterwards the trustee in bankruptcy sought to recover it. It was held that the money was advanced to the bankrupt for the special purpose of enabling his creditors to be paid, was impressed with a trust for the purpose and never became the property of the bankrupt. Lindley LJ decided the case on principle but said at 248 that if authority was needed it would be found in *Toovey v Milne* (1819) 2 B & Ald 683 and other cases. Bowen LJ said at 248 that the money came to the bankrupt's hands impressed with a trust and did not become the property of the bankrupt divisible amongst his creditors, and the judgment of Kay LJ at 249 was to a similar effect.

These cases have the support of longevity, authority, consistency and, I would add, good sense. But they are not binding on your Lordships and it is necessary to consider such arguments as have been put why they should be departed from or distinguished ...

The second, and main, argument for the appellant was of a more sophisticated character. The transaction, it was said, between the respondents and Rolls Razor Ltd., was one of loan, giving rise to a legal action of debt. This necessarily excluded the implication of any trust, enforceable in equity, in the respondents' favour: a transaction may attract one action or the other, it could not admit of both.

My Lords, I must say that I find this argument unattractive. Let us see what it involves. It means that the law does not permit an arrangement to be made by which one person agrees to advance money to another, on terms that the money is to be used exclusively to pay debts of the latter, and if, and so far as not so used, rather than becoming a general asset of the latter available to his creditors at large, is to be returned to the lender. The lender is obliged, in such a case, because he is a lender, to accept, whatever the mutual wishes of lender and borrower may be, that the money he was willing to make available for one purpose only shall be freely available for others of the borrower's creditors for whom he has not the slightest desire to provide.

I should be surprised if an argument of this kind — so conceptualist in character — had ever been accepted. In truth it has plainly been rejected by the eminent judges who from 1819 onwards have permitted arrangements of this type to be enforced, and have approved them as being for the benefit of creditors and all concerned. There is surely no difficulty in recognising the co-existence in one transaction of legal and equitable rights and remedies: when the money is advanced, the lender acquires an equitable right to see that it is applied for the primary designated purpose (see *Re Rogers* (1891) 8 Morr 243 where both Lindley LJ and Kay LJ recognised this): when the purpose has been carried out (i.e., the debt paid) the lender has his remedy against the borrower in debt; if the primary purpose cannot be carried out, the question arises if a secondary purpose (i.e., repayment to the lender) has been agreed, expressly or by implication: if it has, the remedies of equity may be invoked to give effect to it, if it has not (and the money is intended to fall within the general fund of the debtor's assets) then there is the appropriate remedy for recovery of a loan. I can appreciate no reason why the flexible interplay of law and equity cannot let in these practical arrangements, and other variations if desired: it would be to the discredit of both systems if they could not. In the present case the intention to create a secondary trust for the benefit of the lender, to arise if the primary trust, to pay the dividend, could not be carried out, is clear and I can find no reason why the law should not give effect to it.

I pass to the second question, that of notice. I can deal with this briefly because I am in agreement with the manner in which it has been disposed of by all three members of the Court of Appeal. I am prepared, for this purpose, to accept, by way of assumption, the position most favourable to the bank, i.e., that it is necessary to show that the bank had notice of the trust or of the circumstances giving rise to the trust, at the time when they received the money, viz., on July 15, 1964, and that notice on a later date, even though they had not in any real sense given value when they received the money or thereafter changed their position, will not do. It is common ground, and I think right, that a mere request to put the money into a separate account is not sufficient to constitute notice. But on July 15, 1964, the bank, when it received the cheque, also received the covering letter of that date which I have set out above; previously there had been the telephone conversation between Mr. Goldbart and Mr. Parker, to which I have also referred. From these there is no doubt that the bank was told that the money had been provided on loan by a third person and was to be used only for the purpose of paying the dividend. This was sufficient to give them notice that it was trust money and not assets of Rolls Razor Ltd.: the fact, if it be so, that they were unaware of the lender's identity (though the respondent's name as drawer was on the cheque) is of no significance. I may add to this, as having some bearing on the merits of the case, that it is quite apparent from earlier documents that the bank were aware that Rolls Razor Ltd. could not provide the money for the dividend and that this would have to come from an outside source and that they never contemplated that the money so provided could be used to reduce the existing overdraft. They were in fact insisting that other or additional arrangements should be made for that purpose. As was appropriately said by Russell LJ [1968] Ch 540 at 563F, [1968] 1 All ER 613 at 620, it would be giving a complete windfall to the bank if they had established a right to retain the money.

In my opinion, the decision of the Court of Appeal was correct on all points and the appeal should be dismissed.[11]

(b) Antecedent Debt

In **Carreras Rothmans Ltd v Freeman Mathews Treasure Ltd** [1985] Ch 207, [1985] 1 All ER 155, the plaintiff (CR) manufactured cigarettes and tobacco. This was advertised widely in the press by the defendants (FMT), who managed the advertising, and contracted as principals with production agencies and advertising media, thereby incurring substantial liabilities to media creditors (X). FMT paid the accounts, having been put in funds by CR. FMT was in financial difficulties, and CR became concerned that FMT might fail, leaving the debts to X unpaid. CR foresaw that X would have sufficient power to compel it to meet FMT's liabilities to X, even though CR was not legally responsible for them. As a result CR would have to pay the same sum twice, once to FMT and once to X. Accordingly in July 1983, CR agreed with FMT that a special bank account should be established in FMT's name, to be used "only for the purposes of meeting the accounts of the media and production fees of third parties directly attributable to CR's involvement with the agency". The bank was aware of this agreement.

FMT went into liquidation in August, at a time when there was a substantial sum in the special account which had not yet been paid over to X. As foreseen, X called upon CR to meet FMT's liabilities in full, threatening to interrupt CR's new advertising campaign if it did not pay. CR thereupon paid X's debts and took assignments from X of their rights against FMT.

CR sought a declaration that the moneys in the special bank account were held on trust for the sole purpose of paying X and for them to be repaid to CR.

---

11 (1980) 43 MLR 489 (W. Goodhart and G. Jones); [1992] 12 LS 333 (M. Bridge); *Re Kayford Ltd* [1975] 1 WLR 279, [1975] 1 All ER 604 (purchase money retained in separate account by mail-order company held in trust for customers); *Re Chelsea Cloisters Ltd* (1980) 41 P & CR 98 (tenants' damage deposit account moneys held on trust by company landlord in liquidation); cf. *Re Multi Guarantee Co Ltd* [1987] BCLC 257 (no trust of insurance premium moneys transferred to solicitors' joint deposit account); (1988) 85 LSG 14 (I.M. Hardcastle); *Aluminium Industrie Vaassen BV v Romalpa Aluminium Ltd* [1976] 1 WLR 676, [1976] 2 All ER 552; (1976) 92 LQR 360, 528 (R.M. Goode), p. 896, post; *Swiss Bank Corpn v Lloyds Bank Ltd* [1982] AC 584, [1981] 2 All ER 449; (1980) 96 LQR 483 (proceeds of sale of foreign securities kept in separate account); cf. *Mac-Jordan Construction Ltd v Brookmount Erostin Ltd* [1992] BCLC 350. See also *Hussey v Palmer* [1972] 1 WLR 1286, [1972] 3 All ER 744; *Re Sharpe* [1980] 1 WLR 219, [1980] 1 All ER 198; *Rowlandson v National Westminster Bank Ltd* [1978] 1 WLR 798, [1978] 3 All ER 370; *Borden (UK) Ltd v Scottish Timber Products Ltd* [1981] Ch 25, [1979] 3 All ER 961, cf. *Potters v Loppert* [1973] Ch 399, [1973] 1 All ER 658 (estate agent held entitled to retain interest earned by deposit held as stakeholder). See now Estate Agents Act 1979, s. 13.

In holding that there was such a valid trust, PETER GIBSON J said at 220, at 164:

"Mr. Millett and Mr. Higham for the plaintiff contended that the language of the contract letter was apt to create a trust and that such trust was fully constituted as to the moneys in the special account when the defendant agreed to the terms of the contract letter and received the moneys from the plaintiff. They relied on the line of cases of which *Barclays Bank Ltd v Quistclose Investments Ltd* [1970] AC 567, [1968] 3 All ER 651, p. 13 ante, is the highest authority. Mr. Potts denied that any enforceable trust was created. He submitted that the language of the contract letter was apt to create obligations of a contractual nature only in relation to the moneys to be paid into the special account, that the *Quistclose* line of cases was distinguishable ...

The July agreement was plainly intended to vary the contractual position of the parties as to how, as the contract letter put it, payments made by the plaintiff to the defendant for purely onwards transmission, in effect, to the third party creditors, would be dealt with. If one looks objectively at the genesis of the variation, the plaintiff was concerned about the adverse effect on it if the defendant, which the plaintiff knew to have financial problems, ceased trading and the third party creditors of the defendant were not paid at a time when the defendant had been put in funds by the plaintiff. The objective was accurately described by Mr. Higgs in his informal letter of 19 July as to protect the interests of the plaintiff and the third parties. For this purpose a special account was to be set up with a special designation. The moneys payable by the plaintiff were to be paid not to the defendant beneficially but directly into that account so that the defendant was never free to deal as it pleased with the moneys so paid. The moneys were to be used only for the specific purpose of paying the third parties and as the cheque letter indicated, the amount paid matched the specific invoices presented by the defendant to the plaintiff. The account was intended to be little more than a conduit pipe, but the intention was plain that whilst in the conduit pipe the moneys should be protected. There was even a provision covering the possibility (though what actual situation it was intended to meet it is hard to conceive) that there might be a balance left after payment and in that event the balance was to be paid to the plaintiff and not kept by the defendant. It was thus clearly intended that the moneys once paid would never become the property of the defendant. That was the last thing the plaintiff wanted in view of its concern about the defendant's financial position. As a further precaution the bank was to be put on notice of the conditions and purpose of the account. I infer that this was to prevent the bank attempting to exercise any rights of set off against the moneys in the account.

Only two matters were relied on as indicating that no trust was intended. One was the consideration fee; but the presence of consideration does not negative a trust. The other was the express reference in the penultimate paragraph in relation to placements and forward media options with which was contrasted the absence of the word 'trust' in relation to the moneys in the account. But I regard that as of minimal significance when I consider all the other indications as to the capacity in which the defendant was to hold any moneys in the account. In my judgment even in the absence of authority it is manifest that the defendant was intended to act in relation to those moneys in a fiduciary capacity only.

There is of course ample authority that moneys paid by A to B for a specific purpose which has been made known to B are clothed with a trust. In the *Quistclose* case [1970] AC 567, 580, [1968] 3 All ER 651, 654, Lord Wilberforce referred to the recognition, in a series of cases over some 150 years, that arrangements for the payment of a person's creditors by a third person gives rise to

'a relationship of a fiduciary character or trust, in favour, as a primary trust, of the creditors, and secondarily, if the primary trust fails, of the third person ... '

Lord Wilberforce in describing the facts of the *Quistclose* case said a little earlier on p. 580, p. 654, that the mutual intention of the provider of the moneys and of the recipient of the moneys and the essence of the bargain was that the moneys should not become part of the assets of the recipient but should be used exclusively for payment of a particular class of its creditors. That description seems to me to be apt in relation to the facts of the present case too ...

It is of course true that there are factual differences between the *Quistclose* case and the present case. The transaction there was one of loan with no contractual obligation on the part of the lender to make payment prior to the agreement for the loan. In the present case there is no loan but there is an antecedent debt owed by the plaintiff. I doubt if it is helpful to analyse the *Quistclose* type of case in terms of the constituent parts of a conventional settlement, though it may of course be crucial to ascertain in whose favour the secondary trust operates (as in the *Quistclose* case itself) and who has an enforceable right. In my judgment the principle in all these cases is that equity fastens on the conscience of the person who receives from another property transferred for a specific purpose only and not therefore for the recipient's own purposes, so that such person will not be permitted to treat the property as his own or to use it for other than the stated purpose. Most of the cases in this line are cases where there has been an agreement for consideration so that in one sense each party has contributed to providing the property. But if the common intention is that property is transferred for a specific purpose and not so as to become the property of the transferee, the transferee cannot keep the property if for any reason that purpose cannot be fulfilled. I am left in no doubt that the provider of the moneys in the present case was the plaintiff. True it is that its own witnesses said that if the defendant had not agreed to the terms of the contract letter, the plaintiff would not have broken its contract but would have paid its debt to the defendant, but the fact remains that the plaintiff made its payment on the terms of that letter and the defendant received the moneys only for the stipulated purpose. That purpose was expressed to relate only to the moneys in the account. In my judgment therefore the plaintiff can be equated with the lender in *Quistclose* as having an enforceable right to compel the carrying out of the primary trust.

Mr. Potts also submitted that the third party creditors had no enforceable rights and that where the beneficiaries under the primary trust have no enforceable rights, no trust is created. Mr Millet and Mr. Higham also submitted that the third party creditors had no enforceable rights, though that submission was made primarily with an eye to an argument relevant to the section 95 point that the beneficial interest in the moneys paid into the special account always remained in the plaintiffs. In none of the many reported cases in the *Quistclose* line of cases, so far as I am aware, has any consideration been given to the question whether the person intended to benefit from the carrying out of the specific purpose which created the trust had enforceable rights. Thus the existence of enforceable rights in such persons has not been treated as crucial to the existence of a trust. Further in the one case in which so far as I am aware the question who, in addition to the provider of the property, had enforceable rights was determined by the court, it was held that the persons intended to benefit from the carrying out of the primary trust did have enforceable rights. That case is the decision of Sir Robert Megarry V-C in *Re Northern Developments (Holdings) Ltd* (6 October 1978, unreported). In that case the eponymous company (Northern) was the parent company of a group of companies including one (Kelly) which was in financial straits. Seventeen banks agreed to put up a fund in excess of a half a million pounds in an attempt to rescue Kelly. The banks already had other companies in the group as customers. They paid the moneys into an account in Northern's name for the express purpose of providing moneys for Kelly's unsecured creditors and for no other purpose, the amounts advanced being treated as advances to the banks' other customers in the group. The fund was used to sustain Kelly for a time, but then Kelly was put into receivership at a time when a little over half the fund remained unexpended. One of the questions for the court was who was entitled to that balance. Sir Robert Megarry V-C held that there was a *Quistclose* type of trust attaching to the fund, that trust was a purpose trust but enforceable by identifiable individuals, namely the banks as lenders, Kelly, for whose immediate benefit the fund was established, and Kelly's creditors. The reason given by Sir Robert Megarry V-C for holding that Kelly's creditors had enforceable rights were the words of Lord Wilberforce in the *Quistclose* case at p. 580, at p. 654, which I have already cited, describing the *Quistclose* type of trust as giving rise to a relationship of a fiduciary character or trust in favour of the creditors. However, Sir Robert Megarry V-C went on to describe the interests of the creditors in this way:

> 'The fund was established not with the object of vesting the beneficial interest in them, but in order to confer a benefit on Kelly (and so, consequentially, on the rest of the group and the bankers) by ensuring that Kelly's creditors would be paid in an orderly manner. There is perhaps some parallel in the position of a beneficiary entitled to a share of residue under a will. What he has is not a beneficial interest in any asset forming part of residue, but a right to compel the executor to administer the assets of the deceased properly. It seems to me that it is that sort of right which the creditors of Kelly had.'

The interest of the banks was held to be under the secondary trust if the primary trust failed. In the light of that authority I cannot accept the joint submission that the third party creditors for the payment of whose debts the plaintiff had paid the moneys in the special account had no enforceable rights. In any event I do not comprehend how a trust, which on no footing could the plaintiff revoke unilaterally, and which was expressed as a trust to pay third parties and was still capable of performance, could nevertheless leave the beneficial interest in the plaintiff which had parted with the moneys. On Sir Robert Megarry V-C's analysis the beneficial interest is in suspense until the payment is made.''[12]

(c) Loan Paid but Purpose Not Achieved

In **Re EVTR** [1987] BCLC 646, the company was in financial difficulties. The appellant (Barber) "who had just won a very substantial prize on premium

---

12 Claims based on economic duress and fraudulent preference (see now Insolvency Act 1986, s. 239) were abandoned during the trial. (1985) 101 LQR 269 (P.J. Millett); [1985] All ER Rev 316 (P.J. Clarke); (1991) 107 LQR 608 (C. Rickett).

R.T.C. LIBRARY, LETTERKENNY 346 .057

bonds", agreed to assist it in purchasing from Quantel Ltd some new equipment (the Encore System) to enable it to carry on business. To this end Barber deposited £60,000 with EVTR's solicitors (Knapp-Fishers). EVTR also entered into a contract with Concord Leasing Company, whereby that company agreed to take over EVTR's obligations under the purchase agreement, to buy the Encore System itself, and to lease it to EVTR. Barber then authorised Knapp-Fishers to release the £60,000 "for the sole purpose of buying new equipment"; £21,000 was paid to Contract Leasing Company, and £39,000 to Quantel Ltd. Before the Encore System was due for delivery, receivers were appointed in respect of EVTR, which then ceased trading. Since the equipment could no longer be delivered, the £60,000, less agreed deductions, was transferred to the receivers. The trial judge held that these moneys were part of the general assets of EVTR and were not impressed with a trust in favour of Barber.

In reversing the trial judge, DILLON LJ said at 649:

"In the forefront of the appellant's case counsel for the appellant (Mr Jackson) refers to the decision of the House of Lords in *Barclays Bank Ltd v Quistclose Investments Ltd* [1970] AC 567, [1968] 3 All ER 651. There, Quistclose had lent money to a company (Rolls Razor Ltd) on an agreed condition that the money be used only for the purpose of paying a particular dividend which the company had declared. In the event the company went into liquidation, after receiving Quistclose's money, but without having paid the dividend. It was held that Quistclose could claim the whole of the money back, as on a resulting trust, the specific purpose having failed, and Quistclose was not limited to proving as an unsecured creditor in the liquidation of the company.

In the present case the £60,000 was released by Knapp-Fishers to the company on the appellant's instructions for a specific purpose only, namely the sole purpose of buying new equipment. Accordingly, I have no doubt, in the light of *Quistclose*, that, if the company had gone into liquidation, or the receivers had been appointed, and the scheme had become abortive before the £60,000 had been disbursed by the company, the appellant would have been entitled to recover his full £60,000, as between himself and the company, on the footing that it was impliedly held by the company on a resulting trust for him as the particular purpose of the loan had failed.

At the other end of the spectrum, if after the £60,000 had been expended by the company as it was, the Encore System had been duly delivered to, and accepted by, the company, there could be no doubt that the appellant's only right would have been as an unsecured creditor of the company for the £60,000. There would have been no question of the Encore System, or any interest in it, being held on any sort of trust for the appellant, and if, after it had been delivered and installed, the company had sold the system, the appellant could have had no claim whatsoever to the proceeds of sale as trust moneys held in trust for him.

The present case lies on its facts between those two extremes of the spectrum. Other scenarios between the extremes could equally be written, e.g. if, after the £60,000 had been paid by the company, Quantel had been injuncted by a third party from supplying the Encore System on the ground that the Encore System infringed patent rights or copyright of the third party and Quantel had thereupon refunded the £60,000, or if the Encore system was supplied but proved totally useless for its purpose and was therefore rejected and the money was returned ...

On *Quistclose* principles, a resulting trust in favour of the provider of the money arises when money is provided for a particular purpose only, and that purpose fails. In the present case, the purpose for which the £60,000 was provided by the appellant to the company was, as appears from the authority to Knapp-Fishers, the purpose of [the company] buying new equipment. But in any realistic sense of the words that purpose has failed in that the company has never acquired any new equipment, whether the Encore System which was then in mind or anything else. True it is that the £60,000 was paid out by the company with a view to the acquisition of new equipment, but that was only at half-time, and I do not see why the final whistle should be blown at half-time. The proposed acquisition proved abortive and a large part of the £60,000 has therefore been repaid by the payees. The repayments were made because of, or on account of, the payments which made up the £60,000 and those were payments of trust moneys. It is a long-established principle of equity that, if a person who is a trustee receives money or property because of, or in respect of, trust property, he will hold what he receives as a constructive trustee on the trusts of the original trust property. An early application of this principle is the well-known case of *Keech v Sandford* (1726) Sel Cas Ch 61, p 829 post, but the instances in the books are legion. See also *Chelsea Estates Investment Trust Co Ltd v Marche* [1955] Ch 328, [1955] 1 All ER 195 where somewhat similar reasoning applied to a mortgagee. It follows, in my judgment, that the repayments made to the receivers are subject to the same trusts as the original £60,000 in the hands of the company. There is now, of course, no question of the £48,536[13] being applied in the purchase of new equipment for the company, and accordingly, in my judgment, it is now held on a resulting trust for the appellant.''

BINGHAM LJ said at 652:

"It would, I think, strike most people as very hard if the appellant were in this situation to be confined to a claim as an unsecured creditor of the company. While it is literally true that the fund which he provided was applied to the stipulated purpose, the object of the payment was not achieved and that was why the balance was repaid to the respondents. My doubt has been whether the law as it stands enables effect to be given to what I can see as the common fairness of the situation. Our attention has not, I think, been drawn to any case closely analogous to the present. But the company certainly held the fund on trust in the first instance. The purpose for which the fund was paid out partially failed. The repayment to the respondents was a direct result of the company's original holding of the fund as trustee. The balance which was recovered may reasonably be regarded as not having been paid out at all. I am happy to be persuaded that the sums repaid are to be treated as held on the same trusts as the original £60,000 and, in present circumstances, on a resulting trust for the appellant.

I accordingly agree that the appeal should be allowed. I have had the advantage of reading in draft the judgment of Dillon LJ, and am in full agreement with both his reasoning and his conclusion.''

QUESTIONS

1. Do you agree with the decisions in *Barclays Bank Ltd v Quistclose Investments Ltd* [1970] AC 567, [1968] 3 All ER 651, p. 13 ante; *Carreras*

---

13 I.e. £60,000 less agreed deductions.

Rothmans Ltd v Freeman Mathews Treasure Ltd [1985] Ch 207, [1985] 1 All ER 155, p. 16 ante; *Re EVTR* [1987] BCLC 646, p. 19 ante?

2. If a powerful lender were able to make a loan on the basis of its being for a particular purpose only, what would be the position of other, less powerful, creditors if the borrower subsequently becomes insolvent? See Heydon, Gummow and Austin, *Cases and Materials on Equity and Trusts* (4th edn), p. 475 (suggesting that *Re Kayford Ltd* [1975] 1 WLR 279, [1975] 1 All ER 604 and "the *Quistclose* case provide startling opportunities for well-advised lenders to obtain protection against the prospect of the borrower's insolvency"); *Re EVTR* [1987] BCLC 646 at 652, per BINGHAM LJ, supra.)

ii. CONTRACTS FOR THE BENEFIT OF A THIRD PARTY[14]

The English rule of privity of contract requires that only the parties to a contract may sue or be sued upon it. There are of course many exceptions.[15] And there have been many attempts to circumvent the rule, and to change it. One such attempt is based upon the theory that a third party may sue upon a contract if one of the parties contracted as trustee for the third party; the third party then becomes a beneficiary of a trust of the promise, a chose in action; he can require his trustee to sue upon it,[16] and a successful action by the trustee will recover damages for the injury suffered by the third party.[17] This theory has met with success in some cases, but is now discredited as a method of enabling a third party to sue upon a contract.[18] The main reason for its failure was the difficulty of deciding whether there was or was not a trust of a promise. There is no difficulty, as will be seen,[19] in creating a trust of a promise, or of a chose in action. A trust of a debt, or of a bank account are simple examples. The difficulty arose in the "third party contract" situation because of the attempts by the common law courts to find that a trust existed in some situations in which the basic requirement for the creation of a trust was not met. That requirement, as will be seen,[20] is that there should be a manifestation of an intention to create a trust.

The problem of the enforcement of a contract by a person who is not a party to it is not therefore a situation in which there is a difficulty of determining whether there is a contract or a trust. So far as the third party is concerned,

---

14 Cheshire Fifoot & Furmston, *Law of Contract* (12th edn), pp. 450 et seq.; Treitel, *Law of Contract* (9th edn), pp. 534 et seq.; (1930) 46 LQR 12 (A.L. Corbin).

15 In 1991 the Law Commission issued a Consultation Paper: Privity of Contract: Contracts for the Benefit of Third Parties (Law Com No. 121), recommending that third parties should be able to sue if the contracting parties intended them to have enforceable rights; Law Commission Sixth Programme of Law Reform 1995 (Law Com No. 234), Item 1, p. 25. For recent judicial criticism of the privity rule, see *Woodar Investment Development Ltd v Wimpey Construction (UK) Ltd* [1980] 1 WLR 277 at 300, [1980] 1 All ER 571 at 591, per Lord SCARMAN; *Swain v Law Society* [1983] 1 AC 598 at 611, [1982] 2 All ER 827 at 832, per Lord DIPLOCK; *Darlington Borough Council v Wiltshier Northern Ltd* [1995] 1 WLR 68 at 77, per STEYN LJ. See also McGregor, *Contract Code* (1993), paras. 641–649.

16 *Tomlinson v Gill* (1756) Amb 330; *Affréteurs Réunis SA v Leopold Walford (London) Ltd* [1919] AC 801.

17 *Lloyd's v Harper* (1880) 16 ChD 290.

18 *Beswick v Beswick* [1968] AC 58, [1967] 2 All ER 1197; *Woodar Investment Development Ltd v Wimpey Construction (UK) Ltd* supra.

19 See p. 132, post.

20 See p. 132, post.

there is no contract, because of the privity rule. The question is whether or not there was an intention to create a trust of a promise. This is more relevant to Chapter 2.

iii. UNINCORPORATED ASSOCIATIONS

An unincorporated association is not a "legal person", and questions arise as to the means by which the property of such an association is held. Is it owned by the members jointly? Or held by the committee members or club officials on trust for the members? Or for the purposes of the association? Or held by them subject to contractual rights in favour of the members?

The answers to these questions can determine the validity of a gift to an unincorporated association, and are also relevant to the solution of problems concerning the disposal of assets on a dissolution. They are discussed in Chapters 2 and 6.

iv. SETTLEMENTS AND COVENANTS TO SETTLE

It is important also to distinguish between the creation of a trust or settlement and a covenant or contract to create one. Once a settlement is created, the beneficiaries become owners in equity of their share of the settled property. But if the settlor has covenanted to create a settlement or to add property to an existing settlement, the rights of the intended beneficiaries depend on whether or not they can compel the settlor to complete the settlement. Generally, they cannot do so if they are volunteers; for equity does not assist a volunteer. The matter is discussed in detail in Chapter 3.

v. CONTRACTUAL LICENCES

In the context of the rights of a contractual licence to occupy land, there is some authority for imposing a constructive trust where justice and good conscience require it. This is so where land subject to a contractual licence is sold to a third party, and the courts have sought to avoid the result that the purchaser, not being bound by the contract, can evict the licensee, by imposing a constructive trust upon him. This is discussed in Chapter 7.

D. Conditions and Charges[1]

In **Attorney-General v The Cordwainers' Co** (1833) 3 My & K 534,[2] the testator, by his will dated March 31, 1547, devised the Falcon Inn and adjoining premises in Fleet St. to the Cordwainers' Company "for the only interest, use and performance of this my last will and testament ... " The will required the Cordwainers' Company to pay £6 a year to the testator's brother David and after David's death to his widow; to make certain payments to charity and to the officers of the company for attending certain masses; a gift over to David in fee,

---

1 H & M, pp. 53–54; P & M, p. 23; Underhill, pp. 25–27; [1952] 11 CLJ 240 (T.C. Thomas).
2 See also *Re Oliver* (1890) 62 LT 533 (devise of real estate to nephew, "he also paying thereout" certain legacies. Held to create a charge and not a trust. The nephew not obligated to account for surplus).

on failure by the Company to carry out the terms of the will, the company then
"to be clearly expelled, discharged, and put out of the premises".

The rents of the premises were £12 6s. 8d. in 1547. They had risen to £358 in
1833. The question was whether the Company, having carried out the terms of
the will, was entitled to the surplus, or whether they held the premises as
trustees, and were obligated to hold the surplus on charitable trusts. The
Master of the Rolls (Sir John LEACH) held that they held the premises subject
to a condition, and, upon due performance of the condition, were entitled to
keep the surplus beneficially. He said at 542:

"The first question is whether this testator intended the corporation to take
as mere trustees, or whether he intended to give them any beneficial interest.
The next consideration is whether, if the corporation were to take as trustees,
they were to be trustees for mere charitable purposes.

It does not appear to me that the words of this devise do constitute this
corporation mere trustees. The estate is absolutely given to them; not upon
trust, but for the use, interest, and performance of the testator's will. It is rather
a gift upon condition, than a gift upon trust. They are to take the estate so
devised to them, upon condition that they perform the duties which by the
terms of the will are imposed upon them. Those duties are not for mere
charitable purposes. Half the property that this testator disposes of is disposed
of to his brother; an annuity of £6 is given to his brother for his life; and after
his brother's death there is no disposition of this annuity, except that £2 a year
are given to his widow if she survived him. These are not charitable purposes.
It is plain that a beneficial estate was intended to be given to the Cordwainers'
Company, because the testator expressly declares that, if the condition upon
which this estate is devised to the corporation be not performed, the brother
shall enter and defeat the estate given to the Cordwainers' Company. Defeat
what estate? An estate given to them in mere trust, from which they were to
derive no benefit? Is it to be supposed that this was considered by the testator
in the nature of a penalty? The imposition of a penalty for non-performance of
the condition implies a benefit, if the condition be performed, and is
inconsistent with any other intention, than that the testator meant to give a
beneficial interest to the company upon the terms of complying with the
directions contained in his will. There is, therefore, no trust, either express or
implied, for charitable purposes further than to the extent of the special
charge imposed; and, upon all the principles applied in this Court to such a
case, this information must be dismissed."

In **Re Frame** [1939] Ch 700, [1939] 2 All ER 865,[3] a testator bequeathed
property to Mrs. Ada Taylor, his housekeeper "on condition that she adopts
my daughter Alma Edwards and also gives to my daughters Jessie Edwards and
May Alice Edwards the sum of 5*l.* each, and a like sum of 5*l.* to my son
Alexander Edwards." SIMONDS J construed this gift as a trust for the
maintenance of Alma, and held that Mrs. Taylor was bound to provide
maintenance for her even if, as happened, she was unsuccessful in an
application to adopt her. In considering the effect of the words quoted above,
he said at 703, at 867:

3 Cf *Re Brace* [1954] 1 WLR 955, [1954] 2 All ER 354 ("on condition that she will always provide
a house for my daughter Doris at...").

"The question is what those words mean. I have listened to an able and interesting argument on these questions: Whether the condition is a condition subsequent or a condition precedent; whether, if it be a condition precedent, the condition has become impossible of performance, and whether, if so, the gift fails; whether, if it be a condition subsequent, the donee has failed, through no fault of her own, to comply with the condition, and whether, in that event, the gift has failed. As I listened to that argument it impressed itself more and more on me that, after all, this was not a condition at all, for, in my view, on the true construction of this clause, the word 'condition' is not used in its strict legal sense. It is a gift to Mrs. Taylor on condition, in the sense of on the terms or on the trust that she does certain things, and that, I think, becomes clearer when it is realized that the condition relates not only to the adoption of one daughter, but to the payment of certain sums to other daughters. A devise, or bequest, on condition that the devisee or legatee makes certain payments does not import a condition in the strict sense of the word, but a trust, so that, though the devisee or legatee dies before the testator and the gift does not take effect, yet the payments must be made; for it is a trust, and no trust fails for want of trustees. When I come to look at the condition, it seems clear that what the testator intended was that Mrs. Taylor should receive certain moneys on the term that she performed certain acts. Much argument has been directed to what is involved in the condition that 'she adopts my daughter'. It seems clear that whether or not an adoption under the authority of an order made under the Adoption of Children Act 1926 is necessary, what is intended is not any single formal act, but a series of acts to establish as between Mrs Taylor and the testator's daughter the relationship of parent and child — in a word, Mrs. Taylor was to treat the child as if she were her daughter, because that is what adoption means. Is that a trust which the Court can enforce? It includes not only the parental duties of care, advice, and affection, but also the duty of maintenance. This Court cannot compel, so far as adoption involves the giving of care, advice and affection that such things be given. But, seeing that it involves the duty of maintenance, that is a trust which the Court can enforce, directing, if necessary, an inquiry in that regard. It will not allow the whole trust to fail because in part it cannot be enforced.

Therefore, I come to the conclusion that the gift to Mrs. Taylor of all the money and insurance policies — what that means will have to be considered — on condition 'that she adopts my daughter' involves that she receives those things, whatever they may be, on trust to make proper provision for the maintenance of the child as her adopted daughter. That is a trust which can be enforced, and, if necessary, an inquiry can be directed in regard to it."

E. Interests Under a Will or Intestacy[4]

i. THE DISTINCTION BETWEEN A PERSONAL REPRESENTATIVE AND A TRUSTEE

ATTENBOROUGH v SOLOMON
[1913] AC 76 (HL, Viscount HALDANE, Lords ATKINSON and SHAW OF DUNFERMLINE)

The testator, who died on March 20, 1878, devised and bequeathed his residuary estate to his two sons, A.A. Solomon ("A.A.") and J.D. Solomon

---

4 H & M, pp. 54–61; K & S, pp. 13–14; P & M, pp. 19–22; Pettit, pp. 34–37, Snell, pp. 98–100; Underhill, pp. 13–15; (1955) 19 Conv (NS) 199 (B.S. Ker); [1984] Conv 423 (C. Stebbings); [1990] Conv 257 (C. Stebbings); (1991) 11 OJLS 609 (C. Stebbings)

upon trust to sell, and to divide the proceeds of sale among his children equally. Within a year, the debts and legacies had been paid, and the residuary account passed, but the estate had not been finally distributed.

In 1892, A.A. pledged some silver plate, part of the residuary estate, with George Attenborough and Sons, pawnbrokers, the appellants, to secure a personal loan. The appellants had no reason to believe that A.A. was not the absolute owner. The matter came to light when A.A. died in 1907.

The question was whether the appellants obtained any rights over the plate, as pawnbrokers. They would do so if A.A. had acted as an executor, since the power of disposal of personalty by executors is *several*, but not if A.A. were a trustee, because the trustee's power of disposal is *joint*.[5]

Held. The appellants obtained no title because A.A. was a trustee.

VISCOUNT HALDANE LC: The general principles of law which govern this case are not doubtful. The position of an executor is a peculiar one. He is appointed by the will, but then, by virtue of his office, by the operation of law and not under the bequest in the will, he takes a title to the personal property of the testator, which vests him with the plenum dominium over the testator's chattels. He takes that, I say, by virtue of his office. The will becomes operative so far as its dispositions of personalty are concerned only if and when the executor assents to those dispositions. It is true that by virtue of his office he has a general power to sell or pledge for the purpose of paying debts and getting in the money value of the estate. He is executor and he remains executor for an indefinite time. Authorities were cited to us by [counsel for the appellants] to the effect that an executor can sell at a period long after the death of the testator, and that where it is a question of conveyancing, as for instance in the case of the sale of leaseholds by the executor, the purchaser is not entitled to make requisitions as to whether debts remain unpaid, because the executor's office remains intact and he may exercise his functions at any time. That is true as a general principle, and I have no comment to make upon it except that it is qualified by another principle, which is this: The office of executor remains, with its powers attached, but the property which he had originally in the chattels that devolved upon him, and over which these powers extended, does not necessarily remain. So soon as he has assented, and this he may do informally and the assent may be inferred from his conduct, the dispositions of the will become operative, and then the beneficiaries have vested in them the property in those chattels. The transfer is made not by the mere force of the assent of the executor, but by virtue of the dispositions of the will which have become operative because of this assent.

Now, my Lords, in view of the residuary account passed as it was and in the form it was, in view of the evidence of Mr. J.D. Solomon, and in view of the fourteen years which had passed since the testator died before the time when Mr. A.A. Solomon made the pledge to the appellants in 1892, I am of opinion that the true inference to be drawn from the facts is that the executors considered that they had done all that was due from them as executors by 1879, and were content when the residuary account was passed that the dispositions of the will should take effect. That is the inference I draw from the form of the

5 Law Reform Committee 23rd Report (The Powers and Duties of Trustees) 1982, Cmnd 8733, para. 7.12 recommends that "personal representatives should be placed under a duty to act unanimously (subject to any contrary provision in the will) when disposing a property from the deceased's estate." See also Law Commission Report: Title on Death 1989 (Law Com. No. 184), paras. 2.10–2.19 and Law of Property (Miscellaneous Provisions) Act 1994, s. 16.

residuary account; and the inference is strengthened when I consider the lapse of time since then, and that in the interval nothing was done by them purporting to be an exercise of power as executors. My Lords, if this be so, this appeal must be disposed of on the footing that in point of fact the executors assented at a very early date to the dispositions of the will taking effect. It follows that under these dispositions the residuary estate, including the chattels in question, become vested in the trustees as trustees. That they were the same persons as the executors does not affect the point, or in my opinion present the least obstacle to the inference. But if that was so, then the title to the silver plate of A.A. Solomon as executor had ceased to exist before he made the pledge of 1892. What then was the position of the appellants? By the law of England the property in a chattel must always be in one person or body of persons. When the person who owns the chattel makes a pledge of it to a pawnbroker he is not purporting to part with the full property or giving any thing which is in the nature of a title to that property to the pawnee, excepting to a limited extent. The expression has been used that the pawnee in such a case has got a special property in the chattel. My Lords, that is true in this sense, that the pawnbroker is entitled to hold the chattel upon the terms that when the possession has been lawfully given to him it is not to be taken away from him, and that if default is made in the redemption of the pledge, or it may be in the payment of interest, he may go further and by virtue of his contract, assuming it to be valid, sell the chattel. But the contract of pawn is simply an illustration of that contract of bailment of which Holt CJ gave the famous exposition in the great case of *Coggs v Bernard* (1703) 2 Ld Raym 909; and it rests upon this foundation, that the property remains in the bailor, and that the bailee, whether it be a bailment by way of pawn or in any other form, simply takes at the outside a right to the possession dependent on the validity of the title of the bailor with the other rights possibly superadded to which I have referred. If that be true, upon no hypothesis did the appellants get a legal title to the property in the plate. When A.A. Solomon handed over these articles of silver to Messrs. Attenborough he had no property to pass as executor; and they got no contractual rights which could prevail against the trustees. The latter were the true owners and they are now in a position to maintain an action, which under the old forms would have been an action of trover or detinue, to recover possession of the chattels free from the restrictions on the right to reclaim possession which were sought to be imposed by the contract between A.A. Solomon and the appellants. My Lords, the property, if I am right in the inference which I draw from the circumstances of the case, was vested not in A.A. Solomon, but in A.A. Solomon and his co-trustee jointly in 1892, when the attempted pledge was made; and I see no answer to the case made for the respondents that the present trustees, in whom that property is now vested, are entitled to recover it.

In **Re King's Will Trusts** [1964] Ch 542, [1964] 1 All ER 833, PENNYCUICK J held that personal representatives could not exercise the statutory powers of appointing new trustees nor could they rely upon the provisions of Trustee Act 1925, s. 40,[6] to vest realty in newly appointed trustees, unless they had assented

---

6 See p. 622, post.

in writing in accordance with the Administration of Estates Act 1925, s. 36 (4), to the vesting of the realty in themselves as trustees.

The testatrix, by her will dated June 12, 1939, appointed X, Y and Z to be her executors, and X and Y her trustees. The estate contained land. As a result of various deaths and purported appointments of new trustees, Mr. Assheton, the plaintiff, claimed that he was the sole surviving trustee, and that the legal estate was vested in him. The defendant was the sole surviving personal representative (by representation). The question was whether the various appointments of trustees by X and Y and their successors were valid appointments; and whether, if they were valid, the legal estate was now vested, by virtue of Trustee Act 1925, s. 40, in the plaintiff.

PENNYCUICK J decided that the legal estate was in the defendant. Before personal representatives could become trustees of land, it was necessary that they should formally assent in writing in their own favour under s. 36 (4), just as they would in favour of other persons. The deed of appointment of new trustees did not operate as such assent.

With personalty, therefore, an assent can be implied. With realty, it must be in writing. *Re King's Will Trusts* is contrary to the earlier practice of many conveyancers,[7] but in the absence of evidence of widespread problems resulting from this decision, the Law Commission recommended that no change be made.[8]

ii. THE NATURE OF THE INTEREST OF A LEGATEE OR DEVISEE

COMMISSIONER OF STAMP DUTIES (QUEENSLAND) v LIVINGSTON[9]
[1965] AC 694, [1964] 3 All ER 692 (PC, Viscount RADCLIFFE, Lords REID, EVERSHED, PEARCE and UPJOHN)

A testator, H.D. Livingston, died domiciled in New South Wales, leaving to his widow absolutely an estate which consisted of real and personal property in Queensland and in New South Wales.

While the estate was still in the course of administration, the widow (Mrs. Coulson) died intestate, also domiciled in New South Wales.

---

7 (1964) 28 Conv (NS) 298 (J.F. Garner); (1964) 108 SJ 698 at 719; (1964) 80 LQR 328 (R.R.A. Walker); (1976) 29 CLP 60 (E.C. Ryder); see also *Williams on Title* (4th edn), pp. 360 et seq.; Barnsley, *Conveyancing Law and Practice* (3rd edn), pp. 292–284; *Emmet on Title* 11.121–11.122; Farrand, *Contract and Conveyance* (4th edn), p. 10. The requirement of an assent is however supported by Key and Elphinstone, *Conveyancing Precedents* (15th edn), vol. 1, p. 238 (§14) and p. 248 (note *p*); Prideaux, *Conveyancing Forms and Precedents* (25th end), vol. 3, p. 909; Wolstenholme and Cherry, *Conveyancing Statutes* (12th edn), vol. 2, p. 1470, but the support is qualified in 13th edn, Vol. 5, p. 61 (ed. J.T. Farrand).

The equitable beneficial interest may still pass under an implied assent by a personal representative: *Re Edwards' Will Trusts* [1982] Ch 30, [1981] 2 All ER 941; [1981] Conv 450 (G. Shindler); [1982] Conv 4 (P.W. Smith).

8 Law Commission Report: Title on Death 1989 (Law Com No 184); para. 1.5–1.6, rejecting the view in its Working Paper No. 105 (1987), paras 4.23, 42.4. that an assent should be deemed to have been made under certain conditions.

9 [1965] CLJ 44 (S.J. Bailey); *Crowden v Aldridge* [1993] 1 WLR 433, [1993] 3 All ER 603; [1994] Conv 446 (J.G. Ross Martyn). See also *Official Receiver in Bankruptcy v Schutz* (1990) 170 CLR 306; [1992] Conv 92 (J.K. Maxton).

One question was whether succession duty was payable on the widow's death in respect of the Queensland property left to her in the will. Under the relevant Queensland statute succession duty was payable in respect of "every devolution by law of any beneficial interest in property ... upon the death of any person ...".

Held. No duty was payable in Queensland. The widow did not hold a beneficial interest in the property, but merely a chose in action which was situated in New South Wales.

VISCOUNT RADCLIFFE: When Mrs. Coulson died she had the interest of a residuary legatee in the testator's unadministered estate. The nature of that interest has been conclusively defined by decisions of long-established authority, and its definition no doubt depends upon the peculiar status which the law accorded to an executor for the purposes of carrying out his duties of administration. There were special rules which long prevailed about the devolution of freehold land and its liability for the debts of a deceased, but subject to the working of these rules whatever property came to the executor virtute officii came to him in full ownership, without distinction between legal and equitable interests. The whole property was his. He held it for the purpose of carrying out the functions and duties of administration, not for his own benefit; and these duties would be enforced upon him by the Court of Chancery, if application had to be made for that purpose by a creditor or beneficiary interested in the estate. Certainly, therefore, he was in a fiduciary position with regard to the assets that came to him in the right of his office, and for certain purposes and in some aspects he was treated by the court as a trustee. "An executor," said Kay J in *Re Marsden* (1884) 26 ChD 783 at 789, "is personally liable in equity for all breaches of the ordinary trusts which in Courts of Equity are considered to arise from his office." He is a trustee "in this sense".

It may not be possible to state exhaustively what those trusts are at any one moment. Essentially, they are trusts to preserve the assets, to deal properly with them, and to apply them in a due course of administration for the benefit of those interested according to that course, creditors, the death duty authorities, legatees of various sorts, and the residuary beneficiaries. They might just as well have been termed "duties in respect of the assets" as trusts. What equity did not do was to recognise or create for residuary legatees a beneficial interest in the assets in the executor's hands during the course of administration. Conceivably, this could have been done, in the sense that the assets, whatever they might be from time to time, could have been treated as a present, though fluctuating, trust fund held for the benefit of all those interested in the estate according to the measure of their respective interests. But it never was done. It would have been a clumsy and unsatisfactory device from a practical point of view; and, indeed, it would have been in plain conflict with the basic conception of equity that to impose the fetters of a trust upon property, with the resulting creation of equitable interests in that property, there had to be specific subjects identifiable as the trust fund. An unadministered estate was incapable of satisfying this requirement. The assets as a whole were in the hands of the executor, his property; and until administration was complete no one was in a position to say what items of property would need to be realised for the purposes of that administration or of what the residue, when ascertained, would consist or what its value would be. Even in modern economies, when the ready marketability of many forms of property can almost be assumed, valuation and realisation are very far from being interchangeable terms.

At the date of Mrs. Coulson's death, therefore, there was no trust fund consisting of Mr. Livingston's residuary estate in which she could be said to have any beneficial interest, because no trust had as yet come into existence to affect the assets of his estate. The relation of her estate to his was exactly the same as that of Mrs. Tollemache's estate to that of her deceased husband's, as analysed in the well-known decision of *Lord Sudeley v A-G* [1897] AC 11. Just as Mr. Tollemache's rights in the mortgages of New Zealand land were the property of his executors for the purposes of the administration of his estate, and no one else had any property interest in them, so Mr. Livingston's property in Queensland, real or personal, was vested in his executors in full right, and no beneficial property interest in any item of it belonged to Mrs. Coulson at the date of her death. In their Lordships' opinion the decision of the *Sudeley* case is conclusive on this issue. It is sufficient to quote the words of Lord Herschell, which do no more than reflect the reasoning and views of all the members of the House who took part in the decision. "I do not think," he said at 18, speaking of Mrs. Tollemache's executors, "that they have any estate, right, or interest, legal or equitable, in these New Zealand mortgages so as to make them an asset of her estate."

It is evident that there would not have been the divisions of opinion in the Australian courts that have arisen in this case, if the proposition laid down by the *Sudeley* decision had always been regarded as being as final and comprehensive as, in their Lordships' opinion, it was intended to be. There has been a reluctance to accept Lord Herschell's words at their face value and, it would seem, a feeling that they ought to be treated as subject to some limitation that does justice to the "interest" that a residuary legatee possesses in his testator's estate. The judgment of Jordan CJ in *McCaughey v Stamp Duties Comr* (1945) 46 NSWR 192 contains a reasoned statement of some of these misgivings, which were again referred to in the High Court of Australia in *Smith v Layh* (1953) 90 CLR 102 at 108–109; and cases in England such as *Re Cunliffe-Owen, Mountain v IRC* [1953] Ch 545, [1953] 2 All ER 196 indicate a certain unease at relating *Sudeley* to other English decisions. Basically, these criticisms appear to arise from an incomplete assessment of the legal position of assets which belong to an executor for the purposes of his administration and from a use of the word "interest" that is not sufficiently precise to meet the requirements of a taxing Act to which questions of locality and valuation are all important. But since these criticisms have been made, it is desirable that this opinion should notice and comment upon them ...

... their Lordships regard it as clearly established that Mrs. Coulson was not entitled to any beneficial interest in any property in Queensland at the date of her death. What she was entitled to in respect of her rights under her deceased husband's will was a chose in action, capable of being invoked for any purpose connected with the proper administration of his estate; and the local situation of this asset, as much under Queensland law as any other law, was in New South Wales, where the testator had been domiciled and his executors resided and which constituted the proper forum of administration of his estate.

In **Lall v Lall** [1965] 1 WLR 1249, [1965] 3 All ER 330, the question was whether the right of a widow under the Intestates' Estates Act 1952 to require the matrimonial home to be appropriated towards the satisfaction of her share of an intestate's estate gave the widow standing to defend an action for possession of the house. No grant of administration had been made. BUCKLEY J held, following *Commissioner of Stamp Duties (Queensland) v Livingston*, that it did not.

In **Eastbourne Mutual Building Society v Hastings Corporation** [1965] 1 WLR 861, [1965] 1 All ER 779, PLOWMAN J quoted Viscount RADCLIFFE to summarise the principle of the *Livingston* case as follows:

"Therefore, while it may well be said in a general way that a residuary legatee has an interest in the totality of the assets … it is in their Lordships' opinion inadmissible to proceed from that to the statement that such a person has an equitable interest in any particular one of those assets, for such a statement is in conflict with the authority of both *Sudeley* [1897] AC 11 and *Barnardo* [1921] 2 AC 1 and is excluded by the very premise on which those decisions were based."

(1970) 86 LQR 20 (P.V.B.)

"In **Re Leigh's Will Trusts** [1970] Ch 277, [1969] 3 All ER 432, a testatrix specifically bequeathed 'all shares which I hold and any other interest or assets which I may have' in a named company. The testatrix never had any shares or interest of her own in the company, but both at the time she made her will and at her death she was the sole administratrix and beneficiary of her intestate husband's unadministered estate. That estate included some shares in and a debt due from the company. The question for Buckley J was whether those shares and debt passed under the bequest. The testatrix could not have bequeathed them in her capacity of administratrix, but what of her position as sole beneficiary?

The position of a person entitled to the residue or upon an intestacy while the administration is continuing was reviewed by Viscount Radcliffe in *Commissioner of Stamp Duties (Queensland) v Livingston* [1965] AC 694 and, as Buckley J observed, may be summarised in four propositions:

(1) The entire ownership of the assets of the estate remains during the course of administration in the personal representative;

(2) No person entitled to residue or upon an intestacy has any proprietary interest in any particular asset in the estate;

(3) Each such person has a right to require the deceased's estate to be duly administered;[10]

(4) That right is a chose in action which is transmissible.

It follows that the only disposable interest which the testatrix had was the chose in action which could be transmitted to one or more beneficiaries. Buckley J held that the testatrix had 'an interest in the company both in respect of the shares and of the debt sufficient to answer the description in the specific bequest to the [specific legatee], which was accordingly effective to entitle [him] to receive such of the shares and so much of the debt as in the due administration of [the husband's] estate should eventually fall into the possession of the executors of the testatrix' (p. 654).

This decision is understandable on the facts of the case but may be difficult to apply in other circumstances. Suppose that the testatrix already had some

10 See *Passant v Jackson* [1986] STC 164 at 167, per SLADE LJ

shares in the company. Would the gift in the will have carried the additional shares comprised in the unadministered estate? Then again, suppose that the shares had been sold to pay the husband's debts. Could the specific legatee have recourse to the doctrine of marshalling and require to be compensated out of other assets of the husband's estate? And if they had not been sold, how far do the executors have to go to procure them? Buckley J said: 'What she could transmit was her own right to require the administrator of her husband's estate, whoever he might be, to administer his estate in any manner she or her personal representative might require consistent with the rights of any other persons having rights against the estate. This right she could transmit to her executor, coupled with a duty to exercise it in a particular manner. By her will she has, in my judgment, clearly indicated that her executor should so exercise this right as to procure the 51 shares, and the company's indebtedness should to the largest possible extent become available to satisfy the specific bequest' (p. 654). Is the executor bound, if necessary to save the shares, to use the testatrix's own estate to pay off the husband's debts? Alternatively, does the doctrine of ademption apply to any extent if the shares are sold (a) before the testatrix makes her will, or (b) before she dies, or (c) after her death? It may be some time before the implications of this decision are fully worked out."[11]

iii. Executor's Duty is to the Estate as a Whole

In **Re Hayes' Will Trusts** [1971] 1 WLR 758, [1971] 2 All ER 341[12], the testator appointed four persons to be executors and trustees of his will, of whom the testator's son was one. The will gave to the executors a power to sell certain land, expressly authorising sale to his son "despite his being a trustee, and in his case at the value placed upon the same for purposes of estate duty."

The executors agreed to sell the land to the son at the agreed estate duty valuation. The other beneficiaries objected that the sale price was too low.

Ungoed-Thomas J held that the executors were under no duty to agree an estate duty valuation which held an even balance between the beneficiaries, as trustees would have to do. Their duty was to the estate as a whole, and the estate duty valuation should be agreed in the ordinary way. He said at 764, at 346:

"It is of course rightly common ground that 'my trustees' in agreeing the estate duty valuation were acting as executors under statutory powers conferred by section 15 (*f*) of the Trustee Act 1925. They were not acting under any powers conferred by the will, including in particular clause 5 (iii). I am completely satisfied that in fixing and agreeing the amount of the estate duty valuation Mr. Cooper, who was acting for the executors, was completely unaffected by the existence of the power to sell to the son. So this power to agree the estate duty valuation is to be considered as a purely personal representative administration power. It is well established that the estate being administered by a personal representative is the personal representative's property. Of course he has fiduciary duties with regard to it and their performance will be secured by the court; and he may be made liable for breaches of his fiduciary duties. But no legatee, devisee or next-of-kin has any beneficial interests in the assets being administered. His position is quite

---

11 Cf. *Re K* [1986] Ch 180, [1985] 2 All ER 833, p. 288 post, where residuary beneficiaries under an unadministered estate had not acquired "an interest in property" under Forfeiture Act 1982, s. 2(7).

12 (1971) 36 Conv (NS) 136 (J.F. Mummery).

different from that of a trustee, who holds property for beneficiaries and has a duty to hold the balance evenly between the beneficiaries to whom the property belongs and for whom the trustee holds it. It does not necessarily follow that the duty of an executor in the course of administering the estate is subject to the trustee's duty of holding the balance evenly between the beneficiaries. Whether he has such a duty has to be independently considered in the light of his own different fiduciary functions and obligations: see *Commissioner of Stamp Duties (Queensland) v Livingston* [1965] AC 694 at 707, 708. Those functions are to get in the testator's estate, preserve its properties, discharge its liabilities and distribute the resulting net assets. The legal personal representatives would in due course be concerned to obtain a proper discharge for the net assets and thus to ascertain who were entitled to them and to ensure that the assets were distributed to those entitled. But even then they would not be concerned in the course of acting as legal personal representatives with any conflicting interests of beneficiaries under testamentary trusts but only with the trustees of that trust; and not the less so even if they themselves happen to be such trustees. In our case there is not even the possibility of argument that the farms were in the personal representatives' hands freed of administration and merely held for distribution; and therefore held by the legal personal representative on trust for the beneficiaries. Such an argument would be plainly contrary to the established facts. So the legal personal representative functions, so far at any rate as they arise in our case, are functions which relate to the process of ascertaining the net assets available for distribution and not at all functions in the distribution itself.

Much the most important authority on this part of this case is *Re Charteris* [1917] 2 Ch 379. It appears from the recital of facts in the report supplemented by Swinfen Eady LJ's references in the course of his judgment, that a testatrix gave her residue to her executors and trustees upon trust for sale and to raise a legacy to be held by them on trust for A for life and over. She gave them power to appropriate in satisfaction of the legacy and to postpone sale: and she provided that interest on the amount of the legacy in so far as there was no appropriation should be at $3\frac{1}{2}$ per cent. and in so far as there was appropriation the interest would be the income of the appropriated investments. The balance of residue she gave to residuary legatees. It seems that the powers of the executors and trustees to postpone the sale of residue out of whose proceeds the legacy was to be paid and to appropriate it to the legacy were powers given to them in their capacity as executors: but even if they were given to them as trustees then a fortiori the observations made in the judgment would be applicable to them as executors, because, as already indicated, the fiduciary nexus between trustees and beneficiaries fastens directly on the trust property and is in that respect stronger than the fiduciary nexus between executor and beneficiary.

The executors decided to postpone sale and thus not to appropriate investments to the legacy. As the life tenant's interest on appropriated investments would be higher than the $3\frac{1}{2}$ per cent. interest on the amount of the legacy, the life tenant objected to this course. The postponement in itself operated, as was fully realised by the executors when they made their decision, wholly in the interests of the residuary legatee and contrary to the interests of the pecuniary legatee. The bona fides of the executors was not questioned. The objection failed ...

The most likely price, in the absence of consultation between the valuers representing conflicting interests, would presumably be the mean price. The habitual well-recognised process of arriving at that price is for executors to put in the lowest price within the range and then to confer with the district valuer who acts to safeguard the revenue. Such has been the accepted process of arriving at the price which the 'property would fetch if sold in the open market' and it seems to me to be as likely as any to arrive at that price within the margin which is the price most likely to be the market price. That was what was done in our case: and Mr. Cooper's evidence, which I accept, is that the price agreed was the fair and proper price and was in fact in this case the mean price within the marginal limits ranging from 10 per cent. above to 10 per cent. below it.''

F. Powers[13]

A trust is imperative; a power discretionary. A trustee must perform the duties connected with his trust. A power, whether held in a fiduciary capacity or otherwise, may be exercised or not at the discretion of the donee of the power.[14] Whether a particular disposition creates a power or a trust is a question of the intention of the settlor as ascertained from a construction of the language of the instrument.

Under a trust, the beneficiaries are the owners of the property. Under a power, the objects own nothing; they merely have a hope that the power will be exercised in their favour. Until it is exercised, equitable ownership is in those who will take in default of the exercise of the power; their interest is subject to defeasance on such exercise.

The distinction between trust and power becomes blurred in the case of discretionary trusts,[15] especially in the case of "non-exhaustive" discretionary trusts — those in which the trustees may decide not to distribute any income at all, but rather to accumulate it. With an "exhaustive" discretionary trust, it is the duty of the trustees to exercise their discretion in favour of one or more members of the class of beneficiaries. If they fail to do so, the court will make an order for equal division among the beneficiaries, or in such proportions as is appropriate in the circumstances.[16] Further, the class of beneficiaries, if they are of full age and under no disability, and if between them they are entitled to the whole of the beneficial interest, may terminate the trust.[17]

The analysis is all the more difficult with non-exhaustive discretionary trusts. As Pettit says[18] "It is submitted that the term 'non-exhaustive discretionary

---

13 H & M, pp. 61–67, 169–188; K & S, pp. 15–17, P & M, pp. 23–25, Pettit, pp. 26–34; Riddall, pp. 212–227; Snell, pp. 96–98; Underhill, pp. 20–23; *Farwell on Powers* (3rd edn); Maclean, *Trusts and Powers* (1989); (1957) 35 Can BR 1060 (O.R. Marshall); (1953) 69 LQR 334 (D.M. Gordon); (1949) 13 Conv (NS) 20 (J.G. Fleming); (1954) 18 Conv (NS) 565 (F.R. Crane); [1971] CLJ 68 (J.A. Hopkins); (1971) 87 LQR 31 (J.W. Harris); (1976) 54 Can BR 229 (M.C. Cullity); (1977) 3 Mon LR 210 (Y. Grbich); (1982) 98 LQR 551 (C.T. Emery).

14 For the distinction between a fiduciary power and a mere power, see H & M, p. 170; *Re Gulbenkian's Settlements* [1970] AC 508 at 518 per Lord REID; *Re Hay's Settlement Trusts* [1982] 1 WLR 202 at 209, [1981] 3 All ER 786 at 792, p. 39, post, per MEGARRY V-C; *Turner v Turner* [1983] 2 All ER 745, p. 44, post.

15 See also (1970) ASCL 187 (J.D. Davies); (1974) 37 MLR 643 (Y. Grbich). On discretionary trusts generally, see H & M, pp. 199–214; K & S, pp. 165–167; P & M, pp. 136–160; Pettit, pp. 67–72; Riddall, pp. 228–230; Snell, pp. 135–137; Underhill, pp. 20–23.

16 *McPhail v Doulton* [1971] AC 424, [1970] 2 All ER 228; *Re Locker's Settlement Trusts* [1977] 1 WLR 1323, [1978] 1 All ER 216, p. 78, n. 10, post.

17 *Re Smith* [1928] Ch 915, p. 37; post.

18 At p. 69.

trust' in fact conceals the two alternatives referred to by Lord Wilberforce in *McPhail v Doulton*[19] viz. a power of distribution coupled with a trust to dispose of the undistributed surplus, by accumulation or otherwise, and a trust for distribution coupled with a power to withhold a portion and accumulate or otherwise dispose of it. The distinction between these alternatives does not appear to have been raised in *Gartside v IRC*[20] and it is submitted that it is only if the provision there in question was construed in the latter sense that it should properly have been called a discretionary trust. It was in fact consistently so called by their Lordships, though the language of the will is similar to that given as a typical example of a mere power by Russell LJ in *Re Baden's Deed Trusts*."[1]

Finally, it may be added that most of the cases upon the distinction between trusts and powers have arisen in connection with the question whether a disposition is void for uncertainty. These cases are now mentioned only in a footnote,[2] because it was decided in *McPhail v Doulton*[3] that the test of certainty of objects in the case of discretionary trusts should be the same as that established for powers in *Re Gulbenkian's Settlements*.[4]

i. DISCRETIONARY TRUSTS AND POWERS

In **Burrough v Philcox** (1840) 5 My & Cr 72, John Walton, the testator, gave life interests in a trust fund to his two children with remainders to their issue, but if each of the children should die without leaving lawful issue (as happened), then the survivor of the children should have power to dispose, by will, "amongst my nephews and nieces, or their children, either all to one of them or to as many of them as my surviving child shall think proper". There was no gift over in default.

The question was whether this language created a trust in favour of the nephews and nieces, or whether it was a power.

Lord COTTENHAM held that it was a trust. The living nephews and nieces took in equal shares. He said at 89:

"The question is, whether these nephews and nieces and their children, take any interest in the property, independently of the power; that is, whether the power given to the survivor of the son and daughter is a mere power, and the

---

19 [1971] AC 424 at 448, [1970] 2 All ER 228 at 240.
20 [1968] AC 553, [1968] 1 All ER 121. Cf *Pearson v IRC* [1981] AC 753, [1980] 2 All ER 479, p. 582 post (decided by a bare majority in HL, which disagreed with all the judges below). There seems much to be said for the dissenting speech of Lord RUSSELL OF KILLOWEN. The analysis of trust law by Fox J at first instance [1980] Ch 1 at 14–15, [1979] 1 All ER 273 at 281–282, repays study. As pointed out by VINELOTT J in *IRC v Berrill* [1981] 1 WLR 1449, [1982] 1 All ER 867 there is nothing in the speeches in HL casting any doubt on its accuracy or completeness.
1 [1969] 2 Ch 388 at 401, [1969] 1 All ER 1016 at 1022. In *Re Weir's Settlement Trusts* [1971] Ch 145 at 164, [1970] 1 All ER 297 at 300, RUSSELL LJ referred to *Gartside v IRC* as "a case of a non-exhaustive discretionary power or trust."
2 *IRC v Broadway Cottages Trust* [1955] Ch 20, [1954] 3 All ER 120; *Re Hooper's Settlement* (1955) 34 ATC 3; *Re Sayer Trust* [1957] Ch 423, [1956] 3 All ER 600; *Re Eden* [1957] 1 WLR 788, [1957] 2 All ER 430; *Re Saxone Shoe Co Ltd's Trust Deed* [1962] 1 WLR 943, [1962] 2 All ER 904; *Re Leek* [1969] 1 Ch 563, [1968] 1 All ER 793.
3 [1971] AC 424, [1970] 2 All ER 228, p. 71, post.
4 [1970] AC 508, [1968] 3 All ER 785, p. 38, post.

interests of the nephews and nieces and their children were, therefore, to depend upon the exercise of it, or whether there was a gift to them, subject only to the power of selection given to the survivor of the son and daughter.

[His Lordship referred to *Duke of Marlborough v Lord Godolphin* (1750) 2 Ves Sen 61; *Brown v Higgs* (1800) 5 Ves 495 at 506; *Harding v Glyn* (1739) 1 Atk 469, and *Witts v Boddington* (1790) 3 Bro CC 95, and continued:] These and other cases shew that when there appears a general intention in favour of a class, and a particular intention in favour of individuals of a class to be selected by another person, and the particular intention fails, from that selection not being made, the Court will carry into effect the general intention in favour of the class. When such an intention appears, the case arises, as stated by Lord *Eldon* in *Brown v Higgs* (1803) 8 Ves 561 at 574, of the power being so given as to make it the duty of the donee to execute it; and, in such case, the Court will not permit the objects of the power to suffer by the negligence or conduct of the donee, but fastens upon the property a trust for their benefit.''

In **Re Weekes' Settlement** [1897] 1 Ch 289, Mrs. Slade, by her will, gave a life interest in certain property to her husband ''and I give to him power to dispose of all such property by will amongst our children ...'' The will contained no gift in default of appointment.

The husband failed to make any appointment. The question was whether the children were entitled in equal shares or whether the property passed to the heir at law of Mrs. Slade. ROMER J held that the heir at law was entitled. He said at 292:

''Now, apart from the authorities, I should gather from the terms of the will that it was a mere power that was conferred on the husband, and not one coupled with a trust that he was bound to exercise. I see no words in the will to justify me in holding that the testatrix intended that the children should take if her husband did not execute the power.

This is not a case of a gift to the children with power to the husband to select, or to such of the children as the husband should select by exercising the power.

If in this case the testatrix really intended to give a life interest to her husband and a mere power to appoint if he chose, and intended if he did not think fit to appoint that the property should go as in default of appointment according to the settlement, why should she be bound to say more than she has said in this will?

I come to the conclusion on the words of this will that the testatrix only intended to give a life interest and a power to her husband – certainly she has not said more than that.

Am I then bound by the authorities to hold otherwise? I think I am not. The authorities do not shew, in my opinion, that there is a hard and fast rule that a gift to A for life with power to A to appoint among a class and nothing more must, if there is no gift over in the will, be held a gift by implication to the class in default of the power being exercised. In my opinion the cases shew (though there may be found here and there certain remarks of a few learned judges which, if not interpreted by the facts of the particular case before them, might seem to have a more extended operation) that you must find in the will an indication that the testatrix did intend the class or some of the class to take — intended in fact that the power should be regarded in the nature of a trust —

only a power of selection being given, as, for example, a gift to A for life with a gift over to such of a class as A shall appoint.''

ii. TERMINATION OF A DISCRETIONARY TRUST BY ALL MEMBERS OF THE CLASS OF BENEFICIARIES

In **Re Smith** [1928] Ch 915, a fund was held by trustees upon trust ''to pay or apply the whole or any part of the annual income . . . thereof or if they shall think fit from time to time any part of the capital thereof unto and for the maintenance and personal support and benefit of . . . Lilian Aspinall''. There was provision for accumulation of the surplus, the accumulations and the remainder after her death to be held in trust for such of her sons as should attain the age of twenty-one years and such of her daughters as should attain that age or marry.

Mrs. Aspinall had three children, all of whom attained the age of twenty-one years, and one of whom had died. Mrs. Aspinall was past the age of child-bearing.

Mrs. Aspinall, her two surviving children and the legal representatives of her deceased child, mortgaged to the Legal and General Assurance Co. their interests under the trust. The question was whether the trustees should pay the income of the trust to the mortgagees, or whether they retained the discretion to pay to Mrs. Aspinall.

ROMER J held that the mortgage to the Legal and General Assurance Co. was valid. He said at 917:

''The question I have to determine is whether the Legal and General Assurance Company are now entitled to call upon the trustees to pay the whole of the income to them. It will be observed from what I have said that the whole of this share is now held by the trustees upon trusts under which they are bound to apply the whole income and eventually pay over or apply the whole capital to Mrs. Aspinall and the three children or some or one of them. So far as the income is concerned they are obliged to pay it or apply it for her benefit or to pay it or apply it for the benefit of the children. So far as regards the capital they have a discretion to pay it and to apply it for her benefit and subject to that, they must hold it upon trust for the children. Mrs. Aspinall, the two surviving children and the representatives of the deceased child are between them entitled to the whole fund. In those circumstances it appears to me, notwithstanding the discretion which is reposed in the trustees, under which discretion they could select one or more of the people I have mentioned as recipients of the income, and might apply part of the capital for the benefit of Mrs. Aspinall and so take it away from the children, that the four of them, if they were all living, could come to the Court and say to the trustees: 'Hand over the fund to us.' It appears to me that that is in accordance with the decision of the Court of Appeal in a case of *Re Nelson* [1928] Ch 920n, of which a transcript of the judgments has been handed to me, and is in accordance with principle. What is the principle? As I understand it it is this. Where there is a trust under which trustees have a discretion as to applying the whole or part of a fund to or for the benefit of a particular person, that particular person cannot come to the trustees and demand the fund; for the whole fund has not been given to him but only so much as the trustees think fit to let him have. But when the trustees have no discretion as to the amount of the fund to be applied, the fact that the trustees have a discretion as to the method in which the whole of the fund shall be applied for the benefit of the particular person does not prevent that particular person from coming and saying: 'Hand over the fund to me.' That appears to be the result of the two cases which were cited to me: *Green v Spicer* (1830) 1 Russ & M 395 and *Younghusband v Gisborne* (1844) 1 Coll 400.

Now this third case arises. What is to happen where the trustees have a discretion whether they will apply the whole or only a portion of the fund for the benefit of one person, but are obliged to apply the rest of the fund, so far as not applied for the benefit of the first named person, to or for the benefit of a second named person? There, two people together are the sole objects of the discretionary trust and, between them, are entitled to have the whole fund applied to them or for their benefit. It has been laid down by the Court of Appeal in the case to which I have referred that, in such a case as that you treat all the people put together just as though they formed one person, for whose benefit the trustees were directed to apply the whole of a particular fund. The case before the Court of Appeal was this: A testator had directed his trustees to stand possessed of one-third of his residuary estate upon trust during the lifetime of the testator's son Arthur Hector Nelson: 'to apply the income thereof for the benefit of himself and his wife and child or children or of any such persons to the exclusion of the others or other of them as my trustees shall think fit.' What happened was something very similar to what happened in the case before me. Hector Nelson, his wife and the only existing child of the marriage joined together in asking the trustees to hand over the income to them, and it was held by the Court of Appeal that the trustees were obliged to comply with the request, in other words, to treat all those persons who were the only members of the class for whose benefit the income could be applied as forming together an individual for whose benefit a fund has to be applied by the trustees without any discretion as to the amount so to be applied."

iii. Certainty

In the past twenty-five years, important changes have been made in the rules relating to the certainty of identification of objects of a power and beneficiaries of a trust. Certainty in relation to beneficiaries of a trust is dealt with below;[5] and it will there be seen that the rule laid down in *Re Gulbenkian's Settlements* [1970] AC 508, [1968] 3 All ER 785 in relation to powers, has been adopted in the case of discretionary trusts; but not for fixed trusts. Here we are concerned only with the development of the rule relating to powers.

In **Re Gulbenkian's Settlements** [1970] AC 508, [1968] 3 All ER 785, a settlement contained a power to appoint in favour of Nubar Gulbenkian any wife and his children or remoter issue ... and any person ... in whose house or apartments or in whose company or under whose care or control or by or with whom [he] may from time to time be employed or residing." The question was whether the power was void for uncertainty. In was unanimously upheld by the House of Lords. A power is valid if it could be said with certainty whether any given individual was or was not a member of the class. Lord UPJOHN said at 523, at 791:

"In my opinion, this clause is not void for uncertainty, and the Court of Appeal were quite right to overrule the decision of Harman J in *Re Gresham's*

---

5 See p. 70, post.

Settlement [1956] 1 WLR 573, [1956] 2 All ER 193, where he held a similar clause was void on that ground.

My Lords, that is sufficient to dispose of the appeal, but, as I have mentioned earlier, the reasons of two members of the Court of Appeal went further and have been supported by counsel for the respondents with much force and so must be examined.

The Master of the Rolls [1968] Ch 126 at 134E, [1967] 3 All ER 15 at 18, propounded a test in the case of powers collateral, namely, that if you can say of one particular person meaning thereby, apparently, any one person only that he is clearly within the category the whole power is good though it may be difficult to say in other cases whether a person is or is not within the category, and he supported that view by reference to authority. Winn LJ at 138E, at 21 said that where there was not a complete failure by reason of ambiguity and uncertainty the court would give effect to the power as valid rather than hold it defeated since it will have wholly failed, which put — though more broadly — the view expressed by the Master of the Rolls. Counsel for the respondents in his second line of argument relied upon these observations as a matter of principle but he candidly admitted that he could not rely upon any authority. Moreover, the Master of the Rolls at 133B, at 18, expressed the view that the different doctrine with regard to trust powers should be brought into line with the rule with regard to conditions precedent and powers collateral ...

But with respect to mere powers, while the court cannot compel the trustees to exercise their powers, yet those entitled to the fund in default must clearly be entitled to restrain the trustees from exercising it save among those within the power. So the trustees or the court must be able to say with certainty who is within and who is without the power. It is for this reason that I find myself unable to accept the broader proposition advanced by Lord Denning MR and Winn LJ mentioned earlier, and agree with the proposition as enunciated in *Re Gestetner Settlement* [1953] Ch 672, [1953] 1 All ER 1150 and the later cases.''

In **Re Hay's Settlement Trusts** [1982] 1 WLR 202, [1981] 3 All ER 786,[6] under clause 4 of a settlement made in 1958, trustees held the trust fund "for such persons or purposes as the trustees shall by deed ... executed within 21 years from the date hereof appoint." The trustees were prohibited from appointing the settlor, her husband or any past or present trustee.

During the first five years any undisposed of income was to be accumulated and capitalised. Thereafter the income was to be held on a discretionary trust, until the power was exercised or exhausted (whichever was the first to occur).

In 1969 the trustees purported to exercise their power under clause 4 by a deed of appointment. Clause 1 of the deed of appointment gave to the trustees power to hold the fund "for such ... persons and such purposes as shall be appointed", and clause 2 divided the undisposed of income to be held on an intermediate discretionary trust, similar to the power in clause 4 of the settlement, "for the benefit of any ... persons whatsoever (the settlor, her husband or any past or present trustee excepted) as the trustees shall appoint."

6 [1982] Conv 432 (A. Grubb).

Sir Robert MEGARRY V-C held that the intermediate power to appoint under clause 4 of the 1958 settlement was valid, but that the discretionary trust of income created under clause 2 of the 1969 deed of appointment was void. He said at 207, at 791:

"The starting point must be to consider whether the power created by the first limb of clause 4 of the settlement is valid. The essential point is whether a power for trustees to appoint to anyone in the world except a handful of specified persons is valid. Such a power will be perfectly valid if given to a person who is not in a fiduciary position: the difficulty arises when it is given to trustees, for they are under certain fiduciary duties in relation to the power, and to a limited degree they are subject to the control of the courts. At the centre of the dispute there are *Re Manisty's Settlement* [1974] Ch 17, [1973] 2 All ER 1203 (in which Templeman J differed from part of what was said in the Court of Appeal in *Blausten v IRC* [1972] Ch 256, [1972] 1 All ER 41), *McPhail v Doulton* [1971] AC 424, [1970] 2 All ER 228 (which I shall call *Re Baden (No 1)*) and *Re Baden's Deed Trusts (No 2)* [1973] Ch 9, [1972] 2 All ER 1304 (which I shall call *Re Baden (No 2)*).[7] Mr. Child, I may say, strongly contended that *Re Manisty's Settlement* was wrongly decided.

In *Re Manisty's Settlement* [1974] Ch 17, [1973] 2 All ER 1203,[8] a settlement gave trustees a discretionary power to apply the trust fund for the benefit of a small class of the settlor's near relations, save that any member of a smaller 'excepted class' was to be excluded from the class of beneficiaries. The trustees were also given power at their absolute discretion to declare that any person, corporation or charity (except a member of the excepted class or a trustee) should be included in the class of beneficiaries. Templeman J held that this power to extend the class of beneficiaries was valid.

In *Blausten v IRC* [1972] Ch 256, [1972] 1 All ER 41, which had been decided some 18 months earlier, the settlement created a discretionary trust of income for members of a 'specified class' and a power to pay or apply capital to be held on trust for them. The settlement also gave the trustees power 'with the previous consent in writing of the settlor' (at 272, at 49) to appoint any other person or persons (except the settlor) to be included in the 'specified class'. The Court of Appeal decided the case on a point of construction; but Buckley LJ, at 271, at 49, also considered a contention that the trustees' power to add to the 'specified class' was so wide that it was bad for uncertainty, since the power would enable anyone in the world save the settlor to be included. He rejected this contention on the ground that the settlor's prior written consent was requisite to any addition to the 'specified class'; but for this, it seems plain that he would have held the power void for uncertainty. Orr LJ, at 274, at 51, simply concurred, but Salmon LJ, at 274, at 51, expressly confined himself to the point of construction, and said nothing about the power to add to the 'specified class'. In *Re Manisty's Settlement* [1974] Ch 17 at 29, [1973] 2 All ER 1203 at 1213, Templeman J rejected the view of Buckley LJ on this point on the ground that *Re Gestetner Settlement* [1953] Ch 672, [1953] 1 All ER 1150; *Re Gulbenkian's Settlements* [1970] AC 508, [1968] 3 All ER 785 and the two *Baden* cases did not appear to have been fully explored in the *Blausten* case, and the case did not involve any final pronouncement on the point. In general I respectfully agree with Templeman J.

---

7 For *Re Baden (No 1)* and *Re Baden (No 2)*, see pp. 70–87, post.
8 (1973) 37 Conv NS 355 (F.R. Crane); [1974] CLJ 66 (J.A. Hopkins).

I propose to approach the matter by stages. First, it is plain that if a power of appointment is given to a person who is not in a fiduciary position, there is nothing in the width of the power which invalidates it per se. The power may be a special power with a large class of persons as objects; the power may be what is called a 'hybrid' power, or an 'intermediate' power, authorising appointment to anyone save a specified number or class of persons; or the power may be a general power. Whichever it is, there is nothing in the number of persons to whom an appointment may be made which will invalidate it. The difficulty comes when the power is given to trustees as such, in that the number of objects may interact with the fiduciary duties of the trustees and their control by the court. Mr. Child's argument carried him to the extent of asserting that no valid intermediate or general power could be vested in trustees.

That brings me to the second point, namely, the extent of the fiduciary obligations of trustees who have a mere power vested in them, and how far the court exercises control over them in relation to that power. In the case of a trust, of course, the trustee is bound to execute it, and if he does not, the court will see to its execution. A mere power is very different. Normally the trustee is not bound to exercise it, and the court will not compel him to do so. That, however, does not mean that he can simply fold his hands and ignore it, for normally he must from time to time consider whether or not to exercise the power, and the court may direct him to do this.

When he does exercise the power, he must, of course (as in the case of all trusts and powers) confine himself to what is authorised, and not go beyond it. But that is not the only restriction. Whereas a person who is not in a fiduciary position is free to exercise the power in any way that he wishes, unhampered by any fiduciary duties, a trustee to whom, as such, a power is given is bound by the duties of his office in exercising that power to do so in a responsible manner according to its purpose. It is not enough for him to refrain from acting capriciously; he must do more. He must 'make such a survey of the range of objects or possible beneficiaries . . . ' as will enable him to carry out his fiduciary duty. He must find out 'the permissible area of selection and then consider responsibly, in individual cases, whether a contemplated beneficiary was within the power and whether, in relation to other possible claimants, a particular grant was appropriate': *Re Baden (No 1)* [1971] AC 424, at 449, 457, [1970] 2 All ER 228 at 240, 247, per Lord Wilberforce . . .[9]

That brings me to the third point. How is the duty of making a responsible survey and selection to be carried out in the absence of any complete list of objects? This question was considered by the Court of Appeal in *Re Baden (No 2)* [1973] Ch 9, [1972] 2 All ER 1304. That case was concerned with what, after some divergencies of judicial opinion, was held to be a discretionary trust and not a mere power, but plainly the requirements for a mere power cannot be more stringent than those for a discretionary trust. The duty, I think, may be expressed along the following lines: I venture a modest degree of amplification and exegesis of what was said on pp. 20, 27, pp. 1310, 1315. The trustee must not simply proceed to exercise the power in favour of such of the objects as happen to be at hand or claim his attention. He must first consider what persons or classes of persons are objects of the power within the definition in the settlement or will. In doing this, there is no need to compile a complete list

---

9 See also *Vestey v IRC (No 2)* [1979] Ch 198 at 205–206, [1979] 2 All ER 225 at 235–236, per WALTON J; *Turner v Turner* [1984] Ch 100, [1983] 2 All ER 745, p. 44, post.

of the objects, or even to make an accurate assessment of the number of them: what is needed is an appreciation of the width of the field, and thus whether a selection is to be made merely from a dozen or, instead, from thousands or millions ... Only when the trustee has applied his mind to 'the size of the problem' should he then consider in individual cases whether in relation to other possible claimants, a particular grant is appropriate. In doing this, no doubt he should not prefer the undeserving to the deserving; but he is not required to make an exact calculation whether, as between deserving claimants, A is more deserving than B: see *Re Gestetner Settlement* [1953] Ch 672 at 688, [1953] 1 All ER 1150 at 1155, approved in *Re Baden (No 1)* [1971] AC 424 at 453, [1970] 2 All ER 228 at 243–244.

If I am right in these views, the duties of a trustee which are specific to a mere power seem to be threefold. Apart from the obvious duty of obeying the trust instrument, and in particular of making no appointment that is not authorised by it, the trustee must, first, consider periodically whether or not he should exercise the power; second, consider the range of objects of the power; and third, consider the appropriateness of individual appointments. I do not assert that this list is exhaustive; but as the authorities stand it seems to me to include the essentials, so far as relevant to the case before me ....

On this footing, the question is thus whether there is something in the nature of an intermediate power which conflicts with these duties in such a way as to invalidate the power if it is vested in a trustee. The case that there is rests in the main on *Blausten v IRC* [1972] Ch 256, [1972] 1 All ER 41, which I have already summarised. The power there was plainly a mere power, and it authorised the trustees, with the settlor's previous consent in writing, to add any other person or persons (except the settlor) to the specified class.

In that case Buckley LJ referred to the power as being one the exercise of which the trustees were under a duty to consider from time to time, and said, at 272, at 50:

'If the class of persons to whose possible claims they would have to give consideration were so wide that it really did not amount to a class in any true sense at all no doubt that would be a duty which it would be impossible for them to perform and the power could be said to be invalid on that ground. But here, although they may introduce to the specified class any other person or persons except the settlor, the power is one which can only be exercised with the previous consent in writing of the settlor ...

Therefore on analysis the power is not a power to introduce anyone in the world to the specified class, but only anyone proposed by the trustees and approved by the settlor. This is not a case in which it could be said that the settlor in this respect has not set any metes and bounds to the beneficial interests which he intended to create or permit to be created under this settlement.'

After referring to *Re Park* [1932] 1 Ch 580 at 583, Buckley LJ went on, at 273, at 50:

' ... this is not a power which suffers from the sort of uncertainty which results from the trustees being given a power of so wide an extent that it would be impossible for the court to say whether or not they were properly exercising it and so wide that it would be impossible for the trustees to consider in any sensible manner how they should exercise it, if at all, from time to time. The trustees would, no doubt, take into consideration the possible claims of anyone having any claim upon the beneficence of the settlor. That is not a class of persons so wide or so indefinite that the trustees would not be able rationally to exercise their duty to consider from time to time whether or not they should exercise the power.'

It seems quite plain that Buckley LJ considered that the power was saved from invalidity only by the requirement for the consent of the settlor. The reason for saying that in the absence of such a requirement the power would have been invalid seems to be twofold. First, the class of persons to whose possible claims the trustees would be duty-bound to give consideration was so wide as not to form a trust class, and this would make it impossible for the trustees to perform their duty of considering from time to time whether to exercise the power.

I feel considerable difficulty in accepting this view. First, I do not see how mere numbers can inhibit the trustees from considering whether or not to exercise the power, as distinct from deciding in whose favour to exercise it. Second, I cannot see how the requirement of the settlor's consent will result in any 'class' being narrowed from one that is too wide to one that is small enough. Such a requirement makes no difference whatever to the number of persons potentially included: the only exclusion is still the settlor. Thirdly, in any case I cannot see how the requirement of the settlor's consent could make it possible to treat 'anyone in the world save X' as constituting any real sort of a 'class', as that term is usually understood.

The second ground of invalidity if there is no requirement for the settlor's consent seems to be that the power is so wide that it would be impossible for the trustees to consider in any sensible manner how to exercise it, and also impossible for the court to say whether or not they were properly exercising it. With respect, I do not see how that follows. If I have correctly stated the extent of the duties of trustees in whom a mere power is vested, I do not see what there is to prevent the trustees from performing these duties. It must be remembered that Buckley LJ, though speaking after *Re Gulbenkian's Settlements* [1970] AC 508, [1968] 3 All ER 785 and *Re Baden (No 1)* [1971] AC 424, [1970] 2 All ER 228 had been decided, lacked the advantage of considering *Re Baden (No 2)* [1973] Ch 9, [1972] 2 All ER 1304, which was not decided until some five months later. He thus did not have before him the explanation in that case of how the trustees should make a survey and consider individual appointments in cases where no complete list of objects could be compiled. I also have in mind that the settlor in the present case is still alive, though I do not rest my decision on that.

From what I have said it will be seen that I cannot see any ground upon which the power in question can be said to be void. Certainly it is not void for linguistic or semantic uncertainty; there is no room for doubt in the definition of those who are or are not objects of the power. Nor can I see that the power is administratively unworkable. The words of Lord Wilberforce in *Re Baden (No 1)* at 457, at 247 are directed to discretionary trusts, not powers. Nor do I think that the power is void as being capricious. In *Re Manisty's Settlement* [1974] Ch 17 at 27, [1973] 2 All ER 1203 at 1211, Templeman J appears to be suggesting that a power to benefit 'residents of Greater London' is void as being capricious 'because the terms of the power negative any sensible intention on the part of the settlor.' In saying that, I do not think that the judge had in mind a case in which the settlor was, for instance, a former chairman of the Greater London Council, as subsequent words of his on that page indicate. In any case, as he pointed out earlier in the page, this consideration does not apply to intermediate powers, where no class which could be regarded as capricious has been laid down. Nor do I see how the power in the present case could be invalidated as being too vague, a possible ground of invalidity considered in *Re Manisty's Settlement*, at 24, at 1208. Of course, if there is some real vice in a power, and there are real problems of administration or execution, the court may have to hold the power invalid: but I think that the court should be slow to do this. Dispositions ought if possible to be upheld, and the court ought not to be astute to find grounds upon which a power can be invalidated. Naturally, if it is shown that a power offends against some rule of law or equity, then it will be held to be void: but a power should not be held void upon a peradventure. In my judgment, the power conferred by clause 4 of the settlement is valid.

With that, I turn to the discretionary trust of income under clause 2 of the deed of appointment.

[His Lordship held that this discretionary trust of income was void as an excessive execution of the power since trustees cannot delegate their powers unless authorised (p. 745, post), and continued:]

That, I think, suffices to dispose of the case. I have not dealt with the submission which Mr. Child put in the forefront of his argument. This was that even if the power had been wide enough to authorise the creation of the discretionary trust, that trust was nevertheless bad as being a trust in favour of 'so hopelessly wide' a definition of beneficiaries 'as not to form "anything like a class" so that the trust is administratively unworkable': see *Re Baden (No 1)* at 457, at 247 per Lord Wilberforce. I do not propose to go into the authorities on this point. I consider that the duties of trustees under a discretionary trust are more stringent that those of trustees under a power of appointment (see, for example, *Re Baden (No 1)* at 457, at 247), and as at present advised I think that I would, if necessary, hold that an intermediate trust such as that in the present case is void as being administratively unworkable. In my view there is a difference between a power and a trust in this respect. The essence of that difference, I think, is that beneficiaries under a trust have rights of enforcement which mere objects of a power lack. But in this difficult branch of the law I consider that I should refrain from exploring without good reason any matters which do not have to be decided."

In **Turner v Turner** [1984] Ch 100, [1983] 2 All ER 745, three appointments made by family trustees under a fiduciary power were held void. MERVYN DAVIES J said at 106, at 749:

"The question is whether or not the trustees so far failed to direct their minds to the matter of their discretionary powers of appointment that the deeds of appointment ought not to be regarded as an exercise of the powers of appointment. To see such a question asked is at first sight surprising but the evidence given in this case shows good reason for it . . . It is quite clear from the correspondence that the trustees were no more than ciphers.

[His Lordship quoted from MEGARRY V-C in *Re Hay's Settlement Trusts* [1982] 1 WLR 202 at 209, [1981] 3 All ER 786 at 792, p. 39 ante, and continued:]

Accordingly the trustees exercising a power come under a duty to consider. It is plain on the evidence that here the trustees did not in any way 'consider' in the course of signing the three deeds in question. They did not know they had any discretion during the settlor's lifetime, they did not read or understand the effect of the documents they were signing and what they were doing was not preceded by any decision. They merely signed when requested. The trustees

therefore made the appointments in breach of their duty, in that it was their duty to 'consider' before appointing, and this they did not do . . . .
[His Lordship referred to *Pilkington v IRC* [1964] AC 612, [1962] 3 All ER 622, p 772, post; *Re Abrahams' Will Trusts* [1969] 1 Ch 463, [1967] 2 All ER 1175, and continued:]
The authorities I have mentioned, including *Re Hastings-Bass* [1975] Ch 25, [1974] 2 All ER 193, permit the inference that, in a clear case on the facts, the court can put aside the purported exercise of a fiduciary power, if satisfied that the trustees never applied their minds at all to the exercise of the discretion entrusted to them. If appointors fail altogether to exercise the duties of consideration referred to by Sir Robert Megarry V-C then there is no exercise of the power and the purported appointment is a nullity. Applying those principles to this case I am satisfied on the evidence that all three purported appointments ought to be set aside.''

iv. INTERVENTION OF THE COURT

METTOY PENSION TRUSTEES LTD v EVANS[10]
[1990] 1 WLR 1587, [1991] 2 All ER 513 (Ch D, WARNER J)

Mettoy Company Plc, whose main business was the manufacture of "Corgi" toys at Swansea, set up a pension fund for its employees. Under rule 13(5) the company had a power of appointment in favour of the pensioners, with a gift over to itself in default of appointment. A separate trustee company was trustee of the fund. The company went into liquidation with a substantial surplus in the fund. The main question was whether the liquidator could release the power and thus secure the surplus for the general creditors.
Held. The liquidator could not. (i) The power was fiduciary; (ii) it could not be released by the liquidator because he would be in a position where his duty and interest conflicted;[11] and (iii) the court could intervene to protect the pensioners.
WARNER J: Mr. Walker suggested a classification, which I accept, of fiduciary discretions into four categories. In this classification, category 1 comprises any power given to a person to determine the destination of trust property without that person being under any obligation to exercise the power or to preserve it. Typical of powers in this category is a special power of appointment given to an individual where there is a trust in default of appointment. In such a case the donee of the power owes a duty to the beneficiaries under that trust not to misuse the power, but he owes no duty to the objects of the power. He may therefore release the power but he may not enter into any transaction that would amount to a fraud on the power, a fraud on the power being a wrong committed against the beneficiaries under the trust in default of appointment: see *Re Mills* [1930] 1 Ch 654 and *Re Greaves* [1954] Ch 434, [1954] 1 All ER 771. It seems to me to follow that, where the donee of the power is the only person entitled under the trust in default of appointment, the power is not a fiduciary power at all, because then the donee owes no duty to anyone. That was the position in *Re Mills* [1930] 1 Ch 654 and will be the position here if the

---

10 [1991] Conv 364 (J.E. Martin); [1991] All ER Rev 203 (P.J. Clarke); (1991) 106 LQR 214 (S. Gardner); (1990) 53 MLR 377 (R. Nobles).
11 See Social Security Act 1990, Sched. 4. para. 1.

discretion in the last paragraph of rule 13(5) of the 1983 rules is in category 1. Category 2 comprises any power conferred on the trustees of the property or on any other person as a trustee of the power itself: per Romer LJ, at p. 669. I will, as Chitty J did in *Re Somes* [1896] 1 Ch 250, 255, call a power in this category "a fiduciary power in the full sense." Mr. Walker suggested as an example of such powers vested in persons other than the trustees of the property the powers of the managers of a unit trust. A power in this category cannot be released: the donee of it owes a duty to the objects of the power to consider, as and when may be appropriate, whether and if so how he ought to exercise it: and he is to some extent subject to the control of the courts in relation to its exercise: see, for instance, *Re Abrahams' Will Trusts* [1969] 1 Ch 463, 474, [1967] 2 All ER 1175, 1183–1184, per Cross J; *Re Manisty's Settlement* [1974] Ch 17, 24, [1973] 2 All ER 1203, 1209, p. 40 ante, per Templeman J; and *Re Hay's Settlement Trusts* [1982] 1 WLR 202, 210, [1981] 3 All ER 786, p. 39 ante, per Sir Robert Megarry V-C. Category 3 comprises any discretion which is really a duty to form a judgment as to the existence or otherwise of particular circumstances giving rise to particular consequences. Into this category fall the discretions that were in question in such cases as *Weller v Kerr* (1866) LR 1 Sc & Div 11; *Dundee General Hospitals Board of Management v Walker* [1952] 1 All ER 896 and the two cases reported by Lexis that I have already mentioned, namely *Kerr v British Leyland (Staff) Trustees Ltd* CA Transcript 286 and *Mihlenstedt v Barclays Bank International Ltd* [1989] IRLR 522. Category 4 comprises discretionary trusts, that is to say cases where someone, usually but not necessarily the trustees, is under a duty to select from among a class of beneficiaries those who are to receive, and the proportions in which they are to receive, income or capital of the trust property. Mr Walker urged me to eschew the phrases "trust power," "power coupled with a duty," "power coupled with a trust" and "power in the nature of a trust," which, as he demonstrated by means of an impressive survey of reported cases, have been variously used to describe discretions in categories 2, 3 and 4.

In the present case the question is whether the discretion given to the employer by the last paragraph of rule 13(5) of the 1983 rules is in category 1 or category 2.

I have come to the conclusion that the discretion conferred on the employer by the last paragraph of rule 13(5) of the 1983 rules is a fiduciary power in the full sense. The considerations that have led me to that conclusion are these. If that discretion is not such a fiduciary power it is, from the point of view of the beneficiaries under the scheme, illusory. As I have pointed out, the words conferring the power mean no more, on that construction of them, than that the employer is free to make gifts to those beneficiaries out of property of which it is the absolute beneficial owner, so that at best those words amount to what Hutchison J in *El Awadi v Bank of Credit and Commerce International SA Ltd* [1990] 1 QB 606, 617, [1989] 1 All ER 242, 248 called "a true but pointless assertion." The *Courage Group* case [1987] 1 WLR 495, [1987] 1 All ER 528, illustrates one possible consequence of the discretion being of that nature. If the employer were acquired by a take-over raider (to use Millet J's expression in that case) there would be nothing whatever to prevent that raider from rendering itself entitled to the entire surplus. On the simple cesser of the employer's business at a time when the employer was solvent, the position would be governed (in 1983) by the principle of *Parke v Daily News Ltd* [1962] Ch 927, [1962] 2 All ER 929 as modified by section 74 of the Companies Act 1980. The exercise of the discretion would accordingly in general require the

R.T.C.
LETTER...NY

approval of a resolution of the shareholders, and it is doubtful if such a resolution could approve its exercise in favour of beneficiaries other than employees or former employees, for instance their widows. If, as has happened in this case, the employer should become insolvent, the discretion would inevitably not be exercised, because it would become exercisable on behalf of the employer by someone, be he receiver or liquidator, whose duties to creditors required him to refrain from exercising it. . . .

The question then arises, if the discretion is a fiduciary power which cannot be exercised either by the receivers or by the liquidator, who is to exercise it? I heard submissions on that point. The discretion cannot be exercised by the directors of the company, because on the appointment of the liquidator all the powers of the directors ceased. I was referred to a number of authorities on the circumstances in which the court may interfere with or give directions as to the exercise of discretions vested in trustees, namely *Gisborne v Gisborne* (1877) 2 App Cas 300; *Re Hodges* (1878) 7 Ch D 754; *Tabor v Brooks* (1878) 10 Ch D 273; *Klug v Klug* [1918] 2 Ch 67; *Re Allen-Meyrick's Will Trusts* [1966] 1 WLR 499, [1966] 1 All ER 740; *McPhail v Doulton* [1971] AC 424, [1970] 2 All ER 228; p. 71 post; *Re Manisty's Settlement* [1974] Ch 17, 25–26, [1973] 2 All ER 1203, 1209–1211; and *Re Locker's Settlement* [1977] 1 WLR 1323, [1978] 1 All ER 216, p. 78. n. 10, post. None of those cases deals directly with a situation in which a fiduciary power is left with no one to exercise it. They point however to the conclusion that in that situation the court must step in. Mr. Inglis-Jones and Mr. Walker urged me to say that in this case the court should step in by giving directions to the trustees as to the distribution of the surplus in the pension fund. They relied in particular on the passage in *McPhail v Doulton*, where Lord Wilberforce said: at 456, 457, at 247, "As to powers, I agree with my noble and learned friend Lord Upjohn in *Re Gulbenkian's Settlements* [1970] AC 508, [1968] 3 All ER 785, p. 38 ante, that although the trustees may, and normally will, be under a fiduciary duty to consider whether or in what way they should exercise their power, the court will not normally compel its exercise. It will intervene if the trustees exceed their powers, and possibly if they are proved to have exercised it capriciously. But in the case of a trust power, if the trustees do not exercise it, the court will: I respectfully adopt as to this the statement in Lord Upjohn's opinion (at 525, at 793). I would venture to amplify this by saying that the court, if called upon to execute the trust power, will do so in the manner best calculated to give effect to the settlor's or testator's intentions. It may do so by appointing new trustees, or by authorising or directing representative persons of the classes of beneficiaries to prepare a scheme of distribution, or even, should the proper basis for distribution appear by itself directing the trustees so to distribute. The books give many instances where this has been done, and I see no reason in principle why they should not do so in the modern field of discretionary trusts."

Clearly, in the first two sentences of that passage Lord Wilberforce was referring to a discretion in category 2 and in the following part of it to a discretion in category 4. In that latter part he was indicating how the court might give effect to a discretionary trust when called on to execute it. It seems to me however that the methods he indicated could be equally appropriate in a case where the court was called on to intervene in the exercise of a discretion in category 2. In saying that, I do not overlook that, in *Re Manisty's Settlement* [1974] Ch 17, 25, [1973] 2 All ER 1203, 1210. Templeman J expressed the view that the only right and the only remedy of an object of the power who was aggrieved by the trustees' conduct would be to apply to the court to remove the trustees and appoint others in their place. However, the earlier authorities to which I was referred, such as *Re Hodges* (1878) 7 Ch D 754 and *Klug v Klug* [1918] 2 Ch 67, had not been cited to Templeman J. I conclude that, in a situation such as this, it is open to the court to adopt whichever of the methods indicated by Lord Wilberforce appears most appropriate in the circumstances.

That brings me back to the question what should be done about its exercise, a question which I dealt with in part earlier, when I concluded that the court could adopt any of the methods indicated by Lord Wilberforce in *McPhail v Doulton* [1971] AC 424, 457, [1970] 2 All ER 228, 247. No one suggests that I should, in this case, appoint new trustees. So the question is what directions I should give under paragraph (3) of the originating summons. That is a question on which, as I mentioned earlier, I have heard some evidence, particularly evidence from the actuaries, but on which further evidence will be necessary, and on which I have heard no submissions. When counsel have had an opportunity of considering my judgment, I will hear them as to the form of the order I should make at this stage.

[1991] Conv 364, at 365–366 (J E Martin)

"Previous authorities have suggested that the only way the court can intervene in the case of a power is by the appointment of new trustees.[12] This, for some reason, has not been requested in the present case.[13] In upholding the possibility of a more positive intervention, Warner J relied on *Klug v Klug*,[14] where the court in effect directed the exercise of the power of advancement. The appropriate manner of intervention in the present case was deferred until further evidence and submissions had been heard."

G. Where the Crown is Trustee[15]

In considering the use of the term "trust" in relation to the Crown, Lord SELBORNE LC said in **Kinloch v Secretary of State for India** (1882) 7 App Cas 619 at 625:

"Now the words 'in trust for' are quite consistent with, and indeed are the proper manner of expressing, every species of trust — a trust not only as regards those matters which are the proper subjects for an equitable jurisdiction to administer, but as respects higher matters, such as might take place between the Crown and public officers discharging, under the directions of the Crown, duties or functions belonging to the prerogative and to the

12 See *Re Manisty's Settlement* [1974] Ch 17, [1973] 2 All ER 1203.
13 See (1991) 107 LQR 214 (S. Gardner), suggesting that the trustee company was the obvious substitute, and that this would have been the most appropriate means of intervention. Gardner also suggests that one result of the assimilation of remedies might be that "administrative unworkability" now applies to fiduciary powers as well as to discretionary trusts. There would have been no problem in *Mettoy* itself because the class of pensioners would not give rise to difficulty under this principle.
14 [1918] 2 Ch 67, not cited in *Re Manisty's Settlement*, supra. But see (1991) 107 LQR 214 (S. Gardner), where it is considered that the older cases relied on, such as *Klug*, do not give great support to the judicial exercise of fiduciary discretions.
15 H & M, pp. 73–74; Underhill, p. 5.

authority of the Crown. In the lower sense they are matters within the jurisdiction of, and to be administered by, the ordinary courts of equity; in the higher sense they are not. What their sense is here, is the question to be determined, looking at the whole instrument and its nature and effect."

And Lord DIPLOCK in **Town Investments Ltd v Department of the Environment** [1978] AC 359 at 382, [1977] 1 All ER 813 at 819:

"My Lords, I would not exclude the possibility that an officer of state, even though acting in his official capacity, may in some circumstances hold property subject to a trust in private law for the benefit of a subject; but clear words would be required to do this and, even where the person to be benefited is a subject, the use of the expression 'in trust' to describe the capacity in which the property is granted to an officer of state is not conclusive that a trust in private law was intended; for 'trust' is not a term of art in public law and when used in relation to matters which lie within the field of public law the words 'in trust' may do no more than indicate the existence of a duty owed to the Crown by the officer of state, as servant of the Crown, to deal with the property for the benefit of the subject for whom it is expressed to be held in trust, each duty being enforceable administratively by disciplinary sanctions and not otherwise: *Kinloch v Secretary of State for India* (1882) 7 App Cas 619, per Lord Selborne LC, at 625–626. But even if the legal relationship of trustee and cestui qui trust under a trust in private law is capable of existing between an officer of state in his official capacity and a subject, the concept of such relationship being capable of existing between him as trustee and the Crown as cestui qui trust is in my view wholly irreconcilable with the legal nature in public law of the relationship between the Crown and its servants or, in more modern parlance, the government and the ministers who form part of it."[16]

V. Recognition of Trusts by Non-Trust States[17]

The concept of a trust originated in England and followed the flag to all common law jurisdictions. Civil law states have never adopted trusts,[18] but the 1984 Hague Convention on the Law applicable to Trusts and their Recognition seeks to bring about international recognition of the concept. It does so by establishing uniform conflict of laws rules (reflecting those of England and Wales), which are to be applied by all signatories.[19] Accordingly, the trust concept is not introduced into the domestic law of non-trust states.

The Recognition of Trusts Act 1987 enabled the United Kingdom to ratify the Convention.

16 See also *Tito v Waddell (No 2)* [1977] Ch 106 at 210–226, [1977] 3 All ER 129 at 216–228, per MEGARRY V-C.
17 H&M, p.45; Pettit, pp. 20–21; Underhill, pp. 938–956; (1987) 36 ICLQ 260 (D.J. Hayton); (1987) 35 AJCL 307 (E. Gaillard and D. Trautman); (1987) 131 SJ 827 (T. Prime); (1987) 36 ICLQ 454 (A. Wallace); (1989) BTR 41, 65 (J.F. Avery Jones et al).
18 On the proposed new law of trusts in France, see [1992] Conv 407 (H. Dyson); Bérando, *Les Trusts Anglo-Saxon et le Droit Français* (1992). On Roman Law, see Johnston, *The Roman Law of Trusts* (1988).
19 The applicable law is set out in Chap II of the Convention.

RECOGNITION OF TRUSTS ACT 1987[20]

1. Applicable law and recognition of trusts — (1) The provisions of the Convention set out in the Schedule to this Act shall have the force of law in the United Kingdom.

(2) Those provisions shall, so far as applicable, have effect not only in relation to the trusts described in Articles 2 and 3 of the Convention but also in relation to any other trusts of property arising under the law of any part of the United Kingdom or by virtue of a judicial decision whether in the United Kingdom or elsewhere.

SCHEDULE

Section 1

CONVENTION ON THE LAW APPLICABLE TO TRUSTS AND ON THEIR
RECOGNITION

CHAPTER I — SCOPE

Article 1

This Convention specifies the law applicable to trusts and governs their recognition.

Article 2

For the purposes of this Convention, the term "trust" refers to the legal relationship created — inter vivos or on death — by a person, the settlor, when assets have been placed under the control of a trustee for the benefit of a beneficiary or for a specified purpose.

A trust has the following characteristics —
   (a) the assets constitute a separate fund and are not a part of the trustee's own estate;
   (b) title to the trust assets stands in the name of the trustee or in the name of another person on behalf of the trustee;
   (c) the trustee has the power and the duty, in respect of which he is accountable, to manage, employ or dispose of the assets in accordance with the terms of the trust and the special duties imposed upon him by law.

The reservation by the settlor of certain rights and powers, and the fact that the trustee may himself have rights as beneficiary, are not necessarily inconsistent with the existence of a trust.

Article 3

The Convention applies only to trusts created voluntarily and evidenced in writing.

CHAPTER III — RECOGNITION

Article 11

A trust created in accordance with the law specified by the preceding Chapter shall be recognised as a trust.

---

20 Recognition of Trusts Act 1987 (Overseas Territories) Order 1989 (SI 673).

Such recognition shall imply, as a minimum, that the trust property constitutes a separate fund, that the trustee may sue and be sued in his capacity as trustee, and that he may appear or act in this capacity before a notary or any person acting in an official capacity.

In so far as the law applicable to the trust requires or provides, such recognition shall imply in particular —

(a) that personal creditors of the trustee shall have no recourse against the trust assets;

(b) that the trust assets shall not form part of the trustee's estate upon his insolvency or bankruptcy;

(c) that the trust assets shall not form part of the matrimonial property of the trustee or his spouse nor part of the trustee's estate upon his death;

(d) that the trust assets may be recovered when the trustee, in breach of trust, has mingled trust assets with his own property or has alienated trust assets. However, the rights and obligations of any third party holder of the assets shall remain subject to the law determined by the choice of law rules of the forum.

Article 14

The Convention shall not prevent the application of rules of law more favourable to the recognition of trusts.

CHAPTER IV — GENERAL CLAUSES

Article 17

In the Convention the word 'law' means the rules of law in force in a State other than its rules of conflict of laws.[1]

Article 18

The provisions of the Convention may be disregarded when their application would be manifestly incompatible with public policy.

Article 22

The Convention applies to trusts regardless of the date on which they were created.

---

1 Thus excluding the doctrine of renvoi.

2. The Requirements of a Trust

The essential factor in the creation of a trust is a manifestation of an intention by the settlor to create a trust.

There are however other factors.

I. Formalities[1]

A. Inter Vivos

i. DECLARATION AND DISPOSITION

LAW OF PROPERTY ACT 1925
53. Instruments required to be in writing. — (1) Subject to the provisions hereinafter contained with respect to the creation of interests in land by parol—

> (b) a declaration of trust respecting any land or any interest therein[2] must be manifested and proved by some writing signed by some person who is able to declare such trust or by his will;

---

1 H & M, pp. 80–94; K & S, pp. 77–84; P & M, pp. 34–45; Pettit, pp. 77–89; Riddall, pp. 35–45; Snell, pp. 106–108; Underhill, pp. 205–219. The Law Commission intends to publish a Consultation Paper on Formalities in 1996: Sixth Programme of Law Reform (Law Com. No. 234), Item 7, p. 32.

2 Writing is not essential for trusts of pure personalty: *Re Kayford Ltd* [1975] 1 WLR 279, [1975] 1 All ER 604; *Paul v Constance* [1977] 1 WLR 527, [1977] 1 All ER 195.

(*c*) a disposition of an equitable interest or trust subsisting at the time of the disposition, must be in writing[3] signed by the person disposing of the same,[4] or by his agent thereunto lawfully authorised in writing or by will.

(2) This section does not affect the creation or operation of resulting, implied or constructive trusts.[5]

ii. METHODS OF DISPOSITION

It will be seen that the application of section 53 (1) (*c*) in different types of situation has been inconsistent.[6]

(*a*) *Assignment of Equitable Interest*

In **Re Danish Bacon Co Ltd Staff Pension Fund Trusts** [1971] 1 WLR 248, [1971] 1 All ER 486, an employee had the right to nominate a person to receive benefits due under the company's pension fund in the case of death before qualifying for a pension. An employee had, in the approved form, duly signed and witnessed, nominated his wife. He then, by letter to the company, changed the nomination. The question was whether, on the assumption that s.53 (1) (*c*) applied, the documents together could supply the necessary writing. MEGARRY J said at 254, at 492:

"I have been referred to no authority on the point relating to the words in section 53 (1) (*c*) which run 'a disposition . . . must be in writing . . . '; indeed, despite the riches of authority on this point under section 40, section 53 (1) (*c*) appears to be wholly barren. However, if a statutory requirement that a 'memorandum' shall be 'in writing' may be satisfied by two or more documents, I do not see why two or more documents should not satisfy the requirement that a 'disposition' shall be 'in writing'. True, section 40 (1) is merely directed to providing written evidence of a transaction,[7] whereas under section 53 (1) (*c*) (unlike section 53 (1) (*b*)) the matter is one not merely of evidence but of the disposition itself. Yet two documents are used in constituting a strict settlement of land or establishing a trust for sale of land, and there are well-established rules for the incorporation of documents in a will; and if two or more documents, when read together, dispose of an equitable interest, I do not see why the court should insist on separating them and subjecting each separately to the test of section 53 (1) (*c*)."[8]

---

3 The writing need not contain details of the trust where the assignee is to hold in a fiduciary capacity: *Re Tyler* [1967] 1 WLR 1269, [1967] 3 All ER 389; see p. 60, post.

4 This may be satisfied by joinder of documents: *Re Danish Bacon Co Ltd Staff Pension Fund Trusts* [1971] 1 WLR 248, [1971] 1 All ER 486; see p. 61, post.

5 *Bannister v Bannister* [1948] 2 All ER 133; *Oughtred v IRC* [1960] AC 206, [1959] 3 All ER 623, see p. 57, post; *Hodgson v Marks* [1971] Ch 892, [1971] 2 All ER 684; (1971) 35 Conv (NS) 255, at 260–266 (I. Leeming); *Binions v Evans* [1972] Ch 359, [1972] 2 All ER 70; *Ottaway v Norman* [1972] Ch 698, [1971] 3 All ER 1325, p. 151, post.

6 See generally [1979] Conv 17; (1975) 7 Ottawa LR 483 (G. Battersby); (1984) 47 MLR 385 (B. Green).

7 See LR (Miscellaneous Provisions) Act 1989 s. 2, which repeals and replaces LPA 1925, s. 40 by a requirement that a contract for the sale or other disposition of land can *only* be made *in* writing; Cheshire and Burn, *Modern Law of Real Property* (15th edn), pp. 121–124.

8 See *Crowden v Aldridge* [1993] 1 WLR 433, [1993] 3 All ER 603.

(b)   Direction to Trustees to Hold on Trust for Another

In **Grey v Inland Revenue Commissioners** [1960] AC 1, [1959] 3 All ER 603,[9] the question was whether an instruction by a beneficiary to the trustees to hold upon different trusts was a "disposition" within Law of Property Act 1925, s. 53 (1) (*c*). As it was put in argument by Pennycuick QC at 4: "If X holds property in trust for A as absolute equitable owner and A then directs X to hold the property on the settlement of trusts for the benefit of B, C and D, and X accepts the trust, is that direction a 'disposition' of a subsisting equitable interest within the meaning of section 53?"

The settlor, Mr. Hunter, had made six settlements of nominal sums in favour of grandchildren. Subsequently he transferred substantial blocks of shares to the trustees, which they held on trust for him. Then he orally instructed the trustees to hold the shares upon the trusts of the six settlements. Finally, documents were executed in confirmation of the oral declaration, and these were executed by Mr. Hunter. The question was whether the trusts of the shares were created by the oral declaration or by the later documents.

Upon this depended the liability to stamp duty. Stamp duty is payable *ad valorem* upon a "conveyance on sale", which includes "every instrument ... whereby any property, or any estate or interest in any property, upon the sale thereof is transferred to or vested in a purchaser, or any other person on his behalf or by his direction".[10] Thus "the thing which is made liable to the duty is an 'instrument'. If a contract or purchase and sale, or conveyance by way of purchase and sale, can be, or is carried out without an instrument, the case is not within the section, and no tax is imposed. It is not the transaction of purchase and sale which is struck at; it is the instrument whereby the purchase and sale are effected which is struck at."[11]

Whether the trusts of the shares in *Grey v IRC* were created by the oral direction or by the later documents depended on whether the oral declaration was valid. It would be valid as an oral *declaration* of a trust of personalty; but not if it was a *disposition* of an equitable interest.

The House of Lords decided that it was a disposition. The equitable interest was to pass from Mr. Hunter to the beneficiaries. That "amounted in any ordinary sense of the words to a 'disposition of an equitable interest or trust subsisting at the time of the disposition,'" per Lord RADCLIFFE at 15, at 607. There was no necessity to construe the word "disposition" in the light of the language of the earlier Statute of Frauds, which dealt with "grants and assignments". The passing of the interest could only be effected by an instrument in writing. It was thus effected by the later document, and that document was liable to *ad valorem* stamp duty.[12]

(c)   Conveyance of Legal Estate by Nominee

In **Vandervell v Inland Revenue Commissioners** [1967] 2 AC 291, [1967] 1 All ER 1,[13] Vandervell decided to give to the Royal College of Surgeons sufficient money to endow a Chair of Pharmacology. This was to be done by transferring

9 [1960] CLJ 31 (J.W.A. Thornely).
10 Stamp Act 1891, s. 54.
11 Per Lord ESHER in *IRC v Angus* (1889) 23 QBD 579 at 589.
12 Followed by PC in *Baird v Baird* [1990] 2 AC 548, [1990] 2 All ER 300; [1990] Conv 458 (G. Kodilinye).
13 [1966] 24 CLJ 19 (G.H. Jones); (1967) 31 Conv (NS) 175 (S.M. Spencer); (1967) 30 MLR 461 (N. Strauss); *IRC v Hood Barrs (No 2)* (1963) 41 TC 339.

a holding of shares in Vandervell Products Ltd., which were vested in the National Provincial Bank Ltd. on trust for Vandervell, to the Royal College of Surgeons, and then declaring dividends on the shares, for which the Royal College would be free of liability to tax because it is a charity. An option to re-purchase the shares for £5,000 was given to Vandervell Trustees Ltd., a company which acted as trustee for the Vandervell family trusts. The Bank transferred the shares, and the dividends were declared.

The Revenue assessed Vandervell to surtax on the dividends on the ground that he had not absolutely divested himself of all interest in the shares.[14] This was upheld. Vandervell Trustees Ltd. held the option on a resulting trust for Vandervell. One argument for the Revenue was that the Bank had conveyed only the legal estate in the shares to the Royal College of Surgeons; the equitable interest remained in Vandervell because he had failed to effect its disposition in writing as required by s. 53 (1) (*c*). In rejecting this argument, Lord UPJOHN said at 311, at 7:

"[Section 53 (1) (*c*) was] applied in *Grey* [1960] AC 1, [1959] 3 All ER 603, p. 54 ante, and *Oughtred* [1960] AC 206, [1959] 3 All ER 623, p. 57 post, to cases where the legal estate remained outstanding in a trustee and the beneficial owner was dealing and dealing only with the equitable estate. That is understandable; the object of the section, as was the object of the old Statute of Frauds, is to prevent hidden oral transactions in equitable interests in fraud of those truly entitled, and making it difficult, if not impossible, for the trustees to ascertain who are in truth his beneficiaries. But when the beneficial owner owns the whole beneficial estate and is in a position to give directions to his bare trustee with regard to the legal as well as the equitable estate there can be no possible ground for invoking the section where the beneficial owner wants to deal with the legal estate as well as the equitable estate . . .

Counsel for the Crown admitted that where the legal and beneficial estate was vested in the legal owner and he desired to transfer the whole legal and beneficial estate to another he did not have to do more than transfer the legal estate and he did not have to comply with section 53 (1) (*c*); and I can see no relevant difference between that case and this."

(d) Declaration of Trust with Consent of Beneficial Owner

In 1961 Vandervell Trustees Ltd. exercised the option, taking £5,000 from the Vandervell children's settlement for the purpose. The Royal College of Surgeons transferred the shares to Vandervell Trustees Ltd. The Revenue made a further claim on the ground that Vandervell Trustees Ltd. had held the shares on trust for Vandervell. In 1965 Vandervell executed a deed, formally transferring to the children's settlement any right or interest which he might still have in the shares.

Vandervell having died, his estate sued Vandervell Trustees Ltd. for the return of the dividends paid on the shares since 1961. They succeeded before MEGARRY J, but failed in the Court of Appeal in **Re Vandervell's Trusts (No 2)** [1974] Ch 269, [1974] 3 All ER 205.[15] On the question of the way in which the equitable interest, previously enjoyed in the option, had left Vandervell, Lord DENNING said at 320, at 211:

"Mr Balcombe for the executors admitted that the intention of Mr. Vandervell and the trustee company was that the shares should be held on trust

---

14 See ITA 1952, s. 415; now ICTA 1988, ss. 684, 685; p. 556, post.
15 (1974) 38 Conv 405 (P.J. Clarke); (1975) 38 MLR 557 (J.W. Harris).

for the children's settlement. But he said that this intention was of no avail. He said that during the first period, Mr. Vandervell had an equitable interest in the property, namely, a resulting trust; that he never disposed of this equitable interest (because he never knew he had it): and that in any case it was the disposition of an equitable interest which, under section 53 of the Law of Property Act 1925, had to be in writing, signed by him or his agent, lawfully authorised by him in writing (and there was no such writing produced). He cited *Grey v IRC* [1960] AC 1, [1959] 3 All ER 603 and *Oughtred v IRC* [1960] AC 206, [1959] 3 All ER 623.

There is a complete fallacy in that argument. A resulting trust for the settlor is born and dies without any writing at all. It comes into existence whenever there is a gap in the beneficial ownership. It ceases to exist whenever that gap is filled by someone becoming beneficially entitled. As soon as the gap is filled by the creation or declaration of a valid trust, the resulting trust comes to an end. In this case, before the option was exercised, there was a gap in the beneficial ownership. So there was a resulting trust for Mr. Vandervell. But, as soon as the option was exercised and the shares registered in the trustees' name, there was created a valid trust of the shares in favour of the children's settlement. Not being a trust of land, it could be created without any writing. A trust of personalty can be created without writing. Both Mr Vandervell and the trustee company had done everything which needed to be done to make the settlement of these shares binding on them. So, there was a valid trust: see *Milroy v Lord* (1862) 4 De GF & J 264 at 274, per Turner LJ.''

But STEPHENSON LJ had doubts. He said at 322, at 213:

"To expound my doubts would serve no useful purpose; to state them shortly may do no harm. The cause of all the trouble is what the judge called [1974] Ch 269 at 298, [1974] 1 All ER 47 at 72, 'this ill-fated option' and its incorporation in a deed which was 'too short and simple' to rid Mr. Vandervell of the beneficial interest in the disputed shares, as a bare majority of the House of Lords held, not without fluctuation of mind on the part of one of them (Lord Upjohn), in *Vandervell v IRC* [1967] 2 AC 291 at 314–317, [1967] 1 All ER 1 at 9–11. The operation of law or equity kept for Mr. Vandervell or gave him back an equitable interest which he did not want and would have thought he had disposed of if he had ever known it existed. It is therefore difficult to infer that he intended to dispose or ever did dispose of something he did not know he had until the judgment of Plowman J in *Vandervell v IRC* [1966] Ch 261 at 273, which led to the deed of 1965, enlightened him, or to find a disposition of it in the exercise by the trustee company in 1961 of its option to purchase the shares. And even if he had disposed of his interest, he did not dispose of it by any writing sufficient to comply with section 53 (1) (*c*) of the Law of Property Act 1925.''

(e)   Declaration by Equitable Owner of Himself as Trustee

(1958) 74 LQR 180 at 182 (P.V.B.)

"Does a declaration of trust [by an equitable owner] operate to transfer the equitable interest from donor to donee? It is suggested that when the donor declares himself a trustee of his equitable interest, he retains his equitable interest but a subsidiary equitable interest becomes vested in the donee. He might well have active duties, if, for example, he had declared a discretionary trust. Trusts of equitable interests do not seem to have received much attention in this country but are well recognised on the other side of the Atlantic and referred to in *Scott on Trusts* (2nd edn, 1956), p. 645 as subtrusts. Thus the *Restatement of the Law of Trusts*, Vol. 1, s. 83 declares that 'an equitable interest, if transferable, can be held in trust' and gives the following illustration: 'A, the owner of a bond, declares himself a trustee of it for B. B declares himself a trustee for C of his interest in the bond. B is trustee for C of his equitable interest in the bond.' On the other hand, when the donor directs the trustees to hold property on trust for the donee, the donor does indeed disappear from the picture. Whether he says to the trustees, 'I assign my equitable interest to you to hold upon the trusts of the settlements,' so that it merges in the legal interest, or says more simply, 'I direct you to hold the property' upon such trusts, he has, it would seem, purported to assign or dispose of his equitable interest in the property, which he cannot do orally."[16]

(f)   Oral Contract for the Sale of Shares

OUGHTRED v INLAND REVENUE COMMISSIONERS
[1960] AC 206, [1959] 3 All ER 623 (HL, Viscount Radcliffe, Lords Cohen, Keith of Avonholm, Denning and Jenkins)

100,000 preference shares and 100,000 ordinary shares in William Jackson and Son Ltd. were held upon trust for Mrs. Oughtred for life and after her death on trust for her son Peter absolutely. Mrs Oughtred also held 72,700 shares absolutely.

On Mrs. Oughtred's death, estate duty would be payable at the rate applicable to the aggregated value of the settled property and her own free estate. In order to reduce the liability to estate duty,[17] Mrs. Oughtred and Peter orally agreed that she would transfer to him her 72,700 shares, and Peter would release to his mother his remainder interest in the 200,000 preference and ordinary shares. Subsequently, documents covering these transfers were executed. The Revenue claimed stamp duty upon the transfer of Peter's interest in the 200,000 shares.

Held (Viscount Radcliffe and Lord Cohen dissenting). Stamp duty was payable.

Lord Jenkins: It is said further that in the present case the disputed transfer transferred nothing beyond a bare legal estate, because, in accordance with the well-settled principle applicable to contracts of sale, between contract and completion the appellant became under the oral agreement beneficially entitled in equity to the settled shares, subject to the due satisfaction by her of the purchase consideration, and accordingly the entire beneficial interest in the settled shares had already passed to her at the time of the execution of the disputed transfer, and there was nothing left upon which the disputed transfer could operate except the bare legal estate.

The Commissioners of Inland Revenue seek to meet this argument by reference to section 53 (1) (*c*) of the Law of Property Act, 1925. They contend that as the agreement of June 18, 1956, was an oral agreement it could not, in view of section 53 (1) (*c*), effect a disposition of a subsisting equitable interest or trust, and accordingly that Peter's subsisting equitable interest under the trusts of the settlement, in the shape of his reversionary interest, remained vested in him until the execution of the disputed transfer, which in these

---

16 See *Grainge v Wilberforce* (1889) 5 TLR 436; *DHN Food Distributors Ltd v Tower Hamlets London Borough Council* [1976] 1 WLR 852, [1976] 3 All ER 462; (1977) 93 LQR 171 (D. Sugarman and F. Webb).

17 Estate duty has been replaced by inheritance tax. See chap. 15, post.

circumstances operated as a transfer on sale to the appellant of Peter's reversionary interest and additionally as a transfer not on sale to the appellant of the legal interest in the settled shares. It was by this process of reasoning that the Commissioners arrived at the opinion expressed in the case stated that the disputed transfer attracted both the ad valorem duty exigible on a transfer on sale of the reversionary interest and also the fixed duty of 10s.

This argument is attacked on the appellant's side by reference to subsection (2) of section 53 of the Act of 1925, which excludes the creation or operation of resulting, implied or constructive trusts from the provisions of subsection (1). It is said that inasmuch as the oral agreement was an agreement of sale and purchase it gave rise, on the principle to which I have already adverted, to a constructive trust of the reversionary interest in favour of the appellant subject to performance by her of her obligation to transfer to Peter the free shares forming the consideration for the sale. It is said that this trust, being constructive, was untouched by section 53 (1) (c) in view of the exemption afforded by section 53 (2), and that the appellant's primary argument still holds good.

I find it unnecessary to decide whether section 53 (2) has the effect of excluding the present transaction from the operation of section 53 (1) (c), for, assuming in the appellant's favour that the oral contract did have the effect in equity of raising a constructive trust of the settled shares for her untouched by section 53 (1) (c), I am unable to accept the conclusion that the disputed transfer was prevented from being a transfer of the shares to the appellant on sale because the entire beneficial interest in the settled shares was already vested in the appellant under the constructive trust, and there was accordingly nothing left for the disputed transfer to pass to the appellant except the bare legal estate. The constructive trust in favour of a purchaser which arises on the conclusion of a contract for sale is founded upon the purchaser's right to enforce the contract in proceedings for specific performance. In other words, he is treated in equity as entitled by virtue of the contract to the property which the vendor is bound under the contract to convey to him. This interest under the contract is no doubt a proprietary interest of a sort, which arises, so to speak, in anticipation of the execution of the transfer for which the purchaser is entitled to call. But its existence has never (so far as I know) been held to prevent a subsequent transfer, in performance of the contract, of the property contracted to be sold from constituting for stamp duty purposes a transfer on sale of the property in question. Take the simple case of a contract for the sale of land. In such a case a constructive trust in favour of the purchaser arises on the conclusion of the contract for sale, but (so far as I know) it has never been held on this account that a conveyance subsequently executed in performance of the contract is not stampable ad valorem as a transfer on sale. Similarly, in a case like the present one, but uncomplicated by the existence of successive interests, a transfer to a purchaser of the investments comprised in a trust fund could not, in my judgment, be prevented from constituting a transfer on sale for the purposes of stamp duty by reason of the fact that the actual transfer had been preceded by an oral agreement for sale.

In truth, the title secured by a purchaser by means of an actual transfer is different in kind from, and may well be far superior to, the special form of proprietary interest which equity confers on a purchaser in anticipation of such transfer.

This difference is of particular importance in the case of property such as shares in a limited company. Under the contract the purchaser is no doubt entitled in equity as between himself and the vendor to the beneficial interest in the shares, and (subject to due payment of the purchase consideration) to call for a transfer of them from the vendor as trustee for him. But it is only on the execution of the actual transfer that he becomes entitled to be registered as a member, to attend and vote at meetings, to effect transfers on the register, or to receive dividends otherwise than through the vendor as his trustee.

VISCOUNT RADCLIFFE (dissenting): The reason of the whole matter, as I see it, is as follows: On June 18, 1956, the son owned an equitable reversionary interest in the settled shares: by his oral agreement of that date he created in his mother an equitable interest in his reversion, since the subject-matter of the agreement was property of which specific performance would normally be decreed by the court. He thus became a trustee for her of that interest sub modo: having regard to subsection (2) of section 53 of the Law of Property Act, 1925, subsection (1) of that section did not operate to prevent that trusteeship arising by operation of law. On June 26 Mrs. Oughtred transferred to her son the shares which were the consideration for her acquisition of his equitable interest: upon this transfer he became in a full sense and without more the trustee of his interest for her. She was the effective owner of all outstanding equitable interests. It was thus correct to recite in the deed of release to the trustees of the settlement, which was to wind up their trust, that the trust fund was by then held upon trust for her absolutely. There was, in fact, no equity to the shares that could be asserted against her, and it was open to her, if she so wished, to let the matter rest without calling for a written assignment from her son. Given that the trustees were apprised of the making of the oral agreement and of Mrs. Oughtred's satisfaction of the consideration to be given by her, the trustees had no more to do than to transfer their legal title to her or as she might direct. This and no more is what they did.

It follows that, in my view, this transfer cannot be treated as a conveyance of the son's equitable reversion at all. The trustees had not got it: he never transferred or released it to them: how then could they convey it? With all respect to those who think otherwise, it is incorrect to say that the trustees' transfer was made either with his authority or at his discretion. If the recital as to Mrs. Oughtred's rights was correct, as I think that it was, he had no remaining authority to give or direction to issue. A release is, after all, the normal instrument for winding up a trust when all the equitable rights are vested and the legal estate is called for from the trustees who hold it. What the release gave the trustees from him was acquittance for the trust administration and accounts to date, and the fact that he gave it in consideration of the legal interest in the shares being vested in his mother adds nothing on this point. Nor does it, with respect, advance the matter to say, correctly, that at the end of the day Mrs. Oughtred was the absolute owner of the shares, legal and equitable. I think that she was: but that is description, not analysis. The question that is relevant for the purpose of this appeal is how she came to occupy that position; a position which, under English law, could be reached by more than one road.

In **Neville v Wilson** (1996) Times, 8 April NOURSE LJ, giving the judgment of the court, said that "in 1969 the shareholders had entered into an agreement with one another for the informal liquidation of the company and thus, as part of it, for the division of the company's equitable interest in the shares in Universal Engineering in proportions corresponding to their existing shareholdings.

The question, which involved consideration of section 53 of the 1925 Act and a point left open by the House of Lords in *Oughtred v IRC* ([1960] AC 206, [1959] 3 All ER 623), was whether the agreement had had the effect of disposing of the company's interest.

Each shareholder had collectively agreed to assign his interest in the other shares of the company's equitable interest in exchange for the assignment by the other shareholders of their interests in his own aliquot share. Each individual agreement having been a disposition of a subsisting equitable interest not made in writing, there thus arose the question whether it was rendered ineffectual by section 53.

The simple view was that the effect of each individual agreement was to constitute the shareholder an implied or constructive trustee for the other shareholders, so that the requirement for writing in section 53(1)(c) was dispensed with by subsection (2). That was the view taken by Upjohn J at first instance in *Oughtred v IRC* ([1958] Ch 383, 390, [1958] 1 All ER 252, 254) and by Lord Radcliffe in the House of Lords (at p. 227, at p. 625).

There was nothing in the speeches in the House of Lords preventing the court from holding that the effect of each individual agreement was to constitute the shareholder an implied or constructive trustee for the other shareholders.

The analysis of Lord Radcliffe, based on the proposition that a specifically enforceable agreement to assign an interest in property created an equitable interest in the assignee, was unquestionably correct: see *London and South Western Railway Co v Gomm* ((1882) 20 ChD 563, 581). A greater difficulty was caused by Lord Denning's outright rejection of the application of section 53(2), with which Lord Cohen had appeared to agree.

Section 53(2) said that subsection (1)(c) did not affect the creation or operation of implied or constructive trusts. Just as in *Oughtred v IRC* the son's oral agreement created a constructive trust in favour of the mother, so here each shareholder's oral or implied agreement created an implied or constructive trust in favour of the other shareholders.

Why then should section 53(2) not apply? No convincing reason had been suggested or had occurred to the court. Moreover, to deny its application would be to restrict the effect of general words when no restriction was called for and to lay the ground for fine distinctions in the future. Subsection (2) applied to an agreement such as there was in the instant case.

Thus the agreement entered into by the shareholders was not ineffectual and the plaintiffs were entitled to relief accordingly. That meant that the company's equitable interest in the 120 shares did not vest in the Crown as bona vacantia when the company was struck off the register in 1970, and cash now representing the shares would be divided proportionately between the plaintiffs and the defendants.

On grounds not argued before the judge the appeal was allowed.''

(g) Disposition to Fiduciary

In **Re Tyler** [1967] 1 WLR 1269, [1967] 3 All ER 389, Miss Tyler, by her will, appointed Mr. King and Mrs. Green her executors. Shortly after its execution, she placed £1,500 in the hands of Mr. King, and on May 9, 1951 she wrote a letter instructing him to use as much of the money, income or capital, as was needed to provide reasonable care and comfort for Mrs. Green; and to dispose of the surplus at Mrs. Green's death as the testatrix had previously indicated to Mr. King. The testatrix died, then Mr. King and then Mrs. Green.

The instructions for disposal of the surplus on Mrs. Green's death were that £500 should be paid to Mr. King's executors if (as happened) he should die before Mrs. Green, and the rest divided among a number of charitable institutions.

This summons was brought to determine on what trusts the fund was held on Mrs. Green's death.

PENNYCUICK J held that the evidence to support the executors' claim to £500 was insufficient, and that that sum was held on a resulting trust for Miss Tyler's estate. The balance of the fund went to charity. On the question of the observance of the necessary formalities, he said at 1274, at 391:

"We do not know whether there was an interval of time between the payment by Miss Tyler to Mr. King of the £1,500 and the statement by her to him of her wishes with regard to it. On that footing there would have been an interval of time during which Mr. King held the £1,500 on a resulting trust for Miss Tyler. The first question which has been argued is whether a trust was validly constituted as regards formalities, having regard, in particular, to section 53 of the Law of Property Act, 1925, which contains the following provision: ...

It is now well established that the requirement applies to equitable interest in personalty as well as in land. It seems to me that, even on the view of the facts most unfavourable to the creation of a valid trust for this purpose, that is that there was a payment to Mr. King before any trusts were declared, there has been in this case sufficient compliance with the requirements of section 53. The letter of May 9 constitutes, it seems to me, a valid assignment in writing of an equitable interest by Miss Tyler to Mr. King, assuming that such an equitable interest existed. There is nothing in section 53 which requires that, where the assignee is to hold in a fiduciary capacity, the writing shall comprise the particulars of the trust. I conclude, then, that in May, 1951, a trust was validly created so far as formality is concerned."

(h) Under Variation of Trusts Act 1958

The question of the operation of section 53 (1) (c) in relation to the equitable interests of consenting adults when a variation of a trust is effected under the Variation of Trusts Act 1958 was discussed in *Re Holt's Settlement* [1969] 1 Ch 100, [1968] 1 All ER 470. This is dealt with in Chapter 19, below.

(i) Right of Nomination of Benefits under Staff Pension Fund

In **Re Danish Bacon Co Ltd Staff Pension Fund Trusts** [1971] 1 WLR 248, [1971] 1 All ER 486, p. 53, ante, it was not necessary to decide whether the interest was one to which section 53 (1) (c) applied. MEGARRY J said at 255, at 493:

"Whether section 53 (1) (c) does apply is a matter upon which I am by no means clear; and in view of what I have already decided on the section, I do not have to resolve that point. However, it has been extensively argued, and I think I should give some indication of my views. What I am concerned with is a transaction whereby the deceased dealt with something which ex hypothesi could never be his. He was not disposing of his pension, nor of his right to the contributions and interest if he left the company's service. He was dealing merely with a state of affairs that would arise if he died while in the company's pensionable service, or after he had left it without becoming entitled to a pension. If he did this, then the contributions and interest would, by force of the rules, go either to his nominee, if he had made a valid nomination, or to his personal representatives, if he had not. If he made a nomination, it was revocable at any time before his death.

The question is thus whether an instrument with this selective, contingent and defeasible quality, which takes effect only on the death of the person signing it, can fairly be said to be 'a disposition of an equitable interest or trust subsisting at the time of the disposition'. Mr. Ferris put much emphasis on the word 'subsisting': however wide the word 'disposition' might be in its meaning, there was no disposition of a subsisting equity, he said. I should hesitate to describe an instrument which has a mere possibility of becoming a 'disposition' as being in itself a disposition ab initio; and I agree that the word 'subsisting' also seems to point against the nomination falling within section 53 (1) (*c*) ... I very much doubt whether the nomination falls within section 53 (1) (*c*); but as I have indicated, I do not have to decide that point, and I do not do so.''

(*j*) *Disclaimer of Beneficial Interest*

In **Re Paradise Motor Co Ltd** [1968] 1 WLR 1125, [1968] 2 All ER 625, the question arose whether the disclaimer of a beneficial interest in shares was required to be evidenced in writing under section 53 (1) (*c*). In holding that it did not, DANCKWERTS LJ said at 1143, at 632:

"The ... argument was that there could here be no disclaimer of the beneficial interest in the shares because a disclaimer would, by re-transfer, be a disposition of an equitable interest in property, and neither of the suggested disclaimers was in writing signed by [the disclaimant]: see the Law of Property Act, 1925, section 53 (2). We think that the short answer to this is that a disclaimer operates by way of avoidance and not by way of disposition. For the general aspects of disclaimer we refer briefly to the discussion in *Re Stratton's Disclaimer* [1958] Ch 42, [1957] 2 All ER 594.''[18]

B. By Will[19]

WILLS ACT 1837

9. Signing and attestation of wills. — No will shall be valid unless —

   (*a*) it is in writing, and signed by the testator, or by some other person in his presence and by his direction; and

   (*b*) it appears that the testator intended by his signature to give effect to the will; and

---

18 A disclaimer is not treated as a disposition for the purposes of inheritance tax: IHTA 1984 s. 17.

19 H & M, pp. 93–94; K & S, p. 84; P & M, p. 44, Pettit, p. 89; Snell, p. 107; Underhill, p. 205. For detailed commentary on this section, see Mellows, *Law of Succession* (5th edn) chaps. 6, 7; *Theobald on Wills* (15th edn) chap. 4; *Williams on Wills* (7th edn) chaps. 10–16. And for its relation to secret trusts, see pp. 150–169, post. For testamentary formalities in the conflict of laws, see Wills Act 1963.

(c) the signature is made or acknowledged by the testator in the presence of two or more witnesses present at the same time; and

(d) each witness either –
  (i) attests and signs the will; or
  (ii) acknowledges his signature, in the presence of the testator (but not necessarily in the presence of any other witness),

but no form of attestation shall be necessary.[20]

QUESTION

How would you have decided
  (a) *Oughtred v IRC* [1960] AC 206, [1959] 3 All ER 623, p. 57, ante; [1979] Conv 14, at pp. 26–31 (G. Battersby)?
  (b) *Re Vandervell's Trusts* (*No 2*) [1974] Ch 269, [1974] 3 All ER 205, p. 187, ante; [1979] Conv 14, at pp. 31–37; (1974) Conv (NS) 405 (P.J. Clarke); (1975) 38 MLR 557 (J.W. Harris)?

II. Certainty[1]

There can be no trust unless there is certainty in respect of the intention to create a trust, and in respect of the property which is the subject matter of the trust, and (charitable trusts apart) in respect of the beneficiaries. These are the "three certainties".[2] The principles to be applied in solving problems which arise in this context can be extracted from the cases; but each question can only be answered by careful construction of the language of the instrument under consideration.

The three aspects of the "certainty" problem are here treated separately. In many cases, however, they overlap. Thus, "uncertainty in the subject of the gift has a reflex action upon the previous words, and throws doubt upon the intention of the testator, and seems to shew that he could not possibly have intended his words of confidence, hope, or whatever they may be — his appeal to the conscience of the first taker — to be imperative words."[3] Similarly, a division of property among various claimants may create uncertainty as to both the property and the claimants.[4]

There is sometimes confusion between these rules of certainty and some related rules. First, the certainty rules apply quite differently to charitable trusts[5]. There, the requirement is that the trust must be exclusively charitable; there must be no doubt about that. But there is no need to specify which

---

20 As substituted by AJA 1982, s. 17. See Law Reform Committee 22nd Report (Cmnd 7902), Part II.

1 H & M, pp. 94–112; K & S, pp. 112–121; P & M, pp. 90–111; Pettit, pp. 40–50; Riddall, pp. 18–35; Snell, pp. 113–117; Underhill, pp. 57–124.

2 *Knight v Knight* (1840) 3 Beav 148 at 173, per Lord LANGDALE MR.

3 *Mussoorie Bank v Raynor* (1882) 7 App Cas 321 at 331, per Sir Arthur HOBHOUSE; *Re Adams and the Kensington Vestry* (1884) 27 ChD 394. See pp. 65 et seq, post.

4 *Boyce v Boyce* (1849) 16 Sim 476.

5 See pp. 336, 459, post.

particular charity is to benefit. Second, the rule that the objects of a trust (the beneficiaries) must be certain leaves open the question, discussed below[6], whether there can be a non-charitable purpose trust, without human beneficiaries. In so far as this is possible, the purposes must be sufficiently certain[7]. Third, it is important to appreciate the relationship between these rules and discretionary trusts[8]. It is possible to leave uncertain which members of a group of beneficiaries will benefit and which share any one will receive; provided that the property available for distribution is certain, the class of beneficiaries is sufficiently certain, and the discretionary power of selection is vested in some person or persons. If no provision is made for the exercise of the discretion, the disposition is void for uncertainty[9]. Fourth, problems of uncertainty also arise where the gift is to ascertainable beneficiaries, but their qualification is subjected to a condition.[10]

A. Certainty of Intention

As MEGARRY J said in **Re Kayford Ltd** [1975] 1 WLR 279 at 282, [1975] 1 All ER 604 at 607;
      "It is well settled that a trust can be created without using the word 'trust' or 'confidence' or the like: the question is whether in substance a sufficient intention to create a trust has been manifested."
      This requirement is strictly applied[11]. A testator may say that he "hopes" or "expects" or "has full confidence" that a legatee will apply property for the benefit of others. Somehow a line has to be drawn between requests and obligations. The approach of the courts has varied on this question. In the early 19th century, an intention to create a trust would readily be found[12]. Later a stricter construction was applied, the turning point being usually said to be the Court of Appeal decision in *Lambe v Eames* in 1871.[13]

RE ADAMS AND THE KENSINGTON VESTRY
(1884) 27 ChD 394 (CA, BAGGALLAY, COTTON AND LINDLEY LJJ)

George Smith, the testator, provided in his will as follows: "I give, devise, and bequeath all my real and personal estate and effects whatsoever and wheresoever unto and to the absolute use of my wife, Harriet Smith, her

---

6 See pp. 306 et seq, post.
7 *Re Astor's Settlement Trusts* [1952] Ch 534, [1952] 1 All ER 1067, see p. 312, post.
8 See p. 70, post.
9 *Sprange v Barnard* (1789) 2 Bro CC 585.
10 *Re Allen* [1953] Ch 810, [1953] 2 All ER 898; *Re Tuck's Settlement Trusts* [1978] Ch 49, [1978] 1 All ER 1047, p. 652, post; *Re Barlow's Will Trusts* [1979] 1 WLR 278, [1979] 1 All ER 296, p. 87, post. For problems of uncertainty in connection with conditions subsequent, see *Clayton v Ramsden* [1943] AC 320, [1943] 1 All ER 16; *Blathwayt v Lord Cawley* [1976] AC 397, [1975] 3 All ER 625; *Re Jones* [1953] Ch 125, [1953] 1 All ER 357, p. 652 post. See generally H & M, pp. 334–340; Cheshire and Burn, *Modern Law of Real Property* (15th edn), pp. 339–351.
11 *Jones v Lock* (1865) 1 Ch App 25, p. 120, post; *Swiss Bank Corpn v Lloyds Bank Ltd* [1982] AC 584, [1981] 2 All ER 449; *Re Multi Guarantee Co Ltd* [1987] BCLC 257. For a less strict approach, see *Paul v Constance* [1977] 1 WLR 527, [1977] 1 All ER 195, p. 122, post.
12 H & M, pp. 95–96.
13 (1871) 6 Ch App 597; for other cases where it was held that no trust was created, see *Mussoorie Bank Ltd v Raynor* (1882) 7 App Cas 321 ("feeling confident that she will act justly to our children in dividing the same when no longer required by her"); *Re Diggles* (1888) 39 ChD 253 ("it is my desire that she allows A.G. an annuity of £25 during her life"); *Re Hamilton* [1895] 2

executors, administrators and assigns, in full confidence that she will do what is right as to the disposal thereof between my children, either in her lifetime or by will after her decease.''

The question was whether this was an absolute gift, or whether the property was subject to a trust in favour of the children.

Held. The widow took absolutely.

COTTON LJ: The question before us is whether, upon the true construction of the will of *George Smith*, he imposed upon his wife *Harriet* a trust. Now just let us look at it, in the first instance, alone, and see what we can spell out of it, and what was expressed by the will. Reading that will, and I will not repeat it, because it has been already read, it seems to me perfectly clear what the testator intended. He leaves his wife his property absolutely, but what was in his mind was this: "I am the head of the family, and it is laid upon me to provide properly for the members of my family — my children: my widow will succeed me when I die, and I wish to put her in the position I occupied as the person who is to provide for my children." Not that he entails upon her any trust so as to bind her, but he simply says, in giving her this, I express to her, and call to her attention, the moral obligation which I myself had and which I feel that she is going to discharge. The motive of the gift is, in my opinion, not a trust imposed upon her by the gift in the will. He leaves the property to her; he knows that she will do what is right, and carry out the moral obligation which he thought lay on him, and on her if she survived him, to provide for the children. But it is said that the testator would be very much astonished if he found that he had given his wife power to leave the property away. That is a proposition which I should express in a different way. He would be much surprised if the wife to whom he had left his property absolutely should so act as not to provide for the children, that is to say, not to do what is right. That is a very different thing. He would have said: "I expected that she would do what was right, and therefore I left it to her absolutely. I find she has not done what I think is right, but I cannot help it, I am very sorry that she has done so." That would be the surprise, I think, that he would express, and feel, if he could do either, if the wife did what was unreasonable as regards the children.

But, then, it is said there is authority against that, and I am in no way disposed, if there be any definite canon or rule of construction established, to depart from that, because that must introduce great uncertainty. But undoubtedly, to my mind, in the later cases, especially *Lambe v Eames* (1871) 6 Ch App 597 and *Re Hutchinson and Tenant* (1878) 8 ChD 540, both the Court of Appeal and the late Master of the Rolls shewed a desire really to find out what,

Ch 370 ("I wish them to bequeath the same equally between the families of O and P''); *Re Williams* [1897] 2 Ch 12 ("in the fullest trust and confidence that she will carry out my wishes in the following particulars"); *Re Johnson* [1939] 2 All ER 458 ("I request that C on her death leave her property to my four sisters"); *Swain v Law Society* [1983] 1 AC 598, [1982] 2 All ER 827 ("on behalf of all solicitors"). See also, in the context of secret trusts, *Re Snowden* [1979] Ch 528, [1979] 2 All ER 172, p. 155, post. Contrast *Comiskey v Bowring-Hanbury* [1905] AC 84 (testator gave to his wife "the whole of my real and personal estate . . . in full confidence that she will make such use of it as I should have made myself and that at her death she will devise it to such one or more of my nieces as she may think fit and in default of any disposition by her thereof by her will . . . I hereby direct that all my estate and property acquired by her under this my will shall at her death be equally divided among the surviving said nieces"). H.L. held by a majority that there was an intention to make a gift to the wife, with an executory gift over of the whole property at her death to such of her nieces as should survive her, shared according to the wife's will, and otherwise equally. Lord LINDLEY (dissenting) construed the limitation as showing an intention to make an absolute gift to the wife.

upon the true construction, was the meaning of the testator, rather than to lay hold of certain words which in other wills had been held to create a trust, although on the will before them they were satisfied that that was not the intention. I have no hesitation in saying myself, that I think some of the older authorities went a great deal too far in holding that some particular words appearing in a will were sufficient to create a trust. Undoubtedly confidence, if the rest of the context shews that a trust is intended, may make a trust, but what we have to look at is the whole of the will which we have to construe, and if the confidence is that she will do what is right as regards the disposal of the property, I cannot say that that is, on the true construction of the will, a trust imposed upon her. Having regard to the later decisions, we must not extend the old cases in any way, or rely upon the mere use of any particular words, but, considering all the words which are used, we have to see what is their true effect, and what was the intention of the testator as expressed in his will. In my opinion, here he has expressed his will in such a way as not to shew an intention of imposing a trust on the wife, but on the contrary, in my opinion, he has shewn an intention to leave the property, as he says he does, to her absolutely.

In **Re Steele's Will Trusts**[14] [1948] Ch 603, [1948] 2 All ER 193, the testatrix, who died in 1929, provided by clause 2 of her will as follows: "I give my diamond necklace to my son to go and be held as an heirloom by him and by his eldest son on his decease and to go and descend to the eldest son of such eldest son and so on to the eldest son of his descendants as far as the rules of law and equity will permit (and I request my said son to do all in his power by his will or otherwise to give effect to this my wish)." This provision was basically the same as that which had been held in *Shelley v Shelley* (1868) LR 6 Eq 540 to create a trust.

WYNN-PARRY J, while noting the extent to which the construction placed upon precatory expressions had changed since 1868, upheld it. He said at 609, at 196:

"The case of *Shelley v Shelley* has stood for eighty years and I have before me a will which, as I have already observed, is, as regards the relevant passage, couched in exactly the same language mutatis mutandis as that which was considered by Wood V-C in *Shelley v Shelley*. That appears to me to afford the strongest indication that the testatrix in this case, by her will, which appears clearly upon the face of it to have been a will prepared with professional aid, indicated that the diamond necklace in question should devolve in the same manner as the jewellery was directed to devolve by the order in *Shelley v Shelley*. Having regard to that strong indication of intention, and having regard to the fact that I cannot see any good reason why, notwithstanding the admitted trend of modern decisions, I should treat *Shelley v Shelley* as wrongly decided and therefore a case which I ought not to follow, I come to the conclusion that I must declare that upon the true construction of the will of the testatrix the diamond necklace should have been held upon trust for Charles Steele for his life and after his death for the second plaintiff Charles Ronald Steele for his life and after his death for David Steele, the third plaintiff, for his life and after the death of the survivor of them upon trust for the eldest son or grandson of the

14 (1968) 32 Conv (NS) 361 (P. St. J. Langan); Pettit, p. 42.

third plaintiff David Steele and otherwise in the manner decided in *Shelley v Shelley* including the ultimate trust in default of any male issue of David Steele (who takes an absolutely vested interest) in favour of Charles Steele absolutely and that the order in this case will follow mutatis mutandis the minutes which appear in the case of *Shelley v Shelley.*''

B. Certainty of Subject Matter

In **Palmer v Simmonds** (1854) 2 Drew 221, the testatrix, by her will, gave her residuary estate to Thomas Harrison "for his own use and benefit, as I have full confidence in him, that if he should die without lawful issue he will ... leave the bulk of my said residuary estate unto" certain named persons.

The expression of confidence was sufficient, according to the practice at that time, to manifest an intention to create a trust. The question was whether the subject matter of the trust was sufficiently certain. KINDERSLEY V-C held that it was not. He said at 227:

"What is the meaning then of bulk? The appropriate meaning, according to its derivation, is something which bulges out, &c. [His Honour referred to *Todd's Johnson and Richardson's Dictionary* for the different meanings and etymology of the word.] Its popular meaning we all know. When a person is said to have given the bulk of his property, what is meant is not the whole but the greater part, and that is in fact consistent with its classical meaning. When, therefore, the testatrix uses that term, can I say she has used a term expressing a definite, clear, certain part of her estate, or the whole of her estate? I am bound to say she has not designated the subject as to which she expresses her confidence; and I am therefore of opinion that there is no trust created; that *Harrison* took absolutely, and those claiming under him now take."

RE GOLAYS' WILL TRUSTS[15]
[1965] 1 WLR 969, [1965] 2 All ER 660 (ChD, UNGOED-THOMAS J)

By his will, the testator directed his executors "to let Tossy — [whom he named] — to enjoy one of my flats during her lifetime and to receive a reasonable income from my other properties ...."

The question was whether the gift of the income was void for uncertainty.

Held. The gift was valid.

UNGOED-THOMAS J: Another question that arises is whether this gift of reasonable income fails for uncertainty.

There are two classes of case with which I am concerned in interpreting this particular provision in the will: the first is where a discretion is given to specified persons to quantify the amount; the other class of case is where no such discretion is expressly conferred upon any specified person.

The question therefore comes to this: Whether the testator by the words "reasonable income" has given a sufficient indication of his intention to provide an effective determinant of what he intends so that the court in applying that determinant can give effect to the testator's intention.

Whether the yardstick of "reasonable income" were applied by trustees under a discretion given to them by a testator or applied by a court in course of

---

15 (1965) 81 LQR 481 (R.E.M.). For other testamentary gifts which failed, see *Sprange v Barnard* (1789) 2 Bro CC 585 ("the remaining part of what is left"); *Boyce v Boyce* (1849) 16 Sim 476 ("all my other houses"); *Re Jones* [1898] 1 Ch 438 ("such parts of my ... estate as she shall not have sold"); *Re Last* [1958] P. 137, [1958] 1 All ER 316 ("anything that is left").

interpreting and applying the words "reasonable income" in a will, the yardstick sought to be applied by the trustees in the one case and the court in the other case would be identical. The trustees might be other than the original trustees named by the testator and the trustees could even surrender their discretion to the court. It would seem to me to be drawing too fine a distinction to conclude that an objective yardstick which different persons sought to apply would be too uncertain, not because of uncertainty in the yardstick but as between those who seek to apply it.

In this case, however, the yardstick indicated by the testator is not what he or some other specified person subjectively considers to be reasonable but what he identifies objectively as "reasonable income". The court is constantly involved in making such objective assessments of what is reasonable and it is not to be deterred from doing so because subjective influences can never be wholly excluded. In my view the testator intended by "reasonable income" the yardstick which the court could and would apply in quantifying the amount so that the direction in the will is not in my view defeated by uncertainty.

In **Hunter v Moss** [1994] 1 WLR 452, [1994] 3 All ER 215,[16] the defendant was the registered owner of 950 shares in a company with an issued share capital of 1,000 shares. He made an oral declaration of trust in favour of the plaintiff in respect of 5 per cent of the company's issued share capital (i.e. 50 shares). The Court of Appeal, upholding the judge of first instance [1993] 1 WLR 934,[17] but with different reasons, held that the trust was not void for uncertainty.

Parker and Mellows, *Modern Law of Trusts* (6th edn), pp. 95–97.

"Problems have also arisen in connection with attempts to declare trusts of some certain but unidentified part of a larger holding. In *Re London Wine Co (Shippers) Ltd* [1986] PCC 121, wine dealers sent letters to purchasers of wine confirming that they were the sole beneficial owners of the wine which they had bought and paid for; however, no steps were taken to segregate the wine in question from the general mass of stock held by the dealers. It was held that no trust had arisen so that the purchasers had no proprietary rights in the wine as against the holders of a floating charge which the dealers had granted over their entire assets. However, this decision was subsequently distinguished in *Hunter v Moss*, where a declaration of trust in respect of fifty shares in a company in which the settlor held nine hundred and fifty shares was upheld on the basis that any identification of the particular fifty shares held on trust was unnecessary and irrelevant. At first instance, the principle enunciated in *Re London Wine Co (Shippers) Ltd* was confined to tangible property, since 'ostensibly similar or identical assets may in fact have characteristics which distinguish them from other assets in the class' (at p. 940) — as the judge[18] said, some of the wine may have become corked or may have deteriorated in some

---

16 (1994) 110 LQR 335 (D. Hayton); (1995) 48 CLP 113 (P.J. Clarke); (1995) 48 CLP 113 (A. Clarke); [1994] All ER Rev 249 (P.J. Clarke); [1994] CLJ 448 (M. Ockelton); [1996] Conv 223 (J. Martin). See also *Re Goldcorp Exchange Ltd* [1995] 1 AC 74, [1994] 2 All ER 806; *Re Stapylton Fletcher Ltd* [1994] 1 WLR 1181, [1995] 1 All ER 192.
17 [1993] Conv 466 (A. Jones).
18 Colin Rimer QC sitting as a Deputy High Court Judge.

other way. He then went on to state that a declaration of trust in respect of £1,000 in a bank account with a current balance superior to £1,000 would also be effectual. Although the principle thus enunciated must clearly be confined to intangible property similar to the choses in action held by the settlor in respect of the shares and the imaginary bank account, it nevertheless caused some surprise. It has hitherto been thought that trusts of such choses in action would only be valid if the settlor declared a trust either of his entire interest in the chose in action or of a fixed proportion thereof[19] (in other words, on the facts of *Hunter v Moss*, a trust of one-nineteenth of the shares held in the company in question) so that thereafter they would be held on trust for the settlor and the beneficiary in the appropriate proportions. In the Court of Appeal, Dillon LJ[20] simply held that *Re London Wine Co (Shippers) Ltd* was 'a long way from the present' case and concluded that 'just as a person can give by will a specified number of his shares in a certain company, so equally, in my judgment, he can declare himself a trustee of 50 of his ordinary shares ... and that is effective to give a beneficial proprietary interest to the beneficiary under the trust.' This analogy between a bequest and a declaration of trust has been the subject of fierce criticism.[1] The effect of a will is to vest the whole estate of the testator in his executors to be administered; consequently, a legatee acquires merely an equitable chose in action until the administration has been completed, at which point he will receive whatever shares are allocated to him by the executors. The effect of a declaration of trust, on the other hand, is to vest an immediate proprietary interest in the beneficiary; this necessitates some immediate means of determining which shares are subject to the trust. How otherwise can it be determined, in the event that the trustee subsequently deals with the shares by, for example, selling fifty of them, with whose shares he has actually dealt — his own, those of the beneficiary, or a rateable proportion of the shares of each of them? Whether or not these criticisms are actually justified, there can be no doubt that the decision in *Hunter v Moss* has left the law in a somewhat uncertain state. Dillon LJ made no reference whatever to the distinction between tangible and intangible property adopted at first instance. Is this indeed the distinction between *Re London Wine Co (Shippers) Ltd* and *Hunter v Moss*? If not, what is? Since leave to appeal to the House of Lords was refused in *Hunter v Moss*, only future litigation is likely to provide the answer to this question and, consequently, determine whether, as suggested at first instance, it is now possible to declare a trust of a fixed sum in a bank account with a balance superior to that amount."[2]

19 See Underhill, (14th edn.) p. 105.
20 [1994] 1 WLR 452 at 458, 459, [1994] 3 All ER 215, at 221. This was an unreserved judgment with which the other two members of the court simply agreed.
1 By D.J. Hayton in (1994) 110 LQR 335.
2 In *Mac-Jordan Construction Ltd v Brookmount Erostin* (1991) 56 BLR 1, retention money was to be held on trust for sub-contractors but was not set aside as a separate fund. The Court of Appeal held that there were no identifiable assets impressed with the trust. However, this case is not decisive of the question posed in the text since no trust of the retained funds was ever actually declared.
See Sale of Goods Act 1979, sections 20A and 20B (added by Sale of Goods (Amendment) Act 1995), which provide that a buyer, who has prepaid for a specified quantity of unascertained goods forming part of an identified bulk, may acquire an undivided share in the bulk and become a common owner with other such buyers but before his goods have been ascertained.

C. Certainty of Objects

Prior to *McPhail v Doulton* [1971] AC 424, [1970] 2 All ER 228, p. 71, post the requirement of certainty was expressed by one rule for powers and another rule for trusts. As explained above,[3] powers and trusts are different concepts. It is not inevitable that the test for validity on the grounds of certainty should be the same for each. The rule for powers was settled in *Re Gulbenkian's Settlements* [1970] AC 508, [1968] 3 All ER 785, p. 38, ante, which laid down that the requirement of certainty was met if it was possible to determine with certainty whether any given individual was or was not a member of the class.[4]

The rule for trusts, before *McPhail v Doulton*, was stricter. It had been laid down in *IRC v Broadway Cottages Trust* [1955] Ch 20, [1954] 3 All ER 120 that a trust was void unless it was possible to make, at the time when the trust came into operation, a list of all the beneficiaries. This rule was thought to be necessary in order to make a distribution possible if the trustees, in breach of their duty, failed to make a selection. The method of distribution, it was said, would be by equal division among the members of the class of beneficiaries on the principle that Equality is Equity; and equal division was only possible if it was known how many shares there would be.[5] As will be seen, *McPhail v Doulton* applied, as the test for certainty of beneficiaries under a *discretionary* trust, the test which had been applied to powers in *Re Gulbenkian's Settlements*. The problem of determining the division if the trustees failed to select was not insuperable: the court would find a way. The problem was artificial, in that it had never arisen in the form of trustees refusing to select; rather in their asking whether a selection would be valid. Reluctant trustees could in any case be replaced. And, in modern trusts with the employees of a business tycoon as beneficiaries, and not merely members of the family, as was usually the case with older trusts, equal division would be absurd.

The older, stricter, rule, however, still applies to fixed trusts.

A fixed trust is a trust where the interest or share of a beneficiary is laid down in the trust instrument: for example, "on trust for my children in equal shares". A discretionary trust is a trust in which the share of each member of the class of beneficiaries is determined by the discretion of the trustees; but there is still an obligation upon the trustees to make the division; for example: "on trust for such of my children as my trustees shall select." A power enables the donee of the power to make a gift by exercising the power if he thinks fit: for example, "with power to appoint in favour of such of my children and in such proportions as he shall think fit"; or, to give a more sophisticated example: "to my children, grandchildren and their spouses and the employees and ex-employees and their dependants of X Company and in such proportions ... etc.". In the case both of a power to appoint among such a group and also in the case of a discretionary trust in favour of such a group, the test of certainty is that laid down in *Re Gulbenkian's Settlements* and in *McPhail v Doulton*. If the trust were a *fixed* trust, and the trust property were to be divided among such a group in equal shares, it could, as a practical matter, only be shared equally among the members of the group of beneficiaries if it was

---

3 See p. 34, ante.
4 Following the formulation of the rule in *Re Gestetner Settlement* [1953] Ch 672 at 688, [1953] 1 All ER 1150 at 1155, per HARMAN J: "whether any given postulant is a member of the specified class"; see p. 34, ante.
5 *Burrough v Philcox* (1840) 5 My & Cr 72, p. 35, ante.

possible to make an exact and precise list of the members. In the case of a fixed trust, therefore, the rule of *Broadway Cottages* must apply. This point should be borne in mind when reading *McPhail v Doulton.*

Finally, a word of warning on terminology. The language of the cases dealing with the requirement of certainty in trusts and powers must be read with some care. The dividing line between trusts and powers is not always made clear; the very use of phrases such as "trust powers" and "powers in the nature of a trust" shows this. Such phrases refer to trusts in which the trustees have a power of selection; as in a discretionary trust.[6]

i. DISCRETIONARY TRUST

(*a*) *The Is or Is Not Test*

McPHAIL v DOULTON[7]
[1971] AC 424, [1970] 2 All ER 228 (HL, Lords REID, HODSON, Viscount DILHORNE, Lords GUEST and WILBERFORCE)

A deed, executed on July 17, 1941, by the settlor, Mr. Bertram Baden, provided that a fund was to be held upon certain trusts in favour of the staff of Matthew Hall and Co. Ltd. and their relatives and dependants.

The deed provided (clause 9 (*a*)) that the trustees should apply the net income in making grants at their absolute discretion "to or for the benefit of any of the officers and employees or ex-officers or ex-employees of the company or to any relatives or dependants of any such persons in such amounts at such times and on such conditions (if any) as they think fit ... "

The trustees were under no obligation to exhaust the income in any one year. They could realise capital for the purpose of making such grants if the income was insufficient. It was also provided (clause 10) that "no person shall have any right title or interest in the fund otherwise than pursuant to the exercise of such discretion."

Two main questions arose: whether the deed created a power or a trust; and whether it was void for uncertainty. At first instance,[8] GOFF J held that it was a power and not a trust and that it was valid: applying as the test of certainty that applied by the Court of Appeal in *Re Gulbenkian's Settlements*:[9] namely, that a power was valid if it was sufficiently certain to enable any one claimant to show that he comes within the description.

The Court of Appeal [1969] 2 Ch 388, [1969] 1 All ER 1016 agreed (HARMAN and KARMINSKI LJJ, RUSSELL LJ dissenting) that it was a power and

---

6 See [1984] Conv 227 (R. Bartlett and C. Stebbings).
7 (1970) 34 Conv (NS) 287 (F.R. Crane); (1971) CLJ 68 (J. Hopkins); (1971) CLP 133 (H. Cohen); (1971) 87 LQR 31 (J.W. Harris); (1973) 5 NZULR 348; (1974) 37 MLR 643 (Y.F.R. Grbich); (1973) 7 VUWLR 258 (L. McKay); (1975) 4 Anglo-American LR 442 (S. Fradley); (1982) 98 LQR 551 (C.T. Emery); [1984] Conv 22 (P. Matthews), 304 (J. Marlin), 307 (D. Hayton). Law Commission 8th Annual Report 1972–1973 (Law Com 1973 No. 58), para. 68.
8 [1967] 1 WLR 1457, [1967] 3 All ER 159.
9 [1968] Ch 126, [1967] 3 All ER 15, following *Re Allen* [1953] Ch 810, [1953] 2 All ER 898; *Re Leek* [1967] Ch 1061, [1967] 2 All ER 1160; affd [1969] 1 Ch 563, [1968] 1 All ER 793; *Re Gibbard's Will Trusts* [1967] 1 WLR 42, [1966] 1 All ER 273.

not a trust; but remitted the case to the Chancery Division to determine the validity upon the application of the test for certainty of powers which had been laid down by the House of Lords in *Re Gulbenkian's Settlements* [1970] AC 508, [1968] 3 All ER 785, p. 38, ante.

Held. (i) The deed created a trust and not a power; (ii) (Lords HODSON and GUEST dissenting). The test for certainty was the same as that for powers: i.e. whether it could be said with certainty that any given individual was or was not a member of the class.

The case was remitted to the Chancery Division for a determination of validity upon this basis. In *Re Baden's Deed Trusts (No 2)* [1973] Ch 9, [1972] 2 All ER 1304, p. 79, post, the Court of Appeal, affirming BRIGHTMAN J, upheld it.

LORD WILBERFORCE: In this House, the appellants contend, and this is the first question for consideration, that the provisions of clause 9 (a) constitute a trust and not a power. If that is held to be the correct result, both sides agree that the case must return to the Chancery Division for consideration, on this footing, whether this trust is valid. But here comes a complication. In the present state of authority, the decision as to validity would turn on the question whether a complete list (or on another view a list complete for practical purposes) can be drawn up of all possible beneficiaries. This follows from the Court of Appeal's decision in *IRC v Broadway Cottages Trust* [1955] Ch 20, [1954] 3 All ER 120 as applied in later cases by which, unless this House decides otherwise, the Court of Chancery would be bound. The respondents invite your Lordships to review this decision and challenge its correctness. So the second issue which arises, if clause 9 (a) amounts to a trust, is whether the existing test for its validity is right in law and, if not, what the test ought to be.

Before dealing with these two questions some general observations, or reflections, may be permissible. It is striking how narrow and in a sense artificial is the distinction, in cases such as the present, between trusts or as the particular type of trust is called, trust powers, and powers. It is only necessary to read the learned judgments in the Court of Appeal to see that what to one mind may appear as a power of distribution coupled with a trust to dispose of the undistributed surplus, by accumulation or otherwise, may to another appear as a trust for distribution coupled with a power to withhold a portion and accumulate or otherwise dispose of it. A layman and, I suspect, also a logician would find it hard to understand what difference there is.

It does not seem satisfactory that the entire validity of a disposition should depend on such delicate shading. And if one considers how in practice reasonable and competent trustees would act, and ought to act, in the two cases, surely a matter very relevant to the question of validity, the distinction appears even less significant. To say that there is no obligation to exercise a mere power and that no court will intervene to compel it, whereas a trust is mandatory and its execution may be compelled, may be legally correct enough but the proposition does not contain an exhaustive comparison of the duties of persons who are trustees in the two cases. A trustee of an employees' benefit fund, whether given a power or a trust power, is still a trustee and he would surely consider in either case that he has a fiduciary duty: he is most likely to have been selected as a suitable person to administer it from his knowledge and experience, and would consider he has a responsibility to do so according to its purpose. It would be a complete misdescription of his position to say that, if what he has is a power unaccompanied by an imperative trust to distribute, he cannot be controlled by the court unless he exercised it capriciously, or outside the field permitted by the trust (cf. *Farwell on Powers*, 3rd edn, p. 524). Any trustee would surely make it his duty to know what is the permissible area of selection and then consider responsibly, in individual cases, whether a contemplated beneficiary was within the power and whether, in relation to other possible claimants, a particular grant was appropriate.

Correspondingly a trustee with a duty to distribute, particularly among a potentially very large class, would surely never require the preparation of a complete list of names, which anyhow would tell him little that he needs to know. He would examine the field, by class and category; might indeed make diligent and careful inquiries, depending on how much money he had to give away and the means at his disposal, as to the composition and needs of particular categories and of individuals within them; decide upon certain priorities or proportions, and then select individuals according to their needs or qualifications. If he acts in this manner, can it really be said that he is not carrying out the trust?

Differences there certainly are between trust (trust powers) and powers, but as regards validity, should they be so great as that in one case complete, or practically complete, ascertainment is needed, but not in the other? Such distinction as there is would seem to lie in the extent of the survey which the trustee is required to carry out: if he has to distribute the whole of a fund's income, he must necessarily make a wider and more systematic survey than if his duty is expressed in terms of a power to make grants. But just as, in the case of a power, it is possible to underestimate the fiduciary obligation of the trustee to whom it is given, so, in the case of a trust (trust power), the danger lies in overstating what the trustee requires to know or to inquire into before he can properly execute his trust. The difference may be one of degree rather than of principle: in the well-known words of Sir George Farwell, *Farwell on Powers*, 3rd edn (1916), p. 10, trusts and powers are often blended, and the mixture may vary in its ingredients.

With this background I now consider whether the provisions of clause 9 (a) constitute a trust or a power. I do so briefly because this is not a matter on which I or, I understand, any of your Lordships have any doubt. Indeed, a reading of the judgments of Goff J and of the majority in the Court of Appeal leave the strong impression that, if it had not been for their leaning in favour of possible validity and the state of the authorities, these learned judges would have found in favour of a trust. Naturally read, the intention of the deed seems to me clear: clause 9 (a), whose language is mandatory ("shall"), creates, together with a power of selection, a trust for distribution of the income, the strictness of which is qualified by clause 9 (b), which allows the income of any one year to be held up and (under clause 6 (a)) either placed, for the time, with a bank, or, if thought fit, invested. Whether there is, in any technical sense, an accumulation seems to me in the present context a jejune inquiry: what is relevant is that clause 9 (c) marks the difference between "accumulations" of income and the capital of the fund: the former can be distributed by a majority of the trustees, the latter cannot. As to clause 10, I do not find in it any decisive indication. If anything, it seems to point in favour of a trust, but both this and other points of detail are insignificant in the face of the clearly expressed scheme of clause 9. I therefore agree with Russell LJ and would to that extent allow the appeal, declare that the provisions of clause 9 (a) constitute a trust and remit the case to the Chancery Division for determination whether on this basis clause 9 is (subject to the effects of section 164 of the Law of Property Act, 1925) valid or void for uncertainty.

This makes it necessary to consider whether, in so doing, the court should proceed on the basis that the relevant test is that laid down in *IRC v Broadway Cottages Trust* [1955] Ch 20, [1954] 3 All ER 120 or some other test.

That decision gave the authority of the Court of Appeal to the distinction between cases where trustees are given a *power* of selection and those where they are bound by a *trust* for selection. In the former case the position, as decided by this House, is that the power is valid if it can be said with certainty whether any given individual is or is not a member of the class and does not fail simply because it is impossible to ascertain every member of the class: *Re Gulbenkian's Settlements* [1970] AC 508. But in the latter case it is said to be necessary, for the trust to be valid, that the whole range of objects (I use the language of the Court of Appeal) should be ascertained or capable of ascertainment.

The respondents invited your Lordships to assimilate the validity test for trusts to that which applies to powers. Alternatively they contended that in any event the test laid down in the *Broadway Cottages* case was too rigid, and that a trust should be upheld if there is sufficient practical certainty in its definition for it to be carried out, if necessary with the administrative assistance of the court, according to the expressed intention of the settlor. I would agree with this, but this does not dispense from examination of the wider argument. The basis for the *Broadway Cottages* principle is stated to be that a trust cannot be valid unless, if need be, it can be executed by the court, and (though it is not quite clear from the judgment where argument ends and decision begins) that the court can only execute it by ordering an equal distribution in which every beneficiary shares. So it is necessary to examine the authority and reason for this supposed rule as to the execution of trusts by the court.

Assuming, as I am prepared to do for present purposes, that the test of validity is whether the trust can be executed by the court, it does not follow that execution is impossible unless there can be equal division.

As a matter of reason, to hold that a principle of equal division applies to trusts such as the present is certainly paradoxical. Equal division is surely the last thing the settlor ever intended: equal division among all may, probably would, produce a result beneficial to none. Why suppose that the court would lend itself to a whimsical execution? And as regards authority, I do not find that the nature of the trust, and of the court's powers over trusts, calls for any such rigid rule. Equal division may be sensible and has been decreed, in cases of family trusts, for a limited class; here there is life in the maxim "equality is equity", but the cases provide numerous examples where this has not been so, and a different type of execution has been ordered, appropriate to the circumstances.

Mosely v Moseley (1673) Cas temp Finch 53 is an early example, from the time of equity's architect, where the court assumed power (if the executors did not act) to nominate from the sons of a named person as it should think fit and most worthy and hopeful, the testator's intention being that the estate should not be divided. In *Clarke v Turner* (1694) Freem Ch 198, on a discretionary trust for relations, the court decreed conveyance to the heir-at-law judging it "most reputable for the family that the heir-at-law should have it." In *Warburton v Warburton* (1702) 4 Bro Parl Cas 1, on a discretionary trust to distribute between a number of the testator's children, the House of Lords affirmed a decree of Lord Keeper Wright that the eldest son and heir, regarded as necessitous, should have a double share, the court exercising its own discretionary judgment against equal division.

These are examples of family trusts but in *Richardson v Chapman* (1760) 7 Bro Parl Cas 318 the same principle is shown working in a different field. There was a discretionary trust of the testator's "options" (namely, rights of presentation to benefices or dignities in the Church) between a number of named or specified persons, including present and former chaplains and other domestics; also "my worthy friends and acquaintance, particularly the Reverend Dr. Richardson of Cambridge." The House of Lords (reversing Lord Keeper Henley) set aside a "corrupt" presentation and ordered the trustees to present Dr. Richardson as the most suitable person. The grounds of decision in this House, in accordance with the prevailing practice, were not reported, but it may be supposed that the reported argument was accepted that where the court sets aside the act of the trustee, it can at the same time decree the proper act to be done, not by referring the matter to the trustee's discretion, but by directing him to perform as a mere instrument the thing decreed (ibid., 326, 327). This shows that the court can in a suitable case execute a discretionary trust according to the perceived intention of the trustee. It is interesting also to see that it does not seem to have been contended that the trust was void because of the uncertainty of the words "my worthy friends and acquaintance". There was no doubt that Dr. Richardson came within the designation.

In the time of Lord Eldon, the Court of Chancery adopted a less flexible practice: in *Kemp v Kemp* (1801) 5 Ves 849 Sir Richard Arden MR, commenting on *Warburton v Warburton* (1702) 4 Bro Parl Cas 1 ("a very extraordinary" case), said that the court now disclaims the right to execute a power (i.e., a trust power) and gives the fund equally. But I do not think that this change of attitude, or practice, affects the principle that a discretionary trust *can*, in a suitable case, be executed according to its merits and otherwise than by equal division. I prefer not to suppose that the great masters of equity, if faced with the modern trust for employees, would have failed to adapt their creation to its practical and commercial character. Lord Eldon himself, in *Morice v Bishop of Durham* (1805) 10 Ves 522, laid down clearly enough that a trust fails if the object is insufficiently described or if it cannot be carried out, but these principles may be fully applied to trust powers without requiring a complete ascertainment of all possible objects. His earlier judgment in the leading, and much litigated, case of *Brown v Higgs* (1803) 8 Ves 561 shows that he was far from fastening any rigid test of validity upon trust powers. After stating the distinction, which has ever since been followed, between powers, which the court will not require the donee to execute, and powers in the nature of a trust, or trust powers, he says of the latter that if the trustee does not discharge it, the court will, *to a certain extent*, discharge the duty in his room and place. To support this, he cites *Harding v Glyn* (1739) 1 Atk 469, an early case where the court executed a discretionary trust for "relations" by distributing to the next-of-kin.

I dwell for a moment upon this point because, not only was *Harding v Glyn* described by Lord Eldon 8 Ves 561 at 570 as having been treated as a clear authority in his experience for a long period, but the principle of it was adopted in several nineteenth-century authorities. When the *Broadway Cottages Trust* case came to be decided in 1955, these cases were put aside as anomalous (see [1955] Ch 20 at 33, 35, [1954] 3 All ER 120 at 126, 128), but I think they illustrate the flexible manner in which the court, if called on, executes trust powers for a class. At least they seem to prove that the supposed rule as to equal division does not rest on any principle inherent in the nature of a trust. They prompt me to ask why a practice, or rule, which has been long followed and found useful in "relations" cases should not also serve in regard to "employees", or "employees and their relatives", and whether a decision which says the contrary is acceptable.

I now consider the modern English authorities, particularly those relied on to show that complete ascertainment of the class must be possible before it can be said that a discretionary trust is valid.

Re Ogden [1933] Ch 678 is not a case which I find of great assistance. The argument seems to have turned mainly on the question whether the trust was a purpose trust or a trust for ascertained objects. The latter was held to be the case and the court then held that all the objects of the discretionary gift could be ascertained. It is weak authority for the requirement of complete ascertainment.

The modern shape of the rule derives from *Re Gestetner Settlement* [1953] Ch 672, [1953] 1 All ER 1150, where the judgment of Harman J, to his later regret, established the distinction between discretionary powers and discretionary trusts. The focus of this case was upon powers. The judgment first establishes a distinction between, on the one hand, a power collateral, or appurtenant, or other powers "which do not impose a trust on the conscience of the donee" (at 684, at 1153), and on the other hand a trust imposing a duty to distribute. As to the first, the learned judge said: "I do not think it can be the law that it is necessary to know of all the objects in order to appoint to one of them." As to the latter he uses these words, at 685, at 1153: "It seems to me there is much to be said for the view that he must be able to review the whole field in order to exercise his judgment properly." He then considers authority on the validity of powers, the main stumbling-block in the way of his own view being some words used by Fry J in *Blight v Hartnoll* (1881) 19 ChD 294 at 301, which had been adversely commented on in *Farwell on Powers* (3rd edn, at pp. 168, 169), and I think it worth while quoting the words of his conclusion. He says [1953] Ch 672 at 688, 689, [1953] 1 All ER 1150 at 1155, 1156:

"The settlor had good reason, I have no doubt, to trust the persons whom he appointed trustees; but I cannot see here that there is such a duty as makes it essential for these trustees, before parting with any income or capital, to survey the whole field, and to consider whether A is more deserving of bounty than B. That is a task which was and which must have been known to the settlor to be impossible, having regard to the ramifications of the persons who might become members of this class.

"If, therefore, there be no duty to distribute, but only a duty to consider, it does not seem to me that there is any authority binding on me to say that this whole trust is bad. In fact, there is no difficulty, as has been admitted, in ascertaining whether any given postulant is a member of the specified class. Of course, if that could not be ascertained the matter would be quite different, but of John Doe or Richard Roe it can be postulated easily enough whether he is or is not eligible to receive the settlor's bounty. There being no uncertainty in that sense, I am reluctant to introduce a notion of uncertainty in the other sense, by saying that the trustees must worry their heads to survey the world from China to Peru, when there are perfectly good objects of the class in England."

Subject to one point which was cleared up in this House in *Re Gulbenkian's Settlements* [1970] AC 508, [1968] 3 All ER 785, all of this, if I may say so, seems impeccably good sense, and I do not understand the learned judge to have later repented of it. If the judgment was in any way the cause of future difficulties, it was in the indication given — not by way of decision, for the point did not arise — that there was a distinction between the kind of certainty required for powers and that required for trusts. There is a difference perhaps but the difference is a narrow one, and if one is looking to reality one could hardly find better words than those I have just quoted to describe what trustees, in either case, ought to know. A second look at this case, while fully justifying the decision, suggests to me that it does not discourage the application of a similar test for the validity of trusts.

So I come to *IRC v Broadway Cottages Trust* [1955] Ch 20, [1954] 3 All ER 120. This was certainly a case of trust, and it proceeded on the basis of an admission, in the words of the judgment, "that the class of 'beneficiaries' is incapable of ascertainment". In addition to the discretionary trust of income, there was a trust of capital for all the beneficiaries living or existing at the terminal date. This necessarily involved equal division and it seems to have been accepted that it was void for uncertainty since there cannot be equal division among a class unless all the members of the class are known. The Court of Appeal applied this proposition to the discretionary trust of income, on the basis that execution by the court was only possible on the same basis of equal division. They rejected the argument that the trust could be executed by changing the trusteeship, and found the relations cases of no assistance as being in a class by themselves. The court could not create an arbitrarily restricted trust to take effect in default of distribution by the trustees. Finally they rejected the submission that the trust could take effect as a power: a valid power could not be spelt out of an invalid trust.

My Lords, it will have become apparent that there is much in this which I find out of line with principle and authority but before I come to a conclusion on it, I must examine the decision of this House in *Re Gulbenkian's Settlements* on which the appellants placed much reliance as amounting to an endorsement of the *Broadway Cottages* case. But is this really so?

[His Lordship examined the case and continued:] What this does say, and I respectfully agree, is that, in the case of a trust, the trustees must select from the class. What it does not say, as I read it, or imply, is that in order to carry out their duty of selection they must have before them, or be able to get, a complete list of all possible objects.

So I think that we are free to review the *Broadway Cottages* case. The conclusion which I would reach, implicit in the previous discussion, is that the wide distinction between the validity test for powers and that for trust powers is unfortunate and wrong, that the rule recently fastened upon the courts by *IRC v Broadway Cottages Trust* ought to be discarded, and that the test for the validity of trust powers ought to be similar to that accepted by this House in *Re Gulbenkian's Settlements* for powers, namely, that the trust is valid if it can be said with certainty that any given individual is or is not a member of the class.

I am interested, and encouraged, to find that the conclusion I had reached by the end of the argument is supported by distinguished American authority. Professor Scott in his well-known book on trusts (*Scott on Trusts* (1939)) discusses the suggested distinction as regards validity between trusts and powers and expresses the opinion that this would be "highly technical" (s. 122, p. 613). Later in the second *Restatement of Trusts* (1959), s. 122 (which *Restatement* aims at stating the better modern view and which annotates the *Broadway Cottages* case), a common test of invalidity is taken, whether trustees are "authorised" or "directed": this is that the class must not be so indefinite that it cannot be ascertained whether any person falls within it. The reporter is

Professor Austin Scott. In his abridgment, published in 1960 (*Scott's Abridgment of The Law of Trusts*, s. 122, p. 239), Professor Scott maintains the same position:

> "It would seem that if a power of appointment among the members of an indefinite class is valid, the mere fact that the testator intended not merely to confer a power but to impose a duty to make such an appointment should not preclude the making of such an appointment. It would seem to be the height of technicality that if a testator *authorises* a legatee to divide the property among such of the testator's friends as he might select, he can properly do so, but that if he *directs* him to make such a selection, he will not be permitted to do so."

Assimilation of the validity test does not involve the complete assimilation of trust powers with powers. As to powers, I agree with my noble and learned friend Lord Upjohn in *Re Gulbenkian's Settlements* that although the trustees may, and normally will, be under a fiduciary duty to consider whether or in what way they should exercise their power, the court will not normally compel its exercise. It will intervene if the trustees exceed their powers, and possibly if they are proved to have exercised it capriciously. But in the case of a trust power, if the trustees do not exercise it, the court will: I respectfully adopt as to this the statement in Lord Upjohn's opinion at 525, at 793. I would venture to amplify this by saying that the court, if called upon to execute the trust power, will do so in the manner best calculated to give effect to the settlor's or testator's intentions. It may do so by appointing new trustees, or by authorising or directing representative persons of the classes of beneficiaries to prepare a scheme of distribution, or even, should the proper basis for distribution appear by itself directing the trustees so to distribute.[10] The books give many instances where this has been done, and I see no reason in principle why they should not do so in the modern field of discretionary trusts (see *Brunsden v Woolredge* (1765) Amb 507; *Supple v Lowson* (1773) Amb 729; *Liley v Hey* (1842) 1 Hare 580 and *Lewin on Trusts*, 16th edn (1964), p. 630). Then, as to the trustees' duty of inquiry or ascertainment, in each case the trustees ought to make such a survey of the range of objects or possible beneficiaries as will enable them to carry out their fiduciary duty (cf. *Liley v Hey*). A wider and more comprehensive range of inquiry is called for in the case of trust powers than in the case of powers.

Two final points: first, as to the question of certainty. I desire to emphasise the distinction clearly made and explained by Lord Upjohn at 524, at 793 between linguistic or semantic uncertainty which, if unresolved by the court, renders the gift void, and the difficulty of ascertaining the existence or whereabouts of members of the class, a matter with which the court can appropriately deal on an application for directions. There may be a third case where the meaning of the words used is clear but the definition of beneficiaries is so hopelessly wide as not to form "anything like a class" so that the trust is administratively unworkable or in Lord Eldon's words one that cannot be

---

10 *Re Locker's Settlement* [1977] 1 WLR 1323, [1978] 1 All ER 216, where the existing trustees of an exhaustive discretionary trust, who had failed to make annual distribution of income, were nevertheless allowed to apply their discretion in the distribution of the income, but "only in favour of such objects or some or one of them as would have been objects of the said discretion had it been exercised within a reasonable time after receipt of the income" (per GOULDING J at 1327, at 219); [1978] Conv 166 (F.R. Crane); (1978) 94 LQR 177. The court has similar powers of intervention in the case of a fiduciary power: *Mettoy Pension Trustees Ltd v Evans* [1990] 1 WLR 1587, [1991] 2 All ER 513, p. 45 ante.

executed: *Morice v Bishop of Durham* (1805) 10 Ves 522 at 527. I hesitate to give examples for they may prejudice future cases, but perhaps "all the residents of Greater London" will serve. I do not think that a discretionary trust for "relatives" even of a living person falls within this category.[11]

I would allow the appeal . . . .

On remittance to the Chancery Division, BRIGHTMAN J and the Court of Appeal (SACHS, MEGAW and STAMP LJJ) (in **Re Baden's Deed Trusts (No 2)** [1973] Ch 9, [1972] 2 All ER 1304[12]) found that the test of certainty was satisfied. The wide differences in their application of the test demonstrates how difficult it may prove to be in practice.

SACHS LJ: The next point as regards approach that requires consideration is the contention, strongly pressed by Mr. Vinelott, that the court must always be able to say whether any given postulant is *not* within the relevant class as well as being able to say whether he is within it. In construing the words already cited from the speech of Lord Wilberforce in the *Baden* case (as well as those of Lord Reid and Lord Upjohn in the *Gulbenkian* case), it is essential to bear in mind the difference between conceptual uncertainty and evidential difficulties . . .[13]

As Mr. Vinelott himself rightly observed, "the court is never defeated by evidential uncertainty," and it is in my judgment clear that it is conceptual certainty to which reference was made when the "is or is not a member of the class" test was enunciated. (Conceptual uncertainty was in the course of argument conveniently exemplified, rightly or wrongly matters not, by the phrase "someone under a moral obligation" and contrasted with the certainty of the words "first cousins.") Once the class of person to be benefitted is conceptually certain it then becomes a question of fact to be determined on evidence whether any postulant has on inquiry been proved to be within it: if he is not so proved, then he is not in it. That position remains the same whether the class to be benefited happens to be small (such as "first cousins") or large (such as "members of the X Trade Union" or "those who have served in the Royal Navy"). The suggestion that such trusts could be invalid because it might be impossible to prove of a given individual that he was *not* in the

---

11 See *Blausten v IRC* [1972] Ch 256 at 271–273, [1972] 1 All ER 41 at 49–51, where some of these points are further discussed; *Re Manisty's Settlement* [1974] Ch 17 at 27–29, [1973] 2 All ER 1203, at 1211–1213, where TEMPLEMAN J, discussing this point in the context of intermediate powers, said, at 27, at 1211: "A power to benefit 'residents of Greater London' is capricious because the terms of the power negative any sensible intention on the part of the settlor."; (1974) 38 Conv (NS) 269 (L. McKay); *Re Hay's Settlement Trusts* [1982] 1 WLR 202, [1981] 3 All ER 786, p. 39 ante (where MEGARRY V-C "thought that he would, if necessary, hold" that an intermediate discretionary trust would be void for administrative unworkability); [1982] Conv 432 (A. Grubb); *R v District Auditor, ex p West Yorkshire Metropolitan County Council* [1986] RVR 24, p. 84, post.

12 (1973) 36 Conv (NS) 351 (D.J. Hayton); [1973] CLJ 36 (J.A. Hopkins); *Re Bethel* (1971) 17 DLR (3d) 652; (1971) ASCL 377; (1981) 9 Syd LR 58 (R.P. Austin).

13 In *Re Tuck's Settlement Trusts* [1978] Ch 49 at 60, [1978] 1 All ER 1047 at 1052, Lord DENNING MR described this distinction as a "deplorable dichotomy", serving only to defeat the settlor's intention. But this distinction was acknowledged by HL in *Blathwayt v Lord Cawley* [1976] AC 397 at 425, [1975] 3 All ER 625 at 635.

relevant class is wholly fallacious — and only Mr. Vinelott's persuasiveness has prevented me from saying that the contention is almost unarguable . . .

In agreement with the practical approach of Brightman J [1972] Ch 607 at 625, [1971] 3 All ER 985 at 995, I consider that the trustees, or if necessary the court, are quite capable of coming to a conclusion in any given case as to whether or not a particular candidate could properly be described as a dependant — a word that, as the judge said, "conjures up a sufficiently distinct picture". I agree, too, that any one wholly or partly dependent on the means of another is a "dependant". There is thus no conceptual uncertainty inherent in that word and the executors' contentions as to the effect of its use fail.

As regards "relatives" Brightman J, after stating, at 625, at 995, "It is not in dispute that a person is a relative of an . . . employee . . . , if both trace legal descent from a common ancestor:" a little later said: "In practice, the use of the expression 'relatives' cannot cause the slightest difficulty." With that view I agree for the reasons he gave when he correctly set out the evidential position.

MEGAW LJ: The main argument of Mr. Vinelott was founded upon a strict and literal interpretation of the words in which the decision of the House of Lords in *Re Gulbenkian's Settlements* [1970] AC 508, [1968] 3 All ER 785 was expressed. That decision laid down the test for the validity of powers of selection. It is relevant for the present case, because in the previous excursion of this case to the House of Lords [1971] AC 424, [1970] 2 All ER 228 it was held that there is no relevant difference in the test of validity, whether the trustees are given a power of selection or, as was held by their Lordships to be the case in this trust deed, a trust for selection. The test in either case is what may be called the *Gulbenkian* test. The *Gulbenkian* test, as expressed by Lord Wilberforce at 450, at 244, and again in almost identical words at 454, at 246 is this:

" . . . the power is valid if it can be said with certainty whether any given individual is or is not a member of the class and does not fail simply because it is impossible to ascertain every member of the class."

The executors' argument concentrates on the words "or is not" in the first of the two limbs of the sentence quoted above: "if it can be said with certainty whether any given individual is *or is not* a member of the class". It is said that those words have been used deliberately, and have only one possible meaning; and that, however startling or drastic or unsatisfactory the result may be – and Mr. Vinelott does not shrink from saying that the consequence is drastic – this court is bound to give effect to the words used in the House of Lords' definition of the test. It would be quite impracticable for the trustees to ascertain in many cases whether a particular person was *not* a relative of an employee. The most that could be said is: "There is no proof that he is a relative." But there would still be no "certainty" that such a person was not a relative. Hence, so it is said, the test laid down by the House of Lords is not satisfied, and the trust is void. For it cannot be said with certainty, in relation to any individual, that he is not a relative.

I do not think it was contemplated that the words "or is not" would produce that result. It would, as I see it, involve an inconsistency with the latter part of the same sentence: "does not fail simply because it is impossible to ascertain every member of the class". The executors' contention, in substance and reality, is that it *does* fail "simply because it is impossible to ascertain every member of the class".

The same verbal difficulty, as I see it, emerges also when one considers the words of the suggested test which the House of Lords expressly rejected. That is set out by Lord Wilberforce in a passage immediately following the sentence which I have already quoted. The rejected test was in these terms [1971] AC 424 at 450, [1970] 2 All ER 228 at 241: " . . . it is said to be necessary . . . that the whole range of objects . . . should be ascertained or capable of ascertainment". Since that test was rejected, the resulting affirmative proposition, which by implication must have been accepted by their Lordships, is this: a trust for selection will not fail simply because the whole range of objects cannot be ascertained. In the present case, the trustees could ascertain, by investigation and evidence, many of the objects: as to many other theoretically possible claimants, they could not be certain. Is it to be said that the trust fails because it cannot be said with certainty that such persons are not members of the class? If so, is that not the application of the rejected test: the trust failing because "the whole range of objects cannot be ascertained"?

In my judgment, much too great emphasis is placed in the executor's argument on the words "or is not". To my mind, the test is satisfied if, as regards at least a substantial number of objects, it can be said with certainty that they fall within the trust; even though, as regards a substantial number of other persons, if they ever for some fanciful reason fell to be considered, the answer would have to be, not "they are outside the trust", but "it is not proven whether they are in or out". What is a "substantial number" may well be a question of common sense and of degree in relation to the particular trust: particularly where, as here, it would be fantasy, to use a mild word, to suggest that any practical difficulty would arise in the fair, proper and sensible administration of this trust in respect of relatives and dependants.

I do not think that this involves, as Mr. Vinelott suggested, a return by this court to its former view which was rejected by the House of Lords in the *Gulbenkian* case. If I did so think, I should, however reluctantly, accept Mr. Vinelott's argument and its consequences. But as I read it, the criticism in the House of Lords of the decision of this court in that case related to this court's acceptance of the view that it would be sufficient if it could be shown that *one single person* fell within the scope of the power or trust. The essence of the decision of the House of Lords in the *Gulbenkian* case, as I see it, is *not* that it must be possible to show with certainty that any given person is *or is not* within the trust; but that it is not, or may not be, sufficient to be able to show that one individual person is within it. If it does not mean that, I do not know where the line is supposed to be drawn, having regard to the clarity and emphasis with which the House of Lords has laid down that the trust does not fail because the whole range of objects cannot be ascertained.

I would dismiss the appeal.

STAMP LJ: Mr. Vinelott, fastening on those words, "if it can be said with certainty that any given individual is or is not a member of the class", submitted in this court that a trust for distribution among officers and employees or ex-officers or ex-employees or any of their relatives or dependants does not satisfy the test. You may say with certainty that any given individual is or is not an officer, employee, ex-officer or ex-employee. You may say with certainty that a very large number of given individuals are relatives of one of them; but, so the argument runs, you will never be able to say with certainty of many given individuals that they are not. I am bound to say that I had thought at one stage of Mr. Vinelott's able argument that this was no more than an exercise in semantics and that the phrase on which he relies indicated no more than that the trust was valid if there was such certainty in the definition of membership of the class that you could say with certainty that some individuals were members of it: that it was sufficient that you should be satisfied that a given individual presenting himself has or has not passed the test and that it matters not that having failed to establish his membership — here his relationship — you may, perhaps wrongly, reject him. There are, however, in my judgment serious difficulties in the way of a rejection of Mr. Vinelott's submission.

The first difficulty, as I see it, is that the rejection of Mr. Vinelott's submission involves holding that the trust is good if there are individuals — or even one — of whom you can say with certainty that he is a member of the class. That was the test adopted by and the decision of the Court of Appeal in the *Gulbenkian* case where what was under consideration was a power of distribution among a class conferred upon trustees as distinct from a trust for distribution: but when the *Gulbenkian* case came before the House of Lords that test was decisively rejected and the more stringent test upon which Mr. Vinelott insists was adopted. Clearly Lord Wilberforce in expressing the view that the test of validity of a discretionary trust ought to be similar to that accepted by the House of Lords in the *Gulbenkian* case did not take the view that it was sufficient that you could find individuals who were clearly members of the class; for he himself remarked, towards the end of his speech as to the trustees' duty of inquiring or ascertaining, that in each case the trustees ought to make such a survey of the range of objects or possible beneficiaries as will enable them to carry out their fiduciary duty. It is not enough that trustees should do nothing but distribute the fund among those objects of the trust who happen to be at hand or present themselves. Lord Wilberforce, after citing that passage which I have already quoted from the speech of Lord Upjohn in the *Gulbenkian* case, put it more succinctly by remarking that what this did say (and he agreed) was that the trustees must select from the class, but that passage did not mean (as had been contended) that they must be able to get a complete list of all possible objects. I have already called attention to Lord Wilberforce's opinion that the trustees ought to make such a survey of the range of objects or possible beneficiaries as will enable them to carry out their fiduciary duty, and I ought perhaps to add that he indicated that a wider and more comprehensive range of inquiry is called for in the case of what I have called discretionary trusts than in the case of fiduciary powers. But, as I understand it, having made the appropriate survey, it matters not that it is not complete or fails to yield a result enabling you to lay out a list or particulars of every single beneficiary. Having done the best they can, the trustees may proceed upon the basis similar to that adopted by the court where all the beneficiaries cannot be ascertained and distribute upon the footing that they have been: see, for example, *Re Benjamin* [1902] 1 Ch 723. What was referred to as "the complete ascertainment test" laid down by this court in the *Broadway Cottages* case is rejected. So also is the test laid down by this court in the *Gulbenkian* case. Validity or invalidity is to depend upon whether you can say of any individual — and the accent must be upon that word "any", for it is not simply the individual whose claim you are considering who is spoken of — "is or is not a member of the class", for only thus can you make a survey of the range of objects or possible beneficiaries.

If the matter rested there, it would in my judgment follow that, treating the word "relatives" as meaning descendants from a common ancestor, a trust for distribution such as is here in question would not be valid. Any "survey of the range of the objects or possible beneficiaries" would certainly be incomplete, and I am able to discern no principle upon which such a survey could be conducted or where it should start or finish. The most you could do, so far as regards relatives, would be to find individuals who are clearly members of the class — the test which was accepted in the Court of Appeal, but rejected in the House of Lords, in the *Gulbenkian* case.

The matter does not, however, rest there ... *Harding v Glyn* (1739) 1 Atk 469 ... was an early case where the court executed a discretionary trust for "relations" — and it is a discretionary trust for relations that I am considering — by distributing to the next of kin in equal shares[14] ...

Harding v Glyn accordingly cannot be regarded simply as a case where in default of appointment a gift to the next of kin is to be implied as a matter of construction, but as authority endorsed by the decision of the House of Lords [1971] AC 424, [1970] 2 All ER 228, that a discretionary trust for "relations" was a valid trust to be executed by the court by distribution to the next of kin. The class of beneficiaries thus becomes a clearly defined class and there is no difficulty in determining whether a given individual is within it or without it.

Does it then make any difference that here the discretionary trust for relations was a reference not to the relations of a deceased person but of one who was living? I think not. The next of kin of a living person are as readily ascertainable at any given time as the next of kin of one who is dead.

Hackney: *Understanding Equity and Trusts* (1987), pp. 58–59.

"Since courts are prepared to strike down dispositions in favour of classes of objects on the grounds that the objects are too uncertain, they have signalled that the settlor's views, or those of the trustees, are not conclusive on the question of validity. Here, as in the matter of intention and subject matter, a number of interests are at stake, some of them conflicting. Settlors have their own conflicting interests. In general terms they want a relaxed test, as that will result in a greater chance of their dispositions being held valid. But they do not want too relaxed a test, as they do not want trustees to be able to play fast and loose with their intentions. Objects or potential objects (those within range of the settlor's benevolent intentions) have a similar dilemma: wide tests will increase their chances of qualifying, but once qualified they will not want a test so wide that they cannot easily calculate their chances of success if they wish to challenge a particular appointment by a trustee on the grounds that the appointee was a non-object. The trustee's selfish interest is in a tightly drawn test. He must administer the trust properly, according to its terms. A conscientious trustee will want a test that allows him to do that with a minimum of doubt, and of course he faces the unique difficulty that if he pays to the wrong objects either on a valid or invalid trust or power, he will have to make good the deficit, and though courts have power to excuse him, they do not always do so. A trustee in sympathy with the aims of the settlor will be likely to want a test which is less strict, and so he too will settle for a compromise. The public interest is in having a test which does not result in continuous litigation. Litigation is a particular evil in this part of the law, which is overwhelmingly

---

14 Cf *Re Barlow's Will Trusts* [1979] 1 WLR 278, [1979] 1 All ER 296, p. 87, post, where "relations" was held to mean everyone related by blood to the testatrix.

dominated by planning considerations. The ideal is that the law should be capable of formulation in such a way that legal advisers can produce instruments that are free of legal defect and which can operate entirely outside the court. Until court lists are much reduced, courts have better things to do than involve themselves in the luxury of avoidable disputes about certainty of objects, which both hold up other business and cost money to beneficiaries. It is an abuse of judicial power for a judge to say he is happy to have a relaxed test in the interests of enhancing settlors' wishes, and that if anyone has any problem with operating it, all they have to do is go along to see him. The public also presumably has some input in the kind of freedom of disposition which they are happy for settlors to have, and this may differ from the freedom they might themselves wish, were they not considering the public interest.''

(b)   Administrative Unworkability. Capriciousness

In **R v District Auditor, ex p West Yorkshire Metropolitan County Council** [1986] RVR 24,[15] a local authority resolved to create a trust under which the trustees were ''to apply and expend the Trust Fund for the benefit of any or all or some of the inhabitants of the County of West Yorkshire'' in four specified ways. It was conceded that this was not a charitable trust, because one of its objects, the dissemination of information about the proposed abolition of the metropolitan county councils, was not charitable. In holding that the trust could not take effect as an express private trust, LLOYD LJ said at 26:

''Counsel for the county council did not seek to argue that the trust is valid as a charitable trust, though he did not concede the point in case he should have second thoughts in a higher court. His case was that the trust could take effect as an express private trust. For the creation of an express private trust three things are required. First, there must be a clear intention to create the trust. Secondly there must be certainty as to the subject matter of the trust; and thirdly there must be certainty as to the persons intended to benefit. Two of the three certainties, as they are familiarly called, were present here. Was the third? He argued that the beneficiaries of the trust were all or some of the inhabitants of the county of West Yorkshire. The class might be on the large side, containing as it does some $2\frac{1}{2}$ m potential beneficiaries. But the definition, it was said, is straightforward and clear cut. There is no uncertainty as to the concept. If anyone were to come forward and claim to be a beneficiary, it could be said of him at once whether he was within the class or not.

I cannot accept counsel for the county council's argument. I am prepared to assume in favour of the council, without deciding, that the class is defined with sufficient clarity. I do not decide the point because it might, as it seems to me, be open to argument what is meant by ''an inhabitant'' of the county of West Yorkshire. But I put that difficulty on one side. For there is to my mind a more fundamental difficulty. A trust with as many as $2\frac{1}{2}$m potential beneficiaries is, in my judgment, quite simply unworkable. The class is far too large. In *Re Gulbenkian's Settlements* [1970] AC 508, [1968] 3 All ER 785 Lord Reid said at 518, at 787:

'It may be that there is a class of case where, although the description of a class of beneficiaries is clear enough, any attempt to apply it to the facts would lead to such administrative difficulties that it would for that reason be held to be invalid.'

15 [1986] CLJ 391 (C. Harpum).

[His Lordship quoted Lord WILBERFORCE's final paragraph in *McPhail v Doulton* [1971] AC 424 at 457, [1970] 2 All ER 228 at 247, p. 79, ante, and continued:]

It seems to me that the present trust comes within the third case to which Lord Wilberforce refers. I hope I am not guilty of being prejudiced by the example which he gave. But it could hardly be more apt, or fit the facts of the present case more precisely.

I mention the subsequent decisions in *Re Baden's Deed Trusts (No 2)* [1972] Ch 607, [1971] 3 All ER 985, and on appeal [1973] Ch 9, [1972] 2 All ER 1304, p. 79, ante, and *Re Manisty's Settlement* [1974] Ch 17, [1973] 2 All ER 1203, p. 40, ante, with misgiving, since they were not cited in argument. The latter was a case of an intermediate power, that is to say, a power exercisable by trustees in favour of all the world, other than members of an excepted class.

After referring to *Gulbenkian* and the two *Baden* cases, Templeman J (as he then was) said:

'I conclude ... that a power cannot be uncertain merely because it is wide in ambit.'

A power to benefit, for example, the residents of Greater London might, he thought, be bad, not on the ground of its width but on the ground of capriciousness, since the settlor could have no sensible intention to benefit 'an accidental conglomeration of persons' who had 'no discernible link with the settlor'. But that objection could not apply here. The council had every reason for wishing to benefit the inhabitants of West Yorkshire.

Lord Wilberforce's dictum has also been the subject of a good deal of academic comment and criticism, noticeably by L McKay (1974) 38 Conv 269 and CT Emery (1982) 98 LQR 551. I should have welcomed further argument on these matters, but through no fault of counsel for the county council this was not possible. So I have to do the best I can.

My conclusion is that the dictum of Lord Wilberforce remains of high persuasive authority, despite *Re Manisty*. *Manisty's* case was concerned with a power, where the function of the court is more restricted. In the case of a trust, the court may have to execute the trust. Not so in the case of a power. That there may still be a distinction between trusts and powers in this connection was recognised by Templeman J himself in the sentence immediately following his quotation of Lord Wilberforce's dictum, when he said:

'In these guarded terms Lord Wilberforce appears to refer to trusts which may have to be executed and administered by the court and not to powers where the court has a very much more limited function.'

There can be no doubt that the declaration of trust in the present case created a trust and not a power. Following Lord Wilberforce's dictum, I would hold that the definition of the beneficiaries of the trust is 'so hopelessly wide' as to be incapable of forming 'anything like a class'. I would therefore reject counsel for the county council's argument that the declaration of trust can take effect as an express private trust.

Since, as I have already said, it was not argued that the trust can take effect as a valid charitable trust, it follows that the declaration of trust is ineffective. What we have here, in a nutshell, is a non-charitable purpose trust. It is clear law that, subject to certain exceptions, such trusts are void: see *Lewin on Trusts*, 16th edn, pp. 17–19. The present case does not come within any of the established exceptions. Nor can it be brought within the scope of such recent decisions as *Re Denley's Trust Deed* [1969] 1 Ch 373, [1968] 3 All ER 65, p. 322, post and *Re Lipinski's Will Trusts* [1976] Ch 235, [1977] 1 All ER 33, p. 319, post, since there are, for the reasons I have given, no ascertained or ascertainable beneficiaries."[16]

(c) *Many Certain Categories; One Uncertain*

Hanbury & Martin: *Modern Equity* (14th edn) p. 110

"Further difficulties could arise with a definition of a class of beneficiaries which contained a long series of categories which complied with the *McPhail v Doulton* test, but to which there was added one category which did not. What, for example, would the court say to a trust in the same language as that in *McPhail v Doulton* but to which there was added 'any person to whom I may be under a moral obligation and any of my old friends? ... which is, let it be assumed, conceptually uncertain. The same problem as we have seen could arise in a case of power.

In this situation, the class as a whole does not satisfy the test. It would however be unfortunate to declare the whole trust void because of the final addition. After all, the trust is eminently workable as it is. Such a trust, however, may be held void unless it is possible to excise the offending phrase by the operation of a species of severance; a suggestion which is made on more than one occasion."[17]

ii. Gift Subject to a Condition Precedent

In **Re Barlow's Will Trusts** [1979] 1 WLR 278, [1979] 1 All ER 296,[18] the testatrix died in 1975, owning a large collection of valuable pictures. By her will she gave some of them to her executor upon trust for sale, and added a direction to him "to allow any member of my family and any friends of mine who may wish to do so to purchase any of such pictures" at a valuation made in 1970 or at probate value whichever should be the lower.

In holding that the direction was valid, Browne-Wilkinson J said at 280, at 298:

"The main questions which arise for my decision are (a) whether the direction to allow members of the family and friends to purchase the pictures is void for uncertainty since the meaning of the word 'friends' is too vague to be given legal effect; and (b) what persons are to be treated as being members of the testatrix's family. I will deal first with the question of uncertainty.

Those arguing against the validity of the gift in favour of the friends contend that, in the absence of any guidance from the testatrix, the question 'Who were her friends?' is incapable of being answered. The word is said to be 'conceptually uncertain' since there are so many different degrees of friendship and it is impossible to say which degree the testatrix had in mind. In

16 See *Re Beatty* [1990] 1 WLR 1503, p. 307 post (fiduciary power given to trustees in favour of "such person or persons as they think fit" held valid without consideration of administrative unworkability); [1991] Conv 138 (J. Martin).
17 Per Sachs LJ in *Re Leek* [1969] 1 Ch 563 at 586, [1968] 1 All ER 793 at 801; and in the case of a power by Winn LJ in *Re Gulbenkian's Settlements* [1968] Ch 126 at 138, [1967] 3 All ER 15 at 21; cf. decisions on trusts which are not exclusively charitable, p. 459, post.
18 [1980] Conv 263 (L. McKay); (1982) 126 SJ 518 (N.D.M. Parry); (1982) 98 LQR 551, 562–567 (C.T. Emery).

support of this argument they rely on Lord Upjohn's remarks in *Re Gulbenkian's Settlements* [1970] AC 508, [1968] 3 All ER 785, and the decision of the House of Lords in *Re Baden's Deed Trusts* [1971] AC 424, [1970] 2 All ER 228, to the effect that it must be possible to say who is within and who without the class of friends. They say that since the testatrix intended all her friends to have the opportunity to acquire a picture, it is necessary to be able to ascertain with certainty all the members of that class.

Mr. Shillingford, who argued in favour of the validity of the gift, contended that the test laid down in the *Gulbenkian* and *Baden* cases was not applicable to this case; the test, he says, is that laid down by the Court of Appeal in *Re Allen* [1953] Ch 810, [1953] 2 All ER 898, as appropriate in cases where the validity of a condition precedent or description is in issue, namely, that the gift is valid if it is possible to say of one or more persons that he or they undoubtedly qualify even though it may be difficult to say of others whether or not they qualify.

The distinction between the *Gulbenkian* test and the *Re Allen* test is, in my judgment, well exemplified by the word 'friends'. The word has a great range of meanings; indeed, its exact meaning probably varies slightly from person to person. Some would include only those with whom they had been on intimate terms over a long period; others would include acquaintances whom they liked. Some would include people with whom their relationship was primarily one of business; others would not. Indeed, many people, if asked to draw up a complete list of their friends, would probably have some difficulty in deciding whether certain of the people they knew were really 'friends' as opposed to 'acquaintances.' Therefore, if the nature of the gift was such that it was legally necessary to draw up a complete list of 'friends' of the testatrix, or to be able to say of any person that 'he is not a friend', the whole gift would probably fail even as to those who, by any conceivable test, were friends.

But in the case of a gift of a kind which does not require one to establish all the members of the class (e.g. 'a gift of £10 to each of my friends'), it may be possible to say of some people that on any test, they qualify. Thus in *Re Allen* at 817, at 901, Sir Raymond Evershed MR took the example of a gift to X 'if he is a tall man'; a man 6 ft. 6 ins. tall could be said on any reasonable basis to satisfy the test, although it might be impossible to say whether a man, say, 5ft. 10ins. high satisfied the requirement.

So in this case, in my judgment, there are acquaintances of a kind so close that, on any reasonable basis, anyone would treat them as being 'friends'. Therefore, by allowing the disposition to take effect in their favour, one would certainly be giving effect to part of the testatrix's intention even though as to others it is impossible to say whether or not they satisfy the test.

In my judgment, it is clear that Lord Upjohn in *Re Gulbenkian's Settlements* [1970] AC 508, [1968] 3 All ER 785 was considering only cases where it was necessary to establish all the members of the class. He makes it clear, at 524, at 793, that the reason for the rule is that in a gift which requires one to establish all the members of the class (e.g. 'a gift to my friends in equal shares') you cannot hold the gift good in part, since the quantum of each friend's share depends on how many friends there are. So all persons intended to benefit by the donor must be ascertained if any effect is to be given to the gift. In my judgment, the adoption of Lord Upjohn's test by the House of Lords in the *Baden* case is based on the same reasoning, even though in that case the House of Lords held that it was only necessary to be able to survey the class of objects of a power of appointment and not to establish who all the members are.

But such reasoning has no application to a case where there is a condition or description attached to one or more individual gifts; in such cases, uncertainty as to some other persons who may have been intended to take does not in any way affect the quantum of the gift to persons who undoubtedly possess the qualification. Hence, in my judgment, the different test laid down in *Re Allen* [1953] Ch 810, [1953] 2 All ER 898.

The recent decision of the Court of Appeal in *Re Tuck's Settlement Trusts* [1978] Ch 49, [1978] 1 All ER 1047, p. 652, post establishes that the test in *Re Allen* is still the appropriate test in considering such gifts, notwithstanding the *Gulbenkian* and *Baden* decisions: see per Lord Russell of Killowen at 65, at 1056.

Accordingly, in my judgment, the proper result in this case depends on whether the disposition in clause 5 (a) is properly to be regarded as a series of individual gifts to persons answering the description 'friend' (in which case it will be valid), or a gift which requires the whole class of friends to be established (in which case it will probably fail).

The effect of clause 5 (a) is to confer on friends of the testatrix a series of options to purchase. Although it is obviously desirable as a practical matter that steps should be taken to inform those entitled to the options of their rights, it is common ground that there is no legal necessity to do so. Therefore, each person coming forward to exercise the option has to prove that he is a friend; it is not legally necessary, in my judgment, to discover who all the friends are. In order to decide whether an individual is entitled to purchase, all that is required is that the executors should be able to say of that individual whether he has proved that he is a friend. The world 'friend', therefore, is a description or qualification of the option holder.

It was suggested that by allowing undoubted friends to take I would be altering the testatrix's intentions. It is said that she intended all her friends to have a chance to buy any given picture, and since some people she might have regarded as friends will not be able to apply, the number of competitors for that picture will be reduced. This may be so; but I cannot regard this factor as making it legally necessary to establish the whole class of friends. The testatrix's intention was that a friend should acquire a picture. My decision gives effect to that intention.

I therefore hold that the disposition does not fail for uncertainty, but that anyone who can prove that by any reasonable test he or she must have been a friend of the testatrix is entitled to exercise the option. Without seeking to lay down any exhaustive definition of such test, it may be helpful if I indicate certain minimum requirements: (a) the relationship must have been a longstanding one. (b) The relationship must have been a social relationship as opposed to a business or professional relationship. (c) Although there may have been long periods when circumstances prevented the testatrix and the applicant from meeting, when circumstances did permit they must have met frequently. If in any case the executors entertain any real doubt whether an applicant qualifies, they can apply to the court to decide the issue.

Finally on this aspect of the case I should notice two further cases to which I was referred. The first is *Re Gibbard's Will Trusts* [1967] 1 WLR 42, [1966] 1 All ER 273 in which Plowman J upheld the validity of a power to appoint to 'any of my old friends'. It is not necessary for me to decide whether that decision is still good law, in that it applied the *Re Allen* test to powers of appointment. But it does show that, if the *Re Allen* test is the correct test, the word 'friends' is not too uncertain to be given effect.

Secondly, in *Re Lloyd's Trust Instruments* (24 June 1970, unreported) but extracts from which are to be found in *Brown v Gould* [1972] Ch 53, 56–57 [1971] 2 All ER 1505, 1507–1508, Megarry J stated, at 57, at 1508:

'If there is a trust for "my old friends", all concerned are faced with uncertainty as to the concept or idea enshrined in those words. It may not be difficult to resolve that "old" means not "aged" but "of long standing"; but then there is the question of how long is "long". Friendship, too, is a concept with almost infinite shades of meaning. Where the concept is uncertain, the gift is void. Where the concept is certain, then mere difficulty in tracing and discovering those who are entitled normally does not invalidate the gift.'

The extract that I have read itself shows that Megarry J was considering a trust for 'my old friends' (which required the whole class to be ascertained) and not such a case as I have to deal with. In my judgment, that dictum was not intended to apply to such a case as I have before me.

I turn now to the question who are to be treated as 'members of my family.' It is not suggested that this class is too uncertain. The contest is between those who say that only the next of kin of the testatrix are entitled, and those who say that everyone related by blood to the testatrix are included."

[His Lordship then held that everyone related by blood to the testatrix was included].

D. Absence of Certainties

Snell, *Principles of Equity* (29th edn 1980), p. 117.

"The effect of the absence of any of the certainties may be summarised as follows. The paramount certainty is that of subject-matter, in the first sense; if there is no certainty as to the property to be held upon trust, the entire transaction is nugatory. Next, if that certainty is present but there is no certainty of words, the person entitled to the trust property holds free from any trust. Finally, if both these certainties are present but there is uncertainty of objects, there is a resulting trust for the settlor, for 'once establish that a trust [of definite property] was intended, and the legatee cannot take beneficially';[19] the same applies where there is uncertainty of the subject-matter as regards the beneficial interest, unless one of the beneficiaries can establish a claim to the whole.

It will be noticed that the order in which these points should be considered is the natural order of any limitation in trust, e.g. where trustees hold 'Blackacre in trust for A and B equally.' "

---

19 *Briggs v Penny* (1851) 3 Mac & G 546 at 557, per Lord TRURO LC.

1   Read again the sections on Powers (pp. 34–48 ante) and on Certainty of
     Objects (pp. 70–90 ante), and then tabulate the duties of trustees/
     donees of powers, and the tests for certainty of objects, in each of the
     following categories:
     (a) Fixed trusts
     (b) Trusts with a power of selection: e.g. *Burrough v Philcox* (1840) 5 My
         & Cr 72, p. 35 ante.
     (c) Trust powers/Discretionary trusts
         (i)   exhaustive
         (ii) non-exhaustive
     (d) Fiduciary powers
     (e) Non-fiduciary/mere powers
     (f) Gifts subject to a condition
     See H & M, pp. 61–68, 99–112, 209–214.
     How do you account for the differences?

2.   Do you think that the test for certainty laid down in *Re Gulbenkian's
     Settlements* and *McPhail v Doulton* is sound? How would you formulate the
     test after reading *Re Baden's Deed Trusts (No 2)* [1973] Ch 9, [1972] 2 All
     ER 1304? See H & M, pp. 66–67, 99–112.

3.   How far can questions of uncertainty be solved by a third party whom
     the settlor or testator has made an arbiter of the matter? *Re Tuck's
     Settlement Trusts* [1978] Ch 49, [1978] 1 All ER 1047, p. 652, post; *Re Leek*
     [1969] 1 Ch 563, [1968] 1 All ER 793; *Re Coates* [1955] Ch 495, [1955]
     1 All ER 26 (forgotten friends); *Re Wright's Will Trusts* [1981] LS Gaz R
     841, where Judge Blackett-Ord V-C opined that a residuary gift to
     trustees "to use the same at their absolute discretion for such people
     and institutions as they think may have helped me or my late husband"
     would be void for being conceptually uncertain or impracticable; *Re
     Tepper's Will Trusts* [1987] Ch 358, [1987] 1 All ER 970, p. 653, n. 7, post;
     Underhill, p. 81; (1983) 133 NLJ 915 (P. Matthews).

4.   To what extent does a trustee of a discretionary trust run the risk of
     personal liability if he disposes of the fund without considering a
     beneficiary of whom he was unaware? How should he protect himself?
     (1970) 34 Conv (NS) 287 (F. R. Crane); TA 1925, s. 61; p. 676, post.

5.   Do you think that *Re Barlow's Will Trusts* [1979] 1 WLR 278, [1979] 1 All
     ER 296, p. 87, ante, was rightly decided on the basis of (a) authority and
     (b) policy? [1980] Conv 263 (L. McKay); (1982) 126 SJ 518
     (N.D.M. Parry); (1982) 98 LQR 551, 562–567 (C. T. Emery); Underhill,
     pp. 80–82.

6.   Does administrative unworkability invalidate
     (a) powers
     (b) fixed trusts
     as well as discretionary trusts?
     H & M, p. 107, n. 7; P & M, pp. 108–109; Riddall, p. 24; (1991) 107 LQR
     214 (S. Gardner).
        Consider in this context *Re Beatty* [1990] 1 WLR 1503, [1990] 3 All ER
     844, p. 307 post; *Mettoy Pension Trustees Ltd v Evans* [1990] 1 WLR 1587,
     [1991] 2 All ER 513, p. 45 ante.

III. A Special Problem Relating to Unincorporated Associations[20]

A. General

A corporation, like a human being, is a legal person, and can own property. An unincorporated association is not a legal person; but many unincorporated associations exist and operate, and have done so for many years. In *Conservative and Unionist Central Office v Burrell* [1982] 1 WLR 522 at 525, [1982] 2 All ER 1 at 4, p. 101 post LAWTON LJ defined an unincorporated association as "two or more persons bound together for one or more common purposes, not being business purposes, by mutual undertakings each having mutual duties and obligations, in an organisation which has rules which identify in whom control of it and its funds rests and on what terms and which can be joined or left at will". Hence an organisation which is not incorporated may fail to satisfy the requirements of an unincorporated association.[1] The question which must be investigated now is this: what is the proper legal analysis of the way in which they hold property?

The variety of unincorporated associations is limitless. In order to determine into which category any particular association fits, it is necessary for the court to construe the language of its constitution or rules or of the instrument which created it. Certain types may be categorised in order to show some of the possibilities.

(i) An unincorporated association or group of trustees holding property on trusts for charitable purposes; as, for example, on trust for the relief of poverty. This is valid. It is exempt from most forms of taxation, and may continue for ever. Charitable trusts are discussed in Chapter 9.

(ii) An unincorporated association whose funds are required by its rules to be applied for non-charitable purposes. For example: a trust for the preservation of the independence and integrity of newspapers. Generally speaking, a trust for non-charitable purposes is void. The matter is discussed in Chapter 8.

(iii) An unincorporated association whose committee or officers hold property on trust for the members of the association; for example, to the Treasurer for the time being of a school old boys' society.[2] This may be construed as an ordinary trust for beneficiaries. But difficulties can arise in connection with the following questions: whether beneficiaries are sufficiently ascertainable; whether such a beneficial interest under a trust can be obtained or released by joining or leaving an association; and whether the rule against

---

20 H & M, pp. 365–371; K & S, pp. 149–152; P & M, pp. 123–129, Pettit, pp. 54–57; Riddall, pp. 183–184; Snell, pp. 159–160; Underhill, pp. 102–108. See Morris and Leach, *Rule Against Perpetuities* (2nd edn), pp. 313–318; Maudsley, *Modern Law of Perpetuities*, pp. 171–176; Ford, *Unincorporated Non-Profit Associations*, pp. 1–49; Warburton, *Unincorporated Associations: Law and Practice* (2nd edn); [1985] Conv 415; Conv Prec 15–4; [1992] Conv 41 (S. Gardner); [1995] Conv 302 (P. Matthews).

1 The case was concerned with the meaning of "unincorporated association" for the purposes of ICTA 1970 (now ICTA 1988), but it would seem that the definition is of general application: H & M pp. 370–371. See also *Re Koeppler's Will Trust* [1986] Ch 423 at 431, [1985] 2 All ER 869 at 874, per SLADE LJ: "an association of persons bound together by identifiable rules and having an identifiable membership." See also *J H Rayner (Mincing Lane) Ltd v Department of Trade and Industry* [1989] Ch 72, [1988] 3 All ER 257 (International Tin Council).

2 See *Re Drummond* [1914] 2 Ch 90, as discussed in *Leahy v A-G for New South Wales* [1959] AC 457 at 479, [1959] 2 All ER 300 at 307, p. 94, post.

perpetuities applies so as to render void the beneficial interest of any member who joins outside the period.

(iv) An unincorporated association in which the members have a right based upon contract to claim a share of the property. For example, a members' club, such as a golf club. This situation is outside the law of trusts, but it is mentioned here in order to complete the categories by including an explanation of the most common type of unincorporated association. Legal difficulties can of course arise in this analysis. In many cases the members of the association will be unaware of the existence or the terms of the contract. And other difficulties arise if members are minors.

The subject of unincorporated associations is included here, because in some of the categories, especially category (iii), questions arise relating to the requirements of a trust. This aspect of the problem is quite recent. Prior to the decision of the Privy Council in *Leahy v A-G for New South Wales* [1959] AC 457, [1959] 2 All ER 300, p. 94 post, the courts did not analyse the theoretical basis of property holding by unincorporated associations in terms of category (iii), and did not in consequence put such an unincorporated association "at risk" of invalidity by reason of failure to comply with the requirements of a trust for beneficiaries. Before 1959, the courts seemed satisfied so long as the society could, by its rules, alienate its property and did not create a perpetuity.[3] The matter, and the earlier cases,[4] are discussed in *Leahy*, below.

But the analysis of an unincorporated association on the basis of a trust was sometimes made in the context of a resulting trust arising upon the *dissolution* of the society, and the disposal of the surplus funds. This question is related to the one under discussion here, but its detailed consideration is postponed to the chapter on Resulting Trusts, Chapter 6. It will there be seen that the disposal of the surplus can depend on the question whether the situation is analysed as being one where the property is held on trust, or whether it is held subject to the contractual rights of the members. Where a friendly society, a mutual insurance society, a golf club, or whatever, is wound up, and there is a surplus, should the surplus be paid out to the existing members? Or to past and present members? Or to those who contributed the funds, whether they are members or not? And whether they can be identified or not? Or, should the surplus be treated as one without a claimant, and paid to the Crown as *bona vacantia*? It will be seen in Chapter 6 that each of these solutions has at times been applied. Again, much depends on whether the situation is analysed as one of contract or trust.

B. Theoretical Basis of Property Holding

In **Neville Estates Ltd v Madden** [1962] Ch 832, [1961] 3 All ER 769,[5] the trustees of Catford Synagogue entered into a contract to sell some land. The question arose whether the consent of the Charity Commissioners was required. Consent would be required if the land was held upon charitable

---

3 *Carne v Long* (1860) 2 De GF & J 75.
4 *Re Drummond* [1914] 2 Ch 90; *Re Patten* [1929] 2 Ch 276; *Re Prevost* [1930] 2 Ch 383; (1937) 53 LQR 24 at p. 46 (W.O. Hart); *Re Price* [1943] Ch 422, [1943] 2 All ER 505; *Re Macaulay's Estate*, [1943] Ch 435n.
5 See also *Re Recher's Will Trusts* [1972] Ch 526 at 538, [1971] 3 All ER 401 at 407, p. 99, post.

trusts and if the Charitable Trusts Act 1853, s. 62[6] did not apply. The members of the Synagogue claimed that they were entitled to the purchase money.

CROSS J decided that the land was held on charitable trusts and that consent was required. In considering the claim of the members, he discussed the question of the nature of gifts in favour of unincorporated associations. He said at 849, at 778:

"I turn now at last to the legal issues involved. The question of the construction and effect of gifts to or in trust for unincorporated associations was recently considered by the Privy Council in *Leahy v A-G for New South Wales* [1959] AC 457, [1959] 2 All ER 300. The position, as I understand it, is as follows. Such a gift may take effect in one or other of three quite different ways. In the first place, it may, on its true construction, be a gift to the members of the association at the relevant date as joint tenants, so that any member can sever his share and claim it whether or not he continues to be a member of the association. Secondly, it may be a gift to the existing members not as joint tenants, but subject to their respective contractual rights and liabilities towards one another as members of the association. In such a case a member cannot sever his share. It will accrue to the other members on his death or resignation, even though such members include persons who became members after the gift took effect. If this is the effect of the gift, it will not be open to objection on the score of perpetuity or uncertainty unless there is something in its terms or circumstances or in the rules of the association which precludes the members at any given time from dividing the subject of the gift between them on the footing that they are solely entitled to it in equity.

Thirdly, the terms or circumstances of the gift or the rules of the association may show that the property in question is not to be at the disposal of the members for the time being, but is to be held in trust for or applied for the purposes of the association as a quasi-corporate entity. In this case the gift will fail unless the association is a charitable body. If the gift is of the second class, i.e., one which the members of the association for the time being are entitled to divide among themselves, then, even if the objects of the association are in themselves charitable, the gift would not, I think, be a charitable gift. If, for example, a number of persons formed themselves into an association with a charitable object — say the relief of poverty in some district — but it was part of the contract between them that, if a majority of the members so desired, the association should be dissolved and its property divided between the members at the date of dissolution, a gift to the association as part of its general funds would not, I conceive, be a charitable gift."

i. PROPERTY HELD ON TRUST FOR MEMBERS

LEAHY v ATTORNEY-GENERAL FOR NEW SOUTH WALES[7]

[1959] AC 457, [1959] 2 All ER 300 (PC, Viscount SIMONDS, Lords MORTON OF HENRYTON, COHEN, SOMERVELL OF HARROW and DENNING)

An Australian testator provided by clause 3 of his will, inter alia, that his property, known as "Elmslea", should be held upon trust for "such order of

---

6 Which exempts charities which are wholly or partly maintained by voluntary subscription.
7 See *Bacon v Pianta* (1966) 114 CLR 634 ("The Communist Party of Australia"); (1971) 8 Melbourne LR1, (P.W. Hogg).

nuns of the Catholic Church or the Christian Brothers as my executors and trustees shall select''. The gift was not a valid charitable trust, because such orders included some purely contemplative orders, which were not "charitable" in law.

The New South Wales Conveyancing Act 1919–54, s. 37 (D) provided that a trust should not be invalid on the ground that the property might be applicable to objects some of which were charitable and some of which were not.

The question was whether the property could be applied, as being a valid private trust, in favour of the individual members of contemplative orders. Or whether it should be treated as an endowment of the orders selected; and valid only, as a charitable trust, under the New South Wales Conveyancing Act 1919–54, s. 37 (D);[8] and, as such, applicable only in favour of such orders as were charitable.

Held. The trust was intended as an endowment of the orders selected. It could not take effect as a private trust, but was validated by the New South Wales Conveyancing Act.

VISCOUNT SIMONDS: The disposition made by clause 3 must now be considered. As has already been pointed out, it will in any case be saved by the section so far as Orders other than Contemplative Orders are concerned, but the trustees are anxious to preserve their right to select such Orders. They can only do so if the gift is what is called an absolute gift to the selected Order, an expression which may require examination.

Upon this question there has been a sharp division of opinion in the High Court. Williams and Webb JJ agreed with Myers J that the disposition by clause 3 was valid. They held that it provided for an immediate gift to the particular religious community selected by the trustees and that it was immaterial whether the Order was charitable or not because the gift was not a gift in perpetuity. "It is given" they said (and these are the significant words) "to the individuals comprising the community selected by the trustees at the date of the death of the testator. It is given to them for the benefit of the community''. Kitto J reached the same conclusion. He thought that the selected Order would take the gift immediately and absolutely and could expend immediately the whole of what it received. "There is," he said, "no attempt to create a perpetual endowment''. A different view was taken by the Chief Justice and McTiernan J. After an exhaustive examination of the problem and of the relevant authorities they concluded that the provision made by clause 3 was intended as a trust operating for the furtherance of the purpose of the Order as a body of religious women or, in the case of the Christian Brothers, as a teaching Order. "The membership of any Order chosen," they said, "would be indeterminate and the trust was intended to apply to those who should become members at any time. There was no intention to restrain the operation of the trust to those presently members or to make the alienation of the property a question for a Governing Body of the Order chosen or any section or part of that Order.'' They therefore held that unless the trust could be supported as a charity it must fail.

The brief passages that have been cited from the judgments in the High Court sufficiently indicate the question that must be answered and the difficulty of solving it. It arises out of the artificial and anomalous conception of an unincorporated society which, though it is not a separate entity in law, is

8 See p. 464, post.

yet for many purposes regarded as a continuing entity and, however inaccurately, as something other than an aggregate of its members. In law a gift to such a society simpliciter (i.e., where to use the words of Lord Parker in *Bowman v Secular Society Ltd* [1917] AC 406 at 437, neither the circumstances of the gift nor the directions given nor the objects expressed impose on the donee the character of a trustee) is nothing else than a gift to its members at the date of the gift as joint tenants or tenants in common. It is for this reason that the prudent conveyancer provides that a receipt by the treasurer or other proper officer of the recipient society for a legacy to the society shall be a sufficient discharge to executors. If it were not so, the executors could only get a valid discharge by obtaining a receipt from every member. This must be qualified by saying that by their rules the members might have authorised one of themselves to receive a gift on behalf of them all.

It is in the light of this fundamental proposition that the statements, to which reference has been made, must be examined. What is meant when it is said that a gift is made to the individuals comprising the community and the words are added "it is given to them for the benefit of the community"? If it is a gift to individuals, each of them is entitled to his distributive share (unless he has previously bound himself by the rules of the society that it shall be devoted to some other purpose). It is difficult to see what is added by the words "for the benefit of the community." If they are intended to import a trust, who are the beneficiaries? If the present members are the beneficiaries, the words add nothing and are meaningless. If some other persons or purposes are intended, the conclusion cannot be avoided that the gift is void. For it is uncertain, and beyond doubt tends to a perpetuity.

The question then appears to be whether, even if the gift to a selected Order of Nuns is prima facie a gift to the individual members of that Order, there are other considerations arising out of the terms of the will, or the nature of the society, its organisation and rules, or the subject-matter of the gift which should lead the court to conclude that, though prima facie the gift is an absolute one (absolute both in quality of estate and in freedom from restriction) to individual nuns, yet it is invalid because it is in the nature of an endowment and tends to a perpetuity or for any other reason. This raises a problem which is not easy to solve, as the divergent opinions in the High Court indicate.

The prima facie validity of such a gift (by which term their Lordships intend a bequest or devise[9]) is a convenient starting point for the examination of the relevant law. For as Lord Tomlin (sitting at first instance in the Chancery Division) said in *Re Ogden* [1933] Ch 678, a gift to a voluntary association of persons for the general purposes of the association is an absolute gift and prima facie a good gift. He was echoing the words of Lord Parker in *Bowman's* case [1917] AC 406 at 442, that a gift to an unincorporated association for the attainment of its purposes "may ... be upheld as an absolute gift to its members". These words must receive careful consideration, for it is to be noted that it is because the gift can be upheld as a gift to the individual members that it is valid, even though it is given for the general purposes of the association. If the words "for the general purposes of the association" were held to import a trust, the question would have to be asked, what is the trust and who are the beneficiaries? A gift can be made to persons (including a corporation) but it cannot be made to a purpose or to an object: so also, a trust

---

9 The report says demise; but presumably devise is intended.

may be created for the benefit of persons as cestuis que trust but not for a purpose or object unless the purpose or object be charitable. [His Lordship referred to *Cocks v Manners* (1871) LR 12 Eq 574 (a share of residue to the "Dominican Convent at Carisbrooke payable to the Superior for the time being"); *Re Smith* [1914] 1 Ch 937 (bequest to "the society or institution known as the Franciscan Friars of Clevedon County of Somerset"); *Re Clarke* [1901] 2 Ch 110 (bequest to "the committee for the time being of the Corps of Commissionaires in London"); *Re Drummond* [1914] 2 Ch 90 (residuary testamentary gift upon trust for "the Old Bradfordians Club, London"); *Re Taylor* [1940] Ch 481, [1940] 2 All ER 637 (residuary testamentary gift upon trust for "the Midland Bank Staff Association, Liverpool and District Centre"); *Re Price* [1943] Ch 422, [1943] 2 All ER 505 (residuary testamentary gift to "the Anthroposophical Society in Great Britain"); *Re Prevost* [1930] 2 Ch 383 (residuary testamentary gift to "the trustees of the London Library"); *Re Ray's Will Trusts* [1936] Ch 520, [1936] 2 All ER 93 (bequest to "the person who, at the time of my death, shall be or shall act as the abbess of the Franciscan Convent, Woodchester, Gloucestershire") and continued:]

The cases that have been referred to (and many others might have been referred to in the courts of Australia, England and Ireland) are all cases in which gifts have been upheld as valid either on the ground that, where a society has been named as legatee, its members could demand that the gift should be dealt with as they should together think fit; or on the ground that a trust had been established (as in *Re Drummond* [1914] 2 Ch 90) which did not create a perpetuity. It will be sufficient to mention one only of the cases in which a different conclusion has been reached, before coming to a recent decision of the House of Lords which must be regarded as of paramount authority. In *Carne v Long* (1860) 2 De GF & J 75 the testator devised his mansion-house after the death of his wife to the trustees of the Penzance Public Library to hold to them and their successors for ever for the use, benefit, maintenance and support of the said library. It appeared that the library was established and kept on foot by the subscriptions of certain inhabitants of Penzance, that the subscribers were elected by ballot and the library managed by officers chosen from amongst themselves by the subscribers, that the property in the books and everything else belonging to the library was vested in trustees for the subscribers and that it was provided that the institution should not be broken up so long as 10 members remained. It was urged that the gift was to a number of private persons and there were in truth no other beneficiaries. But Campbell LC rejected the plea in words which, often though they have been cited, will bear repetition (ibid., at 79): "If the devise had been in favour of the existing members of the society, and they had been at liberty to dispose of the property as they might think fit, then it might, I think, have been a lawful disposition and not tending to a perpetuity. But looking to the language of the rules of this society, it is clear that the library was intended to be a perpetual institution, and the testator must be presumed to have known what the regulations were." This was perhaps a clear case where both from the terms of the gift and the nature of the society a perpetuity was indicated.

Their Lordships must now turn to the recent case of *Re Macaulay's Estate*, which appears to be reported only in a footnote to *Re Price* [1943] Ch 422 at 435, [1943] 2 All ER 505. There the gift was to the Folkestone Lodge of the Theosophical Society absolutely for the maintenance and improvement of the Theosophical Lodge at Folkestone. It was assumed that the donee, "the Lodge," was a body of persons. The decision of the House of Lords in July

1933, to which both Lord Buckmaster and Lord Tomlin were parties, was that the gift was invalid. A portion of Lord Buckmaster's speech may well be quoted. He had previously referred to *Re Drummond* [1914] 2 Ch 90 and *Carne v Long* (1860) 2 De GF & J 75. "A group of people," he said, "defined and bound together by rules and called by a distinctive name can be the subject of gift as well as any individual or incorporated body. The real question is what is the actual purpose for which the gift is made. There is no perpetuity if the gift is for the individual members for their own benefit, but that, I think, is clearly not the meaning of this gift. Nor again is there a perpetuity if the society is at liberty in accordance with the terms of the gift to spend both capital and income as they think fit ... If the gift is to be for the endowment of the society to be held as an endowment and the society is according to its form perpetual, the gift is bad: but, if the gift is an immediate beneficial legacy, it is good." In the result he held the gift for the maintenance and improvement of the Theosophical Lodge at Folkestone to be invalid. Their Lordships respectfully doubt whether the passage in Lord Buckmaster's speech in which he suggests the alternative ground of validity: viz., that the society is at liberty in accordance with the terms of the gift to spend both capital and income as they think fit, presents a true alternative. It is only because the society, i.e., the individuals constituting it, are beneficiaries, that they can dispose of the gift. Lord Tomlin came to the same conclusion. He found in the words of the will "for the maintenance and improvement" a sufficient indication that it was the permanence of the Lodge at Folkestone that the testatrix was seeking to secure and this, he thought, necessarily involved endowment. Therefore a perpetuity was created. A passage from the judgment of Lord Hanworth MR (which has been obtained from the records) may usefully be cited. He said: "The problem may be stated in this way. If the gift is in truth to the present members of the society described by their society name so that they have the beneficial use of the property and can, if they please, alienate and put the proceeds in their own pocket, then there is a present gift to individuals which is good: but if the gift is intended for the good not only of the present but of future members so that the present members are in the position of trustees and have no right to appropriate the property or its proceeds for their personal benefit then the gift is invalid. It may be invalid by reason of there being a trust created, or it may be by reason of the terms that the period allowed by the rule against perpetuities would be exceeded."

It is not very clear what is intended by the dichotomy suggested in the last sentence of the citation, but the penultimate sentence goes to the root of the matter. At the risk of repetition their Lordships would point out that, if a gift is made to individuals, whether under their own names or in the name of their society, and the conclusion is reached that they are not intended to take beneficially, then thay take as trustees. If so, it must be ascertained who are the beneficiaries ... [10].

It must now be asked, then, whether in the present case there are sufficient indications to displace the prima facie conclusion that the gift made by clause 3 of the will is to the individual members of the selected Order of Nuns at the date of the testator's death so that they can together dispose of it as they think fit. It appears to their Lordships that such indications are ample.

10 Which would now be decided according to the test laid down in *McPhail v Doulton* [1971] AC 424, [1970] 2 All ER 228; p. 71, ante.

In the first place, it is not altogether irrelevant that the gift is in terms upon trust for a selected Order. It is true that this can in law be regarded as a trust in favour of each and every member of the Order. But at least the form of the gift is not to the members, and it may be questioned whether the testator understood the niceties of the law. In the second place, the members of the selected Order may be numerous, very numerous perhaps, and they may be spread over the world. If the gift is to the individuals it is to all the members who were living at the death of the testator, but only to them. It is not easy to believe that the testator intended an "immediate beneficial legacy" (to use the words of Lord Buckmaster) to such a body of beneficiaries. In the third place, the subject-matter of the gift cannot be ignored. It appears from the evidence filed in the suit that Elmslea is a grazing property of about 730 acres, with a furnished homestead containing 20 rooms and a number of outbuildings. With the greatest respect to those judges who have taken a different view, their Lordships do not find it possible to regard all the individual members of an Order as intended to become the beneficial owners of such a property. Little or no evidence has been given about the organisation and rules of the several Orders, but it is at least permissible to doubt whether it is a common feature of them, that all their members regard themselves or are to be regarded as having the capacity of (say) the Corps of Commissionaires (see *Re Clarke* [1901] 2 Ch 110) to put an end to their association and distribute its assets. On the contrary, it seems reasonably clear that, however little the testator understood the effect in law of a gift to an unincorporated body of persons by their society name, his intention was to create a trust, not merely for the benefit of the existing members of the selected Order, but for its benefit as a continuing society and for the furtherance of its work.

Different views have been held upon the question whether the legal title remains in the will trustees after they have selected an Order. Kitto J (expressly) and Williams and Webb JJ (by implication) held that "when a body is selected by the trustees the property will be at home" and will vest presumably in some authorised person or persons. (The Roman Catholic Charities Land Act of 1942 was not invoked in the High Court and becomes irrelevant if the chosen Order is not a charity.) The Chief Justice and McTiernan J were of opinion that the trustees were intended, subject to the power of sale, to remain the repository of the whole legal title and to administer the trust by affording the enjoyment to the selected Order. The latter view is attractive if only because of the difficulty of transferring title when the above-mentioned Act does not apply. But their Lordships do not think it necessary for the purpose of this case to decide the question. No difficulty will arise if only a charitable body can be selected. If the choice is wider, the question will not arise. The dominant and sufficiently expressed intention of the testator is in their opinion (again in the words of Lord Buckmaster) that "the gift is to be an endowment of the society to be held as an endowment", and that "as the society is according to its form perpetual" the gift must, if it is to a non-charitable body, fail.

Their Lordships, therefore, humbly advise her Majesty that the appeal should be dismissed, but that the gift made by clause 3 of the will is valid by reason only of the provisions of section 37 (D) of the Conveyancing Act, 1919–54, and that the power of selection thereby given to the trustees does not extend to Contemplative Orders of Nuns. The costs of all parties will be paid out of the estate of the testator. The costs of all the respondents will be taxed as between solicitor and clients.

ii. Ownership by Members on Contractual Basis

In **Re Recher's Will Trusts** [1972] Ch 526, [1971] 3 All ER 401,[11] one question was whether a gift to the London and Provincial Anti-Vivisection Society was valid. The society was unincorporated.[12] Its main object[13] was to secure the total abolition of vivisection. It consisted of ordinary and life members, and the constitution was laid down in its Rules.

BRIGHTMAN J considered the various ways in which the property of the society could be held, and continued at 538, at 407:

"Having reached the conclusion that the gift in question is not a gift to the members of the London & Provincial society at the date of death, as joint tenants or tenants in common, so as to entitle a member as of right to a distributive share, nor an attempted gift to present and future members beneficially, and is not a gift in trust for the purposes of the society, I must now consider how otherwise, if at all, it is capable of taking effect.

As I have already mentioned, the rules of the London & Provincial society do not purport to create any trusts except in so far as the honorary trustees are not beneficial owners of the assets of the society, but are trustees upon trust to deal with such assets according to the directions of the committee.

A trust for non-charitable purposes, as distinct from a trust for individuals, is clearly void because there is no beneficiary. It does not, however, follow that persons cannot band themselves together as an association or society, pay subscriptions and validly devote their funds in pursuit of some lawful non-charitable purpose. An obvious example is a members' social club. But it is not essential that the members should only intend to secure direct personal advantages to themselves. The association may be one in which personal advantages to the members are combined with the pursuit of some outside purpose. Or the association may be one which offers no personal benefit at all to the members, the funds of the association being applied exclusively to the pursuit of some outside purpose. Such an association of persons is bound, I would think, to have some sort of constitution; that is to say, the rights and liabilities of the members of the association will inevitably depend on some form of contract inter se, usually evidenced by a set of rules. In the present case it appears to me clear that the life members, the ordinary members and the associate members of the London & Provincial society were bound together by a contract inter se. Any such member was entitled to the rights and subject to the liabilities defined by the rules. If the committee acted contrary to the rules, an individual member would be entitled to take proceedings in the courts to compel observance of the rules or to recover damages for any loss he had suffered as a result of the breach of contract. As and when a member paid his subscription to the association, he would be subjecting his money to the disposition and expenditure thereof laid down by the rules. That is to say, the member would be bound to permit, and entitled to require, the honorary trustees and other members of the society to deal with that subscription in accordance with the lawful directions of the committee. Those directions

---

11 (1971) 35 Conv (NS) 381 (J. Mummery); (1971) 8 MULR 1 (P.W Hogg); (1973) 47 ALJ 305 (R. Baxt); *Re Bucks Constabulary Widows' and Orphans' Fund Friendly Society (No 2)* [1979] 1 WLR 936, [1979] 1 All ER 623, p. 204, post. See also [1995] Conv 302 (P. Matthews).
12 It merged with the National Anti-Vivisection Society on 1 January, 1957, and in 1963 was incorporated as The National Anti-Vivisection Society Ltd.
13 Which is not charitable: *National Anti-Vivisection Society v IRC* [1948] AC 31, [1947] 2 All ER 217, p. 408, post.

would include the expenditure of that subscription, as part of the general funds of the association, in furthering the objects of the association. The resultant situation, on analysis, is that the London & Provincial society represented an organisation of individuals bound together by a contract under which their subscriptions became, as it were, mandated towards a certain type of expenditure as adumbrated in rule 1. Just as the two parties to a bi-partite bargain can vary or terminate their contract by mutual assent, so it must follow that the life members, ordinary members and associated members of the London & Provincial society could, at any moment of time, by unanimous agreement (or by majority vote, if the rules so prescribe), vary or terminate their multi–partite contract. There would be no limit to the type of variation or termination to which all might agree. There is no private trust or trust for charitable purposes or other trust to hinder the process. It follows that if all members agreed, they could decide to wind up the London & Provincial society and divide the net assets among themselves beneficially. No one would have any locus standi to stop them so doing. The contract is the same as any other contract and concerns only those who are parties to it, that is to say, the members of the society.

The funds of such an association may, of course, be derived not only from the subscriptions of the contracting parties but also from donations from non-contracting parties and legacies from persons who have died. In the case of a donation which is not accompanied by any words which purport to impose a trust, it seems to me that the gift takes effect in favour of the existing members of the association as an accretion to the funds which are the subject-matter of the contract which such members have made inter se, and falls to be dealt with in precisely the same way as the funds which the members themselves have subscribed. So, in the case of a legacy. In the absence of words which purport to impose a trust, the legacy is a gift to the members beneficially, not as joint tenants or as tenants in common so as to entitle each member to an immediate distributive share, but as an accretion to the funds which are the subject-matter of the contract which the members have made inter se.

In my judgment the legacy in the present case to the London & Provincial society ought to be construed as a legacy of that type, that is to say, a legacy to the members beneficially as an accretion to the funds subject to the contract which they had made inter se. Of course, the testatrix did not intend the members of the society to divide her bounty between themselves, and doubtless she was ignorant of that remote but theoretical possibility. Her knowledge or absence of knowledge of the true legal analysis of the gift is irrelevant. The legacy is accordingly in my view valid, subject only to the effect of the events of January 1, 1957.[13a]

A strong argument has been presented to me against this conclusion and I have been taken through most, if not all, of the cases which are referred to in *Leahy's* case [1959] AC 457, [1959] 2 All ER 300, as well as later authorities. It has been urged upon me that if the gift is not a purpose gift, there is no halfway house between, on the one hand, a legacy to the members of the London & Provincial society at the date of death, as joint tenants beneficially, or as tenants in common beneficially, and, on the other hand, a trust for members which is void for perpetuity because no individual member acting by himself can ever obtain his share of the legacy. I do not see why the choice should be

13aWhen the London & Provincial Society was absorbed by the National Society; p.99 n.12, ante.

confined to these two extremes. If the argument were correct it would be difficult, if not impossible, for a person to make a straightforward donation, whether inter vivos or by will, to a club or other non-charitable association which the donor desires to benefit. This conclusion seems to me contrary to common sense."[14]

iii. THE MANDATE OR AGENCY THEORY

In **Conservative and Unionist Central Office v Burrell** [1982] 2 All ER 1[15], BRIGHTMAN LJ said at 6:

"The issue is whether or not the investment income of the Conservative Party Central Office funds during the relevant years was the income of an unincorporated association.[16] The assertion is that Central Office funds are held for the purposes of an organisation known as the Conservative Party, or more fully as the Conservative and Unionist Party, that such organisation has all the necessary requirements for qualifying as an unincorporated association and that the Special Commissioners were justified in finding that it is such an association. The members of the association are said to be (i) all the persons who are members of the local constituency associations (which local associations are themselves unincorporated associations) and (ii) the members of both Houses of Parliament who accept the Conservative Party whip. The contract which is alleged to bind together the members of this unincorporated association known as the Conservative Party is said to consist of the rules forming the constitution of the National Union of Conservative and Unionist Associations, the rules regulating 'party meetings' at which the candidate chosen by the Parliamentary Conservative Party as leader of the party is presented for election as party leader and the rules forming the respective constitutions of the local constituency associations. I agree, for the reasons given by Lawton LJ, that no such overall unincorporated association exists.[17]

Before, however, that conclusion is accepted, I think that a critical observer is entitled to ask the question what, on that hypothesis, would be the legal relationship between a contributor to Central Office funds and the recipient of the contributions so made.

Strictly speaking, this court does not have to answer that question; it has only to decide the issue whether the Special Commissioners were entitled to find that the Conservative Party is an unincorporated association. But, if no realistic legal explanation of the relationship is forthcoming except the existence of an

---

14 *Re Lipinski's Will Trusts* [1976] Ch 235, [1977] 1 All ER 33, p. 319, post; *Universe Tankships Inc of Monrovia v International Transport Workers Federation* [1983] 1 AC 366, [1982] 2 All ER 67 (payment by ship owners of sum into the Federation fund held not to be a contribution on trust and therefore void and so returnable to the shipowners by way of resulting trust, but to be an accretion to the fund by way of outright gift). See also the CA judgment in [1981] ICR 129; (1980) 45 MLR 564; (1983) 46 MLR 36 (B. Green); (1983) 133 NLJ 15 (J. McMullen and A. Grubb).

15 (1983) 133 NLJ 87 (C.T. Emery); [1983] Conv 150 (P. Creighton); [1987] Conv 415 (P. St.J. Smart).

16 And so chargeable to corporation tax as an "unincorporated association" within the meaning of ICTA 1970, s. 526 (5); now ICTA 1988, s. 832(1).

17 See p. 91, ante.

unincorporated association, one might justifiably begin to entertain doubts as to the credibility of the hypothesis on which the question is asked. I will therefore attempt an answer.

If the Conservative Party is rightly described as an unincorporated association with an identifiable membership bound together by identifiable rules, and Central Office funds are funds of the Conservative Party, no problem arises. In that event, decided cases say that the contribution takes effect in favour of the members of the unincorporated association known as the Conservative Party as an accretion to the funds which are the subject matter of the contract which such members have made inter se: see, for example, *Re Recher's Will Trusts* [1972] Ch 526, [1971] 3 All ER 401, p. 99, ante. If, however, the Conservative Party is not an unincorporated association, that easy answer is not available.

I will consider the hypothesis by stages. No legal problem arises if a contributor (as I will call him) hands to a friend (whom I will call the recipient) a sum of money to be applied by the recipient for political purposes indicated by the contributor, or to be chosen at the discretion of the recipient. That would be a simple case of mandate or agency. The recipient would have authority from the contributor to make use of the money, in the indicated way. So far as the money is used within the scope of the mandate, the recipient discharges himself vis-à-vis the contributor. The contributor can at any time demand the return of his money so far as not spent, unless the mandate is irrevocable, as it might be or become in certain circumstances. But once the money is spent, the contributor can demand nothing back, only an account of the manner of expenditure. No trust arises, except the fiduciary relationship inherent in the relationship of principal and agent. If, however, the recipient were to apply the money for some purpose outside the scope of the mandate, clearly the recipient would not be discharged. The recipient could be restrained, like any other agent, from a threatened misapplication of the money entrusted to him, and like any other agent could be required to replace any money misapplied.

The next stage is to suppose that the recipient is the treasurer of an organisation which receives and applies funds from multifarious sources for certain political purposes. If the contributor pays money to that treasurer, the treasurer has clear authority to add the contribution to the mixed fund (as I will call it) that he holds. At that stage I think the mandate becomes irrevocable. That is to say, the contributor has no right to demand his contribution back, once it has been mixed with other money under the authority of the contributor. The contributor has no legal right to require the mixed fund to be unscrambled for his benefit. This does not mean, however, that all contributors lose all rights once their cheques are cashed, with the absurd result that the treasurer or other officers can run off with the mixed fund with impunity. I have no doubt that any contributor has a remedy against the recipient (ie the treasurer, or the officials at whose direction the treasurer acts) to restrain or make good a misapplication of the mixed fund *except* so far as it may appear on ordinary accounting principles that the plaintiff's own contribution was spent before the threatened or actual misapplication. In the latter event the mandate given by the contributor will not have been breached. A complaining contributor might encounter problems under the law of contract after a change of the office holder to whom his mandate was originally given. Perhaps only the original recipient can be sued for the malpractices of his successors. It is not necessary to explore such procedural intricacies.

So in the present case it seems to me that the status of a contribution to the Conservative Party central funds is this. The contributor draws a cheque (for example) in favour of, or hands it to, the treasurers. The treasurers are impliedly authorised by the contributor to present the cheque for encashment and to add the contribution to Central Office funds. Central Office funds are the subject matter of a mandate which permits them to be used for the purposes of the Conservative Party as directed by the leader of the party. The contributor cannot demand his money back once it has been added to Central Office funds. He could object if Central Office funds were used or threatened to be used otherwise than in accordance with their declared purposes, unless it is correct to say, on ordinary accounting principles, that his contribution has already passed out of Central Office funds.

This discussion of mandates, and complaining contributors, is all very remote and theoretical. No contributor to Central Office funds will view his contribution in this way, or contemplate even the remotest prospect of legal action on his part. He believes he is making an out and out contribution or gift to a political party. And so he is in practical terms. The only justification for embarking on a close analysis of the situation is the challenge, which was thrown down by counsel for the Crown in opening, to suggest any legal framework which fits the undoubted fact that funds are held by the Central Office and are administered for the use and benefit of the Conservative Party, except the supposition that the Conservative Party is an unincorporated association.

I see no legal difficulty in the mandate theory. It is not necessary to invent an unincorporated association in order to explain the situation. The only problem which might arise in practice under the mandate theory would be the case of an attempted bequest to Central Office funds, or to the treasurers thereof, or to the Conservative Party, since no agency could be set up at the moment of death between a testator and his chosen agent. A discussion of this problem is outside the scope of this appeal and, although I think that the answer is not difficult to find, I do not wish to prejudge it.

I would dismiss the appeal.''

Compare the analysis given by Vinelott J at first instance [1980] 3 All ER 42 at 62:[18]

"It appears to me that if someone invites subscriptions on the representation that he will use the fund subscribed for a particular purpose, he undertakes to use the fund for that purpose and for no other and to keep the subscribed fund and any accretions to it (including any income earned by investing the fund pending its application in pursuance of the stated purpose) separate from his own moneys. I can see no reason why if the purpose is sufficiently well defined, and if the order would not necessitate constant and possibly ineffective supervision by the court, the court should not make an order directing him to apply the subscribed fund and any accretions to it for the stated purpose ... Apart from the possible remedy of specific performance I can see no reason why the court should not restrain the recipient of such a fund from applying it (or any accretions to it such as income of investments made with it) otherwise than in pursuance of the stated purpose. If that is so, then it appears to me that

18 The CA judgments, although affirming the decision, do not refer to this analysis.

the recipient of the fund is clearly not the beneficial owner of it and that the income of it is not part of his total income for tax purposes. Equally, whilst the purpose remains unperformed and capable of performance the subscribers are clearly not the beneficial owners of the fund or of the income (if any) derived from it. If the stated purpose proves impossible to achieve or if there is any surplus remaining after it has been accomplished there will be an implied obligation to return the fund and any accretions thereto to the subscribers in proportion to their original contributions, save that a proportion of the fund representing subscriptions made anonymously or in circumstances in which the subscribers receive some benefit (for instance, by subscription to a whist drive or raffle) might then devolve as bona vacantia ... A testamentary gift to a named society which is not an incorporated body must fail unless it can be construed as a gift to the members of an unincorporated association either as joint tenants or as an accretion to the funds of the association to be applied in accordance with its rules (commonly with a view to the furtherance of its objects). But in the case of a testamentary gift there is no room for the implication of any contract between the testator and the persons who are to receive the bequest. In the case of an inter vivos subscription the intention of the subscriber can be given effect by the implication of contractual undertakings of the kind I have described. On further consideration that seems to me to be the proper explanation of the status of the subscriptions made by members of the Chertsey and Walton Constituency Labour Party on which I made some observations in *Re Grant's Will Trusts* [1980] 1 WLR 360, [1979] 3 All ER 359, p. 105, post. The right of subscribers to the return of their subscriptions so far as not used for the purposes for which they were subscribed rests on an implied contractual term and not on a resulting trust.''

———————

[1983] Conv. 150, at p. 154 (P. Creighton)
"It remains to be considered whether and how the mandate analysis is likely to be utilised in the future. For example, should a gift to an unincorporated association be construed as creating in the members a mandate to apply the property for the association's purposes? Brightman LJ would evidently discourage such a development, preferring the solution he pioneered in *Re Recher*. But what of cases like *Re Gillingham* [1959] Ch 62, [1958] 2 All ER 749, p. 197, post, or *Re Denley* [1969] 1 Ch 373, [1968] 3 All ER 65, p. 322, post, where property was donated for particular purposes, quite independent of any association? In principle, whether the recipient is a trustee or agent depends upon the intention of the donor. So, for example, if the terms of the gift describe the recipient as a trustee, or title to land is vested in his name (as in *Re Denley*), then the likely inference is that a trust is intended. But in circumstances where the donor's precise intention is not evident, a court will have some flexibility in determining which analysis to apply. It would still seem preferable to treat the recipients as trustees for the relevant purpose, provided that such a trust would not be void. Where that construction would only lead to invalidating the gift, it might be possible to salvage the disposition by treating it as a power. But where the donor's intention appears obligatory rather than merely permissive, excluding the possibility of a mere power, *Re Endacott* [1960] Ch 232, [1959] 3 All ER 562, p. 315, post, it might then be appropriate to resort to the mandate analysis, at least where the gift was made inter vivos. A valid agency might be spelled out to allow funds to be applied towards a

purpose where a trust for that purpose would have failed. To the extent that it prevents the initial invalidity of such a gift, the mandate concept might be considered a useful alternative to the purpose trust. But consideration of the limited scope of its possible application, and the measure of control over the funds that it permits, suggests that it cannot provide a general framework for explaining gifts for non-charitable purposes. Indeed, as an explanation, it seems scarcely adequate to save the Conservative Party from corporation tax."[19]

iv. Requirements for Validity of Gift

In **Re Grant's Will Trusts** [1980] 1 WLR 360, [1979] 3 All ER 359,[20] a testator left all his real and personal estate "to the Labour Party property committee for the benefit of the Chertsey headquarters of the Chertsey and Walton Constituency Labour Party". In holding that the gift failed and devolved as on intestacy, Vinelott J said at 364, at 363:

"The question raised by the summons is whether the gift in the will of the testator's real and personal estate is a valid gift, or is void for uncertainty or for perpetuity or otherwise; and if it is a valid gift, who are the persons entitled to benefit thereunder?

Before turning to this question, it will be convenient to explain what are in my judgment the principles which govern the validity of a gift to an unincorporated association. A convenient starting point is a passage in the decision of Cross J in *Neville Estates Ltd v Madden* [1962] Ch 832 at 849, [1961] 3 All ER 769 at 778 which is often cited. [His Lordship quoted the extract set out at p. 93, ante, and continued:] This statement, though it may require amplification in the light of subsequent authorities, is still, as I see it, an accurate statement of the law.

In a case in the first category, that is a gift which, on its true construction, is a gift to members of an association who take as joint tenants, any member being able to sever his share, the association is used in effect as a convenient label or definition of the class which is intended to take; but, the class being ascertained, each member takes as joint tenant free from any contractual fetter. So, for instance, a testator might give a legacy or share of residue to a dining or social club of which he had been a member with the intention of giving to each of the other members an interest as joint tenant, capable of being severed in the subject-matter of the gift. Cases within this category are relatively uncommon. A gift to an association will be more frequently found to fall within the second category. There the gift is to members of an association, but the property is given as an accretion to the funds of the association so that the property becomes subject to the contract (normally evidenced by the rules of the association) which govern the rights of the members inter se. Each member is thus in a position to ensure that the subject-matter of the gift is

---

19 And for the possible use of the mandate analysis in *Universe Tankships Inc of Monrovia v International Transport Workers Federation* [1983] 1 AC 366, [1982] 2 All ER 67, p. 101, n. 14, ante, see (1983) 133 NLJ 515 (J. McMullen and A. Grubb). See also *Roche v Sherrington* [1982] 1 WLR 599, [1982] 2 All ER 426, where Slade J held that a special fiduciary relationship could in principle exist between a contributing member of an unincorporated association and the recipient members for the time being at the date of a transaction challenged on the ground of undue influence (Opus Dei). RSC Ord. 15, r. 12.

20 (1980) 43 MLR 459 (B. Green); [1980] Conv 80 (G.A. Shindler).

applied in accordance with the rules of the association, in the same way as any other funds of the association. This category is well illustrated by the decision of Brightman J in *Re Recher's Will Trusts* [1972] Ch 526, [1971] 3 All ER 401. There a share of residue was given to 'The Anti-Vivisection Society, 76 Victoria Street, London, S.W.1.' The society in fact ceased to exist, being amalgamated with another society, during the testatrix's lifetime. Brightman J first examined whether the gift would have been valid if the society had continued to exist. He said at 538, at 365:

[His Lordship quoted the extract set out at p. 99, ante, and continued:]

Two points should be noted. First, as Brightman J pointed out, it is immaterial in considering whether a gift falls within this category that the members of an association have not joined together for a social and recreational purpose, or to secure some personal advantage, but in pursuit of some altruistic purpose. The motive which led the testator to make the gift may have been, indeed most frequently will have been, a desire to further that purpose. It may be said that in that sense the gift is made for the furtherance of the purpose. But the testator has chosen as the means of furthering the purpose to make a gift to an association formed for the pursuit of that purpose in the expectation that the subject-matter of the gift will be so used, without imposing or attempting to impose any trust or obligation on the members, or the trustees, or the committee of the association. Indeed, there are cases where the gift has been expressed as a gift for the purposes, or one of the purposes, of the association, and nonetheless has been held not to impose any purported trust. Two examples will suffice.

[His Lordship referred to *Re Turkington* [1937] 4 All ER 501 (gift expressed as a gift to the Staffordshire Knot Masonic Lodge as a fund to build a suitable temple in Stafford was construed by LUXMOORE J as a gift to the members of the Lodge) and to *Re Lipinski's Will Trusts* [1976] Ch 235, [1977] 1 All ER 33, p. 319, post, and continued:]

That leads to the second point. It must, as I see it, be a necessary characteristic of any gift within the second category that the members of the association can by an appropriate majority, if the rules so provide, or acting unanimously if they do not, alter their rules so as to provide that the funds, or part of them, should be applied for some new purpose, or even distributed amongst the members for their own benefit. For the validity of a gift within this category rests essentially upon the fact that the testator has set out to further a purpose by making a gift to the members of an association formed for the furtherance of that purpose in the expectation that although the members at the date when the gift takes effect will be free, by a majority if the rules so provide or acting unanimously if they do not, to dispose of the fund in any way they may think fit, they and any future members of the association will not in fact do so but will employ the property in the furtherance of the purpose of the association and will honour any special condition attached to the gift.

Turning to the third category, the testator may seek to further the purpose by giving a legacy to an association as a quasi-corporate entity, that is, to present and future members indefinitely, or by purporting to impose a trust. In the former case the gift will fail for perpetuity unless confined within an appropriate period; though if it is so confined and if the members for the time being within the perpetuity period are free to alter the purposes for which the property is to be used and to distribute the income amongst themselves it will not, as I see it, fail upon any other ground. In the latter case, the gift will fail upon the ground that the court cannot compel the use of the property in furtherance of a stated purpose unless, of course, the purpose is a charitable one. As Viscount Simonds said in *Leahy v A-G for New South Wales* [1959] AC 457 at 478, [1959] 2 All ER 300 at 307:

'If the words "for the general purposes of the association" were held to import a trust, the question would have to be asked, what is the trust and who are the beneficiaries? A gift can be made to persons (including a corporation) but it cannot be made to a purpose or to an object: so also, a trust may be created for the benefit of persons as cestuis que trust but not for a purpose or object unless the purpose or object be charitable. For a purpose or object cannot sue, but, if it be charitable, the Attorney-General can sue to enforce it. (Upon this point something will be said later.) It is therefore by disregarding the words "for the general purposes of the association" (which are assumed not to be charitable purposes) and treating the gift as an absolute gift to individuals that it can be sustained.'

There are two cases in which, if this analysis is correct, the reasons given for the decision, though possibly not the decision itself, are not well-founded. [His Lordship referred to *Re Drummond* [1914] 2 Ch 90, and *Re Price* [1943] Ch 422, [1943] 2 All ER 505, and continued:]

I have been referred to the recent decision of Goff J in *Re Denley's Trust Deed* [1969] 1 Ch 373, [1968] 3 All ER 65.[1] There by clause 2 of a trust deed trustees were given powers of sale over land held by them and were directed to hold the land while unsold during a defined perpetuity period on trust, that

'(c) The said land shall be maintained and used as and for the purpose of a recreation or sports ground primarily for the benefit of the employees of the company and secondarily for the benefit of such other person or persons (if any) as the trustees may allow to use the same ... '

Goff J, having held that the words 'secondarily for the benefit of such other person or persons if any as the trustees may allow to use the same,' conferred on the trustees a power operating in partial defeasance of a trust in favour of the employees, held that the trust deed created a valid trust for the benefit of the employees, the benefit being the right to use the land subject to and in accordance with the rules made by the trustees. That case on a proper analysis, in my judgment, falls altogether outside the categories of gifts to unincorporated association and purpose trusts. I can see no distinction in principle between a trust to permit a class defined by reference to employment to use and enjoy land in accordance with rules to be made at the discretion of trustees on the one hand, and, on the other hand, a trust to distribute income at the discretion of trustees amongst a class, defined by reference to, for example, relationship to the settlor. In both cases the benefit to be taken by any member of the class is at the discretion of the trustees, but any member of the class can apply to the court to compel the trustees to administer the trust in accordance with its terms. As Goff J pointed out, at 388, at 72:

'The same kind of problem is equally capable of arising in the case of a trust to permit a number of persons — for example, all the unmarried children of a testator or settlor — to use or occupy a house or to have the use of certain chattels; nor can I assume that in such cases agreement between the parties concerned would be more likely, even if that be a

---

1 See (1977) 41 Conv (NS) 179 (K. Widdows); (1980) 39 CLJ 88 (C.E.F. Rickett); [1985] Conv 318 (J. Warburton).

sufficient distinction, yet no one would suggest, I fancy, that such a trust would be void.'

With those principles in mind, I return to the testator's will . . .

Reading the gift in the will in the light of the rules governing the Chertsey and Walton CLP, it is, in my judgment, impossible to construe the gift as a gift made to the members of the Chertsey and Walton CLP at the date of the testator's death with the intention that it should belong to them as a collection of individuals, though in the expectation that they and any other members subsequently admitted would ensure that it was in fact used for what in broad terms has been labelled 'headquarters' purposes' of the Chertsey and Walton CLP.

I base this conclusion on two grounds. First, the members of the Chertsey and Walton CLP do not control the property, given by subscription or otherwise, to the CLP. The rules which govern the CLP are capable of being altered by an outside body which could direct an alteration under which the general committee of the CLP would be bound to transfer any property for the time being held for the benefit of the CLP to the National Labour Party for national purposes. The members of the Chertsey and Walton CLP could not alter the rules so as to make the property bequeathed by the testator applicable for some purpose other than that provided by the rules; nor could they direct that property to be divided amongst themselves beneficially.

Brightman J observed in *Re Recher's Will Trusts* [1972] Ch 526 at 536, [1971] 3 All ER 401 at 405:

'It would astonish the layman to be told there was a difficulty in his giving a legacy to an unincorporated non-charitable society which he had, or could have, supported without trouble during his lifetime.'

The answer to this apparent paradox is, it seems to me, that subscriptions by members of the Chertsey and Walton CLP must be taken as made upon terms that they will be applied by the general committee in accordance with the rules for the time being including any modifications imposed by the Annual Party Conference or the National Executive Committee. In the event of the dissolution of the Chertsey and Walton CLP any remaining fund representing subscriptions would (as the rules now stand) be held on a resulting trust for the original subscribers. Thus, although the members of the CLP may not be able themselves to alter the purposes for which a fund representing subscriptions is to be used or to alter the rules so as to make such a fund divisible amongst themselves, the ultimate proprietary right of the original subscribers remains. There is, therefore, no perpetuity and no non-charitable purpose trust. But if that analysis of the terms on which subscriptions are held is correct, it is fatal to the argument that the gift in the testator's will should be construed as a gift to the members of the Chertsey and Walton CLP at the testator's death, subject to a direction not amounting to a trust that it be used for headquarters' purposes. Equally it is in my judgment impossible, in particular having regard to the gift over to the National Labour Party, to read the gift as a gift to the members of the National Labour Party at the testator's death, with a direction not amounting to a trust, for the National Party to permit it to be used by the Chertsey and Walton CLP for headquarters' purposes.

That first ground is of itself conclusive, but there is another ground which reinforces this conclusion. The gift is not in terms a gift to the Chertsey and Walton CLP, but to the Labour Party property committee, who are to hold the property for the benefit of, that is in trust for, the Chertsey headquarters of the Chertsey and Walton CLP. The fact that a gift is a gift to trustees and not in terms of an unincorporated association, militates against construing it as a gift to the members of the association at the date when the gift takes effect, and against construing the words indicating the purposes for which the property is to be used as expressing the testator's intention or motive in making the gift and not as imposing any trust. This was, indeed, one of the considerations which led the Privy Council in *Leahy*'s case to hold that the gift ' . . . upon trust for such Order of Nuns of the Catholic Church or the Christian Brothers as my executors and trustees should elect' would, apart from the Australian equivalent of the Charitable Trusts Validation Act, have been invalid.

I am therefore, compelled to the conclusion that the gift of the testator's estate fails, and that his estate accordingly devolves as on intestacy."[2]

QUESTION

Take as an example any club that you know; or of which you are a member. Then consider who is the legal owner of the land or premises occupied by the club, of any investments held, and of its current bank account. Could each member claim a share now? On the ground that he is a beneficial owner? Or on a basis of a contract? Could each member claim a share of the assets on a dissolution? If so, on what basis? See p. 199, post.

---

2 Cf *News Group Newspapers Ltd v SOGAT 82* [1986] ICR 716, where the members of a local branch of a trade union controlled the branch assets and could in theory secede from the union and divide the assets.

3. The Constitution of Trusts. Volunteers[1]

An express trust only exists where the trust property is vested in the trustee and the terms of the trust have been properly declared. Questions relating to the rules concerning the declaration of trusts have been considered. We are now concerned with the further requirement that the trust property must be vested in the trustee.

I. Transfer of the Trust Property to Trustees[2]

The method of transfer varies with the property in question. A legal estate in unregistered land must be transferred by deed,[3] in registered land by registration;[4] stocks and shares by an appropriate form of transfer;[5] equitable interests[6] and copyright by writing;[7] chattels by deed of gift[8] or by an intention to give coupled with a delivery of possession;[9] a bill of exchange by indorsement;[10] and various other types of property by their own special procedure. The vesting of the trust property in the trustee *constitutes* the trust. In a completely constituted trust, there is no need for consideration; and the question of whether a beneficiary is a volunteer is immaterial.

---

1 H & M, pp. 113–145; K & S, pp. 102–111; P & M, pp. 58–90; Pettit, pp. 90–115; Riddall, pp. 71–90; Snell, pp. 119–127; Underhill, pp. 124–159.
2 H & M, pp. 113–121; K & S, pp. 102–107; P & M, pp. 58–62; Riddall, pp. 71–74; Snell, pp. 121–123; Underhill, pp. 129–143.
3 LPA 1925, s. 52 (1).
4 LRA 1925, ss. 5, 9, 20, 23, 69; *Mascall v Mascall* (1984) 50 P & CR 119, p. 119, post.
5 See Companies Act 1985 ss. 182, 183; Stock Transfer Act 1963, s. 1.
6 LPA 1925, s. 53 (1), p. 52, ante.
7 Copyright, Designs and Patents Act 1988, s. 90 (3).
8 *Jaffa v Taylor Gallery Ltd* (1990) Times, 21 March (trust of painting validly constituted without physical delivery to the trustees (one of whom was in Ireland) on the ground that the formal declaration of trust contained in the deed transferred the property in the painting to the trustees, each of whom had a copy of the document and agreed to act).
9 *Ryall v Rowles* (1750) 1 Ves Sen 348; *Irons v Smallpiece* (1819) 2 B & Ald 551; *Cochrane v Moore* (1890) 25 QBD 57; *Lock v Heath* (1892) 8 TLR 295; *Kilpin v Ratley* [1892] 1 QB 582; *Re Cole* [1964] Ch 175, [1963] 3 All ER 433; *Thomas v Times Book Co Ltd* [1966] 1 WLR 911, [1966] 2 All ER 241 (the original manuscript of *Under Milk Wood*). See (1964) 27 MLR 357 (A.C. Diamond); [1953] CLJ 355 (J.W.A. Thornely).
10 Bills of Exchange Act 1882, s. 31; *Whistler v Forster* (1863) 14 CBNS 248; see, however, Cheques Act 1957, ss. 1, 2.

A. Legal Interests

MILROY v LORD
(1862) 4 De GF & J 264 (CA in Ch, KNIGHT BRUCE AND TURNER LJJ)

The settlor executed a voluntary deed, purporting to transfer fifty shares in the Bank of Louisiana to Samuel Lord to be held on trust for the plaintiffs, and later handed to him the share certificates. At the time, Lord held a general power of attorney, which would have entitled him to transfer the settlor's shares. However the shares could only be transferred by registration of the transferee in the books of the bank, and this was never done. The question was whether a trust of the shares had been created in favour of the plaintiffs.

Held (reversing STUART V-C). No trust existed.

TURNER LJ: Under the circumstances of this case, it would be difficult not to feel a strong disposition to give effect to this settlement to the fullest extent, and certainly I spared no pains to find the means of doing so, consistently with what I apprehend to be the law of the Court; but, after full and anxious consideration, I find myself unable to do so. I take the law of this Court to be well settled, that, in order to render a voluntary settlement valid and effectual, the settlor must have done everything which, according to the nature of the property comprised in the settlement, was necessary to be done in order to transfer the property and render the settlement binding upon him. He may of course do this by actually transferring the property to the persons for whom he intends to provide, and the provision will then be effectual, and it will be equally effectual if he transfers the property to a trustee for the purposes of the settlement, or declares that he himself holds it in trust for those purposes; and if the property be personal, the trust may, as I apprehend, be declared either in writing or by parol; but, in order to render the settlement binding, one or other of these modes must, as I understand the law of this Court, be resorted to, for there is no equity in this Court to perfect an imperfect gift. The cases I think go further to this extent, that if the settlement is intended to be effectuated by one of the modes to which I have referred, the Court will not give effect to it by applying another of those modes. If it is intended to take effect by transfer, the Court will not hold the intended transfer to operate as a declaration of trust, for then every imperfect instrument would be made effectual by being converted into a perfect trust. These are the principles by which, as I conceive, this case must be tried.

Applying, then, these principles to the case, there is not here any transfer either of the one class of shares or of the other to the objects of the settlement, and the question therefore must be, whether a valid and effectual trust in favour of those objects was created in the defendant *Samuel Lord* or in the settlor himself as to all or any of these shares. Now it is plain that it was not the purpose of this settlement, or the intention of the settlor, to constitute himself a trustee of the bank shares. The intention was that the trust should be vested in the defendant *Samuel Lord*, and I think therefore that we should not be justified in holding that by the settlement, or by any parol declaration made by the settlor, he himself became a trustee of these shares for the purposes of the settlement. By doing so we should be converting the settlement or the parol declaration to a purpose wholly different from that which was intended to be effected by it, and, as I have said, creating a perfect trust out of an imperfect transaction . . . .

The more difficult question is, whether the Defendant *Samuel Lord* did not become a trustee of these shares? Upon this question I have felt considerable doubt; but in the result, I have come to the conclusion that no perfect trust was ever created in him. The shares, it is clear, were never legally vested in him; and the only ground on which he can be held to have become a trustee of them is, that he held a power of attorney under which he might have transferred them into his own name; but he held that power of attorney as the agent of the settlor; and if he had been sued by the Plaintiffs as trustee of the settlement for an account under the trust, and to compel him to transfer the shares into his own name as trustee, I think he might well have said — These shares are not vested in me; I have no power over them except as the agent of the settlor, and without his express directions I cannot be justified in making the proposed transfer, in converting an intended into an actual settlement. A Court of Equity could not, I think, decree the agent of the settlor to make the transfer, unless it could decree the settlor himself to do so, and it is plain that no such decree could have been made against the settlor. In my opinion, therefore, this decree cannot be maintained as to the fifty *Louisiana Bank* shares.

In **Paul v Paul** (1882) 20 ChD 742,[11] property was settled, in a marriage settlement, upon the spouses successively for life, with remainder to the children of the marriage. If there were no children of the marriage, the wife took absolutely on surviving the husband; and, if she died in his lifetime, she was given a power to appoint by will, and in default of appointment, the property passed to the wife's next of kin excluding the husband.

There were no children of the marriage. The spouses asked that the capital of the fund should be paid to them because the only persons who had any interest therein were the next of kin who were volunteers, and whose interest the wife could defeat by exercising her power of appointment, or by surviving her husband.

The Court of Appeal refused the application. The funds were settled. The trust in favour of the next of kin was constituted. It was immaterial that they were volunteers.

In **Re Bowden** [1936] Ch 71,[12] a settlor, by a voluntary settlement executed in 1868, prior to becoming a nun, purported to convey to trustees all the property to which she might become entitled under her father's will. This could not create a trust, because there was no existing trust property.[13] However, the settlor's father died in 1869, and, during the next five years, the settlor's share of her father's estate was transferred to the trustees. In 1935, the settlor requested the trustees to return to her the funds then representing the property. BENNETT J refused. The property had been effectively settled, and was held upon the trusts of the settlement.

---

11 See also *Jefferys v Jefferys* (1841) Cr & Ph 138.
12 See also *Re Adlard* [1954] Ch 29, [1953] 2 All ER 1437 (covenant to settle).
13 See pp. 134–140, post. *Re Ellenborough* [1903] 1 Ch 697.

RE RALLI'S WILL TRUSTS
[1964] Ch 288, [1963] 3 All ER 940 (ChD, Buckley J)

A testator, who died in 1899, left his residuary estate on trust for his wife for life, and then for his two daughters, Helen and Irene absolutely.

Helen, by her marriage settlement, covenanted to settle after-acquired property in favour, in the events which happened, of the children of Irene.

On the death of Helen and of the testator's widow, the plaintiff, who was Irene's husband, was sole surviving trustee, both of the testator's will and of the marriage settlement; and Helen's share of the residuary estate was thus vested in him. The question was whether the plaintiff held it on trust for those interested under Helen's will, or on the trusts of Helen's marriage settlement.

Held. The plaintiff held Helen's share upon the trusts of the marriage settlement. The property was vested in the trustee of the marriage settlement, and it made no difference that it came to him in his capacity as trustee of the will trusts.

BUCKLEY J: The investments representing the share of residue in question, which I shall call "the fund", stand in the name of the plaintiff. This is because he is now the sole surviving trustee of the testator's will. Therefore, say the defendants, he holds the fund primarily on the trusts of the will, that is to say, in trust for them as part of Helen's estate. The plaintiff is, however, also the sole surviving covenantee under clause 7 of the settlement as well as the sole surviving trustee of that settlement. This, however, affords him no answer, say the defendants, to their claim under the will unless the plaintiff, having transferred the fund to them in pursuance of the trusts of the will, could compel them to return it in pursuance of their obligation under the covenant, and this, they say, he could not do. In support of this last contention they rely on *Re Plumptre's Marriage Settlement* [1910] 1 Ch 609; *Re Pryce* [1917] 1 Ch 234 and *Re Kay's Settlement* [1939] Ch 329, [1939] 1 All ER 245, p. 125 post.

The plaintiff, on the other hand, contends that, as he already holds the fund, no question of his having to enforce the covenant arises. The fund, having come without impropriety into his hands, is now, he says, impressed in his hands with the trusts upon which he ought to hold it under the settlement; and because of the covenant it does not lie in the mouth of the defendants to say that he should hold the fund in trust for Helen's estate. He relies on *Re Bowden* [1936] Ch 71, p. 113, ante ... The plaintiff also relies on *Re Adlard* [1954] Ch 29, [1953] 2 All ER 1437, where Vaisey J followed *Re Bowden*, and on the observations of Upjohn J in *Re Burton's Settlements* [1955] Ch 82 at 104, [1954] 3 All ER 193 at 204.

Mr. Goff for the defendants says that *Re Bowden* and *Re Adlard* are distinguishable from the present case because in each of those cases the fund had reached the hands of the trustees of the relevant settlement and was held by them in that capacity, whereas in the present case the fund is, as he maintains, in the hands of the plaintiff in the capacity of trustee of the will and not in the capacity of trustee of the settlement. He says that *Re Burton's Settlements*, the complicated facts of which I forbear to set out here, should be distinguished on the ground that, when the settlement there in question was made, the trustee of that settlement and the trustee of the settlement under which the settlor had expectations was the same, so that the settlor by her settlement gave directions to the trustee of the settlement under which she had expectations, who then already held the relevant fund.

Sir Milner Holland, for the plaintiff, says that the capacity in which the trustee has become possessed of the fund is irrelevant. Thus in *Strong v Bird* (1874) LR 18 Eq 315 an imperfect gift was held to be completed by the donee obtaining probate of the donor's will of which he was executor, notwithstanding that the donor died intestate as to her residue and that the donee was not a person entitled as on her intestacy. Similarly in *Re James* [1935] Ch 449 a grant of administration to two administrators was held to perfect an imperfect gift by the intestate to one of them, who had no beneficial interest in the intestate's estate.

In my judgment the circumstance that the plaintiff holds the fund because he was appointed a trustee of the will is irrelevant. He is at law the owner of the fund, and the means by which he became so have no effect upon the quality of his legal ownership. The question is: For whom, if anyone, does he hold the fund in equity? In other words, who can successfully assert an equity against him disentitling him to stand upon his legal right? It seems to me to be indisputable that Helen, if she were alive, could not do so, for she has solemnly covenanted under seal to assign the fund to the plaintiff, and the defendants can stand in no better position. It is, of course, true that the object of the covenant was not that the plaintiff should retain the property for his own benefit, but that he should hold it on the trusts of the settlement. It is also true that, if it were necessary to enforce performance of the covenant, equity would not assist the beneficiaries under the settlement, because they are mere volunteers; and that for the same reason the plaintiff, as trustee of the settlement, would not be bound to enforce the covenant and would not be constrained by the court to do so, and indeed, it seems, might be constrained by the court not to do so. As matters stand, however, there is no occasion to invoke the assistance of equity to enforce the performance of the covenant. It is for the defendants to invoke the assistance of equity to make good their claim to the fund. To do so successfully they must show that the plaintiff cannot conscientiously withhold it from them. When they seek to do this, he can point to the covenant which, in my judgment, relieves him from any fiduciary obligation he would otherwise owe to the defendants as Helen's representatives. In so doing the plaintiff is not seeking to enforce an equitable remedy against the defendants on behalf of persons who could not enforce such a remedy themselves: he is relying upon the combined effect of his legal ownership of the fund and his rights under the covenant. That an action on the covenant might be statute-barred is irrelevant, for there is no occasion for such an action.[14]

BUCKLEY J also held that a clause in the settlement providing that "all the property comprised within the terms of [the covenant] shall become subject in equity to the settlement hereby covenanted to be made thereof" had the effect of imposing a trust independently of the vesting of the property in the trustee. It is difficult, however, to see that the provision could be more than a future declaration of a trust of unascertained property, and therefore void. See *Re Anstis* (1886) 31 ChD 596.

14 Cf. *Re Brooks' Settlement Trusts* [1939] Ch 993, [1939] 3 All ER 920, p. 136 post.

B. Equitable Interests

A trust of an equitable interest may be constituted by an assignment of that interest to trustees; being a disposition of an equitable interest, it must be in writing under section 53(1)(c) of the Law of Property Act 1925 (p. 53 ante).

In **Kekewich v Manning** (1851) 1 De GM & G 176,[14a] trustees held shares on trust for A for life remainder to B absolutely. B assigned his equitable interest to C to hold on trust for D. This was held to create a trust of B's equitable interest in remainder.

C. Act of Third Party Necessary to Perfect Legal Title

There are difficulties where the act of a third party is required to perfect a transfer of the legal title.

RE ROSE[15]
[1952] Ch 499, [1952] 1 All ER 1217 (CA, EVERSHED MR, JENKINS and MORRIS LJJ)

On March 30, 1943 the settlor made two transfers of shares in an unlimited company in the form required by its Articles of Association. The directors of the company could, under the Articles, refuse, at their discretion, to register a transfer. The transfers were registered on June 30, 1943. The settlor died at a time at which estate duty would be payable on the shares if the effective date of the transfer was June 30, but not if it was March 30. The Crown claimed the duty.[16]

Held (affirming ROXBURGH J). No duty payable. The settlor had done everything in his power to effect the transfer.

EVERSHED MR: The burden of the case presented by the Crown may be briefly put as it was formulated in reply by Mr. Pennycuick. This document, he said, on the face of it, was intended to operate and operated, if it operated at all, as a transfer. If for any reason it was at its date incapable of so operating, it is not legitimate, either by reference to the expressed intention in the document or on well-established principles of law, to extract from it a wholly different transaction — that is, to make it take effect not as a transfer but as a declaration of trust. Now I agree that on the face of the document it was obviously intended (if you take the words used) to operate and operate immediately as a transfer — "I do hereby transfer to the transferee" these shares "to hold unto the said transferee, subject to the several conditions on which I held the same at the time of the execution hereof". It plainly was intended to operate immediately as a transfer of rights. To some extent at least,

---

14a *Gilbert v Overton* (1864) 2 Hem & M 110 (assignment of agreement for lease).
15 (1976) 40 Conv (NS) 139 (L. McKay), where the reasoning of the decision is criticised. *Re Rose* was described in *Rowlandson v National Westminster Bank Ltd* [1978] 1 WLR 798 at 802, [1978] 3 All ER 370 at 377, as "a gloss" on the principle of perfect gifts. See *Re Fry* [1946] Ch 312, [1946] 2 All ER 106; *Re Paradise Motor Co Ltd* [1968] 1 WLR 1125, [1968] 2 All ER 625; *Vandervell v IRC* [1967] 2 AC 291 at 330, [1967] 1 All ER 1 at 18; *Tett v Phoenix Property and Investment Co Ltd* [1984] BCLC 599; *Mascall v Mascall* (1984) 50 P & CR 119, p. 119, post; *Brown & Root Technology Ltd v Sun Alliance and London Assurance Co Ltd* [1995] 3 WLR 558.
16 Estate duty was replaced by capital transfer tax, itself replaced by inheritance tax in IHTA 1984, p. 569, post.

it is said, it could not possibly do so. To revert to the illustration which has throughout been taken, if the company had declared a dividend during this interregnum, it is not open to question that the company must have paid that dividend to the deceased. So that vis-à-vis the company, this document did not, and could not, operate to transfer to Mrs. Rose the right against the company to claim and receive that dividend. Shares, Mr. Pennycuick says, are property of a peculiar character consisting, as it is sometimes put, of a bundle of rights — that is, rights against or in the company. It has followed from his argument that if such a dividend had been paid, the deceased could, consistently with the document to which he has set his hand and seal, have retained that dividend, and, if he had handed it over to his wife, it would have been an independent gift. I think myself that such a conclusion is startling. Indeed, I venture to doubt whether to anybody but a lawyer such a conclusion would even be comprehensible — at least without a considerable amount of explanation. That again is not conclusive; but I confess that I approach a matter of this kind with a pre-conceived notion that a conclusion that offends common sense, so much as this would prima facie do, ought not to be the right conclusion.

[His Lordship examined *Milroy v Lord* in detail, and referred to the dictum of TURNER LJ which is reprinted above at p. 112.]

Those last few sentences form the gist of the Crown's argument and on it is founded the broad, general proposition that if a document is expressed as, and on the face of it intended to operate as, a transfer, it cannot in any respect take effect by way of trust — so far I understand the argument to go. In my judgment, that statement is too broad and involves too great a simplification of the problem; and is not warranted by authority. I agree that if a man purporting to transfer property executes documents which are not apt to effect that purpose, the court cannot then extract from those documents some quite different transaction and say that they were intended merely to operate as a declaration of trust, which ex facie they were not: but if a document is apt and proper to transfer the property — is in truth the appropriate way in which the property must be transferred — then it does not seem to me to follow from the statement of Turner LJ that, as a result, either during some limited period or otherwise, a trust may not arise, for the purpose of giving effect to the transfer. The simplest case will, perhaps, provide an illustration. If a man executes a document transferring all his equitable interest, say, in shares, that document, operating, and intended to operate, as a transfer, will give rise to and take effect as a trust; for the assignor will then be a trustee of the legal estate in the shares for the person in whose favour he has made an assignment of his beneficial interest. And, for my part, I do not think that the case of *Milroy v Lord* (1862) 4 De GF & J 264 is an authority which compels this court to hold that in this case — where, in the terms of Turner LJ's judgment, the settlor did everything which, according to the nature of the property comprised in the settlement, was necessary to be done by him in order to transfer the property — the result necessarily negatives the conclusion that, pending registration, the settlor was a trustee of the legal interest for the transferee.

The view of the limitations of *Milroy v Lord*, which I have tried to express, was much better expressed by Jenkins J in the recent case which also bears the same name of *Re Rose* [1949] Ch 78, [1948] 2 All ER 971 (though that is a coincidence). It is true that the main point, the essential question to be determined, was whether there had been a transfer eo nomine of certain shares within the meaning of a will. The testator in that case, Rose, by his will had given a number of shares to one Hook but the gift was subject to this qualification, "if such shares have not been transferred to him previously to my death". The question was, had the shares been transferred to him in these circumstances? He had executed (as had this Mr. Rose) a transfer in appropriate form and handed the transfer and the certificate to Hook; but, at the time of his death, the transfer had not been registered. It was said, therefore, that there had been no transfer; and (following Mr. Pennycuick's argument) there had been no passing to Hook of any interest, legal or beneficial, whatever, by the time the testator died. If that view were right then, of course, Hook would be entitled to the shares under the will. But my brother went a little more closely into the matter, because it was obvious that on one view of it, if it were held that there was a "transfer" within the terms of the will, though the transfer was inoperative in the eye of the law and not capable of being completed after the death, then Mr. Hook suffered the misfortune of getting the shares neither by gift inter vivos nor by testamentary benefaction. Therefore, my brother considered the case of *Milroy v Lord*, and in regard to it he used this language [1949] Ch 78 at 89, [1948] 2 All ER 971 at 978; "I was referred on that to the well known case of *Milroy v Lord*, and also to the recent case of *Re Fry* [1946] Ch 312, [1946] 2 All ER 106. Those cases, as I understand them, turn on the fact that the deceased donor had not done all in his power, according to the nature of the property given, to vest the legal interest in the property in the donee. In such circumstances it is, of course, well settled that there is no equity to complete the imperfect gift. If any act remained to be done by the donor to complete the gift at the date of the donor's death the court will not compel his personal representatives to do that act and the gift remains incomplete and fails. In *Milroy v Lord* the imperfection was due to the fact that the wrong form of transfer was used for the purpose of transferring certain bank shares. The document was not the appropriate document to pass any interest in the property at all." Then he refers to *Re Fry*, which is another illustration.[17] "In this case, as I understand it, the testator had done everything in his power to divest himself of the shares in question to Mr. Hook. He had executed a transfer. It is not suggested that the transfer was not in accordance with the company's regulations. He had handed that transfer together with the certificate to Mr. Hook. There was nothing else the testator could do." I venture respectfully to adopt the whole of the passage I have read which, in my judgment, is a correct statement of the law. If that be so, then it seems to me that it cannot be asserted on the authority of *Milroy v Lord*, and I venture to think it also cannot be asserted as a matter of logic and good sense or principle, that because, by the regulations of the company, there had to be a gap before Mrs. Rose could, as between herself and the company, claim the rights which the shares gave her vis-à-vis the company, the deceased was not in the meantime a trustee for her of all his rights and benefits under the shares. That he intended to pass all those rights, as I have said, seems to be too plain for argument. I think the matter might be put perhaps in a somewhat different fashion, though it reaches the same end. Whatever might be the position during the period between the execution of this document and the registration of the shares, the transfers were on June 30, 1943, registered. After registration, the title of Mrs. Rose was beyond doubt complete in every respect; and if the deceased had received a dividend between execution and registration and Mrs. Rose had claimed to have that dividend handed to her, what would have been the deceased's answer? It could no longer be that the

17 See also *Re Transatlantic Life Assurance Co Ltd* [1980] 1 WLR 79, [1979] 3 All ER 352.

purported gift was imperfect; it had been made perfect. I am not suggesting that the perfection was retroactive. But what else could he say? How could he, in the face of his own statement under seal, deny the proposition that he had, on March 30, 1943, transferred the shares to his wife? — and by the phrase "transfer the shares" surely must be meant transfer to her "the shares and all my right title and interest thereunder." Nothing else could sensibly have been meant. Nor can he, I think, make much of the fact that this was a voluntary settlement on his part. Being a case of an unlimited company, as I have said, Mrs. Rose had herself to undertake by covenant to accept the shares subject to their burdens — in other words, to relieve the deceased of his liability as a corporator. I find it unnecessary to pursue the question of consideration, but it is, I think, another feature which would make exceedingly difficult and, sensibly impossible, the assertion on the deceased's part of any right to retain any such dividend. Nor is the Crown's argument made any easier by the circumstance that another emanation of the Crown has adjudicated that stamp duty ad valorem under section 74 of the Act of 1910 was payable upon this transfer as a disposition of the subject-matter transferred.[18]

In **Mascall v Mascall** (1984) 50 P & CR 119[19] the plaintiff executed a transfer of a house with registered title in favour of his son, and also handed the land certificate to him. Before the documents were sent to the Land Registry for the registration of the son as proprietor, the plaintiff and his son had a serious row. The plaintiff then sought a declaration that the transfer was void. In holding that there had been an effective gift to the son, LAWTON LJ referred to *Milroy v Lord* and *Re Rose* and said at 125:

"In my judgment, that is the situation here. The plaintiff had done everything in his power to transfer the house to the defendant. He had intended to do it. He had handed over the land certificate. He had executed the transfer and all that remained was for the defendant, in the ordinary way of conveyancing, to submit the transfer for stamping and then to ask the Land Registry to register his title. Mr. Pearson sought to say that, in relation to registered land, if not to unregistered land, the plaintiff could have done more because he himself, pursuant to section 18 of the Land Registration Act 1925, could have asked the Land Registry to register the transfer and he had not done so; therefore he had not done everything within his power. In my judgment, that is a fallacious argument. He had done everything in his power in the ordinary way of the transfer of registered property and, in the ordinary way, it was for the defendant to get the Land Registry to register him as the proprietor of the property. In those circumstances, it seems to me that the deputy judge's judgment was correct and I would dismiss the appeal."

---

18 See *Mallott v Wilson* [1903] 2 Ch 494, where BYRNE J held that, where an intended trustee disclaimed an interest transferred on trust as soon as he knew of it, the transfer constituted the trust until disclaimer, whereupon the legal estate, now clothed with the trusts, revested in the settlor. For criticism, see [1981] Conv 141 (P. Matthews).
19 (1985) 82 LSG 1629 (H. Wilkinson).

II. Declaration of Self as Trustee[20]

If the settlor declares himself trustee, there is no problem of constitution of the trust. The property is already vested in the settlor. The problem in this context relates to the *declaration* of the trust. "Men often mean to give things to their kinsfolk, they do not often mean to constitute themselves trustees."[1] It is necessary to show that the settlor manifested an intention to declare himself trustee. Nothing else will do. An intention to give will not be construed as an intention to declare himself trustee. "An imperfect gift is no declaration of trust."[1]

JONES v LOCK
(1865) 1 Ch App 25 (CA in Ch, Lord CRANWORTH LC)

On returning from a business visit to Birmingham, Robert Jones was reproved by his family for not bringing a present for his baby son. He produced a cheque for £900 payable to himself, and said: "Look you here, I give this to baby; it is for himself, and I am going to put it away for him, and will give him a great deal more along with it." He placed the cheque in the baby's hand. His wife feared that the baby might tear it, and Jones added: "Never mind if he does; it is his own, and he may do what he likes with it." He then took the cheque back and locked it in the safe. Six days later he died. The question was whether the baby was entitled to the cheque.

Held. There had been no gift to the baby;[2] and no declaration of trust in his favour.

LORD CRANWORTH LC: This is a special case, in which I regret to say that I cannot bring myself to think that, either on principle or on authority, there has been any gift or any valid declaration of trust. No doubt a gift may be made by any person *sui juris* and *compos mentis*, by conveyance of a real estate or by delivery of a chattel; and there is no doubt also that, by some decisions, unfortunate I must think them, a parol declaration of trust of personalty may be perfectly valid even when voluntary. If I give any chattel that, of course, passes by delivery, and if I say, expressly or impliedly, that I constitute myself a trustee of personalty, that is a trust executed, and capable of being enforced without consideration. I do not think it necessary to go into any of the authorities cited before me; they all turn upon the question, whether what has been said was a declaration of trust or an imperfect gift. In the latter case the parties would receive no aid from a Court of equity if they claimed as volunteers. But when there has been a declaration of trust, then it will be enforced, whether there has been consideration or not. Therefore the question in each case is one of fact; has there been a gift or not, or has there been a declaration of trust or not? I should have every inclination to sustain this gift, but unfortunately I am unable to do so; the case turns on the very short question whether *Jones* intended to make a declaration that he held the

---

20 H & M, pp. 121–124; K & S, pp. 107–108; P & M, pp. 62–66; Pettit, pp. 94–95; Riddall, p. 74; Snell, pp. 123–124; Underhill, pp. 125–129.

1 Maitland, *Equity* (2nd Edn) p. 72.

2 Because the gift of a non-bearer cheque requires endorsement. Under Cheques Act 1957, s. 2, endorsements in blank of cheques payable to order are no longer necessary as far as the rights of a collecting bank are concerned; and under Cheques Act 1992, s. 1, a cheque is not transferable if it is crossed and bears the words "account payee" across its face.

property in trust for the child; and I cannot come to any other conclusion than that he did not. I think it would be of very dangerous example if loose conversations of this sort, in important transactions of this kind, should have the effect of declarations of trust.

[His Lordship then commented on the evidence, and said that no doubt it was a fair representation of what actually took place, and that the father really had an intention of settling something on the child, and that his giving the note to the child was symbolical of what he meant to do; but it was not his meaning to enable the child, by his next friend, to bring an action of trover for the cheque or file a bill for the £900, but he merely meant to say that now he could make a provision for the boy; and what he said to the solicitor was quite consistent with it.]

It was all quite natural, but the testator would have been very much surprised if he had been told that he had parted with the £900, and could no longer dispose of it. It all turns upon the facts, which do not lead me to the conclusion that the testator meant to deprive himself of all property in the note, or to declare himself a trustee of the money for the child. I extremely regret this result, because it is obvious that, by the act of God, this unfortunate child has been deprived of a provision which his father meant to make for him.

RICHARDS v DELBRIDGE
(1874) LR 18 Eq 11 (Chancery, Sir George JESSEL MR)

John Delbridge was tenant of premises where he carried on business as a bone manure merchant. He was assisted by Edward Bennetto Richards, who was his infant grandson. Shortly before Delbridge's death, he indorsed on the lease, and signed the following memorandum: "This deed and all thereto belonging I give to *Edward Bennetto Richards* from this time forth, with all the stock-in-trade." He delivered the document to Richards' mother to hold for him, and then died, making no mention of this property in his will. The question was whether, on Delbridge's death, the lease and business passed to Richards, or whether it passed under the will.

Held. It passed under the will. There was no conveyance to, or declaration of trust in favour of, Richards.

SIR GEORGE JESSEL MR: The principle is a very simple one. A man may transfer his property, without valuable consideration, in one of two ways: he may either do such acts as amount in law to a conveyance or assignment of the property, and thus completely divest himself of the legal ownership, in which case the person who by those acts acquires the property takes it beneficially, or on trust, as the case may be; or the legal owner of the property may, by one or other of the modes recognised as amounting to a valid declaration of trust, constitute himself a trustee, and, without an actual transfer of the legal title, may so deal with the property as to deprive himself of its beneficial ownership, and declare that he will hold it from that time forward on trust for the other person. It is true he need not use the words, "I declare myself a trustee," but he must do something which is equivalent to it, and use expressions which have that meaning; for, however anxious the Court may be to carry out a man's intention, it is not at liberty to construe words otherwise than according to their proper meaning . . . .

The true distinction appears to me to be plain, and beyond dispute: for a man to make himself a trustee there must be an expression of intention to become a trustee, whereas words of present gift shew an intention to give over property to another, and not retain it in the donor's own hands for any purpose, fiduciary or otherwise.

In *Milroy v Lord* (1862) 4 De GF & J 264 at 274, Lord Justice *Turner*, after referring to the two modes of making a voluntary settlement valid and effectual, adds these words: "The cases, I think, go further, to this extent, that if the settlement is intended to be effectuated by one of the modes to which I have referred, the Court will not give effect to it by applying another of those modes. If it is intended to take effect by transfer, the Court will not hold the intended transfer to operate as a declaration of trust, for then every imperfect instrument would be made effectual by being converted into a perfect trust."

In **Middleton v Pollock** (1876) 2 ChD 104,[3] Mr. Pollock, a solicitor, received money for investment from various clients. The money was so intermingled that it was impossible to trace that invested by each client. Pollock died heavily insolvent.

Before his death, he made declarations of trust in favour of selected clients, mostly relatives and friends. The one selected for trial as a representative case was that of a relative, Miss Elliott.

Miss Elliott's money had never been invested. Before he died, Pollock indorsed a bill of exchange in her favour, and signed a declaration that he held certain leaseholds on trust for her to secure the repayment to her of the money owed, plus interest. Miss Elliott knew nothing of this. The question was whether Miss Elliott (and the others similarly placed) was entitled to the property in preference to the general creditors. Sir George JESSEL MR held that she was, as there had been a valid declaration of trust in favour of Miss Elliott. The trust could not be avoided as a fraudulent preference under 13 Eliz. c. 5, p. 178 post, as it was made bona fide and for valuable consideration.

In **Paul v Constance** [1977] 1 WLR 527, [1977] 1 All ER 195,[4] Mr. Constance was separated from his wife and lived with the plaintiff. He received £950 as damages resulting from an injury at work, and he and the plaintiff decided to put it into a deposit account at Lloyds Bank.

Because of the embarrassment which would be caused by having an account in two different names, the account was opened in Mr. Constance's name only. He indicated on various occasions that he wished it to be hers as much as his. On his death, Mrs. Constance claimed the deposit as part of her husband's estate. The plaintiff sought a declaration that the deposit was held on trust for her.

In finding for the plaintiff, SCARMAN LJ, after referring to *Jones v Lock* (1865) 1 Ch App 25, p. 120, ante, and *Richards v Delbridge* (1874) LR 18 Eq 11, p. 121, ante, said at 531, at 198:

"There is no suggestion of a gift by transfer in the present case. The facts of the two cases do not, therefore, very much help the submission of Mr. Blythe

---

3 *Gee v Liddell* (1866) 35 Beav 621.
4 Criticised in Heydon, Gummow and Austin, *Cases and Materials on Equity and Trusts* (4th edn), pp. 142–144.

but he was able to extract from them this principle: that there must be a clear declaration of trust and that means there must be clear evidence from what is said or done of an intention to create a trust — or, as Mr. Blythe put it, 'an intention to dispose of a property or a fund so that somebody else to the exclusion of the disponent acquires the beneficial interest in it'. He submitted that there was no such evidence.

When one looks at the detailed evidence to see whether it goes as far as that — and I think that the evidence does have to go as far as that — one finds that from the time that the deceased received his damages right up to his death he was saying, on occasions, that the money was as much the plaintiff's as his. When they discussed the damages, how to invest them or what to do with them and when they discussed the bank account, he would say to her: 'The money is as much yours as mine'.

The judge, rightly treating the basic problem in the case as a question of fact, reached this conclusion. He said: 'I have read through my notes and I am quite satisfied that it was the intention of Mrs. Paul and Mr. Constance to create a trust in which both of them were interested.'

In this court the issue becomes: was there sufficient evidence to justify the judge in reaching that conclusion of fact? In submitting that there was, Mr. Wilson draws attention first and foremost to the words used. When one bears in mind the unsophisticated character of the deceased and his relationship with the plaintiff during the last few years of his life, Mr. Wilson submits that the words that he did use on more than one occasion, 'This money is as much yours as mine', convey clearly a present declaration that the existing fund was as much the plaintiff's as his own. The judge accepted that conclusion. I think that he was well justified in doing so and, indeed, I think that he was right to do so.

It might, however, be thought that this was a borderline case, since it is not easy to pin-point a specific moment of declaration, and one must exclude from one's mind any case built upon the existence of an implied or constructive trust, for this case was put forward at the trial and is now argued by the plaintiff as one of express declaration of trust. It was so pleaded and it is only as such that it may be considered in this court. The question, therefore, is whether, in all the circumstances, the use of those words on numerous occasions as between the deceased and the plaintiff constituted an express declaration of trust. The judge found that they did. For myself, I think that he was right so to find. I therefore would dismiss the appeal."[5]

---

5 See *Re Vandervell's Trusts (No 2)* [1974] Ch 269, [1974] 1 All ER 47, p. 188, *post*, where the declaration was made by the trustees with the consent of the beneficial owner.

III. Covenants to Settle[6]

A. Unenforceable by Volunteers

Where there is no settlement, but only a covenant to settle, consideration becomes material. Persons who have given consideration (including those within the marriage consideration) may enforce a covenant. Volunteers may not.

The question commonly arises in connection with family settlements; either where the covenantor has failed to comply with a covenant to establish a settlement, or where a spouse, being a beneficiary under a marriage settlement, covenants to settle after-acquired property and fails to do so. Some writers are critical of the law which leaves covenants unenforceable by volunteers. Various suggestions have been made for overcoming it, and these will be considered.

PULLAN v KOE[7]
[1913] 1 Ch 9 (ChD, SWINFEN EADY J)

A marriage settlement dated May 1859, which settled property on trusts for a husband and wife and prospective children, contained a provision that the wife should settle after-acquired property of the value of £100 or upwards.

In 1879, she received a present of £285 from her mother. The money was paid into her husband's bank account, on which she had power to draw. Part was then invested in Cape of Good Hope bearer bonds or debentures; and the interest paid to the account. The bonds remained at the bank.

In 1909, the husband died. The trustees of the settlement, acting on behalf of the wife and children, claimed the bonds from the husband's executor. The defendants relied on the Statutes of Limitation.

Held. The trustees succeeded. The £285 was subject to a trust in favour of those within the marriage consideration, and was now represented by the bonds.

SWINFEN EADY J: It was contended that the bonds never in fact became trust property, as both the wife and husband were only liable in damages for breach of covenant, and that the case was different from cases where property which has once admittedly become subject to the trusts of an instrument has been improperly dealt with, and is sought to be recovered. In my opinion as soon as the 285*l.* was paid to the wife it became in equity bound by and subject to the trusts of the settlement. The trustees could have claimed that particular sum, could have obtained at once the appointment of a receiver of it, if they could

---

6 H & M, pp. 134–135; K & S, pp. 101–104; P & M, pp. 77–90; Pettit, pp. 95–108; Riddall, pp. 78–85; Snell, pp. 120–127; Underhill, pp. 144–159. See also (1960) 76 LQR 100 (D.W. Elliott); (1962) 78 LQR 228 (J.A. Hornby); [1965] 23 CLJ 46 (G.H. Jones); (1966) 29 MLR 397 (D. Matheson); (1966) 8 Malaya LR 153 (M. Scott); [1967] ASCL 387 (J.D. Davies); (1969) 85 LQR 213 (W.A. Lee); (1975) 91 LQR 236 (J.L. Barton); (1976) 92 LQR 427 (R.P. Meagher and J.R.F. Lehane); (1979) 32 CLP 1; (1981) 34 CLP 189 (C.E.F. Rickett); [1982] Conv 280 (M.W. Friend), 352 (S. Smith); (1982) 98 LQR 17 (J.D. Feltham); (1986) 60 ALJ 387 (S. Lindsay and P. Ziegler); *Perspectives of Law*, p. 240 (R.H. Maudsley); Gardner, *An Introduction to the Law of Trusts*, chap. 4.

7 *Re D'Angibau* (1880) 15 ChD 228; *Re Plumptre's Marriage Settlement* [1910] 1 Ch 609; *Re Cook's Settlement Trusts* [1965] Ch 902, [1964] 3 All ER 898, p. 127, post; cf. *Paul v Paul* (1882) 20 ChD 742.

have shewn a case of jeopardy, and, if it had been invested and the investment could be traced, could have followed the money and claimed the investment.

This point was dealt with by Jessel MR in *Smith v Lucas* (1881) 18 ChD 531 at 543, where he said: "What is the effect of such a covenant in equity? It has been said that the effect in equity of the covenant of the wife, as far as she is concerned, is that it does not affect her personally, but that it binds the property: that is to say, it binds the property under the doctrine of equity that that is to be considered as done which ought to be done. That is in the nature of specific performance of the contract no doubt. If, therefore, this is a covenant to settle the future-acquired property of the wife, and nothing more is done by her, the covenant will bind the property."

Again in *Collyer v Isaacs* (1881) 19 ChD 342 at 351, Jessel MR said: "A man can contract to assign property which is to come into existence in the future, and when it has come into existence, equity, treating as done that which ought to be done, fastens upon that property, and the contract to assign thus becomes a complete assignment. If a person contract for value, e.g., in his marriage settlement, to settle all such real estate as his father shall leave him by will, or purports actually to convey by the deed all such real estate, the effect is the same. It is a contract for value which will bind the property if the father leaves any property to his son."

The property being thus bound, these bonds became trust property, and can be followed by the trustees and claimed from a volunteer.

Again the trustees are entitled to come into a Court of Equity to enforce a contract to create a trust, contained in a marriage settlement, for the benefit of the wife and the issue of the marriage, all of whom are within the marriage consideration. The husband covenanted that he and his heirs, executors, and administrators should, as soon as circumstances would admit, convey, assign, and surrender to the trustees the real or personal property to which his wife should become beneficially entitled. The trustees are entitled to have that covenant specifically enforced by a Court of Equity. In *Re D'Angibau* (1880) 15 ChD 228 at 242 and in *Re Plumptre's Marriage Settlement* [1910] 1 Ch 609 at 616 it was held that the Court would not interfere in favour of volunteers, not within the marriage consideration, but here the plaintiffs are the contracting parties and the object of the proceeding is to benefit the wife and issue of the marriage.

RE KAY'S SETTLEMENT
[1939] Ch 329, [1939] 1 All ER 245 (ChD, Simonds J)

In 1907 Mary Winifred Kay, a spinster, executed a voluntary conveyance in favour of herself for life and after her death for her issue, containing a covenant to settle after-acquired property. She married and had three children and became entitled to other property. She refused a request by the trustees of the settlement to bring in the property on the ground that, as the settlement was purely voluntary, they ought not to take steps to enforce the covenant or to recover damages.

Held. Trustees directed not to take any such steps.

Simonds J: The trustees have issued this summons, making as parties to it, first, the settlor herself and, secondly, her infant children, who are beneficiaries under the settlement. But, be it observed, though beneficiaries, her children are, for the purpose of this settlement, to be regarded as volunteers, there being no marriage consideration, which would have entitled them to sue, though they are parties to this application. The trustees ask whether, in the event which has happened of the settlor having become entitled to certain property, they should take proceedings against her to compel performance of the covenant or to recover damages on her failure to implement it .... The settlor has appeared by Mr. Evershed and has contended, as she was entitled to contend, that the only question before the Court was whether the trustees ought to be directed to take such proceedings; that is to say, she contended that the only question before the Court was precisely that question which Eve J had to deal with in *Re Pryce* [1917] 1 Ch 234. She has said that the question before me is not primarily whether, if she were sued, such an action would succeed (as to which she might have a defence, I know not what), but whether, in the circumstances as they are stated to the Court, the trustees ought to be directed to take proceedings against her.

As to that, the argument before me has been, on behalf of the children of the marriage, beneficiaries under the settlement, that, although it is conceded that the trustees could not successfully take proceedings for specific performance of the agreements contained in the settlement, yet they could successfully, and ought to be directed to, take proceedings at law to recover damages for the non-observance of the agreements contained in the settlement .... In the circumstances I must say that I felt considerable sympathy for the argument which was put before me by Mr. Winterbotham on behalf of the children, that there was, at any rate, on the evidence before the Court to-day, no reason why the trustees should not be directed to take proceedings to recover what damages might be recoverable at law for breach of the agreements entered into by the settlor in her settlement. But on a consideration of *Re Pryce* it seemed to me that so far as this Court was concerned the matter was concluded and that I ought not to give any directions to the trustees to take the suggested proceedings.

In *Re Pryce* the circumstances appear to me to have been in no wise different from those which obtain in the case which I have to consider. In that case there was a marriage settlement made in 1887. It contained a covenant to settle the wife's after-acquired property ....

[His Lordship set out the after-acquired property and continued:] The husband died in 1907, and there was no issue of the marriage. Subject to his widow's life interest in both funds, the ultimate residue of the wife's fund was held in trust for her statutory next of kin, and the husband's fund was held in trust for him absolutely. The widow was also tenant for life under her husband's will. The trustees of the marriage settlement in that case took out a summons "to have it determined whether these interests and funds were caught by the provisions of the settlement, and, if so, whether they should take proceedings to enforce them" ....

Eve J, in a considered judgment, held that although the interests to which I have referred were caught by the covenant of the wife and the agreement by the husband respectively, yet the trustees ought not to take any steps to recover any of them. In the case of the wife's fund he said that her next of kin were volunteers, who could neither maintain an action to enforce the covenant nor for damages for breach of it, and that the Court would not give them by indirect means what they could not obtain by direct procedure; therefore he declined to direct the trustees to take proceedings either to have the covenant specifically enforced or to recover damages at law. The learned judge, as I have said, took time to consider his judgment. Many of the cases which have been cited to me, though not all of them apparently, were cited to him, and after deciding that no steps should be taken to enforce specific performance of the covenant he used these words [1917] 1 Ch at 214: "The position of the wife's fund is somewhat different, in that her next of kin would be entitled to it on her death; but they are volunteers, and although the Court would probably compel fulfilment of the contract to settle at the instance of any persons within the marriage consideration — see per Cotton LJ in *Re D'Angibau* (1880) 15 ChD 228 at 242 — and in their favour will treat the outstanding property as subjected to an enforceable trust — *Pullan v Koe* [1913] 1 Ch 9 — 'volunteers have no right whatever to obtain specific performance of a mere covenant which has remained as a covenant and has never been performed'; see per James LJ in *Re D'Angibau* at 246. Nor could damages be awarded either in this Court, or, I apprehend, at law, where, since the Supreme Court of Judicature Act, 1873,[8] the same defences would be available to the defendant as would be raised in an action brought in this Court for specific performance or damages."

That is the exact point which has been urged on me with great insistence by Mr. Winterbotham. Whatever sympathy I might feel for his argument, I am not justified in departing in any way from this decision, which is now twenty-one years old. The learned judge went on: "In these circumstances, seeing that the next of kin could neither maintain an action to enforce the covenant nor for damages for breach of it, and that the settlement is not a declaration of trust constituting the relationship of trustee and cestui que trust between the defendant and the next of kin, in which case effect could be given to the trusts even in favour of volunteers, but is a mere voluntary contract to create a trust, ought the Court now for the sole benefit of these volunteers to direct the trustees to take proceedings to enforce the defendant's covenant? I think it ought not; to do so would be to give the next of kin by indirect means relief they cannot obtain by any direct procedure, and would in effect be enforcing the settlement as against the defendant's legal right to payment and transfer from the trustees of the parents' marriage settlement." It is true that in those last words the learned judge does not specifically refer to an action for damages, but it is clear that he has in his mind directions both with regard to an action for specific performance and an action to recover damages at law — or, now, in this Court.

In those circumstances it appears to me that I must follow the learned judge's decision and I must direct the trustees not to take any steps either to compel performance of the covenant or to recover damages through her failure to implement it.

RE COOK'S SETTLEMENT TRUSTS
[1965] Ch 902, [1964] 3 All ER 898 (ChD, Buckley J)

In 1934, by an agreement and subsequent settlement of family property, made between Sir Herbert Cook Bart., Sir Francis Cook (his son) and the trustees of the settlement, certain pictures became the absolute property of Sir Francis Cook. In the settlement, Sir Francis covenanted (cl. 6) for valuable consideration that if any of those pictures should be sold during his lifetime, the net proceeds of sale should be paid to the trustees of the settlement to be held upon the trusts of the settlement.

8 Now Supreme Court Act 1981, s. 49.

In 1962, Sir Francis gave a Rembrandt (a picture of Titus) to his wife. She desired to sell it. The question was whether, on the sale of the Rembrandt, the trustees were obligated to take steps to enforce the performance of the covenant.

Held. As the beneficiaries had given no consideration for the covenant, they could not require the trustees to take steps to enforce it. Nor were they beneficiaries of a trust of the promise.[9]

BUCKLEY J: Mr. Goff, appearing for Sir Francis, has submitted first that, as a matter of law, the covenant contained in clause 6 of the settlement is not enforceable against him by the trustees of the settlement... [He] submits that the covenant was a voluntary and executory contract to make a settlement in a future event and was not a settlement of a covenant to pay a sum of money to the trustees. He further submits that as regards the covenant all the beneficiaries under the settlement are volunteers, with the consequence that not only should the court not direct the trustees to take proceedings on the covenant but it should positively direct them not to take proceedings. He relies upon *Re Pryce* [1917] 1 Ch 234 and *Re Kay's Settlement* [1939] Ch 329, [1939] 1 All ER 245.

Counsel for the second and third defendants have contended that on the true view of the facts there was an immediate settlement of the obligation created by the covenant, and not merely a covenant to settle something in the future. It was said, as Mr. Monckton put it, that by the agreement Sir Herbert bought the rights arising under the covenant for the benefit of the cestuis que trustent under the settlement and that, the covenant being made in favour of the trustees, these rights became assets of the trust. He relied on *Fletcher v Fletcher* (1844) 4 Hare 67; *Williamson v Codrington* (1750) 1 Ves Sen 511 and *Re Cavendish Browne's Settlement Trusts* [1916] WN 341. I am not able to accept this argument. The covenant with which I am concerned did not, in my opinion, create a debt enforceable at law, that is to say, a property right, which, although to bear fruit only in the future and upon a contingency, was capable of being made the subject of an immediate trust, as was held to be the case in *Fletcher v Fletcher*. Nor is this covenant associated with property which was the subject of an immediate trust as in *Williamson v Codrington*. Nor did the covenant relate to property which then belonged to the covenantor, as in *Re Cavendish Browne's Settlement Trusts*. In contrast to all these cases, this covenant upon its true construction is, in my opinion, an executory contract to settle a particular fund or particular funds of money which at the date of the covenant did not exist and which might never come into existence. It is analogous to a covenant to settle an expectation or to settle after-acquired property. The case, in my judgment, involves the law of contract, not the law of trusts.

As an alternative argument, Mr. Brightman formulated this proposition, which he admitted not to be directly supported by any authority, but he claimed to conflict with none: that where a covenantor has for consideration moving from a third party covenanted with trustees to make a settlement of property, the court will assist an intended beneficiary who is a volunteer to enforce the covenant if he is specially an object of the intended trust or (which Mr. Brightman says is the same thing) is within the consideration of the deed. In formulating this proposition Mr. Brightman bases himself on language used by Cotton LJ in *Re D'Angibau* (1880) 15 ChD 228 at 242 and by Romer J in

---

9 Appeal compromised. The picture was later sold at Christies for 760,000 guineas. See Times, 7 November, 1964, p. 5 and 20 March, 1965, p. 10.

Cannon v Hartley [1949] Ch 213 at 223, [1949] 1 All ER 50 at 58. As an example of a case to which the proposition would apply, Mr. Brightman supposes a father having two sons who enters into an agreement with his elder son and with trustees whereby the father agrees to convey an estate to his elder son absolutely in consideration of the son covenanting with his father and the trustees, or with the trustees alone, to settle an expectation on trusts for the benefit of the younger son. The younger son is a stranger to the transaction, but he is also the primary (and special) beneficiary of the intended settlement. A court of equity should, and would, Mr. Brightman contends, assist the younger son to enforce his brother's covenant and should not permit the elder son to frustrate the purposes of the agreement by refusing to implement his covenant although he has secured the valuable consideration given for it. The submission is not without attraction, for it is not to be denied that, generally speaking, the conduct of a man who, having pledged his word for valuable consideration, takes the benefits he has so obtained and then fails to do his part, commands no admiration. I have, therefore, given careful consideration to this part of the argument to see whether the state of the law is such as might justify me (subject to the construction point) in dealing with the case on some such grounds.

There was no consideration for Sir Francis's covenant moving from the trustees; nor, of course, was there any consideration moving from Sir Francis's children. [His Lordship referred to *A-G v Jacobs-Smith* [1895] 2 QB 341 at 353; *Hill v Gomme* (1839) 5 My & Cr 250 at 254; *Harvey v Ashley* (1748) 3 Atk 607 at 610; *Re D'Angibau* (1880) 15 ChD 228; *Green v Paterson* (1886) 32 ChD 95, and continued:]

These authorities show that there is an equitable exception to the general rule of law which I have mentioned where the contract is made in consideration of marriage and the intended beneficiary who seeks to have the contract enforced is within the marriage consideration. They do not support the existence of any wider exception save perhaps in the case of a beneficiary who is not within the marriage consideration but whose interests under the intended trusts are closely interwoven with interests of others who are within that consideration. They do not support the view that any such exception exists in favour of a person who was not a party to the contract and is not to be treated as though he had been and who has given no consideration and is not to be treated as if he had given consideration. Where the obligation to settle property has been assumed voluntarily it is clear that no object of the intended trusts can enforce the obligation. Thus in *Re Kay's Settlement* [1939] Ch 329, [1939] 1 All ER 245, a spinster made a voluntary settlement in favour of herself and her issue which contained a covenant to settle after-acquired property. She later married and had children who, as volunteers, were held to have no right to enforce the covenant. Mr. Brightman distinguishes that case from the present on the ground that in *Re Kay's Settlement* the settlement and covenant were entirely voluntary, whereas Sir Francis received consideration from Sir Herbert; but Sir Francis received no consideration from his own children. Why, it may be asked, should they be accorded an indulgence in a court of equity which they would not have been accorded had Sir Herbert given no consideration? As regards them the covenant must, in my judgment, be regarded as having been given voluntarily. A plaintiff is not entitled to claim equitable relief against another merely because the latter's conduct is unmeritorious. Conduct by A which is unconscientious in relation to B so as to entitle B to equitable relief may not be unconscientious in relation to C so that

C will have no standing to claim relief notwithstanding that the conduct in question may affect C. The father in Mr. Brightman's fictitious illustration could after performing his part of the contract release his elder son from the latter's covenant with him to make a settlement on the younger son, and the younger son could, I think, not complain. Only the covenant with the trustees would then remain, but this covenant would be a voluntary one, the trustees having given no consideration. I can see no reason why in these circumstances the court should assist the younger son to enforce the covenant with the trustees. But the right of the younger son to require the trustees to enforce their covenant, could not, I think, depend on whether the father had or had not released his covenant. Therefore, as it seems to me, on principle the younger son would not in any event have an equitable right to require the trustees to enforce their covenant. In other words, the arrangement between the father and his elder son would not have conferred any equitable right or interest upon his younger son.

I reach the conclusion that Mr. Brightman's proposition is not well-founded. There is no authority to support it and *Green v Paterson* (1886) 32 ChD 95 is, I think, authority the other way. Accordingly, the second and third defendants are not, in my judgment, entitled to require the trustees to take proceedings to enforce the covenant even if it is capable of being construed in a manner favourable to them.

[His Lordship then held that the words "in case any of such pictures shall be sold" in clause 6 of the settlement following the covenant that Sir Francis would not during his lifetime sell without previous notice in writing to the trustees, only referred to a sale by Sir Francis and did not contain any embargo on a disposition of the works of art in any other way, e.g., by gift.]

In **Cannon v Hartley** [1949] Ch 213, [1949] 1 All ER 50, a deed of separation, dated 1941, executed by the husband (the defendant) the wife and the daughter, provided that the defendant would settle, in favour of the wife and daughter, half of what the husband should receive under the will of either of his parents, being worth more than £1,000.

In 1944, the defendant inherited property in excess of £1,000, but failed to make the settlement. In 1946, the wife died. The daughter sued, as a party to the deed of separation, for damages for breach of covenant, and succeeded. She would have been unable, as a volunteer, to insist on the property being settled.

B. Should Volunteers be Able to Enforce?

i. ACTION FOR DAMAGES BY TRUSTEES

Pettit: *Equity and the Law of Trusts* (7th edn), pp. 98–99

"(ii) *Cestui que trust a volunteer*
The fact that the obligation is contained in a deed makes no difference in equity which has no special regard to the form of a seal.[10] It may well be asked, however, whether the trustees with whom the covenant is made can, or should,

---

10 See e.g. *Jefferys v Jefferys* (1841) Cr & Ph 138; *Kekewich v Manning* (1851) 1 De GM & G 176.

bring an action at law for damages since the common law regards consideration and a seal as alternative requirements. On this question it has been held that volunteers cannot compel trustees to take proceedings for damages, and further, that if the trustees ask the court for directions as to what they should do, they will be directed not to take any steps either to compel performance of the covenant or to recover damages through the failure to implement it. Thus in the leading case of *Re Pryce*[11] there was a marriage settlement under which the wife covenanted to settle after-acquired property. The beneficial limitations of funds brought into the settlement by the wife (including any after-acquired property) were successive life interests to the wife and the husband, remainder to the children of the marriage (of whom there were never in fact any), and an ultimate remainder to the wife's next-of-kin, who were of course volunteers. The husband was dead and the wife did not wish the covenant to be enforced. The court held that the trustees *ought* not to take any steps to compel the transfer or payment to them of the after-acquired property. The principle of *Re Pryce* has been strongly criticised by Professor Elliott,[12] who argues that the trustees should merely have been directed that they *need* not sue, leaving them with a discretion to sue for damages for breach of covenant if they wished. Professor Hornby[13] goes further, and contends that the court should have directed them to sue, on the ground that there was a completely constituted trust of the benefit of the covenant. Since these critical articles, however, *Re Pryce*[14] and *Re Kay's Settlement*[15] have been followed in *Re Cook's Settlement Trusts*,[16] where Sir Francis Cook covenanted with the trustees of a re-settlement that in case certain assets should be sold (including Rembrandt's 'Titus'), the proceeds of sale should be paid to them on trust for his children, who were volunteers. It was held that the trustees ought not to take any proceedings against Sir Francis consequent upon a sale.

On the cases as they stand there is no clear authority as to the position if the trustees do not ask the court for directions, but choose to bring an action. Professor Elliott takes the view that if an action would lie any damages recovered would become trust property, and that such damages would be substantial.[17] The authorities for this view are not very weighty, and even if valid as regards a covenant to pay money or transfer specific property, do not establish the point in the case of a covenant to settle after-acquired property.[18] Lee considers that any damages recovered would be held on a resulting trust for the settlor.

(iii) *Cestui que trust a covenantee*

Even where the *cestui que trust* is a volunteer, there is a clear decision at first instance,[19] that if the covenant is made with him, there is no answer to an action

---

11 [1917] 1 Ch 234; *Re Kay's Settlement* [1939] Ch 329, [1939] 1 All ER 245, p. 125, ante. See generally *Perspectives of Law*, p. 240 (R.H. Maudsley).
12 (1960) 76 LQR 100.
13 (1962) 78 LQR 228.
14 [1917] 1 Ch 234.
15 [1939] Ch 329, [1939] 1 All ER 245.
16 [1965] Ch 902, [1964] 3 All ER 898. These cases have found some academic support: [1967] ASCL 387 (J.D. Davies); (1969) 85 LQR 213 (W.A. Lee); but have also met with further severe academic criticism (1975) 91 LQR 236 (J.L. Barton); (1976) 92 LQR 427 (R.P. Meagher and J.R.F. Lehane). Cf. *Re Ralli's Will Trusts* [1964] Ch 288, [1963] 3 All ER 940, p. 113, ante.
17 See (1960) 76 LQR 100 (D.W. Elliott), citing, inter alia, *Re Cavendish Browne's Settlement Trusts* [1916] WN 341. See also [1988] Conv 18 (D. Goddard).
18 See R.H. Maudsley, op. cit, p. 244, and J.D. Davies, op cit, p. 392.
19 *Cannon v Hartley* [1949] Ch 213, [1949] 1 All ER 50, p. 130, ante.

by him at common law on the covenant, and substantial damages for breach thereof will be awarded. But, as a volunteer, he will not be able to obtain the equitable remedy of specific performance.[20]

(iv) *Performance of unenforceable covenant*
It is clear that if the settlor has in fact transferred property to trustees in compliance with an unenforceable covenant to settle the same in favour of volunteers, he thereby completely constitutes the trust, and cannot thereafter claim to recover the property, which must be held by the trustees on the declared trusts."[1]

In **Re Cavendish Browne's Settlement Trusts** [1916] WN 341, Catherine Penelope Cavendish Browne made a voluntary settlement containing a covenant "to convey and transfer to the trustees all the property, both real and personal, to which she was absolutely entitled by virtue of the joint operation of the wills of" J.H. and A.C.B. When Catherine died, she had not yet assured to the trustees a share of unconverted real estate in Canada, to which she had become entitled under the two wills. The question was whether the value of the share or any part of it ought to be paid to the trustees by way of damages for breach of covenant. YOUNGER J "without delivering a final judgment, held on the authority of *Williamson v Codrington* (1750) 1 Ves Sen 511; *Cox v Barnard* (1850) 8 Hare 310; *Fletcher v Fletcher* (1844) 4 Hare 67; *Re Parkin* [1892] 3 Ch 510; *Ward v Audland* (1847) 16 M & W 862; *Lloyd's v Harper* (1880) 16 ChD 290; *Davenport v Bishopp* (1843) 2 Y & C Ch Cas 451; *Clough v Lambert* (1839) 10 Sim 174; *Synge v Synge* [1894] 1 QB 466; *Spickernell v Hotham* (1854) Kay 669; *Re Plumptre's Marriage Settlement* [1910] 1 Ch 609 that the trustees were entitled to recover [from Catherine's administrators] substantial damages for breach of the covenant to assure, and that the measure of damages was the value of the property which would have come to the hands of the trustees if the covenant had been duly performed."[2]

ii. TRUST OF THE PROMISE

If there was a trust of the promise, there would be a constituted trust of a chose in action, and such a trust could be enforced by the trustee for the benefit of the beneficiary,[3] or by the beneficiary for his own benefit, joining the trustee as co-plaintiff or as defendant.[4]

---

20 See (1988) 8 LS 172 (M.R.T. McNair), suggesting historical support for allowing specific performance of covenants in favour of volunteers.
1 *Paul v Paul* (1882) 20 ChD 742 p. 113 ante; *Re Adlard* [1954] Ch 29, [1953] 2 All ER 1437; *Re Ralli's Will Trusts* [1964] Ch 288, [1963] 3 All ER 940, p. 113, ante.
2 See also *Jackson v Horizon Holidays Ltd* [1975] 1 WLR 1468, [1975] 3 All ER 92, where it was held that a husband, who contracted with the defendants for a holiday abroad for himself and his wife and family, could recover damages in respect of the loss suffered by all, when the defendants failed to provide the facilities promised. The reasoning in this decision was disapproved in *Woodar Investment Development Ltd v Wimpey Construction (UK) Ltd* [1980] 1 WLR 277, [1980] 1 All ER 571; [1981] Conv. 386 (K. Hodkinson). See also (1976) 39 MLR 202 (D. Yates); (1986) 37 NILQ 211 (G. Samuel); (1987) 103 LQR 564 (R. Flannigan); (1988) 8 LS 14 (N.H. Andrews); (1988) 13 NZULR 68 (S. Stoljar).
3 *Lloyd's v Harper* (1880) 16 ChD 290. See also *Barclays Bank plc v Willowbrook International Ltd* [1987] FTLR 386; *Harrison v Tew* [1989] QB 307, [1987] 3 All ER 865.
4 *Affréteurs Réunis SA v Leopold Walford (London) Ltd* [1919] AC 801.

FLETCHER v FLETCHER
(1844) 4 Hare 67 (Chancery, Wigram V-C)

By a voluntary deed, Ellis Fletcher covenanted with trustees to pay to them £60,000, which the trustees were to hold upon trust for, in the events which happened, Ellis's illegitimate son, Jacob. The trustees were unaware of the deed, which was found among Ellis's papers after his death. The trustees did not wish to establish the trust except under an order of the court. The question was whether Jacob could enforce the covenant against the executor of Ellis.

Held. Jacob was entitled to enforce the covenant, although it was voluntary.

Wigram V-C: It is not denied that, if the Plaintiff in this case had brought an action in the name of the trustees, he might have recovered the money; and it is not suggested, that if the trustees had simply allowed their name to be used in the action, their conduct could have been impeached. There are two classes of cases, one of which is in favour of, and the other, if applicable, against, the Plaintiff's claim. The question is, to which of the two classes it belongs.

In trying the equitable question I shall assume the validity of the instrument at law. If there was any doubt of that it would be reasonable to allow the Plaintiff to try the right by suing in the name of the surviving trustee. The first proposition relied upon against the claim in equity was, that equity will not interfere in favour of a volunteer. That proposition, though true in many cases, has been too largely stated. A court of equity, for example, will not, in favour of a volunteer, enforce the performance of a contract in specie. That it will, however, sometimes act in favour of a volunteer is proved by the common case of a volunteer on a bond who may prove his bond against the assets. Again, where the relation of trustee and *cestui que trust* is constituted, as where property is transferred from the author of the trust into the name of a trustee, so that he has lost all power of disposition over it, and the transaction is complete as regards him, the trustee, having accepted the trust, cannot say he holds it, except for the purposes of the trust; and the Court will enforce the trust at the suit of a volunteer. According to the authorities, I cannot, I admit, do anything to perfect the liability of the author of the trust, if it is not already perfect. This covenant, however, is already perfect. The covenantor is liable at law, and the Court is not called upon to do any act to perfect it. One question made in argument has been, whether there can be a trust of a covenant the benefit of which shall belong to a third party; but I cannot think there is any difficulty in that. Suppose, in the case of a personal covenant to pay a certain annual sum for the benefit of a third person, the trustee were to bring an action against the covenantor; would he be afterwards allowed to say he was not a trustee? If he cannot do so after once acknowledging the trust, then there is a case in which there is a trust of a covenant for another. In the case of *Clough v Lambert* (1839) 10 Sim 174 the question arose; the point does not appear to have been taken during the argument, but the Vice-Chancellor of England was of opinion that the covenant bound the party; that the *cestui que trust* was entitled to the benefit of it; and that the mere intervention of a trustee made no difference. The proposition, therefore, that in no case can there be a trust of a covenant is clearly too large, and the real question is whether the relation of trustee and *cestui que trust* is established in the present case.

Perspectives of Law (ed. R. Pound), p. 248

"There was, then, a trust of the promise, and the plaintiff as beneficiary of this trust, could enforce it. But it seems to me that there are one or two difficulties in holding that a trust of a chose in action was created on the facts of this particular case.[5] In the first place, positive evidence of intention is lacking. Ellis Fletcher, the covenantor, covenanted that he would pay the £60,000 to trustees 'to be held on the following trusts'. There is clearly a trust which will affect the money once it is received by the trustee, but no manifestation of an intention by either party to create a trust of a chose in action. Secondly . . . it seems to me that a trust of this nature should be created, if at all, by the obligee and not by the obligor; and there was evidence of the fact that the trustee did not enter into the arrangement intending to be a trustee of a promise, for he did not know about it, and wished to decline the trust as soon as he did hear about it. A trust of tangible property is declared by the owner of the property, whether he keeps the property himself or transfers it to another on trust; a trust of a debt is declared by the creditor. A covenantor should not claim, at one swoop, to burden himself with the promise of the payment of money to a promisee, and impose trusts upon the promisee behind his back. It is not as if he were assigning the benefit of a promise, or transferring the money; in such cases he could of course impose trusts on the promise or on the money. The logic of the matter seems to me to be that if A covenants to pay money to B which B is to hold on trust for C, the trusts on which money will be held, when paid over, can be declared by A; but a trust of A's promise should be declared by the person who has the benefit of the promise, namely B; and this will usually be proved by showing that B contracted as trustee for the persons nominated by the covenantor. Both these difficulties are overcome by the rules of the Restatement that the inference in these cases is that the promisee becomes trustee of his rights under the promise, and that, in the case of a voluntary covenant to settle, the settlor is the promisor."[6]

IV. Trusts of Future Property[7]

In **Norman v Federal Commissioner of Taxation** (1963) 109 CLR 9, WINDEYER J said, at 24:

"As to attempted assignments of things not yet in existence:

As it is impossible for anyone to own something that does not exist, it is impossible for anyone to make a present gift of such a thing to another person, however sure he may be that it will come into existence and will then be his to give. He can, of course, promise that when the thing is his he will make it over

---

5 For difficulties in deciding whether in any particular case there is a manifestation of the intention to create a trust, see *Re Engelbach's Estate* [1924] 2 Ch 348; *Vandepitte v Preferred Accident Insurance Corpn of New York* [1933] AC 70; *Re Schebsman* [1944] Ch 83, [1943] 2 All ER 768; *Green v Russell* [1959] 2 QB 226, [1959] 2 All ER 525; *Scruttons Ltd v Midland Silicones Ltd* [1962] AC 446, [1962] 1 All ER 1; *Beswick v Beswick* [1968] AC 58, [1967] 2 All ER 1197; *Woodar Investment Development Ltd v Wimpey Construction (UK) Ltd* [1980] 1 WLR 277, [1980] 1 All ER 571; *Forster v Silvermere Golf and Equestrian Centre Ltd* (1981) 42 P & CR 255. See also (1982) 98 LQR 17 (J.D. Feltham).

6 §26, Comment (*n*).

7 H & M, pp. 136–138; Riddall, pp. 69–70; Snell, pp. 82–84; Underhill, pp. 159–161; (1966) 30 Conv (NS) 286 (M.C. Cullity and H.A.J. Ford).

to the intended donee. But in the meantime he may change his mind and when the time comes refuse to carry out his promise, even though it were by deed. A court of law could not compel him to perform it. A court of equity would not. Courts of equity never had the objections to all agreements about future interests that, until the seventeenth century, were deeply rooted in the common law. Equity did not share the view that such agreements were void on the ground of maintenance. But things not yet in existence could only be the subject of agreement, not of present disposition. And, in relation to promises and agreements, equity has been faithful to its maxim that it does not come to the aid of volunteers. For equity a deed does not make good a want of consideration.

If we turn from attempted gifts of future property to purported dispositions of it for value, the picture changes completely. The common law objection remains. But in equity a would-be present assignment of something to be acquired in the future is, when made for value, construed as an agreement to assign the thing when it is acquired. A court of equity will ensure that the would-be assignor performs this agreement, his conscience being bound by the consideration. The purported assignee thus gets an equitable interest in the property immediately the legal ownership of it is acquired by the assignor, assuming it to have been sufficiently described to be then identifiable. The prospective interest of the assignee is in the meantime protected by equity. These principles, which now govern assignments for value of property to be acquired in the future, have been developed and established by a line of well-known cases, of which *Holroyd v Marshall* (1862) 10 HL Cas 191; *Collyer v Isaacs* (1881) 19 ChD 342; *Tailby v Official Receiver* (1888) 13 App Cas 523, and *Re Lind* [1915] 2 Ch 345 are the most important. 'And so', to use *Maitland's* words, 'lawyers easily slipped into the way of saying that in equity one could make an assignment of goods hereafter to be acquired though one could not do so at law. This was a compendious way of putting the matter and was not likely to deceive any equity lawyer': *Maitland, Equity*, 2nd edn (1936) p. 150.''

RE ELLENBOROUGH
[1903] 1 Ch 697 (ChD, BUCKLEY J)

By a voluntary settlement, Miss Emily Towry Law, a sister of Lord Ellenborough, purported to assign to the trustees the property to which she might become entitled under the wills of her brother and her sister. She received property under her sister's will and conveyed it to the trustees. On her brother's death in 1902, she received property under his will, and declined to transfer it to the trustees. The question was whether she was obligated to do so.

Held. She could not be compelled to hand over the property.

BUCKLEY J: The question is whether a volunteer can enforce a contract made by deed to dispose of an expectancy. It cannot be and is not disputed that if the deed had been for value the trustees could have enforced it. If value be given, it is immaterial what is the form of assurance by which the disposition is made, or whether the subject of the disposition is capable of being thereby disposed of or not. An assignment for value binds the conscience of the assignor. A Court of Equity as against him will compel him to do that which ex hypothesi he has not yet effectually done. Future property, possibilities, and expectancies are all assignable in equity for value: *Tailby v Official Receiver* (1888) 13 App Cas 523 at 543. But when the assurance is not for value, a Court of Equity will not assist a volunteer. In *Meek v Kettlewell* (1842) 1 Hare 464, affirmed by Lord Lyndhust (1843) 1 Ph 342, the exact point arose which I have here to decide, and it was held that a voluntary assignment of an expectancy, even though under seal, would not be enforced by a Court of Equity. "The assignment of an expectancy", says Lord Lyndhurst (1843) 1 Ph at 347, "such as this is, cannot be supported unless made for a valuable consideration." It is however suggested that that decision was overruled or affected by the decision of the Court of Appeal in *Kekewich v Manning* (1851) 1 De GM & G 176 at 187, and a passage in White and Tudor's Leading Cases in Equity, 7th edn, vol. ii, p. 851, was referred to upon the point. In my opinion *Kekewich v Manning* has no bearing upon that which was decided in *Meek v Kettlewell*. The assignment in *Kekewich v Manning* was not of an expectancy, but of property. "It is on legal and equitable principles", said Knight Bruce LJ, "we apprehend, clear that a person sui juris, acting freely, fairly, and with sufficient knowledge, ought to have and has it in his power to make, in a binding and effectual manner, a voluntary gift of any part of his property, whether capable or incapable of manual delivery, whether in possession or reversionary, and howsoever circumstanced." The important words there are "of his property". The point of *Meek v Kettlewell* and of the case before me is that the assignment was not of property, but of a mere expectancy. On December 22, 1893, that with which the grantor was dealing was not her property in any sense. She had nothing more than an expectancy. In *Re Tilt* (1896) 74 LT 163 there was again a voluntary assignment of an expectancy, and the point was not regarded as arguable. "It was rightly admitted" said Chitty J "that as, when this plaintiff executed the deed of 1880, she had no interest whatever in the fund in question, which was a mere expectancy, the deed was wholly inoperative both at law and in equity, being entirely voluntary." By "wholly inoperative" there the learned judge of course did not mean that if the voluntary settlor had handed over the funds the trustees would not have held them upon the trusts, but that the grantees under the deed could not enforce it as against the settlor in a Court of Equity or elsewhere. In my judgment the interest of the plaintiff as sole heiress-at-law and next of kin of the late Lord Ellenborough was not effectually assigned to the trustees by the deed, and the trustees cannot call upon her to grant, assign, transfer, or pay over to them his residuary real and personal estate.

In **Re Brooks' Settlement Trusts** [1939] Ch 993, [1939] 3 All ER 920, property was held under a marriage settlement on trust for X for life, and after her death on trust for such of her issue as she might by deed or will appoint, and in default of appointment on trust for her children in equal shares. One child, A, conveyed to trustees "all the part or share . . . and other interest whether vested or contingent to which the settlor is now or may at any time hereafter become entitled whether in default of appointment or under any appointment hereafter to be made". X appointed the sum of £3,517 to A. The question was whether the trustees of the marriage settlement, who were also the trustees of A's settlement, should pay the money to A. FARWELL J held that they should pay. A could not settle property to which he might become entitled under a future appointment; for in that property he had only an expectancy. He could settle property to which he would become entitled in default of appointment; for in that property he had a vested interest subject to divestment.

This case does not appear to have been cited in *Re Ralli's Will Trusts* [1964]
Ch 288, [1963] 3 All ER 940; p. 113, ante.

————————

In **Williams v Commissioner of Inland Revenue** [1965] NZLR 395,[8] Williams,
who had a life interest under a trust, executed a voluntary deed, in which "the
assignor by way of gift hereby assigns to the assignee for the religious purposes
of the Parish of the Holy Trinity Gisborne for the four years commencing on 30
June, 1960 the first £500 of the net income which shall accrue to the assignor
personally while he lives in each of the said four years from the Trust ... And
the assignor hereby declares that he is trustee for the sole use and benefit of
the assignee for the purpose aforesaid of so much (if any) of the said income
as may not be capable of assignment (or may come to his hands)."

The question arose whether Williams had effectively divested himself of his
interest in the £500 so as not to be liable for income tax on it. The New Zealand
Court of Appeal held that he had not.

TURNER J (delivering the judgment of NORTH P and himself) said: "Mr.
Thorp, for the appellant, submitted that what was assigned by this document
was a defined share in the existing life estate of the assignor in the trust
property, and hence that the deed of assignment took effect, as at its date, to
divest the assignor of the annual sums of £500 so that he did not thereafter
derive them for taxation purposes in the years under consideration. For the
respondent Commissioner it was contended that the deed was ineffective to
divest the assignor of the sums, and that its effect was no more than that of an
order upon the trustees still revocable by the assignor until payment.

The life interest of the appellant in the trust was at the date of the execution
of the deed an existing equitable interest. This cannot be doubted, and it was
so conceded by the learned Solicitor-General. Being an existing interest, it was
capable in equity of immediate effective assignment. Such an assignment
could be made without consideration, if it immediately passed the equitable
estate: *Kekewich v Manning* (1851) 1 De GM & G 176. There is no doubt that if
the deed before us had purported to assign, not 'the first £500', but the whole
of the appellant's life interest under the trust, such an assignment would have
been good in equity.

But while equity will recognise a voluntary assignment of an existing
equitable interest, it will refuse to recognise in favour of a volunteer an
assignment of an interest, either legal or equitable, not existing at the date of
the assignment, but to arise in the future. Not yet existing, such property
cannot be owned, and what may not be owned may not be effectively assigned:
Holroyd v Marshall (1862) 10 HL Cas 191 at 210, per Lord Westbury LC. If, not
effectively assigned, it is made the subject of an agreement to assign it, such an
agreement may be good in equity, and become effective upon the property
coming into existence (ibid., 211) but if, and only if, the agreement is made for
consideration (as in *Spratt v Comr of Inland Revenue* [1964] NZLR 272), for
equity will not assist a volunteer: *Re Ellenborough* [1903] 1 Ch 697.

The deed on which this appeal is founded was not made for consideration.
The simple question is therefore — was that which it purported to assign (viz.
'the first five hundred pounds of the net income which shall accrue') an

————————

8 (1965) ASCL 328 (J.D. Davies); see also *Shepherd v Federal Taxation Comr* (1965) 113 CLR 385.

existing property right, or was it a mere expectancy, a future right not yet in existence? If the former, counsel agree that the deed was effective as an immediate assignment: if the latter, it is conceded by Mr. Thorp that it could not in the circumstances of this case have effect.

What then was it that the assignor purported to assign? What he had was the life interest of a *cestui que trust* in a property or partnership adventure vested in or carried on by trustees for his benefit. Such a life interest exists in equity as soon as the deed of trust creating it is executed and delivered. Existing, it is capable of immediate assignment. We do not doubt that where it is possible to assign a right completely it is possible to assign an undivided interest in it. The learned Solicitor-General was therefore right, in our opinion, in conceding that if here, instead of purporting to assign 'the first £500 of the income', the assignor had purported to assign (say) an undivided one-fourth share in his life estate, then he would have assigned an existing right, and in the circumstances effectively.

But in our view, as soon as he quantified the sum in the way here attempted, the assignment became one not of a share or a part of his right, but of moneys which should arise from it. Whether the sums mentioned were ever to come into existence in whole or in part could not at the date of assignment be certain. In any or all of the years designated the net income might conceivably be less than five hundred pounds; in some or all of them the operations of the trust might indeed result in a loss. The first £500 of the net income, then, might or might not (judging the matter on the date of execution of the deed) in fact have any existence.

We accordingly reject Mr. Thorp's argument that what was here assigned was a part or share of the existing equitable right of the assignor. He did not assign part of his right to income; he assigned a right to a part of the income, a different thing. The £500 which was the subject of the purported assignment was five hundred pounds *out of the net income.* There could be no such income for any year until the operations of that year were complete, and it became apparent what debits were to be set off against the gross receipts. For these reasons we are of opinion that what was assigned here was money; and that was something which was not presently owned by the assignor. He had no more than an expectation of it, to arise, it is true, from an existing equitable interest — but that interest he did not purport to assign . . . .

It was argued in the alternative by Mr. Thorp, but somewhat faintly, that if the document were not effective as an assignment it was effective as a declaration of trust, and that this result was sufficient to divest the appellant of the enjoyment of the annual sums so that he did not derive them as income. It will be recalled in this regard that the text of the deed includes an express declaration of trust. Mr. Thorp's submission was that this express declaration is effective even if the assignment fails. We agree that there may be circumstances in which a purported assignment, ineffective for insufficiency of form or perhaps through lack of notice, may yet perhaps be given effect by equity by reason of the assignor having declared himself to be a trustee; but it is useless to seek to use this device in the circumstances of the present case. Property which is not presently owned cannot presently be impressed with a trust any more than it can be effectively assigned; property which is not yet in existence may be the subject of a present agreement to impress it with a trust when it comes into the hands of the donor; but equity will not enforce such an agreement at the instance of the *cestui que trust* in the absence of consideration: *Ellison v Ellison* (1802) 6 Ves 656 at 662, per Lord Eldon LC; *Brennan v Morphett* (1908) 6 CLR 22 at 30 per Griffith CJ; cf. *Underhill's Law of Trusts and Trustees*, 11th edn 43. For the same reasons therefore as apply in this case to the argument on assignment, Mr. Thorp's second alternative submission must also fail.''

Perspectives of Law (ed. R. Pound), p. 250

"A contract for consideration to convey future property to trustees upon trust is valid[9] and, in most cases, specifically enforceable.[10] A gratuitous covenant under seal to convey property to trustees is actionable at the instance of the beneficiary, if the court finds, on a proper construction of the situation, that the promisee became trustee of the promise for the beneficiaries.[11] A purported assignment of an expectancy cannot be a conveyance because there is nothing to convey. If consideration is given for the purported conveyance, it will be construed as a contract to assign and enforceable as such.[12] But if it is made gratuitously it is a nullity.[13] In *Re Ellenborough*,[14] the sister of Lord Ellenborough purported to convey by voluntary settlement the property which she would receive under her brother's will. On his death she declined to transfer the property to the trustees, and Buckley J held that the trustees could not compel her to do so.

The question is whether such a gratuitous covenant or assignment in respect of future property can ever be effective as a declaration of trust, so that the trust will become effective when the property vests in the trustee. The situation can arise if the property, on falling in, is transferred to trustees without a further declaration of the trusts, or where the property vests in the settlor after he has declared the trusts on which he is to hold it.

We have seen that, in England, a covenant in a marriage settlement to settle after-acquired property is not enforceable at the suit of the next of kin because they are volunteers;[15] and it is clear that a deed purporting to grant future property on trust is ineffective.[16] But if, in either of these cases, the property found its way into the hands of the trustees, it would presumably be held upon the trusts declared in the relevant documents.[17] If the settlor, in either case, conveyed the property to the trustees, that action could be construed as a further declaration of the trusts; but if the property reaches the trustees by another route, being conveyed perhaps by the executors of the testator from whom the property came, or coming into the hands of the trustee in a different capacity,[18] the possibility of finding that there was a further declaration of trust is less strong. There appear to be three possible solutions to such a case: that the trustees take beneficially, that they hold on trust for the settlor, or that they

---

9 *Re Lind* [1915] 2 Ch 345; *Re Gillott's Settlement* [1934] Ch 97; *Re Haynes' Will Trusts* [1949] Ch 5, [1948] 2 All ER 423.

10 *Pullan v Koe* [1913] 1 Ch 9, p. 124, ante.

11 *Fletcher v Fletcher* (1844) 4 Hare 67, p. 132, ante.

12 Snell, *Equity* (26th edn), p. 91.

13 *Meek v Kettlewell* (1842) 1 Hare 464; *Re Ellenborough* [1903] 1 Ch 697; *Re Brooks' Settlement Trusts* [1939] Ch 993, [1939] 3 All ER 920, p. 136, ante.

14 [1903] 1 Ch 697, p. 135, ante.

15 *Re D'Angibau* (1880) 15 ChD 228; *Re Plumptre's Marriage Settlement* [1910] 1 Ch 609.

16 *Re Ellenborough* [1903] 1 Ch 697; *Re Brooks' Settlement Trusts* [1939] Ch 993, [1939] 3 All ER 920.

17 *Re Ellenborough*, supra; Miss Emily Towry Law had already handed over to the trustees the property which she received under her sister's will and no attempt was made to recover it; *Re Adlard* [1954] Ch 29, [1953] 2 All ER 1437; *Re Ralli's Will Trusts* [1964] Ch 288, [1963] 3 All ER 940, p. 113, ante.

18 *Re Ralli's Will Trusts*, supra.

hold on the trusts declared in the previous document. The first is obviously unsatisfactory; the second involves the proposition that the settlor could claim back in equity property which he had covenanted or purported to settle. The third avoids the necessity of making the ultimate destination of the property depend upon the route by which it reached the trustees; it is consistent with the expressed intention of the parties, and appears to be the most satisfactory solution.[19]

Where the property comes to the settlor himself, it is possible for the court to hold that a previous declaration of trust, followed by the vesting of the property in himself as trustee, constitutes the trust. The question is whether he will be treated as making the declaration at the moment he receives the property.[20] It is clear that a previous declaration is not of itself sufficient,[1] subsequent confirmation of a previous declaration is sufficient.[2] In less obvious cases it is no doubt a question of construction to determine whether or not the settlor is to be taken to have made a subsequent declaration or to have affirmed a previous one. If he made the declaration every day, the last declaration being made the moment before he received the property, this would no doubt be sufficient. But in the absence of authority, in England at least, it is unsafe to predict to what extent an argument on these lines might be acceptable. What is clear in these cases . . . is that the beneficiaries must show that the trust was properly declared and properly constituted. In connection with the declaration, there are again very difficult points of construction, the solution of which will largely depend on the view the court takes on the policy question whether or not trusts ought to be created in this way. There appears to be nothing intrinsically wrong in holding that the declaration of a trust may precede its constitution.''

QUESTIONS

1. Consider whether the doctrine expounded by EVERSHED MR in *Re Rose* [1952] Ch 499, [1952] 1 All ER 1217, p. 116, ante, is inconsistent with the principles laid down in other parts of this chapter. Would it apply if the transfer was never registered? Do you think that the transfer of shares is a special situation? *Mascall v Mascall* (1984) 50 P & CR 119, p. 119 ante; H & M, pp. 118-121; Underhill, pp. 133–136.

2. What would be the result in *Re Ellenborough* [1903] 1 Ch 697, p. 135, ante, if Miss Towry Law had, instead of purporting to assign what she would receive under her brother's will, declared herself a trustee of it? *Matter of Gurlitz* 105 Misc 30, 172 NY Supp 523 (1918); *Brennan v Morphett* (1908) 6 CLR 22; *Williams v Comr of Inland Revenue* [1965] NZLR 395, p. 136, ante; *Re Northcliffe* [1925] Ch 651; *Perspectives of Law*, pp. 257–258.

3. It appears from cases in section III that Equity will not assist a volunteer (nor direct his trustees) to enforce a covenant to settle after-acquired property. Consider the effect of the House of Lords decision in *Beswick v Beswick* [1968] AC 58, [1967] 2 All ER 1197 on this; and, in particular, where the settlor has given valuable consideration, and an attempt to enforce the covenant is made by

19 *Re Ralli's Will Trusts*, supra.
20 Restatement of Trusts 2d § 26, Comments *k* and *l*; § 86, Comment *c*.
1 *Matter of Gurlitz* 105 Misc 30, 172 NY Supp 523 (1918); *Brennan v Morphett* (1908) 6 CLR 22.
2 *Re Northcliffe* [1925] Ch 651.

a)   the settlor, or his estate,
b)   the trustees,
c)   a beneficiary who is a volunteer.
Re Cook's Settlement Trusts [1965] Ch 902, [1964] 3 All ER 898; *Coulls v Bagot's Executor and Trustee Co* (1967) 40 ALJR 471 at 477; cases in note 5, p. 133, ante; H & M, pp. 132–135; P & M, pp. 77–90; Pettit, pp. 101–103; [1967] ASCL 387–396 (J.D. Davies); (1978) CLJ 301 (B. Coote); Treitel, *Law of Contract* (9th edn 1995), pp. 577–582.

4.   After reading the articles quoted on p. 123, note 6, what do you think of *Re Pryce* and *Re Kay's Settlement?*

5.   What exceptions exist to the rule that Equity will not assist a volunteer? H & M, pp. 138–145; K & S, pp. 105–107; P & M, pp. 63–77; Pettit, pp. 108–115; Riddall, pp. 86–90; Snell, pp. 124–125, 380–386; Underhill, pp. 135–143.

On donatio mortis causa, see *Sen v Headley* [1991] Ch 425, [1991] 2 All ER 636; [1991] Conv 307 (M. Halliwell); (1991) 50 CLJ 404 (J. Thornely); [1991] All ER Rev 207 (P. Clarke); (1991) 1 Carib.LR 100 (G. Kodilinye); (1993) 109 LQR 19 (P. Baker); *Woodard v Woodard* [1995] 3 All ER 980; [1992] Conv 53 (J. Martin).

6.   What is the relationship between the rule in *Strong v Bird* (1874) LR 18 Eq 315 and *Re Ralli's Will Trusts* [1964] Ch 288, [1963] 3 All ER 940, p. 113, ante? See *Re Gonin* [1979] Ch 16, [1977] 2 All ER 720; (1977) 93 LQR 485; [1982] Conv 14 (G. Kodilinye); *Re Brooks' Settlement Trusts* [1939] Ch 993, [1939] 3 All ER 920, p. 136, ante; Underhill, pp. 142–143.

4. Testamentary Dispositions which Fail to Comply with the Wills Act 1837[1]

I. Introduction

Section 9 of the Wills Act 1837[2] prescribes the formalities which are necessary for the validity of a testamentary disposition. It is important that strict formalities should attend a will. If a problem should arise, the testator is no longer with us and cannot be consulted. The imposition of certain formalities reduces the chance of mistake, or of ill-considered and hasty dispositions. There are many decisions on the question whether the formalities have been observed, but they do not concern us here.[3] It should, however, be said that wills of members of the armed forces made on active service are not required to observe the same formalities.[4]

What should be done however if the testator's intention is obvious, but a formality is lacking? Perhaps there was only one witness; or perhaps two witnesses attested the will, but not in the presence of the testator. In this situation, the well-intentioned formalities become a burden, unnecessarily invalidating the will. Further, what should the court do if a beneficiary fraudulently obtains a benefit for himself? — as by promising orally that he

---

1 H & M, pp. 146–168; K & S, pp. 84–99; P & M, pp. 44–55; Pettit, pp. 116–123; Riddall, pp. 52–59, 83–86; Snell, pp. 108–113; Underhill, pp. 222–237; (1915) 28 HLR 236, 366 (G.P. Costigan); (1937) 53 LQR 501 (W.S. Holdsworth); (1947) 12 Conv (NS) 28 (J.G. Flemming); (1951) 67 LQR 314 (L.A. Sheridan); (1963) 27 Conv (NS) 92 (J.A. Andrews); (1972) 36 Conv (NS) 113 (R. Burgess); (1972) 23 NILQ 263 (R. Burgess); [1979] Conv. 360 (P. Matthews); [1980] Conv 341 (D.R. Hodge); [1981] Conv 335 (T.G. Watkin); [1985] Conv 248 (B. Perrins); [1995] Conv 366 (D. Wilde); Oakley, *Constructive Trusts* (2nd edn), chap. 5; Miller, *Machinery of Succession*, (2nd edn) pp. 223–230; *Theobald on Wills* (15th edn), chaps. 6, 11; *Williams on Wills* (7th edn), chap. 36.

2 As substituted by AJA 1982, s. 17, p. 62, ante, which relaxes to some extent the formality requirements. See Law Reform Committee 22nd Report 1980 (Cmnd 7902), Part II.

3 See p. 62, n. 19, ante.

4 Wills Act 1837, s. 11 (as amended).

would hold certain property, left to him in the will, on trust for another?[5] Equity strives, where possible, to prevent a statute being used as a cloak for fraud. The secret trust doctrines grew up in this context,[6] and reasonably clear rules were laid down to meet the situation where, by the terms of the will, the gift was made to a legatee absolutely (a "fully secret" trust); for there was in that situation a possibility of fraud. The problem is more difficult where the gift is to a legatee "on such trusts as I have declared (or shall declare)" (a "half-secret" trust). The legatee here takes in a fiduciary capacity, and cannot fraudulently claim for himself. It would be strange if the mention of the trust *prevented* its being enforced as a secret trust; but, there being no possibility of fraud, its enforcement must be based upon some doctrine other than that of fraud.

Secret trusts however are only one of various methods of effecting testamentary dispositions without spelling out the disposition in the will. They will be considered in order.

II. Incorporation by Reference

IN THE GOODS OF SMART[7]
[1902] P 238 (PD, GORELL BARNES J)

By a will made in 1895, the testatrix directed that, after a life interest, her trustees should give to such of her friends as she might designate certain articles to be specified in a book or memorandum to be found with her will.

Such a book or memorandum was prepared in 1898 or 1899. Subsequently (July 27, 1900) a codicil was executed which confirmed the will, but did not refer to the book.

Held. The "book or memorandum" was referred to as a future document and could not be admitted to probate.

GORELL BARNES J: The question is, therefore, whether the book, so far as it is referred to, if referred to at all, in that clause which I read from the will, is to be incorporated with the will and codicil. I have already practically intimated my view that it ought not to be incorporated, and I might have contented myself with saying that I come to that conclusion in consequence, principally, of a decision of the President in the case of *Durham v Northen* [1895] P 66, but

---

5 A similar problem arises where land is conveyed inter vivos to a donee on an oral trust for a third party; thus failing to comply with LPA 1925, s. 53 (1) (*b*), p. 52, ante. An oral trust will be enforced where this is necessary to prevent fraud: *Taylor v Salmon* (1838) 4 My & Cr 134; *Davies v Otty (No 2)* (1865) 35 Beav 208; *Rochefoucauld v Boustead* [1897] 1 Ch 196; *Bannister v Bannister* [1948] 2 All ER 133; *Re Nichols* [1974] 1 WLR 296 at 301, [1973] 3 All ER 632 at 637; [1984] CLJ 306 (T.E. Youdan); [1986] 36 NILQ 358 (M.P. Thompson); [1987] Conv 246 (J.D. Feltham); [1988] Conv 267 (T.G. Youdan); *Du Boulay v Raggett* (1988) 58 P & CR 138.

6 *McCormick v Grogan* (1869) LR 4 HL 82 at 88, 89, 97, p. 152, post. See also *Thynn v Thynn* (1684) 1 Vern 296; *Crook v Brooking* (1688) 2 Vern 50 per Lord JEFFREYS LC; *Drakeford v Wilks* (1747) 3 Atk 539. See now *Re Snowden* [1979] Ch 528, [1979] 2 All ER 172, p. 155, post, per MEGARRY V-C.

7 *Allen v Maddock* (1858) 11 Moo PCC 427; *Re Jones* [1942] Ch 328, [1942] 1 All ER 642; *Re Edwards' Will Trusts* [1948] Ch 440, [1948] 1 All ER 821, p. 146, post; *Re Schintz's Will Trusts* [1951] Ch 870, [1951] 1 All ER 1095; *Re Tyler* [1967] 1 WLR 1269, [1967] 3 All ER 389; *Re Berger* [1990] Ch 118, [1989] 1 All ER 591; cf *In the Goods of Lady Truro* (1866) LR 1 P & D 201; *Jarman on Wills* (8th edn) p. 154.

Mr. Deane argued that that case was inconsistent with other authorities, and that the authorities were in conflict amongst themselves; so I desired to look through them to see if that contention could be properly supported. Before referring very briefly to the cases, it seems to me desirable to state how the principle upon which this matter ought to be decided appears to my mind. It seems to me that it has been established that if a testator, in a testamentary paper duly executed, refers to an existing unattested testamentary paper, the instrument so referred to becomes part of his will; in other words, it is incorporated into it; but it is clear that, in order that the informal document should be incorporated in the validly executed document, the latter must refer to the former as a written instrument then existing — that is, at the time of execution — in such terms that it may be ascertained. A leading case upon this subject is *Allen v Maddock* (1858) 11 Moo PCC 427, and it is desirable also to refer to *In the Goods of Mary Sunderland* (1866) LR 1 P & D 198. It will be seen from a statement of the principle in the form I have just given, that the document which it is sought to incorporate must be existing at the time of the execution of the document into which it is to be incorporated, and there must be a reference in the properly executed document to the informal document as an existing one, and not as a future document. If the document is not existing at the time of the will, but comes into existence afterwards, and then, after that again, there is a codicil confirming the will, the question arises, as it has done in a number of these cases, whether that document is incorporated. It appears to me that, following out the principle which I have already referred to, the will may be treated, by the confirmation given by the codicil, as executed again, and as speaking from the date of the codicil, and if the informal document is existing then, and is referred to in the will as existing, so as to identify it, there will be incorporation; but if the will, treated as being re-executed at the date of the codicil, still speaks in terms which shew that it is referring to a future document, then it appears to me there is no incorporation. I might put a clear concrete case. Suppose that the will said, ''I wish certain articles to be disposed of by my executors in accordance with a list which I shall hereafter write'', and the testator then wrote a list such as was contemplated, and then, after that, a codicil was made confirming the will, one of the conditions at the date of the codicil which is necessary for incorporation would be fulfilled, namely, the execution of a document; but the other condition would not be fulfilled, because the will, even speaking from the date of its so-called re-execution by that confirmation by the codicil, would still in terms refer to something which even then was future. I have, perhaps, stated a little more fully than is necessary what was very clearly and shortly said by the President (Sir F.H. Jeune) in the case to which I have referred . . . [8]

Therefore, to my mind, it is clear that if the terms of the reference in this case indicate a document of a future character there is no incorporation. The words are: ''I direct my trustees to give to such of my friends as I may designate in a book or memorandum that will be found with this will.'' That reference, made at the date of the will, was, I think, clearly made as to a future document. A document next comes into existence, and a codicil is afterwards made; but if you treat the will according to the cases, as speaking at the date of the codicil, the reference is still in terms to a document which, even then, is future, and therefore does not comply with one of the necessary conditions, namely, that

8 *Durham v Northen* [1895] P 66.

it must refer to a document as existing at the date when the will is reexecuted.

III. Facts of Independent Legal Significance

Jarman on Wills (8th edn) p. 153

"In *Stubbs v Sargon*[9] it was contended that, on the same principle, a devise of realty to 'the persons who shall be in co-partnership with me at the time of my decease, or to whom I shall have disposed of my business' was void, as leaving it for the testator by some further act, not authorised by the Statute of Frauds, to select the devise. But Lord Langdale, and on appeal Lord Cottenham, held the devise good. Lord Cottenham compared the case to that of a father having two sons, and devising his property to such one of them as should not become entitled to an estate from a third person; here the act of a third person determines who shall take the father's estate. But the act is not testamentary; if it were, one man would be making another man's will. And if not testamentary when done by a third person, it cannot be so when done by the testator himself; otherwise a testator could not devise to such person as, at his death, should be his wife or servant. And Lord Langdale said, if the description was such as to distinguish the devisee from every other person, it was sufficient without entering into the question whether the description was acquired by the devisee after the date of the will, or by the testator's own act in the ordinary course of his affairs, or in the management of his property.

The question is, therefore: Is the supplementary act testamentary? If it is, the devise is void; if it is not, then, although it is the sole act of the testator, the devise is good.

The point frequently arises where a testator by his will directs part of his property to be disposed of in such way as he shall by letter, memorandum, etc., or the like, direct; it is clear that no such document can have any testamentary operation, unless executed as a will, or incorporated by a subsequent will or codicil[10]."

Scott: *Trusts* (4th edn) §54.2.

"*Where disposition is determined by facts of independent significance.* There is another doctrine of the law of wills which is sometimes confused with the doctrine of incorporation by reference. Even though a disposition cannot be fully ascertained from the terms of the will, it is not invalid if it can be ascertained from facts which have significance apart from their effect upon the disposition in the will. Indeed it is frequently necessary to resort to extrinsic evidence to identify the persons who are to take or the subject matter of a disposition. Thus a bequest to the children or the heirs or next of kin of a named person requires a resort to extrinsic evidence to establish their identity, but it is of course valid. So also a disposition in favor of persons who are in the employ of the testator

9 (1837) 2 Keen 255; on appeal (1838) 3 My & Cr 507.
10 See *Re Jones* [1942] Ch 328, [1942] 1 All ER 642, p. 147, post.

at the time of his death, or a disposition in favor of such person or institution as may care for the testator during his old age or last illness, is valid. So too the property given may be ascertained by extrinsic facts; thus a bequest of money in banks, securities in a safe-deposit box, or furniture in a designated room or house, is valid. On the other hand, the disposition is invalid where the facts from which it is to be ascertained have no independent significance; thus a disposition in favor of such persons as may be named in an unattested memorandum, or such property as may be designated in such a memorandum, is invalid unless it can be upheld on the doctrine of incorporation by reference, since the designation in the memorandum has no significance apart from the disposition of the property by the will ... this doctrine, like that of incorporation by reference, is a general doctrine of the law of wills ... ''

IV. Gifts to Trustees of an Existing Settlement

A testamentary gift may be made as an addition to an existing settlement by "incorporating" the settlement into the will by reference in accordance with the principles explained in Section II. But difficulties will obviously arise where the settlement is amended; for the amended settlement will be a new document. If the rules of the doctrine of incorporation by reference are strictly observed, it seems that the only alternative solutions are either to hold that the settlement is void, or to enforce it in its *un*amended form. Neither solution is satisfactory.

In **Re Edwards' Will Trusts** [1948] Ch 440, [1948] 1 All ER 821,[11] a settlor, in 1935, made a 'pilot' settlement of £100, the fund to be held upon trust, as to income and capital, for such persons as the settlor should by a memorandum direct, and subject thereto, upon trust for his wife and children. By his will, made on the same date but afterwards, the settlor directed that his residuary estate should be held upon the trusts of the settlement "so far as such trusts and provisions are subsisting and capable of taking effect."

By a subsequent memorandum dated November 1937, he laid down certain trusts upon which part of the fund was to be held. Seven years later, he died. The question was whether the residuary estate was held upon the trusts of the settlement; and, if so, whether these were the original trusts, or those laid down in the memorandum of 1937. The Court of Appeal held that the will incorporated the settlement in its original unamended form. Lord GREENE MR said at 446, at 823:

"The settlement here is a document which can be perfectly well identified, and there is no rule of law to the contrary. It can accordingly be incorporated as a piece of writing into the testamentary disposition. Indeed, if the settlement, instead of being a thing having value and force in itself, had been

---

11 *Re Jones* [1942] Ch 328, [1942] 1 All ER 642; *Re Schintz's Will Trusts* [1951] Ch 870, [1951] 1 All ER 1095; *Re Cooper* [1939] Ch 811, [1939] 3 All ER 586, p. 163, post.

merely a memorandum previously executed to which, in his will, he referred, it could perfectly well have been admitted to probate as a testamentary instrument. The question then would have arisen, what provisions in this instrument are valid and what are invalid? I start then with the proposition that the incorporation of this document into the will is a permissible and easy matter. When I say incorporation, I am referring to what I may perhaps call the mechanical act of incorporation by reading the language of it into the will itself. We have now got therefore to a stage where there is a will, part of the directions of which cannot operate any more than they could operate if they had been contained, as in the case of *Re Jones* [1942] Ch 328, [1942] 1 All ER 642, in the will itself. The presence of that invalid provision in the case of *Re Jones* did not involve its being struck out of the probate and treated as not being part of the will, nor do I see any reason why the invalidity of a provision contained in this settlement should be any reason for excluding it from the testamentary directions of the deceased. The result of his having in that identifiable document included something which the law does not allow to have effect, is a matter to be considered after probate when the question of the validity of his testamentary dispositions arises. The result therefore is that there is here a composite will consisting of a combination of the actual will itself plus the provisions of the settlement ...

It seems to me that the directions for incorporation are directions to read into the will the entirety of a document which the testator no doubt thought would be effective. But if, on writing them into the will, it turns out that part of them is invalid from some rule of law, as in the present case, I cannot read the testator's directions as meaning that, therefore, the whole process of incorporation must be abandoned. I think that the effect of it is that so much of the settlement as can validly have operation as part of a testamentary disposition is left to take effect according to its true construction. I have formed that view quite apart from a point which appears to me to confirm it, namely, that in cl. 2 of the will, after the direction that the residuary estate is to be held upon the trusts of the settlement, appear the words 'so far as such trusts, powers and provisions are subsisting and capable of having effect'. I see no reason myself for reading those words as not extending to a case where some of the trusts are invalid through a rule of law. When the settlement is written into the will there are a string of trusts. Some of them are capable of taking effect; some are incapable of taking effect. It is perfectly true that this form of phrase generally operates in the common case where some trusts in the document referred to have expired through the effluxion of time or the extinction of a family or the birth of children, or something of that kind. But I do not read the words as limited to that class of case. I think a trust which is prevented from operating by a rule of law is a trust which can be fairly described as a trust which is not subsisting and capable of taking effect. I have come to the same conclusion without reference to those words, but I think their presence confirms the view that I have taken.''

Miller: *The Machinery of Succession* (2nd edn 1996) pp. 228–230

''Facts of Independent Legal Significance
An alternative approach to testamentary gifts on the trusts of inter vivos settlements has been advocated and has been widely accepted in the United

States.[12] The proponents of this approach point out that there are a number of situations where it is necessary and permissible to have regard to acts or events occurring either before or after the execution of a will in order to identify a legatee or the subject matter of a legacy. Thus, if a testator makes a gift to the persons who are in his employment at the time of his death, it is necessary to have regard to the facts existing at his death in order to ascertain the beneficiaries. Extrinsic evidence as to the identity of such persons is admissible for such facts have significance apart from their relevance to the testamentary gift. It is possible for the testator during his lifetime to discharge employees and to employ other persons, and such acts will have the effect of modifying the testamentary disposition. However, such acts are not testamentary for they were not done for the purpose of supplementing the will. They are relevant to ascertaining the persons who are to take under the testamentary gift, but they also have independent legal significance.

In the same way, it is argued that the terms of a testamentary gift can be regarded as determined by a fact of independent legal significance, namely, the inter vivos trust as it exists at the date of death, i.e., even though modified after the date of the will. Again, it can be argued that, although modifications of the inter vivos trust effected after the date of the will have the effect of modifying the terms of the testamentary gift, such modifications should not be regarded as testamentary acts for they were not done for the purpose of supplementing the will, but for the purpose of modifying the terms of the inter vivos trust. In other words, they have a significance independent of their effect on the will.[13]

In the United States the Uniform Probate Code contains a provision authorising gifts by will to the trustees of a trust established, or to be established, by the testator or another, if the trust is identified in the will and its terms are set forth in a written instrument, other than a will, executed before, concurrently with, or after the execution of the testator's will or in another individual's will if that individual has predeceased the testator.[14] The gift is not invalid because the trust is liable to amendment or revocation or because it was amended after the execution of the will or after the death of the testator. Unless the testator's will otherwise provides, the property so given is not deemed to be held under a testamentary trust of the testator, but becomes a part of the trust to which it is given.[15]

Such an approach has not been accepted, at least openly, in England. Professor Scott stated that there were numerous English cases in which, after creating a trust inter vivos, the settlor had by will left property upon the same trust, merely making reference to the prior disposition. He argued that in many of these cases there was no reference to a particular instrument so that the doctrine of incorporation by reference was inapplicable.[16] It is true that in

12 See Scott, *Trusts and the Statute of Wills* (1930) 43 Harvard LR 521, at 544 et seq.; Evans, *Non-testamentary Acts and Incorporation by Reference* (1949) 16 Univ of Chicago LR 635. See also Uniform Probate Code, s. 2–512.

13 See the survey and criticism by Lauritzen, *Can a Revocable Trust be Incorporated by Reference?* (1950) 45 North Western Univ LR 583.

14 Section 2–511. There is a separate section dealing with Events of Independent Significance: s. 2–512.

15 Regardless of the existence, size or character of the corpus of the Trust. See also the Report of the Ontario Law Commission Relating to Testamentary Additions to Trusts; Appendix V to the Proceedings of the 49th Meeting of the Conference of Commissions of Uniformity of Legislation in Canada.

16 (1930) 43 Harvard LR 521 at 547.

the cases cited by him the words used to refer to the existing trust may in some respects leave room for debate, but in each case the trust referred to had been created prior to the execution of the will and was irrevocable.[17] Some support for the approach may perhaps be found in *Re Playfair*[18] where the testator bequeathed £20,000 to trustees to be held on the trusts of a marriage settlement. The testator's son, who had a vested interest under the marriage settlement, predeceased the testator so that it was necessary to consider whether his estate could derive any benefit from the disposition in the will. If the marriage settlement had been incorporated into the will, then as a purely testamentary gift it would have lapsed. However, it was held that the gift was an addition to the funds of the marriage settlement so that the gift did not lapse and the son's estate was entitled. In this case too the settlement was not liable to amendment.

The adoption of such an approach is not without difficulty. Professor Scott acknowledged that if the inter vivos trust was of a nominal sum and was created simply for the purpose of avoiding the necessity of spelling out the trusts in the will it would not in substance be a fact of independent legal significance.[19] How substantial must the inter vivos trust be to have independent legal significance? Looked at in another way it could present the difficult question of deciding whether a particular amendment of the inter vivos trust was testamentary or not.[20]

In considering the extent to which effect should be given to gifts by will on the trusts of an inter vivos settlement liable to amendment, the potential threat to the policy of the Wills Act must be borne in mind. This applies as much to any extension of the doctrine of incorporation by reference as to any development of the doctrine of facts of independent legal significance. How far should a testator be permitted to reserve for himself or herself a power to make future dispositions which do not comply with the Wills Act? If the trustee of the inter vivos trust is a trust corporation, and if the signatures are all carefully witnessed, then it can be argued that the evils which the Wills Act seeks to prevent have been successfully guarded against. On the other hand if the trustee is the testator himself or herself, and the inter vivos settlement is at all times subject to his unfettered control, there is a real danger of the underlying policy of the Wills Act being thwarted."[1]

American Uniform Testamentary Additions to Trusts Act 1960

Section 1. Testamentary Additions to Trusts. — A devise or bequest, the validity of which is determinable by the law of this state, may be made by a will to the trustee or trustees of a trust established or to be established by the testator or by the testator and some other person or persons or by some other person or persons (including a funded or unfunded life insurance trust, although the trustor has reserved any or all rights of ownership of the insurance contracts)

17 *Berchtoldt v Hertford* (1844) 7 Beav 172; *Ford v Ruxton* (1844) 1 Coll 403; *Re Finch and Chew's Contract* [1903] 2 Ch 86; *Re Beaumont* [1913] 1 Ch 325; *Re Powell* [1918] 1 Ch 407; *Re Gooch* [1929] 1 Ch 740; *Re Shelton's Settled Estates* [1945] Ch 158, [1945] 1 All ER 283.
18 [1951] Ch 4, [1950] 2 All ER 285.
19 Loc cit., p. 549.
20 See Lauritzen, loc. cit., pp. 609–610.
 1 See Lauritzen, loc. cit., pp. 612–613.

if the trust is identified in the testator's will and its terms are set forth in a written instrument (other than a will) executed before or concurrently with the execution of the testator's will or in the valid last will of a person who has predeceased the testator (regardless of the existence, size, or character of the corpus of the trust). The devise or bequest shall not be invalid because the trust is amendable or revocable, or both, or because the trust was amended after the execution of the will or after the death of the testator. Unless the testator's will provides otherwise, the property so devised or bequeathed (a) shall not be deemed to be held under a testamentary trust of the testator but shall become a part of the trust to which it is given and (b) shall be administered and disposed of in accordance with the provisions of the instrument or will setting forth the terms of the trust, including any amendments thereto made before the death of the testator (regardless of whether made before or after the execution of the testator's will), and, if the testator's will so provides, including any amendments to the trust made after the death of the testator. A revocation or termination of the trust before the death of the testator shall cause the devise or bequest to lapse.

Section 2. Effect on Prior Wills. — This Act shall have no effect upon any devise or bequest made by a will executed prior to the effective date of this Act.

Section 3. Uniformity of Interpretation. — This Act shall be so construed as to effectuate its general purpose to make uniform the law of those states which enact it.

v. Secret Trusts[2]

A. Fully Secret Trusts

A testator sometimes makes a gift by will which is absolute on its face, but which is intended to be held by the legatee (or devisee) upon trust. This may be, as was commonly the situation in the older cases, a method of giving property to a mistress or to an illegitimate child, without the fact being made public by inclusion in the will. The testator could give the legacy to a trusted friend, absolutely, relying on the friend to hand over the legacy as required. The situation commonly arises also where an aged testatrix is unable to make up her mind as to her wishes, usually in relation to trinkets; she leaves the property to a solicitor, and he will see to its disposal according to later verbal instructions.[3]

The difficulty is that such intended trusts do not comply with the necessary formalities of the Wills Act 1837. If they are not to be enforced in favour of the intended beneficiaries, what should happen? It is inequitable for the legatee to keep it for himself. Equity will not allow a statute to be used as an engine of fraud. Fraud would be prevented if the legatee was required to hold upon a resulting trust for the estate. But this of course is a denial of the testator's

2 H & M, pp. 152–168; K & S, pp. 84–99; P & M, pp. 44–55; Pettit, pp. 116–123; Riddall, pp. 52–59, 85–86; Snell, pp. 108–113; Underhill, pp. 227–237; see articles referred to at p. 142, note 1, ante.

3 See e.g. *Re Snowden* [1979] Ch 528, [1979] 2 All ER 172, p. 155, post.

intention. Provided that the intended trusts are communicated to the legatee *prior to* the testator's death, such trusts are enforced in favour of the intended beneficiary.[4]

THYNN v THYNN
(1684) 1 Vern 296 (Chancery, Earl of GUILDFORD, Lord Keeper)

The Case was, that Mr. *Thynn,* of *Eagham,* Deceased, having made a Will, and thereby made his Wife sole Executrix; the Defendant Mr. *Thynn* the Son, hearing of this Will, came to his Mother in the Life-time of his Father, and perswaded her, that there being many Debts, the Executorship would be troublesome to her; and desired that he might be nam'd Executor;[5] — for that he by reason of his Privilege of Parliament could struggle the better with the Creditors, and perswaded his Mother to move his Father in it; declaring that he would be only an Executor in Trust for her: And the Mother accordingly prevails on the Father that it might be so: And thereupon Mr. *Thynn* the Son gets a new Will drawn, whereby a Legacy of 50*l.* only is given to his Mother, and therein he makes himself sole Executor; and cancels the former Will, tho' the Father opposed the doing thereof; and the last Will was read over so low, that the Testator could not hear it; and when he called to have it read louder, the Scrivenor cried, he was afraid of disturbing his Worship. The Defendant having thus made himself sole Executor, and procured this Will to be executed, where only a Legacy of 50*l.* was given to his Mother, set up for himself, and denied the Trust for his Mother: And in his two first Answers he denied the Will was drawn by his Directions, and that the 50*l.* therein given to his Mother was without the Testator's Privity; but in his third Answer he confessed it.

Upon the whole Matter, it appeared to be, as well as a Fraud, as also a Trust, the Lord *Keeper,* notwithstanding the Statute of *Frauds* and *Perjuries,* tho' no Trust was declar'd in Writing, decreed it for the Plaintiff, and Order'd that the Defendant should be examined on Interrogatories for discovery of the Estate.

i. INFORMAL DISCLOSURE OF EXISTENCE AND TERMS OF TRUST

OTTAWAY v NORMAN
[1972] Ch 698, [1971] 3 All ER 1325[6] (ChD, BRIGHTMAN J)

By his will, dated March 8, 1960, Harry Ottaway devised his freehold bungalow, called "Ashcroft" and its contents to Miss Hodges, his housekeeper; and one half of his residuary estate to her, and the other half to his son, William.

During his lifetime Harry orally communicated his intention to Miss Hodges that she should leave the bungalow and its contents, and it was alleged, so

---

4 The same principle applies where an existing legacy is not revoked: *Chamberlaine v Chamberlaine* (1678) Freem Ch 34; *Moss v Cooper* (1861) 1 John & H 352; and where an intestate, in reliance upon the undertaking of next of kin, fails to make a will: *Stickland v Aldridge* (1804) 9 Ves 516, and where a legatee undertakes to dispose of property on death in a particular manner: *Ottaway v Norman* [1972] Ch 698, [1971] 3 All ER 1325, infra.

5 Before the Executors Act 1830, an executor was permitted to retain beneficially property not otherwise disposed of by the will.

6 (1972) 36 Conv (NS) 113 (R. Burgess), 129 (D.J. Hayton); (1973) 36 MLR 210 (S.M. Bandali) p. 277, post; [1971] ASCL 384 (J. Hackney).

much of her residuary estate as should remain undisposed of at her death, to the plaintiffs, William and William's wife Dorothy.

A few months after Harry's death in 1963, Miss Hodges made a will which accorded with this arrangement. But in 1967 she made a new will in which she devised the bungalow to the defendant and his wife. The plaintiff alleged that Miss Hodges had agreed to leave the bungalow, its contents and her residuary estate to them, and brought an action for a declaration that the defendant, who was Miss Hodges's executor, held the property on a constructive trust for them. In the evidence, the undertaking in respect of the bungalow was established, but not that in respect of the residuary estate.

Held. The defendant held the bungalow on a constructive trust for the plaintiffs.

BRIGHTMAN J: It will be convenient to call the person upon whom such a trust is imposed the "primary donee" and the beneficiary under that trust the "secondary donee." The essential elements which must be proved to exist are: (i) the intention of the testator to subject the primary donee to an obligation in favour of the secondary donee; (ii) communication of that intention to the primary donee; and (iii) the acceptance of that obligation by the primary donee either expressly or by acquiescence. It is immaterial whether these elements precede or succeed the will of the donor. I am informed that there is no recent reported case where the obligation imposed on the primary donee is an obligation to make a will in favour of the secondary donee as distinct from some form of inter vivos transfer. But it does not seem to me that there can really be any distinction which can validly be taken on behalf of the defendant in the present case. The basis of the doctrine of a secret trust is the obligation imposed on the conscience of the primary donee and it does not seem to me that there is any materiality in the machinery by which the donor intends that that obligation shall be carried out.

Mr. Buckle, for Mr. Norman, relied strongly on *McCormick v Grogan* (1869) LR 4 HL 82. In that case a testator in 1851 had left all his property by a three line will to his friend Mr. Grogan. In 1854 the testator was struck down by cholera. With only a few hours to live he sent for Mr. Grogan. He told Mr. Grogan in effect that his will and a letter would be found in his desk. The letter named various intended beneficiaries and the intended gifts to them. The letter concluded with the words:

"I do not wish you to act strictly on the foregoing instructions, but leave it entirely to your own good judgment to do as you think I would, if living, and as the parties are deserving;"

An intended beneficiary whom Mr. Grogan thought it right to exclude sued. I will read an extract from the speech of Lord Westbury, at 97, because Mr. Buckle relied much upon it.

" ... the jurisdiction which is invoked here by the appellant is founded altogether on personal fraud. It is a jurisdiction by which a Court of Equity, proceeding on the ground of fraud, converts the party who has committed it into a trustee for the party who is injured by that fraud. Now, being a jurisdiction founded on personal fraud, it is incumbent on the court to see that a fraud, a malus animus, is proved by the clearest and most indisputable evidence."

Lord Westbury continued, at 97:

"You are obliged, therefore, to shew most clearly and distinctly that the person you wish to convert into a trustee acted malo animo. You must shew distinctly that he knew that the testator or the intestate was beguiled and deceived by his conduct. If you are not in a condition to affirm that without any misgiving, or possibility of mistake, you are not warranted in affixing on the individual the delictum of fraud, which you must do before you convert him into a trustee. Now are there any indicia of fraud in this case?''

Lord Westbury then examined the facts with which that case was concerned.

Founding himself on Lord Westbury Mr. Buckle sought at one stage to deploy an argument that a person could never succeed in establishing a secret trust unless he could show that the primary donee was guilty of deliberate and conscious wrongdoing of which he said there was no evidence in the case before me. That proposition, if correct, would lead to the surprising result that if the primary donee faithfully observed the obligation imposed on him there would not ever have been a trust at any time in existence. The argument was discarded, and I think rightly. Mr. Buckle then fastened on the words "clearest and most indisputable evidence" and he submitted that an exceptionally high standard of proof was needed to establish a secret trust. I do not think that Lord Westbury's words mean more than this: that if a will contains a gift which is in terms absolute, clear evidence is needed before the court will assume that the testator did not mean what he said. It is perhaps analogous to the standard of proof which this court requires before it will rectify a written instrument, for there again a party is saying that neither meant what they have written ...[7]

Having heard the evidence I have no doubt in my mind that I have received an accurate account of all essential facts from William and Mrs. Dorothy Ottaway (the plaintiffs). I find as a fact that Mr. Harry Ottaway intended that Miss Hodges should be obliged to dispose of the bungalow in favour of the plaintiffs at her death; that Mr. Harry Ottaway communicated that intention to Miss Hodges; and that Miss Hodges accepted the obligation. I find the same facts in relation to the furniture, fixtures and fittings which passed to Miss Hodges under clause 4 of Mr. Harry Ottaway's will. I am not satisfied that any similar obligation was imposed and accepted as regards any contents of the bungalow which had not devolved on Miss Hodges under clause 4 of Mr. Harry Ottaway's will.

I turn to the question of money. In cross-examination William said the trust extended to the house, furniture and money:

"Everything my father left to Miss Hodges was to be in the trust. The trust comprised the lot. She could use the money as she liked. She had to leave my wife and me whatever money was left."

In cross-examination Mrs. Dorothy Ottaway said that her understanding was that Miss Hodges was bound to make a will giving her and her husband the bungalow, contents and any money she had left. "She could please herself about the money. She did not have to save it for us. She was free to spend it."

It seems to me that two questions arise. First, as a matter of fact, what did the parties intend should be comprised in Miss Hodges's obligation? All money which Miss Hodges had at her death including both money which she had acquired before Mr. Harry Ottaway's death and money she acquired after his death from all sources? Or only money acquired under Mr. Harry Ottaway's will? Secondly, as a matter of law, if such an obligation existed would it create

---

7 Not followed in *Re Snowden* [1979] Ch 528 at 534–537, [1979] 2 All ER 172 at 176–179, p. 155 post, where MEGARRY V-C applied the ordinary civil standard of proof on a balance of probabilities, unless fraud was alleged against the alleged trustee.

a valid trust? On the second question I am content to assume for present purposes but without so deciding that if property is given to the primary donee on the understanding that the primary donee will dispose by his will of such assets, if any, as he may have at his command at his death in favour of the secondary donee, a valid trust is created in favour of the secondary donee which is in suspense during the lifetime of the primary donee, but attaches to the estate of the primary donee at the moment of the latter's death. There would seem to be at least some support for this proposition in an Australian case to which I was referred: *Birmingham v Renfrew* (1937) 57 CLR 666[8]. I accept that the parties mentioned money on at least some occasions when they talked about Mr. Harry Ottaway's intentions for the future disposition of Ashcroft. I do not, however, find sufficient evidence that it was the intention of Mr. Harry Ottaway that Miss Hodges should be compelled to leave all her money, from whatever source derived, to the plaintiffs. This would seem to preclude her giving even a small pecuniary legacy to any friend or relative. I do not think it is clear that Mr. Harry Ottaway intended to extract any such far-reaching undertaking from Miss Hodges or that she intended to accept such a wide obligation herself. Therefore the obligation, if any, is in my view, to be confined to money derived under Mr. Harry Ottaway's will. If the obligation is confined to money derived under Mr. Harry Ottaway's will, the obligation is meaningless and unworkable unless it includes the requirement that she shall keep such money separate and distinct from her own money. I am certain that no such requirement was ever discussed or intended. If she had the right to mingle her own money with that derived from Mr. Harry Ottaway, there would be no ascertainable property upon which the trust could bite at her death. This aspect distinguishes this case from *Re Gardner* [1920] 2 Ch 523.

There is another difficulty. Does money in this context include only cash or cash and investments, or all movable property of any description? The evidence is quite inconclusive. In my judgment the plaintiff's claim succeeds in relation to the bungalow and in relation to the furniture, fixtures and fittings which devolved under paragraph 4 of Mr. Harry Ottaway's will subject, of course, to normal wastage, fair wear and tear, but not to any other assets.

In **Re Boyes** (1884) 26 ChD 531, a legacy was given to the testator's solicitor, who was told that it was to be held upon trust, but he was not informed, until after the testator's death, what the trusts were. Among the testator's papers, a letter was found which said that the residuary estate was to be held on trust for a lady to whom the testator was not married. The solicitor desired to carry out the testator's wishes.

KAY J held that he took as trustee, holding on a resulting trust for the testator's next of kin, and said at 536:

'The essence of all those decisions is that the devisee or legatee accepts a particular trust which thereupon becomes binding upon him, and which it would be a fraud in him not to carry into effect . . . The defendant is a trustee

---

8   See also *Re Cleaver* [1981] 1 WLR 939, [1981] 2 All ER 1018, p. 279, post, where NOURSE J relied on *Birmingham v Renfrew* in the context of mutual wills and cited extracts from the judgment of DIXON J.

of this property for the next of kin of the testator. I can only hope that they will consider the claim which this lady has upon their generosity."

The delivery of a sealed letter during the testator's lifetime is a sufficient communication provided that it is known to contain the terms of a trust and is accepted as such. For "a ship which sails under sealed orders, is sailing under orders though the exact terms are not ascertained by the captain till later."[9]

ii. STANDARD OF PROOF

In **Re Snowden** [1979] Ch 528, [1979] 2 All ER 172,[10] the testatrix aged 86 made her will six days before she died; she left her residuary estate to her brother Bert absolutely. Bert died six days after the testatrix, leaving all his property to his son. Evidence was given by members of the firm of solicitors who had prepared and witnessed the will that the testatrix "wished to be fair to everyone", and that she wanted Bert to "look after the division for her".

SIR ROBERT MEGARRY V-C held there was no secret trust but only a moral obligation on Bert, and therefore his son was absolutely entitled to the residue. He said at 534, at 176:

"One question that arises is whether the standard of proof required to establish a secret trust is merely the ordinary civil standard of proof, or whether it is a higher and more cogent standard. If it is the latter, I feel no doubt that the claim that there is a secret trust must fail. On this question, *Ottaway v Norman* [1972] Ch 698, [1971] 3 All ER 1325, p. 151, ante, was cited; it was, indeed, the only authority that was put before me. According to the headnote, the standard of proof 'was not an exceptionally high one but was analogous to that required before the court would rectify a written instrument.' When one turns to the judgment, one finds that what Brightman J said at 712, at 1333, was that Lord Westbury's words in *McCormick v Grogan* (1869) LR 4 HL 82 at 97, a case on secret trusts, did not mean that an exceptionally high standard of proof was needed, but meant no more than that:

'if a will contains a gift which is in terms absolute, clear evidence is needed before the court will assume that the testator did not mean what he said. It is perhaps analogous to the standard of proof which this court requires before it will rectify a written instrument, for there again a party is saying that neither meant what they have written.'

[His Lordship referred to *Ottaway v Norman* and continued:]

I feel some doubt about how far rectification is a fair analogy to secret trusts in this respect. Many cases of rectification do of course involve a party in saying that neither meant what they have written, and requiring that what they have written should be altered. On the other hand, the whole basis of secret trusts, as I understand it, is that they operate outside the will, changing nothing that is written in it, and allowing it to operate according to its tenor, but then fastening a trust on to the property in the hands of the recipient. It is at least

---

9 *Re Keen* [1937] Ch 236 at 242, per Lord WRIGHT MR; *Re Boyes* (1884) 26 ChD 531 at 536.
10 [1979] Conv 448 (F.R. Crane); [1979] 38 CLJ 26 (C.E.F. Rickett); (1991) 107 LQR 194 (B. Robertson). See also *Re Cleaver* [1981] 1 WLR 939 at 947–948, [1981] 2 All ER 1018 at 1023–4, p. 279, post, where NOURSE J held that mutual wills need only be proved on the balance of probabilities.

possible that very different standards of proof may be appropriate for cases where the words of a formal document have to be altered and for cases where there is no such alteration but merely a question whether, when the document has been given effect to, there will be some trust of the property with which it dealt .... I am not sure that it is right to assume that there is a single, uniform standard of proof for all secret trusts. The proposition of Lord Westbury in *McCormick v Grogan* with which Brightman J was pressed in *Ottaway v Norman* was that the jurisdiction in cases of secret trust was

> 'founded altogether on personal fraud. It is a jurisdiction by which a Court of Equity, proceeding on the ground of fraud, converts the party who has committed it into a trustee for the party who is injured by that fraud. Now, being a jurisdiction founded on personal fraud, it is incumbent on the court to see that a fraud, a malus animus, is proved by the clearest and most indisputable evidence.'

Of that, it is right to say that the law on the subject has not stood still since 1869, and that it is now clear that secret trusts may be established in cases where there is no possibility of fraud. *McCormick v Grogan* has to be read in the light both of earlier cases that were not cited, and also of subsequent cases, in particular *Blackwell v Blackwell* [1929] AC 318. It seems to me that fraud comes into the matter in two ways. First, it provides an historical explanation of the doctrine of secret trusts; the doctrine was evolved as a means of preventing fraud. That, however, does not mean that fraud is an essential ingredient for the application of the doctrine; the reason for the rule is not part of the rule itself. Second, there are some cases within the doctrine where fraud is indeed involved. There are cases where for the legatee to assert that he is a beneficial owner, free from any trust, would be a fraud on his part.

It is to this latter aspect of fraud that it seems to me that Lord Westbury's words are applicable. If a secret trust can be held to exist in a particular case only by holding the legatee guilty of fraud, then no secret trust should be found unless the standard of proof suffices for fraud. On the other hand, if there is no question of fraud, why should so high a standard apply? In such a case, I find it difficult to see why the mere fact that the historical origin of the doctrine lay in the prevention of fraud should impose the high standard of proof for fraud in a case in which no issue of fraud arises. In accordance with the general rule of evidence, the standard of proof should vary with the nature of the issue and its gravity: see *Hornal v Neuberger Products Ltd* [1957] 1 QB 247, [1956] 3 All ER 970.

Now in the present case there is no question of fraud. The will directed the residue to be held in trust for the brother absolutely, and the only question is whether or not the beneficial interest thus given to him has been subjected to a trust, and if so, what that trust is. The trust, if it is one, is plainly one which required the brother to carry it out: it was he who was to distribute the money and see that everything was dealt with properly, and not the trustees of the will. There was thus no attempt to cancel the testamentary trust of residue for the brother and require the trustees of the will to hold the residue on the secret trust instead. Accordingly I cannot see that rectification provides any real analogy. The question is simply that of the ordinary standard of evidence required to establish a trust.

I therefore hold that in order to establish a secret trust where no question of fraud arises, the standard of proof is the ordinary civil standard of proof that is required to establish an ordinary trust. I am conscious that this does not accord with what was said in *Ottaway v Norman* [1972] Ch 698, [1971] 3 All ER 1325;

but I think the point was taken somewhat shortly there, and the judge does not seem to have had the advantage of having cited to him the authorities that I have considered. For those reasons I have overcome my hesitation in differing from him. I cannot therefore dispose of the case summarily on the footing that a high standard of proof has plainly not been achieved, but I must consider the evidence in some detail to see whether the ordinary standard of proof has been satisfied. The initial question, of course, is whether the brother was bound by a secret trust, or whether he was subject to no more than a moral obligation. [His Lordship considered the evidence and continued:]

The general picture which seems to me to emerge from the evidence is of a testatrix who for long had been worrying about how to divide her residue and who was still undecided. She had a brother whom she trusted implicitly and who knew her general views about her relations and her property. She therefore left her residue to him in the faith that he would, in due time and in accordance with her general wishes, make in her stead the detailed decisions about the distribution of her residue which had for so long troubled her and on which she was still undecided. He was her trusted brother, more wealthy than she, and a little older. There was thus no need to bind him by any legally enforceable trust; and I cannot see any real indication that she had any thought of doing this. Instead, she simply left him, as a matter of family confidence and probity, to do what he thought she would have done if she had ever finally made up her mind. In short, to revert to the language of Christian LJ in *McCormick v Grogan* (1867) IR 1 Eq 313 at 328, I cannot see any real evidence that she intended the sanction to be the authority of a court of justice and not merely the conscience of her brother. I therefore hold that her brother took the residue free from any trust.''

B. Half-Secret Trusts

The gift may be to a legatee, not absolutely, but in a fiduciary capacity. Different questions then arise. If the legacy is "to X upon such trusts as I have orally declared (or shall orally declare) to him", it is clear that X can never claim beneficially. The property is given to him as trustee. We saw that the reason which the judges gave for enforcing fully secret trusts was the prevention of fraud. If, in a half-secret trust, there is no possibility of fraud, how can the court justify the imposition of a trust on that ground?

One possible solution is to refuse to enforce half-secret trusts and to hold that the beneficial interest returns to the testator's estate by way of resulting trust.

It would however be a strange rule of law which says that a gift to X absolutely (on a fully secret trust) makes X hold upon trust for Y; yet a gift to X *upon trust* (on a half-secret trust) will be held on a resulting trust. That would mean that the mention of the intended trust in the will would prevent its taking effect.

It seems therefore that (a) half-secret trusts should be no less readily enforced than fully secret trusts; (b) fraud is not an adequate basis for the enforcement of half-secret trusts: (c) some other and better rationale is required. The cases will show that some courts have used the analogy of the doctrine of incorporation by reference to meet this problem; with the result that half-secret trusts communicated before or at the time of the will may be enforced; but not those communicated between the date of the will and the death of the testator. Clearly this is inadequate. An attempt is made at the end of this chapter to suggest a theory which is capable of providing a rational basis for the enforcement of secret trusts.[11]

But the problem is wider than this. The question is not merely: on what basis can we enforce these trusts? The question should be: bearing in mind the sound policy in favour of formalities in wills, and the express terms of the Wills Act 1837, s. 9, are the reasons for the enforcement of informal dispositions so compelling that it is necessary to enforce them, or some of them? Having answered that question, the earlier one becomes relevant.

BLACKWELL v BLACKWELL
[1929] AC 318 (HL, Lord HAILSHAM LC, Viscount SUMNER, Lords BUCKMASTER, CARSON and WARRINGTON)

The testator, John Duncan Blackwell, by a codicil to his will, gave to five persons the sum of £12,000, the income to be applied "for the purposes indicated by me to them," with power to apply £8,000 of the capital "to such person or persons indicated by me to them", as they thought fit.

The objects of the trust were communicated orally to the trustees, and accepted by them prior to the execution of the codicil. These were in favour of a lady and her illegitimate son. The widow challenged the validity of the trust and claimed the £12,000 as part of the residue.

Held. The trust was valid, and oral evidence was admissible to prove it.

VISCOUNT SUMNER: In itself the doctrine of equity, by which parol evidence is admissible to prove what is called "fraud" in connection with secret trusts, and effect is given to such trusts when established, would not seem to conflict with any of the Acts under which from time to time the Legislature has regulated the right of testamentary disposition. A Court of conscience finds a man in the position of an absolute legal owner of a sum of money, which has been bequeathed to him under a valid will, and it declares that, on proof of certain facts relating to the motives and actions of the testator, it will not allow the legal owner to exercise his legal right to do what he will with his own. This seems to be a perfectly normal exercise of general equitable jurisdiction. The facts commonly but not necessarily involve some immoral and selfish conduct on the part of the legal owner. The necessary elements, on which the question turns, are intention, communication, and acquiescence. The testator intends his absolute gift to be employed as he and not as the donee desires; he tells the proposed donee of this intention and, either by express promise or by the tacit promise, which is signified by acquiescence, the proposed donee encourages him to bequeath the money in the faith that his intentions will be carried out. The special circumstance, that the gift is by bequest only makes this rule a special case of the exercise of a general jurisdiction, but in its application to a bequest the doctrine must in principle rest on the assumption that the will has first operated according to its terms. It is because there is no one to whom the

---

11 See [1979] Conv 360 (P. Matthews) where it is argued that the incorporation by reference doctrine is the true basis of half-secret trusts; [1980] Conv 341 (D.R. Hodge) where it is argued that the fraud theory is the true basis of *all* secret trusts: "the essence of the fraud being found, not in the element of personal gain in the secret trustee, but in the facts that the deceased's confidence is being betrayed and the secret beneficiaries being deprived of benefits which, but for the trustee's action, would have been secured to them by other means" (p. 348).

law can give relief in the premises, that relief, if any, must be sought in equity. So far, and in the bare case of a legacy absolute on the face of it, I do not see how the statute-law relating to the form of a valid will is concerned at all, and the expressions, in which the doctrine has been habitually described, seem to bear this out. For the prevention of fraud equity fastens on the conscience of the legatee a trust, a trust, that is, which otherwise would be inoperative; in other words it makes him do what the will in itself has nothing to do with; it lets him take what the will gives him and then makes him apply it, as the Court of conscience directs, and it does so in order to give effect to wishes of the testator, which would not otherwise be effectual.

To this two circumstances must be added to bring the present case to the test of the general doctrine, first, that the will states on its face that the legacy is given on trust but does not state what the trusts are, and further contains a residuary bequest, and, second, that the legatees are acting with perfect honesty, seek no advantage to themselves, and only desire, if the Court will permit them, to do what in other circumstances the Court would have fastened it on their conscience to perform.

Since the current of decisions down to *Re Fleetwood* (1880) 15 ChD 594 and *Re Huxtable* [1902] 2 Ch 793 has established that the principles of equity apply equally when these circumstances are present as in cases where they are not, the material question is whether and how the Wills Act affects this case. It seems to me that, apart from legislation, the application of the principle of equity, which was made in *Fleetwood's* and *Huxtable's* cases, was logical, and was justified by the same considerations as in the cases of fraud and absolute gifts. Why should equity forbid an honest trustee to give effect to his promise, made to a deceased testator, and compel him to pay another legatee, about whom it is quite certain that the testator did not mean to make him the object of this bounty? In both cases the testator's wishes are incompletely expressed in his will. Why should equity, over a mere matter of words, give effect to them in one case and frustrate them in the other? No doubt the words 'in trust' prevent the legatee from taking beneficially, whether they have simply been declared in conversation or written in the will, but the fraud, when the trustee, so called in the will, is also the residuary legatee, is the same as when he is only declared a trustee by word of mouth accepted by him. I recoil from interfering with decisions of long standing, which reject this anomaly, unless constrained by statute.

The answer is put in the phrase, "this is making the testator's will for him", instead, that is, of limiting him to the will made in statutory form. What then of the legislation? Great authorities seem to have expressed an opinion, that this equitable principle, as a whole, conflicts with s. 9 of the Wills Act. Lord Cairns in 1868 says that when a devisee seeks to apply what has been devised to him otherwise than in accordance with the testator's intentions, communicated by him and accepted, "it is in effect a case of trust, and in such case the Court will not allow the devisee to set up the Statute of Frauds, or, rather, the Statute of Wills .... But in this the Court does not violate the spirit of the statutes; but for the ... prevention of fraud, it engrafts the trusts on the devise by admitting evidence which the statute would in terms exclude, in order to prevent a devisee from applying property to a purpose foreign to that for which he undertook to hold it": *Jones v Badley* (1868) 3 Ch App 362 at 364.

In the following year in *McCormick v Grogan* (1869) LR 4 HL 82... [His Lordship discussed the relationship between the equitable principle and the Wills Act 1837, s. 9, and continued:] Accordingly, I think the conclusion is confirmed, which the frame of s. 9 of the Wills Act seems to me to carry on its face, that the legislation did not purport to interfere with the exercise of a general equitable jurisdiction, even in connection with secret dispositions of a testator, except in so far as reinforcement of the formalities required for a valid will might indirectly limit it. The effect, therefore, of a bequest being made in terms on trust, without any statement in the will to show what the trust is, remains to be decided by the law as laid down by the Courts before and since the Act and does not depend on the Act itself.

The limits, beyond which the rules as to unspecified trusts must not be carried, have often been discussed. A testator cannot reserve to himself a power of making future unwitnessed dispositions by merely naming a trustee and leaving the purposes of the trust to be supplied afterwards, nor can a legatee give testamentary validity to an unexecuted codicil by accepting an indefinite trust, never communicated to him in the testator's lifetime: *Johnson v Ball* (1851) 5 De G & Sm 85; *Re Boyes* (1884) 26 ChD 531; *Riordan v Banon* (1876) IR 10 Eq 469; *Re Hetley* [1902] 2 Ch 866. To hold otherwise would indeed be to enable the testator to "give the go-by" to the requirements of the Wills Act, because he did not choose to comply with them. It is communication of the purpose to the legatee, coupled with acquiescence or promise on his part, that removes the matter from the provision of the Wills Act and brings it within the law of trusts, as applied in this instance to trustees, who happen also to be legatees. If I am right in thinking that there is no contradiction of the Wills Act in applying the same rule, whether the trustee is or is not so described in the will, and the whole topic is detached from the enforcement of the Wills Act itself, then, whether the decisions in equity are or are not open to doubt in themselves, I think that, in view of the subject-matter of these decisions and the length of time during which they have been acquiesced in, your Lordships may well in accordance with precedent refuse to overrule them lest titles should be rendered insecure and settlements, entered into in reliance on their authority, should now be disturbed. It is to be remembered that the rule as to trusts not expressed in a will is not limited to relations such as the testator in this case was concerned to provide for, but may have been applied in many other connections. I pretend to no means of knowledge of my own, but it seems to me probable that effect has been given to these cases to a substantial extent and therefore that, to avoid possible injustice, your Lordships should refuse to interfere with them now. Accordingly in my opinion the appeal fails on all grounds.

i. TIME OF COMMUNICATION AND ACCEPTANCE

RE KEEN
[1937] Ch 236, [1937] 1 All ER 452 (CA, Lords WRIGHT MR, GREENE and ROMER LJJ)

A testator, Harry Augustus Keen, by clause 5 of his will, gave £10,000 to trustees "to be held upon trust and disposed of by them among such person, persons or charities as may be notified by me to them ... during my lifetime".

Prior to the execution of the will, he handed to one of the trustees a sealed envelope, containing the name of a lady who was to be the beneficiary. The trustee did not open the envelope until after the testator's death, but he was aware of the fact that it contained the beneficiary's name.

Held. The reservation of a power to make future unattested dispositions is contrary to the Wills Act 1837. Furthermore, the communication, being prior to the execution of the will, was inconsistent with the terms of the will. The legacy therefore fell into residue.

LORD WRIGHT MR: The summons came before Farwell J, who decided adversely to the claims of the lady on the short ground that she could not prove that she was a person notified to the trustees by the testator during his lifetime within the words of clause 5. His opinion seems to be that the clause required the name and identity of the lady to be expressly disclosed to the trustees during the testator's lifetime so that it was not sufficient to place these particulars in the physical possession of the trustees or one of them in the form of a memorandum which they were not to read till the testator's death.

I am unable to accept this conclusion, which appears to me to put too narrow a construction on the word "notified" as used in clause 5 in all the circumstances of the case. To take a parallel, a ship which sails under sealed orders, is sailing under orders though the exact terms are not ascertained by the captain till later. I note that the case of a trust put into writing which is placed in the trustees' hands in a sealed envelope, was hypothetically treated by Kay J as possibly constituting a communication in a case of this nature: *Re Boyes* (1884) 26 ChD 531 at 536. This, so far as it goes, seems to support my conclusion. The trustees had the means of knowledge available whenever it became necessary and proper to open the envelope. I think Mr. Evershed was right in understanding that the giving of the sealed envelope was a notification within clause 5.

This makes it necessary to examine the matter on a wider basis, and to consider the principles of law which were argued both before Farwell J and this Court, but which the judge found it merely necessary to mention. There are two main questions: first, how far parol evidence is admissible to define the trust under such a clause as this, and, secondly and in particular, how far such evidence if admissible at all would be excluded on the ground that it would be inconsistent with the true meaning of clause 5.

It is first necessary to state what, in my opinion, is the true construction of the words of the clause.

These words, in my opinion, can only be considered as referring to a definition of trusts which have not yet at the date of the will been established and which between that date and the testator's death may or may not be established. Mr. Roxburgh has strenuously argued, basing himself in particular on the word "may", that the clause even though it covers future dispositions, also includes a disposition antecedent to or contemporaneous with the execution of the will. I do not think that even so wide a construction of the word "may" would enable Mr. Roxburgh's contention to succeed, but in any case I do not feel able to accept it. The words of the clause seem to me to refer only to something future and hypothetical, to something as to which the testator is reserving an option whether to do or not to do it . . . .

The principles of law or equity relevant in a question of this nature have now been authoritatively settled or discussed by the House of Lords in *Blackwell v Blackwell* [1929] AC 318. In 1869 in *McCormick v Grogan* (1869) LR 4 HL 82 the House of Lords had held that a secret trust, that is a trust created by an expression of the testator's wishes communicated to and accepted by the legatee, bound the conscience of the legatee, though in the terms of the will the bequest was absolute. Such a trust was held to be altogether outside the will; the will took effect according to its terms and the property passed absolutely to the legatee: but the Court, it was held, would compel the legatee to apply that property according to the undertaking he had assumed to carry out the wishes of the testator. It would be a fraud or breach of faith not to fulfil the undertaking which the legatee had given to carry out the purposes for which the bequest to him was made.

No complication was involved in such a case by reason of s. 9 of the Wills Act, 1837. The testamentary disposition, which had been duly attested, received full effect. But a different question had to be considered when in the will itself the property was left to the legatee in trust, but neither the nature of the trust nor its beneficiaries were defined in the will. That was the case decided in *Blackwell v Blackwell* . . . .

As in my judgment clause 5 should be considered as contemplating future dispositions and as reserving to the testator the power of making such dispositions without a duly attested codicil simply by notifying them during his lifetime, the principles laid down by Lord Sumner must be fatal to the appellant's claim. Indeed they would be equally fatal even on the construction for which Mr. Roxburgh contended, that the clause covered both anterior or contemporaneous notifications as well as future notifications. The clause would be equally invalid, but, as already explained, I cannot accept that construction. In *Blackwell v Blackwell* [1929] AC 318; *Re Fleetwood* (1880) 15 Ch D 594 and *Re Huxtable* [1902] 2 Ch 793 the trusts had been specifically declared to some or all of the trustees at or before the execution of the will and the language of the will was consistent with that fact. There was in these cases no reservation of a future power to change the trusts, in whole or in part. Such a power would involve a power to change a testamentary disposition by an unexecuted codicil and would violate s. 9 of the Wills Act. This was so held in *Re Hetley* [1902] 2 Ch 866. *Johnson v Ball* (1851) 5 De G & Sm 85 is again a somewhat different example of the rule against dispositions made subsequently to the date of the will in cases where the will in terms leaves the property on trust, and shows that the position may be different from the position where the will in terms leaves the gift absolutely. The trusts referred to but undefined in the will must be described in the will as established prior to or at least contemporaneously with its execution.

But there is still a further objection which in the present case renders the appellant's claim unenforceable; the trusts which it is sought to establish by parol evidence would be inconsistent with the express terms of the will. That such an objection is fatal appears from the cases already cited, such as *Re Huxtable*. In that case an undefined trust of money for charitable purposes was declared in the will as in respect of the whole corpus, and accordingly evidence was held inadmissible that the charitable trust was limited to the legatee's life so that he was free to dispose of the corpus after his death. Similarly in *Johnson v Ball* the testator by the will left the property to trustees upon the uses contained in a letter signed "by them and myself": it was held that evidence was not admissible to show that though no such letter was in existence at the date of the will, the testator had made a subsequent declaration of trust; the Court held that these trusts could not be enforced. Lord Buckmaster in *Blackwell's* case [1929] AC 318 at 331 described *Johnson v Ball* as an authority pointing to "a case where the actual trusts were left over after the date of the will to be subsequently determined by the testator". That in his opinion would be a contravention of the Wills Act. I know of no authority which would justify such a contravention. Lord Buckmaster also quotes at 330 the grounds on which Parker V-C based his decision as being both "that the letter referred to in the will had no existence at the time when the will was made and that supposing it referred to a letter afterwards signed it is impossible to give effect to it as a declaration of the trusts, since it would admit the document as part of the will and it was unattested''.

In the present case, while clause 5 refers solely to a future definition or to future definitions of the trust subsequent to the date of the will, the sealed letter relied on as notifying the trust was communicated (as I find the facts) before the date of the will. That it was communicated to one trustee only and not to both would not, I think, be an objection (see Lord Warrington's observation in the *Blackwell* case at 341). But the objection remains that the notification sought to be put in evidence was anterior to the will and hence not within the language of clause 5, and inadmissible simply on that ground as being inconsistent with what the will prescribes.

It is always with reluctance that a Court refuses to give effect to the proved intention of the testator. In the present case it may be said that the objection is merely a matter of drafting and that the decision in *Blackwell v Blackwell* would have been applicable if only clause 5 had been worded as applying to trusts previously indicated by the testator. The sealed letter would then have been admissible, subject to proof of the communication and acceptance of the trust. This may be true, but the Court must deal with the matter as in fact it is. It would be impossible to give effect to the appellant's contention without not merely extending the rule laid down in *Blackwell v Blackwell*, but actually contravening the limitations which have been placed on that rule as necessarily arising from the Wills Act and, in addition, from the fact that the conditions prescribed by the will cannot be contradicted.

The appeal must be dismissed and the decision of Farwell J affirmed.

In **Re Bateman's Will Trusts** [1970] 1 WLR 1463, [1970] 3 All ER 817, a testator directed his trustee to set aside £24,000 and pay the income "to such persons and in such proportions as shall be stated by me in a sealed letter in my own handwriting addressed to my trustees." There was no evidence as to whether a sealed letter had been written and addressed to the trustees by the testator at the date of the will. PENNYCUICK V-C held that the direction was invalid, and said at 1468, at 820:

"These words clearly, I think, import that the testator may, in the future, after the date of the will, give a sealed letter to his trustees. It is impossible to confine the words to a sealed letter already so given. If that is the true construction of the wording, it is not in dispute that the direction is invalid.

I was referred to one or two cases on the point, in particular, *Re Keen's Estate* [1937] Ch 236, [1937] 1 All ER 452 in the Court of Appeal, and *Re Jones* [1942] Ch 328, [1942] 1 All ER 642, per Simonds J. I do not think it necessary to go further into those cases because it is really clear and not in dispute that once one must construe the direction as admitting of a future letter then the direction is invalid, as an attempt to dispose of the estate by a non-testamentary instrument.''[12]

---

12 *Riordan v Banon* (1876) IR 10 Eq 469; cf. *Balfe v Halpenny* [1904] 1 IR 486; *Re Browne* [1944] IR 90; (1951) 67 LQR 413 (L.A. Sheridan); [1992] Conv 202 (J. Mee) and (1991) 5 Trust Law International 69 (P. Couglan); *Re Prendiville* (5 December 1990, unreported).

ii. Alterations to the Trust Property

In **Re Cooper** [1939] Ch 811, [1939] 3 All ER 586, a testator left £5,000 to two trustees, to whom he communicated the terms of the trust before he had executed his will in February 1938. The trustees acquiesced. By a later will in March, the testator purported to cancel the earlier will except for certain bequests, and then added: "The sum of £5,000 bequeathed to my trustees in the will now cancelled is to be increased to £10,000, they knowing my wishes regarding that sum." This increase was never communicated by the testator to the trustees. The Court of Appeal held that the first £5,000 was subject to a secret trust, but that the additional £5,000 went on a resulting trust. Sir Wilfred Greene MR said at 817, at 589:

"The substance of the matter is that, having imposed on the conscience of these two trustees the trust in relation to the legacy of 5000*l.* and having written that legacy into his will of February, 1938, by this will he in effect is giving another legacy of the same amount to be held upon the same trusts. It seems to me that upon the facts of this case it is impossible to say that the acceptance by the trustees of the onus of trusteeship in relation to the first and earlier legacy is something which must be treated as having been repeated in reference to the second legacy or the increased legacy, whichever way one chooses to describe it. In order that a secret trust might be made effective with regard to that added sum in my opinion precisely the same factors were necessary as were required to validate the original trusts, namely, communication, acceptance or acquiescence, and the making of the will on the faith of such acceptance or acquiescence. None of these elements, as I have said, were present. It is not possible, in my opinion, to treat the figure of 5000*l.* in relation to which the consent of the trustees was originally obtained as something of no essential importance. I cannot myself see that the arrangement between the testator and the trustees can be construed as though it had meant '5000*l.* or whatever sum I may hereafter choose to bequeath.' That is not what was said and it was not with regard to any sum other than the 5000*l.* that the consciences of the trustees (to use a technical phrase) were burdened. It must not be thought from what I have been saying that some trifling excess of the sum actually bequeathed over the figure mentioned in the first bequest to the trustees would necessarily not be caught. Such an addition might come within the rule of de minimis if the facts justified it. Similarly it must not be thought that, if a testator, having declared to his trustees trusts in relation to a specified sum, afterwards in his will inserts a lesser sum, that lesser sum would not be caught by the trusts. In such a case the greater would I apprehend be held to include the less."

iii. Surplus After Performing the Trust

In **Re Rees** [1950] Ch 204, [1949] 2 All ER 1003, a testator, the Reverend Thomas Rees, appointed his solicitor and Thomas Hopkins as executors and trustees of his will, and in clause 3 left the whole of his property "unto my trustees absolutely they well knowing my wishes concerning the same". At the execution of the will the testator told his trustees that he left his estate to them on their assurance that they would make certain payments out of it "and on the understanding that any surplus was to be retained by them for their own use."

On the death of the testator in 1944, the payments were made, leaving a substantial surplus in the hands of the trustees. The Court of Appeal, affirming

VAISEY J [1949] Ch 541, held that the surplus did not vest in the trustees absolutely and beneficially, but went on a resulting trust for the testator's next of kin. EVERSHED MR said at 207, at 1004:

"There are two distinct points. The first is one of the construction of the will. On its true interpretation, does cl. 3 confer on the persons named as trustees an interest in the property on trust only, or does it give the property to those two persons conditionally on their discharging the wishes communicated to them? The second point which arises, if the first is decided adversely to the plaintiff, is this: although the form of the will on its proper reading, creates only a trust estate in the trustees, can they, nevertheless, by oral evidence, prove that they held it on trust, having discharged the several payments to which I have already alluded, for the two trustees beneficially or the survivor of them? I will deal with the two questions in that order.

[His Lordship construed the clause as conferring upon the trustees an interest in trust only, and continued:]

"That makes it necessary to consider the second question. As I have already indicated, I agree with the judge that to admit evidence to the effect that the testator informed one of the executors — or, I will assume in Mr. Milner Holland's favour, both of the executors — that he intended them to take beneficial interests and that his wishes included that intention, would be to conflict with the terms of the will as I have construed them; for the inevitable result of admitting that evidence and giving effect to it would be that the will would be regarded not as conferring a trust estate only upon the two trustees, but as giving them a conditional gift which on construction is the thing which, if I am right, it does not do."[13]

C. Tenants in Common and Joint Tenants

In **Re Stead** [1900] 1 Ch 237, FARWELL J had to consider a gift by will to two persons as joint tenants which had been made upon the faith of an antecedent promise by one of them to hold upon secret trusts. He said at 241:

"If A induces B either to make, or to leave unrevoked, a will leaving property to A and C as tenants in common, by expressly promising, or tacitly consenting, that he and C will carry out the testator's wishes, and C knows nothing of the matter until after A's death, A is bound, but C is not bound: *Tee v Ferris* (1856) 2 K & J 357; the reason stated at 368 being, that to hold otherwise would enable one beneficiary to deprive the rest of their benefits by setting up a secret trust. If, however, the gift were to A and C as joint tenants, the authorities have established a distinction between those cases in which the will is made on the faith of the antecedent promise by A and those in which the will is left unrevoked on the faith of a subsequent promise. In the former case, the trust binds both A and C: *Russell v Jackson* (1852) 10 Hare 204; *Jones v Badley* (1868) 3 Ch App 362, the reason stated being that no person can claim an interest under a fraud committed by another; in the latter case A and not C is bound: *Burney v Macdonald* (1845) 15 Sim 6 and *Moss v Cooper* (1861) 1 John & H 352, the reason stated at 367 being that the gift is not tainted with any fraud in procuring the execution of the will. Personally I am unable to see any difference between a gift made on the faith of an antecedent promise and a gift

---

13 See *Re Tyler* [1967] 1 WLR 1269 at 1277, [1967] 3 All ER 389 at 394, where PENNYCUICK J said "I will make no pretence of finding that reasoning easy."

left unrevoked on the faith of a subsequent promise to carry out the testator's wishes; but apparently a distinction has been made by the various judges who have had to consider the question. I am bound, therefore, to decide in accordance with these authorities . . . ."

(1972) 88 LQR at 228 (B. Perrins)

"The 'reasons stated' by Farwell J in *Re Stead* are at first sight contradictory. One consideration is that a person must not be allowed, by falsely setting up a secret trust, to deprive another of his benefits under the will. Apparently this is decisive if the parties are tenants in common but not if they are joint tenants. On the other hand one person must not profit by the fraud of another. Apparently this is decisive only if the parties are joint tenants and not if they are tenants in common. Yet again it is apparently only fraud in procuring the execution of a will that is relevant, and not fraud in inducing a testator not to revoke a will already made. All very confusing, but add *Huguenin v Baseley* (1807) 14 Ves 273 and the whole picture springs into focus and the confusion disappears. Returning to A and C, whether they are tenants in common or joint tenants, C is not bound *if his gift was not induced by the promise of A* because to hold otherwise would be to enable A to deprive C of his benefit by setting up a secret trust; but C is bound *if his gift was induced by the promise of A* because he cannot profit by the fraud of another; and if the trust was communicated to A after the will was made, then C takes free *if his gift was not induced by the promise of A* because if there is no inducement there is no fraud affecting C.

This, it is submitted, is what was decided by the cases cited in Farwell J's judgment."

D. Theoretical Basis of Secret Trusts[14]

In **Re Young** [1951] Ch 344, [1950] 2 All ER 1245, a testator made a bequest to his wife, and imposed a condition that she should, inter alia, make certain bequests which he had communicated to her. One of them was a gift of £2,000 in favour of Thomas Cobb, the testator's chauffeur. Cobb attested the will. An attesting witness cannot receive a legacy under the will.[15] DANCKWERTS J held that Cobb was entitled to the £2,000. This was a gift to him under an oral trust declared by the testator and not a bequest under the will. He said at 350, at 1250:

"There is one other point, which is rather interesting, concerning the validity of one of these legacies. The widow has testified that the testator's intention, as communicated to her, was that the man who had been employed by the testator for many years as chauffeur and general factotum should receive a legacy of £2,000. The chauffeur was one of the two attesting witnesses to the will, and if he takes the legacy under the terms of the will the result of s. 15 of the Wills Act, 1837, is to make his legacy ineffective. The question is whether he takes the legacy under the will. Mr. Christie, on behalf of the next-of-kin, referred to *Re Fleetwood* (1880) 15 ChD 594, a case of a secret trust,

---

14 See articles referred to at p. 142, note 1, ante.
15 Wills Act 1837, s. 15, modified by Wills Act 1968 which allows the attesting witness-legatee to take if the will was duly executed without his attestation.

decided by Hall V-C, where it was held that, as a woman intended to be a beneficiary was one of the attesting witnesses to the fourth codicil, the trust for her failed as to her beneficial interest, as it would have done, Hall V-C said, had it been declared in the codicil. It appears that the point was not argued in that particular case, which was concerned with a number of other points; and it seems to me that that particular decision is contrary to principle. The whole theory of the formation of a secret trust is that the Wills Act has nothing to do with the matter because the forms required by the Wills Act are entirely disregarded, since the persons do not take by virtue of the gift in the will, but by virtue of the secret trusts imposed upon the beneficiary, who does in fact take under the will.

In the Irish case of *O'Brien v Condon* [1905] 1 IR 51 Sir Andrew Porter MR had to consider the matter with the decision of *Re Fleetwood* before him. He pointed out in a judgment which seems to me to be entirely in accordance with principle and common sense that *Re Fleetwood* was inconsistent with the principle of the matter, and inconsistent with certain other cases, one of which was a decision of the House of Lords on an Irish appeal, namely *Cullen v A-G for Ireland* (1866) LR 1 HL 190. Sir Andrew Porter MR pointed out in *O'Brien v Condon* at 59 that the point was not argued before Hall V-C in *Re Fleetwood*, and accordingly he decided to differ from the decision in *Re Fleetwood* and to apply what seems to me to be the proper statement of the principle. I agree with the decision in *O'Brien v Condon* and I think it right to follow it in the circumstances of this case, because the particular point was not argued before Hall V-C and I think that his judgment on it was given per incuriam.

It seems to me that according to *Cullen v A-G for Ireland*, and the later decision of *Re Gardner* [1923] 2 Ch 230, every consideration connected with this principle requires me to reach the conclusion that a beneficiary under a secret trust does not take under the will, and that he is not, therefore, affected by s. 15 of the Wills Act, 1837.''

Hanbury & Martin: *Modern Equity* (14th edn), pp. 164–165.

"It is one thing to say that the trust operates outside the will, but it is another to say just how and when the trust takes effect. . . . the most natural way for this to occur is to treat the communication to the trustee as the declaration of trust, and the vesting of the property in the trustee by the will as the constitution of the trust. If this is so, the declaration is *inter vivos*, the Wills Act has no effect upon it, and the only statutory formalities that are relevant are Law of Property Act 1925, s. 53 (1) (b)[16], which requires that declarations of trusts of land should be evidenced in writing; but this would not affect the rule requiring a fraudulent trustee in a fully secret trust of land to hold on a constructive trust.[17] There would be no awkward distinction between declarations prior to and subsequent to the will in half-secret trusts,[18] the sole question would be

---

16 See p. 52 ante; *Re Baillie* (1886) 2 TLR 660 at 661. But there was no writing in *Ottaway v Norman* [1972] Ch 698, [1971] 3 All ER 1325.
17 LPA 1925, s. 53 (2).
18 *Re Keen* [1937] Ch 236, p. 160, ante; *Re Bateman's Will Trusts* [1970] 1 WLR 1463, [1970] 3 All ER 817, p. 163, ante.

whether or not a trust was declared of the property before the death, and whether that trust became properly constituted by the vesting of the property in the trustee.

We have seen that the usual rule in the case of property coming to a person who had previously declared himself trustee of it was that the trust did not become constituted without a further manifestation of intention.[19] It was submitted that where a third person accepted an instruction to hold the property on certain trusts and the settlor subsequently transferred the property to him without further declaration, the trust would be constituted. It should make no difference whether the property passed to the trustee by conveyance *inter vivos* or by a will.[20] It will probably fail however if the trustee predeceases the testator at any rate in the case of a fully secret trust.[1] Assuming its terms were known, it may be that a half-secret trust could be saved by the maxim 'a trust does not fail for want of a trustee'.[2]

Until the property has so vested, there is no completely constituted trust; the declaration can have no effect and cannot create property rights. The will can be revoked or altered, or the property may be disposed of during the testator's lifetime. The testator can revoke his instructions to the secret trustee at any time,[3] and if he acts as if he had forgotten the declaration or assumed it to be no longer existent, it will be treated as having expired. And no rational theory, it is suggested, can be found which will justify the remarkable decision in *Re Gardner (No 2)*.[4] We have seen that a wife left her estate to her husband for life,[5] and that after his death, it was to be held on secret trust for five named beneficiaries. One of the beneficiaries predeceased the wife. The representatives of the deceased beneficiary successfully claimed the share.

A gift by will normally lapses if the donee predeceases the testator,[6] and the estate of the donee can only claim if the donee acquired some interest in the property before he died. No such interest could exist in this case; and the theory which suggests that a secret trust can be treated as a declaration of trust *inter vivos* does not suggest that any interest is obtained by any beneficiary prior to the constitution of the trust by vesting of the legal estate in the trustee.''

---

19 See p. 119, ante; *Brennan v Morphett* (1908) 6 CLR 22; *Matter of Gurlitz* 105 Misc 30, 172 NY Supp 523 (1918); *Re Northcliffe* [1925] Ch 651.

20 As with the property received by Miss Towry Law from her sister and conveyed to the trustees; *Re Ellenborough* [1903] 1 Ch 697, p. 135, ante; *Re Adlard* [1954] Ch 29, [1953] 2 All ER 1437; *Re Ralli's Will Trusts* [1964] Ch 288, [1963] 3 All ER 940, p. 113, ante.

1 Per COZENS-HARDY LJ in *Re Maddock* [1902] 2 Ch 220 at 251; Oakley, *Constructive Trusts* (2nd edn), p. 120.

2 Unless the particular trustee is regarded as essential to the trust. For an example in another context, see *Re Lysaght* [1966] Ch 191, [1965] 2 All ER 888.

3 But any substituted instructions given after the will is executed will be invalid in the case of a half secret trust.

4 [1923] 2 Ch 230. See Oakley, p. 121, suggesting that there is no clear rule against a non-testamentary trust for a dead person. This is doubtful, as such a beneficiary has no legal personality, unless it is clear that his estate is intended to take.

5 *Re Gardner (No 1)* [1920] 2 Ch 523.

6 A special exception is made in the case of children of the testator who predecease him, leaving issue: Wills Act 1837, s. 33; as amended by AJA 1982, s. 19. Such a gift takes effect in favour of the issue.

QUESTIONS

1. Should secret trusts be classified as express, implied or constructive trusts? Why? Is this a matter of practical significance? p. 292 post; H & M pp. 167–168; P & M, pp. 54–55; Pettit, pp. 118–119; Riddall, pp. 58–59; (1951) 67 LQR 314 at 323 et seq. (L.A. Sheridan); [1979] Conv 341 at 348 (D.R. Hodge); Oakley, *Constructive Trusts* (2nd edn), pp. 129–130; *Ottaway v Norman* [1972] Ch 698, [1971] 3 All ER 1325; *Re Baillie* (1886) 2 TLR 660 at 661.

2. Can you suggest any rational ground to support *Re Gardner* (*No 2*) [1923] 2 Ch 230: H & M, p. 166; Underhill, pp. 234–236.

3. Is it advisable, as a matter of policy to enforce (a) fully secret trusts, (b) half-secret trusts? H & M, p. 168; (1951) 67 LQR 314 at 328; [1981] Conv 335 (T.G. Watkin); Scott, *Trusts* (3rd edn) §55.9.

4. "The fraud theory is, consistently with the authorities, available to justify the enforcement of all secret trusts." (D.R. Hodge in [1980] Conv 341 at 348) "The ghost of fraudulent behaviour in the area of secret trusts still lingers. It should be exorcised once and for all." (C.E.F. Rickett in (1979) 38 CLJ 260 at 264).

   What is meant by fraud? Does the ghost still linger, and, if so, should it be exorcised?

5. Why is the rule in half-secret trusts for the time of communication and acceptance different from that in fully secret trusts? Should it be?

6. To what extent does the doctrine of secret trusts apply to inter vivos dispositions? (1951) 67 LQR 314 at 323; *Re Tyler* [1967] 1 WLR 1269 at 1275, [1967] 3 All ER 389 at 392.

   V sells and conveys two cottages to P. By a separate oral agreement P allows V to occupy one of the cottages rent free for so long as he desires. Consider how V can be protected if P claims possession. By a constructive trust (*Bannister v Bannister* [1948] 2 All ER 133)? By an estoppel licence? If both methods are applicable, which is to be preferred? Maudsley and Burn, *Land Law: Cases and Materials* (6th edn), pp. 604–605.

7. Would you recommend legislation in England on the lines of the American Uniform Testamentary Additions to Trusts Act (p. 149, et seq. ante)?

5. Trusts and Creditors

I. Introduction

Property which a debtor owns beneficially is normally available to his creditors for the payment of his debts. A settlor, on setting up a trust, intends however to benefit the beneficiaries, and not to give the money to their creditors. We consider in Section II the extent to which a trust can be created so as to deprive the creditors of the beneficiary from recourse to the fund. But it may be that the settlor is worried about his own creditors. To what extent can he escape from them by creating trusts of his property in favour of members of his family? That is the subject of Section III.

II. Protective Trusts[1]

A. General

A protective trust is a useful way of protecting a beneficiary against the effects of misfortune or his own extravagance. It represents a compromise between two forces: the desire on the one hand to make a man's property available for his creditors; and on the other to enable family property to be available for the support of the family in the event of the insolvency of the head of the family. As here described, a protective trust shows the furthest extent to which English law will permit property to be denied to creditors. Most American jurisdictions allow beneficial interests under trusts to be inalienable, and this has allowed the development of what they call "spendthrift trusts".[2]

The basis of a protective trust is a determinable life interest,[3] determinable upon a stated event, which is usually any situation in which the income or any

---

1 H & M, pp. 188–198; K & S, pp. 335–336; P & M, pp. 182–188; Pettit, pp. 72–74; Riddall, pp. 230–233; Snell, pp. 137–140; Underhill, pp. 183–189; (1957) 21 Conv (NS) 110, 323 (L.A. Sheridan); (1967) 31 Conv (NS) 117 (A.J. Hawkins).

2 Scott, *Law of Trusts*, § 152, p. 183 post; Griswold, *Spendthrift Trusts* (2nd edn, 1947); Keeton, *Modern Developments in the Law of Trusts*, chap. 15. In England it was possible from the early 19th century to 1935 to create a trust for the separate use of a married woman and to impose a restraint upon anticipation or alienation. See Law Reform (Married Women and Tortfeasors) Act 1935 and Married Women (Restraint upon Anticipation) Act 1949.

3 Which must be distinguished from a gift subject to a condition subsequent: *Brandon v Robinson* (1811) 18 Ves 429; *Rochford v Hackman* (1852) 9 Hare 475.

part of it becomes payable to anyone other than the beneficiary. A settlor cannot create in himself an interest which is determinable upon his own bankruptcy.[4] He may make it determinable upon any event *other than* bankruptcy.[5] And he may create an interest in *another* person which is determinable upon that other's bankruptcy.

When the determining event occurs, the life interest is forfeited. That is not necessarily a disaster; forfeiture means that the life tenant is no longer entitled; therefore, his creditors (or the trustee in bankruptcy) cannot claim. But on the forfeiture of the life interest, other trusts then arise; which, in the case of the protective trust provisions contained in Trustee Act 1925, s. 33, will be discretionary trusts, with the original life tenant a member of the class of beneficiaries.

As will be seen, a settlor may spell out the terms of a protective trust. But, since 1925, he may take advantage of Trustee Act 1925, s. 33, and declare that property is held "on protective trusts".[6]

B. Trustee Act 1925, s. 33

TRUSTEE ACT 1925

33. Protective Trusts. — (1) Where any income, including an annuity or other periodical income payment, is directed to be held on protective trusts for the benefit of any person (in this section called "the principal beneficiary") for the period of his life or for any less period, then, during that period (in this section called the "trust period") the said income shall, without prejudice to any prior interest, be held on the following trusts, namely:

    (i) Upon trust for the principal beneficiary during the trust period or until he, whether before or after the termination of any prior interest, does or attempts to do or suffers any act or thing, or until any event happens, other than an advance under any statutory or express power, whereby, if the said income were payable during the trust period to the principal beneficiary absolutely during that period, he would be deprived of the right to receive the same or any part thereof,[7] in any of which cases, as well as on the termination of the trust period, whichever first happens, this trust of the said income shall fail or determine:

    (ii) If the trust aforesaid fails or determines during the subsistence of the trust period, then, during the residue of that period, the said income shall be held upon trust for the application thereof for the maintenance or support, or otherwise for the benefit, of all or any one or more exclusively of the other or others of the following persons[8] (that is to say) —

---

4 *Re Burroughs-Fowler* [1916] 2 Ch 251; Trustee Act 1925, s. 33 (3), p. 172, post.
5 *Re Detmold* (1889) 40 ChD 585, p. 172, post.
6 Or words making clear that this was intended; *Re Wittke* [1944] Ch 166 ("upon protective trusts for the benefit of my sister"); *Re Platt* [1950] CLY 4386 ("for protective life interest").
7 *Re Smith's Will Trusts* (1981) 131 NLJ 292, p. 173, post.
8 See Family Law Reform Act 1987, s. 1, Sched. 2, para 2. Relationships are to be construed without regard to illegitimacy.

(*a*) the principal beneficiary and his or her wife or husband, if any, and his or her children or more remote issue, if any; or

(*b*) if there is no wife or husband or issue of the principal beneficiary in existence, the principal beneficiary and the persons who would, if he were actually dead, be entitled to the trust property or the income thereof or to the annuity fund, if any, or arrears of the annuity, as the case may be;

as the trustees in their absolute discretion, without being liable to account for the exercise of such discretion, think fit.

(2) This section does not apply to trusts coming into operation before the commencement of this Act, and has effect subject to any variation of the implied trusts aforesaid contained in the instrument creating the trust.

(3) Nothing in this section operates to validate any trust which would, if contained in the instrument creating the trust, be liable to be set aside.

C. Forfeiture

The courts have often had to determine whether or not a particular event has effected a forfeiture. When the question arises upon an express trust, the result depends, of course, upon a construction of the language of the forfeiture provisions, which may or may not differ materially from the Trustee Act 1925, s. 33. It will be seen that in some of the cases it is to the advantage of the life tenant to establish that there was a forfeiture; sometimes not.

In **Re Detmold** (1889) 40 ChD 585, under a marriage settlement of the settlor's own property, the income was payable to himself "during his life, or till he shall become bankrupt, or shall . . . suffer something whereby [the income], or some part thereof, would . . . by operation or process of law, if belonging absolutely to him, become vested in or payable to some other person", and after the determination of the trust in favour of the settlor, upon trust to pay the income to his wife. In July 1888 an order was made appointing a judgment creditor of the settlor to be receiver of the income; and in September 1888 the settlor was adjudicated bankrupt.

NORTH J, in holding that the wife was entitled to the income, said at 588:

"The limitation of the life interest to the settlor was validly determined by the fact that, in consequence of the order appointing the receiver, he ceased to be entitled to receive the income. This took place before the bankruptcy, and, therefore, the forfeiture is valid against the trustee in bankruptcy."

In **Re Balfour's Settlement** [1938] Ch 928, [1938] 3 All ER 259, the income of a settled fund was payable to Nigel Balfour for life or until he should "do or suffer something whereby the same or some part thereof would through his act or default or by operation or process of law or otherwise if belonging absolutely to him become vested in or payable to some other person", with a discretionary trust over. During 1933 to 1936 the sole trustee advanced to him part of the capital at his request and in breach of trust. Balfour was then adjudicated bankrupt. FARWELL J held that his interest had determined, because the trustees had asserted their right to impound the income prior to the date of the bankruptcy; and therefore nothing passed to the trustee in bankruptcy.[9]

In **Re Baring's Settlement Trusts** [1940] Ch 737, [1940] 3 All ER 20, under a family settlement a wife had a protected life interest with the income payable to her "until some event should happen whereby the income . . . would become . . . payable to . . . some other person", with a discretionary trust over. Her husband obtained a sequestration order against her property on her failure to obey a court order to return her infant children to the jurisdiction of the court. When she eventually returned with the children, the question arose whether the life interest was forfeited. MORTON J held that it was, although the sequestration order was only temporary. He said at 753, at 30 that the settlor "intended that there should be a continuous benefit to the beneficiaries so that either the tenant for life should be in a position to have the income or the discretionary trust should arise".

In **Re Dennis's Settlement Trusts** [1942] Ch 283, [1942] 1 All ER 520,[10] under a family settlement of 1923 the settlor's son, then an infant, was given a protected life interest "until any act or event should happen whereby the income would . . . become vested in . . . some other person." On his attaining twenty-one in 1935, a supplemental deed was executed providing that for the next six years the trustees should pay to him only part of the income and accumulate the balance for him. FARWELL J held that this rearrangement caused a forfeiture.

In **Re Smith's Will Trusts** (1981) 131 NLJ 292, a trustee bank held the residue of a testator's estate on trusts, inter alia, (a) to pay to the testator's daughter "for her own absolute use and benefit" up to £10,000, if she so requested, and (b) to hold the income of the residue and of the balance, after any payments to her under (a), on protective trusts for her life. In 1976 she requested and received £10,000 for the purchase of a house. MEGARRY V-C held that the life interest of the daughter determined under Trustee Act 1925, s. 33 (1) (i). When the payment was made, she was "deprived of the right to receive part of the income" from the residue "directed to be held on protective trusts".

In **Gibbon v Mitchell** [1990] 1 WLR 1304, [1990] 3 All ER 338, Mr Gibbon purported to surrender his protected life interest in favour of his two children, with a view to reducing the effect of inheritance tax. He was not advised that the effect of the deed would be to forfeit his life interest and to bring into operation the discretionary trusts: under section 33, unless an order of the court was first obtained under the Variation of Trusts Act 1958 (p. 781 post),

---

9 Cf. *Re Brewer's Settlement* [1896] 2 Ch 503, where the bankruptcy took place before the trustees exercised their right.
10 (1942) 58 LQR 312 (R.E.M.).

which would remove the protection annexed to the life interest. MILLETT J ordered that the deed should be set aside for mistake.

In **Re Tancred's Settlement** [1903] 1 Ch 715 at 723, Sir Seymer Tancred was entitled under a deed of 1891 to income for life or "until he should dispose or attempt to dispose of the ... income ... or do something whereby the income ... would become payable to or vested in some other person". In 1896 he assigned his life interest to the trustees of his marriage settlement, of which he was tenant for life and solely entitled to the income, and appointed them his attorneys to receive the income; and authorised them to charge their expenses to the fund. BUCKLEY J held that there was no forfeiture.

In **Re Westby's Settlement** [1950] Ch 296, [1950] 1 All ER 479, the Court of Appeal held that there was no forfeiture where the tenant for life under a protective trust was of unsound mind, and fees became payable out of the estate to the Supreme Court Funds under section 148 (3) of the Lunacy Act 1890.[11]

In **Re Oppenheim's Will Trusts** [1950] Ch 633, [1950] 2 All ER 86, HARMAN J, in holding that, where a tenant for life under a protective trust was certified as a person of unsound mind, the appointment of a receiver did not effect a forfeiture, said at 636, at 88:

"I think that a man who has a statutory agent, as this man has, can give by his agent a personal discharge no less than ... if he were on the top of Mount Everest, his banker could give a personal discharge on his behalf. It seems to me also that the forfeiture was not intended to operate in a case of this kind where no one else will be entitled to the benefit of the income in the event which has happened. It was intended to prevent the income from getting into other hands. That does not occur in the present case."

In **Re Longman** [1955] 1 WLR 197, [1955] 1 All ER 455, a son was entitled to the income from a trust fund subject to a forfeiture "if he should commit any act whereby any part of the income ... became vested in or payable to any other person". In 1953 he authorised his trustees to pay money to his creditors "from the dividend due to me in July next from [a certain company]". The company, however, did not declare a dividend. DANCKWERTS J held that this prevented a forfeiture and said at 199, at 456:

"It seems to me that the authorities given by the son were completely nugatory, and that there was nothing on which they could operate and they never did operate on anything."

---

11 See now Mental Health Act 1983, s. 106 (6).

In **Re Mair** [1935] Ch 562, FARWELL J held that an order made under section 57 of the Trustee Act 1925,[12] authorising the trustees to raise money to enable a tenant for life under a protective trust to "pay certain pressing liabilities" did not effect a forfeiture. He said at 565:

"If and when the Court sanctions an arrangement or transaction under s. 57, it must be taken to have done it as though the power which is being put into operation had been inserted in the trust instrument as an overriding power . . . The forfeiture clause remains attached to the income which is payable to the tenant for life from time to time . . .

It must, however, be remembered that if a scheme sanctioned by the court involves, as in *Re Salting* [1932] 2 Ch 57, an agreement or covenant by the tenant for life to pay premiums on policies or other like payments with a proviso that if they are not duly paid the trustees are to pay them out of income, the failure to pay by the tenant for life will create a forfeiture, since it will be that act or omission of the tenant for life that creates the forfeiture and not the exercise by the Court of its overriding power."

Hanbury & Martin. *Modern Equity* (14th edn), pp. 196–197

"It is not clear whether a forfeiture is effected when an order is made in the Family Division of the High Court which alters a protected life interest under a marriage settlement.[13] In *Re Richardson's Will Trusts*,[14] the court ordered that the principal beneficiary should charge his interest with an annual payment of £50 in favour of his divorced wife. The charge was held to create a forfeiture. On the other hand, in *General Accident Fire and Life Assurance Corpn Ltd v IRC*[15] an order of the Divorce Court diverting part of the income from the life tenant in favour of a former wife was held not to effect a forfeiture.

These cases are distinguishable on a narrow ground of construction of section 33.[16] But the broader ground of the decision, that this situation has no relevance to the real purpose of protective trusts, would seem to apply to the charge in *Re Richardson's Will Trusts* as much as to the diversion of part of the income in the *General Accident* case. It is submitted that the principle of the *General Accident* case is sound. As Donovan LJ said,[17] '. . . the section is intended as a protection to spendthrift or improvident or weak life tenants. But it can give . . . no protection against the effect of a court order such as was made here. Furthermore, if such an order involves a forfeiture much injustice could be

---

12 See p. 782, post.
13 Which the court has power to do under Matrimonial Causes Act 1973, s. 24 (1), p. 787, post.
14 [1958] Ch 504, [1958] 1 All ER 538; *Edmonds v Edmonds* [1965] 1 WLR 58, [1965] 1 All ER 379n. *Re Richardson* illustrates the advantage of establishing a series of protective trusts, "one set until the beneficiary is twenty-five, another from twenty-five to thirty-five, a third from thirty-five to forty-five, and another for the rest of his life." A forfeiture of, or a charge upon, the principal beneficiary's interest in one of the trusts would not affect his interest in subsequent trusts. He would get a fresh start. (1958) 74 L.Q.R. 182 (R.E.M.).
15 [1963] 1 WLR 1207, [1963] 3 All ER 259.
16 Ibid., see DONOVAN LJ at 1217, at 262 and RUSSELL LJ at 1221, at 264; (1963) 27 Conv (NS) 517 (F.R. Crane).
17 [1963] 1 WLR 1207 at 1218, [1963] 3 All ER 259 at 262.

done.' Perhaps the problem can be rationalised with the cases on section 57 by saying with Russell LJ, who made clear, however, that he did not rest his decision on this approach: 'the settlement throughout was potentially subject in all its trusts to such an order as was made.[18] *Re Richardson's Will Trusts* was not mentioned; but an earlier case on the Matrimonial Causes Act 1859 in favour of forfeiture, *Re Carew*,[19] was overruled. It is tempting to say that *Re Richardson's Will Trusts* is wrong; but it should be noted that in that case, as in *Re Carew*, the decision in favour of forfeiture forwarded the broad policy of section 33; for the forfeiture in those cases allowed the discretionary trusts to operate when otherwise the trustee in bankruptcy would have claimed the interest.''

(1958) 74 LQR 184 (R.E.M.)

"This sequence of events points a moral for draftsmen. Hitherto the normal course of drafting has been to give a life interest simply 'on protective trusts', with or without variations. The result is that a single mistaken act by the beneficiary may deprive him of his determinable life interest and reduce him for the rest of his life to the status of merely one of the beneficiaries of a discretionary trust. *Re Richardson* suggests that there may be advantages in setting up a series of protective trusts, e.g., one set until the beneficiary is twenty-five, another from twenty-five to thirty-five, a third from thirty-five to forty-five, and another for the rest of his life. The result would be that a youthful indiscretion at say, twenty-two, would not irretrievably condemn the beneficiary to the mere hopes of a beneficiary under a discretionary trust, dependent upon the exercise of the trustees' discretion, but would give him a fresh start when he was twenty-five. Again, a bankruptcy at the age of thirty would not per se mean that when he was twice that age he would still have not an income as of right, but a mere hope of a well-exercised discretion. Indeed, instead of relating the stages to the age of the beneficiary, they might be related to a period of time (e.g. five years) after the occurrence of any event which had made the initial trust pass from Stage 1 to Stage 2. England lacks the device of the spendthrift trust in the American sense, but it is far from clear that the fullest possible use is being made of the existing machinery of protective and discretionary trusts.''

D. The Effect of Forfeiture

In **Re Gourju's Will Trusts** [1943] Ch 24, [1942] 2 All ER 605, Mrs. Gourju was a protected life tenant under her husband's will. She resided at Nice. That part of France was occupied by the Germans in June, 1940. By the Trading with the Enemy Act 1939 and Orders made thereunder,[20] she became disentitled to

---

18   Ibid., at 1222, at 266.
19   (1910) 103 LT 658.
20   Trading With the Enemy (Custodian) Order 1939 (S.R. & O. 1939 No. 1198). Later Orders contained a proviso that vesting in the Custodian of Enemy Property should not take place if it would cause a forfeiture.

receive the income of the fund, and her protected life interest was forfeited. The Custodian of Enemy Property could not claim the income, for he had no better claim than Mrs. Gourju. The discretionary trusts came into effect. The trustees wished to accumulate the income and pay it at the end of the war to Mrs. Gourju. SIMONDS J held that they could not do so. Their duty was to pay to one or more of the members of the discretionary class.

Underhill and Hayton: *Law Relating to Trusts and Trustees* (15th edn) p. 187

"Another point that not infrequently arises is whether, under a discretionary trust (such as the statutory trust above set forth) *where the settlor is a third party*, and the defeasible life interest has been forfeited either by bankruptcy or alienation (voluntary or involuntary), the trustees can, *under the discretion* vested in them, continue to pay the income to the person whose life interest has determined. Obviously the object of such trusts is to enable this to be done if it can be. The authorities are, however, against the right of the trustees to do this,[1] on the ground apparently that the life tenant, being bound to hand over to his creditor or assignee whatever his interest in the income may be, is none the less bound with regard to such part of the income as may be paid to him by the trustees in the exercise of their discretion; and that they, having notice of this equity, are equally bound not to pay him. This may seem to be a reductio ad absurdum, since the trustees could not under any circumstances pay any part of the income to the creditor or assignee,[2] so that it is difficult to see how the latter could suffer by the payment being made to the life tenant himself, or what claim he could have upon the trustees. Nevertheless, trustees under such circumstances have been made liable to the creditor or assignee,[3] although, curiously enough, it is well settled that they are at liberty to *expend* the income for his benefit.[4] In one case it was held that the trustees might apply such part as they thought fit of the income for the benefit of the person whose life interest had determined without reference to any debt which such person might owe to the trust estate.[5] This case is distinct from that which has been more frequently before the courts where the contest is between the tenant of a protected life interest and his own assignee. The law is, therefore, in an anomalous and unsatisfactory state; and it is not considered that it has been in any way altered by the introduction by section 33 of the Trustee Act 1925[6] of the statutory 'protective trusts'.

---

1 *Re Coleman* (1888) 39 ChD 443; *Re Neil* (1890) 62 LT 649, explained by STIRLING LJ in *Re Fitzgerald* [1904] 1 Ch 573 at 593.
2 *Re Bullock* (1891) 64 LT 736; *Train v Clapperton* [1908] AC 342; *Re Laye* [1913] 1 Ch 298; *Re Hamilton* (1921) 124 LT 737. But cf. *Lord v Bunn* (1843) 2 Y & C Ch Cas 98, which seems contra at first sight, but really turned on a question of construction.
3 *Re Coleman*, supra; *Re Neil*, supra, explained by STIRLING LJ in *Re Fitzgerald*, supra.
4 *Re Bullock*, supra and cf. *Re Coleman*, supra; and *Re Neil*, supra. But see *Re Ashby* [1892] 1 QB 872, where VAUGHAN WILLIAMS J thought that the bankrupt might be liable to account for sums paid to him, though, perhaps, just for the surplus above that needed for his mere support. See also *Re Allen-Meyrick's Will Trusts* [1966] 1 WLR 499 at 503, [1966] 1 All ER 740 at 743.
5 *Re Eiser's Will Trusts* [1937] 1 All ER 244.
6 See p. 171, ante.

It needs scarcely be said that, until they have notice of an act amounting to forfeiture, the trustees are justified in paying the income to the first beneficiary."[7]

III. Attempts to Deprive Creditors of the Settlor[8]

We discussed in Section II the extent to which it was possible to give to a person an interest which would be kept from his creditors on his bankruptcy. We now consider the extent to which creditors can claim property which the debtor has given away in the form of a transaction at an undervalue.

A. Transactions Defrauding Creditors

INSOLVENCY ACT 1986

423. Transactions defrauding creditors.[9] — (1) This section relates to transactions entered into at an undervalue; and a person enters into such a transaction with another person[10] if —

(*a*) he makes a gift to the other person or he otherwise enters into a transaction with the other on terms that provide for him to receive no consideration;

(*b*) he enters into a transaction with the other in consideration of marriage;[11] or

(*c*) he enters into a transaction with the other for a consideration the value of which, in money or money's worth, is significantly less than the value, in money or money's worth, of the consideration provided by himself.[12]

(2) Where a person has entered into such a transaction, the court may, if satisfied under the next subsection, make such order as it thinks fit[13] for —

(*a*) restoring the position to what it would have been if the transaction had not been entered into, and

---

7 *Re Long* [1901] WN 166.

8 H & M, pp. 344–352; K & S, pp. 158–165; P & M, pp. 175–181; Pettit, pp. 208–211; Riddall, pp. 49–50; Snell, pp. 128–135; Underhill, pp. 264–267; Muir Hunter on *Personal Insolvency* 3-292–3-301, 3-466–3-470; Insolvency Law and Practice: Report of the Review Committee 1982 (Cmnd. 8558), chap. 28.

9 Replacing LPA 1925, s. 172, which replaced 13 Eliz I, c. 5.

10 A person may be an individual or a corporate body: Insolvency Act 1986, s. 207.

11 In *Re Densham* [1975] 1 WLR 1519 at 1527, [1975] 3 All ER 726 at 734, GOFF J required three tests to be satisfied: "(1) it must be made on the occasion of the marriage; (2) it must be conditional only to take effect on the marriage taking place; (3) it must be made by a person for the purpose of or with a view to encouraging or facilitating the marriage." Only (1) was satisfied in *Re Densham*. See *IRC v Lord Rennell* [1964] AC 173 at 202, 208, [1963] 1 All ER 803 at 813, 816.

12 *Agricultural Mortgage Corpn plc v Woodward* [1995] 1 EGLR 1 (creation of tenancy for wife set aside, even though it was at full value, since wife achieved benefits greater than those conferred by the tenancy itself). Cf. *Menzies v National Bank of Kuwait SAK* [1994] BCC 119 (letter giving instructions as to allocation of money due under a contract not a transaction at an undervalue as company did not provide any consideration in giving the instructions).

13 Section 425 (1) sets out specific orders which the court may make "without prejudice to the generality of section 423".

(*b*) protecting the interests of persons who are victims of the transaction.[14]

(3) In the case of a person entering into such a transaction, an order shall only be made if the court is satisfied that it was entered into by him for the purpose[15] —

(*a*) of putting assets beyond the reach of a person who is making, or may at some time make, a claim against him, or

(*b*) of otherwise prejudicing the interests of such a person in relation to the claim which he is making or may make ...

(5) In relation to a transaction at an undervalue, references here and below to a victim of the transaction are to a person who is, or is capable of being, prejudiced by it; and in the following two sections the person entering into the transaction is referred to as "the debtor".

424. Those who may apply for an order under s. 423. — (1) An application for an order under section 423 shall not be made in relation to a transaction except —

(*a*) in a case where the debtor has been adjudged bankrupt or is a body corporate which is being wound up or in relation to which an administration order is in force, by the official receiver, by the trustee of the bankrupt's estate or the liquidator or administrator of the body corporate or (with the leave of the court) by a victim of the transaction ...

(*c*) in any other case, by a victim of the transaction.

(2) An application made under any of the paragraphs of subsection (1) is to be treated as made on behalf of every victim of the transaction.

425. Provision which may be made by order under s. 423. — (2) An order under section 423 may affect the property of, or impose any obligation on, any person whether or not he is the person with whom the debtor entered into the transaction; but such an order —

(*a*) shall not prejudice any interest in property which was acquired from a person other than the debtor and was acquired in good faith, for value and without notice[16] of the relevant circumstances, or prejudice any interest deriving from such an interest, and

(*b*) shall not require a person who received a benefit from the transaction in good faith, for value and without notice of the relevant circumstances to pay any sum unless he was a party to the transaction.

(3) For the purposes of this section the relevant circumstances in relation to a transaction are the circumstances by virtue of which an order under section 423 may be made in respect of the transaction.

---

14 See *Chohan v Saggar* [1994] BCC 134.

15 In *Royscott Spa Leasing v Lovett* [1994] NPC 146, CA assumed, without deciding, that it was enough for the purpose to be "substantial" rather than "dominant". It did not have to be a "sole" purpose. See also *Chohan v Saggar* [1992] BCC 306 at 323; *Midland Bank plc v Wyatt* [1995] 3 FCR 11; *Pinewood Joinery v Starelm Properties Ltd* [1994] BCC 569 (dominant purpose not to put hostel beyond reach of creditors, but to gain tax advantage successfully negotiated with Inspector of Taxes).

16 Notice will include constructive notice: cf. *Lloyds Bank Ltd v Marcan* [1973] 1 WLR 339 at 345, [1973] 2 All ER 359 at 369 per PENNYCUICK V-C (decided under LPA 1925, s. 172).

B. Bankruptcy Provisions

The bankruptcy provisions operate in harmony with those regarding transactions at an undervalue independent of bankruptcy. They are similar but not identical. In particular, section 339 only applies where there is a bankruptcy and on the application of the trustee in bankruptcy; and when the transaction has occurred not more than five years before bankruptcy; there is no need to establish intent. Section 423, however, applies irrespective of bankruptcy, on the application of any person prejudiced; there is no statutory time limit, and intent must be established.[17]

INSOLVENCY ACT 1986

339. Transactions at an undervalue.[18] — (1) Subject as follows in this section and sections 341 and 342, where an individual is adjudged bankrupt and he has at a relevant time (defined in section 341) entered into a transaction with any person at an undervalue, the trustee of the bankrupt's estate may apply to the court for an order under this section.

(2) The court shall, on such an application, make such order as it thinks fit[19] for restoring the position to what it would have been if that individual had not entered into that transaction.

(3) For the purposes of this section and sections 341 and 342, an individual enters into a transaction with a person at an undervalue if —

(a) he makes a gift to that person or he otherwise enters into a transaction with that person on terms that provide for him to receive no consideration,

(b) he enters into a transaction with that person in consideration of marriage, or

(c) he enters into a transaction with that person for a consideration the value of which, in money or money's worth, is significantly less than the value, in money or money's worth, of the consideration provided by the individual.[20]

341. "Relevant time" under ss. 339, 340.[1] — (1) Subject as follows, the time at which an individual enters into a transaction at an undervalue . . . is a relevant time if the transaction is entered into or the preference given —

(a) in the case of a transaction at an undervalue at a time in the period of 5 years ending with the day of the presentation of the bankruptcy petition on which the individual is adjudged bankrupt . . .

(2) Where an individual enters into a transaction at an undervalue . . . at a time mentioned in paragraph (a) . . . of subsection (1) (not being, in the case of a transaction at an undervalue, a time less than 2 years before the end of the period mentioned in paragraph (a)), that time is not a relevant time for the purposes of section 339 . . . unless the individual —

---

17 On the position with respect to land, see (1987) 84 LSG 2257–2258; (1988) 85 LSG No 7, p. 17 (I. Storey); No 34, p. 3.

18 Replacing Bankruptcy Act 1914, s.42. For similar provisions in the case of corporate insolvency, see ss. 239–241; *Re MC Bacon Ltd* [1990] BCLC 324; *Re Paramount Airways Ltd* [1993] Ch 223, [1992] 3 All ER 1 (the section has extra-territorial effect).

19 Section 342 (1) sets out specific orders which the court may make "without prejuduce to the generality of 339(2)."

20 *Re Kumar* [1993] 1 WLR 224, [1993] 2 All ER 700 (property adjustment order on divorce set aside); cf *Re Abbott* [1983] Ch 45, [1982] 3 All ER 181.

1 Section 340 deals with preferences.

(*a*) is insolvent at that time, or

(*b*) becomes insolvent in consequence of the transaction ... but the requirements of this subsection are presumed to be satisfied, unless the contrary is shown, in relation to any transaction at an undervalue which is entered into by an individual with a person who is an associate of his (otherwise than by reason only of being his employee).

(3) For the purposes of subsection (2), an individual is insolvent if —

(*a*) he is unable to pay his debts as they fall due, or

(*b*) the value of his assets is less than the amount of his liabilities, taking into account his contingent and prospective liabilities.

342. Orders under ss. 339, 340. — (2) An order under section 339 or 340 may affect the property of, or impose any obligation on, any person whether or not he is the person with whom the individual in question entered into the transaction ... but such an order —

(*a*) shall not prejudice any interest in property which was acquired from a person other than that individual and was acquired in good faith and for value, or prejudice any interest deriving from such an interest, and

(*b*) shall not require a person who received a benefit from the transaction ... in good faith and for value to pay a sum to the trustee of the bankrupt's estate, except where he was a party to the transaction ...

(2A)[2] Where a person has acquired an interest in property from a person other than the individual in question, or has received a benefit from the transaction or preference, and at the time of that acquisition or receipt —

(*a*) he had notice of the relevant surrounding circumstances and of the relevant proceedings, or

(*b*) he was an associate of, or was connected with, either the individual in question or the person with whom that individual entered into the transaction or to whom that individual gave the preference,

then, unless the contrary is shown, it shall be presumed for the purposes of paragraph (a) or (as the case may be) paragraph (b) of subsection (2) that the interest was acquired or the benefit was received otherwise than in good faith.

(4)[2] For the purposes of subsection (2A)(a), the relevant surrounding circumstances are (as the case may require) —

(*a*) the fact that the individual in question entered into the transaction at an undervalue; or

(*b*) the circumstances which amounted to the giving of the preference by the individual in question.

(5)[2] For the purposes of subsection (2A)(a), a person has notice of the relevant proceedings if he has notice —

(*a*) of the fact that the petition on which the individual in question is adjudged bankrupt has been presented; or

(*b*) of the fact that the individual in question has been adjudged bankrupt.

---

2 As inserted by Insolvency (No 2) Act 1994, s. 2, on which see Current Law Statutes, annotated by P.H. Kenny; (1995) LSG 92/35, p. 31 (C. Maggs).

R.T.C. LIBRARY, LETTERKENNY

C. Meaning of Undervalue

In **Re MC Bacon Ltd** [1990] BCLC 324, the question arose whether the granting of a debenture by a company (which had diversified from traditional bacon into the supply of pre-packaged manufactured products such as gammon steaks, gammon joints and rashered bacon) in favour of a bank to secure an overdraft was a transaction at an undervalue under section 238 (6) of the Insolvency Act 1986 (which is similar to section 423, p. 178 ante). In holding that it was not at an undervalue, MILLETT J said at 340:[3]

"The granting of the debenture was not a gift, nor was it without consideration. The consideration consisted of the bank's forbearance from calling in the overdraft and its honouring of cheques and making of fresh advances to the company during the continuance of the facility. The applicant relies therefore on para (*b*).[3a]

To come within that paragraph the transaction must be (i) entered into by the company; (ii) for a consideration; (iii) the value of which measured in money or money's worth; (iv) is significantly less than the value; (v) also measured in money or money's worth; (vi) of the consideration provided by the company. It requires a comparison to be made between the value obtained by the company for the transaction and the value of consideration provided by the company. Both values must be measurable in money or money's worth and both must be considered from the company's point of view.

In my judgment, the applicant's claim to characterise the granting of the bank's debenture as a transaction at an undervalue is misconceived. The mere creation of a security over a company's assets does not deplete them and does not come within the paragraph. By charging its assets the company appropriates them to meet the liabilities due to the secured creditor and adversely affects the rights of other creditors in the event of insolvency. But it does not deplete its assets or diminish their value. It retains the right to redeem and the right to sell or remortgage the charged assets. All it loses is the ability to apply the proceeds otherwise than in satisfaction of the secured debt. That is not something capable of valuation in monetary terms and is not customarily disposed of for value.

In the present case the company did not suffer that loss by reason of the grant of the debenture. Once the bank had demanded a debenture the company could not have sold or charged its assets without applying the proceeds in reduction of the overdraft; had it attempted to do so, the bank would at once have called in the overdraft. By granting the debenture the company parted with nothing of value, and the value of the consideration which it received in return was incapable of being measured in money or money's worth.

Counsel for the applicant (Mr Vos) submitted that the consideration which the company received was, with hindsight, of no value. It merely gained time and with it the opportunity to lose more money. But he could not and did not claim that the company ought to have received a fee or other capital sum in return for the debenture. That gives the game away. The applicant's real

---

3 This passage was cited with approval by CA in *Menzies v National Bank of Kuwait* SAK [1994] BCC 119 at 128–129, per BALCOMBE LJ; and in *Agricultural Mortgage Corpn plc v Woodward* [1995] 1 EGLR 1 at 3, per Sir Christopher SLADE.
3a This is para. (c) in s. 423.

complaint is not that the company entered into the transaction at an undervalue but that it entered into it at all.''

QUESTION

The Restatement of Trusts § 152 provides: "(1) Except as stated in § 156 [where the settlor is a beneficiary] and 157 [particular classes of claimants], if by the terms of a trust the beneficiary is entitled to the income from the trust property for life or for a term of years and it is provided that his interest shall not be transferable by him and shall not be subject to the claims of his creditors, the restraint on the voluntary and involuntary transfer of his right to the income accruing during his life is valid. (2) A trust in which by the terms of the trust or by statute a valid restraint on the voluntary and involuntary transfer of the interest of the beneficiary is imposed is a spendthrift trust."

In some American jurisdictions, statutes provide that only that part of a beneficiary's interest which is required for his education and support shall be protected against his creditors.

Consider the differences between the American spendthrift trusts and the English protective trust developments. Would you favour the introduction of spendthrift trusts in England? (Scott: *Trusts* (4th edn), § 151; *Cases on Trusts* (5th edn), p. 381).

6. Resulting Trusts[1]

I. General

This chapter will deal with a miscellaneous group of situations in which the settlor has transferred property to other persons, but the beneficial interest returns, or "results" to the settlor. It was at one time common to say that trusts arose as a result of the presumed or implied intention of the settlor. But that explanation is clearly inadequate in cases, such as *Vandervell v IRC*[2] where the existence of a resulting trust imposed a serious fiscal burden on the grantor. That was the last thing he intended.

The modern classification divides resulting trusts into "automatic" and "presumed" resulting trusts.[3] The first category is that in which property has been conveyed to trustees, and the beneficial interest has not been wholly disposed of. The trustees cannot enjoy it, and inevitably a resulting trust arises in favour of the settlor. The second category is that in which the conveyance is not made expressly upon trust; but, by reason of certain presumptions established by the law, the legal owner is required to hold the property upon trust for the settlor.

The presumptions are always rebuttable by evidence, and they may indeed give way to contrary, stronger presumptions, such as the presumption of advancement in favour of a person to whom the donor stood *in loco parentis*. The presumptions were developed in earlier centuries; they are not always consistent with modern ideas of property ownership, and are easily displaced. As Lord UPJOHN said in *Vandervell v IRC*:[4] "In reality the so-called presumption of a resulting trust is no more than a long-stop to provide the answer where the relevant facts and circumstances fail to reach a solution". There is no difference between an "automatic" and a "presumed" resulting trust once the trust has been established. The merit of the classification is that it provides

---

1 H & M, pp. 233–259; K & S, pp. 189–214; P & M, pp. 181–208; Pettit, pp. 128–156; Riddall, pp. 191–207; Snell, pp. 175–190; Underhill, pp. 301–304.
2 [1967] 2 AC 291, [1967] 1 All ER 1; p. 185, post.
3 See *Re Vandervell's Trusts (No 2)* [1974] Ch 269 at 294, [1974] 1 All ER 47 at 68; p. 187, post.
4 [1967] 2 AC 291 at 312, 313, [1967] 1 All ER 1 at 8.

an explanation for the existence of a resulting trust where there is no presumption, or evidence of intention to support it.

Finally, it should be noted that resulting trusts overlap with constructive trusts, in that they are imposed in some cases in order to achieve a just result. Thus, if a person obtains legal title to property by fraud, he will be compelled to hold it on trust for the transferor;[5] this may be regarded as a constructive trust or a resulting trust. As Lord DENNING MR said in *Hussey v Palmer:*[6] "Although the plaintiff alleged that there was a resulting trust, I should have thought that the trust in this case, if there was one, was more in the nature of a constructive trust; but this is more a matter of words than anything else. The two run together."[7]

II. Conveyance to Trustees

A. No Declaration of Trust

VANDERVELL v INLAND REVENUE COMMISSIONERS
[1967] 2 AC 291, [1967] 1 All ER 1 (HL, Lords REID, PEARCE, UPJOHN, DONOVAN and WILBERFORCE)

RE VANDERVELL'S TRUSTS (No 2)
[1974] Ch 269, [1974] 3 All ER 205 (CA, Lord DENNING MR, STEPHENSON and LAWTON LJJ)

Guy Anthony Vandervell decided to make a gift of money to the Royal College of Surgeons for the purpose of founding a Chair of Pharmacology. His plan was to arrange the transfer to the College of a block of shares in Vandervell Products Ltd., which were held by the National Provincial Bank as his nominee; to provide the bulk of the endowment by declaring dividends on those shares; and to enable Vandervell Trustees Ltd. (a private trustee company which acted as trustee for the Vandervell children's trust, among other private trusts) to re-purchase the shares for £5,000. In this way the dividends would not be taxable in the hands of the charity; and the shares would return after the payment of the dividends to the family's control.

The shares were transferred in 1958, and the dividends amounting to £266,000 gross were declared on the shares. But no express provision was made to declare the trusts on which Vandervell Trustees Ltd. held the option. If the option was held on trust for Vandervell, the settlor, he would be liable to pay surtax upon the whole of the dividends paid to the College, because he had failed to divest himself absolutely of all interest in the property within the Income Tax Act 1952, s. 415 (2).[8]

On receiving an assessment to surtax, Vandervell arranged, in October 1961, for Vandervell Trustees Ltd. to exercise the option. They did so, using £5,000

---

5 See p. 292, n. 16, post.
6 [1972] 1 WLR 1286 at 1289, [1972] 3 All ER 744 at 747. See pp. 293 et seq., post.
7 See also *Passee v Passee* [1988] 1 FLR 263 at 269, where NICHOLLS LJ suggested that a trust arising from a contribution to the acquisition of a matrimonial home could be called implied, constructive or resulting, the latter being not inappropriate.
8 Now ICTA 1988, s. 685, p. 556, post.

from the children's settlement for the purchase. The shares were transferred. Vandervell Trustees Ltd. treated them as being held on trust for the children's settlement, and paid to that settlement all dividends received during 1961–1965.

Vandervell was then assessed to surtax on these dividends, on the ground that the shares were, like the option, held on resulting trust for him. At last, on January 19, 1965, he executed a deed transferring to the trusts of the children's settlement any interest which he might have in the shares. He died in March 1967.

Before the assessment for 1961–1965 was settled, Vandervell's executors started an action against the trustee company, claiming that the dividends belonged to Vandervell. The Revenue asked to be joined as a party, but, on objection by the trustee company, was excluded: *Re Vandervell's Trusts* [1971] AC 912, [1970] 3 All ER 16. The executors succeeded before MEGARRY J, but failed in the Court of Appeal.

In the first of the cases, **Vandervell v IRC** [1967] 2 AC 291, [1967] 1 All ER 1[9] the House of Lords, dealing with the position prior to the exercise of the option, examined three solutions: that the option was held on trust for the children's settlement; that Vandervell Trustees Ltd. held it beneficially; and that it was held on resulting trust for Vandervell. The third solution was chosen.

LORD WILBERFORCE: On these findings it was, in my opinion, at once clear that the appellant's contention that the option became subject to the trusts of the children's settlement of 1949 must fail, for the reason that it was not the intention of the settlor, or of his plenipotentiary, Mr. Robins, at the time the option was exercised that this should be so. I need not elaborate this point since I understand that there is no disagreement about it. This was the appellant's main (if not the sole) contention before the special commissioners and Plowman J and it remained his first contention on this appeal. The alternative which ... is expressed in the printed case as being that the option was held by the trustee company in equity as well as in law as the absolute owner thereof for the purposes of its business, is, of course, one which the appellant is entitled to put forward, as a contention of law, at any stage, provided that it is consistent with the facts as found by the special commissioners. It is on that contention that the appellant ultimately fell back. For my part, I cannot find that it is so consistent ...

Correspondingly, the evidence points clearly away from any conclusion that the trustee company held beneficially, or for the purpose of its business. It had no business, no function, except as a trustee; no assets, except as a trustee. The £5,000 to be paid if the option was to be exercised was, as a term of the arrangement between Mr. Vandervell and the college, part of the £150,000 benefaction; how could that come from the company's own resources? To extract from the findings a conclusion that the trustee company was to hold free from any trust but possibly subject to some understanding or gentleman's agreement seems to me, rather than even a benevolent interpretation of the evidence, a reconstruction of it. I may add that had this contention been put forward at the hearing before the special commissioners the Revenue might

---

9 (1964) 24 CLJ 19 (G.H. Jones); (1967) 31 Conv (NS) 175 (S.M. Spencer); (1967) 30 MLR 461 (N. Strauss).

well have been tempted to explore, by cross-examination, the real control of the trustee company and to argue that the case came within section 415 (2) of the Income Tax Act 1952.

If, then, as I think, both the first two alternatives fail, there remains only the third, which, to my mind, corresponds exactly with Mr. Robins' intentions, namely, that the option was held by the trustee company on trusts which were undefined, or in the air.

As to the consequences, there has been some difference and possibly lack of clarity below. The special commissioners held that the initially undefined trusts could be defined later in a way which might benefit the appellant, and they found the benefit to the appellant in this circumstance. The Court of Appeal, starting from the fact that the trustee company took the option as a volunteer, thought that this was a case where the presumption of a resulting trust arose and was not displaced. For my part, I prefer a slightly different and simpler approach. The transaction has been investigated on the evidence of the settlor and his agent and the facts have been found. There is no need, or room, as I see it, to invoke a presumption. The conclusion, on the facts found, is simply that the option was vested in the trustee company as a trustee on trusts, not defined at the time, possibly to be defined later. But the equitable, or beneficial interest, cannot remain in the air: the consequence in law must be that it remains in the settlor. There is no need to consider some of the more refined intellectualities of the doctrine of resulting trust, nor to speculate whether, in possible circumstances, the shares might be applicable for Mr. Vandervell's benefit: he had, as the direct result of the option and of the failure to place the beneficial interest in it securely away from him, not divested himself absolutely of the shares which it controlled.

In the later case, **Re Vandervell's Trusts (No 2)** dealing with the position after the exercise of the option and prior to the 1965 deed, the width of the difference of the analysis of MEGARRY J [1974] Ch 269, [1974] 1 All ER 47 and that of the Court of Appeal [1974] Ch 269, 308, [1974] 3 All ER 205 makes it necessary to include extracts from the judgments in both courts. On the executors' failure to recover the money representing the dividends for 1961–1965, the Revenue accepted the situation, and the assessment was withdrawn.

MEGARRY J: It seems to me that the relevant points on resulting trusts may be put in a series of propositions which, so far as not directly supported, appear at least to be consistent with Lord Wilberforce's speech, and reconcilable with the true intent of Lord Upjohn's speech, though it may not be with all his words on a literal reading. The propositions are the broadest of generalisations, and do not purport to cover the exceptions and qualifications that doubtless exist. Nevertheless, these generalisations at least provide a starting point for the classification of a corner of equity which might benefit from some attempt at classification. The propositions are as follows.

(1) If a transaction fails to make any effective disposition of any interest it does nothing. This is so at law and in equity, and has nothing to do with resulting trusts. (2) Normally the mere existence of some unexpressed intention in the breast of the owner of the property does nothing: there must

at least be some expression of that intention before it can effect any result. To yearn is not to transfer. (3) Before any doctrine of resulting trust can come into play, there must at least be some effective transaction which transfers or creates some interest in property. (4) Where A effectually transfers to B (or creates in his favour) any interest in any property, whether legal or equitable, a resulting trust for A may arise in two distinct classes of case. For simplicity, I shall confine my statement to cases in which the transfer or creation is made without B providing any valuable consideration, and where no presumption of advancement can arise; and I shall state the position for transfers without specific mention of the creation of new interests.

(a) The first class of case is where the transfer to B is not made on any trust. If, of course, it appears from the transfer that B is intended to hold on certain trusts, that will be decisive, and the case is not within this category; and similarly if it appears that B is intended to take beneficially. But in other cases there is a rebuttable presumption that B holds on a resulting trust for A. The question is not one of the automatic consequences of a dispositive failure by A, but one of presumption: the property has been carried to B, and from the absence of consideration and any presumption of advancement B is presumed not only to hold the entire interest on trust, but also to hold the beneficial interest for A absolutely. The presumption thus establishes both that B is to take on trust and also what that trust is. Such resulting trusts may be called "presumed resulting trusts".

(b) The second class of case is where the transfer to B is made on trusts which leave some or all of the beneficial interest undisposed of. Here B automatically holds on a resulting trust for A to the extent that the beneficial interest has not been carried to him or others. The resulting trust here does not depend on any intentions or presumptions, but is the automatic consequence of A's failure to dispose of what is vested in him. Since ex hypothesi the transfer is on trust, the resulting trust does not establish the trust but merely carries back to A the beneficial interest that has not been disposed of. Such resulting trusts may be called "automatic resulting trusts".

(5) Where trustees hold property in trust for A, and it is they who, at A's direction, make the transfer to B, similar principles apply, even though on the face of the transaction the transferor appears to be the trustees and not A. If the transfer to B is on trust, B will hold any beneficial interest that has not been effectually disposed of on an automatic resulting trust for the true transferor, A. If the transfer to B is not on trust, there will be a rebuttable presumption that B holds on a resulting trust for A.

I turn to the speech of Lord Wilberforce. At the outset (at 324, at 15) he stated his concurrence with the view taken below, based on Mr. Vandervell's failure to divest himself of all interest in the option, and said that but for the division of opinion in the House he would have thought it sufficient to express his concurrence. He then turned to the facts, and after discussing them at some length, he rejected the contention that the option had become subject to the trusts of the children's settlement. He did this because it was not the intention of Mr. Vandervell or Mr. Robins "at the time the option was exercised that this should be so" (at 327, at 17). I think that the word "exercised" probably should be read as "granted", for there does not seem to have been any evidence before the House as to the intentions which Mr. Vandervell or Mr. Robins had when the option was exercised in 1961; and, I may add, the reference on p. 327, p. 17 to the alternative "numbered 3 above" is plainly not to the Arabic (3) on p. 326 but to the Roman (iii) on p. 325. Lord

Wilberforce held that on the evidence the defendant company held the option not beneficially, subject to some understanding or gentleman's agreement, but on "trusts which were undefined, or in the air" (at 328, at 17). He then referred to the decision of the Court of Appeal as being one where, starting from the fact that the defendant company took the option as a volunteer, the court thought that the presumptions of a resulting trust arose and was not displaced. Lord Wilberforce then said, at 329, at 18: [quoted p. 188, ante].

Now as it seems to me this passage shows Lord Wilberforce as rejecting the application of what I have called the "presumption" class of resulting trust and accepting that the case falls into what I have called the "automatic" class. The grant of the option to the defendant company was, as he had held, on trust. There was thus no need, nor, indeed, any reason to consider whether the option was granted to the defendant company beneficially, or whether there was any presumption of a resulting trust, for that question had been foreclosed by the decision that the defendant company did not take beneficially but held on trust. The only question was whether Mr. Vandervell had ever effectually disposed of the beneficial interest that the defendant company, holding on trust, must hold on a resulting trust for him unless and until an effective trust for some other beneficiary was constituted. This had not been done, and so the defendant company continued to hold on a resulting trust for Mr. Vandervell.

If one bears in mind Lord Wilberforce's speech and the principles that I have tried to state it seems to me that when one looks again at Lord Upjohn's speech it is at least possible to read it as supporting what seems to me to be the right analysis of the case, namely, that the true grantor of the option was Mr. Vandervell, that the option was granted to the defendant company on trust, that no effective trusts were ever declared, and so the defendant company held the option on an automatic resulting trust for Mr. Vandervell. Indeed, that is what I think he was laying down. The question is whether, on the evidence before me, I ought to reach any other conclusion.

... My conclusion is that there is nothing in the evidence before me that warrants any conclusion different from that reached in *Vandervell No. 1*, namely, that the option was granted to the defendant company on trust, but that no effective trusts were ever established and so the defendant company held the option on a resulting trust for Mr. Vandervell.

(3) *Effect of children's £5,000.* The third issue is that of the effect of exercising the option with £5,000 of the moneys held by the defendant company on the trusts of the children's settlement. I shall deal with this main issue before I turn to estoppel and acquiescence. That issue is, in essence, whether trustees who hold an option on trust for X will hold the shares obtained by exercising that option on trust for Y merely because they used Y's money in exercising the option. Authority apart, my answer would be an unhesitating No. The option belongs to X beneficially, and the money merely exercises rights which belong to X. Let the shares be worth £50,000, so that an option to purchase those shares for £5,000 is worth £45,000, and it will at once be seen what a monstrous result would be produced by allowing trustees to divert from their beneficiary X the benefits of what they hold in trust for him merely because they used Y's money instead of X's ...

I need only say that the consequences of recognising any rule to the effect that trustees of more than one trust can in effect transfer the assets of one trust to another trust simply by expending the money of that other trust on improving the assets seems to me to be incalculable ... I merely add that, as I have already mentioned, Mr. Balcombe has throughout accepted what he has pleaded, namely, that the plaintiff's right to the shares is subject to a lien in favour of the children's settlement for the £5,000 paid for exercising the option with interest. This in effect will restore the status quo ante as regards this payment.

[His Lordship then considered the effect of acquiescence and estoppel and concluded that the plaintiff's claim was not affected on either of these grounds.]

In the Court of Appeal [1974] Ch 269, 308, [1974] 3 All ER 205.[10]

LORD DENNING MR:

Summary of the claims
The root cause of all the litigation is the claim of the revenue authorities.

The first period—1958–1961: The revenue authorities claimed that Mr. Vandervell was the beneficial owner of the *option* and was liable for surtax on the dividends declared from 1958 to 1961. This came to £250,000. The claim of the revenue was upheld by the House of Lords: see *Vandervell v IRC* [1967] 2 AC 291, [1967] 1 All ER 1.

The second period—1961–1965: The revenue authorities claimed that Mr. Vandervell was the beneficial owner of the *shares*. They assessed him for surtax in respect of the dividends from October 11, 1961, to January 19, 1965, amounting to £628, 229. The executors dispute the claim of the revenue. They appealed against the assessments. But the appeal was, by agreement, stood over pending the case now before us. The executors have brought this action against the trustee company. They seek a declaration that, during the second period, the dividends belonged to Mr. Vandervell himself, and they ask for an account of them. The revenue asked to be joined as parties to the action. The court did join them (see *Re Vandervell's Trusts* [1970] Ch 44, [1969] 3 All ER 496); but the House of Lords reversed the decision (see [1971] AC 912, [1970] 3 All ER 16). So this action has continued — without the presence of the revenue, whose claim to £628,229 has caused all the trouble.

The third period—1965–1967: The revenue agreed that they have no claim against the estate for this period.

The law for the first period
The first period was considered by the House of Lords in *Vandervell v IRC* [1967] 2 AC 291, [1967] 1 All ER 1. They held, by a majority of three to two, that, during this period, the trustee company held the option as a trustee. The terms of the trust were stated in two ways. Lord Upjohn (with the agreement of Lord Pearce) said that the proper inference was that "the trustee company should hold as trustee upon such trusts as he [Mr. Vandervell] or the trust company should from time to time declare" (see pp. 309, 315, 317, pp. 6, 9, 11). Lord Wilberforce said "that the option was held by the trustee company on trusts" "not at the time determined, but to be decided on a later date" (see pp. 328, 325, pp. 17, 16).

The trouble about the trust so stated was that it was too uncertain. The trusts were not declared or defined with sufficient precision for the trustees to ascertain who the beneficiaries were. It is clear law that a trust (other than a

---

10 (1974) 38 Conv (NS) 405 (P.J. Clarke); (1975) 38 MLR 557 (J.W. Harris); (1975) 7 Ottawa LR 483 (G. Battersby).

charitable trust) must be for ascertainable beneficiaries: see *Re Gulbenkian's Settlements* [1970] AC 508 at 523–524, [1968] 3 All ER 785 at 792–793, per Lord Upjohn. Seeing that there were no ascertainable beneficiaries, there was a resulting trust for Mr. Vandervell. But if and when Mr. Vandervell should declare any defined trusts, the resulting trust would come to an end. As Lord Upjohn said [1967] 2 AC 291 at 317, [1967] 1 All ER 1 at 11: " . . . until these trusts should be declared, there was a resulting trust for [Mr. Vandervell]."

During the first period, however, Mr. Vandervell did not declare any defined trusts. The option was, therefore, held on a resulting trust for him. He had not divested himself absolutely of the shares. He was, therefore, liable to pay surtax on the dividends.

The law for the second period
In October and November 1961, the trustee company exercised the option. They paid £5,000 out of the children's settlement. The Royal College of Surgeons transferred the legal estate in the 100,000 "A" shares to the trustee company. Thereupon the trustee company became the legal owner of the shares. This was a different kind of property altogether. Whereas previously the trustee company had only a chose in action of one kind — an option — it now had a chose in action of a different kind — the actual shares. This trust property was not held by the trustee company beneficially. It was held by them on trust. On this occasion a valid trust was created at the time of the transfer. It was manifested in clear and unmistakable fashion. It was precisely defined. The shares were to be held on the trusts of the children's settlement. The evidence of intention is indisputable: (i) The trustee company used the children's money — £5,000 — with which to acquire the shares. This would be a breach of trust unless they intended the shares to be an addition to the children's settlement. (ii) The trustee company wrote to the revenue authorities the letter of November 2, 1961, declaring expressly that the shares "will henceforth be held by them upon the trusts of the [children's] settlement." (iii) Thenceforward all the dividends received by the trustees were paid by them to the children's settlement and treated as part of the funds of the settlement. This was all done with the full assent of Mr. Vandervell. Such being the intention, clear and manifest, at the time when the shares were conveyed to the trustee company, it is sufficient to create a trust.

Mr. Balcombe for the executors admitted that the intention of Mr. Vandervell and the trustee company was that the shares should be held on trust for the children's settlement. But he said that this intention was of no avail. He said that during the first period, Mr. Vandervell had an equitable interest in the property, namely, a resulting trust; that he never disposed of this equitable interest (because he never knew he had it): and that in any case it was the disposition of an equitable interest which, under section 53 of the Law of Property Act 1925, had to be in writing, signed by him or his agent, lawfully authorised by him in writing (and there was no such writing produced). He cited *Grey v IRC* [1960] AC 1, [1959] 3 All ER 603, p. 54, ante, and *Oughtred v IRC* [1960] AC 206, [1959] 3 All ER 623, p. 57, ante.

There is a complete fallacy in that argument. A resulting trust for the settlor is born and dies without any writing at all. It comes into existence whenever there is a gap in the beneficial ownership. It ceases to exist whenever that gap is filled by someone becoming beneficially entitled. As soon as the gap is filled by the creation or declaration of a valid trust, the resulting trust comes to an end. In this case, before the option was exercised, there was a gap in the beneficial ownership. So there was a resulting trust for Mr. Vandervell. But, as soon as the option was exercised and the shares registered in the trustees' name, there was created a valid trust of the shares in favour of the children's settlement. Not being a trust of land, it could be created without any writing. A trust of personalty can be created without any writing. Both Mr. Vandervell and the trustee company had done everything which needed to be done to make the settlement of these shares binding on them. So there was a valid trust: see *Milroy v Lord* (1862) 4 De GF & J 264 at 274, per Turner LJ.

The law as to the third period

The executors admit that from January 19, 1965, Mr. Vandervell had no interest whatsoever in the shares. The deed of that date operated so as to transfer all his interest thenceforward to the trustee company to be held by them on trust for the children. I asked Mr. Balcombe: What is the difference between the events of October and November 1961, and the event of January 19, 1965? He said that it lay in the writing. In 1965, Mr. Vandervell disposed of his equitable interest in writing: whereas in 1961 there was no writing. There was only conduct or word of mouth. That was insufficient. And, therefore, his executors were not bound by it.

The answer to this argument is what I have said. Mr. Vandervell did not dispose in 1961 of any equitable interest. All that happened was that his resulting trust came to an end — because there was created a new valid trust of the shares for the children's settlement.

STEPHENSON LJ: I have had more doubt than Lord Denning MR and Lawton LJ whether we can overturn the judgment of Megarry J (p. 187, ante) in what I have not found an easy case. Indeed, treading a (to me) dark and unfamiliar path, I had parted from both my fellow-travellers and following the windings of Mr. Balcombe's argument had nearly reached a different terminus before the light which they threw upon the journey enabled me to join them at the same conclusion.

To expound my doubts would serve no useful purpose; to state them shortly may do no harm. The cause of all the trouble is what the judge called [1974] Ch 269 at 298, [1974] 1 All ER 47 at 72 "this ill-fated option" and its incorporation in a deed which was "too short and simple" to rid Mr. Vandervell of the beneficial interest in the disputed shares, as a bare majority of the House of Lords held, not without fluctuation of mind on the part of one of them (Lord Upjohn), in *Vandervell v IRC* [1967] 2 AC 291 at 314–317, [1967] 1 All ER 1 at 9–11. The operation of law or equity kept for Mr. Vandervell or gave him back an equitable interest which he did not want and would have thought he had disposed of if he had ever known it existed. It is therefore difficult to infer that he intended to dispose or ever did dispose of something he did not know he had until the judgment of Plowman J in *Vandervell v IRC* [1966] Ch 261 at 273, which led to the deed of 1965, enlightened him, or to find a disposition of it in the exercise by the trustee company in 1961 of its option to purchase the shares. And even if he had disposed of his interest, he did not dispose of it by any writing sufficient to comply with section 53 (1) (*c*) of the Law of Property Act 1925.

But Lord Denning MR and Lawton LJ are able to hold that no such disposition is needed because (1) the option was held on such trusts as might thereafter be declared by the trustee company or Mr. Vandervell himself, and (2) the trustee company has declared that it holds the shares in the children's settlement. I do not doubt the first, because it was apparently the view of the majority of the House of Lords in *Vandervell v IRC* [1967] 2 AC 291, [1967] 1 All ER 1. I should be more confident of the second if it had been pleaded or argued either here or below and we had had the benefit of Megarry J's views upon it. If counsel for the trustee company in the court below had thought that the evidence supported it, he would not, I think, have sought and obtained the amendment of the defence which he did to allege what the judge rejected as an unusual and improbable form of trust which was not supported by the evidence. If counsel for the trustee company in this court had accepted it, I do not think that he would have opened this appeal as he did with references to perfecting or completing the trust but none to declaring it. I see, as perhaps did counsel, difficulties in the way of a limited company declaring a trust by parole or conduct and without resolution of the board of directors, and difficulties also in the way of finding any declaration of trust by Mr. Vandervell himself in October or November 1961, or any conduct then or later which would in law or equity estop him from denying that he made one.

However, Lord Denning MR and Lawton LJ are of the opinion that these difficulties, if not imaginary, are not insuperable and that these shares went into the children's settlement in 1961 in accordance with the intention of Mr. Vandervell and the trustee company — a result with which I am happy to agree as it seems to me to be in accordance with the justice and the reality of the case.

B. Where an Express Trust Fails

In **Essery v Cowlard** (1884) 26 ChD 191, a marriage settlement of 1877 declared that certain property of the intended wife had been transferred to trustees to be held by them in trust for herself, her intended husband and the issue of the marriage. The marriage never took place. The parties cohabited, and children were born. PEARSON J held that the contract for marriage had been rescinded. The trusts failed. Illegitimate children would not in those days have been able to take, nor could they be legitimated by the subsequent marriage of their parents. The trustees held on a resulting trust for the settlor (the intended wife), who could claim the return of the property.

RE AMES' SETTLEMENT
[1946] Ch 217, [1946] 1 All ER 689 (ChD, VAISEY J)

John Ames and Miss Hamilton married in 1908. Ames' father transferred £10,000 to trustees to be held on the usual trusts of a marriage settlement. The parties lived together for a number of years in England and Kenya. In 1926, the Supreme Court of Kenya declared the marriage null and void. The wife surrendered all her interests under the settlement. There was no issue. On the death of John Ames in 1945, the question was whether the £10,000 should be paid to those entitled under the settlement in default of issue, or to the representatives of the settlor.

Held. The marriage being void *ab initio*,[11] the fund was held on resulting trust for the settlor.

---

11 A decree of nullity in England granted after July 31, 1971 in respect of a voidable marriage has prospective and not retrospective effect: Matrimonial Causes Act 1973, s. 16; see also s. 24, under which the court has power to make property adjustment orders.

VAISEY J: I regard the contest as merely this: the plaintiffs hold certain funds in their hands, and they ask to which of the alternative claimants they ought to make those funds over. I think it would not be incorrect to say that the problem is really which of those parties has the better equity. The persons who constitute the hypothetical next-of-kin say "Look at the deed of settlement. We are the persons there designated to take the fund, and there is no reason why we should not do so," and therefore claim to have the better equity. On the other hand it is said "But that trust, with the other trusts, were all based on the consideration and contemplation of a valid marriage, and now that it has been judicially decided that there never was a marriage that trust cannot possibly form the foundation of a good equitable right." The settlor's representatives say that theirs is the better equity because the money was only parted with by their testator on a consideration which was expressed but which in fact completely failed. It seems to me that the claim of the executors of the settlor in this case must succeed. I think that the case is, having regard to the wording of the settlement, a simple case of money paid on a consideration which failed. I do not think that that hypothetical class of next-of-kin (who were only brought in, so to speak, and given an interest in the fund on the basis and footing that there was going to be a valid marriage between John Ames and Miss Hamilton) have really any merits in equity, and I do not see how they can claim under the express terms of a document which, so far as regards the persons with whom the marriage consideration was concerned, has utterly and completely failed. If their claim be good, it is difficult to see at what precise period of time their interest became an interest in possession. But I hold that their claim is not good, and that they have not been able to establish it.[12]

A similar principle has been held to apply where property is transferred under a void contract. In **Westdeutsche Landesbank Girozentrale v Islington London Borough Council** [1994] 1 WLR 938, [1994] 4 All ER 890 money was paid by the bank to the local authority under an "interest rate swaps" contract which was ultra vires and void. Legal title to the money had passed even though the contract was void. The Court of Appeal held, as an alternative to recovery at common law on restitutionary principles, that the local authority held the money on resulting trust for the bank because the purpose had wholly failed. Applying *Sinclair v Brougham* [1914] AC 398, the money remained the bank's in equity.[13]

C. Incomplete Disposal of Beneficial Interest

i. SURPLUS FUNDS

In **Re Cochrane** [1955] Ch 309, [1955] 1 All ER 222, a marriage settlement provided for funds to be held on trust for the wife "during her life so long as

---

12 See also *Morice v Bishop of Durham* (1804) 9 Ves 399; on appeal (1805) 10 Ves 522, and *Chichester Diocesan Fund and Board of Finance Inc v Simpson* [1944] AC 341, [1944] 2 All ER 60, being examples of resulting trusts arising where an intended charitable trust failed. Similarly, if a gift fails for lack of mental capacity: *Simpson v Simpson* [1989] Fam Law 20.
13 Criticised in [1994] 2 RLR 73 (W. Swadling) and [1994] Conv 395 (S. Evans). An appeal to the House of Lords is pending.

she shall continue to reside with the said W.J.B. Cochrane ... and after [her] decease or the prior determination of the trust in her favour ... upon trust to pay the said income to the said W.J.B.Cochrane (if then living) during his life and after the decease of the survivor of them ... in trust for'' such of their issue as they should jointly or as the survivor of them should appoint, and in default of appointment equally at the age of 21, or in the case of daughters, earlier marriage.

The wife ceased to reside with the husband. Her interest thus terminated and the income was paid to the husband. In 1953 the husband died. No appointment in favour of the children had been made. The question was whether the claim of the children was accelerated, or whether the fund was held on a resulting trust during the gap in the beneficial limitations following the husband's death.

HARMAN J, holding that a resulting trust arose, said at 315, at 226: ''Is it clear not only that something has been left out, but what it is that ought to be put in? — the second, of course, being much the more difficult part. One can see that the limitations over do not marry with the prior trusts. It should have been obvious to the draftsman that the event might happen which in fact has happened. But is it clear that the gift over ought, so to speak, to be accelerated? I do not think so on this particular deed, and I base that decision on this: that I cannot see clearly what it is which should have been put in. There is a power for the spouses to appoint to issue; there is a power for the survivor to appoint. Now, it is clear and conceded that the wife, notwithstanding that she forfeited her interest in her husband's lifetime, still has for the rest of her life — or had, at any rate, after her husband's death — power to dispose of the fund as the survivor of the two, either by deed or by will. That power clearly did not stop with the cesser of her interest, so that she could alter the beneficial trust by appointing away from the children in favour of the grandchildren or by making an unequal division between her daughters; and it seems to me in the face of that that it is impossible to say that the gift over took effect at the date of the ceasing of her husband's interest.

It was admitted in fact before me that the fund could not be disturbed so long as the power of appointment was outstanding in the survivor of the two spouses, and that alone seems to me to show that it could not be true to say that the gift over could operate until the event had happened which is stated to be the event in the deed; namely, the death of the survivor of the husband and wife.

The result of that is that the draftsman has failed to provide for the event which has happened. A resulting trust is the last resort to which the law has recourse when the draftsman has made a blunder or failed to dispose of that which he has set out to dispose of, but that seems to have happened here, and until the death of the survivor I think that there is a resulting trust of the income of the fund in favour of the settlors in proportion to their several interests.''

RE THE TRUSTS OF THE ABBOTT FUND
[1900] 2 Ch 326 (ChD, STIRLING J)

Dr. Abbott, of Cambridge, died in 1844, leaving ample funds for the support of his family, including two daughters, Frederica and Katherine, who were deaf and dumb. But on the death of Dr. Abbott's surviving trustee in 1889, it was learned that all the money had disappeared.

Dr. Fawcett, and subsequently Mr. Smith, issued appeals to friends who subscribed money to a fund for the support of the two ladies. No provision was made for the disposal of the fund on the death of the survivor. This occurred in 1899, and there was then a surplus of £366 13s 9d.

Held. The fund was held upon a resulting trust for the subscribers.

STIRLING J: It seems to me . . . that I may treat the fund which was collected by Dr. Fawcett as really applicable to the same purposes, for that is the effect of it, as that which was subscribed in response to the circular issued by Mr. Smith. The ladies are both dead, and the question is whether so far as this fund has not been applied for their benefit, there is a resulting trust of it for the subscribers. I cannot believe that it was ever intended to become the absolute property of the ladies so that they should be in a position to demand a transfer of it to themselves, or so that if they became bankrupt the trustee in the bankruptcy should be able to claim it. I believe it was intended that it should be administered by Mr. Smith, or the trustees who had been nominated in pursuance of the circular. I do not think the ladies ever became absolute owners of this fund. I think that the trustee or trustees were intended to have a wide discretion as to whether any, and if any what, part of the fund should be applied for the benefit of the ladies and how the application should be made. That view would not deprive them of all right in the fund, because if the trustees had not done their duty — if they either failed to exercise their discretion or exercised it improperly — the ladies might successfully have applied to the court to have the fund administered according to the terms of the circular. In the result, therefore, there must be a declaration that there is a resulting trust of the moneys remaining unapplied for the benefit of the subscribers to the Abbott fund.

In other cases it is possible to find that the gift, although expressed as applicable to a particular purpose only, was in fact intended to take effect as a gift to the beneficiary absolutely.

In **Re Osoba** [1979] 1 WLR 247, [1979] 2 All ER 393,[14] the testator left property to his widow on trust to be used "for her maintenance and for the training of my daughter up to university grade and for the maintenance of my aged mother". The mother predeceased the testator. The widow died in 1970, and the daughter completed her university education in 1975. The surplus was claimed by the testator's children by a previous marriage on intestacy. The Court of Appeal held that the testator's intention was to make absolute gifts to the beneficiaries, the references to maintenance and education being expressions of motive. BUCKLEY LJ said at 257, at 402:

"If a testator has given the whole of a fund, whether of capital or income, to a beneficiary, whether directly or through the medium of a trustee, he is regarded, in the absence of any contraindication, as having manifested an

---

14 [1978] CLJ 219 (C.E.F. Rickett). See also *Re Andrew's Trust* [1905] 2 Ch 48 (surplus from fund for education of children of a deceased clergyman held payable to the children. The gift was construed as a gift to them, applicable primarily for their education). See also *Re Foord* [1922] 2 Ch 519; *Re Denley's Trust Deed* [1969] 1 Ch 373, [1968] 3 All ER 65; *Re Lipinski's Will Trusts* [1976] Ch 235, [1977] 1 All ER 33, p. 319, post.

intention to benefit that person to the full extent of the subject matter, notwithstanding that he may have expressly stated that the gift is made for a particular purpose, which may prove to be impossible of performance or which may not exhaust the subject matter. This is because the testator has given the whole fund; he has not given so much of the fund as a trustee or anyone else should determine, but the whole fund. This must be reconciled with the testator's having specified the purpose for which the gift is made. This reconciliation is achieved by treating the reference to the purpose as merely a statement of the testator's motive in making the gift. Any other interpretation of the gift would frustrate the testator's expressed intention that the whole subject matter shall be applied for the benefit of the beneficiary. These considerations have, I think, added force where the subject matter is the testator's residue, so that any failure of the gift would result in intestacy. The specified purpose is regarded as of less significance than the dispositive act of the testator, which sets the measure of the extent to which the testator intends to benefit the beneficiary.''

[His Lordship held that, in the absence of words of severance, the beneficiaries took as joint tenants, so that on the widow's death the daughter became entitled to the whole.]

RE GILLINGHAM BUS DISASTER FUND
[1958] Ch 300, [1958] 1 All ER 37 (ChD, HARMAN J)[15]

In 1951, a squad of Royal Marine cadets was marching through a street in Gillingham, when a bus, out of control, struck them in the rear, killing 24, and injuring several others. A memorial fund was established by the Mayors of Gillingham, Rochester and Chatham, which was stated to be devoted ''among other things, to defraying the funeral expenses, caring for the boys who may be disabled, and then to such worthy cause or causes ... as the Mayors may determine.''

The public contributed about £9,000, partly in identifiable sums from individual subscribers, but mainly from street collections and other untraceable sources. Various payments were made from the fund toward expenditure not covered by the common law liability accepted by the driver of the bus and his employers. There was a surplus, and the question arose as to its disposal.

Held. The surplus was held on a resulting trust for the donors.

HARMAN J: I have already decided that the surplus of this fund now in the hands of the plaintiffs as trustees ought not to be devoted to charitable purposes under a cy-près scheme. There arises now a further question, namely, whether, as the Treasury Solicitor claims, this surplus should be paid to the Crown as bona vacantia, or whether there is a resulting trust in favour of the subscribers, who are here represented by the Official Solicitor. The general principle must be that where money is held upon trust and the trusts declared do not exhaust the fund it will revert to the donor or settlor under what is called a resulting trust. The reasoning behind this is that the settlor or donor

---

15 Cf. *Re West Sussex Constabulary's Widows, Children and Benevolent (1930) Fund Trusts* [1971] Ch 1, [1970] 1 All ER 544, p. 200, post.

did not part with his money absolutely out and out but only sub modo to the intent that his wishes as declared by the declaration of trust should be carried into effect. When, therefore, this has been done any surplus still belongs to him. This doctrine does not, in my judgment, rest on any evidence of the state of mind of the settlor, for in the vast majority of cases no doubt he does not expect to see his money back: he has created a trust which so far as he can see will absorb the whole of it. The resulting trust arises where that expectation is for some unforeseen reason cheated of fruition, and is an inference of law based on after-knowledge of the event.

Counsel for the Crown admitted that it was for him to show that this principle did not apply to the present case. Counsel for the subscribers cited to me *Re Abbott* [1900] 2 Ch 326 ... Stirling J had no difficulty in coming to the conclusion that the ladies were not intended to become the absolute owners of the fund and therefore their personal representatives had no claim. It was never suggested in this case that any claim by the Crown to bona vacantia might arise. A similar result was reached in *Re Hobourn Aero Components Air Raid Distress Fund* [1946] Ch 86, [1945] 2 All ER 711 where the judge found that though the objects of the fund were charitable no general charitable intent was shown in the absence of any element of public benefit and decided that the money belonged to the subscribers upon a resulting trust. Here again no claim was made on behalf of the Crown that the surplus constituted bona vacantia.

I was referred to two cases where a claim was made to bona vacantia and succeeded. The first of these was *Cunnack v Edwards* [1896] 2 Ch 679. This was a case of a society formed to raise a fund by subscriptions and so forth from the members to provide for widows of deceased members. Upon the death of the last widow of a member it was found that there was a surplus. It was held by the Court of Appeal that no question of charity arose, that there was no resulting trust in favour of the subscribers, but that the surplus passed to the Crown as bona vacantia ....

The ratio decidendi seems to have been that having regard to the constitution of the fund no interest could possibly be held to remain in the contributor who had parted with his money once and for all under a contract for the benefit of his widow. When this contract had been carried into effect the contributor had received all that he contracted to get for his money and could not ask for any more.

A similar result was reached in the case of *Smith v Cooke* [1891] AC 297, cited by A.L. Smith LJ [1896] 2 Ch 679 at 683, though it does not appear from the report what the result was. Another case cited to me was *Braithwaite v A-G* [1909] 1 Ch 510. Here again it was held that there was no room for a resulting trust and the claim to bona vacantia succeeded. The opponents there, it appears, were the last two surviving annuitants. Their claim was rejected on the ground that they had had or were having everything for which the contract provided. The claim of the Attorney-General on behalf of charity was rejected, it being held that there was no charity. A different result was reached by Kekewich J in *Re Buck* [1896] 2 Ch 727, but it was on the ground that the society was a charity and the money was therefore directed to be applied cy-près ....

[His Lordship referred to "the three hospital cases": *Re Welsh Hospital (Netley) Fund* [1921] 1 Ch 655, p. 203 post; *Re Hillier's Trusts* [1954] 1 WLR 9, [1953] 2 All ER 1547,[16] and *Re Ulverston and District New Hospital Building Trusts* [1956] Ch 622, [1956] 3 All ER 164, p. 204 post and continued:]

16 On appeal [1954] 1 WLR 700, [1954] 2 All ER 59, p. 203, post.

It was argued for the Crown that the subscribers to this fund must be taken to have parted with their money out and out, and that there was here, as in *Cunnack v Edwards* [1896] 2 Ch 679 and *Braithwaite v A-G* [1909] 1 Ch 510, no room for a resulting trust. But there is a difference between those cases and this in that they were cases of contract and this is not. Further, it seems to me that the hospital cases are not of great help because the argument centred round general charitable intent, a point which cannot arise unless the immediate object be a charity. I have already held there is no such question here. In my judgment the nearest case is the *Hobourn* case [1946] Ch 86, [1945] 2 All ER 711, which, however, is no authority for the present because no claim for bona vacantia was made.

In my judgment the Crown has failed to show that this case should not follow the ordinary rule merely because there was a number of donors who, I will assume, are unascertainable. I see no reason myself to suppose that the small giver who is anonymous has any wider intention than the large giver who can be named. They all give for the one object. If they can be found by inquiry the resulting trust can be executed in their favour. If they cannot I do not see how the money could then, with all respect to Jenkins LJ, change its destination and become bona vacantia. It will be merely money held upon a trust for which no beneficiary can be found. Such cases are common and where it is known that there are beneficiaries the fact that they cannot be ascertained does not entitle the Crown to come in and claim. The trustees must pay the money into court like any other trustee who cannot find his beneficiary. I conclude, therefore, that there must be an inquiry for the subscribers to this fund[17].

ii. MEMBERS' CLUBS AND ASSOCIATIONS

Where members contribute to the funds or property of a club or society which is established for non-charitable purposes, the question arises as to the entitlement to its assets when the club or association is dissolved[18]. The various solutions are that the members are entitled under the doctrine of resulting trusts, or that the members are contractually entitled, or that the property is *bona vacantia*, to which the Crown is entitled[19]. It may be that persons other than the members have also contributed to the funds, as in *Re West Sussex Constabulary's Widows, Children and Benevolent (1930) Fund Trusts* [1971] Ch 1, [1970] 1 All ER 544, p. 200, post, in which case it must be decided whether they have any entitlement under a resulting trust. The earlier decisions display no uniformity of approach[20], and should be read in the light of the analysis of WALTON J in *Re Bucks Constabulary Widows' and Orphans' Fund Friendly Society (No 2)* [1979] 1 WLR 936, [1979] 1 All ER 623, p. 204, post.

17 The fund was wound up in 1965, when the remainder of the money was paid into court. It was announced on 5 April, 1993 that this money (£7,300 uninvested) was to be spent on a memorial to the victims. Cf. Charities Act 1993, s. 14, p. 495, post, which provides for the application cy-près of money given to charity, and obtained from gifts by unknown donors, even where it was given for a specific purpose only.
18 As to when there is a dissolution so as to render the unspent assets distributable, see *Re William Denby & Sons Ltd Sick and Benevolent Fund* [1971] 1 WLR 973, [1971] 2 All ER 1196; *Re GKN Bolts and Nuts Ltd (Automotive Division) Birmingham Works Sports and Social Club* [1982] 1 WLR 774, [1982] 2 All ER 855. See generally Warburton, *Unincorporated Associations: Law and Practice* (2nd edn 1992).
19 Ing, *Bona Vacantia* (1971), pp. 180 et seq.
20 See (1973) 92 Law Notes 297, 330 (A. Cooklin).

His Lordship held that the surplus belonged to the members by contract, to the exclusion of any resulting trust or any entitlement of the Crown on the basis of *bona vacantia*. This decision was cited but not referred to in the judgment of SCOTT J in *Davis v Richards and Wallington Industries Ltd* [1990] 1 WLR 1511, [1991] 2 All ER 563, p. 000 post. It was there considered that the contractual background did not preclude the finding of a resulting trust. However, any resulting trust for members was excluded by a contrary intention, so that their share would have devolved as *bona vacantia* had it not been held that the employers were entitled under the terms of the trust deed.[1]

In **Cunnack v Edwards** [1896] 2 Ch 679, a society governed by the Friendly Societies Act 1829,[2] was formed to raise funds, by the subscription, fines and forfeitures of its members to provide annuities for the widows of those members who died. By 1879, all the members had died, and by 1892, the last widow died. There was then a surplus of £1,250.

The Court of Appeal, reversing CHITTY J, held that the Crown took the fund as *bona vacantia*. There was no room for a resulting trust because each member had paid his contributions without reserving any beneficial interest to himself. A.L. SMITH LJ said at 683:

"As the member paid his money to the society, so he divested himself of all interest in this money for ever, with this one reservation, that if the member left a widow she was to be provided for during her widowhood. Except as to this he abandoned and gave up the money for ever". The benefits were for the widows and not for the members.

RE WEST SUSSEX CONSTABULARY'S WIDOWS, CHILDREN AND BENEVOLENT (1930) FUND TRUSTS[3]
[1971] Ch 1, [1970] 1 All ER 544 (ChD, GOFF J)

A fund was established for the purpose of providing payments to widows and certain dependants of deceased members of the West Sussex Constabulary. Clause 10 of the rules provided that, with exceptions, a member who resigned should forfeit all claims to the fund. Receipts to the fund came from members' subscriptions, the proceeds of entertainments, sweepstakes, raffles and collecting boxes and various donations and legacies. On the amalgamation of the constabulary with other police forces as from January 1, 1968 the operation of the fund came to an end. The question arose as to the distribution of the fund.

Held. (i) Where a donation or legacy was made for the specific purpose of the fund, the donor was entitled under a resulting trust. (ii) Money received from all other sources passed to the Crown as *bona vacantia*.

GOFF J: First, it was submitted that the fund belongs exclusively and in equal shares to all those persons now living who were members on December 31,

---

1 Criticised at [1991] Conv 366 (J. Martin); [1992] Conv 41 (S. Gardner); (1992) 6 Trust Law International 119 at 124 (Lord BROWNE-WILKINSON); (1994) 8 Trust Law International 35 (VINELOTT J).
2 On friendly societies, see Warburton, supra, pp. 5–6.
3 (1971) 87 LQR 464 (M.J. Albery).

1967, and the personal representatives off all the then members since deceased, to all of whom I will refer collectively as "the surviving members." That argument is based on the analogy of the members' club cases, and the decisions in *Re Printers and Transferrers Amalgamated Trades Protection Society* [1899] 2 Ch 184; *Re Lead Co's Workmen's Fund Society* [1904] 2 Ch 196 and the Irish case of *Tierney v Tough* [1914] 1 IR 142. The ratio decidendi of the first two of those cases was that there was a resulting trust, but that would not give the whole fund to the surviving members, unless rule 10 of the fund's rules could somehow be made to carry to them the contributions of the former members despite the failure of the purposes of the fund (as was pointed out by O'Connor MR in *Tierney v Tough* at 155), and unless indeed the moneys raised from outside sources also could somehow be made to accrue to the surviving members. I agree with Ungoed-Thomas J that the ratio decidendi of *Tierney v Tough* is to be preferred: see *Re St Andrew's Allotment Association* [1969] 1 WLR 229 at 238, [1969] 1 All ER 147 at 154.

This brings one back to the principle of the members' clubs, and I cannot accept that as applicable for three reasons; First, it simply does not look like it; this was nothing but a pensions or dependent relatives fund not at all akin to a club; secondly, in all the cases where the surviving members have taken, with the sole exception of *Tierney v Tough*, the club society or organisation existed for the benefit of the members for the time being exclusively, whereas in the present case, as in *Cunnack v Edwards* [1896] 2 Ch 679, only third parties could benefit. Moreover, in *Tierney v Tough* the exception was minimal and discretionary and can, I think, fairly be disregarded. Finally, this very argument was advanced and rejected by Chitty J in *Cunnack v Edwards* at first instance [1895] 1 Ch 489 at 496, and was abandoned on the hearing of the appeal. That judgment also disposes of the further argument that the surviving members of the fund had power to amend the rules under rule 14 and could therefore have reduced the fund into possession, and so ought to be treated as the owners of it or the persons for whose benefit it existed at the crucial moment. They had the power but they did not exercise it, and it is now too late.

Then it was argued that there is a resulting trust, with several possible consequences. If this be the right view there must be a primary division of the fund into three parts, one representing contributions from former members, another contributions from the surviving members, and the third moneys raised from outside sources. The surviving members then take the second, and possibly by virtue of rule 10, the first also. That rule is as follows:

"Any member who voluntarily terminates his membership shall forfeit all claim against the fund, except in the case of a member transferring to a similar fund of another force, in which instance the contributions paid by the member to the West Sussex Constabulary's Widows, Children and Benevolent (1930) Fund may be paid into the fund of the force to which the member transfers."

Alternatively, the first part may belong to the past members on the footing that rule 10 is operative so long only as the fund is a going concern, or may be bona vacantia. The third is distributable in whole or in part between those who provided the money, or again is bona vacantia.

In my judgment the doctrine of resulting trust is clearly inapplicable to the contributions of both classes. Those persons who remained members until their deaths are in any event excluded because they have had all they contracted for, either because their widows and dependants have received or are in receipt of the prescribed benefits, or because they did not have a widow or dependants. In my view that is inherent in all the speeches in the Court of Appeal in *Cunnack v Edwards* [1896] 2 Ch 679. Further, whatever the effect of the fund's rule 10 may be upon the contributions of those members who left prematurely, they and the surviving members alike are also in my judgment unable to claim under a resulting trust because they put their money on a contractual basis and not one of trust: see per Harman J in *Re Gillingham Bus Disaster Fund* [1958] Ch 300 at 314, [1958] 1 All ER 37 at 43. The only case which has given me difficulty on this aspect of the matter is *Re Hobourn Aero Components Ltd's Air Raid Distress Fund* [1946] Ch 86, [1945] 2 All ER 711, where in somewhat similar circumstances it was held there was a resulting trust. The argument postulated, I think, the distinction between contract and trust but in another connection, namely, whether the fund was charitable: see pp. 89 and 90. There was in that case a resolution to wind up but that was not, at all events as expressed, the ratio decidendi: see per Cohen J at 97, at 718, but, as Cohen J observed, there was no argument for bona vacantia. Moreover, no rules or regulations were ever made and although in fact £1 per month was paid or saved for each member serving with the forces, there was no prescribed contractual benefits. In my judgment that case is therefore distinguishable.

Accordingly, in my judgment all the contributions of both classes are bona vacantia, but I must make a reservation with respect to possible contractual rights. In *Cunnack v Edwards* [1895] 1 Ch 489 and *Braithwaite v A-G* [1909] 1 Ch 510 all the members had received, or provision had been made for, all the contractual benefits. Here the matter has been cut short. Those persons who died whilst still in membership cannot, I conceive, have any rights because in their case the contract has been fully worked out, and on a contractual basis I would think that members who retired would be precluded from making any claim by rule 10, although that is perhaps more arguable. The surviving members, on the other hand, may well have a right in contract on the ground of frustration or total failure of consideration, and that right may embrace contributions made by past members, though I do not see how it could apply to moneys raised from outside sources. I have not, however, heard any argument based on contract and therefore the declarations I propose to make will be subject to the reservation which I will later formulate. This will not prevent those parts of the fund which are bona vacantia from being paid over to the Crown as it has offered to give a full indemnity to the trustees.

I must now turn to the moneys raised from outside sources. Counsel for the Treasury Solicitor made an overriding general submission that there cannot be a resulting trust of any of the outside moneys because in the circumstances it is impossible to identify the trust property; no doubt something could be achieved by complicated accounting, but this, he submitted, would not be identification but notional reconstruction. I cannot accept that argument. In my judgment, in a case like the present, equity will cut the Gordian knot by simply dividing the ultimate surplus in proportion to the sources from which it has arisen. Chitty J in *Cunnack v Edwards* at first instance [1895] 1 Ch 489, particularly at 497 and 498, was prepared to order an inquiry, notwithstanding the difficulty that it involved, going back over many years, and despite the fact that the early records were not available; but that was a difficulty of ascertaining the original contributions, not of working out surpluses or interest calculations year by year. Similarly it was not suggested that any such operation ought to be carried out, or that the necessity for it prevented the doctrine of resulting trust being applied in the *Re Printers and Transferrers* case [1899] 2 Ch 184. Yet in both those cases, although the matter was not further complicated by outside contributions, the problem of interest on invested funds, and of contributions and expenditure made at different times, must have presented itself. Again, in the *Printers* case, fines and forfeitures were ignored: see pp. 189 and 190. There may be cases of tolerable simplicity where the court will be more refined, but in general, where a fund has been raised from mixed sources, interest has been earned over the years and income — and possibly capital — expenditure has been made indiscriminately out of the fund as an entirety, and then the venture comes to an end prematurely or otherwise, the court will not find itself baffled but will cut the Gordian knot as I have said.

Then counsel divided the outside moneys into three categories, first, the proceeds of entertainments, raffles and sweepstakes, secondly, the proceeds of collecting-boxes; and, thirdly, donations, including legacies if any, and he took particular objections to each.

I agree that there cannot be any resulting trust with respect to the first category. I am not certain whether Harman J in *Re Gillingham Bus Disaster Fund* [1958] Ch 300, [1958] 1 All ER 37 meant to decide otherwise. In stating the facts at 304, at 39, he referred to "street collections and so forth". In the further argument at 309 there is mention of whist drives and concerts but the judge himself did not speak of anything other than gifts. If, however, he did, I must respectfully decline to follow his judgment in that regard, for whatever may be the true position with regard to collecting-boxes, it appears to me to be impossible to apply the doctrine of resulting trust to the proceeds of entertainments and sweepstakes and such-like money-raising operations for two reasons: first, the relationship is one of contract and not of trust; the purchaser of a ticket may have the motive of aiding the cause or he may not; he may purchase a ticket merely because he wishes to attend the particular entertainment or to try for the prize, but whichever it be, he pays his money as the price of what is offered and what he receives; secondly, there is in such cases no direct contribution to the fund at all; it is only the profit, if any, which is ultimately received and there may even be none.

In any event, the first category cannot be any more susceptible to the doctrine than the second to which I now turn. Here one starts with the well-known dictum of P.O. Lawrence J in *Re Welsh Hospital (Netley) Fund* [1921] 1 Ch 655 at 660 where he said:

"So far as regards the contributors to entertainments, street collections etc., I have no hesitation in holding that they must be taken to have parted with their money out-and-out. It is inconceivable that any person paying for a concert ticket or placing a coin in a collecting-box presented to him in the street should have intended that any part of the money so contributed should be returned to him when the immediate object for which the concert was given or the collection made had come to an end. To draw such an inference would be absurd on the face of it."

This was adopted by Upjohn J in *Re Hillier's Trusts* [1954] 1 WLR 9, [1953] 2 All ER 1547, where the point was actually decided . . . .

[The analysis of Upjohn J] was approved by Denning LJ in the Court of Appeal [1954] 1 WLR 700, [1954] 2 All ER 59 although it is true he went on to say that the law makes a presumption of charity. I quote from 714, 70:

"Let me first state the law as I understand it in regard to money collected for a specified charity by means of a church collection, a flag day, a whist drive, a dance, or some such activity. When a man gives money on such an occasion, he gives it, I think, beyond recall. He parts with the money out-and-out . . . "

In *Re Ulverston and District New Hospital Building Trusts* [1956] Ch 622 at 633, [1956] 3 All ER 164 at 170 Jenkins LJ threw out a suggestion that there might be a distinction in the case of a person who could prove that he put a specified sum in a collecting-box, and, in the *Gillingham* case [1958] Ch 300, [1958] 1 All ER 37, Harman J after noting this, decided that there was a resulting trust with respect to the proceeds of collections. He said at 314, at 43: [quoting the last paragraph extracted, p. 199, ante:]

It will be observed that Harman J considered that *Re Welsh Hospital (Netley) Fund* [1921] 1 Ch 655; *Re Hillier's Trusts* and *Re Ulverston and District New Hospital Building Trusts* did not help him greatly because they were charity cases. It is true that they were, and, as will presently appear, that is in my view very significant in relation to the third category, but I do not think it was a valid objection with respect to the second, and for my part I cannot reconcile the decision of Upjohn J in *Re Hillier's Trusts* with that of Harman J in the *Gillingham* case. As I see it, therefore, I have to choose between them. On the one hand it may be said that Harman J had the advantage, which Upjohn J had not, of considering the suggestion made by Jenkins LJ. On the other hand that suggestion with all respect, seems to me somewhat fanciful and unreal. I agree that all who put their money into collecting-boxes should be taken to have the same intention, but why should they not all be regarded as intending to part with their money out and out absolutely in all circumstances? I observe that P.O. Lawrence J in *Re Welsh Hospital* [1921] 1 Ch 655 at 661 used very strong words. He said any other view was inconceivable and absurd on the face of it. That commends itself to my humble judgment, and I therefore prefer and follow the judgment of Upjohn J in *Re Hillier's Trusts* .... [His Lordship referred to *Re Hillier's Trusts*, and continued:] Therefore, where, as in the present case, the object was neither equivocal nor charitable, I can see no justification for infecting the third category with the weaknesses of the first and second, and I cannot distinguish this part of the case from *Re Abbott Fund Trusts* [1900] 2 Ch 326, p. 195, ante.

[His Lordship directed certain inquiries, and continued:]

And I make the following declarations: First, that the portion attributable to donations and legacies is held on a resulting trust for the donors or their estates and the estates of the respective testators; secondly, that the remainder of the fund is bona vacantia.

These declarations are, however, without prejudice to (1) Any claim which may be made in contract by any person or the personal representatives of any person who was at any time a member, and (2) Any right or claim of the trustees to be indemnified against any such claim out of the whole fund including the portion attributable to donations and legacies.

Finally there will, of course, be general liberty to apply.

RE BUCKS CONSTABULARY WIDOWS' AND ORPHANS' FUND FRIENDLY SOCIETY (No 2)[4]
[1979] 1 WLR 936, [1979] 1 All ER 623 (Ch D, WALTON J)

The Bucks Constabulary Fund, which was registered under the Friendly Societies Act 1896, was established to provide, by voluntary contributions from its members, for the relief of widows and orphans of deceased members of the Bucks Constabulary. By section 49 (1) of the 1896 Act, the property of such a

---

4 [1980] 39 CLJ 88 (C.E.F. Rickett); (1980) 43 MLR 626 (B. Green).

society vested in its trustees for the benefit of the society and its members. In 1968 the Constabulary amalgamated with others and the society was wound up. Its rules did not provide for the distribution of its assets on dissolution. The main issue was whether the assets should be distributed among the persons who were members at the date of dissolution, or whether they should pass to the Crown as *bona vacantia*.

Held. As there were members in existence at the dissolution, the assets belonged to those members to the total exclusion of any claim by the Crown.

WALTON J: Before I turn to a consideration of the authorities, it is I think pertinent to observe that all unincorporated societies rest in contract to this extent, but there is an implied contract between all of the members inter se governed by the rules of the society. In default of any rule to the contrary — and it will seldom, if ever, be that there is such a rule — when a member ceases to be a member of the association he ipso facto ceases to have any interest in its funds. Once again, so far as friendly societies are concerned, it is made very clear by section 49 (1), that it is the members, the present members, who, alone, have any right in the assets. As membership always ceases on death, past members or the estates of deceased members therefore have no interest in the assets. Further, unless expressly so provided by the rules, unincorporated societies are not really tontine societies intended to provide benefits for the longest liver of the members. Therefore, although it is difficult to say in any given case precisely when a society becomes moribund, it is quite clear that if a society is reduced to a single member neither he, nor still less his personal representatives on his behalf, can say he is or was the society and therefore entitled solely to its fund. It may be that it will be sufficient for the society's continued existence if there are two members, but if there is only one the society as such must cease to exist. There is no association, since one can hardly associate with oneself or enjoy one's own society. And so indeed the assets have become ownerless.

[His Lordship distinguished *Cunnack v Edwards* [1896] 2 Ch 679, p. 200, ante on the ground that the combined effect of the rules of the society and the Friendly Societies Act 1892 precluded any argument in favour of distribution among the members' estates, and continued:]

The next case to which I was referred was *Re Printers and Transferrers Amalgamated Trades Protection Society* [1899] 2 Ch 184. I am afraid that I get little assistance from that case. There, there was no claim by the Crown to the assets as bona vacantia, obviously correctly, but the distribution which was ordered was on the basis of a resulting trust apparently influenced by Chitty J's decision at first instance in the case just cited. With all respect to Byrne J who decided that case, I do not think that the method of distribution employed could, in the light of the judgment in the Court of Appeal in *Cunnack v Edwards* [1896] 2 Ch 679, ever have been correct.

The next case was *Braithwaite v A-G* [1909] 1 Ch 510. Although it is undeniably correct that no mention was made at any point in the case of the fact in express terms, the society there in question having been established as a friendly society in 1808 and actually registered under the Act of 1793, was, like the society in *Cunnack v Edwards* [1896] 2 Ch 679, governed by the provisions of the Act of 1829. It is therefore hardly surprising that, after deciding the new point namely that the contributions of honorary members were absolute gifts to the society and could not be recovered, it was held that the benefited members, of whom there were just two surviving both drawing annuities, did not take the fund. This was a straight following of *Cunnack v Edwards* on identical legislation. The rules made no further provision for benefited members and hence it is not to be wondered at that Swinfen Eady J summed the matter up in three pithy paragraphs, at 520:

"In the present case the two surviving benefited members are entitled to the annuities for which their contract of membership provides, but not to any other interest in the funds. The entire beneficial interest has been exhausted in respect of each deceased benefited member, and when the annuities to the two surviving members cease to be payable upon their respective deaths, they too will have exhausted all their beneficial interest in the funds. All possible claimants to the fund having now been disposed of, I decide that the surplus of the benefited members' fund and the children's fund belong to the Crown as bona vacantia."

The next case is one from Ireland, *Tierney v Tough* [1914] 1 IR 142. O'Connor MR, though concurring in the decision, criticised the reasoning in the *Printers'* case [1899] 2 Ch 184 along the lines which appeal to me and which I have already noted. It is true that he did not in any way allude to the statutory provisions which appear to me to have played so large a part in *Cunnack v Edwards*, but the basis upon which he rested his decision is short, simple and wholly convincing. It must be borne in mind that this was simply the case of an unincorporated association. No question of the statutory provisions arose. O'Connor MR put it thus, at 155:

"The conclusion which I have arrived at in the present case is, that the fund belongs to the existing members, and I think that the true reason is to be found in the fact that the accumulated fund is the property of the society, which is composed of individual members. The society is only the aggregation of those individuals, and the property of the former is the property of the latter. This is not a case in which all the members have disappeared, and their claims have been satisfied, or never arose, as in *Cunnack v Edwards*. There are here existing members with unsatisfied claims against the fund. As I said before, and I think this cannot be controverted, if the existing members, with the assent of their committee and their trustee, agreed to divide the fund among themselves, there is no person qualified to call them to account for so doing. The fund is a private one. On the authorities it is clear that there is no charitable trust attaching to it, and I think I have shown that the fund cannot be regarded as bona vacantia. The Attorney-General then has no claim."

The next case was *Re Customs and Excise Officers' Mutual Guarantee Fund* [1917] 2 Ch 18. I do not consider that this case adds anything by way of theory to the matter. The fund there in question became wholly unnecessary as a result of changes in excise practice on December 31, 1914, when there were still members of the fund in existence and it was held to be distributable amongst the members then living accordingly. Although the decision in *Re St Andrew's Allotment Association* [1969] 1 WLR 229, [1969] 1 All ER 147 is fully in line with the analysis which I have made, I do not think it in fact adds anything thereto. In *Re William Denby & Sons Ltd Sick and Benevolent Fund* [1971] 1 WLR 973, [1971] 2 All ER 1196, the main finding was that, as the substratum of the association had not gone, it continued, but Brightman J said, at 978, at 1201:

"One matter is common ground. It is accepted by all counsel that a fund of this sort is founded in contract and not in trust. That is to say, the right of a member of the fund to receive benefits is a contractual right and the member ceases to have any interest in the fund if and when he has received the totality of the benefits to which he was contractually entitled. In other words, there is no possible claim by any member, founded on a resulting trust. I turn to the question whether the fund has already been dissolved or terminated so that its assets have already become distributable. If it has been dissolved or terminated, the members entitled to participate would prima facie be those persons who were members at the date of dissolution or termination . . . ''

and he refers to the *Printers and Transferrers'* case [1899] 2 Ch 184; *Re Lead Co's Workmen's Fund Society* [1904] 2 Ch 196, 207 and *Re St Andrew's Allotment Association* [1969] 1 WLR 229, [1969] 1 All ER 147. Once again, this is fully in line with the principle of the cases as I see them.

Finally, although there is at any rate one later case, for the purpose of this review there comes a case which gives me great concern, *Re West Sussex Constabulary's Widows, Children and Benevolent (1930) Fund Trusts* [1971] Ch 1, [1970] 1 All ER 544, p. 200, ante. The case is indeed easily distinguishable from the present case in that what was there under consideration was a simple unincorporated association and not a friendly society, so that the provisions of section 49 (1) of the Act of 1896 do not apply. Otherwise the facts in that case present remarkable parallels to the facts in the present case. Goff J decided that the surplus funds had become bona vacantia. [His Lordship read extracts from the case and continued:]

It will be observed that the first reason given by Goff J for his decision is that he could not accept the principle of the members' clubs as applicable. This is a very interesting reason because it is flatly contrary to the successful argument of Mr. Ingle Joyce in the case Goff J purported to follow, *Cunnack v Edwards* [1895] 1 Ch 489, at 494 where he said:

"This society was nothing more than a club, in which the members had no transmissible interest: *Re St James' Club* (1852) 2 De GM & G 383, 387. Whatever the members, or even the surviving member, might have done while alive, when they died their interest in the assets of the club died with them."

And in the Court of Appeal [1896] 2 Ch 679 he used the arguments he had used below. If all that Goff J meant was that the purposes of the fund before him were totally different from those of a members' club then of course one must agree, but if he meant to imply that there was some totally different principle of law applicable one must ask why that should be. His second reason is that in all the cases where the surviving members had taken, the organisation existed for the benefit of the members for the time being exclusively. This may be so, so far as actual decisions go, but what is the principle? Why are the members not in control, complete control, save as to any existing contractual rights, of the assets belonging to their organisation? One could understand the position being different if valid trusts had been declared of the assets in favour of third parties, for example charities, but that this was emphatically not the case was demonstrated by the fact that Goff J recognised that the members could have altered the rules prior to dissolution and put the assets into their own pockets. If there was no obstacle to their doing this, it shows in my judgment quite clearly that the money was theirs all the time. Finally, he purports to follow *Cunnack v Edwards* [1896] 2 Ch 679 and it will be seen from the analysis which I have already made of that case that it was extremely special in its facts, resting on a curious provision of the Act of 1829 which is no longer applicable. As I have already indicated, in the light of section 49 (1) of the Act of 1896 the case before Goff J is readily distinguishable, but I regret that, quite apart from that, I am wholly unable to square it with the relevant principles of law applicable.

The conclusion therefore is that, as on dissolution there were members of the society here in question in existence, its assets are held on trust for such members to the total exclusion of any claim on behalf of the Crown. The remaining question under this head which falls now to be argued is, of course, whether they are simply held per capita, or, as suggested in some of the cases, in proportion to the contributions made by each.

DAVIS v RICHARDS & WALLINGTON INDUSTRIES LTD
[1990] 1 WLR 1511, [1991] 2 All ER 563 (Ch D, Scott J)

On the winding up of a pension fund the question arose as to the entitlement to a surplus of some £3m. The fund derived from contributions from employers and employees and from funds transferred from other schemes. There was some doubt as to the validity of the trust deed, which provided that the employers were entitled to any surplus.

Held. The trust deed was valid and so the employers were entitled to the surplus. Had the deed been invalid, any part of the surplus attributable to the contributions of the employees would have devolved as *bona vacantia*, as the resulting trust which would otherwise have arisen was excluded by a contrary intention.

Scott J: Finally I must address myself to the arguments on resulting trust. These arguments arise only if the definitive deed was ineffective and its inefficacy cannot be remedied by the execution of the executory trust.

Mr Charles, arguing for bona vacantia, has drawn a distinction between payments made under contract and payments made under a trust. He suggested that rights arising under pension schemes were, basically, rights of a contractual character rather than equitable rights arising under a trust. As I understood the argument, if the context in which the rights arise is mainly or exclusively contractual, then a resulting trust will be excluded; but, if the context is mainly or exclusively that of trust, a resulting trust may apply. Unincorporated associations, he said, were based in contract, a pension scheme was a species of unincorporated association, the contributions to pension schemes by employees and employers alike were made under contract with one another; so there was no room for any resulting trust to apply to the surplus produced by the contributions.

[His Lordship referred to *Kerr v British Leyland (Staff) Trustees Ltd* [1986] CA Transcript 286; *Mihlenstedt v Barclays Bank International Ltd* [1989] IRLR 522 and *Palmer v Abney Park Cemetery Co Ltd* (4 July 1985, unreported), and continued:]

In my opinion, the contractual origin of rights under a pension scheme, although relevant to the question whether a resulting trust applies to surplus, is not conclusive. There are a number of authorities where the courts have had to deal with the question whether the assets of a defunct association or the surplus assets of a pension scheme had become bona vacantia or were held on resulting trusts for the subscribers or members.

I can start with *Re West Sussex Constabulary's Widows, Children and Benevolent (1930) Fund Trusts* [1971] Ch 1, [1970] 1 All ER 544. The case concerned a benevolent fund raised from various sources, including raffles, sweepstakes, street collections, legacies and donations. The fund had to be wound up and the question was its destination. Goff J held that so much of the fund as derived from raffles, sweepstakes, street collections and the like was not the subject of any resulting trust and was bona vacantia, but that there was a resulting trust in respect of the legacies and donations. As to the proceeds of the raffles and sweepstakes, Goff J said at 11, at 548:

> "it appears to me to be impossible to apply the doctrine of resulting trust to the proceeds of entertainments and sweepstakes and such-like money raising operations for two reasons. First, the relationship is one of contract and not of trust. The purchaser of a ticket may have the motive of aiding the cause or he may not. He may purchase a ticket merely because he wishes to attend the particular entertainment or to try for the prize, but whichever it be, he pays his money as the price of what is offered and what he receives ... "

Mr Charles draws attention to the reference to contract. As to the proceeds of the collecting boxes, Goff J referred to various authorities, including, in particular, Harman J's decision in *Re Gillingham Bus Disaster Fund* [1958] Ch 300, [1958] 1 All ER 37 and Upjohn J's decision in *Re Hillier* [1954] 1 WLR 9, [1953] 2 All ER 1547. He expressed a preference for the latter decision and said at 13, at 550:

> "I agree that all who put their money into collecting boxes should be taken to have the same intention, but why should they not all be regarded as intending to part with their money out and out, absolutely, in all circumstances?"

On that ground he held that a resulting trust did not apply to the proceeds of collecting boxes and that the proceeds were bona vacantia. He declined, however, when dealing with legacies and donations to draw the same inference of intention to part out and out with the money that he had drawn in respect of the collecting boxes and held that resulting trust applied to the part of the fund attributable to legacies and donations.

[His Lordship referred to *Jones v Williams* (15 March 1988, unreported), where Knox J held that a resulting trust could be excluded by a clause in the trust deed, and continued:]

I respectfully agree with Knox J's approach. I would, however, venture one qualification. The provision in a trust deed necessary to exclude a resulting trust need not, in my opinion, be express. In the absence of an express provision it would, I think, often be very difficult for a sufficiently clear intention to exclude a resulting trust to be established. But, in general, any term that can be expressed can also, in suitable circumstances, be implied. In my opinion, a resulting trust will be excluded not only by an express provision but also if its exclusion is to be implied. If the intention of a contributor that a resulting trust should not apply is the proper conclusion, it would not be right, in my opinion, for the law to contradict that intention.

In my judgment, therefore, the fact that a payment to a fund has been made under contract and that the payer has obtained all that he or she bargained for under the contract is not necessarily a decisive argument against a resulting trust.

I must apply these principles to the surplus in the present case. The fund was, as I have said, fed from three sources: employees' contributions, transfers from other pension schemes and employers' contributions. The employees' contributions were made under contract. Employees were obliged to contribute 5 per cent of salary. They were entitled, in return, to the specified pension and other benefits. The funds from other pension schemes, too, were transferred under contract. There would have been three parties to all these contracts, namely the trustees of the transferred scheme, the trustees of the 1975 scheme and the transferring members themselves. Perhaps the employer company would have been a party as well. The transfer would certainly have been made with its consent. Under these contracts, by implication if not expressly, the transferor trustees would have been discharged from liability in respect of the transferred funds, whether liability to the transferring employee members or liability to the employer company. Finally there are the employers. They, too, made their contributions under contract; they made them under the contracts of employment between themselves and their employees. But there is a very important difference between the contractual obligation of the employees and that of the employers. The employees' contractual obligation was specific in amount, 5 per cent of salary. The employers' contractual obligation was conceptually certain but the amount was inherently uncertain. The obligation was to pay whatever was necessary to fund the scheme. The terms of rule 3 of Pt II of the 1975 rules describe accurately, in my opinion, the contractual obligation of the employers:

"The employer will pay to the trustees such amounts as may from time to time be required to enable the trustees to maintain the benefits . . . "

In practice, the amount of the employers' contributions in respect of each employee was actuarily calculated. The calculations were based on assumptions as to the time when the benefits would become payable and as to the amount of the employee's final salary at that time. If the scheme should terminate before that time, the amount paid would be bound to have been more than needed to have been paid in order to fund the employee's benefits as at the date of termination.

Two separate questions seem to me to require to be answered. First, to what extent should the surplus, the £3m-odd, be regarded as derived from each of these three sources? One possible answer is that there should be a calculation of the total amount of employees' contributions, the total amount of funds transferred from other companies' pension schemes and the total amount of employers' contributions, and that the surplus should be regarded as derived from these three sources in the same proportions as the three totals bear to one another.

I do not accept that this is right. It ignores the different bases on which these contributions were paid. Since the employers' obligation was to pay whatever was from time to time necessary to fund the various scheme benefits and since the employees' 5 per cent contributions and the amount of the transferred funds constituted the base from which the amount of the employers' contributions would from time to time have to be assessed, it is logical, in my judgment, to treat the scheme benefits as funded first by the employees' contributions and the transferred funds, and only secondarily by the employers' contributions, and, correspondingly, to treat the surplus as provided first by the employers' contributions and only secondarily by the employees' contributions and the transferred funds.

There are two possible factual situations to be considered. It is possible (although, I think, very unlikely) that the employees' contributions and the funds transferred from the pension schemes of other companies would, without there having been any contribution at all from the employers, have been sufficient to provide in full for all the scheme benefits and, perhaps, still to have left some surplus. If that is the position, it would follow that, with the advantage of hindsight, the employers need not have made any contributions at all in order to have funded the benefits. This situation would, in my judgment, require that that surplus (which would be bound, I think, to be very small) should be regarded as derived from the employees' contributions and the transferred funds and that the balance of the surplus should be regarded as derived from the employers' contributions.

The much more likely situation is that some contribution at least was required from the employers in order to produce assets sufficient to provide all the scheme benefits to which employees became entitled on 31 July 1982. In that event the whole of the surplus, in my judgment, should be regarded as derived from the employers' contributions. This conclusion is, to my mind, in accordance both with logic and with equity. The actuarial calculations on which the employers' actual contributions were based were themselves based upon a series of assumptions. The termination of the scheme invalidated the assumptions. The employers had, in the event, made payments exceeding the amount necessary to discharge their obligation to fund the benefits to which the employees eventually became entitled. There is a well-established equity that enables accounts drawn up under a mistake to be reopened (see Goff and Jones, *The Law of Restitution* (3rd edn, 1986) p 199). In cases such as the present there was no mistake at the time the contributions were assessed and paid. The actuarial calculations were, I am sure, impeccable. But subsequent events having invalidated some of the assumptions underlying the calculations, the case is, in my opinion, strongly analogous to that of an account drawn up under a mistake. In my opinion, equity should treat the employers as entitled to claim the surplus, or so much of it as derived from the overpayments.

The second question is whether a resulting trust applies to the surplus, or to so much of the surplus as was derived from each of the three sources to which I have referred. As to the surplus derived from the employers' contributions, I can see no basis on which a resulting trust can be excluded. The equity to which I referred in the previous paragraph demands, in my judgment, the conclusion that the trustees hold the surplus derived from the employers' contributions upon trust for the employers. There is no express provision excluding a resulting trust and no circumstances from which, in my opinion, an implication to that effect could be drawn. On the other hand, in my judgment, the circumstances of the case seem to me to point firmly and clearly to the conclusion that a resulting trust in favour of the employees is excluded.

The circumstances are these.

(i) Each employee paid his or her contributions in return for specific financial benefits from the fund. The value of these benefits would be different for each employee, depending on how long he had served, how old he was when he joined and how old he was when he left. Two employees might have paid identical sums in contributions but have become entitled to benefits of a very different value. The point is particularly striking in respect of the employees, (and there were several of them,) who exercised their option to a refund of contributions. How can a resulting trust work as between the various employees inter se? I do not think it can and I do not see why equity should impute to them an intention that would lead to an unworkable result. (ii) The scheme was established to take advantage of the legislation relevant to an exempt approved scheme and a contracted-out scheme. The legislative requirements placed a maximum on the financial return from the fund to which each employee would become entitled. The proposed rules would have preserved the statutory requirements. A resulting trust cannot do so. In my judgment, the relevant legislative requirements prevent imputing to the employees an intention that the surplus of the fund derived from their contributions should be returned to them under a resulting trust.

In my judgment, therefore, there is no resulting trust for the employees.

iii. METHOD OF DISTRIBUTION AMONG MEMBERS

If (as will usually be the case) the Crown cannot establish any entitlement to the surplus assets of a dissolved association, then the question arises as to the proper manner of distribution among the members. Some of the earlier cases have favoured the resulting trust solution but, as will be seen, the modern approach proceeds on the basis of a contractual entitlement. Of course, the question will not arise if the rules of the association provide for the destination of the assets on a dissolution.

If the resulting trust solution is adopted the assets should be distributed among past and present members, in shares proportionate to their contributions, as in *Re Hobourn Aero Components Air Raid Distress Fund* [1946] Ch 86, [1945] 2 All ER 711; affirmed [1946] Ch 194, [1946] 1 All ER 501. Sometimes the distribution has been confined to those who were members at the dissolution, which is a more convenient solution where the ascertainment of the true entitlements would otherwise be too difficult. This was done in *Re Printers and Transferrers Amalgamated Trades Protection Society* [1899] 2 Ch 184.

The modern cases show that the members' entitlement is much more likely to be upon the basis of contractual rights. The distribution will be *per capita*, and confined to those who were members at the time of the dissolution.

RE SICK AND FUNERAL SOCIETY OF ST. JOHN'S SUNDAY SCHOOL, GOLCAR[5]
[1973] Ch 51, [1972] 2 All ER 439 (ChD, MEGARRY J)

In 1866 a society was formed at a Sunday school near Huddersfield to provide for sickness and death benefits for its members. Teachers and children could join, and subscriptions were based on a sliding scale according to age; those under 13 paying $\frac{1}{2}$d. per week (Rule 9) and those over 12 paying 1d. The benefits for those paying the full subscription were twice those of the smaller subscribers (Rules 12, 14).

On December 12, 1966, a meeting unanimously decided to wind up the Society as from December 31. No further subscriptions were paid. There was some £4,000 of surplus assets.

Before the assets were distributed among the current members, four ex-members, who had been excluded from membership for failure to pay subscriptions since 1963 (Rules 9, 17), claimed to pay up their arrears and to participate. A further meeting was held in September 1968 in which it was again resolved to wind up the Society and to distribute the assets among the

---

5 Applied in *Re Bucks Constabulary Widows' and Orphans' Fund Friendly Society (No 2)* [1979] 1 WLR 936, [1979] 1 All ER 623, p. 204, ante; *Re GKN Bolts and Nuts Ltd (Automotive Division) Birmingham Works Sports and Social Club* [1982] 1 WLR 774, [1982] 2 All ER 855; [1983] Conv 315 (R. Griffith); cf. *Davis v Richards and Wallington Industries Ltd* [1990] 1 WLR 1511, [1991] 2 All ER 563, p. 208 ante.

persons who were members on December 31, 1966, and the personal representatives of such members who had subsequently died.

Held. Distribution accordingly; with full shares for full members and half shares for the children. The ex-members were excluded.

MEGARRY J (having held that the resolution of December 1966 was a valid resolution to wind up the Society): In my judgment the substantive rights of all concerned crystallised on December 31, 1966, when, in accordance with the resolution of December 12, 1966, the society ceased all its activities ... Accordingly, in my judgment the personal representatives of each deceased member are entitled to the share to which that member would have been entitled had he lived ...

I turn to question 2. This relates to the basis of distribution. Is each member entitled to an equal share, or is there to be a division into full shares and half-shares, with those paying $\frac{1}{2}$d. a week entitled only to a half-share, and those paying 1d. a week a full share? Or is the basis of distribution to be proportionate to the amounts respectively contributed by each member? The first step, in my view, is to decide between the first two contentions on the one hand and the third on the other: is the proper basis that of division per capita, whether in full or half-shares, or that of division in proportion to the amounts contributed? In discussing this, I speak, of course, in general terms, and subject to any other basis for division that is to be discerned in the rules or any other source.

The authorities are in a curious state. In *Re Printers and Transferrers Amalgamated Trades Protection Society* [1899] 2 Ch 184, Byrne J applied the amounts-contributed basis to a trade union, putting matters on the footing of a resulting trust, and directing division on that basis among the members existing at the time of the resolution for dissolution. In *Re Lead Company's Workmen's Fund Society* [1904] 2 Ch 196, Warrington J followed this decision in the case of an unregistered friendly society. In these cases payments for forfeitures, fines, sick benefits and so on, were disregarded. In *Tierney v Tough* [1914] 1 IR 142, another case of an unregistered friendly society, O'Connor MR was critical of the application of the law relating to resulting trusts to such cases. Despite his criticism, however, he directed division on the basis of the amounts contributed. On the other hand, in the case of clubs, *Brown v Dale* (1878) 9 ChD 78 supports the per capita basis, though it is so shortly reported as to provoke more questions than it answers. *Feeney and Shannon v MacManus* [1937] IR 23, another club case, also supports the same basis. The case is a little remarkable in that the headnote proclaims that *Tierney v Tough* [1914] 1 IR 142 was "applied"; and it appears from page 33 that the basis of the decision was not so much that equal division was right, but that equality was necessary because ascertaining the proportionate contributions was an impossibility. Finally, in *Re St Andrew's Allotment Association* [1969] 1 WLR 229, [1969] 1 All ER 147, concerning an allotment association, Ungoed-Thomas J considered these cases, together with *Re Blue Albion Cattle Society* [1966] CLY 1274, The Guardian, May 28, 1966, where Cross J had applied the per capita basis to a cattle-breeding society. In the *St Andrew's* case Ungoed-Thomas J said at 238, at 154:

> "If the true principle is that laid down in *Tierney v Tough* [1914] 1 IR 142 and that principle certainly seems to me preferable to the principle of the resulting trust adopted in *Re Printers and Transferrers Amalgamated Trades Protection Society* [1899] 2 Ch 184, then it would seem to me that prima facie the assets are distributable between members at the relevant date per

capita. It is conceivable that a basis for distinguishing the friendly and mutual benefit society cases may be that, whereas in the club cases enjoyment ab initio and equality are contemplated, yet in the friendly and mutual benefit society cases what are contemplated are advantages related to contributions.''

The reference to the principle laid down in *Tierney v Tough* must, I think, be to the comments of O'Connor MR which rejected the concept of resulting trust, rather than to the actual decision, which was on the basis of the proportionate contributions that flow from the concept of resulting trust.

It seems to me, with all respect, that much of the difficulty arises from confusing property with contract. A resulting trust is essentially a property concept: any property that a man does not effectually dispose of remains his own. If, then, there is a true resulting trust in respect of an unexpended balance of payments made to some club or association, there will be a resulting trust in respect of that unexpended balance, and the beneficiaries under that trust will be those who made the payments. If any are dead, the trusts will be for their estates; death does not deprive a man of his beneficial interest. Yet in what I may call "the resulting trust cases," the beneficiaries who were held to be entitled were the members living at the time of the dissolution, to the exclusion of those who died or otherwise ceased to be members. If, then, there were any resulting trust, it must be a trust modified in some way, perhaps by some unexplained implied term, that distinguishes between the quick and the dead. It cannot be merely an ordinary resulting trust.

On the other hand, membership of a club or association is primarily a matter of contract. The members make their payments, and in return they become entitled to the benefits of membership in accordance with the rules. The sums they pay cease to be their individual property, and so cease to be subject to any concept of resulting trust. Instead, they become the property, through the trustees of the club or association, of all the members for the time being, including themselves. A member who, by death or otherwise, ceases to be a member thereby ceases to be the part owner of any of the club's property: those who remain continue owners. If, then, dissolution ensues, there must be a division of the property of the club or association among those alone who are owners of that property, to the exclusion of former members. In that division, I cannot see what relevance there can be in the respective amounts of the contributions. The newest member, who has made a single payment when he joined only a year ago, is as much a part owner of the property of the club or association as a member who has been making payments for 50 years. Each has had what he has paid for: the newest member has had the benefits of membership for a year or so and the oldest member for 50 years. Why should the latter, who for his money has had the benefits of membership for 50 times as long as the former, get the further benefit of receiving 50 times as much in the winding up?

I have, of course, been speaking in the broadest of outlines; but I must say that the view taken on principle by O'Connor MR in *Tierney v Tough* [1914] 1 IR 142 and by Ungoed-Thomas J in *Re St Andrew's Allotment Association* [1969] 1 WLR 229, [1969] 1 All ER 147 seem to me to be preferable to the other view, despite certain difficulties in the basis of distinction between the club cases and the others tentatively suggested by Ungoed-Thomas J in the passage that I have read: at 238, at 154. Accordingly, I reject the basis of proportionate division in favour of equality, or division per capita. But then the second question arises, namely, whether the principle of equality prevails not only when there is no more than one class of members but when there are two or more classes. Is the proposed division into shares and half-shares sound, or ought it to be rejected in favour of equality throughout?

On the footing that the rules of a club or association form the basis of the contract between all the members, I must look at the rules of the society to see whether they indicate any basis other than that of equality. It seems to me that they do. Those aged from five to 12 years old pay contributions at half the rate (rule 9), and correspondingly their allowances (rule 12) and death benefit (rule 14) are also paid at half the rate. Where the rules have written into them the basis of inequality among different classes of members in relation to the principal contractual burdens and benefits of membership, it seems to me to follow that this inequality ought also to be applied to the surplus property of the society. A distinction between classes of members is quite different from a distinction between individual members of the same class based on the amounts contributed by each member. At any given moment one can say that the rights and liabilities of all the members of one class differ in the same way from the rights and liabilities of all the members of the other class, irrespective of the length of membership or anything else. It was indeed suggested that the words ''two classes of subscribers'' in rule 9 did not mean that there were two classes of members, the word ''subscribers'' being in contrast with the word ''member'' used in the next sentence. But the rules are too ill-drafted for any such inferences to be drawn; and rule 5, providing for special meetings of the committee when requested by three ''subscribers,'' and a general meeting if required by 20 of the ''members,'' strongly suggests that the terms are used interchangeably. At any rate, I have heard no sensible explanations of the distinction ...

[His Lordship then rejected the claims of the ex members.]

QUESTIONS

1. How would you have decided *Re Vandervell's Trusts* (*No 2*) if it had gone on appeal to the House of Lords, and you had been sitting?
2. Re-examine the situations in which the court has found a solution based upon (i) a resulting trust, (ii) a contractual right, (iii) bona vacantia. Do you think that the choice was based upon logical analysis, or upon convenience of result, or upon chance?

III. The Presumptions[6]

A. Presumption of Resulting Trust

i. VOLUNTARY CONVEYANCES

Where property is transferred for no consideration to a stranger (that is, to a person who is not the wife or child of the transferor) a rebuttable presumption arises that the transferee holds on a resulting trust for the transferor. This presumption used to apply equally to land and personalty, but, as a result of section 60 (3) of the Law of Property Act 1925, this is no longer so.

---

6 H & M, pp. 249–259; K & S, pp. 189–214; P & M, pp. 189–201; Pettit, pp. 128–142; Riddall, pp. 193–197, 204–207; Snell, pp. 177–184; Underhill, pp. 317–334.

(a) Land

LAW OF PROPERTY ACT 1925

60. Abolition of technicalities in regard to conveyancing and deeds.
(3) In a voluntary conveyance a resulting trust for the grantor shall not be implied merely by reason that the property is not expressed to be conveyed for the use or benefit of the grantee.

The effect of section 60 (3) is that a voluntary conveyance of land takes effect as expressed, unless there is evidence of a contrary intention.

In **Hodgson v Marks** [1971] Ch 892, [1971] 2 All ER 684, Mrs. Hodgson, a widow and 83 years of age, was the owner of a house. Mr. Evans was her lodger. He gained her trust and affection, and supervised the investment of her money. A nephew of Mrs. Hodgson was suspicious of Mr. Evans and tried to persuade her to turn him out. In order to protect Mr. Evans, she transferred the house to him, under an oral agreement that she would continue to be the beneficial owner. Mr. Evans was registered as the absolute owner. He later sold it to Mr. Marks. The question was whether Mrs. Hodgson was entitled to protection against Mr. Marks as the owner of an overriding interest on the ground that she was a person in actual occupation of the land. The Court of Appeal held that Mr. Evans held the house upon a resulting trust for her and that she was, therefore, equitable owner of the house. Her right to the house constituted an overriding interest under Land Registration Act 1925, s. 70 (1) (*g*).

(b) Personalty

In **Re Vinogradoff** [1935] WN 68,[6a] Mrs Vinogradoff, in 1926, gratuitously transferred a sum of £800 War Loan into the joint names of herself and of her infant granddaughter, Laura Jackson. The question was whether the stock was owned, on Mrs. Vinogradoff's death, by her estate or by Laura Jackson.

FARWELL J decided that it was held upon a resulting trust for the estate of Mrs. Vinogradoff. Section 20 of the Law Property act 1925, under which the appointment of an infant as trustee is void, did not affect the presumption of a resulting trust. "The stock was not the property of the infant, but formed part of the estate of the testatrix."

ii. PRESUMPTION IN FAVOUR OF A PURCHASER: PURCHASE IN THE NAME OF ANOTHER, AND JOINT PURCHASE IN THE NAME OF ONE

In **Dyer v Dyer** (1788) 2 Cox Eq Cas 92, EYRE CB explained the principle at 93:
"The clear result of all the cases, without a single exception, is, that the trust of a legal estate, whether freehold, copyhold, or leasehold; whether taken in the names of the purchasers and others jointly, or in the name of others without that of the purchaser; whether in one name or several; whether jointly or *successive*, results to the man who advances the purchase-money. This is a general proposition supported by all the cases, and there is nothing to

---

6a See also *Thavorn v Bank of Credit and Commerce International SA* [1985] 1 Lloyd's Rep 259 (resulting trust where aunt opened bank account in name of 15 year old nephew).

contradict it; and it goes on a strict analogy to the rule of the common law, that where a feoffment is made without consideration, the use results to the feoffor".[7]

FOWKES v PASCOE[8]
(1875) 10 Ch App 343 (CA in Ch, JAMES AND MELLISH LJJ)

Mrs. Baker made various purchases of $3\frac{1}{4}$ per cent. Annuities, amounting in all to £7,000 in the joint names of herself and John Pascoe, who was the son of Mrs. Baker's daughter-in-law.

By her will, Mrs. Baker gave her residuary estate to the daughter-in-law for life and after her death to John Pascoe and his sister in equal shares.

John Pascoe claimed to be entitled both to the capital sum and to the dividends due at Mrs. Baker's death, and afterwards received by him.

Held. Pascoe was entitled to the capital, but not to the dividends.

MELLISH LJ: Now, the presumption must, beyond all question, be of very different weight in different cases. In some cases it would be very strong indeed. If, for instance, a man invested a sum of stock in the name of himself and his solicitor, the inference would be very strong indeed that it was intended solely for the purpose of a trust, and the Court would require very strong evidence on the part of the solicitor to prove that it was intended as a gift; and certainly his own evidence would not be sufficient. On the other hand a man may make an investment of stock in the name of himself and some person, although not a child or wife, yet in such a position to him as to make it extremely probable that the investment was intended as a gift. In such a case, although the rule of law, if there was no evidence at all, would compel the Court to say that the presumption of trust must prevail, even if the Court might not believe that the fact was in accordance with the presumption, yet, if there is evidence to rebut the presumption, then, in my opinion, the Court must go into the actual facts. And if we are to go into the actual facts, and look at the circumstances of this investment, it appears to me utterly impossible, as the Lord Justice has said, to come to any other conclusion than that the first investment was made for the purpose of gift and not for the purpose of trust. It was either for the purpose of trust or else for the purpose of gift; and therefore any evidence which shews it was not for the purpose of trust is evidence to shew that it was for the purpose of gift. We find a lady of considerable fortune, having no nearer connections than Mr. *Pascoe*, who was then a young man living in her house, and for whom she was providing. We find her, manifestly out of her savings, buying a sum of £250 stock in the joint names of herself and him, and at the same time buying another sum of £250 stock, on the very same day, in the joint names of herself and a lady who was living with her as a companion. Then, applying one's common sense to that transaction, what inference is it possible to draw, except that the purchases were intended for the purpose of gifts? If they were intended for the purpose of trusts, what possible reason was there why the two sums were not invested in the same names? Besides, at the very same time the lady had a large sum of stock in her own name, and could anything be more absurd than to suppose that a lady with £4,000 or £5,000 in her own name at that time in the same stock, and having a sum of £500 to invest out of her savings, should go and

---

7 LPA 1925, s. 60 (3) does not apply, as the conveyance is not voluntary.
8 *Young v Sealey* [1949] Ch 278, [1949] 1 All ER 92; (1969) 85 LQR 530 (M.C. Cullity).

invest £250 in the name of herself and a young gentleman who was living in her house, and another £250 in the name of herself and her companion, and yet intend the whole to be for herself? I cannot come to any other conclusion than that it must have been intended by way of a present after her death.

Then, when we have once arrived at the conclusion that the first investment was intended as a gift (and the second was exactly similar), and when we find that the account was opened for the purpose of gift, those facts appear to me to rebut the presumption altogether, because when an account is once found to be opened for the purpose of gift there is very strong reason to suppose that everything added to that account was intended for the purpose of gift also. Assuming the testatrix to know that she had made a gift, and had invested a sum of money in stock in the joint names of herself and *Pascoe* for the purpose of making a present to him, it would certainly be a very extraordinary thing that she should go and add other large sums to that account, not for the purpose of making a present to him, but for the purpose of his being a trustee. I cannot help coming to the conclusion that, as a matter of fact, these investments were intended for the purpose of gift.

There were one or two facts relied on against this conclusion. It was said that Mr. *Pascoe* kept the matter secret for a great number of years, and never revealed it. I do not greatly rely on that. Every one who has experience knows that some persons are very reticent about their affairs, and some persons are always talking about them. You cannot form any inference as to that. If he really and bona fide believed, and had no doubt that it was intended for a gift, and for his use, I do not see that there was anything extraordinary in his not mentioning it to the persons who now say it was not mentioned to them. The only fact that in the least degree, in my opinion, went against him was his not accounting for the dividend which was due at the death of the testatrix. I think it is not at all impossible that he might have honestly believed that that was his, although I entirely agree that in point of law it was not so; therefore on the whole I come to the same conclusion as the Lord Justice.[9]

B. Presumption of Advancement

Where a voluntary conveyance is made to the wife[10] or child of the donor, or to a person to whom he stands *in loco parentis*, the presumption is that a gift was

---

9 See also *Crane v Davis* (1981) Times, 13 May, where the defendant registered the title of a house in Walton Street, Oxford, in the name of his company, having purchased it with money given to him by the plaintiff for its purchase on her behalf. FALCONER J held, following dicta in *Seldon v Davidson* [1968] 1 WLR 1083, [1968] 2 All ER 755, that the house was held on a resulting trust for the plaintiff.

10 Or fiancée: Law Reform (Miscellaneous Provisions) Act 1970, s. 2(1); *Mossop v Mossop* [1989] Fam 77, [1988] 2 All ER 202; [1988] Conv 284 (J. Martin); cf. *Bernard v Josephs* [1982] Ch 391, [1982] 3 All ER 162.

But there is no presumption where a man puts property into the name of his mistress: *Diwell v Farnes* [1959] 1 WLR 624, [1959] 2 All ER 379; nor where a wife puts property into the name of her husband: *Mercier v Mercier* [1903] 2 Ch 98; *Heseltine v Heseltine* [1971] 1 WLR 342, [1971] 1 All ER 952. The Law Commission Report: Matrimonial Property 1988 (Law Com No. 175) considers that the law which presumes an advancement upon a transfer from husband to wife, but not vice versa, is out of date. It proposes that, where property other than land (or a life assurance policy) is purchased by one spouse for the joint use or benefit of both, it should be jointly owned in the absence of a contrary intention. Where land or other property is transferred by one spouse (whether husband or wife) to the other, it should be owned by the transferee, unless it was transferred for their joint use or benefit, in which case it should be jointly owned.

intended. This is the presumption of advancement. It is a stronger presumption than the so-called presumption of a resulting trust, as is made clear in *Shephard v Cartwright*.[11] But it can be rebutted by comparatively slight evidence of a contrary intention.[12]

In **Bennet v Bennet** (1879) 10 ChD 474, JESSEL MR said at 476.[13]

"The doctrine of equity as regards presumption of gifts is this, that where one person stands in such a relation to another that there is an obligation on that person to make a provision for the other, and we find either a purchase or investment in the name of the other, or in the joint names of the person and the other, of an amount which would constitute a provision for the other, the presumption arises of an intention on the part of the person to discharge the obligation to the other; and therefore, in the absence of evidence to the contrary, that purchase or investment is held to be in itself evidence of a gift.

In other words, the presumption of gift arises from the moral obligation to give.

That reconciles all the cases upon the subject but one, because nothing is better established than this, that as regards a child, a person not the father of the child may put himself in the position of one *in loco parentis* to the child, and so incur the obligation to make a provision for the child . . . .

A person *in loco parentis* means a person taking upon himself the duty of a father of a child to make a provision for that child. It is clear that in that case the presumption can only arise from the obligation, and therefore in that case the doctrine can only have reference to the obligation of a father to provide for his child, and nothing else.

But the father is under that obligation from the mere fact of his being the father, and therefore no evidence is necessary to shew the obligation to provide for his child, because that is part of his duty. In the case of a father, you have only to prove the fact that he is the father, and when you have done that the obligation at once arises; but in the case of a person *in loco parentis* you must prove that he took upon himself the obligation."

SHEPHARD v CARTWRIGHT

[1955] AC 431, [1954] 3 All ER 649 (HL, VISCOUNT SIMONDS, Lords MORTON OF HENRYTON, REID, TUCKER and SOMERVELL OF HARROW)

In 1929 Philip Edward Shephard established certain private companies which prospered.The shares in these companies were divided among his three children, the appellants, one of whom was an infant. One reason for so dividing the shares was to obtain certain tax advantages.

In 1934 he formed a public company which took over the private companies, paying £300,000 in cash and £400,000 in shares. The Shephard children signed the necessary documents at the request of their father.

Shephard in effect controlled the cash and the shares and obtained the children's signatures to all necessary documents, without their knowing what they were signing. By 1936 all the money properly due to the children was

---

11 [1955] AC 431, [1954] 3 All ER 649, infra.
12 *McGrath v Wallis* [1995] 2 FLR 114.
13 See also *Re Paradise Motor Co Ltd* [1968] 1 WLR 1125, [1968] 2 All ER 625.

exhausted. On Shephard's death in 1949, the children sued the executors for an account. The defendants argued that the intention of the father since 1929 indicated clearly that he intended to treat the money and shares as his own.

Held. The estate was liable. The shares and money were owned beneficially by the children. Evidence of the activities of the father subsequent to the transfer of the shares to the children was not admissible in his favour.

VISCOUNT SIMONDS: I think it well to pause in this year 1929 and to ask what was the result in law or equity of the registration, in the names of his children of shares for which he supplied the cash, and I pause in order to examine the law, because it appears to me that the only two facts which are at this stage relied on to rebut the presumption of advancement, viz., that the children were ignorant and that certificates were not given to them, are of negligible value.

My Lords, I do not distinguish between the purchase of shares and the acquisition of shares upon allotment, and I think that the law is clear that on the one hand where a man purchases shares and they are registered in the name of a stranger there is a resulting trust in favour of the purchaser; on the other hand, if they are registered in the name of a child or one to whom the purchaser then stood *in loco parentis*, there is no such resulting trust but a presumption of advancement. Equally it is clear that the presumption may be rebutted but should not, as Lord Eldon said, give way to slight circumstances: *Finch v Finch* (1808) 15 Ves 43.

It must then be asked by what evidence can the presumption be rebutted, and it would, I think, be very unfortunate if any doubt were cast (as I think it has been by certain passages in the judgments under review) upon the well-settled law on this subject. It is, I think, correctly stated in substantially the same terms in every textbook that I have consulted and supported by authority extending over a long period of time. I will take, as an example, a passage from Snell's Equity, 24th Edn., p. 153, which is as follows:

"The acts and declarations of the parties before or at the time of the purchase, or so immediately after it as to constitute a part of the transaction, are admissible in evidence either for or against the party who did the act or made the declaration ... But subsequent declarations are admissible as evidence only against the party who made them, and not in his favour."

I do not think it necessary to review the numerous cases of high authority upon which this statement is founded. It is possible to find in some earlier judgments reference to "subsequent" events without the qualifications contained in the textbook statement: it may even be possible to wonder in some cases how in the narration of facts certain events were admitted to consideration. But the burden of authority in favour of the broad proposition as stated in the passage I have cited is overwhelming and should not be disturbed.

But although the applicable law is not in doubt, the application of it is not always easy. There must often be room for argument whether a subsequent act is part of the same transaction as the original purchase or transfer, and equally whether subsequent acts which it is sought to adduce in evidence ought to be regarded as admissions by the party so acting, and if they are so admitted, further facts should be admitted by way of qualification of those admissions.

The first question, then, is whether any subsequent events are admissible as part of the original transaction to prove that the deceased had not in 1929 the intention of advancement which the law presumes. My Lords, for nearly five years nothing happened which could by any means be regarded as throwing light upon his original intention, but an event did happen which would amply explain a change in that intention. For within a short time of their promotion the businesses of the six companies were prosperous beyond all expectation. In the year 1931 their combined profits were £57,780, in 1932 £128,525 and in 1933 £344,671. It is not surprising that in the light of this great success the deceased and his co-adventurer, Meyer, should form a public company to acquire all the shares of all the six companies. This they did.

[His Lordship reviewed the events subsequent to 1929, and continued:]

I have omitted to state one fact subsequent to the original transaction which, whether or not it is to be regarded as part of it and admissible in evidence under that head, is clearly admissible as an admission by the deceased against interest. Shortly before the completion of the agreement with the new company and no doubt as part of the arrangement, one of the old companies, New Ideal Homesteads Ltd., declared and paid a dividend of £25 12s. per share. The deceased, acting presumably under the power of attorney to which I have referred, received the dividend attributable to the appellants' shares and, though retaining it for his own use, instructed the respondent Dunk, an accountant who acted for the deceased in the preparation of his income tax returns, that the dividend was the income of the appellants. It was so treated by Dunk, whose integrity has not been challenged. Similar information and instructions were given by the deceased to Dunk in regard to the sums placed to the deposit account of the appellants with Barclays Bank Ltd., and to the untaxed interest payable in respect of those sums, and were acted on by him.

I turn, then, again to ask how these facts which I have briefly narrated can be adduced in evidence by the deceased or his estate. And I think it convenient at this stage to refer to a matter in which, with great respect, I think the Master of the Rolls fell into an error and, moreover, into an error which largely influenced him in the conclusion to which he came. For he treated the appellants' claim merely as a claim against a dead man's estate, and therefore (as he says and reiterates) as a claim in which a heavy onus lay on the claimants. But that is not, in my opinion, the way in which the claim should be regarded. It starts with the fact that in 1929 certain shares were placed by their father in the names of the appellants, and, that fact being admitted or proved, a presumption at once arises which it is for the respondents to rebut. They as executors are in no stronger position than their testator would be in if he were alive.

My Lords, at the outset of this opinion I said that there must often be room for argument whether subsequent events can be regarded as forming part of the original transaction so as to be admissible evidence of intention and in this case it has certainly been vigorously argued that they can. But, though I know of no universal criterion by which a link can for this purpose be established between one event and another, here I see insuperable difficulty in finding any link at all. The time factor alone of nearly five years is almost decisive, but, apart from that, the events of 1934 and 1935, whether taken singly or in their sum, appear to me to be wholly independent of the original transaction. It is in fact fair to say that, so far from flowing naturally and inevitably from it, they probably never would have happened but for the phenomenal success of the enterprise. Nor can I give any weight to the argument much pressed upon us that the deceased was an honourable man and therefore could not have acted as he did, if he had in 1929 intended to give the shares outright to his children.

I assume that he was an honourable man as well in the directions in regard to income tax that he gave to Mr. Dunk as otherwise, but I think that he may well have deemed it consistent with honourable conduct and with paternal benevolence to take back part of what he had given when the magnitude of the gift so far surpassed his expectation.

If, then, these events cannot be admitted in evidence as part of the original transaction, can they be admitted to rebut the presumption on the ground that they are admissions by the appellants against interest? I conceive it possible, and this view is supported by authority, that there might be such a course of conduct by a child after a presumed advancement as to constitute an admission by him of his parent's original intention, though such evidence should be regarded jealously. But it appears to me to be an indispensable condition of such conduct being admissible that it should be performed with knowledge of the material facts. In the present case the undisputed fact that the appellants under their father's guidance did what they were told without inquiry or knowledge precludes the admission in evidence of their conduct and, if it were admitted, would deprive it of all probative value. It is otherwise, however, with the conduct of the deceased. I have already made it clear that the respondents have failed to discharge the burden which rests on them of rebutting the presumption of advancement. The appellants, therefore, in my opinion, need no reinforcement from subsequent events. But, since inevitably in a complex case like this, either upon the footing of being examined de bene esse or because they have been admitted for some other purpose than the proof of intention, all the facts relevant or irrelevant have been reviewed, I do not hesitate to say that the only conclusion which I can form about the deceased's original intention is that he meant the provision he then made for his children to be for their permanent advancement. He may well have changed his mind at a later date, but it was too late. He may have thought that, having made an absolute gift, he could yet revoke it. This is something that no one will ever know. The presumption which the law makes is not to be thus rebutted. If it were my duty to speculate upon these matters, my final question would be why the deceased should have put these several parcels of shares in six different companies into the names of his wife and three children unless he meant to make provision for them, and since counsel have not been able to suggest any, much less any plausible, reason why he should have done so, I shall conclude that the intention which the law imputes to him was in fact his intention. The reasoning which made so strong an appeal to Mellish LJ in *Fowkes v Pascoe* (1875) 10 Ch App 343 has in this case also particular weight.

In my opinion, then, this appeal succeeds on the main question that has been argued before us.[14]

---

14 For the operation of the principle of advancement in the case of a joint banking account, see *Marshal v Crutwell* (1875) LR 20 Eq 328; *Re Roberts* [1946] Ch 1; *Hoddinott v Hoddinott* [1949] 2 KB 406; *Jones v Maynard* [1951] Ch 572, [1951] 1 All ER 802; *Re Bishop* [1965] Ch 450, [1965] 1 All ER 249; *Re Figgis* [1969] 1 Ch 123, [1968] 1 All ER 999; *Thompson v Thompson* (1970) 114 SJ 455; *McHardy and Sons v Warren* [1994] 2 FLR 338; Cretney and Masson, *Principles of Family Law* (5th edn), pp. 254–255. The problem of housekeeping money was dealt with by Married Women's Property Act 1964, under which equality of ownership is presumed in the absence of other evidence.

WARREN v GURNEY
[1944] 2 All ER 472 (CA, Lord GREENE MR, FINLAY and MORTON LJJ)

In 1929, Elijah Gurney purchased a house, "Fairview", for £300. It was conveyed to his daughter, who was about to be married to Denis Warren. Elijah retained the title deeds.

In 1943 Elijah signed a document headed "my wish", in which he stated that the house was to be divided between his three daughters. No provision was made in his will. He died in 1944, and Catherine Warren, claiming to be absolute owner of "Fairview", sued Elijah's executors to recover possession of the deeds.

Held. Catherine held "Fairview" on trust for her father. The presumption of advancement was rebutted by the contemporaneous declarations of Elijah. The document headed "my wish" was inadmissible.

MORTON LJ: It is well established that when a parent buys a property and has it conveyed into the name of his child, there arises a presumption that the parents intended to make a gift or advancement to the child of that property. Of course, that is a presumption which can be rebutted by evidence that that was not the father's intention. The father retained the title deeds of the property and he still had them in his possession when he died in the year 1944.

Three points were taken by counsel for the appellant. First of all, he contended that the judge was wrong in admitting as evidence a document headed "my wish", which he held was signed by Elijah Gurney, which was dated September 6, 1943. In my view counsel's contention under that heading was quite correct. The document headed "my wish" was not admissible in evidence. It was in the nature of a subsequent declaration by the alleged donor, which was not against his own interest, and it is clearly established that subsequent declarations by the alleged donor are only admissible if they are against his interest. The reason for that is quite obvious. If the rule were otherwise it would be extremely easy for persons to manufacture evidence, even although at the time when they made the purchase they in fact intended the child to have the gift of the property.

The second contention put forward by counsel for the appellants was that, on the admissible evidence, the judge was not justified in coming to the conclusion that the defendants had rebutted the presumption of advancement. In my view, there was ample evidence to justify that conclusion of the judge. In the first place, there is the fact that the father retained the title deeds from the time of purchase to the time of his death. I think that is a very significant fact, because title deeds, as it was said in COKE ON LITTLETON, are "sinews of the land". One would have expected the father to have handed them over, either to the plaintiff or her husband, if he had intended the gift. It is to be noted that the judge accepted the evidence given by the plaintiff's mother, Mary Ann Gurney, and by her brother, Meyrick George Gurney, and rejected the evidence of Denis Warren, the plaintiff's husband, where it conflicted with that given by those two witnesses.

I do not intend to travel all through the evidence given before the county court judge, but I wish to read one portion of it only, which, it seems to me, is of the utmost importance. Meyrick George Gurney gave evidence as follows:

"I am the son of Elijah Gurney and his executor. In 1929 father said he had thought of buying one of the properties for plaintiff: asked me which I thought best."

Pausing there, the words, "for plaintiff" might, if they had stood alone, seem to indicate that a gift was intended, but that possible meaning is displaced by what follows:

"I said 'Fairview'. Father said he had been talking to Warren. Father said Warren had said if father bought the house he would pay for the house as he could. I went with father to Wadeson, the solicitor. Father required property made in my sister's name, so that there could be no trouble at a later date, as Warren had to pay for it at a later date. Father said he should keep the deeds as security."

There are other passages of importance in the evidence. There are passages in the evidence of Mary Ann Gurney, containing statements as to contemporaneous declarations by the testator. There are certain statements made by the plaintiff herself against her own interest: for instance, the statement that she had not enough money to pay any rent. But I need not go further into the evidence. It seems to me, on the passages which I have referred to alone, the county court judge was fully justified in coming to his conclusion. The passage I have read from the evidence of Meyrick Gurney is a passage of the evidence of a witness whom the judge believed, and it seems to me that those contemporaneous declarations are quite sufficient to rebut the presumption even if they stood alone.

It is quite clear that contemporaneous declarations by the alleged donor are admissible in evidence. I am satisfied that there was ample evidence upon which the judge could found his conclusion, and, indeed, it is difficult to see how, on the evidence which he believed, he could have reached any other conclusion.

The last point raised by counsel for the appellant was this. He said that, on the evidence, and on the findings of the judge, his client was entitled to become the absolute owner of this property on the payment of a sum of £250 into the estate. I express no view as to whether that contention is or is not correct, because, even if it were correct, if would clearly not justify the plaintiff's claim to be handed the title deeds now. If that contention were correct she could only have them on payment of £250, which has never in fact been paid.

For these reasons, I think that this appeal should be dismissed with costs.

———————

Where a house has been acquired for joint occupation but conveyed into the name of one party, the presumption of advancement is a last resort, and is rebuttable by comparatively slight evidence whether the relationship is husband and wife or father and child.

In **McGrath v Wallis** [1995] 2 FLR 114, a house was acquired as a family home for the occupation of the parents and their son and daughter. As the father was not employed, it was conveyed into the son's name, as only he was acceptable as a mortgagor. Solicitors drew up a declaration of trust indicating that the father had a share of 80 per cent and the son 20 per cent. This was never sent to the father for signature and was found in the solicitors' files. There was no reason why the father should have wished to give the house to the son. The Court of Appeal held that the evidence was ample to rebut the presumption. As the contributions were in fact 70 per cent and 30 per cent, the father's estate was entitled to a 70 per cent share. The observations in *Pettitt v Pettitt* [1970] AC 777 at 793, 811, 824, [1969] 2 All ER 385 at 388, 404, 415, as to the weakness of the presumption with regard to the family home, applied equally to father and son.

Where property has been transferred for an unlawful purpose, for example to keep it safe from the transferor's creditors, the question arises whether the transferor can invoke or rebut the presumptions in order to support his claim to beneficial ownership. It has long been established that the presumption of advancement cannot be rebutted by evidence of an unlawful purpose. Thus in **Gascoigne v Gascoigne** [1918] 1 KB 223 a husband who took a lease of land in his wife's name in order to keep it from his creditors could not rebut the presumption of advancement.

The House of Lords reviewed the position in **Tinsley v Milligan** [1994] 1 AC 340, [1993] 3 All ER 65.[15] Two women purchased a house jointly but agreed that it should be in the name of the appellant in order to facilitate false claims to housing benefit by the respondent. Both were parties to the fraud, which was carried out over several years. Subsequently the parties fell out and the appellant moved out of the house. She brought an action seeking possession and the respondent counterclaimed for a declaration that the appellant held the house on trust for both parties equally. A majority of the House of Lords (Lords JAUNCEY OF TULLICHETTLE, LOWRY and BROWNE-WILKINSON) upheld the counterclaim, Lords KEITH OF KINKEL and GOFF OF CHIEVELEY dissenting. The principle upheld by the majority was that a transferor was entitled to succeed if he could establish his title without relying on his own illegality. Lord JAUNCEY OF TULLICHETTLE, said at 366, at 82;

"At the outset it seems to me to be important to distinguish between the enforcement of executory provisions arising under an illegal contract or other transaction and the enforcement of rights already acquired under the completed provisions of such a contract or transaction. Your Lordships were referred to a very considerable number of authorities, both ancient and modern, from which certain propositions may be derived.

First, it is trite law that the court will not give its assistance to the enforcement of executory provisions of an unlawful contract whether the illegality is apparent ex facie the document or whether the illegality of purpose of what would otherwise be a lawful contract emerges during the course of the trial: *Holman v Johnson* (1775) 1 Cowp 341 at 343, per Lord Mansfield CJ; *Pearce v Brooks* (1866) LR 1 Exch 213 at 217–218, per Pollock CB; *Alexander v Rayson* [1936] 1 KB 169 at 182, and *Bowmakers Ltd v Barnet Instruments Ltd.* [1945] KB 65 at 70, [1944] 2 All ER 579 at 582.

Second, it is well established that a party is not entitled to rely on his own fraud or illegality in order to assist a claim or rebut a presumption. Thus when money or property has been transferred by a man to his wife or children for the purpose of defrauding creditors and the transferee resists his claim for recovery he cannot be heard to rely on his illegal purpose in order to rebut the presumption of advancement; *Gascoigne v Gascoigne* [1918] 1 KB 223 at 226; *Chettiar v Chettiar* [1962] AC 294 at 302, [1962] 1 All ER 494 at 498 and *Tinker v Tinker* [1970] P 136 at 143, [1970] 1 All ER 540 at 543, per Salmon LJ.

---

15 [1993] CLJ 394 (R. Thornton); (1993) 143 NLJ 1577 (B. Council); (1993) 7 Trust Law International 114 (M. Lunney); [1994] Conv 62 (M. Halliwell); (1994) 57 MLR 441 (H. Stowe); (1994) 110 LQR 3 (R. Buckley); (1995) 111 LQR 135 (N. Enonchong). See Law Commission Report: Sixth Programme of Law Reform 1995 (Law Com No 234), Item 4.

Third, it has, however, for some years been recognised that a completely executed transfer of property or of an interest in property made in pursuance of an unlawful agreement is valid and the court will assist the transferee in the protection of his interest provided that he does not require to found on the unlawful agreement: *Ayerst v Jenkins* (1873) LR 16 Eq 275 at 283; *Alexander v Rayson* [1936] 1 KB 169 at 184–185; *Bowmakers Ltd v Barnet Instruments Ltd* [1945] KB 65, [1944] 2 All ER 579; *Sajan Singh v Sardara Ali* [1960] AC 167 at 176, [1960] 1 All ER 269 at 272–273. To the extent, at least, of his third proposition it would appear that there has been some modification over the years of Lord Eldon LC's principles.[15a]

The ultimate question in this appeal is, in my view, whether the respondent in claiming the existence of a resulting trust in her favour is seeking to enforce unperformed provisions of an unlawful transaction or whether she is simply relying on an equitable proprietary interest that she has already acquired under such a transaction.

[His Lordship referred to *Gissing v Gissing* [1971] AC 886, [1970] 2 All ER 780, and continued:]

I find this a very narrow question but I have come to the conclusion that the transaction whereby the claimed resulting trust in favour of the respondent was created was the agreement between the parties that, although funds were to be provided by both of them, nevertheless the title to the house was to be in the sole name of the appellant for the unlawful purpose of defrauding the Department of Social Security. So long as that agreement remained unperformed neither party could have enforced it against the other. However, as soon as the agreement was implemented by the sale to the appellant alone she became trustee for the respondent who can now rely on the equitable proprietary interest which has thereby been presumed to have been created in her favour and has no need to rely on the illegal transaction which led to its creation."

Lord BROWNE-WILKINSON said at 371, at 87:

"A presumption of resulting trust also arises in equity when A transfers personalty or money to B: see *Snell's Equity* (29th edn, 1990) pp 183–184; *Standing v Bowring* (1885) 31 Ch D 282 at 287, per Cotton LJ and *Dewar v Dewar* [1975] 1 WLR 1532 at 1537, [1975] 2 All ER 728 at 732. Before 1925 there was also a presumption of resulting trust when land was voluntarily transferred by A to B; it is arguable, however, that the position has been altered by the 1925 property legislation: see *Snell's Equity* p 182. The presumption of a resulting trust is, in my view, crucial in considering the authorities. On that presumption (and on the contrary presumption of advancement) hinges the answer to the crucial question: does a plaintiff claiming under a resulting trust have to rely on the underlying illegality? Where the presumption of resulting trust applies, the plaintiff does not have to rely on the illegality. If he proves that the property is vested in the defendant alone but that the plaintiff provided part of the purchase money, or voluntarily transferred the property to the defendant, the plaintiff establishes his claim under a resulting trust unless either the contrary presumption of advancement displaces the presumption of resulting trust or the defendant leads evidence to rebut the presumption of resulting trust. Therefore, in cases where the presumption of advancement does not apply, a

15a "To a fraudulent plaintiff seeking relief the court would say 'Let the estate lie where it falls' ": *Muckleston v Brown* (1801) 6 Ves 52 at 68–69.

plaintiff can establish his equitable interest in the property without relying in any way on the underlying illegal transaction. In this case the respondent as defendant simply pleaded the common intention that the property should belong to both of them and that she contributed to the purchase price: she claimed that in consequence the property belonged to them equally. To the same effect was her evidence-in-chief. Therefore the respondent was not forced to rely on the illegality to prove her equitable interest. Only in the reply and the course of the respondent's cross-examination did such illegality emerge: it was the appellant who had to rely on that illegality.

Although the presumption of advancement does not directly arise for consideration in this case, it is important when considering the decided cases to understand its operation. On a transfer from a man to his wife, children or others to whom he stands in loco parentis, equity presumes an intention to make a gift. Therefore in such a case, unlike the case where the presumption of resulting trust applies, in order to establish any claim the plaintiff has himself to lead evidence sufficient to rebut the presumption of gift and in so doing will normally have to plead, and give evidence of, the underlying illegal purpose.

[His Lordship reviewed the authorities and continued:]

The majority of cases have been those in which the presumption of advancement applied: in those authorities the rule has been stated as being that a plaintiff cannot rely on evidence of his own illegality to rebut the presumption applicable in such cases that the plaintiff intended to make a gift of the property to the transferee. Thus in *Gascoigne v Gascoigne* [1918] 1 KB 223; *McEvoy v Belfast Banking Co Ltd* [1934] NI 67; *Re Emery's Investments' Trusts* [1959] Ch 410, [1959] 1 All ER 577, *Chettiar v Chettiar* [1962] AC 294, [1962] 1 All ER 494 and *Tinker v Tinker* [1970] P 136 at 141–142, [1970] 1 All ER 540 at 542–543, the crucial point was said to be the inability of the plaintiff to lead evidence rebutting the presumption of advancement. In each case the plaintiff was claiming to recover property voluntarily transferred to, or purchased in the name of, a wife or child, for an illegal purpose. Although reference was made to Lord Eldon LC's principle, none of those cases was decided on the simple ground (if it were good law) that equity would not in any circumstances enforce a resulting trust in such circumstances. On the contrary in each case the rule was stated to be that the plaintiff could not recover because he had to rely on the illegality to rebut the presumption of advancement.

In my judgment, the explanation for this departure from Lord Eldon LC's absolute rule is that the fusion of the administration of law and equity has led the courts to adopt a single rule (applicable both at law and in equity) as to the circumstances in which the court will enforce property interests acquired in pursuance of an illegal transaction, viz the *Bowmakers* rule: [1945] KB 65, [1944] 2 All ER 579. A party to an illegality can recover by virtue of a legal or equitable property interest if, but only if, he can establish his title without relying on his own illegality. In cases where the presumption of advancement applies, the plaintiff is faced with the presumption of gift and therefore cannot claim under a resulting trust unless and until he has rebutted that presumption of gift: for those purposes the plaintiff does have to rely on the underlying illegality and therefore fails.''

Lord GOFF OF CHIEVELEY (dissenting) said at 357, at 74:
"The reason why the court of equity will not assist the claimant to recover his property or to assert his interest in it has been variously stated. It is sometimes

said that it is because he has not come to equity with clean hands. This was the reason given by Alexander CB in *Groves v Groves* (1828) 3 Y & J 163 at 174, and by Salmon LJ (with whom Cross LJ agreed) in *Tinker v Tinker* [1970] P 136 at 143, [1970] 1 All ER 540 at 543. Sometimes it is said that the claimant cannot be heard or allowed to assert his claim to an equitable interest, as in *Curtis v Perry* (1802) 6 Ves 739 at 746, per Lord Eldon LC: *Childers v Childers* (1857) 3 K & J 310 at 315, per Page-Wood V-C and *Cantor v Cox* (1976) 239 Estates Gazette 121 at 122 per Plowman V-C. But this is, as I see it, another way of saying that the claimant must fail because he has not come to the court with clean hands. It follows that in these cases the requirements necessary to give rise to an equitable interest are present; it is simply that the claimant is precluded from asserting them. This explains why, in cases where the unlawful purpose has not been carried into effect, the court is able to hold that, despite the illegality, there is an equitable interest to which the claimant is entitled.

Another conclusion follows from the identification of the basis upon which equity refuses its assistance in these cases. This is that the circumstances in which the court refuses to assist the claimant in asserting his equitable interest are not limited to cases in which there is a presumption of advancement in favour of the transferee. If that was the case, the principle could be said to be limited to those cases in which the transferor has to rely upon the illegal transaction in order to rebut the presumption; in other words the cases could be said to fall within what is sometimes called the *Bowmakers* rule, under which a claimant's claim is unenforceable when he has either to found his claim on an illegal transaction or to plead its illegality in order to support his claim: *Bowmakers Ltd v Barnet Instruments Ltd* [1945] KB 65, [1944] 2 All ER 579. Of course, in a number of cases of this kind, especially in modern times, the presumption of advancement does apply, because many cases are concerned with a man hiding away his assets in order to escape his creditors, or for some other similar purpose, by transferring them to his wife or to one of his children. But there are cases in which the principle has been applied, or has been recognised, where there was no presumption of advancement. Examples are *Curtis v Perry* (1802) 6 Ves 739; *Ex p Yallop* (1808) 15 Ves 60; *Roberts v Roberts* (1818) Dan 143; *Groves v Groves* (1828) 3 Y & J 163; *Haigh v Kaye* (1872) 7 Ch App 469; *Re Great Berlin Steamboat Co* (1884) 26 Ch D 616 and *Cantor v Cox* (1976) 239 Estates Gazette 121. Of course, where the presumption of advancement does apply, and the illegality is not established from another source, for example by the defendant, the claimant will be in the particular difficulty that, in order to rebut the presumption, he will have to rely upon the underlying transaction and so will of necessity have to disclose his own illegality. This is what happened in *Chettiar v Chettiar* [1962] AC 294, [1962] 1 All ER 494, where the property in question had been transferred by the claimant to his son, who, having fallen ill, took no part in the hearing and so himself gave no evidence of the illegality; even so, the father's claim failed because he was unable to rebut the presumption of advancement without relying upon the illegal transaction. But the case does not decide that the principle only applies where it is necessary to rebut the presumption of advancement; and, as I have already stated, there are many cases in which the principle has been recognised or applied where there was no such presumption. Furthermore, if for example the defendant proves that the property was transferred to him for a fraudulent or illegal purpose, a court of equity will refuse to assist the claimant when asserting his interest in it, even though the claimant's case can be, and was, advanced, without reference to the underlying legal purpose, for example on the simple basis that the transfer of the property to the defendant was without consideration. This conclusion follows inevitably from the nature of the principle, and the grounds upon which equity refuses its assistance; it is at least implicit in a number of cases, such as *Platamone v Staple* (1815) Coop G 250; *Groves v Groves* (1828) 3 Y & J 163, and *Haigh v Kaye* (1872) 7 Ch App 469. It follows that the so-called *Bowmakers* rule does not apply in cases concerned with the principle under discussion, because, once it comes to the attention of a court of equity that the claimant has not come to the court with clean hands, the court will refuse to assist the claimant, even though the claimant can prima facie establish his claim without recourse to the underlying fraudulent or illegal purpose. This is a point to which I will return when I come to consider the judgment of Lloyd LJ in the present case.

[His Lordship reviewed the decision of the Court of Appeal and continued:]

Lloyd LJ held that it was not the respondent, but the appellant, who had relied on the illegality in the present; and that accordingly, on the *Bowmakers* rule ([1945] KB 65, [1944] 2 All ER 579), the respondent was entitled to succeed in her claim for an equitable interest in the house. This theme is developed in the speech of my noble and learned friend Lord Browne-Wilkinson, who has discerned a development in the law since the late 19th century which supports this approach.

For reasons which I have already given, I have been unable to discover any such development in the law. As I read the authorities, they reveal a consistent application of the principle, subject only to the recognition of a locus poenitentiae for the claimant where the illegal purpose has not been carried into effect. Furthermore, the invocation by Lloyd LJ of the *Bowmakers* rule is, as I have already indicated, inconsistent with principle and authority. This conclusion flows from the nature of the principle itself, which is that a court of equity will not assist a claimant who does not come to equity with clean hands. This equitable maxim is more broadly based than the *Bowmakers* rule. It is founded on the principle that he who has committed iniquity shall not have equity; and what is required to invoke the maxim is no more than that the alleged misconduct has 'an immediate and necessary relation to the equity sued for': see *Dering v Earl of Winchelsea* (1787) 1 Cox Eq Cas 318 at 319–320, and *Snell's Equity* (29th edn, 1990) p 32.''

It was subsequently held by the Court of Appeal in **Tribe v Tribe**[16] that a person who has transferred property for an unlawful purpose may rely on his own illegality to rebut the presumption of advancement if the unlawful purpose has not been carried. *Tinsley v Milligan* did not decide that there was no exception to the rule that a person may not found an action on his own unlawful act. Thus a father who transferred shares to his son in order to deceive creditors was able to rebut the presumption of advancement where the share transfer was never shown to any creditor. It was emphasised, however, that evidence that property was transferred to protect it from creditors would not on its own rebut the presumption of advancement because the only way to

---

16 [1995] 3 WLR 913, [1995] 4 All ER 236; (1996) 26 Fam Law 3. (S. Cretney). This approach is not new. See *Symes v Hughes* (1870) LR 9 Eq 475; *Sekhon v Alissa* [1989] 2 FLR 94.

protect property from creditors was for the transferor to divest himself of his beneficial interest. Such a motive would normally reinforce the presumption. To rebut it, the transferor must show that he intended to retain an interest and conceal it from his creditors. The court would need compelling evidence, and would be unlikely to conclude that this was the transferor's intention where there was no imminent threat from known creditors at the time of the transfer.

IV. Family Property[17]

Problems of resulting trusts have commonly arisen in recent years in the context of the ownership of the matrimonial home, or of the home occupied by an unmarried cohabiting couple. In the case of spouses the dispute is likely to arise when the marriage has broken down. In such circumstances the ascertainment of the beneficial ownership of the home is only the first stage, as the court has a wide jurisdiction to make property adjustment orders under the Matrimonial Causes Act 1973. No such jurisdiction exists in the case of unmarried couples, whose entitlement is determined by the law of trusts.

Beneficial ownership is ascertained by applying the principles of both resulting and constructive trusts, but the presumption of advancement now plays little part. For convenience, the topic will be examined only in this chapter.

The principles were reviewed by the House of Lords in *Lloyds Bank plc v Rosset* [1991] 1 AC 107, [1990] 1 All ER 1111, p. 232 post.[18] It was considered that, in the absence of a declaration of trust evidenced in writing (p. 52, ante), there are two ways of acquiring a beneficial interest. The first is to establish that the parties expressed a common intention to share the beneficial interest, followed by detrimental reliance by the claimant, as in *Grant v Edwards* [1986] Ch 638, [1986] 2 All ER 426, p. 240, post. Alternatively, the court must be able to infer that the parties had a common intention to share. Such an inference can be drawn, it was said, only where the claimant has contributed directly to the purchase price, either initially or by payment of mortgage instalments. It was doubted whether indirect contributions would suffice. Direct contributions were regarded as giving rise to a constructive trust, although traditionally such contributions give rise to a presumption of a resulting trust.[19]

The rejection of the view, expressed in earlier cases,[20] that an indirect contribution can suffice without the necessity of finding an express common intention to share, is capable of producing injustice, as where the wife pays

---

17 See generally H & M, pp. 260–290; Bromley, *Family Law* (8th edn, 1992), chap. 18; Cretney and Masson, *Principles of Family Law* (5th edn, 1990) chap. 11.

18 (1990) 106 LQR 539 (J. Davies); [1990] Conv 314 (M. Thompson), [1990] All ER Rev 138 (S. Cretney); [1991] CLJ 38 (M. Dixon); (1991) 54 MLR 126 (S. Gardner); (1993) 23 Fam Law 231 (J. Dewar).

19 Later payments of mortgage instalments, without any liability to make them, do not found a presumption of a resulting trust, although a constructive trust can arise; (1994) 8 Trust Law International 43 (P. Matthews).

20 *Gissing v Gissing* [1971] AC 886, [1970] 2 All ER 780; *Burns v Burns* [1984] Ch 317, [1984] 1 All ER 244, p. 235; *Grant v Edwards* [1986] Ch 638, [1986] 2 All ER 426, p. 240 post.

household bills, thereby enabling her husband to pay the mortgage instalments.[1] Some Commonwealth jurisdictions have resolved this problem by legislation[2] or by applying the principles of unjust enrichment, and are rejecting the view, illustrated by *Burns v Burns* [1984] Ch 317, [1984] 1 All ER 244, p. 000, post, that domestic duties must be left out of account.[3] Another approach is to invoke the more flexible principles of proprietary estoppel, where the act of detrimental reliance need not involve expenditure, and which does not require a search for an artificial common intention.[4] The process of assimilating the doctrines of proprietary estoppel and constructive trust has begun, but is not complete.[5] Another view is that the relationship of the parties should itself generate the claim.[6]

The principles laid down in *Lloyds Bank plc v Rosset* have since been applied by the lower courts on several occasions. A council tenant's discount under the "right to buy" legislation has been regarded as a direct contribution.[7] An indirect contribution consisting of working in a business for pocket money only has been held insufficient in the absence of an express common intention.[8]

In **Hammond v Mitchell** [1991] 1 WLR 1127, [1992] 2 All ER 109[9] a man owned a bungalow in England and a house in Spain. An express common intention to share was established in relation to the bungalow but not the house. The woman had acted as the man's unpaid business assistant in addition to domestic duties at both properties. This sufficed to give her a share of the bungalow but not the house. Similar principles apply where property is in joint names but the documents are silent as to the beneficial interest.[10]

In the case of direct contributions, the beneficial interest acquired will normally be proportionate to the contribution, but there is more flexibility where there is an express common intention coupled with detrimental reliance. If the parties have agreed to share but have not agreed the size of their shares, the court will determine what is a "fair share".[11]

Finally, a husband or wife who has made a substantial contribution in money or money's worth to the improvement of property in which either or both of

1 Such a contribution may suffice under the "reasonable expectation" approach in New Zealand; *Lankow v Rose* [1995] 1 NZLR 277.

2 De Facto Relationships Act 1984 (NSW); (1994) 8 Trust Law International 74 (M. Bryan). A Law Commission consultation paper on the Property Rights of Unmarried Cohabitants is planned in 1996; Law Com No 232, 29th Annual Report, paras 2.78– 2.79.

3 See *Peter v Beblow* (1993) 101 DLR (4th) 621.

4 [1990] Conv 370 (D. Hayton); (1993) 109 LQR 114 (P. Ferguson) and 485 (D. Hayton); (1993) 3 Carib LR 96 (R. Smith).

5 *Grant v Edwards*; *Lloyds Bank plc v Rosset*, supra; *Stokes v Anderson* [1991] 1 FLR 391.

6 (1993) 109 LQR 263 (S. Gardner).

7 *Springette v Defoe* (1992) 65 P & CR 1.

8 *Ivin v Blake* (1993) 67 P & CR 263.

9 [1992] All ER Rev 210 (P. Clarke); [1992] Conv 218 (A. Lawson); (1993) 56 MLR 224 (P. O'Hagan). See also *Risch v McFee* (1990) 61 P & CR 42; *Windeler v Whitehall* [1990] 2 FLR 505; *McHardy and Sons v Warren* [1994] 2 FLR 338.

10 *Springette v Defoe* supra; *Savill v Goodall* [1993] 1 FLR 705. A declaration in the title documents is conclusive in the absence of fraud or mistake.

11 *Stokes v Anderson* [1991] 1 FLR 391; *Drake v Whipp* (1995) Times, 19 December, p. 246, post. See also *Midland Bank plc v Cooke* [1995] 4 All ER 562, p. 245, post (the court may infer an agreement as to the proportions of the parties' shares on general equitable principles, and is not bound to find that the shares are proportionate to the direct contributions).

them has a beneficial interest, is treated as having a share or an enlarged share in that beneficial interest.[12]

LLOYDS BANK PLC v ROSSET
[1991] 1 AC 107, [1990] 1 All ER 1111 (HL, Lords Bridge of Harwich, Griffiths, Ackner, Oliver of Aylmerton and Jauncy of Tullichettle

A semi-derelict farmhouse was purchased as a family home with funds from the husband's family trust and (without the wife's knowledge) with a bank loan secured on the property, which was conveyed into the husband's sole name. The vendor permitted builders to enter and do works before completion. During this period the wife spent nearly every day at the property. supervising the builders. She also helped her husband to plan the renovation and did some decorating. Subsequently the husband was unable to repay the bank loan and the bank took possession proceedings. The wife claimed that she had a share of the beneficial interest, and that this was enforceable against the bank.
Held The wife had no beneficial interest. The question of priorities did not, therefore, arise.
LORD BRIDGE OF HARWICH: Even if there had been the clearest oral agreement between Mr and Mrs Rosset that Mr Rosset was to hold the property in trust for them both as tenants in common, this would, of course, have been ineffective since a valid declaration of trust by way of gift of a beneficial interest in land is required by s 53(1) of the Law of Property Act 1925 to be in writing. But if Mrs Rosset had, as pleaded, altered her position in reliance on the agreement this could have given rise to an enforceable interest in her favour by way either of a constructive trust or of a proprietary estoppel.

Having rejected the contention that there had been any concluded agreement, arrangement or any common intention formed before contracts for the purchase of the property were exchanged on 23 November 1982 that Mrs Rosset should have any beneficial interest, the judge concentrated his attention on Mrs Rosset's activities in connection with the renovation works as a possible basis from which to infer such a common intention. He described what she did up to the date of completion as follows:

"Up to 17 December 1982 [Mrs Rosset's] contribution to the venture was: (1) to urge on the builders and to attempt to co-ordinate their work, until her husband insisted that he alone should give instructions; (2) to go to builders' merchants and obtain material required by the builders ... and to deliver the materials to the site. This was of some importance because Mr Griffin and his employees did not know the Thanet area; (3) to assist her husband in planning the renovation and decoration of the house. In this, she had some skill over and above that acquired by most housewives. She was a skilled painter and decorator who enjoyed wallpapering and decorating, and, as her husband acknowledged, she had good ideas about his work. In connection with this, she advised on the

---

12 Matrimonial Proceedings and Property Act 1970, s. 37. This is subject to any contrary intention. See *Thomas v Fuller-Brown* [1988] 1 FLR 237 (where the claim failed because the inference was that the expenditure was in return for rent-free accommodation; *Cadman v Bell* [1988] EGCS 139 (licence for life); *Passee v Passee* [1988] 1 FLR 263; [1988] Conv 361 (J. Warburton). It is otherwise if the money was advanced as a loan; *Spence v Brown* [1988] Fam Law 291; cf *Hussey v Palmer* [1972] 1 WLR 1286, p. 295, post.

position of electric plugs and radiators and planned the design of the large breakfast room and the small kitchen of the house; (4) to carry out the wallpapering of Natasha's bedroom and her own bedroom, after preparing the surfaces of the walls and clearing up the rooms concerned before the papering began; (5) to begin the preparation of the surfaces of the walls of her son's bedroom, the den, the upstairs lavatory and the downstairs washroom for papering. All this wallpapering was completed after 17 December 1982 but by 31 December 1982; (6) to assist in arranging the insurance of the house by the Minister Insurance Co Ltd home cover policy, in force from 3 November 1982; (7) to assist in arranging a crime prevention survey on 23 November 1982; (8) to assist in arranging the installation of burglar alarms described in a specification dated 3 December 1982.''

Later the judge said:

''I am satisfied that in 1982 the common intention expressed by [Mr and Mrs Rosset] in conversation between themselves was that Vincent Farmhouse should be purchased in the name of [Mr Rosset] alone, because funds would not be made available from [his] family trust in Switzerland unless the purchase was made only in his name. In addition, however, it was their common intention that the renovation of the house should be a joint venture, after which the house was to become a family home to be shared by [the parties] and their children.''

I pause to observe that neither a common intention by spouses that a house is to be renovated as a 'joint venture' nor a common intention that the house is to be shared by parents and children as a family home throws any light on their intentions with respect to the beneficial ownership of the property.

[His Lordship cited further passages from the judgment of the trial judge and continued:]

It is clear from these passages in the judgment that the judge based his inference of a common intention that Mrs Rosset should have a beneficial interest in the property under a constructive trust essentially on what Mrs Rosset did in and about assisting in the renovation of the property between the beginning of November 1982 and the date of completion on 17 December 1982. Yet by itself this activity, it seems to me, could not possibly justify any such inference. It was common ground that Mrs Rosset was extremely anxious that the new matrimonial home should be ready for occupation before Christmas if possible. In these circumstances, it would seem the most natural thing in the world for any wife, in the absence of her husband abroad, to spend all the time she could spare and to employ any skills she might have, such as the ability to decorate a room, in doing all she could to accelerate progress of the work quite irrespective of any expectation she might have of enjoying a beneficial interest in the property. The judge's view that some of this work was work 'on which she could not reasonably have been expected to embark unless she was to have an interest in the house' seems to me, with respect, quite untenable. The impression that the judge may have thought that the share of the equity to which he held Mrs Rosset to be entitled had been 'earned' by her work in connection with the renovation is emphasised by his reference in the concluding sentence of his judgment to the extent to which her 'qualifying contribution' reduced the cost of the renovation.

On any view the monetary value of Mrs Rosset's work expressed as a contribution to a property acquired at a cost exceeding £70,000 must have been so trifling as to be almost de minimis. I should myself have had considerable doubt whether Mrs Rosset's contribution to the work of renovation was sufficient to support a claim to a constructive trust in the absence of writing to satisfy the requirements of s. 53(1) of the Law of Property Act 1925 even if her husband's intention to make a gift to her of half or any other share in the equity of the property had been clearly established or if he had clearly represented to her that that was what he intended. But here the conversations with her husband on which Mrs Rosset relied, all of which took place before November 1982, were incapable of lending support to the conclusion of a constructive trust in the light of the judge's finding that by that date there had been no decision that she was to have any interest in the property. The finding that the discussions 'did not exclude the possibility' that she should have an interest does not seem to me to add anything of significance.

These considerations lead me to the conclusion that the judge's finding that Mr Rosset held the property as constructive trustee for himself and his wife cannot be supported and it is on this short ground that I would allow the appeal. In the course of the argument your Lordships had the benefit of elaborate submissions as to the test to be applied to determine the circumstances in which the sole legal proprietor of a dwelling house can properly be held to have become a constructive trustee of a share in the beneficial interest in the house for the benefit of the partner with whom he or she has cohabited in the house as their shared home. Having in this case reached a conclusion on the facts which, although at variance with the views of the courts below, does not seem to depend on any nice legal distinction and with which, I understand, all your Lordships agree, I cannot help doubting whether it would contribute anything to the illumination of the law if I were to attempt an elaborate and exhaustive analysis of the relevant law to add to the many already to be found in the authorities to which our attention was directed in the course of the argument. I do, however, draw attention to one critical distinction which any judge required to resolve a dispute between former partners as to the beneficial interest in the home they formerly shared should always have in the forefront of his mind.

The first and fundamental question which must always be resolved is whether, independently of any inference to be drawn from the conduct of the parties in the course of sharing the house as their home and managing their joint affairs, there has at any time prior to acquisition, or exceptionally at some later date, been any agreement, arrangement or understanding reached between them that the property is to be shared beneficially. The finding of an agreement or arrangement to share in this sense can only, I think, be based on evidence of express discussions between the partners, however imperfectly remembered and however imprecise their terms may have been. Once a finding to this effect is made it will only be necessary for the partner asserting a claim to a beneficial interest against the partner entitled to the legal estate to show that he or she has acted to his or her detriment or significantly altered his or her position in reliance on the agreement in order to give rise to a constructive trust or proprietary estoppel.

In sharp contrast with this situation is the very different one where there is no evidence to support a finding of an agreement or arrangement to share, however reasonable it might have been for the parties to reach such an arrangement if they had applied their minds to the question, and where the court must rely entirely on the conduct of the parties both as the basis from which to infer a common intention to share the property beneficially and as the conduct relied on to give rise to a constructive trust. In this situation direct contributions to the purchase price by the partner who is not the legal owner, whether initially or by payment of mortgage instalments, will readily justify the inference necessary to the creation of a constructive trust. But, as I read the authorities, it is at least extremely doubtful whether anything less will do.

The leading cases in your Lordships' House are *Pettitt v Pettitt* [1970] AC 777, [1969] 2 All ER 385, and *Gissing v Gissing* [1971] AC 886, [1970] 2 All ER 780. Both demonstrate situations in the second category to which I have referred and their Lordships discuss at great length the difficulties to which these situations give rise. The effect of these two decisions is very helpfully analysed in the judgment of Lord MacDermott LCJ in *McFarlane v McFarlane* [1972] NI 59.

Outstanding examples on the other hand of cases giving rise to situations in the first category are *Eves v Eves* [1975] 1 WLR 1338, [1975] 3 All ER 768 and *Grant v Edwards* [1986] Ch 638, [1986] 2 All ER 426. In both these cases, where the parties who had cohabited were unmarried, the female partner had been clearly led by the male partner to believe, when they set up home together, that the property would belong to them jointly. In *Eves v Eves* the male partner had told the female partner that the only reason why the property was to be acquired in his name alone was because she was under 21 and that, but for her age, he would have had the house put into their joint names. He admitted in evidence that this was simply an 'excuse'. Similarly, in *Grant v Edwards* the female partner was told by the male partner that the only reason for not acquiring the property in joint names was because she was involved in divorce proceedings and that, if the property were acquired jointly, this might operate to her prejudice in those proceedings. As Nourse LJ put it [1986] Ch 638 at 649, [1986] 2 All ER 426 at 433:

"Just as in *Eves v Eves*, these facts appear to me to raise a clear inference that there was an understanding between the plaintiff and the defendant, or a common intention, that the plaintiff was to have some sort of proprietary interest in the house; otherwise no excuse for not putting her name onto the title would have been needed."

The subsequent conduct of the female partner in each of these cases, which the court rightly held sufficient to give rise to a constructive trust or proprietary estoppel supporting her claim to an interest in the property, fell far short of such conduct as would by itself have supported the claim in the absence of an express representation by the male partner that she was to have such an interest. It is significant to note that the share to which the female partners in *Eves v Eves* and *Grant v Edwards* were held entitled were one-quarter and one-half respectively. In no sense could these shares have been regarded as proportionate to what the judge in the instant case described as a 'qualifying contribution' in terms of the indirect contributions to the acquisition or enhancement of the value of the houses made by the female partners.

I cannot help thinking that the judge in the instant case would not have fallen into error if he had kept clearly in mind the distinction between the effect of evidence on the one hand which was capable of establishing an express agreement or an express representation that Mrs Rosset was to have an interest in the property and evidence on the other hand of conduct alone as a basis for an inference of the necessary common intention ...

For the reasons I have indicated I would allow the appeal ...

BURNS v BURNS[13]
[1984] Ch 317, [1984] 1 All ER 244 (CA, WALLER, FOX and MAY LJJ)

The plaintiff and defendant lived together but were not married. The defendant bought a house in 1963 which was conveyed into his sole name. The plaintiff made no direct contributions to the purchase price or mortgage payments, but looked after the children and the home. When she started working in 1975, the defendant did not ask her to contribute to the household expenses. She did, however, pay the rates and telephone bills, and purchased some domestic goods. She also did some decorating. In 1980 the plaintiff left the defendant, and claimed a beneficial interest in the house.

Held. The plaintiff had not established any trust in her favour.

Fox LJ: The house with which we are concerned in this case was purchased in the name of the defendant and the freehold was conveyed to him absolutely. That was in 1963. If, therefore, the plaintiff is to establish that she has a beneficial interest in the property she must establish that the defendant holds the legal estate upon trust to give effect to that interest. That follows from *Gissing v Gissing* [1971] AC 886, [1970] 2 All ER 780. For present purposes I think that such a trust could only arise (a) by express declaration or agreement *or* (b) by way of a resulting trust where the claimant has directly provided part of the purchase price *or* (c) from the common intention of the parties.

In the present case (a) and (b) can be ruled out. There was no express trust of an interest in the property for the benefit of the plaintiff; and there was no express agreement to create such an interest. And the plaintiff made no direct contribution to the purchase price. Her case, therefore, must depend upon showing a common intention that she should have a beneficial interest in the property. Whether the trust which would arise in such circumstances is described as implied, constructive or resulting does not greatly matter. If the intention is inferred from the fact that some indirect contribution is made to the purchase price, the term "resulting trust" is probably not inappropriate. Be that as it may, the basis of such a claim, in any case, is that it would be inequitable for the holder of the legal estate to deny the claimant's right to a beneficial interest.

In determining whether such common intention exists it is, normally, the intention of the parties when the property was purchased that is important. As to that I agree with the observations of Griffiths LJ in *Bernard v Josephs* [1982] Ch 391, 404, [1982] 3 All ER 162, 170–171. As I understand it, that does not mean that for the purpose of determining the ultimate shares in the property one looks simply at the factual position as it was at the date of acquisition. It is necessary for the court to consider all the evidence, including the contribution of the parties, down to the date of separation (which in the case of man and mistress will generally, though not always, be the relevant date). Thus the law proceeds on the basis that there is nothing inherently improbable in the parties acting on the understanding that the woman

"should be entitled to a share which was not to be quantified immediately upon the acquisition of the home but should be left to be determined when the mortgage was repaid or the property disposed of, on the basis of

13 (1984) 47 MLR 341 (N.V. Lowe and A.Smith), 735 (J. Dewar); [1984] Conv 381 (S. Coneys); (1984) 43 CLJ 277 (R. Ingleby); [1984] All ER Rev 167 (R. Deech).

what would be fair having regard to the total contributions, direct or indirect, which each spouse had made by that date," (see *Gissing v Gissing* [1971] AC 886, 909, [1970] 2 All ER 780, 793, per Lord Diplock).

That approach does not, however, in my view preclude the possibility that while, initially, there was no intention that the claimant should have any interest in the property, circumstances may subsequently arise from which the intention to confer an equitable interest upon the claimant may arise (e.g., the discharge of a mortgage or the effecting of capital improvements to the house at his or her expense). Further, subsequent events may throw light on the initial intention.

Looking at the position at the time of the acquisition of the house in 1963, I see nothing at all to indicate any intention by the parties that the plaintiff should have an interest in it. The price of the house was £4,900. Of that, about £4,500 was raised by the defendant on a mortgage. The mortgage was in his own name; he assumed responsibility for the debt. The balance of the purchase price and the costs of the purchase were paid by the defendant out of his own moneys. The plaintiff made no financial contribution; she had nothing to contribute. As to the reason for buying the house the judge said that he had no doubt that it was an important factor in the decision that the defendant realised that it was much better use of money to buy an asset — a house — rather than rent a flat (which was what he was doing previously).

It seems to me that at the time of the acquisition of the house nothing occurred between the parties to raise an equity which would prevent the defendant denying the plaintiff's claim. She provided no money for the purchase; she assumed no liability in respect of the mortgage; there was no understanding or arrangement that the plaintiff would go out to work to assist with the family finances; the defendant did nothing to lead her to change her position in the belief that she would have an interest in the house. It is true that she contemplated living with the defendant in the house and, no doubt, that she would do housekeeping and look after the children. But those facts do not carry with them any implication of a common intention that the plaintiff should have an interest in the house. Taken by themselves they are simply not strong enough to bear such an implication.

I come then to the position in the year after the house was purchased. I will deal with them under three heads, namely financial contributions, work on the house and finally housekeeping. There is some overlapping in these categories.

So far as financial contributions are concerned, the plaintiff's position really did not change during the 1960's. She had no money of her own and could not contribute financially to the household. All the mortgage instalments were paid by the defendant alone. By the end of the 1960's as a result of qualifying as an instructor in flower arrangement she was able to earn a little by giving lessons in flower arrangements. But as I understand the judgment, the amounts were small particularly since lessons had to be given in the evening with the result that the plaintiff had to have a baby sitter.

Then in 1972 the plaintiff took flying lessons and qualified as a pilot of light aircraft in 1973. But that was simply a pastime and neither produced nor was intended to produce any addition to the family budget; it was, in fact, an expense.

The plaintiff's driving instruction business did produce an income. It started in 1972 and to begin with was on a small scale. The business increased and, after 1975, the plaintiff "was earning a certain amount" from it according to the judge's finding. By the time she left the defendant in 1980 she was earning, in all, about £60 per week (which we were told during the hearing was net of expenses). It looks as though she was earning at this rate from about 1977 or 1978 onwards.

There was never any question of the plaintiff being asked by the defendant to apply her earnings to household expenses so as to relieve him. She was free to do what she liked with her earnings.

The judge's findings as to expenditure by the plaintiff were as follows. (i) She made gifts of clothing and other things to the defendant and the children. (ii) She paid for the housekeeping. The defendant allowed her, latterly, £60 per week for housekeeping. It seems to be accepted that the defendant was generous with money and the plaintiff was not kept short as regards housekeeping money. (iii) She paid the rates. The housekeeping payments made by the defendant were, however, fixed at an amount which took account of this. (iv) She paid the telephone bills. That was a matter of agreement between her and the defendant because she spent a lot of time on the telephone talking to her friends. (v) She bought a number of chattels for domestic use; a dishwasher, a washing machine, a tumble dryer and either a drawing room suite or three armchairs and a bed for her separate room. The bed, the dishwasher and the chairs she took with her when she left in 1980. (vi) She provided some doorknobs and door furnishings of no great value.

None of this expenditure, in my opinion, indicates the existence of the common intention which the plaintiff has to prove. What is needed, I think, is evidence of a payment or payments by the plaintiff which it can be inferred was referable to the acquisition of the house. Lord Denning MR in *Hazell v Hazell* [1972] 1 WLR 301, 304, [1972] 1 All ER 923, 926, thought that expression, which appears in the speech of Lord Diplock in *Gissing v Gissing* [1971] AC 886, 909, [1970] 2 All ER 780, 793 was being over-used. He said quoting from *Falconer v Falconer* [1970] 1 WLR 1333, 1336, [1970] 3 All ER 449, 452, that if there was a substantial financial contribution towards the family expenses that would raise an inference of a trust. I do not think that formulation alters the essence of the matter for present purposes. If there is a substantial contribution by the woman to family expenses, and the house was purchased on a mortgage, her contribution is, indirectly, referable to the acquisition of the house since, in one way or another, it enables the family to pay the mortgage instalments. Thus, a payment could be said to be referable to the acquisition of the house if, for example, the payer either (a) pays part of the purchase price or (b) contributes regularly to the mortgage instalments or (c) pays off part of the mortgage or (d) makes a substantial financial contribution to the family expenses so as to enable the mortgage instalments to be paid.

But if a payment cannot be said to be, in a real sense, referable to the acquisition of the house it is difficult to see how, in such a case as the present, it can base a claim for an interest in the house. Looking at the items which I have listed above, and leaving aside, for the present, the housekeeping which I will deal with separately, none of the items can be said to be referable to the acquisition of the house. The making of ordinary gifts between members of a family certainly is not. Nor, in the circumstances as found by the judge, are the payments of rates or of the telephone bills. The provision of the door knobs etc. is of very small consequence. As regards the purchase of chattels for domestic use, the plaintiff must, I think, have regarded at any rate some of these as her own property since she took them away with her when she left. But quite apart from that I do not think that the provision of chattels, by itself, is evidence of any common intention that the plaintiff should have a beneficial interest in the house. In *Gissing v Gissing* [1971] AC 886, [1970] 2 All ER 780 Viscount Dilhorne, after referring to the requirement of a common intention that the wife should have an interest in the house, said, at p. 900, at p. 786:

"To establish this intention there must be some evidence which points to its existence. It would not, for instance, suffice if the wife just made a mortgage payment while her husband was abroad. Payment for a lawn and provision of some furniture and equipment for the house does not itself point to the conclusion that there was such an intention."

Lord Diplock said, at p. 910, at p. 794: "The court is not entitled to infer a common intention ... from the mere fact that she provided chattels for joint use in the new matrimonial home; ... "

It is to be borne in mind that the judge found that if the plaintiff wanted more money at any time from the defendant she could have had it. She was, no doubt, happy to use her own money to buy things for the house but, against the financial background, such purchases are no indication of a common intention that she was to have an interest in the house.

As regard work on the house, in 1971 a fairly substantial improvement was made to the house; the attic was converted into a bedroom with a bathroom en suite. That was paid for wholly by the defendant.

In 1977 or 1978 the plaintiff decorated the house throughout internally because she wished the house to be wallpapered and not painted. I do not think that carries her case any further. Thus in *Pettitt v Pettitt* [1970] AC 777, 826, [1969] 2 All ER 385, 416 Lord Diplock said:

"If the husband likes to occupy his leisure by laying a new lawn in the garden or building a fitted wardrobe in the bedroom while the wife does the shopping, cooks the family dinner and bathes the children, I, for my part, find it quite impossible to impute to them as reasonable husband and wife any common intention that these domestic activities or any of them are to have any effect upon the existing proprietary rights in the family home ..."

Accordingly I think that the decoration undertaken by the plaintiff gives no indication of any such common intention as she must assert.

There remains the question of housekeeping and domestic duties. So far as housekeeping expenses are concerned, I do not doubt that (the house being bought in the man's name) if the woman goes out to work in order to provide money for the family expenses, as a result of which she spends her earnings on the housekeeping and the man is thus able to pay the mortgage instalments and other expenses out of his earnings, it can be inferred that there was a common intention that the woman should have an interest in the house— since she will have made an indirect financial contribution to the mortgage instalments. But this is not this case.

During the greater part of the period when the plaintiff and the defendant were living together she was not in employment or, if she was, she was not earning amounts of any consequence and provided no money towards the family expenses. Nor is it suggested that the defendant ever asked her to. He provided, and was always ready to provide, all the money that she wanted for housekeeping. The house was not bought in the contemplation that the plaintiff would, at some time, contribute to the cost of its acquisition. She worked to suit herself. And if toward the very end of the relationship she had money to spare she spent it entirely as she chose. It was in no sense "joint" money. It was her own; she was not expected and was not asked to spend it on the household.

I think it would be quite unreal to say that, overall, she made a substantial financial contribution towards the family expenses. That is not in any way a criticism of her; it is simply the factual position.

But, one asks, can the fact that the plaintiff performed domestic duties in the house and looked after the children be taken into account? I think it is necessary to keep in mind the nature of the right which is being asserted. The court has no jurisdiction to make such order as it might think fair; the powers conferred by the Matrimonial Causes Act 1973 in relation to the property of married persons do not apply to unmarried couples. The house was bought by the defendant in his own name and, prima facie, he is the absolute beneficial owner. If the plaintiff, or anybody else, claims to take it from him, it must be proved the claimant has, by some process of law, acquired an interest in the house. What is asserted here is the creation of a trust arising by common intention of the parties. That common intention may be inferred where there has been a financial contribution, direct or indirect, do the acquisition of the house. But the mere fact that parties live together and do the ordinary domestic tasks is, in my view, no indication at all that they thereby intended to alter the existing property rights of either of them.

[His Lordship referred to *Pettitt v Pettitt* [1970] AC 777, [1969] 2 All ER 385; *Button v Button* [1968] 1 WLR 457, [1968] 1 All ER 1064; *Hall v Hall* (1981) 3 FLR 379; *Gissing v Gissing* [1971] AC 886, [1970] 2 All ER 780; *Falconer v Falconer* [1970] 1 WLR 1333, [1970] 3 All ER 449; *Cooke v Head* [1972] 1 WLR 518, [1972] 2 All ER 38; and *Bernard v Josephs* [1982] Ch 391, [1982] 3 All ER 162, and continued:]

For the reasons which I have given I think that the appeal must be dismissed. I only add this. The plaintiff entered upon her relationship with the defendant knowing that there was no prospect of him marrying her. And it is evident that in a number of respects he treated her very well. He was generous to her, in terms of money, while the relationship continued. And, what in the long term is probably more important, he encouraged her to develop her abilities in a number of ways with the result that she built up the successful driving instruction business. Nevertheless, she lived with him for 18 years as man and wife, and, at the end of it, has no rights against him. But the unfairness of that is not a matter which the courts can control. It is a matter for Parliament.

GRANT v EDWARDS[14]

[1986] Ch 638, [1986] 2 All ER 426 (CA, Sir NICOLAS BROWNE-WILKINSON V-C, MUSTILL and NOURSE LJJ)

The plaintiff and the defendant, who were not married, set up home together. The defendant bought a house which was conveyed into the joint names of the defendant and his brother, who had no beneficial interest. The defendant told the plaintiff that her name was not on the title because it would be detrimental in the divorce proceedings pending against her husband. The defendant paid the deposit and mortgage instalments while the plaintiff made substantial contributions to the household expenses. When the parties separated the plaintiff claimed a beneficial interest in the house.

Held. The plaintiff was entitled to a half share in the house.

---

14 [1986] Conv 291 (J. Warburton); (1986) 45 CLJ 394 (D.J. Hayton); (1986) 136 NLJ 324; (1987) 50 MLR 94 (B.Sufrin); [1987] Conv 16 (J. Montgomery), 93 (J. Eekelaar).

NOURSE LJ: In order to decide whether the plaintiff has a beneficial interest in 96, Hewitt Road we must climb again the familiar ground which slopes down from the twin peaks of *Pettitt v Pettitt* [1970] AC 777, [1969] 2 All ER 385 and *Gissing v Gissing* [1971] AC 886, [1970] 2 All ER 780. In a case such as the present, where there has been no written declaration or agreement, nor any direct provisions by the plaintiff of part of the purchase price so as to give rise to a resulting trust in her favour, she must establish a common intention between her and the defendant, acted upon by her, that she should have a beneficial interest in the property. If she can do that, equity will not allow the defendant to deny that interest and will construct a trust to give effect to it.

In most of these cases the fundamental, and invariably the most difficult, question is to decide whether there was the necessary common intention, being something which can only be inferred from the conduct of the parties, almost always from the expenditure incurred by them respectively. In this regard the court has to look for expenditure which is referable to the acquisition of the house: see per Fox LJ in *Burns v Burns* [1984] Ch 317, 328H–329C, [1984] 1 All ER 244, 252. If it is found to have been incurred, such expenditure will perform the twofold function of establishing the common intention and showing that the claimant has acted upon it.

There is another and rarer class of case, of which the present may be one, where although there has been no writing, the parties have orally declared themselves in such a way as to make their common intention plain. Here the court does not have to look for conduct from which the intention can be inferred, but only for conduct which amounts to an acting upon it by the claimant. And although that conduct can undoubtedly be the incurring of expenditure which is referable to the acquisition of the house, it need not necessarily be so.

The clearest example of this rarer class of case is *Eves v Eves* [1975] 1 WLR 1338, [1975] 3 All ER 768. That was a case of an unmarried couple where the conveyance of the house was taken in the name of the man alone. At the time of the purchase he told the woman that if she had been 21 years of age, he would have put the house into their joint names, because it was to be their joint home. He admitted in evidence that that was an excuse for not putting the house into their joint names, and this court inferred that there was an understanding between them, or a common intention that the woman was to have some sort of proprietary interest in it; otherwise no excuse would have been needed. After they had moved in, the woman did extensive decorative work to the downstairs rooms and generally cleaned the whole house. She painted the brickwork of the front of the house. She also broke up with a 14-lb. sledge hammer the concrete surface which covered the whole of the front garden and disposed of the rubble into a skip, worked in the back garden and, together with the man, demolished a shed there and put up a new shed. She also prepared the front garden for turfing. Pennycuick V-C at first instance, being unable to find any link between the common intention and the woman's activities after the purchase, held that she had not acquired a beneficial interest in the house. On an appeal to this court the decision was unanimously reversed, by Lord Denning MR on a ground which I respectfully think was at variance with the principles stated in *Gissing v Gissing* [1971] AC 886, [1970] 2 All ER 780 and by Browne LJ and Brightman J on a ground which was stated by Brightman J [1975] 1 WLR 1338, 1345, [1975] 3 All ER 768, 774:

"The defendant clearly led the plaintiff to believe that she was to have some undefined interest in the property, and that her name was only omitted from the conveyance because of her age. This, of course, is not enough by itself to create a beneficial interest in her favour; there would at best be a mere 'voluntary declaration of trust' which would be 'unenforceable for want of writing': per Lord Diplock in *Gissing v Gissing* [1971] AC 886, 905, [1970] 2 All ER 780, 790. If, however, it was part of the bargain between the parties, expressed or to be implied, that the plaintiff should contribute her labour towards the reparation of a house in which she was to have some beneficial interest, then I think that the arrangement becomes one to which the law can give effect. This seems to be consistent with the reasoning of the speeches in *Gissing v Gissing.*"

He added that he did not find much difficulty in inferring the link which Pennycuick V-C had been unable to find, observing in the process that he found it difficult to suppose that the woman would have been wielding the 14-lb sledge hammer and so forth except in pursuance of some expressed or implied arrangement and on the understanding that she was helping to improve a house in which she was to all practical intents and purposes promised that she had an interest. Browne LJ, at p. 1343, at p. 773, agreed with Brightman J about the basis for the court's decision in favour of the woman and was prepared to draw the inference that the link was there.

About that case the following observations may be made. First, as Brightman J himself observed, if the work had not been done the common intention would not have been enough. Secondly, if the common intention had not been orally made plain, the work would not have been conduct from which it could be inferred. That, I think, is the effect of the actual decision in *Pettitt v Pettitt* [1970] AC 777, [1969] 2 All ER 385. Thirdly, and on the other hand, the work was conduct which amounted to an acting upon the common intention by the woman.

It seems therefore, on the authorities as they stand, that a distinction is to be made between conduct from which the common intention can be inferred on the one hand and conduct which amounts to an acting upon it on the other. There remains this difficult question: what is the quality of conduct required for the latter purpose? The difficulty is caused, I think because although the common intention has been made plain, everything else remains a matter of inference. Let me illustrate it in this way. It would be possible to take the view that the mere moving into the house by the woman amounted to an acting upon the common intention. But that was evidently not the view of the majority in *Eves v Eves* [1975] 1 WLR 1338, [1975] 3 All ER 768. And the reason for that may be that, in the absence of evidence, the law is not so cynical as to infer that a woman will only go to live with a man to whom she is not married if she understands that she is to have an interest in their home. So what sort of conduct is required? In my judgment it must be conduct on which the woman could not reasonably have been expected to embark unless she was to have an interest in the house. If she was not to have such an interest, she could reasonably be expected to go and live with her lover, but not, for example, to wield a 14-lb sledge hammer in the front garden. In adopting the latter kind of conduct she is seen to act to her detriment on the faith of the common intention.

In order to see how the present case stands in the light of the views above expressed, I must summarise the crucial facts as found, expressly or impliedly, by the judge. They are the following. (1) The defendant told the plaintiff that her name was not going onto the title because it would cause some prejudice in the matrimonial proceedings between her and her husband. The defendant never had any real intention of replacing his brother with the plaintiff when those proceedings were at an end. Just as in *Eves v Eves* [1975] 1 WLR 1338, [1975] 3 All ER 768, these facts appear to me to raise a clear inference that there was an understanding between the plaintiff and the defendant, or a common intention, that the plaintiff was to have some sort of proprietary interest in the house; otherwise no excuse for not putting her name onto the title would have been needed. (2) Except for any instalments under the second mortgage which may have been paid by the plaintiff as part of the general expenses of the household, all the instalments under both mortgages were paid by the defendant. Between February 1970 and October 1974 the total amount paid in respect of the second mortgage was £812 at a rate of about £162 each year. Between 1972 and 1980 the defendant paid off £4,745 under the first mortgage at an average rate of £527 per year. (3) The £6 per week which the defendant admitted that the plaintiff paid to him, at least for a time after they moved into the house, was not paid as rent and must therefore have been paid as a contribution to general expenses. (4) From August 1972 onwards the plaintiff was getting the same sort of wage as the defendant, i.e. an annual wage of about £1,200 in 1973, out of which she made a very substantial contribution to the housekeeping and to the feeding and bringing up of the children. From June 1973 onwards she also received £5 a week from her former husband which went towards the maintenance of her two elder sons.

As stated under (1) above, it is clear that there was a common intention that the plaintiff was to have some sort of proprietary interest in 96, Hewitt Road. The more difficult question is whether there was conduct on her part which amounted to an acting upon that intention or, to put it more precisely, conduct on which she could not reasonably have been expected to embark unless she was to have an interest in the house.

From the above facts and figures it is in my view an inevitable inference that the very substantial contribution which the plaintiff made out of her earnings after August 1972 to the housekeeping and to the feeding and to the bringing up of the children enabled the defendant to keep down the instalments payable under both mortgages out of his own income and, moreover, that he could not have done that if he had had to bear the whole of the other expenses as well. For example, in 1973, when he and the plaintiff were earning about £1,200 each, the defendant had to find a total of about £643 between the two mortgages. I do not see how he would have been able to do that had it not been for the plaintiff's very substantial contribution to the other expenses. There is certainly no evidence that there was any money to spare on either side and the natural inference is to the contrary. In this connection, it is interesting to note that when dealing with the moneys in the Leeds Permanent Building Society account the judge said:

"They lived from hand to mouth, as I see it. They put their money in, and when there was some money to spare, they would share it out in this way."

In the circumstances, it seems that it may properly be inferred that the plaintiff did make substantial contributions to the instalments payable under both mortgages. This is a point which seems to have escaped the judge, but I think that there is an explanation for that. He was concentrating, as no doubt were counsel, on the plaintiff's claim that she herself had paid all the instalments under the second mortgage. It seems very likely that the indirect consequence of her very substantial contribution to the other expenses were not fully explored.

Was the conduct of the plaintiff in making substantial indirect contributions to the instalments payable under both mortgages conduct upon which she could not reasonably have been expected to embark unless she was to have an interest in the house? I answer that question in the affirmative. I cannot see upon what other basis she could reasonably have been expected to give the defendant such substantial assistance in paying off mortgages on his house. I therefore conclude that the plaintiff did act to her detriment on the faith of the common intention between her and the defendant that she was to have some sort of proprietary interest in the house.

I should add that, although *Eves v Eves* [1975] 1 WLR 1338, [1975] 3 All ER 768, was cited to the judge, I think it doubtful whether the significance of it was fully brought to his attention. He appears to have assumed that the plaintiff could only establish the necessary common intention if she could point to expenditure from which it could be inferred. I do not find it necessary to decide whether, if the common intention had not been orally made plain, the expenditure in the present case would have been sufficient for that purpose. That raises a difficult and still unresolved question of general importance which depends primarily on a close consideration of the speeches of their Lordships in *Gissing v Gissing* [1971] AC 886, [1970] 2 All ER 780 and the judgments of Fox and May LJJ in *Burns v Burns* [1984] Ch 317, [1984] 1 All ER 244, p. 235, ante. If it be objected that the views which I have expressed will expose the possibility of further fine distinctions on these intellectual steeps, I must answer that that is something which is inherent in the decision of the majority of this court in *Eves v Eves* [1975] 1 WLR 1338, [1975] 3 All ER 768. Be that as it may, I am in no doubt that that authority is a sure foundation for a just decision of the present case, a justness which was fully demonstrated in the concise and commonsensical argument of Mr. St. Ville on behalf of the plaintiff in this court.

[His Lordship then considered the quantum of the plaintiff's share, and held that she was entitled to a half].[15]

SIR NICOLAS BROWNE-WILKINSON V-C: I suggest that in other cases of this kind, useful guidance may in the future be obtained from the principles underlying the law of proprietary estoppel which in my judgment are closely akin to those laid down in *Gissing v Gissing* [1971] AC 886, [1970] 2 All ER 780. In both, the claimant must to the knowledge of the legal owner have acted in the belief that the claimant has or will obtain an interest in the property. In both, the claimant must have acted to his or her detriment in reliance on such belief. In both, equity acts on the conscience of the legal owner to prevent him from acting in an unconscionable manner by defeating the common intention. The two principles have been developed separately without cross-fertilisation between them: but they rest on the same foundation and have on all other matters reached the same conclusions.

In many cases of the present sort, it is impossible to say whether or not the claimant would have done the acts relied on as a detriment even if she thought she had no interest in the house. Setting up house together, having a baby, making payments to general housekeeping expenses (not strictly necessary to enable the mortgage to be paid) may all be referable to the mutual love and affection of the parties and not specifically referable to the claimant's belief

---

15 On size of the share, see generally H & M, pp. 269– 270; Cheshire & Burn, *Modern Law of Real Property* (15th Edn), p. 240.

that she has an interest in the house. As at present advised, once it has been shown that there was a common intention that the claimant should have an interest in the house, any act done by her to her detriment relating to the joint lives of the parties is, in my judgment, sufficient detriment to qualify. The acts do not have to be inherently referable to the house: see *Jones (A.E) v Jones (F.W.)* [1977] 1 WLR 438, [1977] 2 All ER 231, and *Pascoe v Turner* [1979] 1 WLR 431, [1979] 2 All ER 945. The holding out to the claimant that she had a beneficial interest in the house is an act of such a nature as to be part of the inducement to her to do the acts relied on. Accordingly, in the absence of evidence to the contrary, the right inference is that the claimant acted in reliance on such holding out and the burden lies on the legal owner to show that she did not do so: see *Greasley v Cooke* [1980] 1 WLR 1306, [1980] 3 All ER 710.

The possible analogy with proprietary estoppel was raised in argument. However, the point was not fully argued and since the case can be decided without relying on such analogy, it is unsafe for me to rest my judgment on that point. I decide the case on the narrow ground already mentioned.

[His Lordship then considered the quantum of the plaintiff's share and held that she was entitled to a half.]

Some recent cases in the Court of Appeal display a more flexible approach to direct contributions than might have been anticipated from a strict interpretation of the principles laid down by the House of Lords in *Lloyds Bank plc v Rosset* [1991] 1 AC 107, [1990] 1 All ER 1111, p. 232, ante.

In **McHardy and Sons v Warren** (1994) 2 FLR 338, the husband's parents paid a deposit of £650 as a wedding present to the couple. The husband executed a charge on the house, which was in his sole name, in favour of the plaintiffs, who were trade creditors. The plaintiffs argued that the wife was entitled to (at most) a share of 8.97%, which represented the proportion which half the deposit bore to the purchase price. The Court of Appeal held that she was entitled to a half share.

DILLON LJ said at 340: "To my mind it is the irresistible conclusion that where a parent pays the deposit, either directly or to the solicitors or to the bride and groom, it matters not which, on the purchase of their first matrimonial home, it is the intention of all three of them that the bride and groom should have equal interests in the matrimonial home, not interests measured by reference to the percentage half the deposit [bears] to the full price..."

In **Midland Bank plc v Cooke** [1995] 4 All ER 562, a house was bought in the husband's name with a mortgage loan of £6,450, his savings of £950 and a gift of £1,100 from his parents to the couple. The wife did not pay the mortgage directly but paid other outgoings from her earnings. Both stated that they never discussed their shares. A later mortgage was executed in favour of the plaintiff, and the house was subsequently put into the joint names of the couple. In possession proceedings brought by the plaintiff, the Court of Appeal held that if an equitable interest has been acquired by direct contribution (the money derived from the gift) and there is no express evidence of intention, the court will assess the proportions the parties are assumed to have intended by surveying the course of dealing between them, their sharing of the burdens and benefits of the property, and all conduct throwing light on the question. The court is not bound to find that the shares are proportionate to direct contributions on a strict resulting trust basis and is free to infer an intention to share differently on general equitable principles. On that basis the parties took in equal shares.

WAITE LJ said at 576: "One could hardly have a clearer example of a couple who had agreed to share everything equally: the profits of his business while it prospered, and the risks of indebtedness suffered through its failure; the upbringing of their children; the rewards of her own career as a teacher; and, most relevantly, a home into which he had put his savings and to which she was to give over the years the benefit of the maintenance and improvement contribution. When to all that is added the fact (still an important one) that this was a couple who had chosen to introduce into their relationship the additional commitment which marriage involves, the conclusion becomes inescapable that their presumed intention was to share the beneficial interest in the property in equal shares."

Similarly in **Drake v Whipp** (1995) Times, 19 December, where the woman made a direct contribution of about one fifth to the purchase and conversion of a barn. The parties had a common intention that she should have a beneficial interest, which the Court of Appeal determined as one third, adopting a "broad brush" approach, and emphasising the need to distinguish constructive and resulting trust principles. Thus the finding of a common intention may enable the court to fix a fair share which differs from the proportionate resulting trust.[16]

QUESTIONS

1. What part do presumptions play in this field today? What is their relevance where property has been transferred for an illegal purpose?
2. Should Parliament intervene to assist claimants such as the plaintiff in *Burns v Burns*? If so, how should this be done?
3. What kind of act must be shown (a) to found an inference of a common intention to share the beneficial interest in the home; (b) to establish detrimental reliance upon an express oral common intention? What is the significance of indirect contributions in the light of *Lloyds Bank plc v Rosset* [1991] 1 AC 107, [1990] 1 All ER 1111, p. 232 ante?

---

16 Cf. *Killey v Clough* [1996] NPC 38, where CA held that, if co-habitees have formed a common intention to hold a family home in equal shares, it cannot substitute some other proportion.

7. Constructive Trusts[1]

I. General

A constructive trust is one which arises by operation of law. It can arise in a wide variety of circumstances. There is little agreement among writers as to the proper categories. There is much inconsistency in the use of terminology, and there are many situations involving overlap between the categories into which trusts are usually classified. Many of the issues which arise in this area appear also in other contexts. It is important for these reasons, among others, to clarify a few general points upon which the present account is based.

It is often assumed that a constructive trust, like any other trust, is a situation in which specific property is vested in a trustee on trust for ascertained beneficiaries. This is not always so; there are many differences between constructive trusts and others. A constructive trustee may not know that he is a trustee. Where the trust arises because a fiduciary has received a benefit in breach of a fiduciary obligation, it may be difficult to say what the trust property is. In many cases, the duty of a constructive trustee is less onerous than that of an express trustee; he is under no obligation to invest in authorised securities, nor to observe the usual duty of *exacta diligentia*. It would be unreasonable to impose such obligations in cases in which he did not know he was a trustee.

It is sometimes difficult to see the distinction between a constructive trust and a duty to account. Where an agent has obtained illegal profits, should we say that he is a constructive trustee, or that he is under a duty to account? The former involves a proprietary claim by the plaintiff, the latter a personal claim. The difference may be considerable, but the terminology is indiscriminate.[2]

---

1 H & M, pp. 291–330; K & S, pp. 215–248; P & M, pp. 209–285; Pettit, pp. 157–177; Riddall, pp. 380–394; Snell, pp. 192–197; Underhill, pp. 345–432. See generally (1913–14) 27 Harv LR 125: (1955) 71 LQR 39 (A.W. Scott); Waters, *The Constructive Trust* (1964); Oakley, *Constructive Trusts* (2nd edn. 1987); Elias, *Explaining Constructive Trusts.*

2 *Boardman v Phipps* [1967] 2 AC 46, [1966] 3 All ER 721; *A-G's Reference (No 1 of 1985)* [1986] QB 491 at 503, [1986] 2 All ER 219 at 223; Sir Christopher SLADE: *The Informal Creation of Interests in Land* (1984) Child & Co Oxford Lecture, p.4.

This means that there is much confusion between cases of constructive trust and cases of the liability of fiduciaries.[3] So long as the defendant can pay, it makes little difference whether the claim is proprietary or personal. But if the defendant is insolvent, and the plaintiff can only be satisfied by a claim in priority to the general creditors, the distinction is crucial; just as it is in cases which are usually discussed in the context of the beneficiaries' right to "trace", or to "follow the trust property," or to make a "claim *in rem*." By making a proprietary claim, the plaintiff can take any property which he can show to be his in equity; and he can make a claim in priority to the general creditors upon a mixed fund of money or investments. Further, if the investments have appreciated, he may wish to claim a share of the fund at this higher value.

We cannot explore these matters in detail now;[4] our present point is to indicate the connection between them. A claim involving only the defendant's personal liability to account has nothing to do with a constructive trust. A proprietary claim against a fiduciary may be a claim in respect of a specific item, but is more commonly against a fund, usually a mixed fund. The plaintiff may wish to have a charge on the fund to give him priority over the general creditors or he may, because of the increase in the value of the fund, wish to claim a share. Here we have a mixture of "constructive trust", "liability of fiduciaries" and "tracing". These are all inter-connected.

The distinction between constructive and resulting trusts is less clear than it used to be. Traditionally resulting trusts arose where there was a failure to dispose of the whole beneficial interest, while constructive trusts were imposed to prevent unconscionable conduct. But some modern decisions show a tendency to merge the two concepts.[5] This has little practical significance (for example, no formalities are required for the creation of either resulting or constructive trusts[6]) but adds to the existing difficulties in attempting to define the constructive trust.

Another question is whether the constructive trust is a "remedy" or an "institution".[7] If it is simply a means of demanding the return of the property to which the plaintiff is entitled in equity, and which is wrongly held by the defendant, then it looks like a proprietary remedy (and this is the way in which constructive trusts are regarded in most jurisdictions in the United States of America). The "remedial" constructive trust is widely accepted in Australia, New Zealand and Canada.[8] Such a trust can be imposed *de novo* as the foundation for the grant of an equitable remedy, and does not involve the vindication of some pre-existing proprietary right of the plaintiff. It may operate only from the date of the court order, and thus not affect third parties.[9] English law, however, has not yet followed other jurisdictions and the

---

3 See pp. 257, 259 post.

4 See pp. 891 et seq, post.

5 See Lord DENNING MR in *Hussey v Palmer* [1972] 1 WLR 1286 at 1290, [1972] 3 All ER 744 at 747, "Although the plaintiff alleged that there was a resulting trust, I should have thought that the trust ... was more in the nature of a constructive trust; but this is more a matter of words than anything else. The two run together." A resulting trust, however, creates a share proportionate to the contribution, which may not be the case with a constructive trust; p. 245, ante.

6 See pp. 53 et seq, ante. See, however, *Macmillan Inc v Bishopsgate Investment Trust plc (No 3)* [1995] 1 WLR 978, [1975] 3 All ER 747 (distinctions in the conflict of laws).

7 H & M, pp. 296–298.

8 *Muschinski v Dodds* (1985) 160 CLR 583; *Powell v Thompson* [1991] 1 NZLR 597; *Pettkus v Becker* (1980) 117 DLR (3d) 257.

9 *Muschinski v Dodds*, supra.

concept of the constructive trust as a universal remedy for unjust enrichment has been rejected by the Court of Appeal. In *Halifax Building Society v Thomas*,[10] where a mortgage loan was obtained from the plaintiff by fraudulent misrepresentation, the argument that a profit derived from fraud was held on constructive trust for the victim of the fraud did not succeed. The unjust enrichment was not at the expense of the plaintiff, whose loan had been fully repaid out of the proceeds of sale of the mortgaged property. Thus the plaintiff was not entitled to the surplus proceeds of sale. The legislative solution was the court's power to confiscate the benefits derived from crime.[11] Sir Peter MILLETT has recently said that "there is neither room nor need for the remedial constructive trust. In my view it is a counsel of despair which too readily concedes the impossibility of propounding a general rationale for the availability of proprietary remedies.[12]"

The "institutional" constructive trust vindicates the beneficiary's pre-existing proprietary right and, being operative before the date of the court order which confirms it, can affect third parties. This is the way in which the English cases have traditionally regarded the constructive trust,[13] although, as mentioned above, the duties of a constructive trustee are not necessarily the same as those of an express trustee, and have not been fully worked out.

Finally, it may be asked whether we can find a general principle which will determine the circumstances in which a constructive trust will exist. This would be a great improvement over the present miscellany. Some find this in the principle of unjust enrichment, arguing that where the defendant is unjustly enriched at the expense of the plaintiff, he should disgorge; and that, as the defendant should never have had the property, his creditors should not be entitled to share it. Some decisions in the era of Lord Denning MR went further, treating a constructive trust as a doctrine which permits a desired result to be reached on a principle of justice and good conscience, regardless of the effect upon the rights of third parties of using a proprietary remedy to reach the solution.[14] This view of the constructive trust has lost momentum. This question will be taken up infra, p. 292. We must first examine the situations in which it has long been established that a constructive trust arises.

II. Categories of Constructive Trusts

A. Unauthorised Profit by a Trustee or Fiduciary

The principle is that a person in a fiduciary position may not make use of his position to gain a benefit for himself. He must not put himself in a position where his interest and duty might conflict. In addition to express trustees, the

---

10 [1996] 2 WLR 63, [1995] 4 All ER 673: cf. *Metall und Rohstoff AG v Donaldson Lufkin & Jenrette Inc* [1990] 1 QB 391 at 497, [1989] 3 All ER 14 at 57 (good arguable case for remedial constructive trust).
11 Criminal Justice Act 1988. Part VI.
12 (1995) 9 Trust Law International 35 at 40.
13 See *Re Sharpe* [1980] 1 WLR 219, [1980] 1 All ER 198.
14 [1973] CLP 17 (A.J. Oakley); (1977) 28 NILQ 123 (R.H. Maudsley).

rule applies to other fiduciaries such as personal representatives, company directors, partners and agents. The category of fiduciaries is not closed.[15]

Examples of the operation of this principle include the following: where a lease is held on trust, the trustee must not renew it in his own favour;[16] or purchase the reversion;[17] he must not purchase the trust property;[18] nor must he make any incidental profits out of his position.[19] These matters are fully dealt with in Chapter 20 under the heading of liability of fiduciaries.[20]

B. Strangers to the Trust. Trustees de Son Tort[1]

Third parties who have not been appointed trustees may incur liability if they receive or deal with trust property for their own benefit with actual or constructive notice that it is trust property transferred in breach of trust, or if, without necessarily receiving the property, they assist the trustees in a breach of trust.

As submitted above, a distinction should be made between (a) the personal liability of a fiduciary to account and (b) a constructive trust. The distinction becomes clear when the remedies of the beneficiaries are considered; the distinction between proceeding against the plaintiff personally and against the property in his hands then becomes obvious. In many factual situations, these two basic kinds of liability will overlap. Knowing receipt or dealing with trust property is properly a case of constructive trusteeship so long as the property or its proceeds are retained (after which any liability must be personal), while assistance in a breach of trust, without receiving the trust property, can only give rise to a personal liability to account. It must be said however that many judicial formulations treat both types of situation as cases of constructive trust.

The main difficulty which has been encountered has been in determining the standard of conduct required to found liability in the assistance and receipt cases. Is dishonesty required, or is it sufficient that the third party ought reasonably to have known that he was assisting in a breach of trust or receiving trust property? In the receipt category, can a case be made out for strict liability where the recipient is a volunteer?

In the case of assisting in a breach of trust opinions have differed as to whether dishonesty is a prerequisite to liability or whether negligence suffices, but the matter can now be regarded as settled by the Privy Council in *Royal Brunei Airlines Sdn Bhd v Tan* [1995] 2 AC 378, [1995] 3 All ER 97, p. 252 post,

---

15 *English v Dedham Vale Properties Ltd* [1978] 1 WLR 93, [1978] 1 All ER 382. See also *Reading v A-G* [1951] AC 507, [1951] 1 All ER 617; *Swain v Law Society* [1983] 1 AC 598, [1982] 2 All ER 827; *Mathew v TM Sutton Ltd* [1994] 1 WLR 1455, [1994] 4 All ER 793. Cf. *Appleby v Cowley* (1982) Times, 14 April (head of barristers' chambers in Nottingham held by MEGARRY V-C not to hold them on any form of trust or fiduciary obligation towards the members).

16 *Keech v Sandford* (1726) Sel Cas Ch 61, p. 829, post

17 *Protheroe v Protheroe* [1968] 1 WLR 519, [1968] 1 All ER 1111, p. 831, post.

18 See p. 824, post.

19 *Boardman v Phipps* [1967] 2 AC 46, [1966] 3 All ER 721, p. 844, post.

20 Pp. 829, et seq.

1 H & M, pp. 300–311; K & S, pp. 235–241; P & M, pp. 251–271; Pettit, pp. 166–176; Snell, pp. 193–194; Underhill, pp. 408–432; Oakley, *Constructive Trusts* (2nd edn), pp. 85–111. See generally (1986) 102 LQR 114, 267 (C. Harpum); (1989) 9 OJLS 261 (P.L. Loughlan). Birks ed. *The Frontiers of Liability* (1994), vol 1, Part I, Knowing Assistance and Knowing Receipt (papers by C. Harpum, Sir Leonard HOFFMANN and W. Swadling); (1996) 112 LQR 56 (S. Gardner).

where the English and Commonwealth decisions are fully reviewed. It was there held that dishonesty is a necessary ingredient of accessory liability. It was further held that, contrary to the previous understanding, there is no requirement that the breach of trust in which the third party assisted should involve any dishonesty on the part of the trustees.

Where the claim is based on knowing receipt or dealing with trust property, a distinction must be drawn between the situation where the defendant retains the property or its proceeds and where he does not. In the former case, he takes subject to the trust by the ordinary principles of property law unless he can show that he was a bona fide purchaser of the legal estate for value without notice, actual, constructive or imputed. Thus he holds the property as constructive trustee, and a tracing action will lie in respect of the identifiable proceeds if he has disposed of it. Where, however, neither the property nor its proceeds remain, the question is whether the defendant is personally liable to account for its value.

The degree of knowledge sufficient to found personal liability is not yet settled. Sir Robert MEGARRY V-C in *Re Montagu's Settlement Trusts* [1987] Ch 264, [1992] 4 All ER 308 held that actual knowledge is required. This approach has not found favour, and the weight of authority supports the view that constructive notice suffices (see p. 260, post). Applying the principles of restitution, liability is receipt-based, not fault-based.[2] This being so, it is strongly arguable that a volunteer should be personally liable even if he received the trust property without notice. This is the position with the common law action for money had and received, as shown by *Lipkin Gorman v Karpnale Ltd* [1991] 2 AC 548, [1992] 4 All ER 512.

Finally, whether the case is one of assisting in a breach of trust or receipt of trust property, the existence of the trust must be established. Knowledge of a "doubtful equity" does not suffice.[3]

i. ASSISTANCE IN A BREACH OF TRUST

As mentioned above, one ground of liability (which is personal liability to account rather than constructive trusteeship) arises where a third party assists the trustees in a breach of trust. Opinions have varied as to the degree of knowledge of the breach of trust which is required to found liability. Clearly an innocent third party with no reason to suspect the breach will not be liable. The question is whether dishonesty is required or whether negligence suffices. UNGOED-THOMAS J in *Selangor United Rubber Estates Ltd v Cradock (No 3)* [1968] 1 WLR 1555, [1968] 2 All ER 1073 and BRIGHTMAN J in *Karak Rubber Co Ltd v Burden (No 2)* [1972] 1 WLR 602, [1972] 1 All ER 1210 held that constructive notice of the breach of trust sufficed.[4] But the Court of Appeal in *Carl Zeiss Stiftung v Herbert Smith & Co (No 2)* [1969] 2 Ch 276, [1969] 2 All ER 367 considered that "want of probity" must be established. This approach was preferred by the Court of Appeal in *Belmont Finance Corpn Ltd v Williams*

---

2 This distinction was recently affirmed by the Privy Council in *Royal Brunei Airlines Sdn Bhd v Tan* [1995] 2 AC 378, [1995] 3 All ER 97.

3 *Carl Zeiss Stiftung v Herbert Smith & Co (No 2)* [1969] 2 Ch 276, [1969] 2 All ER 367; *Brinks Ltd v Abu-Saleh (No. 3)* (1995) Times, 23 October. A solicitor in doubt as to possible liability should apply to the court for directions: *Finers v Miro* [1991] 1 WLR 35, [1991] 1 All ER 182.

4 Followed in *Baden v Société Générale pour Favoriser le Développement du Commerce et de l'Industrie en France SA* [1993] 1 WLR 509n, [1992] 4 All ER 161.

Furniture Ltd [1979] Ch 250, [1979] 1 All ER 118; *Lipkin Gorman v Karpnale Ltd* [1989] 1 WLR 1340, [1992] 4 All ER 409, p 260, post, and *Polly Peck International plc v Nadir (No 2)* [1992] 4 All ER 769. MILLETT J in *Agip (Africa) Ltd v Jackson* [1990] Ch 265, [1992] 4 All ER 385, p 258, post, held that dishonesty was required, and the decision was upheld by the Court of Appeal at [1991] Ch 547, [1992] 4 All ER 451, although, as the defendants would have been liable on either view, the matter was dealt with briefly. The requirement of dishonesty has recently been confirmed by the Privy Council in *Royal Brunei Airlines Sdn Bhd v Tan* [1995] 2 AC 378, [1995] 3 All ER 97, infra. It was also held that the breach of trust in which the third party assisted need not itself have been fraudulent. This overturns the previous rule, deriving from *Barnes v Addy* (1874) 9 Ch App 244, that there must have been a dishonest and fraudulent design on the part of the trustees. Lord NICHOLLS, delivering the judgment of the Board, also considered that the term "knowing assistance", used throughout the caselaw, should be avoided, as the work "knowing" was an inapt criterion. Dishonesty was the touchstone of liability. His Lordship further suggested that in this context the five categories of knowledge laid down by PETER GIBSON J in *Baden v Société Générale pour Favoriser le Développement du Commerce et de l'Industrie en France SA* [1993] 1 WLR 509n, [1992] 4 All ER 161[5] were "best forgotten."

ROYAL BRUNEI AIRLINES SDN BHD v TAN[5a]

[1995] 2 AC 378, [1995] 3 All ER 97 (PC, Lords GOFF OF CHIEVELEY, ACKNER, NICHOLLS of BIRKENHEAD and STEYN and SIR John MAY

The plaintiff airline appointed Borneo Leisure Travel Sdn Bhd ("BLT") to act as its general travel agent. BLT was required to account to the plaintiff for the proceeds of ticket sales, after deducting commission. The terms of the agreement constituted BLT a trustee of the money for the plaintiff. The money was not paid into a separate bank account but was used in the business of BLT, which was conceded to be a breach of trust. BLT fell into arrears in accounting to the plaintiff and the agreement was terminated. As BLT was insolvent, the plaintiff sought a remedy against Tan, who was the principal shareholder and director of BLT. It was conceded that Tan had assisted in the breach of trust with actual knowledge. The Court of Appeal of Brunei Darussalam held him not liable on the ground that the breach of trust in which he had assisted had not been shown to be a dishonest and fraudulent design on the part of BLT, which was considered essential to accessory liability in cases of long standing and high authority. In fact BLT's breach was dishonest, because Tan's state of mind was to be imputed to the company.[6] The issue on appeal to the Privy Council was whether the breach of trust which is a prerequisite to accessory liability must itself be a dishonest and fraudulent breach by the trustee, a view deriving from a dictum of Lord Selborne LC in *Barnes v Addy* (1874) 9 Ch App 244 at 251–252. The resolution of this issue also required consideration of the

---

5 Set out in *Re Montagu's Settlement Trusts* [1987] Ch 264, [1992] 4 All ER 308, p. 261, post.

5a (1995) 111 LQR 545 (C. Harpum); Conv 338 (M. Halliwell); CLJ 505 (R. Nolan); 3 RLR 105 (J. Stevens); 145 NLJ 1379 (C. Passmore and N. Sieve); 9 Trust Law International 102 (G. McCormack); (1996) 112 LQR 56 (S. Gardner); (1996) 59 MLR 443 (A. Berg).

6 This was accepted by the Privy Council. See *El Ajou v Dollar Land Holdings plc* [1994] 2 All ER 685, p. 266, post.

question whether the person assisting in the breach of trust must have acted dishonestly (as opposed to negligently) in order to incur liability, and a consideration of the meaning of "dishonesty".

Held: Tan was personally liable for dishonestly assisting in BLT's breach of trust. There was no further requirement of dishonesty on the part of BLT.

LORD NICHOLLS OF BIRKENHEAD:

The honest trustee and the dishonest third party
  It must be noted at once that there is a difficulty with the approach adopted on this point in the *Belmont*[7] case. Take the simple example of an honest trustee and a dishonest third party. Take a case where a dishonest solicitor persuades a trustee to apply trust property in a way the trustee honestly believes is permissible but which the solicitor knows full well is a clear breach of trust. The solicitor deliberately conceals this from the trustee. In consequence, the beneficiaries suffer a substantial loss. It cannot be right that in such a case the accessory liability principle would be inapplicable because of the innocence of the trustee. In ordinary parlance, the beneficiaries have been defrauded by the solicitor. If there is to be an accessory liability principle at all, whereby in appropriate circumstances beneficiaries may have direct recourse against a third party, the principle must surely be applicable in such a case, just as much as in a case where both the trustee and the third party have been dishonest. Indeed, if anything, the case for liability of the dishonest third party seems stronger where the trustee is innocent, because in such a case the third party alone was dishonest and that was the cause of the subsequent misapplication of the trust property.
  The position would be the same if, instead of *procuring* the breach, the third party dishonestly *assisted* in the breach. Change the facts slightly. A trustee is proposing to make a payment out of the trust fund to a particular person. He honestly believes he is authorised to do so by the terms of the trust deed. He asks a solicitor to carry through the transaction. The solicitor well knows that the proposed payment would be a plain breach of trust. He also well knows that the trustee mistakenly believes otherwise. Dishonestly he leaves the trustee under his misapprehension and prepares the necessary documentation. Again, if the accessory principle is not to be artificially constricted, it ought to be applicable in such a case.
  These examples suggest that what matters is the state of mind of the third party sought to be made liable, not the state of mind of the trustee. The trustee will be liable in any event for the breach of trust, even if he acted innocently, unless excused by an exemption clause in the trust instrument or relieved by the court. But *his* state of mind is essentially irrelevant to the question whether the *third party* should be made liable to the beneficiaries for the breach of trust. If the liability of the third party is fault-based, what matters is the nature of his fault, not that of the trustee. In this regard dishonesty on the part of the third party would seem to be a sufficient basis for his liability, irrespective of the state of mind of the trustee who is in breach of trust. It is difficult to see why, if the

---

7 *Belmont Finance Corpn Ltd v Williams Furniture Ltd* [1979] Ch 250, [1979] 1 All ER 118, upholding Lord SELBORNE's principle.

third party dishonestly assisted in a breach, there should be a further prerequisite to his liability, namely, that the trustee also must have been acting dishonestly. The alternative view would mean that a dishonest third party is liable if the trustee is dishonest, but if the trustee did not act dishonestly that of itself would excuse a dishonest third party from liability. That would make no sense.

Earlier authority

The view that the accessory liability principle cannot be restricted to fraudulent breaches of trust is not to be approached with suspicion as a latter-day novelty. Before the accessory principle donned its *Barnes v Addy* straitjacket, judges seem not to have regarded the principle as confined in this way.

[His Lordship considered *Fyler v Fyler* (1841) 3 Beav 550; *A-G v Leicester Corpn* (1844) 7 Beav 176 and *Eaves v Hickson* (1861) 30 Beav 136, and continued:]

What has gone wrong? Their Lordships venture to think that the reason is that ever since the *Selangor* case highlighted the potential uses of equitable remedies in connection with misapplied company funds, there has been a tendency to cite and interpret and apply Lord Selborne's formulation in *Barnes v Addy* (1874) 9 Ch App 244, 251–252 as though it were a statute. This has particularly been so with the accessory limb of Lord Selborne LC's apothegm. This approach has been inimical to analysis of the underlying concept. Working within this constraint, the courts have found themselves wrestling with the interpretation of the individual ingredients, especially "knowingly" but also "dishonest and fraudulent design on the part of the trustees", without examining the underlying reason why a third party who has received no trust property is being made liable at all. One notable exception is the judgment of Thomas J in *Powell v Thompson* [1991] 1 NZLR 597, 610–615. On this point he observed at p. 613:

"Once a breach of trust has been committed, the commission of which has involved a third party, the question which arises is one as between the beneficiary and that third party. If the third party's conduct has been unconscionable, then irrespective of the degree of impropriety in the trustee's conduct, the third party is liable to be held accountable to the beneficiary as if he or she were a trustee."

To resolve this issue it is necessary to take an overall look at the accessory liability principle. A conclusion cannot be reached on the nature of the breach of trust which may trigger accessory liability without at the same time considering the other ingredients including, in particular, the state of mind of the third party. It is not necessary, however, to look even more widely and consider the essential ingredients of recipient liability. The issue on this appeal concerns only the accessory liability principle. Different considerations apply to the two heads of liability. Recipient liability is restitution-based, accessory liability is not.

No liability

The starting point for any analysis must be to consider the extreme possibility: that a third party who does not receive trust property ought never to be liable directly to the beneficiaries merely because he assisted the trustee to commit a breach of trust or procured him to do so. This possibility can be dismissed summarily. On this the position which the law has long adopted is clear and makes good sense. Stated in the simplest terms, a trust is a relationship which exists when one person holds property on behalf of another. If, for his own purposes, a third party deliberately interferes in that relationship by assisting the trustee in depriving the beneficiary of the property held for him by the trustee, the beneficiary should be able to look for recompense to the third party as well as the trustee. Affording the beneficiary a remedy against the third party serves the dual purpose of making good the beneficiary's loss should the trustee lack financial means and imposing a liability which will discourage others from behaving in a similar fashion.

The rationale is not far to seek. Beneficiaries are entitled to expect that those who become trustees will fulfil their obligations. They are also entitled to expect, and this is only a short step further, that those who become trustees will be permitted to fulfil their obligations without deliberate intervention from third parties. They are entitled to expect that third parties will refrain from intentionally intruding in the trustee-beneficiary relationship and thereby hindering a beneficiary from receiving his entitlement in accordance with the terms of the trust instrument. There is here a close analogy with breach of contract. A person who knowingly procures a breach of contract, or knowingly interferes with the due performance of a contract, is liable to the innocent party. The underlying rationale is the same.

Strict liability
The other extreme possibility can also be rejected out of hand. This is the case where a third party deals with a trustee without knowing, or having any reason to suspect, that he is a trustee. Or the case where a third party is aware he is dealing with a trustee but has no reason to know or suspect that their transaction is inconsistent with the terms of the trust. The law has never gone so far as to give a beneficiary a remedy against a non-recipient third party in such circumstances. Within defined limits, proprietary rights, whether legal or equitable, endure against third parties who were unaware of their existence. But accessory liability is concerned with the liability of a person who has not received any property. His liability is not property-based. His only sin is that he interfered with the due performance by the trustee of the fiduciary obligations undertaken by the trustee. These are personal obligations. They are, in this respect, analogous to the personal obligations undertaken by the parties to a contract. But ordinary, every day business would become impossible if third parties were to be held liable for *unknowingly* interfering in the due performance of such personal obligations. Beneficiaries could not reasonably expect that third parties should deal with trustees at their peril, to the extent that they should become liable to the beneficiaries even when they received no trust property and even when they were unaware and had no reason to suppose that they were dealing with trustees.

Fault-based liability
Given, then, that in some circumstances a third party may be liable directly to a beneficiary, but given also that the liability is not so strict that there would be liability even when the third party was wholly unaware of the existence of the trust, the next step is to seek to identify the touchstone of liability. By common accord dishonesty fulfils this role. Whether, in addition, negligence will suffice is an issue on which there has been a well-known difference of judicial opinion. The *Selangor* decision [1968] 1 WLR 1555, [1968] 2 All ER 1073 in 1968 was the first modern decision on this point. Ungoed-Thomas J at 1590, at 1104, held that the touchstone was whether the third party had knowledge of

circumstances which would indicate to "an honest, reasonable man" that the breach in question was being committed or would put him on enquiry. Brightman J reached the same conclusion in *Karak Rubber Co Ltd v Burden (No 2)* [1972] 1 WLR 602, [1972] 1 All ER 1210. So did Peter Gibson J in 1983 in the *Baden* case [1993] 1 WLR 509n, [1992] 4 All ER 161. In that case the judge accepted a five-point scale of knowledge which had been formulated by counsel.

Meanwhile doubts had been expressed about this test by Buckley LJ and Goff LJ in the *Belmont* case [1979] Ch 250, 267, 275, [1979] 1 All ER 118, 130, 136. Similar doubts were expressed in Australia by Jacobs P in *DPC Estates Pty Ltd v Grey* [1974] 1 NSWLR 443, 459. When that decision reached the High Court of Australia, the doubts were echoed by Barwick CJ, Gibbs J and Stephen J: see *Consul Development Pty Ltd v DPC Estates Pty Ltd* (1975) 132 CLR 373, 376, 398, and 412.

Since then the tide in England has flowed strongly in favour of the test being one of dishonesty: see, for instance, Sir Robert Megarry V-C in *Re Montagu's Settlement Trusts* [1987] Ch 264, 285, [1992] 4 All ER 308, 330, and Millett J in *Agip (Africa) Ltd v Jackson* [1990], Ch 265, 293, [1992] 4 All ER 385, 405. In *Eagle Trust plc v SBC Securities Ltd* [1993] 1 WLR 484, 495, [1992] 4 All ER 488, 499, Vinelott J stated that it could be taken as settled law that want of probity was a prerequisite to liability. This received the imprimatur of the Court of Appeal in *Polly Peck International plc v Nadir (No 2)* [1992] 4 All ER 769, 777, per Scott LJ. [His Lordship then considered the divergent judicial views in New Zealand and continued:]

Dishonesty

Before considering this issue further it will be helpful to define the terms being used by looking more closely at what dishonesty means in this context. Whatever may be the position in some criminal or other contexts (see, for instance, *R v Ghosh* [1982] QB 1053, [1982] 2 All ER 689), in the context of the accessory liability principle acting dishonestly, or with a lack of probity, which is synonymous, means simply not acting as an honest person would in the circumstances. This is an objective standard. At first sight this may seem surprising. Honesty has a connotation of subjectivity, as distinct from the objectivity of negligence. Honesty, indeed, does have a strong subjective element in that it is a description of a type of conduct assessed in the light of what a person actually knew at the time, as distinct from what a reasonable person would have known or appreciated. Further, honesty and its counterpart dishonesty are mostly concerned with advertent conduct, not inadvertent conduct. Carelessness is not dishonesty. Thus for the most part dishonesty is to be equated with conscious impropriety.

However, these subjective characteristics of honesty do not mean that individuals are free to set their own standards of honesty in particular circumstances. The standard of what constitutes honest conduct is not subjective. Honesty is not an optional scale, with higher or lower values according to the moral standards of each individual. If a person knowingly appropriates another's property, he will not escape a finding of dishonesty simply because he sees nothing wrong in such behaviour. ...

Negligence

It is against this background that the question of negligence is to be addressed. This question, it should be remembered, is directed at whether an honest third party who receives no trust property should be liable if he procures or assists in a breach of trust of which he would have become aware had he exercised reasonable diligence. Should he be liable to the beneficiaries for the loss they suffer from the breach of trust?

The majority of persons falling into this category will be the hosts of people who act for trustees in various ways: as advisers, consultants, bankers, and agents of many kinds. This category also includes officers and employees of companies, in respect of the application of company funds. All these people will be accountable to the trustees for their conduct. For the most part they will owe to the trustees a duty to exercise reasonable skill and care. When that is so, the rights flowing from that duty form part of the trust property. As such they can be enforced by the beneficiaries in a suitable case if the trustees are unable or unwilling to do so. That being so, it is difficult to identify a compelling reason why, in addition to the duty of skill and care vis-à-vis the trustees which the third parties have accepted, or which the law has imposed upon them, third parties should also owe a duty of care directly to the beneficiaries. They have undertaken work for the trustees. They must carry out that work properly. If they fail to do so, they will be liable to make good the loss suffered by the trustees in consequence. This will include, where appropriate, the loss suffered by the trustees being exposed to claims for breach of trust.

Outside this category of persons who owe duties of skill and care to the trustees, there are others who will deal with trustees. If they have not accepted, and the law has not imposed upon them, any such duties in favour of the trustees, it is difficult to discern a good reason why they should nevertheless owe such duties to the beneficiaries.

There remains to be considered the position where third parties are acting for, or dealing with, dishonest trustees. In such cases the trustees would have no claims against the third party. The trustees would suffer no loss by reason of the third party's failure to discover what was going on. The question is whether in this type of situation the third party owes a duty of care to the beneficiaries to, in effect, check that a trustee is not misbehaving. The third party must act honestly. The question is whether that is enough.

In agreement with the preponderant view, their Lordships consider that dishonesty is an essential ingredient here. There may be cases where, in the light of the particular facts, a third party will owe a duty of care to the beneficiaries. As a general proposition, however, beneficiaries cannot reasonably expect that all the world dealing with their trustees should owe them a duty to take care lest the trustees are behaving dishonestly.

Unconscionable conduct

Mention, finally, must be made of the suggestion that the test for liability is that of unconscionable conduct. Unconscionable is a word of immediate appeal to an equity lawyer. Equity is rooted historically in the concept of the Lord Chancellor, as the keeper of the Royal Conscience, concerning himself with conduct which was contrary to good conscience. It must be recognised, however, that unconscionable is not a word in everyday use by non-lawyers. If it is to be used in this context, and if it is to be the touchstone for liability as an accessory, it is essential to be clear on what, *in this context*, unconscionable *means*. If unconscionable means no more than dishonesty, then dishonesty is the preferable label. If unconscionable means something different, it must be said that it is not clear what that something different is. Either way, therefore, the term is better avoided in this context.

The accessory liability principle

Drawing the threads together, their Lordships' overall conclusion is that dishonesty is a necessary ingredient of accessory liability. It is also a sufficient ingredient. A liability in equity to make good resulting loss attaches to a person who dishonestly procures or assists in a breach of trust or fiduciary obligation. It is not necessary that, in addition, the trustee or fiduciary was acting dishonestly, although this will usually be so where the third party who is assisting him is acting dishonestly. "Knowingly" is better avoided as a defining ingredient of the principle, and in the context of this principle the *Baden* scale of knowledge is best forgotten.

In **Agip (Africa) Ltd v Jackson**,[8] payment orders from Agip to third parties were fraudulently altered by Agip's accountant, who changed the names of the payees to those of companies formed by the defendants, who were two accountants in partnership and their employee. The money was transferred to the accounts of the companies and ultimately paid to third parties abroad, from whom it was irrecoverable. Agip sought to recover from the defendants, who had throughout followed the instructions of their client, a French lawyer acting for unknown principals. At first instance [1990] Ch 265, [1992] 4 All ER 385, Millett J held that dishonesty was the test for accessory liability and that the defendants, who had acted with at least reckless indifference, were accordingly liable for assisting in the fraudulent breach of fiduciary duty by Agip's accountant[9]. This was upheld by the Court of Appeal [1991] Ch 547, [1992] 4 All ER 451, although uncritical reference was made to the *Selangor* line of cases.

MILLETT J said at 294, at 406:

"Mr Jackson and Mr Griffin are professional men. They obviously knew that they were laundering money. There were consciously helping their clients to make arrangements designed for the purpose of concealment from, inter alios, the plaintiff. It must have been obvious to them that their clients could not afford their activities to see the light of day. Secrecy is the badge of fraud. They must have realised at least that their clients *might* be involved in a fraud on the plaintiffs.

Can Mr Jackson and Mr Griffin possibly have believed that their arrangements had an honest purpose? They pleaded no such belief. They have given no evidence. On their behalf it was submitted that they were entitled to be reassured by the fact that they were taking over arrangements which had been established for some years, that they were introduced to them by a partner in a well-known and reputable firm of chartered accountants and that, if there was any wrongdoing, it would surely have come to light long before. Had Mr Jackson and Mr Griffin given evidence to this effect, I might or might not have believed it. But I will not assume it when they do not tell me so . . . .

I am led to the conclusion that Mr Jackson and Mr Griffin were at best indifferent to the possibility of fraud. They made no inquiries of the plaintiffs because they thought that it was none of their business. That is not honest

---

8 (1991) 50 CLJ 409 (C. Harpum); [1992] Conv 367 (S. Goulding); (1992) 12 LS 332 (H. Norman); (1993–94) 4 KCLJ 82 (P. Oliver).
9 Two were personally liable and the third was vicariously liable; p. 274, post.

behaviour. The sooner that those who provide the services of nominee companies for the purpose of enabling their clients to keep their activities secret realise it, the better. In my judgment, it is quite enough to make them liable to account as constructive trustees.''

In the Court of Appeal Fox LJ said at 567, at 467:

"The degree of knowledge required was described by Ungoed-Thomas J in *Selangor United Rubber Estates Ltd v Cradock (No 3)* [1968] 1 WLR 1555, 1590 [1968] 2 All ER 1073, 1104, as knowledge of circumstances which would indicate to an honest and reasonable man that such a design was being committed or would put him on inquiry whether it was being committed.

Peter Gibson J in *Baden v Société Générale pour Favoriser le Développement du Commerce et de l'Industrie en France SA* [1993] 1 WLR 509n at 576, [1992] 4 All ER 161 at 235 gave a more expanded description of the circumstances constituting the necessary knowledge under five heads as follows: (i) actual knowledge; (ii) wilfully shutting one's eyes to the obvious; (iii) wilfully and recklessly failing to make such inquiries as an honest and reasonable man would make; (iv) knowledge of any circumstances which would indicate the facts to an honest and reasonable man; and (v) knowledge of circumstances which would put an honest and reasonable man on inquiry. I accept that formulation. It is, however, only an explanation of the general principle and is not necessarily comprehensive.

The judge held, and it is not challenged, that Mr Bowers did not participate in the furtherance of the fraud at all; although he was a partner in Jackson & Co he played no part in the movement of the money and gave no instructions about it. Mr Jackson and Mr Griffin are in quite a different position. Mr Jackson set up the company structures. Mr Jackson and Mr Griffin controlled the movement of the money from the time it reached Baker Oil to the time it was paid out of the account of Jackson & Co in the Isle of Man bank. On the evidence, and in the absence of evidence from Mr Jackson and Mr Griffin themselves, I agree with the judge that both of them must be regarded as having assisted in the fraud. That, however, by no means concludes the matter. There remains the question of their state of mind. Did they have the necessary degree of knowledge?

[His Lordship reviewed the evidence and concluded:]

In the circumstances I think that the judge rightly came to the conclusion that they must have known they were laundering money, and were consequently helping their clients to make arrangements to conceal some dispositions of money which had such a degree of impropriety that neither they nor their clients could afford to have them disclosed. . . .

In the end, it seems to me that the most striking feature in the case is that in August 1984 Mr Jackson and Mr Griffin were being given advice on the possibility that a payment or payments might involve a fraud on Agip. Having got to that point it seems to me that persons acting honestly would have pursued the matter with a view to satisfying themselves that there was no fraud. But there is nothing to show that they did that. They made no inquiries of Agip at all. They let matters continue. In the circumstances, I conclude that Mr Jackson and Mr Griffin are liable as constructive trustees. Mr Bowers is liable for the acts of Mr Jackson, who was his partner, and of Mr Griffin, who was employed by the partnership.

Accordingly, I think that the judge came to the right conclusion and I would dismiss the appeal."

In **Lipkin Gorman v Karpnale Ltd** [1989] 1 WLR 1340, [1992] 4 All ER 409, a partner in a firm of solicitors fraudulently withdrew £200,000 from the firm's client account at Lloyds Bank plc (the second defendant) and lost the money gambling at the Playboy Club (owned by the first defendant). The solicitors sued the bank for assisting in the partner's breach of fiduciary duty and the club for money had and received. The action against the club proceeded to the House of Lords (p. 260 post). The Court of Appeal held the bank not liable. MAY LJ contrasted the *Selangor* and *Karak* decisions with *Carl Zeiss Stiftung v Herbert Smith & Co (No 2)* [1969] 2 Ch 276, [1969] 2 All ER 367, p. 251 ante and *Belmont Finance Corpn Ltd v Williams Furniture Ltd* [1979] Ch 250, [1979] 1 All ER 118, p. 251 ante and concluded at 1355, at 420, that there was "at least strong persuasive authority" for the proposition that constructive knowledge of the breach did not suffice.

ii. KNOWING RECEIPT OR DEALING

Where a person, not appointed as trustee, has received trust property for his own benefit[10] with knowledge that it is trust property transferred in breach of trust, or has acquired knowledge after such receipt and then dealt with the property inconsistently with the trust, he is liable as a constructive trustee. He may be described as a trustee *de son tort*, an expression borrowed from the law of executors (see *Re Barney* [1892] 2 Ch 265). There is no significance today in the distinction between constructive trustees and trustees *de son tort*. The question whether the property received by the third party is that of the beneficiary will be resolved by the principles of tracing, explained in chapter 21.

As indicated above, the question whether the third party takes subject to the trust is governed by the doctrine of notice. Only a purchaser of the legal estate without notice, actual, constructive or imputed, can take free of the claims of the beneficiaries. An innocent volunteer, for example, although without notice of any kind, cannot take free of the trust because he is not a purchaser. His position, as shown by *Re Diplock* [1948] Ch 465, [1948] 2 All ER 318, p. 904, post, is that the beneficiaries may exercise the remedy of "tracing" against him if he still has the property or its identifiable proceeds.

Where the third party no longer has the property or its proceeds, the question arises as to whether he is personally liable to account for its value. The real difficulty is as to whether a third party with constructive, but not actual, knowledge is liable.

If the principles of unjust enrichment are applied, there seems no good reason why actual notice should be a condition of liability. Indeed, an innocent volunteer is unjustly enriched if he has had the benefit of another's property

---

10 Liability cannot arise in this category for receipt and dealing as agent for another: *Agip (Africa) Ltd v Jackson* [1991] Ch 547, [1992] 4 All ER 451; *Polly Peck International plc v Nadir (No 2)* [1992] 4 All ER 769.

even though he received it without notice of any kind.[11] Such a volunteer is personally liable at common law for money had and received, as in *Lipkin Gorman v Karpnale Ltd* [1991] 2 AC 548, [1992] 4 All ER 512, and in equity for receipt of another's property in the administration of an estate, as in *Ministry of Health v Simpson* [1951] AC 251, [1950] 2 All ER 1137 (the *Diplock* litigation). The harshness of any such rule is mitigated by the defence of change of position, recognised by the House of Lords in *Lipkin Gorman v Karpnale Ltd.* However, the authorities do not yet establish strict liability for innocent volunteers. Most modern judicial formulations support the view that knowledge is required, but that constructive knowledge suffices[12]. Clearly a purchaser without notice of trust property transferred in breach of trust is no more liable to a personal action than he is to a tracing claim. He will be personally liable if he took with notice, but the courts have emphasised that a purchaser acting in an arm's length commercial transaction not involving title to land has no duty to investigate[13]. Thus there is less scope for the doctrine of constructive notice.

(a) Actual or Constructive Knowledge

The following extracts illustrate the differing views on the degree of knowledge required for personal liability.

RE MONTAGU'S SETTLEMENT TRUSTS[14]
[1987] Ch 264, [1992] 4 All ER 308 (Ch D, Sɪʀ Rᴏʙᴇʀᴛ Mᴇɢᴀʀʀʏ V-C)

Trustees transferred certain settled chattels to the beneficiary, the tenth Duke, absolutely. The transfer, which was the result of an honest mistake, was in breach of trust. The Duke's solicitor had at an earlier stage known of the terms of the settlement. The Duke disposed of a number of the chattels during his lifetime. After his death, the eleventh Duke claimed that his predecessor had become a constructive trustee of the chattels, and was therefore personally accountable for the value of any chattels which had been disposed of.
Held. While the tenth Duke's estate must return any remaining chattels or their traceable proceeds, the Duke had incurred no personal liability as constructive trustee.
Sɪʀ Rᴏʙᴇʀᴛ Mᴇɢᴀʀʀʏ V-C: That brings me to the essential question for decision. The core of the question (and I put it very broadly) is what suffices to

---

11 (1989) 105 LQR 528 (P. Birks); (1991) 107 LQR 71 (P. Millett); [1992] All ER Rev 270–272 (W. Swadling); (1994) 57 MLR 38 (S. Fennell); Goff and Jones, *The Law of Restitution* (4th edn), p 673.

12 *Belmont Finance Corpn Ltd v Williams Furniture Ltd (No 2)* [1980] 1 All ER 393; *International Sales and Agencies Ltd v Marcus* [1982] 3 All ER 551; *Agip (Africa) Ltd v Jackson* [1990] Ch 265, [1992] 4 All ER 385 (not dealt with on appeal); *Polly Peck International plc v Nadir (No 2)* [1992] 4 All ER 769; (1990) 49 CLJ 217 (C. Harpum); (1993) 109 LQR 368 (M. Bryan); *El Ajou v Dollar Land Holdings plc* [1993] 3 All ER 717 (reversed on a different point at [1994] 2 All ER 685). Similarly in New Zealand; *Powell v Thompson* [1991] 1 NZLR 597; *Equiticorp Industries Group Ltd v Hawkins* [1991] 3 NZLR 700.

13 *Polly Peck International plc v Nadir (No 2)*, supra and *(No 3)* [1994] 1 BCLC 661 supra; *Eagle Trust plc v SBC Securities Ltd* [1993] 1 WLR 484, [1992] 4 All ER 488; *Cowan de Groot Properties Ltd v Eagle Trust plc* [1992] 4 All ER 700; *El Ajou v Dollar Land Holdings plc*, supra.

14 This was followed by Aʟʟɪᴏᴛᴛ J in *Lipkin Gorman v Karpnale Ltd* [1987] 1 WLR 987, [1992] 4 All ER 331, but the higher courts decided on other grounds. See also *Barclays Bank plc v Quincecare Ltd* [1992] 4 All ER 363 (decided 1988).

constitute a recipient of trust property a constructive trustee of it. I can leave on one side the equitable doctrine of tracing: if the recipient of trust property still has the property or its traceable proceeds in his possession, he is liable to restore it unless he is a purchaser without notice. But liability as a constructive trustee is wider, and does not depend upon the recipient still having the property or its traceable proceeds. Does it suffice if the recipient had "notice" that the property he was receiving was trust property, or must he have not merely notice of this, but knowledge, or "cognizance," as it has been put?

In my previous judgment I provisionally took the view that mere notice was not enough, and that what was required was knowledge or cognizance. In saying this, I very much had in mind what was said in the Court of Appeal in *Carl Zeiss Stiftung v Herbert Smith & Co (No 2)* [1969] 2 Ch 276, [1969] 2 All ER 367, and I shall not repeat what I have already said about that case. It is that question which Mr. Taylor and Mr. Chadwick have now explored before me, with an ample and helpful citation of authority, most of which had not been cited previously. It was common ground that it was impossible to contend that the law to be found in the cases was clear and not in something of a muddle. Part of the difficulty arises from the fact that in cases on constructive trusts in which there is clearly knowledge the term "notice" is often convenient to use, without any distinction between notice and knowledge being intended.

At the outset, I think that I should refer to *Baden, Delvaux and Lecuit v Société Générale pour Favoriser le Développement du Commerce et de l'Industrie en France SA* [1993] 1 WLR 509n, [1992] 4 All ER 161, a case which for obvious reasons I shall call "the *Baden*" case. That case took 105 days to hear, spread over 7 months, and the judgment of Peter Gibson J is over 120 pages long. It was a "knowing assistance" type of constructive trust, as distinct from the "knowing receipt or dealing" type which is in issue before me. I use these terms as a convenient shorthand for two of the principle types of constructive trust. Put shortly, under the first of these heads a person becomes liable as a constructive trustee if he knowingly assists in some fraudulent design[15] on the part of a trustee. Under the second head, a person also becomes liable as a constructive trustee if he either receives trust property with knowledge that the transfer is a breach of trust, or else deals with the property in a manner inconsistent with the trust after acquiring knowledge of the trust. It will be seen that the word "knowledge" occurs under each head; and in the *Baden* case, at p. 575, at p. 235, the judge in effect said that "knowledge" had the same meaning under each head.

I pause at that point. In the books and the authorities the word "notice" is often used in place of the word "knowledge", usually without any real explanation of its meaning. This seems to me to be a fertile source of confusion; for whatever meaning the layman may attach to those words, centuries of equity jurisprudence have attached a detailed and technical meaning to the term "notice", without doing the same for "knowledge." The classification of "notice" into actual notice, constructive notice and imputed notice has been developed in relation to the doctrine that a bona fide purchaser for value of a legal estate takes free from any equitable interests of which he has no notice. I need not discuss this classification beyond saying that I use the term "imputed notice" as meaning any actual or constructive notice that a solicitor or other agent for the purchaser acquires in the course of the

---

15 It has since been decided that the breach of trust need not be fraudulent: *Royal Brunei Airlines Sdn Bhd v Tan* [1995] 2 AC 378, [1995] 3 All ER 97, p. 252 ante.

transaction in question, such notice being imputed to the purchaser. Some of the cases describe any constructive notice that a purchaser himself obtains as being "imputed" to him; but I confine "imputed" to notice obtained by another which equity imputes to the purchaser.

Now until recently I do not think there had been any classification of "knowledge" which corresponded with the classification of "notice." However, in the *Baden* case, at p. 575, at p. 235, the judgment sets out five categories of knowledge, or of the circumstances in which the court may treat a person as having knowledge. Counsel in that case were substantially in agreement in treating all five types as being relevant for the purpose of a constructive trust; and the judge agreed with them: at 582, at 243. These categories are (i) actual knowledge; (ii) wilfully shutting one's eyes to the obvious; (iii) wilfully and recklessly failing to make such inquiries as an honest and reasonable man would make; (iv) knowledge of circumstances which would indicate the facts to an honest and reasonable man; and (v) knowing of circumstances which would put an honest and reasonable man on inquiry. If I pause there, it can be said that these categories of knowledge correspond to two categories of notice: Type (i) corresponds to actual notice, and types (ii), (iii), (iv) and (v) correspond to constructive notice. Nothing, however, is said (at least in terms) about imputed knowledge. This is important, because in the case before me Mr. Taylor strongly contended that Mr. Lickfold's knowledge must be imputed to the Duke, and that this was of the essence of his case.

It seems to me that one must be very careful about applying to constructive trusts either the accepted concepts of notice or any analogy to them. In determining whether a constructive trust has been created, the fundamental question is whether the conscience of the recipient is bound in such a way as to justify equity in imposing a trust on him. The rules concerning a purchaser without notice seem to me to provide little guidance on this and to be liable to be misleading. First, they are irrelevant unless there is a purchase. A volunteer is bound by an equitable interest even if he has no notice of it; but, in many cases of alleged constructive trusts, the disposition has been voluntary and not for value, and yet notice or knowledge is plainly relevant. Second, although a purchaser normally employs solicitors, and so questions of imputed notice may arise, it is unusual for a volunteer to employ solicitors when about to receive bounty. Even if he does, he is unlikely to employ them in order to investigate the right of the donor to make the gift or of the trustees or personal representatives to make the distribution; and until this case came before me I had never heard it suggested that a volunteer would be fixed with imputed notice of all that his solicitors would have discovered had he employed solicitors and had instructed them to investigate his right to receive the property.

Third, there seems to me to be a fundamental difference between the questions that arise in respect of the doctrine of purchaser without notice and constructive trusts. As I said in my previous judgment, ante, pp. 272h–273b, p. 320:

"The former is concerned with the question whether a person takes property subject to or free from some equity. The latter is concerned with whether or not a person is to have imposed upon him the personal burdens and obligations of trusteeship. I do not see why one of the touchstones for determining the burdens on property should be the same as that for deciding whether to impose a personal obligation on a man. The cold calculus of constructive and imputed notice does not seem to me to be an appropriate instrument for deciding whether a man's conscience is sufficiently affected for it to be right to bind him by the obligations of a constructive trustee."

I can see no reason to resile from that statement, save that to meet possible susceptibilities I would alter "man" to "person." I would only add that there is more to being made a trustee than merely taking property subject to an equity.

(1991) 107 LQR 71 at p. 80–82 (Sir Peter MILLETT)

"Unfortunately, the law has been thrown into confusion in England by the judgment of Sir Robert Megarry V-C in *Re Montagu's Settlement Trusts*,[16] where he doubted whether constructive notice is sufficient, and expressed his own view that dishonesty or want of probity is required.[17]

Before the degree of knowledge that is required is considered, there is a threshhold question to be resolved: whether (as is commonly assumed) the liability, if any, of the recipient to account after he has parted with the property derives from the trust upon which he held the property while it was still in his possession. Sir Robert Megarry denied that this was so. 'The equitable doctrine of tracing,' he said, 'and the imposition of a constructive trust by reason of the knowing receipt of trust property are governed by different rules and must be kept distinct. Tracing is primarily a means of determining the rights of property, whereas the imposition of a constructive trust creates personal obligations that go beyond mere property rights ... Whether a constructive trust arises in such a case primarily depends on the knowledge of the recipient.'[18]

In the writer's view, this is profoundly mistaken.[19] It is necessary to return to first principles. A tracing claim leads to the application of the law governing priorities, by which a beneficiary has priority over an innocent volunteer who receives trust property transferred to him in breach of trust. Notice is irrelevant; receipt by a volunteer, without more, constitutes the recipient a trustee for the true owner. He holds the property on a resulting trust. As a trustee, he is liable not only to the true owner's proprietary remedies but also to the ordinary personal obligation of a trustee to account. If he parts with the trust property, he necessarily deprives the true owner of any proprietary remedy against him, but one would not expect his personal liability to determine. It does not follow that he *does* remain liable; but it is surely more appropriate to refer the source of his continuing liability, if any, to the substantive trust in respect of which he was formerly a trustee than to some remedial constructive trust imposed *de novo* by the Court.

16 [1987] Ch 264, [1992] 4 All ER 308. See, too, Hayton (1985) 27 Malaya L. Rev. 313, which supports Sir Robert MEGARRY's approach.
17 At p. 285, at p. 329, following Professor Austin in *Essays in Equity* ed. Finn (1985) 196 at p. 228. The reasoning has been adopted in the new edition of Underhill and Hayton, *Law Relating to Trusts and Trustees* (14th ed.), at pp. 353–355.
18 At p. 285, at p. 329.
19 It appears to rest on a passage in *Re Diplock* [1948] Ch 465, at pp. 478–9 [1948] 2 All ER 318 at pp. 479–480 taken out of context.

It is submitted that, whether the recipient has retained or parted with the property, the source of his liability is the same, *i.e.* the receipt of trust property to which he was not entitled.[20] Even if, having parted with the property, his liability is necessarily only a personal one, it still arises in the context of competing proprietary claims. In both cases, liability should be receipt-based, not fault-based. It does not follow that the rules governing liability are the same in the two cases. It would be unduly harsh to deny a defence to the unwitting trustee who acted both honestly and reasonably in parting with the trust property; but there is no warrant for introducing a requirement of dishonesty in order to found liability.

Of course, a donee does not look a gift horse in the mouth; and a casino does not inquire into its client's title to the money which he stakes. Such considerations often lead to the objection that the doctrine of constructive notice is out of place in such cases. This is a confusion of thought. Unless the circumstances are such as to put a reasonable man on inquiry, there can be no question of the recipient being fixed with constructive notice. It will only be in exceptional circumstances that such notice can be established on the part of a volunteer. But if it can be established he ought to be liable.

The last question is whether, in the absence of constructive notice, the innocent volunteer who has parted with the trust property can be made liable. The traditional view is that he cannot. If the authorities which support this view are examined, however, it will be found that most of them are not concerned with volunteers at all, but with banks or other creditors who have received trust money in reduction or discharge of debts owed to them. Such recipients are not volunteers, and cannot be made liable in the absence of constructive notice.[1] It does not follow that a volunteer cannot be liable in the absence of notice.

If, as is suggested, the liability is receipt-based, it should logically be strict. The absence of notice on the part of a volunteer is normally irrelevant. It does not help him if he retains the property. Why should it provide him with a defence if he has parted with it, albeit in breach of a trust of whose existence he had no reason to be aware? The answer, it is suggested, is that this is not the true nature of the volunteer's defence. His defence is based on having parted with the property, not on the absence of constructive notice. That is a necessary, but not necessarily a sufficient, condition for the defence to operate. The defence itself is based on change of position. But in those countries like the United States of America where this defence is recognised, it is not established by the mere fact that the defendant parted with the money before acquiring notice of the facts.[2] It is no defence, for example, if he spent the money on ordinary living expenses; there must have been some extraordinary expenditure which he would not have incurred if he had not received the money. This, it is suggested, rather than that indicated by *Re Montagu's Settlement Trusts*, is the direction in which equity should develop.''

---

20 See C. Harpum, (1986) 102 LQR 114 at p. 290.
1 *Thomson v Clydesdale Bank Ltd* [1893] AC 282; *Westpac Banking Corpn v Savin* [1985] 2 NZLR 41.
2 See *Scott on Trusts* (4th edn.) para. 292.2.

In **Agip (Africa) Ltd v Jackson** [1990] Ch 265, [1992] 4 All ER 385,[3] where the defendants were held liable on the basis of knowing assistance in a breach of trust, MILLETT J analysed the "knowing receipt" category at 291, at 403:

"In my judgment, much confusion has been caused by treating this as a single category and by failing to differentiate between a number of different situations. Without attempting an exhaustive classification, it is necessary to distinguish between two main classes of case under this heading.

The first is concerned with the person who receives for his own benefit trust property transferred to him in breach of trust. He is liable as a constructive trustee if he received it with notice, actual or constructive, that it was trust property and that the transfer to him was a breach of trust; or if he received it without such notice but subsequently discovered the facts. In either case he is liable to account for the property, in the first case as from the time he received the property, and in the second as from the time he acquired notice.

The second and, in my judgment, distinct class of case is that of the person, usually an agent of the trustees, who receives the trust property lawfully and not for his own benefit but who then either misappropriates it or otherwise deals with it in a manner which is inconsistent with the trust. He is liable to account as a constructive trustee if he received the property knowing it to be such, though he will not necessarily be required in all circumstances to have known the exact terms of the trust . . . .

In either class of case it is immaterial whether the breach of trust was fraudulent or not. The essential feature of the first class is that the recipient must have received the property for his own use and benefit. This is why neither the paying nor the collecting bank can normally be brought within it. In paying or collecting money for a customer the bank acts only as his agent. It is otherwise, however, if the collecting bank uses the money to reduce or discharge the customer's overdraft. In doing so it receives the money for its own benefit."

In **El Ajou v Dollar Land Holdings plc** [1993] 3 All ER 717 the plaintiff, the victim of a fraud, sought redress against the defendant company, which had received some of the proceeds of the fraud as a purchaser. One basis of the claim was "knowing receipt". MILLETT J considered the principles at 738:

"The plaintiff seeks a personal remedy based on 'knowing receipt'. As I have previously pointed out, this is the counterpart in equity of the common law claim for money had and received. The latter, at least, is a receipt-based claim to restitution, and the cause of action is complete when the money is received: see *Lipkin Gorman v Karpnale Ltd* [1991] 2 AC 548 at 572, [1992] 4 All ER 512 at 527. So, in my judgment, is the former, unless arbitrary and anomalous distinctions between the common law and equitable claims are to be insisted upon. But it is necessary at the outset to identify the assets which DLH received, and the occasions upon which it received them. The plaintiff alleges that DLH received the sum of £270,000 in March 1986, and a further £1,030,000 in June 1986.

[His Lordship reviewed the facts and continued:]

---

3 CA dealt only with the "assistance" category: [1991] Ch 547, [1992] 4 All ER 451.

DLH claims to be a bona fide purchaser for value without notice. Unfortunately, the nature of the knowledge required is highly controversial, at least where the recipient is a volunteer and the plaintiff brings a personal claim. In *Re Montagu's Settlement Trusts* [1987] Ch 264 at 285, [1992] 4 All ER 308 at 330, p. 261 ante, Megarry V-C expressed the view obiter that, in such a case, dishonesty or want of probity involving actual knowledge or wilful blindness is required. In *Agip (Africa) Ltd v Jackson* [1991] Ch 547 at 567, [1992] 4 All ER 451 at 467, Fox LJ expressed the view that dishonesty is not required, and that knowledge of any circumstances which would indicate the facts to an honest and reasonable man, and knowledge of circumstances which would put an honest and reasonable man on inquiry, are sufficient.

That was a case of knowing assistance, not knowing receipt, and it is not clear whether Fox LJ's remarks were intended to apply to the former. But they must at least cover the latter. In *Eagle Trust plc v SBC Securities Ltd* [1993] 1 WLR 484 at 506–507, [1992] 4 All ER 488 at 509–510, Vinelott J based liability firmly on inferred knowledge and not on constructive notice. For my own part I agree that even where the plaintiff's claim is a proprietary one, and the defendant raises the defence of bona fide purchaser for value without notice, there is no room for the doctrine of constructive notice in the strict conveyancing sense in a factual situation where it is not the custom and practice to make inquiry. But it does not follow that there is no room for an analogous doctrine in a situation in which any honest and reasonable man would have made inquiry. Vinelott J held that knowledge might be inferred if the circumstances were such that an honest and reasonable man would have inferred that the moneys were probably trust moneys and were being misapplied. He left open the question whether a recipient might escape liability if the court was satisfied that, although an honest and reasonable man would have realised this, through foolishness or inexperience he did not in fact suspect it.

That question does not arise in the present case. In the absence of full argument I am content to assume, without deciding, that dishonesty or want of probity involving actual knowledge (whether proved or inferred) is not a precondition of liability; but that a recipient is not expected to be unduly suspicious and is not to be held liable unless he went ahead without further inquiry in circumstances in which an honest and reasonable man would have realised that the money was probably trust money and was being misapplied. That approach is in accordance with the preponderance of judicial authority in this country and New Zealand, and is consistent with an analysis of the underlying trust as a subsisting trust. Moreover, I do not see how it would be possible to develop any logical and coherent system of restitution if there were different requirements in respect of knowledge for the common law claim for money had and received, the personal claim for an account in equity against a knowing recipient and the equitable proprietary claim. In the present case, for example, it would be illogical and undesirable to require the plaintiff to assert a proprietary claim he does not need in order to avoid the burden of having to prove dishonesty or ask the court to infer it.''

[His Lordship held that the defendant company was not liable because, although F, its chairman and non-executive director, had actual knowledge, this could not be attributed to the company. The Court of Appeal reversed this decision at [1994] 2 All ER 685, holding that F was the "directing mind and will" of the company. The degree of knowledge required for "knowing receipt" was not discussed. The case was remitted to the High Court on the issue of quantum of the plaintiff's claim. ROBERT WALKER J held that, where the plaintiff is one of several victims of a fraud, there may be cases where the property received by the defendant would be treated as not solely that of the plaintiff, but that this was not such a case. *El Ajou v Dollar Land Holdings plc (No 2)* [1995] 2 All ER 213].

(b) Position at Common Law

Where a person has received property to which he is not entitled and no longer possesses it or its traceable proceeds, the common law equivalent to the equitable action for "knowing receipt" is the action for money had and received. This action lies against an innocent volunteer who had no notice of any kind of the plaintiff's entitlement, although a bona fide purchaser has a defence. The plaintiff must establish legal title to the property in question. The defence of change of position is available to an innocent defendant (but not to a wrongdoer) who has so changed his position that it would be inequitable to require restitution. A comparison of the common law and equitable actions lends support to the view that personal liability in equity for receipt of trust property should not require knowledge, as both actions are restitutionary.

LIPKIN GORMAN v KARPNALE LTD[4]
[1991] 2 AC 548, [1992] 4 All ER 512 (HL, Lords BRIDGE OF HARWICH, TEMPLEMAN, GRIFFITHS, ACKNER and GOFF OF CHIEVELEY).

A firm of solicitors sought to recover money paid to the Playboy Club (owned by the defendant) by a partner in the firm (Cass) who had wrongly withdrawn it from the firm's client account and spent it on gambling. (The claim against the bank for assistance in a breach of trust failed in the Court of Appeal, p. 260 ante). The Club had received the money without notice of its source, but, as the gambling contract was unenforceable, had given no consideration.

Held The club was personally liable at common law for money had and received, but could invoke change of position as a partial defence to the extent that it had paid out winnings to Cass.

LORD GOFF OF CHIEVELEY: It is well established that a legal owner is entitled to trace his property into its product, provided that the latter is indeed identifiable as the product of his property. Thus, in *Taylor v Plumer* (1815) 3 M & S 562, where Sir Thomas Plumer gave a draft to a stockbroker for the purpose of buying exchequer bills, and the stockbroker instead used the draft for buying American securities and doubloons for his own purposes, Sir Thomas was able to trace his property into the securities and doubloons in the hands of the stockbroker, and so defeat a claim made to them by the stockbroker's assignees in bankruptcy. Of course, "tracing" or "following" property into its product involves a decision by the owner of the original

---

4 (1991) 107 LQR 527 (P. Watts); [1991] CLJ 407 (W.R. Cornish); [1992] Conv 124 (M. Halliwell); (1992) 55 MLR 377 (E. McKendrick); [1992] All ER Rev 202 (P.J. Clarke); 255 (W.J. Swadling); (1994) 57 MLR 38 (S. Fennell). On change of position, see further *South Tyneside Metropolitan Borough Council v Svenska International plc* [1995] 1 All ER 545; (1994) 58 MLR 505 (P. Key).

property to assert his title to the product in place of his original property. This is sometimes referred to as ratification. I myself would not so describe it; but it has, in my opinion, at least one feature in common with ratification, that it cannot be relied upon so as to render an innocent recipient a wrongdoer (cf *Bolton Partners v Lambert* (1889) 41 Ch D 295 at 307 per Cotton LJ: " . . . an act lawful at the time of its performance [cannot] be rendered unlawful, by the application of the doctrine of ratification.")

I return to the present case. Before Cass drew upon the solicitors' client account at the bank, there was of course no question of the solicitors having any legal property in any cash lying at the bank. The relationship of the bank with the solicitors was essentially that of debtor and creditor; and, since the client account was at all material times in credit, the bank was the debtor and the solicitors were its creditors. Such a debt constitutes a chose in action, which is a species of property; and, since the debt was enforceable at common law, the chose in action was legal property belonging to the solicitors at common law.

There is in my opinion no reason why the solicitors should not be able to trace their property at common law in that chose in action, or in any part of it, into its product, ie cash drawn by Cass from their client account at the bank. Such a claim is consistent with their assertion that the money so obtained by Cass was their property at common law. Further, in claiming the money as money had and received, the solicitors have not sought to make the club liable on the basis of any wrong, a point which will be of relevance at a later stage, when I come to consider the defence of change of position.

[His Lordship rejected the argument that the Club had given consideration, and continued:]

Change of position

I turn then to the last point on which the club relied to defeat the solicitors' claim for the money. This was that the claim advanced by the solicitors was in the form of an action for money had and received, and that such a claim should only succeed where the defendant was unjustly enriched at the expense of the plaintiff. If it would be unjust or unfair to order restitution, the claim should fail. It was for the court to consider the question of injustice or unfairness, on broad grounds. If the court thought that it would be unjust or unfair to hold the club liable to the solicitors, it should deny the solicitors recovery. Mr Lightman QC, for the club, listed a number of reasons why, in his submission, it would be unfair to hold the club liable. These were: (1) the club acted throughout in good faith, ignorant of the fact that the money had been stolen by Cass; (2) although the gaming contracts entered into by the club with Cass were all void, nevertheless the club honoured all those contracts; (3) Cass was allowed to keep his winnings (to the extent that he did not gamble them away); (4) the gaming contracts were merely void not illegal; and (5) the solicitors' claim was no different in principle from a claim to recover against an innocent third party to whom the money was given and who no longer retained it.

I accept that the solicitors' claim in the present case is founded upon the unjust enrichment of the club, and can only succeed if, in accordance with the principles of the law of restitution, the club were indeed unjustly enriched at the expense of the solicitors. The claim for money had and received is not, as I have previously mentioned, founded upon any wrong committed by the club against the solicitors. But it does not, in my opinion, follow that the court has carte blanche to reject the solicitors' claim simply because it thinks it unfair or unjust in the circumstances to grant recovery. The recovery of money in restitution is not, as a general rule, a matter of discretion for the court. A claim to recover money at common law is made as a matter of right; and, even though the underlying principle of recovery is the principle of unjust enrichment, nevertheless, where recovery is denied, it is denied on the basis of legal principle.

It is therefore necessary to consider whether Mr Lightman's submission can be upheld on the basis of legal principle. In my opinion it is plain, from the nature of his submission, that he is in fact seeking to invoke a principle of change of position, asserting that recovery should be denied because of the change in position of the club, who acted in good faith throughout.

Whether change of position is, or should be, recognised as a defence to claims in restitution is a subject which has been much debated in the books. It is, however, a matter on which there is a remarkable unanimity of view, the consensus being to the effect that such a defence should be recognised in English law. I myself am under no doubt that this is right.

Historically, despite broad statements of Lord Mansfield to the effect that an action for money had and received will only lie where it is inequitable for the defendant to retain the money (see in particular *Moses v Macferlan* (1760) 2 Burr 1005), the defence has received at most only partial recognition in English law. I refer to two groups of cases which can arguably be said to rest upon change of position: (1) where an agent can defeat a claim to restitution on the ground that, before learning of the plaintiff's claim, he has paid the money over to his principal or otherwise altered his position in relation to his principal on the faith of the payment; and (2) certain cases concerned with bills of exchange, in which money paid under forged bills has been held irrecoverable on grounds which may, on one possible view, be rationalised in terms of change of position: see eg *Price v Neal* (1762) 3 Burr 1354, and *London and River Plate Bank Ltd v Bank of Liverpool Ltd* [1896] 1 QB 7. There has, however, been no general recognition of any defence of change of position as such; indeed, any such defence is inconsistent with the decisions of the Exchequer Division in *Durrant v Ecclesiastical Comrs for England and Wales* (1880) 6 QBD 234, and of the Court of Appeal in *Baylis v Bishop of London* [1913] 1 Ch 127. Instead, where change of position has been relied upon by the defendant, it has been usual to approach the problem as one of estoppel: see eg *R E Jones Ltd v Waring & Gillow Ltd* [1926] AC 670, and *Avon County Council v Howlett* [1983] 1 WLR 605, [1983] 1 All ER 1073. But it is difficult to see the justification for such a rationalisation. First, estoppel normally depends upon the existence of a representation by one party, in reliance upon which the representee has so changed his position that it is inequitable for the representor to go back upon his representation. But, in cases of restitution, the requirement of a representation appears to be unnecessary. It is true that, in cases where the plaintiff has paid money directly to the defendant, it has been argued (though with difficulty) that the plaintiff has represented to the defendant that he is entitled to the money; but in a case such as the present, in which the money is paid to an innocent donee by a thief, the true owner has made no representation whatever to the defendant. Again, it was held by the Court of Appeal in *Avon County Council v Howlett* that estoppel cannot operate pro tanto, with the effect that if, for example, the defendant has innocently changed his position by disposing of part of the money, a defence of estoppel would provide him with a defence to the whole of the claim. Considerations such as these provide a strong indication that, in many cases, estoppel is not an appropriate concept to deal with the problem.

In these circumstances, it is right that we should ask ourselves: why do we feel that it would be unjust to allow restitution in cases such as these? The answer must be that, where an innocent defendant's position is so changed that he will suffer an injustice if called upon to repay or to repay in full, the injustice of requiring him so to repay outweighs the injustice of denying the plaintiff restitution. If the plaintiff pays money to the defendant under a mistake of fact, and the defendant then, acting in good faith, pays the money or part of it to charity, it is unjust to require the defendant to make restitution to the extent that he has so changed his position. Likewise, on facts such as those in the present case, if a thief steals my money and pays it to a third party who gives it away to charity, that third party should have a good defence to an action for money had and received. In other words, bona fide change of position should of itself be a good defence in such cases as these. The principle is widely recognised throughout the common law world. It is recognised in the United States of America (see the American Law Institute's *Restatement of the Law, Restitution* (1937) section 142, pp. 567–578 and Palmer, *The Law of Restitution* (1978) vol III, para. 16.8); it has been judicially recognised by the Supreme Court of Canada (see *Storthoaks Rural Municipality v Mobil Oil Canada Ltd* (1975) 55 DLR (3d) 1); it has been introduced by statute in New Zealand (Judicature Act 1908, s. 94B (as amended)) and in Western Australia (see Western Australia Law Reform (Property, Perpetuities and Succession) Act 1962, s 24, and Western Australia Trustee Act 1962, s 65(8)), and it has been judicially recognised by the Supreme Court of Victoria (see *Bank of New South Wales v Murphett* [1983] 1 VR 489). In the important case of *Australia and New Zealand Banking Group Ltd v Westpac Banking Corpn* (1988) 78 ALR 157, there are strong indications that the High Court of Australia may be moving towards the same destination (see especially at pp. 162 and 168, per curiam). The time for its recognition in this country is, in my opinion, long overdue.

I am most anxious that, in recognising this defence to actions of restitution, nothing should be said at this stage to inhibit the development of the defence on a case by case basis, in the usual way. It is, of course, plain that the defence is not open to one who has changed his position in bad faith, as where the defendant has paid away the money with knowledge of the facts entitling the plaintiff to restitution; and it is commonly accepted that the defence should not be open to a wrongdoer. There are matters which can, in due course, be considered in depth in cases where they arise for consideration. They do not arise in the present case. Here there is no doubt that the club have acted in good faith throughout, and the action is not founded upon any wrongdoing of the club. It is not, however, appropriate in the present case to attempt to identify all those actions in restitution to which change of position may be a defence. A prominent example will, no doubt, be found in those cases where the plaintiff is seeking repayment of money paid under a mistake of fact; but I can see no reason why the defence should not also be available in principle in a case such as the present, where the plaintiff's money has been paid by a thief to an innocent donee, and the plaintiff then seeks repayment from the donee in an action for money had and received. At present I do not wish to state the principle any less broadly than this: that the defence is available to a person whose position has so changed that it would be inequitable in all the circumstances to require him to make restitution, or alternatively to make restitution in full. I wish to stress, however, that the mere fact that the defendant has spent the money, in whole or in part, does not of itself render it inequitable that he should be called upon to repay, because the expenditure might in any event have been incurred by him in the ordinary course of things. I fear that the mistaken assumption that mere expenditure of money may be regarded as amounting to a change of position for present purposes has led in the past to opposition by some to recognition of a defence which in fact is likely to be available only on comparatively rare occasions. In this connection I have particularly in mind the speech of Lord Simonds in *Ministry of Health v Simpson* [1951] AC 251 at 276, [1950] 2 All ER 1137 at 1147.

I wish to add two further footnotes. The defence of change of position is akin to the defence of bona fide purchase; but we cannot simply say that bona fide purchase is a species of change of position. This is because change of position will only avail a defendant to the extent that his position has been changed; whereas, where bona fide purchase is invoked, no inquiry is made (in most cases) into the adequacy of the consideration. Even so, the recognition of change of position as a defence should be doubly beneficial. It will enable a more generous approach to be taken to the recognition of the right to restitution, in the knowledge that the defence is, in appropriate cases, available; and, while recognising the different functions of property at law and in equity, there may also in due course develop a more consistent approach to tracing claims, in which common defences are recognised as available to such claims, whether advanced at law or in equity.

[His Lordship then concluded that the solicitors were entitled to £154,695, being the Club's net winnings from Cass].

iii. Agent Assuming Trustee's Duties

An agent of the trustees, such as a solicitor or banker, will not incur liability as constructive trustee merely by reason of being in possession of trust property knowing it to be such. His receipt is merely ministerial and the transfer is not normally a breach of trust. He may, of course, be liable if he has received for his own benefit property transferred to him in breach of trust or if he assists the trustees in a breach of trust, as discussed above. The cases suggest that he will not be liable if he acts honestly and in accordance with the instructions of his principal[5]. A fortiori where the existence of the trust is not established.[6]

In **Williams-Ashman v Price and Williams** [1942] Ch 219, [1942] 1 All ER 310, solicitors had received trust money into the firm's account and, on the trustee's instructions, in some cases those of a sole trustee, made unauthorised investments. Bennett J said at 228, at 313:

---

5 *Morgan v Stephens* (1861) 3 Giff 226; *Barnes v Addy* (1874) 9 Ch App 244; *Mara v Browne* [1896] 1 Ch 199; *Competitive Insurance Co Ltd v Davies Investments Ltd* [1975] 1 WLR 1240, [1975] 3 All ER 254 (a liquidator unaware of the trust). See generally (1986) 102 LQR 111 at pp. 130 et seq (C. Harpum).

6 *Carl Zeiss Stiftung v Herbert Smith & Co (No 2)* [1969] 2 Ch 276, [1969] 2 All ER 367 (solicitors not liable to account for monies received as costs and expenses paid by client for work in defending action in which plaintiff was attempting to establish that the client was constructive trustee of all its assets. Knowledge of a "doubtful equity" did not suffice).

"*Mara v Browne* [1896] 1 Ch 199 seems to me to be a decision that an agent in possession of money which he knows to be trust money, so long as he acts honestly, is not accountable to the beneficiaries interested in the trust money unless he intermeddles in the trust by doing acts characteristic of a trustee and outside the duties of an agent. After all, the beneficiaries have their remedy against the persons who are the real trustees. I have stated that, in my opinion, Mr. Alfred Williams acted throughout the transactions honestly. Indeed, the contrary is not suggested. He acted throughout on the instructions of his principals. He never intermeddled in the trust. He has, I think, acted incautiously. Many people might take the view that he ought to have ascertained by reference to the declaration of trust what the trusts were before he did what he was asked to do first by Dr. MacGowan and Mr. Streather [the trustees] and afterwards, when Mr. Streather had died, by Dr. MacGowan alone. But considerations of this kind do not assist the plaintiff unless he can establish that when the money came into the possession of the firm, Mr. Alfred Williams or the firm came under a duty to him as a beneficiary interested in the trust fund. It is only if the plaintiff can establish the existence of such a duty that he can establish a liability on the firm arising out of the breaches of trust committed by the express trustees.

The plaintiff is, I think, trying to use the passage from Stirling J's judgment and the statement from Underhill's Law of Trusts and Trustees to support a proposition which neither Stirling J nor the late Sir Arthur Underhill could have had in mind when they used the words relied on.[7]

Blyth v Fladgate [1891] 1 Ch 337 was plainly a case where the defendants, a firm of solicitors, were saddled with the liability of trustees because they had dealt with trust moneys in breach of trust and without instructions from their principals. The facts were that at a time when there was but one trustee of a marriage settlement, trust moneys had been invested in exchequer bills which had been deposited with the bankers of the solicitors and were so deposited when the sole trustee died. Afterwards, while there was no trustee, the bills were sold and the proceeds of sale were placed to the credit of the solicitors with their bankers and afterwards paid by the solicitors to a mortgagor who, as security for their repayment, executed a mortgage in favour of three persons who were subsequently appointed to be trustees of the settlement. The advance on this mortgage was held improper and a breach of trust, and for this breach the solicitors were held to be responsible as constructive trustees because, having in their possession money which they knew was trust money, they had made an improper investment of it without instructions from or the authority of any principal. Stirling J's observations must be read in relation to the facts with which he was dealing. In *Mara v Browne* [1896] 1 Ch 199 the Court of Appeal laid down clearly the principles which govern the rights of the plaintiff and defendant firm in respect of the two sums of 200*l.* and 700*l.* received by the firm from Miss Pullen. On the facts, as I find them to be, the firm is not responsible to the plaintiff for the breaches of trust committed by the express trustees of the declaration of trust in respect of these two sums. The result is that the action fails and must be dismissed with costs.''

---

7 "Where the trust funds come into the custody and under the control of a solicitor, or indeed of any one else, with notice of the trusts, he can only discharge himself of liability by showing that the property was duly applied in accordance with the trusts": Underhill (9th edn.), p. 548, and relied on by STIRLING J in *Blyth v Fladgate* [1891] 1 Ch 337.

iv. Liability of Partner of Constructive Trustee

Another question which arises concerns the liability of persons in partnership with someone who is held to have become a constructive trustee. Where a partner in a firm of solicitors incurs liability as a constructive trustee, his partners do not incur liability merely by reason of the fact that monies received and paid in breach of trust have passed through the firm's client account.

In **Re Bell's Indenture** [1980] 1 WLR 1217, [1980] 3 All ER 425, trustee-beneficiaries misapplied nearly £30,000 of the trust fund with the knowledge and assistance of H, a partner in a firm of solicitors acting for the trustees. The misapplied monies passed through the firm's client account. H's liability was not disputed, but the beneficiaries sought to make H's partner liable also as constructive trustee. It was conceded that H's partner had acted honestly and reasonably throughout. VINELOTT J held that while a solicitor has the implied authority to accept trust monies as agent of the trustees, he has no such authority to accept office as trustee, nor to constitute himself a constructive trustee and so make his partners liable for any misapplication of the trust money. The monies had not been received by the partnership as trustees. *Blyth v Fladgate* [1891] 1 Ch 337, where the solicitor's partners were held liable in similar circumstances, was distinguished on the ground that the partners there became trustees and could not be considered merely as agents of the trustees, as there were no trustees when the money was paid into the firm's account. Thus H's partner was not liable as constructive trustee.[8]

C. Mutual Wills[9]

Where two persons by agreement make wills which give the property of the first to die to the survivor, and after the survivor's death to agreed legatees, they are said to make mutual wills. The parties are commonly husband and wife, but not necessarily so. The survivor may be given a life interest with remainders over to the agreed legatees; or perhaps an absolute interest with a substitutionary gift to the agreed legatees.[10] It is now established that the doctrine applies even where no property is left to the survivor.

Assume that the first to die, the husband, dies with a will which takes effect in the agreed form. The widow then re-marries and decides to leave all her estate to her new husband. This would be a breach of the agreement. But the agreed legatees cannot sue (even if they knew about the agreement) because they were not parties to the agreement. Nor can the widow be prevented from making a new will, for an existing will is always revocable.[11] It is not right that

---

8 See [1981] Conv 310 (P. Luxton). Nor was he liable under the Partnership Act 1890. See also *Mara v Browne* [1896] 1 Ch 199 at 208. Cf. *Agip (Africa) Ltd v Jackson* [1991] Ch 547, [1992] 4 All ER 451, where an accountant was held vicariously liable for the acts of his partner, who was liable as constructive trustee in the "assistance" category; *Re Bell's Indenture* was not cited.

9 H & M pp. 311–317; K & S, pp. 204–207; P & M, pp. 285–291; Pettit, pp. 124–127; Riddall, pp. 207–211; Snell, pp. 193–201; Underhill, pp. 390–394; Mellows: *Law of Succession* (5th edn), pp. 27–36; *Williams on Wills* (7th edn), chap. 2; (1951) 14 MLR 136 (J.D.B. Mitchell); (1951) 15 Conv (NS) 28 (G.B. Graham); (1970) 34 Conv (NS) 230 (R. Burgess); (1977) 15 Alberta LR 211 (L.A. Sheridan); (1979) University of Toronto LJ 390 (T.G. Youdan); [1982] Conv 228 (K. Hodkinson); (1989) 105 LQR 534; (1991) 54 MLR 581 (C.F. Rickett); Conv Precedents 4–4.

10 *Re Green* [1951] Ch 148, [1950] 2 All ER 913.

11 *Re Hey* [1914] P. 192.

the widow should be able to ignore the obligations of the contract, even if she has taken no benefit. It is established that a trust is imposed in favour of the agreed legatees. But that simple solution leaves a number of questions unanswered.

1. Is this an express trust, or a constructive trust? If an express trust, who declared it, and when, and in respect of which identifiable property?

If a constructive trust, upon what ground? The failure to carry out the contract is not a sufficient justification. The receipt of benefits under the first will would be; but it has been held that such receipt is not necessary.[12] Is fraud the basis?

2. To what property does the trust attach?[13] To that (if any) received by the survivor from the first to die? To that owned by the survivor at the date of the first death? To all property owned by the survivor at the date of his death?

3. When does that trust come into effect? On the first death (which would prevent a lapse of the interest of one of the agreed beneficiaries)? Or on the second death, at which time the property which is the subject of the trust would be identifiable?

4. Could the estate of the first to die take proceedings to enforce the agreement on the principle of *Beswick v Beswick*? [1968] AC 58, [1967] 2 All ER 1197; H & M, p. 313; *Re Dale* [1994] Ch 31, [1993] 4 All ER 129, p. 281 post.

(1951) 14 MLR 136 at p. 139 (J.D.B. Mitchell).

"Scope of the Trust

The date of creation has important consequences on the scope of the trust. It is obvious that where the first testator's will only gives a life interest to the survivor, no question arises in relation to that estate. It must be held upon trust to give effect to the whole will including the ultimate dispositions. Similarly even if it apparently gives an absolute interest, yet the survivor holds all that he receives thereunder on trust for himself for life and then for the ultimate beneficiaries.[14] The trust, however, where the doctrine applies, affects not only the estate of the first testator but also that of the survivor. The question is as to the extent to which it does so. Is the entirety comprised in it and if so is it the entirety as at the first death or does the trust also comprise after-acquired property?

The short answer would simply be that the extent of the trust is defined by the agreement. Thus in *Re Green* the trust was to operate on property received from the other party and on property which was derived from another trust.[15] The definition might be express, as in that case, or implied, by reason, for example, of the fact that the ultimate gifts are set out in specific sums and not as residuary dispositions. This short answer is not, judging from the few

---

12 *Re Dale*, [1994] Ch 31, [1993] 4 All ER 129, p. 281, post.
13 (1951) 14 MLR 136 at 139, 140 (J.D.B. Mitchell), infra.
14 *Re Green* [1951] Ch 148, [1950] 2 All ER 913.
15 In this respect *Re Green* does nothing more than make clear the effect of the agreement, which was implicit in earlier decisions, such as *Re Hagger* [1930] 2 Ch 190 at 195, or *Re Oldham* [1925] Ch 75 where, had the trust been regarded as effective, there would nevertheless have been some free property. The arrangement in *Dufour v Pereira* (1769) 1 Dick 419 seems only to have covered residue. See 2 Hargr Jurid Arg, p. 305.

reported cases, satisfactory since the agreement is often silent or ambiguous on the point. In one case[16] the trust apparently only affected property held by the survivor at the first death. That restriction was perhaps dictated by the fact that the mutual wills were only intended to deal with the assets of the two testators which resulted from a business they had carried on together. It was therefore reasonable to allow the survivor a free hand with the fruits of his unaided labour. In *Re Oldham*[17] Astbury J seemed disposed to hold that the trust only binds the property held by the survivor at the time of his death, thus leaving unimpaired the power of disposition inter vivos. This seems to conflict with the decision as to lapse in *Re Hagger*, which implies that the interest of the beneficiaries is vested during the lifetime of the survivor. Moreover a devise to A with a direction to settle 'so much as he shall die seised of' has, by reason of uncertainty, been held incapable of creating a trust.[18] Yet, in effect, that is what the view of Astbury J amounts to. The significance of this question lies of course in the powers of the survivor over his own property during his life. It would seem absurd if the court is prepared to prevent his breaking faith with the first testator only to the extent of preventing inconsistent testamentary dispositions thus allowing him to make the arrangement nugatory by dispositions inter vivos. It seems, therefore, that the two arguments of certainty and good faith lead to the conclusions that, in the absence of any definition, the trust of the survivor's property must be treated as embracing that which he holds at the death of the first testator together with subsequently acquired property; though clearly he will be entitled to deal freely with the income of the fund and accumulations of the income. Such indeed seems to be the implication to be drawn from Lord Camden's direction for accounts to be taken in *Dufour v Pereira*, and to have been the opinion of Lord Loughborough. It was one of his objections to finding an agreement in *Lord Walpole v Lord Orford*[19] that it would have resulted in an inability of the survivor to raise portions for his daughters by mortgage. This breadth of the scope of the trust, or at least the possibility of it, affords another reason for delimiting it in the agreement.''

In **Re Hagger** [1930] 2 Ch 190, a husband and wife made a joint will (to which the same principles apply) by which, inter alia, the survivor was given a life interest in the whole of their estate, and after the survivor's death, their property at Wandsworth was to be held on trust for sale, with Eleanor Palmer as one of nine beneficiaries. The wife died in 1904, Eleanor Palmer in 1923, and the husband in 1928. By his will the husband left all his property on different trusts.

The questions were whether the beneficiaries under the joint will could take on the husband's death; and, if so, whether Eleanor Palmer's interest lapsed by reason of her death before the husband. CLAUSON J held that all the beneficiaries, including Eleanor, could claim. He said at 195:

"To my mind *Dufour v Pereira* (1769) 1 Dick 419, decides that where there is a joint will such as this, on the death of the first testator the position as regards

16 *Re Hagger* [1930] 2 Ch 190.
17 [1925] Ch 75 at 88.
18 *Bland v Bland* (1745) 2 Cox Eq Cas 349. See also *Re Jones* [1898] 1 Ch 438.
19 (1797) 3 Ves 402 at 417. For the opposed view see, however, DIXON J in *Birmingham v Renfrew* (1937) 57 CLR 666 at 689. See also *Re Cleaver* [1981] 1 WLR 939, [1981] 2 All ER 1018, p. 279, post.

that part of the property which belongs to the survivor is that the survivor will be treated in this Court as holding the property on trust to apply it so as to carry out the effect of the joint will. As I read Lord Camden's judgment in *Dufour v Pereira* that would be so, even though the survivor did not signify his election to give effect to the will by taking benefits under it. But in any case it is clear that Lord Camden has decided that if the survivor takes a benefit conferred on him by the joint will he will be treated as a trustee in this Court, and he will not be allowed to do anything inconsistent with the provisions of the joint will. It is not necessary for me to consider the reasons on which Lord Camden based his judgment. The case must be accepted in this Court as binding. Therefore I am bound to hold that from the death of the wife the husband held the property, according to the tenor of the will, subject to the trusts thereby imposed upon it, at all events if he took advantage of the provisions of the will. In my view he did take advantage of those provisions.

The effect of the will was that the husband and wife agreed that the property should on the death of the first of them to die pass to trustees to hold on trusts inconsistent with the right of survivorship, and therefore the will effected a severance of the joint interest of the husband and wife. By the will they made a provision which was inconsistent with the survivor taking by survivorship. Therefore the property at the moment when, on the wife's death, it came within the ambit of the will ceased to be held by the two jointly, and the husband had no title to the wife's interest on her dying in his lifetime, save in so far as he took a life interest under the joint will. From the moment of the wife's death the Wandsworth property was held on trust for the husband for life with a vested interest in remainder as to one-sixth in E. Palmer. So far as the husband's interest in the property is concerned the will operated as a trust from the date of the wife's death. There is, accordingly, no lapse by reason of Eleanor Palmer's death in the husband's lifetime, but after the wife's death."

Similar questions arise, where, as in *Ottaway v Norman* [1972] Ch 698, [1971] 3 All ER 1325, property is left to a legatee upon a secret trust to leave it by will to another. BRIGHTMAN J , as has been seen,[20] upheld the trust.

(1973) 36 MLR 210 at pp. 212–214 (S.M. Bandali)

"On the evidence [in *Ottaway v Norman*] Brightman J found that the residue was not intended to be subject to trust. However, he went on to state a new principle, while making clear that this was obiter. 'I am content to assume for present purposes but without so deciding that if property is given to the primary donee on the understanding that the primary donee will dispose by will of such assets, if any, as he may have at his command at his death in favour of the secondary donee, a valid trust is created in favour of the secondary donee which is in suspense during the lifetime of the primary donee, but attached to the estate of the primary donee at the moment of the latter's death.'[1] In the present case on the evidence there had been no such 'far-reaching undertaking' and, therefore, no trust arose as regards Eva's [the

20 See p. 151, ante.
1 *Ottaway v Norman* [1972] Ch 698 at 713, [1971] 3 All ER 1325 at 1334.

house-keeper's] residuary estate. Moreover, no obligation had been undertaken by Eva as regards the money she had received under H's will. Such an obligation could be binding provided the donor and donee had discussed and intended that the donee should keep the money distinct from her own money, but there was no such evidence here.[2] However, the above doctrine of a 'trust in suspense' calls for analysis, for apart from being a salutary, if bad, attempt at indicating the potential dynamism of equitable principles, the opinion ignores some difficulties.

There is no clear English authority on this concept. The court referred to *Birmingham v Renfrew*,[3] an Australian decision, as giving some support to the proposition. This was a case of mutual wills where the survivor-husband revoked his will in breach of the undertaking he had given to his wife, and the High Court held that the agreement between them had created a constructive trust not of any specific property but of any residue of property, of whatever character, at the time of the survivor's death. The obligation was a 'floating obligation, suspended, so to speak, during the lifetime of the survivor [and] can descend upon the assets at his death and crystallise into a trust.'[4] Let us consider theoretical difficulties.

First, there is the problem of determining the ownership of property in the interval. Is the property (i.e. which 'he may have at his command at his death') during the intervening period vested in the primary donee or the secondary donee? If the former, then the legal owner should logically be able to dispose of it subject to any possible remedy for a breach of contract which, again, would be subject to the rules of privity and consideration. If the ownership is vested in the secondary donee, then there is an immediate trust. But, according to Brightman J, the trust 'attaches ... at the moment of the [primary donee's] death.' It is submitted that the difficulty cannot be avoided by holding that, in such circumstances, the primary donee has a life interest in such assets, for the fact is that the donor has been given a promise that property would be given 'if any' is left at the donee's death; this suggests that the donee is free to do what he likes with the property.[5] Moreover, if the trust attaches when the primary donee dies, what property could be subject to a life interest before that event?

Secondly, such an undertaking would in all probability fail to satisfy the requirement of certainty of the subject matter of a trust. This requirement has to be satisfied at the time the trust comes into operation. Brightman J's words that the trust is, during the intervening period, in suspense suggests that the trust has its existence at the time the donor dies, though it does not 'bite' until the primary donee dies. If so, such a trust would fail to meet the test of certainty. The primary donee should then take the property absolutely. Moreover, the trust is open to the charge of inconsistency of directions if the primary donee is entitled to do what he likes with the property during his lifetime (an absolute ownership) but is bound by a promise to leave any

---

2 The absence of this intention to keep the money distinct was, according to BRIGHTMAN J, the distinguishing factor from *Re Gardner* [1920] 2 Ch 523, where the half-secret trust clearly showed that the donee only had a life interest in the personal estate of the donor.

3 (1937) 57 CLR 666.

4 Ibid., per DIXON J at 689.

5 Presumably, if the trust arises at the death of the donee, and if the ultimate beneficiary predeceases the donee then, unlike in *Re Gardner* [1923] 2 Ch 230, the trust fails. Who would then be entitled to the property?

residue of that property in a particular way at his death.[6] It is therefore submitted that the trust concept cannot legitimately be extended to deal with the situation envisaged by Brightman J. It would be theoretically better if the situation is left to be dealt with by the law of contract, i.e. the estate of the promisor should be subject to contractual obligation undertaken by the promisor.

In **Re Cleaver** [1981] 1 WLR 939, [1981] 2 All ER 1018,[6a] an elderly couple married in 1967 and made wills in each other's favour, with a substitutionary gift to the husband's three children. After the husband's death, the wife made a new will, leaving the property to one child only. NOURSE J held that, on the balance of probabilities, there had been an agreement to make mutual wills, and therefore a constructive trust arose. Following *Birmingham v Renfrew* (1937) 57 CLR 666, it was held that the trust attached to the survivor's assets, allowing her to enjoy the property subject to a fiduciary duty which crystallised on her death and disabled her only from voluntary dispositions inter vivos calculated to defeat the agreement. There would be no objection to ordinary gifts of small value.

NOURSE J, having referred to *Dufour v Pereira* (1769) 1 Dick 419 and *Re Oldham* [1925] Ch 75, said at 945, at 1023:

"I do not find it necessary to refer to any other English case, but I have derived great assistance from the decision of the High Court of Australia in *Birmingham v Renfrew* (1937) 57 CLR 666. That was a case where the available extrinsic evidence was held to be sufficient to establish the necessary agreement between two spouses. It is chiefly of interest because both Sir John Latham CJ and more especially Dixon J examined with some care the whole nature of the legal theory on which these and other similar cases proceed. I would like to read three passages from the judgment of Dixon J which state, with all the clarity and learning for which the judgments of that most eminent judge are renowned, what I believe to be a correct analysis of the principles on which a case of enforceable mutual wills depends. The first passage reads, at 682–683:

'I think the legal result was a contract between husband and wife. The contract bound him, I think, during her lifetime not to revoke his will without notice to her. If she died without altering her will then he was bound after her death not to revoke his will at all. She on her part afforded the consideration for his promise by making her will. His obligation not to revoke his will during her life without notice to her is to be implied. For I think the express promise should be understood as meaning that if she died leaving her will unrevoked then he would not revoke his. But the agreement really assumes that neither party will alter his or her will without the knowledge of the other. It has long been established that a contract between persons to make corresponding wills gives rise to equitable obligations when one acts on the faith of such an agreement and dies leaving his will unrevoked so that the other takes property under its dispositions. It operates to impose upon the survivor an obligation

---

6 Cf. *Re Golay's Will Trusts* [1965] 1 WLR 969, [1965] 2 All ER 660 and *Re Jones* [1898] 1 Ch 438.

6a *Goodchild v Goodchild* [1996] 1 WLR 694 [1996] 1 All ER 670.

regarded as specifically enforceable. It is true that he cannot be compelled to make and leave unrevoked a testamentary document and if he dies leaving a last will containing provisions inconsistent with his agreement it is nevertheless valid as a testamentary act. But the doctrines of equity attach the obligation to the property. The effect is, I think, that the survivor becomes a constructive trustee and the terms of the trust are those of the will which he undertook would be his last will.'

Next, at 689:

'There is a third element which appears to me to be inherent in the nature of such a contract or agreement, although I do not think it has been expressly considered. The purpose of an agreement for corresponding wills must often be, as in this case, to enable the survivor during his life to deal as absolute owner with the property passing under the will of the party first dying. That is to say, the object of the transaction is to put the survivor in a position to enjoy for his own benefit the full ownership so that, for instance, he may convert it and expend the proceeds if he choose. But when he dies he is to bequeath what is left in the manner agreed upon. It is only by the special doctrines of equity that such a floating obligation, suspended, so to speak, during the lifetime of the survivor can descend upon the assets at his death and crystallise into a trust. No doubt gifts and settlements, inter vivos, if calculated to defeat the intention of the compact, could not be made by the survivor and his right of disposition, inter vivos, is, therefore, not unqualified. But, substantially, the purpose of the arrangement will often be to allow full enjoyment for the survivor's own benefit and advantage upon condition that at his death the residue shall pass as arranged.'

Finally, at 690:

'In *Re Oldham* [1925] Ch 75 Astbury J pointed out, in dealing with the question whether an agreement should be inferred, that in *Dufour v Pereira* (1769) 1 Dick 419 the compact was that the survivor should take a life estate only in the combined property. It was therefore, easy to fix the corpus with a trust as from the death of the survivor. But I do not see any difficulty in modern equity in attaching to the assets a constructive trust which allowed the survivor to enjoy the property subject to a fiduciary duty which, so to speak, crystallised on his death and disabled him from voluntary dispositions inter vivos.'

I interject to say that Dixon J was there clearly referring only to voluntary dispositions inter vivos which are calculated to defeat the intention of the compact. No objection could normally be taken to ordinary gifts of small value. He went on:

'On the contrary, as I have said, it seems rather to provide a reason for the intervention of equity. The objection that the intended beneficiaries could not enforce a contract is met by the fact that a constructive trust arises from the contract and the fact that testamentary dispositions made upon the faith of it have taken effect. It is the constructive trust and not the contract that they are entitled to enforce.'

It is also clear from *Birmingham v Renfrew* that these cases of mutual wills are only one example of a wider category of cases, for example secret trusts, in which a court of equity will intervene to impose a constructive trust. A helpful and interesting summary of that wider category of cases will be found in the argument of Mr. Nugee in *Ottaway v Norman* [1972] Ch 698, 701–702, [1971] 3 All ER 1325. The principle of all these cases is that a court of equity will not permit a person to whom property is transferred by way of gift, but on the faith of an agreement or clear understanding that it is to be dealt with in a particular way for the benefit of a third person, to deal with the property inconsistently with that agreement or understanding. If he attempts to do so after having received the benefit of the gift equity will intervene by imposing a constructive trust on the property which is the subject matter of the agreement or understanding. I take that statement of principle, and much else which is of assistance in this case, from the judgment of Slade J in *Re Pearson Fund Trusts* (21 October 1977 unreported). The statement of principle is at p. 52 of the official transcript. The judgment of Brightman J in *Ottaway v Norman* is to much the same effect.

I would emphasise that the agreement or understanding must be such as to impose on the donee a legally binding obligation to deal with the property in the particular way and that the other two certainties, namely, those as to the subject matter of the trust and the persons intended to benefit under it, are as essential to this species of trust as they are to any other. In spite of an argument by Mr. Keenan, who appears for Mr. and Mrs. Noble, to the contrary, I find it hard to see how there could be any difficulty about the second or third certainties in a case of mutual wills unless it was in the terms of the wills themselves. There, as in this case, the principal difficulty is always whether there was a legally binding obligation or merely what Lord Loughborough LC in *Lord Walpole v Lord Orford* (1797) 3 Ves 402 at 419, described as an honourable engagement.

Before turning in detail to the evidence which relates to the question whether there was a legally binding obligation on the testatrix in the present case or not I must return once more to *Birmingham v Renfrew*. It is clear from that case, if from nowhere else, that an enforceable agreement to dispose of property in pursuance of mutual wills can be established only by clear and satisfactory evidence. That seems to me to be no more than a particular application of the general rule that all claims to the property of deceased persons must be scrutinised with very great care. However, that does not mean that there has to be a departure from the ordinary standard of proof required in civil proceedings. I have to be satisfied on the balance of probabilities that the alleged agreement was made, but before I can be satisfied of that I must find clear and satisfactory evidence to that effect.''

RE DALE[7]
[1994] Ch 31, [1993] 4 All ER 129 (Ch D, MORRITT J)

A husband and wife agreed that each would leave his or her estate to their son and daughter equally. The husband died first, leaving his estate of £18,500 accordingly. The wife made a new will leaving £300 to her daughter and the rest of her estate of £19,000 to her son.
Held. The son, as executor, held the estate on trust for himself and the daughter equally. Benefit by the survivor was not necessary to the doctrine of mutual wills.
MORRITT J: There is no doubt that for the doctrine to apply there must be a contract at law. It is apparent from all the cases to which I shall refer later, but

7 (1993) 7 Trust Law International 18 (D. Brown); [1993] All ER Rev 415 (C. Sherrin); (1994) 144 NLJ 1272 (P. O'Hagan); (1995) 58 MLR 95 (A. Brierley).

in particular from *Gray v Perpetual Trustee Co Ltd* [1928] AC 391, that it is necessary to establish an agreement to make and not revoke mutual wills, some understanding or arrangement being insufficient—"without such a definite agreement there can no more be a trust in equity than a right to damages at law:" see per Viscount Haldane, at p. 400. Thus, as the defendant submitted, it is necessary to find consideration sufficient to support a contract at law. The defendant accepted that such consideration may be executory if the promise when performed would confer a benefit on the promisee or constitute a detriment to the promisor. But, it was submitted, the promise to make and not revoke a mutual will could not constitute a detriment to the first testator because he would be leaving his property in the way that he wished and because he would be able, on giving notice to the second testator, to revoke his will and make another if he changed his mind. Accordingly, it was argued, consideration for the contract had to take the form of a benefit to the second testator.

I do not accept this submission. It is to be assumed that the first testator and the second testator had agreed to make and not to revoke the mutual wills in question. The performance of that promise by the execution of the will by the first testator is in my judgment sufficient consideration by itself. But, in addition, to determine whether a promise can constitute consideration it is necessary to consider whether its performance would have been so regarded: cf. *Chitty on Contracts*, 26th ed. (1989), vol. 1, p. 160, para. 161. Thus it is to be assumed that the first testator did not revoke the mutual will notwithstanding his legal right to do so. In my judgment, this too is sufficient detriment to the first testator to constitute consideration. Thus mutual benefit is not necessary for the purpose of the requisite contract. What is necessary to obtain a decree of specific performance of a contract in favour of a third party is not, in my judgment, a relevant question when considering the doctrine of mutual wills. A will is by its very nature revocable: cf. *Re Heys' Estate* [1914] P 192. It seems to me to be inconceivable that the court would order the second testator to execute a will in accordance with the agreement at the suit of the personal representatives of the first testator or to grant an injunction restraining the second testator from revoking it. The principles on which the court acts in imposing the trust to give effect to the agreement to make and not revoke mutual wills must be found in the cases dealing with that topic, not with those dealing with the availability of the remedy of specific performance.

The origin of the doctrine of mutual wills is the decision of Lord Camden LC in *Dufour v Pereira* (1769) 1 Dick 419. His judgment has been variously described as "energetic and eloquent:" *Hargrave, Juridical Arguments and Collections* (1799), vol. 2, p. 311; "ingenious and eloquent:" *Lord Walpole v Lord Orford* (1797) 3 Ves 402, 416; "very alluring:" *Re Oldham* [1925] Ch 75, 84, and "with robust simplicity:" *Birmingham v Renfrew* (1937) 57 CLR 666, 676. But there are at least two versions of it which are not in the same terms. The case concerned a joint will made pursuant to an agreement between husband and wife whereby the residuary estate of each of them was to constitute a common fund to be held for the survivor for his or her life with remainders over. On the death of the husband the wife, who was one of his executors, proved the will. Thereafter she took possession of her husband's property and enjoyed the benefit of his residuary estate together with her separate property for many years, but on the death of the wife it was found that her last will disregarded the provisions of the joint will and left her estate to her daughter, the defendant, Mrs. Pereira. The plaintiffs were the beneficiaries under the joint will and claimed that the wife's personal estate was held in trust for them. The relevant passage in the judgment of Lord Camden LC, 1 Dick 419, 420, is in the following terms:

"Consider how far the mutual will is binding, and whether the accepting of the legacies under it by the survivor is not a confirmation of it. I am of the opinion it is. It might have been revoked by both jointly; it might have been revoked separately, provided the party intending it, had given notice to the other of such revocation. But I cannot be of opinion, that either of them, could, during their joint lives, do it secretly; or that after the death of either, it could be done by the survivor by another will.

It is a contract between the parties, which cannot be rescinded, but by the consent of both. The first that dies, carries his part of the contract into execution. Will the court afterwards permit the other to break the contract? Certainly not.

The defendant Camilla Rancer has taken the benefit of the bequest in her favour by the mutual will; and has proved it as such; she has thereby certainly confirmed it; and therefore I am of the opinion, the last will of the wife, so far as it breaks in upon the mutual will, is void. And declare that Mrs. Camilla Rancer having proved the mutual will, after her husband's death; and having possessed all his personal estate, and enjoyed the interest thereof during her life, has by those acts bound her assets to make good all her bequests in the said mutual will; and therefore let the necessary accounts be taken."

In *Lord Walpole v Lord Orford* (1797) 3 Ves. 402, the judgment of Lord Camden LC was read from a note by the Solicitor-General which Lord Loughborough LC, who had appeared as counsel in *Dufour v Pereira*, described as most accurate. His description, at p. 417, was that "There was no probate of it"–that is the joint will–was her will: but on the contrary the will, she made, was proved."

He continued:

"Therefore the court considered it not as her testament, but as a contract with her husband for valuable consideration; under which she acted for 16 or 17 years; that she had taken the benefit of it for her whole life. Therefore she had accepted the terms; and had bound herself to the conditions under which all the property was given by the will of her husband."

After referring to the pleadings Lord Loughborough LC said, at p. 417:

"The effect of the agreement was, that the wife had the enjoyment during life, and limited to that, of all the specific interests: she had a limited power of disposing of part of that property: but all, she had, was upon condition, that she should dispose of her own property, that she might have acquired after his death (and she did increase it), upon the dispositions of that will. Suppose, she had rejected instead of proving the will of her husband, and had property distinct from that subject to the operation of this contract, and an attempt had been made to bind her by it: I do not apprehend, that Lord Camden would have said, that merely by the chance of her surviving, she a feme covert would have been bound by the contract with her husband."

He described Lord Camden LC's decision in the following terms, at p. 418:

"he determined, that she was bound; and that her husband's will must rule hers; she having enjoyed all the benefit; and the will being perfectly defined."

But in *Hargrave, Juridical Arguments and Collections*, vol. 2, in a dissertation on *Walpole's* case, Mr. Hargrave quotes extensively from a manuscript copied from Lord Camden LC's own handwriting which he describes, at p. 306, as "entered," seemingly in the decree. This source was described as authoritative by Viscount Haldane in *Gray v Perpetual Trustee Co Ltd* [1928] AC 391, 399 and is, in my judgment, to be preferred because it is much fuller. In *Hargrave*, at pp. 304–306, the facts are set out. At p. 306, Lord Camden LC recorded that mutual wills were unknown in England but that the case must be decided in accordance with English law. He stated, at p. 307:

"And I trust, that the everlasting maxims of equity and conscience, upon which the jurisdiction of this court is built, are capacious enough, not only to comprehend this, but every other case that may happen; and that the justice of this court is co-extensive with every possible variety of human transactions. Consider it in two views. First, how far the mutual will shall operate as a binding engagement, independent of any confirmation by accepting the legacy under it. Secondly, whether the survivor can depart from this engagement, after she has accepted a benefit under it."

Lord Camden LC's decision on the first point should be read in full. He said, at pp. 307–311:

"It was said upon the first point, and Mr. Skynner cited an authority to prove it, that where two had made a mutual will either of them might cheat his partner, foeda machinatione, by a secret will to disappoint the joint disposition, because they are two distinct instruments. *Hall and Bickerstaff* to the same purpose.

The law of these countries then must be very defective, and totally destitute of the principles of equity and good conscience: for nothing can be more barbarous, than a law, which does permit in the very text of it one man to defraud another. The equity of this court abhors the principle. A mutual will is a mutual agreement. A mutual will is a revocable act. It may be revoked by joint consent clearly.— By one only, if he give notice, I can admit. But to affirm, that the survivor (who has deluded his partner into this will upon the faith and persuasion that he would perform his part) may legally recall his contract, either secretly during the joint lives, or after at his pleasure; I cannot allow. The mutual will is in the whole and every part mutually upon condition, that the whole shall be the will.— There is a reciprocity, that runs through the instrument. The property of both is put into a common fund and every devise is the joint devise of both. This is a contract. If not revoked during the joint lives by any open act, he that dies first dies with the promise of the survivor, that the joint will shall stand. It is too late afterwards for the survivor to change his mind: because the first to die's will is then irrevocable, which would otherwise have been differently framed, if that testator had been appraised of this dissent. Thus is the first testator drawn in and seduced by the fraud of the other, to make a disposition in his favour, which but for such a false promise he would never have consented to.

It was argued however, that the parties knowing that all testaments were in their nature revocable, were aware of this consequence, and must therefore be presumed to contract upon this hazard. There cannot be a more absurd presumption than to suppose two persons, while they are contracting, to give each a licence to impose upon the other. Though a will is always revocable, and the last must always be the testator's will; yet a man may so bind his assets by agreement, that his will shall be a trustee for performance of his agreement. A covenant to leave so much to his wife or daughter, etc. Or suppose he makes his will, and covenants not to revoke it. These cases are common; and there is no difference between promising to make a will in such a form and making his will with a promise not to revoke it. This court does not set aside the will but makes the devisee heir or executor trustee to perform the contract. Suppose the husband had so devised after the wife's promise, that he would devise in like manner. A man intends to devise for the benefit of A and B promises that if he will him his executor, A shall have his legacy. *Thynn v Thynn* (1684) 1 Vern 296; *Devenish v Baines* (1689) Prec Ch 3, testator, persuaded by his wife to give his copyhold, which he intended to devise to his godson. *Chamberlaine's* case cited. A man persuaded his father not to make a will, promising his brother and sisters should have the provision intended. This court bound the will with the promise, and raised a trust in the devisee. The act done by one is a good consideration for the performance of the other.

This case stands upon the very same principle. The parties by the mutual will do each of them devise, upon the engagement of the other, that he will likewise devise in manner therein mentioned. The instrument itself is the evidence of the agreement; and he, that dies first, does by his death carry the agreement on his part into execution. If the other then refuses, he is guilty of a fraud, can never unbind himself, and becomes a trustee of course. For no man shall deceive another to his prejudice. By engaging to do something that is in his power, he is made a trustee for the performance, and transmits that trust to those that claim under him. The court is never deceived by the form of instruments. The actions of men here are stripped of their legal clothing, and appear in their first naked simplicity. Good faith and conscience are the rules, by which every transaction is judged in this court; and there is not an instance to be found since the jurisdiction was established, where one man has ever been released from his engagement, after the other has performed his part."

Only in the sentence at p. 308 is there any reference to the first testator conferring a benefit on the second testator. The rest of the judgment on the first point emphasises more than once that there is a contract between the testators which, on the death of the first testator, is carried into effect by him, that the first testator dies with the promise of the second testator that the agreement will stand, and that it would be a fraud on the first testator to allow the second testator to disregard the contract which became irrevocable on the death of the first testator. In my judgment the essence of the decision is contained in the passage at p. 310:

"he, that dies first, does by his death carry the agreement on his part into execution. If the other then refuses, he is guilty of a fraud, can never unbind himself, and becomes a trustee of course. For no man shall deceive another to his prejudice."

In my judgment, it is no part of the principle there expressed that the first testator must have conferred a benefit on the second testator by his will. If he has, the principle will apply a fortiori, but it may apply even if he has not.

Lord Camden LC's judgment on the second question appears at p. 311, in the following terms:

"I have perhaps given myself more trouble than was necessary upon this point; because, if it could be doubtful, whether after the husband's death his wife could be at liberty to revoke her part of the mutual will, it is most clear, that she has estopped herself to this defence by an actual confirmation of the mutual will, not only by proving it, but by accepting and enjoying an interest under it. She receives this benefit, takes possession of all her husband's estates, submits to the mutual will as long as she lives, and then breaks the agreement after her death. In this view the case falls within the rule of *Noys v Mordaunt* (1706) 2 Vern 581. She takes under the joint will and can take no otherwise."

In my view the emphasis in this passage on proving the joint will and accepting and enjoying an interest under it underlines the fact that Lord Camden did not regard those matters as relevant to the application of the principle enunciated on the first question.

My conclusion on the defendant's submission based on this authority is that it does not establish that the doctrine of mutual wills can only apply if the testators confer mutual benefits on each other. In my judgment it establishes, subject to later authorities, that such mutual benefit is a sufficient but not a necessary condition.

[His Lordship referred to *Lord Walpole v Lord Orford* (1797) 3 Ves 402; *Re Wilford's Estate* (1879) 11 Ch D 267; *Stone v Hoskins* [1905] P 194; *Re Heys' Estate* [1914] P. 192; *Re Oldham* [1925] Ch 75; *Gray v Perpetual Trustee Co Ltd* [1928] AC 391; *Re Hagger* [1930] 2 Ch 190, p. 276 ante; *Birmingham v Renfrew* (1937) 57 CLR 666; *Re Cleaver* [1981] 1 WLR 939, [1981] 2 All ER 1018, p. 279 ante, *Re Basham* [1986] 1 WLR 1498, [1987] 1 All ER 405, and continued:]

Having concluded the survey of the authorities to which I was so helpfully referred by counsel, I should now express my conclusion and my reasons for it. My conclusion is that I should answer the preliminary issue in the negative. It is clear from the decision of Lord Camden on the first question in *Dufour v Pereira* that there must be a legally binding contract to make and not to revoke mutual wills and that the first testator has died having performed his part of the agreement. The basis of the doctrine, at p. 310 in *Hargrave, Juridical Arguments and Collections*, vol. 2, is:

"If the other then refuses, he is guilty of a fraud, can never unbind himself, and becomes a trustee of course. For no man shall deceive another to his prejudice. By engaging to do something that is in his power, he is made a trustee for the performance, and transmits that trust to those that claim under him."

As all the cases show, the doctrine applies when the second testator benefits under the will of the first testator. But I am unable to see why it should be any the less a fraud on the first testator if the agreement was that each testator should leave his or her property to particular beneficiaries, for example their children, rather than to each other. It should be assumed that they had good reason for doing so and in any event that is what the parties bargained for. In each case there is the binding contract. In each case it has been performed by the first testator on the faith of the promise of the second testator and in each case the second testator would have deceived the first testator to the detriment of the first testator if he, the second testator, were permitted to go back on his agreement. I see no reason why the doctrine should be confined to cases where the second testator benefits when the aim of the principle is to prevent the first testator from being defrauded. A fraud on the first testator will include cases where the second testator benefits, but I see no reason why the principle should be confined to such cases. In my judgment so to hold is consistent with all the authorities, supported by some of them, and is in furtherance of equity's original jurisdiction to intervene in cases of fraud.

D. The Vendor under a Contract for the Sale of Land[8]

In **Rayner v Preston**[9] (1881) 18 ChD 1, Preston agreed in 1878 to sell to Rayner for £3,100 a house in Suffolk Street, Liverpool, which had been insured by Preston against fire. The contract did not refer to the insurance. After the date of the contract but before the time fixed for completion, the house was damaged by fire to the amount of £330, and this sum was paid by the insurers to Preston. Rayner brought an action to establish his right to the sum, or to have it applied in repairing the house. The Court of Appeal held that Rayner was not entitled to the benefit of the insurance as against Preston.

The law on this point was changed by Law of Property Act 1925, s.47, under which a purchaser may, on completion, recover from the vendor any money due under an insurance policy "in respect of any damage or destruction of property included in the contract". COTTON LJ[10] said at 6:

"It was said that the vendor is, between the time of the contract being made and being completed by conveyance, a trustee of the property for the purchaser, and that as, but for the fact of the legal ownership of the building insured being vested in him, he could not have recovered on the policy, he must be considered a trustee of the money recovered. In my opinion, this cannot be maintained. An unpaid vendor is a trustee in a qualified sense only, and is so only because he has made a contract which a Court of Equity will give effect to by transferring the property sold to the purchaser, and so far as he is a trustee he is so only in respect of the property contracted to be sold. Of this the policy is not a part. A vendor is in no way a trustee for the purchaser of rents accruing before the time fixed for completion, and here the fire occurred and the right to recover the money accrued before the day fixed for completion. The argument that the money is received in respect of property which is trust property is, in my opinion, fallacious. The money is received by virtue or in respect of the contract of insurance, and though the fact that the insured had parted with all interest in the property insured would be an answer to the claim, on the principle that the contract is one of indemnity only, this is very different from the proposition that the money is received by reason of his legal interest in the property."

In **Shaw v Foster** (1872) LR 5 HL 321, LORD CAIRNS said at 338:

"The vendor was a trustee of the property for the purchaser; the purchaser was the real beneficial owner in the eye of a Court of Equity of the property subject only to this observation, that the vendor, whom I have called the trustee, was not a mere dormant trustee, he was a trustee having a personal and substantial interest in the property, a right to protect that interest, and an active right to assert that interest if anything should be done in derogation of it. The relation, therefore, of trustee and *cestui que trust* subsisted, but subsisted

---

8 H & M, pp. 317–320; K & S, pp. 218–220; P & M, pp. 292–293; Pettit, pp. 176–177; Snell, p. 195; Underhill, pp. 399–405; Farrand, *Contract and Conveyance* (4th edn, 1983), pp. 167–173; [1959] 23 Conv (NS) 173 (V.G. Wellings). The principle also applies to personalty if the contract is specifically enforceable. See further Law Commission Report: *Risk of Damage after Contract for Sale* 1990 (Law Com. No. 191).

9 *Lake v Bayliss* [1974] 1 WLR 1073, [1974] 2 All ER 1114; (1974) 38 Conv (NS) 357 (F.R. Crane); *Freevale Ltd v Metrostore (Holdings) Ltd* [1984] Ch 199, [1984] 1 All ER 495.

10 BRETT LJ and JAMES LJ (who dissented) expressed different views.

subject to the paramount right of the vendor and trustee to protect his own interest as vendor of the property."[11]

E. Acquisition of Property by Killing

In the case of **Re Crippen** [1911] P 108, Crippen murdered his wife, who died intestate, and was hanged. Crippen's will left his property to his mistress. Was the mistress entitled to the wife's estate? No, because Crippen was never entitled to it (and it accordingly devolved upon the wife's next of kin). Thus equity imposes a constructive trust[12] where a beneficiary seeks to benefit from the will (or intestacy) of the person he has killed. Similarly where the killer seeks to benefit from an insurance policy on the victim's life,[13] or claims a widow's pension after killing her husband.[14]

The principle is not confined to murder. It extends to manslaughter,[15] but it is uncertain whether it applies to any other criminal killings, such as causing death by reckless driving.

(1973) 89 LQR 235 (T.G. Youdan)

"Introduction

It is a well-established general principle that a person who kills another is not entitled to enjoy any property which he would otherwise have acquired as a result of that death. However, the limits of the principle are ill-defined and the English courts have worked out no rational theory for their actions in depriving killers—actions that might seem to conflict with other well-established principles and, in many cases, might seem to contravene the language of the legislature.[16]

It is the purpose of this article to examine the practical effect and theoretical basis of the principle. This examination will involve consideration of certain problems of causation; the types of killing that invoke the principle; and the

---

11 See also *Lysaght v Edwards* (1876) 2 ChD 499 at 506, per Jessel MR ("The position of the vendor is something between what is called a naked or bare trustee, or a mere trustee (that is, a person without beneficial interest), and a mortgagee who is not, in equity (any more than a vendor), the owner of the estate, but is, in certain events, entitled to what the unpaid vendor is, viz, possession of the estate and a charge upon the estate for his purchase-money."); *Royal Bristol Permanent Building Society v Bomash* (1887) 35 ChD 390 at 397, per Kekewich J ("Of course we all know that he is only a trustee in a modified sense"); *Cumberland Consolidated Holdings Ltd v Ireland* [1946] KB 264 at 269, [1946] 1 All ER 284 at 286, per Lord Greene MR ("His position is that of a quasi-trustee for the purchaser"). The vendor owes no fiduciary duty to a sub-purchaser: *Berkley v Poulett* (1976) 242 EG 39.
12 This will be necessary only where the killer actually acquires the property in question. In most cases it is withheld from him. See generally *Williams on Wills* (7th edn), pp. 89–94.
13 *Cleaver v Mutual Reserve Fund Life Association Ltd* [1892] 1 QB 147. *Davitt v Titcumb* [1990] Ch 110, [1989] 3 All ER 417 (mortgage protection policy).
14 *R v Chief National Insurance Comr, ex p Connor* [1981] QB 758, [1981] 1 All ER 769; (1981) 44 MLR 718 (St. J. Robilliard).
15 *Re Giles* [1972] Ch 544, [1971] 3 All ER 1141 (diminished responsibility. Cf. an acquittal by reason of insanity); *Re K* [1986] Ch 180, [1985] 2 All ER 833; *Re H* [1990] 1 FLR 441; [1991] Conv 48 (J. Martin); (1995) 111 LQR 196 (R. Buckley); *Jones v Roberts* [1995] 2 FLR 422.
16 For an early review of this topic, see Chadwick, A Testator's Bounty to his Slayer (1914) 30 LQR 211. See also Toohey, "Killing the Goose that lays the Golden Eggs" (1958) 23 ALJ 14.

different ways that acquisitions may be brought about by killing. Once the practical application of the principle has thus been clarified it will be shown that the principle is simply an example of the use of the constructive trust to prevent unjust enrichment. It will then be convenient to deal with the difficult question of who should benefit from the court's deprivation of the killer, i.e. who is the beneficiary of the constructive trust . . .

A THEORETICAL BASIS

Ames, in his famous article 'Can a Murderer acquire Title by his Crime and keep it'?,[17] said that three results were possible where a person acquires property by killing: (i) the legal title does not pass to the killer; (ii) the legal title passes to the killer, and he may retain it in spite of his crime; or (iii) the legal title passes to the killer, but equity will treat him as a constructive trustee of the title because of the unconscionable mode of its acquisition.[18]

It has been shown that English courts have rejected the second possibility and generally they have considered that the killer does not gain legal title. However, there has been little discussion of the theoretical basis for a deprivation that in most cases might appear to contravene legislative provisions. There are two methods that have been used to justify this result. Both methods are sometimes employed in the same judgment and the difference between them is more superficial than real. The first approach is to say that all laws—whether made by statute or judicial precedent—must conform to a 'higher law.' The second approach is to interpret the law so as to make it conform to the judge's conception of what it should be. A case which is a good example of the former approach is *Riggs v Palmer*[19] where the New York Court of Appeals held that a legatee did not gain title to property which he would have received as the result of murdering his testator. Earl J said that there are certain principles that 'have their foundation in universal law administered in all civilised countries' and that 'all laws, as well as all contracts, may be controlled in their operation and effect by general, fundamental maxims of the common law.'[20] This approach is, however, generally recognized as being too open an example of judicial law-making and the courts that consider the killer does not acquire legal title usually arrive at such a result by liberal statutory interpretation. . .[1]

The constructive trust approach to this situation has received considerable recognition in the United States[2] and, moreover, in the joint tenancy context courts in Canada,[3] Australia,[4] and New Zealand,[5] finding it impossible to hold that the right of survivorship does not operate at common law, have accepted

---

17 Lectures on Legal History, at p. 310.
18 Ibid., at p. 311.
19 115 NY 506, 22 NE 188 (1889).
20 Ibid., at p. 190.
1 See Woerner, "Self-made Heirship through Murder" (1925) 10 St Louis Law Rev 34; a note "Succession by Murder—Applicability of the Constructive Trust" (1931) 29 Mich L Rev 745 at 746.
2 Scott, *Trusts* (3rd edn), s. 492; Restatement: Restitution, §. 187. See also *Ellerson v Westcott* 148 NY 149, 42 NE 540 (1896), where ANDREWS CJ rationalised *Riggs v Palmer* 115 NY 506, 22 NE 188 (1889) on the constructive trust theory.
3 *Schobelt v Barber* (1966) 60 DLR (2d) 519.
4 *Rasmanis v Jurewitsch* (1970) 70 SRNSW 407. But cf. *Re Barrowcliff* [1927] SASR 147; *Kemp v Public Curator of Queensland* [1969] Qd R 145.
5 *Re Pechar* [1969] NZLR 574.

the constructive trust as the appropriate way to prevent the unjust enrichment of the killer ...

THE EFFECT OF THE KILLER'S DEPRIVATION

As the English courts have worked out no suitable justification for depriving the wrongdoer of property acquired as the result of the killing so no rational theory has been devised for working out who becomes entitled to the property.[6] However, if it is accepted that it is the constructive trust which is used to prevent the unjust enrichment of the wrongdoer the confusion is reduced and the person who is entitled to the property—the beneficiary of the constructive trust—is the person who, in the eyes of equity, has the best right to it.[7] Now, it might be argued that this simply begs the question which is, who has the best right to the property? The reply is that though the process for determining the answer to that question is equitable and therefore flexible nevertheless guide-lines are to be found from the other situations where the constructive trust is similarly employed,[8] and from the decisions in this situation which, though generally unsupported by any or by inadequate reasoning, have achieved equitable results.

The principle is, it is suggested, that where there are circumstances showing that a particular person has a better equity than anybody else the property should be given to that person but otherwise it should be given to the estate of the victim[9] for lack of 'any other suitable recipient,'[10] and in all cases the wrongdoer or anyone (except a bona fide purchaser) claiming through him should be excluded. It will be convenient now to examine this principle in the context of each of the methods of acquisition discussed in this article ... ''[11]

The Forfeiture Act 1982[12] gives the court power to grant total or partial relief from forfeiture of inheritance and related rights to persons guilty of unlawful killing other than murder, where the court is satisfied that the justice of the case requires it. The killer must bring proceedings for this purpose within three months of any conviction.[13] The Act applies to killings before and after its coming into operation, unless the property has already been acquired by someone else before that date in consequence of the forfeiture principle.

FORFEITURE ACT 1982

1. The "forfeiture rule".—(1) In this Act, the "forfeiture rule" means the rule of public policy which in certain circumstances precludes a person who has

---

6 See *Re Callaway* [1956] Ch 559, [1956] 2 All ER 451; *Re Peacock* [1957] Ch 310, [1957] 2 All ER 98.

7 See Costigan (1915) 9 Ill L Rev 505.

8 It is arguable that the constructive trust is similarly employed in other situations where a person would be unjustly enriched by the acquisition or retention of property, e.g. where he acquires it as the result of a secret trust arrangement; a mutual will arrangement; an informal inter vivos arrangement which does not comply with the required formalities; or acquiescence.

9 In the unusual situation where a remainderman kills the *cestui que vie* of a prior life interest the beneficiary would not be the victim but the tenant *pur autre vie*.

10 *Rasmanis v Jurewitsch* [1968] 2 NSWR 166 at 169, per STREET J (affd (1970) 70 SRNSW 407).

11 See also *Davis v Worthington* [1978] WAR 144; (1979) 123 SJ 729 (H.E. Markson).

12 (1983) 46 MLR 66 (P.H. Kenny).

13 The doctrine does not require a criminal conviction: *Gray v Barr* [1971] 2 QB 554, [1971] 2 All ER 949 (acquittal but lower standard of proof in civil action).

unlawfully killed another from acquiring a benefit in consequence of the killing.

(2) References in this Act to a person who has unlawfully killed another include a reference to a person who has unlawfully aided, abetted, counselled or procured the death of that other and references in this Act to unlawful killing shall be interpreted accordingly.

2. Power to modify the rule.—(1) Where a court determines that the forfeiture rule has precluded a person (in this section referred to as "the offender") who has unlawfully killed another from acquiring any interest in property mentioned in subsection (4) below, the court may make an order under this section modifying the effect of that rule.

(2) The court shall not make an order under this section modifying the effect of the forfeiture rule in any case unless it is satisfied that, having regard to the conduct of the offender and of the deceased and to such other circumstances as appear to the court to be material, the justice of the case requires the effect of the rule to be so modified in that case.[14]

(3) In any case where a person stands convicted of an offence of which unlawful killing is an element, the court shall not make an order under this section modifying the effect of the forfeiture rule in that case unless proceedings for the purpose are brought before the expiry of the period of three months beginning with his conviction.

(4) The interests in property referred to in subsection (1) above are—

(*a*) any beneficial interest in property which (apart from the forfeiture rule) the offender would have acquired—

(i) under the deceased's will ... or the law relating to intestacy ...;

(ii) on the nomination of the deceased in accordance with the provisions of any enactment;

(iii) as a donatio mortis causa made by the deceased; ...

(*b*) any beneficial interest in property which (apart from the forfeiture rule) the offender would have acquired in consequence of the death of the deceased, being property which, before the death, was held on trust for any person.

(5) An order under this section may modify the effect of the forfeiture rule in respect of any interest in property to which the determination referred to in subsection (1) above relates and may do so in either or both of the following ways, that is—

(*a*) where there is more than one such interest, by excluding the application of the rule in respect of any (but not all) of those interests; and

(*b*) in the case of any such interest in property, by excluding the application of the rule in respect of part of the property.

(6) On the making of an order under this section, the forfeiture rule shall have effect for all purposes (including purposes relating to anything done before the order is made) subject to the modifications made by the order.

(7) The court shall not make an order under this section modifying the effect of the forfeiture rule in respect of any interest in property which, in consequence of the rule, has been acquired before the coming into force of

---

14 See *Re K* [1986] Ch 180, [1985] 2 All ER 833; *Re H* [1990] 1 FLR 441 (degree of moral blame significant).

this section by a person other than the offender or a person claiming through him.[15]

(8) In this section—

"property" includes any chose in action or incorporeal moveable property; and

"will" includes codicil.

5. Exclusion of murderers.—Nothing in this Act or in any order made under section 2 or referred to in section 3 (1) of this Act shall affect the application of the forfeiture rule in the case of a person who stands convicted of murder.

F. Secret Trusts[16]

It is unsettled whether secret trusts are to be regarded as express or constructive. The practical significance of the classification is that constructive trusts of land are exempted from the requirement of written evidence by section 53 (2) of the Law of Property Act 1925. If a secret trust is to be analysed as a declaration operating outside the will, then it looks like an express trust, particularly if it is a half-secret trust, where the intention to create a trust is expressed in the will. Fully secret trusts may be easier to classify as constructive, as they are enforceable on the ground of fraud: *McCormick v Grogan* (1869) LR 4 HL 82, which cannot be perpetrated by a half-secret trustee.[17] There is little authority on the point. In *Ottaway v Norman* [1972] Ch 698, [1971] 3 All ER 1325, p.151, ante, an oral fully secret trust of land was upheld without discussing this matter, whereas in *Re Baillie* (1886) 2 TLR 660 a half-secret trust of land was held to require written evidence. But if a fully secret trust of land were to fail for lack of writing on the ground that it was express, the secret trustee, having accepted the trust, would not hold for his own benefit, but for the residuary legatee or next-of-kin. Any other result would amount to using the statute as an instrument of fraud.

G. Justice and Good Conscience[18]

In some modern cases, especially in the context of parties' rights in a family home, or of the rights of a licensee to occupy land, constructive trusts have been imposed on the ground that justice and good conscience so require. This was a theory pioneered primarily by Lord Denning MR. The most recent

---

15 *Re K*, supra (property not "acquired" if held by personal representatives who have not completed administration).

16 Chap 4, ante. See H & M pp. 167–168; Snell p. 112; P & M pp. 54–55; Pettit p. 118; Underhill, pp. 227–237; Oakley, *Constructive Trusts* (2nd edn), pp. 129–130; (1972) 23 NILQ 263 (R. Burgess); (1951) 67 LQR 34 (L.A. Sheridan); *Brown v Pourau* [1995] 1 NZLR 352.

17 Save in the sense of defeating the expectations of the testator. See [1980] Conv 341 (D.R. Hodge); *Re Dale* [1994] Ch 31, [1993] 4 All ER 129, p. 281 ante.

18 H & M, pp. 323–330; Pettit, pp. 178–182.

decisions, however, lend little support to such a wide jurisdiction.[19] Instead, more specific guidelines have been laid down for the imposition of constructive trusts. As far as interests in the home are concerned, we saw in Chapter 6 that the House of Lords in *Lloyds Bank plc v Rosset* [1991] 1 AC 107, [1990] 1 All ER 1111, p. 232 ante held that, in the absence of a written declaration or a direct contribution to the price, a claimant could only succeed by proving a common intention to share, which had been acted upon. Such a common intention (if not express) could be inferred only from a direct contribution to the price. In the context of contractual licences, the question whether a third party acquiring the land from the licensor holds on constructive trust for the licensee has been clarified by the Court of Appeal in *Ashburn Anstalt v Arnold* [1989] Ch 1, [1988] 2 All ER 147, p. 299 post.

The following extracts reveal the varying attitudes of the courts to the "new model" constructive trust over the past twenty-five years.

i. FAMILY ARRANGEMENTS

In **Eves v Eves** [1975] 1 WLR 1338, [1975] 3 All ER 768, Lord DENNING MR said at 1340, at 769:

"I will call her Janet because she has had four surnames already. She was married for the first time at the age of 19; but that marriage only lasted about a year. Next at the age of 19 she met a man, Stuart Eves. He was a married man. They could not marry. So they started living together. She took his name and had two children by him. After $4\frac{1}{2}$ years that relationship broke down. Now both have got divorces from their former spouses and have remarried. The question arises now as to the house where they lived ...

The problem in this case is a familiar one. It often happens that a man and a woman set up house together and have children. They cannot marry because one or other or both are already married. But they intend to marry as soon as they are free to do so. She takes his name. They live as husband and wife. They are known to their neighbours as husband and wife. They get a house; but it is put in his name alone. Then, before they get married, the relationship breaks down. In strict law she has no claim on him whatever. She is not his wife. He is not bound to provide a roof over her head. He can turn her into the street. She is not entitled to any maintenance from him for herself. All she can do is to go to the magistrates and ask for an affiliation order against him on the footing that she is a 'single woman': and get an order for him to pay maintenance for the children. If he does not pay, she may have great difficulty in getting any money out of him, even for the children. Such is the strict law. And a few years ago even equity would not have helped her. But things have altered now. Equity is not past the age of child bearing. One of her latest progeny is a constructive trust of a new model. Lord Diplock brought it into the world and we have nourished it. In *Gissing v Gissing* [1971] AC 886, [1970] 2 All ER 780, Lord Diplock said at 905, at 790:

---

19 Similarly in the Commonwealth; see *Allen v Snyder* [1977] 2 NSWLR 685; *Carly v Farrelly* [1975] 1 NZLR 356; *Muschinski v Dodds* (1985) 62 ALR 429; *cf Pettkus v Becker* (1980) 117 DLR (3d) 257; (1982) 12 Fam Law 21 (M. Bryan). See also *Baumgartner v Baumgartner* (1987) 62 ALJR. 29; [1988] Conv 259 (D. Hayton); *Peter v Beblow* (1993) 101 DLR (4th) 621.

See further (1978) 94 LQR 351 (W.M. Gummow); (1975) 53 CBR 366 (D. Waters); [1982] Conv 424 (F. Bates); [1983] Conv 420 (K. Hodkinson); [1989] Conv 418 (P.T. Evans); Birks ed. *The Frontiers of Liability* (1994), vol 2, Part III, The Remedial Constructive Trust (papers by D.W.M. Waters, S. Gardner, J. Eekelaar, P. Birks and J.D. Davies).

'A resulting, implied or constructive trust—and it is unnecessary for present purposes to distinguish between these three classes of trust—is created by a transaction between the trustee and the cestui que trust in connection with the acquisition by the trustee of a legal estate in land, whenever the trustee has so conducted himself that it would be inequitable to allow him to deny to the cestui que trust a beneficial interest in the land acquired. And he will be held so to have conducted himself if by his words or conduct he has induced the cestui que trust to act to his own detriment in the reasonable belief that by so acting he was acquiring a beneficial interest in the land.'

We have followed this advice in several cases, notably in *Binions v Evans* [1972] Ch 359, [1972] 2 All ER 70; *Cooke v Head* [1972] 1 WLR 518, [1972] 2 All ER 38 and *Hussey v Palmer* [1972] 1 WLR 1286, [1972] 3 All ER 744. I would specially mention *Cooke v Head* because there too a man and woman set up home without being married. I ventured to suggest, at 520, at 41:

' . . . whenever two parties by their joint efforts acquire property to be used for their joint benefit, the courts may impose or impute a constructive or resulting trust. The legal owner is bound to hold the property on trust for them both. This trust does not need any writing. It can be enforced by an order for sale, but in a proper case the sale can be postponed indefinitely. It applies to husband and wife, to engaged couples, and to man and mistress, and maybe to other relationships too.'

This principle was considered by Walton J in *Richards v Dove* [1974] 1 All ER 888. But that case turned on its own special circumstances and is not of any general application.

The principle does apply in the present case. Although Janet did not make any financial contribution, it seems to me that this property was acquired and maintained by both by their joint efforts with the intention that it should be used for their joint benefit until they were married and thereafter as long as the marriage continued. At any rate, Stuart Eves cannot be heard to say to the contrary. He told her that it was to be their home for them and their children. He gained her confidence by telling her that he intended to put it in their joint names (just as married couples often do) but that it was not possible until she was 21. The judge described this as a 'trick', and said that it 'did not do him much credit as a man of honour'. The man never intended to put it in joint names but always determined to have it in his own name. It seems to me that he should be judged by what he told her—by what he led her to believe—and not by his own intent which he kept to himself. Lord Diplock made this clear in *Gissing v Gissing* [1971] AC 886 at 906, [1970] 2 All ER 780 at 790.

It seems to me that this conduct by Mr. Eves amounted to a recognition by him that, in all fairness, she was entitled to a share in the house, equivalent in some way to a declaration of trust; not for a particular share, but for such share as was fair in view of all she had done and was doing for him and the children and would thereafter do. By so doing he gained her confidence. She trusted him. She did not make any financial contribution but she contributed in many other ways. She did much work in the house and garden. She looked after him and cared for the children. It is clear that her contribution was such that if she had been a wife she would have had a good claim to have a share in it on a divorce: see *Wachtel v Wachtel* [1973] Fam 72 at 92–94, [1973] 1 All ER 829 at 837–839.

In view of his conduct, it would, I think, be most inequitable for him to deny her any share in the house. The law will impute or impose a constructive trust by which he was to hold it in trust for them both. But what should be the shares? I think one half would be too much. I suggest it should be one quarter of the equity . . . .

I would therefore allow the appeal and declare that the defendant holds the legal estate on trust for sale but the benefit in proportion of the shares of one quarter to Janet and three quarters to Mr. Eves."[20]

The Court of Appeal in **Grant v Edwards** [1986] Ch 638, [1986] 2 All ER 426, p. 240, ante, agreed with the result in *Eves v Eves* but rejected Lord Denning's wide statements.[1] NOURSE LJ at 647, at 432, said that Lord Denning's ground for decision was at variance with the principles stated in *Gissing v Gissing* [1971] AC 886, [1970] 2 All ER 780, and continued:

"About that case [*Eves v Eves*] the following observations may be made. First, as Brightman J himself observed, if the work had not been done the common intention would not have been enough. Second, if the common intention had not been orally made plain, the work would not have been conduct from which it could be inferred. That, I think, is the effect of the actual decision in *Pettitt v Pettitt* [1970] AC 777, [1969] 2 All ER 385. Third, and on the other hand, the work was conduct which amounted to an acting on the common intention by the woman."

In **Hussey v Palmer** [1972] 1 WLR 1286, [1972] 3 All ER 744,[2] Mrs. Hussey, an elderly widow, was invited to live with her daughter and son-in-law. The house was too small, and an additional bedroom was added, at a cost of £607, which Mrs. Hussey paid.

Differences arose, and Mrs. Hussey left the house. She claimed the £607 on the basis of a resulting trust.

Lord DENNING MR said at 1289, at 747:

"Although the plaintiff alleged that there was a resulting trust, I should have thought that the trust in this case, if there was one, was more in the nature of a constructive trust; but that is more a matter of words than anything else. The two run together. By whatever name it is described, it is a trust imposed by law whenever justice and good conscience require it. It is a liberal process, founded upon large principles of equity, to be applied in cases where the legal owner cannot conscientiously keep the property for himself alone, but ought to allow another to have the property or the benefit of it or a share in it. The trust may arise at the outset when the property is acquired, or later on, as the circumstances may require. It is an equitable remedy by which the court can enable an aggrieved party to obtain restitution. It is comparable to the legal remedy of money had and received which, as Lord Mansfield said, is 'very beneficial and therefore, much encouraged' [*Moses v MacFerlan* (1760) 2 Burr 1005 at 1012]. Thus we have

20 For a different reasoning leading to the same conclusion, see the judgments of BROWNE LJ and BRIGHTMAN J. See also *Cooke v Head* [1972] 1 WLR 518, [1972] 2 All ER 38, where a mistress, who had made no financial contribution but had done a lot of heavy building work, was awarded a one third share under a resulting or constructive trust which arose whenever two parties by their joint efforts acquired property to be used for their joint benefit.
1 The decision was approved by HL in *Lloyds Bank plc v Rosset* [1991] 1 AC 107, [1990] 1 All ER 1111, without reference to Lord DENNING's approach.
2 (1973) 89 LQR 2; (1973) 37 Conv (NS) 65 (D.J. Hayton).

repeatedly held that when one person contributes towards the purchase price of a house, the owner holds it on a constructive trust for him, proportionate to his contribution, even though there is no agreement between them, and no declaration of trust to be found, and no evidence of any intention to create a trust. Instances are numerous where a wife has contributed money to the initial purchase of a house or property; or later on to the payment of mortgage instalments; or has helped in business: see *Falconer v Falconer* [1970] 1 WLR 1333, [1970] 3 All ER 449; *Heseltine v Heseltine* [1971] 1 WLR 342, [1971] 1 All ER 952 and *Re Cummins* [1972] Ch 62, [1971] 3 All ER 782. Similarly, when a mistress has contributed money, or money's worth, to the building of a house: *Cooke v Head* [1972] 1 WLR 518, [1972] 2 All ER 38. Very recently we held that a purchaser, who bought a cottage subject to the rights of an occupier, held it on trust for her benefit: *Binions v Evans* [1972] Ch 359, [1972] 2 All ER 70. In all those cases it would have been quite inequitable for the legal owner to take the property for himself and exclude the other from it. So the law imputed or imposed a trust for his or her benefit.

The present case is well within the principles of those cases. Just as a person, who pays part of the purchase price, acquires an equitable interest in the house, so also he does when he pays for an extension to be added to it. [His Lordship considered *Unity Joint Stock Mutual Banking Association v King* (1858) 25 Beav 72; *Chalmers v Pardoe* [1963] 1 WLR 677, [1963] 3 All ER 552 and *Inwards v Baker* [1965] 2 QB 29, [1965] 1 All ER 446, and continued:] In those cases it was emphasised that the court must look at the circumstances of each case to decide in what way the equity can be satisfied. In some by an equitable lien. In others by a constructive trust. But in either case it is because justice and good conscience so require.

In the present case Mrs. Hussey paid £607 to a builder for the erection of this extension. It may well be, as the defendant says, that there was no contract to repay it at all. It was not a loan to the son-in-law. She could not sue him for repayment. He could not have turned her out. If she had stayed there until she died, the extension would undoubtedly have belonged beneficially to the son-in-law. If, during her lifetime, he had sold the house, together with the extension, she would be entitled to be repaid the £607 out of the proceeds. He admits this himself. But he has not sold the house. She has left, and the son-in-law has the extension for his own benefit and could sell the whole if he so desired. It seems to me to be entirely against conscience that he should retain the whole house and not allow Mrs. Hussey any interest in it, or any charge upon it. The court should, and will, impose or impute a trust by which Mr. Palmer is to hold the property on terms under which, in the circumstances that have happened, she has an interest in the property proportionate to the £607 which she put into it. She is quite content if he repays her the £607. If he does not repay the £607, she can apply for an order for sale, so that the sum can be paid to her. But the simplest way for him would be to raise the £607 on mortgage and pay it to her. But, on the legal point raised, I have no doubt there was a resulting trust, or, more accurately, a constructive trust, for her, and I would so declare. I would allow the appeal, accordingly.''[3]

---

3 PHILLIMORE LJ held that a resulting trust arose; CAIRNS LJ dissented. Cf. *Spence v Brown* [1988] Fam Law 291.

In **Heseltine v Heseltine** [1971] 1 WLR 342, [1971] 1 All ER 952, a wealthy wife, on her husband's advice, advanced large sums of money to her husband, partly to avoid estate duty and partly to enable him to qualify as an underwriter at Lloyd's (where underwriters must own assets to a certain value). After they separated she claimed the return of the money. If the doctrine of resulting trusts were strictly applied, it would seem that her claim would fail, as the presumption of a resulting trust in her favour would be rebutted by the evidence as to the purpose of the transactions: no estate duty would be saved, nor would the husband have qualified at Lloyd's, if her intention had been to retain the beneficial ownership. Yet the Court of Appeal upheld the wife's claim. Lord Denning said, at 346, at 955:

"If the conduct of the husband is such that it would be inequitable for him to claim the property beneficially as his own, then, although it is transferred into his name, the court will impose on him a trust to hold it for them both jointly, or for her alone, as the circumstances of the case may require. Applying this principle, it would plainly be inequitable that the husband should hold this £40,000 beneficially as his own. The wife put it into his name for the sake of them all, for his and her sake and all the family, because she trusted him".

Constructive trusts have also been invoked to remedy the situation where a promise to leave property by will has not been fulfilled. In *Layton v Martin* [1986] 2 FLR 227 a man promised to provide for his mistress by will, but failed to do so. Her claim to an interest under a constructive trust was rejected because she had made no contribution to the acquisition or preservation of the man's assets. But the claim succeeded in *Re Basham* [1986] 1 WLR 1498, [1987] 1 All ER 405,[4] where a stepdaughter acted to her detriment in reliance upon her stepfather's assurances that he would leave her his property. However, he died intestate. There was little authority for the application of the proprietary estoppel doctrine where the belief related to a future right and to non-specific assets. Edward Nugee QC overcame these possible difficulties by holding that a constructive trust arose where the belief related to a future right. An analogy could then be drawn with the mutual wills doctrine, which was not confined to present rights in specific assets.[5]

ii. LICENCES

A licence to occupy land is traditionally regarded as creating a personal right only.[6] This is clearly so in the case of a gratuitous licence (unless the circumstances give rise to an estoppel, which is capable of binding third parties). Where the licence is contractual, the proper remedy is upon the contract. This may work hardship in cases where the land is sold to a third party, and the courts have sought to avoid the result that the purchaser, not being bound by the contract, can evict the licensee, by imposing a constructive trust on him.

---

4 [1987] Conv 211 (J. Martin); (1987) 46 CLJ 215 (D. Hayton); [1987] All ER Rev 156 (P.J. Clarke); 263 (C.H. Sherrin).
5 *Re Cleaver* [1981] 1 WLR 939, [1981] 2 All ER 1018, p. 279 ante.
6 *King v David Allen & Sons Billposting Ltd* [1916] 2 AC 54; *Clore v Theatrical Properties Ltd* [1936] 3 All ER 483. On licences generally, see Cheshire and Burn, *Modern Law of Real Property* (15th edn), chap. 18; H & M, chap. 27.

The authorities were reviewed by the Court of Appeal in *Ashburn Anstalt v Arnold.*[7] This is set out below, after the extracts from earlier decisions.

In **Binions v Evans** [1972] Ch 359, [1972] 2 All ER 70,[8] a widow occupied land under an informal arrangement. The property was sold to a purchaser at a low price, expressly subject to her rights, but the purchaser sought to evict her. The majority of the Court of Appeal, following *Bannister v Bannister* [1948] 2 All ER 133, construed her interest as a life interest under the Settled Land Act 1925, which accordingly bound a purchaser with notice.[9] Lord DENNING MR regarded the widow as a contractual licensee, and held that the purchaser took subject to a constructive trust in her favour. He said at 368, at 76:

"In these circumstances, this court will impose on the [purchaser] a constructive trust for her benefit; for the simple reason that it would be utterly inequitable for the [purchaser] to turn the widow out contrary to the stipulation subject to which he took the premises. That seems to me clear from the important decision of *Bannister v Bannister* [1948] 2 All ER 133, which was applied by the judge, and which I gladly follow.

This imposing of a constructive trust is entirely in accord with the precepts of equity. As Cardozo J once put it: 'A constructive trust is the formula through which the conscience of equity finds expression'; see *Beatty v Guggenheim Exploration Co* 225 NY 380 (1919) at 386 or, as Lord Diplock put it quite recently in *Gissing v Gissing* [1971] AC 886 at 905, [1970] 2 All ER 780 at 790, a constructive trust is created 'whenever the trustee has so conducted himself that it would be inequitable to allow him to deny to the cestui que trust a beneficial interest in the land acquired'.

I know that there are some who have doubted whether a contractual licensee has any protection against a purchaser, even one who takes with full notice. We were referred in this connection to Professor Wade's article in the Law Quarterly Review in (1952) 68 LQR 337, and to the judgment of Goff J in *Re Solomon* [1967] Ch 573, [1966] 3 All ER 255. None of these doubts can prevail, however, when the situation gives rise to a constructive trust.[10]"

In **Re Sharpe** [1980] 1 WLR 219, [1980] 1 All ER 198, an aunt lent money to her nephew under an agreement whereby she was to be entitled to live in his house for the rest of her life. On the nephew's bankruptcy, his trustee in bankruptcy claimed possession of the house. It was held that the circumstances gave rise to a constructive trust in the aunt's favour, which conferred on her an interest binding on the trustee in bankruptcy. BROWNE-WILKINSON J, however, felt some reservation about the constructive trust solution. He said at 223, at 201:

---

7 [1989] Ch 1, [1988] 2 All ER 147, p. 299 post. See (1988) 104 LQR 175 (P. Sparkes); (1988) 51 MLR 226 (J. Hill); [1988] Conv 201 (M.P. Thompson); [1988] CLJ 353 (A.J. Oakley); [1988] All ER Rev 177 (P.J. Clarke); *IDC Group Ltd v Clarke* [1992] 1 EGLR at 189 (not discussed on appeal at (1993) 65 P & CR 172).
8 Maudsley and Burn, *Land Law: Cases and Materials* (6th edn), pp. 555–557.
9 Cf. *Dodsworth v Dodsworth* (1973) 228 EG 1115; Maudsley and Burn, supra, pp. 598–599; *Costello v Costello* (1994) 27 HLR 12.
10 [1973] CLJ 123 (R.J. Smith); (1972) 37 Conv (NS) 266 (J. Martin).

"This right is based upon the line of recent Court of Appeal decisions which has spelt out irrevocable licences from informal family arrangements, and in some cases characterised such licences as conferring some equity or equitable interest under a constructive trust. I do not think that the principles lying behind these decisions have yet been fully explored and on occasion it seems that such rights are found to exist simply on the ground that to hold otherwise would be a hardship to the plaintiff."[11]

In **Ashburn Anstalt v Arnold** [1989] Ch 1, [1988] 2 All ER 147, the question was whether the plaintiff purchaser took the land subject to the interest of the defendant. The Court of Appeal held that the defendant had a lease which was binding on the plaintiff under the normal rules of property law.[12] The court, however, considered what the position would have been if the defendant had been only a contractual licensee. After concluding that such a licence could not bind a purchaser in the absence of a constructive trust, Fox LJ at 23, at 165 examined the circumstances in which a constructive trust could be imposed for the protection of the licensee:
"We come then to four cases in which the application of the principle to particular facts has been considered.
In *Binions v Evans* [1972] Ch 359, [1972] 2 All ER 70, the defendant's husband was employed by an estate and lived rent free in a cottage owned by the estate. The husband died when the defendant was 73. The trustees of the estate then entered into an agreement with the defendant that she could continue to live in the cottage during her lifetime as tenant at will rent free; she undertook to keep the cottage in good condition and repair. Subsequently the estate sold the cottage to the plaintiffs. The contract provided that the property was sold subject to the tenancy. In consequence of that provision the plaintiffs paid a reduced price for the cottage. The plaintiffs sought to eject the defendant, claiming that she was a tenant at will. That claim failed. In the Court of Appeal Megaw and Stephenson LJJ decided the case on the ground that the defendant was a tenant for life under the Settled Land Act 1925. Lord Denning MR did not agree with that. He held that the plaintiffs took the property subject to a constructive trust for the defendant's benefit. In our view that is a legitimate application of the doctrine of constructive trusts. The estate would certainly have allowed the defendant to live in the house during her life in accordance with their agreement with her. They provided the plaintiffs with a copy of the agreement they made. The agreement for sale was subject to the agreement, and they accepted a lower purchase price in consequence. In the circumstances it was a proper inference that on the sale to the plaintiffs, the intention of the estate and the plaintiffs was that the plaintiffs should give effect to the tenancy agreement. If they had failed to do so, the estate would have been liable in damages to the defendant.
In *DHN Food Distributors Ltd v Tower Hamlets Borough Council* [1976] 1 WLR 852, [1976] 3 All ER 462, premises were owned by Bronze Investments Ltd. but occupied by an associated company (D.H.N.) under an informal agreement between them—they were part of a group. The premises were subsequently

---

11 [1980] Conv 207 (J. Martin), suggesting proprietary estoppel as a preferable basis for the decision; (1980) 96 LQR 336 (G. Woodman).
12 Overruled on this point in *Prudential Assurance Co Ltd v London Residuary Body* [1992] 2 AC 386, [1992] 3 All ER 504.

purchased by the council and the issue was compensation for disturbance. It was said that Bronze was not disturbed and that D.H.N. had no interest in the property. The Court of Appeal held that D.H.N. had an irrevocable licence to occupy the land. Lord Denning MR said, at 859, at 466:

'It was equivalent to a contract between the two companies whereby Bronze granted an irrevocable licence to D.H.N. to carry on their business on the premises. In this situation Mr. Dobry cited to us *Binions v Evans* to which I would add *Bannister v Bannister* [1948] 2 All ER 133 and *Siew Soon Wah v Yong Tong Hong* [1973] AC 836. Those cases show that a contractual licence (under which a person has a right to occupy premises indefinitely) gives rise to a constructive trust, under which the legal owner is not allowed to turn out the licensee. So, here. This irrevocable licence gave to D.H.N. a sufficient interest in the land to qualify them for compensation for disturbance.'

Goff LJ made this a ground for his decision also.

On that authority, Browne-Wilkinson J in *Re Sharpe* [1980] 1 WLR 219, [1980] 1 All ER 198, felt bound to conclude that, without more, an irrevocable licence to occupy gave rise to a property interest. He evidently did so with hesitation. For the reasons which we have already indicated, we prefer the line of authorities which determine that a contractual licence does not create a property interest. We do not think that the argument is assisted by the bare assertion that the interest arises under a constructive trust.

In *Lyus v Prowsa Developments Ltd* [1982] 1 WLR 1044, [1982] 2 All ER 953, p. 303, post, the plaintiffs contracted to buy a plot of registered land which was part of an estate being developed by the vendor company. A house was to be built which would then be occupied by the plaintiffs. The plaintiffs paid a deposit to the company, which afterwards became insolvent before the house was built. The company's bank held a legal charge, granted before the plaintiff's contract, over the whole estate. The bank was under no liability to complete the plaintiffs' contract. The bank, as mortgagee, sold the land to the first defendant. By the contract of sale it was provided that the land was sold subject to and with the benefit of the plaintiff's contract. Subsequently, the first defendant contracted to sell the plot to the second defendant. The contract provided that the land was sold subject to the plaintiffs' contract so far, if at all, as it might be enforceable against the first defendant. The contract was duly completed. In the action the plaintiffs sought a declaration that their contract was binding on the defendants and an order for specific performance. The action succeeded. This again seems to us to be a case where a constructive trust could justifiably be imposed. The bank were selling, as mortgagees under a charge prior in date to the contract. They were therefore not bound by the contract and on any view could give a title which was free from it. There was, therefore, no point in making the conveyance subject to the contract unless the parties intended the purchaser to give effect to the contract. Further, on the sale by the bank a letter had been written to the bank's agents, Messrs. Strutt & Parker, by the first defendant's solicitors, giving an assurance that their client would take reasonable steps to make sure the interests of contractual purchasers were dealt with quickly and to their satisfaction. How far any constructive trust so arising was on the facts of that case enforceable by the plaintiffs against owners for the time being of the land we do not need to consider.

Re Sharpe seems to us a much more difficult case in which to imply a constructive trust against the trustee in bankruptcy and his successors, and we do not think it could be done. Browne-Wilkinson J did not, in fact, do so. He felt (understandably, we think) bound by authority to hold that an irrevocable licence to occupy was a property interest. In *Re Sharpe* although the aunt provided money for the purchase of the house, she did not thereby acquire any property interest in the ordinary sense, since the judge held that it was advanced by way of a loan, though, no doubt, she may have had some rights of occupation as against the debtor. And when the trustee in bankruptcy, before entering into the contract of sale, wrote to the aunt to find out what rights, if any, she claimed in consequence of the provision of funds by her, she did not reply. The trustee in bankruptcy then sold with vacant possession. These facts do not suggest a need in equity to impose constructive trust obligations on the trustee or his successors.

We come to the present case. It is said that when a person sells lands and stipulates that the sale should be 'subject to' a contractual licence, the court will impose a constructive trust upon the purchaser to give effect to the licence: see *Binions v Evans* [1972] Ch 359, 368, [1972] 2 All ER 70, 76, per Lord Denning MR. We do not feel able to accept that as a general proposition. We agree with the observations of Dillon J in *Lyus v Prowsa Developments Ltd* [1982] 1 WLR 1044, 1051, [1982] 2 All ER 953, 959:

'By contrast, there are many cases in which land is expressly conveyed subject to possible incumbrances when there is no thought at all of conferring any fresh rights on third parties who may be entitled to the benefit of the incumbrances. The land is expressed to be sold subject to incumbrances known to him, and to protect the vendor against any possible claim by the purchaser .... So, for instance, land may be contracted to be sold and may be expressed to be conveyed subject to the restrictive covenants contained in a conveyance some 60 or 90 years old. No one would suggest that by accepting such a form of contract or conveyance a purchaser is assuming a new liability in favour of third parties to observe the covenants if there was for any reason before the contract or conveyance no one who could make out a title as against the purchaser to the benefit of the covenants.'

The court will not impose a constructive trust unless it is satisfied that the conscience of the estate owner is affected. The mere fact that that land is expressed to be conveyed 'subject to' a contract does not necessarily imply that the grantee is to be under an obligation, not otherwise existing, to give effect to the provisions of the contract. The fact that the conveyance is expressed to be subject to the contract may often, for the reasons indicated by Dillon J, be at least as consistent with an intention merely to protect the grantor against claims by the grantee as an intention to impose an obligation on the grantee. The words 'subject to' will, of course, impose notice. But notice is not enough to impose on somebody an obligation to give effect to a contract into which he did not enter. Thus, mere notice of a restrictive covenant is not enough to impose upon the estate owner an obligation or equity to give effect to it: *LCC v Allen* [1914] 3 KB 642.

The material facts in the present case are as follows. (i) There is no finding that the plaintiff paid a lower price in consequence of the provision that the sale was subject to the 1973 agreement. (ii) The 1973 agreement was not contractually enforceable against Legal & General, which was not, therefore, exposed to the risk of any contractual claim for damages if the agreement was not complied with. The 1973 agreement was enforceable against Cavendish and it seems that in 1973 Cavendish was owned by Legal & General. There is no finding as to the relationship between Cavendish and Legal & General in August 1985, when Legal & General sold to the plaintiff. And there is no evidence before the deputy judge as to the circumstances or the arrangements attending the transfer by Cavendish to Legal & General. (iii) Whilst the letter of 7 February 1985 is not precisely worded, it seems that Legal & General was itself prepared to give effect to the 1973 agreement.

In matters relating to the title to land, certainty is of prime importance. We do not think it desirable that constructive trusts of land should be imposed in reliance on inferences from slender materials. In our opinion the available evidence in the present case is insufficient. The deputy judge, while he did not have to decide the matter, was not disposed to infer a constructive trust, and we agree with him.''

iii. REGISTERED LAND

The constructive trust doctrine has even been applied to registered land, in favour of persons who have failed to protect their interests on the register, as required by the Land Registration Act 1925.

In **Peffer v Rigg** [1977] 1 WLR 285, [1978] 3 All ER 745,[13] a purchaser with notice of an interest under a trust for sale (a minor interest) was held to take subject to it, applying general equitable principles. By section 20 (1) of the Land Registration Act 1925, a transferee for valuable consideration takes free from unprotected minor interests. GRAHAM J held that the requirement of good faith could be read into this provision, so that a transferee with notice of the minor interest could not rely on it,[14] but the same result could be achieved by utilising the constructive trust. He said at 294, at 752:

''On the evidence of this case I have found that the second defendant knew quite well that the first defendant held the property on trust for himself and the plaintiff in equal shares. The second defendant knew this was so and that the property was trust property when the transfer was made to her, and therefore she took the property on a constructive trust in accordance with general equitable principles: see *Snell's Principles of Equity*, 27th edn (1973), pp. 98–99. This is a new trust imposed by equity and is distinct from the trust which bound the first defendant. Even if, therefore, I am wrong as to the proper construction of sections 20 and 59, when read together, and even if section 20 strikes off the shackles of the express trust which bound the first defendant, this cannot invalidate the new trust imposed on the second defendant''.[15]

The House of Lords, however, has since confirmed that the doctrine of notice has no relevance to registered land: ''The only kind of notice recognised is by

13 Maudsley and Burn, *Land Law: Cases and Materials* (6th edn), pp. 112–114, 160.
14 But see LRA 1925, ss. 59 (6) and 74.
15 (1977) 93 LQR 341 (R.J. Smith); [1977] CLJ 227 (D.J. Hayton); (1977) 40 MLR 602 (S. Anderson); [1978] Conv 52 (J. Martin).

entry on the register".[16] This does not exclude the possibility of a constructive trust arising where a purchaser seeks to use the Land Registration Act as an instrument of fraud.

In **Lyus v Prowsa Developments Ltd** [1982] 1 WLR 1044, [1982] 2 All ER 953,[17] land was bought expressly subject to the plaintiff's contractual rights, but the defendants sought to defeat them by relying on the provisions of the Land Registration Act 1925.[18] DILLON J, in imposing a constructive trust on the defendants on the ground that the statute is not to be used as an instrument of fraud, said at 1054, at 962:

"It has been pointed out by Lord Wilberforce in *Midland Bank Trust Co Ltd v Green* [1981] AC 513 at 531, [1981] 1 All ER 153 at 159, that it is not fraud to rely on legal rights conferred by Act of Parliament. Under section 20 [of the Land Registration Act 1925], the effect of the registration of the transferee of a freehold title is to confer an absolute title subject to entries on the register and overriding interests, but, 'free from all other estates and interests whatsoever, including estates and interests of His Majesty ...'

[His Lordship considered *Miles v Bull (No 2)* [1969] 3 All ER 1585, and continued:]

It seems to me that the fraud on the part of the defendants in the present case lies not just in relying on the legal rights conferred by an Act of Parliament, but in the first defendant reneging on a positive stipulation in favour of the plaintiffs in the bargain under which the first defendant acquired the land. That makes, as it seems to me, all the difference. It has long since been held, for instance, in *Rochefoucauld v Boustead* [1897] 1 Ch 196, that the provisions of the Statute of Frauds 1677, now incorporated in certain sections of the Law of Property Act 1925, cannot be used as an instrument of fraud, and that it is fraud for a person to whom land is agreed to be conveyed as trustee for another to deny the trust and relying on the terms of the statute to claim the land for himself. *Rochefoucauld v Boustead* was one of the authorities on which the judgment in *Bannister v Bannister* [1948] 2 All ER 133 was founded.

It seems to me that the same considerations are applicable in relation to the Land Registration Act 1925. If, for instance, the agreement of October 18, 1979, between the bank and the first defendant had expressly stated that the first defendant would hold Plot 29 upon trust to give effect for the benefit of the plaintiffs to the plaintiffs' agreement with the vendor company, it would be difficult to say that the express trust was overreached and rendered nugatory by the Land Registration Act 1925. The Land Registration Act 1925 does not, therefore, affect the conclusion which I would otherwise have reached in reliance on *Bannister v Bannister* and the judgment of Lord Denning MR in *Binions v Evans* [1972] Ch 359, [1972] 2 All ER 70, p. 298, ante, had Plot 29 been unregistered land."

---

16 *Williams & Glyn's Bank Ltd v Boland* [1981] AC 487 at 504, [1980] 2 All ER 408 at 412, per Lord WILBERFORCE. See also, on unregistered land, *Midland Bank Trust Co Ltd v Green* [1981] AC 513, [1981] 1 All ER 153; *Hollington Bros Ltd v Rhodes* [1951] 2 All ER 578n, [1951] 2 TLR 691.
17 (1983) 46 MLR 96 (P.H. Kenny); [1983] Conv 64 (P. Jackson); [1983] CLJ 54 (C. Harpum); [1984] 47 MLR 476 (P. Bennett); [1985] CLJ 280 (M.P. Thompson). The decision was approved by CA in *Ashburn Anstalt v Arnold* [1989] Ch 1, [1988] 2 All ER 147, p. 299, ante.
18 Sections 29, 34 (4).

iv. SUMMARY

Parker and Mellows, *Modern Law of Trusts* (6th edn), pp. 278–279.

"The Legacy of the 'new model' Constructive Trust[19]
Until relatively recently the courts limited the imposition of constructive trusts for the purpose of granting relief against fraudulent and unconscionable conduct to the extreme situations which have been considered so far. However, in the years immediately before and after 1970, a series of decisions emanating from the Court of Appeal imposed constructive trusts of this type not only as a result of fraudulent or unconscionable conduct but also as a result of conduct which the individual judges were prepared to classify merely as inequitable. The underlying and indeed often expressed objective of the judges in question was to prevent results which would otherwise have been inequitable. If application of the basic principles of property law led to a result which, in the view of the court in question, was contrary to good conscience, that court acted upon the conscience of the party who would otherwise have obtained this unjust benefit and imposed a constructive trust upon him to bring the result into line with the requirements of justice. This approach was, of course, much closer to the American attitude to the constructive trust and was thought to be symptomatic of a general change of attitude towards the constructive trust. However, subsequent decisions have rejected the approach manifested in this series of cases and English law seems for the moment to have reverted to its traditional position. The recent acceptance by the Court of Appeal that 'there is a good arguable case' for the existence of a remedial constructive trust[20] may well indicate the possibility of a move towards a more remedial approach but this is likely to be of a much more limited nature than the attempt made in the years immediately before and after 1970 to convert the constructive trust into a general equitable remedy capable of doing justice in any individual case. This does not mean, however, that the series of decisions handed down at that time can be wholly ignored. While their influence on the law governing contractual licences has, admittedly, been almost wholly negated, their influence on the law governing joint enterprises entered into by the members of a family unit has undoubtedly played some part in the development of what some commentators now call 'the common intention constructive trust.'[1]"*

QUESTIONS

1. What subject matter would you include in a chapter on Constructive Trusts?
    Consider now whether:
    (a) secret trusts
    (b) mutual wills
    (c) land subject to a contract for sale

---

19 This expression was coined by Lord DENNING MR in *Eves v Eves* [1975] 1 WLR 1338, [1975] 3 All ER 768.
20 In *Metall und Rohstoff AG v Donaldson Lufkin & Jenrette Inc* [1990] 1 QB 391, 479, [1989] 3 All ER 14, 57.
1 See particularly [1990] Conv 370 (D.J. Hayton).

(d) cases like *Binions v Evans* [1972] Ch 359, [1972] 2 All ER 70, p. 298, ante; *Hussey v Palmer* [1972] 1 WLR 1286, [1972] 3 All ER 744, p. 295, ante; *Re Sharpe* [1980] 1 WLR 219, [1980] 1 All ER 198, p. 298, ante, and *Lyus v Prowsa Developments Ltd* [1982] 1 WLR 1044, [1982] 2 All ER 953, p. 303, ante.

(e) benefits acquired by a killer

are instances of constructive trusts.

2. Consider the distinction made above (p. 247, ante) between accountability and constructive trusteeship. Is the distinction important? Are *Re Montagu's Settlement Trusts* [1987] Ch 264, [1992] 4 All ER 308, p. 261, ante, and *Boardman v Phipps* [1967] 2 AC 46, [1966] 3 All ER 721, p. 844, post cases on constructive trusts?

3. What degree of knowledge is necessary to found personal liability for receiving trust property and for assisting in a breach of trust? Should there be any distinction between the two categories? Should the former category be governed by the principles of unjust enrichment, and, if so, how would this affect the position of an innocent volunteer?

4. In what circumstances will a constructive trust be imposed for the protection of a contractual licensee? *Ashburn Anstalt v Arnold* [1989] Ch 1, [1988] 2 All ER 147, p. 299, ante.

5. Is the "new model" constructive trust (*Eves v Eves* [1975] 1 WLR 1338, [1975] 3 All ER 768, p. 293, ante) a desirable development? Is it likely to survive?

8. Non-Charitable Purpose Trusts[1]

I. General Principles

The orthodox view is that a private trust can only exist if the trustees hold the trust property on trust for ascertainable individuals – or for such as will be ascertained during the period of perpetuity.[2] Various reasons are given. The beneficial interest must be vested in somebody within the period of perpetuity. The court must be able to enforce a trust, and there must therefore be ascertainable persons in whose favour the court can decree performance. A trust is obligatory; and there cannot be an obligation unless there is a corresponding right. And, of course, a purpose must be sufficiently certain. "Benevolent" or "patriotic" or "public" purposes are too vague. None of these reasons applies of course to charitable trusts. Charitable trusts are a special type of purpose trust,[3] one which is of special importance to society, and one which is therefore given special privileges in terms of perpetuity, taxation and enforcement. The Attorney-General is charged with the duty of enforcement of charitable trusts.

The reasons given for disallowing non-charitable purpose trusts can all be challenged.[4] Supporters of such trusts point out that enforcement should be no problem; for in every case which has been litigated, the trustees have been willing to perform. Those entitled in default could complain in a case of misapplication. If a question of enforcement should arise, this is no more of a problem than the enforcement of charitable trusts; if it is a matter of social importance to enforce a particular purpose trust, an officer or Department of

---

1 H & M, pp. 353–379; K & S, pp. 149–158; P & M, pp. 111–129, 159–161; Pettit, pp. 49–57; Riddall, pp. 175–182; Snell, pp. 102–103; Underhill, pp. 91–108; Maudsley, *Modern Law of Perpetuities*, pp. 166–178; Morris and Leach, *Rule Against Perpetuities* (2nd edn, 1962), chap. 12; Gray, *Rule against Perpetuities*, Appendix H § 894–909; Scott, *Trusts* (4th edn) § 119, 123–124; (1892) 5 HLR 389 (J.B. Ames); (1953) 17 Conv (NS) 46 (L.A. Sheridan); (1953) 6 CLP 151 (O.R. Marshall); (1958) 4 University of Western Australia LR 235 (L.A. Sheridan); (1970) 34 Conv (NS) 77 (P.A. Lovell); (1971) 87 LQR 31 (J.W. Harris); (1973) 37 Conv (NS) 420 (L. McKay).

2 *Re Flavel's Will Trusts* [1969] 1 WLR 444, especially at 446–447, [1969] 2 All ER 232 at 233–234.

3 See Part II, pp. 333 et seq., post.

4 See Morris and Leach, p. 307, note 1; H & M, pp. 346–349; (1977) 40 MLR 397 (N.P. Gravells).

State could be instructed to undertake it. Further, the requirement of ascertainable beneficiaries is a rule of *private* trusts in favour of *beneficiaries*. That rule should not be relevant to a purpose trust. If it is insisted that, charitable trusts always excepted, a trust *must* have a beneficiary who can enforce the trust, then purpose trusts could be treated as powers.[5] It is not asking very much to suggest that a disposition which calls itself a trust but fails to provide persons capable of enforcing the obligation should be treated as a power. To say that trustees cannot be *compelled* to perform, is not to say that they *must not* perform.[6]

The courts have also said that the power of testamentary disposition is a personal one which cannot be delegated to another; and, that, with the exception of charitable gifts and general and special powers of appointment,[7] a testator cannot leave it to someone else to make a will for him. This supposed anti-delegation rule does not apply to trusts created inter vivos, and was rejected in *Re Beatty*[8] by HOFFMANN J in the case of a testamentary disposition to trustees to allocate to or among such person or persons as they think fit. "The common law rule ... is a chimera, a shadow cast by the rule of certainty, having no independent existence."[9]

Some cases at first instance have upheld non-charitable purpose trusts. The modern trend however is to declare them void; and the court will not extend the confines of existing decisions. Even those have been described by HARMAN LJ as "troublesome, anomalous and aberrant".[10] We will consider in Section VII the ways in which it is possible to achieve a non-charitable purpose without setting up a trust.

In **Morice v Bishop of Durham** (1804) 9 Ves 399; affd (1805) 10 Ves 522, there was a bequest to the Bishop upon trust for "such objects of benevolence and liberality as the Bishop of Durham in his own discretion shall most approve of". This was held not to be a charitable trust. As there were no ascertainable beneficiaries the trust failed. Sir William GRANT MR said at 404:

"The only question is whether the Trust, upon which the residue of the personal Estate is bequeathed, be a trust for charitable purposes. That it is upon some trust, and not for the personal benefit of the Bishop is clear from the words of the Will; and is admitted by his Lordship; who expressly disclaims any beneficial interest. That it is a Trust, unless it be of a charitable nature, too indefinite to be executed by this Court, has not been, and cannot be denied. There can be no Trust over the exercise of which this Court will not assume a

---

5 Ames, *Lectures on Legal History*, p. 285; Morris and Leach, pp. 319–321.
6 Scott, *Trusts* (4th edn) §§ 123, 124; *IRC v Broadway Cottages Trust* [1955] Ch 20, [1954] 3 All ER 120, is Court of Appeal authority against this view.
7 *Re Park* [1932] 1 Ch 580; *Re Abraham's Will Trusts* [1969] 1 Ch 463, [1967] 2 All ER 1175; *Re Gulbenkian's Settlements*, [1970] AC 508, [1968] 3 All ER 785; *Re Manisty's Settlement* [1974] Ch 17, [1973] 2 All ER 1203; *Re Hay's Settlement Trusts* [1982] 1 WLR 202, [1981] 3 All ER 786.
8 [1990] 1 WLR 1503, [1990] 3 All ER 844, explaining *Chichester Diocesan Fund and Board of Finance Inc v Simpson* [1944] AC 341, [1944] 2 All ER 60; (1991) 107 LQR 211 (J.D. Davies).
9 At 1509, at 849. The power was an intermediary or hybrid power: it was not a general power because of its fiduciary nature; nor a special power because there was no class; [1991] Conv 138 (J. Martin).
10 *Re Endacott* [1960] Ch 232 at 251, [1959] 3 All ER 562 at 571; *Re Wood* [1949] Ch 498, [1949] 1 All ER 1100 (The Week's Good Cause).

control; for an uncontrollable power of disposition would be Ownership, and not Trust. If there be a clear Trust, but for uncertain objects, the property, that is the subject of the trust, is undisposed of, and the benefit of such Trust must result to those, to whom the Law gives Ownership in default of disposition by the former owner. But this doctrine does not hold good with regard to Trusts for Charity. Every other Trust must have a definite object. There must be somebody, in whose favour the Court can decree performance."

It must not however be assumed that it is always a simple matter to *classify* a trust as being a trust for persons, or a trust for purposes. The problem has been seen in the earlier discussion[11] of unincorporated associations. A gift of property to an unincorporated association raises the question of the identification of the beneficial ownership. We saw that such a gift may be construed as a gift to the present members beneficially, or to those persons who may be members at any particular time; and that the claim of each member may be based upon the contractual rights controlling his membership, or upon rights arising under trusts on which the property is held. If the rights are based upon a trust, there are, as we have seen, problems relating to the nature of the ownership among the members; whether each one can sever and claim his share,[12] and problems of perpetuity. The real problem arises however where the gift cannot be construed as one to which the members are entitled; as where the gift was not intended to be for their personal benefit,[13] or where there is no list kept of the members; or, more especially, where the object of the association is the promotion of a purpose, as opposed to the benefit of the members. Then the problem is the same as that of an express trust for purposes. "It is at this point that the cases on gifts to unincorporated associations become relevant to the question whether there can be a trust without a *cestui que trust.* It would certainly seem strange if a testator could give property to an unincorporated anti-vivisection society to be applied for its purposes, but could not give property to an individual trustee to be applied by him for the purpose of anti-vivisection."[14] But a gift to an anti-vivisection society may be construed as a gift to its members.[15] And a gift which is to benefit specified persons by the use of property in a particular manner may be construed as a trust for those persons and not a trust for purposes.[16] This question is discussed in Section IV. The non-charitable purpose trust will first be examined.

---

11 See p. 91, ante.

12 See p. 91, ante. *Neville Estates Ltd v Madden* [1962] Ch 832, [1961] 3 All ER 769.

13 *Leahy v A-G for New South Wales* [1959] AC 457, [1959] 2 All ER 300, p. 94, ante; *Re Smith* [1914] 1 Ch 937; *R v District Auditor, ex p West Yorkshire Metropolitan County Council* [1986] RVR 24, p. 84, ante.

14 Morris and Leach, p. 317.

15 *Re Recher's Will Trusts* [1972] Ch 526, [1971] 3 All ER 401, p. 59, ante.

16 *Re Denley's Trust Deed* [1969] 1 Ch 373, [1968] 3 All ER 65 (recreation ground for benefit of employees); [1968] ASCL 437 (J.D. Davies); (1969) 32 MLR 96 (J.M. Evans); (1970) 34 Conv (NS) 77 (P.A. Lovell); *Re Lipinski's Will Trusts* [1976] Ch 235, [1977] 1 All ER 33, p. 319, post (buildings for Jewish Association for benefit of members); (1977) 93 LQR 167; cf. *Re Grant's Will Trusts* [1980] 1 WLR 360, [1979] 3 All ER 359, p. 105, ante.

II. Anomalous Cases of Purpose Trusts being Enforced

Most of the successful purpose trusts in England have been concerned with the care of particular animals,[17] and a few for the erection or maintenance of tombs or monuments.[18]

RE DEAN
(1889) 41 ChD 552 (ChD, NORTH J)

A testator charged his freehold estates with the payment of £750 per annum to his trustees for the period of fifty years if any of his horses and hounds should so long live, and declared that the trustees should apply the money in the maintenance of his horses and hounds; but without imposing upon them any obligation to render any account.

Held. This was a valid non-charitable trust, although there was no one who could enforce it.

NORTH J: The first question is as to the validity of the provision made by the testator in favour of his horses and dogs. It is said that it is not valid; because (for this is the principal ground upon which it is put) neither a horse nor a dog could enforce the trust; and there is no person who could enforce it. It is obviously not a charity, because it is intended for the benefit of the particular animals mentioned and not for the benefit of animals generally, and it is quite distinguishable from the gift made in a subsequent part of the will to the *Royal Society for the Prevention of Cruelty to Animals,* which may well be a charity. In my opinion this provision for the particular horses and hounds referred to in the will is not, in any sense, a charity, ...

Then it is said, that there is no *cestui que trust* who can enforce the trust, and that the Court will not recognise a trust unless it is capable of being enforced by some one. I do not assent to that view. There is not the least doubt that a man may if he pleases, give a legacy to trustees, upon trust to apply it in erecting a monument to himself, either in a church or in a churchyard, or even in unconsecrated ground, and I am not aware that such a trust is in any way invalid, although it is difficult to say who would be the *cestui que trust* of the monument. In the same way I know of nothing to prevent a gift of a sum of money to trustees, upon trust to apply it for the repair of such a monument. In my opinion such a trust would be good, although the testator must be careful to limit the time for which it is to last, because, as it is not a charitable trust, unless it is to come to an end within the limits fixed by the rule against perpetuities, it would be illegal. But a trust to lay out a certain sum in building a monument, and the gift of another sum in trust to apply the same to keeping that monument in repair, say, for ten years, is in my opinion, a perfectly good trust, although I do not see who could ask the Court to enforce it. If persons beneficially interested in the estate could do so, then the present Plaintiff can do so; but, if such persons could not enforce the trust, still it cannot be said that the trust must fail because there is no one who can actively enforce it.

---

17 *Pettingall v Pettingall* (1842) 11 LJ Ch 176; *Re Dean* (1889) 41 ChD 552; *Re Haines* (1952) Times, 7 November; (1983) 80 LSG 2451 (P. Matthews). See also *Re Thompson* [1934] Ch 342, p. 311, post.
18 *Trimmer v Danby* (1856) 25 LJ Ch 424, p. 311, post; *Mussett v Bingle* [1876] WN 170, p. 311, post; *Pirbright v Salwey* [1896] WN 86; *Re Hooper* [1932] 1 Ch 38, p. 310, post.

Is there then anything illegal or obnoxious to the law in the nature of the provision, that is, in the fact that it is not for human beings, but for horses and dogs? It is clearly settled by authority that a charity may be established for the benefit of horses and dogs, and, therefore, the making of a provision for horses and dogs, which is not a charity, cannot of itself be obnoxious to the law, provided, of course, that it is not to last for too long a period. Then there is what I consider an express authority upon this point in *Mitford v Reynolds* (1848) 16 Sim 105.

RE HOOPER
[1932] 1 Ch 38 (ChD, MAUGHAM J)

A testator gave a sum of money to trustees for the care and upkeep of certain family graves and monuments, and a tablet and a window in a church for "so far as [the trustees] legally can do so". The question was whether the gift was valid.

Held. The trust for the upkeep of the graves and monuments, not being charitable, was valid for 21 years.

MAUGHAM J: This point is one to my mind of doubt, and I should have felt some difficulty in deciding it if it were not for *Pirbright v Salwey* [1896] WN 86, a decision of Stirling J, which unfortunately is reported, as far as I know, only in the Weekly Notes. The report is as follows: "A testator, after expressing his wish to be buried in the inclosure in which his child lay in the churchyard of E., bequeathed to the rector and church-wardens for the time being of the parish church 800*l.* Consols, to be invested in their joint names, the interest and dividends to be derived therefrom to be applied, so long as the law for the time being permitted, in keeping up the inclosure and decorating the same with flowers: *Held,* that the gift was valid for at least a period of 21 years from the testator's death, and *semble* that it was not charitable."

That was a decision arrived at by Stirling J, after argument by very eminent counsel. The case does not appear to have attracted much attention in text-books, but it does not appear to have been commented upon adversely, and I shall follow it.

The trustees here have the sum of 1000*l.* which they have to hold upon trust to "invest the same and to the intent that so far as they legally can do so and in any manner that they may in their discretion arrange they will out of the annual income thereof" do substantially four things: first, provide for the care and upkeep of the grave and monument in the Torquay cemetery; secondly, for the care and upkeep of a vault and monument there in which lie the remains of the testator's wife and daughter; thirdly, for the care and upkeep of a grave and monument in Shotley churchyard near Ipswich, where the testator's son lies buried; and, fourthly, for the care and upkeep of the tablet in Saint Matthias' Church at Ilsham to the memories of the testator's wife and children and the window in the same church to the memory of his late father. All those four things have to be done expressly according to an arrangement made in the discretion of the trustees and so far as they legally can do so. I do not think that is distinguishable from the phrase "so long as the law for the time being permits," and the conclusion at which I arrive, following the decision I have mentioned, is that this trust is valid for a period of twenty-one years from the testator's death so far as regards the three matters which involve the upkeep of graves or vaults or monuments in the churchyard or in the cemetery. As regards the tablet in St. Matthias' Church and the window in the same church there is no question but that that is a good charitable gift, and, therefore, the rule against perpetuities does not apply.

Something has been said with regard to apportionment. To my mind there is no room for a legal apportionment, because it is left to the discretion of the trustees to arrange how much they will out of this income apply during the twenty-one years to the four objects in question. At the end of the twenty-one years any part which is not applied for the upkeep of the tablet and the window in St. Matthias' Church will, of course, be undisposed of and will fall, unless some other event happens, into residue.

In **Trimmer v Danby** (1856) 25 LJ Ch 424, the testator gave £1,000 to his executors, "and I do direct them to lay out and expend the same to erect a monument to my memory in St. Paul's Cathedral, among those of my brothers in art." The bequest was upheld by KINDERSLEY V-C, who said at 427:

"I do not suppose that there would be anyone who could compel the executors to carry out this bequest and raise the monument; but if the residuary legatees or the trustees insist upon the trust being executed, my opinion is that this Court is bound to see it carried out. I think, therefore, that as the trustees insist upon the sum of 1000*l.* being laid out according to the directions in the will, that sum must be set apart for the purpose."

In **Mussett v Bingle** [1876] WN 170, the testator gave £300 to be applied in the erection of a monument to his wife's first husband, and £200 the interest of which was to be applied in keeping up the monument. It was admitted that the latter direction was void for perpetuity. The former was upheld; HALL V-C saying that the direction was one which the executors "were ready to perform, and it must be performed accordingly".

PARISH COUNCILS AND BURIAL AUTHORITIES (MISCELLANEOUS PROVISIONS) ACT 1970

1. Maintenance of private graves.—(1) A burial authority or a local authority may agree with any person in consideration of the payment of a sum by him, to maintain—
   (*a*) a grave, vault, tombstone, or other memorial in a burial ground or crematorium provided or maintained by the authority;
   (*b*) a monument or other memorial to any person situated in any place within the area of the authority to which the authority have a right of access;
so, however, that no agreement ... made under this subsection by any authority with respect to a particular grave, vault, tombstone, monument or other memorial may impose on the authority an obligation with respect to maintenance for a period exceeding 99 years from the date of that agreement.

In **Re Thompson** [1934] Ch 342, the testator, an alumnus of Trinity Hall, Cambridge, gave a legacy of £1,000 to a friend George William Lloyd, to be applied by him towards the promotion and furthering of fox-hunting. Trinity Hall was the residuary legatee. Both parties desired to carry out the testator's wishes, so far as they could legally do so, but Trinity Hall felt obligated, as a charity, to make objections to the enforcement of the trust. CLAUSON J upheld the gift; "following the example of Knight Bruce V-C in *Pettingall v Pettingall* (1842) 11 LJ Ch 176, to order that, upon the defendant Mr. Lloyd giving an undertaking (which I understand he is willing to give) to apply the legacy when received by him towards the object expressed in the testator's will, the plaintiffs do pay to the defendant Mr. Lloyd the legacy of 1000*l.*; and that, in case the legacy should be applied by him otherwise than towards the promotion and furthering of fox-hunting, the residuary legatees are to be at liberty to apply."

III. The Requirement of Ascertainable Beneficiaries

RE ASTOR'S SETTLEMENT TRUSTS[19]
[1952] Ch 534, [1952] 1 All ER 1067 (ChD, ROXBURGH J)

An inter vivos settlement was made in 1945, expressly limited to the perpetuity period, under which substantially all the issued shares in The Observer Ltd were held by the trustees upon trust for various non-charitable purposes; which included, among others, 1. The maintenance ... of good understanding sympathy and co-operation between nations. 2. The preservation of the independence and integrity of newspapers. 4. The control publication ... financing or management of any newspapers periodicals books pamphlets or publications. 5. The protection of newspapers ... from being absorbed ... by combines or being tied by finance or otherwise to special ... views ... inconsistent with the highest integrity and independence. It was conceded that the trusts were not charitable.

Held. The trusts were invalid; because (i) they were non-charitable purpose trusts which no-one could enforce; (ii) the trusts included objects which were too uncertain.

ROXBURGH J: The question upon which I am giving this reserved judgment is whether the non-charitable trusts of income during "the specified period" declared by clause 5 and the third schedule of the settlement of 1945 are void. Mr. Jennings and Mr. Buckley have submitted that they are void on two grounds: (1) that they are not trusts for the benefit of individuals; (2) that they are void for uncertainty.

Lord Parker considered the first of these two questions in his speech in *Bowman v Secular Society Ltd* [1917] AC 406 and I will cite two important passages. The first is at 437: "The question whether a trust be legal or illegal or be in accordance with or contrary to the policy of the law, only arises when it has been determined that a trust has been created, and is then only part of the larger question whether the trust is enforceable. For, as will presently appear, trusts may be unenforceable and therefore void, not only because they are illegal or contrary to the policy of the law, but for other reasons." The second is at 441: "A trust to be valid must be for the benefit of individuals, which this

---

19 (1952) 68 LQR 449 (R.E.M.); (1953) 6 CLP 151 (O.R. Marshall); (1953) 17 Conv (NS) 46
(L.A. Sheridan); (1955) 18 MLR 120 (L.H. Leigh).

is certainly not, or must be in that class of gifts for the benefit of the public which the courts in this country recognize as charitable in the legal as opposed to the popular sense of that term."

Commenting on those passages Mr. Gray observed that *Bowman v Secular Society Ltd* arose out of a will and he asked me to hold that Lord Parker intended them to be confined to cases arising under a will. But they were, I think, intended to be quite general in character. Further, Mr. Gray pointed out that Lord Parker made no mention of the exceptions or apparent exceptions which undoubtedly exist, and from this he asked me to infer that no such general principle can be laid down. The question is whether those cases are to be regarded as exceptional and anomalous or whether they are destructive of the supposed principle. I must later analyse them. But I will first consider whether Lord Parker's propositions can be attacked from a base of principle.

The typical case of a trust is one in which the legal owner of property is constrained by a court of equity so to deal with it as to give effect to the equitable rights of another. These equitable rights have been hammered out in the process of litigation in which a claimant on equitable grounds has successfully asserted rights against a legal owner or other person in control of property. Prima facie, therefore, a trustee would not be expected to be subject to an equitable obligation unless there was somebody who could enforce a correlative equitable right, and the nature and extent of that obligation would be worked out in proceedings for enforcement. This is what I understand by Lord Parker's first proposition. At an early stage, however, the courts were confronted with attempts to create trusts for charitable purposes which there was no equitable owner to enforce. Lord Eldon explained in *A-G v Brown* (1818) 1 Swan 265 at 290 how this difficulty was dealt with: "It is the duty of a court of equity, a main part, originally almost the whole, of its jurisdiction, to administer trusts; to protect not the visible owner, who alone can proceed at law, but the individual equitably, though not legally, entitled. From this principle has arisen the practice of administering the trust of a public charity: persons possessed of funds appropriate to such purposes are within the general rule; but no one being entitled by an immediate and peculiar interest to prefer a complaint, who is to compel the performance of their obligations, and to enforce their responsibility? It is the duty of the King, as parens patriae, to protect property devoted to charitable uses; and that duty is executed by the officer who represents the Crown for all forensic purposes. On this foundation rests the right of the Attorney-General in such cases to obtain by information the interposition of a court of equity...." But if the purposes are not charitable, great difficulties arise both in theory and in practice. In theory, because having regard to the historical origins of equity it is difficult to visualise the growth of equitable obligations which nobody can enforce, and in practice, because it is not possible to contemplate with equanimity the creation of large funds devoted to non-charitable purposes which no court and no department of state can control, or in the case of maladministration reform. Therefore, Lord Parker's second proposition would prima facie appear to be well founded. Moreover, it gains no little support from the practical considerations that no officer has ever been constituted to take, in the case of non-charitable purposes, the position held by the Attorney-General in connexion with charitable purposes, and no case has been found in the reports in which the court has ever directly enforced a non-charitable purpose against a trustee. Indeed where, as in the present case, the only beneficiaries are purposes and an at present unascertainable person, it is difficult to see who could initiate such proceedings. If the purposes are valid trusts, the settlors have retained no beneficial interest and could not initiate them. It was suggested that the trustees might proceed ex parte to enforce the trusts against themselves. I doubt that, but at any rate nobody could enforce the trusts against them. This point, in my judgment, is of importance, because in most of the cases which are put forward to disprove Lord Parker's propositions the court had indirect means of enforcing the execution of the non-charitable purpose.

These cases I must now consider. First of all, there is a group relating to horses, dogs, graves and monuments, among which I was referred to *Pettingall v Pettingall* (1842) 11 LJ Ch 176; *Mitford v Reynolds* (1848) 16 Sim 105; *Re Dean* (1889) 41 ChD 552; *Pirbright v Salwey* [1896] WN 86, and *Re Hooper* [1932] 1 Ch 38.

[His Lordship examined these cases, and also *Re Thompson* [1934] Ch 342, and *Re Price* [1943] Ch 422, [1943] 2 All ER 505, and continued:]

Let me then sum up the position so far. On the one side there are Lord Parker's two propositions with which I began. These were not new, but merely re-echoed what Sir William Grant had said as Master of the Rolls in *Morice v Bishop of Durham* (1804) 9 Ves 399 at 405 as long ago as 1804: "There must be somebody, in whose favour the court can decree performance." The position was recently restated by Harman J in *Re Wood* [1949] Ch 498 at 501, [1949] 1 All ER 1100 at 1101: "A gift on trust must have a cestui que trust", and this seems to be in accord with principle. On the other side is a group of cases relating to horses and dogs, graves and monuments—matters arising under wills and intimately connected with the deceased—in which the courts have found means of escape from these general propositions and also *Re Thompson* [1934] Ch 342 and *Re Price* [1943] Ch 422, [1943] 2 All ER 505 which I have endeavoured to explain. *Re Price* belongs to another field. The rest may, I think, properly be regarded as anomalous and exceptional and in no way destructive of the proposition which traces descent from or through Sir William Grant through Lord Parker to Harman J. Perhaps the late Sir Arthur Underhill was right in suggesting that they may be concessions to human weakness or sentiment (see Law of Trusts, 8th edn, p. 79) . They cannot, in my judgment, of themselves (and no other justification has been suggested to me) justify the conclusion that a Court of Equity will recognise as an equitable obligation affecting the income of large funds in the hands of trustees a direction to apply it in furtherance of enumerated non-charitable purposes in a manner which no court or department can control or enforce. I hold that the trusts here in question are void on the first of the grounds submitted by Mr. Jennings and Mr. Buckley.

The second ground upon which the relevant trusts are challenged is uncertainty. If (contrary to my view) an enumeration of purposes outside the realm of charities can take the place of an enumeration of beneficiaries, the purposes must, in my judgment, be stated in phrases which embody definite concepts and the means by which the trustees are to try to attain them must also be prescribed with a sufficient degree of certainty. The test to be applied is stated by Lord Eldon in *Morice v Bishop of Durham* (1805) 10 Ves 522 at 539 as follows: "As it is a maxim, that the execution of a trust shall be under the control of the court, it must be of such a nature, that it can be under that control; so that the administration of it can be reviewed by the court; or, if the trustee dies, the court itself can execute the trust: a trust therefore, which, in case of mal-administration could be reformed; and a due administration directed; and then, unless the subject and the objects can be ascertained, upon principles, familiar in other cases, it must be decided, that the court can neither reform mal-administration, nor direct a due administration." See also *Re Macduff* [1896] 2 Ch 451 at 463.

Mr. Gray argued that this test was not properly applicable to trusts declared by deed, but I can see no distinction between a will and a deed in this respect.

Applying this test, I find many uncertain phrases in the enumeration of purposes, for example, "different sections of people in any nation or community" in paragraph 1 of the third schedule, "constructive policies" in paragraph 2, "integrity of the press" in paragraph 3, "combines" in paragraph 5, "the restoration ... of the independence of ... writers in newspapers" in paragraph 6, and "benevolent schemes" in paragraph 7. Mr. Gray suggested that in view of the unlimited discretion bestowed upon the trustees (subject only to directions from the settlors) the trustees would be justified in excluding from their purview purposes indicated by the settlors but insufficiently defined by them. But I cannot accept this argument. The purposes must be so defined that if the trustees surrendered their discretion, the court could carry out the purposes declared, not a selection of them arrived at by eliminating those which are too uncertain to be carried out. If, for example, I were to eliminate all the purposes except those declared in paragraph 4, but to decree that those declared in paragraph 4 ought to be performed, should I be executing the trusts of this settlement?

But how in any case could I decree in what manner the trusts applicable to income were to be performed? The settlement gives no guidance at all. Mr. Hunt suggested that the trustees might apply to the court ex parte for a scheme. It is not, I think, a mere coincidence that no case has been found outside the realm of charity in which the court has yet devised a scheme of ways and means for attaining enumerated trust purposes. If it were to assume this (as I think) novel jurisdiction over public but not charitable trusts it would, I believe, necessarily require the assistance of a custodian of the public interest analogous to the Attorney-General in charity cases, who would not only help to formulate schemes but could be charged with the duty of enforcing them and preventing mal-administration. There is no such person. Accordingly, in my judgment, the trusts for the application of income during "the specified period" are also void for uncertainty.

But while I have reached my decision on two separate grounds, both, I think, have their origin in a single principle, namely, that a court of equity does not recognise as valid a trust which it cannot both enforce and control. This seems to me to be good equity and good sense.

I dealt at the hearing with the trusts for accumulation and the trusts to take effect at the end of "the specified period", and the order will be drawn up accordingly.

RE ENDACOTT
[1960] Ch 232, [1959] 3 All ER 562 (CA, Lord EVERSHED MR, SELLERS and HARMAN LJJ)

The testator gave his residuary estate "to North Tawton Devon Parish Council for the purpose of providing some useful memorial to myself . . . " The value of the residuary estate was approximately £20,000. The question was whether the gift was valid.

Held. The gift, not being beneficial to the Council, nor to the inhabitants, and not being charitable, was void.

LORD EVERSHED MR [Having held that the language of the will showed an intention to impose a trust; and that the trust was not charitable]:

I now turn to Mr. Arnold's alternative argument based on the view that there is here a trust and a trust of a public character, but not a charitable trust. What he says is, that the trust is in line with the trusts which were rendered effective in those cases which I have called "anomalous", and many of which are referred to in Roxburgh J's decision, beginning with *Pettingall v Pettingall* (1842) 11 LJ Ch 176. I include in that list cases such as the three to which we have had our attention particularly drawn today. The argument is that assuming the non-charitable but public nature of this trust, still it is of a character which the court can efficiently, and will, enforce. It must be said that these cases are of a somewhat anomalous kind. They are classified in the recent book written by Mr. J.H.C. Morris and Professor Barton Leach, The Rule Against Perpetuities (1956) (p. 298). "We proceed", say the authors, "to examine these 'anomalous' exceptions. It will be found that they fall into the following groups: (1) trusts for the erection or maintenance of monuments or graves; (2) trusts for the saying of masses, in jurisdictions where such trusts are not regarded as charitable; (3) trusts for the maintenance of particular animals; (4) trusts for the benefit of unincorporated associations (though this group is more doubtful); (5) miscellaneous cases." I am prepared to accept, for the purposes of the argument, that it does not matter that the trusts here are attached to residue and not to a legacy; that is to say, it does not matter that the persons who would come to the court and either complain if the trusts were not being carried out, or claim the money on the footing that they had not been carried out, are next-of-kin rather than residuary legatees. Still, in my judgment, the scope of these cases ... ought not to be extended. So to do would be to validate almost limitless heads of non-charitable trusts, even though they were not (strictly speaking) public trusts, so long only as the question of perpetuities did not arise; and, in my judgment, that result would be out of harmony with the principles of our law. No principle perhaps has greater sanction of authority behind it than the general proposition that a trust by English law, not being a charitable trust, in order to be effective, must have ascertained or ascertainable beneficiaries. These cases constitute an exception to that general rule. The general rule, having such authority as that of Lord Eldon, Lord Parker and my predecessor, Lord Greene MR, behind it, was most recently referred to in the Privy Council in *Leahy v A-G for New South Wales* [1959] AC 457, [1959] 2 All ER 300. I add also that, in my judgment, the proposition stated in Mr. Morris and Professor Barton Leach's book (p. 308) that if these trusts should fail as trusts they may survive as powers, is not one which I think can be treated as accepted in English law.

I therefore, so far as this case is concerned, conclude (having already stated my view of the meaning of the words) that, though this trust is specific, in the sense that it indicates a purpose capable of expression, yet it is of far too wide and uncertain a nature to qualify within the class of cases cited. It would go far beyond any fair analogy to any of those decisions.

HARMAN LJ: I cannot think that charity has anything to do with this bequest. As for establishing it without the crutch of charity, I applaud the orthodox sentiments expressed by Roxburgh J in the *Astor* case [1952] Ch 534, [1952] 1 All ER 1067, and I think, as I think he did, that though one knows there have been decisions at times which are not really to be satisfactorily classified, but are perhaps merely occasions when Homer has nodded, at any rate these cases stand by themselves and ought not to be increased in number, nor indeed followed, except where the one is exactly like another. Whether it would be better that some authority now should say those cases were wrong, this perhaps is not the moment to consider. At any rate, I cannot think a case of this kind, the case of providing outside a church an unspecified and unidentified memorial, is the kind of instance which should be allowed to add to those troublesome, anomalous and aberrant cases.

In my judgment, Danckwerts J came to the right conclusion, and this appeal ought to be dismissed.

In **Re Shaw** [1957] 1 WLR 729, [1957] 1 All ER 745, the question arose as to the validity of a residuary gift under the will of George Bernard Shaw, which provided that the residue of his estate should be applied towards the institution of a 40-letter alphabet in the place of the present 26-letter alphabet. Harman J decided that the trusts were not charitable; nor could they be enforced as purpose trusts or as powers.[20]

By way of background, Harman J said at 731, at 747:

"All his long life Bernard Shaw was an indefatigable reformer. He was already well known when the present century dawned, as novelist, critic, pamphleteer, playwright, and during the ensuing half-century he continued to act as a kind of itching powder to the British public, to the English-speaking peoples, and, indeed to an even wider audience, castigating their follies, their foibles and their fallacies, and bombarding them with a combination of paradox and wit that earned him in the course of years the status of an oracle: the Shavian oracle; and the rare distinction of adding a word to the language. Many of his projects he lived to see gain acceptance and carried into effect and become normal. It was natural that he should be interested in English orthography and pronunciation. These are obvious targets for the reformer. It is as difficult for the native to defend the one as it is for the foreigner to compass the other. The evidence shows that Shaw had for many years been interested in the subject. Perhaps his best known excursion in this field is 'Pygmalion', in which the protagonist is a professor of phonetics: this was produced as a play in 1914 and has held the stage ever since and invaded the world of the film. It is, indeed, a curious reflection that this same work, tagged with versicles which I suppose Shaw would have detested, and tricked out with music which he would have eschewed (see the preface to the 'Admirable Bashville'), is now charming huge audiences on the other side of the Atlantic and has given birth to the present proceedings. I am told that the receipts from this source have enabled the executor to get on terms with the existing death duties payable on the estate, thus bringing the interpretation of the will into the realm of practical politics.

The testator, whatever his other qualifications, was the master of a pellucid style, and the reader embarks on his will confident of finding no difficulty in understanding the objects which the testator had in mind. This document, moreover, was evidently originally the work of a skilled equity draftsman. As such I doubt not it was easily to be understood if not of the vulgar at any rate by

20 Mrs. Shaw's will was held to be valid, p. 369, post.

the initiate. Unfortunately the will bears ample internal evidence of being in part the testator's own work. The two styles, as ever, make an unfortunate mixture. It is always a marriage of incompatibles: the delicate testamentary machinery devised by the conveyancer can but suffer when subjected to the cacoethes scribendi of the author, even though the latter's language, if it stood alone, might be a literary masterpiece."

[And on purpose trusts:] "The principle has been recently restated by Roxburgh J in *Re Astor Settlement Trusts* [1952] Ch 534, [1952] 1 All ER 1067, where the authorities are elaborately reviewed. An object cannot complain to the court, which therefore cannot control the trust, and, therefore, will not allow it to continue. I must confess that I feel some reluctance to come to this conclusion. I agree at once that, if the persons to take in remainder are unascertainable, the court is deprived of any means of controlling such a trust, but if, as here, the persons taking the ultimate residue are ascertained, I do not feel the force of this objection. They are entitled to the estate except in so far as it has been devoted to the indicated purposes, and in so far as it is not devoted to those purposes, the money being spent is the money of the residuary legatees of the ultimate remaindermen, and they can come to the court and sue the executor for a devastavit, or the trustee for a breach of trust, and thus, though not themselves interested in the purposes, enable the court indirectly to control them. This line of reasoning is not, I think, open to me. See, for instance, the statement by Lord Greene MR in *Re Diplock* [1941] Ch 253 at 259, [1941] 1 All ER 193 at 198. 'Those principles,' he says, dealing with uncertainty, 'I apprehend are really nothing more than the application of a fundamental principle of the law relating to trusts. In order that a trust may be properly constituted, there must be a beneficiary. The beneficiary must be ascertained or must be ascertainable. In the case of what I may call impersonal trusts, such as a gift to charitable purposes, or to benevolent purposes, there is no class of beneficiary which can be defined in the same sense as a class of beneficiaries such as a class of relatives. In the latter case, although no particular person in the class may be able to say that at any given moment he is entitled to anything out of the trust, the class as a whole can enforce the trust. Now in the case of charitable trusts in which no defined class is specified, nevertheless owing to the particular principles which have come to be applied to charitable gifts, the courts have not treated the trust as failing for that reason. There is a very good ground for that, namely that the Crown, as parens patriae taking all charities under its protection, is in a position to enforce the trust; and therefore, although there may be no specified charitable beneficiary who can come to the court and insist on having the trust performed, nevertheless the Attorney-General can appear and is entitled to insist on the trust being carried out, if necessary, by a scheme cy près. But that exception to the general rule, that there must be beneficiaries ascertained or ascertainable — if I may call it an exception — does not extend beyond what falls within the legal class of charity. It does not extend to other public spirited purposes.' The same view is taken in the judgment of Jenkins LJ in *IRC v Broadway Cottages Trusts* [1955] Ch 20, [1954] 3 All ER 120.

I should have wished to regard this bequest as a gift to the ultimate residuary legatees subject to a condition by which they cannot complain of income during the first 21 years after the testator's death being devoted to the alphabet project. This apparently might be the way in which the matter would be viewed in the United States, for I find in Morris and Leach's work on the Rule against Perpetuities (1956), at p. 308, the following passage quoted from the American

Law Institute's Restatement of Trusts.[1] 'Where the owner of property transfers it upon an intended trust for a specific non-charitable purpose, and there is no definite or definitely ascertainable beneficiary designated, no trust is created; but the transferee has power to apply the property to the designated purpose, unless he is authorized so to apply the property beyond the period of the rule against perpetuities, or the purpose is capricious'. As the authors point out, this is to treat a trust of this sort as a power, for clearly there is no one who can directly enforce the trust, and if the trustees choose to pay the whole moneys to the residuary legatees, no one can complain. All that can be done is to control the trustees indirectly in the exercise of their power. In my judgment, I am not at liberty to validate this trust, by treating it as a power. (See per Jenkins LJ in *Sunnylands* case above [1955] Ch at 36, [1954] 3 All ER at 128. 'We do not think that a valid power is to be spelt out of an invalid trust'. This also was the view of the learned author of Gray on Perpetuities (4th edn), the leading work on the subject (See Appendix H), and I feel bound to accept it).

The result is that the alphabet trusts are, in my judgment, invalid, and must fail. It seems that their begotter suspected as much, hence his jibe about failure by judicial decision. I answer that it is not the fault of the law, but of the testator, who failed almost for the first time in his life to grasp the legal problem or to make up his mind what he wanted.'[2]

IV. Trusts for Persons or Purposes

A gift which is to benefit specified persons by the use of property in a particular manner may be construed as a trust for persons and not for purposes.

RE LIPINSKI'S WILL TRUSTS[3]
[1976] Ch 235, [1977] 1 All ER 33 (ChD, Oliver J)

In 1967 the testator bequeathed his residuary estate to trustees on trust as to one half for the Hull Judeans (Maccabi) Association "in memory of my late wife to be used solely in the work of constructing the new buildings for the association and/or improvements to the said buildings". The objects of the Association included "(a) To promote the interest, and the active participation of Anglo-Jewish youth, of both sexes, in amateur sports, in all forms of cultural, and in non-political, communal activities. (b) To inculcate within its ranks a team spirit, a conception of fair play, good citizenship and self-discipline ... (d) To promote and foster the interest to cultivate a knowledge of Jewish history, of the Hebrew language and national traditions". On a summons to determine the effect of the trust.

---

1 1st edn. For 2nd edn § 124, see p. 329, post.
2 "It is understood that the case was compromised on appeal and that the alphabet trusts are being carried out; see [1958] 1 All ER 245." Morris and Leach, p. 310. See (1957) 73 LQR 305 (R.E.M.). See Holroyd, *The Shaw Companion* (1992), vol. 4, pp. 3–26 and Appx B for a detailed discussion of the compromise and the full text of the will.
3 [1976] ASCL 419 (J. Hackney); (1977) 93 LQR 167; (1977) 41 Conv (NS) 139 (F.R. Crane), 179 (K. Widdows); (1977) 40 MLR 231 (N.P. Gravells); (1977) 9 Victoria University of Wellington LR 1 (L. McKay); cf. *R v District Auditor, ex p West Yorkshire Metropolitan County Council* [1986] RVR 24, p. 84 ante (no ascertained or ascertainable beneficiaries); [1986] CLJ 391 (C. Harpum).

Held. It was valid. It was a trust for the members of the Association, who were ascertained or ascertainable.

OLIVER J: I approach question 1 of the summons, therefore, on the footing that this is a gift to an unincorporated non-charitable association. Such a gift, if it is an absolute and beneficial one, is of course perfectly good: see, for instance, the gift to the Corps of Commissionaires in *Re Clarke* [1901] 2 Ch 110. What I have to consider, however, is the effect of the specification by the testator of the purposes for which the legacy was to be applied.

The principles applicable to this type of case were stated by Cross J in *Neville Estates Ltd v Madden* [1962] Ch 832 at 849, [1961] 3 All ER 769 at 778, p. 93, ante, and they are conveniently summarised in *Tudor, Charities*, 6th edn (1967), p. 150, where it is said:

> "In *Neville Estates Ltd v Madden* Cross J expressed the opinion (which is respectfully accepted as correct) that every such gift might, according to the actual words used, be construed in one of three quite different ways: (*a*) As a gift to the members of the association at the date of the gift as joint tenants so that any member could sever his share and claim it whether or not he continued to be a member. (*b*) As a gift to the members of the association at the date of the gift not as joint tenants, but subject to their contractual rights and liabilities towards one another as members of the association. In such a case a member cannot sever his share. It will accrue to the other members on his death or resignation, even though such members include persons who become members after the gift took effect. If this is the effect of the gift, it will not be open to objection on the score of perpetuity or uncertainty unless there is something in its terms or circumstances or in the rules of the association which precludes the members at any given time from dividing the subject of the gift between them on the footing that they are solely entitled to it in equity. (*c*) The terms or circumstances of the gift or the rules of the association may show that the property in question — i.e., the subject of the gift — is not to be at the disposal of the members for the time being but is to be held in trust for or applied for the purposes of the association as a quasi-corporate entity. In this case the gift will fail unless the association is a charitable body."

That summary may require, I think, a certain amount of qualification in the light of subsequent authority, but for present purposes I can adopt it as a working guide. Mr. Blackburne, for the next-of-kin, argues that the gift in the present case clearly does not fall within the first category, and that the addition of the specific direction as to its employment by the association prevents it from falling into the second category. This is, therefore, he says, a purpose trust and fails both for that reason and because the purpose is perpetuitous. He relies upon this passage from the judgment of the Board in *Leahy v A-G for New South Wales* [1959] AC 457 at 478, [1959] 2 All ER 300 at 307:

> "If the words 'for the general purposes of the association' were held to import a trust, the question would have to be asked, what is the trust and who are the beneficiaries? A gift can be made to persons (including a corporation) but it cannot be made to a purpose or to an object: so also, a trust may be created for the benefit of persons as cestuis que trust but not for a purpose or object unless the purpose or object be charitable. For a purpose or object cannot sue, but, if it be charitable, the Attorney-General can sue to enforce it." ...

I accept Mr. Blackburne's submission that the designation of the sole purpose of the gift makes it impossible to construe the gift as one falling into the first of Cross J's categories, even if that were otherwise possible. But I am not impressed by the argument that the gift shows an intention of continuity. Mr. Blackburne prays in aid *Re Macaulay's Estate* [1943] Ch 435n which is reported as a note to *Re Price* [1943] Ch 422, [1943] 2 All ER 505, where the gift was for the "maintenance and improvement of the Theosophical Lodge at Folkestone". The House of Lords held that it failed for perpetuity, the donee being a non-charitable body. But it is clear from the speeches of both Lord Buckmaster and Lord Tomlin that their Lordships derived the intention of continuity from the reference to "maintenance". Here it is quite evident that the association was to be free to spend the capital of the legacy. As Lord Buckmaster said in *Re Macaulay's Estate* at 436:

"In the first place it is clear that the mere fact that the beneficiary is an unincorporated society in no way affects the validity of the gift ... The real question is what is the actual purpose for which the gift is made. There is no perpetuity if the gift were for the individual members for their own benefit, but that, I think, is clearly not the meaning of this gift. Nor again is there a perpetuity if the society is at liberty in accordance with the terms of the gift, to spend both capital and income as they think fit."

Re Price itself is authority for the proposition that a gift to an unincorporated non-charitable association for objects upon which the association is at liberty to spend both capital and income will not fail for perpetuity, although the actual conclusion in that case has been criticised—the point that the trust there (the carrying on of the teachings of Rudolf Steiner) was a "purpose trust" and thus unenforceable on that ground was not argued.[4] It does not seem to me, therefore, that in the present case there is a valid ground for saying that the gift fails for perpetuity.

But that is not the end of the matter. If the gift were to the association simpliciter, it would, I think, clearly fall within the second category of Cross J's categories. At first sight, however, there appears to be a difficulty in arguing that the gift is to members of the association subject to their contractual rights inter se when there is a specific direction or limitation sought to be imposed upon those contractual rights as to the manner in which the subject matter of the gift is to be dealt with. This, says Mr. Blackburne, is a pure "purpose trust" and is invalid on that ground, quite apart from any question of perpetuity. I am not sure, however, that it is sufficient merely to demonstrate that a trust is a "purpose" trust. With the greatest deference, I wonder whether the dichotomy postulated in the passage which I have referred to in the judgment of the Board in *Leahy's* case [1959] AC 457 at 478, [1959] 2 All ER 300 at 307 is not an over-simplification. Indeed, I am not convinced that it was intended as an exhaustive statement or to do more than indicate the broad division of trusts into those where there are ascertainable beneficiaries (whether for particular purposes or not) and trusts where there are none ...

There would seem to me to be, as a matter of common sense, a clear distinction between the case where a purpose is prescribed which is clearly intended for the benefit of ascertained or ascertainable beneficiaries, particularly where those beneficiaries have the power to make the capital their own, and the case where no beneficiary at all is intended (for instance, a memorial to a favourite pet) or where the beneficiaries are unascertainable: as in the case, for instance, of *Re Price* [1943] Ch 422, [1943] 2 All ER 505. If a valid gift may be made to an unincorporated body as a simple accretion to the

---

4 See *Re Grant's Will Trusts* [1980] 1 WLR 360 at 369, [1979] 3 All ER 359 at 367, p. 105 ante.

funds which are the subject matter of the contract which the members have made inter se—and *Neville Estates Ltd v Madden* [1962] Ch 832, [1961] 3 All ER 769, and *Re Recher's Will Trusts* [1972] Ch 526, [1971] 3 All ER 401, p. 99, ante, show that it may—I do not really see why such a gift, which specifies a purpose which is within the powers of the association and of which the members of the association are the beneficiaries, should fail. Why are not the beneficiaries able to enforce the trust or, indeed, in the exercise of their contractual rights, to terminate the trust for their own benefit? Where the donee association is itself the beneficiary of the prescribed purpose, there seems to me to be the strongest argument in common sense for saying that the gift should be construed as an absolute one within the second category—the more so where, if the purpose is carried out, the members can by appropriate action vest the resulting property in themselves, for here the trustees and the beneficiaries are the same persons.

Is such a distinction as I have suggested borne out by the authorities? The answer is, I think, "not in terms," until recently. But the cases appear to me to be at least consistent with this. For instance *Re Clarke* [1901] 2 Ch 110 (the case of the Corps of Commissionaires); *Re Drummond* [1914] 2 Ch 90 (the case of the Old Bradfordians)[5] and *Re Taylor* [1940] Ch 481, [1940] 2 All ER 637 (the case of the Midland Bank Staff Association), in all of which the testator had prescribed purposes for which the gifts were to be used, and in all of which the gifts were upheld, were all cases where there were ascertainable beneficiaries; whereas in *Re Wood* [1949] Ch 498, [1949] 1 All ER 1100, and *Leahy's* case (where the gifts failed) there were none. *Re Price* is perhaps out of line, because there was no ascertained beneficiary and yet Cohen J was prepared to uphold the gift even on the supposition that (contrary to his own conclusion) the purpose was non-charitable. But, as I have mentioned, the point about the trust being a purpose trust was not argued before him.

A striking case which seems to be not far from the present is *Re Turkington* [1937] 4 All ER 501, where the gift was to a masonic lodge "as a fund to build a suitable temple in Stafford". The members of the lodge being both the trustees and the beneficiaries of the temple, Luxmoore J construed the gift as an absolute one to the members of the lodge for the time being.

Directly in point is the more recent decision of Goff J in *Re Denley's Trust Deed* [1969] 1 Ch 373, [1968] 3 All ER 65, where the question arose as to the validity of a deed under which land was held by trustees as a sports ground:

> "primarily for the benefit of employees of [a particular company] and secondarily for the benefit of such other person or persons ... as the trustees may allow to use the same ... "

The latter provision was construed by Goff J as a power and not a trust. The same deed conferred on the employees a right to use and enjoy the land subject to regulations made by the trustees. Goff J held that the rule against enforceability of non-charitable "purpose or object" trusts was confined to those which were abstract or impersonal in nature where there was no beneficiary or cestui que trust. A trust which, though expressed as a purpose, was directly or indirectly for the benefit of an individual or individuals was valid provided that those individuals were ascertainable at any one time and the trust was not otherwise void for uncertainty. Goff J said at 382, at 69:

---

5 The reasons given for the decision were doubted by VINELOTT J in *Re Grant's Will Trusts* [1980] 1 WLR 360 at 369, [1979] 3 All ER 359 at 367.

"I think there may be a purpose or object trust, the carrying out of which would benefit an individual or individuals, where that benefit is so indirect or intangible or which is otherwise so framed as not to give those persons any locus standi to apply to the court to enforce the trust, in which case the beneficiary principle would, as it seems to me, apply to invalidate the trust, quite apart from any question of uncertainty or perpetuity. Such cases can be considered if and when they arise. The present is not, in my judgment, of that character, and it will be seen that clause 2 (d) of the trust deed expressly states that, subject to any rules and regulations made by the trustees, the employees of the company shall be entitled to the use and enjoyment of the land. Apart from this possible exception, in my judgment the beneficiary principle of *Re Astor's Settlement Trusts* [1952] Ch 534, [1952] 1 All ER 1067, which was approved in *Re Endacott* [1960] Ch 232, [1959] 3 All ER 562—see particularly by Harman LJ, at 250, at 570—is confined to purpose or object trusts which are abstract or impersonal. The objection is not that the trust is for a purpose or object per se, but that there is no beneficiary or cestui que trust.... Where, then, the trust, though expressed as a purpose, is directly or indirectly for the benefit of an individual or individuals, it seems to me that it is in general outside the mischief of the beneficiary principle."

I respectfully adopt this, as it seems to me to accord both with authority and with common sense.

If this is the right principle, then on which side of the line does the present case fall? Mr. Morritt has submitted in the course of his argument in favour of charity that the testator's express purpose "solely in the work of constructing the new buildings for the association" referred and could only refer to the youth centre project, which was the only project for the erection of buildings which was under consideration at the material time. If this is right, then the trust must, I think, fail, for it is quite clear that the project as ultimately conceived embraced not only the members of the association, but the whole Jewish community in Hull, and it would be difficult to argue that there was any ascertainable beneficiary. I do not, however, so construe the testator's intention. The evidence is that the testator knew the association's position and that he took a keen interest in it. I infer that he was kept informed of its current plans. The one thing that is quite clear from the minutes is that from 1965 right up to the testator's death there was great uncertainty about what was going to be done. There was a specific project for the purchase of a house in 1965. By early 1966 the youth centre was back in favour. By October 1966 it was being suggested that the association should stay where they were in their rented premises. The meeting of March 21 is, I think, very significant because it shows that they were again thinking in terms of their own exclusive building and that the patrons (of whom the testator was one) would donate the money when it was needed. At the date of the will, the association had rejected the youth centre plans and were contemplating again the purchase of premises of their own; and thereafter interest shifted to the community centre. I am unable to conclude that the testator had any specific building in mind; and, in my judgment, the reference to "the" buildings for the association means no more than whatever buildings the association may have or may choose to erect or acquire. The reference to improvements reflects, I think, the testator's contemplation that the association might purchase or might, at his death, already have purchased an existing structure which might require improvement or conversion, or even that they might, as had at one time been suggested, expend money in improving the premises which they rented from the Jewish Institute. The association was to have the legacy to spend in this way for the benefit of its members.

I have already said that, in my judgment, no question of perpetuity arises here, and accordingly the case appears to me to be one of the specification of a particular purpose for the benefit of ascertained beneficiaries, the members of the association for the time being. There is an additional factor. This is a case in which, under the constitution of the association, the members could, by the appropriate majority, alter their constitution so as to provide, if they wished, for the division of the association's assets among themselves. This has, I think, a significance. I have considered whether anything turns in this case upon the testator's direction that the legacy shall be used "solely" for one or other of the specified purposes. Mr. Rossdale has referred me to a number of cases where legacies have been bequeathed for particular purposes and in which the beneficiaries have been held entitled to override the purpose, even though expressed in mandatory terms.

Perhaps the most striking in the present context is *Re Bowes* [1896] 1 Ch 507, where money was directed to be laid out in the planting of trees on a settled estate. That was a "purpose" trust, but there were ascertainable beneficiaries, the owners for the time being of the estate; and North J held that the persons entitled to the settled estate were entitled to have the money whether or not it was laid out as directed by the testator....

I can see no reason why the same reasoning should not apply in the present case simply because the beneficiary is an unincorporated non-charitable association. I do not think the fact that the testator has directed the application "solely" for the specified purpose adds any legal force to the direction. The beneficiaries, the members of the association for the time being, are the persons who could enforce the purpose and they must, as it seems to me, be entitled not to enforce it or, indeed, to vary it.

Thus, it seems to me that whether one treats the gift as a "purpose" trust or as an absolute gift with a superadded direction or, on the analogy of *Re Turkington* [1937] 4 All ER 501 as a gift where the trustees and the beneficiaries are the same persons, all roads lead to the same conclusion.

In my judgment, the gift is a valid gift.[6]

v. Useless or Capricious Purposes

If there is a theory upon which purpose trusts are valid, will this cover trusts for every purpose? Or will there be exceptions for illegal, immoral, wasteful or useless purposes?

In **Brown v Burdett** (1882) 21 ChD 667, the testatrix devised a freehold house upon trust to block up all the rooms of the house[7], except four which

6 See *Re Grant's Will Trusts* [1980] 1 WLR 360, [1979] 3 All ER 359, p. 105, ante, where VINELOTT J held, as a second ground for his decision, that the gift was a trust for non-charitable purposes and therefore void for perpetuity; (1980) 43 MLR 459 (B. Green).
7 The method is described in some detail at pp. 668–670 of the report.

were to be set aside for a house-keeper and his wife for twenty years, and subject thereto upon trust for Richard Burdett for life and after his death to Thomas Baxter in fee. BACON V-C had no difficulty in holding that the provisions for blocking up the house were void. The whole judgment states: "I think I must 'unseal' this useless, undisposed of property. There will be a declaration that the house and premises were undisposed of by the will, for the term of twenty years from the testatrix's death."

The M'Caigs of Oban could not resist the attractions of posthumous greatness. John Stuart M'Caig provided in his will that the income of his whole estate should be used for the purpose of building statues of himself and his family and the building of "artistic towers" at prominent points on his estates. Miss Catherine M'Caig, who was his sister and also his heir, succeeded in having the trust set aside on the ground that, under Scots law, an heir can only be disinherited by a beneficial gift to someone else: **M'Caig v University of Glasgow** 1907 SC 231. On the question whether the doctrine of public policy would have destroyed the trust, Lord KYLLACHY said at 242:
"I have, I confess, much sympathy with that argument. For I consider that if it is not unlawful, it ought to be unlawful, to dedicate by testamentary disposition, for all time, or for a length of time, the whole income of a large estate—real and personal—to objects of no utility, private or public, objects which benefit nobody, and which have no other purpose or use than that of perpetuating at great cost, and in an absurd manner, the idiosyncracies of an eccentric testator. I doubt much whether a bequest of that character is a lawful exercise of the *testamenti factio*. Indeed, I suppose it would be hardly contended to be so if the purposes, say of the trust here, were to be slightly varied, and the trustees were, for instance, directed to lay the truster's estate waste, and to keep it so; or to turn the income of the estate into money, and throw the money yearly into the sea; or to expend income in annual or monthly funeral services in the testator's memory; or to expend it in discharging from prominent points upon the estate, salvoes of artillery upon the birthdays of the testator, and his brothers and sisters. Such purposes would hardly, I think, be alleged to be consistent with public policy; and I am by no means satisfied that the purposes which we have here before us are in a better position."

In her turn, Miss Catherine M'Caig provided in her will for the erection of eleven bronze statues of her parents and their nine children, each to cost not less than £1,000. This failed in **M'Caig's Trustees v Kirk-Session of United Free Church of Lismore** 1915 SC 426. Lord SALVESEN declared it void on grounds of public policy and said at 434:
"In the first place, I think it is so because it involves a sheer waste of money, and not the less so that the expenditure would give employment to a number of sculptors and workmen, for it must be assumed that their labour could be usefully employed in other ways. I think, further, that it would be a dangerous thing to support a bequest of this kind which can only gratify the vanity of testators, who have no claim to be immortalised, but who possess the means by which they can provide for more substantial monuments to themselves than many that are erected to famous persons by public subscription. A man may, of course, do with his money what he pleases while he is alive, but he is generally

restrained from wasteful expenditure by a desire to enjoy his property, or to accumulate it, during his lifetime. The actings of the two M'Caigs form an excellent illustration of this principle of human conduct. For many years they had apparently contemplated the erection of similar statues, but they could not bring themselves to part with the money during their own lifetimes ... The prospect of Scotland being dotted with monuments to obscure persons who happened to have amassed a sufficiency of means, and cumbered with trusts for the purposes of maintaining these monuments in all time coming, appears to me to be little less than appalling ... ''[8]

VI. Rule against Perpetuities

The rule against perpetuities may affect the duration as well as the commencement of purpose trusts. Thus, a purpose trust is void, not only if it fails to vest within the perpetuity period,[9] but also if, by its terms, the income or capital are required to be tied up for a time in excess of the perpetuity period.[10] The latter is the rule against excessive duration. It is not applicable to trusts for charitable purposes; the community interest is that charitable trusts should last for ever.

There seems to be no reason why purpose trusts should not be drafted so as to continue for the full period of lives in being plus 21 years. No English case, however, has upheld a purpose trust for more than 21 years.[11] The trust in *Re Astor's Settlement Trusts*[12] was designed to continue for lives in being plus 21 years; and, though the trust failed, no objection was taken on this point; indeed, counsel pointed out that "such a trust could continue for 100 years". If the trust provides for its continuation "so long as the law allows", or for some similar period, it will be valid for 21 years.[13] In *Re Dean*,[14] a trust for the maintenance of the testator's horses and hounds "for the period of 50 years if any should so long live" was upheld, presumably on the ground that it must end within 21 years. Certainly, the animals could not be used as lives in being: as MEREDITH J said in *Re Kelly*:[15] "There can be no doubt that 'lives' means lives of human beings, not animals or trees in California."

---

8 See also *Aitken's Trustees v Aitken* 1927 SC 374 (massive bronze equestrian statue of artistic merit); *Mackintosh's Judicial Factor v Lord Advocate* 1935 SC 406 (erection of vault); *Lindsay's Executor v Forsyth* 1940 SC 568 (£1,000 on trust to provide a weekly supply of fresh flowers on the grave of my mother and my own).
9 Before 1964, the rule was that it was void unless it must vest, if it vest at all, within the period; Perpetuities and Accumulations Act 1964. See generally H & M, pp. 371–374; Cheshire and Burn, *Modern Law of Real Property* (15th edn, 1994), pp. 286, et seq.; Megarry & Wade, *Law of Real Property* (5th edn, 1984), pp. 238 et seq.; Morris & Leach, *Rule against Perpetuities* (2nd edn, 1962 and Supplement); Maudsley, *Modern Law of Perpetuities* (1979).
10 See *Re Lipinski's Will Trusts* [1976] Ch 235, [1977] 1 All ER 33, p. 319, ante.
11 See *Re Khoo Cheng Teow* [1932] Straits Settlement Reports 226, infra.
12 [1952] Ch 534, [1952] 1 All ER 1067, p. 312, ante.
13 *Re Hooper* [1932] 1 Ch 38, p. 310, ante.
14 (1889) 41 ChD 552, p. 309, ante.
15 [1932] IR 255 at 260–261; Maudsley and Burn, *Land Law: Cases and Materials* (6th edn), p. 356.

In **Re Khoo Cheng Teow** [1932] Straits Settlement Reports 226, a Chinese testator devised No. 56 Church Street, Singapore to the British Malaya Trustee and Executor Co. Ltd. as trustees, with a direction to let the premises and to apply the net rents "in the performance of the religious ceremonies according to the custom of the Chinese called *Sin Chew* to perpetuate my memory". The period specified was "during the lives of Her Majesty Queen Victoria and her descendants now living and during the lives and life of the survivors and survivor of them and during the period of twenty-one years after the death of such survivor." TERRELL J, in declaring the trust valid, held that the rule against perpetuities applied to the Straits Settlements, and that the gift for Sin Chew ceremonies was not charitable, and said at 228: "It is clear that the devise does not offend the rule against perpetuities".

PERPETUITIES AND ACCUMULATIONS ACT 1964

15. Short title, interpretation and extent.—(4) Nothing in this Act shall affect the operation of the rule of law rendering void for remoteness certain dispositions under which property is limited to be applied for purposes other than the benefit of any person or class of persons in cases where the property may be so applied after the end of the perpetuity period.

Hanbury & Maudsley: *Modern Equity* (11th edn, 1981), p. 439

"The provision is susceptible of two constructions. First, the orthodox view, that it means, in short, that the Act is to make no change to the law relating to the duration of purpose trusts. On the other hand, under the terms of the section, what is unaffected is the 'operation of the rule of law rendering void ... certain dispositions ... where the property may be so applied after the end of the perpetuity period.' In short, a purpose trust still remains void if it may last beyond the perpetuity period. But, what is the perpetuity period? Section 1 says that the perpetuity period 'applicable to [a] disposition ... shall be of a duration equal to such number of years not exceeding eighty as is specified ... in the instrument.'

So construed, the subsection means that purpose trusts existing beyond the perpetuity period are void; but the perpetuity period may be either the usual period measured by life in being plus 21 years; or a period of years not exceeding 80 as may be specified in the instrument; and it would seem therefore that a testator could specify such a period. Eighty years is of course longer than many would think to be the ideal period. But it is an improvement on royal lives; and it is submitted that the second interpretation is open to the courts, and that it should be applied."[16]

NEW ZEALAND PERPETUITIES ACT 1964[17]

20. Rule against inalienability.—(1) Except as provided in subsection (2) of this section, nothing in this Act shall affect the operation of the rule of law

---

16 Maudsley, *Modern Law of Perpetuities* (1978), pp. 177–178; (1965) 29 Conv (NS) 165 (J.A. Andrews). Cf. H & M (14th edn), p. 374 which prefers the orthodox view; Underhill, p. 178.
17 See also Victoria Perpetuities and Accumulations Act 1968, s. 18.

rendering non-charitable purpose trusts void for remoteness in cases where the trust property may be applied for the purposes of the trusts after the end of the perpetuity period.

(2) If any such trust is not otherwise void, the provision of section 8 of this Act [Necessity to wait and see] shall apply to it, and the property subject to the trust may be applied for the purposes of the trust during the perpetuity period, but not thereafter.

VII. How to Achieve a Non-Charitable Purpose

A. By Incorporation

Report of the Goodman Committee on Charity Law and Voluntary Organisations 1976, para. 24.

"Purpose Trusts
24. The point made about those trusts whose purposes are held not to be charitable because they fail on grounds of legal uncertainty is one of substance. The legal argument is that these trusts fail because the beneficiaries are a fluctuating class and therefore uncertain, or because their objects are uncertain. This can in fact be obviated by careful drafting through the medium of a company. A simple and common course is to form a company limited by guarantee with the desired non-charitable objects and this will be perfectly valid. The long-standing invalidity of non-charitable purpose trusts now serves as a trap for the unwary and has led to much litigation. A will which provides money for the fulfilment of a purpose the testator has in mind may be attacked by disappointed beneficiaries on the grounds that the gift is void. The question before the court is whether the declared purpose is charitable, or whether the testator has declared a charitable intent. If so, the gift is valid but, if not, void. This involves the trustees in much expense and if the gift is held invalid, the clearly stated intentions of the testator will have been defeated. Since the testator's object could have been achieved by adopting a different technique, there seems no purpose in maintaining the rule as it stands. Accordingly, our recommendation is that further consideration be given by government to the validation of such 'purpose trusts'."

B. By Legislation

ONTARIO PERPETUITIES ACT 1966[18]

16. Specific non-charitable trusts.—(1) A trust for a specific non-charitable purpose that creates no enforceable equitable interest in a specific person shall be construed as a power to appoint the income or the capital, as the case may be, and, unless the trust is created for an illegal purpose or a purpose contrary to public policy, the trust is valid so long as and to the extent that it is exercised either by the original trustee or his successor, within a period of twenty-one years, notwithstanding that the limitation creating the trust manifested an

18 See [1967] ASCL, pp. 378–380 (J.D. Davies).

intention, either expressly or by implication, that the trust should or might continue for a period in excess of that period, but, in the case of such a trust that is expressed to be of perpetual duration, the court may declare the limitation to be void if the court is of opinion that by so doing the result would more closely approximate the intention of the creator of the trust than the period of validity provided by this section.

(2) To the extent that the income or capital of a trust for a specific non-charitable purpose is not fully expended within a period of twenty-one years, or within any annual or other recurring period within which the limitation creating the trust provided for the expenditure of all or a specified portion of the income or the capital, the person or persons, or his or their successors, who would have been entitled to the property comprised in the trust if the trust had been invalid from the time of its creation, are entitled to such unexpended income or capital.[19]

C. Construe or Draft as a Power

American Law Institute: Restatement of the Law of Trusts (2d) §124

"Where the owner of property transfers it in trust for a specific non-charitable purpose, and there is no definite or definitely ascertainable beneficiary designated, no enforceable trust is created; but the transferee has power to apply the property to the designated purpose, unless such application is authorized or directed to be made beyond the period of the rule against perpetuities, or the purpose is capricious."

Although the courts have ruled[20] that "a valid power is not to be spelt out of an invalid trust", there appears to be no objection to drafting the purpose as a power instead of as a trust, i.e., by giving the property not to a trustee upon trust, but to the ultimate beneficiary subject to a power in a third party to apply the property for the non-charitable purpose for the perpetuity period.

Morris and Leach: *Rule Against Perpetuities* (2nd edn, 1965), p. 320

"No case decides that a power to apply property towards a specific non-charitable purpose must be treated as void. Such authority as exists suggests that it may well be valid. It is now clear that the law recognises the validity of powers of appointment which cannot be described as either general or special powers. Moreover, a power to appoint to such charitable institutions (including two named unincorporated associations) as the donee should nominate has been upheld, notwithstanding that the two named institutions were not charitable.[1] It is not a long step from this to hold that a power to

---

19 See also New Zealand Perpetuities Act 1964, s. 20; Belize Trusts Act 1992.
20 *IRC v Broadway Cottages Trust* [1955] Ch 20, [1954] 3 All ER 120, per JENKINS LJ. See also *Re Shaw* [1957] 1 WLR 729 at 746, [1957] 1 All ER 745 at 759, p. 317, ante, where HARMAN J followed the Court of Appeal with apparent reluctance; Scott, *Trusts* §§ 124 where this question is asked: "Should the failure of the duty drag down with it the power?".
1 *Re Douglas* (1887) 35 ChD 472; (1902) 15 HLR 67 (J.C. Gray); (1958) 4 UWALR 235 at p. 260 (L.A. Sheridan).

appoint for a specific non-charitable purpose is valid, even though a trust for such a purpose is void ... It may well be, therefore, that if testators or settlors express their wishes in the form of a power and not in the form of a trust, they may be able to accomplish their non-charitable purposes. No question of enforcement would arise, for to the extent that the power was not exercised, there would be a resulting trust for the persons entitled in default of appointment. Of course the power, being more analogous to a special than to a general power of appointment, would have to be exercisable only within the limits of perpetuity. But subject to this, the only question would be one of policy. It is not desirable that eccentric or vainglorious testators should be allowed to give large sums of money for the purpose of erecting costly monuments to themselves or to seal up their houses for twenty years or to order their property to be thrown into the sea. But is there anything contrary to public policy in permitting testators to indulge such human desires as to bequeath a moderate sum of money for the maintenance of their pet animals or the repair of their graves within the period of perpetuities? The present authors conclude that there is not.''

D. Draft as a Gift to a Group of Persons, such as an Unincorporated Association, and Not for Purposes Only

Re Recher's Will Trusts [1972] Ch 526, [1971] 3 All ER 401, p. 99, ante.
Re Denley's Trust Deed [1969] 1 Ch 373, [1968] 3 All ER 65, p. 322, ante.
Re Lipinski's Will Trusts [1976] Ch 235, [1977] 1 All ER 33, p. 319, ante.

E. Conveyancing Device

If there is a gift to one charity followed by a gift over to another charity upon an event which may happen outside the perpetuity period, the gift over to the second charity is valid. Advantage was taken of this rule to achieve a non-charitable purpose in *Re Tyler*.[2]

RE TYLER
[1891] 3 Ch 252 (CA, LINDLEY, FRY and LOPES LJJ)

Sir James Tyler, who died in 1890, bequeathed £42,000 Russian 5 per cent. stock to the trustees of the London Missionary Society and committed to their care and charge the keys of his family vault at Highgate Cemetery "the same to be kept in good repair, and name legible, and to rebuild when it shall require: failing to comply with this request, the money to go to the Blue Coat School, Newgate Street, London".

Held. The gift and gift over were valid.

FRY LJ: In this case the testator has given a sum of money to one charity with a gift over to another charity upon the happening of a certain event. That event, no doubt, is such as to create an inducement or motive on the part of the first donee, the *London Missionary Society*, to repair the family tomb of the testator. Inasmuch as both the donees of this fund, the first donee and the second, are charitable bodies, and are created for the purposes of charity, the rule of law against perpetuities has nothing whatever to do with the donees.

2 See also [1987] Conv 415 (P. St. J. Smart).

Does the rule of law against perpetuities create any objection to the nature of the condition? If the testator had required the first donee, the *London Missionary Society*, to apply any portions of the fund towards the repair of the family tomb, that would, in all probability, at any rate, to the extent of the sum required, have been void as a perpetuity which was not charity. But he has done nothing of the sort. He has given the first donee no power to apply any part of the money. He has only created a condition that the sum shall go over to *Christ's Hospital* if the *London Missionary Society* do not keep the tomb in repair. Keeping the tomb in repair is not an illegal object. If it were, the condition tending to bring about an illegal act would itself be illegal; but to repair the tomb is a perfectly lawful thing. All that can be said is that it is not lawful to tie up property for that purpose. But the rule of law against perpetuities applies to property, not motives; and I know of no rule which says that you may not try to enforce a condition creating a perpetual inducement to do a thing which is lawful. That is this case.

Then it is said by Mr. *Buckley*, "But if the gift had been to the *London Missionary Society* simply, they might have spent the money; by imposing this condition you require them to keep that invested, because it may have to go over at any moment to *Christ's Hospital*." What is the harm of that? Being a charity, and not affected by the rule against perpetuities, whether you direct them to keep the money invested in plain words, or whether you impose the condition which renders it necessary to keep it invested, seems to me the same thing and to be equally harmless, and not affected by the law against perpetuities.

I think the learned Judge in the Court below was quite right, and that this appeal must be dismissed.

In **Re Dalziel** [1943] Ch 277, [1943] 2 All ER 656, a testatrix gave £20,000 to the governors of St. Bartholomew's Hospital "subject to the condition that they shall use the income" for the upkeep and repair of the mausoleum and surrounding garden in Highgate Cemetery, with a gift over to another charity "subject to the above conditions" if they failed to do so.

COHEN J held that both the gift and the gift over were void, and said at 282, at 660:

"Lady Dalziel has not only given power, but directed the trustees to apply part of this gift or, if necessary, the whole of this gift in the maintenance of the tomb".

QUESTIONS

1. "There are difficulties in reconciling *Re Denley's Trust Deed* with dicta in *Leahy v A-G for New South Wales*" (Pettit, p. 51, n. 15). Should we now add *Re Recher's Will Trusts* [1972] Ch 526, [1971] 3 All ER 401, p. 99, ante?

   What would you say of the following purpose in *Re Astor's Settlement Trusts* [1952] Ch 534, [1952] 1 All ER 1067. "7. The establishment ... or support of any charitable public or benevolent schemes ... for or in connection with (a) the improvement of newspapers or journalism or (b) the relief or benefit of persons (or the families or dependents of persons) actually or formerly engaged in journalism or in the newspaper business."?

2. Consider *Oppenheim v Tobacco Securities Trust Co Ltd* [1951] AC 297, [1951] 1 All ER 31 , p. 385, post. Must such a gift be void, whether as a charitable or a non-charitable purpose trust?

3. How would you advise a client who wanted to provide for the application of money to encourage the sport of fishing?

4. Assuming that purpose trusts are enforceable upon one theory or another, do you consider that it will be necessary to determine a dividing line between those which are useful to the public and those which are useless or harmful? How would you draw such a line? Is the theory of *Brown v Burdett* (1882) 21 ChD 667, p. 324, ante, adequate? Before finally reaching a conclusion on this, read the material on the definition of legal charity (pp. 339, et seq., post), and observe the difficulties that have been experienced in drawing a line between "charitable purposes" and "useful" or "benevolent purposes". Royal Commission on the Taxation of Profits and Income, paras. 168–175 (1955) Cmd 9474; (1956) 72 LQR 187 (G. Cross); *Dingle v Turner* [1972] AC 601, [1972] 1 All ER 878, p. 356, post, per Lord CROSS OF CHELSEA.

5. Consider the perpetuity problem raised in *Re Dean* (1889) 41 ChD 552, p. 309, ante. How would this be affected by the Perpetuities and Accumulations Act 1964? Morris and Leach, p. 322; *Re Kelly* [1932] IR 255; *Re Searight's Estate*, 95 NE 2d 779, 87 Ohio App 417, (1950); Scott, *Cases on Trusts* (5th edn), p. 351; H & M, pp. 359–360, 371–374; Maudsley, *Modern Law of Perpetuities*, pp. 166–178.

Part Two. Charities

9. Charitable Trusts[1]

---

1 H & M, pp. 380–465; K & S, pp. 169–188; P & M, pp. 296–359; Pettit, pp. 216–315; Riddall, pp. 91–144; Snell, pp. 143–174. See generally *Tudor on Charities* (8th edn, 1995), which contains the text of the Charities Act 1993; Cairns, *Charities: Law and Practice* (2nd edn 1993); Cracknell, *Charities Law and Practice* (1994); Cracknell, *Charities* (4th edn 1996); Sheridan and Keeton, *The Modern Law of Charities* (4th edn, 1992); Picarda, *The Law and Practice Relating to Charities* (2nd edn, 1995); *Williams on Wills* (7th edn 1995), pp. 887–915; Nightingale, *Charities* (1973); Whitaker, *The Foundations* (1974); Chesterman, *Charities, Trusts and Social Welfare* (1979); Gladstone, *Charity Law and Social Justice* (1982); Phillips, *Charitable Status* (2nd edn, 1982). See also the Annual Reports of the Charity Commissioners for England and Wales; the Decisions of the Charity Commissioners (which began in 1993); and their Publications (listed in Annual Report for 1993 Appx A); the Annual Charity and Appeals Supplements of the Solicitor's Journal and the Annual Charities Review and Christmas Appeals Supplements of the New Law Journal; and the Charity Law & Practice Review (which began in 1992).

For important reviews of the law and practice, see 10th Report from the Expenditure Committee of the House of Commons: Charity Commissioners and their Accountability 1974–1975, vol. I, Report, vol. II, Minutes of Evidence and Appendices; the Goodman Committee Report on Charity Law and Voluntary Organisations (1976); Annual Report of Charity Commissioners for 1976, paras. 7–14; (1976) 39 MLR 77 (M. Partington); (1976) 5 Anglo-American Law Review 153 (L.A. Sheridan); the Wolfenden Committee Report on the Future of Voluntary Organisations; 16th Report from the Committee of Public Accounts 1987–88, Monitoring and Control of Charities in England and Wales (1988); The Woodfield Committee Report on Efficiency Scrutiny of the Supervision of Charities (1987); Charities: A Framework for the Future (1989) Cm 694 (White Paper by the Secretary of State for the Home Department). On the history of charity, see Jones, *History of the Law of Charity* (1969).

For developments in Europe, see Annual Report for 1989, paras. 16–25; 1991, paras. 17–22 (European Associations); 1992, paras. 16–25.

I. Introduction

A trust by the terms of which the income is to be applied exclusively for charitable purposes is treated with special favour by the law. Such a trust is valid, although it is a purpose trust; the Attorney-General is charged with the duty of enforcing it in the name of the Crown, although, as we shall see, the general administration of charitable trusts is carried out by the Charity Commissioners.[2] It may exist perpetually; indeed, many trusts currently in existence were founded some 500 years ago. It is no objection that the trust fails to provide with reasonable certainty what are the charitable purposes for which the money must be applied; certainty of intention to apply it for charitable purposes is sufficient. If there is doubt as to the particular charitable purposes, the Charity Commissioners or the court, or in some cases the Crown, will prepare a scheme. And, last but by no means least, a charitable trust is free from liability to income tax[3] and corporation tax,[4] and from capital gains tax,[5] and stamp duty;[6] it is also entitled to 80 per cent relief in respect of non-domestic rates; further relief being at the discretion of the local authority.[7] A

---

2 Charities Act 1993, ss. 1 (4), 33, p. 501 post. Any person interested in the charity may take legal proceedings under s. 33; *Brooks v Richardson* [1986] 1 WLR 385, [1986] 1 All ER 952; *Bradshaw v University College of Wales, Aberystwyth* [1988] 1 WLR 190, [1987] 3 All ER 200; *Re Hampton Fuel Allotment Charity* [1989] Ch 484; [1988] 2 All ER 761; *Haslemere Estates Ltd v Baker* [1982] 1 WLR 1109, [1982] 3 All ER 525; *Gunning v Buckfast Abbey Trustees Registered* (1994) Times, 9 June (fee-paying parents at preparatory school run as part of a charitable trust); (1995) 9 Trust Law International 13. (R. Nolan).

3 ICTA 1988, s. 505 as amended by FA 1996, s. 146. Profits from a trade are not exempt, unless the trade is exercised in the course of the actual carrying out of a primary purpose of the charity, or the work in connection with the trade is mainly carried out by beneficiaries of the charity: ibid., s. 505 (1) (e). See *IRC v Educational Grants Association Ltd* [1967] Ch 993, [1967] 2 All ER 893; *IRC v Helen Slater Charitable Trust Ltd* [1982] Ch 49, [1981] 3 All ER 98; Annual Report for 1981, paras. 5–12 (trading by or on behalf of charities); FA 1986, s. 30 (1); Inland Revenue Booklet CS2 (Trading by Charities); (1995/96) 3 CL & PR 149 (J. Kessler).

4 ICTA 1988, ss. 505 (1), 506 (1); similarly for a charitable corporation: s. 9 (4).

5 TCGA 1992, s. 256.

6 FA 1982, s. 129, exempting all instruments conveying, transferring or leasing assets to charities, as from March 22, 1982.

7 Local Government Finance Act 1988, s. 47.

charity is liable to value added tax on all goods and services purchased.[8] There are reliefs given to donors of single cash gifts ("Gift Aid")[9] to charity; gifts of any amount in favour of a charity are exempt from capital gains tax,[10] and from inheritance tax.[11] There are also tax advantages both to a charity and to a donor in respect of annual covenants which are made for a period exceeding three years.[12] There are similar advantages to a company which gives to charity,[13] and to its employees who give under a company payroll deduction scheme.[14] This is a formidable list of fiscal advantages.[15] The more significant it becomes, the more insistent is the Revenue to challenge particular claims to relief.[16]

The attitude of the courts to gifts for charitable purposes has varied. In 1908, Lord LOREBURN said: "Now there is no better rule than that a benignant construction will be placed upon charitable bequests."[17] But since the 1940s when taxation became penal the courts have been astute to restrict the scope of charity especially by emphasising the requirement of public benefit.[18] In 1982, however, Lord HAILSHAM OF ST. MARYLEBONE referred to Lord Loreburn's dictum and said "In construing trust deeds the intention of which is to set up a charitable trust, and in others too, where it can be claimed that there is an ambiguity, a benignant construction should be given if possible."[19]

8 VATA 1994, s. 30. There is no general relief from value added tax for charities, but there are some specific reliefs: the zero rate is applied to the supply of some goods *to* charities in prescribed circumstances (for example, medical or scientific equipment solely for use in medical research, diagnosis or treatment), and to the supply *by* certain charities (for example, those established primarily for the relief of distress or for the protection or benefit of animals) of some, but not all, donated goods: Sch 8, Group 15. Certain services are exempt from VAT, for example, the provision of education and health and welfare services: ss. 8, 31, Sch 9; [1995–96] 3 CL & PR 37 (J. Warburton).

9 The gift must exceed £250: FA 1990, s. 25 (1), (2) (*a*) (*g*), as amended by FA 1993, s. 67 (2).

10 TCGA 1992, s. 257.

11 IHTA 1984, ss. 23 (gift by individual during lifetime or on death); 76 (property passing from a discretionary trust). Transfers from a charitable trust are also exempt, s. 58 (1) (*a*).

12 ICTA 1988, s. 660 (3); FA 1989, s. 59. The charity can claim the basic income tax deducted by the donor, and the donor can claim relief against higher rate income tax: ICTA 1988, s. 683; FA 1989, s. 56. On the background, see [1986] BTR 101 (D. Stopforth); and, generally, [1989] Conv 321 (D. Morris).

13 Ibid ss. 505 (1), 506 (1). The charity can claim the corporation tax deducted by the company. A company may also make a deductible, one-off payment, not exceeding 3 per cent of its dividends.

14 Ibid, s. 202. Such donations (up to £900 per annum: FA 1989, s. 58 as amended by FA 1993, s. 68) are deductible expenses of the donor and are paid gross to an approved charitable agent to pay to the charity: Charitable Deductions (Approved Schemes) Regs 1986 (SI 2211).

15 For a review and criticism of fiscal advantages, see Goodman Committee, chap. 5; [1972] BTR 346 (G.N. Glover). See generally Tudor, chap. 8; Picarda, chaps. 48, 49; see Inland Revenue Statistics 1995: 10.1 (Covenants to charities) gross amount for 1994/1995 £875m; cost of tax relief £245m: 10.2 (Gift aid) amount donated in 1994 £329.3m; tax repayments £109.9m; 10.4 (Payroll gift scheme) gross amount deducted £16m; cost of tax relief £4m.

16 Measures were introduced by FA 1986, ss. 31, 33 to prevent abuse of tax advantages; see also ICTA 1988, ss. 339, 427, 505, 506, 683.

17 *Weir v Crum-Brown* [1908] AC 162 at 167.

18 The Royal Commission on the Taxation of Profits and Income (1955) Cmnd. 9474, recommended (paras. 168–175) that some charitable trusts should be subject to tax liability, and others, measured by a stricter definition, should be entitled to the present exemptions. See the different views expressed in the House of Lords on this question in *Dingle v Turner* [1972] AC 601, [1972] 1 All ER 878, p. 356, post.

19 *IRC v McMullen* [1981] AC 1 at 14, [1980] 1 All ER 884 at 890, p. 374, post; *Re Koeppler Will Trusts* [1986] Ch 423 at 438, [1985] 2 All ER 869 at 878, p. 372, post; *Re Hetherington* [1990] Ch 1, [1989] 2 All ER 129, p. 406 post; *Guild v IRC* [1992] 2 AC 310, [1992] 2 All ER 10, p. 423 post.

Similarly, the Government's intention is to encourage the liberality of the donor, and within the present financial restraints, the development of the voluntary sector as a whole.

A study of the material in this Part will indicate the many problems which are faced in keeping this area of the law in line with modern developments. Much of the work previously done by voluntary bodies is now undertaken by the Government. It is no small problem to make the law of charity adjust to the pattern of the modern welfare state.

The role of the Charity Commissioners is all important and all pervasive. They produce annually a Report on their activities, and, since 1993, a separate Report of their important Decisions. Their functions are set out in the Charities Act 1993, which consolidates the Charities Acts 1960 and 1992.[19a] The 1992 Act has had a profound effect on the work of the Commission.[19b] Its main thrust is to increase the powers of the Commission to protect charities and the obligations of charities to account to the public. The effect of the Act is to increase the duty of trustees to prepare and submit annual accounts, to disqualify certain persons from trusteeship, to control fundraising and public charitable collections, and to provide more effective means of enforcement.

Annual Report of the Charity Commissioners for England and Wales, 1989, para. 7.

"7. We are appointed under the Charities Act 1960 principally to further the work of charities by giving advice and information and investigating and checking abuses. We function in three different ways. First, we act in a pro-judicial capacity on behalf of the Courts. Our decisions can be challenged, even by Government, only in the Courts. Secondly, we act on behalf of Government, fulfilling the will of Parliament in respect of charities. Thirdly, we act as managers of a business operation. Our functions in relation to the first two, accordingly, are:

On behalf of the Courts
- to determine whether trusts or institutions are charitable in law and so define charitable status;
- to make schemes and orders in order that charitable property may be more effectively used;
- to give consent to transactions proposed by charity trustees where they are in the interests of a charity;
- to give advice to charity trustees to make the administration of their charity more effective;
- to act where there is evidence of maladministration or misapplication of the property of a charity to correct the abuse and to protect or recover the property.
- to secure the vesting of the property of a charity in the charity trustees, the Official Custodian or other person authorised to hold it in order to protect it from loss;
- to give directions and to make orders for obtaining accounts and other information relating to a charity to enable us to carry out our functions.

19a See chap 11 infra.
19b Annual Report for 1992, paras 3–18; (1992) CL & PR 15 (H. Picarda).

On behalf of Parliament
- to maintain an up-to-date and accurate Register of Charities available to the public;
- to receive charity accounts and make them available to the public in order to enhance the accountability of trustees; to provide information about the resources of charities and how they are used; and to enable a charity's affairs to be examined;
- to monitor registered charities to discover cause for investigation;
- to investigate misapplication, maladministration and other forms of abuse and take or recommend remedial action;
- to stimulate and promote reviews of local charities to secure the best use of charitable resources for the benefit of the community;
- to promote the sound administration of charities by trustees.''

II. Definition of Charity[20]

With so much at stake, one would hope for a precise definition of charity. Instead, the courts have sought a satisfactory one for nearly 400 years. The recommendation of the Nathan Committee in 1952 that a new statutory definition of charity should be enacted was not implemented.[1] In 1976 the Goodman Committee recommended that the categories of charities should be re-stated in simple and modern language replacing that of the Charitable Uses Act of 1601 and extending these to include objects now considered to be within the scope of charity.[2] In 1980 and 1989, however, the Government decided not to promote a legislative definition.[3] The scope of charity today is based upon a large number of decisions, themselves based on the spirit and intendment of the preamble to the Charitable Uses Act 1601. These decisions may be either those of the courts or those of the Charity Commissioners on an application for registration under the Charities Act 1993.[4]

A. The Preamble to the Charitable Uses Act 1601

43 Eliz. I, c. 4: The Preamble
WHEREAS Lands, Tenements, Rents, Annuities, Profits, Hereditaments, Goods, Chattels, Money and Stocks of Money, have been heretofore given, limited, appointed and assigned, as well by the Queen's most excellent Majesty, and her most noble Progenitors, as by sundry other well disposed Persons; some for

---

20 H & M, pp. 388–391; K & S, pp. 170–173; S & K, pp. 1–63; P & M, pp. 301–304; Pettit, pp. 226–230; Riddall, pp. 91–97; Snell, pp. 143–146; Tudor, pp. 1–8; Picarda, pp. 3–11. See also (1945) 61 LQR 268 (J. Brunyate); (1956) 72 LQR 187 (G. Cross).
1 Report of the Committee on the Law and Practice relating to Charitable Trusts (1952 Cmd. 8710), paras. 120–140. See also SACHS LJ in *Incorporated Council of Law Reporting for England and Wales v A-G* [1972] Ch 73 at 94, [1971] 3 All ER 1029 at 1041 ("Any statutory definition might well merely produce a fresh spate of litigation and provide a set of undesirable artificial distinctions"); Annual Report for 1970, para. 25; 1973, paras. 1–3.
2 Page 16; p. 342, post. See also the House of Commons Report, Vol. 1, paras. 24–34; Vol. II, pp. 13, 23–25, 48– 56, 67, 116–117, 149, 155–156, 172–175, 287; Annual Report for 1973, paras. 2–5.
3 White Paper, paras 2.7–2.17.
4 Charities Act 1993, s. 3; p. 503, post.

Relief of aged, impotent and poor People, some for Maintenance of sick and maimed Soldiers and Mariners, Schools of Learning, Free Schools, and Scholars in Universities, some for Repair of Bridges, Ports, Havens, Causways, Churches, Sea-Banks and Highways, some for Education and Preferment of Orphans, some for or towards Relief, Stock or Maintenance for Houses of Correction, some for Marriages of poor Maids, some for Supportation, Aid and Help of young Tradesmen, Handicraftsmen and Persons decayed, and others for Relief or Redemption of Prisoners or Captives, and for Aid or Ease of any poor Inhabitants concerning Payments of Fifteens,[5] setting out of Soldiers and other Taxes; which Lands, Tenements, Rents, Annuities, Profits, Hereditaments, Goods, Chattels, Money and Stocks of Money, nevertheless have not been employed according to the charitable Intent of the givers and Founders thereof, by reason of Frauds, Breaches of Trust, and Negligence in those that should pay, deliver and employ the same: For Redress and Remedy whereof, Be it enacted ... ''

Tudor on Charities (6th edn, 1967) p. 2.

"The Charitable Uses Act, 1601[6] will usually be referred to in this work as 'the Statute of Elizabeth I'. The Statute of Elizabeth I was not directed so much to the definition of charity as to the correction of abuses which had grown up in the administration of trusts of a charitable nature. But the Court of Chancery used the preamble to the statute in order to simplify its task of determining what purposes were charitable and what were not. The preamble to the statute contained a comprehensive list of objects which in 1601 were recognised as charitable. The court never regarded the list as exhaustive. It treated the objects enumerated in the preamble as particular instance to which additions might properly be made from time to time. It became the practice of the court to refer to the preamble as a sort of index or chart[7] in order to determine whether or not a given purpose was charitable. That which began as a rule of practice became in course of time a rule of law, and in 1805 Sir William Grant MR was able to declare that 'those purposes are charitable which that Statute enumerates or which by analogies are deemed within its spirit and intendment.'[8] But objects which are neither enumerated in the preamble nor by analogy deemed to be within its spirit and intendment are not charitable, even though such objects are beneficial to the public.''[9]

---

5 A tax on movable property originating in the twelfth century and last heard of in the reign of James I. See I Bl Com. 309; Jowitt, *Dictionary of English Law* (1976) Vol. I, p. 789.
6 43 Eliz. I, c. 4.
7 *Income Tax Special Purposes Comrs v Pemsel* [1891] AC 531 at 581, per Lord MACNAGHTEN.
8 *Morice v Bishop of Durham* (1804) 9 Ves 399 at 405.
9 *Gilmour v Coats* [1949] AC 426 at 443, [1949] 1 All ER 848 at 852, per Viscount SIMONDS; *A-G v National Provincial and Union Bank of England* [1924] AC 262 at 265, per Viscount CAVE LC; *Houston v Burns* [1918] AC 337; *Re Macduff* [1896] 2 Ch 451 at 466, per LINDLEY LJ; *Dunne v Byrne* [1912] AC 407 at 411, per Lord MACNAGHTEN; *Farley v Westminster Bank Ltd* [1939] AC 430, [1939] 3 All ER 491. This is only a selection from among the many cases that might have been cited.

In **Commissioners for Special Purposes of Income Tax v Pemsel** [1891] AC 531, Lord MACNAGHTEN summarised the scope of charity[10] at 583:

"No doubt the popular meaning of the words 'charity' and 'charitable' does not coincide with their legal meaning;[11] and no doubt it is easy enough to collect from the books a few decisions which seem to push the doctrine of the court to the extreme, and to present a contrast between the two meanings in an aspect almost ludicrous. But still it is difficult to fix the point of divergence, and no one as yet has succeeded in defining the popular meaning of the word 'charity'.... How far then, it may be asked, does the popular meaning of the word 'charity' correspond with its legal meaning? 'Charity' in its legal sense comprises four principal divisions: trusts for the relief of poverty; trusts for the advancement of education; trusts for the advancement of religion; and trusts for other purposes beneficial to the community, not falling under any of the preceding heads."

The preamble to 43 Eliz. I, c. 4, was repealed by s. 38 (1)[12] of the Charities Act 1960; however, for a trust to be charitable, its purposes must still be within the spirit and intendment of the preamble. In **Scottish Burial Reform and Cremation Society v Glasgow Corpn** [1968] AC 138, [1967] 3 All ER 215, Lord WILBERFORCE spoke of the legal test of charitable purposes at 154, at 223:

"On this subject, the law of England, though no doubt not very satisfactory and in need of rationalisation, is tolerably clear. The purposes in question, to be charitable, must be shown to be for the benefit of the public, or the community, in a sense or manner within the intendment of the preamble to the statute 43 Eliz. I, c. 4. The latter requirement does not mean quite what it says; for it is now accepted that what must be regarded is not the wording of the preamble itself, but the effect of decisions given by the courts as to its scope, decisions which have endeavoured to keep the law as to charities moving according as new social needs arise or old ones become obsolete or satisfied. Lord Macnaghten's grouping of the heads of recognised charity in *Pemsel's* case[13] is one that has proved to be of value and there are many problems which it solves. But three things may be said about it, which its author would surely not have denied: first that, since it is a classification of convenience, there may well be purposes which do not fit neatly into one or other of the headings; secondly, that the words used must not be given the force of a statute to be construed; and thirdly, that the law of charity is a moving subject which may well have evolved even since 1891."[14]

---

10 The classification originated in the argument of Sir Samuel Romilly in *Morice v Bishop of Durham* (1805) 10 Ves 522 at 523; *Ashfield Municipal Council v Joyce* [1978] AC 122.
11 "The words 'charity' and 'charitable' bear, for the purposes of English law and equity, meanings totally different from the senses in which they are used in ordinary educated speech, or, for instance, in the Authorised Version of the Bible"; *IRC v McMullen* [1981] AC 1 at 15, [1980] 1 All ER 884 at 890, per Lord HAILSHAM OF ST. MARYLEBONE.
12 Itself repealed as spent by Education Act 1973, Sch. 2, Part I. See also Charities Act 1993, ss. 96 and 97.
13 [1891] AC 531 at 583.
14 See also Lord REID at 146, at 218 and Lord UPJOHN at 153, at 221, p. 411, post; and RUSSELL LJ in *Incorporated Council of Law Reporting for England and Wales v A-G* [1972] Ch 73 at 88–89, [1971] 3 All ER 1029 at 1035, p. 434, post.

Section III of this chapter sets out the detail of trusts which fall within each of Lord MACNAGHTEN's four principal divisions,[15] and Section III of chapter 11 gives the numbers and scope of charities now being registered by the Charity Commissioners under the Charities Act 1993.[16]

B. Criteria for Charitable Status

For a trust to be charitable it must not only be within the spirit and intendment of the preamble to the Act of 1601; it must also satisfy the requirement of public benefit.[17] It will be seen that each of the four heads of Lord MACNAGHTEN's classification involves two elements; that of benefit, and that of public benefit. There is no need to prove that the relief of poverty, the advancement of education, or the advancement of religion are beneficial. They are. The question of proving that the purposes of a trust are beneficial arises only under the fourth head. A trust for the advancement of education, or advancement of religion among a selected few, is not charitable. The problem is to determine the proper test for the identification of the public; or that part of the public which the law requires to be benefited.

This requirement of public benefit will be illustrated in the context of each of the four heads. It varies from head to head. The variation is most marked in the context of trusts for the relief of poverty.

Report of the Goodman Committee: Charity Law and Voluntary Organisations (1976), paras. 16–17, 21–22, 26–29, 32.[18]

"Importance of Charitable Status

16. One of the questions to which we have given a great deal of attention is whether there is a better way of defining the scope and ambit of charity but before we can come to that we have to consider whether the result of the cases is satisfactory; whether there should be amendments in detail; or whether the whole concept is wrong and charity should either be narrowed or expanded in some more fundamental way....

17. On the one hand, we had evidence suggesting that the scope of charities should be restricted to what is said to be its meaning as generally understood in its ordinary sense. In short, that it should be restricted to the relief of the poor and of people suffering from deprivation of one sort or another. On the

---

15 P. 345. There are many charitable purposes which overlap; for example, a gift for "the preparation of poor students for the Ministry" might come under all four of Lord MACNAGHTEN's divisions: H & M, p. 388, n. 71.

16 Pp. 508–511, post.

17 H & M, pp. 419–430; K & S, p. 170; S & K, pp. 16– 55; P & M, pp. 305–311; Pettit, pp. 252–260; Riddall, pp. 114–122; Snell, pp. 152–154; Tudor, pp. 5–7; Picarda, pp. 16–28. (1953) 31 Can BR 537 (G.H.L. Fridman); (1956) 72 LQR 187 (G. Cross); (1958) 21 MLR 138 (P.S. Atiyah); [1947] CLJ 63 (G.H. Jones); (1975) 39 Conv (NS) 183 (S. Plowright); (1976) 27 NILQ 198 (J.C. Brady); (1977) 40 MLR 397 (N.P. Gravells); (1983) 36 CLP 241 (H. Cohen); [1989] Conv 28 (S. Bright); (1990) 64 ALJ 404 (P.L. Hemphill). Goodman Report, chap. 2 (Benefit to the "Community"), chap. 3 ("Benefit" to the Community).

18 See also House of Commons Report (1975) vol. I, paras. 24–62, which proposes that the head "Beneficial to the Community" should be made the governing criterion in all cases. Nightingale, *Charities*, pp. 34–68.

other hand, we have had evidence suggesting that the benefits accorded to charities should be extended to other voluntary bodies which have not so far been considered to come at all within the ambit of charities. Such bodies include pressure groups and, in fact, any voluntary organisation, political or otherwise. We do not agree with either of these views and we feel that at the outset we should make clear our reasons.

21. There are many fields where the control which tends to go with state assistance can be unwelcome and this applies especially to the arts and provision for cultural and recreational facilities. Charity is increasingly moving into these fields and this is a development which in our opinion is to be welcomed.

Should the Concept of Charity be Expanded?

22. But then comes the question where is it to stop? Parallel to the pressure to restrict the ambit of charity, there is also the desire to extend it and to afford to all 'Non-Profit Distributing Organisations' (NPDOs) the privileges afforded to charities.[19] There would have to be stringent provisions to avoid abuse but otherwise the objects and activities of the NPDO would be irrelevant. Thus professional bodies, political parties and pressure groups of all sorts could be accorded the privileges now confined to charities.... While, therefore, we believe that the ambit of charity should remain flexible and capable of growth (and as a corollary that some objects may with time cease to be charitable), we think that the existing concept should remain despite the difficulties of definition.

Criteria for Charitable Status

26. We have now reached the position that the scope of charity should not be restricted (except perhaps in so far as objects which once were accepted as charitable may have in the course of time ceased to have the relevant characteristics of charity); that it should continue its natural process of development, but that it should not include all voluntary activities. How then can we distinguish charitable objects from other objects? Is it possible to frame the definition which will neatly include every object which ought to be regarded as charitable and as neatly exclude everything which ought not to be so regarded, or can we at least point to the general criteria which should govern the decision whether an object is charitable or not and leave it to the Charity Commissioners and the courts to develop the concept as they have done in the past, or is there any other way?

Benefit to the Community

27. It is clear that there must be a desire to benefit the community but many things which are far removed from charity may benefit the community. For instance, a highly successful commercial venture, generating exports and providing massive employment is of immense benefit to the community but it is not charitable. Conversely, the importance of the tax factors to charities has led some to suggest that one should first consider what purposes or activities should be subsidised and to define charity to conform to the answer so found.

19 This approach was advocated by the Charity Law Reform Committee. See a similar rejection in the House of Common Report, vol. I, paras. 31–32, vol. II, pp. 48 et seq.

To argue thus turns the argument upside down. If the field open for tax benefits is undefined, it follows that any purpose which some may consider deserving of subsidy would qualify to be regarded as charitable. But the government may choose to subsidise certain types of industry and lame ducks and public utilities which cannot be run at a profit and although these might in 1601, when they were provided, if at all, by private enterprise have been regarded as charitable, they cannot now be so regarded. It would seem therefore that the concept of charity must be confined to an object to benefit the community in certain particular ways, such as relief of distress, or deprivation, and, in its more modern manifestations, the improvement of the quality of life in relation to the arts, recreation, amenities and our national heritage.

Altruism

28. Although altruism is not definable in legal terms it is nevertheless an important element in our social thinking which makes for a better quality of life. Generally speaking, it may be said that charity and the private profit of the donor are mutually exclusive and it is for this reason that at a later part in this report we have suggested that gifts to relatives or to employees of the donor even for the relief of poverty should no longer be regarded as charitable. . . .

Definition of Charity

29. Given these two criteria of benefit to the community and altruism, the decision in particular cases is at present left to the Charity Commissioners and the court, who refer to the preamble to the Act of 1601 as summarised by Lord Macnaghten in the Pemsel case and to as many of the hundreds of decided cases as they may feel to be relevant to the case before them. There has never been a definition of charity and many people believe that the time has come to formulate one. Others point out that to define is to confine believing the very flexibility of the law in relation to charities is, and should continue to be, its strength. They emphasise the difficulty of finding a definition in sufficiently wide terms to encompass all that is now considered charitable, or may in the future be so considered and nothing else. There has been much concern too that if any new definition were adopted, the entire body of case law established over the centuries would cease to be relevant. On the other hand, it is said that the cases have established law which is unsatisfactory in that it is out of tune with modern modes of thought and social needs and that it is inflexible . . . We do not believe that it is possible to formulate a definition of this sort, and we are comforted by the fact that the same conclusion was reached in the debates leading to the passing of the 1960 Act. For instance, in relation to the element of public benefit, there are a large number of cases which consider the degree of public benefit required and the nature of that public benefit whether direct or indirect. We do not think that all these cases should be swept aside, nor would it be possible without a complete codification to incorporate them in a statute. What we have done in the succeeding chapters is to consider some of the fields in which the existing case law is the subject of criticism and to suggest a number of amendments of a specific nature which could be made.

Categories of Charity

32. We have also given particular consideration to the question whether a greater degree of certainty can be introduced in relation to the categories of

objects which should qualify as charitable. The preamble to the Act of 1601 is written in language inappropriate to contemporary concepts and it has led, and will lead, to mental gymnastics if it is to encompass within its terms the many forms of human endeavour now or hereafter deserving to fall within the scope of charity, while excluding those which should lie outside. What we suggest therefore would be beneficial would be to produce an updated version of the preamble to the Act of 1601 and we have therefore produced a list, in general terms, of objects deemed to be charitable (see Appendix 1).[20] It is based upon the Pemsel classification extended by references in relation to the fourth head to objects which are now considered to be within the scope of charity. It is, we hope, formulated in modern and simple language. We place particular emphasis on ensuring the continued flexibility of the law in this respect and propose that the formulation should be such as not to close the categories of charity and thus crystallise and prevent the future development of the scope of charity. As it would be made clear that this new classification is an updated version of the old classification, we do not think that the existing case law would become irrelevant."[1]

The Tenth Report from the Expenditure Committee of the House of Commons recommended, in 1975, as follows:
"34. We recommend, therefore, that legislation should be introduced whereby all Charities should be required to satisfy the test of purposes beneficial to the community. In the case of those Charities formerly admitted under one of the other heads, namely, the relief of poverty, the advancement of education and the advancement of religion, they should continue to qualify only if they also satisfy the main criterion. We do not believe such a change would affect the great majority of Charities in any way; but we do believe it would act as a check to abuse at the fringe."

III. The Four Heads of Charity

A. The Relief of Aged, Impotent and Poor People[2]

i. Disjunctive Construction

It is not necessary that the trust should be for the relief of persons in all three categories. Any one category will do. But the trust must be within the spirit and intendment of the Preamble, and it must be for the relief of such persons, and not merely for their benefit.

---

20 Which is too long for inclusion here.
1 See also the Minority Report, pp. 143 et seq.
2 H & M, pp. 391–393, 408–409, 420–422; K & S, p. 176; S & K, pp. 140–175; P & M, pp. 309–310, 311–313; Pettit, pp. 230–232, 258–259; Riddall, pp. 98–100, 116; Snell, pp. 146–147, 154; Tudor, pp. 20–39; Picarda, pp. 29–39; Goodman Report, paras. 45 (Self-Help Organisations), 55– 59 (Poverty Prevention).

(a) Aged

JOSEPH ROWNTREE MEMORIAL TRUST HOUSING ASSOCIATION LTD v ATTORNEY-GENERAL[3]

[1983] Ch 159, [1983] 1 All ER 288 (ChD, PETER GIBSON J)

A charitable housing association wished to build small self-contained dwellings for sale to elderly people on long leases in consideration of a capital payment. Five schemes were designed to provide accommodation to meet the disabilities and requirements of the elderly. All applicants were required to be 65 if male, and 60 if female, to be able to pay the service charge, to lead an independent life and to be in need of the type of accommodation provided.

The schemes were based on the National Federation of Housing Associations' standard scheme called "The Leasehold Scheme for the Elderly." They differed in detail. In one scheme, the tenant would pay a premium of 70 per cent of the cost of the premises, the remaining 30 per cent being met by Housing Association Grant under the Housing Act 1980. On death the lease was assignable to the tenant's spouse or relative if living at the premises when the tenant died. Failing such assignment, or if the tenant became incapable, the lease would revert to the Association, and the tenant or his estate would receive 70 per cent of the then value of the property.

The question was whether the schemes were charitable.

Held (reversing the Charity Commissioners). Valid charitable schemes for the aged.

PETER GIBSON J: I hope I summarise the objections of the Charity Commissioners fairly as being the following: (1) the schemes provide for the aged only by way of bargain on a contractual basis rather than by way of bounty. (2) The benefits provided are not capable of being withdrawn at any time if the beneficiary subsequently ceases to qualify. (3) The schemes are for the benefit of private individuals, not for a charitable class. (4) The schemes are a commercial enterprise capable of producing profit for the beneficiary.

Before I deal with these objections it is appropriate to consider the scope of the charitable purpose which the plaintiffs claim the scheme carries out, that is to say in the words of the preamble to the Statute of Elizabeth I (1601) "the relief of aged persons." That purpose is indeed part of the very first set of charitable purposes contained in the preamble: "the relief of aged, impotent and poor people." Looking at those words without going to authority and attempting to give them their natural meaning, I would have thought that two inferences therefrom were tolerably clear. First, the words "aged, impotent and poor" must be read disjunctively. It would be as absurd to require that the aged must be impotent or poor as it would be to require the impotent to be aged or poor, or the poor to be aged or impotent. There will no doubt be many cases where the objects of charity prove to have two or more of the three qualities at the same time. Second, essential to the charitable purpose is that it should relieve aged, impotent and poor people. The word "relief" implies that the persons in question have a need attributable to their condition as aged, impotent or poor persons which requires alleviating, and which those persons could not alleviate, or would find difficulty in alleviating, themselves from their own resources. The word "relief" is not synonymous with "benefit."

---

3 (1983) 46 MLR 782 (R. Nobles); [1983] All ER Rev 356 (P.J. Clarke). Joseph Rowntree was the Quaker philanthropist and cocoa manufacturer. On charitable housing associations and shared ownership (DIYSO Schemes), see Annual Report for 1993, paras. 98–102.

Those inferences are in substance what both Mr. Nugee for the plaintiffs and Mr. McCall for the Attorney-General submit are the true principles governing the charitable purpose of the relief of aged persons. Mr. Nugee stresses that any benefit provided must be related to the needs of the aged. Thus a gift of money to the aged millionaires of Mayfair would not relieve a need of theirs as aged persons.[4] Mr. McCall similarly emphasises that to relieve a need of the aged attributable to their age would be charitable only if the means employed are appropriate to the need. He also points out that an element of public benefit must be found if the purpose is to be charitable. I turn then to authority to see if there is anything that compels a different conclusion.

[His Lordship referred to *Re Lucas* [1922] 2 Ch 52 (bequest to the oldest respectable inhabitants of Gunville of the amount of 5s per week); *Re Glyn* (1950) 66 (pt 2) TLR 510 (bequest for building cottages for old women of the working classes of the age of 60 years or upwards[5]); *Re Bradbury* [1950] 2 All ER 1150n (bequest to pay sums for the maintenance of an aged person or persons in a nursing home approved by my trustees); *Re Robinson* [1951] Ch 198, [1950] 2 All ER 1148 (bequest to the old people over 65 years of Hazel Slade near Hednesford to be given as my trustees think best); *Re Cottam* [1955] 1 WLR 1299, [1955] 3 All ER 704 (gift to provide flats for persons over 65 to be let at economic rents[6]); *Re Lewis* [1955] Ch 104, [1954] 3 All ER 257 (gift to 10 blind girls and 10 blind boys, Tottenham residents if possible, the sum of £100 each) and continued:]

In *Re Neal* (1966) 110 SJ 549, a testator provided a gift for the founding of a home for old persons. Further directions provided for fees to be charged sufficient to maintain the home with sufficient staff to run it and cover the costs of the trustees. Goff J, in a very briefly reported judgment, said that in order to conclude whether a trust was charitable or not it was not necessary to find in it an element of relief against poverty, but it was sufficient to find an intention to relieve aged persons. The form of the gift and directions were a provision for succouring and supplying such needs of old persons as they had because they were old persons. Therefore he held it was a charitable bequest.

[His Lordship referred to *Re Resch's Will Trusts* [1969] 1 AC 514, [1967] 3 All ER 915 and quoted from Lord WILBERFORCE at 542, 544, at 922, 923, cited p. 426, post, and continued:]

These authorities convincingly confirm the correctness of the proposition that the relief of the aged does not have to be relief for the aged poor. In other words the phrase "aged, impotent and poor people" in the preamble must be read disjunctively. The decisions in *Re Glyn, Re Bradbury, Re Robinson, Re Cottam* and *Re Lewis* give support to the view that it is a sufficient charitable purpose to benefit the aged, or the impotent, without more. But these are all decisions at first instance and with great respect to the judges who decided them they appear to me to pay no regard to the word "relief". I have no hesitation in preferring the approach adopted in *Re Neal* and *Re Resch's Will Trusts* that there must be a need which is to be relieved by the charitable gift, such need being attributable to the aged or impotent condition of the person to be benefited.

4 (1955) 75 LQR 12 (R.E. Megarry); (1958) 21 MLR at pp. 140–141 (P.S. Atiyah).
5 In *Re Wall* (1889) 42 ChD 510, the age of 50 years was accepted as a qualification for "aged".
6 *Re Payling's Will Trusts* [1969] 1 WLR 1595, [1969] 3 All ER 698, where BUCKLEY J upheld a gift of a house "to be used as a home for aged persons ... as Mansfield Corporation in their absolute discretion may decide". The accommodation was to be free, but the occupiers had to provide for their own maintenance. Cf. *Re Martin* (1977) 121 SJ 828; Times, 17 November.

My attention was drawn to Picarda, *The Law and Practice Relating to Charities* (1977), p. 79 where a similar approach is adopted by the author.

In any event in the present case, as I have indicated, the plaintiffs do not submit that the proposed schemes are charitable simply because they are for the benefit of the aged. The plaintiffs have identified a particular need for special housing to be provided for the elderly in the ways proposed and it seems to me that on any view of the matter that is a charitable purpose, unless the fundamental objections of the Charity Commissioners to which I have referred are correct. To these I now turn.

The first objection is, as I have stated, that the scheme makes provision for the aged on a contractual basis as a bargain rather than by way of bounty. This objection is sometimes expressed in the form that relief is charitable only where it is given by way of bounty and not by way of bargain: see *Halsbury's Laws of England*, 4th edn, vol. 5 (1974), para. 516. But as the editors recognise this does not mean that a gift cannot be charitable if it provides for the beneficiaries to contribute to the cost of the benefits they receive. There are numerous cases where beneficiaries only receive benefits from a charity by way of bargain. *Re Cottam* [1955] 1 WLR 1299, [1955] 3 All ER 704 and *Re Resch's Will Trusts* [1969] 1 AC 514, [1967] 3 All ER 915 provide examples. Another class of cases relates to fee-paying schools: see for example *Abbey Malvern Wells Ltd v Ministry of Local Government and Planning* [1951] Ch 728, [1951] 2 All ER 154. Another example relates to a gift for the provision of homes of rest for lady teachers at a rent: *Re Estlin* (1903) 89 LT 88. It is of course crucial in all these cases that the services provided by the gift are not provided for the private profit of the individuals providing the services.

The source of the statement that charity must be provided by way of bounty and not bargain is to be found in some remarks of Rowlatt J in *IRC v Society for the Relief of Widows and Orphans of Medical Men* (1926) 11 TC 1. This was a case relating to the statutory provisions allowing tax relief for income applicable to charitable purposes only of trusts or bodies established for charitable purposes only. Rowlatt J said, at 22:

> "It seems to me that when it is said that the relief of poverty is a charity within the meaning of the rule which we are discussing that does mean the relief of poverty by way of bounty; it does not mean the relief of poverty by way of bargain. A purely mutual society among very poor people whose dependants would quite clearly always be very poor would not, I think, be a charity; it would be a business arrangement as has been said in one of the cases, whereby contractual benefits accrued to people whose poverty makes them very much in need of them. That would not be a charity. I think, therefore, that the crux of this case is whether this is a case of that sort."

He went on to hold that the case before him was not that of a mutual society: the beneficiaries had no right to anything.

In my judgment Rowlatt J's remarks must be understood in their limited context. They are entirely appropriate in determining whether a mutual society conferring rights on members is charitable. If a housing association were a co-operative under which the persons requiring the dwellings provided by the housing association had by the association's constitution contractual rights to the dwellings, that would no doubt not be charitable, but that is quite different from bodies set up like the trust and the association. The applicants for dwellings under the schemes which I am considering would have no right to any dwelling when they apply. The fact that the benefit given to them is in the form of a contract is immaterial to the charitable purpose in making the benefit available. I see nothing in this objection of the Charity Commissioners.[7]

The second objection was that the schemes do not satisfy the requirement that the benefits they provide must be capable of being withdrawn at any time if the beneficiary ceases to qualify. No doubt charities will, so far as practical and compatible with the identified need which they seek to alleviate, try to secure that their housing stock becomes available if the circumstances of the persons occupying the premises change. But it does not seem to me to be an essential part of the charitable purpose to secure that this should always be so. The nature of some benefits may be such that it will endure for some time, if benefits in that form are required to meet the particular need that has been identified. Thus in *Re Monk* [1927] 2 Ch 197,[8] a testatrix set up a loan fund whereby loans for up to nine years were to be made available to the poor. This was held to be charitable. No doubt the circumstances of the borrower might change whilst the loan was outstanding. If the grant of a long-term leasehold interest with the concomitant security of tenure that such an interest would give to the elderly is necessary to meet the identified needs of the elderly then in my judgment that is no objection to such a grant. The plaintiffs have put in evidence that they oppose the inclusion in a lease of any provision entitling the plaintiffs to determine the lease in the event of a change in financial circumstances of the tenant. Their main reason—which to my mind is a cogent one—is the unsettling effect it could have on aged tenants. In any event the distinction between what prima facie is a short term letting and a long lease has been rendered somewhat illusory by statute. A charity may find it no less difficult to recover possession from weekly tenants whose circumstances have changed than it would to recover possession from a tenant under a long lease.

The third objection was that the schemes were for the benefit of private individuals and not for a charitable class. I cannot accept that. The schemes are for the benefit of a charitable class, that is to say the aged having certain needs requiring relief therefrom. The fact that, once the association and the trust have selected individuals to benefit from the housing, those individuals are identified private individuals does not seem to me to make the purpose in providing the housing a non-charitable one any more than a trust for the relief of poverty ceases to be a charitable purpose when individual poor recipients of bounty are selected.

The fourth objection was that the schemes were a commercial enterprise capable of producing a profit for the beneficiary. I have already discussed the cases which show that the charging of an economic consideration for a charitable service that is provided does not make the purpose in providing the service non-charitable, provided of course that no profits accrue to the provider of the service. It is true that a tenant under the schemes may recover more than he or she has put in, but that is at most incidental to the charitable purpose. It is not a primary objective. The profit—if it be right to call the increased value of the equity a profit as distinct from a mere increase avoiding the effects of inflation, as was intended—is not a profit at the expense of the

---

7 See (1990) 134 SJ 946 (R. Venables); [1991] Conv 419 (J. Warburton and D. Morris); [1993] 1 Ch Com Rep 18.

8 Annual Report for 1990, Appx A (*e*) (Garfield Property Trust, involving loans to assist in provision of accommodation for poor members of the Exclusive Brethren).

charity, and indeed it might be thought improper, if there be a profit, that it should accrue to the charity which has provided no capital and not to the tenant which has provided most if not all the capital. Again, I cannot see that this objection defeats the charitable character of the schemes.

[His Lordship considered the schemes and continued:]

In my judgment the trustees may provide accommodation in the form of small self-contained dwellings for aged persons in need of such accommodation by granting it to them in consideration of the payment to the trustees of the whole or a substantial part of the cost or market value of such dwellings in accordance with the schemes. The presence or absence of the following provisions is not essential to the charitable nature of the scheme, that is to say (1) the H.A.G. contribution; (2) the provision of warden services, provided that the accommodation is designed to meet the special needs of the elderly tenants; (3) the prohibition of any assignment except on the death of the tenant to his spouse or qualified member of the family or household; (4) the right of the landlords to determine the lease on the death of the tenant or on the tenant becoming incapable of managing his or her own affairs; (5) the right of the tenant to surrender the lease.

(b) Impotent

Tudor on Charities (8th edn, 1995), p. 26

"The word 'impotent' has never been defined by the Court, but it has been interpreted fairly liberally.[9] It is defined in the Oxford English Dictionary as meaning 'physically weak, without bodily strength; unable to use one's limbs; helpless, decrepit,' a definition sufficiently wide to cover not only those suffering from permanent disability, whether of body or mind, but those temporarily incapacitated by injury or illness, or in need of rest, and young children incapable of protecting themselves from the consequences of cruelty or neglect. The cases show that this definition, or something like it, has guided the Courts. Thus gifts for the benefit of the blind,[10] the sick and wounded,[11] including former enemies who have been wounded,[12] the prevention of cruelty to children,[13] and faith-healing,[14] have been held to be charitable.

9 See resettlement and rehabilitation, p. 97; care of children, p. 98, and Recreational Charities Act 1958, p. 112.
10 *Re Fraser* (1883) 22 Ch D 827; *Re Lewis* [1955] Ch 104, [1954] 3 All ER 257 and see *Re Elliott* (1910) 102 LT 528, 530; *Barber v Chudley* (1922) 128 LT 766; see also *Re Spence's Will Trusts* [1979] Ch 483, [1978] 3 All ER 92.
11 *Re Hillier* [1944] 1 All ER 480. The sick or wounded may be abroad: Annual Report for 1990, para. 32 (The Gdansk Hospice Fund).
12 *Re Robinson* [1931] 2 Ch 122 (Gift for disabled German Soldiers).
13 *Comrs for the Special Purposes of Income Tax v Pemsel* [1891] AC 531, 572. It may be that the prevention of cruelty to children is also charitable on another ground, namely, that such gifts are calculated to promote public morality by encouraging kindness, discouraging cruelty and stimulating humane sentiments for the benefit of mankind: see and compare *Re Wedgwood* [1915] 1 Ch 113; *Re Moss* [1949] 1 All ER 495, p. 415 post. In *Re Cole* [1958] Ch 877, [1958] 3 All ER 102, CA held by a majority (ROMER and ORMEROD LJJ, Lord EVERSHED MR dissenting), affirming the decision of HARMAN J, that a trust to apply the income derived from two freehold houses for the general benefit and general welfare of the children for the time being in a particular home maintained by a local authority was not charitable but they did not hold that the home was not a charity; applied in *Re Sahal's Will Trusts* [1958] 1 WLR 1243, [1958] 3 All ER 428.
14 *Re Kerin* (1966) Times, 24 May: GOFF J held that faith-healing was for the relief of impotent persons or for the advancement of religion or for both purposes; *Funnell v Stewart* [1996] 1 WLR 288.

Although in *Re Roadley*[15] a trust to apply income in payment of the expenses and maintenance of patients in a hospital was upheld on the ground that it was for the relief of persons who were both impotent and poor, it is now clear[16] that (given always the necessary element of public benefit) gifts for the establishment or support of hospitals and nursing homes are charitable as being for the relief of impotent persons who need not necessarily be poor. Furthermore, a gift to provide accommodation for relations coming from a distance to visit patients critically ill in hospital is charitable.[17]

Gifts for the establishment or support of homes of rest are also charitable. The term 'home of rest' connotes not primarily a home for persons who are old or worn out and so permanently in need of rest, but rather a convalescent home to which persons ordinarily actively employed in their various pursuits are enabled to retire."[18]

(c) Poor

Tudor on Charities (8th edn, 1995), p. 29

" 'Poor' is a relative term[19] and an individual need not be destitute in order to qualify as a poor person within the meaning of the preamble to the Statute of Charitable Uses 1601.[20] The Courts have never defined 'poor': its meaning has to be ascertained from the reported cases, which show that an individual is considered to be poor if he is in genuinely straitened circumstances and unable to maintain a very modest standard of living for himself and the persons (if any) dependent upon him."[1]

(1956) 72 LQR 187 at pp. 206–207 (G. Cross)
"Poverty ... is a vague word which has meant different things at different times and in different places ... "

In **Re Coulthurst** [1951] Ch 661, [1951] 1 All ER 774 Sir Raymond Evershed said at 665, at 776:
"It is quite clearly established that poverty does not mean destitution; it is a word of wide and somewhat indefinite import; it may not unfairly be

---

15 [1930] 1 Ch 524.
16 See *Re Adams* [1968] Ch 80, [1967] 3 All ER 285 (reversing in part [1967] 1 WLR 162, [1966] 3 All ER 825); *Re Resch's Will Trusts* [1969] 1 AC 514, [1967] 3 All ER 915, p. 426 post; see also *Liverpool and District Hospital for Diseases of the Heart v A-G* [1981] Ch 193, [1981] 1 All ER 994.
17 *Re Dean's Will Trusts* [1950] 1 All ER 882.
18 *Re White's Will Trusts* [1951] 1 All ER 528, 529. See also *IRC v Roberts Marine Mansions Trustees* (1927) 11 TC 425.
19 *Mary Clark Home Trustees v Anderson* [1904] 2 KB 645 at 655 per Channell J; *Re Clarke* [1923] 2 Ch 407 at 411, 412 per Romer J.
20 *Re Clarke* [1933] Ch 103 at 108 per Maugham J. See also (1956) 72 LQR 182, 206 (G. Cross).
1 *Mary Clark Home Trustees v Anderson*, supra; *Re Gardom* [1914] 1 Ch 662 (reversed, but not on this point, by the House of Lords (1915) 84 LJ Ch 749); *Shaw v Halifax Corpn* [1915] 2 KB 170; *Re Clarke* [1923] 2 Ch 407; *Re De Carteret*, supra. p. 353, post. See Annual Report for 1991, Appx A (*b*), reproducing CC leaflet on Charities for the Relief of the Poor, especially on assisting those who receive state benefit and on ways in which trustees can apply income for the relief of poverty.

paraphrased for present purposes as meaning persons who have to 'go short' in the ordinary acceptation of that term, due regard being had to their status in life, and so forth."

Tudor on Charities (8th edn, 1995), p. 30

"A charitable gift for the poor may be expressed in general and indefinite language,[2] or may be for the poor of a particular defined area (parish, town or other place),[3] or poor persons of a particular religious denomination attending a specified chapel or chapels,[4] or the poor of a particular regiment,[5] or families of men or women (not being commissioned) in the armed forces,[6] or a particular class of poor people, such as poor gentlewomen,[7] distressed gentlefolk,[8] or persons of moderate[9] or limited[10] means, who are not self-supporting,[11] or housekeepers,[12] or tradesmen of a particular kind,[13] or unsuccessful literary men,[14] or servants,[15] or 'poor struggling youths of merit',[16] or poor pious persons,[17] or poor emigrants,[18] or persons descended from residents of a named borough in a particular year needing assistance to

---

2 *A-G v Peacock* (1676) Finch 245 (for the good of poor people for ever); *A-G v Rance* (1728) cited in (1762) Amb 422; *Nash v Morley* (1842) 5 Beav 177; *Re Darling* [1896] 1 Ch 50 (to the poor and the service of God, following *Powerscourt v Powerscourt* (1824) 1 Mol 616).

3 *Woodford Inhabitants v Parkhurst* (1639) Duke 70; *A-G v Pearce* (1740) 2 Atk 87; *A-G v Clarke* (1762) Amb 422; *A-G v Exeter Corpn* (1826) 2 Russ 45, (1827) 3 Russ 395; *A-G v Wilkinson* (1839) 1 Beav 370; *A-G v Bovill* (1840) 1 Ph 762; *Salter v Farey* (1843) 7 Jur 831; *Re Lambeth Charities* (1853) 22 LJ Ch 959; *A-G v Blizard* (1855) 21 Beav 233; *Russell v Kellett* (1855) 3 Sm & G 264; *Re Lousada* (1887) 82 LT Jo 358 (London Poor); *Re St Alphage, London Wall* (1888) 59 LT 614; *Re Lucas* [1922] 2 Ch 52 (poor inhabitants of Gunville, a small town); *Re Monk* [1927] 2 Ch 197 (gift of income of a fund set aside out of residue to buy coal for distribution among poor and deserving inhabitants of a particular parish and to apply the rest of the residue, capital and income, in making loans of interest to poor and deserving inhabitants of that parish); *Re Roadley* [1930] 1 Ch 524 (poor of two named parishes). *Guinness Trust (London Fund) Founded 1890, Registered 1902 v West Ham Corpn* [1959] 1 WLR 233, [1959] 1 All ER 482; *Re Lepton's Charity* [1972] Ch 276, [1971] 1 All ER 799. The place may be abroad; *Re Niyazi's Will Trusts* [1978] 1 WLR 910, [1978] 3 All ER 785, p. 354 post (Famagusta).

4 *Re Wall* (1889) 42 ChD 510.

5 *Re Donald* [1909] 2 Ch 410.

6 *Soldiers', Sailors' and Airmen's Families Association v A-G* [1968] 1 WLR 313, [1968] 1 All ER 448n.

7 *A-G v Power* (1809) 1 Ball & B 145; *Mary Clark Home Trustees v Anderson* [1904] 2 KB 645; *Re Gardom* [1914] 1 Ch 662; *Shaw v Halifax Corpn* [1915] 2 KB 170.

8 *Re Young* [1951] Ch 344.

9 *Re Clarke* [1923] 2 Ch 407.

10 *Re De Carteret* [1933] Ch 103.

11 *Re Central Employment Bureau for Women and Students' Careers Association* [1942] 1 All ER 232.

12 *A-G v Pearce* (1740) 2 Akt 87. 'Housekeeper' is a word now used to denote a domestic servant who looks after the house of another, but in the case of old charities it sometimes means a person who is housebound, and sometimes a householder.

13 *Re White's Trusts* (1886) 33 ChD 449.

14 *Thompson v Thompson* (1844) 1 Coll 381 at 395.

15 *Reeve v A-G* (1843) 3 Hare 191; *Loscombe v Wintringham* (1850) 13 Beav 87.

16 *Milne's Executors v Aberdeen University Court* (1905) 7 F 642.

17 *Nash v Morley* (1842) 5 Beav 177.

18 *Barclay v Maskelyne* (1858) 32 LTOS 205. But a gift 'for emigration uses' is not charitable: see *Re Sidney* [1908] 1 Ch 488.

improve their condition in life by emigrating,[19] or inmates of a workhouse,[20] or patients in a hospital,[1] or debtors,[2] or fifty needy and deserving old men and fifty needy and deserving old women of a particular place,[3] or widows and orphans of poor clergymen,[4] or seamen of a particular port,[5] or victims of a particular disaster,[6] or widows and orphans of a particular parish,[7] or indigent bachelors and widowers 'who have shown sympathy with science',[8] or the relief of domestic distress."[9]

In **Re De Carteret** [1933] Ch 103, a trust, created by the will of a Bishop of Jamaica, provided for the payment of "annual allowances of forty pounds each to widows or spinsters in England whose income otherwise shall not be less than eighty or more than one hundred and twenty pounds per annum". Preference was to "be given to widows with young children dependent on them". This was held to be a valid charitable trust for the relief of poverty. It was no objection that there was a minimum income qualification for the persons to be benefited.[10] Emphasis was placed by MAUGHAM J on the fact that the preference was to be given to widows with young children dependent upon them. "I should have hesitated to hold that it was a good charitable gift had it merely been for 'widows and spinsters'; but I think that, in confining it, as I do, in effect, to widows with young children dependent on them, I am within the decisions to which I have referred."

In **Re Sanders' Will Trusts** [1954] Ch 265, [1954] 1 All ER 667, a codicil gave money "to provide or assist in providing dwellings for the working classes and their families resident in the area of Pembroke Dock ... or within a radius of five miles therefrom ... "

19 *Re Tree* [1945] Ch 325, [1945] 2 All ER 65 (Hastings). For the grounds on which EVERSHED J distinguished *Re Compton* [1945] Ch 123, [1945] 1 All ER 198; see [1945] Ch 325 at 328–332, [1945] 2 All ER 65 at 68–70; and see (1956) 72 LQR 182 (G. Cross), at p. 190, n. 8. In *Re Tree* the element of poverty was present. It is doubtful whether the decision could have been justified if that element had been absent: see *Davies v Perpetual Trustee Co Ltd* [1959] AC 439 at 456, [1959] 2 All ER 128 at 132.
20 *A-G v Vint* (1850) 3 De G & Sm 704.
 1 *Reading Corpn v Lane* (1601) Toth 32; see also *Re Roadley* [1930] 1 Ch 524.
 2 *A-G v Painter-Stainers' Co* (1788) 2 Cox Eq Cas 51; *A-G v Ironmongers' Co* (1834) 2 My & K 576.
 3 *Re Reed* (1893) 10 TLR 87; and see also *Re Wall* (1889) 42 ChD 510.
 4 *Waldo v Caley* (1809) 16 Ves 206; and see *Re Friend of the Clergy's Charters* [1921] 1 Ch 409, where this was assumed without argument.
 5 *Powell v A-G* (1817) 3 Mer 48.
 6 *Pease v Pattinson* (1886) 32 ChD 154; *Re Hartley Colliery Accident Relief Fund* (1908) 102 LT 165n; *Cross v Lloyd-Greame* (1909) 102 LT 163 (where there were only six victims); *Re North Devon and West Somerset Relief Fund Trusts* [1953] 1 WLR 1260, [1953] 2 All ER 1032 (flood disaster). It is suggested, however, that disaster relief funds fall more naturally under the fourth head of charities, as those relieved need not necessarily be poor. The emphasis of such a fund is need for 'relief'.
 7 *A-G v Comber* (1824) 2 Sim & St 93; *Russell v Kellett* (1855) 3 Sm & G 264.
 8 *Weir v Crum-Brown* [1908] AC 162 (on appeal from the Court of Session).
 9 *Kendall v Granger* (1842) 5 Beav 300 at 303.
10 Following *Spiller v Maude* (1881) 32 ChD 158n ("incapacitated actors"); *Re Lacy* [1899] 2 Ch 149; *Re Gardom* [1914] 1 Ch 662 (where the gift was "for the maintenance of a temporary house of residence for ladies of limited means"); cf. *Over Seventies Housing Association v Westminter City Council* [1974] RA 247.

HARMAN J held that the gift was not a charitable trust because the expression "the working classes" did not indicate poor persons.[11]

In **Re Niyazi's Will Trusts** [1978] 1 WLR 910, [1978] 3 All ER 785, the testator gave his residuary estate worth about £15,000 for "the construction of or as a contribution towards the cost of a working men's hostel" to be created in Famagusta, Cyprus. MEGARRY V-C held that this was a charitable trust and said at 915, at 789:

"The word 'hostel' has to my mind a strong flavour of a building which provides somewhat modest accommodation for those who have some temporary need for it and are willing to accept accommodation of that standard in order to meet the need. When 'hostel' is prefixed by the expression 'working mens,' then the further restriction is introduced of the hostel being intended for those with a relatively low income who work for their living, especially as manual workers.[12] The need, in other words, is to be the need of working men, and not of students or battered wives or anything else. Furthermore, the need will not be the need of the better paid working men who can afford something superior to mere hostel accommodation, but the need of the lower end of the financial scale of working men, who cannot compete for the better accommodation but have to content themselves with the economies and shortcomings of hostel life. It seems to me that the word 'hostel' in this case is significantly different from the word 'dwellings' in *Re Sanders' Will Trusts* [1954] Ch 265, [1954] 1 All ER 667, a word which is appropriate to ordinary houses in which the well-to-do may live, as well as the relatively poor.

Has the expression 'working mens hostel' a sufficient connotation of poverty in it to satisfy the requirements of charity? On any footing the case is desperately near the border-line, and I have hesitated in reaching my conclusion. On the whole, however, for the reasons that I have been discussing, I think that the trust is charitable, though by no great margin. This view is in my judgment supported by two further considerations. First, there is the amount of the trust fund, which in 1969 was a little under £15,000. I think one is entitled to assume that a testator has at least some idea of the probable value of his estate. The money is given for the purpose 'of the construction of or as a contribution towards the cost of the construction of a working mens hostel.' £15,000 will not go very far in such a project . . .

The other consideration is that of the state of housing in Famagusta. Where the trust is to erect a building in a particular area, I think it is legitimate, in construing the trust, to have some regard to the physical conditions existing in that area. Quite apart from any question of the size of the gift, I think that a trust to erect a hostel in a slum or in an area of acute housing need may have to be construed differently from a trust to erect a hostel in an area of housing affluence or plenty. Where there is a grave housing shortage, it is plain that the

---

11 The case was settled on appeal; (1954) Times, July 22. Some homes for working classes have been registered as charities, where there were other factors which indicated a requirement of poverty: Annual Report for 1965, Appendix C, para. I. A. 9; Goodman Report, paras. 75–78 (Housing).

12 On the meaning of "working classes", see *Westminster City Council v Duke of Westminster* [1991] 4 All ER 136 (reversed (1992) 24 HLR 572).

poor are likely to suffer more than the prosperous, and that the provision of a 'working mens hostel' is likely to help the poor and not the rich. In the result, then, I hold that the trust is charitable.''

In **Biscoe v Jackson** (1887) 35 ChD 460, the testator gave a sum of money out of his residuary estate to be applied in the establishment of a soup kitchen[13] for the parish of Shoreditch and of a cottage hospital adjoining thereto. This was held to be a charitable trust for the relief of poverty.

In **Re Coulthurst** [1951] Ch 661, [1951] 1 All ER 774, a testator provided a fund to be applied "to or for the benefit of such ... of the ... widows and orphaned children of deceased officers and deceased ex-officers of Coutts & Co ... as the bank shall in its absolute discretion consider by reason of his her or their financial circumstances to be most deserving of such assistance''. This was held by the Court of Appeal to create a valid trust for the relief of poverty.[14]

In **Re Gwyon** [1930] 1 Ch 255, the testator established a fund, to be called "Gwyon's Boys Clothing Foundation''. The income of the fund was to be applied in providing knickers ("loose fitting breeches, gathered in at the knee"[15]) for boys of Farnham and district, with certain qualifications expressed by Eve J in the extract below. No preference was indicated in favour of children of poor parents. In holding that the trust was not charitable, but void, Eve J said at 260:

"The question is whether the testator has effectively created such a charity as he contemplated, a charity in the legal sense of the word. Is the object of his benefaction the relief of poverty, are the gifts for the benefit of the poor and needy? I do not think they are. Apart from residential and age qualifications, the only conditions imposed on a recipient are (1) that he shall not belong to or be supported by any charitable institution, (2) that neither he nor his parents shall be in receipt of parochial relief, (3) that he shall not be black,[16] (4) that on a second or subsequent application he shall not have disposed of any garment received within the then preceding year from the Foundation and that when he comes for a new pair of knickers or trousers the legend 'Gwyon's Present' shall still be decipherable on the waistband of his old ones.

13 Mrs Beeton's recipe for "Benevolent Soup, suitable for a Soup Kitchen, at any time, average cost 2d per pint," included "half an ox cheek; four onions, two turnips, one cabbage, a bunch of herbs, one and a half pints of lentils, 10 quarts of water. Simmer for four hours." See Times for 2 January 1800, 5 January and 7 January 1985.
14 On the element of public benefit in the definition of the class to be benefited, cf. *Re Compton* [1945] Ch 123, [1945] 1 All ER 198; *Oppenheim v Tobacco Securities Trust Co Ltd* [1951] AC 297, [1951] 1 All ER 31, p. 385, post; *Gibson v South American Stores (Gath and Chaves) Ltd* [1950] Ch 177, [1949] 2 All ER 985, (necessitous and deserving employees, ex-employees and their dependents); *Dingle v Turner* [1972] AC 601, [1972] 1 All ER 878, p. 356, post; *Re Denison* (1974) 42 DLR (3d) 652 ("relief of impoverished or indigent members of the Law Society of Upper Canada and of their wives, widows and children" held charitable).
15 *Shorter Oxford English Dictionary.* See *The Ballad of the Reverend John Gwyon,* by P. Hawkins; (1990) 109 Law Notes 166.
16 See p. 484, n. 13, post.

None of these conditions necessarily imports poverty nor could the recipients be accurately described as a class of aged, impotent or poor persons. The references to the receipt of parochial relief and to the possibility of last year's garment having been disposed of show, no doubt, that the testator contemplated that candidates might be forthcoming from a class of society where incidents of this nature might occur, but although a gift to or for the poor other than those who were in receipt of parochial relief—that is, paupers—would be a good charitable gift, it does not follow that a gift to all and sundry in a particular locality and not expressed to be for the poor ought to be construed as evidencing an intention to relieve poverty merely because the testator is minded to exclude paupers. I think that according to the true construction of these testamentary documents the benevolence of the testator was intended for all eligible boys other than paupers, and I cannot spell out of them any indication which would justify the Foundation Trustees refusing an applicant otherwise eligible on the ground that his material circumstances were of too affluent a character. In these circumstances I cannot hold this trust to be within the description of a legal charitable trust.''

ii. PUBLIC BENEFIT

DINGLE v TURNER[17]
[1972] AC 601, [1972] 1 All ER 878 (HL, Viscount DILHORNE, Lords MACDERMOTT, HODSON, SIMON OF GLAISDALE and CROSS OF CHELSEA)

Frank Hanscombe Dingle, the testator, directed the trustees of his will to pay the income of his residuary estate to his wife for her life, and after her death to invest a capital sum in the names of the "pension fund trustees" upon trust "to apply the income thereof in paying pensions to poor employees of E. Dingle and Co Ltd" who were aged or incapacitated. The ultimate residue of the estate was to be held on similar trusts. At the date of the testator's death in 1950, the company had over 600 employees and there was a substantial number of ex-employees. The widow died in 1966.

Held (affirming MEGARRY J). The will created a valid charitable trust.

LORD CROSS OF CHELSEA: By his judgment given on April 2, 1971, Megarry J held inter alia, following the decision of the Court of Appeal in *Gibson v South American Stores (Gath and Chaves) Ltd* [1950] Ch 177, [1949] 2 All ER 985, that the trust declared by clause 8 (e) was a valid charitable trust but, on the application of the appellant Betty Mary Dingle, one of the persons interested under an intestacy, he granted a certificate under section 12 of the Administration of Justice Act 1969 enabling her to apply to this House directly for leave to appeal against that part of his judgment and on May 17, 1971, the House gave her leave to appeal.

Your Lordships, therefore, are now called upon to give to the old "poor relations" cases and the more modern "poor employees" cases that careful consideration which, in his speech in *Oppenheim v Tobacco Securities Trust Co Ltd*

---

17 [1974] CLJ 3 (G.H. Jones); (1972) 36 Conv (NS) 209 (D.J. Hayton); (1973) 36 MLR 532 (S.E.A. Johnson); [1978] Conv 277 (T.G. Watkin); Goodman Report, paras. 37 (Poor Relations Cases), 38–39 (Trusts for Employees) recommends that the poverty exception for poor relations and poor employees should be abolished. As a background to the problem discussed in this case by Lord CROSS OF CHELSEA, see p. 357, post.

[1951] AC 297 at 313, [1951] 1 All ER 31 at 38, p. 385, post, Lord Morton of Henryton said that they might one day require.

The contentions of the appellant and the respondents may be stated broadly as follows. The appellant says that in the *Oppenheim* case this House decided that in principle a trust ought not to be regarded as charitable if the benefits under it are confined either to the descendants of a named individual or individuals or to the employees of a given individual or company and that though the "poor relations" cases may have to be left standing as an anomalous exception to the general rule because their validity has been recognised for so long the exception ought not to be extended to "poor employees" trusts which had not been recognised for long before their status as charitable trusts began to be called in question. The respondents, on the other hand, say, first, that the rule laid down in the *Oppenheim* case with regard to educational trusts ought not to be regarded as a rule applicable in principle to all kinds of charitable trust, and, secondly, that in any case it is impossible to draw any logical distinction between "poor relations" trusts and "poor employees" trusts, and that, as the former cannot be held invalid today after having been recognised as valid for so long, the latter must be regarded as valid also. . . .

Most of the cases on the subject were decided in the 18th or early 19th centuries and are very inadequately reported, but two things at least were clear. First, that it never occurred to the judges who decided them that in the field of "poverty" a trust could not be a charitable trust if the class of beneficiaries was defined by reference to descent from a common ancestor. Secondly, that the courts did not treat a gift or trust as necessarily charitable because the objects of it had to be poor in order to qualify, for in some of the cases the trust was treated as a private trust and not a charity. The problem in *Re Scarisbrick's Will Trusts* [1951] Ch 622, [1951] 1 All ER 822, p. 361, post, was to determine on what basis the distinction was drawn. . . . The Court of Appeal . . . held that in this field the distinction between a public or charitable trust and a private trust depended on whether as a matter of construction the gift was for the relief of poverty amongst a particular description of poor people or was merely a gift to particular poor persons, the relief of poverty among them being the motive of the gift. The fact that the gift took the form of a perpetual trust would no doubt indicate that the intention of the donor could not have been to confer private benefits on particular people whose possible necessities he had in mind; but the fact that the capital of the gift was to be distributed at once did not necessarily show that the gift was a private trust.

[His Lordship reviewed the earlier cases, referring to *Spiller v Maude* (1881) reported at (1886) 32 ChD 158n; *Pease v Pattinson* (1886) 32 ChD 154; *Re Buck* [1896] 2 Ch 727; *Re Gosling* (1900) 48 WR 300; *Re Drummond* [1914] 2 Ch 90; *Re Sir Robert Laidlaw*, unreported, but explained at [1950] Ch 177 at 195; *Re Compton* [1945] Ch 123, [1945] 1 All ER 198; *Re Hobourn Aero Components Ltd's Air Raid Distress Fund* [1946] Ch 194, [1946] 1 All ER 501; *Gibson v South American Stores (Gath and Chaves) Ltd* [1950] Ch 177, [1949] 2 All ER 985; *Oppenheim v Tobacco Securities Trust Co Ltd* [1951] AC 297, [1951] 1 All ER 31; *Re Cox* [1955] AC 627, [1955] 2 All ER 550; *Re Young* [1955] 1 WLR 1269, [1955] 3 All ER 689 and *Davies v Perpetual Trustee Co Ltd* [1959] AC 439, [1959] 2 All ER 128 and continued:] After this long—but I hope not unduly long—recital of the decided cases, I turn to consider the arguments advanced by the appellant in support of the appeal. Even on [the assumption that the "poor relations" cases, the "poor members" cases and the "poor employees" cases are all anomalous] the appeal must fail. The status of some of the "poor relations" trusts as valid charitable trusts was recognised more than 200 years ago and a few of those then recognised are still being administered as charities today. In *Re Compton* Lord Greene MR said, at 139, at 206, that it was "quite impossible" for the Court of Appeal to overrule such old decisions and in *Oppenheim* Lord Simonds in speaking of them remarked, at 309, at 35, on the unwisdom of casting doubt on "decisions of respectable antiquity in order to introduce a greater harmony into the law of charity as a whole". Indeed, counsel for the appellant hardly ventured to suggest that we should overrule the "poor relations" cases. His submission was that which was accepted by the Court of Appeal for Ontario in *Re Cox* [1951] OR 205—namely that while the "poor relations" cases might have to be left as long standing anomalies there was no good reason for sparing the "poor employees" cases which only date from *Re Gosling* (1900) 48 WR 300 and which have been under suspicion ever since the decision in *Re Compton* [1945] Ch 123, [1945] 1 All ER 198. But the "poor members" and the "poor employees" decisions were a natural development of the "poor relations" decisions and to draw a distinction between different sorts of "poverty" trusts would be quite illogical and could certainly not be said to be introducing "greater harmony" into the law of charity. Moreover, though not as old as the "poor relations" trusts "poor employees" trusts have been recognised as charities for many years; there are now a large number of such trusts in existence; and assuming, as one must, that they are properly administered in the sense that benefits under them are only given to people who can fairly be said to be, according to current standards, "poor persons", to treat such trusts as charities is not open to any practical objection. So as it seems to me it must be accepted that wherever else it may hold sway the *Compton* rule has no application in the field of trusts for the relief of poverty and that there the dividing line between a charitable trust and a private trust lies where the Court of Appeal drew it in *Re Scarisbrick's Will Trusts* [1951] Ch 622, [1951] 1 All ER 822.

Oppenheim [1951] AC 297, [1951] 1 All ER 31 was a case of an educational trust and though the majority evidently agreed with the view expressed by the Court of Appeal in the *Hobourn Aero* case [1946] Ch 194, [1946] 1 All ER 501 that the *Compton* rule was of universal application outside the field of poverty it would no doubt be open to this House without overruling *Oppenheim* to hold that the scope of the rule was more limited. If ever I should be called upon to pronounce on this question—which does not arise in this appeal—I would as at present advised be inclined to draw a distinction between the practical merits of the *Compton* rule and the reasoning by which Lord Greene MR sought to justify it. That reasoning—based on the distinction between personal and impersonal relationships—has never seemed to me very satisfactory and I have always—if I may say so—felt the force of the criticism to which my noble and learned friend Lord MacDermott subjected it in his dissenting speech in *Oppenheim*. For my part I would prefer to approach the problem on far broader lines. The phrase a "section of the public" is in truth a vague phrase which may mean different things to different people. In the law of charity judges have sought to elucidate its meaning by contrasting it with another phrase: "a fluctuating body of private individuals". But I get little help from the supposed contrast for as I see it one and the same aggregate of persons may well be describable both as a section of the public and as a fluctuating body of private individuals. The ratepayers of the Royal Borough of Kensington and Chelsea, for example, certainly constitute a section of the public; but would it be a misuse of language to describe them as a "fluctuating body of private individuals"? After all, every part of the public is composed of individuals and being susceptible of increase or decrease is fluctuating. So at the end of the day one is left where one started with the bare contrast between "public" and "private". No doubt some classes are more naturally describable as sections of the public than as private classes while other classes are more naturally describable as private classes than as sections of the public. The blind, for example, can naturally be described as a section of the public; but what they have in common—their blindness—does not join them together in such a way that they could be called a private class. On the other hand, the descendants of Mr. Gladstone might more reasonably be described as a "private class" than as a section of the public, and in the field of common employment the same might well be said of the employees in some fairly small firm. But if one turns to large companies employing many thousands of men and women most of whom are quite unknown to one another and to the directors the answer is by no means so clear. One might say that in such a case the distinction between a section of the public and a private class is not applicable at all or even that the employees in such concerns as I.C.I. or G.E.C. are just as much "sections of the public" as the residents in some geographical area. In truth the question whether or not the potential beneficiaries of a trust can fairly be said to constitute a section of the public is a question of degree and cannot be by itself decisive of the question whether the trust is a charity. Much must depend on the purpose of the trust. It may well be that, on the one hand, a trust to promote some purpose, prima facie charitable, will constitute a charity even though the class of potential beneficiaries might fairly be called a private class and that, on the other hand, a trust to promote another purpose, also prima facie charitable, will not constitute a charity even though the class of potential beneficiaries might seem to some people fairly describable as a section of the public. In answering the question whether any given trust is a charitable trust the courts—as I see it—cannot avoid having regard to the fiscal privileges accorded to charities. As counsel for the Attorney-General remarked in the course of the argument the law of charity is bedevilled by the fact that charitable trusts enjoy two quite different sorts of privilege. On the one hand, they enjoy immunity from the rules against perpetuity and uncertainty and though individual potential beneficiaries cannot sue to enforce them the public interest arising under them is protected by the Attorney-General. If this was all there would be no reason for the courts not to look favourably on the claim of any "purpose" trust to be considered as a charity if it seemed calculated to confer some real benefit on those intended to benefit by it whoever they might be and if it would fail if not held to be a charity. But that is not all. Charities automatically enjoy fiscal privileges which with the increased burden of taxation have become more and more important and in deciding that such and such a trust is a charitable trust the court is endowing it with a substantial annual subsidy at the expense of the taxpayer.[18] Indeed, claims of trusts to rank as charities are just as often challenged by the revenue as by those who would take the fund if the trust was invalid. It is, of course, unfortunate that the recognition of any trust as a valid charitable trust should automatically attract fiscal privileges, for the question whether a trust to

18 See at p. 610, where counsel for the Attorney-General stated that in 1972 the annual estimated income of trusts for poor employees, poor members of associations, or professional groups was £4,690,000, and the income for poor relations was £3,400.

further some purpose is so little likely to benefit the public that it ought to be declared invalid and the question whether it is likely to confer such great benefits on the public that it should enjoy fiscal immunity are really two quite different questions. The logical solution would be to separate them and to say—as the Radcliffe Commission[19] proposed—that only some charities should enjoy fiscal privileges. But, as things are, validity and fiscal immunity march hand in hand and the decisions in the *Compton* [1945] Ch 123, [1945] 1 All ER 198 and *Oppenheim* [1951] AC 297, [1951] 1 All ER 31 cases were pretty obviously influenced by the consideration that if such trusts as were there in question were held valid they would enjoy an undeserved fiscal immunity. To establish a trust for the education of the children of employees in a company in which you are interested is no doubt a meritorious act; but however numerous the employees may be the purpose which you are seeking to achieve is not a public purpose.[20] It is a company purpose and there is no reason why your fellow taxpayers should contribute to a scheme which by providing "fringe benefits" for your employees will benefit the company by making their conditions of employment more attractive. The temptation to enlist the assistance of the law of charity in private endeavours of this sort is considerable—witness the recent case of the Metal Box scholarships—*IRC v Educational Grants Association Ltd* [1967] Ch 993, [1967] 2 All ER 893—and the courts must do what they can to discourage such attempts. In the field of poverty the danger is not so great as in the field of education—for while people are keenly alive to the need to give their children a good education and to the expense of doing so they are generally optimistic enough not to entertain serious fears of falling on evil days much before they fall on them. Consequently the existence of company "benevolent funds" the income of which is free of tax does not constitute a very attractive "fringe benefit". This is a practical justification—though not, of course, the historical explanation— for the special treatment accorded to poverty trusts in charity law. For the same sort of reason a trust to promote some religion among the employees of a company might perhaps safely be held to be charitable provided that it was clear that the benefits were to be purely spiritual. On the other hand, many "purpose" trusts falling under Lord Macnaghten's fourth head (*Income Tax Special Purposes Comrs v Pemsel* [1891] AC 531 at 583) if confined to a class of employees would clearly be open to the same sort of objection as educational trusts. As I see it, it is on these broad lines rather than for the reasons actually given by Lord Greene MR that the *Compton* rule [1945] Ch 123, [1945] 1 All ER 198 can best be justified.

My Lords, for the reasons given earlier in this speech I would dismiss this appeal; but as the view was expressed in the *Oppenheim* case [1951] AC 297, [1951] 1 All ER 31 that the question of the validity of trusts for poor relations and poor employees ought some day to be considered by this House and as the fund in dispute in this case is substantial your Lordships may perhaps think it proper to direct that the cost of all parties to the appeal be paid out of it.

LORD HODSON: My Lords, I agree with my noble and learned friend, Lord Cross of Chelsea, that this appeal should be dismissed and with his reasons for that conclusion. With this reservation: that I share the doubts expressed by my noble and learned friends, Lord MacDermott and Viscount Dilhorne, as to the

19 Royal Commission on the Taxation of Profits and Income (1955) Cmd. 9474, chap. 7; see also (1956) 72 LQR 187 (G. Cross); (1977) 40 MLR 397 (N.P. Gravells).
20 For criticism of this approach, see [1978] Conv 277 (T.G. Watkin).

relevance of fiscal considerations in deciding whether a gift or trust is charitable.

iii. IMMEDIATE DISTRIBUTION. SELECTION BY TRUSTEES

A trust may be charitable even though the trustees may distribute the capital and even though the persons to be benefited are selected at the discretion of the trustees.

In **Re Scarisbrick** [1951] Ch 622, [1951] 1 All ER 822, a testatrix provided that, after the death of her children, the residue of her estate should be held upon trust "for such relations of my said son and daughters as in the opinion of the survivor of my said son and daughters shall be in needy circumstances and for such charitable objects either in Germany or ... Great Britain ... for such interests and in such proportions ... as the survivor of my said son and daughters shall by deed or will appoint."

The parties agreed that one half of the fund was effectively devoted to charity. The question arose in respect of the gifts in favour of the relations. No appointment was ever made by the survivor of the children. The Court of Appeal (reversing ROXBURGH J) upheld the gift.

JENKINS LJ, after laying down a number of general propositions relating to the requirement of public benefit in charitable trusts, and referring to the exceptional case of a trust for poor relations, said at 650, at 837:

"Applying these general propositions to the present case, I ask myself whether the trust in cl. 11 for 'such relations ... as in the opinion of the survivor of ' the testatrix's 'son and daughters shall be in needy circumstances for such interests and in such proportions ... as the survivor ... shall by deed or will appoint' is a trust for the relief of poverty. If it is such a trust, then, as I understand the exception above referred to, it matters not that the potential objects of such trust are confined to relations of the son and daughters. If language means anything, a person in needy circumstances is a person who is poor and as such a proper object of charity, and no one can take under this trust who is not in needy circumstances. I do not think that the effect of the expression in 'needy circumstances' is materially altered by the qualifying words 'in the opinion of the survivor....'

'Poverty' is necessarily to some extent a relative matter, a matter of opinion, and it is not to be assumed that the person made the judge of 'needy circumstances' in the present case would have acted otherwise than in accordance with an opinion fairly and honestly formed as to the circumstances, needy or otherwise, of anyone coming into consideration as a potential object of the power. Under a similar trust which did not expressly make the appointor's opinion the test of eligibility, the appointor would in practice have to make the selection according to the best of his or her opinion or judgment. The express reference to the appointor's opinion merely serves to reduce the possibility of dispute as to the eligibility or otherwise of any particular individual on the score of needy circumstances. Accordingly, I dismiss the words 'in the opinion of the survivor' as having no material bearing on the character of this trust. In so doing, I am fortified by the similar conclusion reached in this court as to the effect of the words 'in the opinion of the London Board' in *Gibson v South American Stores (Gath and Chaves) Ltd* [1950] Ch 177 at 185, [1949] 2 All ER 985 at 989.

[His Lordship discussed the cases relating to the requirement of public benefit in relation to gifts in favour of poor relations, and continued:]

Accordingly, in the view I take, this is a trust for the relief of poverty in the charitable sense amongst the class of relations described, and, being a trust for the relief of poverty, is in view of the exception above stated, not disqualified from ranking as a legally charitable trust by the circumstances that its application is confined to a class of relations (albeit a wide class), with the result that its potential beneficiaries do not comprise the public or a section thereof under the decisions to which I have referred.

I am accordingly of opinion that as the law now stands the trust in question should be upheld as a valid charitable trust for the relief of poverty.

The judge took a different view ...

I find myself unable to accept the judge's view as to the effect of the authorities. I think the true question in each case has really been whether the gift was for the relief of poverty amongst a class of persons, or rather, as Sir William Grant MR put it,[1] a particular description of poor, or was merely a gift to individuals, albeit with relief of poverty amongst those individuals as the motive of the gift, or with a selective preference for the poor or poorest amongst those individuals. If the gift is perpetual in character, that no doubt is an important circumstance as demonstrating that the intention cannot have been merely to benefit the statutory next of kin of the propositus or other particular individuals identified by the gift. Moreover, the gift, if perpetual, can only be supported on the footing that it is charitable—an illogical though in past practice probably a persuasive reason for holding it such.

But I see no sufficient ground in the authorities for holding that a gift for the benefit of poor relations qualifies as charitable only if it is perpetual in character. I do not think that the observation of Sir William Grant MR above referred to goes by any means as far as that. It is fully satisfied if taken as meaning that an immediate bequest of a sum to be distributed among poor relations may on its true construction be no more than a gift to particular individuals (i.e., the next of kin of the propositus), whereas a gift having perpetual continuance cannot be so confirmed. If a gift or trust on its true construction does extend to those in need amongst relations in every degree, even though it provides for immediate distribution, then, inasmuch as the class of potential beneficiaries becomes so wide as to be incapable of exhaustive ascertainment, the impersonal quality, if I may so describe it, supplied in continuing gifts by the element of perpetuity, is equally present."[2]

QUESTIONS

1. Can you formulate a satisfactory definition of poverty?

    Should this be sought in terms of persons who pay no income tax, receive public assistance, or are entitled to legal aid? (Tudor, p. 29; (1965) 72 LQR 187 at pp. 206–207; Nathan Report, paras. 120–140).

    Or should it be limited to persons who, for one reason or another, are ineligible to obtain relief from the State?

2. What advice would you give for the drawing up of a public appeal and trust deed following a tragic accident or disaster? CC Leaflet 40 (Disaster Appeals); Annual Report for 1965, paras. 54–58; 1981, para. 8, Appendix A; (1982) 132 NLJ 223 (H. Picarda), discussing the Penlee

---

1 In *A-G v Price* (1810) 17 Ves 371 at 374. See *Re Segelman* [1996] 2 WLR 173.
2 *Re Cohen* [1973] 1 WLR 415, [1973] 1 All ER 889 (trust "for or towards the maintenance and benefit of any relative of mine whom my trustees shall consider to be in special need" held charitable).

Lifeboat Disaster Fund and the Penlee Fishermen's Fund; Annual Report for 1982, paras. 31–35 (South Atlantic Fund for the benefit of members of the Falklands Task Force serving in one of the three services or the Merchant Marine, and their dependants); 1985, para. 19 (Bradford City Disaster Charitable Trust); 1988, para. 25 (Armenian earthquake and Philippines Ferry); 1989, paras. 36, 37 (Clapham Junction and Hillsborough); Cairns, *Charities Law and Practice* (2nd edn), pp. 173–177, which includes the A-G's guidelines; H & M, pp. 438–439; Riddall, pp. 136–137.

B. The Advancement of Education[3]

i. GENERAL

The concept of education has progressed a long way since the Preamble to the Statute of Elizabeth I spoke of "the maintenance of schools of learning, free schools and scholars in universities" and "the education and preferment of orphans". As BUCKLEY LJ said in *Incorporated Council of Law Reporting for England and Wales v A-G*, it now extends "to the improvement of a useful branch of human knowledge and its public dissemination."[4] The main areas of controversy in the modern law will be discussed in the cases which follow. The concept includes of course "satellite" purposes such as the payment of teachers and administrative staff,[5] and an educational institution may be charitable, although a private company, so long as it does not operate for profit.[6]

It was in this area that the modern emphasis on the necessity for "public benefit" first came to the fore. Apart from the fourth category (p. 408, post), the question was hardly material in the low-tax days before 1939. If it was charitable to advance education among the many, why was it not charitable to advance education among the few? Indeed, the highly selective system of British education assumes this. Scholarships for boys born in particular villages, or for boys to be educated at particular schools, have been upheld for centuries, as have "closed" scholarships to individual Colleges at Oxford or Cambridge. The fiscal exemptions which charities enjoy and the dramatic increase in the rates of taxation from 1939 and the emphasis upon equality in education rather than selectivity prompt the asking of a different question: Even if the provision of money for the education of a selected few is to be encouraged, how is it possible to justify the tax free status of such money? In short, the law of charity must not be allowed to develop into a tax-planning

---

3 H & M, pp. 394–405, 422–426; K & S, pp. 170–171; S & K, pp. 97–118; P & M, pp. 305–307, 314–318; Pettit, pp. 232–235, 252–258; Riddall, pp. 100–102, 116–118; Snell, pp. 147–148, 152–153; Tudor, pp. 39–61; Picarda, pp. 40– 61; Goodman Report, paras. 62 (The Arts), 63 (Research), 64–67 (Learned Societies), 68 (Propaganda); Charity Commissioners Leaflet on Education Charities, reproduced in Annual Report for 1986, Appx A.

4 [1972] Ch 73 at 102, [1971] 3 All ER 1029 at 1046.

5 *Case of Christ's College, Cambridge* (1757) 1 Wm Bl 90.

6 *Abbey Malvern Wells Ltd v Ministry of Local Government and Planning* [1951] Ch 728, [1951] 2 All ER 154; *Re Girls' Public Day School Trust* [1951] Ch 400, where a girls' school carried on by private company was held not to be a charity because profits could benefit the shareholders. See *Butterworth v Keeler* 219 NY 446, 114 NE 308 (1916); Scott, *Cases on Trusts* (5th edn), pp. 678–679.

device for the tax free education of the children of the wealthy;[7] nor must
employers, by setting up educational trusts for the children of their employees,
be able to use it for commercial advantage.[8] The same sort of concept carried
over to religious trusts. We have seen that the problem has been avoided in the
case of trusts for the relief of poverty.

ii. EDUCATION IS NOT LIMITED TO TEACHING

In **Royal Choral Society v Inland Revenue Commissioners** [1943] 2 All ER 101,
the question was whether the appellants were a society "established for
charitable purposes only" and thus entitled to exemption from income tax.
The objects of the society were "to form and maintain a choir in order to
promote the practice and performance of choral works, whether by way of
concerts or choral pageants in the Royal Albert Hall or as otherwise decided
from time to time".

The Court of Appeal held that the Society was charitable as being established
for the purposes of the advancement of aesthetic education. Lord GREENE MR
said at 104:

"Dealing with the educational aspect from the point of view of the public
who hear music, the Solicitor-General argued that nothing could be
educational which did not involve teaching—as I understood him, teaching in
the sense of a master teaching a class. He said that in the domain of art the only
thing that could be educational in a charitable sense would be the education of
the executants: the teaching of the painter, the training of the musician, and so
forth. I protest against that narrow conception of education when one is
dealing with aesthetic education. Very few people can become executants, or
at any rate executants who can give pleasure either to themselves or to others;
but a very large number of people can become instructed listeners with a
trained and cultivated taste. In my opinion, a body of persons established for
the purpose of raising the artistic taste of the country and established by an
appropriate document which confines them to that purpose, is established for
educational purposes, because the education of artistic taste is one of the most
important things in the development of a civilised human being."[9]

In **Commissioners of Inland Revenue v White** [1980] TR 155,[10] the principal
object of the Clerkenwell Green Association for Craftsmen was "to promote

7 Goodman Report, paras. 47 (Costly Services), 60–61 (Education), p. 145; House of Commons
   Report, vol. I, paras. 45–52, vol. II, pp. 39–43, 93, 164–165, 249–271.
8 See *Wicks v Firth* [1983] 2 AC 214, [1983] 1 All ER 151 (scholarships paid by trustees of Imperial
   Chemical Industries Educational Trust to children of higher-paid employees of ICI held (Lord
   TEMPLEMAN dissenting) not taxable as emoluments of the fathers' employments). The effect of
   the decision was reversed by FA 1983, s. 20, in respect of scholarships awarded after 15 March,
   1983. See now ICTA 1988, ss. 331, 165; *Glynn v IRC* [1990] 2 AC 298 (school fees of taxpayer's
   daughter at Roedean paid directly by employer pursuant to taxpayer's contract of service held
   to be perquisite of employment and therefore taxable). See also *Sherdley v Sherdley* [1988] AC
   213, [1987] 2 All ER 54 (taxpayer held entitled to apply against himself for an order under
   Matrimonial Causes Act 1973, s. 23 (1) (*d*) that he pay school fees for the benefit of his infant
   children; the sole purpose of the application was to obtain tax advantages).
9 Annual Report for 1991, para. 76, Appx D (*b*) (Promotions of the Arts without reference to
   education held to be charitable).
10 Annual Report for 1980, paras. 66–73; p. 437, post.

any charitable purpose which will encourage the exercise and maintain the standards of crafts both ancient and modern, preserve and improve craftsmanship and foster, promote and increase the interest of the public therein''. The Association had converted two buildings for use as workshops by craftsmen, who included a hand engraver, antique furniture restorer, clock maker, silversmith, polisher and plater, musical instrument maker, glass polisher, manufacturing jeweller, diamond mounter, watch repairer, general engraver, printer and fashion designer. Fox J held that the purpose was charitable and said at 158:

"The word 'craftsmanship', in its general use in the English language, suggests a degree of quality of workmanship ... There is, in my opinion, a substantial range of activity which would foster, promote and increase the interest of the public in craftsmanship and which would itself be charitable.... It seems to me that there is a wide field of high quality craftsmanship where there could be no doubt as to the educative value to the public of increased information."[11]

In **Re Dupree's Deed Trusts** [1945] Ch 16, [1944] 2 All ER 443, a trust with capital of £5,000 was established for the purpose of providing an annual chess tournament for boys and young men under the age of 21 resident in the city of Portsmouth.[12] In spite of the argument of counsel for the next-of-kin that the encouragement of "the playing of chess in schools would not be altogether desirable. It might take pupils away from cricket, football and athletic pursuits generally", the trust was upheld as an educational charitable trust. VAISEY J however had some anxiety as to the problem of drawing the right line in these cases. He said at 20, at 445:

"One feels, perhaps, that one is on rather a slippery slope. If chess, why not draughts? If draughts, why not bezique, and so on, through to bridge and whist, and, by another route, to stamp collecting and the acquisition of birds' eggs? Those pursuits will have to be dealt with if and when they come up for consideration ... "

RE HOPKINS' WILL TRUSTS[13]
[1965] Ch 669, [1964] 3 All ER 46 (ChD, WILBERFORCE J)

The testatrix gave one third part of her estate to "the Francis Bacon Society Inc. ... to be earmarked and applied towards finding the Bacon-Shakespeare manuscripts and in the event of the same having been discovered by the date of my death then for the general purposes of the work and propaganda of the society".

The objects of the Society were: "(1) To encourage the study of the works of Francis Bacon as philosopher, lawyer, statesman and poet; also his character,

---

11 Ibid., 1990 Appx A (*f*) (Community Computing in Newcastle).
12 This is not contrary to Sex Discrimination Act 1975. Charities are expressly excepted: s. 43; Sex Discrimination Act 1975 (Amendment of Section 43) Order 1977, S.I. 1977 No. 528. In 1976 a Phyllis Loe Chess Tournament for Girls Trust was established for girls below the age of 18 educated in Portsmouth. See (1977) 41 Conv (NS) 8.
13 (1965) 29 Conv (NS) 368 (M. Newark and A. Samuels).

genius and life; his influence on his own and succeeding times, and the tendencies and results of his writings. (2) To encourage the general study of evidence in favour of Francis Bacon's authorship of the plays commonly ascribed to Shakespeare, and to investigate his connection with other works of the Elizabethan period.'' The Society was registered as a charity under the Charities Act 1960.

Held. A valid educational charitable trust.[14]

WILBERFORCE J [commenting that the society was a registered charity under Charities Act 1960 and so was conclusively presumed to be a charity[15] continued:] Miss Hopkins could have given the money to the society during her life and the society under its constitution could have spent it for the purposes stated in the will. But the validity of her testamentary disposition is questioned. The basis for the challenge is that this is a gift to the society not absolutely but upon a stated trust, so that it is necessary to see whether the trust is valid. It cannot be upheld as a gift upon valid but non-charitable trusts, and the society does not seek so to uphold it. It can only be supported if it is a valid charitable trust. Whether it is so is what the court has to decide ...

Let me say at once that no determination of the authorship of the "Shakespeare" plays, or even of any subsidiary question relating to it, falls to be made in the present proceedings. The court is only concerned, at this point, with the practicability and later with the legality of carrying Miss Hopkins' wishes into effect, and it must decide this, one way or the other, upon the evidence of the experts which is before it.

[His Lordship reviewed the evidence and continued:] On this evidence, should the conclusion be reached that the search for the Bacon-Shakespeare manuscripts is so manifestly futile that the court should not allow this bequest to be spent upon it as upon an object devoid of the possibility of any result? I think not. The evidence shows that the discovery of any manuscript of the plays is unlikely; but so are many discoveries before they are made (one may think of the Codex Sinaiticus, or the Tomb of Tutankhamen, or the Dead Sea Scrolls); I do not think that that degree of improbability has been reached which justifies the court in placing an initial interdict on the testatrix's benefaction.

I come, then, to the only question of law: is the gift of a charitable character? The society has put its case in the alternative under the two headings of education and of general benefit to the community and has argued separately for each. This compartmentalisation is derived from the accepted classification into four groups of the miscellany found in the Statute of Elizabeth (43 Eliz. I, c. 4). That Statute, preserved as to the preamble only by the Mortmain and Charitable Uses Act, 1888, lost even that precarious hold on the Statute Book when the Act of 1888 was repealed by the Charities Act, 1960, but the somewhat ossificatory classification to which it gave rise survives in the decided cases. It is unsatisfactory because the frontiers of "educational purposes" (as of the other divisions) have been extended and are not easy to trace with precision, and because, under the fourth head, it has been held necessary for the court to find a benefit to the public within the spirit and intendment of the obsolete Elizabethan statute. The difficulty of achieving that, while at the same time keeping the law's view of what is charitable reasonably in line with modern requirements, explains what Lord Simonds accepted as the case-to-case

14 The gift was also valid under the fourth head.
15 See Charities Act 1993, s. 4(1), p. 507.

approach of the courts: see *National Anti-Vivisection Society v IRC* [1948] AC 31, [1947] 2 All ER 217. There are, in fact, examples of accepted charities which do not decisively fit into one rather than the other category. Examples are institutes for scientific research (see the *National Anti-Vivisection* case, per Lord Wright at 42, at 220), museums (see *Re Pinion* [1965] Ch 85 at 104, [1964] 1 All ER 890 at 892), the preservation of ancient cottages (*Re Cranstoun* [1932] 1 Ch 537), and even the promotion of Shakespearian drama (*Re Shakespeare Memorial Trust* [1923] 2 Ch 398). The present may be such a case.

Accepting, as I have the authority of Lord Simonds for so doing, that the court must decide each case as best it can, on the evidence available to it, as to benefit, and within the moving spirit of decided cases, it would seem to me that a bequest for the purpose of search, or research, for the original manuscripts of England's greatest dramatist (whoever he was) would be well within the law's conception of charitable purposes. The discovery of such manuscripts, or of one such manuscript, would be of the highest value to history and to literature. It is objected, against this, that as we already have the text of the plays, from an almost contemporary date, the discovery of a manuscript would add nothing worth while. This I utterly decline to accept. Without any undue exercise of the imagination, it would surely be a reasonable expectation that the revelation of a manuscript would contribute, probably decisively, to a solution of the authorship problem, and this alone is benefit enough. It might also lead to improvements in the text. It might lead to more accurate dating.

Is there any authority, then, which should lead me to hold that a bequest to achieve this objective is not charitable? By Mr. Fox, for the next-of-kin, much reliance was placed on the decision on Bernard Shaw's will, the *"British Alphabet"* case (*Re Shaw* [1957] 1 WLR 729, [1957] 1 All ER 745, p. 317, ante). Harman J held that the gift was not educational because it merely tended to the increase of knowledge and that it was not within the fourth charitable category because it was not itself for a beneficial purpose but for the purpose of persuading the public by propaganda that it was beneficial. The gift was very different from the gift here. But the judge did say this at 737, at 752: "if the object be merely the increase of knowledge, that is not in itself a charitable object unless it be combined with teaching or education"; and he referred to the House of Lords decision, *Whicker v Hume* (1858) 7 HL Cas 124, where, in relation to a gift for advancement of education and learning, two of the Lords read "learning" as equivalent to "teaching", thereby in his view implying that learning, in its ordinary meaning, is not a charitable purpose.

This decision certainly seems to place some limits upon the extent to which a gift for research may be regarded as charitable. Those limits are that either it must be "combined with teaching or education", if it is to fall under the third head, or it must be beneficial to the community in a way regarded by the law as charitable, if it is to fall within the fourth category. The words "combined with teaching or education", though well explaining what the judge had in mind when he rejected the gift in *Shaw's* case [1957] 1 WLR 729, [1957] 1 All ER 745, are not easy to interpret in relation to other facts. I should be unwilling to treat them as meaning that the promotion of academic research is not a charitable purpose unless the researcher were engaged in teaching or education in the conventional meaning; and I am encouraged in this view by some words of Lord Greene MR in *Re Compton* [1945] Ch 123 at 127, [1945] 1 All ER 198 at 200. The testatrix there had forbidden the income of the bequest to be used for research, and Lord Greene MR treated this as a negative definition of the education to be provided. It would, he said, exclude a grant to enable a beneficiary to conduct research on some point of history or science. This shows that Lord Greene MR considered that historic research might fall within the description of "education". I think, therefore, that the word "education" as used by Harman J in *Re Shaw* must be used in a wide sense, certainly extending beyond teaching, and that the requirement is that, in order to be charitable, research must either be of educational value to the researcher or must be so directed as to lead to something which will pass into the store of educational material, or so as to improve the sum of communicable knowledge in an area which education may cover—education in this last context extending to the formation of literary taste and appreciation (compare *Royal Choral Society v IRC* [1943] 2 All ER 101, p. 364, ante). Whether or not the test is wider than this, it is, as I have stated it, amply wide enough to include the purposes of the gift in this case.

As regards the fourth category, Harman J is evidently leaving it open to the court to hold, on the facts, that research of a particular kind may be beneficial to the community in a way which the law regards as charitable, "beneficial" here not being limited to the production of material benefit (as through medical or scientific research) but including at least benefit in the intellectual or artistic fields.

So I find nothing in this authority to prevent me from finding that the gift falls under either the third or fourth head of the classification of charitable purposes.

On the other side there is *Re British School of Egyptian Archaeology* [1954] 1 WLR 546, [1954] 1 All ER 887, also a decision of Harman J, a case much closer to the present. The trusts there were to excavate, to discover antiquities, to hold exhibitions, to publish works and to promote the training and assistance of students—all in relation to Egypt. Harman J held that the purposes were charitable, as being educational. The society was one for the diffusion of a certain branch of knowledge, namely, knowledge of the ancient past of Egypt; and it also had a direct educational purpose, namely, to train students. The conclusion reached that there was an educational charity was greatly helped by the reference to students, but it seems that Harman J must have accepted that the other objects—those of archaeological research—were charitable, too. They were quite independent objects on which the whole of the society's funds could have been spent, and the language "the school has a direct educational purpose, namely, to train students" seems to show that the judge was independently upholding each set of objects.

Mr. Fox correctly pointed out that in that case there was a direct obligation to diffuse the results of the society's research and said that it was this that justified the finding that the archaeological purposes were charitable. I accept that research of a private character, for the benefit only of the members of a society, would not normally be educational—or otherwise charitable—as did Harman J [1954] 1 WLR 546 at 551, [1954] 1 All ER 887 at 890, but I do not think that the research in the present case can be said to be of a private character, for it is inherently inevitable, and manifestly intended, that the result of any discovery should be published to the world . I think, therefore, that the *British School of Egyptian Archaeology* case supports the society's contentions.

A number of other authorities were referred to as illustrating the wide variety of objects which have been accepted as educational or as falling under the fourth category but, since none of them is close to the present, I shall not refer to them. They are well enough listed in the standard authorities.

One final reference is appropriate: to *Re Shakespeare Memorial Trust* [1923] 2 Ch 398. The scheme there was for a number of objects which included the performance of Shakespearian and other classical English plays, and stimulating the art of acting. I refer to it for two purposes, first as an example of a case where the court upheld the gift either as educational or as for purposes beneficial to the community—an approach which commends itself to me here—and secondly as illustrative of the educational and public benefit accepted by the court as flowing from a scheme designed to spread the influence of Shakespeare as the author of the plays. This gift is not that, but it lies in the same field, for the improving of our literary heritage, and my judgment is for upholding it.

In **Re Besterman's Will Trusts** (1980) Times, 21 January,[16] SLADE J, in upholding a trust for completing research on Voltaire and Rousseau, said:

"(1) A trust for research will ordinarily qualify as a charitable trust if, but only if (a) the subject matter of the proposed research is a useful subject of study; and (b) it is contemplated that knowledge acquired as a result of the research will be disseminated to others; and (c) the trust is for the benefit of the public, or a sufficiently important section of the public. (2) In the absence of a contrary context, however, the court will be readily inclined to construe a trust for research as importing subsequent dissemination of the results thereof. (3) Furthermore, if a trust for research is to constitute a valid trust for the advancement of education, it is not necessary either (a) that a teacher/pupil relationship should be in contemplation, or (b) that the persons to benefit from the knowledge to be acquired should be persons who are already in the course of receiving 'education' in the conventional sense. (4) In any case where the court has to determine whether a bequest for the purposes of research is or is not of a charitable nature, it must pay due regard to any admissible extrinsic evidence which is available to explain the wording of the will in question or the circumstances in which it was made."

In **Re Shaw's Will Trusts** [1952] Ch 163, [1952] 1 All ER 49,[17] the testatrix, who was the widow of George Bernard Shaw, bequeathed the residue of her estate upon the following trusts: "The making of grants contributions and payments to any foundation ... having for its objects the bringing of the masterpieces of fine art within the reach of the people of Ireland of all classes in their own country.... The teaching promotion and encouragement in Ireland of self control, elocution, oratory, deportment, the arts of personal contact, of social intercourse, and the other arts of public, private, professional and business life ..."

VAISEY J upheld the gift as an educational charitable trust. It was "a sort of finishing school for the Irish people". "I think" he said at 172, at 55, "that 'education' includes ... not only teaching, but the promotion or encouragement of these arts and graces of life which are, after all, perhaps the

---

16 Applied in *McGovern v A-G* [1982] Ch 321 at 352, [1981] 3 All ER 493 at 518, p. 446, post (research into the maintenance and observance of human rights).
17 See Holroyd, *The Shaw Companion* (1992), vol. 4, pp. 6–9 for a discussion of the case and a full text of the will.

finest and best part of the human character ... It is education of a desirable sort, and which, if corrected and augmented and amplified by other kinds of teaching and instruction, might have most beneficial results."

In **Incorporated Council of Law Reporting for England and Wales v Attorney-General**[18] [1972] Ch 73, [1971] 3 All ER 1029, the Court of Appeal unanimously held that the Council was charitable under the fourth head of Lord MACNAGHTEN's classification.[19] Two of the judges, SACHS and BUCKLEY LJJ held that it was charitable also as being for the advancement of education. BUCKLEY LJ said at 101, at 1045:

"Foster J declined to accept the view that the council's objects are educational, mainly, I think, upon the ground that in many respects they are not used for instructional purposes. He did, however, take the view that they are charitable on the ground that the purpose of the publication of The Law Reports is to enable judge-made law to be properly developed and administered by the courts, a purpose beneficial to the community and within the spirit of the preamble.

What then does the evidence establish about the need for reliable law reports and the reasons for publishing them? As the uncontradicted evidence of Professor Goodhart makes clear, in a legal system such as ours, in which judges' decisions are governed by precedents, reported decisions are the means by which legal principles (other than those laid down by statutes) are developed, established and made known, and by which the application of those legal principles to particular kinds of facts are illustrated and explained. Reported decisions may be said to be the tissue of the body of our non-statutory law. Whoever, therefore, would carry out any anatomical researches upon our non-statutory corpus juris must do so by research amongst, and study of, reported cases.

Professor Goodhart recalls that Sir Frederick Pollock in his paper entitled *The Science of Case Law* published in 1882 pointed out that the study of law is a science in the same sense as physics or chemistry are sciences, and that the material with which it is concerned consists of individual cases which must be analysed and measured as carefully as is the material in the other sciences. At about the same time the 'case system' of teaching law was introduced at the Harvard Law School, which has since become generally adopted. Accurate and authoritative law reports are thus seen to be essential both for the advancement of legal education and the proper administration of justice. As Professor Goodhart says: 'Accuracy in The Law Reports is, therefore, as important for the science of law as is the accuracy of instruments in the physical sciences.'

The legal profession has from times long past been termed a learned profession, and rightly so, for no man can properly practise or apply the law who is not learned in that field of law with which he is concerned. He must have more than an aptitude and more than a skill. He must be learned in a sense importing true scholarship. In a system of law such as we have in this country this scholarship can only be acquired and maintained by a continual study of case law.

---

18 See pp. 434, 462, post.
19 See also *Incorporated Council of Law Reporting of the State of Queensland v Commissioner of Taxation* (1971) 45 ALJR 552; (1972) 88 LQR 171.

I agree with Foster J in thinking that, when counsel in court cites a case to a judge, counsel is not in any real sense 'educating' the judge, counsel performing the role of a teacher and the judge filling the role of a pupil; but I do not agree with him that the process should not be regarded as falling under the charitable head of 'the advancement of education'.

In a number of cases learned societies have been held to be charitable. Sometimes the case has been classified under Lord Macnaghten's fourth head, sometimes under the second. It does not really matter under which head such a case is placed, but for my own part I prefer to treat the present case as falling within the class of purposes for the advancement of education rather than within the final class of other purposes for the benefit of the community. For the present purpose the second head should be regarded as extending to the improvement of a useful branch of human knowledge and its public dissemination.

[His Lordship referred to *Beaumont v Oliveira* (1869) 4 Ch App 309, where bequests to the Royal Society whose object is 'improving natural knowledge' and the Royal Geographical Society 'the improvement and diffusion of geographical knowledge' were held charitable under the fourth head of charity; *Royal College of Surgeons of England v National Provincial Bank Ltd* [1952] AC 631, [1952] 1 All ER 984, where the objects were 'the encouragement of the study and practice of the art and science of surgery'; *Re Lopes* [1931] 2 Ch 130, a gift to the Zoological Society of London whose objects are 'the advancement of Zoology and animal physiology and the introduction of new and curious subjects of the animal kingdom'; and *Re British School of Egyptian Archaeology* [1954] 1 WLR 546, [1954] 1 All ER 887, p. 368, ante), where gifts were upheld as being for the advancement of education; and continued:]

The fact that the council's publications can be regarded as a necessary part of a practising lawyer's equipment does not prevent the council from being established exclusively for charitable purposes. The practising lawyer and the judge must both be lifelong students in that field of scholarship for the study of which The Law Reports provide essential material and a necessary service. The benefit which the council confers upon members of the legal profession in making accurate reports available is that it facilitates the study and ascertainment of the law. It also helps the lawyer to earn his livelihood, but that is incidental to or consequential on the primary scholastic function of advancing and disseminating knowledge of the law, and does not detract from the exclusively charitable character of the council's objects: compare *Royal College of Surgeons of England v National Provincial Bank Ltd* [1952] AC 631, [1952] 1 All ER 984 and *Royal College of Nursing v St Marylebone Corpn* [1959] 1 WLR 1077, [1959] 3 All ER 663.

The service which publication of The Law Reports provides benefits not only those actively engaged in the practice and administration of the law, but also those whose business it is to study and teach law academically, and many others who need to study the law for the purposes of their trades, businesses, professions or affairs. In all these fields, however, the nature of the service is the same: it enables the reader to study, and by study to acquaint himself with and instruct himself in the law of this country. There is nothing here which negatives an exclusively charitable purpose.

Although the objects of the council are commercial in the sense that the council exists to publish and sell its publications, they are unself-regarding. The members are prohibited from deriving any profit from the council's activities, and the council itself, although not debarred from making a profit out of its business, can only apply any such profit in the further pursuit of its objects. The council is consequently not prevented from being a charity by reason of any commercial element in its activities.

I therefore reach the conclusion that the council is a body established exclusively for charitable purposes and is entitled to be registered under the Act of 1960."

In **Re South Place Ethical Society** [1980] 1 WLR 1565, [1980] 3 All ER 918, the objects of the Society were "the study and dissemination of ethical principles and the cultivation of a rational religious sentiment." DILLON J held that the trust was for the advancement of education, and said at 1576, at 928:

"The first part of the objects is the study and dissemination of ethical principles. Dissemination, I think, includes dissemination of the fruits of the study, and I have no doubt that that part of the objects satisfies the criterion of charity as being for the advancement of education. The second part, the cultivation of a rational religious sentiment, is considerably more difficult. As I have already said, I do not think that the cultivation is limited to cultivation of the requisite sentiment in the members of the society and in no one else. In the context the society is outward looking, and the cultivation would extend to all members of the public whom the society's teachings may reach. The sentiment or state of mind is to be rational, that is to say founded in reason. As I see it, a sentiment or attitude of mind founded in reason can only be cultivated or encouraged to grow by educational methods, including music, and the development of the appreciation of music by performances of high quality. The difficulty in this part of the society's objects lies in expressing a very lofty and possibly unattainable ideal in a very few words, and the difficulty is compounded by the choice of the word 'religious', which while giving the flavour of what is in mind, is not in my view used in its correct sense."[20]

In **Re Koeppler Will Trusts** [1986] Ch 423, [1985] 2 All ER 869,[1] the testator left a share of his residuary estate "for the warden and the chairman of the academic advisory council ... of the institution known as Wilton Park ... for the benefit at their discretion of the said institution as long as Wilton Park remains a British contribution to the formation of an informed international public opinion and to the promotion of greater co-operation in Europe and the West in general". In holding that the gift in favour of Wilton Park was charitable, SLADE LJ said at 435, at 877:

"Concluding, therefore, as I do, that the gift falls to be construed as a 'purpose trust' for the furtherance of the work of the Wilton Park project, in the form which that work took at the date of the death, were those purposes of an exclusively charitable nature? The evidence as to the nature of the work of the Wilton Park project is to be found summarised fully and accurately in the judge's judgment [1984] Ch 243, [1984] 2 All ER 111 and I propose merely to draw attention to certain particular points.

---

20 P. 396 post; [1993] Ch Com Rep 1 (Cult Information Centre, for the education of the public, mainly students, about techniques used for recruitment into alternative or unconventional religious or contemporary sects sometimes known as "new religious movements" held to be charitable).
1 [1985] Conv 412 (T.G. Watkin).

The organisation and conduct of the conferences which had been held since 1950 at Wiston House were clearly the central features of the Wilton Park project. The 'specific aspects' dealt with at each conference covered a wide range of topics. Examples of these specific aspects are to be found in the programmes for the four conferences immediately preceding the date of the testator's will and those for the four conferences immediately preceding his death. They were:

'(1) An inquiry into the "quality of life," ecology and the environment; participation in government and industry; tensions in free societies; (2) Europe and the emergent patterns and super-power relationships; (3) the unification of Europe; a balance-sheet; (4) the requirements of Western defence and the possibilities of arms control; (5) the European Community and its external relations; (6) the media, public opinion and the decisionmaking process in government; (7) security issues as a factor in domestic and international politics; (8) labour and capital and the future of industrial society.'

As the judge observed, those specific themes are self-evidently matters on which persons of differing political persuasions might have differing views and some of the speakers invited to speak at plenary sessions of the conferences were politicians. However, he found, at 251D, at 117, that 'it is clear that Wilton Park has taken pains to avoid inculcating any particular political viewpoint.' There is therefore no question of the Wilton Park conferences being intended to further the interests of a particular political party.

No one would suggest that the mere organisation and conduct of conferences, albeit dealing with topics of public interest, would necessarily constitute a charitable activity. If such activities are to be charitable, they must be shown to be for the benefit of the public, or the community, in a sense or manner within the intendment of the preamble to the statute 43 Eliz. 1, c. 4. The possibly relevant head of charity in the present case is that of the advancement of education.

In the context of the activities of the Wilton Park project, the judge had this to say, at 261F-G, at 125:

'Let me consider first whether the Wilton Park process can properly be described as educational. Mr. McCall submitted, and I accept, that the following salient points emerged from the evidence: (i) the conferences sought to improve the minds of participants, not necessarily by adding to their factual knowledge but by expanding their wisdom and capacity to understand; (ii) the subjects discussed at conferences were recognised academic subjects in higher education; (iii) the conferences operated by a process of discussion designed to elicit an exchange of views in a manner familiar in places of higher education; (iv) the conferences were designed to capitalise on the expertise of participants who were there both to learn and to instruct.'

Having considered certain arguments to the contrary submitted by Mr. Farrow on behalf of the second defendant, the judge concluded, at p. 262F: 'the Wilton Park process can be described as educational' and, I think, by necessary inference, that when looked at on its own it can properly be described as charitable.

As I understood Mr. Farrow's argument, he did not seek to challenge this conclusion before this court. He conceded that if, on the true construction of the will, the purpose of the gift is the furtherance of the Wilton Park project, then that is an educational purpose and the gift is of a charitable nature. The essential point of his argument was that the purpose of the gift is furtherance of the formation end and the promotion end—an argument which, for the reasons already given, I would reject.

I think that this concession made on behalf of the second defendant was rightly made. As the judge said, at 262A, at 126:
'the concept of education is now wide enough to cover the intensive discussion process adopted by Wilton Park in relation to a somewhat special class of adults, persons influencing opinion in their own countries, designed (as I was told Sir Heinz put it) to dent opinions and to cross-fertilise ideas.'

Mr. McCall referred us to what was said by Lord Hailsham of St. Marylebone LC in *IRC v McMullen* [1981] AC 1 at 15, [1980] 1 All ER 884 at 890: 'both the legal conception of charity, and within it the educated man's ideas about education, are not static, but moving and changing.' As to the element of public benefit, the participants in the courses appear to have been selected from widely drawn categories, as persons likely to influence opinion in their own country. Like the judge, I find little difficulty in inferring that not only they themselves are likely to benefit from the courses, but are likely to pass on such benefits to others."

iii. SPECIAL SCHOOL AND UNIVERSITY ACTIVITIES

Some activities, not otherwise educational, are treated as being for the advancement of education if they are carried out as part of school or university activities.[2]

INLAND REVENUE COMMISSIONERS v McMULLEN
[1981] AC 1, [1980] 1 All ER 884 (HL, Lord HAILSHAM OF ST MARYLEBONE LC, Lords DIPLOCK, SALMON, RUSSELL OF KILLOWEN and KEITH OF KINKEL)

In 1972 the Football Association created a trust, the objects of which were stated in clause 3 (a) of the deed to be, inter alia, "to organise or provide or assist in the organisation and provision of facilities which will enable and encourage pupils of schools and universities in any part of the United Kingdom to play association football or other games or sports and thereby to assist in ensuring that due attention is given to the physical education and development of such pupils as well as to the development and occupation of their minds." There were then set out various methods to be adopted to further these objects.

The Charity Commissioners registered the trust as a charity under Charities Act 1960, s. 4. An appeal against registration was allowed by WALTON J [1978] 1 WLR 664, [1978] 1 All ER 230, and the Court of Appeal by a majority (STAMP and ORR LJJ, BRIDGE LJ dissenting) [1979] 1 WLR 130, [1979] 1 All ER 588. On appeal by the trustees.

Held (reversing Court of Appeal) A valid educational charitable trust.

LORD HAILSHAM OF ST MARYLEBONE LC: Four questions arose for decision below. In the first place neither the parties nor the judgment below were in agreement as to the proper construction of the trust deed itself. Clearly this is a preliminary debate which must be settled before the remaining questions are

---

2 Similarly *Re Gray* [1925] Ch 362, p. 430, post (sport in the Army). See also *Re Lipinski's Will Trusts* [1976] Ch 235 at 242, [1977] 1 All ER 33 at 39.

even capable of decision. In the second place the appellants contend and the respondents dispute that, on the correct construction of the deed, the trust is charitable as being for the advancement of education. Thirdly, the appellants contend and the respondents dispute that if they are wrong on the second question the trust is charitable at least because it falls within the fourth class of Lord Macnaghten's categories as enumerated in *Income Tax Special Purposes Comrs v Pemsel* [1891] AC 531 at 583, p. 341 ante, as a trust beneficial to the community within the spirit and intendment of the preamble to the statute 43 Eliz. 1, c. 4. Fourthly the appellants contend and the respondents dispute that, even if not otherwise charitable, the trust is a valid charitable trust falling within section 1 of the Recreational Charities Act 1958 (p. 422 post), that is a trust to provide or to assist in the provision of facilities for recreation or other leisure time occupation provided in the interests of social welfare. . . .

Since we have reached the view that the trust is a valid educational charity their Lordships have not sought to hear argument nor, therefore, to reach a conclusion on any but the first two disputed questions in the dispute. Speaking for myself, however, I do not wish my absence of decision on the third or fourth points to be interpreted as an indorsement of the majority judgments in the Court of Appeal nor as necessarily dissenting from the contrary views contained in the minority judgment of Bridge LJ.[2a] For me at least the answers to the third and fourth questions are still left entirely undecided.

I now turn to the question of construction.

[His Lordship held that the deed meant that the "purpose of the settlor is to promote the physical education and development of pupils at schools and universities as an addition to such part of their education as relates to their mental education by providing the facilities and assistance to games and sports in the manner set out at greater length and in greater detail in the enumerated subclauses of clause 3 (a) of the deed," and continued:]

On a proper analysis, therefore, I do not find clause 3 (a) ambiguous. But, before I part with the question of construction, I would wish to express agreement with a contention made on behalf of the appellants and of the Attorney-General, but not agreed to on behalf of the respondents, that in construing trust deeds the intention of which is to set up a charitable trust, and in others too, where it can be claimed that there is an ambiguity, a benignant construction should be given if possible.[3] This was the maxim of the civil law: "semper in dubiis benigniora praeferenda sunt." There is a similar maxim in English law: "ut res magis valeat quam pereat." It certainly applies to charities when the question is one of uncertainty (*Weir v Crum-Brown* [1908] AC 162, 167), and, I think, also where a gift is capable of two constructions one of which would make it void and the other effectual (cf. *Bruce v Deer Presbytery* (1867) LR 1 Sc & Div 96, 97; *Houston v Burns* [1918] AC 337, per Lord Finlay LC, at 341–2, and cf. also *Re Bain* [1930] 1 Ch 224, 230). In the present case I do not find it necessary to resort to benignancy in order to construe the clause, but, had I been in doubt, I would certainly have been prepared to do so.

I must now turn to the deed, construed in the manner in which I have found it necessary to construe it, to consider whether it sets up a valid charitable trust for the advancement of education.

It is admitted, of course, that the words "charity" and "charitable" bear, for the purposes of English law and equity, meanings totally different from the

---

2a Now upheld in *Guild v IRC* [1992] 2 AC 310, [1992] 2 All ER 10, p. 423, post.
3 P. 337, ante.

senses in which they are used in ordinary educated speech or, for instance, in the Authorised Version of the Bible (contrast, for instance, the expression "cold as charity" with the Authorised Version of I Corinthians xiii and both of these with the decisions in *Incorporated Council of Law Reporting for England and Wales v A-G* [1972] Ch 73, [1971] 3 All ER 1029, p. 370, ante; *IRC v Yorkshire Agricultural Society* [1928] 1 KB 611; *Brisbane City Council v A-G for Queensland* [1979] AC 411, [1978] 3 All ER 30; but I do not share the view, implied by Stamp LJ and Orr LJ in the instant case [1979] 1 WLR 130, 139, [1979] 1 All ER 588, 594, that the words "education" and "educational" bear, or can bear, for the purposes of the law of charity, meanings different from those current in present-day educated English speech. I do not believe that there is such a difference. What has to be remembered, however, is that, as Lord Wilberforce pointed out in *Re Hopkins' Will Trusts* [1965] Ch 669, 678, [1964] 3 All ER 46, 51, and in *Scottish Burial Reform and Cremation Society Ltd v Glasgow City Corpn* [1968] AC 138, [1967] 3 All ER 215, especially at 154, at 223, both the legal conception of charity, and within it the educated man's ideas about education, are not static, but moving and changing. Both change with changes in ideas about social values. Both have evolved with the years. In particular in applying the law to contemporary circumstances it is extremely dangerous to forget that thoughts concerning the scope and width of education differed in the past greatly from those which are now generally accepted.

In saying this I do not in the least wish to cast doubt on *Re Nottage* [1895] 2 Ch 649, p. 430 post, which was referred to in both courts below and largely relied on by the respondents here. Strictly speaking *Re Nottage* was not a case about education at all. The issue there was whether the bequest came into the fourth class of charity categorised in Lord Macnaghten's classification of 1891. The mere playing of games or enjoyment of amusement or competition is not per se charitable, nor necessarily educational, though they may (or may not) have an educational or beneficial effect if diligently practised. Neither am I deciding in the present case even that a gift for physical education per se and not associated with persons of school age or just above would necessarily be a good charitable gift. That is a question which the courts may have to face at some time in the future. But in deciding what is or is not an educational purpose for the young in 1980 it is not irrelevant to point out what Parliament considered to be educational for the young in 1944 when, by the Education Act of that year, in sections 7 and 53 (which are still on the statute book), Parliament attempted to lay down what was then intended to be the statutory system of education organised by the state, and the duties of the local education authorities and the minister in establishing and maintaining the system. Those sections are so germane to the present issue that I cannot forbear to quote them both. Section 7 provides (in each of the sections the emphasis being mine):

> "The statutory system of public education shall be organised in three progressive stages to be known as primary education, secondary education, and further education; and it shall be the duty of the local education authority for every area, so far as their powers extend, to contribute towards *the spiritual, moral, mental, and physical development of the community by securing that efficient education throughout those stages shall be available to meet the needs of the population of their area.*"

[His Lordship quoted 53 (1) and (2) of the same Act and continued:]

There is no trace in these sections of an idea of education limited to the development of mental, vocational or practical skills, to grounds or facilities the special perquisite of particular schools, or of any schools or colleges, or term-time, or particular localities, and there is express recognition of the contribution which extra-curricular activities and voluntary societies or bodies can make even in the promotion of the purely statutory system envisaged by the Act. In the light of section 7 in particular I would be very reluctant to confine the meaning of education to formal instruction in the classroom or even the playground, and I consider it sufficiently wide to cover all the activities envisaged by the settlor in the present case. One of the affidavits filed on the part of the respondent referred to the practices of ancient Sparta. I am not sure that this particular precedent is an entirely happy one, but from a careful perusal of *Plato's Republic* I doubt whether its author would have agreed with Stamp LJ in regarding "physical education and development" as an elusive phrase, or as other than an educational charity, at least when used in association with the formal education of the young during the period when they are pupils of schools or in statu pupillari at universities.

It is, of course, true that no authority exactly in point could be found which is binding on your Lordships in the instant appeal. Nevertheless, I find the first instance case of *Re Mariette* [1915] 2 Ch 284, a decision of Eve J, both stimulating and instructive. Counsel for the respondents properly reminded us that this concerned a bequest effectively tied to a particular institution. Nevertheless, I cannot forbear to quote a phrase from the judgment, always bearing in mind the danger of quoting out of context. Eve J said at 288:

"No one of sense could be found to suggest that between those ages" (10 to 19) "any boy can be properly educated unless at least as much attention is given to the development of his body as is given to the development of his mind."[4]

Apart from the limitation to the particular institution I would think that these words apply as well to the settlor's intention in the instant appeal as to the testator's in *Re Mariette*, and I regard the limitation to the pupils of schools and universities in the instant case as a sufficient association with the provision of formal education to prevent any danger or vagueness in the object of the trust or irresponsibility or capriciousness in application by the trustees. I am far from suggesting that the concept either of education or of physical education even for the young is capable of indefinite extension. On the contrary, I do not think that the courts have as yet explored the extent to which elements of organisation, instruction, or the disciplined inculcation of information, instruction or skill may limit the whole concept of education. I believe that in some ways it will prove more extensive, in others more restrictive than has been thought hitherto. But it is clear at least to me that the decision in *Re Mariette* is not to be read in a sense which confines its application for ever to gifts to a particular institution. It has been extended already in *Re Mellody* [1918] 1 Ch 228 to gifts for annual treats for schoolchildren in a particular locality (another decision of Eve J);[5] to playgrounds for children (*Re Chesters* 25 July 1934, unreported), and possibly *not* educational, but referred to in *IRC v Baddeley* [1955] AC 572, 596, [1955] 1 All ER 525, 536); to a children's outing (*Re Ward's*

4 Bequest of £1,000 to the Governing Body of Aldenham School for the purpose of building Eton fives courts or squash rackets courts held to be valid charitable gift. EVE J added: "To leave 200 boys at large and to their own devices during their leisure hours would be to court catastrophe; it would not be educating them, but would probably result in their quickly relapsing into something approaching barbarism"; Annual Report for 1991, para. 74 (Cliff Richard Tennis Development Trust held to be charitable).

5 This was also held to be valid as a gift under the fourth head, p. 408, post.

Estate (1937) 81 SJ 397); to a prize for chess to boys and young men resident in the city of Portsmouth (*Re Dupree's Deed Trusts* [1945] Ch 16, [1944] 2 All ER 443, p. 365 ante (a decision of Vaisey J) and for the furthering of the Boy Scouts movement by helping to purchase sites for camping, outfits, etc. (*Re Webber* [1954] 1 WLR 1500, [1954] 3 All ER 712; another decision of Vaisey J). In that case Vaisey J is reported as saying, at 1501, at 713:

> "I am bound to say that I am surprised to hear that anyone suggests that the Boy Scouts movement,[6] as distinguished from the Boy Scout Association, or the Boy Scouts organisation, or any other form of words, is other than an educational charity. I should have thought that it was well settled and well understood that the objects of the organisation of boy scouts is an education of a very special kind no doubt, but still, none the less, educational."

It is important to remember that in the instant appeal we are dealing with the concept of physical education and development of the young deliberately associated by the settlor with the status of pupilage in schools or universities (of which, according to the evidence, about 95 per cent. are within the age group 17 to 22). We are not dealing with adult education, physical or otherwise, as to which some considerations may be different. Whether one looks at the statute or the cases, the picture of education when applied to the young which emerges is complex and varied, but not, to borrow Stamp LJ's epithet [1979] 1 WLR 130, 134H, [1979] 1 All ER 588, 591, "elusive". It is the picture of a balanced and systematic process of instruction, training and practice containing, to borrow from section 7 of the Act of 1944, both spiritual, moral, mental and physical elements, the totality of which in any given case may vary with, for instance, the availability of teachers and facilities, and the potentialities, limitations and individual preferences of the pupils. But the totality of the process consists as much in the balance between each of the elements as in the enumeration of the things learned or the places in which the activities are carried on. I reject any idea which would cramp the education of the young within the school or university syllabus, confine it within the school or university campus, limit it to formal instruction, or render it devoid of pleasure in the exercise of skill. It is expressly acknowledged to be a subject in which the voluntary donor can exercise his generosity, and I can find nothing contrary to the law of charity which prevents a donor providing a trust which is designed to improve the balance between the various elements which go into the education of the young. That is what in my view the object of the instant settlement seeks to do.

I am at pains to disclaim the view that the conception of this evolving, and therefore not static, view of education is capable of infinite abuse or, even worse, proving void for uncertainty. . . .

I also wish to be on my guard against the "slippery slope" argument of which I see a reflection in Stamp LJ's reference to "hunting, shooting and fishing." It seems to me that that is an argument with which Vaisey J dealt effectively in *Re Dupree's Deed Trusts* [1945] Ch 16, [1944] 2 All ER 443, in which he validated the chess prize.

[His Lordship quoted from VAISEY J at 20, set out at p. 365, ante, and continued]

---

6 Its purpose is stated in its charter to be the instruction of "boys of all classes in the principles of discipline, loyalty and good citizenship."

My Lords, for these reasons I reach the conclusion that the trust is a valid charitable gift for the advancement of education, which, after all, is what it claims to be. The conclusion follows that the appeal should be allowed, the judgments appealed from be reversed and the order for registration made by the commissioners be restored.

Report of the Charity Commissioners for England and Wales for 1984, paras. 19, 21

The Oxford Ice Skating Association Limited

"19. The objects of the Company were to provide or assist in the provision of facilities for recreation or other leisure-time occupation in the interests of social welfare as defined in the Recreational Charities Act 1958 in any part of the United Kingdom and in furtherance of that object and without prejudice to its generality to provide or assist in the provision of facilities for an ice skating rink in the City of Oxford or its environs to be available to the members of the public at large and to promote certain further objects which were clearly within the charitable purposes set out in the 1958 Act.

21. The Inland Revenue did not rely on the principle which had emerged from *Re Nottage* [1895] 2 Ch 649 that encouragement of a 'mere sport' is not charitable. Nevertheless, in deciding whether the provision of an ice skating rink was charitable, we considered whether the case was authority for a distinction between the promotion of a single sport and several sports. We agreed that the word 'mere' in that context was intended to mean 'nothing but' and referred to 'sport pure and simple'. The number of sports to be promoted was irrelevant; and in our view, the conclusion to be drawn from *Re Nottage* is that the promotion of sport can be charitable only if it is directed to some other end which benefits the public. Support for this view could be found in *Re Gray* [1925] Ch 362, p. 430 post, in which a gift for the promotion of shooting, fishing, cricket, football and polo in a regiment was held to be charitable not because the trust was for the promotion of more than one sport but because it promoted the efficiency of the Army. And in *Re Hadden* [1932] 1 Ch 133 a gift for providing playing fields, parks, gymnasiums and other 'plans' was held to be charitable because it promoted the health and welfare of the working classes. We also agreed that *Re Hadden* and *Re Morgan* [1955] 1 WLR 738, [1955] 2 All ER 632[7] were authority for the proposition that although the promotion of sport in itself is not charitable, the provision *for the public* of land, with or without buildings, for carrying on sport is charitable. Accordingly the provision of a public ice skating rink is charitable without need to rely on the Recreational Charities Act 1958."

---

7 *IRC v Baddeley* [1955] AC 572 at 589, 615, [1955] 1 All ER 525; Annual Report for 1965, para. 25 (King George's Fields Foundation); *R v Doncaster Metropolitan Borough Council* (1986) 57 P & CR 1; *Oldham Borough Council v A-G* [1993] Ch 210, [1993] 2 All ER 432; *cf. Liverpool City Council v A-G*, (1992) Times, 1 May (covenant by council to use donated land as recreation ground held not charitable); *Barrett (Manchester) Ltd v Bolton Metropolitan Borough Council* (1991, unreported); (1992) 142 NLJ 687 (C. Crawford).

The Commissioners also held that the objects were charitable under the Act, having regard to the evidence of public benefit (at least 50,000 people would use the ice-rink each week); p. 422 post."

iv. EVALUATION OF AESTHETIC MERIT

Even within a school curriculum, there may be doubt whether a particular subject is educational in the legal sense. The question is all the more difficult outside the school context. The acceptance of aesthetic and artistic subjects as being educational brings the court face to face with the problem of selecting which activities qualify. Not all noise-making qualifies as educational music; not every collection of junk as a museum of art. And what qualifies in one age may fail in the next, and vice-versa. The policy of the law is to encourage the promotion of artistic work of quality; but it is an extreme step to permit the promotion, free of tax and permanently, of the work of a particular artist. The same problem arises in other fields of charity. Indeed it is at the back of many of the decisions under the fourth head.[8] How should the selection be determined, and by whom? In *Re Shaw's Will Trusts* [1952] Ch 163, [1952] 1 All ER 49, VAISEY J said at 168, at 53: "The court ought not to weigh the respective merits of particular educational methods"; and at 172, at 55: "Whatever may be my own personal views about this type of education, they have nothing to do with the case."

RE DELIUS
[1957] Ch 299, [1957] 1 All ER 854 (ChD, ROXBURGH J)

The widow of the composer Frederick Delius gave her residuary estate upon various trusts for the advancement of Delius's musical works. The most significant clause was clause 12 by which the trustees were to "apply the royalties income and the income of my residuary trust fund for or towards the advancement ... of the musical works of my late husband ... under conditions in which the making of profit is not the object to be attained and which might be economically impossible by any concert operatic or other organisation ..." and then suggested ways in which this should be achieved. The question was whether the will created a charitable trust.

Held. A valid charitable trust for the advancement of education.

ROXBURGH J: First of all, I have to decide what is the purpose of this trust. In arriving at a conclusion on that point, I must have regard not only to the language in which the purpose is expressed (and, indeed, that is of itself reasonably clear) but also to the means which are indicated for achieving that purpose, which make the position even clearer. It seems to me that in very truth the purpose is the spreading and establishment of knowledge and appreciation of Delius's works amongst the public of the world. It is, indeed, remarkable to what extent that objective has been achieved in the 21 years or so since the widow died. The copyrights in Delius's works were valued at the date of her death at £1,483, and at that time formed a comparatively small portion of his residuary estate. The royalties received in the year ending April

---

8 Cf. *National Anti-Vivisection Society v IRC* [1948] AC 31, [1947] 2 All ER 217, p. 408, post.

5, 1936, amounted to £103, in the year 1946 they amounted to £2,233, and in the year 1956 they amounted to £7,278; which is no doubt largely to be attributed to Sir Thomas Beecham.

The position is now that certain of Delius's works are so well known that no guarantee is required by the recording companies in respect thereof, but the trustees are now advised that some of the lesser-known works which were recorded in the early history of the trust should be re-recorded if the work of the trust can continue to be carried on. Sir Thomas Beecham has been engaged for some years on the task of editing the whole of the compositions of Delius, with a view to the publication and issue of a uniform edition of the whole body of his musical works in accordance with the provisions of clause 12 of the will, but the printing and publication of the major portion of this edition has been held in abeyance pending the decision of this court whether after the period of 21 years from the death of the testatrix the trusts declared in clause 12 constitute valid and effectual charitable trusts, or are void as infringing the rule against perpetuities or otherwise.

I have stated what I understand to be the purpose of the trusts, and the question is whether that purpose is charitable in the eye of the law? I can do no better in this connexion than to read certain passages from the judgment of Lord Greene MR in *Royal Choral Society v IRC* [1943] 2 All ER 101. There are, of course, certain points which necessarily occur to the mind in connexion with a musical composition. It might be suggested as regards some music, at any rate, that its purpose was limited to giving pleasure, and as regards all music it must be said that it gives pleasure. That is a feature about music. When I say "all music", I mean all that can be truly called music. Indeed, a lot of pleasure is derived by some from something which can hardly be truly called music, but, at any rate, pleasure is a circumstance intimately connected with music. But that in itself does not operate to destroy the charitable character of a bequest for the advancement of the art of music. I adopt, with great satisfaction, the words of Lord Greene [1943] 2 All ER 101 at 104: "Curiously enough, some people find pleasure in providing education. Still more curiously, some people find pleasure in being educated: but the element of pleasure in those processes is not the purpose of them, but what may be called a by-product which is necessarily there." That seems to me to be all that need be said about the aspect of pleasure connected with the music of Delius.

Lord Greene proceeded: [His Lordship quoted the extract at p. 364, ante; and continued:] Those words have been freely adopted in subsequent cases, and I adopt them and also hold that they are directly applicable to this trust.

I do not find it necessary to consider what the position might be if the trusts were for the promotion of the works of some inadequate composer. It has been suggested that perhaps I should have no option but to give effect even to such a trust. I do not know, but I need not investigate that problem, because counsel who have argued before me have been unanimous in the view that the standard of Delius's work is so high that that question does not arise in the present case.

The point which has been made—and it is one of interest and importance—is, that first of all this trust is not a trust for the promotion of music in general but the music of a particular individual composer. That could not of itself vitiate the charitable nature of the trust, because, after all, aesthetic appreciation of music in a broad sense can only be derived from aesthetic appreciation of the works of a large number of composers. It is the aggregate of the work of a large number of composers which is the basis of the aesthetic appreciation, and, therefore, if it is charitable to promote music in general it must be charitable to promote the music of a particular composer, presupposing (as in this case I can assume) that the composer is one whose music is worth appreciating.

In order to make that plain, I would refer to *Re Shakespeare Memorial Trust* [1923] 2 Ch 398, where the charitable trust was, to put it shortly, to promote the works of Shakespeare. I cannot conceive that anybody would doubt that a trust to promote the works of Beethoven would be charitable, but the real strength of the point put in this case arises from the fact that this trust was created by the widow of Delius, and nobody would doubt that, amongst the many motives which actuated her, affection for her deceased husband was to be found. But one must be careful to distinguish motive from purpose, because motive is not relevant in these cases except in so far as it is incorporated into the purpose. Considering the purposes, it is possible to approach the purposes upon the hypothesis that their intention was, as Mr. Browne-Wilkinson put it, to enhance her husband's reputation.

This is, of course, rather subtle. It is a question which is the cart and which is the horse, because, of course, the more aesthetic appreciation of Delius's music is achieved the more Delius's reputation will necessarily be enhanced. The two things fit together, and there is no doubt whatever that both objects have in fact already been to a large extent achieved. But, in my judgment, it is not fair to approach the problem from that point of view. I think that there is every reason to suppose that the testatrix took the view, and was well advised to take it, that if the work of Delius was brought before the public in an efficient manner, the aesthetic appreciation of the public would grow and, inherent in that growth, would be the enhancement of Delius's reputation, which was in itself a desirable thing, and I for my part refuse to disentangle it. There is no reliable evidence on which I can disentangle it. What is quite clear to me is that these purposes would plainly be charitable if for the name "Delius" the name "Beethoven" were substituted and, in my judgment, they do not cease to be charitable because in this context the name is "Delius" and not "Beethoven".

RE PINION
[1965] Ch 85, [1964] 1 All ER 890 (CA, HARMAN, DAVIES and RUSSELL LJJ)

By his will, the testator, Arthur Watson Hyde Pinion, gave the income of the residue of his estate to his sister Edith for her life and after her death provided that his studio and contents, which included pictures, furniture, china, glass and objets d'art should be offered to the National Trust and kept intact in the studio and displayed to the public. A custodian was appointed, the post to be offered to Edith and after her death to a blood relation. Goods and chattels not of an antique nature could be disposed of. By a codicil he revoked his sister's life interest and provided that if, as happened, the National Trust was not prepared to observe the provisions of the will, his executors should maintain the studio and contents as a museum.

Held (reversing WILBERFORCE J). The trust was not for the advancement of education and was void.

HARMAN LJ: This appeal concerns the testamentary dispositions of Arthur Watson Hyde Pinion, who died in the year 1961, having, by his will made in 1956 as varied by a codicil made in 1961, sought to devote almost the whole of his not inconsiderable estate to a project designed to keep himself and his family for all time before the public eye by allowing the public to view without cost his studio, situate at 22A Pembridge Villas, Notting Hill, intact with its entire contents. These treasures are to be entrusted to a custodian, first his sister and subsequently a blood relation of his, who are to be paid and housed out of his estate. The question is whether he was entitled to saddle his property with this chimaera to the deprivation of his next-of-kin and this, the judge has held, he was entitled to do at the instance of the Attorney-General, who persuaded him, though hardly, that the testator has created a valid charitable trust.

The will and codicil are rambling and half coherent documents reduced to some semblance of order by the judge but his summary is, I think, perhaps too neat and logical and the actual words should be read to convey its authentic flavour. It starts by conferring a life interest in the whole estate on his sister, the first defendant, who is also his sole next-of-kin, and proceeds. [His Lordship then read passages of the will and codicils and continued:] I construe this farrago as meaning that the entire contents of the studio, which housed all the articles referred to, are to be exhibited as a whole and, as he says, "to be kept intact in the studio". The only exception is that articles "not of an antique nature" may be disposed of. I assume that the revocation of the sister's life interest accelerated the gift to the National Trust, which has refused the bequest, and that the authority to his executors to appoint a trust to carry out the bequest is in fact mandatory, the contrary not having been argued.

In this court the Attorney-General did not seek to support the gift as being beneficial in a general sense to the public, but confined his pleas to that head of charity which is characterised as the advancement of education. He argued both here and below that no evidence was receivable on this subject. A museum, he said, is a place which the law assumes to have an educational value and purpose. The cases on this subject to be found in Tudor on Charities, 5th edition (1929), are not very satisfactory. It would appear that a gift to an established museum is charitable: see *British Museum Trustees v White* (1826) 2 Sim & St 594. In *Re Holburne* (1885) 53 LT 212 a gift to trustees of objects of art to form an art museum in Bath open to the public and a fund to endow it was held a valid charitable gift as being of public utility or benefit. No question was there raised as to the merit of the collection. It must have been agreed that such merit existed, for everyone assumed it, including the judge. I conclude that a gift to found a public museum may be assumed to be charitable as of public utility if no one questions it. So in a case about religion, such as *Thornton v Howe* (1862) 31 Beav 14, the case about Joanna Southcote, the court will assume without inquiry that the teaching may do some good if not shown to be subversive of morality. Where the object is to found a school the court will not study the methods of education provided that on the face of them they are proper: *Re Shaw's Will Trusts* [1952] Ch 163, [1952] 1 All ER 49. A school for prostitutes or pickpockets would obviously fail. A case about education is *Re Hummeltenberg* [1923] 1 Ch 237, where the headnote reads: "To be valid a charitable bequest must be for the public benefit, and the trust must be capable of being administered and controlled by the court. The opinion of the donor of a gift or the creator of a trust that the gift or trust is for the public benefit does not make it so, the matter is one to be determined by the court on the evidence before it."

The bequest in that case was connected with spiritualism and the point to which I draw attention is that the judge (the late Lord Russell of Killowen, then Russell J) said it must be decided on the evidence. There is a passage in his judgment as follows [1923] 1 Ch at 242: "It was contended" (says he) "that the court was not the tribunal to determine whether a gift or trust was or was not a gift or a trust for the benefit of the public. It was said that the only judge of this was the donor of the gift or the creator of the trust. For this view reliance was placed on the views expressed by the Master of the Rolls [Porter MR] and by some members of the Court of Appeal in Ireland in *Re Cranston* [1898] 1 IR 431 at 446. Reliance was also placed on a sentence in the judgment of Chitty J in *Re Foveaux* [1895] 2 Ch 501. So far as the views so expressed declare that the personal or private opinion of the judge is immaterial, I agree; but so far as they lay down or suggest that the donor of the gift or the creator of the trust is to determine whether the purpose is beneficial to the public, I respectfully disagree. If a testator by stating or indicating his view that a trust is beneficial to the public can establish that fact beyond question, trusts might be established in perpetuity for the promotion of all kinds of fantastic (though not unlawful) objects, of which the training of poodles to dance might be a mild example. In my opinion the question whether a gift is or may be operative for the public benefit is a question to be answered by the court by forming an opinion upon the evidence before it."

Where a museum is concerned and the utility of the gift is brought in question it is, in my opinion, and herein I agree with the judge, essential to know at least something of the quality of the proposed exhibits in order to judge whether they will be conducive to the education of the public. So I think with a public library, such a place if found to be devoted entirely to works of pornography or of a corrupting nature, would not be allowable. Here it is suggested that education in the fine arts is the object. For myself a reading of the will leads me rather to the view that the testator's object was not to educate anyone, but to perpetuate his own name and the repute of his family, hence perhaps the direction that the custodian should be a blood relation of his. However that may be, there is a strong body of evidence here that as a means of education this collection is worthless. The testator's own paintings, of which there are over 50, are said by competent persons to be in an academic style and "atrociously bad" and the other pictures without exception worthless. Even the so-called "Lely" turns out to be a 20th century copy.

Apart from pictures there is a haphazard assembly—it does not merit the name collection, for no purpose emerges, no time nor style is illustrated—of furniture and objects of so-called "art" about which expert opinion is unanimous that nothing beyond the third-rate is to be found. Indeed one of the experts expresses his surprise that so voracious a collector should not by hazard have picked up even one meritorious object. The most that skilful cross-examination extracted from the expert witnesses was that there were a dozen chairs which might perhaps be acceptable to a minor provincial museum and perhaps another dozen not altogether worthless, but two dozen chairs do not make a museum and they must, to accord with the will, be exhibited stifled by a large number of absolutely worthless pictures and objects.

It was said that this is a matter of taste, and de gustibus non est disputandum, but here I agree with the judge that there is an accepted canon of taste on which the court must rely, for it has itself no judicial knowledge of such matters, and the unanimous verdict of the experts is as I have stated. The judge with great hesitation concluded that there was that scintilla of merit which was sufficient to save the rest. I find myself on the other side of the line. I can conceive of no useful object to be served in foisting upon the public this mass of junk. It has neither public utility nor educative value. I would hold that the testator's project ought not to be carried into effect and that his next-of kin is entitled to the residue of his estate.

v. PUBLIC BENEFIT

OPPENHEIM v TOBACCO SECURITIES TRUST CO LTD[9]

[1951] AC 297, [1951] 1 All ER 31 (HL, Lords SIMONDS, NORMAND, OAKSEY, MORTON OF HENRYTON and MACDERMOTT)

The income of a trust fund was directed to be applied "in providing for . . . the education of children of employees or former employees of the British-American Tobacco Co, Ltd . . . or any of its subsidiary or allied companies in such manner . . . as the acting trustees shall in their absolute discretion . . . think fit" with power also to apply the capital for the like purposes.

The number of employees of the company and their subsidiary and allied companies exceeded 110,000.

The question was whether the class to be benefited was a sufficient section of the public.

Held. (Lord MACDERMOTT dissenting). Because the qualification to benefit was based upon a personal nexus, the class of beneficiaries was not a section of the public; and the trust was void.

LORD SIMONDS: My Lords, once more your Lordships have to consider the difficult subject of charitable trusts, and this time a question is asked to which no wholly satisfactory answer can be given.

Before I turn to the authorities I will make some preliminary observations. It is a clearly established principle of the law of charity that a trust is not charitable unless it is directed to the public benefit. This is sometimes stated in the proposition that it must benefit the community or a section of the community. Negatively it is said that a trust is not charitable if it confers only private benefits. In the recent case of *Gilmour v Coats* [1949] AC 426, [1949] 1 All ER 848, p. 400, post, this principle was reasserted. It is easy to state and has been stated in a variety of ways, the earliest statement that I find being in *Jones v Williams* (1767) Amb 651 in which Lord Hardwicke LC is briefly reported as follows: "Definition of charity: a gift to a general public use, which extends to the poor as well as to the rich . . . ". With a single exception, to which I shall refer, this applies to all charities. We are apt now to classify them by reference to Lord Macnaghten's division in *Income Tax Comrs v Pemsel* [1891] AC 531 at 538, and, as I have elsewhere pointed out, it was at one time suggested that the element of public benefit was not essential except for charities falling within the fourth class, "other purposes beneficial to the community". This is certainly wrong except in the anomalous case of trusts for the relief of poverty with which I must specifically deal. In the case of trusts for educational purposes the condition of public benefit must be satisfied. The difficulty lies in

9 (1951) 67 LQR 162 (R.E.M.), 164 (A.L.G.); *Caffoor v Income Tax Comr, Colombo* [1961] AC 584 at 602, [1961] 2 All ER 436 at 443, per Lord RADCLIFFE. See also *Davies v Perpetual Trustee Co Ltd* [1959] AC 439, [1959] 2 All ER 128 (a gift of land in Sydney, New South Wales "to the Presbyterians the descendants of those settled in the Colony hailing from or born in the North of Ireland to be held in trust for the purpose of establishing a college for the education and tuition of their youth in the standards of the Westminster Divines as taught in the Holy Scriptures" held void by Privy Council. The class of persons was "a fluctuating body of private individuals", and in no sense "a section of the community").

determining what is sufficient to satisfy the test, and there is little to help your Lordships to solve it.

If I may begin at the bottom of the scale, a trust established by a father for the education of his son is not a charity. The public element, as I will call it, is not supplied by the fact that from that son's education all may benefit. At the other end of the scale the establishment of a college or university is beyond doubt a charity. "Schools of learning and free schools and scholars of universities" are the very words of the preamble to the Statute of Elizabeth. So also the endowment of a college, university or school by the creation of scholarships or bursaries is a charity and none the less because competition may be limited to a particular class of persons. It is upon this ground, as Lord Greene MR pointed out in *Re Compton* [1945] Ch 123 at 136, [1945] 1 All ER 198 at 205 that the so-called Founder's Kin cases can be rested. The difficulty arises where the trust is not for the benefit of any institution either then existing or by the terms of the trust to be brought into existence, but for the benefit of a class of persons at large. Then the question is whether that class of persons can be regarded as such a "section of the community" as to satisfy the test of public benefit. These words "section of the community" have no special sanctity, but they conveniently indicate first, that the possible (I emphasize the word "possible") beneficiaries must not be numerically negligible, and secondly, that the quality which distinguishes them from other members of the community, so that they form by themselves a section of it, must be a quality which does not depend on their relationship to a particular individual. It is for this reason that a trust for the education of members of a family or, as in *Re Compton*, of a number of families cannot be regarded as charitable. A group of persons may be numerous but, if the nexus between them is their personal relationship to a single propositus or to several propositi, they are neither the community nor a section of the community for charitable purposes.

I come, then, to the present case where the class of beneficiaries is numerous but the difficulty arises in regard to their common and distinguishing quality. That quality is being children of employees of one or other of a group of companies. I can make no distinction between children of employees and the employees themselves. In both cases the common quality is found in employment by particular employers. The latter of the two cases by which the Court of Appeal held itself to be bound, *Re Hobourn Aero Components Ltd's Air Raid Distress Fund* [1946] Ch 194, [1946] 1 All ER 501, is a direct authority for saying that such a common quality does not constitute its possessors a section of the public for charitable purposes. In the former case, *Re Compton*, Lord Greene MR had by way of illustration placed members of a family and employees of a particular employer on the same footing, finding neither in common kinship nor in common employment the sort of nexus which is sufficient. My Lords, I am so fully in agreement with what was said by Lord Greene in both cases and by my noble and learned friend, then Morton LJ in the *Hobourn* case, that I am in danger of repeating without improving upon their words. No one who has been versed for many years in this difficult and very artificial branch of the law can be unaware of its illogicalities, but I join with my noble and learned friend in echoing the observations which he cited [1946] Ch at 208, [1946] 1 All ER at 510 from the judgment of Russell LJ in *Re Grove-Grady* [1929] 1 Ch 557 at 582, and I agree with him that the decision in *Re Drummond* [1914] 2 Ch 90 "imposed a very healthy check upon the extension of the legal definition of 'charity' ". It appears to me that it would be an extension, for which there is no justification in principle or authority, to regard common employment as a quality which constitutes those employed a section of the community. It must not, I think, be forgotten that charitable institutions enjoy rare and increasing privileges, and that the claim to come within that privileged class should be clearly established. With the single exception of *Re Rayner* (1920) 89 LJCh 369, which I must regard as of doubtful authority, no case has been brought to the notice of the House in which such a claim as this has been made, where there is no element of poverty in the beneficiaries, but just this and no more, that they are the children of those in a common employment.

Learned counsel for the appellant sought to fortify his case by pointing to the anomalies that would ensue from the rejection of his argument. For, he said, admittedly those who follow a profession or calling, clergymen, lawyers, colliers, tobacco-workers and so on, are a section of the public; how strange then it would be if, as in the case of railwaymen, those who follow a particular calling are all employed by one employer. Would a trust for the education of railwaymen be charitable, but a trust for the education of men employed on the railways by the Transport Board not be charitable? And what of service of the Crown whether in the civil service or the armed forces? Is there a difference between soldiers and soldiers of the King? My Lords, I am not impressed by this sort of argument and will consider on its merits, if the occasion should arise, the case where the description of the occupation and the employment is in effect the same, where in a word, if you know what a man does, you know who employs him to do it. It is to me a far more cogent argument, as it was to my noble and learned friend in the *Hobourn* case, that if a section of the public is constituted by the personal relation of employment, it is impossible to say that it is not constituted by 1,000 as by 100,000 employees, and, if by 1,000, then by 100, and, if by 100, then by 10. I do not mean merely that there is a difficulty in drawing the line, though that too is significant: I have it also in mind that, though the actual number of employees at any one moment might be small, it might increase to any extent, just as, being large, it might decrease to any extent. If the number of employees is the test of validity, must the court take into account potential increase or decrease, and, if so, as at what date? ...

I would also, as I have previously indicated, say a word about the so called "poor relations" cases. I do so only because they have once more been brought forward as an argument in favour of a more generous view of what may be charitable. It would not be right for me to affirm or to denounce or to justify these decisions: I am concerned only to say that the law of charity, so far as it relates to "the relief of aged, impotent and poor people" (I quote from the statute) and to poverty in general, has followed its own line, and that it is not useful to try to harmonize decisions on that branch of the law with the broad proposition on which the determination of this case must rest. It is not for me to say what fate might await those cases if in a poverty case this House had to consider them...[10]

The appeal should in my opinion be dismissed with costs.

LORD MACDERMOTT (dissenting): My Lords, it is not disputed that this trust is for the advancement of education. The question is whether it is of a public nature, whether, in the words of Lord Wrenbury in *Verge v Somerville* [1924] AC 496 at 499, "it is for the benefit of the community or of an appreciably important class of the community". The relevant class here is that from which

---

10 Their fate was decided in favour of charity in *Dingle v Turner* [1972] AC 601, [1972] 1 All ER 878, p. 356, ante.

those to be educated are to be selected. The appellant contends that this class is public in character; the respondent bank (as personal representative of the last surviving settlor) denies this and says that the class is no more than a group of private individuals.

Until comparatively recently the usual way of approaching an issue of this sort, at any rate where educational trusts were concerned, was, I believe, to regard the facts of each case and to treat the matter very much as one of degree. No definition of what constituted a sufficient section of the public for the purpose was applied, for none existed; and the process seems to have been one of reaching a conclusion on a general survey of the circumstances and considerations regarded as relevant rather than of making a single, conclusive test. The investigation left the course of the dividing line between what was and what was not a section of the community unexplored, and was concluded when it had gone far enough to establish to the satisfaction of the court whether or not the trust was public; and the decision as to that was, I think, very often reached by determining whether or not the trust was private.

If it is still permissible to conduct the present inquiry on these broad if imprecise lines, I would hold with the appellant. The numerical strength of the class is considerable on any showing. The employees concerned number over 110,000, and it may reasonably be assumed that the children, who constitute the class in question, are no fewer. The large size of the class is not, of course, decisive but in my view it cannot be left out of account when the problem is approached in this way. Then it must be observed that the propositi are not limited to those presently employed. They include former employees (not reckoned in the figure I have given) and are, therefore, a more stable category than would otherwise be the case. And, further, the employees concerned are not limited to those in the service of the "British American Tobacco Co Ltd or any of its subsidiary or allied companies"—itself a description of great width— but include the employees, in the event of the British American Tobacco Co Ltd being reconstructed or merged on amalgamation, of the reconstructed or amalgamated company or any of its subsidiary companies. No doubt the settlors here had a special interest in the welfare of the class they described, but, apart from the fact that this may serve to explain the particular form of their bounty, I do not think it material to the question in hand. What is material, as I regard the matter, is that they have chosen to benefit a class which is, in fact, substantial in point of size and importance and have done so in a manner which, to my mind, manifests an intention to advance the interests of the class described as a class rather than as a collection or succession of particular individuals. . . .

The respondent bank, however, contends that the inquiry should be of quite a different character to that which I have been discussing. It advances as the sole criterion a narrower test derived from the decisions of the Court of Appeal in *Re Compton* [1945] Ch 123, [1945] 1 All ER 198, and *Re Hobourn Aero Components Ltd's Air Raid Distress Fund* [1946] Ch 194, [1946] 1 All ER 501.

The test [there] propounded focuses upon the common quality which unites those within the class concerned and asks whether that quality is essentially impersonal or essentially personal. If the former, the class will rank as a section of the public and the trust will have the element common to and necessary for all legal charities; but, if the latter, the trust will be private and not charitable. It is suggested in the passage just quoted, and made clear beyond doubt in *Re Hobourn* that in the opinion of the Court of Appeal employment by a designated employer must be regarded for this purpose as a personal and not as an impersonal bond of union. In this connexion and as illustrating the discriminating character of what I may call "the *Compton* test" reference should be made to that part of the judgment of the learned Master of the Rolls in *Re Hobourn* [1946] Ch 194 at 206, [1946] 1 All ER 501 at 509 in which he speaks of the decision in *Hall v Derby Borough Urban Sanitary Authority* (1885) 16 QBD 163. The passage runs thus: "That related to a trust for railway servants. It is said that if a trust for railway servants can be a good charity, so too a trust for railway servants in the employment of a particular railway company is a good charity. That is not so. The reason, I think, is that in the one case the trust is for railway servants in general and in the other case it is for employees of a particular company, a fact which limits the potential beneficiaries to a class ascertained on a purely personal basis."

My Lords, I do not quarrel with the result arrived at in the *Compton* and *Hobourn* cases, and I do not doubt that the *Compton* test may often prove of value and lead to a correct determination. But, with the great respect due to those who have formulated this test, I find myself unable to regard it as a criterion of general applicability and conclusiveness. In the first place I see much difficulty in dividing the qualities or attributes, which may serve to bind human beings into classes, into two mutually exclusive groups, the one involving individual status and purely personal, the other disregarding such status and quite impersonal. As a task this seems to me no less baffling and elusive than the problem to which it is directed, namely, the determination of what is and what is not a section of the public for the purposes of this branch of the law. After all, what is more personal than poverty or blindness or ignorance? Yet none would deny that a gift for the education of the children of the poor or blind was charitable; and I doubt if there is any less certainty about the charitable nature of a gift for, say, the education of children who satisfy a specified examining body that they need and would benefit by a course of special instruction designed to remedy their educational defects.

But can any really fundamental distinction, as respects the personal or impersonal nature of the common link, be drawn between those employed, for example, by a particular university and those whom the same university has put in a certain category as the result of individual examination and assessment? Again, if the bond between those employed by a particular railway is purely personal, why should the bond between those who are employed as railway men be so essentially different? Is a distinction to be drawn in this respect between those who are employed in a particular industry before it is nationalized and whose who are employed therein after that process has been completed and one employer has taken the place of many? Are miners in the service of the National Coal Board now in one category and miners at a particular pit or of a particular district in another? Is the relationship between those in the service of the Crown to be distinguished from that obtaining between those in the service of some other employer? Or, if not, are the children of, say, soldiers or civil servants to be regarded as not constituting a sufficient section of the public to make a trust for their education charitable?

It was conceded in the course of the argument that, had the present trust been framed so as to provide for the education of the children of those engaged in the tobacco industry in a named county or town, it would have been a good charitable disposition, and that even though the class to be benefited would have been appreciably smaller and no more important than is the class here. That concession follows from what the Court of Appeal has said. But if it is sound and a personal or impersonal relationship remains the universal criterion I think it shows, no less than the queries I have just raised in indicating some of the difficulties of the problem, that the *Compton* test is a very arbitrary and artificial rule. This leads me to the second difficulty that I have regarding it. If I understand it aright it necessarily makes the quantum of public benefit a consideration of little moment; the size of the class becomes immaterial and the need of its members and the public advantage of having that need met appear alike to be irrelevant. To my mind these are considerations of some account in the sphere of educational trusts for, as already indicated, I think the educational value and scope of the work actually to be done must have a bearing on the question of public benefit.

Finally, it seems to me that, far from settling the state of the law on this particular subject, the *Compton* test is more likely to create confusion and doubt in the case of many trusts and institutions of a character whose legal standing as charities has never been in question. I have particularly in mind gifts for the education of certain special classes such, for example, as the daughters of missionaries, the children of those professing a particular faith or accepted as ministers of a particular denomination, or those whose parents have sent them to a particular school for the earlier stages of their training. I cannot but think that in cases of this sort an analysis of the common quality binding the class to be benefited may reveal a relationship no less personal than that existing between an employer and those in his service. Take, for instance, a trust for the provision of university education for boys coming from a particular school. The common quality binding the members of that class seems to reside in the fact that their parents or guardians all contracted for their schooling with the same establishment or body. That the school in such a case may itself be a charitable foundation seems altogether beside the point and quite insufficient to hold the *Compton* test at bay if it is well founded in law.

My Lords, counsel for the appellant and for the Attorney-General adumbrated several other tests for establishing the presence or absence of the necessary public element. I have given these my careful consideration and I do not find them any more sound or satisfactory than the *Compton* test. I therefore return to what I think was the process followed before the decision in *Compton's* case, and, for the reasons already given, I would hold the present trust charitable and allow the appeal. I have only to add that I recognize the imperfections and uncertainties of that process. They are as evident as the difficulties of finding something better. But I venture to doubt if it is in the power of the courts to resolve those difficulties satisfactorily as matters stand. It is a long cry to the age of Elizabeth and I think what is needed is a fresh start from a new statute.

INLAND REVENUE COMMISSIONERS v EDUCATIONAL GRANTS ASSOCIATION LTD

[1967] Ch 123, [1966] 3 All ER 708 (ChD, Pennycuick J)

The Educational Grants Association Ltd was an association established for the advancement of education. It had a close relation with the Metal Box Co Ltd, and the bulk of its income came from a deed of covenant executed in its favour by the Metal Box Co Ltd.

In the years relevant to the present claim for repayment of income tax, between 76 per cent. and 85 per cent. of the income of the Association was applied for the education of children of persons connected with the Metal Box Co Ltd.

The claim for repayment raised the question whether the Association was established for charitable purposes only, and whether the income was applied "for charitable purposes only" with in s. 447 (1) (*b*) of the Income Tax Act 1952.[11]

Held. The claim failed because the income was not applied for charitable purposes only.

PENNYCUICK J: . . . The objects of the corporation, in order that they may be exclusively charitable, must be confined to objects for the public benefit. Equally, the application of the income, if it is to be within those objects, must be for the public benefit. Conversely, the application of income otherwise than for the public benefit must be outside the objects and ultra vires. For example, under an object for the advancement of education, once that is accepted as an exclusively charitable object, the income must be applied for the advancement of education by way of public benefit. An application of income for the advancement of education by way of private benefit would be ultra vires, and nonetheless so by reason that, in the nature of things, the members of a private class are included in the public as a whole. This may perhaps explain the repetition of the words "for charitable purposes only" in the second requirement of the subsection.

Mr. Talbot, for the association, advanced a simple and formidable argument: namely, (i) the association is established for specified educational purposes; (ii) those purposes are admittedly charitable purposes, so the first requirement is satisfied; (iii) the income has been applied for the specified educational purposes; and (iv) therefore the income has been applied for charitable purposes, and the second requirement is satisfied. It seems to me that this argument leaves out of account the element of public benefit. It is true that it is claimed by the association and admitted by the revenue that the educational purposes specified in the association's memorandum are charitable purposes, but this by definition implies that the purposes are for the public benefit. In order that the second requirement may be satisfied, it must equally be shown that its income has been applied not merely for educational purposes as expressed in the memorandum, but for those educational purposes by way of public benefit. An application of income by way of private benefit would be ultra vires. It is not open to the association first to set up a claim which can only be sustained on the basis that the purposes expressed in the memorandum are for the public benefit, and then, when it comes to the application of income, to look only to the purposes expressed in the memorandum, leaving the element of public benefit out of account. This point may be illustrated by considering the familiar example of a case in which a fund is settled upon trust for the advancement of education in general terms and the income is applied for the education of the settlor's children. Mr. Talbot does not shrink from the conclusion that such an application comes within the terms of the trust and satisfies the second requirement of the subsection. I think it does neither.

I understand from Mr. Talbot that he advanced the foregoing contention— and, I think, only this contention—before the special commissioners, although it is not very clearly reflected in their findings. The special commissioners were

11 See now ICTA 1988, s. 505 (1) (*c*).

evidently much pre-occupied by *Re Koettgen's Will Trusts* [1954] Ch 252, [1954] 1 All ER 581, to which I shall refer in a moment. It was substantially the only argument which Mr. Talbot advanced before me as to the construction of the section.

Mr. Goulding, for the Inland Revenue Commissioners, based his argument upon construction broadly on the lines which I have indicated above as being correct. He devoted much of his argument to repelling the application of the *Koettgen* case to the present one. The headnote in the *Koettgen* case is as follows:

"A testatrix bequeathed her residuary estate on trust 'for the promotion and furtherance of commercial education . . . ' The will provided that 'The persons eligible as beneficiaries under the fund shall be persons of either sex who are British-born subjects and who are desirous of educating themselves or obtaining tuition for a higher commercial career but whose means are insufficient or will not allow of their obtaining such education or tuition at their own expense. . . . ' She further directed that in selecting the beneficiaries 'it is my wish that the . . . trustees shall give a preference to any employees of John Batt & Co (London) Ltd or any members of the families of such employees; failing a sufficient number of beneficiaries under such description then the persons eligible shall be any persons of British birth as the . . . trustees may select Provided that the total income to be available for benefiting the preferred beneficiaries shall not in any one year be more than 75 per cent. of the total available income for that year.' In the event of the failure of those trusts there was a gift over to a named charity. It was admitted that the trust was for the advancement of education, but it was contended for the charity that having regard to the direction to prefer a limited class of persons the trusts were not of a sufficiently public nature to constitute valid charitable trusts:—

"*Held*, that the gift to the primary class from whom the trustees could select beneficiaries contained the necessary element of benefit to the public, and that it was when that class was ascertained that the validity of the trust had to be determined; so that the subsequent direction to prefer, as to 75 per cent. of the income, a limited class did not affect the validity of the trust, which was accordingly a valid and effective charitable trust. *Oppenheim v Tobacco Securities Trust Co Ltd* [1951] AC 297, [1951] 1 All ER 31 distinguished."

That headnote, I think, accurately represents the effect of what the judge decided.

The other case considered by the special commissioners was *Caffoor v Income Tax Comr, Colombo* [1961] AC 584, [1961] 2 All ER 436, in the Privy Council. The headnote, so far as now relevant, is as follows:

"By the terms of a trust deed executed in Ceylon in 1942 the trust income after the death of the grantor was to be applied by the board of trustees, the appellants, in their absolute discretion for all or any of a number of purposes which included '(2) . . . (b) the education instruction or training in England or elsewhere abroad of deserving youths of the Islamic Faith' in any department of human activity. 'The recipients of the benefits . . . shall be selected by the board from the following classes of persons and in the following order:—(i) male descendants along either the male or female line of the grantor or of any of his brothers or sisters failing whom' youths of the Islamic faith born of Moslem parents of the Ceylon Moorish community permanently resident in Colombo or elsewhere in Ceylon . . .

Held, . . . (2) that in view of what was in effect the absolute priority to the benefit of the trust income which was conferred on the grantor's own family by clause (2) (b) (i) of the trust deed this was a family trust and not a trust of a public character solely for charitable purposes, and the income thereof was accordingly not entitled to the exemption claimed. . . ." *Re Compton* [1945] Ch 123, [1945] 1 All ER 198, *Oppenheim v Tobacco Securities Trust Co Ltd* [1951] AC 297, [1951] 1 All ER 31 and *Re Koettgen's Will Trusts* [1954] Ch 252, [1954] 1 All ER 581 considered. . . ."

I think it right, however, to add that for myself I find considerable difficulty in the *Koettgen* decision. I should have thought that a trust for the public with preference for a private class comprised in the public might be regarded as a trust for the application of income at the discretion of the trustees between charitable and non-charitable objects. However, I am not concerned here to dispute the validity of the *Koettgen* decision. I only mention the difficulty I feel as affording some additional reason for not applying the *Koettgen* decision by analogy in connection with the second requirement of the subsection.

I return now to the present case. The association has claimed that the purposes of the association are exclusively charitable, which imports that the purposes must be for the public benefit. The revenue have admitted that claim. I have then to consider whether the association has applied its income within its expressed objects and by way of public benefit. There is no doubt that the application has been within its expressed objects, but has it been by way of public benefit? In order to answer this question, I must, I think, look at the individuals and institutions for whose benefit the income has been applied, and seek to discern whether these individuals and institutions possess any, and, if so, what, relevant characteristics by virtue of which the income has been applied for their benefit. One may for this purpose look at the minutes of the council, circular letters and so forth. Mr. Goulding at one time appeared to suggest that one might look at the actual intention of the members of the council. I do not think that is so.

When one makes this inquiry, one finds that between 75 per cent. and 85 per cent. of the income of the association has been expended upon the education of children connected with Metal Box. The association is intimately connected with Metal Box in the many respects found in the case stated. It derives most of its income from Metal Box. The council of management, as the special commissioners found, has followed a policy of seeking applications for grants from employees and ex-employees of Metal Box, though these applications are not, of course, always successful. The inference is inescapable that this part of the association's income—i.e., 75 per cent. to 85 per cent.—has been expended for the benefit of these children by virtue of a private characteristic; i.e., their connection with Metal Box. Such an application is not by way of public benefit. It is on all fours with an application of 75 per cent. to 85 per cent. of the income of a trust fund upon the education of a settlor's children. It follows, in my judgment, that, as regards the income which has been applied for the education of children connected with Metal Box, the association has failed to satisfy the second requirement in the subsection, and that the claim for relief fails. No reason has been suggested why the association should not obtain relief in respect of income applied for the benefit of institutions and outside individuals: see the words "so far as" in the section.

I recognise that this conclusion involves a finding that the council of management has acted ultra vires in applying the income of the association as it has done, albeit within the expressed objects of the association memorandum. This conclusion follows from the basis on which the association has framed its objects and based its claim. It is of course open to a comparable body to frame its objects so as to make clear that its income may be applied for private as well as public purposes, but in that case it may not obtain tax relief. It does not seem to me that such a body can have it both ways. I propose, therefore, to allow this appeal.[12]

QUESTIONS

1. Consider the difficulties with which a court is faced when compelled to make a value judgment upon artistic matters. What would you say of a gift
   (*a*) to promote the music of the "Blithe Spirits" (an unknown but promising Pop Group)?
   (*b*) to the Plantagenet Society for the purpose of establishing that Henry VII was responsible for the deaths of the Princes in the Tower?
   (*c*) for sex education in primary schools?
   (*d*) for the provision in schools of instruction on driving automobiles?

2. Do you think that the provision of sports facilities generally for the young should be charitable per se? *IRC v McMullen* [1979] 1 WLR 130 (CA); [1981] AC 1, [1980] 1 All ER 884 (HL) (where the point was expressly left open).

3. The disagreement between Lord SIMONDS and Lord MACDERMOTT on the question of the ascertainment of the test of public benefit was discussed by Lord CROSS OF CHELSEA in *Dingle v Turner* (p. 356, ante). Where do you stand on this controversy? How would *Oppenheim v Tobacco Securities Trust Co Ltd* (p. 385, ante) be decided if it arose today? [1974] CLJ 63 (G.H. Jones); Annual Report for 1971, para. 21; (1993–94) 2 CL & PR 203 (J. Callman).

4. (After reading Section C) Compare the test of public benefit in trusts for the advancement of education and trusts for the advancement of religion.

C. The Advancement of Religion[13]

i. GENERAL

The charitable nature of the third head of charity is based on nothing more specific than the inclusion in the Preamble of "the repair of churches".[14] The

---

12 See Annual Report for 1976, paras. 45–49 (The Cowen Charitable Trust); Annual Report for 1978, paras. 86–89 (where the Charity Commissioners followed *Re Koettgen's Will Trusts* [1954] Ch 252, [1954] 1 All ER 581 in three cases; 75 per cent, 65 per cent and 75 per cent.); *Re Martin* (1977) 121 SJ 828, Times, November 17.

13 H & M, pp. 401–405, 426–428; K & S, pp. 173–174; S & K, pp. 64–96; P & M, pp. 319–322; Pettit, pp. 235–240, 256; Riddall, pp. 102–105; Snell, pp. 148–149, 152; Tudor, pp. 62–87; Picarda, pp. 62–104; Goodman Report, paras. 40–41, 51–57; House of Commons Report, vol. 1, paras. 53–58, vol II, pp. 191–217, 313–316, 362–364; White Paper, paras. 2.18–2.36. See generally Crowther, *Religious Trusts* (1954). On the history, see Holdsworth, *H.E.L.* viii, pp. 402–410; (1930) 45 LQR 293, at p. 305 (Sir F. Pollock).

14 On the use of church halls for other charitable purposes, see Annual Report for 1984, Appx A.

concept has widened with the spread of religious toleration. It is not confined to the Established Church; or even to the Christian religion.[15] The boundaries are ill-defined, and many of the cases are conflicting. The extracts which follow are chosen as illustrations of significant issues which arise in this field.

Again, it is necessary to show a benefit to the public or a section of the public. This must be proved by evidence which is acceptable to the court; the faith of a particular religion that prayer and intercession will confer a benefit on the public is not sufficient. It seems that the concept of public benefit under this head is similar to that in the case of education, but not identical,[16] for while the pupils of a private school form a section of the public for the purposes of education, the same is not true of the members of a cloistered order in the context of religion.

ii. WHAT IS RELIGION?

Tudor on Charities (8th edn, 1995), p. 62

'' 'Religion' has been defined as meaning 'A particular system of faith and worship' and 'Recognition on the part of man of some higher unseen power as having control of his destiny, and as being entitled to obedience, reverence, and worship';[17] and numerous cases concerned with gifts and trusts for the advancement of religion show that this is the meaning accepted by the court. Hence the advancement or promotion of religion means, according to Lord Hanworth MR in *Keren Kayemeth Le Jisroel Ltd v IRC*[18] 'the promotion of spiritual teaching in a wide sense, and the maintenance of the doctrines on which it rests, and the observances that serve to promote and manifest it.' In *United Grand Lodge of Ancient Free and Accepted Masons of England v Holborn Borough Council*[19] Donovan J said: 'To advance religion means to promote it, to spread its message ever wider among mankind; to take some positive steps to sustain and increase religious belief; and these things are done in a variety of ways which may be comprehensively described as pastoral and missionary.' In *Re South Place Ethical Society*[20] Dillion J said: 'It seems to me that two of the essential attributes of religion are faith and worship; faith in a god and worship of that god,' and he referred to the definition quoted above.''

---

15 *Gilmour v Coats* [1949] AC 426 at 457, 458, [1949] 1 All ER 848 at 861, 862, per Lord REID; *Neville Estates Ltd v Madden* [1962] Ch 832 at 853, [1961] 3 All ER 769 at 781, per CROSS J.
16 See *Dingle v Turner* [1972] AC 601 at 625, [1972] 1 All ER 878 at 889, p. 356, ante, per Lord CROSS OF CHELSEA.
17 *Oxford English Dictionary*. In *Bowman v Secular Society Ltd* [1917] AC 406, 458, 459, Lord PARKER OF WADDINGTON said: ''Trusts for the purpose of religion have always been recognised in equity as good charitable trusts, but so far as I am aware there is no express authority dealing with the question what constitutes religion for the purpose of this rule,'' and proceeded to trace the history of religion in England from before the Reformation, indicating how religious trusts had been affected by the penal statutes and later by toleration. For a concise summary of the legislation whereby religious bodies other than the established church obtained equality before the law, see *Tyssen's Charitable Bequests* (2nd ed), p. 95.
18 [1931] 2 KB 465, 477 (affd [1932] AC 650).
19 [1957] 1 WLR 1080, 1090, [1957] 3 All ER 281, 285, infra.
20 [1980] 1 WLR 1565, 1572, [1980] 3 All ER 918, infra. See also *R v Registrar General, ex p Segerdal* [1970] 2 QB 697, 709, [1970] 3 All ER 886, 889, per BUCKLEY LJ and see *Church of the New Faith v Commissioner of Pay-Roll Tax* (1982) 154 CLR 120, p. 397, post.

In the **United Grand Lodge** case [1957] 1 WLR 1080, [1957] 3 All ER 281, DONOVAN J, in holding that the objects of freemasonry were not "charitable or otherwise concerned with the advancement of religion" within Rating and Valuation (Miscellaneous Provisions) Act 1955, s. 8 (1) (*a*), said at 1090, at 285:

"Accordingly, one cannot really begin to argue that the main object of freemasonry is to advance religion, except perhaps by saying that religion can be advanced by example as well as by precept, so that the spectacle of a man leading an upright moral life may persuade others to do likewise. The appellants did not in fact advance this argument, but even if it were accepted, it leads to no useful conclusion here. For a man may persuade his neighbour by example to lead a good life without at the same time leading him to religion. And there is nothing in the constitution, nor, apparently, in the evidence tendered to the appeals committee, to support the view that the main object of masonry is to encourage masons to go out in the world and by their example lead persons to some religion or another.

When one considers the work done by organizations which admittedly do set out to advance religion, the contrast with masonry is striking. To advance religion means to promote it, to spread its message ever wider among mankind; to take some positive steps to sustain and increase religious belief; and these things are done in a variety of ways which may be comprehensively described as pastoral and missionary. There is nothing comparable to that in masonry. This is not said by way of criticism. For masonry really does something different. It says to a man, 'Whatever your religion or your mode of worship, believe in a Supreme Creator and lead a good moral life.' Laudable as this precept is, it does not appear to us to be the same thing as the advancement of religion. There is no religious instruction, no programme for the persuasion of unbelievers, no religious supervision to see that its members remain active and constant in the various religions they may profess, no holding of religious services, no pastoral or missionary work of any kind."

In **Re South Place Ethical Society** [1980] 1 WLR 1565, [1980] 3 All ER 918,[1] the objects of the Society were "the study and dissemination of ethical principles and the cultivation of a rational religious sentiment". DILLON J held that these were not for the advancement of religion, and said at 1571, at 924:

"In a free country—and I have no reason to suppose that this country is less free than the United States of America—it is natural that the court should desire not to discriminate between beliefs deeply and sincerely held, whether they are beliefs in a god or in the excellence of man or in ethical principles or in Platonism or some other scheme of philosophy. But I do not see that that warrants extending the meaning of the word 'religion' so as to embrace all other beliefs and philosophies. Religion, as I see it, is concerned with man's relations with God, and ethics are concerned with man's relations with man. The two are not the same, and are not made the same by sincere inquiry into the question: what is God? If reason leads people not to accept Christianity or any known religion, but they do believe in the excellence of qualities such as truth, beauty and love, or believe in the platonic concept of the ideal, their

---

1 [1981] Conv 150 (St. J. Robilliard). Cf. *United States v Seeger*, 380 US 163 (1965); (1978) 91 HLR 1056.

beliefs may be to them the equivalent of a religion, but viewed objectively they are not religion. The ground of the opinion of the court, in the United States Supreme Court, that any belief occupying in the life of its possessor a place parallel to that occupied by belief in God in the minds of theists prompts the comment that parallels, by definition, never meet.''

In **Church of the New Faith v Commissioner of Pay-Roll Tax (Victoria)** (1982) 154 CLR 120, the High Court of Australia held that Scientology as exemplified by the Church of New Faith was a religion, and was therefore exempt from pay-roll tax under the Pay-roll Tax Act 1971 (Victoria).

MASON ACJ and BRENNAN J said at 136:
"We would therefore hold that, for the purposes of the law, the criteria of religion are twofold: first, belief in a supernatural Being, Thing or Principle; and second, the acceptance of canons of conduct in order to give effect to that belief, though canons of conduct which offend against the ordinary laws are outside the area of any immunity, privilege or right conferred on the grounds of religion. Those criteria may vary in their comparative importance, and there may be a different intensity of belief or of acceptance of canons of conduct among religions or among the adherents to a religion. The tenets of a religion may give primacy to one particular belief or to one particular canon of conduct. Variations in emphasis may distinguish one religion from other religions, but they are irrelevant to the determination of an individual's or a group's freedom to profess and exercise the religion of his, or their choice.''

WILSON J and DEANE J said at 174:
"One of the more important indicia of 'religion' is that the particular collection of ideas and/or practices involves belief in the supernatural, that is to say, belief that reality extends beyond that which is capable of perception by the senses. If that be absent, it is unlikely that one has a 'religion'. Another is that the ideas relate to man's nature and place in the universe and his relation to things supernatural. A third is that the ideas are accepted by adherents as requiring or encouraging them to observe particular standards or codes of conduct or to participate in specific practices having supernatural significance. A fourth is that, however loosely knit and varying in beliefs and practices adherents may be, they constitute an identifiable group or identifiable groups. A fifth, and perhaps more controversial, indicium (cf. *Malnak v Yogi* 592 F 2d 197 (1979)) is that the adherents themselves see the collection of ideas and/or practices as constituting a religion.

As has been said, no one of the above indicia is necessarily determinative of the question whether a particular collection of ideas and/or practices should be objectively characterized as 'a religion'. They are no more than aids in determining that question and the assistance to be derived from them will vary according to the context in which the question arises. All of those indicia are, however, satisfied by most or all leading religions.''[2]

Pettit: *Equity and the Law of Trusts* (7th edn, 1993), pp. 235–236.

It is generally accepted that 'the Court of Chancery makes no distinction between one religion and another ... [or] one sect and another ... [unless]

---

2 See also MURPHY J at 151: (1984) 14 Melbourne ULR 539 (M. Darian-Smith).

the tenets of a particular sect inculcate doctrines adverse to the very foundations of all religion and . . . subversive of all morality . . . If the tendency were not immoral and although this Court might consider the opinions sought to be propagated foolish or even devoid of foundation' the trust would nevertheless be charitable.[3] 'As between different religions the law stands neutral, but it assumes that any religion is at least likely to be better than none.'[4] The courts are understandably reluctant to judge the relative worth of different religions or the truth of competing religious doctrines, all of which may have a place in a tolerant and culturally diverse society.

These propositions are undoubtedly true so far as the various Christian denominations are concerned; there is no doubt as to the charitable character of religious trusts not only for the established church, but also for nonconformist bodies,[5] Unitarians,[6] Roman Catholics,[7] and the Exclusive Brethren.[8] More controversially two trusts associated with the Unification Church[9] have been registered as charitable, as has a trust for the publication of the works of Joanna Southcote.[10] Similarly with regard to organisations which exist for the advancement of religion, such as the Church Army,[11] the Salvation Army,[12] the Church Missionary Society,[13] the Society for the Propagation of the Gospel in Foreign Parts,[14] the Sunday School Association,[15] the Protestant Alliance and kindred institutions,[16] and even, it has been held, a society of clergymen, in connection with a trust to provide dinners, on the ground that the free meals would increase the usefulness of the society by attracting a

---

3 Per ROMILLY MR in *Thornton v Howe* (1862) 31 Beav 14 at 19; *Gilmour v Coats* [1949] AC 426, [1949] 1 All ER 848, p. 400 post; *Re Watson* [1973] 1 WLR 1472, [1973] 3 All ER 678, p. 399 post.

4 Per CROSS J in *Neville Estates Ltd v Madden* [1962] Ch 832 at 853, [1961] 3 All ER 769 at 781.

5 Since the Toleration Act 1688. See eg *Re Strickland's Will Trusts* [1936] 3 All ER 1027; appeal dismissed by consent [1937] 3 All ER 676 (Baptist); *Re Manser* [1905] 1 Ch 68 (Quakers). [On gifts by will to non-conformist churches, see (1985) NLJ Annual Charities Reviews (H.W. Wilkinson)].

6 Since the Unitarian Relief Act 1813. Eg *Re Nesbitt's Will Trusts* [1953] 1 All ER 936.

7 Since the Roman Catholic Charities Act 1832. Eg *Dunne v Byrne* [1912] AC 407; *Re Flinn* [1948] Ch 241, [1948] 1 All ER 541. As to whether there has been, or now is, an anti-Roman Catholic bias, see (1981) 2 JLH 207 (M. Blakeney); [1990] Conv 34 (C.E.F. Rickett).

8 *Holmes v A-G* (1981) Times, 12 February; [Annual Report for 1981, paras. 22–31 (Exclusive Brethren formerly Plymouth Brethren), [1995] 3 Ch Com Rep p. 7 (relief of poor members of Exclusive Brethren); *Broxtowe Borough Council v Birch* [1981] RA 215].

9 Popularly known as the Moonies. The Attorney General appealed against the refusal of the Charity Commissioners to accede to his request to remove the trusts from the register, but the appeal was eventually discontinued; see the statement of the Attorney General in Hansard, 3 Feb 1988, 977 et seq, and the debate in the Lords, 10 Feb, 247 et seq.

10 *Thornton v Howe*, supra; Joanna Southcote claimed that she was with child by the Holy Ghost, and would give birth to a second Messiah. As the law then was, the effect of holding the gift charitable was that, being given out of land, it failed by reason of the Statute of Mortmain and went to the heir-at-law.

11 *Re Smith* (1938) 54 TLR 851.

12 *Re Fowler* (1914) 31 TLR 102; *Re Smith*, supra.

13 *Re The Clergy Society* (1856) 2 K & J 615.

14 *Re Maguire* (1870) LR 9 Eq 632.

15 *R v Special Comrs of Income Tax* [1911] 2 KB 434.

16 *Re Delmar Charitable Trust* [1897] 2 Ch 163 (societies having as their object 'to maintain and defend the doctrines of the Reformation, and the principles of civil and religious liberty against the advance of Popery').

greater number of clergymen to the meetings.[17] But not, it has been decided, the Oxford Group Movement.[18]

Beyond the Christian religion, trusts for the advancement of the Jewish religion are undoubtedly charitable.[19] So far as wholly distinct religions such as Islam or Buddhism are concerned, there are clear dicta[20] in favour of charitable status, and this is assumed in regulations[1] made under the Charities Act 1993. Moreover the Charity Commissions have registered trusts for the advancement of the Hindu, Sikh, Islamic and Buddhist religions. Neither the objects of the Theosophical Society[2] nor those of the South Place Ethical Society[3] or the Church of Scientology[4] are for the advancement of religion, and it has not been thought arguable that gifts for the maintenance of a masonic temple[5] or a college for training spiritualistic mediums[6] are charitable on this ground, and the same must surely be true of an atheistic society."[7]

In **Re Watson** [1973] 1 WLR 1472, [1973] 3 All ER 678,[8] PLOWMAN J had to consider the validity of a gift in a will "for the continuance of the work of God as it has been maintained by Mr. H.G. Hobbs and myself since 1942 by God's

---

17 *Re Charlesworth* (1910) 26 TLR 214.

18 *Re Thackrah* [1939] 2 All ER 4; *Oxford Group v IRC* [1949] 2 All ER 537 (the movement is probably a social movement founded on Christian ethics rather than a movement for the advancement of religion).

19 Since the Religious Disabilities Act 1846, according, inter alia, to *Neville Estates Ltd v Madden* [1962] Ch 832, [1961] 3 All ER 769. But a Jewish religious trust was held charitable in *Straus v Goldsmid* (1837) 8 Sim 614, not following Lord HARDWICKE's decision in *De Costa v De Paz* (1754) 2 Swan 487n.

20 *Re South Place Ethical Society* [1980] 1 WLR 1565, [1980] 3 All ER 918 where two of the essential attributes of religion were said to be faith and worship—faith in a god and worship of that god. Buddhism seems to be regarded as a religion whether or not it has these attributes. This was said to be too narrow a test by the High Court of Australia in *Church of the New Faith v Comr for Pay-Roll Tax* (1982) 57 ALJR 785, noted (1984) 100 LQR 340; (1984) 14 MULR 539 (M. Darian Smith); [1984] Conv 449 (St John Robilliard), where Scientology was held to be a religion in Victoria. The wider Australian view has been applied in New Zealand—*Centrepoint Community Growth Trust v IRC* [1985] 1 NZLR 673. See (1981) 131 NLJ 436 (H Picarda); (1989) 63 ALJ 834 (W. Sadurski).

1 SI 1962 No. 1421; SI 1963 No. 2074; SI 1996 No. 180. [Many immigrant religious organisations have been recognised as charitable. However, "many Hindu, Sikh, and Moslem organisations which are basically religious also have social, cultural and educational functions which have a greater importance than is the case with comparable Christian communities". Annual Report for 1976, para. 109. For the position of Rastafarians, see *Crown Suppliers (PSA) Ltd v Dawkins* [1993] ICR 517; SI 1996 No. 180.]

2 *Re Macaulay's Estate* [1943] Ch 435n ("to form a nucleus of Universal Brotherhood of Humanity without distinction of race, creed, caste or colour"). Cf *Re Price* [1943] Ch 422; [1943] 2 All ER 505 (Anthroposophical Society).

3 *Re South Place Ethical Society*, supra ("the study and dissemination of ethical principles" and "the cultivation of a rational religious sentiment"—society concerned with man's relations with man, not man's relations with God: nor did it have attributes referred to in n. 11, supra). See (1981) 131 NLJ 761 (A. Hoffer).

4 *R v Registrar General, ex p Segerdal* [1970] 2 QB 697, [1970] 3 All ER 886, but see supra n. 20.

5 *Re Porter* [1925] 1 Ch 746.

6 *Re Hummeltenberg* [1923] 1 Ch 237.

7 The point did not arise in *Bowman v Secular Society Ltd* [1917] AC 406, where it was held that there is nothing contrary to law in an attack on or a denial of the truth of Christianity unaccompanied by vilification, ridicule or irreverence. Christianity is not part of the law of England.

8 (1974) 90 LQR 4; [1973] ASCL 468 (J. Hackney). On fringe religious organisations, see Annual Report for 1976, paras 103–108; and on Exorcism, paras 65–67.

enabling ... in propagating the truth as given in the Holy Bible''. The testatrix and Mr. Hobbs were members of a very small group of undenominational Christians, who met at Long Melford, Suffolk, and which apparently contained no member outside their immediate families. Mr. Hobbs had written and distributed a large number of religious books and tracts mainly at the expense of the testatrix. Expert evidence was given that their intrinsic worth was nil. The trust was upheld.

iii. PUBLIC BENEFIT

GILMOUR v COATS

[1949] AC 426, [1949] 1 All ER 848 (HL, Lords SIMONDS, DU PARCQ, NORMAND, MORTON OF HENRYTON and REID)

A gift of £500 was made in trust for the purposes of the Carmelite Priory, St Charles' Square, Notting Hill, if those purposes were charitable.

The Priory was a community of strictly cloistered nuns, who devoted their lives to prayer, contemplation, penance and self-sanctification. They engaged in no works outside the convent.

An affidavit of Cardinal Griffin, Roman Catholic Archbishop of Westminster, stated that, according to the doctrine of the Roman Catholic Church, the work of such a community conferred benefits, not only upon the participants, but upon the public generally.

Held. The purposes of the Priory lacked the element of public benefit which was necessary to make them charitable.[9]

LORD SIMONDS: It is the established belief of the Roman Catholic Church, as appears from the Apostolic Constitution "Umbratilem", that the prayers and other spiritual penances and exercises, in which the nuns engage for the benefit of the public, in fact benefit the public by drawing down upon them grace from God, which enables those who are not yet Christians to embrace the Christian religion and those who are already Christians to practise Christianity more fully and fruitfully, and, further that the prayers and other spiritual exercises of the nuns are the more efficacious by virtue of the fact that they devote their lives with especial devotion to the service of God. It is this benefit to all the world, arising from the value of their intercessory prayers, that the appellant puts in the forefront of her case in urging the charitable purpose of the trust.

Nor is it only on the intercessory value of prayer that the appellant relies for the element of public benefit in their lives. For it is the evidence of Cardinal Griffin—and I do not pause to ask whether it is evidence of fact or opinion—that the practice of the religious life by the Carmelite nuns and other religions is a source of great edification to other Catholics—and indeed in innumerable cases to non-Catholics—leading them to a higher estimation of spiritual things and to a greater striving after their own spiritual perfection and that the knowledge that there are men and women who are prepared to sacrifice all that the worldly in man holds dear in order to attain a greater love of God and

---

9 Local Government Finance Act 1988, s. 2, Sch. 1, para. 7 gives exemption from community charge to a member of a religious community whose principal occupation is prayer, contemplation ... , and who has no income or capital of his own and is dependent on the community concerned for his material needs. Only a place of public religious worship is exempt from local non-domestic rating: ibid., s. 51, Sch. 5, para. 11.

union with Him inculcates in them a greater estimation of the value and importance of the things which are eternal than they would have if they had not these examples before them. Here then is the second element of public benefit on which the appellant relies, the edification of a wider public by the example of lives devoted to prayer.

I will reserve for final consideration an argument which was not urged in the courts below; that the trusts declared by the settlement are beneficial to the public, in that qualification for admission to the community is not limited to any private group of persons but any person being a female Roman Catholic may be accepted, and therefore those trusts provide facilities for the intensified and most complete practice of religion by those members of the public who have a vocation for it. Your Lordships were reluctant to listen to an argument on which you have not the advantage of the opinions of the learned judges in the courts below, but in the special circumstances of this case thought fit to admit it.

I turn then to the question whether, apart from this final consideration, the appellant has established that there is in the trusts which govern this community the element of public benefit which is the necessary condition of legal charity ...

I need not go beyond the case of *Cocks v Manners* (1871) LR 12 Eq 574 which was decided nearly eighty years ago by Wickens V-C. In that case the testatrix left her residuary estate between a number of religious institutions, one of them being the Dominican Convent at Carisbrooke, a community not differing in any material respect from the community of nuns now under consideration. The learned judge who was, I suppose, as deeply versed in this branch of the law as any judge before or since (for he had been for many years junior counsel to the Attorney-General in equity cases), used these words, which I venture to repeat, though they have already been cited in the courts below (1871) LR 12 Eq at 585: "On the Act [sc. the Statute of Elizabeth] unaffected by authority I should certainly hold that the gift to the Dominican Convent is neither within the letter nor the spirit of it; and no decision has been referred to which compels me to adopt a different conclusion. A voluntary association of women for the purpose of working out their own salvation by religious exercises and self denial seems to me to have none of the requisites of a charitable institution, whether the word 'charitable' is used in its popular sense or in its legal sense. It is said, in some of the cases, that religious purposes are charitable, but that can only be true as to religious services tending directly or indirectly towards the instruction or the edification of the public; an annuity to an individual, so long as he spent his time in retirement and constant devotion, would not be charitable, nor would a gift to ten persons, so long as they lived together in retirement and performed acts of devotion, be charitable. Therefore the gift to the Dominican Convent is not, in my opinion, a gift on a charitable trust." No case, said the learned Vice-Chancellor, had been cited to compel him to come to a contrary conclusion, nor has any such case been cited to your Lordships. Nor have my own researches discovered one. But since that date the decision in *Cocks v Manners* has been accepted and approved in numerous cases. They are referred to in the judgment of Jenkins J and I need only remind your Lordships, first, that Lindsey LJ in *Re White* [1893] 2 Ch 41 at 51 used these words: "A society for the promotion of private prayer and devotion by its own members, and which has no wider scope, no public element, no purposes of general utility would be a 'religious' society, but not a 'charitable' one: see *Cocks v Manners*," and, secondly, that in *Dunne v Byrne* [1912] AC 407 at 410 Lord Macnaghten in delivering the judgment of the Privy Council refers to *Cocks v Manners* as the exemplar of a case in which the purpose would be considered by a devout Catholic to be conducive to the good of religion but which is "certainly not charitable". I have thus stated the law as it was universally accepted in case-law (except some recent Irish cases) and also in all text-books of authority at the date when these proceedings were begun, and I now ask what is the argument upon which your Lordships are invited to unsettle it.

Apart from what I have called the final argument, which I will deal with later, the contention of the appellant rests not on any change in the lives of the members of such a community as this nor, from a wider aspect, on the emergence of any new conception of the public good, but solely on the fact that for the first time certain evidence of the value of such lives to a wider public together with new arguments based upon that evidence has been presented to the court. Never before, it was urged, has the benefit to be derived from intercessory prayer and from edification been brought to the attention of the court; if it had been, the decision in *Cocks v Manners* (1871) LR 12 Eq 574 would, or at least should, have been otherwise. I have examined the records of *Cocks v Manners* which were supplied to me by the Record Office and I find that the case has been fully and accurately reported. There was no such evidence as was adduced in this case by the appellant and Cardinal Griffin. Nor, as appears from the report, was any argument addressed to this specific point nor any judgment on it. What weight is to be attributed to this, which is the mainstay of the appellant's case? To me, my Lords, despite the admirable argument of Mr. Charles Russell, the weight is negligible. True it is that Wickens V-C emphasised that aspect of the religious life which is admittedly its more important aim, "the love and contemplation of divine things" (1871) LR 12 Eq at 585. But "its secondary aim the apostolate, particularly all that pertains to our neighbour's salvation" (I use the appellant's words) is no new thing and I cannot suppose that it was absent from the learned judge's mind that those, who devote their lives to prayer, pray not for themselves alone, or that they believe that their prayers are not in vain. Nor, as I think, can he have been unaware of the effect which the example of their lives may have upon others. As I venture to think, these aspects of the case were neither insisted on in evidence or argument nor discussed by the learned judge because they do not afford any real support for the contention that there is in the purpose of the community the element of public benefit which is the condition of legal charity.

My Lords, I would speak with all respect and reverence of those who spend their lives in cloistered piety, and in this House of Lords Spiritual and Temporal, which daily commences its proceedings with intercessory prayers, how can I deny that the Divine Being may in His wisdom think fit to answer them? But, my Lords, whether I affirm or deny, whether I believe or disbelieve, what has that to do with the proof which the court demands that a particular purpose satisfies the test of benefit to the community? Here is something which is manifestly not susceptible of proof. But, then it is said, this is a matter not of proof but of belief: for the value of intercessory prayer is a tenet of the Catholic faith, therefore in such prayer there is benefit to the community. But it is just at this "therefore" that I must pause. It is, no doubt, true that the advancement of religion is, generally speaking, one of the heads of charity. But it does not follow from this that the court must accept as proved whatever a particular church believes. The faithful must embrace their faith believing where they cannot prove; the court can act only on proof. A gift to two or ten or a hundred cloistered nuns in the belief that their prayers will benefit the world at large does not from that belief alone derive validity any more than does the belief of any other donor for any other purpose. The importance of this case leads me to state my opinion in my own words but, having read again the judgment of the learned Master of the Rolls, I will add that I am in full agreement with what he says on this part of the case.[10]

I turn to the second of the alleged elements of public benefit, edification by example. And I think that this argument can be dealt with very shortly. It is in my opinion sufficient to say that this is something too vague and intangible to satisfy the prescribed test. The test of public benefit has, I think, been developed in the last two centuries. To-day it is beyond doubt that that element must be present. No court would be rash enough to attempt to define precisely or exhaustively what its content must be. But it would assume a burden which it could not discharge if now for the first time it admitted into the category of public benefit something so indirect, remote, imponderable and, I would add, controversial as the benefit which may be derived by others from the example of pious lives. The appellant called in aid the use by Wickens V-C of the word "indirectly" in the passage that I have cited from his judgment in *Cocks v Manners* (1871) LR 12 Eq 574 at 585, but I see no reason to suppose that that learned judge had in mind any such question as your Lordships have to determine. . . .

It remains finally to deal with an argument which, as I have said, was not presented to the Court of Appeal but appears in the appellant's formal case. It is that the element of public benefit is supplied by the fact that qualification for admission to membership of the community is not limited to any group of persons but is open to any woman in the wide world who has the necessary vocation. Thus, it is said, just as the endowment of a scholarship open to public competition is a charity, so also is a gift to enable any woman (or, presumably, any man) to enter a fuller religious life a charity. To this argument which, it must be admitted, has a speciously logical appearance, the first answer is that which I have indicated earlier in this opinion. There is no novelty in the idea that a community of nuns must, if it is to continue, from time to time obtain fresh recruits from the outside world. That is why a perpetuity is involved in a gift for the benefit of such a community and it is not to be supposed that, to mention only three masters of this branch of the law, Wickens V-C, Lord Lindsey, or Lord Macnaghten failed to appreciate the point. Yet by direct decision or by way of emphatic example a community such as this is by them regarded as the very type of religious institution which is not charitable. I know of no consideration applicable to this case which would justify this House in unsettling a rule of law which has been established so long and by such high authority. But that is not the only, nor indeed the most cogent, reason why I cannot accede to the appellant's argument. It is a trite saying that the law is life, not logic. But it is, I think, conspicuously true of the law of charity that it has been built up not logically but empirically. It would not, therefore, be surprising to find that, while in every category of legal charity some element of public benefit must be present, the court had not adopted the same measure in regard to different categories, but had accepted one standard in regard to

---

10 [1948] Ch 340, [1948] 1 All ER 521. "They are to be paid, not to do good, but to be good", at 353, at 528, per GREENE MR. See Annual Report for 1990, para. 56 (Society of the Precious Blood).

those gifts which are alleged to be for the advancement of education and another for those which are alleged to be for the advancement of religion, and it may be yet another in regard to the relief of poverty. To argue by a method of syllogism or analogy from the category of education to that of religion ignores the historical process of the law. Nor would there be lack of justification for the divergence of treatment which is here assumed. For there is a legislative and political background peculiar to so-called religious trusts, which has I think influenced the development of the law in this matter. Thus, even if the simple argument that, if education is a good thing, then the more education the better, may appear to be irrefutable, to repeat that argument substituting "religion" for "education" is to ignore the principle which I understand to be conceded that not all religious purposes are charitable purposes. It was, no doubt, this consideration which led Wickens V-C to say (1871) LR 12 Eq 574 at 585 that a gift to a Dominican convent was "one of the last gifts which the legislature which passed the Act would have thought of including in it". Upon this final argument I would add this observation. I have stressed the empirical development of the law of charity and your Lordships may detect some inconsistency in an attempt to rationalise it. But it appears to me that it would be irrational to the point of absurdity on the one hand to deny to a community of contemplative nuns the character of a charitable institution but on the other to accept as a charitable trust a gift which had no other object than to enable it to be maintained in perpetuity by recruitment from the outside world.

Finally I would say this. I have assumed for the purpose of testing this argument that it is a valid contention that a gift for the advancement of education is necessarily charitable if it is not confined within too narrow limits. But that assumption is itself difficult to justify. It may well be that the generality of the proposition is subject to at least two limitations. The first of them is implicit in the decision of Russell J in *Re Hummeltenberg* [1923] 1 Ch 237: the second is one that is not in the nature of things likely to occur, but, if it can be imagined that it was made a condition of a gift for the advancement of education that its beneficiaries should lead a cloistered life and communicate to no one, and leave no record of, the fruits of their study, I do not think that the charitable character of the gift could be sustained.

For the reasons that I have given I am of opinion that this appeal should be dismissed.

In **Neville Estates Ltd v Madden** [1962] Ch 832, [1961] 3 All ER 769, the trustees of the Catford Synagogue entered into a contract to sell two plots of land to the plaintiffs for £10,000. The plaintiffs obtained detailed planning permission for the building thereon of flats and garages. The value of the land increased and the Charity Commissioners refused their permission to sell.

The plaintiffs brought an action for specific performance arguing, inter alia, that the land was not held on charitable trusts, and that the permission of the Charity Commissioners was not therefore necessary.

The argument was that the trustees held the land upon trust for the advancement of religion among a private group of persons only. In holding that the purposes were charitable, CROSS J said at 852, at 780:

"I turn now to the argument that this is a private, not a public trust ... The trust with which I am concerned resembles that in *Gilmour v Coats* [1949] AC 426, [1949] 1 All ER 848 in this, that the persons immediately benefited by it are not a section of the public but the members of a private body. All persons of the Jewish faith living in or about Catford might well constitute a section of the public, but the members for the time being of the Catford Synagogue are no more a section of the public than the members for the time being of a Carmelite Priory. The two cases, however, differ from one another in that the members of the Catford Synagogue spend their lives in the world, whereas the members of a Carmelite Priory live secluded from the world. If once one refuses to pay any regard—as the courts refused to pay any regard—to the influence which these nuns living in seclusion might have on the outside world, then it must follow that no public benefit is involved in a trust to support a Carmelite Priory. As Lord Greene said in the Court of Appeal [1948] Ch 340 at 345, [1948] 1 All ER 521 at 525: 'Having regard to the way in which the lives of the members are spent, the benefit is a purely private one.' But the court is, I think, entitled to assume that some benefit accrues to the public from the attendance at places of worship of persons who live in this world and mix with their fellow citizens. As between different religions the law stands neutral, but it assumes that any religion is at least likely to be better than none.

But then it is said—and it is this part of the argument that has caused me the greatest difficulty: 'But this is a case of self-help.' Suppose that a body of persons, being dissatisfied with the facilities for the education of small children provided in their district, form an association for the education of the children of members. A committee is formed; each member pays a subscription; the funds of the society are employed in hiring premises and paying a teacher; and the rules provide that the association cannot be dissolved by the members at any given moment but is to continue for the benefit of the members existing from time to time. No doubt the public benefits by the fact that the children of the members receive an education. But could it possibly be argued that the association was a charity and was entitled to the great fiscal advantages which a charity enjoys? Or would it make any difference if the committee allowed the children of non-members to attend the classes free of charge if there was room for them, in the same way as members of the public, though having no right to enter the synagogue, are not in practice refused admission?

I feel the force of this analogy; but, as Lord Simonds pointed out in *Gilmour v Coats* [1949] AC 426 at 449, [1949] 1 All ER 848 at 856, it is dangerous to reason by analogy from one head of charity to another. After the passing of the Toleration Acts, dissenting chapels sprang up all over the country. As can be deduced from the language of section 1 of the Trustees Appointment Act, 1850 (see Sir Morton Peto's Act), the chapel was normally vested in trustees for the particular congregation or society of dissenters in question. In course of time disputes sometimes arose between rival groups, some members alleging that others had ceased to hold the tenets laid down in the trust deed and were not entitled to its benefits. A typical example of such a dispute is to be found in *A-G v Bunce* (1868) LR 6 Eq 563. No one, so far as I know, ever questioned that trusts for such dissenting bodies were charitable trusts provided that the members for the time being could not put an end to them. What the position would be if the members for the time being could divide the property among themselves was expressly left open by Sir George Jessel MR in *Bunting v Sargent* (1879) 13 ChD 330 at 337.

Section 4 of the Religious Disabilities Act, 1846, provided that Her Majesty's subjects professing the Jewish religion in respect of their schools, places of religious worship, education and charitable purposes and the property held therewith, should be subject to the same laws as Her Majesty's Protestant subjects dissenting from the Church of England were subject to and not further or otherwise. From that time it has, I think, always been assumed by lawyers that trusts for the benefit of a congregation of Jews attending a synagogue were charitable trusts. It is, for example, obvious that Parliament and the Charity Commissioners assumed in 1870 that the four synagogues which became the constituent synagogues of the United Synagogue were charitable bodies. Yet it is equally clear from clause 6a of this scheme that the constituent synagogues have not been open to all persons of the Jewish faith, but were unincorporated associations with a list of members.

Generally speaking, no doubt, an association which is supported by its members for the purposes of providing benefits for themselves will not be a charity. But I do not think that this principle can apply with full force in the case of trusts for religious purposes. As Lord Simonds pointed out, the law of charity has been built up not logically but empirically, and there is a political background peculiar to religious trusts which may well have influenced the development of the law with regard to them.

In my judgment, this trust with which I am concerned in this case is a charitable trust''.

In **Re Hetherington**, [1990] Ch1, [1989] 2 All ER 129,[11] the testatrix left £2,000 to "the Roman Catholic Church Bishop of Westminster for the repose of the souls of my husband and my parents and my sisters and also myself when I die'', and her residuary estate "to the Roman Catholic Church St Edwards Golders Green for Masses for my soul''. In holding that both gifts were charitable, Sir Nicolas BROWNE-WILKINSON V-C said at 12, at 134:

"The grounds on which the trust in the present case can be attacked are that there is no *express* requirement that the Masses for souls which are to be celebrated are to be celebrated in public. The evidence shows that celebration in public is the invariable practice but there is no requirement of Canon law to that effect. Therefore it is said the money could be applied to saying Masses in private which would not be charitable since there would be no sufficient element of public benefit.

In my judgment the cases establish the following propositions.

(1) A trust for the advancement of education, the relief of poverty or the advancement of religion is prima facie charitable and assumed to be for the public benefit. *National Anti-vivisection Society v IRC* [1948] AC 31, 42 and 65, [1947] 2 All ER 217, 220, 233, p. 408, post. This assumption of public benefit can be rebutted by showing that in fact the particular trust in question cannot operate so as to confer a legally recognised benefit on the public, as in *Gilmour v Coats* [1949] AC 426, [1949] 1 All ER 848, p. 400 ante.

(2) The celebration of a religious rite in public does confer a sufficient public benefit because of the edifying and improving effect of such celebration on the members of the public who attend. As Lord Reid said in *Gilmour v Coats* at 459, at 862:

'A religion can be regarded as beneficial without it being necessary to assume that all its beliefs are true, and a religious service can be regarded

---

11 [1989] CLJ 373 (J. Hopkins); [1989] Con 453 (N.D.M. Parry); [1989] All ER Rev 181 (P.J. Clarke); (1989) 139 NLJ 1767 (J.M.Q. Hepworth); (1990) 22 Mal LR 114 (C.H. Sherrin).

as beneficial to all those who attend it without it being necessary to determine the spiritual efficacy of that service or to accept any particular belief about it.'

(3) The celebration of a religious rite in private does not contain the necessary element of public benefit since any benefit by prayer or example is incapable of proof in the legal sense, and any element of edification is limited to a private, not public, class of those present at the celebration: see *Gilmour v Coats; Yeap Cheah Neo v Ong Cheng Neo* (1875) LR 6 PC 381 and *Hoare v Hoare* (1886) 56 LT 147.

Where there is a gift for a religious purpose which could be carried out in a way which is beneficial to the public (i.e. by public Masses) but could also be carried out in a way which would not have sufficient element of public benefit (i.e. by private masses) the gift is to be construed as a gift to be carried out only by the methods that are charitable, all non-charitable methods being excluded: see *Re White* [1893] 2 Ch 41, 52–53; and *Re Banfield* [1968] 1 WLR 846, [1968] 2 All ER 276.

Applying those principles to the present case, a gift for the saying of Masses is prima facie charitable, being for a religious purpose. In practice, those Masses will be celebrated in public which provides a sufficient element of public benefit. The provision of stipends for priests saying the Masses, by relieving the Roman Catholic Church pro tanto of the liability to provide such stipends, is a further benefit. The gift is to be construed as a gift for public Masses only on the principle of *Re White*, private Masses not being permissible since it would not be a charitable application of the fund for a religious purpose.

I will therefore declare that both gifts are valid charitable trusts for the saying of Masses in public. The pecuniary legacy should be paid to the Archbishop of Westminster who is plainly the person referred to as the Bishop of Westminster, to be held by him on those trusts. Since the will appoints no trustee of the residuary gift, the residuary gift will be dealt with by the Crown under a scheme made under the Sign Manual.''[12]

QUESTIONS

1. How would you define religion?
2. Now compare the differences in the requirements of public benefit between religious and educational trusts.
   What would you say of
   (*a*) a trust for the provision of a private chapel in a preparatory school?
   (*b*) a trust to provide religious services for long-term prisoners in the maximum security wing of a prison?
   (*c*) a trust to provide a church for Methodists and for persons likely to become Methodists in West Ham? (see *IRC v Baddeley* [1955] AC 572, [1955] 1 All ER 525, p. 419, post).
3. Would there have been a different result in *Gilmour v Coats* if it had been shown that a number of nuns retired periodically and returned to life outside the convent? See CROSS J in *Neville Estates Ltd v Madden* [1962] Ch 832 at 853, [1961] 3 All ER 769 at 781.

12 On Sign Manual generally, see Tudor, pp. 325–328.

D. Other Purposes Beneficial to the Community[13]

This is the residual head of charity, and most new registrations by the Charity Commissioners are made under it.[14]

i. GENERAL

(a) The Test is what the Law Treats as Charitable

The test is what the law treats as charitable, and not what the testator thought was charitable. This question may however make it necessary for the court to make a subjective decision in the determination of what is beneficial.

NATIONAL ANTI-VIVISECTION SOCIETY v INLAND REVENUE COMMISSIONERS
[1948] AC 31, [1947] 2 All ER 217 (HL, Viscount SIMON, Lords WRIGHT, SIMONDS, NORMAND and PORTER)

The appellants were a society whose object was the suppression of vivisection. They claimed exemption from income tax on the ground that they were "a body of persons ... established for charitable purposes only" within the Income Tax Act 1918, s. 37 (1) (*b*).[15]

Held. (Lord PORTER dissenting.) The Society was not established for charitable purposes only, and was not therefore within this exemption.

LORD SIMONDS: My Lords, the question raised in this appeal is whether the National Anti-Vivisection Society, which I will call "the society," is a body of persons established for charitable purposes only within the meaning of s. 37 of the Income Tax Act, 1918, and, accordingly, entitled to exemption from income tax on the income of its investments. Before I refer to the cases and to the judgments in the courts below I will state the two questions which appear to me to be raised in this appeal. The first and shorter point is whether a main purpose of the society is of such a political character that the court cannot regard it as charitable. To this point little attention was directed in the courts below. It is mentioned only in the judgment of the learned Master of the Rolls. As will appear in the course of this opinion, it is worthy of more serious debate (p. 442 post). The second point is fundamental. It is at the very root of the law of charity as administered by the Court of Chancery and its successor, the Chancery Division of the High Court of Justice. It is whether the court, for the purpose of determining whether the object of the society is charitable may disregard the finding of fact that any assumed public benefit in the direction of the advancement of morals and education was far outweighed by the detriment to medical science and research and consequently to the public health which would result if the society succeeded in achieving its object, and that on balance, the object of the society, so far from being for the public benefit, was gravely injurious thereto. The society says that the court must

---

13 H & M, pp. 405–419, 428–431; K & S, pp. 176–177; S & K, pp. 119–139, 183–200; P & M, pp. 323–333; Pettit, pp. 240–252; Riddall, pp. 105–144; Snell, pp. 149–152; Tudor, pp. 88–120; Picarda, pp. 105–169. See generally (1983) 36 CLP 241 (H. Cohen).
14 Annual Report for 1985, para. 8.
15 See now ICTA 1988, s. 505 (1) (*c*).

disregard this fact, arguing that evidence of disadvantages or evils which would or might result from the stopping of vivisection is irrelevant and inadmissible.

The second question raised in this appeal, which I have already tried to formulate, is of wider importance, and I must say at once that I cannot reconcile it with my conception of a court of equity that it should take under its care and administer a trust, however well-intentioned its creator, of which the consequence would be calamitous to the community. I would not weary your Lordships with a historical excursion into the origin of the equitable jurisdiction in matters of charity, one of the "heads of equity" as Lord Macnaghten called it in *Pemsel's* case [1891] AC 531 ...

My Lords, this then being the position, that the court determined "one by one" whether particular named purposes were charitable, applying always the overriding test whether the purpose was for the public benefit, and that the King as parens patriae intervened pro bono publico for the protection of charities, what room is there for the doctrine which has found favour with the learned Master of the Rolls and has been so vigorously supported at the bar of the House, that the court may disregard the evils that will ensue from the achievement by the society of its ends? It is to me a strange and bewildering idea that the court must look so far and no farther, must see a charitable purpose in the intention of the society to benefit animals and thus elevate the moral character of men but must shut its eyes to the injurious results to the whole human and animal creation. I will readily concede that, if the purpose is within one of the heads of charity forming the first three classes in the classification which Lord Macnaghten borrowed from Sir Samuel Romilly's argument in *Morice v Bishop of Durham* (1805) 10 Ves 522, the court will easily conclude that it is a charitable purpose. But even here to give the purpose the name of "religious" or "education" is not to conclude the matter. It may yet not be charitable, if the religious purpose is illegal or the educational purpose is contrary to public policy. Still there remains the overriding question: Is it pro bono publico? It would be another strange mis-reading of Lord Macnaghten's speech in *Pemsel's* case [1891] AC 531 (one was pointed out in *Re Macduff* [1896] 2 Ch 451) to suggest that he intended anything to the contrary. I would rather say that, when a purpose appears broadly to fall within one of the familiar categories of charity, the court will assume it to be for the benefit of the community and, therefore, charitable, unless the contrary is shown, and further that the court will not be astute in such a case to defeat on doubtful evidence the avowed benevolent intention of a donor. But, my Lords, the next step is one that I cannot take. Where on the evidence before it the court concludes that, however well-intentioned the donor, the achievement of his object will be greatly to the public disadvantage, there can be no justification for saying that it is a charitable object. If and so far as there is any judicial decision to the contrary, it must, in my opinion, be regarded as inconsistent with principle and be overruled. This proposition is clearly stated by Russell J in *Re Hummeltenberg* [1923] 1 Ch 237 at 242. "In my opinion," he said, "the question whether a gift is or may be operative for the public benefit is a question to be answered by the court forming an opinion upon the evidence before it." This statement of that very learned judge follows immediately upon some observations on the cases of *Re Foveaux* [1895] 2 Ch 501 and *Re Cranston* [1898] 1 IR 431 which were the mainstay of the appellant's argument ...

[His Lordship examined these cases and *A-G v Marchant* (1866) LR 3 Eq 424 and *Re Campden Charities* (1881) 18 ChD 310, and continued:]

My Lords, what I have said is enough to conclude this case. But there is an important passage in the judgment of the Master of the Rolls, which I ought not to ignore. "I do not see," he says [1946] KB 185, 205, [1946] 1 All ER 205, 212, "how at this time of day it can be asserted that a particular exemplification of those objects is not beneficial merely because in that particular case the achievement of those objects would deprive mankind of certain consequential benefits however important those benefits may be. If this were not so, it would always be possible, by adducing evidence which was not before the court on the original occasion to attack the status of an established charitable object to the great confusion of trustees and all others concerned. Many existing charities would no doubt fall if such a criterion were to be adopted." I venture with great respect to think that this confuses two things. A purpose regarded in one age as charitable may in another be regarded differently. I need not repeat what was said by Jessel MR in *Re Campden Charities* (1881) 18 ChD 310. A bequest in the will of a testator dying in 1700 might be held valid on the evidence then before the court but on different evidence held invalid if he died in 1900. So, too, I conceive that an antivivisection society might at different times be differently regarded. But this is not to say that a charitable trust, when it has once been established, can ever fail. If by a change in social habits and needs, or, it may be, by a change in the law the purpose of an established charity becomes superfluous or even illegal, or if with increasing knowledge it appears that a purpose once thought beneficial is truly detrimental to the community, it is the duty of trustees of an established charity to apply to the court or in suitable cases to the charity commissioners ... and ask that a cy-près scheme may be established. And I can well conceive that there might be cases in which the Attorney-General would think it his duty to intervene to that end. A charity once established does not die, though its nature may be changed. But it is wholly consistent with this that in a later age the court should decline to regard as charitable a purpose, to which in an earlier age that quality would have been ascribed, with the result that (unless a general charitable intention could be found) a gift for that purpose would fail. I cannot share the apprehension of the Master of the Rolls that great confusion will be caused if the court declines to be bound by the beliefs and knowledge of a past age in considering whether a particular purpose is to-day for the benefit of the community. But if it is so, then I say that it is the lesser of two evils.

American Law Institute: Restatement of the Law of Trusts (2nd edn) § 374*l*

"The courts do not take sides or attempt to decide which of two conflicting views of promoting the social interest of the community is the better adapted to the purpose, even though the views are opposed to each other. Thus, a trust to promote peace by disarmament, as well as a trust to promote peace by preparedness for war, is charitable. See Comment *d*."

(b)   The Spirit and Intendment of the Preamble

The benefit to the public must be within the spirit and intendment of the Preamble; or at least within the cases previously decided. It is easier of course for a trust to qualify if its purpose is one expressly mentioned in the Preamble.

WILLIAMS' TRUSTEES v INLAND REVENUE COMMISSIONERS
[1947] AC 447, [1947] 1 All ER 513 (HL, Viscount SIMON, Lords WRIGHT, PORTER, SIMONDS and NORMAND)

A trust was established for the purpose of promoting Welsh interests in London by various methods: by social contacts, the study of the Welsh language, literature, and art, the maintenance of a library of literature on the Welsh language or relating to Wales. The trustees were also empowered to maintain an institute for the benefit of the Welsh people in London "with a view to creating a centre in London for promoting the moral social spiritual and educational welfare of Welsh people and fostering the study of the Welsh language and of Welsh history literature music and art." No alcoholic liquor was to be sold or consumed on any part of the premises. The question was whether the trust was exempt from income tax.

Held. Not being charitable, the trust was liable to pay income tax.

LORD SIMONDS: My Lords, there are, I think, two propositions which must ever be borne in mind in any case in which the question is whether a trust is charitable. The first is that it is still the general law that a trust is not charitable and entitled to the privileges which charity confers, unless it is within the spirit and intendment of the preamble to the statute of Elizabeth (43 Eliz. c. 4), which is expressly preserved by s. 13, sub-s. 3 of the Mortmain and Charitable Uses Act 1888.[16] The second is that the classification of charity in its legal sense into four principal divisions by Lord Macnaghten in *Income Tax Comrs v Pemsel* [1891] AC 531 at 583 must always be read subject to the qualification appearing in the judgment of Lindsey LJ in *Re Macduff* [1896] 2 Ch 451 at 466: "Now Sir Samuel Romilly did not mean, and I am certain Lord Macnaghten did not mean, to say that every object of public general utility must necessarily be a charity. Some may be, and some may not be." This observation has been expanded by Lord Cave LC in this House in these words: "Lord Macnaghten did not mean that all trusts for purposes beneficial to the community are charitable, but that there were certain beneficial trusts which fell within that category; and accordingly to argue that because a trust is for a purpose beneficial to the community it is therefore a charitable trust is to turn round his sentence and to give it a different meaning. So here it is not enough to say that the trust in question is for public purposes beneficial to the community or for the public welfare; you must also show it to be a charitable trust. See *A-G v National Provincial and Union Bank of England* [1924] AC 262 at 265".[17] But it is just because the purpose of the trust deed in this case is said to be beneficial to the community or a section of the community and for no other reason that its charitable character is asserted. It is not alleged that the trust is (*a*) for the benefit of the community and (*b*) beneficial in a way which the law regards as

---

16 Repealed by the Charities Act 1960, s. 38 (1), p. 341, ante.
17 This approach of precedent and analogy was followed by DILLON J in *Re South Place Ethical Society* [1980] 1 WLR 1565 at 1575, [1980] 3 All ER 918 at 926. But cf. the less restrictive approach of RUSSELL LJ in *Incorporated Council of Law Reporting for England and Wales v A-G* [1972] Ch 73 at 88–89, [1971] 3 All ER 1029 at 1035. See also Lord WILBERFORCE in *Brisbane City Council v A-G for Queensland* [1979] AC 411 at 422, [1978] 3 All ER 30 at 33; Annual Report for 1985, paras 24–27 (analogy required, but strict approach to it undesirable: "We should act constructively and imaginatively"); [1994] Ch Com Rep 5 (Public Concern at Work held charitable).

charitable. Therefore, as it seems to me, in its mere statement the claim is imperfect and must fail.

My Lords, the cases in which the question of charity has come before the courts are legion and no one who is versed in them will pretend that all the decisions even of the highest authority are easy to reconcile, but I will venture to refer to one or two of them to make good the importance of my two general propositions. In *Houston v Burns* [1918] AC 337 the question was as to the validity of a gift "for such public, benevolent, or charitable purposes in connexion with the parish of Lesmahagow or the neighbourhood" as might be thought proper. This was a Scotch case but upon the point now under consideration there is no difference between English and Scotch law. It was argued that the limitation of the purpose to a particular locality was sufficient to validate the gift, that is to say, though purposes beneficial to the community might fail, yet purposes beneficial to a localized section of the community were charitable. That argument was rejected by this House. If the purposes are not charitable per se, the localization of them will not make them charitable. It is noticeable that Lord Finlay LC expressly overrules a decision or dictum of Lord Romilly [1918] AC 337 at 341 to the contrary effect in *Dolan v Macdermot* (1867) LR 5 Eq 60. Next I will refer to a case in the Privy Council which is the more valuable because Lord Macnaghten himself delivered the judgment of the Board. In that case the question was of the validity of a residuary gift "to the Roman Catholic Archbishop of Brisbane and his successors to be used and expended wholly or in part as such Archbishop may judge most conducive to the good of religion in this diocese." What could have been easier than to say that such a trust was beneficial to the community, and moreover to a section of the community sufficiently defined by a reference to the diocese, and was therefore charitable? Yet the only argument was that the benefit to the community was of a character which fell within the preamble to the Statute of Elizabeth, i.e., for religious purposes, and therefore was charitable. And it is to be observed that this contention was rejected on the narrow ground that the terms of the bequest were not identical with religious purposes. "The language of the bequest" said Lord Macnaghten, "would (to quote Lord Langdale's words) be open to such latitude of construction as to raise no trust which a Court of Equity could carry into execution": *Dunne v Byrne* [1912] AC 407 at 411. One more decision out of many to the same effect may be cited. In *Earley v Westminster Bank* [1939] AC 430, [1939] 3 All ER 491 a testatrix had bequeathed the residue of her estate in equal shares to the respective vicars and churchwardens of two named churches "for parish work". Could it be doubted that the purpose of the gift was beneficial to the community? It could fairly be described in the very words in which the appellants here assert the charitable nature of their trust. Yet the gift failed. It was, in the words of Lord Russell of Killowen at 437, at 494 "for the assistance and furtherance of those various activities connected with the parish church which are to be found in . . . every parish". It would be unduly cynical to say that that is not a purpose beneficial to the community. Yet it failed. And it failed because it did not fall within the spirit and intendment of the preamble to the Statute of Elizabeth.

My Lords, I must mention another aspect of this case, which was discussed in the Court of Appeal and in the argument at your Lordships' bar. It is not expressly stated in the preamble to the statute, but it was established in the Court of Chancery, and, so far as I am aware, the principle has been consistently maintained, that a trust in order to be charitable must be of a public character. It must not be merely for the benefit of particular private individuals: if it is, it will not be in law a charity though the benefit taken by those individuals is of the very character stated in the preamble. The rule is thus stated by Lord Wrenbury in *Verge v Somerville* [1924] AC 496 at 499: "To ascertain whether a gift constitutes a valid charitable trust so as to escape being void on the ground of perpetuity, a first inquiry must be whether it is public— whether it is for the benefit of the community or of an appreciably important class of the community. The inhabitants of a parish or town, or any particular class of such inhabitants, may for instance, be the objects of such a gift, but private individuals, or a fluctuating body of private individuals, cannot." It is, I think, obvious that this rule, necessary as it is, must often be difficult of application and so the courts have found. Fortunately perhaps, though Lord Wrenbury put it first, the question does not arise at all, if the purpose of the gift whether for the benefit of a class of inhabitants or of a fluctuating body of private individuals is not itself charitable. I may however refer to a recent case in this House which in some aspects resembles the present case. In *Keren Kayemeth le Jisroel Ltd v IRC* [1932] AC 650 a company had been formed which had as its main object (to put it shortly) the purchase of land in Palestine, Syria or other parts of Turkey in Asia and the peninsula of Sinai for the purpose of settling Jews on such lands. In its memorandum it took numerous other powers which were to be exercised only in such a way as should in the opinion of the company be conducive to the attainment of the primary object. No part of the income of the company was distributable among its members. It was urged that the company was established for charitable purposes for numerous reasons, with only one of which I will trouble your Lordships, namely, that it was established for the benefit of the community or of a section of the community, namely, Jews, whether the association was for the benefit of Jews all over the world or of the Jews repatriated in the Promised Land. Lord Tomlin dealing with the argument that I have just mentioned upon the footing that, if benefit to "a community" could be established the purpose might be charitable, proceeded to examine the problem in that aspect and sought to identify the community. He failed to do so, finding it neither in the community of all Jews throughout the world nor in that of the Jews in the region prescribed for settlement. It is perhaps unnecessary to pursue the matter. Each case must be judged on its own facts and the dividing line is not easily drawn. But the difficulty of finding the community in the present case, when the definition of "Welsh people" in the first deed is remembered, would not I think be less than that of finding the community of Jews in *Keren's case*.[18]

In **Scottish Burial Reform and Cremation Society v Glasgow Corporation** [1968] AC 138, [1967] 3 All ER 215, the question was whether the appellant Society was a charity and therefore entitled to partial exemption from rates under the Local Government (Financial Provisions, etc.) (Scotland) Act 1962, s. 4 (2) (*a*). The objects of the Society so far as relevant were:

---

18 See, however, Annual Report for 1977, para 79, where the Charity Commissioners, when subsequently registering the trust as a charity under Validation of Trusts Act 1954, held, citing *Idle v Tree* [1945] Ch 325, that the definition of the beneficiary class in *Williams' Trustees v IRC* nevertheless did comprise a sufficient section of the public, p. 464, post.

"(*a*) To promote reform in the present methods of burial in Scotland both as regards the expense involved and the dangerous effects on the public health.

(*b*)To promote inexpensive and at the same time sanitary methods of disposal of the dead, which shall best tend to render the remains innocuous; and, in particular, to promote the method known as cremation."

The Society charged fees, but was non-profit making.

The House of Lords held that the objects were for the benefit of the public and also within the spirit and intendment of the statute of Elizabeth, and were charitable. On the latter point Lord REID said at 146, at 218:

"But the appellants must also show that the public benefit is of a kind within the spirit and intendment of the Statute of Elizabeth I. The preamble specifies a number of objects which were then recognised as charitable. But in more recent times a wide variety of other objects have come to be recognised as also being charitable. The courts appear to have proceeded first by seeking some analogy between an object mentioned in the preamble and the object with regard to which they had to reach a decision. And then they appear to have gone further and to have been satisfied if they could find an analogy between an object already held to be charitable and the new object claimed to be charitable. And this gradual extension has proceeded so far that there are few modern reported cases where a bequest or donation was made or an institution was being carried on for a clearly specified object which was for the benefit of the public at large and not of individuals, and yet the object was held not to be within the spirit and intendment of the Statute of Elizabeth I. Counsel in the present case were invited to search for any case having even the remotest resemblance to this case in which an object was held to be for the public benefit but yet not to be within that spirit and intendment. But no such case could be found.

There is, however, another line of cases where the bequest did not clearly specify the precise object to which it was to be applied but left a discretion to trustees or others to choose objects within a certain field. There the courts have been much more strict, so that if it is possible that those entrusted with the discretion could, without infringing the testator's directions, apply the bequest in any way which would not be charitable (for example, because it did not benefit a sufficiently large section of the public) then the claim that the bequest is charitable fails. But that line of cases can have no application to the present case, and it is easy to fall into error if one tries to apply to a case like the present judicial observations made in a case where there was a discretion which could go beyond objects strictly charitable."

And Lord UPJOHN at 153, at 222:

"My Lords, I conclude by saying that the authorities show that the 'spirit and intendment' of the preamble to the Statute of Elizabeth have been stretched almost to breaking point. In the nineteenth and early twentieth centuries this was often due to a desire on the part of the courts to save the intentions of the settlor or testator from failure from some technical rule of law. Now that it is used so frequently to avoid the common man's liability to rates or taxes, this generous trend of the law may one day require reconsideration."[19]

---

19 See also *Incorporated Council of Law Reporting for England and Wales v A-G* [1972] Ch 73 at 88, [1971] 3 All ER 1029 at 1035, per RUSSELL LJ, p. 434, post.

ii. ANIMALS[20]

In **Re Wedgwood** [1915] 1 Ch 113, the testatrix gave the residue of her estate to her brother Cecil upon an oral understanding that he would apply it for the protection and benefit of animals. One aspect of such work—and one in which the testatrix was particularly interested—was the improvement of methods of slaughtering animals.

The Court of Appeal held this to be a valid charitable trust. The protection of animals was calculated to protect public morality by checking the innate tendency to cruelty.

In **Re Moss** [1949] 1 All ER 495, the testatrix made gifts to a friend, Violet Harvey, "for her to use at her discretion for her work for the welfare of cats and kittens needing care and attention". ROMER J held this to be a valid charitable trust.[1]

RE GROVE-GRADY[2]
[1929] 1 Ch 557 (CA, Lord HANWORTH MR, LAWRENCE and RUSSELL LJJ)

The testatrix gave her residuary estate upon trust to found the "Beaumont Animals Benevolent Society", whose objects included (object No. 1) the acquisition of land "for the purpose of providing a refuge or refuges for the preservation of all animals birds or other creatures not human ... and so that all such animals birds or other creatures not human shall there be safe from molestation or destruction by man ... "

Held (LAWRENCE LJ dissenting; and reversing ROMER J). The trust was not charitable because it lacked the necessary element of benefit to the community.

RUSSELL LJ: There can be no doubt that upon the authorities as they stand a trust in perpetuity for the benefit of animals may be a valid charitable trust if in the execution of the trust there is necessarily involved benefit to the public; for if this be a necessary result of the execution of the trust, the trust will fall within Lord Macnaghten's fourth class in *Pemsel's* case [1891] AC 531 at 583—namely, "trusts for other purposes beneficial to the community."

So far as I know there is no decision which upholds a trust in perpetuity in favour of animals upon any other ground than this, that the execution of the trust in the manner defined by the creator of the trust must produce some benefit to mankind. I cannot help feeling that in some instances matters have been stretched in favour of charities almost to bursting point: and that a decision benevolent to one doubtful charity has too often been the basis of a subsequent decision still more benevolent in favour of another.

---

20 Goodman Report, pages 72–73 (Animal Charities); House of Commons Report, vol. II, pp. 133–134, 140–144 (Memorandum of Evidence of RSPCA).
1 *Re Douglas* (1887) 35 ChD 472 (home for lost dogs); *Re Cranston* [1898] 1 IR 431 (to promote vegetarianism); *Marsh v Means* (1857) 3 Jur NS 790 (to finance propaganda against cruelty to animals); *Tatham v Drummond* (1864) 4 De GJ & Sm 484 (Royal Society for the Prevention of Cruelty to Animals); *University of London v Yarrow* (1857) 1 De G & J 72 (hospital for animals useful to mankind); *National Anti-Vivisection Society v IRC* [1948] AC 31 at 45, [1947] 2 All ER 217 at 222, per Lord WRIGHT; *Re Green's Will Trust* [1985] 3 All ER 455 (rescue, maintenance and benefit of cruelly treated animals and the prevention of cruelty to animals).
2 Compromised in the House of Lords sub nom *A-G v Plowden* [1931] WN 89.

The cases have accordingly run to fine distinctions, and speaking for myself I doubt whether some dispositions in favour of animals held to be charitable under former decisions would be held charitable to-day. For instance, anti-vivisection societies, which were held to be charities by Chitty J in *Re Foveaux*,[3] and were described by him as near the border line, might possibly in the light of later knowledge in regard to the benefits accruing to mankind from vivisection be held not to be charities.

The difficulty arises when you apply the test of benefit to the public to each particular case. The will of Mrs. Grove-Grady is no exception, for it presents a very difficult problem. . . .

Assuming that I have correctly interpreted object No. 1, it comes down to this, that the residuary estate may be applied in acquiring a tract of land, in turning it into an animal sanctuary, and keeping a staff of employees to ensure that no human being shall ever molest or destroy any of the animals there. Is that a good charitable trust within the authorities?

In my opinion it is not. It is merely a trust to secure that all animals within the area shall be free from molestation or destruction by man. It is not a trust directed to ensure absence or diminution of pain or cruelty in the destruction of animal life. If this trust is carried out according to its tenor, no animal within the area may be destroyed by man no matter how necessary that destruction may be in the interests of mankind or in the interests of the other denizens of the area or in the interests of the animal itself; and no matter how painlessly such destruction may be brought about. It seems to me impossible to say that the carrying out of such a trust necessarily involves benefit to the public. Beyond perhaps hearing of the existence of the enclosure the public does not come into the matter at all. Consistently with the trust the public could be excluded from entering the area or even looking into it. All that the public need know about the matter would be that one or more areas existed in which all animals (whether good or bad from mankind's point of view) were allowed to live free from any risk of being molested or killed by man; though liable to be molested and killed by other denizens of the area. For myself I feel quite unable to say that any benefit to the community will necessarily result from applying the trust fund to the purposes indicated in the first object.

If then benefit to the community as a necessary result of the execution of the trust is essential, this trust is not charitable. It is well settled that if consistently with the trust the funds may be applied for a purpose not charitable, the trust will fail for perpetuity notwithstanding that the funds might under the trust have been applied for purposes strictly charitable.

[His Lordship referred to *Re Wedgwood* [1915] 1 Ch 113 and continued:]

It was a peculiar case in this, that the trust was a secret trust declared orally. To ascertain the scope of the trust all the verbal statements made by the testatrix had to be regarded. The testatrix had explained the nature of the methods by which she desired her estate to be applied for the protection and benefit of animals—namely, in obtaining for them the benefit of humane slaughtering, i.e. avoidance of cruelty. All the members of the Court refer to that fact in their judgments; and from that they were able to spell out public benefit. Except for that purpose, there was no occasion to refer to that fact at all. Lord Cozens-Hardy says [1915] 1 Ch 113 at 117: "It tends to promote public morality by checking the innate tendency to cruelty." Kennedy LJ at

---

3 [1895] 2 Ch 501 at 507; overruled in *National Anti-Vivisection Society v IRC* [1948] AC 31, [1947] 2 All ER 217, p. 408, ante.

120, 121, in reviewing what he calls the particularly pertinent decisions, relies on those in which it is pointed out that the prevention of cruelty to animals is for the benefit of the public. Swinfen Eady LJ seems quite clear on the point. After referring to the explanation of the testatrix above mentioned he uses this language at 122: "The object of the trust being thus ascertained and defined, the question arises, is this a valid charitable trust?" He says that it is, because it is a gift for a general public purpose beneficial to the community. He arrives at that view, because (amongst other things) the discouragement of cruelty promotes humane sentiments in man towards the lower animals and elevates the human race. It seems to me that the decision in *Re Wedgwood* is definitely based on the view that the object of the trust being discouragement of cruelty to lower animals, that, upon the existing authorities, involved benefit to the community.

The Court in *Re Wedgwood* was certainly not purporting to lay down any new law. It is not, in my opinion, a decision either (1) that every trust for the benefit of animals necessarily involves benefit to the community, or (2) that a trust for the benefit of animals which involves no such benefit is a charitable trust.

In my opinion, the Court must determine in each case whether the trusts are such that benefit to the community must necessarily result from their execution.

In the present case I cannot persuade myself that the trusts described by the testatrix under the head of the first object fulfil that description. To do so would go beyond any decided case. The authorities have, in my opinion, reached the furthest admissible point of benevolence in construing, as charitable, gifts in favour of animals, and for myself, I am not prepared to go any further.

In **Re Murawski's Will Trust** [1971] 1 WLR 707, [1971] 2 All ER 328, a gift to the Bleakholt Animal Sanctuary, whose objects were "the provision of care and shelter for stray, neglected and unwanted animals of all kinds and the protection of animals from ill-usage, cruelty and suffering" was held to be charitable.[4]

Purposes connected with animals may be charitable if expressed in terms of education[5] or of environmental preservation.[6] As FARWELL J said in **Re Lopes** [1931] 2 Ch 130 at 136:
"A ride on an elephant may be educational".

Report of the Charity Commissioners for England and Wales for the year 1973, para. 40.
"40. Concern for the protection of the environment was the motive for the establishment of a number of new charities. As an example, the Advisory Committee on Oil Pollution of the Sea was registered in October. Its objects include the preservation of the seas of the world in general and the seas

---

4 See Annual Report for 1971, para. 26 (Home of Rest for Horses); [1994] 2 Ch Com Rep 1 (Animal Abuse, Injustice and Defence Society).
5 *Re Lopes* [1931] 2 Ch 130.
6 *Re Verrall* [1916] 1 Ch 100 (National Trust).

adjacent to the United Kingdom in particular from pollution by human activities and the promotion of research into the causes and effects of such pollution and the means by which the injurious effects of pollution may be prevented or reduced. The establishment of the original Committee in 1952 was due to concern about the plight of oiled sea birds but the Committee are now proposing to increase the scope of their activities and money has been raised for research into the causes of pollution as well as the rehabilitation of sea birds."[7]

iii. SOCIAL, SPORTING AND RECREATIONAL TRUSTS

A trust to provide sporting facilities is not charitable per se.[8] However, if the facilities are for pupils of schools or universities, or if the game itself is of an educational nature, the trusts will be charitable for the advancement of education; and if the facilities are within the armed forces, they contribute to the safety and protection of the country and will be charitable under the fourth head.

In **Inland Revenue Commissioners v City of Glasgow Police Athletic Association** [1953] AC 380, [1953] 1 All ER 747, p. 434, post, the question was whether the Association was entitled to exemption from income tax on the ground that it was a body of persons established for charitable purposes only.

The object of the Association was "to encourage and promote all forms of athletic sports and general pastimes".

Nearly every member of the Glasgow police force was a member. The Association provided athletic, social and recreational facilities. It played a valuable part in maintaining health, morale and *esprit de corps* in the force, promoted good relations between the force and the public and increased the efficiency of the force generally.

The House of Lords (Lords NORMAND, MORTON OF HENRYTON, REID and COHEN, with Lord OAKSEY dissenting) held that the Association was not entitled to exemption. A trust for the promotion of the efficiency of the force would be charitable; but the provision of recreation was not. Lord NORMAND said at 395, at 752: "The Special Commissioners had evidence before them which entitled them to find that, among its purposes, were the encouragement of recruiting, the improvement of the efficiency of the force, and the public advantage. This is a purpose which the Special Commissioners were entitled to

---

7 Report for 1979 paras 61–65 (Rebecca charity for purchasing Porthmadog Embankment and its tolls); *Re Cranstoun* [1932] 1 Ch 537 (preservation of two Elizabethan cotttages); Annual Report for 1990, Appx A(*b*) (Seattle and Carlisle Railway Trust); 1991, para. 73 (Wilderness Trust to advance the education of the public on its conservation and inter-relationship with the environment generally).

8 The point was left open in *IRC v McMullen* [1981] AC 1 at 15, [1980] 1 All ER 884 at 887; *Re Nottage* [1895] 2 Ch 649, p. 430, post (prize for a yacht race); *Re Clifford* (1912) 106 LT 14 (Oxford Angling and Preservation Society); *Re Patten* [1929] 2 Ch 276 (not even for the Sussex County Cricket Club); Annual Report for 1984, paras 18–25 (Oxford Ice Skating Association Ltd), p. 379 ante: cf. *Re Laidlaw Foundation* (1985) 13 DLR (4th) 491 (foundation to promote amateur athletic sports held charitable as promoting health); doubted in Annual Report 1989, para. 53, where Birchfield Harriers Athletic Club was refused registration. See (1956) CLP 39 (O.R. Marshall); (1988) 52 NLJ Annual Charities Review iv (H. Picarda).

hold in law to be a public charitable purpose. But there remains the non-charitable purpose of providing recreation to the members. The question is whether this non-charitable purpose is incidental to the public charitable purpose. If not, it cannot be said that the association was a body established for charitable purposes only ... The private advantage of members is a purpose for which the association is established and it therefore cannot be said that this is an association established for a public charitable purpose only.''

INLAND REVENUE COMMISSIONERS v BADDELEY [9]
[1955] AC 572, [1955] 1 All ER 525 (HL, Viscount SIMONDS, Lords PORTER, REID, TUCKER and SOMERVELL OF HARROW)

Two conveyances of land were made to the respondent trustees on similar but not identical terms. In the first deed land, on which were a mission church, lecture room and store, was conveyed upon trust to permit the property to be "used by the leaders for the time being of the Stratford Newtown Methodist Mission for the promotion of the religious social and physical well-being of persons resident in the County Boroughs of West Ham and Leyton ... by the provision of facilities for religious services and instruction and for the social and physical training and recreation of such aforementioned persons who for the time being are in the opinion of such leaders members or likely to become members of the Methodist Church and of insufficient means otherwise to enjoy the advantages provided ... and by promoting and encouraging all forms of such activities as are calculated to contribute to the health and well-being of such persons". (Clause 2 (a)). In the second deed four pieces of land laid out as playing-fields were conveyed upon similar trusts, the main difference being that the trustees were to permit them to be used for the moral (instead of religious) social and physical well-being of the same class of persons.

The question was whether the conveyances could be stamped at the reduced rate on the ground that the purposes were charitable.

Held. (Lord REID dissenting). The purposes were not charitable, because: (i) The purposes were wide enough to include non-charitable purposes; (ii) (Lords TUCKER and PORTER expressing no opinion) The requirement of public benefit was not satisfied.

VISCOUNT SIMONDS: I find it convenient, my Lords, to examine the two deeds separately, and take first a deed of conveyance to the respondents as trustees of certain land at Stratford, in the county of Essex, of an area of about 680 square yards with a mission church, lecture room and store erected on some part thereof. So far as relevant (omitting certain words which admittedly were inserted in error) the trusts of this property were as follows: [His Lordship read clause 2 (*a*) and continued:] This main trust is followed by certain ancillary provisions which cannot, I think, affect the question whether it is a charitable trust. It is at once apparent that the document is not skillfully drawn. It is presumably *all* the persons resident in the specified boroughs whose religious, social and physical well-being is to be promoted, but this is to be achieved by providing certain facilities for religious services and instruction and for the social and physical training and recreation of "such aforementioned persons," i.e., such residents, as are for the time being "in the opinion of such leaders members or likely to become members of the

---

9 See also *D'Aguiar v Guyana IRC* [1970] TR 31 (Citizens' Advice and Aid Service of Georgetown held non-charitable by Privy Council).

Methodist Church and of insufficient means ... to enjoy the advantages provided by these presents". This awkward phraseology leaves me in doubt whether the beneficiaries under this trust are to be all the residents in a certain area or only such of the residents as satisfy two conditions, first that they are Methodists or in the opinion of the leaders potential Methodists, and secondly, that they are of limited means. It might even be that upon a true interpretation of the deed some benefits are open to all the residents, others to a more limited class. Fortunately I do not find it necessary to determine this question, for I think that, whatever view may be taken of it, this case is governed by the recent decision of this House in *Williams' Trustees v IRC* [1947] AC 447, [1947] 1 All ER 513, p. 411 ante....

Other aspects of the trust established by the first deed were discussed and it is right that I should make some observations upon them, but before doing so I will turn to the second deed.... [His Lordship held that this trust also failed for vagueness and generality, and continued:].

This brings me to another aspect of the case, which was argued at great length and to me at least presents the most difficult of the many difficult problems in this branch of the law. Suppose that, contrary to the view that I have expressed, the trust would be a valid charitable trust, if the beneficiaries were the community at large or a section of the community defined by some geographical limits, is it the less a valid trust if it is confined to members or potential members of a particular church within a limited geographical area?

The starting point of the argument must be, that this charity (if it be a charity) falls within the fourth class in Lord Macnaghten's classification. It must therefore be a trust which is, to use the words of Sir Samuel Romilly in *Morice v Bishop of Durham* (1805) 10 Ves 522 at 532, of "general public utility," and the question is what these words mean. It is, indeed, an essential feature of all "charity" in the legal sense that there must be in it some element of public benefit, whether the purpose is educational, religious or eleemosynary: see the recent case of *Oppenheim v Tobacco Securities Trust Co Ltd* [1951] AC 297, [1951] 1 All ER 31, p. 385 ante, and, as I have said elsewhere, it is possible, particularly in view of the so-called "poor relations' cases," the scope of which may one day have to be considered, that a different degree of public benefit is requisite according to the class in which the charity is said to fall. But it is said that if a charity falls within the fourth class, it must be for the benefit of the whole community or at least of all the inhabitants of a sufficient area. And it has been urged with much force that, if as Lord Greene said in *Re Strakosch* [1949] Ch 529, [1949] 2 All ER 6, p. 439 post, this fourth class is represented in the preamble to the Statute of Elizabeth by the repair of bridges, etc., and possibly by the maintenance of Houses of Correction, the class of beneficiaries or potential beneficiaries cannot be further narrowed down. Some confusion has arisen from the fact that a trust of general public utility, however general and however public, cannot be of equal utility to all and may be of immediate utility to few. A sea wall, the prototype of this class in the preamble, is of remote, if any, utility to those who live in the heart of the Midlands. But there is no doubt that a trust for the maintenance of sea walls generally or along a particular stretch of coast is a good charitable trust. Nor, as it appears to me, is the validity of a trust affected by the fact that by its very nature only a limited number of people are likely to avail themselves, or are perhaps even capable of availing themselves, of its benefits. It is easy, for instance, to imagine a charity which has for its object some form of child welfare, of which the immediate beneficiaries could only be persons of tender age. Yet this would satisfy any test of general public utility. It may be said that it would satisfy the test because the indirect benefit of such a charity would extend far beyond its direct beneficiaries, and that aspect of the matter has probably not been out of sight. Indirect benefit is certainly an aspect which must have influenced the decision of the "cruelty to animals" cases. But, I doubt whether this sort of rationalisation helps to explain a branch of the law which has developed empirically and by analogy upon analogy.

It is, however, in my opinion, particularly important in cases falling within the fourth category to keep firmly in mind the necessity of the element of general public utility, and I would not relax this rule. For here is a slippery slope. In the case under appeal the intended beneficiaries are a class within a class; they are those of the inhabitants of a particular area who are members of a particular church: the area is comparatively large and populous and the members may be numerous. But, if this trust is charitable for them, does it cease to be charitable as the area narrows down and the numbers diminish? Suppose the area is confined to a single street and the beneficiaries to those whose creed commands few adherents: or suppose the class is one that is determined not by religious belief but by membership of a particular profession or by pursuit of a particular trade. These were considerations which influenced the House in the recent case of *Oppenheim* [1951] AC 297, [1951] 1 All ER 31. That was a case of an educational trust, but I think that they have even greater weight in the case of trusts which by their nominal classification depend for their validity upon general public utility.

It is pertinent, then, to ask how far your Lordships might regard yourselves bound by authority to hold the trusts now under review valid charitable trusts, if the only question in issue was the sufficiency of the public element. I do not repeat what I said in the case of *Williams' Trustees v IRC* [1947] AC 447, [1947] 1 All ER 513, p. 411 ante, about *Goodman v Mayor of Saltash* (1882) 7 App Cas 633 and the cases that closely followed it.[10] Further consideration of them does not change the view that I then expressed, which in effect endorsed the opinion of the learned editor of the last edition of Tudor on Charities. More relevant is the case of *Verge v Somerville* [1924] AC 496. In that case, in which the issue was as to the validity of a gift "to the trustees of the Repatriation Fund or other similar fund for the benefit of New South Wales returned soldiers," Lord Wrenbury, delivering the judgment of the Judicial Committee, said at 499 that, to be a charity, a trust must be "for the benefit of the community or of an appreciably important class of the community. The inhabitants", he said, "of a parish or town or any particular class of such inhabitants, may, for instance, be the objects of such a gift, but private individuals, or a fluctuating body of private individuals, cannot." Here, my Lords, are two expressions: "an appreciably important class of the community" and "any particular class of such inhabitants," to which in any case it is not easy to give a precise quantitative or qualitative meaning. But I think that in the consideration of them the difficulty has sometimes been increased by failing to observe the distinction, at which I hinted earlier in this opinion, between a form of relief extended to the whole community yet by its very nature advantageous only to the few and a form of relief accorded to a selected few out of a larger number equally willing and able to take advantage of it. Of the former type repatriated

10 *Peggs v Lamb* [1994] Ch 172, [1994] 2 All ER 15. On trusts for the benefit of a locality, see H & M, pp. 431–432; Picarda, 132–133; Tudor, pp. 105–108.

New South Wales soldiers would serve as a clear example. To me it would not seem arguable that they did not form an adequate class of the community for the purpose of the particular charity that was being established. It was with this type of case that Lord Wrenbury was dealing, and his words are apt to deal with it. Somewhat different considerations arise if the form, which the purporting charity takes, is something of general utility which is nevertheless made available not to the whole public but only to a selected body of the public—an important class of the public it may be. For example, a bridge which is available for all the public may undoubtedly be a charity and it is indifferent how many people use it. But confine its use to a selected number of persons, however numerous and important: it is then clearly not a charity. It is not of general public utility: for it does not serve the public purpose which its nature qualifies it to serve.

Bearing this distinction in mind, though I am well aware that in its application it may often be very difficult to draw the line between public and private purposes, I should in the present case conclude that a trust cannot qualify as a charity within the fourth class in *Income Tax Comrs v Pemsel* [1891] AC 531 if the beneficiaries are a class of persons not only confined to a particular area but selected from within it by reference to a particular creed. The Master of the Rolls in his judgment cites a rhetorical question asked by Mr. Stamp in argument [1953] Ch 504 at 519, [1953] 2 All ER 233 at 239. "Who has ever heard of a bridge to be crossed only by impecunious Methodists?" The reductio ad absurdum is sometimes a cogent form of argument, and this illustration serves to show the danger of conceding the quality of charity to a purpose which is not a public purpose. What is true of a bridge for Methodists is equally true of any other public purpose falling within the fourth class and of the adherents of any other creed.

The passage that I have cited from *Verge v Somerville* [1924] AC 496 at 499 refers also (not, I think, for the first time) to "private individuals" or a "fluctuating body of private individuals" in contradistinction to a class of the community or of the inhabitants of a locality. This is a difficult conception to grasp: the distinction between a class of the community and the private individuals from time to time composing it is elusive. But, if it has any bearing on the present case, I would suppose that the beneficiaries, a body of persons arbitrarily chosen and impermanent, fall more easily into the latter than the former category.

I conclude that on this ground also I should decide this case against the respondents even if I were otherwise in their favour, and will only add that in coming to this conclusion I find myself in agreement with Babington LJ in the *Londonderry* case[11] to which I have already referred.

I move that the appeals be allowed accordingly. The costs of all parties will be paid by the appellants in accordance with the undertaking previously given.

The charitable status of various associations, such as Women's Institutes, Boys' Clubs and the National Playing Fields Association, which had for many years been assumed to be charitable, was put in doubt as a result of these decisions.

----

11 *Londonderry Presbyterian Church House Trustees v IRC* [1946] NI 178.

The Recreational Charities Act 1958 soon followed; but it may well be thought to have created as many problems as it solved.

_____

RECREATIONAL CHARITIES ACT 1958[12]

1. General provision as to recreational and similar trusts, etc.—(1) Subject to the provisions of this Act, it shall be and be deemed always to have been charitable to provide, or assist in the provision of, facilities for recreation or other leisure-time occupation, if the facilities are provided in the interests of social welfare:

Provided that nothing in this section shall be taken to derogate from the principle that a trust or institution to be charitable must be for the public benefit.

(2) The requirement of the foregoing subsection that the facilities are provided in the interests of social welfare shall not be treated as satisfied unless—

 (_a_) the facilities are provided with the object of improving the conditions of life for the persons for whom the facilities are primarily intended; and

 (_b_) either—

    (i) those persons have need of such facilities as aforesaid by reason of their youth, age, infirmity or disablement, poverty or social and economic circumstances; or

    (ii) the facilities are to be available to the members or female members of the public at large.

(3) Subject to the said requirement, subsection (1) of this section applies in particular to the provision of facilities at village halls, community centres and women's institutes, and to the provision and maintenance of grounds and buildings to be used for purposes of recreation or leisure-time occupation, and extends to the provision of facilities for those purposes by the organising of any activity.

2. Miners' welfare trusts.—(1) Where trusts declared before the seventeenth day of December, nineteen hundred and fifty-seven, required or purported to require property to be held for the purpose of activities which are social welfare activities within the meaning of the Miners' Welfare Act, 1952, and at that date the whole or part of the property held on those trusts or of any property held with that property represented an application of moneys standing to the credit of the miners' welfare fund or moneys provided by the Coal Industry Social Welfare Organisation, those trusts shall be treated as if they were and always had been charitable.

(2) For the purposes of this section property held on the same trusts as other property shall be deemed to be held with it, though vested in different trustees.[13]

_____

12 (1959) 23 Con (NS) 15 (S.G. Maurice); (1958) 21 MLR 534 (L. Price); [1980] Conv 173 (J. Warburton); Goodman Report, paras. 69–71 (Sport).
13 Section 3 provides a number of savings and other provisions relating to past transactions.

In **Guild v Inland Revenue Commissioners**[14] [1992] 2 AC 310, [1992] 2 All ER 10, the House of Lords held that a bequest "to the town council of North Berwick for the use in connection with the sports centre in North Berwick or some similar purpose in connection with sport" was charitable under section 1 (1) and (2) of the Recreational Charities Act 1958, and therefore exempt from capital transfer tax. Lord KEITH OF KINKEL said at 318; at 15:

"In the course of his argument in relation to the first branch of the bequest counsel for the commissioners accepted that it assisted in the provision of facilities for recreation or other leisure time occupation within the meaning of subsection (1) of section 1 of the Act, and also that the requirement of public benefit in the proviso to the subsection was satisfied. It was further accepted that the facilities of the sports centre were available to the public at large so that the condition of subsection (2)(b)(ii) was satisfied. It was maintained, however, that these facilities were not provided 'in the interests of social welfare' as required by subsection (1), because they did not meet the condition laid down in subsection (2)(a), namely that they should be 'provided with the object of improving the conditions of life for the persons for whom the facilities are primarily intended.' The reason why it was said that this condition was not met was that on a proper construction it involved that the facilities should be provided with the object of meeting a need for such facilities in people who suffered from a position of relative social disadvantage. Reliance was placed on a passage from the judgment of Walton J in *Inland Revenue Commissioners v McMullen* [1978] 1 WLR 664, [1978] 1 All ER 230. That was a case where the Football Association had set up a trust to provide facilities to encourage pupils of schools and universities in the United Kingdom to play association football and other games and sports. Walton J held that the trust was not valid as one for the advancement of education nor did it satisfy section 1 of the Act of 1958. He said, at 675, at 241, in relation to the words 'social welfare' in subsection (1):

'In my view, however, these words in themselves indicate that there is some kind of deprivation—not, of course, by any means necessarily of money—which falls to be alleviated; and I think that this is made even clearer by the terms of subsection (2)(a). The facilities must be provided with the object of improving the conditions of life for persons for whom the facilities are primarily intended. In other words, they must be to some extent and in some way deprived persons.'

When the case went to the Court of Appeal [1979] 1 WLR 130, [1979] 1 All ER 588 the majority (Stamp and Orr LJJ) affirmed the judgment of Walton J on both points, but Bridge LJ dissented. As regards the Recreational Charities Act 1958 point he said, at 142–143, at 597–598:

'I turn therefore to consider whether the object defined by clause 3(a) is charitable under the express terms of section 1 of the Recreational Charities Act 1958. Are the facilities for recreation contemplated in this clause to be "provided in the interests of social welfare" under section 1(1)? If this phrase stood without further statutory elaboration, I should not hesitate to decide that sporting facilities for persons undergoing any formal process of education are provided in the interests of social welfare. Save in the sense that the interests of social welfare can only be served by the meeting of some social need, I cannot accept the judge's view that the

---

14 [1992] Conv 361 (H. Norman); (1992) 51 CLJ 429 (J. Hopkins); [1992] All ER Rev 213 (P.J. Clarke); [1992–93] 1 CL & PR 45 (D. Morris).

interests of social welfare can only be served in relation to some "deprived" class. The judge found this view reinforced by the requirement of subsection (2)(*a*) of section 1 that the facilities must be provided "with the object of improving the conditions of life for the persons for whom the facilities are primarily intended; . . ." Here again I can see no reason to conclude that only the deprived can have their conditions of life improved. Hyde Park improves the conditions of life for residents in Mayfair and Belgravia as much as for those in Pimlico or the Portobello Road, and the village hall may improve the conditions of life for the squire and his family as well as for the cottagers. The persons for whom the facilities here are primarily intended are pupils of schools and universities, as defined in the trust deed, and these facilities are in my judgment unquestionably to be provided with the object of improving their conditions of life. Accordingly the ultimate question on which the application of the statute to this trust depends, is whether the requirements of section 1(2)(*b*)(i) are satisfied on the grounds that such pupils as a class have need of facilities for games or sports which will promote their physical education and development by reason either of their youth or of their social and economic circumstances, or both. The overwhelming majority of pupils within the definition are young persons and the tiny minority of mature students can be ignored as de minimis. There cannot surely be any doubt that young persons as part of their education do need facilities for organised games and sports both by reason of their youth and by reason of their social and economic circumstances. They cannot provide such facilities for themselves but are dependent on what is provided for them.'

In the House of Lords [1981] AC 1, [1980] 1 All ER 884 the case was decided against the Crown upon the ground that the trust was one for the advancement of education, opinion being reserved on the point under the Recreational Charities Act 1958. Lord Hailsham of St Marylebone LC said, at 11, at 887:

' . . . I do not wish my absence of decision on the third or fourth points to be interpreted as an endorsement of the majority judgments in the Court of Appeal nor as necessarily dissenting from the contrary views contained in the minority judgment of Bridge LJ'

[His Lordship referred to *National Deposit Friendly Society Trustees v Skegness Urban District Council* [1959] AC 293, [1958] 2 All ER 601; *Commissioner of Valuation for Northern Ireland v Lurgan Borough Council* [1968] NI 104, and continued:]

The fact is that persons in all walks of life and all kinds of circumstances may have their conditions of life improved by the provision of recreational facilities of suitable character. The proviso requiring public benefit excludes facilities of an undesirable nature. In my opinion the view expressed by Bridge LJ in *Inland Revenue Commissioners v McMullen* is clearly correct and that of Walton J in the same case is incorrect. I would therefore reject the argument that the facilities are not provided in the interests of social welfare unless they are provided with the object of improving the conditions of life for persons who suffer from some form of social disadvantage. It suffices if they are provided with the object of improving the conditions of life for members of the community generally. The Lord President, whose opinion contains a description of the facilities available at the sports centre which it is unnecessary to repeat, took the view that they were so provided. I respectfully agree, and indeed the contrary was not seriously maintained.

It remains to consider the point upon which the executor was unsuccessful before the First Division, namely whether or not the second branch of the bequest of residue, referring to 'some similar purpose in connection with sport,' is so widely expressed as to admit of the funds being applied in some manner which falls outside the requirements of section 1 of the Act of 1958...

The matter for decision turns upon the ascertainment of the intention of the testator in using the words he did. The adjective 'similar' connotes that there are points of resemblance between one thing and another. The points of resemblance here with the sports centre cannot be related only to location in North Berwick or to connection with sport. The first of these is plainly to be implied from the fact of the gift being to the town council of North Berwick and the second is expressly stated in the words under construction. So the resemblance to the sports centre which the testator had in mind must be ascertained by reference to some other characteristics possessed by it. The leading characteristics of the sports centre lie in the nature of the facilities which are provided there and the fact that those facilities are available to the public at large. These are the characteristics which enable it so satisfy section 1 of the Act of 1958. Adopting so far as necessary a benignant construction, I infer that the intention of the testator was that any other purpose to which the town council might apply the bequest or any part of it should also display those characteristics. In the result I am of opinion, the first part of the bequest having been found to be charitable within the meaning of section 1 of the Act of 1958, that the same is true of the second part, so that the funds in question qualify for exemption from capital transfer tax."

QUESTIONS

1. What is the effect of the Recreational Charities Act 1958 on the *Glasgow Police* and *Baddeley* cases? H & M, pp. 401–402.
2. Consider the test for a sufficient section of the public under each of the four heads of charity. See especially *Re Dunlop* [1984] NI 408 where a trust "to found or help to found a home for Old Presbyterian persons" was held to be charitable; [1987] Conv 114 (N. Dawson).

iv. HOSPITALS[15]

RE RESCH'S WILL TRUSTS
[1969] 1 AC 514, [1967] 3 All ER 915 (PC, Lords HODSON, GUEST, DONOVAN, WILBERFORCE and Sir Alfred NORTH)

A number of questions arose under the will of Edmund Resch, who died in 1963, leaving a residuary estate worth A $8,000,000. The relevant question was whether a gift to a private non-profit-making hospital was a charitable gift. The gift was of income "to the Sisters of Charity for a period of 200 years or for so long as they shall conduct St Vincent's Private Hospital whichever shall be the shorter period, to be applied for the general purposes of such hospital and upon the expiration of the said period of 200 years or upon the said Sisters of

---

15   CC Leaflet 6 (Charities for the Relief of Sickness); [1995] Ch Com Rep. 35 (Funds Raised and Donated to NHS Hospitals); *NHS Charitable Funds: a Guide* (1994): Annual Report for 1994, p. 7; Goodman Report, paras. 47 (Costly Services), 48–49 (Hospitals).

Charity ceasing to conduct such hospital" to pay the income to named charities.

Held. A valid charitable gift.

LORD WILBERFORCE: St Vincent's Private Hospital was inaugurated in 1909, when the present building, called by that name, was converted to that purpose, having previously been used as a Hospice for the Dying. The hospital was established and has since 1909 been conducted by the Sisters of Charity, a voluntary association or congregation of women, governed by their constitution under which they devote themselves without reward to good works. The Sisters also conducted in 1909 and still conduct the adjacent St Vincent's Hospital which is a public hospital within the Public Hospitals Act, 1929–59. The evidence shows that the reason for the establishment of the private hospital was to relieve the pressing demand of the public for admission to the general hospital which was quite inadequate to the demand upon it. Another reason was that there were many persons who needed hospital nursing and attention who were not willing to enter a public hospital but were willing and desirous of having hospital accommodation with more privacy and comfort than would be possible in the general hospital. The establishment of an adjacent private hospital would enable the honorary medical staff in the general hospital to admit for treatment under their care in the private hospital patients who were reluctant to enter the general hospital and were able and willing to pay reasonable and proper fees for admission and treatment in a private hospital. The private hospital has 82 beds as compared with over 500 in the general hospital. . . .

A gift for the purposes of a hospital is prima facie a good charitable gift. This is now clearly established both in Australia and in England, not merely because of the use of the word "impotent" in the preamble to 43 Eliz. c. 4, though the process of referring to the preamble is one often used for reassurance, but because the provision of medical care for the sick is, in modern times, accepted as a public benefit suitable to attract the privileges given to charitable institutions. This has been recognised in the High Court in Australia in *Taylor v Taylor*[16] and *Kytherian Association of Queensland v Sklavos* (1958) 101 CLR 56: in England in *Re Smith* [1962] 1 WLR 763, [1962] 2 All ER 563.

In spite of this general proposition, there may be certain hospitals, or categories of hospitals, which are not charitable institutions (see *Re Smith*). Disqualifying indicia may be either that the hospital is carried on commercially, i.e., with a view to making profits for private individuals, or that the benefits it provides are not for the public, or a sufficiently large class of the public to satisfy the necessary tests of public character. Each class of objection is taken in the present case. As regards the first, it is accepted that the private hospital is not run for the profit, in any ordinary sense, of individuals. Moreover, if the purposes of the hospital are otherwise charitable, they do not lose this character merely because charges are made to the recipients of benefits—see *IRC v Falkirk Temperance Café Trust* 1927 SC 261; *Salvation Army (Victoria) Property Trust v Fern Tree Gully Corpn* (1951) 85 CLR 159 at 173. But what is said is that surpluses are made and are used for the general purposes of the Sisters of Charity. This association, while in a broad sense philanthropic, has objects which may not be charitable in the legal sense. Furthermore its purposes, though stated in its "constitutions" are not limited by law, other than the canon law of the Roman Catholic Church, and under this, they are

---

16 (1910) 10 CLR 218 at 227, per GRIFFITH CJ.

empowered, and may be obliged, to alter their purposes so as to include other objects which may not be strictly charitable.

Their Lordships do not consider it necessary to enter upon these latter considerations. For whatever the Sisters of Charity may be empowered to do with regard to their general property, as regards the share of income of the residuary estate, given to them as trustees, they are bound by the trusts declared in the will under which any money received by them must be applied exclusively for the general purposes of the private hospital as above defined. As regards these purposes, it appears, from the evidence already summarised, that the making of profits for the benefit of individuals is not among them. The most that is shown is that, on a cash basis, and without making such adjustments as would be required for commercial accounting, a net surplus is produced over the years which in fact has been applied largely, though not exclusively for hospital purposes. The share of income given by the will must be devoted entirely to the purposes of the private hospital. The character, charitable or otherwise, of the general activities of the Sisters, is not therefore a material consideration ...

Their Lordships turn to the second objection. This, in substance, is that the private hospital is not carried on for purposes "beneficial to the community" because it provides only for persons of means who are capable of paying the substantial fees required as a condition of admission.

In dealing with this objection, it is necessary first to dispose of a misapprehension. It is not a condition of validity of a trust for the relief of the sick that it should be limited to the poor sick. Whether one regards the charitable character of trusts for the relief of the sick as flowing from the word "impotent" ("aged, impotent and poor people") in the preamble to 43 Eliz. c. 4 or more broadly as derived from the conception of benefit to the community, there is no warrant for adding to the condition of sickness that of poverty. As early as *IRC v Pemsel* Lord Herschell was able to say [1891] AC 531 at 571:

> "I am unable to agree with the view that the sense in which 'charities' and 'charitable purpose' are popularly used is so restricted as this. I certainly cannot think that they are limited to the relief of wants occasioned by lack of pecuniary means. Many examples may, I think, be given of endowments for the relief of human necessities, which would be as generally termed charities as hospitals or almshouses, where, nevertheless, the necessities to be relieved do not result from poverty in its limited sense of the lack of money."

Similarly in *Verge v Somerville* [1924] AC 496 Lord Wrenbury, delivering the judgment of this Board on an appeal from New South Wales, pointed out that trusts for education and religion do not require any qualification of poverty to be introduced to give them validity and held generally that poverty is not a necessary qualification in trusts beneficial to the community. The proposition that relief of sickness was a sufficient purpose without adding poverty was accepted by the Court of Appeal in *Re Smith* [1962] 1 WLR 763, [1962] 2 All ER 563. The appellants did not really contest this. They based their argument on the narrower proposition that a trust could not be charitable which excluded the poor from participation in its benefits. The purposes of the private hospital were, they said, to provide facilities for the well-to-do: an important section of the community was excluded: the trusts could not therefore be said to be for the benefit of the community. There was not sufficient "public element".

To support this, they appealed to some well-known authorities. [His Lordship referred to *Jones v Williams* (1767) Amb 651 and *Re Macduff* [1896] 2 Ch 451, where] in a general discussion of such expressions as "charitable" or "philanthropic", Lindsey LJ said at 464:

> "I am quite aware that a trust may be charitable though not confined to the poor; but I doubt very much whether a trust would be declared to be charitable which excluded the poor."

... Their Lordships accept the correctness of what has been said in those cases, but they must be rightly understood. It would be a wrong conclusion from them to state that a trust for the provision of medical facilities would necessarily fail to be charitable merely because by reason of expense they could only be made use of by persons of some means. To provide, in response to public need, medical treatment otherwise inaccessible but in its nature expensive, without any profit motive, might well be charitable: on the other hand to limit admission to a nursing home to the rich would not be so. The test is essentially one of public benefit, and indirect as well as direct benefit enters into the account. In the present case, the element of public benefit is strongly present. It is not disputed that a need exists to provide accommodation and medical treatment in conditions of greater privacy and relaxation than would be possible in a general hospital and as a supplement to the facilities of a general hospital. This is what the private hospital does and it does so at, approximately, cost price. The service is needed by all, not only by the well-to-do. So far as its nature permits it is open to all: the charges are not low, but the evidence shows that it cannot be said that the poor are excluded: such exclusion as there is, is of some of the poor—namely, those who have (a) not contributed sufficiently to a medical benefit scheme or (b) need to stay longer in the hospital than their benefit will cover or (c) cannot get a reduction of or exemption from the charges. The general benefit to the community of such facilities results from the beds and medical staff of the general hospital, the availability of a particular type of nursing and treatment which supplements that provided by the general hospital and the benefit to the standard of medical care in the general hospital which arises from the juxtaposition of the two institutions ...

[Their Lordships] ... hold ... that the gift in favour of the Sisters of Charity is a valid charitable bequest.[17]

Report of the Charity Commissioners for England and Wales for the year 1975, para. 70.

"*Charities engaged in fringe medicine*

70. As a result of our considerations of the New Age Healing Trust mentioned in paragraphs 68 and 69 above[18] we considered the practical difficulties involved and the principles which should be followed in considering applications for the registration of institutions set up to promote and/or

17 *Joseph Rowntree Memorial Trust Housing Association Ltd v A-G* [1983] Ch 159, [1983] 1 All ER 288, p. 346, ante.

18 An application to register a trust for "the practising for the public benefit of New Age Healing for the relief of the sick and persons in ill-health" was rejected. But the Yoga for Health Foundation is a registered charity; the trust is "for the purpose of research into the therapeutic benefits to be obtained by the practice of Yoga both mentally and physically and the promotion of such benefits": *Yoga for Health Foundation v Customs and Excise Comrs* [1984] STC 630.

practice unorthodox methods of healing. The main problem was the need to make value judgments in such cases. For this purpose we would require evidence to satisfy us that an unusual form of treatment had some merit, in the same way as the court would require evidence if the case had been brought before them. An organisation proposing to engage in such well known therapeutic activities as acupuncture, osteopathy and faith healing would not necessarily be required to submit evidence concerning the effectiveness of its activities. In other cases, however, evidence would be required concerning the nature of the healing method proposed and the therapeutic result of that method. The effectiveness of proposed treatment could be a matter of special knowledge derived from a study of cases or from other sources. It could also be provided by evidence that the treatment was generally acceptable to the medical profession. This did not mean that every institution practising in the field of fringe medicine must necessarily use methods acceptable to the generality of the medical profession if it were to obtain charitable status, but there might be grounds for reasonable doubt if no medically qualified persons were prepared to testify to the beneficial results of the treatment. We concluded that where therapeutic methods and results were common knowledge evidence on these points would not be required before registration but, where they were not, the applicant should be required to submit evidence, and a decision whether to register the institution should be based on a study of that evidence as well as of the stated objects."[19]

v. MISCELLANEOUS

It is impossible to include or even to foresee all the areas which could be included under the fourth head. This section will present a miscellaneous collection of cases which help to illustrate the borderlines of this class.

(a) The Services[20]

In **Re Gray** [1925] Ch 362, the testator gave sums of money for the establishment of a regimental fund for the Carabiniers to be called "the Gray

---

19 See Annual Report for 1978, paras. 61–63, Appendix B, suggesting ways in which the income for charities for the relief of sickness may be applied; paras. 82–85 (British Pregnancy Advisory Service).

20 *Re Stephens* (1892) 8 TLR 792 (gift to the National Rifle Association "for the teaching of shooting at moving objects so as to prevent as far as possible a catastrophe similar to that at Majuba Hill" held charitable); *Re Lord Stratheden and Campbell* [1894] 3 Ch 265 ("an annuity of £100 to be provided to the Central London Rangers on the appointment of the next lieutenant-colonel." The gift was held to be charitable but void for perpetuity); H & M, p. 384; *Re Good* [1905] 2 Ch 60 (trust for the "maintenance of a library for the officers' mess of the 2nd Battalion 14th Regiment of Foot now at Natal" held charitable); *Re Donald* [1909] 2 Ch 410 (gift "to the officer commanding the Northamptonshire Militia for the mess of that regiment or for the poor of the regiment" held charitable); *Re Barker* (1909) 25 TLR 753 (gift to the Royal Engineers' Institute to provide prizes for competition among Royal Engineer cadets or officers held charitable); *Re Corbyn* [1941] Ch 400, [1941] 2 All ER 160 (trust for the benefit of boys from the training ship Exmouth "to be trained to become officers in His Majesty's Navy (Britannic) or the British Mercantile Marine" held charitable); *Re Driffill* [1950] Ch 92, [1949] 2 All ER 933 (trust to be applied "in whatever manner the trustees may consider desirable to promote the defence of the United Kingdom against the attack of hostile aircraft" held charitable). See also *The City of London Rifle and Pistol Club and Burnley Rifle Club* [1993] 1 Ch Com Rep 4, p. 432 post, where applications for charity registration from two rifle clubs on the basis that in modern conditions they do not promote the defence of the realm were rejected.

Fund". Its objects were "the promotion of sport (including in that term only shooting fishing cricket football and polo)".

ROMER J held that the gifts were charitable, as they promoted the physical efficiency of the Army. He said at 365:

"It is contended on behalf of the persons entitled to the residue that those two legacies were given on trusts which are not charitable. It is said that the object of the testator was merely to encourage sport. If that were so the gifts would no doubt be given on trusts which were not charitable: see *Re Nottage* [1895] 2 Ch 649, where a gift for purposes of encouraging yacht racing was held not to be a charitable legacy. But in my opinion it was not the object of the testator in the present case to encourage or promote either sport in general or any sport in particular. I think it is reasonably clear that it was his intention to benefit the officers and men of the Carabiniers by giving them an opportunity of indulging in healthy sport. It is to be observed that the particular sports specified were all healthy outdoor sports, indulgence in which might reasonably be supposed to encourage physical efficiency. That I think was his object even though he refers to the fund as the 'Sporting Fund'. This case, therefore, does not, in my opinion, fall within *Re Nottage*.

I realise the truth of what Eve J said in *Re Mariette* [1915] 2 Ch 284, p. 377 ante, as to the natural inclination of the Court, if possible, to give effect to a gift of this sort and the danger of allowing that natural inclination to induce one to disregard established principles. But I am glad to find that there is an established principle enabling me to give effect to the gifts in the present case. This principle was established by Farwell J in *Re Good* [1905] 2 Ch 60 at 66, 67, a case that as far as I know has never been questioned in any way. In that case the testator gave his residuary personalty upon trust for the officers' mess of his regiment, to be invested and the income to be applied in maintaining a library for the officers' mess for ever, any surplus to be expended in the purchase of plate for the mess. According to the headnote of the report of that case it was held that the gift to maintain the library and to purchase plate for the officers' mess, being for a general public purpose tending to increase the efficiency of the army and aid taxation, was a good charitable bequest. It was also held that the gift might be supported as a 'setting out of soldiers' within the meaning of those words in the statute of Elizabeth. But the judgment of Farwell J was based primarily on the ground that the gift on trust for the maintenance of the library was a gift tending to increase the efficiency of the army, and he referred, only as a possible alternative ground, to the fact that the trust tended to aid taxation.

In the course of his judgment he said, referring to the argument, for the Attorney-General: 'Now Mr. Parker has put his argument on two grounds. First, he says that anything that improves the efficiency of the army is charitable within the meaning of the Act, because it is for a public purpose—a purpose in which the public are interested. Secondly, he says that it also comes within the last clause of the preamble of the statute of Elizabeth: "The aid or ease of any poor inhabitants concerning payments of fifteens, setting out of soldiers and other taxes," because it will relieve the taxation of the public ... I think it would be difficult to say that money given to be expended in terms in some specific way in order to increase the efficiency of a regiment in a particular mode is not a good charity. This gift, to my mind, does tend to increase the efficiency of the army by giving the officers greater opportunities of providing themselves with literature.' Then, after dealing with the suggestion that the money might conceivably be applied in the purchase of books which were unlikely to increase the efficiency of the army, he says: 'An officer is all the better equipped if he can speak several languages, and if he knows the history and geography of his own nation as well as many other nations, as well as being instructed in the military art, I should be sorry to have to hold that any gift which tends to educational equipment in that way is not a charitable gift.' . . .

In the case before Farwell J the efficiency was mental efficiency, and the only distinction between that case and the present case is that in the present case the efficiency is physical as opposed to mental efficiency. But it is obviously for the benefit of the public that those entrusted with the defence of the realm should be not only mentally but also physically efficient, and I think I am justified in coming to the conclusion that there is no difference between mental and physical efficiency for the present purpose.''[1]

In **The City of London Rifle and Pistol Club and Burnley Rifle Club**[2] (1993) Decisions of the Charity Commissioners, Vol 1, p4, the Charity Commissioners held that the Clubs were not entitled to charitable status. Their objects were: "to encourage skill in shooting by providing instruction and practice in the use of firearms to Her Majesty's subjects so that they will be better fitted to serve their country in the Armed Forces, Territorial Army or any other organisation in which their services may be required in the defence of the Realm in times of peril".

In holding that the activities of the Clubs did not promote the security of the nation and the defence of the realm, the Commissioners distinguished *Re Stephens* [1892] 8 TLR 792, where Kekewich J upheld as charitable a gift under the will of Mr Henry Stephens to the National Rifle Association to form a fund to be called The Stephens' Prize Fund, "to be expended by the Council for the teaching of shooting at moving objects in any manner they may think fit, so as to prevent as far as possible a catastrophe similar to that at Majuba Hill".

They referred to *Re Good* [1905] 2 Ch 60; *Re Driffill* [1950] Ch 92; *Re Lord Stratheden and Campbell* [1894] 3 Ch 265; *Re Gray* [1925] Ch 362; *Re Corbyn* [1941] Ch 400; p. 430, n. 20 ante and continued:

Two particular aspects of the judgment of Kekewich J served to underline the distinction between the purposes of the gift in *Re Stephens* and the purposes of the City Club and Burnley Clubs:

(1) Kekewich J found that the object in the testator's mind was clear. He desired that Englishmen should be taught to shoot with those particular weapons which were used in war for the destruction of their enemies and the protection of themselves.

(2) Kekewich J found that what the testator meant was that accurate shooting was to be taught among Englishmen in general—an object which would be promoted directly or indirectly in the Army—and so a repetition of the catastrophe at Majuba Hill would be adverted.

The answers provided by the City and Burnley Clubs to a questionnaire established that the purpose of the Clubs was not to teach members of the

---

1 Annual Report for 1965, Appendix E; 1977, paras. 123–124 (Old Contemptibles Association, founded in 1925 to foster the spirit of "The Contemptible Little Army of 1914"—a purpose analogous to promoting the efficiency of the Army—wound up in 1977). Cf. Annual Report for 1983, paras. 35–36 (trust to eliminate waste in the public service so as to increase its efficiency not analogous to promotion of efficiency of the armed forces and of the police and so not registered).

2 [1992–93] 2 CL & PR 97 (P.J. Clarke), criticising this unduly restrictive view of the law.

public *in general* to shoot. The answers also established that the purpose of the Clubs was not to teach members of the public in general to shoot with *those particular weapons which were used in times of war*. Evidence revealed that whilst firearms used by the Armed Forces might bear some resemblance to firearms used by civilian shooting clubs, there was nevertheless a substantial difference in equipment and style between military and civilian shooting disciplines.

We concluded that if *Re Stephens* was still to be considered a good authority, it could be only for the proposition that it was charitable to promote the teaching of the general public in the use of weapons used by the Armed Forces and not that institutions in the form of the City and Burnley Clubs were necessarily charitable. That would depend upon the inherent nature of the Clubs themselves.

Even if we were wrong in our view that *Re Stephens* was not authority for the proposition that the City and Burnley Clubs were charitable, we considered that there had been such a radical change in circumstances since the decision in *Re Stephens* that the City and Burnley Clubs could not be regarded as charities for promoting the security of the nation and the defence of the Realm. On the evidence before us, we concluded that that charitable purpose was not carried out in the modern day by the provision of facilities for the instruction and practice in shooting through the medium of rifle and pistol clubs in the form adopted by the City and Burnley Clubs.

It has been judicially recognised that changes in social habits and needs might subsequently lead to reconsideration of the question whether a particular object continued to be charitable in law. (See *National Anti-Vivisection Society v Inland Revenue Commissioners* [1948] AC 31. Lord Simonds at p. 74 and *Gilmour v Coats* [1949] AC 426. Lord Simonds at p. 143).

We considered that the following factors had rendered the decision in *Re Stephens* obsolete in the sense indicated by Lord Simonds in *National Anti-Vivisection Society v Inland Revenue Commissioners* and *Gilmour v Coats*:

(1) The strength of the modern British Army no longer depended on the expert shooting skills of soldiers in the way that it did at the time of the Boer War (and the Battle of Majuba Hill). The tactical and technological advances that had taken place in modern warfare (as exemplified in the recent Falklands and Gulf conflicts) had substantially increased the gulf between fully trained service personnel familiar with the latest communications equipment and technical weaponry and the competent single shot competition shooter.

(2) The social and organisational changes affecting the recruitment and training of men and women for the Armed Forces had rendered it anachronistic to view rifle and pistol clubs as fulfilling the role of a semi-trained third line reserve for the Armed Forces. There was no reason to believe that rifle and pistol clubs would be used as a manpower reserve in times of war or other national emergency . . .

We also considered that the main purpose of each of the Clubs was to benefit their members by providing them with facilities for the enjoyment of shooting as a recreation and the practice of shooting as a sport. In our opinion, any benefit to the public by way of promoting the security of the nation and the defence of the realm was incidental to the benefits to members in the way of affording them recreational and sporting facilities. We concluded, therefore, that the Clubs fell clearly within the decision in *Inland Revenue Commissioners v City of Glasgow Police Athletic Association* and were not established for exclusively charitable purposes.

We also considered that the Clubs could not be regarded as charities either for the advancement of education, or the promotion of public recreation because they lacked the essential element of public benefit. Furthermore, they did not satisfy the condition of section 1(2)(*b*)(ii) of the Recreational Charities Act 1958, p. 422 ante, that the facilities for recreation and other leisure-time occupation should be available to the members or female members of the public at large."

(b) The Police

In **Inland Revenue Commissioners v City of Glasgow Police Athletic Association** [1953] AC 380, [1953] 1 All ER 747, p. 418, ante, Lord NORMAND said at 391, at 749:

"The Special Commissioners, having found these facts, rejected the only contention then put forward on behalf of the Crown that, by reason of the wide nature and extent of the objects of the association, it was not a body of persons established for charitable purposes only. They were aided in arriving at this conclusion by such cases as *Re Good* [1905] 2 Ch 60 and *Re Gray* [1925] Ch 362, p. 430, ante. As I shall not have occasion to refer to these cases again I will say now that so far as they are founded on the principle that gifts exclusively for the purpose of promoting the efficiency of the armed forces are good charitable gifts, they are, in my opinion, unassailable, but that the decision that the actual gifts were of that nature is more doubtful. I would hold further that gifts or contributions exclusively for the purpose of promoting the efficiency of the police forces and the preservation of public order are by analogy charitable gifts."[3]

(c) Miscellaneous Public Purposes

In **Re Wokingham Fire Brigade Trusts** [1951] Ch 373, [1951] 1 All ER 454, a voluntary fire brigade was purchased by the National Fire Service in 1942. DANCKWERTS J held that the provision of a fire brigade was a charitable purpose and that the assets should be applied *cy-près*.[4]

INCORPORATED COUNCIL OF LAW REPORTING FOR ENGLAND AND WALES v ATTORNEY-GENERAL[5]
[1972] Ch 73, [1971] 3 All ER 1029 (CA, RUSSELL, SACHS AND BUCKLEY LJJ)

The Incorporated Council of Law Reporting for England and Wales was incorporated in 1870 with the primary object of "the preparation and

---

3 See also Annual Report for 1984, para. 17 (Police Memorial Trust to commemorate officers killed on duty).

4 Annual Report for 1979 (gift of manor house to Ware UDC for use as a Council Room and offices, and the purposes of a fire brigade registered by Commissioners as charitable). Cf. *London Borough of Richmond-Upon-Thames v A-G* (1982) 81 LGR 156 at 164 where WARNER J said that it was unnecessary for him to decide whether the provision of Municipal Offices or of a Town Hall could be a valid charitable purpose.

5 (1972) 88 LQR 171; *Incorporated Council of Law Reporting of the State of Queensland v Comr of Taxation* (1971) 45 ALJR 552, where the High Court of Australia held that the council was a charitable institution within the Income Tax and Social Services Contribution Assessment Act 1936–62, s. 23 (*e*). BARWICK CJ said at 555: "the production of law reports is clearly beneficial to the whole community because of the universal importance of maintaining the socially sustaining fabric of the law". See also Annual Report for 1980, paras. 78–79 (National Law Library Trust, which is concerned with a computer-assisted information retrieval system for legal information).

publication in a convenient form, at a moderate price, and under gratuitous professional control, of reports of judicial decisions of the superior and appellate courts in England". All income and property were to be applied solely towards the promotion of the Council's objects, and no portion could be paid by way of profit to its members. Payment of remuneration was authorised for editors, reporters and other persons for services rendered.

In 1966 the Council applied to be registered as a charity under s. 4 of the Charities Act 1960. In 1967 the Charity Commissioners refused to register it as a charity. The Council appealed to the High Court under s. 5 (3),[6] joining as parties the Commissioners of Inland Revenue and the Attorney-General.

Held. The Council was entitled to be registered as a charity under the fourth head; and also (RUSSELL LJ dissenting) as a trust for the advancement of education.[7]

RUSSELL LJ: I come now to the question whether, if the main purpose of the council is, as I think it is, to further the sound development and administration of the law in this country, and if, as I think it is, that is a purpose beneficial to the community or of general public utility, that purpose is charitable according to the law of England and Wales.

On this point the law is rooted in the Statute of Elizabeth I, a statute the object of which was the oversight and reform of abuses in the administration of property devoted by donors to purposes which were regarded as worthy of such protection as being charitable. The preamble to the Statute listed certain examples of purposes worthy of such protection. These were from an early stage regarded merely as examples, and have through the centuries been regarded as examples or guideposts for the courts in the differing circumstances of a developing civilisation and economy. Sometimes recourse has been had by the courts to the instances given in the preamble in order to see whether in a given case sufficient analogy may be found with something specifically stated in the preamble, or sufficient analogy with some decided case in which already a previous sufficient analogy has been found. Of this approach perhaps the most obvious example is the provision of crematoria by analogy with the provisions of burial grounds by analogy with the upkeep of churchyards by analogy with the repair of churches. On other occasions a decision in favour or against a purpose being charitable has been based in terms upon a more general question whether the purpose is or is not within "the spirit and intendment" of the Statute of Elizabeth I and in particular its preamble. Again (and at an early stage in development) whether the purpose is within "the equity" or within "the mischief" of the Statute. Again whether the purpose is charitable "in the same sense" as purposes within the preview of the Statute. I have much sympathy with those who say that these phrases do little of themselves to elucidate any particular problem. "Tell me", they say, "what you define when you speak of spirit, intendment, equity, mischief, the same sense, and I will tell you whether a purpose is charitable according to law. But you never define. All you do is sometimes to say that a purpose is none of these things. I can understand it when you say that the preservation of sea walls is for the safety of lives and property, and therefore by analogy the voluntary

---

6 This was the first such application under the Act; Annual Report for 1970, para. 27.
7 See p. 370, ante.

provision of lifeboats and fire brigades are charitable. I can even follow you as far as crematoria. But these other generalities teach me nothing."

I say I have much sympathy for such approach: but it seems to me to be unduly and improperly restrictive. The Statute of Elizabeth I was a statute to reform abuses: in such circumstances and in that age the courts of this country were not inclined to be restricted in their implementation of Parliament's desire for reform to particular examples given by the Statute; and they deliberately kept open their ability to intervene when they thought necessary in cases not specifically mentioned, by applying as the test whether any particular case of abuse of funds or property was within the "mischief" or the "equity" of the Statute.

For myself I believe that this rather vague and undefined approach is the correct one, with analogy, its handmaid, and that when considering Lord Macnaghten's fourth category in *Pemsel's* case [1891] AC 531 at 583 of "other purposes beneficial to the community" (or as phrased by Sir Samuel Romilly (then Mr. Romilly) in argument in *Morice v Bishop of Durham* (1805) 10 Ves 522 at 531: "objects of general public utility") the courts, in consistently saying that not all such are necessarily charitable in law, are in substance accepting that if a purpose is shown to be so beneficial or of such utility it is prima facie charitable in law, but have left open a line of retreat based on the equity of the Statute in case they are faced with a purpose (e.g., a political purpose) which could not have been within the contemplation of the Statute even if the then legislators had been endowed with the gift of foresight into the circumstances of later centuries.

In a case such as the present, in which in my view the object cannot be thought otherwise than beneficial to the community and of general public utility, I believe the proper question to ask is whether there are any grounds for holding it to be outside the equity of the Statute[8] and I think the answer to that is here in the negative. I have already touched upon its essential importance to our rule of law. If I look at the somewhat random examples in the preamble to the Statute I find in the repair of bridges, havens, causeways, sea banks and highways examples of matters which if not looked after by private enterprise must be a proper function and responsibility of government, which would afford strong ground for a statutory expression by Parliament of anxiety to prevent misappropriation of funds voluntarily dedicated to such matters. It cannot I think be doubted that if there were not a competent and reliable set of reports of judicial decisions, it would be a proper function and responsibility of government to secure their provision for the due administration of the law. It was argued that the specific topics in the preamble that I have mentioned are all concerned with concrete matters, and that so also is the judicially accepted opinion that the provision of a court house is a charitable purpose. But whether the search be for analogy or for the equity of the Statute this seems to me to be too narrow or refined an approach. I cannot accept that the provision, in order to facilitate the proper administration of the law, of the walls and other physical facilities of a court house is a charitable purpose, but

---

8 See p. 411, n. 17, ante, and cf. the approach of the High Court of Australia in *Incorporated Council of Law Reporting of the State of Queensland v Comr of Taxation* (1971) 45 ALJR 552 at 555; *Royal National Agricultural and Industrial Association v Chester* (1974) 48 ALJR 304 at 305 ("improving the breeding and racing of Homer pigeons" held not charitable); (1975) 91 LQR 167.

that the dissemination by accurate and selective reporting of knowledge of a most important part of the law to be there administered is not.

Accordingly the purpose for which the association is established is exclusively charitable in the sense of Lord Macnaghten's fourth category. I would not hold that the purpose is purely the advancement of education: but in determining that the purpose is within the equity of the Statute I by no means ignore the function of the purpose in furthering knowledge in legal science.

I would dismiss the appeal.

Report of the Charity Commissioners for England and Wales for the year 1973, paras. 69–70.

"*Council of Industrial Design*
The object of the council of improving the design of industrial products was in our view clearly of benefit to the public not only in the general sense of making industry more efficient and competitive but also more directly in encouraging the production of safer, more effective and more pleasing articles. The spread of knowledge of such articles was also of public benefit. On the other hand the council's activities, through its design centres with their catalogues describing approved products and displaying goods with the manufacturer's name attached, must provide some commercial benefit to the individual firms concerned. Moreover, the advantage was something more than mere advertisement in the sense of publicity: there was the additional publicised advantage of approval by the council, a body subsidised by public funds and so semi-official. However, the industrial firms whose products were exhibited were not members of the institution. Moreover the members of the council were not self-regarding industrialists but the nominees of a Minister of the Crown who had an absolute power to remove them from office. It accordingly appeared to us that it was not a purpose of the council to benefit the firms concerned and we decided that the council was a charity and should be registered.

[The Commissioners referred in para. 70 to the judgment of RUSSELL LJ in *Incorporated Council of Law Reporting for England and Wales v A-G* and continued:]

We were satisfied that in the case of the Council of Industrial Design there was a substantial public benefit which raised a prima facie assumption of charitability and that, applying Lord Justice Russell's test mentioned above, there was nothing in the circumstances of the case to negative the assumption."

In **Commissioners of Inland Revenue v White** [1980] TR 155, p. 364, ante, Fox J held that the provision of workshop accommodation for craftsmen in Clerkenwell, London, was charitable. He referred to *IRC v Yorkshire Agricultural Society* [1928] 1 KB 611 (general improvement of agriculture), *Re Town and Country Planning Act 1947* [1951] Ch 132, [1950] 2 All ER 857 n. (management of Crystal Palace as "a place for education and recreation and for the promotion of industry commerce and art") and *Construction Industry Training Board v A-G* [1971] 1 WLR 1303, [1972] 2 All ER 1339 (training of persons employed in the construction industry), and said at 160:

"[These cases] seem to me to establish that the promotion or advancement of industry (including a particular industry such as agriculture) or of commerce is a charitable object provided that the purpose is the advancement of the benefit of the public at large and not merely the promotion of the interests of those engaged in the manufacture and sale of their particular products.... In my opinion, the fact that individual craftsmen may obtain benefits from the Association's activities is not conclusive on the question of charitable status ... The Association is not a self-regarding body and many of its members are not craftsmen at all ... The benefit of craftsmen is not an object of the Association. The object of the Association is, broadly, the furtherance of crafts and craftsmanship; the benefiting of craftsmen, in so far as it takes place, is just a means to that end ... The authorities, I think, distinguish between cases where benefit to the individual is the purpose of the trust or society and cases where it is merely incidental to that purpose....

It seems to me that the object of encouraging the exercise and maintaining the standards of such crafts as were carried on by the licensees in Cornwall House and Pennybank Chambers is a charitable object by analogy with the principle that the promotion of an industry or of commerce is a charitable object. In my view there is a clear element of public benefit. The crafts concerned—and, indeed, a very wide variety of other modern crafts—are certainly of value to the public. One cannot doubt that their extinction or the erosion of their standards would be a public loss ... Further, to preserve and improve craftsmanship is itself a charitable object. It seems to me that craftsmanship in general is an activity which is of utility to the public, and that it must be for the public benefit in the fullest sense that standards should not be allowed to fall, and should indeed be improved."[9]

(d) Relief of the Unemployed

Report of the Charity Commissioners for England and Wales for the year 1983, paras. 12–14

"12. The relief of poverty among unemployed persons is a clear charitable purpose and in so far as an institution assists people to find employment or to train or re-train them for employment as a means of relieving their poverty, there is no difficulty in the institution obtaining registration as a charity. The establishment in life of young persons is a charitable purpose as is the apprenticing of young persons and the provision of the tools of their trade. Moreover the provision of vocational training is a charitable purpose in itself, and where young people are concerned the provision of opportunity to experience regular work for a limited time might well be a method of training them for life as well as relieving them of poverty, even if the work provided is of an unskilled nature giving little in the way of vocational training. It is less easy, however, to conclude that the purposes of an institution are charitable where it is to employ persons without any educational purpose in view for work which is not itself directed to the achievement of any charitable purpose. But this difficulty does not arise where the work is directed to some charitable purpose in, for example, the field of social welfare or the improvement of the

9 Annual Report 1983, para. 41 (Trireme Trust for the building of a replica of a Greek trireme); 1985, paras. 28–32 (Consumers' Company, publishers of Which); 1987, paras. 16–19 (Business in the Community); 1990, para. 40 (Whitehall and Industry Group Trust).

environment. Trusts to conduct study and research into unemployment, its causes and possible remedy would also be charitable provided that the results are to be made public.

13. It has long been held that the provision of sheltered workshops for disabled persons is a good charitable object. Such provision enables the disabled to earn a living and thereby prevent poverty. We considered whether the same principle could be applied to the relief of involuntary unemployment through non-political, non-profitmaking organisations administered by independent trustees. We find it difficult to see, however, how the prevention of unemployment by the provision of work on a life-time or long-term basis is charitable since the benefits are not commensurate with the needs. Sheltered workshops deal with lifelong disabilities, but the provision of employment for the able bodied from leaving school to retirement age could not be held to be charitable.

14. Unemployment is a great social evil, and we are anxious to assist development of charitable endeavour so far as this is compatible with the law. We are concerned to be flexible in dealing with organisations approaching us and we recognise that it may be possible to accept as charitable the purposes of certain intermediate agencies (i.e. co-ordinating bodies) operating in this field and that in certain circumstances provision of employment could be directed to a charitable purpose. No general guidelines can, however, be laid down at this stage and we shall have to deal with cases on their merits (The North Wales Employment and Advice Centre Limited is dealt with in paragraphs 25 to 27)."[10]

(e) Promotion of Racial Harmony

In **Re Strakosch** [1949] Ch 529, a testator provided a fund "for any purpose which in [the trustees'] opinion is designed to strengthen the bonds of unity between the Union of South Africa and the Mother Country, and which incidentally will conduce to the appeasement of racial feeling between the Dutch and English speaking sections of the South African community."

The Court of Appeal held that this was not a charitable trust. Lord GREENE said at 536:

"Roxburgh J held that it was not a good charitable gift. Before us further evidence was produced consisting of an affidavit by Field Marshal Smuts. We have given this affidavit most careful consideration but we are unable to regard it as affording a reason for coming to a conclusion different from that at which Roxburgh J arrived. We realize the truth of the contention that the objects to which the gift is to be devoted are matters of great public concern both in the Union of South Africa and in the Mother Country. In particular the appeasement of racial feeling in the Union cannot but benefit all inhabitants of the Union, not merely the members of the two sections of the community expressly referred to. But the very wide and vague scope of the gift and the unrestricted latitude of application which its language permits make it impossible in our opinion to find that it falls within the spirit and intendment of the preamble to the Statute of Elizabeth.

... Field Marshal Smuts (than whom no one can speak with greater authority on this subject) expresses a strong opinion that the proper method for the appeasement of racial feeling is education in its widest sense—'students' education, journalistic training, interchange of young men and women between Britain and South Africa, and between young South Africans of

10 See Report for 1988, para. 19 for the registration of the Employment Institute as a charity.

different racial origin.' It is unfortunate if, as may well be, these methods were in the testator's mind that he did not seek to constitute a trust which might well have been valid as an educational trust notwithstanding that the education had the ultimate aim as set out in the will. We, however, find it impossible to construe this trust as one confined to educational purposes."[11]

Report of the Charity Commissioners for England and Wales for the year 1983, paras. 18–20.

"18. The promotion of racial harmony has been considered not to be a charitable purpose largely on the authority of *Re Strakosch* [1949] Ch 529, in which it was held that the appeasement of racial feelings (between the Dutch and English speaking sections of the South African community) was a political purpose and therefore not charitable and arguably because the very wide and vague scope of the gift in that case and the unrestricted latitude of application which its language permitted made it impossible to find that it fell within the spirit and intendment of the preamble to the Statute of Elizabeth. We took the view that *Re Strakosch* did not freeze the appeasement of racial feeling as a political purpose for all time. In England and Wales the question of whether it would be beneficial to the public to appease racial feeling appeared to be no longer a political one as legislation had been passed in an attempt to enforce good race relations and it is unlikely that any substantial body of opinion in England and Wales would not consider the promotion of good race relations to be a purpose beneficial to the community. The fundamental reason why political purposes are not charitable is that the Court has no means of judging whether the proposed change in the law will or will not be for the public benefit. The matter is no longer one for the Court to judge. The nation, through Parliament, has already decided that it is for the public benefit and the matter has ceased to be political. It also seemed to us that the second possible objection would be overcome if Community Relations Councils were able to adopt wording of sufficient precision to express their purposes.

19. We considered that the promotion of racial harmony was undoubtedly for the benefit of the public; but the question to be considered was whether it was also charitable in law. We took the view that the promotion of racial harmony or good race relations is analogous to purposes which the Courts have held to be charitable. We agreed that that purpose was analogous with

(*a*) the preservation of public order and the prevention of breaches of peace (*Inland Revenue Commissioners v City of Glasgow Police Athletic Association* [1953] AC 380, [1953] 1 All ER 747, p. 418, ante);

---

11 Cf. *Re Koeppler Will Trusts* [1986] Ch 423, [1985] 2 All ER 869, p. 372 ante, where a trust for the purpose of the furtherance of a British contribution to the formation of an informed international public opinion and to the promotion of greater co-operation in Europe and the West in general was held to be charitable. SLADE LJ referred to *Re Strakosch*, and said at 439, at 879:

"In the present case, I accept Mr. McCall's submission that there is no sufficient reason why the wide and vague scope of the testator's stated ultimate aims in doing the work which he did, and in making the testamentary gift which he did, should be held to destroy the otherwise admittedly educational nature of that work and that gift. There seems to have been no vagueness about the nature of the work itself. For the reasons which I have given I consider that the trust purpose of that gift was the futherance of the work of the Wilton Park project and that that purpose was charitable as being for the advancement of education."

(*b*) the mental and moral improvement of man on the basis that discrimination on grounds of colour is immoral (*Re Hood* [1931] 1 Ch 240; *Re Price* [1943] Ch 422, [1943] 2 All ER 505 and *Re South Place Ethical Society* [1980] 1 WLR 1565, [1980] 3 All ER 918); and

(*c*) the promotion of equality of women with men (*Halpin v Seear* (27th February 1976) our annual report for 1977, paragraphs 34 to 36).

20. We agreed that although particular applications for registration will have to be considered on their merits, in general we were prepared to accept, subject to consideration of any objection and of course any future decisions of the Courts, that promoting good race relations, endeavouring to eliminate discrimination on grounds of race and encouraging equality of opportunity between persons of different racial groups were charitable purposes.''[12]

(*f*) *Public Memorials*

Report of the Charity Commissioners for England and Wales for the year 1981, paras. 68–70

"*The Earl Mountbatten of Burma Statue Appeal Trust*

68. Following the assassination in 1979 of Admiral of the Fleet, The Earl Mountbatten of Burma, a charitable trust (The Mountbatten Memorial Trust) having wide charitable objects was established. In addition, in July 1981 an appeal was made, including a letter in *The Times* signed by the Prime Minister and other eminent people, for a public memorial to take the form of a statue of the Earl, in naval uniform, to be sited on the Foreign Office green overlooking Horse Guards Parade and the Admiralty, with a maintenance fund for its upkeep and repair. The project was estimated to cost £100,000 and any surplus was to be used for charitable purposes.

69. The law on the charitable status of public memorials is scanty and imprecise. The decision of Mr. Justice Clauson in *Murray v Thomas* [1937] 4 All ER 545 indicated that a war memorial of a substantial kind (in that case a memorial hall) intended not only to commemorate the dead but to serve a useful purpose for the benefit of the community could be charitable; but the judge reserved the question whether funds collected to provide a non-utilitarian object such as a statue might be charitable. We had registered as charities one or two funds for the upkeep and maintenance of statues but we had not previously considered whether a fund for the provision of a statue was charitable. In Halsbury's *Laws of England*, Fourth Edition, Volume 5, page 339, it is stated that 'The erection of a monument, not of the donor, or memorial, may perhaps be charitable' and the footnote numbered 17 adds that 'The Charity Commissioners have treated some such cases as charitable, e.g. the Wellington Monument in Somerset and the Cobden Obelisk at Midhurst'. However, the Wellington Monument was erected on land belonging to the National Trust so that there were other amenity aspects, which made for charitability, and we were unable to trace any papers relating to the Cobden Obelisk.

70. After due consideration, and reference to the law in the U.S.A. (where statues have been accepted as charitable in some States) we concluded that the

---

12 The Inland Revenue has stated that it will not formally object to the registration of organisations with the object of promotion of good race relations: Annual Report for 1987, para. 14.

provision of a statue might be held to have a sufficient element of public benefit where the person being commemorated was nationally, and perhaps internationally, respected and could be said to be a figure of historical importance. In such a case the provision and maintenance of a statue can be held to be charitable as likely to foster patriotism and good citizenship, and to be an incentive to heroic and noble deeds. The Earl Mountbatten of Burma Statue Appeal Trust established by a declaration of trust dated the 9th October 1981 came into this category, its object being 'the commemoration for the benefit of the public of the life and works of (the late Earl) by the erection of a statue ... and by maintaining that memorial', and has been registered as a charity.''[13]

(g) Politics[14]

Political activity is not charitable. Indeed the rule appears to be that an activity whose objective is to change the law is thereby disabled from being a charity. How, it is said, can a trust to change the law be regarded by the law as so beneficial to the community that it deserves the privileges of charity?

1. Political Objectives

In **National Anti-Vivisection Society v Inland Revenue Commissioners** [1948] AC 31, [1947] 2 All ER 217, p. 408, ante, Lord SIMONDS said at 61, at 231:
   "The learned Master of the Rolls cites in his judgment [1946] KB 185 at 207, [1946] 1 All ER 205 at 214, a passage from the speech of Lord Parker in *Bowman v Secular Society Ltd* [1917] AC 406 at 442: 'A trust for the attainment of political objects has always been held invalid, not because it is illegal ... but because the court has no means of judging whether a proposed change in the law will or will not be for the public benefit.' Lord Parker is here considering the possibility of a valid charitable trust and nothing else and when he says 'has always been held invalid' he means 'has always been held not to be a valid charitable trust'. The learned Master of the Rolls found this authoritative statement upon a branch of the law, with which no one was more familiar than Lord Parker, to be inapplicable to the present case for two reasons, first because he felt difficulty in applying the words to 'a change in the law which is in common parlance a "non-political" question,' and secondly, because he thought they could not in any case apply, when the desired legislation is 'merely ancillary to the attainment of what is ex hypothesi a good charitable object'.
   My Lords, if I may deal with this second reason first, I cannot agree that in this case an alteration in the law is merely ancillary to the attainment of a good charitable object. In a sense no doubt, since legislation is not an end in itself every law may be regarded as ancillary to the object which its provisions are intended to achieve. But that is not the sense in which it is said that a society has a political object. Here the finding of the commissioners is itself conclusive

---

13 (1983) 133 NLJ 1107 (H. Picarda). For memorials which are for charitable purposes as being for the advancement of religion see p. 309, ante; for private memorials which are for non charitable purposes, see *Re Endacott* [1960] Ch 232, [1959] 3 All ER 562, p. 315, ante; *M'Caig University of Glasgow* 1907 SC 231, p. 325, ante.
14 Goodman Report, chap 4; House of Commons Report, vol. I, paras. 35–44, vol. II, pp. 23 25–26, 48–83, 117–119, 129–154, 156–159, 214–215, 313–314, 316–317, 349–350, 361–362 (1977) 19 Mal LR 42 (L.A. Sheridan); White Paper, paras. 2.37–2.46.

'We are satisfied,' they say, 'that the main object of the society is the total abolition of vivisection ... and (for that purpose) the repeal of the Cruelty to Animals Act, 1876, and the substitution of a new enactment prohibiting vivisection altogether.' ... Coming to the conclusion that it is a main object, if not the main object, of the society, to obtain an alteration of the law, I ask whether that can be a charitable object, even if its purposes might otherwise be regarded as charitable.

My Lords, I see no reason for supposing that Lord Parker in the cited passage used the expression 'political objects' in any narrow sense or was confining it to objects of acute political controversy. On the contrary he was, I think, propounding familiar doctrine, nowhere better stated than in a textbook, which has long been regarded as of high authority but appears not to have been cited for this purpose to the courts below (as it certainly was not to your Lordships), *Tyssen on Charitable Bequests*, 1st ed. The passage which is at p. 176, is worth repeating at length: 'It is a common practice for a number of individuals amongst us to form an association for the purpose of promoting some change in the law, and it is worth our while to consider the effect of a gift to such an association. It is clear that such an association is not of a charitable nature. However desirable the change may really be, the law could not stultify itself by holding that it was for the public benefit that the law itself should be changed. Each court in deciding on the validity of a gift must decide on the principle that the law is right as it stands. On the other hand, such a gift could not be held void for illegality.' Lord Parker uses slightly different language but means the same thing, when he says that the court has no means of judging whether a proposed change in the law will or will not be for the public benefit. It is not for the court to judge and the court has no means of judging. The same question may be looked at from a slightly different angle. One of the tests, and a crucial test, whether a trust is charitable, lies in the competence of the court to control and reform it. I would remind your Lordships that it is the King as parens patriae who is the guardian of charity and that it is the right and duty of his Attorney-General to intervene and inform the court, if the trustees of a charitable trust fall short of their duty. So too is it his duty to assist the court, if need be, in the formulation of a scheme for the execution of a charitable trust. But, my Lords, is it for a moment to be supposed that it is the function of the Attorney-General on behalf of the Crown to intervene and demand that a trust shall be established and administered by the court, the object of which is to alter the law in a manner highly prejudicial, as he and His Majesty's Government may think, to the welfare of the state? This very case would serve as an example, if upon the footing that it was a charitable trust it became the duty of the Attorney-General on account of its maladministration to intervene. There is undoubtedly a paucity of judicial authority on this point. It may fairly be said that *De Themmines v de Bonneval* (1828) 5 Russ 288, to which Lord Parker referred in *Bowman's* case [1917] AC 406, turned on the fact that the trust there in question was held to be against public policy. In *IRC v Temperance Council of the Christian Churches of England and Wales* (1926) 136 LT 27, the principle was clearly recognised by Rowlatt J, as it was in *Re Hood* [1931] 1 Ch 240 at 250, 252. But in truth the reason of the thing appears to me so clear that I neither expect nor require much authority. I conclude upon this part of the case that a main object of the society is political and for that reason the society is not established for charitable purposes only. I would only add that I would reserve my opinion on the hypothetical example of a private enabling Act, which was suggested in the course of the argument. I do not regard *Re Villers-Wilkes* (1895) 72 LT 323 as a decision that a legacy which had for its main purpose the passing of such an Act is charitable."[15]

2. Political Propaganda Masquerading as Education

A trust for a political party is not charitable. Attempts have been made to establish trusts for political purposes in the form of educational trusts. The dividing line between education in certain political principles and support of a political party is sometimes difficult to draw. A trust for "the furtherance of Conservative principles and religious and mental improvement" was upheld as charitable in *Re Scowcroft* [1898] 2 Ch 638. Since then, however, the courts have been quick to find a political object disguised as education. In the present century, the courts have at least been consistent between the parties.[16]

In **Re Hopkinson** [1949] 1 All ER 346, the testator gave his residuary estate to found an educational fund "for the advancement of adult education with particular reference to ... the education of men and women of all classes (on the lines of the Labour Party's memorandum headed 'A Note on Education in the Labour Party' ...) to a higher conception of social, political and economic ideas and values and of the personal obligations of duty and service which are necessary for the realisation of an improved and enlightened social civilisation."

VAISEY J held that the trust was not charitable. He said at 348:

"In my judgment, there are two ways of reading the words which I have quoted. They may be read, first, as equivalent to a general trust for the advancement of adult education which, standing alone, would admittedly be charitable, the super-added purpose being treated merely as a rough guide to be followed or as a hint to be taken as to the kind of adult education which the testator had in mind, the strictly educational main purpose always being adhered to, or, secondly, they may be read as indicating that the first part is to be taken as a general direction and the second part beginning with the words 'with particular reference to' as the particular direction dominating the whole of the trust. The second of these alternative views seems to me to be the right one. I think that the particular purpose is the main purpose of the trust, that is to say, while every or any kind of adult education is within the discretion reposed in the residuary legatees, the particular purpose referred to is, so to speak, the overriding and essential purpose, on the nature of which the validity of the whole trust depends ...

Political propaganda masquerading—I do not use the word in any sinister sense—as education is not education within the Statute of Elizabeth (43 Eliz., c. 4). In other words, it is not charitable."

---

15 Lord PORTER thought that the rule should apply only to trusts which are purely political. Lord NORMAND would have excluded only trusts whose predominant purpose was political. See also *Re Shaw* [1957] 1 WLR 729, [1957] 1 All ER 745.

16 *Bonar Law Memorial Trust v IRC* (1933) 49 TLR 220 (Conservative); *Re Ogden* [1933] Ch 678 (Liberal); *Re Hopkinson* [1949] 1 All ER 346 (Labour). See also Annual Report for 1982, paras 45–51 (refusal to register Youth Training because of its political purpose to assist the work of the Workers Revolutionary Party); 1991, para. 75 (refusal to register Margaret Thatcher Foundation, as it was concerned with arguing and advancing a particular political viewpoint).

In **Re Bushnell** [1975] 1 WLR 1596, [1975] 1 All ER 721,[17] a testator who died in 1941 gave the residue of his estate, subject to a life interest for his wife, who died in 1972, on trust to apply the income towards "furthering the knowledge of the socialised application of medicine to public and personal health and well-being and to demonstrating that the full advantage of socialised medicine can only be enjoyed in a socialist state" by means of lectures and by publishing and distributing books and literature on socialised medicine. GOULDING J held that the dominant and essential object of the trust was a political one and that it did not constitute a charitable trust.

In **Re Koeppler Will Trusts** [1986] Ch 423, [1985] 2 All ER 869, p. 372, ante, where the facts are given, SLADE LJ said at 437, at 878:

"However, in the present case, as I have already mentioned, the activities of Wilton Park are not of a party political nature. Nor, so far as the evidence shows, are they designed to procure changes in the laws or governmental policy of this or any other country: even when they touch on political matters, they constitute, so far as I can see, no more than genuine attempts in an objective manner to ascertain and disseminate the truth. In these circumstances I think that no objections to the trust arise on a political score, similar to those which arose in the *McGovern* case [1982] Ch 321, [1981] 3 All ER 493, infra. The trust is, in my opinion, entitled to what is sometimes called 'benignant construction,' in the sense that the court is entitled to presume that the trustees will only act in a lawful and proper manner appropriate to the trustees of a charity and not, for example, by the propagation of tendentious political opinions, any more than those running the Wilton Park project so acted in the 33 years preceding the testator's death: compare *McGovern v Attorney-General*, at 353E-F, at 519."

In **Webb v O'Doherty** (1991) Times, 11 February, a students' union was restrained from making payments to the National Student Committee to Stop War in the Gulf. HOFFMANN J said: "The Student Union is an educational charity. Its purposes are wholly charitable and its funds can be devoted to charitable purposes only. Charitable educational purposes undoubtedly include discussion of political issues: *A-G v Ross* [1986] 1 WLR 252 at 263, [1985] 3 All ER 334 at 343, per SCOTT J. There is, however, a clear distinction between the discussion of political matters, or the acquisition of information which may have a political content, and a campaign on a political issue. There is no doubt that campaigning, in the sense of seeking to influence public opinion on political matters, is not a charitable activity. It is, of course, something which students are, like the rest of the population, perfectly at liberty to do in their private capacities, but it is not a proper object of the expenditure of charitable money."

---

17 (1975) 38 MLR 471 (R.M.B. Cotterrell). In *Baldry v Feintuck* [1972] 1 WLR 552, [1972] 2 All ER 81 the students' union of Sussex University was restrained from making payment to a publicity campaign against the abolition of free milk. See also *A-G v Ross* [1986] 1 WLR 252, [1985] 3 All ER 334, p. 463 post.

3. Reform of the Law or Governmental Practices of a Foreign Country

McGOVERN v ATTORNEY-GENERAL
[1982] Ch 321, [1981] 3 All ER 493 (Ch D, SLADE J)[18]

In 1977 a pilot trust was created by Amnesty International, the purposes of which were set out in clause 2 of the trust deed:
"A. The relief of needy persons within any of the following categories:
(i) Prisoners of Conscience
(ii) persons who have recently been Prisoners of Conscience
(iii) persons who would in the opinion of the Trustees be likely to become Prisoners of Conscience if they returned to their country of ordinary residence
(iv) relatives and dependents of the foregoing persons
by the provision of appropriate charitable (and in particular financial educational or rehabilitational) assistance.
B. Attempting to secure the release of Prisoners of Conscience.
C. Procuring the abolition of torture or inhuman or degrading treatment or punishment.
D. The undertaking promotion and commission of research into the maintenance and observance of human rights.
E. The dissemination of the results of such research ...
F. The doing of all other such things as shall further the charitable purposes set out above."
The Charity Commissioners refused to register the trust as a charity. On appeal.
Held. Trust not charitable. Its main purpose was political.
SLADE J: As a a broad proposition, I would accept that a trust for the relief of human suffering and distress would prima facie be capable of being of a charitable nature, within the spirit and intendment of the preamble to the Statute of Elizabeth, as being what Mr. Hoffmann termed a "charity of compassion." It does not, however, follow that a trust established for good compassionate purposes will necessarily qualify as a charity according to English law, any more than it necessarily follows that such a qualification will attach to a trust for the relief of poverty or for the advancement of education or for the advancement of religion.
[His Lordship referred to *Bowman v Secular Society Ltd* [1917] AC 406 at 442, p. 442, ante, per Lord PARKER OF WADDINGTON, and to *National Anti-Vivisection Society v IRC* [1948] AC 31 at 49–50, 62–63, [1947] 2 All ER 217 at 224, 232, p. 408, ante, per Lords WRIGHT and SIMONDS, and continued:]
From the passages from the speeches of Lord Parker, Lord Wright and Lord Simonds which I have read I extract the principle that the court will not regard as charitable a trust of which a main object is to procure an alteration of the law of the United Kingdom for one or both of two reasons: first, the court will ordinarily have no sufficient means of judging as a matter of evidence whether the proposed change will or will not be for the public benefit. Secondly, even if the evidence suffices to enable it to form a prima facie opinion that a change in the law is desirable, it must still decide the case on the principle that the law

18 [1982] Conv 387 (T.G. Watkin); (1982) 45 MLR 704 (R. Nobles); (1982) 10 NZULR 169 (C.E.F. Rickett); (1983) 46 MLR 385 (F. Weiss); [1984] Conv 263 (C.J. Forder). See also Annual Report for 1987, para 12 (trusts for research into human rights registered).

is right as it stands since to do otherwise would usurp the functions of the legislature . . .

I now turn to consider the status of a trust of which a main object is to secure the alteration of the laws of a *foreign* country. The mere fact that the trust was intended to be carried out abroad would not by itself necessarily deprive it of charitable status. A number of trusts to be executed outside this country have been upheld as charities, though the judgment of Sir Raymond Evershed MR in *Camille and Henry Dreyfus Foundation Inc v IRC* [1954] Ch 672, 684–685, [1954] 2 All ER 466, 471–472 illustrates that certain types of trust—for example, trusts for the setting out of soldiers or the repair of bridges or causeways—might be acceptable as charities only if they were to be executed in the United Kingdom. The point with which I am at present concerned is whether a trust of which a direct and main object is to secure a change in the laws of a foreign country can *ever* be regarded as charitable under English law. Though I do not think that any authority cited to me precisely covers the point, I have come to the clear conclusion that it cannot.

I accept that the dangers of the court encroaching on the functions of the legislature or of subjecting its political impartiality to question would not be nearly so great as when similar trusts are to be executed in this country. I also accept that on occasions the court will examine and express an opinion upon the quality of a foreign law. Thus, for example, it has declined to enforce or recognise rights conferred or duties imposed by a foreign law, in certain cases where it has considered that, on the particular facts, enforcement or recognition would be contrary to justice or morality. I therefore accept that the particular point made by Mr. Tyssen (about the law stultifying itself) has no application in this context. There is no obligation on the court to decide on the principle that any foreign law is ex hypothesi right as it stands; it is not obliged for all purposes to blind itself to what it may regard as the injustice of a particular foreign law.

In my judgment, however, there remain overwhelming reasons why such a trust still cannot be regarded as charitable. All the reasoning of Lord Parker of Waddington in *Bowman v Secular Society Ltd* [1917] AC 406 seems to me to apply a fortiori in such a case. A fortiori the court will have no adequate means of judging whether a proposed change in the law of a foreign country will or will not be for the public benefit. Sir Raymond Evershed MR in *Camille and Henry Dreyfus Foundation Inc v Inland Revenue Commissioners* [1954] Ch 672, 684, [1954] 2 All ER 466, 471 expressed the prima facie view that the community which has to be considered in this context, even in the case of a trust to be executed abroad, is the community of the United Kingdom. Assuming that this is the right test, the court in applying it would still be bound to take account of the probable effects of attempts to procure the proposed legislation, or of its actual enactment, on the inhabitants of the country concerned, which would doubtless have a history and social structure quite different from that of the United Kingdom. Whatever might be its view as to the content of the relevant law from the standpoint of an English lawyer, it would, I think, have no satisfactory means of judging such probable effects upon the local community.

Furthermore, before ascribing charitable status to an English trust of which a main object was to secure the alteration of a foreign law, the court would also, I conceive, be bound to consider the consequences for this country as a matter of public policy. In a number of such cases there would arise a substantial prima facie risk that such a trust, if enforced, could prejudice the relations of this country with the foreign country concerned: compare *Habershon v Vardon* (1851) 4 De G & Sm 467. The court would have no satisfactory means of assessing the extent of such risk, which would not be capable of being readily dealt with by evidence and would be a matter more for political than for legal judgment. For all these reasons, I conclude that a trust of which a main purpose is to procure a change in the laws of a foreign country is a trust for the attainment of political objects within the spirit of Lord Parker of Waddington's pronouncement and, as such, is non-charitable.

Thus, far, I have been considering trusts of which a main purpose is to achieve changes in the law itself or which are of a party-political nature. Under any legal system, however, the government and its various authorities, administrative and judicial, will have wide discretionary powers vested in them, within the framework of the existing law. If a principal purpose of a trust is to procure a reversal of government policy or of particular administrative decisions of governmental authorities, does it constitute a trust for political purposes falling within the spirit of Lord Parker's pronouncement? In my judgment it does. If a trust of this nature is to be executed in England, the court will ordinarily have no sufficient means of determining whether the desired reversal would be beneficial to the public, and in any event could not properly encroach on the functions of the executive, acting intra vires, by holding that it should be acting in some other manner. If it is a trust which is to be executed abroad, the court will not have sufficient means of satisfactorily judging, as a matter of evidence, whether the proposed reversal would be beneficial to the community in the relevant sense, after all its consequences, local and international, had been taken into account. It may be added that Lord Normand, in the *National Anti-Vivisection Society* case [1948] AC 31, [1947] 2 All ER 217, specifically equated legislative change and changes by way of government administration in the present context. As he said, at 77, at 240:

"The society seems to me to proclaim that its purpose is a legislative change of policy toward scientific experiments on animals, the consummation of which will be an Act prohibiting all such experiments. I regard it as clear that a society professing these purposes is a political association and not a charity. If for legislative changes a change by means of government administration was substituted the result would be the same."

If the crucial test whether a trust is charitable formulated by Lord Simonds in the same case, at 62, at 232—namely, the competence of the court to control and reform it—is applied, I think one is again driven to the conclusion that trusts of the nature now under discussion, which are to be executed abroad, cannot qualify as charities any more than if they are to be executed in this country. The court, in considering whether particular methods of carrying out or reforming them would be for the public benefit, would be faced with an inescapable dilemma, of which a hypothetical example may be given. It appears from the Amnesty International Report 1978, p. 270, that Islamic law sanctions the death penalty for certain well-defined offences, namely, murder, adultery and brigandage. Let it be supposed that a trust were created of which the object was to secure the abolition of the death penalty for adultery in those countries where Islamic law applies, and to secure a reprieve for those persons who have been sentenced to death for this offence. The court, when invited to enforce or to reform such a trust, would either have to apply English standards as to public benefit, which would not necessarily be at all appropriate in the local conditions, or would have to attempt to apply local standards, of which it knew little or nothing. An English court would not, it seems to me, be competent either to control or reform a trust of this nature, and it would not be appropriate that it should attempt to do so.

Summary of conclusions relating to trusts for political purposes

Founding them principally on the House of Lords decisions in the *Bowman* case [1917] AC 406 and the *National Anti-Vivisection Society* case [1948] AC 31, [1947] 2 All ER 217, I therefore summarise my conclusions in relation to trusts for political purposes as follows. (1) Even if it otherwise appears to fall within the spirit and intendment of the preamble to the Statute of Elizabeth, a trust for political purposes falling within the spirit of Lord Parker's pronouncement in *Bowman's* case can never be regarded as being for the public benefit in the manner which the law regards as charitable. (2) Trusts for political purposes falling within the spirit of this pronouncement include, inter alia, trusts of which a direct and principal purpose is either (i) to further the interests of a particular political party; or (ii) to procure changes in the laws of this country; or (iii) to procure changes in the laws of a foreign country; or (iv) to procure a reversal of government policy or of particular decisions of governmental authorities in this country; or (v) to procure a reversal of governmental policy or of particular decisions of governmental authorities in a foreign country.

This categorisation is not intended to be an exhaustive one, but I think it will suffice for the purposes of this judgment; I would further emphasise that it is directed to trusts of which the *purposes* are political. As will appear later, the mere fact that trustees may be at liberty to employ political *means* in furthering the non-political purposes of a trust does not necessarily render it non-charitable . . .
[His Lordship then considered the requirement that trust purposes must be wholly and exclusively charitable, and continued:]
From all these authorities, I think that two propositions follow in the present case. First, if any one of the main objects of the trusts declared by the trust deed is to be regarded as "political" in the relevant sense, then, the trusts of the trust deed cannot qualify as being charitable. Secondly, however, if all the main objects of the trust are exclusively charitable, the mere fact that the trustees may have incidental powers to employ political means for their furtherance will not deprive them of their charitable status.
After this introduction I now turn to examine these trusts themselves. . . .
It will not be necessary to consider the trusts declared by clause 2A, since it is common ground that, if read in isolation, these trusts are of a charitable nature. Of the remaining sub-clauses, I shall begin by considering the construction and legal effect of clause 2B. . . .
Expressed in one sentence, the main object of the broadly-defined trust contained in clause 2B must in my judgment be regarded as being the procurement of the reversal of the relevant decisions of governments and governmental authorities in those countries where such authorities have decided to detain "prisoners of conscience," whether or not in accordance with the local law. The procurement of the reversal of such decisions cannot, I think, be regarded merely as one possible method of giving effect to the purposes of clause 2B, any more than in the *National Anti-Vivisection Society* case [1948] AC 31, [1947] 2 All ER 217 the alteration of the law could be regarded as merely one method of giving effect to the purpose of abolishing vivisection. On the construction which I place on clause 2B, it is the principal purpose

itself. On this view of the matter, the trust declared by clause 2B cannot in my judgment qualify as a charitable trust. It is a trust for political purposes, within the fifth of the categories listed above. . . .

For these reasons it must in my judgment follow that the trusts of clause 2B are not charitable. Unlike those of clause 2A, they cannot be regarded as purely eleemosynary. It must also follow from this that the trusts of the trust deed as a whole are invalid as not being for exclusively charitable purposes. Nevertheless, having heard full argument as to clause 2C, D and E, I will express my conclusions in relation to them, in case this may be of assistance either to the parties or to a higher court. . . .

I prefer to base my conclusion in relation to the trusts of clause 2C on the wider grounds that they include the procurement not only of changes in the law of the United Kingdom but also of changes in the laws of foreign countries and the reversal of particular decisions of governmental authorities in foreign countries. They are therefore political trusts within the second, third and fifth of the heads categorised above. For these reasons, it must follow that in my judgment the trusts of clause 2C are not charitable. . . .

If sub-clauses D and E had been the only trust purposes contained in the trust deed, I would have held them to be of a charitable nature. The subject matter of the proposed research seems to me manifestly a subject of study which is capable of adding usefully to the store of human knowledge. . . . It appears that the study of human rights has become an accepted academic discipline; the subject is taught in many universities, and is part of the curriculum in departments of many schools. I think that sub-clauses D and E when read together make it clear that it is contemplated that the knowledge acquired as a result of the research would be disseminated to others. Furthermore, if these two sub-clauses had stood in isolation I would have felt little difficulty in holding that the trusts thereby declared were for the benefit of the public. The mere theoretical possibility that the trustees might have implemented them in a political manner would not have rendered them non-charitable; the two sub-clauses would have been entitled to a benignant construction and to the presumption, referred to by Gray J in *Jackson v Phillips* (1867) 96 Mass (14 Allen) 539, that the trustees would only act in lawful and proper manner appropriate to the trustees of a charity and not, for example, by the propagation of tendentious political opinions.

As things are, the trusts of sub-clauses D and E, just as much as the trusts of sub-clauses A and F, must in my judgment fail along with sub-clauses B and C. None of the trusts of this trust deed can be regarded as being charitable.

Conclusion

In eloquent passages at the end of their addresses, Mr. Knox and Mr. Hoffmann made reference to the classic problem facing Antigone, who believed that there are certain laws of men which a higher law may require them to disregard. Mr. Hoffmann, by reference to the various international conventions to which this country has been a party, submitted that it is committed to the elimination of unjust laws and actions wherever these may exist or occur throughout the world.

Indisputably, laws do exist both in this country and in many foreign countries which many reasonable persons consider unjust. No less indisputably, laws themselves will from time to time be administered by governmental authorities in a manner which many reasonable persons consider unjust, inhuman or degrading. Amnesty International, in striving to remedy what it considers to be such injustices, is performing a function which many will regard as being of great value to humanity. Fortunately, the laws of this country place very few restrictions on the rights of philanthropic organisations such as this, or of individuals, to strive for the remedy of what they regard as instances of injustice, whether occurring here or abroad. However, for reasons which I think adequately appear from Lord Parker of Waddington's pronouncement in *Bowman's* case [1917] AC 406, the elimination of injustice has not as such ever been held to be a trust purpose which qualifies for the privileges afforded to charities by English law. I cannot hold it to be a charitable purpose now.

For all these reasons, I must decline to make the declaration sought by the originating summons, namely, that the trust constituted by the trust deed ought to be registered as a charity.[19]

4. Guidelines

(a) Political Activities by Charities

Charity Commissioners for England and Wales: Political Activities and Campaigning by Charities, July 1995 (Leaflet CC 9), paras 2, 5–12 and 14–54.

"**Introduction**

2. Charities must not be political organisations. But they are not precluded from all political activity. A distinction must be made between political purposes and political activities. The Courts have made it clear that a body whose stated purposes include the attainment of a political purpose cannot be charitable. A body whose purposes are charitable, (and therefore do not include a political purpose) may nevertheless engage in activities which are directed at securing, or opposing, changes in the law or in government policy or decisions, whether in this country or abroad. (In this leaflet the expression 'political activities' is used in this sense). But charities cannot engage in such political activities without restraint.

Charitable Status: definition of a political purpose

5. What charities are allowed to do is determined by their 'purposes'—the objects for which they are established, as set out in their governing document. An institution whose stated purposes include the attainment of a political purpose cannot be a charity. This is clear from a number of cases decided by the Courts. The reason for this is that charities must be constituted for the public benefit. The Courts have made it clear that they will not determine whether a political purpose is or is not for the public benefit. Such questions are for political debate and Parliamentary determination.

6. Briefly, the Courts have held that purposes designed to promote the interests of a political party (an expression which is used in this leaflet to mean any local, national or European political grouping), or to seek or oppose changes in the law or government policy or decisions, whether in this country or abroad, are not charitable.

---

19 See also *R v Radio Authority, ex p Bull* [1995] 3 WLR 572, [1995] 4 All ER 481.

Extent to which charities may engage in political activities

7. Although an organisation established for political purposes can never be a charity, the trustees of a charity may do some things of a political nature as a means of achieving the purposes of the charity.

8. This principle, although easy to state, is not always easy to apply in practice. In applying it charity trustees must take particular care since the dividing line between proper debate in the public arena and improper political activity is a difficult one to judge. The guidance given in this leaflet, which is drawn from the principles established by the Courts, is designed to help trustees to determine that line in relation to a range of activities. Any political activity undertaken by trustees must be in furtherance of, and ancillary to, the charity's stated objects and within its powers.

9. To be ancillary, activities must serve and be subordinate to the charity's purposes. They cannot, therefore, be undertaken as an end in themselves and must not be allowed to dominate the activities which the charity undertakes to carry out its charitable purposes directly. The trustees must be able to show that there is a reasonable expectation that the activities will further the purposes of the charity, and so benefit its beneficiaries to an extent justified by the resources devoted to those activities.

10. Where these requirements are met, trustees of charities may properly enter into dialogue with government on matters relating to their purposes or the way in which the trustees carry out their work. They may publish the advice or views they express to Ministers. They may also seek to inform and educate the public on particular issues which are relevant to the charity and its purposes, including information about their experience of the needs met in their field of activities and the solutions they advocate. But they must do so on the basis of a reasoned case and their views must be expressed with a proper sense of proportion.

11. Trustees must not advocate policies, nor seek to inform and educate, on subjects and issues which do not bear on the purposes of their charity. Moreover, the manner and content of any advocacy of, or opposition to, legislative or policy change must be appropriate to a charity.

12. In summary, therefore, a charity can engage in political activity if:
- there is a reasonable expectation that the activity concerned will effectively further the stated purposes of the charity and so benefit its beneficiaries to an extent justified by the resources devoted to the activity;
- the activity is within the powers which the trustees have to achieve those purposes;
- the activity is consistent with these guidelines;
- the views expressed are based on a well-founded and reasoned case and are expressed in a responsible way. . .

14. Because of the need to meet these requirements it is important that any charity undertaking political activities has adequate arrangements in place for the commissioning, control and evaluation of such activities by its trustees (who are, of course, ultimately responsible for ensuring that they are properly conducted).

Campaigning

15. Campaigning by charities to mobilise public opinion to influence government policy can arouse strong feelings. On the one hand, many people think that charities should be allowed, and indeed have a duty, to campaign

freely to change public policy on any issue if it is relevant to their work and if they have direct experience to offer. On the other hand, some argue that such campaigning is a misuse of charity funds, a misdirection of effort by charities and a misuse of the fiscal concessions from which charities benefit. This is particularly so if the charity appears to favour a particular political party or a policy of a political party.

16. By the very nature of their knowledge and social concern, however, some charities are well placed to play a part in public debate on important issues of the day and to make an important contribution to the development of public policy. Others will invariably be drawn into such debate. It would be wrong to think that this cannot and should not happen: it is open to charities to engage in campaigning activities, provided the requirements set out in paras. 7–14 of this leaflet are satisfied.

17. Whether a charity can properly engage in campaigning will therefore depend upon the nature of its purposes, its powers and the way in which it contributes to public debate. Where charities wish to raise issues in a way which will inform public debate and influence decisions of public bodies, great care must be taken to ensure that the issues concerned are relevant to their purposes and that the means by which they raise them are within their powers and consistent with these guidelines.

18. A charity should not seek to organise public opinion to support or oppose a political party which advocates a particular policy favoured or opposed by the charity. It is inevitable that sometimes a policy put forward by a charity coincides with that of a particular political party, or a political party decides to adopt such a policy. It does not follow that the charity is prevented from promoting its policy on the issue. However, it may influence how it does so. In such cases the charity should take particular care—especially to ensure that the independence of its view is explained and understood.

19. Where a charity can properly campaign, the information provided to the public in support of the campaign as a whole must be accurate and sufficiently full to support its position. In arguing its case a charity is not restricted to using print media alone. If it uses a communications medium the nature of which makes it impracticable to set out the full basis of the charity's position, the charity can simply state its position, without the need to set out the full factual basis and argument lying behind that position. It must be able to set out its full position, however, if called upon to do so.

20. Provided all other requirements are met, material produced in support of a campaign may have emotional content. Indeed, the Commission accepts that in the areas in which many charities work it is difficult to avoid engaging the emotions of the public. But it would be unacceptable (except where the nature of the medium makes it impracticable to set out the basis of the charity's position) for a charity to seek to persuade government or the public on the basis of material which was merely emotive.

What political activities are allowed?

21. A charity may undertake only those activities which further its purposes and which are authorised by its governing document. If the activity involves campaigning, then in all cases the manner in which it is conducted must be in accordance with the principles set out in paras. 15–20 of this leaflet.

22. Where this is the case, a charity may engage in activities of the kinds shown below. Examples of activities in which a charity must not engage are shown in *italics*.

Influencing government or public opinion

23. A charity may seek to influence government or public opinion through well-founded, reasoned argument based on research or direct experience on issues either relating directly to the achievement of the charity's own stated purposes or relevant to the wellbeing of the charitable sector.

24. A charity may provide information to its supporters or the public on how individual Members of Parliament or parties have voted on an issue, provided they do so in a way which will enable its supporters or the public to seek to persuade those Members or parties to change their position through well-founded, reasoned argument rather than merely through public pressure.

25. A charity may provide its supporters, or members of the public, with material to send to Members of Parliament or the government, provided that the material amounts to well-founded, reasoned argument.

26. A charity may organise and present a petition to either House of Parliament or to national or local government, provided that the purpose of the petition is stated on each page.

27. *A charity must not base any attempt to influence public opinion or to put pressure on the government, whether directly or indirectly through supporters or members of the public, to legislate or adopt a particular policy on data which it knows (or ought to know) is inaccurate or on a distorted selection of data in support of a preconceived position.*

28. *A charity must not participate in party political demonstrations.*

29. *A charity must not claim evidence of public support for its position on a political issue without adequate justification.*

30. *Except where the nature of the medium being employed makes it impracticable to set out the basis of the charity's position, a charity must not seek to influence government or public opinion on the basis of material which is merely emotive.*

31. *A charity must not invite its supporters, or the public, to take action in support of its position without providing them with sufficient information to enable them to decide whether to give their support and to take the action requested. In particular, a charity must not invite its supporters or the public to write to their Members of Parliament or the government without providing them with sufficient information to enable them to advance a reasoned argument in favour of the charity's position.*

32. *A charity whose stated purposes include the advancement of education must not overstep the boundary between education and propaganda in promoting that purpose. The distinction is between providing balanced information designed to enable people to make up their own mind and providing one-sided information designed to promote a particular point of view.*

Responding to proposed legislation

33. A charity may provide, and publish comments on possible or proposed changes in the law or government policy, whether contained in a Green or White Paper or otherwise.

34. A charity may, in response to a Parliamentary Bill, supply to Members of either House for use in debate such relevant information and reasoned arguments as can reasonably be expected to assist the achievement of its charitable purposes.

Advocating and opposing changes in the law and public policy

35. A charity may advocate a change in the law or public policy which can reasonably be expected to help it to achieve its charitable purposes and may oppose a change in the law or public policy which can reasonably be expected to hinder its ability to do so. In either case the charity can present government

with a reasoned memorandum in support of its position. It may publish its views and may seek to influence public opinion in favour of its position by well-founded reasoned argument.

Supporting, opposing and promoting legislation

36. A charity may support the passage of a Bill which it reasonably believes would help it to achieve its charitable purposes and may oppose the passage of a Bill which it reasonably believes would hinder its ability to do so.

37. A charity may spend its funds on the promotion of public general legislation provided it has the power to do so and the legislation can reasonably be expected to further its charitable purposes.

Commenting on public issues

38. A charity may comment publicly on social, economic and political issues if these relate to its purposes or the way in which the charity is able to carry out its work.

Supporting political parties

39. A charity may advocate a particular solution if it can reasonably be expected to further the purposes of the charity, even though that solution is advocated by a political party. If it does so it must make plain that its view are independent of the political party.

40. *A charity must not support a political party.*

41. A charity may affiliate to a campaigning alliance, even if the alliance includes non-charitable organisations, provided certain conditions are met. First, the charity must carefully consider the alliance's activities, and the implications of the charity's being associated with them, and should only affiliate if affiliation can reasonably be expected to further the charity's own charitable purposes. Second, since a charity may not undertake through an alliance activities which it would be improper for it to undertake directly, if the alliance engages in such activities the charity must dissociate itself from them and take reasonable steps to ensure that its name, and any funds it has contributed, are not used to support them.

Providing information

42. A charity may provide factual information to its members and those interested in its work in seeking to inform their Members of Parliament and others on matters related to the purposes of the charity.

43. A charity may employ Parliamentary staff to inform Members of Parliament on matters relevant to its purposes.

45. *A charity must not provide supporters or members of the public with material specifically designed to underpin a political campaign or for or against a government or particular MPs.*

46. *A charity must not issue material which supports or opposes a particular political party or the Government.*

Forthcoming elections

47. A charity may respond to forthcoming elections, whether local, national or to the European Parliament, by analysing and commenting on the proposals of political parties which relate to its purposes or the way in which it is able to carry out its work, provided that it comments in a way which is consistent with these guidelines and complies with all the relevant provisions of electoral law.

48. A charity may also bring to the attention of prospective candidates issues relating to its purposes or the way in which it is able to carry out its work, and raise public awareness about them generally, provided that the promotional material is educational, informative, reasoned and well-founded.

49. *A charity must not seek to persuade members of the public to vote for or against a candidate or for or against a political party.*

Conducting and publishing research

50. A charity which conducts research must ensure that it is properly conducted using a methodology appropriate to the subject. If the research is undertaken to test a hypothesis arising from a charity's own experience or earlier research, it must be undertaken objectively to test that hypothesis rather than merely to support a preconceived position or objective. The aim in publishing the results of the research must be to inform and educate the public.

51. *A charity must not distort research, or the results of research, to support a preconceived position or objective.*

52. *A charity must not promote the results of research conducted by itself or others which it knows, or ought to know, to be flawed.*

53. A charity must not undertake research for another body where it is clear that body intends to use the research for political or propagandist purposes.

Seeking support for government grants

54. A charity may seek the support of Members of Parliament where a question arises as to whether a government grant to the charity is to be made or continued.''

(b) Expenditure by Student Unions
Report of the Charity Commissioners for England and Wales for the Year 1983, Appendix A.

''Attorney General's Guidance on Expenditure by Student Unions:

The Attorney General, as protector of charities, frequently receives complaints about the use of Student Union funds for purposes which go beyond those permitted for such funds, and he is greatly concerned about those cases in which the complaints turn out to be well founded because the funds have been used for a purpose incompatible with the charitable objects of the Student Union in question.

It has been held in the Courts that a Student Union has charitable objects if it exists to represent and foster the interests of the students at an educational establishment in such a way as to further the educational purposes of the establishment itself. The Attorney General believes that that will be the case with the great majority of Student Unions, including those provided for in the constitutions of their parent establishments (unless those establishments do not themselves have charitable objects). If a Student Union has charitable objects it follows as a matter of law that, whatever may be stated in its constitution, those objects cannot be changed, even by unanimous vote of its members, so as to include non-charitable objects; and Union funds may be spent only on those charitable objects or for properly incidental purposes.

The Attorney General recognises the difficult position in which officers of Student Unions with charitable objects may find themselves. They may have no experience of charity law, and their members may believe that Union funds can be spent on anything that they think to be of general interest. However, the officers are trustees of the funds, and they have a duty to see that the funds are used only for purposes permitted by charity law. The complaints which have been made in recent years contain allegations of considerable expenditure of an improper nature. Such investigation as has been undertaken confirms that there are grounds for concern. Although perhaps the items taken individually appear not to be very great, they represent in total a major abuse of charitable funds.

In the circumstances the Attorney General considers it right that he should issue guidelines to assist Union officers in the discharge of their responsibility for Union funds. In the event of wrongful application of funds, such officers would potentially be at personal risk to a claim that they have been party to a breach of trust, and might well find themselves bound to make good any loss to the funds of their Union at their own expense. It is therefore important that they should be aware of their responsibilities.

The Attorney General considers that expenditure of a Student Union's charitable funds is proper if it can be said to be appropriate for the purpose of representing and furthering the interests of the students at the relevant college (and 'college' here includes 'university') in such a way as to assist in the educational aims of the college—for example, by providing channels for the representation of student views within the college, or by improving the conditions of life of the students and in particular providing facilities for their social and physical well-being.

It is clear, for example, that if a college is to function properly, there is a need for the normal range of clubs and societies so as to enable each student to further the development of his abilities, mental and physical. Equally, it is likely that the college will gain from the fact that the students hold meetings to debate matters of common concern, and publish some form of campus newspaper. Reasonable expenditure on such purposes is, in the view of the Attorney General, plainly permissible for a Student Union.

On the other hand, for the students to offer financial support to a political cause in a foreign country—as opposed to merely debating the merits of that cause—is, in the Attorney General's view, irrelevant to the educational purpose of the college. Such expenditure must accordingly be rejected as improper.

Between these extremes there is a wide range of cases for which the Attorney General believes the best touchstone to be the question: does the matter in issue affect the interests of either students *as such* or the affairs of the college *as such*? If the answer is 'no', then the case is likely to be one on which the students may hold debates and express views but not charge expenditure to the charitable funds of the Union.

A major area of difficulty appears to be that of political issues. While the Attorney General recognises that it is entirely natural that students will wish to express their views on political matters, the law sets strict limits to the expenditure of charitable funds for political purposes. Such expenditure is permissible only if the political purposes are merely *incidental* to the necessarily non-political objects of the charity. Thus, for a Union to expend its charitable funds in supporting a political campaign or demonstration is extremely unlikely to be justifiable unless the issue directly affects students as students. It may be helpful to mention that in this context politics is not to be limited to party politics, but extends essentially to all aspects of the making and changing of laws. Thus it would be no less improper, in the view of the Attorney General, for charitable funds of a Union to be devoted to a campaign for or against the legalisation of drugs, even though this is not a matter of party political debate, than it would be for such funds to be used either in support of or opposition to a campaign concerning, say, nuclear weapons or some controversial parliamentary debate not concerned with the interests of students as such.

Another area of difficulty appears to be that of industrial disputes. The Attorney General accepts that students may often wish to express a view on a current dispute, particularly if it be centred upon the neighbourhood of the college of which they are students. There is, however, in his view no justification for applying charitable funds in support of either side to the dispute. It would be as wrong for charitable funds to be spent on the hire of coaches, say, for the purpose of taking demonstrators to the scene of the dispute as it would be to hire coaches to take students to a demonstration in respect of the political issues referred to in the last paragraph.

There is, of course, no objection whatsoever to students joining together to collect their own moneys for a particular purpose for which Union funds cannot be used. The Attorney General wishes to stress that the objection is not to student participation in activities outside the educational sphere, but to the use of charitable funds for purposes for which they cannot properly be applied according to the law.

In issuing these guidelines the Attorney General is anxious solely to assist those who may find themselves called to account for their actions as trustees of charitable moneys. Officers should, of course, bear in mind that it will be amongst their most important duties to identify and keep proper accounts of all Union funds (including, for example, not merely subscriptions to the Union, but income from Union investments, and profits from Union activities, such as the running of a bar or dance at the expense of the Union and with the assistance of its employees). They have a further duty to ensure that expenditure not only is within the proper bounds within which the funds of their Union can be used, but also has been approved and recorded as the Constitution of the Union requires.

They should also bear in mind that a trustee is at all times entitled to seek advice, if necessary at the expense of the trust fund, on any aspect of his trust which causes him doubt or concern; in particular, under Section 24 of the Charities Act 1960 the Charity Commissioners are empowered on the written application of a charity trustee to give him their opinion or advice on any matter affecting the performance of his duties as such.

The Attorney General would add that he hopes that the senior members of the college concerned will always be willing to assist Student Union officers in considering doubtful items of expenditure. It must be borne in mind that where the parent body is itself a charitable body and thus has a duty to ensure that its funds are properly applied for purposes within, or incidental to, its own charitable educational purposes, it might well be that upon becoming aware of major items of improper expenditure by the Union it ought properly to cease to fund the Union until the position had been rectified.''

QUESTION

Why are trusts for political purposes not charitable? If they were, where would you draw the line?

IV. The Trust Must be Exclusively Charitable[20]

To be charitable, the purpose of a trust must not merely include purposes which are charitable. The purposes must be exclusively charitable. This requirement has appeared in cases previously discussed. It appears dramatically in cases where the purposes are for charitable or some alternative purpose which is wider than legal charity. Thus, "charitable or benevolent" purposes are wider than legal charity. "Charitable and benevolent purposes" are however charitable, because, even though "benevolent" is wider than "charitable",[1] the purposes here must be not only "benevolent" but "charitable" as well.

Where the purposes of a trust extend beyond the limits of legal charity, the court may, on construing the language, reach one of several possible solutions.

(i) That the trust is void. This result seems inevitable if it is possible, consistently with the terms of the trust, to apply the whole of the fund to non-charitable purposes.

(ii) That the non-charitable purposes are incidental only.

(iii) That the fund should be divided into parts; some being applicable to charity and some not. Such a solution can only be reached where the language of the trust instrument can be construed as directing such a division.

A. And/Or Cases[2]

CHICHESTER DIOCESAN FUND AND BOARD OF FINANCE INCORPORATED v SIMPSON
[1944] AC 341, [1944] 2 All ER 60 (HL, Viscount SIMON LC, Lords MACMILLAN, WRIGHT, PORTER and SIMONDS)

Caleb Diplock, the testator, directed his executors to apply the residue of his estate, amounting to more than £250,000 "for such charitable institution or

---

20 H & M, pp. 430–439; K & S, pp. 171–173; S & K, pp. 41–55, 279– 296; P & M, pp. 333–338; Pettit, pp. 216–222; Riddall, pp. 128–138; Snell, pp. 154–159; Tudor, pp. 49–51, 147–155; Picarda, pp. 196–225.

1 See also *Re Atkinson's Will Trusts* [1978] 1 WLR 586, [1978] 1 All ER 1275 ("worthy causes" held not to be exclusively charitable).

2 (*a*) Cases of *Or: Blair v Duncan* [1902] AC 37 ("such charitable or public purposes as my trustee thinks proper"); *Houston v Burns* [1918] AC 337 ("public, benevolent or charitable purposes"); *Re Macduff* [1896] 2 Ch 451 ("some one or more purposes, charitable, philanthropic or ... "). These purposes were all held not charitable. Cf. *Re Bennett* [1920] 1 Ch 305 ("charity, or any other public objects in the parish of Faringdon"); *Guild v IRC* [1992] 2 AC 310, [1992] 2 All ER 10, p. 423 ante (gift to specified charitable purpose "or some similar purpose in connection with it").

(*b*) Cases of *And: Blair v Duncan*, supra, at 44, per Lord DAVEY: "If the words were 'charitable and public purposes', I think effect might be given to them, the words ... being construed to mean charitable purposes of a public character."; *Re Sutton* (1885) 28 ChD 464 ("charitable and deserving objects"); *Re Best* [1904] 2 Ch 354 ("charitable and benevolent institutions"). These purposes were held to be charitable. Cf. *Williams v Kershaw* (1835) 5 Cl & Fin 111n ("benevolent, charitable and religious purposes"); *Re Eades* [1920] 2 Ch 353 ("such religious, charitable and philanthropic objects as X Y and Z shall jointly appoint"). See also *A-G v National Provincial and Union Bank of England* [1924] AC 262 ("such patriotic purposes or objects and such charitable institution or institutions or charitable object or objects in the British Empire as my trustees may select" held void); *A-G of the Bahamas v Royal Trust Co* [1986] 1 WLR 1001, [1986] 3 All ER 423 ("for any purposes for and/or connected with the education and welfare of Bahamian children and young people"); [1986] All ER Rev 202 (P.J. Clarke).

institutions or other charitable or benevolent object or objects in England" as they should in their absolute discretion select.

Held. The gift was void.[3]

LORD SIMONDS: My Lords, the words for your consideration are "charitable or benevolent". The question is whether, in the context in which they are found in this will, these words give to the executors a choice of objects extending beyond that which the law recognizes as charitable. If they do not, that is the end of the matter. The trust is a good charitable trust. If they do, it appears to be conceded by counsel for the appellant institution that the trust is invalid, but, in deference to the argument of the Attorney-General, who invited your Lordships to take a different view, I must say a few words at a later stage. My Lords, of those three words your Lordships will have no doubt what the first, "charitable", means. It is a term of art with a technical meaning and that is the meaning which the testator must be assumed to have intended. If it were not so, if in this will "charitable" were to be given, not its legal, but some popular, meaning, it would not be possible to establish the validity of the bequest. The last of the three words "benevolent" is not a term of art. In its ordinary meaning it has a range in some respects far less wide than legal charity, in others somewhat wider. It is, at least, clear that the two words, the one here used in its technical meaning, the other having only, and, accordingly, here used in, a popular meaning, are by no means coterminous. These two words are joined or separated by the word "or", a particle, of which the primary function is to co-ordinate two or more words between which there is an alternative. It is, I think, the only word in our language apt to have this effect. Its primary and ordinary meaning is the same, whether or not the first alternative is preceded by the word "either".

My Lords, averting my mind from the possible ill effects of an alternative choice between objects "charitable" and objects "benevolent", I cannot doubt that the plain meaning of the testator's words is that he has given this choice, and that, if he intended to give it, he could have used no words more apt to do so. Is there, then, anything in the context which narrows the area of choice by giving to the words "or benevolent" some other meaning than that which they primarily and naturally have? And if so, what is the other meaning which is to be given to them? Let me examine the second question first. Since the test of validity depends on the area of choice not being extended beyond the bounds of legal charity, a meaning must be given to the words "or benevolent" which retains them within these bounds. This result, it has been contended, may be reached by giving to the word "or" not its primary disjunctive meaning but a secondary meaning which may, perhaps, be called exegetical or explanatory. Undoubtedly "or" is capable of this meaning. So used, it is equivalent to "alias" or "otherwise called". The dictionary examples of this use will generally be found to be topographical, as "Papua or New Guinea", but, my Lords, this use of the word "or" is only possible if the words or phrases which it joins connote the same thing and are interchangeable the one with the other. In this case the testator is assumed to use the word "charitable" in its legal sense. I see no possible ground for supposing that he proceeds to explain it by another word which has another meaning and by no means can have that meaning. I must reject the exegetical "or". Then it was suggested that the words "or benevolent" should be construed as equivalent to

---

3 For the sequel, see *Ministry of Health v Simpson* [1951] AC 251, [1950] 2 All ER 1137, p. 904, post.

"provided such objects are also of a benevolent character", that is to say, the objects must be charitable but of that order of charity which is commonly called benevolent. I think that this is only a roundabout way of saying that "or" should be read as "and," that the objects of choice must have the two characteristics of charitable and benevolent. It is possible that a context may justify so drastic a change as that involved in reading the disjunctive as conjunctive. I turn then to the context to see what justification it affords for reading the relevant words in any but their natural meaning. Reading and re-reading them, as your Lordships have so often done in the course of this case, I can find nothing which justifies such a departure. It is true that the word "other" introduces the phrase "charitable or benevolent object or objects" and to this the appellants attached some importance, suggesting that since "other" looked back to "charitable institution or institutions", so all that followed must be of the genus charitable. There can be no substance in this, for in the phrase so introduced the word "charitable" is itself repeated and is followed by the alternative "or benevolent". Apart from this slender point it seemed that the appellants relied on what is called a general, a dominant, an overriding, charitable intention, giving charitable content to a word or phrase which might otherwise not have that quality. That such a result is possible there are cases in the books to show. Some of them have been cited to your Lordships, but here again I look in vain for any such context. On the plain reading of this will I could only come to the conclusion that the testator intended exclusively to benefit charitable objects if I excised the words "or benevolent" which he has used. That I cannot do.

B. Main and Subsidiary Objects[4]

In **Oxford Group v Inland Revenue Commissioners** [1949] 2 All ER 537, the question was whether the Oxford Group, a company limited by guarantee, was exempt from income tax. The objects of the movement, as laid down in its memorandum of association, included—

"3 (A) The advancement of the Christian religion, and, in particular, by the means and in accordance with the principles of the Oxford Group Movement, founded in or about the year 1921 by Frank Nathan Daniel Buchman. (B) The maintenance, support, development and assistance of the Oxford Group Movement in every way ... (C) (9) To establish and support or aid in the establishment and support of any charitable or benevolent associations or institutions, and to subscribe or guarantee money for charitable or benevolent purposes in any way connected with the purposes of the association or calculated to further its objects. (10) To do all such other things as are incidental, or the association may think conducive, to the attainment of the above objects or any of them."

No question arose under 3 (A). The Court of Appeal held however that 3 (B) and 3 (C) (9) and (10) included purposes which were outside the scope of legal charity, and that the Company was not exempt from income tax.

In **General Nursing Council for England and Wales v St Marylebone Borough Council** [1959] AC 540, [1959] 1 All ER 325, the House of Lords, by a majority

4 [1978] Conv 92 (N.P. Gravells).

of 3–2, decided that the General Nursing Council for England and Wales, a body whose main object was the regulation of the nursing profession, was not a charity, nor was it "otherwise concerned with the advancement of . . . social welfare". (Rating and Valuation (Miscellaneous Provisions) Act 1955, s. 8 (1) (*a*)). It was not therefore entitled to rating relief under s. 8 (2).

There may, however, be incidental non-charitable purposes.

In **Re Bernstein's Will Trusts** (1971) 115 SJ 808, the testator, after a life interest to his widow, gave his residuary estate on trust for the Eye, Ear and Throat Infirmary, Liverpool, one quarter of which was to form a nursing staff fund, "for the purpose of providing extra comforts at Christmas time for the nursing staff". UNGOED-THOMAS J held that the trust for the nursing staff was charitable, being subservient to the gift to the hospital.

In **Royal College of Surgeons of England v National Provincial Bank Ltd** [1952] AC 631, [1952] 1 All ER 984, the House of Lords decided, by a majority of 3–2, that the Royal College of Surgeons was a charity. Its object was "the due promotion and encouragement of the study and practice of the . . . art and science [of surgery]". The other activities, which included the professional protection of the members of the profession, were merely ancillary.

In **Re Coxen** [1948] Ch 747, [1948] 2 All ER 492, a trust fund, amounting to some £200,000, was held upon trust for medical charities and provided expressly for the payment of £100 towards a dinner for the Court of Aldermen of the City of London upon their meeting upon the business of the trust, and the payment of one guinea to each Alderman who attended during the whole of a Committee meeting. The trust was upheld on the ground, either that such payments should be treated as being made for the better administration of the trust; or as being incidental and ancillary to it.

In **Incorporated Council of Law Reporting for England and Wales v Attorney-General**[5] [1972] Ch 73, [1971] 3 All ER 1029, p. 370 ante, the Court of Appeal held that the activities of the Council were charitable. BUCKLEY LJ said at 103, at 1047:
"The subsidiary objects, such as printing and publishing statutes, the provision of a noting-up service and so forth, are ancillary to this primary object and do not detract from its exclusively charitable character. Indeed, the publication of the statutes of the realm is itself, I think, a charitable purpose for reasons analogous to those applicable to reporting judicial decisions."

In **London Hospital Medical College v Inland Revenue Commissioners** [1976] 1 WLR 613, [1976] 2 All ER 113, a students' union was held to be a

---

5 Followed by the Charity Commissioners, in deciding that the Commonwealth Magistrates Association should be entered on the register of charities: Annual Report for 1975, para. 63.

charitable trust where its predominant object was to further the educational purposes of the college, even though one of its objects was to confer private and personal benefits on union members.[6]

In **A-G v Ross** [1986] 1 WLR 252, [1985] 3 All ER 334, a students' union was also held to be a charitable trust, even though one of its objects was affiliation to a non-charitable organisation. SCOTT J said at 265, at 345:
"The union was formed and exists for the charitable purpose of furthering the educational function of the [North London] Polytechnic. The non-charitable activities which the union is, under its constitution, authorised to carry on and has carried on are, in my judgment, as a matter of degree no more than ancillary means by which the charitable purpose may be pursued."[7]

C. Severance

In **Salusbury v Denton** (1857) 3 K & J 529, Lynch Burrows bequeathed a fund to his widow to be applied by her in her will, "part to the foundation of a charity school, or such other charitable endowment for the benefit of the poor of Offley as she may prefer ... and the remainder ... to be at her disposal among my relatives, in such proportions as she may be pleased to direct". The widow died without having made a will or appointment. One question was whether the fund was divisible. PAGE-WOOD V-C held that the fund was divisible into two equal parts, one for charitable purposes, and the other for the plaintiff absolutely, as the only person entitled under the Statutes of Distribution. He said at 539:
"Here there is a plain direction to the widow to give a part to the charitable purposes referred to in the will as she may think fit, and the remainder among the testator's relatives as she may direct. And the widow having died without exercising that discretion, the moiety in question must be divided equally."

Equal division may however be inappropriate: *Re Coxen* [1948] Ch 747, [1948] 2 All ER 492, p. 462, ante.

D. Limited Reform

The Charitable Trusts (Validation) Act 1954[8] provided retrospective validation for instruments coming into effect before 16 December, 1952,[9] where,

---

6 See also *IRC v City of Glasgow Police Athletic Association* [1953] AC 380, [1953] 1 All ER 747, p. 418, ante; *Re Lipinski's Will Trusts* [1976] Ch 235, [1977] 1 All ER 33, p. 319, ante; *Re South Place Ethical Society* [1980] 1 WLR 1565, [1980] 3 All ER 918, p. 372, ante (social activities held to be ancillary to objects of ethical humanist society); *Funnell v Stewart* [1996] 1 WLR 288 (private religious services confined to a closed group held to be subsidiary to public spiritual or faith healing part of the group's work); *McGovern v A-G* [1982] Ch 321 at 340–343, [1981] 3 All ER 493 at 509–511, p. 446, ante; *CIR v White* [1980] TR 155, p. 364, ante. See also *The City of London Rifle and Pistol Club and the Burnley Rifle Club* (1993) Decisions of the Charity Commissioners, Vol 1, p 4, p. 432 ante.
7 [1985] All ER Rev 320 (P.J. Clarke).
8 (1954) 18 Conv (NS) 532; (1962) 26 Conv (NS) 200 (S.G. Maurice).
9 The date of the publication of the Report of the Committee on the Law and Practice relating to Charitable Trusts (1952 Cmd. 8710), see chap. 12.

"consistently with the terms of the [trust] provision, the property could be used exclusively for charitable purposes, but could nevertheless be used for purposes which are not charitable". The Act is complex, and produced much litigation.[10] It has no application upon trusts coming into effect after 15 December, 1952. More comprehensive legislation has been enacted in some Commonwealth countries.[11]

v. Charitable Purposes Overseas[12]

Decisions of the Charity Commissioners 1993, vol 1, pp. 16–17.

"Charities Operating Overseas: Charities for Fourth Head Purposes
In our Annual Report for 1963 we reproduced extracts from a letter of advice we had sent to major charities concerned with overseas relief work. Part of that advice was that we had entertained no doubt that the advancement of religion, the advancement of education and the relief of poverty (the first three heads of charity as classified in the well known judgment *Income Tax Special Purposes Comrs v Pemsel* [1891] AC 531) were charitable in whatever part of the world they are carried out, but that charities within the fourth head of the classification in the *Pemsel* case, i.e. for other purposes beneficial to the community, would be charitable only if of benefit to the community of the United Kingdom. We have taken a fresh look at the basis upon which we should consider the charitable status of charities operating overseas.

We take the view that jurisdiction is not an issue. An institution can only be a charity if it is subject to the jurisdiction of the English Courts and only such an institution can be registered by us. That has one important consequence— we are considering only the status of institutions based in the United Kingdom and whether they are charitable or not depends upon English law—see Evershed MR in *Camille and Henry Dreyfus Foundation Incorporated v IRC* [1954] Ch 672 at pages 683, 685 and 687. To be charitable all institutions must be for the public benefit. That test of public benefit has to be the same for all charities whether they operate in the United Kingdom or elsewhere as the Courts cannot judge what is for the public benefit in a foreign country and cannot recognise as charitable an institution which is contrary to the public benefit in the United Kingdom but is for the public benefit elsewhere.

---

10 *Vernon v IRC* [1956] 1 WLR 1169, [1956] 3 All ER 14; *Re Gillingham Bus Disaster Fund* [1959] Ch 62, [1958] 2 All ER 749; (1958) 74 LQR 190, 489 (P.S. Atiyah); [1959] CLJ 41 (S.J. Bailey); *Re Wykes* [1961] Ch 229, [1961] 1 All ER 470; *Re Mead's Trust Deed* [1961] 1 WLR 1244, [1961] 2 All ER 836; *Re Harpur's Will Trusts* [1962] Ch 78, [1961] 3 All ER 588; *Re Chitty's Will Trusts* [1970] Ch 254, [1969] 3 All ER 1492; *Re South Place Ethical Society* [1980] 1 WLR 1565, [1980] 3 All ER 918, p. 372, ante (imperfect trust provision validated). The trust in *Williams' Trustees v IRC* [1947] AC 447, [1947] 1 All ER 513, p. 411 ante, was eventually saved by the Act and registered by the Charity Commissioners in 1977; Annual Report for 1977, paras. 71–80.
11 (New South Wales) Conveyancing Act 1919–1954, s. 37D; (New Zealand) Trustee Act 1956, s. 82; (Victoria) Property Law Act 1958, s. 131; (Western Australia) Trustee Act 1962, s. 102; (1940) 14 ALJ 58; (1946) 62 LQR 325; (1950) 24 ALJ 239 (E.H. Coghill); (1967) 16 ICLQ 464 (M.C. Cullity); (1973) 47 ALJ 68 (I.J. Hardingham); Charities Act (Northern Ireland) 1964, s. 24.
12 H & M, pp. 389–390; P & M, pp. 308–309; Pettit, p. 258; Tudor, p. 6; Picarda, pp. 23–25; (1965) 29 Conv (NS) 123 (D.M. Emrys Evans); Goodman Report, paras. 86–88 (International Activity), 89–92 (Foreign Charities); [1993–94] 2 CL & PR 1 (L. Sheridan).

When considering the charitable status of institutions whose purposes are to be carried out abroad, the first question must still be 'Would the objects of the institution be charitable according to English law if its purposes were to be carried out in England?'. Having established that the objects of the institution are ostensibly charitable the Courts will then look at the overseas dimension. That approach seems to us to be implicit in both *Keren Kayemeth Le Jisroel Ltd v IRC* [1932] AC 650 and in the *Dreyfus Foundation* case.

It appears that if the objects of the institution are for the relief of poverty, the promotion of religion or the advancement of education, the Courts adopt the same approach as they do in relation to charities with those objects operating within the United Kingdom, that is that the public benefit element would be presumed. It is, however, only a presumption. The element of public benefit can be challenged not only in relation to charities operating in the United Kingdom but also to those operating overseas. It seems to us that the criterion for challenging the public benefit element must be the same for all charities, that is it must be the one adopted by the English Courts. We doubt whether the Courts would regard it as charitable to support in a foreign country a religion permitted in that country but deemed, if carried on in the United Kingdom, contrary to the public benefit.

Charities falling under the fourth head of Lord Macnaghten's classification in the *Pemsel* case present a particular difficulty. The criteria of public benefit must be that adopted by the Courts in respect of charities operating in the United Kingdom. We consider, however, that rather than try to develop complex concepts of tangible and intangible benefit to the community of the United Kingdom, there is a simpler approach which is equally consistent with the cited cases. We consider that in determining the charitable status of institutions operating abroad, one should first consider whether they would be regarded as charities if their operations are confined to the United Kingdom. If they would, then they should be presumed also to be charitable even though operating abroad unless it would be contrary to public policy to recognise them. (See *Re Vagliano* (1905) 75 LJ Ch 119; *Armstrong v Reeves* (1890) 25 LR 1r 325; *Re Jackson* (1910) Times 11 June; *Mitford v Reynolds* (1842) 1 Ph 185 and *Re Jacobs* (1970) 114 SJ 515 and also the Canadian case of *Re Levy Estate* (1989) 58 DLR (4th) 375 and the Australian cases of *Re Stone* (1970) 91 WN (NSW) 704 and *Lander v Whitbread* (1982) 2 NSWLR 530). We consider that this approach reconciles the decision in *Keren Kayemeth Le Jisroel Limited* and the comments made in the *Dreyfus Foundation* case. In particular, we noted the words of Lord Evershed MR in the *Dreyfus Foundation* case that 'to such cases the argument of public policy [meaning the United Kingdom public policy] might be the answer' and of Jenkins LJ in that case that 'it is here only necessary for me to observe that it cannot be maintained that no purpose is recognised as charitable under our law unless it is carried out in and for the benefit of the public, or some section of the public, of the United Kingdom'. Illustrations of that principle are provided by *Attorney General v Guise* (1692) 2 Vern 266 (gift for application in Scotland contrary to Scottish law) and *Habershon v Vardon* (1851) 4 De G & Sm 467 (a trust to restore Jews to Jerusalem then under Turkish rule, held as tending to promote revolution in a friendly state. A similar trust has been upheld when Palestine was no longer under Turkish rule, see *Re Rosenblum* (1924) 131 LT 21). We further consider that it is necessary to distinguish carefully between the objects of a charity and the means by which that object is to be carried out. If the object itself is contrary to the laws of the foreign state in which it would operate then the trust will not be charitable. On the other hand, if only the means of carrying out the object is contrary to such laws then there will be a failure in the trusts and a case for a cy-près application."

In **Re Robinson** [1931] 2 Ch 122, MAUGHAM J held that a gift "to the German Government for the time being for the benefit of its soldiers disabled in the late war" was charitable. He said at 126:

"It is abundantly clear that, whatever the construction which might have been placed upon the Statute of Elizabeth when that statute was passed in the forty-third year of the Queen's reign, for at least 200 years the Courts have been in the habit of treating the phrase 'charitable purposes' as not confined to charitable purposes within this realm."[13]

QUESTIONS

1. Does fiscal immunity play too large a part in the law of charities? Should provision be made to validate certain useful and beneficial trusts without giving to them tax-free status? Consider what is said by the House of Lords in *Dingle v Turner* [1972] AC 601, [1972] 1 All ER 878, p. 356, ante; (1956) 72 LQR 187 (G. Cross); Royal Commission on the Taxation of Profits and Income (1955) Cmd. 9474, chap. 7; (1977) 40 MLR 397 (N.P. Gravells); and tie this in with your thoughts on purpose trusts in chapter 9.

2. Note the difference in the requirement of public benefit in each of the heads of Charity.

3. To what extent should relief for the population of developing countries be provided through charitable trusts; and to what extent through foreign aid? Appreciate that the domestic taxpayer contributes in either case.

---

13 See also *Re Vagliano* [1905] WN 179 (trust for the establishment of ... or aids to churches, hospitals and schools, and assistance to poor and aged persons for the time being resident in or natives of Cephalonia held charitable); *Keren Kayemeth Le Jisroel Ltd v IRC* [1932] AC 650, p. 413, ante (trust for the purchase of land in "Palestine, Syria, or other parts of Turkey, in Asia and the peninsula of Sinai for the purpose of settling Jews on such lands" held not charitable); *Re Jacobs* (1970) 114 SJ 515 (trust "for the purpose of planting a grove of trees in Israel to perpetuate my name on the eternal soil of the Holy Land" held charitable; Annual Report for 1970, para. 78); *Re Niyazi's Will Trusts* [1978] 1 WLR 910, [1978] 3 All ER 785, p. 354, ante (trust for "the construction of a working mens hostel" in Famagusta, Cyprus, held charitable; *McGovern v A-G* [1982] Ch 321, [1981] 3 All ER 493, p. 446, ante; *Lander v Whitbread* [1982] 2 NSWLR 530 (trust "for the Government of the State of Israel for the advancement of education in that State" held charitable in New South Wales); *Re Levy Estate* (1989) 58 DLR (4th) 375 held valid in Ontario; *Re Gray* (1990) 73 DLR (4th) 161; (1990) 4 TL & P 74 (G. Kodiline); *Re Stone* (1970) 91 WNNSW 704 at 707.

See also Annual Report for 1990, paras. 32–34 (Gdansk Hospice Fund; Nairobi Hospice Trust; Kuwaiti Support Fund); 1991, paras. 69–70 (Kurdish Charitable Trust; Amar Trust; Independent Iran Fund).

10. Cy-près[1]

I. General

If it should be impossible or impracticable to apply funds for the precise charitable purpose intended by the donor, the question arises whether the trust should fail, or whether the funds should be applied for a slightly different charitable purpose. Where the *cy-près* doctrine operates it makes possible the application of funds to purposes as near as possible to those selected by the donor.

Before the Charities Act 1960 came into force, the *cy-près* doctrine could only be applied if it was "impossible or impracticable" to carry out the purposes of the trust. This requirement, although the word "impossible" was widely construed, caused a number of difficulties; for nothing could be done in cases where the continued administration of the trust was highly inconvenient, but not "impossible"; nor where, perhaps through changes in the needs of society or the value of money, an old charity served no useful purpose in modern times. The whole matter was modernised by the Charities Act 1960, ss. 13 and 14, now Charities Act 1993, ss. 13 and 14.

Before that matter is examined in detail, however, it will be convenient to look at another requirement for the application of the doctrine, namely that, in a case where the problem arises *at the commencement* of the trust, the language of the instrument must show that there was a paramount charitable intention. There is no such requirement in a case of subsequent failure.

In the case of initial failure, the gift will lapse and result to the donor or to his estate, unless there is, on the construction of the instrument, a paramount intention to benefit charity. In the case of subsequent failure, that is to say, after the trust has been in operation, there can be no such resulting trust. As ROMER LJ said in *Re Wright* [1954] Ch 347 at 362, [1954] 2 All ER 98 at 104:

---

1 H & M, pp. 439–455; K & S, pp. 181–187; S & K, pp. 201–276; P & M, pp. 338–349; Pettit, pp. 294–308; Riddall, pp. 145–161; Snell, pp. 161–167; Tudor, pp. 391–445; Picarda, pp. 279–346; *Williams on Wills* (7th edn) pp. 916–932. See, generally, Sheridan and Delany, *The Cy-près Doctrine* (1959); (1968) 6 Alberta Law Review 16; (1972) 1 Anglo-American Law Review 101 (L.A. Sheridan); Report of the Committee on the Law and Practice relating to Charitable Trusts (1952 Cmd. 8710), chap. 9; Goodman Report, paras. 188–192; House of Commons Report, vol I, paras. 63–71, vol. II, pp. 122, 177–178, 200–201; (1987) 50 NLJ Annual Charities Review 34 (P. Luxton); Annual Report for 1989, paras. 73–80, p. 488 post containing guidelines.

"Once money is effectually dedicated to charity, whether in pursuance of a general or particular charitable intent, the testator's next-of-kin or residuary legatees are for ever excluded."

If, however, the donor wants the property to return to himself or to his estate or to pass to a third party, he must expressly so provide by a gift over to take effect within the perpetuity period.[2]

ii. Initial Failure[3]

Where a charitable trust fails at the commencement of the trust, the destiny of the property depends on the width of charitable intent manifested by the donor. If his intention was that the property should be applied to the one purpose or institution selected by him, and that alone, then the gift will lapse. But if his intention was to benefit charity generally, then the property may be applied cy-près.

A. Width of Charitable Intent

RE RYMER

[1895] 1 Ch 19 (CA, Lord HERSCHELL LC, LINDLEY and A.L. SMITH LJJ)

Horatio Rymer bequeathed a legacy of £5,000 "to the rector for the time being of St. Thomas' Seminary for the education of priests in the diocese of Westminster". The testator died in 1893.

At the date of the will St. Thomas' Seminary was in existence and provided education for priests for the diocese of Westminster. But at the date of the testator's death, the seminary ceased to exist, and the students were transferred to a seminary near Birmingham.

The question was whether the legacy lapsed or whether it should be applied cy-près.

Held (affirming CHITTY J). There being no general charitable intent, the legacy lapsed and fell into the testator's estate.

LINDLEY LJ: I think the result at which Mr. Justice Chitty has arrived is right. I have attended to and followed the arguments both of Mr. *Cozens-Hardy* and of Mr. *Ingle Joyce*, and in a great many of those arguments I concur. I think, with Mr. *Joyce*, that it does not do to approach a will of this kind by a short cut by saying there is a lapse, and there is an end of it. It is begging the question whether there is a lapse or not. You must construe the will and see what the real object of the language which you have to interpret is. I will not read the words of this gift again; I have read them very often, and studied them with care. I cannot arrive at the conclusion at which the Appellant's counsel ask me to arrive, that this is in substance and in truth a bequest of £5,000 for the education of the priests in the diocese of *Westminster*. I do not think it is. It is a gift of £5,000 to a particular seminary for the purposes thereof, and I do not

---

2 *Re Peel's Release* [1921] 2 Ch 218; *Re Randell* (1888) 38 ChD 213; *Re Cooper's Conveyance Trusts* [1956] 1 WLR 1096, [1956] 3 All ER 28; Perpetuities and Accumulations Act 1964, ss. 3, 12; Maudsley, *Modern Law of Perpetuities*, p. 190.

3 See generally (1969) 32 MLR 283 (J.B.E. Hutton).

think it is possible to get out of that. I think the context shews it. I refer to the masses, the choice of candidates, and so on. If once you get thus far the question arises, Does that seminary exist? The answer is, It does not. Then you arrive at the result that there is a lapse; and if there is a lapse, is there anything in the doctrine of *cy-près* to prevent the ordinary doctrine of lapse from applying? I think not. Once you arrive at the conclusion that there is a lapse, then all the authorities which are of any value shew that the residuary legatee takes the lapsed gift. We are asked to overrule that doctrine, laid down by Vice-Chancellor Kindersley in *Clark v Taylor* (1853) 1 Drew 642 and followed in *Fisk v A-G* (1867) LR 4 Eq 521. I think that the doctrine is perfectly right. There may be a difficulty in arriving at the conclusion that there is a lapse. But when once you arrive at the conclusion that a gift to a particular seminary or institution, or whatever you may call it, is "for the purposes thereof", and for no other purpose—if you once get to that, and it is proved that the institution or seminary, or whatever it is, has ceased to exist in the lifetime of the testator, you are driven to arrive at the conclusion that there is a lapse, and then the doctrine of *cy-près* is inapplicable. That is in accordance with the law, and in accordance with all the cases that can be cited. I quite agree that in coming to that conclusion you have to consider whether the mode of attaining the object is only machinery, or whether the mode is not the substance of the gift. Here it appears to me the gift to the seminary is the substance of the whole thing. It is the object of the testator. I think that is plain from the language used.

Those are the short grounds of my judgment. I do not comment upon the decisions, because the Lord Chancellor has done that sufficiently.[4]

In **Re Wilson** [1913] 1 Ch 314, a testator, who died in 1870, provided a sum of money as a salary for a school-master, who was to teach at a school to be erected by voluntary subscriptions from landowners in the neighbourhood. There was no reasonable likelihood of such a school being established.

PARKER J was unable to find any general charitable intent. The particular purpose failed, and the gift fell into residue.

In **Re Packe** [1918] 1 Ch 437, the testatrix gave to the Poor Clergy Relief Corporation a cottage and £1,000 upon trust to provide "a holiday home or house of rest for clergymen of the Church of England and their wives"; and provided that if the Corporation should refuse the gift, then the property was to be given to any other society selected by her executors "as a holiday home or house of rest for ladies or gentlemen of limited means". The Corporation renounced the gift, and it was not possible to find any other society willing to carry out the wishes of the testatrix. NEVILLE J held that the gift failed.

In **Re Good's Will Trusts** [1950] 2 All ER 653, the testator provided funds for the purpose of purchasing land, erecting thereon "six or more rest homes

---

4 *Re Crowe* (1979) Annual Report for 1979 paras. 40–45, where SLADE J found no general charitable intention in the case of a trust for a scholarship at the Royal Naval School in the Spanish and Russian languages. "The court could not construct a general charitable intention from mere guess work."

each home consisting of a livingroom, sleeping apartment and usual outside domestic conveniences, all to be on the ground floor and all on one level", and money for paying for the upkeep of the homes. The money was insufficient for the purpose. WYNN-PARRY J held that the language was so particular as to exclude the possibility of finding a general charitable intention. The gift failed.

BISCOE v JACKSON
(1887) 35 ChD 460 (CA, COTTON, LINDSEY and FRY LJJ)

A testator provided that his trustees should set aside, out of such of his personal estate as might by law be bequeathed for charitable purposes, a sum of £10,000, of which £4,000 was to be applied "in the establishment of a soup kitchen for the parish of *Shoreditch*, and of a cottage hospital adjoining thereto ... " and the provision of various related services. It was impossible to obtain the land necessary to carry out the provisions of the will. The next of kin claimed the fund.

Held. The will showed a general charitable intention. A scheme for the application of the funds *cy-près* was directed.

COTTON LJ: This is an appeal from an order made in November by Mr. Justice *Kay*, which directed a reference to settle a scheme to apply a sum of £10,000. For the purpose of this appeal we must assume that the bequest contained in the will could not be carried into effect in accordance with the particular directions contained in the will as was found by the certificate. That certificate was excepted to, and Mr. Justice *Kay* disallowed the exception. For the present purpose the Attorney-General does not press his appeal against the decision of Mr. Justice *Kay*. The real question, therefore, is whether or not the Court can, in a legacy like this, apply the doctrine of *cy-près?* It is clear that when there is a legacy given to a particular legatee, and that legatee fails before the death of the testator—there being only the gift to the particular legatee, even though that legatee is an institution—the legacy fails. But the question which we have now to consider is this, is this to be considered as a legacy to a particular institution which cannot be carried into effect, or do we see here an expressed intention by the testator to benefit the poor of the parish of *Shoreditch*, pointing out a particular mode in which he desires that benefit to be effected? For if the latter be the true view, then if that particular mode cannot have effect given to it, the Court will take hold of the charitable intention to benefit the poor of the parish and will apply the legacy in the best way *cy-près* for their benefit.

Now, in my opinion, notwithstanding the argument which has been addressed to us, I think there is that general intention. It is very true that the testator leaves certain things to be done by the trustees to whom he is giving the sum of £10,000, and if that is to be considered as a gift to an existing institution, or as a gift for that purpose only, it has failed. But then, in my opinion, looking at this whole clause, we see an intention on the part of the testator to give £10,000 to the sick and poor of the parish of *Shoreditch*, pointing out how he desires that to be applied; and that particular mode having failed, as we must for the purposes of this appeal assume to be the case, then the intention to benefit the poor of *Shoreditch*, being a good charitable object, will have effect given to it according to the general principle laid down long ago by this Court, by applying it *cy-près*. If the will had said that the trustees must build the particular building within the parish of *Shoreditch* there might be some difficulty, but what the testator desires to do is to provide a particular kind of hospital and a soup kitchen for the poor of the parish of *Shoreditch*. To my mind that shows that he intends not that it is to be located in a particular place, though that would be a proper mode of giving effect to the particular directions contained, if a place in the parish could be found; but that it is for the benefit of the parish, that is of the poor in the parish of *Shoreditch*. The testator directs that this shall be done by providing them with soup in this kitchen, by providing them with relief in a cottage hospital, and then by a direction that there is to be a woman living in the hospital to look after the inmates in the hospital, and that a sum of money is to be paid to a medical man to attend to them; and then he directs his trustees "to apply the residue of such annual income towards the necessities and for the benefit thereof, and of the patients who shall from time to time be taken into such hospital in such manner in all respects as my trustees or trustee in their or his absolute discretion think fit". Of course we have to determine what is the effect, looking fairly at the words used by the testator, to see what his intention was. To my mind the clear result is that he intended here to provide for the benefit of the poor, which is a good charitable bequest, and to provide for that primarily in the particular way he points out. If that fails then the doctrine applies, and Mr. Justice *Kay* was right in directing a reference to ascertain what was the best means for giving effect to his intentions, having regard to what the testator has said in the will as to the particular mode in which he desires his intentions should have effect given to them. In my opinion this appeal must fail; and that being our decision the other appeal is of course abandoned by the Attorney-General.

B. Defunct or Non-Existent Charity

In **Re Harwood** [1936] Ch 285, a testatrix, by a will made in 1925, left inter alia £200 to the Wisbech Peace Society, Cambridge, and £300 to the Peace Society of Belfast. She died in 1934. The Wisbech Peace Society had existed before 1934 but had ceased to exist by that date; there was no evidence that the Peace Society of Belfast had ever existed. FARWELL J held the second legacy was applicable *cy-près*, but not the first legacy. He said at 286:
   "The first question that I have to determine is whether a gift of 200*l.* 'to the Wisbech Peace Society, Cambridge' fails. The evidence is that this particular society ceased to exist in the testatrix's lifetime. It is said that it is being still carried on as part of the work of the Peace Committee of the Society of Friends. The onus is upon them to show that they are the persons entitled to take. The evidence in this case is so unsatisfactory that I cannot say that that onus has been discharged.
   That leaves the question whether there is any general charitable intent, so as to admit of the application of the cy-près doctrine. In that will there is a long list of various charitable societies including charities whose work is devoted to peace. It is said that as this is one of a long list of charitable legacies there is a general charitable intent. On the other hand, it is said that where there is a gift to a particular society, which once existed but ceased to exist before the death of the testator or testatrix, the gift lapses and there is no room for the cy-près doctrine. I have been referred to *Re Davis* [1902] 1 Ch 876. In that case the learned judge was able to come to the conclusion that as to one particular gift there was a general charitable intent; but in that case no such society as that

named in the will had ever existed. It was not a case of a society which had been in existence and had ceased to exist. I do not propose to decide that it can never be possible for the Court to hold that there is a general charitable intent in a case where the charity named in the will once existed but ceased to exist before the death. Without deciding that, it is enough for me to say that, where the testator selects as the object of his bounty a particular charity and shows in the will itself some care to identify the particular society which he desires to benefit, the difficulty of finding any general charitable intent in such case if the named society once existed, but ceased to exist before the death of the testator, is very great. Here the testatrix has gone out of her way to identify the object of her bounty. In this particular case she has identified it as being 'the Wisbech Peace Society Cambridge (which is a branch of the London Peace Society)'. Under those circumstances, I do not think it is open to me to hold that there is in this case any such general charitable intent as to allow the application of the cy-près doctrine.

Accordingly, in my judgment, the legacy of 200*l.* fails and is undisposed of.

Then there is the gift to the 'Peace Society of Belfast'.

The claimant for this legacy is the Belfast Branch of the League of Nations Union. I am quite unable on the evidence to say that that was the society which this lady intended to benefit, and I doubt whether the lady herself knew exactly what society she did mean to benefit. I think she had a desire to benefit any society which was formed for the purpose of promoting peace and was connected with Belfast. Beyond that, I do not think that she had any very clear idea in her mind. That is rather indicated by the pencil note which was found after her death. At any rate I cannot say that by the description, 'the Peace Society of Belfast,' the lady meant the Belfast Branch of the League of Nations Union; but there is enough in this case to enable me to say that, although there is no gift to any existing society, the gift does not fail. It is a good charitable gift and must be applied cy-près. The evidence suggests that at some time or other, possibly before the late War, there may have been a society called the Peace Society of Belfast. It is all hearsay evidence; there is nothing in the least definite about it, and it does not satisfy me that there ever was any society in existence which exactly fits the description in this case, and there being a clear intention on the part of the lady, as expressed in her will, to benefit societies whose object was the promotion of peace, and there being no such society as that named in her will, in this case there is a general charitable intent, and, accordingly, the doctrine of cy-près applies.''

In **Re Spence** [1979] Ch 483, [1978] 3 All ER 92, a testatrix, who made her will in 1968 and died in 1972, left one moiety of her residue to "the Old Folks Home at Hillworth Lodge Keighley for the benefit of the patients". Hillworth Lodge, originally built as a workhouse, had from 1948 to 1971 been an aged persons' home under the National Assistance Act 1948. It was closed down in 1971 and had since then been used as government offices. The question arose whether the gift was a valid charitable gift. MEGARRY V-C held that the gifts failed, and said at 492, at 98:

"[*Re Harwood* [1936] Ch 285 and cases which apply it, such as *Re Stemson's Will Trusts* [1970] Ch 16, [1969] 2 All ER 517] have been concerned with gifts to institutions, rather than gifts for purposes. The case before me, on the other hand, is a gift for a purpose, namely, the benefit of the patients at a particular

Old Folks Home. It therefore seems to me that I ought to consider the question, of which little or nothing was said in argument, whether the principle in *Re Harwood*, or a parallel principle, has any application to such case. In other words, is a similar distinction to be made between, on the one hand, a case in which the testator has selected a particular charitable purpose, taking some care to identify it, and before the testator dies that purpose has become impracticable or impossible of accomplishment, and on the other hand a case where the charitable purpose has never been possible or practicable?

As at present advised I would answer Yes to that question. I do not think that the reasoning of the *Re Harwood* line of cases is directed to any feature of institutions as distinct from purposes. Instead, I think the essence of the distinction is in the difference between particularity and generality. If a particular institution or purpose is specified, then it is that institution or purpose, and no other, that is to be the object of the benefaction. It is difficult to envisage a testator as being suffused with a general glow of broad charity when he is labouring, and labouring successfully, to identify some particular specified institution or purpose as the object of his bounty. The specific displaces the general. It is otherwise where the testator has been unable to specify any particular charitable institution or practicable purpose, and so, although his intention of charity can be seen, he has failed to provide any way of giving effect to it. There, the absence of the specific leaves the general undisturbed. It follows that in my view in the case before me, where the testatrix has clearly specified a particular charitable purpose which before her death became impossible to carry out, Mr. Mummery has to face that level of great difficulty in demonstrating the existence of a general charitable intention which was indicated by *Re Harwood*. . . .

From what I have said it follows that I have been quite unable to extract from the will, construed in its context, any expression of a general charitable intention which would suffice for the moiety to be applied cy-près. Instead, in my judgment, the moiety was given for a specific charitable purpose which, though possible when the will was made, became impossible before the testatrix died. The gift of the moiety accordingly fails, and it passes as on intestacy."[5]

C. Continuation of Charity in Another Form

Although a particular charity no longer exists in its original form, the court may find that it continues elsewhere.

RE FARAKER[6]
[1912] 2 Ch 488 (CA, COZENS-HARDY MR, FARWELL and KENNEDY LJJ)

Mrs. Faraker, the testatrix, who died in 1911, bequeathed a legacy of £200 to "Mrs Bailey's Charity, Rotherhithe".

---

5 See also pp. 478, 479, post; *Re Finger's Will Trusts* [1972] Ch 286 at 299, [1971] 3 All ER 1050 at 1060, p. 475, post.
6 *Re Lucas* [1948] Ch 424, [1948] 2 All ER 22; cf. *Re Stemson's Will Trusts* [1970] Ch 16, [1969] 2 All ER 517; *Re Slatter's Will Trusts* [1964] Ch 512, [1964] 2 All ER 469; (1964) 28 Conv (NS) 313 (J.T. Farrand).

A charity, known as Hannah Bayly's Charity, had been founded in 1756 by a Mrs. Hannah Bayly for the benefit of poor widows who were resident in and parishioners of Rotherhithe.

A scheme had been made in 1905 by the Charity Commissioners which had consolidated this and a number of charities in Rotherhithe. The funds were to be held upon various trusts for the benefit of the poor of Rotherhithe, no mention being made of widows.

No question was raised as to the spelling of the name Bayly, and it was admitted that the testatrix referred to Hannah Bayly's Charity.

The question was whether the legacy lapsed.

Held (reversing NEVILLE J) . The consolidated charities were entitled to the legacy.

FARWELL LJ: . . . Neville J has held that Hannah Bayly's Charity is no longer in existence. If that be so, I ask myself, How did it come to an end? and the answer suggested is, By the scheme of the Charity Commissioners. The jurisdiction given to the Charity Commissioners is given by the Act of 1860, and they have amongst other authorities the same power that the Court of Chancery had and the Chancery Division has for establishing schemes for the administration of any charity. That administration may, under proper circumstances, be cy-près, but the jurisdiction is for the establishment, encouragement, and continuance of a charity—even going beyond the actual words of the will, if there be an impossibility of carrying out literally the trusts—and a jurisdiction to administer cy-près. In the present case there is no question of a cy-près execution. Nobody suggests that there has been a failure of poor widows in Rotherhithe, and unless and until that happy event happens there will be no case for any cy-près administration. What is said is this: the Commissioners have in fact destroyed this trust because in the scheme which they have issued dealing with the amalgamation of the several charities the objects are stated to be poor persons of good character resident in Rotherhithe, not mentioning widows in particular— not of course excluding them, but not giving them that preference which I agree with the Master of the Rolls in thinking ought to have been given. But to say that this omission has incidentally destroyed the Bayly Trust is a very strained construction of the language and one that entirely fails, because the Charity Commissioners had no jurisdiction whatever to destroy the charity. Suppose the Charity Commissioners or this Court were to declare that a particular existing charitable trust was at an end and extinct, in my opinion they would go beyond their jurisdiction in so doing. They cannot take an existing charity and destroy it; they are obliged to administer it. To say that this pardonable slip (I use the word with all respect to the draftsman) has the effect of destroying the charity appears to me extravagant. In all these cases one has to consider not so much the means to the end as the charitable end which is in view, and so long as that charitable end is well established the means are only machinery, and no alteration of the machinery can destroy the charitable trust for the benefit of which the machinery is provided.

In my opinion it is quite impossible to say here that the widows are excluded, or even if they were in terms excluded, that that would destroy the trust: it could only give grounds for an application to set right that which in any event could only be put in per incuriam. I agree that the appeal must be allowed.

D. Unincorporated and Incorporated Charities[7]

In **Re Finger's Will Trusts** [1972] Ch 286, [1971] 3 All ER 1050,[8] a testatrix left shares of her residuary estate to eleven named charities, of which two were the National Radium Commission, an unincorporated charity, and the other to the National Council for Maternity and Child Welfare, an incorporated charity. Both charities had ceased to exist between the date of the will and the date of death.

GOFF J held that (i) the first gift was valid as a purpose trust and ordered a scheme for its administration;

(ii) the second gift failed, but, since there was a general charitable intention, it was applicable cy-près. He said at 294, at 1056:

"Both gifts therefore fail unless they can be supported as purpose gifts, in which case they will be applicable by way of scheme for the indicated purpose, and if either or both cannot so stand there remains a final question, whether the will discloses a general charitable intention, in which case of course the share or shares will be applicable by scheme cy-près, failing which there is an intestacy.

If the matter were res integra I would have thought that there would be much to be said for the view that the status of the donee, whether corporate or unincorporate, can make no difference to the question whether as a matter of construction a gift is absolute or on trust for purposes. Certainly drawing such a distinction produces anomalous results.

In my judgment, however, on the authorities a distinction between the two is well established, at all events in this court. I refer first to *Re Vernon's Will Trusts* [1972] Ch 300n, [1971] 3 All ER 1061n where Buckley J said at 303C–G, at 1064:

'Every bequest to an unincorporated charity by name without more must take effect as a gift for a charitable purpose. No individual or aggregate of individuals could claim to take such a bequest beneficially. If the gift is to be permitted to take effect at all, it must be as a bequest for a purpose, viz., that charitable purpose which the named charity exists to serve. A bequest which is in terms made for a charitable purpose will not fail for lack of a trustee but will be carried into effect either under the Sign Manual or by means of a scheme. A bequest to a named unincorporated charity, however, may on its true interpretation show that the testator's intention to make the gift at all was dependent upon the named charitable organisation being available at the time when the gift takes effect to serve as the instrument for applying the subject matter of the gift to the charitable purpose for which it is by inference given. If so and the named charity ceases to exist in the lifetime of the testator, the gift fails: *Re Ovey* (1885) 29 ChD 560. A bequest to a corporate body, on the other hand, takes effect simply as a gift to that body beneficially, unless there are circumstances which show that the recipient is to take the gift as a trustee. There is no need in such a case to infer a trust for any particular purpose. The objects to which the corporate body can properly apply its funds may

---

7 For the difference between an unincorporated and an incorporated association, see p. 91, ante.

8 (1972) 36 Conv (NS) 198 (R.B.M. Cotterrell); (1974) 38 Con (NS) 187 (J. Martin); *Re Edis's Declaration of Trust* [1972] 1 WLR 1135, [1972] 2 All ER 769; *Re Koeppler Will Trusts* [1986] Ch 423, [1985] 2 All ER 869, pp. 372, 445, ante. See also *Liverpool and District Hospital for Diseases of the Heart v A-G* [1981] Ch 193, [1981] 1 All ER 994; [1984] Conv 112 (J. Warburton).

be restricted by its constitution, but this does not necessitate inferring as a matter of construction of the testator's will a direction that the bequest is to be held in trust to be applied for those purposes: the natural construction is that the bequest is made to the corporate body as part of its general funds, that is to say, beneficially and without the imposition of any trust. That the testator's motive in making the bequest may have undoubtedly been to assist the work of the incorporated body would be insufficient to create a trust.'

As I read the dictum in *Re Vernon's Will Trusts*, the view of Buckley J was that in the case of an unincorporated body the gift is per se a purpose trust, and provided that the work is still being carried on will have effect given to it by way of scheme notwithstanding the disappearance of the donee in the lifetime of the testator, unless there is something positive to show that the continued existence of the donee was essential to the gift. Then Buckley J put his dictum into practice and decided *Re Morrison* (1967) 111 SJ 758 on that very basis, for there was nothing in that case beyond the bare fact of a gift to a dissolved unincorporated committee. In the case of a corporation, however, *Re Vernon* shows that the position is different as there has to be something positive in the will to create a purpose trust at all.

[His Lordship referred to *Re Meyers* [1951] Ch 534, [1951] 1 All ER 538, *Re Roberts* [1963] 1 WLR 406, [1963] 1 All ER 674, and *Re Morrison* (1967) 111 SJ 758, and continued:]

Accordingly I hold that the bequest to the National Radium Commission being a gift to an unincorporated charity is a purpose trust for the work of the commission which does not fail but is applicable under a scheme, provided (1) there is nothing in the context of the will to show—and I quote from *Re Vernon's Will Trusts*—that the testatrix's intention to make a gift at all was dependent upon the named charitable organisation being available at the time when the gift took effect to serve as the instrument for applying the subject matter of the gift to the charitable purpose for which it was by inference given; (2) *that* charitable purpose still survives; but that the gift to the National Council for Maternity and Child Welfare 117 Piccadilly London being a gift to a corporate body fails, notwithstanding the work continues, unless there is a context in the will to show that the gift was intended to be on trust for that purpose and not an absolute gift to the corporation.

I take first the National Radium Commission and I find in this will no context whatever to make that body of the essence of the gift....

In my judgment, therefore, this is a valid gift for the purposes of the Radium Commission as specified in article 7 of the supplemental charter of July 20, 1939, and I direct that a scheme be settled for the administration of the gift.

I turn to the other gift and here I can find no context from which to imply a purpose trust. Counsel for the Attorney-General relied on *Re Meyers* [1951] Ch 534, [1951] 1 All ER 538, but there the context was absolutely compelling. There were many gifts to hospitals and the case dealt only with the hospitals, and whilst hospitals are not identical, this did mean that all were of the same type and character. Moreover, not only were those gifts both to incorporated and unincorporated hospitals but in some of the corporate cases the name used by the testator was that by which the hospital was generally known to the public but was not the exact title of the corporation. In the present case there are at best three different groups of charities not one; they are not in fact grouped in the order in which they appear in the will, and the particular donees within the respective groups are not all of the same type or character.

Further, and worse, two do not fit into any grouping at all, and for what it is worth they come first in the list. In my judgment, therefore, this case is not comparable with *Re Meyers* and I cannot find a context unless I am prepared—which I am not—to say that the mere fact that residue is given to a number of charities, some of which are incorporated and others not, is of itself a sufficient context to fasten a purpose trust on the corporation.

In my judgment, therefore, the bequest to the National Council for Maternity and Child Welfare fails.

Finally, I must consider, however, whether the share passes on intestacy or whether the will discloses a general charitable intention. Here, of course, I was at once presented with *Re Harwood* [1936] Ch 285, p. 471, ante, and I feel the force of the argument on behalf of the next of kin based on that case, although I confess I have always felt the decision in that case to be rather remarkable. However, Farwell J did not say that it was impossible to find a general charitable intention where there is a gift to an identifiable body which has ceased to exist but only that it would be very difficult. Moreover, I observe that in *Re Roberts* [1963] 1 WLR 406, 416, [1963] 1 All ER 674, 681, Wilberforce J said this about *Re Harwood*:

'Lastly, there is *Re Harwood* a decision of Farwell J, where there was a gift to a very particular society for a very special purpose, the Wisbech Peace Society, where it was not difficult to come to the conclusion that that society having disappeared, the gift lapsed. Though of course I accept—and gladly accept—what Farwell J said, that where the gift is to a particular charity carefully identified it would be very difficult for the court to find a general charitable intent if the named society had ceased to exist at the testator's death, one must consider that in relation to the circumstance of the charity and the information which can be found whether in fact the particular charity has ceased to exist.'

In the present case the circumstances are very special. First, of course, apart from the life interest given to the mother and two small personal legacies, the whole estate is devoted to charity and that is, I think, somewhat emphasised by the specific dedication to charity in the preface:

'And after payment of the said legacies my trustees shall hold the balance then remaining of my residuary estate upon trust to divide the same in equal shares between the following charitable institutions and funds.'

Again, I am I think entitled to take into account the nature of the council, which as I have said was mainly, if not exclusively, a co-ordinating body. I cannot believe that this testatrix meant to benefit that organisation and that alone.

Finally, I am entitled to place myself in the armchair of the testatrix and I have evidence that she regarded herself as having no relatives.

Taking all these matters into account, in my judgment I can and ought to distinguish *Re Harwood* and find—as I do—a general charitable intention. Accordingly, this share is applicable cy-près, and I understand the Attorney-General is willing that it should be paid to the association. That seems to me manifestly the proper thing to do, and therefore I shall order by way of scheme, the Attorney-General not objecting, that this share be paid to the proper officer of the association to be held on trust to apply the same for its general purposes.''

In **Re Spence** [1979] Ch 483, [1978] 3 All ER 92, p. 472, ante, MEGARRY V-C, in holding that there was no general charitable intent, distinguished *Re Finger's Will Trusts*. He referred to the three "very special circumstances" mentioned by GOFF J in respect of the gift to the incorporated charity, and said at 493, at 99:

"In the case before me neither of these last two circumstances applies, nor have any substitute special circumstances been suggested. As for the first, the will before me gives 17 pecuniary legacies to relations and friends, amounting in all to well over one third of the net estate. Further, in *Re Rymer* [1895] 1 Ch 19, which does not appear to have been cited, the will had prefaced the disputed gift by the words 'I give the following charitable legacies to the following institutions and persons respectively.' These words correspond to the direction which in *Re Finger's Will Trusts* was regarded as providing emphasis, and yet they did not suffice to avoid the conclusion of Chitty J and the Court of Appeal that a gift to an institution which had ceased to exist before the testator's death lapsed and could not be applied cy-près. I am not sure that I have been able to appreciate to the full the cogency of the special circumstances that appealed to Goff J; but however that may be, I can see neither those nor any other special circumstances in the present case which would suffice to distinguish *Re Harwood*."

E. Charity by Association

In **Re Jenkins's Will Trusts** [1966] Ch 249, [1966] 1 All ER 926, the testatrix bequeathed her residuary estate to be divided into seven equal parts, one of which was to be held in trust for six charitable institutions and the seventh in trust for "the British Union for the Abolition of Vivisection to do all in its power to urge and get an Act passed prohibiting unnecessary cruelty to animals." The question was whether the seventh share should be held upon charitable trusts on the ground that the will disclosed a general charitable intention. BUCKLEY J held that the gift of the seventh share failed. He said at 256, at 929:

"The principle of noscitur a sociis does not in my judgment entitle one to overlook self-evident facts. If you meet seven men with black hair and one with red hair you are not entitled to say that here are eight men with black hair. Finding one gift for a non-charitable purpose among a number of gifts for charitable purposes the court cannot infer that the testator or testatrix meant the non-charitable gift to take effect as a charitable gift when in the terms it is not charitable, even though the non-charitable gift may have a close relation to the purposes for which the charitable gifts are made."

In **Re Satterthwaite's Will Trusts**[9] [1966] 1 WLR 277, [1966] 1 All ER 919, the testatrix announced to an official of the Bond Street branch of the Midland Bank that she hated the whole human race and wished to leave her estate to animal charities. Nine were selected, apparently from the London telephone directory. Seven of them were animal charities, and the other two were an anti-vivisectionist society and the London Animal Hospital. It was not possible to identify an institution of that name which was in existence at the date of the will. The Court of Appeal (HARMAN, DIPLOCK and RUSSELL LJJ) held that the

---

9 Decided twelve days earlier than, but apparently not cited in, *Re Jenkins's Will Trusts*, supra.

share for the hospital was to be applied cy-près. RUSSELL LJ said at 286, at 925:

"What is the result in law of this? I have already indicated that [the testatrix] is to be taken as intending to benefit a charitable activity. But the organisation picked by name was not such. Prima facie, therefore, the bequest would fail and there would be a lapse, with the result in this case in fact—owing to the incidence of liabilities and death duties—of mere relief of other residuary objects. But my assumption is that the testatrix was pointing to a particular charitable application of this one-ninth of residue. If a particular mode of charitable application is incapable of being performed as such, but it can be discerned from his will that the testator has a charitable intention (commonly referred to as a general charitable intention) which transcends the particular mode of application indicated, the court has jurisdiction to direct application of the bequest to charitable purposes cy-près. Here I have no doubt from the nature of the other dispositions by this testatrix of her residuary estate that a general intention can be discerned in favour of charity through the medium of kindness to animals. I am not in any way deterred from this conclusion by the fact that one-ninth of residue was given to an anti-vivisection society which in law—unknown to the average testator—is not charitable."

In **Re Spence** [1979] Ch 483, [1978] 3 All ER 92, p. 472, ante, MEGARRY V-C held that the doctrine of charity by association was not applicable and said at 494, at 99:

"The other way in which Mr. Mummery sought to meet his difficulty was by relying on *Re Satterthwaite's Will Trusts* (which he said was his best case), and on *Re Knox* [1937] Ch 109, [1936] 3 All ER 623, which I think may possibly be better. The doctrine may for brevity be described as charity by association. If the will gives the residue among a number of charities with kindred objects, but one of the apparent charities does not in fact exist, the court will be ready to find a general charitable intention and so apply the share of the non-existent charity cy-près. I have not been referred to any explicit statement of the underlying principle, but it seems to me that in such cases the court treats the testator as having shown the general intention of giving his residue to promote charities with that type of kindred objects, and then, when he comes to dividing the residue, as casting around for particular charities with that type of objects to name as donees. If one or more of these are non-existent, then the general intention will suffice for a cy-près application. It will be observed that, as stated, the doctrine depends, at least to some extent, upon the detection of 'kindred objects' (a phrase which comes from the judgment of Luxmoore J in *Re Knox* at 113, at 626) in the charities to which the shares of residue are given; in this respect the charities must in some degree be ejusdem generis."

[His Lordship referred to *Re Satterthwaite's Will Trusts*, *Re Knox*, and *Re Hartley* (1978) unreported, and continued:]

"It will be observed that these are all cases of gifts to bodies which did not exist. In such cases, the court is ready to find a general charitable intention: see *Re Davis* [1902] 1 Ch 876, especially at 884. The court is far less ready to find such an intention where the gift is to a body which existed at the date of the will but ceased to exist before the testator died, or, as I have already held, where the gift is for a purpose which, though possible and practicable at the date of the will, has ceased to be so before the testator's death. The case before me is, of course, a case in this latter category, so that Mr. Mummery has to overcome this greater difficulty in finding a general charitable intention.

Not only does Mr. Mummery have this greater difficulty: he also has, I think, less material with which to meet it. He has to extract the general charitable intention for the gift which fails from only one other gift: the residue, of course, was simply divided into two. In *Re Knox* and *Re Hartley* the gifts which failed were each among three other gifts, and in *Re Satterthwaite's Will Trusts* there were seven or eight other gifts. I do not say that a general charitable intention or a genus cannot be extracted from a gift of residue equally between two: but I do say that larger numbers are likely to assist in conveying to the court a sufficient conviction both of the genus and of the generality of the charitable intention.''

III. Subsequent Failure[10]

As has been seen, once money is absolutely and effectively dedicated to charity, the next of kin are for ever excluded. Thus, *cy-près* may apply even if a general charitable intention is lacking.

RE SLEVIN
[1891] 2 Ch 236 (CA, LINDLEY, BOWEN and KAY LJJ)

The testator by his will bequeathed "the pecuniary legacies following", one of which was a legacy of £200 to the Orphanage of St. Dominic's, Newcastle-on-Tyne. That Orphanage was in existence at the testator's death; but it came to an end soon afterwards, and before the legacy was paid.

Held (reversing STIRLING J). The money was applicable *cy-près*.

KAY LJ: The orphanage did come to an end before the legacy was paid over. In the case of a legacy to an individual, if he survived the testator it could not be argued that the legacy would fall into the residue. Even if the legatee died intestate and without next of kin, still the money was his, and the residuary legatee would have no right whatever against the Crown. So, if the legatee were a corporation which was dissolved after the testator's death, the residuary legatee would have no claim.

Obviously it can make no difference that the legatee ceased to exist immediately after the death of the testator. The same law must be applicable whether it was a day, or month, or year, or, as might well happen, ten years after; the legacy not having been paid either from delay occasioned by the administration of the estate or owing to part of the estate not having been got in. The legacy became the property of the legatee upon the death of the testator, though he might not, for some reason, obtain the receipt of it till long after. When once it became the absolute property of the legatee, that is equivalent to saying that it must be provided for; and the residue is only what remains after making such provision. It does not for all purposes cease to be part of the testator's estate until the executors admit assets and appropriate and pay it over; but that is merely for their convenience and that of the estate. The rights as between the particular legatee and the residue are fixed at the testator's death.

10 See generally [1983] Conv 107 (P. Luxton).

These positions are so obvious that it would seem impossible to dispute some authority to the contrary. Is there any such authority? [Having found no such authority, his Lordship continued:] In the present case we think that the Attorney-General must succeed, not on the ground that there is such a general charitable intention that the fund should be administered *cy-près* even if the charity had failed in the testator's lifetime, but because, as the charity existed at the testator's death, this legacy became the property of that charity, and on its ceasing to exist its property falls to be administered by the Crown, who will apply it, according to custom, for some analogous purpose of charity: *A-G v Ironmongers' Co* (1834) 2 My & K 576; *Wilson v Barnes* (1886) 38 Ch D 507; *Tyssen* on Charitable Bequests (at p. 440).

In **Re Wright**[11] [1954] Ch 347, [1954] 2 All ER 98, the testatrix, who died in 1933, provided that her residuary estate, subject to a life interest, should be held on trust to provide and maintain a convalescent home. This would have been practicable in 1933. But, on the death of the life tenant in 1942, the balance of probabilities was against it. The question was whether the test of practicability should be applied at the date of the testatrix's death or at the date when the funds became available. The Court of Appeal (DENNING and ROMER LJJ), following *Re Slevin* [1891] 2 Ch 236, held that the material date was that of the death of the testatrix. ROMER LJ said at 359, at 102:

"Mr. Dillon's argument, on behalf of the testatrix's next-of-kin, was to the effect that the gift in the will was for a special charitable purpose: namely, for the establishment and maintenance of the convalescent home which the testatrix had in mind and which she described with such particularity; and that the gift was dependent and conditional upon it being practicable to carry the purpose, as so described, into effect when the death of the life tenant, Mrs. Webb, made the fund available for the home. It is not so much a question of lapse, he said, as a condition of practicability being attached to the gift, so that if the condition could not be satisfied the bequest would fail. Mr. Buckley, on the other hand, contended that no such condition or contingency as suggested attached to the bequest. He argued that in the case of any charitable gift by will, whether immediate or future, no question of impracticability supervening after the testator's death is of any materiality, provided that the object or purpose to which the gift is to be applied is practicable when the testator died. That is the time, he argued, when the rights of the parties, charity on the one hand and the next-of-kin or other persons taking in default on the other, are to be ascertained and they are to be ascertained at that time once and for all.

In the present case Roxburgh J followed, on the point now under consideration, his earlier decision in *Re Moon* [1948] 1 All ER 300. In that case a testator directed that after the death of his wife his trustees should pay a legacy of '£3,000 to the Trustees of the Gloucester Street Wesleyan Methodist Church at Devonport on trust to invest the same in some Government security and to apply the income thereof to mission work in the district served by the said Gloucester Street Wesleyan Methodist Church including particularly John Street and Moon Street'. When the testator's widow died, it had become impracticable to carry out the mission work which the testator envisaged.

---

11 *Re Tacon* [1958] Ch 447, [1958] 1 All ER 163; *Harris v Sharp* (1987) unreported; [1988] Conv 288 (D. Partington).

Roxburgh J held that the gift was charitable and held further that, although the legacy was a future legacy, the question whether or not the charitable purpose lapsed for impracticability had to be ascertained at the moment when the charity trustees became absolutely entitled to the legacy, that was, at the moment of the testator's death and not at the moment when it became payable. The judge was guided to this conclusion by the reasoning of the judgment of this court in *Re Slevin* [1891] 2 Ch 236, which was delivered by Kay LJ. The testator in that case bequeathed, amongst other 'charitable legacies', a legacy to an orphanage which was in existence at the time of the testator's death but which was discontinued before his assets had been administered and therefore before the legacy was or properly could be paid. The question was whether, in those circumstances, the legacy failed and fell into residue. In the course of the argument Kay LJ rhetorically asked at 237; . . . 'where the charity, the legatee, is in existence at the death of the testator, and has received, or might have received the legacy, does not the legacy by that very fact become impressed with charity which the residuary legatee cannot get rid of?' The judgment of the court gave an affirmative answer to that question."

In **Re King** [1923] 1 Ch 243, a testatrix left residue for the purpose of providing a stained glass window in the church of Irminster to the memory of herself and her relatives. The net residue was £1,094 14s. 4d. and the estimate for the window was between £750 and £800. ROMER J held that the whole residue had been dedicated to charity and directed that the surplus be applied *cy-près*. He said at 246:

"In cases of a gift to a charitable institution, where such institution ceases to exist before the death of the testator the cy-près doctrine does not apply unless a general charitable intention can be found, and it is contended by the next of kin that there is not any difference between such a case and the present case, where the sum is left over after a particular intention has been fulfilled, there being no general charitable intention shown. But in the case of a legacy to a charitable institution that exists at the death of the testator, but ceases to exist after his death and before the legacy is paid over, the legacy is applied cy-près, even in the absence of a general charitable intention: see *Re Slevin* [1891] 2 Ch 236. In Tyssen's Charitable Bequests, 2nd edn p. 202, I find the following statement: 'where a gift is made for a particular charitable purpose which is sufficiently provided for without the gift, the gift will be applied cy-près,' and various authorities are cited in support of this principle. Such authorities and the other authorities cited to me show that the contention of the Attorney-General is well founded, and I therefore hold that the contention on behalf of the next of kin fails, and that the surplus must be applied cy-près. The Attorney-General consenting, this surplus will be applied in the erection of a further stained-glass window or windows in the same church."

IV. Impossibility and Impracticability

A. Before Charities Act 1960

Even if there was a paramount charitable intent or if a charitable trust had once operated, the *cy-près* doctrine could only be applied if the object of the trust became impossible or impracticable in whole or in part. If it became impossible or impracticable to apply the whole of the fund for the charitable purpose, the surplus might be applied *cy-près*. *Cy-près* application was not available where the fund could be more usefully or conveniently applied for other purposes, nor where the objects were outmoded in the sense that they concerned purposes which were once of significance, but which are unrelated to present day conditions; or for purposes which are provided for from other sources. In order to move with the times, the test of impossibility or impracticability was given an increasingly wide construction.

In **Attorney-General v City of London** (1790) 3 Bro CC 171, there was a trust for "the advancement and propagation of the Christian religion among the Infidels in Virginia". Lord THURLOW LC said at 177: "The trusts to the corporation to convert infidels ceasing for want of objects (there being now no infidels) the charity must be applied *de novo.*"

In **Ironmongers' Co v Attorney-General** (1844) 10 Cl & Fin 908, Thomas Belton, by his will of 1723, left the residue of his estate to the Worshipful Company or Corporation of Ironmongers of the City of London upon trust to pay half the income "unto the redemption of British slaves in Turkey or Barbary". In 1833 "the altered circumstances of those countries left little or no demand for the bounty of the testator" and Lord BROUGHAM LC decreed that the fund be applied cy-près.[12]

In **Re Weir Hospital** [1910] 2 Ch 124, Benjamin Weir died in 1902, the owner of two freehold houses, No. 12 Devonshire Road, Balham and The Hawthorns, Streatham. The Hawthorns was subject to a restrictive covenant (which prevented its use as a hospital); but this expired in 1907. The testator devised the houses upon trust; to use No. 12 Devonshire Road as a hospital or convalescent home, to be called the Weir Hospital, and to use The Hawthorns for the same purpose after the expiration of the restrictive covenant, either independently or in conjunction with No. 12 Devonshire Road. The residuary estate was given for the maintenance of the hospital.

In 1907 expert opinion was agreed that The Hawthorns was not a suitable site for a hospital. The Charity Commissioners approved a scheme whereby The Hawthorns would be turned into a home for nurses, and the bulk of the fund applied in enlarging and maintaining the Bolingbroke Hospital, to be renamed the Weir and Bolingbroke Hospital. The Court of Appeal, reversing Eve J, held that the Commissioners had acted *ultra vires*. It was not impracticable to carry out the provisions of the will.

In **Re Robinson** [1923] 2 Ch 332, a testatrix bequeathed £1,500 towards the endowment of an evangelical church in Bournemouth, subject to various

---

12 See *Re Mavrogordato's Trust Deed*; Annual Report for 1979, paras. 52–55 (gift in 1910 to Leper Hospital in Chios, which closed in 1959 on eradication of leprosy in the area; cy-près order made).

conditions, one of which was that a black gown should always be worn (by the preacher) in the pulpit. On a showing that the observance of this condition was likely to alienate the congregation and to defeat the testatrix's main object, P. O. LAWRENCE J deleted the condition on the ground of impracticability.

In **Re Dominion Students' Hall Trust**[13] [1947] Ch 183, a company, limited by guarantee, was established for various charitable purposes, one of which was to promote community of citizenship, culture and tradition among all members of the British Commonwealth of Nations. It maintained a hostel for students in Bloomsbury. The benefit of the charity was restricted to Dominion students of European origin. The court was asked to approve an alteration of the memorandum of the company, deleting the words "of European origin". EVERSHED J, in approving the application, said at 185:

"The purpose of both the petition and the summons is that a restriction which has hitherto been characteristic of the charity, limiting its objects so as to exclude coloured students of the British Empire, should be removed and that the benefits of the charity should be open to all citizens from the Empire without what is commonly known as the 'colour bar.' Having regard to the interest of the Inns of Court in Imperial students, I have thought it right to be particularly careful to see that I have jurisdiction to authorise the scheme and to sanction the petition. The proposed removal of the 'colour bar' restriction has been put to a substantial number of the subscribers. Owing to the necessities of the case, it has not been possible to put it to all, but those to whom it has been put represent over 75 per cent. in value of the subscription and none dissents from what is now proposed.

It is plain that I have to bear in mind the general proposition contained in the head note of *Re Weir Hospital* [1910] 2 Ch 124, which is to the effect that funds given by a testator for a particular charitable purpose cannot be applied cy-près by the court unless it has been shown to be impossible to carry out the testator's intention. True, the present is not a case of a testator and the court is, perhaps, not quite so strictly limited as in the case of a will. It is true, also, that the word 'impossible' should be given a wide significance: see *Re Campden Charities* (1881) 18 ChD 310; *Re Robinson* [1923] 2 Ch 332. It is not necessary to go to the length of saying that the original scheme is absolutely impracticable. Were that so, it would not be possible to establish in the present case that the charity could not be carried on at all if it continued to be so limited as to exclude coloured members of the Empire.

I have, however, to consider the primary intention of the charity. At the time when it came into being, the objects of promoting community of citizenship, culture and tradition among all members of the British Commonwealth of Nations might best have been attained by confining the Hall to members of the Empire of European origin. But times have changed, particularly as a result of the war; and it is said that to retain the condition, so far from furthering the

---

13 "[The Race Relations Act 1976, s. 34 (1)] provides that any discrimination necessary to comply with the terms of the governing instrument of a charity established to confer benefits on persons of a particular racial group shall not be unlawful, but it specifically excludes from this exception any provision which restricts the benefits by reference to colour. Any provision of this latter kind is to operate so as to confer benefits on the class of person which results if the restriction as to colour is disregarded." Annual Report for 1976, para. 20. See [1981] Conv 131 (T.G. Watkins) for a detailed discussion of this section; Annual Report for 1987, para. 14.

charity's main object, might defeat it and would be liable to antagonise those students, both white and coloured, whose support and good-will it is the purpose of the charity to sustain. The case, therefore, can be said to fall within the broad description of impossibility illustrated by *Re Campden Charities* (1881) 18 ChD 310 and *Re Robinson* [1923] 2 Ch 332.''

In **Re Lysaght** [1966] Ch 191, [1965] 2 All ER 888,[14] the testatrix provided funds to found medical studentships within the gift of the Royal College of Surgeons of England. One of the qualifications, Clause 11, was that ''any such student shall be of the male sex and the son of a duly qualified British born medical man . . . and must be a British born subject and not of the Jewish or Roman Catholic faith''.

The Royal College of Surgeons declined to accept the gift since the exclusion of those of the Jewish or Roman Catholic faith was ''so invidious and so alien to the spirit of the College's work as to make the gift inoperable in its present form''. It was however willing to accept it with that paragraph deleted.

BUCKLEY J held that the testatrix's intention was that the gift was conditional upon the College accepting the office of trustee. Their refusal to act would defeat the paramount intention. A scheme should be ordered to provide for the payment of the money to the College to be held on the trusts declared by the will, but omitting the religious disqualification. He said at 202, at 893:

''A general charitable intention, then, may be said to be a paramount intention on the part of a donor to effect some charitable purpose which the court can find a method of putting into operation, notwithstanding that it is impracticable to give effect to some direction by the donor which is not an essential part of his true intention—not, that is to say, part of his paramount intention.

In contrast, a particular charitable intention exists where the donor means his charitable disposition to take effect if, but only if, it can be carried into effect in a particular specified way, for example, in connection with a particular school to be established at a particular place, *Re Wilson* [1913] 1 Ch 314, p. 469, *ante*, or by establishing a home in a particular house, *Re Packe* [1918] 1 Ch 437. The alternatives are neatly stated by Younger LJ in *Re Willis* [1921] 1 Ch 44 at 54:

'The problem which in this case we have to solve is to say by which of two different principles the construction of this gift has to be controlled. The first of these principles is that if a testator has manifested a general intention to give to charity, whether in general terms or to charities of a defined character or quality, the failure of the particular mode in which the charitable intention is to be effectuated shall not imperil the charitable gift. If the substantial intention is charitable the court will substitute some other mode of carrying it into effect. The other principle which I paraphrase from the judgment of Kay J in *Biscoe v Jackson* (1887) 35 Ch D 460 at 463, p. 470, *ante*, is this. If on the proper construction of the will the mode of application is such an essential part of the gift that you cannot distinguish any general purpose of charity but are obliged to say that the

14 *Re Woodhams* [1981] 1 WLR 493, [1981] 1 All ER 202 (restrictions limiting scholarships to absolute orphans from Dr. Barnardo's homes or the Church of England Children's Society homes deleted); *Re JW Laing Trust* [1984] Ch 143, [1984] 1 All ER 50, p. 492, *post* (obligation to distribute capital within ten years of death of settlor deleted).

prescribed mode of doing that charitable act is the only one the testator intended or at all contemplated, then, the court cannot, if that mode fails, apply the money cy-près."

When, therefore, the Attorney-General submits that the primary intention of the testatrix in the present case was to found a medical studentship and that the detailed directions contained in clause 11 are not essential to that intention, he is, I think, contending, notwithstanding his concession to the contrary, that the testatrix had a general charitable intention, that is to say, a paramount intention to which the court can give effect, notwithstanding that it may be impracticable or, as Mr. Clauson suggests, impolitic to give effect to that part of those detailed directions which require religious discrimination. I proceed, therefore, to consider how far (a) the selection of the college as the trustee of the endowment fund and (b) the provision for religious discrimination, are essential parts of the testatrix's intention . . . ''

B. Widening of Cy-près Jurisdiction. Charities Act 1993

The Nathan Committee[15] recommended the relaxation of the requirements of impracticability. Far-reaching reforms were introduced by section 13 of the Charities Act 1960, now section 13 of the Charities Act 1993.

CHARITIES ACT 1993

13. Occasions for applying property cy-près.[16]—(1) Subject to subsection (2) below, the circumstances in which the original purposes of a charitable gift can be altered to allow the property given or part of it to be applied cy-près shall be as follows:—

(a) where the original purposes, in whole or in part,—
  (i) have been as far as may be fulfilled; or
  (ii) cannot be carried out, or not according to the directions given and to the spirit of the gift;[17] or
(b) where the original purposes provided a use for part only of the property available by virtue of the gift;[18] or
(c) where the property available by virtue of the gift and other property applicable for similar purposes can be more effectively used in conjunction, and to that end can suitably, regard being had to the spirit of the gift, be made applicable to common purposes;[19] or
(d) where the original purposes were laid down by reference to an area which then was but has since ceased to be a unit for some other purpose, or by reference to a class of persons or to an area which has for

---

15 Report of the Committee on the Law and Practice relating to Charitable Trusts (1952 Cmd. 8710), para. 365.
16 See Annual Report for 1970, paras. 37-46; 1989, paras. 73–80, p. 566, post.
17 See *Re Robinson* [1923] 2 Ch 332, p. 483 ante; *Re Dominion Students' Hall Trust* [1947] Ch 183, p. 484, ante; *Re Lysaght* [1966] Ch 191, [1965] 2 All ER 888, p. 485, ante.
18 See *Re North Devon and West Somerset Relief Fund* [1953] 1 WLR 1260, [1953] 2 All ER 1032.
19 For the previous powers concerning amalgamation, see TA 1925, s. 57; *Re Harvey* [1941] 3 All ER 284.

any reason since ceased to be suitable, regard being had to the spirit of the gift, or to be practical in administering the gift;[20] or

(e) where the original purposes, in whole or in part, have, since they were laid down—

(i) been adequately provided for by other means; or

(ii) ceased, as being useless or harmful to the community or for other reasons, to be in law charitable;[1] or

(iii) ceased in any other way to provide a suitable and effective method of using the property available by virtue of the gift, regard being had to the spirit of the gift.[2]

(2) Subsection (1) above shall not affect the conditions which must be satisfied in order that property given for charitable purposes may be applied cy-près, except in so far as those conditions require a failure of the original purposes.

(3) References in the foregoing subsections to the original purposes of a gift shall be construed, where the application of the property given has been altered or regulated by a scheme or otherwise, as referring to the purposes for which the property is for the time being applicable.

(4) Without prejudice to the power to make schemes in circumstances falling within subsection (1) above, the court may by scheme made under the court's jurisdiction with respect to charities, in any case where the purposes for which the property is held are laid down by reference to any such area as is mentioned in the first column in Schedule 3[3] to this Act, provide for enlarging the area to any such area as is mentioned in the second column in the same entry in that Schedule.

(5) It is hereby declared that a trust for charitable purposes places a trustee under a duty, where the case permits and requires the property or some part of it to be applied cy-près, to secure its effective use for charity by taking steps to enable it to be so applied.[4]

Report of the Charity Commissioners for England and Wales for the year 1970, paras. 42–43.

''42. The relaxation of the rule relating to failure has enabled us over the last 10 years to assist many charities which wish to serve the local community in more modern and effective ways. As we have indicated above, this process had started 100 years before the Charities Act; but many of the schemes which our predecessors made during that time have in their turn grown out-of-date. The process of modifying the objects of charities, whether local or national, is an ever-continuing process. Thus the original terms of a charitable gift of the 18th century or earlier may have required the trustees to distribute to poor persons

---

20 *Peggs v Lamb* [1994] Ch 172, [1994] 2 All ER 15 (gift for benefit of freemen of ancient borough of Huntingdon, whose qualifying members had been substantially reduced to 15, and whose income had been increased to £13,700 each; scheme ordered to enlarge class to cover inhabitants of borough as a whole).

1 See *National Anti-Vivisection Society v IRC* [1948] AC 31, [1947] 2 All ER 217.

2 *Re JW Laing Trust* [1984] Ch 143, [1984] 1 All ER 50, p. 492, post; Annual Report for 1985, Appx B.

3 As amended by Local Government Act 1972, s. 210 (9) (*f*).

4 See *National Anti-Vivisection Society v IRC* [1984] AC 31, 74, [1947] 2 All ER 217, 238 per Lord SIMONDS.

loaves of bread, candles or particular kinds of clothing. Even by the end of the 19th century many such trusts had failed, but the schemes which we then made prescribed in narrow terms the amounts of income which could be given in direct grants, or the particular institutions (e.g. a hospital or a clothing club) to which subscriptions might be granted, or the particular purposes (e.g., the cost of an outfit on entering a trade or the provision of passage money to aid emigration) to which contributions might be made. The amount of money which might be granted by way of temporary relief in cases of unexpected loss or sudden destitution was always most carefully limited as our predecessors were concerned lest the indiscriminate distribution of gift by a charity might have the effect of pauperizing the beneficiaries. Only too often neither the terms of the original gift nor the terms of the subsequent scheme appear to us to be achieving the basic intention of the donor, which was usually to make a real contribution towards relieving distress. In such cases we substitute more general provisions allowing the trustees to use the charity's resources in ways which will relieve need in whatever form it may still be found to exist. It is therefore our practice to make the provisions of the scheme as wide as possible, but we also add an explanatory note, which is strictly not part of the scheme, to draw the trustees' attention to those ways which we know of at present in which the income may be usefully applied.

43. We have made good use of the power contained in section 13 (1) (*e*) (i) which makes it clear that a cy-près scheme can be made where the original purposes in whole or in part have, since they have been laid down, been adequately provided for by other means. For example, we have made schemes for a number of charities established for the repair of roads and bridges, substituting for those purposes other general purposes for the benefit of local inhabitants which could include, for instance, the promotion of the arts, the provision of seats or shelters, the preservation of old buildings, or the improvement of local amenities.''

Report of the Charity Commissioners for England and Wales for the year 1989, paras. 74–75.

''74. The application of the cy-près doctrine is a legal process involving the establishment of a scheme. The determination of the new purposes to be conferred is essentially a practical issue in which usefulness and practicality as well as proximity to the existing trusts must be taken into account. In determining the appropriate cy-près application, regard must first be had to the trusts of the charity. With these in mind the nearest practicable charitable purpose needs to be ascertained. Consideration must be given to whether that purpose is suitable and effective, bearing in mind the situation of the charity in the community and the needs of that community. If the view is taken that the nearest practical purpose is not suitable or effective, then other purposes may be selected. To choose a purpose which may be the nearest practicable purpose to the original purposes of the charity, but which is already adequately provided for, or which cannot provide a suitable and effective method of using the charity's property, would be to impose purposes which will have already failed within the circumstances laid down in section 13 of the Charities Act 1960. Thus, for example, the proceeds of sale of an almshouse or a school might not be appropriated solely for the relief of poverty or for educational purposes respectively if the area of benefit were already adequately provided with poor or educational charities. Similarly, there would be no point in extending the area of benefit of a charity if the adjoining areas to which it might be extended already had adequate provision in the terms of the charity's purposes. Instead, the purposes might be extended within the existing area of benefit. The physical location of the charity within its existing area of benefit might also be a factor in determining a practical cy-près application: adjoining areas might not be readily combined with the existing area of benefit.

75. In determining the new purposes, it is essential not to erect artificial barriers to a flexible use of the doctrine. Factors which are relevant but not overriding should not be rigidly applied as immutable legal rules or principles. In the course of consultation following the Woodfield Report the following areas were mentioned as giving rise to problems:

(i) The elevation of the Macnaghten classification into a rigid legal definition which creates four distinct and mutually exclusive types of charity.
The Macnaghten classification is not a definition and there is no rule of law which prohibits the charity whose purposes fall within one part of the classification from being schemed so that its new purposes include other areas of the classification. The extent to which a charity's purposes can be altered would depend upon the circumstances pertaining to the charity mentioned in the preceding paragraph. The degree of flexibility which can be applied in altering the purposes of a charity is all the greater when the existing purposes already include elements of more than one part of the classification, for instance trusts for the education of poor persons or a trust for the poor and for the public benefit. Whilst closed schools would normally, on cy-près principles, be schemed for educational purposes, there may be cases where the local nature of the trust is clearly present and the circumstances warrant consideration being given to widening the objects rather than altering the area of benefit.

(ii) The pursuit of ostensible legal points at the expense of practical consideration.
It is claimed that schemes proposing mutually beneficial amalgamations of charities have in the past been turned down because the purposes of the charities were not wholly coincidental. There is no legal rule which restricts amalgamations of charities to those whose purposes are identical. 'Similar' in section 13(1)(c) of the 1960 Act does not mean 'the same'. There is no reason why adjustments cannot be made to beneficiary classes and areas of benefit where the practical considerations are clearly in favour of it.

(iii) The automatic placing of greater weight on one part of a charity's objects than another.
Where the beneficiary class of the charity is defined by reference to a number of components, for instance poor women resident in the parish of X, care should be taken not to attach undue importance to one component as against the remainder. It may be that other factors in the charity's foundation or trust deed will indicate that one element is more important than another but in the absence of any such indication, rules should not be created which would inhibit flexibility.

(iv) The concept that a charity's objects can never be changed so as to exclude any part of its existing purposes.
As a matter of general practice this is a sound rule but if taken to excessive lengths it can effectively frustrate radical reorganisations of trusts where such

reorganisation would be appropriate. It is, for instance, sensible when making regulating schemes for schools to amalgamate the varied and various prize funds into a single fund so that the identity of the separate fund is lost. Such an amalgamation may be administratively and practically sound as the individual prize funds established many years ago may now be insufficient to provide the prizes intended. The process can be applied to other groupings of charities.

(v) The idea that certain elements of a trust are sacrosanct, for instance the age limit included in educational schemes, religious qualifications in essentially secular charities, sex qualifications particularly in relation to schools.
We take the view that no part of a charity's trust is unalterable.''

RE LEPTON'S CHARITY
[1972] Ch 276, [1971] 1 All ER 799 (Ch D, PENNYCUICK V-C)

By his will of November 26, 1715, Joseph Lepton devised land known as "Dickroyd" in Pudsey, Yorkshire, to trustees upon trust to pay £3 per annum "unto such Protestant dissenting minister whether he be Presbiterian or Independant as shall stately preach at the Protestant dissenting meeting place at Pudsey soe long as such minister shall preach there" and to distribute "the overplus of the profitts . . . unto such poor aged and necessitouse people legally settled within the town of Pudsey as shall subsist without the town allowance" at the discretion of the trustees. Lepton died in 1716 when the total income from the rents and profits was £5 per annum. The land was sold and the income in 1970 was £791 14s. 6d. There was one Protestant dissenting meeting place, the Pudsey Congregational Chapel.
   The question arose whether the court had jurisdiction to vary the will by scheme under Charities Act 1960, s. 13 so as to raise the annual payment to £100.
   Held. Scheme so ordered.
   PENNYCUICK V-C: The occasions for applying property cy-près are now set out in section 13 of the Charities Act 1960. It is clear that this section in part restates the principles applied under the existing law, but also extends those principles. The section should be read as a whole, but for the present purpose it will be sufficient to refer specifically only to a few sentences. Section 13 reads:
   "(1) Subject to subsection (2) below, the circumstances in which the original purposes of a charitable gift can be altered to allow the property given or part of it to be applied cy-près shall be as follows:—(*a*) where the original purposes, in whole or in part,— . . . (ii) cannot be carried out, or not according to the directions given and to the spirit of the gift; . . . (*e*) where the original purposes, in whole or in part, have, since they were laid down,— . . . (iii) ceased in any other way to provide a suitable and effective method of using the property available by virtue of the gift, regard being had to the spirit of the gift. (2) Subsection (1) above shall not affect the conditions which must be satisfied in order that property given for charitable purposes may be applied cy-près, except in so far as those conditions require a failure of the original purposes.''
   Subsection (1) (*e*) (iii) appears to be no more than a final writing out large of paragraph (*a*) (ii). The expression "spirit of the gift" may be an echo of words used in the *Campden Charities* case (1881) 18 ChD 310. It must, I think, be

equivalent in meaning to the basic intention underlying the gift, that intention being ascertainable from the terms of the relevant instrument read in the light of admissible evidence.

One must next consider whether in relation to a trust for payment of a fixed annual sum out of the income of a fund to charity A and payment of the residue of that income to charity B the expression "the original purposes of a charitable gift" in section 13 (1) should be construed as referring to the trusts as a whole or must be related severally to the trust for payment of the fixed annual sum and the trust for payment of residuary income. Mr. Browne-Wilkinson contends that the former is the correct view. Mr. Griffith contends that the latter is the correct view.

It seems to me that the words "the original purposes of a charitable gift" are apt to apply to the trusts as a whole in such a case. Where a testator or settlor disposes of the entire income of a fund for charitable purposes, it is natural to speak of the disposition as a single charitable gift, albeit the gift is for more than one charitable purpose. Conversely, it would be rather unnatural to speak of the disposition as constituting two or more several charitable gifts each for a single purpose. Nor, I think, is there any reason why one should put this rather artificial construction on the words. The point can, so far as I can see, only arise as a practical issue in regard to a trust of the present character. A trust for division of income between charities in aliquot shares would give rise to different considerations, inasmuch as even if one treats it as a single gift the possibility or otherwise of carrying out the trusts of one share according to the spirit of the gift could hardly react upon the possibility or otherwise of carrying out the trusts of the other share according to the spirit of the gift. The same is true, mutatis mutandis, of trusts for charities in succession. But in a trust of the present character there is an obvious interrelation between the two trusts in that changes in the amount of the income and the value of money may completely distort the relative benefits taken under the respective trusts. The point is familiar in other instances of fixed annuity and residual income.

Once it is accepted that the words "the original purposes of a charitable gift" bear the meaning which I have put upon them it is to my mind clear that in the circumstances of the present case the original purposes of the gift of Dickroyd cannot be carried out according to the spirit of the gift, or to use the words of paragraph (*e*) (iii) "have ceased . . . to provide a suitable and effective method of using the property . . . regard being had to the spirit of the gift". The intention underlying the gift was to divide a sum which, according to the values of 1715, was modest but not negligible, in such a manner that the minister took what was then a clear three fifths of it. This intention is plainly defeated when in the conditions of today the minister takes a derisory £3 out of a total of £791.

It is not suggested that subsection (2) has any significant bearing upon the present question, for it is precisely the condition requiring the failure of the original purposes that subsection (1) (*a*) (ii) and subsection (1) (*e*) (iii) are concerned to modify.

If, contrary to my view, the words "the original purposes of a charitable gift" must be read severally in relation to the trust for payment of the fixed annual sum and to the trust for payment of residuary income, I think it is no less clear that paragraphs (*a*) (ii) and (*e*) (iii) would have no application. On this footing it would be impossible to maintain in respect of either trust that the original purposes cannot be carried out in the spirit of the gift. The minister is available to receive £3 a year, for what it is worth, and it is conceded by Mr.

Browne-Wilkinson that there are sufficient poor, aged and necessitous people in Pudsey to absorb £788 a year.

Neither counsel sought to derive any assistance from the definitions in sections 45 and 46 of the Act.

I conclude that the new conditions for cy-près applications introduced by section 13 of the Act of 1960 have been satisfied. Mr. Griffith concedes that if it is legitimate to alter the purposes at all then £100 a year is a reasonable amount to be paid to the minister. There was some expert evidence on the value of money into which, for this reason, it is unnecessary to enter.

I propose to make an order by way of scheme accordingly. I should perhaps add, to avoid misunderstanding—and this is not in dispute—that should there cease to be a minister at the chapel with the consequence that the income becomes applicable in accordance with the provisions of the will, limited to take effect upon that event, section 13 will have no application as between the poor of Pudsey and the heirs of the testator.

In **Re J.W. Laing Trust** [1984] Ch 143,[5] [1984] 1 All ER 50, a settlor in 1922 transferred shares worth £15,000 to the plaintiff company as trustee to hold on a charitable trust. Both capital and income were to be wholly distributed in the lifetime of the settlor or within ten years of his death. The settlor died in 1978. By 1982 the capital as yet undistributed was worth £24 million. The plaintiff company applied to the court for the settlement of a scheme enabling the trustee to be discharged from the obligation to distribute capital within ten years of the settlor's death. PETER GIBSON J refused the application under section 13 (1) (*e*) (ii) on the ground that the obligation was an administrative provision and not an "original purpose of a charitable gift". He went on, however, to approve a scheme for the discharge of the obligation in the exercise of the court's inherent jurisdiction. He said at 149, at 53:

"It is necessary to identify the original purposes of the gift. I venture to suggest that, as a matter of ordinary language, those purposes in the present case should be identified as general charitable purposes and nothing further. I would regard it as an abuse of language to describe the requirement as to distribution as a purpose of the gift. Of course, that requirement was one of the provisions which the settlor intended to apply to the gift, but it would, on any natural use of language, be wrong to equate all the express provisions of a gift, which ex hypothesi the settlor intended to apply to the gift, with the purposes of a gift. To my mind the purposes of a charitable gift would ordinarily be understood as meaning those charitable objects on which the property given is to be applied. It is not meaningful to talk of the requirement as to distribution being either charitable or non-charitable. The purposes of a charitable gift correspond to the beneficiaries in the case of a gift by way of a private trust. . . .

I confess that from the outset I have found difficulty in accepting that it is meaningful to talk of a cy-près application of property that has from the date of the gift been devoted both as to capital and income to charitable purposes generally, albeit subject to a direction as to the timing of the capital distributions. No case remotely like the present had been drawn to my attention . . .

5 [1984] Conv 319 (J. Warburton); [1984] All ER Rev 305 (P.J. Clarke); [1985] Conv 313 (P. Luxton).

In the result, despite all the arguments that have been ably advanced, I remain unpersuaded that such a gift is capable of being applied cy-près and, in particular, I am not persuaded that the requirement as to distribution is a purpose within the meaning of section 13. Rather, it seems to me to fall on the administrative side of the line, going, as it does, to the mechanics of how the property devoted to charitable purposes is to be distributed. Accordingly, I must refuse the application so far as it is based on section 13.

In my judgment, the plaintiff has made out a very powerful case for the removal of the requirement as to distribution, which seems to me to be inexpedient in the very altered circumstances of the charity since that requirement was laid down 60 years ago. I take particular account of the fact that this application is one that has the support of the Attorney-General. Although the plaintiff is not fettered by the express terms of the gift as to the charitable purposes for which the charity's funds are to be applied, it is, in my view, proper for the plaintiff to wish to continue to support the causes which the settlor himself wished the charity to support from its inception, and which would suffer if that support was withdrawn as a consequence of the distribution of the charity's assets. I have no hesitation in reaching the conclusion that the court should, in the exercise of its inherent jurisdiction, approve a scheme under which the trustees for the time being of the charity will be discharged from the obligation to distribute the capital within 10 years of the death of the settlor.''

In **Oldham Borough Council v Attorney-General** [1993] Ch 210, [1993] 2 All ER 432[6] land was conveyed in 1962 to the Oldham Borough Council upon trust ''to preserve and manage it at all times hereafter as playing fields to be known as 'the Clayton Playing Fields' for the benefit and enjoyment of the inhabitants of Oldham Chadderton and Royton.''

The question was whether the court had power to authorise the Council to sell the land to developers for a very large price, and to use the proceeds for the acquisition of playing fields with much better facilities than the existing site. The Court of Appeal held that it had power to authorise the sale under its inherent jurisdiction, even though none of the requirements of section 13 (1) was satisfied.

DILLON LJ said at 219, at 436:

''Broadly, the effect of that section is that an alteration of the 'original purposes' of a charitable gift can only be authorised by a scheme for the cy-près application of the trust property and such a scheme can only be made in the circumstances set out in paragraphs (*a*) to (*e*) of section 13 (1).

It follows that if the retention of a particular property is part of the 'original purposes' of a charitable trust, sale of that property would involve an alteration of the original purposes even if the proceeds of the sale were applied in acquiring an alternative property for carrying out the same charitable activities. If so, a sale of the original property could only be ordered as part of a cy-près scheme, and then only if circumstances within one or other of paragraphs (*a*) to (*e*) are made out. The particular bearing of that in the present case is that the council accepts, and the Attorney-General agrees, that the circumstances of this charity do not fall within any of these paragraphs. If, therefore, on a true appreciation of the deed of gift and of section 13, the

6 [1993] All ER Rev 260 (P.J. Clarke).

retention of the existing site is part of the original purposes of the charity, the court cannot authorise any sale. It is necessary, therefore, to look first at the terms of the deed of gift ...

[His Lordship examined the terms and continued:]

On that wording, I have no doubt at all that the original purpose, in ordinary parlance, of the donor was, in one sense, that the particular land conveyed should be used for ever as playing fields for the benefit and enjoyment of the inhabitants of Oldham, Chadderton and Royton ...

As Lord Cranworth LC said in *President and Scholars of the College of St. Mary Magdalen, Oxford v A-G* (1857) 6 HL Cas 189, 205:

> 'it is plain that persons who give lands to a charity, devote them for ever to the purposes of that charity, and such is always the expression used in such gifts, the gifts being made to the charitable object "for ever." With the belief that the charity will endure for ever, it is extremely improbable that they can have contemplated the sale of the lands ... '

I come then to what I regard as the crux of this case, viz., the true construction of the words 'original purposes of a charitable gift' in section 13 of the Act of 1960. Do the 'original purposes' include the intention and purpose of the donor that the land given should be used for ever for the purposes of the charity, or are they limited to the purposes of the charity, in the sense in which Lord Cranworth LC was using these words in the passage just cited?

Certain of the authorities cited to us can be put on one side. Thus in *Re JW Laing Trust* [1984] Ch 143, 153, [1984] 1 All ER 50, 56, p. 492 ante, Peter Gibson J said, plainly correctly:

> 'It cannot be right that any provision, even if only administrative, made applicable by a donor to his gift should be treated as a condition and hence as a purpose.'

In that case, however, the provision, which was held to be administrative and was plainly not a 'purpose,' was a provision that the capital was to be wholly distributed within the settlor's lifetime or within 10 years of his death.

Conversely, there are cases where the donor has imposed a condition, as part of the terms of his gift, which limits the main purpose of the charity in a way which, with the passage of time, has come to militate against the achievement of that main purpose. The condition is there part of the purpose, but the court has found itself able on the facts to cut out the condition by way of a cy-près scheme under the cy-près jurisdiction, on the ground that the subsistence of the condition made the main purpose impossible or impracticable of achievement: see *Re Dominion Students' Hall Trust*, [1947] Ch 183, p. 484 ante, where a condition of a trust for the maintenance of a hostel for male students of the overseas dominions of the British Empire restricted the benefits to dominion students of European origin; and see, also *Re Robinson*; [1923] 2 Ch 332, p. 483 ante, where it was a condition of the gift of an endowment for an evangelical church that the preacher should wear a black gown in the pulpit. But unlike those conditions, the intention or purpose in the present case that the actual land given should be used as playing fields is not a condition qualifying the use of that land as playing fields.

It is necessary, in my judgment, in order to answer the crucial question of the true construction of section 13, to appreciate the legislative purpose of section 13. Pennycuick V-C said in *Re Lepton's Charity* [1972] Ch 276, 284F, [1971] 1 All ER 799, 803 p. 490 ante, that the section 'in part restates the principles applied under the existing law, but also extends those principles.' But the principles with which it is concerned are the principles for applying property cy-près and nothing else. The stringency of those principles, as stated in *Re Weir Hospital* [1910] 2 Ch 124, p. 483 ante, has been somewhat mitigated, but to nothing like the extent contended for by the unsuccessful parties in *Re Weir Hospital*. But there is nothing to suggest any legislative intention, in enacting section 13, to extend the cases where a cy-près scheme is necessary, if anything is to be done, to cases where before the Act of 1960 no scheme was required.

The cases seem to be consistent, before the Act of 1960, that mere sale of charitable property and reinvestment of the proceeds in the acquisition of other property to be held on precisely the same charitable trusts, or for precisely the same charitable purposes, did not require a scheme:
[His Lordship referred to *Re Ashton's Charity* (1856) 22 Beav 288; *Re Parke's Charity* (1842) 12 Sim 329 and *Re North Shields Old Meeting House* (1859) 7 WR 541 and continued:]

This seems to have been the standard practice in the 19th century and I see no reason why Parliament should have intended to alter it by section 13 of the Act of 1960. That section is concerned with the cy-près application of charitable funds, but sales of charitable lands have, in so far as they have been dealt with by Parliament, always been dealt with by other sections not concerned with the cy-près doctrine.

There are, of course, some cases where the qualities of the property which is the subject matter of the gift are themselves the factors which make the purposes of the gift charitable, e.g., where there is a trust to retain for the public benefit a particular house once owned by a particular historical figure or a particular building for its architectural merit or a particular area of land of outstanding natural beauty. In such cases, sale of the house, building or land would necessitate an alteration of the original charitable purposes and, therefore, a cy-près scheme because after a sale the proceeds or any property acquired with the proceeds could not possibly by applied for the original charitable purpose. But that is far away from cases such as the present, where the charitable purpose—playing fields for the benefit and enjoyment of the inhabitants of the districts of the original donees, or it might equally be a museum, school or clinic in a particular town—can be carried on on other land.

Accordingly, I would allow this appeal, set aside the declaration made by the judge, and substitute a declaration to the opposite effect . . .

I should add finally that we were referred by counsel to the provisions of the Charities Act 1992, which have not yet come into force. That Act changes the law in various respects; therefore its provisions cannot help us in deciding the questions with which we have been concerned on this appeal. Equally, however, we have not had to consider whether our decision would have been different if all the provisions of the Act of 1992 had already come into force.''

C. Charity Collections

CHARITIES ACT 1993

14. Application cy-près of gifts of donors unknown or disclaiming.—
(1) Property given for specific charitable purposes which fail shall be applicable cy-près as if given for charitable purposes generally, where it belongs—

(a) to a donor who after—
  (i) the prescribed advertisements and inquiries have been published and made,[7] and
  (ii) the prescribed period beginning with the publications of those advertisements has expired, cannot be identified or cannot be found;[8]
(b) to a donor who has executed a disclaimer in the prescribed form of his right to have the property returned.[9]

(2) Where the prescribed advertisements and inquiries have been published and made by or on behalf of trustees with respect to any such property, the trustees shall not be liable to any person in respect of the property if no claim by him to be interested in it is received by them before the expiry of the period mentioned in subsection (1)(a)(ii) above.

(3) For the purposes of this section property shall be conclusively presumed (without any advertisement or inquiry) to belong to donors who cannot be identified, in so far as it consists—
(a) of the proceeds of cash collections made by means of collecting boxes or by other means not adapted for distinguishing one gift from another; or
(b) of the proceeds of any lottery, competition, entertainment, sale or similar money-raising activity, after allowing for property given to provide prizes or articles for sale or otherwise to enable the activity to be undertaken.

(4) The court may by order direct that property not falling within subsection (3) above shall for the purposes of this section be treated (without any advertisement or inquiry) as belonging to donors who cannot be identified, where it appears to the court either—
(a) that it would be unreasonable, having regard to the amounts likely to be returned to the donors, to incur expense with a view to returning the property; or
(b) that it would be unreasonable, having regard to the nature, circumstances and amounts of the gifts, and to the lapse of time since the gifts were made, for the donors to expect the property to be returned.

(5) Where property is applied cy-près by virtue of this section, the donor shall be deemed to have parted with all his interest at the time when the gift was made; but where property is so applied as belonging to donors who cannot be identified or cannot be found, and is not so applied by virtue of subsection (3) or (4) above,—
(a) the scheme shall specify the total amount of that property; and
(b) the donor of any part of that amount shall be entitled, if he makes a claim not later than six months after the date on which the scheme is made, to recover from the charity for which the property is applied a sum equal to that part, less any expenses properly incurred by the

---

7 Charities (Cy-près Advertisements Inquiries and Disclaimers) Regs 1993.
8 *Re Henry Wood National Memorial Trust* [1966] 1 WLR 1601, [1967] 1 All ER 238n; Annual Report for 1965, paras. 19–21.
9 Annual Report for 1980, paras. 135–136 (South Scarborough Swimming Pool Association); 1981, paras. 62–63 (South Petherton Swimming Pool Fund, Somerset).

charity trustees after that date in connection with claims relating to his gift; and

(c) the scheme may include directions as to the provision to be made for meeting any such claim.

(6) Where—

(a) any sum is, in accordance with any such directions, set aside for meeting any such claims, but

(b) the aggregate amount of any such claims actually made exceeds the relevant amount,

then, if the Commissioners so direct, each of the donors in question shall be entitled only to such proportion of the relevant amount as the amount of his claim bears to the aggregate amount referred to in paragraph (b) above; and for this purpose "the relevant amount" means the amount of the sum so set aside after deduction of any expenses properly incurred by the charity trustees in connection with claims relating to the donors' gifts.

(7) For the purposes of this section, charitable purposes shall be deemed to "fail" where any difficulty in applying property to those purposes makes that property or the part not applicable cy-près available to be returned to the donors.

(10) In this section, except in so far as the context otherwise requires, references to a donor include persons claiming through or under the original donor, and references to property given include the property for the time being representing the property originally given or property derived from it.

(11) This section shall apply to property given for charitable purposes, notwithstanding that it was so given before the commencement of this Act.

D. Small Charities

The Charities Act 1985 enabled trustees of certain small charities in effect to determine their own cy-près application with the concurrence of the Charity Commissioners. The Act was repealed by the Charities Act 1992 and replaced by provisions which extend and simplify the law. This is now consolidated in the Charities Act 1993.

CHARITIES ACT 1993

74. Small charities: power to transfer all property, modify objects etc.—(1) This section applies to a charity if—

(a) its gross income in its last financial year did not exceed £5,000, and

(b) it does not hold any land on trusts which stipulate that the land is to be used for the purposes, or any particular purposes, of the charity,

and it is neither an exempt charity nor a charitable company.

(2) Subject to the following provisions of this section, the charity trustees of a charity to which this section applies may resolve for the purposes of this section—

(a) that all the property of the charity should be transferred to such other charity as is specified in the resolution, being either a registered charity or a charity which is not required to be registered;

(b) that all the property of the charity should be divided, in such manner as is specified in the resolution, between such two or more other charities as are so specified, being in each case either a registered charity or a charity which is not required to be registered;

(c) that the trusts of the charity should be modified by replacing all or any of the purposes of the charity with such other purposes, being in law charitable, as are specified in the resolution;

(d) that any provision of the trusts of the charity—

    (i) relating to any of the powers exercisable by the charity trustees in the administration of the charity, or

    (ii) regulating the procedure to be followed in any respect in connection with its administration,

should be modified in such manner as is specified in the resolution.

(3) Any resolution passed under subsection (2) must be passed by a majority of not less than two-thirds of such charity trustees as vote on the resolution.

(4) The charity trustees of a charity to which this section applies ("the transferor charity") shall not have power to pass a resolution under subsection (2)(a) or (b) unless they are satisfied—

(a) that the existing purposes of the transferor charity have ceased to be conducive to a suitable and effective application of the charity's resources; and

(b) that the purposes of the charity or charities specified in the resolution are as similar in character to the purposes of the transferor charity as is reasonably practicable;

and before passing the resolution they must have received from the charity trustees of the charity, or (as the case may be) of each of the charities, specified in the resolution written confirmation that those trustees are willing to accept a transfer of property under this section.

(5) The charity trustees of any such charity shall not have power to pass a resolution under subsection (2)(c) unless they are satisfied—

(a) that the existing purposes of the charity (or, as the case may be, such of them as it is proposed to replace) have ceased to be conducive to a suitable and effective application of the charity's resources; and

(b) that the purposes specified in the resolution are as similar in character to those existing purposes as is practical in the circumstances.

75. Small charities: power to spend capital—(1) This section applies to a charity if—

(a) it has a permanent endowment which does not consist of or comprise any land, and

(b) its gross income in its last financial year did not exceed £1,000, and it is neither an exempt charity nor a charitable company.

(2) Where the charity trustees of a charity to which this section applies are of the opinion that the property of the charity is too small, in relation to its purposes, for any useful purpose to be achieved by the expenditure of income alone, they may resolve for the purposes of this section that the charity ought to be freed from the restrictions with respect to expenditure of capital to which its permanent endowment is subject.

(3) Any resolution passed under subsection (2) must be passed by a majority of not less than two-thirds of such charity trustees as vote on the resolution.

(4) Before passing such a resolution the charity trustees must consider whether any reasonable possibility exists of effecting a transfer or division of all the charity's property under section 43 (disregarding any such transfer or

division as would, in their opinion, impose on the charity an unacceptable burden of costs).

Under both sections, the trustees must give public notice of their resolution, a copy of which must be sent to the Charity Commissioners for their approval.[10] Neither section applies to an exempt or corporate charity.

QUESTIONS

1. Would it now be possible for gifts such as those in *National Anti-Vivisection Society v IRC* [1948] AC 31, [1947] 2 All ER 217, p. 408, ante, and *Oppenheim v Tobacco Securities Trust Co Ltd* [1951] AC 297, [1951] 1 All ER 31, p. 385, ante, to be saved by Charities Act 1993, s. 13 (1) (*e*) (ii)? H & M, pp. 452–453; (1974) 38 Conv (NS) at p. 233.
2. In what circumstances is proof of a general charitable intent still necessary? Charities Act 1960, s. 13 (2), s. 14; Pettit, pp. 298–301.
3. How do you distinguish between
   (a) *Re Finger's Will Trusts* [1972] Ch 286, [1971] 3 All ER 1050, p. 475, ante, where the gift to the incorporated charity failed and there was a cy-près scheme, and where the gift to the unincorporated charity did not fail and there was a scheme, but not cy-près and *Re Faraker* [1912] 2 Ch 488, p. 473, ante, where the gift did not fail and there was no scheme.
   (b) *Re Jenkins's Will Trusts* [1966] Ch 249, [1966] 1 All ER 926, p. 478, ante and *Re Satterthwaite's Will Trusts* [1966] 1 WLR 277, [1966] 1 All ER 919, p. 478, ante.
4. Now consider *Re Spence* [1979] Ch 483, [1978] 3 All ER 92, where the gift failed and there was no cy-près scheme. Could the gift have been saved by applying *Re Finger's Will Trusts, Re Faraker* or *Re Satterthwaite's Will Trusts*? (1972) 36 Conv NS 198 (R.B.M. Cotterell); (1974) 38 Conv (NS) 187 (J. Martin); Pettit, pp. 301–306; Picarda, pp. 306–307, 318–319, 324–325.

---

10 In 1994 approval was first given to 1,948 resolutions: Annual Report for 1994, p. 10. See CC Leaflet 44 (Small Charities).

11. The Administration of Charities[1]

I. General

The administration of charities is effected more and more through the control and supervision of the Charity Commissioners and less and less by the courts. Prior to 1960 the powers of the administrative authorities were inadequate; but, as we have seen, major reforms in the law relating to *cy-près* were introduced by the Charities Act 1960. The bulk of the Act is concerned with the administration of charities. These matters form the lifeblood of the modern law. Little of this appears in the law reports. Most of this chapter will consist of extracts from the statute and from the valuable Reports produced annually by the Charity Commissioners.

In 1989 the Government published a White Paper directed towards increasing the supervision of charities by the Charity Commissioners with the object of minimising abuse and maladministration by charity trustees.[2]

---

1 H & M, pp. 455–465; K & S, pp. 187–188; S & K, pp. 305–348; P & M, pp. 350–359; Pettit, pp. 262–294; Riddall, pp. 164–170; Snell, pp. 167–174; Tudor, pp. 308–311; Picarda, pp. 379–510.

2 Charities: A Framework for the Future (Cm 694) (White Paper). This is based on National Audit Office Report 1986–87 (HC 380) and on Efficiency Scrutiny of the Supervision of Charities (Woodfield Report) 1987; [1988] Conv 163 (H.W. Wilkinson); [1989] Conv 301; (1989) 133 NLJ 1312 (D.G. Cracknell). See HL debate on the White Paper: Times, 1 December 1989.

This was implemented by the Charities Act 1992. Part I of that Act and the Charities Act 1960 were consolidated in the Charities Act 1993,[2a] but not the whole of charity law. Parts II and III of the 1992 Act on fund-raising and public collections remain separate; as do the Charitable Trusts Validation Act 1954 and the Recreational Charities Act 1958.

II. The Authorities

A. The Charity Commissioners

CHARITIES ACT 1993

1. The Charity Commissioners.—(1) There shall continue to be a body of Charity Commissioners for England and Wales, and they shall have such functions as are conferred on them by this Act in addition to any functions under any other enactment not repealed by this Act.

(2) The provision of Schedule 1 to this Act shall have effect with respect to the constitution and proceedings of the Commissioners and other matters relating to the Commissioners and their officers and employees.

(3) The Commissioners shall (without prejudice to their specific powers and duties under other enactments) have the general function of promoting the effective use of charitable resources by encouraging the development of better methods of administration, by giving charity trustees information or advice on any matter affecting the charity and by investigating and checking abuses.[3]

(4) It shall be the general object of the Commissioners so to act in the case of any charity (unless it is a matter of altering its purposes) as best to promote and make effective the work of the charity in meeting the needs designated by its trusts; but the Commissioners shall not themselves have power to act in the administration of a charity.

(5) The Commissioners shall, as soon as possible after the end of every year, make to the Secretary of State[4] a report on their operations during that year, and he shall lay a copy of the report before each House of Parliament.

SCHEDULE 1.

CONSTITUTION, ETC., OF CHARITY COMMISSIONERS

1.—(1) There shall be a Chief Charity Commissioner, and two other commissioners.

(2) Two at least of the commissioners shall be persons who have a Seven Year qualification.

2aFor a commentary on the 1992 and 1993 Acts by J.Warburton, see Current Law Statutes Annotated 1993; *A Trustees' Guide to the Charities Acts 1992 & 1993*, published by the Charity Commissioners.

3 See Annual Report for 1991, paras. 4–11, on the reorganisation of the Commission into Charity Support and Charity Supervision.

4 The Secretary of State for Home Affairs. See the Annual Reports of the Charity Commissioners for England and Wales. The Report for the year 1970 contains a detailed review of the operation of the Charities Act 1960 during its first ten years; and that for 1985 contains detailed comment on particular aspects of the work of the Commissioners after twenty five years of the Act.

(3) The chief commissioner and the other commissioners shall be appointed by the Secretary of State, and shall be deemed for all purposes to be employed in the civil service of the Crown.

(4) There may be paid to each of the commissioners such salary and allowances as the Secretary of State may with the approval of the Treasury determine.

(5) If at any time it appears to the Secretary of State that there should be more than three commissioners, he may with the approval of the Treasury appoint not more than two additional commissioners.[5]

B. The Official Custodian for Charities

The Official Custodian for Charities holds investments and property in his name on behalf of many charity trustees.[6] He is only allowed to buy or sell investments or property on behalf of a charity if the trustees instruct him to do so. He has no power to manage investments. The Charities Act 1992 section 29 drastically reduced his functions by requiring the divestment of all property other than land and that held following an order under section 20 of the Charities Act 1960.[7]

CHARITIES ACT 1993

2. The official custodian for charities.—(1) There shall continue to be an officer known as the official custodian for charities (in this Act referred to as "the official custodian"), whose function it shall be to act as trustee for charities in the cases provided for by this Act,[8] and the official custodian for charities shall be by that name a corporation sole having perpetual succession and using an official seal, which shall be officially and judicially noticed.

(2) Such officer of the Commissioners as they may from time to time designate shall be the official custodian for charities.

C. The Visitor[9]

The visitor of an ecclesiastical[10] or eleemosynary corporation[11] has exclusive jurisdiction over matters of internal management, such as the admission and

---

5 Two part-time commissioners were appointed in 1988: Woodfield Report, Part 5, Annex C; White paper, para.1.21.

6 See CC Leaflet 13.

7 The divestment of cash and securities has proceeded according to plan. At the outset of 1994, the Official Custodian had responsibility for 700 different securities belonging to 21,216 charities. By the end of the year those figures were reduced to 64 and 1,877 respectively: Annual Report for 1994, p. 22.

8 See ss. 21 and 22.

9 Pettit, pp. 277–283; Tudor, pp. 369–388, Picarda, chap. 41; Mitcheson, *Opinion on the Visitation of Charities* (1887); (1970) 86 LQR 531 (J.W. Bridge); (1981) 97 LQR 610; (1986) 136 NLJ 484, 519, 567, 665. (P.M. Smith).

10 Corporations which exist for the furtherance of religion and the perpetuation of the rites of the church.

11 Originally a corporation whose object was the distribution of free alms, or the relief of individual distress: *Re Armitage* [1972] Ch 438, [1972] 1 All ER 708. For the purpose of visitatorial powers, corporate schools, modern universities and the Inns of Court are included.

removal of students,[12] and the award of degrees and prizes.[13] There is no appeal from his decisions, unless the statutes of the corporation so provide, but he is subject to judicial review, if he has acted outside his jurisdiction or in breach of the rules of natural justice or has abused his powers.[14]

The Education Reform Act 1988 abolished the visitor's jurisdiction in relation to the appointment, employment and dismissal of academic staff.[15]

In **Re Christ Church** (1866) 1 Ch App 526, Lord CRANWORTH LC, representing the Queen as the Visitor of Christ Church, Oxford, sanctioned the appropriation of part of the revenues of the college to augment the stipend of the Regius Professorship of Greek, which was on the same foundation as the college. He said at 527:

"The study of Greek is an important and material element of education, and it is most desirable that a stipend larger than the very inadequate one of £40 per annum should be provided for the professorship. The present application is highly honourable to the Dean and Chapter, and not only receives my ready sanction, but also my hearty approval."

III. The Register[16]

A. The Register

CHARITIES ACT 1993

3. The register of charities—(1) The Commissioners shall continue to keep a register of charities, which shall be kept by them in such manner as they think fit.[17]

(2) There shall be entered in the register every charity not excepted by subsection (5) below; and a charity so excepted (other than one excepted by paragraph (a) of that subsection) may be entered in the register at the request of the charity, but (whether or not it was excepted at the time of registration) may at any time, and shall at the request of the charity, be removed from the register.

(3) The register shall contain—
  (a) the name of every registered charity; and
  (b) such other particulars of, and such other information relating to, every such charity as the Commissioners think fit.

---

12 *Patel v University of Bradford Senate* [1979] 1 WLR 1066, [1979] 2 All ER 582.
13 *R v HM the Queen in Council, ex p Vijayatunga* [1990] 2 QB 444, [1989] 2 All ER 843; *Oakes v Sidney Sussex College, Cambridge* [1988] 1 WLR 431, [1988] 1 All ER 1004.
14 *R v Lord President of the Privy Council, ex p Page* [1993] AC 682, [1993] 1 All ER 97; (1993) 109 LQR 155 (H.W.R. Wade) *R v Visitors to the Inns of Court, ex p Calder* [1994] QB 1, [1993] 2 All ER 876. See also [1992–93] CL & PR 63 (H. Picarda); [1993–94] CL & PR 103 (P.M. Smith).
15 S. 206. The Act applies to publicly funded universities and similar institutions: s. 202; (1991) 54 MLR 137 (P. Pettit).
16 See CC Leaflets 22 (Registration of Religious Charities); 23 (Exempt Charities); 45 (Central Register of Charities); Annual Report for 1970, paras. 17–27; Goodman Report, chap. 6; House of Commons Report, vol. I, paras. 93– 104, 115–117.
17 For the computerisation of the Register, see Annual Report for 1990, paras. 25–28.

(4) Any institution which no longer appears to the Commissioners to be a charity shall be removed from the register, with effect, where the removal is due to any change in its purposes or trusts, from the date of that change; and there shall also be removed from the register any charity which ceases to exist or does not operate.

(5) The following charities are not required to be registered—

(a) any charity comprised in Schedule 2 to this Act (in this Act referred to as an "exempt charity");

(b) any charity which is excepted by order or regulations;[18]

(c) any charity which has neither—

(i) any permanent endowment, nor

(ii) the use or occupation of any land.

and whose income from all sources does not in aggregate amount to more than £1,000 a year;

and no charity is required to be registered in respect of any registered place of worship.[19]

(6) With any application for a charity to be registered there shall be supplied to the Commissioners copies of its trusts (or, if they are not set out in any extant document, particulars of them), and such other documents or information as may be prescribed by regulations made by the Secretary of State or as the Commissioners may require for the purpose of the application.

(7) It shall be the duty—

(a) of the charity trustees of any charity which is not registered nor excepted from registration to apply for it to be registered, and to supply the documents and information required by subsection (6) above; and

(b) of the charity trustees (or last charity trustees) of any institution which is for the time being registered to notify the Commissioners if it ceases to exist, or if there is any change in its trusts or in the particulars of it entered in the register, and to supply to the Commissioners particulars of any such change and copies of any new trusts or alterations of the trusts.

(8) The register (including the entries cancelled when institutions are removed from the register) shall be open to public inspection at all reasonable times; and copies (or particulars) of the trusts of any registered charity as supplied to the Commissioners under this section shall, so long as it remains on the register, be kept by them and be open to public inspection at all reasonable times,[20] except in so far as regulations made by the Secretary of State otherwise provide.

5. Status of registered charity (other than small charity) to appear on official publications etc.—(1) This section applies to a registered charity if its gross income in its last financial year exceeded £5,000.

18 SI 1960 No. 2366 (Voluntary Schools); SI 1996 No. 180 (Religious Charities); SI 1961 No. 1044 (Boy Scouts and Girl Guides); SI 1965 No. 1056 (Armed Forces); SI 1966 No. 965 (Non-exempt Universities).

19 See Places of Worship Registration Act 1855, s. 3 for their registration by the Registrar General.

20 At St. Alban's House, Haymarket, London; Graeme House, Derby Square, Liverpool; and The Deane, Tangier, Taunton, Somerset. The Charities Division of the Inland Revenue's Claims Branch is at Bootle, Merseyside.

(2) Where this section applies to a registered charity, the fact that it is a registered charity shall be stated in English in legible characters—

(a) in all notices, advertisements and other documents issued by or on behalf of the charity and soliciting money or other property for the benefit of the charity;

(b) in all bills of exchange, promissory notes, endorsements, cheques and orders for money or goods purporting to be signed on behalf of the charity; and

(c) in all bills rendered by it and in all its invoices, receipts and letters of credit.

6. Power of Commissioners to require charity's name to be changed—(1) Where this subsection applies to a charity, the commissioners may give a direction requiring the name of the charity to be changed, within such period as is specified in the direction, to such other name as the charity trustees may determine with the approval of the Commissioners.

(2) Subsection (1) above applies to a charity if—

(a) it is a registered charity and its name ("the registered name")—
  (i) is the same as, or
  (ii) is in the opinion of the Commissioners too like,
  the name, at the time when the registered name was entered in the register in respect of the charity, of any other charity (whether registered or not);

(b) the name of the charity is in the opinion of the Commissioners likely to mislead the public as to the true nature—
  (i) of the purposes of the charity as set out in its trusts, or
  (ii) of the activities which the charity carries on under its trusts in pursuit of those purposes;

(c) the name of the charity includes any word or expression for the time being specified in regulations made by the Secretary of State[1] and the inclusion in its name of that word or expression is in the opinion of the Commissioners likely to mislead the public in any respect as to the status of the charity;

(d) the name of the charity is in the opinion of the Commissioners likely to give the impression that the charity is connected in some way with Her Majesty's Government or any local authority, or with any other body of persons or any individual, when it is not so connected; or

(e) the name of the charity is in the opinion of the Commissioners offensive;

and in this subsection any reference to the name of a charity is, in relation to a registered charity, a reference to the name by which it is registered.

SCHEDULE 2
EXEMPT CHARITIES

The following institutions, so far as they are charities, are exempt charities within the meaning of this Act, that is to say—

(a) any institution which, if the Charities Act 1960 had not been passed, would be exempted from the powers and jurisdiction, under the Charitable Trusts Acts 1853 to 1939, of the Commissioners or Minister

1 Charities (Misleading Names) Regs 1992 (SI 1992 No. 1901).

of Education (apart from any power of the Commissioners or Minister
to apply those Acts in whole or in part to charities otherwise exempt) by
the terms of any enactment not contained in those Acts other than
section 9 of the Places of Worship Registration Act 1855;[2]

(b) the universities of Oxford, Cambridge, London, Durham and
    Newcastle, the colleges and halls in the universities of Oxford,
    Cambridge, Durham and Newcastle, Queen Mary and Westfield
    College in the University of London and the colleges of Winchester and
    Eton;

(c) any university, university college, or institution connected with a
    university or university college, which Her Majesty declares by Order in
    Council to be an exempt charity for the purposes of this Act;[3]

(d) a grant-maintained school;[4]

(f) the Curriculum Council for Wales;

(h) a higher education corporation;[5]

(i) a successor company to a higher education corporation (within the
    meaning of section 129(5) of the Education Reform Act 1988) at a time
    when an institution conducted by the company is for the time being
    designated under that section;

(j) a further education corporation;[6]

(k) the Board of Trustees of the Victoria and Albert Museum;

(l) the Board of Trustees of the Science Museum;

(m) the Board of Trustees of the Armouries;

(n) the Board of Trustees of the Royal Botanic Gardens, Kew;

(o) the Board of Trustees of the National Museums and Galleries on
    Merseyside;

(p) the trustees of the British Museum and the trustees of the Natural
    History Museum;

(q) the Board of Trustees of the National Gallery;

(r) the Board of Trustees of the Tate Gallery;

(s) the Board of Trustees of the National Portrait Gallery;

(t) the Board of Trustees of the Wallace Collection;

(u) the Trustees of the Imperial War Museum;

(v) the Trustees of the National Maritime Museum;

(w) any institution which is administered by or on behalf of an institution
    included above and is established for the general purposes of, or for any
    special purpose of or in connection with, the last-mentioned
    institution;

---

2 The institutions referred to are the Universities of: Birmingham (Birmingham University Act
  1900, s. 14); Liverpool (Liverpool University Act 1903, s. 14): Manchester (Victoria University
  of Manchester Act 1904, s. 11); Leeds (University of Leeds Act 1904, s. 12); Sheffield
  (University of Sheffield Act 1905, s. 11); Bristol (University of Bristol Act 1909, s. 12); Reading
  (University of Reading Act 1926, s. 10); Nottingham (University of Nottingham Act 1949, s. 9)
  Southampton (University of Southampton Act 1953, s. 10); The Representative Body of the
  Welsh Church and its property (Welsh Church Act 1914, s. 13, Welsh Church (Temporalities)
  Act 1919, s. 7(1)), and property within the Church Funds Investment Measure 1958.
3 Further universities were added by Exempt Charities Orders 1962 (SI No. 1343), 1965 (SI No.
  1715), 1966 (SI No. 1460), 1967 (SI No. 821), 1969 (SI No. 1496) (The Open University), 1971
  (SI No. 453), 1982 (SI No. 1661); 1983 (SI No. 1516); 1984 (SI No. 1976); 1987 (SI No. 1823);
  1989 (SI No. 2394); 1994 (SI No. 1905); 1994 (SI No. 2956); 1995 (SI No. 1994).
4 Paras. (e) and (g) were repealed by Education Act 1993, s. 351(3). Sch. 21. Pt. II.
5 These are mainly the former polytechnics, the majority of which are now universities.
6 The former sixth form and tertiary colleges.

(x) the Church Commissioners and any institution which is administered by them;

(y) any registered society within the meaning of the Industrial and Provident Societies Act 1965 and any registered society or branch within the meaning of the Friendly Societies Act 1974;

(z) the Board of Governors of the Museum of London;

(za) the British Library Board.

B. Effect of Registration

CHARITIES ACT 1993

4. Effect of, and claims and objections to, registration[7]—(1) An institution shall for all purposes other than rectification of the register be conclusively presumed to be or to have been a charity at any time when it is or was on the register of charities.

(2) Any person who is or may be affected by the registration of an institution as a charity may, on the ground that it is not a charity, object to its being entered by the Commissioners in the register, or apply to them for it to be removed from the register; and provision may be made by regulations made by the Secretary of State as to the manner in which any such objection or application is to be made, prosecuted or dealt with.[8]

(3) An appeal against any decision of the Commissioners to enter or not to enter an institution in the register of charities, or to remove or not to remove an institution from the register, may be brought in the High Court by the Attorney-General, or by the persons who are or claim to be the charity trustees of the institution, or by any person whose objection or application under subsection (2) above is disallowed by the decision.[9]

(5) Any question affecting the registration or removal from the register of an institution may, notwithstanding that it has been determined by a decision on appeal under subsection (3) above, be considered afresh by the Commissioners and shall not be concluded by that decision, if it appears to the Commissioners that there has been a change of circumstances or that the

---

7 (1983) 80 LSG 2142 (J.M. Fryer); *Wynn v Skegness Urban District Council* [1967] 1 WLR 52, [1966] 3 All ER 336; *Finch v Poplar Borough Council* (1967) 66 LGR 324; *Re Murawski's Will Trusts* [1971] 1 WLR 707, [1971] 2 All ER 328, p. 417, *ante*.

8 An application for the removal of the Oxford Literary and Debating Union Charitable Trust was refused: Annual Report for 1976, paras. 54–64. See also Annual Report for 1978, para. 84.

9 The first appeal under this section was heard on November 18, 1970; *Incorporated Council of Law Reporting for England and Wales v A-G* [1971] Ch 626, [1971] 1 All ER 436; affd [1972] Ch 73, [1971] 3 All ER 1029. See also *Re Murawski's Will Trusts* [1971] 1 WLR 707, [1971] 2 All ER 328; *Construction Industry Training Board v A-G* [1973] Ch 173, [1972] 2 All ER 1339, following which decision, most industrial training boards established under the Industrial Training Act 1964 have been registered; Annual Report for 1973, para. 39; *IRC v McMullen* [1981] AC 1, [1980] 1 All ER 884, p. 374, *ante*, where HL upheld the decision of the Commissioners to register (reversing WALTON J and CA). Decisions to register have also been upheld in *IRC v White* [1980] TR 155, p. 364, *ante*; Annual Report for 1980, paras. 66–73; *McGovern v A-G* [1982] Ch 321, [1981] 3 All ER 493, p. 446, *ante*. A decision not to register was reversed in *Joseph Rowntree Memorial Trust Housing Association Ltd v A-G* [1983] Ch 159, [1983] 1 All ER 288, p. 346, *ante*. See also Charities Act 1993, s. 33(5); Annual Report for 1979, paras. 56–68 (Dulwich College Picture Gallery).

For recommendations that appeals be financed from public funds, see Annual Report for 1973, para. 6; Goodman Report, para. 151; House of Commons Report, vol. I, paras, 84–85.

decision is inconsistent with a later judicial decision, whether given on such an appeal or not.

C. Examples of Charities on the Register. Modern Developments

The Annual Report of the Charity Commissioners for 1994 states that at the end of 1994 there were 178,609 charities on the computerised register. It estimates that their gross annual income is £12.8 billion with the upper and lower limits being plus or minus £643 millions.

The following extracts illustrate the pattern of development in the objects of charitable gifts.

Report of the Goodman Committee on Charity Law and Voluntary Organisations (1976), paras. 137–138.

"New Registrations
137. About 3,000 charities are registered each year at present by the Charity Commissioners. Many of these are old charities, i.e., those created before 1960. In 1975, 2,859 charities were registered, of which 2,388 were post-1960 charities. We were given a breakdown of these by the Charity Commissioners, classified according to objects, as follows:

Objects	*Number*
General Charitable Purposes	192
Relief of Poverty	136
Children and Young People	126
Old People	95
Health and Sickness	243
Social Welfare and Culture	572
Moral Welfare and Reform	57
Religion	133
Education	319
Misc. purposes for Benefit of the Community	74
Multiple Objects (2 or more)	441
Total	2,388

The usefulness of this table in giving a picture a new trends in charities is limited. The Commissioners themselves subdivide these categories into a large number of sub-categories and some information as to trends could be gleaned from a breakdown of these sub-categories.

Modern Developments

138. Some of the more unusual types of new charities recently established according to the Commissioners have been in the field of social welfare, to meet current social problems relating to drug addiction and the consequences of the break-up of family life and cultural matters. The formation of charities for the conservation of the environment has also become increasingly popular including, on the one hand, the prevention of pollution and, on the other, the preservation of industrial relics. Particular new developments in the charity field in the past few years have included the establishment of organisations to

help battered wives and their children by providing them with alternative accommodation and in other ways; a charity for artificial kidney users; a disabled drivers' motor club; a charity for providing recorded tapes for the disabled and toy libraries. Another significant new development is the general purposes foundation or trust which collect money for distribution to other charities. Two registered in 1974 were the Charities Aid Foundation and the Charity Stamp Fund. The less fortunate in our community remain the concern of a high proportion of the newly established charities. But the Charity Commissioners note that a changing pattern is evolving. In the past the most usual way of expressing this concern has been for people to give of their personal fortune, often by will, with instructions to trustees to apply the income for these purposes. Now there is an increasing tendency for institutions to be established with little or no permanent endowment, as a result of a small group of people joining together to pursue charitable objects which are of concern to them. The founders bring to the new charities their enthusiasm and perhaps their expertise in a particular subject, but few, or no, funds. They have to depend on the ability of the trustees to raise funds by appeals to the public or to grant-making charities or agencies. One of the fields in which this change is evident is in the number of charities for religious and social welfare purposes which are founded for immigrant communities, pioneered and administered by members of these communities themselves. These examples illustrate how charities arise to meet new needs and carry on pioneering work in fields where the welfare services do not operate or are inadequate. This is a development to be welcomed as explained in Chapter 1.''

New trends have been reported by the Charity Commissioners in recent years. In 1978 new charities were established "for the relief of poverty and distress caused by unemployment, particularly among young people"; and in 1980 "there was an upsurge in the number set up with multiple objects, mainly objects embracing all four principal heads of charity . . . The largest category of new charities, some 22 per cent, had multiple objects. This is a departure from the usual pattern: the largest category is normally that of charities established broadly for the social well-being of the community at large, which this year fell to fewer than 20 per cent."

In 1982 "the new charities continued to reflect a wide range of activities—care for latch key children; victim support schemes; research into the causes of diseases, as well as groups helping to cope with the effects of diseases; groups helping ethnic minorities; the protection of the environment and of historic buildings;—reflecting modern times. We also continued to receive proposals for the formation of charities to help the unemployed, some of which seek to provide training in skills required for the manufacture, use, operation, repair and maintenance of computers, microprocessors and other electronic equipment, and were often able to accept them for registration."[9a]

9a Annual Reports for 1978, para. 60; 1982, para. 30.

Report of the Charity Commissioners for England and Wales for the year 1985, paras. 6–7.

"6. In recent years public expenditure restraint has stimulated the creation of new volunteer organisations within communities to meet the needs of those who whether by ill-health or misfortune are intolerably burdened. During the last five years we have registered some 45 charities concerned to provide support and assistance through the provision of home care attendance to families responsible for the care of those who are physically or mentally disabled. Over recent years we have also registered an increasing number of charities established to help those who have been the unfortunate victims of criminal assault; some 70 victim support groups have been registered in the last two years. Both these types of support schemes use voluntary helpers from the local community to provide a service of practical care and assistance.

7. In a similar way we have recognised as charitable organisations set up to meet new problems arising from changing social needs, for example: means to help latch key children; intermediary bodies which promote the effectiveness of other charities; parent-teacher associations; hospices (an increasing trend); local community and amenity associations; organisations devoted to the screening and improving of women's health, particularly cervical screening; various organisations in the field of care of the mentally handicapped; 'half-way' houses; new ventures in the arts and museums; and help for the young to set up in their own business enterprises."

Report of the Charity Commissioners for England and Wales for the year 1988, para. 24.

"24. New charities continue to reflect changing social needs and circumstances; and the largest group of new registrations relates to social, cultural and educational purposes. We have, for example, registered trusts connected with the Tate Gallery and the National Gallery, one concerned with the acquisition of pictures for exhibition, and the other with advancing education through the publication of material related to the Gallery's paintings. The first two City Technology Colleges have been registered on the basis of a model memorandum and articles of association agreed with us, and we were able to assist with the setting up of the Parliamentary Science and Technology Information Foundation which provides Members of both Houses of Parliament and their constituents with authoritative information and assessments upon scientific and technological research and education relevant to the United Kingdom. We registered after useful discussion the Educational Broadcasting Services Trust which was set up to promote and develop the education of the public through broadcasting. The Trust will work with the BBC, Independent Television, Channel 4, independent local radio, independent production companies and other educational bodies mainly on the commissioning of educational programmes and providing information and promotional support services. We have also registered the British Foundation for the Industrial Space University which advances education in space related studies and promotes academic research in that field. The Foundation will also award scholarships, grants, allowances and prizes to students attending the International Space University of Boston,

Massachusetts, and to other students or persons engaged in research into any branch of space technology and related sciences."

Report of the Charity Commissioners for England and Wales for the year 1989, paras. 28–30.

"28. The voluntary sector has continued to demonstrate a sensitivity to changing needs, whether in this country or abroad, and to develop a capacity to meet those needs. Three areas have been particularly prominent in the registration of new charities: the care of the environment, including the preservation of flora and fauna, the relief of the social problems of persons suffering or recovering from physical or mental illness, and the relief of persons who have suffered physical or mental deprivation.

29. The preservation of the environment, including its flora and fauna, continues to be a major concern. Development has been most marked in the number of charities for the protection of the environment outside the United Kingdom. We have registered charities concerned with the study of marginal regions, and of wetlands in Asia; charities for the conservation of the rain forests and their flora and fauna; charities to stimulate scientific research in waterfowl and their habitats and in the breeding of camelids; and charities to conserve elephants, the rhinoceros, birds in Portugal and the barn owl. More generally we have registered charities to research into waste recycling processes; to promote the protection of endangered flora and fauna; to educate the public in the ecological importance of trees and their planting, care and protection; to advance education and research in the field of energy and energy related subjects, including forms of renewable energy; and to educate the public in the value of clean air and the methods and consequence of air pollution.

30. In this country a charity for the clearance of fallen timber, the treatment of damaged trees and the planting and establishment of new trees was formed at the end of last year. This year the Prince of Wales Royal Park Tree Appeal was registered. Both these charities will have an added relevance following the recent storm damage. In Wales a charity for the conservation of broad leaved woods and trees was formed. We have also registered a charity for the conservation of Highgate Cemetery and its monuments."

Report of the Charity Commissioners for England and Wales for the year 1992, para. 67.

Breakdown of Registered Charities by Object Type

Relief of Poverty	53,435	General	13,920
Education	37,171	Misc	9,749
Social Welfare and Culture	33,511	Elderly	7,022
Health and Sickness	24,080	Overseas	4,274
Children Young People and		Moral Welfare	2,656
Students	21,057	Religion	15,807

Note: Some charities are classified under more than one object type.

D. Charity Commissioners' Decisions

Report of the Charity Commissioners for England and Wales for the year 1966, paras. 28–41.

"The Commissioners' Decisions on Charitable Purposes[10]

28. Section 5 (1) of the Charities Act provides that an institution which is on the register shall be conclusively presumed to be a charity and this has given us power in effect to decide that an institution is a charity, subject only to an appeal to the High Court. We have no similar power to decide that an institution is not a charity, because no conclusive presumptions are to be drawn from its absence from the register, but experience has shown that a decision not to register an institution is likely to result in its losing many of the advantages enjoyed by charities. Thus in the absence of appeals to the court, it has fallen to us . . . to decide whether an existing institution is a charity. Cases not involving existing institutions continue to come before the courts, usually on the construction of a will, in which a decision is reached affecting the law of charitable purposes.

29. It has long been recognised that the court has treated the concept of charity flexibly and has been ready to extend the meaning of "charitable purposes" to meet changed circumstances. It is our belief that when Parliament entrusted us with the duty of registering charities and thereby of determining the charitable status of applicant institutions it expected us to bring to this task the flexibility which the court has already shown. Since Parliament has provided that appeal from our decision lies to the High Court, it is clear that we must reach our decision on charitable status as a matter of law, applying the principles adopted by the court. In doing so, however, we believe that we are entitled and expected to follow the court in extending the field of charity by analogy from cases already decided. It would surely have been a serious and unintended result of the passing of the Charities Act if the field of charity had become fixed and limited by the decisions already reached in the courts and consequently capable of enlargement only on the few occasions when one of the class of cases mentioned at the end of the last paragraph or an appeal against a decision of ours comes before the court.

30. Many cases have already come before us in which new voluntary and non-profit-making bodies have been founded to meet new problems thrown up by changing social needs. Acting on analogy with court decisions in broadly similar cases we have felt it right to regard the field of charity as extending to some of these bodies. We have had as an example the practice of the Chief Inspector of Taxes (Claims Division) in allowing relief from tax to organisations whose claims to be charities did not fall into a category originally recognised as charitable although analogous to a case in some such category. In this the Chief Inspector of Taxes has doubtless been guided by the confidential decisions of the Special Commissioners of Inland Revenue. There have been many instances in which it would have been unreasonable for us not

---

10 House of Commons Report 1975, vol. II, pp. 18, 23–24. See Charity Commissioners' leaflet "Starting a Charity" (CC 21): Annual Report for 1987, Appendix A1.

to have followed the line already adopted by these authorities especially where an institution had long enjoyed relief from income tax.[11]

31. The problem whether a newly formed society is a charity when its purposes are unlike any which the court has already considered can on occasion prove extremely difficult. As the judges themselves have admitted charity law is not always governed by logic nor are the decisions entirely consistent. For instance, it has more than once been stated in judgments that if a purpose is to be regarded as charitable it must fall within the spirit and intendment of the preamble to the Elizabethan Statute of Charitable Uses of 1601 (see, for example, Lord Simonds in *Williams' Trustees v IRC* [1947] AC 447 at 455, [1947] 1 All ER 513 at 518); nor can it be argued that this doctrine is affected by the fact that the Charities Act, in repealing the Mortmain and Charitable Uses Act, 1888, has removed the express preservation of this preamble to which Lord Simonds drew attention. It does appear, however, that almost all the cases in which this doctrine has been mentioned have been cases in which the court decided that the institution before it was not a charity. There are many other cases in which the court, when deciding that some society was a charity, did not pause to trace its connection with the Elizabethan preamble. We believe that, although we must never lose sight of the list of charitable instances in the preamble, we are entitled to enter in the register organisations whose connection with any of them may seem tenuous, provided that the court has given us a lead in a decision about a comparable organisation.

32. Another doctrine in charity law which causes many problems is expressed in the statement that although a charity must be for the benefit of the community, not all purposes that are for the benefit of the community are necessarily charitable: if an institution is to be charitable its purposes must be for the benefit of the community in a way which the law recognises as charitable. This can, however, be interpreted indifferently either as restricting the field of charity within the limits of previous decisions or as permitting an almost unrestricted flexibility. We do not believe that either of these extremes is right; and it is our hope that by constant attention to previous court decisions, we shall succeed in developing from them, with the approval of the court if there is an appeal, such a concept of the field of charity as may meet the needs of the community.

33. We think it important to mention these matters not only by way of explaining how we interpret our duties in deciding whether or not to register organisations as charities, but also because it is clear that in the absence of any regular flow of appeals from our decisions we shall inevitably move further and further away from cases decided by the court. In considering future applications we must necessarily take account of what, acting as a Board of Commissioners, we have previously decided, as the court takes account of its previous decisions, and this cannot but gradually extend the field of charity. Such continual development appears to us to be inevitable as attempts are made within the concepts of charity progressively to meet the needs of a society which is not itself static.

34. It may be useful to mention one or two other matters that arise in connection with our consideration of charitable purposes. We consider that we

11 Under FA 1986, s. 33, the Inland Revenue may pass information to the Charity Commissioners, where it appears that a charity is applying its funds for purposes which are not charitable: Annual Report for 1987, para. 28. See also Charities Act 1993, s. 10.

are bound by the decisions of the courts to base our decision whether an institution is a charity upon the words used in its constitution or other instrument of government, particularly where the words appear in a deed or in the memorandum of association of a company. Words to define a charitable purpose must be clear and certain. Many organisations have applied to us to register objects expressed in terms so obscure and containing so much that is merely emotive that the objects were uncertain or unenforceable.

35. There have been a few cases in which it has become apparent that an institution's activities are in conflict with the words used and are in no sense charitable; in such cases we have preferred, whenever possible, to put a construction on the words which will permit the known activities, even though this has inevitably involved our rejecting the application for registration as a charity. But there have been times when the words have been so free from doubt that we have had no option but to register the institution with the caution that in future its objects must be strictly observed.

36. Some of our non-legal correspondents have questioned the justification for the importance which the law attached to the words used rather than to the institution's activities. It is felt by such correspondents that it should be enough to examine the activities of the institution to decide whether it is a charity and that two organisations both doing the same things should be equally qualified for registration. But this fails to take account of the fact that the law must be concerned principally with the obligation imposed on the institution to pursue certain objects. It is this obligation which established it as a charity; and so long as an institution is free to pursue any activities it wishes it cannot be treated as an established charity, however much its current activities may resemble those of other recognised charities.

37. The problem of interpreting words presents a somewhat different aspect when we are asked to consider draft documents intended to set up proposed charities. It is not unusual to find an attempt to dress up the purposes of the proposed institution in words which it is hoped will be accepted as charitable even though the purposes, so phrased, are quite remote from the true intentions of the promoters. We are convinced that this is a highly unsatisfactory course and that the governing instrument of every institution should show unequivocally what the institution really sets out to achieve. Three particular devices call for comment.

38. The first is the over-working of the word "education". Ingenious draftsmen have found it possible to embrace within this word a vast variety of activities, mainly propagandist, which do not come within the meaning of the "advancement of education" as it is used in charity law. A purpose which is not charitable cannot be made charitable merely by representing it to be a form of education.

39. The second device is the use of very wide general terms. It is of course true that there are some founders of charities, particularly those who are settling part of their own personal fortune, who genuinely expect to apply the settled property for all manner of charitable purposes; in such a case the general words are not intended to conceal a more limited true purpose. But, nonetheless, they may be difficult to interpret and it is undesirable that they should be used in any case where the proposed charity has a more limited purpose, particularly if the charity is intending to appeal to the public and not be merely the vehicle for the founder's own benevolence.

40. The third device is that of enumerating a number of objects, some perhaps charitable and others less obviously so, and then declaring that the

institution is to be confined to carrying out such of the listed objects as are charitable. We have already commented on this device in paragraph 25 of our report for 1964. This approach begs the question, prevents the real purpose of the institution from being readily recognised and quite unnecessarily introduces difficulty in construing and acting upon the documents in which it is used. If a proposed charity shows us a draft instrument incorporating such a phrase we consider ourselves entitled to enquire what are intended to be its activities, with a view to seeing whether those activities can be authorised in terms of clearly defined charitable purposes.

41. As in our reports for the last two years we give a list, in Appendix A, of the cases in which decisions on or affecting charitable status have been reached by us, sitting as a Board.[12] As was to be expected, there were fewer cases considered last year at this level than in previous years, and this reflects both a reduction in the number of institutions applying for registration and the fact that a great deal more work is now done in advising on draft documents. We find that advice given by our staff on a document still in draft is usually readily accepted by those concerned with the foundation of the charity. No problem then arises when the institution applies for registration.''[13]

IV. Co-ordination of Charitable and State Welfare Activities[14]

CHARITIES ACT 1993

76. Local authority's index of local charities.—(1) The council of a county or of a district or London borough and the Common Council of the City of London may maintain an index of local charities or of any class of local charities in the council's area, and may publish information contained in the index, or summaries or extracts taken from it.

77. Reviews of local charities by local authority.—(1) The council of a county or of a district or London borough and the Common Council of the City of London may, subject to the following provisions of this section, initiate, and carry out in co-operation with the charity trustees, a review of the working of any group of local charities with the same or similar purposes in the council's area, and may make to the Commissioners such report on the review and such recommendations arising from it as the council after consultation with the trustees think fit.

---

12 Since 1993 Decisions of the Charity Commissioners have been reported each year separately from the Annual Report.
13 See also Annual Report for 1986, paras. 38–39.
14 Goodman Report, pp. 81–100; House of Commons Report, vol. I, paras. 72–78; vol. II, pp. 20–21, 37, 58, 76, 163–164, 218–248 (criticism by Oxfordshire Charities Review Organiser), 297, 303–304, 351–358, 364–368 (The Charity Commissioners' Reply), 371–372, 382–390. See Annual Report for 1970, paras. 28–36; 1971, paras. 101–107; 1972, para.49; Local Authority Social Services Act 1970; Annual Report for 1976, paras. 78–84 (an example of co-operation between a charity and a local authority); Annual Report for 1977, paras. 51–56 (Motability: charity in partnership with State); paras. 58–62 (care of disabled); Annual Report for 1978, paras. 61–63, App. A and B suggesting ways in which the income of charities for the relief of poverty and sickness may be spent without overlapping the statutory services; CC Leaflets 4 (Charities for the Relief of the Poor); 29 (Charities and Local Authorities).

78. Co-operation between charities, and between charities and local authorities.—(1) Any local council and any joint board discharging any functions of such a council—

(a) may make, with any charity established for purposes similar or complementary to services provided by the council or board, arrangements for co-ordinating the activities of the council or board and those of the charity in the interests of persons who may benefit from those services or from the charity; and

(b) shall be at liberty to disclose to any such charity in the interests of those persons any information obtained in connection with the services provided by the council or board, whether or not arrangements have been made with the charity under this subsection.

In this subsection "local council" means, in relation to England, the council of a county, or of a district, London borough, or parish or (in Wales) community, and includes also the Common Council of the City of London and the Council of the Isles of Scilly and, in relation to Wales, the council of a county, county borough or community.

(2) Charity trustees shall, notwithstanding anything in the trusts of the charity, have power by virtue of this subsection to do all or any of the following things, where it appears to them likely to promote or make more effective the work of the charity, and may defray the expense of so doing out of any income or money applicable as income of the charity, that is to say,—

(a) they may co-operate in any review undertaken under section 77 above or otherwise of the working of charities or any class of charities;

(b) they may make arrangements with an authority acting under subsection (1) above, or with another charity for co-ordinating their activities and those of the authority or of the other charity;

(c) they may publish information of other charities with a view to bringing them to the notice of those for whose benefit they are intended.

10th Report from the Expenditure Committee of the House of Commons (1975), vol. II, pp. 20–21. Memorandum submitted by the Charity Commissioners.

"Local Reviews of Charities

23. The general conclusion reached as a result of the post-war debate on the part which charities should play in the welfare state was that while charities should not withdraw from fields in which they were performing useful services, their special function should be to seek out gaps in the statutory services and to pioneer new services. With these principles in mind sections 10 to 12[14a] of the Act of 1960 contain powers for closer coordination of the work of local charities, and for encouraging co-operation between charities and local authorities, the latter, of course, being responsible for many statutory services which parallel or overlap the work of some charities.

24. In order to enable the situation in each area to be assessed and the necessary steps to achieve these objectives to be formulated, provision was made, in section 11 of the Act, for a review of local charities by the local authority. There is, however, no obligation on local authorities to carry out

---

14a Now Charities Act 1993, ss. 76–78, supra.

such a review or on trustees of charities to take part in a review. At the end of a review the local authority can make recommendations to the Charity Commissioners, but the Commissioners can normally make a scheme for a charity only if they receive an application for that purpose from the trustees of that charity.

25. The starting of local reviews of charities was not possible until the registration of existing charities had reached some degree of finality, but the first reviews started in 1964''.[15]

v. Scheme Making Powers[16]

CHARITIES ACT 1993

16. Concurrent jurisdiction with High Court for certain purposes.[17]—(1) Subject to the provisions of this Act, the Commissioners may by order exercise the same jurisdiction and powers as are exercisable by the High Court in charity proceedings for the following purposes—

(a) establishing a scheme for the administration of a charity;[18]

(b) appointing, discharging or removing a charity trustee or trustee for a charity, or removing an officer or employee;

(c) vesting or transferring property, or requiring or entitling any person to call for or make any transfer of property or any payment.

(2) Where the court directs a scheme for the administration of a charity to be established, the court may by order refer the matter to the Commissioners for them to prepare or settle a scheme in accordance with such directions (if any) as the court sees fit to give, and any such order may provide for the scheme to be put into effect by order of the Commissioners as if prepared under subsection (1) above and without any further order of the court.

---

15 By the end of 1980, 1242 schemes had been made as a result of local reviews: Annual Report for 1980, para. 155. The initiation and progress of local reviews, and the establishment of schemes as a result of such reviews was an annual topic in the Reports between 1963 and 1980. They provide useful guidance to authorities contemplating reviews. See Annual Report 1963, paras. 33–36; 1964, paras. 13–30; 1968, paras. 55–60.

16 See Annual Report for 1970, paras. 47–49; 1976, paras. 69–75; Charities Act 1993, ss. 15 (schemes for charities established or regulated by Royal Charter), 17 (schemes for charities established by statute) 20 (publicity for proceedings), 24 (schemes to establish common investment funds, p. 523, post). For examples, see Annual Report for 1975, paras. 51–61; 1976, paras. 76–95; 1977, paras. 86–153; 1978, paras. 99–145; 1979, paras. 86–113; 1980, paras. 113–149; 1981, paras. 79–93; 1982, paras. 58–74 (including the Armitt Trust, Ambleside, for the exhibition of water-colour drawings by Beatrix Potter); 1983, paras. 45–72 (Guide Dogs for the Blind Association); 1984, paras. 32–34 (Hospital of St. Cross, Winchester); 1985, paras. 36–48; 1986, paras. 22– 25, Appx. B (Royal Academy of Music—John Retson Bequest including three named Stradivarius instruments); 1987, para. 48 (sale of 30 Greek manuscripts by Highgate School); 1988, paras. 49–68; White Paper 1989, paras. 6.14–6.16; Leaflet CC 36 ''Making a Scheme''; Annual Report for 1993, paras 39–49 (schemes approved for Holloway and Bedford New College to sell three paintings by Gainsborough, Turner and Constable) and for Bridge House Estate to spend surplus income for maintenance and repair of bridges over the River Thames on transport and access to it for elderly and disabled people in Greater London or for charitable purposes for the general benefit of its inhabitants.

17 See also Reverter of Sites Act 1987, s. 2; Annual Report for 1988, paras. 78–82; [1993–94] CL & PR 243 (D. Morris).

18 No alteration of the purposes of a charity can be made unless the cyprès doctrine is satisfied. See ss. 13 and 14, p. 486 ante.

(3) The Commissioners shall not have any jurisdiction under this section to try or determine the title at law or in equity to any property as between a charity or trustee for a charity and a person holding or claiming the property or an interest in it adversely to the charity, or to try or determine any question as to the existence or extent of any charge or trust.

(4) Subject to the following subsections the Commissioners shall not exercise their jurisdiction under this section as respects any charity, except—

(a) on the application of the charity; or

(b) on an order of the court under subsection (2) above; or

(c) in the case of a charity other than an exempt charity, on the application of the Attorney General.

(5) In the case of a charity which is not an exempt charity and whose income from all sources does not in aggregate exceed £500 a year, the Commissioners may exercise their jurisdiction under this section on the application—

(a) of any one or more of the charity trustees; or

(b) of any person interested in the charity; or

(c) of any two or more inhabitants of the area of the charity if it is a local charity.

(6) Where in the case of a charity, other than an exempt charity, the Commissioners are satisfied that the charity trustees ought in the interests of the charity to apply for a scheme, but have unreasonably refused or neglected to do so and the Commissioners have given the charity trustees an opportunity to make representations to them, the Commissioners may proceed as if an application for a scheme had been made by the charity but the Commissioners shall not have power in a case where they act by virtue of this subsection to alter the purposes of a charity, unless 40 years have elapsed from the date of its foundation.

(8) The Commissioners may on the application of any charity trustee or trustee for a charity, exercise their jurisdiction under this section for the purpose of discharging him from his trusteeship.

(10) The Commissioners shall not exercise their jurisdiction under this section in any case (not referred to them by order of the court) which, by reason of its contentious character, or of any special question of law or of fact which it may involve, or for other reasons, the Commissioners may consider more fit to be adjudicated on by the court.

(11) An appeal against any order of the Commissioners under this section may be brought in the High Court by the Attorney General.

(12) An appeal against any order of the Commissioners under this section may also, at any time within the three months beginning with the day following that on which the order is published, be brought in the High Court by the charity or any of the charity trustees, or by any person removed from any office or employment by the order (unless he is removed with the concurrence of the charity trustees or with the approval of the special visitor, if any, of the charity).

(13) No appeal shall be brought under subsection (12) above except with a certificate of the Commissioners that it is a proper case for an appeal or with the leave of one of the judges of the High Court attached to the Chancery Division.[19]

(14) Where an order of the Commissioners under this section establishes a scheme for the administration of a charity, any person interested in the charity

19 See *Childs v A-G* [1973] 1 WLR 497, [1973] 2 All ER 108.

shall have the like right of appeal under subsection (12) above as a charity trustee, and so also, in the case of a charity which is a local charity in any area, shall any two or more inhabitants of the area and the council of any parish or (in Wales) any community comprising the area or any part of it.

Report of the Charity Commissioners for England and Wales for the year 1982, para. 52.

"Schemes and Orders

52. One of our most important activities is the constructive task of making schemes and orders to enable trustees to administer their charities more efficiently and use their funds and property more effectively in carrying out their purposes. Schemes may deal with all or any of such matters as the appointment of new bodies of trustees, the vesting of property in new trustees or in a custodian trustee, the amalgamation or grouping of charities under a single body of trustees,[20] the provision of *cy-près* objects in place of objects which are no longer practicable,[1] the enlargement of the beneficial area within which the charity operates, and the erection or improvement of buildings to be used for the purposes of the charity. Schemes dealing with only one or two of these subjects are usually short and simple, whereas others, including some which provide for the complete regulation of a charity or a number of charities, may be long and complicated and involve much discussion with the trustees. During the year we established 852 schemes."[2]

Report of the Charity Commissioners for England and Wales for the year 1976, para. 74.

"Amalgamating Schemes

74. We have referred elsewhere in this and previous reports to schemes which group or amalgamate charities. The grouping of charities under a single body of trustees may be effected in one of three ways depending on the circumstances in each case. Some schemes consolidate the charities into a single new charity, so that the constituent charities thereafter lose their identity for all practical purposes. In other schemes the individual charities retain their identity but are all given the same objects so that they can be managed together efficiently with a single set of minute books, books of account, etc. In other cases again it may be inappropriate, or indeed beyond our powers, to give all the charities identical objects and while most of the grouped charities may be given similar purposes the income of one or two of

---

20 Annual Report for 1978, paras. 132–136 (amalgamation of Cuddesdon and Ripon Theological Colleges). For a scheme extending the trustees' power of investment, see Annual Report for 1979, para. 166 (Investment in the Pooh Properties."Pooh is a great money-spinner and has so far withstood the test of time.").

1 See Annual Report for 1989, paras. 74–75, p. 488 ante. The Court has power to order a cy-près scheme for a charitable company: *Liverpool and District Hospital for Diseases of the Heart v A-G* [1981] Ch 193, [1981] 1 All ER 994, p. 475, n. 8, ante; [1984] Conv 112 (J. Warburton). On the alteration of its objects clause by a charitable company, see Charities Act 1993, s. 64.

2 In 1994, 677 Schemes were made: Annual Report for 1994, p. 10.

them may have to be made applicable for other purposes and accounted for separately. This might happen, for instance, where a scheme is being made to group a number of charities for the relief of the needy but the income of one of the charities is applicable partly for the relief of the needy and partly for the advancement of education or of religion."[3]

VI. Provision of Advice

CHARITIES ACT 1993

29. Power to advise charity trustees[4]—(1) The Commissioners may on the written application of any charity trustee give him their opinion or advice on any matter affecting the performance of his duties as such.

(2) A charity trustee or trustee for a charity acting in accordance with the opinion or advice of the Commissioners given under this section with respect to the charity shall be deemed, as regards his responsibility for so acting, to have acted in accordance with his trust, unless, when he does so, either—

(a) he knows or has reasonable cause to suspect that the opinion or advice was given in ignorance of material facts; or

(b) the decision of the court has been obtained on the matter or proceedings are pending to obtain one.

Report of the Charity Commissioners for England and Wales for the year 1986, paras. 17–19.

"17. Giving advice is an essential part of our work and is a statutory duty. We are charged with the general function of giving charity trustees information and advice on any matter affecting the charity as a means of promoting effective use of its resources. Moreover, section 24 of the Charities Act 1960 contains special provisions enabling a charity trustee to seek the opinion and advice of the Commissioners on any matter affecting the performance of his duties as a trustee. Provided that certain conditions are met, such advice protects the trustees acting upon it from any charge of breach of trust. In addition we may give advice without request to charity trustees in any case where we consider advice should be given in the interests of the charity to ensure proper administration of the charity and to correct or prevent a misapplication of its funds. Advice is often tendered as a preliminary to or in the course of our other work. For instance, in considering circumstances where a scheme or order may be required, registering a charity or engaging in an inquiry.

18. It is important to bear in mind that advising trustees on the proper administration of their trust is an essential part of preventing and checking

---

3 See also *Re Freeston's Charity* [1978] 1 WLR 741, [1979] 1 All ER 51.
4 Annual Report for 1970, para. 64; 1982, paras.24–27; 1986, paras. 17–21; 1989, para. 33. In 1987 the Commissioners advised on nearly 3,000 draft governing instruments for proposed charities; Annual Report for 1987, para.11. Commissioners must exercise reasonable care in giving advice under s. 24, but no individual duty of care is owed to potential objects of charity for wrong advice given: *Mills v Winchester Diocesan Board of Finance* [1989] Ch 428, [1989] 2 All ER 317. See also *Marley v Mutual Security Merchant Bank Co and Trust Ltd* [1991] 3 All ER 198.

maladministration and abuse and is enjoined on us specifically by section 1 (3) of the Charities Act 1960.[5] It would be wrong to concentrate upon the investigation of abuse after it has occurred at the expense of preventative measures.

(19) Other bodies also offer advice. Much general advice is given by voluntary bodies, for example the Charities Aid Foundation, National Council for Voluntary Organisations, National Association of Almshouses, Institute of Charity Fundraising Managers, Schools Associations etc. For our part we have continued to revise and expand the range of advisory leaflets which we make available to charity trustees. We are particularly concerned to raise the quality of trusteeship of the tens of thousands of charities whose trusteeship is undertaken by public spirited people from a wide variety of backgrounds without the assistance of professional staff. Such people undoubtedly bring a wide range of experience and knowledge to the administration of their charities but many have no previous experience of the administration of a trust or the requirements or responsibilities which are peculiar to charitable trustees. We hope, by making information freely available to charity trustees through leaflets, to reduce the number of individual enquiries made to us and so enable us to divert our limited resources to other areas.''[6]

VII. Investment

A. Extended Powers of Investment

Sections 70 and 71 of the Charities Act 1993 (re-enacting sections 38 and 39 of the Charities Act 1992) give charitable trustees wider powers of investment than those available under the Trustee Investments Act 1961 (p. 663 post). These powers are in advance of any general reform of the law in this area.[7]

CHARITIES ACT 1993

70. Relaxation of restrictions on wider-range investments—(1) The Secretary of State may by order made with the consent of the Treasury—
  (a) direct that, in the case of a trust fund consisting of property held by or in trust for a charity, any division of the fund in pursuance of section 2(1) of the Trustee Investments Act 1961 (trust funds to be divided so that wider-range and narrower-range investments are equal in value) shall be made so that the value of the wider-range part at the time of the division bears to the then value of the narrower-range part such proportion as is specified in the order;
  (b) provide that, in its application in relation to such a trust fund, that Act shall have effect subject to such modifications so specified as the

5 Now Charities Act 1993, s. 1(3).
6 See also the various Charity Commissioners explanatory leaflets listed in CC 1 (Charities and the Charity Commission).
7 See CC Leaflet 14 (Investment of Charitable Funds: Basic Principles); 38 (Expenditure and Replacement of Permanent Endowment). On the delegation of investment decisions by Charity Trustees, see [1994] Ch Com Rep vol 2, pp. 28–32. On schemes conferring wider powers of investment, see [1995] Ch Com Rep Vol 3, pp. 18–28. On reform, see [1995/96] 3 CL & PR 65 (H.P. Dale and M. Gwinnell).

Secretary of State considers appropriate in consequence of, or in connection with, any such direction.

(2) Where, before the coming into force of an order under this section, a trust fund consisting of property held by or in trust for a charity has already been divided in pursuance of section 2(1) of that Act, the fund may, notwithstanding anything in that provision, be again divided (once only) in pursuance of that provision during the continuance in force of the order.[8]

71. Extension of powers of investment—(1) The Secretary of State may by regulations made with the consent of the Treasury make, with respect to property held by or in trust for a charity, provision authorising a trustee to invest such property in any manner specified in the regulations, being a manner of investment not for the time being included in any Part of Schedule 1 to the Trustee Investments Act 1961.

(2) Regulations under this section may make such provision—

(a) regulating the investment of property in any manner authorised by virtue of subsection (1) above, and

(b) with respect to the variation and retention of investments so made, as the Secretary of State considers appropriate.

(3) Such regulations may, in particular, make provision—

(a) imposing restrictions with respect to the proportion of the property held by or in trust for a charity which may be invested in any manner authorised by virtue of subsection (1) above, being either restrictions applying to investment in any such manner generally or restrictions applying to investment in any particular such manner;

(b) imposing the like requirements with respect to the obtaining and consideration of advice as are imposed by any of the provisions of section 6 of the Trustee Investments Act 1961 (duty of trustees in choosing investments).

(4) Any power of investment conferred by any regulations under this section—

(a) shall be in addition to, and not in derogation from, any power conferred otherwise than by such regulations; and

(b) shall not be limited by the trusts of a charity (in so far as they are not contained in any Act or instrument made under an enactment) unless it is excluded by those trusts in express terms;

but any such power shall only be exercisable by a trustee in so far as a contrary intention is not expressed in any Act or in any instrument made under an enactment and relating to the powers of the trustee.

B. Common Investment and Deposit Funds[9]

Under section 26 of the Charities Act 1960, power was given to the court or the Commissioners to create common investment schemes under which property transferred to the fund is invested by trustees appointed to manage

---

8 Charities (Trustee Investments Act 1961) Order 1995 (SI 1995 No. 1092) directs that any division of a charitable trust fund shall be made so that the value of the wider-range part at the time of the division bears to the then value of the narrower-range part the proportion of three to one.

9 Annual Report for 1993, paras. 79–81; CC Leaflets 15 (CIF and CDF); 15a (an alphabetical list of available funds).

the fund. The participating charities are entitled to shares related to their contributions. Under this power, the Commissioners established the Charities Official Investment Fund in 1968. The Charities Act 1992 went further and authorised the creation of common deposit schemes. The legislation is now consolidated in the Charities Act 1993.

CHARITIES ACT 1993

24. Schemes to establish common investment funds.—(1) The court or the Commissioners may by order make and bring into effect schemes (in this section referred to as "common investment schemes") for the establishment of common investment funds under trusts which provide—

    (a) for property transferred to the fund by or on behalf of a charity participating in the scheme to be invested under the control of trustees appointed to manage the fund; and

    (b) for the participating charities to be entitled (subject to the provisions of the scheme) to the capital and income of the fund in shares determined by reference to the amount or value of the property transferred to it by or on behalf of each of them and to the value of the fund at the time of the transfers.

(2) The court or the Commissioners may make a common investment scheme on the application of any two or more charities.[10]

(3) A common investment scheme may be made in terms admitting any charity to participate, or the scheme may restrict the right to participate in any manner.

(4) A common investment scheme may make provision for, and for all matters connected with, the establishment, investment, management and winding up of the common investment fund, and may in particular include provision—

    (a) for remunerating persons appointed trustees to hold or manage the fund or any part of it, with or without provision authorising a person to receive the remuneration notwithstanding that he is also a charity trustee of or trustee for a participating charity;

    (b) for restricting the size of the fund, and for regulating as to time, amount or otherwise the right to transfer property to or withdraw it from the fund, and for enabling sums to be advanced out of the fund by way of loan to a participating charity pending the withdrawal of property from the fund by the charity;

    (c) for enabling income to be withheld from distribution with a view to avoiding fluctuations in the amounts distributed, and generally for regulating distributions of income;

    (d) for enabling moneys to be borrowed temporarily for the purpose of meeting payments to be made out of the fund;

    (e) for enabling questions arising under the scheme as to the right of a charity to participate, or as to the rights of participating charities, or as to any other matter, to be conclusively determined by the decision of the trustees managing the fund or in any other manner;

    (f) for regulating the accounts and information to be supplied to participating charities.

10 Even though the trustees of the trust funds are the same: *Re London University's Charitable Trust* [1964] Ch 282, [1963] 3 All ER 859.

(5) A common investment scheme, in addition to the provision for property to be transferred to the fund on the basis that the charity shall be entitled to a share in the capital and income of the fund, may include provision for enabling sums to be deposited by or on behalf of a charity on the basis that (subject to the provisions of the scheme) the charity shall be entitled to repayment of the sums deposited and to interest thereon at a rate determined by or under the scheme; and where a scheme makes any such provision it shall also provide for excluding from the amount of capital and income to be shared between charities participating otherwise than by way of deposit such amounts (not exceeding the amounts properly attributable to the making of deposits) as are from time to time reasonably required in respect of the liabilities of the fund for the repayment of deposits and for the interest on deposits, including amounts required by way of reserve.

25. Schemes to establish common deposit funds—(1) The court or the Commissioners may by order make and bring into effect schemes (in this section referred to as "common deposit schemes") for the establishment of common deposit funds under trusts which provide—

(a) for sums to be deposited by or on behalf of a charity participating in the scheme and invested under the control of trustees appointed to manage the fund; and

(b) for any such charity to be entitled (subject to the provisions of the scheme) to repayment of any sums so deposited and to interest thereon at a rate determined under the scheme.

VIII. Dealings with Charity Property[11]

A. Power to Authorise Dealings

Section 26 of the Charities Act 1993 (re-enacting section 23 of the Charities Act 1960) empowers the Charity Commissioners to authorise transactions beneficial to a charity.

CHARITIES ACT 1993

26. Power to authorise dealings with charity property etc.[12]—(1) Subject to the provisions of this section, where it appears to the commissioners that any action proposed or contemplated in the administration of a charity is expedient in the interests of the charity, they may by order sanction that action, whether or not it would otherwise be within the powers exercisable by the charity trustees in the administration of the charity; and anything done under the authority of such an order shall be deemed to be properly done in the exercise of those powers.

---

11 CC Leaflet 28 (Disposal of Charity Land); 33 (Acquiring Land); HM Land Registry Practice Advice Leaflet No. 1 (Charity Land Transactions) (2nd edn 1993); [1992–93] 1 CL & PR 27 (J. Warburton); (1995) NLJ Christmas Appeals Supplement 14 (P. Luxton). For a precedent for the transfer of freehold land, see (1993) 143 NLJ 1229. 1,083 orders were made in 1994: Annual Report for 1994, p.10.

12 Annual Report for 1989, paras. 112–14; 1992, paras. 54–57 (Central Young Men's Christian Association). On decisions under the earlier law, see Annual Report for 1982, paras. 75–80 (sale of the Old Vic Theatre); 1983 (sale of the Mermaid and Roundhouse Theatres).

(2) An order under this section may be made so as to authorise a particular transaction, compromise or the like, or a particular application of property, or so as to give a more general authority, and (without prejudice to the generality of subsection (1) above) may authorise a charity to use common premises, or employ a common staff, or otherwise combine for any purpose of administration, with any other charity.

B. Restrictions on Dispositions

Part V of the Charities Act 1993 (re-enacting sections 32–37 of the Charities Act 1992) provides that the consent of the Charity Commissioners shall no longer be required by charity trustees to sell charity land, provided that the statutory requirements are satisfied.[13] There are less stringent requirements for leases for seven years or less.

CHARITIES ACT 1993

36. Restrictions on dispositions—(1) Subject to the following provisions of this section and section 40[14] below, no land held by or in trust for a charity shall be sold, leased or otherwise disposed of without an order of the court or of the Commissioners.

(2) Subsection (1) above shall not apply to a disposition of such land if—
  (a) the disposition is made to a person who is not—
    (i) a connected person (as defined in Schedule 5 to this Act), or
    (ii) a trustee for, or nominee of, a connected person; and
  (b) the requirements of subsection (3) or (5) below have been complied with in relation to it.

(3) Except where the proposed disposition is the granting of such a lease as is mentioned in subsection (5) below, the charity trustees must, before entering into an agreement for the sale, or (as the case may be) for a lease or other disposition, of the land—
  (a) obtain and consider a written report on the proposed disposition from a qualified surveyor instructed by the trustees and acting exclusively for the charity;
  (b) advertise the proposed disposition for such period and in such manner as the surveyor has advised in his report (unless he has there advised that it would not be in the best interests of the charity to advertise the proposed disposition); and
  (c) decide that they are satisfied, having considered the surveyor's report, that the terms on which the disposition is proposed to be made are the best that can reasonably be obtained for the charity.

(4) For the purposes of subsection (3) above a person is a qualified surveyor if—
  (a) he is a fellow or professional associate of the Royal Institution of Chartered Surveyors or of the Incorporated Society of Valuers and Auctioneers or satisfies such other requirement or requirements as may be prescribed by regulations made by the Secretary of State;[15]and

---

13 A disposition not complying with s. 36 is valid in favour of a purchaser in good faith for money or money's worth: Charities Act 1993, s. 37(4).
14 Voluntary release of rentcharges by charities.
15 Charities (Qualified Surveyors' Reports) Regs 1992 (SI 1992 No. 2980)

(b) he is reasonably believed by the charity trustees to have ability in, and experience of, the valuation of land of the particular kind, and in the particular area, in question;

and any report prepared for the purposes of that subsection shall contain such information, and deal with such matters, as may be prescribed by regulations so made.

(5) Where the proposed disposition is the granting of a lease for a term ending not more than seven years after it is granted (other than one granted wholly or partly in consideration of a fine), the charity trustees must, before entering into an agreement for the lease—

(a) obtain and consider the advice on the proposed disposition of a person who is reasonably believed by the trustees to have the requisite ability and practical experience to provide them with competent advice on the proposed disposition; and

(b) decide that they are satisfied, having considered that person's advice, that the terms on which the disposition is proposed to be made are the best that can reasonably be obtained for the charity.

(6) Where—

(a) any land is held by or in trust for a charity, and

(b) the trusts on which it is so held stipulate that it is to be used for the purposes, or any particular purposes, of the charity,

then (subject to subsections (7) and (8) below and without prejudice to the operation of the preceding provisions of this section) the land shall not be sold, leased or otherwise disposed of unless the charity trustees have previously—

(i) given public notice of the proposed disposition, inviting representations to be made to them within a time specified in the notice, being not less than one month from the date of the notice; and

(ii) taken into consideration any representations made to them within that time about the proposed disposition.

(7) Subsection (6) above shall not apply to any such disposition of land as is there mentioned if—

(a) the disposition is to be effected with a view to acquiring by way of replacement other property which is to be held on the trusts referred to in paragraph (b) of that subsection; or

(b) the disposition is the granting of a lease for a term ending not more than two years after it is granted (other than one granted wholly or partly in consideration of a fine).

(8) The Commissioners may direct—

(a) that subsection (6) above shall not apply to dispositions of land held by or in trust for a charity or class of charities (whether generally or only in the case of a specified class or dispositions or land, or otherwise as may be provided in the direction), or

(b) that that subsection shall not apply to a particular disposition of land held by or in trust for a charity,

if, on an application made to them in writing by or on behalf of the charity or charities in question, the Commissioners are satisfied that it would be in the interests of the charity or charities for them to give the direction.

(9) The restrictions on disposition imposed by this section apply notwithstanding anything in the trusts of a charity; but nothing in this section applies—

(a) to any disposition for which general or special authority is expressly given (without the authority being made subject to the sanction of an order of the court) by any statutory provision contained in or having effect under an Act of Parliament[16] or by any scheme legally established; or

(b) to any disposition of land held by or in trust for a charity which—
   (i) is made to another charity otherwise than for the best price that can reasonably be obtained, and
   (ii) is authorised to be so made by the trusts of the first-mentioned charity; or

(c) to the granting, by or on behalf of a charity and in accordance with its trusts, of a lease to any beneficiary under those trusts where the lease—
   (i) is granted otherwise than for the best rent that can reasonably be obtained; and
   (ii) is intended to enable the demised premises to be occupied for the purposes, or any particular purposes, of the charity.

(10) Nothing in this section applies—
(a) to any disposition of land held by or in trust for an exempt charity;
(b) to any disposition of land by way of mortgage or other security; or
(c) to any disposition of an advowson.

(11) In this section "land" means land in England or Wales.[17]

IX. Ex Gratia Payments

Section 27 of the Charities Act 1993 (re-enacting section 17 of the Charities Act 1992) extends to the Commissioners the power of the Attorney-General to permit a charity to make an ex gratia payment under his supervision. Guidance as to the circumstances under which this power may be exercised is given in *Re Snowden* and *Re Henderson* [1970] Ch 700.

CHARITIES ACT 1993

27. Power to authorise ex gratia payments etc.—(1) Subject to subsection (3) below, the Commissioners may by order exercise the same power as is exercisable by the Attorney General to authorise the charity trustees of a charity—
(a) to make any application of property of the charity, or
(b) to waive to any extent, on behalf of the charity, its entitlement to receive any property,
in a case where the charity trustees—
   (i) (apart from this section) have no power to do so, but
   (ii) in all the circumstances regard themselves as being under a moral obligation to do so.

(2) The power conferred on the Commissioners by subsection (1) above shall be exercisable by them under the supervision of, and in accordance with

---

16 For example, Housing Associations Act 1985, as amended by Charities Act 1992, s. 78(1) and Sched 6.
17 See also ss. 37 (supplementary provisions); 38–39 (mortgages); Land Registration Rules 1925, rr 60–62, as substituted by Land Registration (Charities) Rules 1993 (SI 1993 No. 1704); and 1995 (SI 1995 No. 140).

such directions as may be given by, the Attorney General; and any such directions may in particular require the Commissioners, in such circumstances as are specified in the directions—
(a) to refrain from exercising that power; or
(b) to consult the Attorney General before exercising it.
(3) Where—
(a) an application is made to the Commissioners for them to exercise that power in a case where they are not precluded from doing so by any such directions, but
(b) they consider that it would nevertheless be desirable for the application to be entertained by the Attorney General rather than by them,
they shall refer the application to the Attorney General.
(4) It is hereby declared that where, in the case of any application made to them as mentioned in subsection (3)(a) above, the Commissioners determine the application by refusing to authorise charity trustees to take any action falling within subsection (1)(a) or (b) above, that refusal shall not preclude the Attorney General, on an application subsequently made to him by the trustees, from authorising the trustees to take that action.

Report of the Charity Commissioners for England and Wales for the year 1969, paras. 27–29.

"27. Briefly summarised the facts in the *Snowden* case were that a testator gave to close relatives all his shares in certain companies with which he had been connected and, after making other legacies, left his residuary estate to a number of charities. Those companies were, however, taken over by a much larger company and all the testator's shares were sold and at the date of his death were represented in his estate by cash. The result was that nothing passed under the gift to the relatives, but the legacies received by the charities under the residuary gift were enhanced to an extent that the testator obviously had not anticipated. Most, but not all, of the charities felt that they were under an obligation to make a payment out of the residuary legacies to the relatives to go some way towards achieving the obvious intention of the testator. It was argued on their behalf that since charities rely for their subscriptions on the recognition by the public of a moral duty to support charities, so also charities cannot and must not ignore moral obligations that are laid on them and should behave in this respect at least as well as a responsible individual.

28. The facts in the Henderson case were different because there were no specific named charities which benefited and which could consider whether or not an ex-gratia payment should be made. In this case the testatrix made a holograph will to which certain words had been added in her handwriting but in a different colour. It was uncertain whether these words had been added before execution and they were not admitted to probate; but in the circumstances they would have had a considerable effect in increasing the size of legacies that were payable to a nephew and niece. The will ended with the words: "Anything over to *Charitys*" (*sic*). The proceedings were brought by the executrix who asked that she might be allowed to make some reasonable payment to provide increased legacies for the nephew and niece to meet the wishes expressed in the written words even though this would reduce the size of the residue falling to be distributed to charities.

29. Mr. Justice Cross delivered a considered judgment in which he reviewed other instances in which persons under disability are expected to recognise moral obligations and considered some old cases where charities were authorised not to press to their full legal claims arising from breaches of trust. He then reached the important conclusion that the court and the Attorney-General had power to give authority to charity trustees to make ex-gratia payments out of funds held on charitable trusts. It is to be noted, however, that the Judge did not suggest that trustees have any power themselves to make such payments without authority. The Judge emphasised that the power to give this authority is not to be exercised on slender grounds but only in cases where it can be fairly said that if the charity were an individual it would be morally wrong for him to refuse to make the payment. He drew the distinction between cases like those which were before him in which the testator never intended the charity to receive so large a gift as it did receive and other cases in which the testator did intend the charity to receive exactly what came to it but the testator's relatives considered that he was not morally justified in leaving his money to a charity rather than to them. In the latter case there would as a rule be no moral obligation resting on the charity and no authority should be given for it to make a payment. There might be some cases where an ex-gratia payment could be justified even though the intentions of the testator had been carried out; for instance the testator in making the gift to the charity might have been breaking a solemn, though not legally enforceable, promise to leave a legacy to someone else. The judge, however, said he thought that instances in which an ex-gratia payment would be justified would be rarer in the cases where the testator clearly intended to leave the money to charity and not to the claimant, than in those in which the testator's obvious intention to benefit the claimant had been frustrated through some oversight or legal technicality."[18]

X. Accounts, Returns and Reports

Part VI of the Charities Act 1993 (re-enacting sections 19 to 27 of the Charities Act 1992) imposes strict duties on trustees [19] to keep annual accounting records, prepare annual accounts, arrange for their audit, and send annual reports to the Commissioners on their activities, with a statement of the accounts and the auditor's report. There are criminal penalties for failure to submit reports and returns.[20]

This was one of the main areas of anxiety stressed by the White Paper.

CHARITIES ACT 1993

41. Duty to keep accounting records—(1) The charity trustees of a charity shall ensure that accounting records are kept in respect of the charity which are sufficient to show and explain all the charity's transactions, and which are such as to—

---

18 See Annual Report for 1970, para. 84; 1976, paras. 114–116; 1977, paras. 154–156.
19 For charitable companies, see Companies Act 1985, ss. 221, 228, 236. Sch 4. Exempt charities are required to keep proper books of account: Charities Act 1993, s. 46.
20 See Statement of Recommended Practice (SORP) on accounts by charities: CC Leaflet 51; (1995) SJ Christmas Charity and Appeals Supplement 22 (D.G. Cracknell).

(a) disclose at any time, with reasonable accuracy, the financial position of the charity at that time, and

(b) enable the trustees to ensure that, where any statements of accounts are prepared by them under section 42(1) below, those statements of accounts comply with the requirements of regulations under that provision.

42. Annual statements of accounts—(1) The charity trustees of a charity shall (subject to subsection (3) below) prepare in respect of each financial year of the charity a statement of accounts complying with such requirements as to its form and contents as may be prescribed by regulations made by the Secretary of State.

(2) Without prejudice to the generality of subsection (1) above, regulations under that subsection may make provision—

(a) for any such statement to be prepared in accordance with such methods and principles as are specified or referred to in the regulations;

(b) as to any information to be provided by way of notes to the accounts;

and regulations under that subsection may also make provision for determining the financial years of a charity for the purposes of this Act and any regulations made under it.

(3) Where a charity's gross income in any financial year does not exceed £100,000,[21] the charity trustees may, in respect of that year, elect to prepare the following, namely—

(a) a receipts and payment account, and

(b) a statement of assets and liabilities,

instead of a statement of accounts under subsection (1) above.

43. Annual audit or examination of charity accounts—(1) Subsection (2) below applies to a financial year of a charity ("the relevant year") if the charity's gross income or total expenditure in any of the following, namely—

(a) the relevant year,

(b) the financial year of the charity immediately preceding the relevant year (if any), and

(c) the financial year of the charity immediately preceding the year specified in paragraph (b) above (if any),

exceeds £250,000.[21]

(2) If this subsection applies to a financial year of a charity, the accounts of the charity for that year shall be audited by a person who—

(a) is, in accordance with section 25 of the Companies Act 1989 (eligibility for appointment) eligible for appointment as a company auditor, or

(b) is a member of a body for the time being specified in regulations under section 44 below and is under the rules of that body eligible for appointment as auditor of the charity.

(3) If subsection (2) above does not apply to a financial year of a charity, then (subject to subsection (4) below) the accounts of the charity for that year shall, at the election of the charity trustees, either—

(a) be examined by an independent examiner, that is to say an independent person who is reasonably believed by the trustees to have

---

21 As substituted by the Charities Act 1993 (Substitution of Sums) Order 1995 (SI 1995 No. 2696).

the requisite ability and practical experience to carry out a competent examination of the accounts, or

(b) be audited by such a person as is mentioned in subsection (2) above.

45. Annual reports—(1) The charity trustees of a charity shall prepare in respect of each financial year of the charity an annual report containing—

(a) such a report by the trustees on the activities of the charity during that year, and

(b) such other information relating to the charity or to its trustees or officers,

as may be prescribed by regulations made by the Secretary of State.

(2) Without prejudice to the generality of subsection (1) above, regulations under that subsection may make provision—

(a) for any such report as is mentioned in paragraph (a) of that subsection to be prepared in accordance with such principles as are specified or referred to in the regulations;

(b) enabling the Commissioners to dispense with any requirement prescribed by virtue of subsection (1)(b) above in the case of a particular charity or a particular class of charities, or in the case of a particular financial year of a charity or of any class of charities.

(3) The annual report required to be prepared under this section in respect of any financial year of a charity shall be transmitted to the Commissioners by the charity trustees. . .

(6) Any annual report transmitted to the Commissioners under subsection (3) above, together with the documents attached to it, shall be kept by the Commissioners for such period as they think fit.

47. Public inspection of annual reports etc.—(1) Any annual report or other document kept by the Commissioners in pursuance of section 45(6) above shall be open to public inspection at all reasonable times—

(a) during the period for which it is so kept; or

(b) if the Commissioners so determine, during such lesser period as they may specify.

48. Annual returns by registered charities—(1) Every registered charity shall prepare in respect of each of its financial years an annual return in such form, and containing such information, as may be prescribed by regulations made by the Commissioners.

49. Offences— Any person who, without reasonable excuse, is persistently in default in relation to any requirement imposed—

(a) by section 45 (3) above (taken with section 45 (4) or (5), as the case may require);[1] or

(b) by section 47 (2)[2] or 48 (2)[3] above,

shall be guilty of an offence and liable on summary conviction to a fine not exceeding level 4 on the standard scale.[4]

---

1 Failure to submit the annual report to the Commissioners.
2 Failure to provide members of the public with copies of accounts.
3 Failure to provide the Commissioners with the annual return.
4 Criminal Justice Act 1982 s. 37(2); the present amount is £2,500. See generally [1992-93] 1 CL & PR 101 (F. Quint).

XI. Inquiries

Section 8 of the Charities Act 1993 sets out the powers of the Commissioners to institute inquiries. An inquiry is necessary before they can exercise their wide powers for the protection of a charity under section 18 (p. 535 post).

CHARITIES ACT 1993

8. General power to institute inquiries[5]—(1) The Commissioners may from time to time institute inquiries with regard to charities or a particular charity or class of charities, either generally or for particular purposes, but no such inquiry shall extend to any exempt charity.

(2) The Commissioners may either conduct such an inquiry themselves or appoint a person to conduct it and make a report to them.

(6) Where an inquiry has been held under this section, the Commissioners may either—

(a) cause the report of the person conducting the inquiry, or such other statement of the results of the inquiry, as they think fit, to be printed and published, or

(b) publish any such report or statement in some other way which is calculated in their opinion to bring it to the attention of persons who may wish to make representations to them about the action to be taken.

———

Report of the Charity Commissioners for England and Wales for the year 1986, para. 44.

"44. Allegations of abuse cover a wide range of problems: alleged misappropriation of funds forms only a small proportion of the cases examined. Complaints cover such matters as unconstitutional behaviour, inadequate financial control, weak administration, unduly high administration or fund-raising costs, factional disputes or personality clashes, political activities, deficiencies in the treatment of beneficiaries,[6] and dubious

---

5 See also ss. 9 (power to call for documents, and search records), 18 (power to act for protection of charities), p. 535 post; CC Leaflet 47 (Investigating Charities); and generally [1992–93] 1. CL & PR 127 (E. Cairns).

6 For the wide scope of an inquiry under the section and its predecessor, Charities Act 1960, s. 6, see Annual Report for 1979, paras. 24–36 (*Rule v Charity Commissioners*). See also Annual Reports for 1973, paras. 87–97; 1974, paras. 78–97; 1975, paras. 74–94; 1976, paras. 125–142; 1977, paras. 159–165; 1978, paras. 162–164; 1979, paras. 125–139; 1980, paras.156–171; 1981, paras. 105–129; 1982, paras. 97–109; 1983, paras. 87–94; 1984, paras. 46–54 (Official Solicitor appointed to act as trustee); 1985, paras. 72–89; 1986, paras. 43–56; 1987, paras. 27–38; 1988, paras. 35–57; 1991, paras. 111–130 (Oxfam and War on Want); 1992, paras. 79–104; (1993) Decisions of Charity Commissioners 24 (Royal British Legion); 1993, paras. 52–60. See *Jones v A-G* (1976) Times, 10 November; Annual Report for 1976, paras. 25–29, p. 633, post.

fund-raising methods.[7] Many complaints are based on misapprehension about trustees' powers; some are trivial or obsessive. All allegations and complaints, whether pointing to a weakness in administration or a breach of trust, are investigated unless they are clearly mistaken, vindictive or repetitive; if they are substantiated, action is taken to remedy the situation if it is possible to do so.''

Report of the Charity Commissioners for England and Wales for the year 1994, pp. 11–12.

"Before opening an inquiry we carry out a short preliminary evaluation to see whether there is a prima facie cause for concern which calls for an investigation or whether the matter at issue could more helpfully be dealt with in another way.

We opened 1,600 evaluation cases during the year, an 85% increase compared with 1993. 909 of these (57%) arose from monitoring and other internal Commission operations, and 691 (43%) from external sources, including public complaints and cases referred by the police. Cases arising from monitoring and internal operations showed an increase of 200% over 1993.

Of the 1,600 evaluations:

691 (43%) revealed no significant causes for concern;

282 (18%) revealed matters which were dealt with by advice and information;

397 (25%) led to inquiries being opened; and

230 (14%) were outstanding at the end of the year.

523 inquiry cases were completed in the year. In 226 of the inquiry cases completed, we were satisfied as a result of our enquiries that no significant cause for concern existed in fact. In 297 cases however significant causes for concern were substantiated:

195 (66%) were concerned with maladministration (e.g. inadequate management or financial controls, misunderstanding difficulties with associated trading organisations);

51 (17%) were concerned with fund-raising abuse;

43 (14%) revealed evidence of deliberate malpractice;

5 (2%) identified improper political activities by charities, and

3 (1%) were concerned with tax abuse.

The Charities Act 1993 gives us a number of protective powers. In the course of our inquiries we took the following actions:

---

7 See Part II of the Charities Act 1992 (Control of Fund-Raising for Charitable Institutions), which introduced a new regime aimed at professional fund-raisers; and Part III (Public Charitable Collections), which repealed earlier legislation and established a single regime for all collections; Charitable Institutions (Fund-Raising) Regs 1994 (SI 1994 No. 3024); CC Leaflet 20 (Fundraising and Charities); [1992–93] 1 CL & PR 35, 147, 233 (P. Luxton).

On fundraising generally see Picarda, chap. 45; Tudor, chap 7; and on fundraising for maintained schools [1995] Conv 453 (D. Morris).

104 Orders or Directions were made to obtain information or documents;
34 bank accounts were frozen;
30 orders were made restricting charity transactions;
11 trustees were appointed (no trustees were removed);
4 receivers and managers were appointed.

We had 708 investigation cases in hand at the end of the year. Our use of the power to appoint receivers and managers is discussed and illustrated on page 16 below.

In cases where a cause for concern was substantiated we were able to record the recovery or protection from actual or potential risk of charity property to an estimated value of £19 million."

XII. Trustees[8]

A. Number

TRUSTEE ACT 1925

34. Limitation of the number of trustees.—(3) This section[9] only applies to settlements and dispositions of land, and the restrictions imposed on the number of trustees do not apply—

(*a*) in the case of land vested in trustees for charitable, ecclesiastical, or public purposes.

B. Acting by Majority

In **Re Whiteley** [1910] 1 Ch 600, one question was whether a decision of the majority of charitable trustees was binding on the whole. Earlier cases[10] had held that the decision of the majority was binding in matters of a public nature. EVE J held that the rule covered decisions of charitable trustees generally, and said at 608:

"It is true that the authorities referred to by the applicants are both concerned with the appointment of a person to discharge the duties of an office of a public nature, but I cannot read the observations of Lord Lyndhurst[11] as limiting the principle there stated to the particular class of case with which he was there dealing; and I think when he speaks of a 'trust of a public nature' he is using an expression equivalent for all practical purposes to 'a trust of a charitable nature'. In other words, I regard the words 'public' and 'charitable' in this connection as synonymous, and, so regarding them, I think that the rule on which the applicants rely is of general application."

---

8 See CC Leaflet 3 (Responsibilities of Charity Trustees). For the personal liability of charity trustees and their right to be indemnified out of the trust fund, see (1979) 95 LQR 99 (A.J. Hawkins).
9 See p. 615, post.
10 *Wilkinson v Malin* (1832) 2 Tyr 544; *Perry v Shipway* (1859) 4 De G & J 353.
11 *Wilkinson v Malin*, supra, at 571.

C. Appointment

CHARITIES ACT 1993

18. Power to act for protection of charities.—
(5) The Commissioners may by order made of their own motion appoint a person to be a charity trustee[12]—
(a) in place of a charity trustee removed by them under this section or otherwise;
(b) where there are no charity trustees, or where by reason of vacancies in their number or the absence or incapacity of any of their number the charity cannot apply for the appointment;
(c) where there is a single charity trustee, not being a corporation aggregate, and the Commissioners are of opinion that it is necessary to increase the number for the proper administration of the charity;
(d) where the Commissioners are of opinion that it is necessary for the proper administration of the charity to have an additional charity trustee because one of the existing charity trustees who ought nevertheless to remain a charity trustee either cannot be found or does not act or is outside England and Wales.
(6) The powers of the Commissioners under this section to remove or appoint charity trustees of their own motion shall include power to make any such order with respect to the vesting in or transfer to the charity trustees of any property as the Commissioners could make on the removal or appointment of a charity trustee by them under section 16 above.[13]
(7) Any order under this section for the removal or appointment of a charity trustee or trustee for a charity, or for the vesting or transfer of any property shall be of the like effect as an order made under section 16 above.
(12) Before exercising any jurisdiction under this section otherwise than by virtue of subsection (1) above, the Commissioners shall give notice of their intention to do so to each of the charity trustees, except any that cannot be found or has no known address in the United Kingdom; and any such notice may be given by post and, if given by post, may be addressed to the recipient's last known address in the United Kingdom.
(16) This section shall not apply to an exempt charity.

16. Concurrent jurisdiction with High Court for certain purposes—(1)(*b*) (p. 517, ante).

83. Transfer and evidence of title to property vested in trustees.—(1) Where, under the trusts of a charity, trustees of property held for the purposes of the charity may be appointed or discharged by resolution of a meeting of the charity trustees, members or other persons, a memorandum declaring a trustee to have been so appointed or discharged shall be sufficient evidence of that fact, if the memorandum is signed either at the meeting by the person presiding or in some other manner directed by the meeting, and is attested by two persons present at the meeting.

---

12 "Means the persons having the general control and management of the administration of a charity", s. 97.
13 P. 517, ante.

(2) A memorandum evidencing the appointment or discharge of a trustee under subsection (1) above, if executed as a deed, shall have the like operation under section 40 of the Trustee Act, 1925[14] (which relates to vesting declarations as respects trust property in deeds appointing or discharging trustees), as if the appointment or discharge were effected by the deed.

D. Retirement

Charity trustees may retire in the same way as trustees of private trusts.[15]

Law Reform Committee 23rd Report (The Powers and Duties of Trustees) 1982 Cmnd. 8733, paras. 9.1., VI, 39, 40.

"39. Section 39 of the Trustee Act 1925 (p. 629, post) should be amended so as to permit a charity trustee to retire on giving formal written notice to his co-trustees (para. 6.2)

40. We also recommend that some provision equivalent to section [83 of the Charities Act 1993] be introduced so that the remaining charity trustees can produce a memorandum which will constitute sufficient evidence of the fact that one of their number has retired. (para. 6.2)"

E. Removal and Suspension

CHARITIES ACT 1993

18. Power to act for protection of charities—(1) Where, at any time after they have instituted an inquiry under section 8 above[16] with respect to any charity, the Commissioners are satisfied—

(a) that there is or has been any misconduct or mismanagement in the administration of the charity; or

(b) that it is necessary or desirable to act for the purpose of protecting the property of the charity or securing a proper application for the purposes of the charity of that property or of property coming to the charity

the Commissioners may of their own motion do one or more of the following things—

(i) by order suspend any trustee, charity trustee, officer, agent or employee of the charity from the exercise of his office or employment pending consideration being given to his removal (whether under this section or otherwise);

(ii) by order appoint such number of additional charity trustees as they consider necessary for the proper administration of the charity;

(iii) by order vest any property held by or in trust for the charity in the official custodian, or require the persons in whom any such property is

14 P. 622, post.
15 P. 629, post.
16 P. 532, ante.

vested to transfer it to him, or appoint any person to transfer any such property to him;
(iv) order any person who holds any property on behalf of the charity, or of any trustee for it, not to part with the property without the approval of the Commissioners;
(v) order any debtor of the charity not to make any payment in or towards the discharge of his liability to the charity without the approval of the Commissioners;
(vi) by order restrict (notwithstanding anything in the trusts of the charity) the transactions which may be entered into, or the nature or amount of the payments which may be made, in the administration of the charity without the approval of the Commissioners;
(vii) by order appoint (in accordance with section 19 below) a receiver and manager in respect of the property and affairs of the charity.[17]
(2) Where, at any time after they have instituted an inquiry under section 8 above with respect to any charity, the Commissioners are satisfied—
(a) that there is or has been any misconduct or mismanagement in the administration of the charity; and
(b) that it is necessary or desirable to act for the purpose of protecting the property of the charity or securing a proper application for the purposes of the charity of that property or of property coming to the charity
the Commissioners may of their own motion do either or both of the following things—
(i) by order remove any trustee, charity trustee, officer, agent or employee of the charity who has been responsible for or privy to the misconduct or mismanagement or has by his conduct contributed to it or facilitated it;[18]
(ii) by order establish a scheme for the administration of the charity.
(3) The references in subsection (1) or (2) above to misconduct or mismanagement shall (notwithstanding anything in the trusts of the charity) extend to the employment for the remuneration or reward of persons acting in the affairs of the charity, or for other administrative purposes, of sums which are excessive in relation to the property which is or is likely to be applied or applicable for the purposes of the charity.
(4) The Commissioners may also remove a charity trustee by order made of their own motion—
(a) where, within the last five years, the trustee—
(i) having previously been adjudged bankrupt or had his estate sequestrated, has been discharged, or
(ii) having previously made a composition or arrangement with, or granted a trust deed for, his creditors, has been discharged in respect of it;

---

17 S. 19 provides supplementary provisions relating to receiver and manager appointed for a charity. See Charities (Receiver and Manager) Regs 1992 (SI 1992 No. 2355; Annual Report for 1994, p. 16).
18 This power was first exercised in 1964 as a result of the report of an accountant appointed under Charities Act 1960, ss. 6, 8; Annual Report for 1964, paras. 12, 57, 58. See also Annual Report for 1971, paras. 90–96 (Sanctuary); 1972, paras. 78–81; 1976, paras. 25–29; *Jones v A-G* (1976) Times, 10 November; Annual Report for 1976, paras. 25–29, p. 000, post; 1977, paras. 31–33 (CA upheld decision of BRIGHTMAN J as "wholly unassailable"); paras. 163–165 (Kidney Machine Fund); 1978, paras. 158–161 (Bedside Bingo).

(b) where the trustee is a corporation in liquidation;
(c) where the trustee is incapable of acting by reason of mental disorder within the meaning of the Mental Health Act 1983;[19]
(d) where the trustee has not acted, and will not declare his willingness or unwillingness to act;
(e) where the trustee is outside England and Wales or cannot be found or does not act, and his absence or failure to act impedes the proper administration of the charity.

(5)(6)(7) p. 535, ante

(11) The power of the Commissioners to make an order under subsection (1)(i) above shall not be exercisable so as to suspend any person from the exercise of his office or employment for a period of more than 12 months; but (without prejudice to the generality of section 89(1) below), any such order made in the case of any person may make provision as respects the period of his suspension for matters arising out of it, and in particular for enabling any person to execute any instrument in his name or otherwise act for him and, in the case of a charity trustee, for adjusting any rules governing the proceedings of the charity trustees to take account of the reduction in the number capable of acting.[20]

16. Concurrent jurisdiction with High Court for certain purposes.—(1)(8) (p. 517, ante)

XIII. Land held by Charitable Trustees is Settled Land[1]

SETTLED LAND ACT 1925

29. Charitable and public trusts.—(1) For the purposes of this section, all land vested or to be vested in trustees on or for charitable, ecclesiastical, or public trusts or purposes shall be deemed to be settled land, and the trustees shall, without constituting them statutory owners, have in reference to the land, all the powers which are by this Act conferred on a tenant for life and on the trustees of a settlement.

In connexion only with the exercise of those powers, and not so as to impose any obligation in respect of or to affect—

(a) the mode of creation or the administration of such trusts; or
(b) the appointment or number of trustees of such trusts;

the statute or other instrument creating the trust or under which it is administered shall be deemed the settlement, and the trustees shall be deemed the trustees of the settlement, and, save where the trust is created by a will coming into operation after the commencement of this Act, a separate instrument shall not be necessary for giving effect to the settlement.

---

19 For the meaning of mental disorder, see Mental Health Act 1983, s. 1(2).
20 On disqualification for acting as a charity trustee, see Charities Act 1993, ss. 72 and 73. On application for waiver under s. 22(1), see [1993] 1 Ch Com Rep 26; [1994] 2 Ch Com Rep 11.
1 See Cheshire and Burn, *Modern Law of Real Property* (15th edn, 1994), pp. 931–939; *Re Booth and Southend-on-Sea Estates Co's Contract* [1927] 1 Ch 579.

Any conveyance of land held on charitable, ecclesiastical or public trusts shall state that the land is held on such trusts, and, where a purchaser has notice that the land is held on charitable, ecclesiastical, or public trusts, he shall be bound to see that any consents or orders requisite for authorising the transaction have been obtained.

———————

Under clause 2 of the Trust of Land and Appointment of Trustees Bill 1995,[2] no new settlements of land under the Settled Land Act 1925 may be created after the commencement of the Act. Accordingly section 29 is repealed, and no land held on charitable, ecclesiastical or public trusts is deemed to be settled land, even if it was so deemed before the commencement of the Act. Instead there is to be trust of land (clause 2(5) as amended on Report in the House of Lords).

2 See Law Commission Report on Trusts of Land 1989 (Law Com No. 181), para. 18.

Part Three. Trusts and Taxes

12. Introduction[1]

I. General

Taxation, according to Jean Baptiste Colbert, writing in the seventeenth century, is like plucking a live goose: the art of it is to get the most feathers with the least hissing.[2] In fact, some geese have never been content with just hissing. They have resorted increasingly to both tax evasion and tax avoidance. Tax evasion, which is the criminal breach of the tax laws, is a practice indulged in on a large scale by all social groups: unofficial estimates suggest that the income on which tax is evaded is of an amount broadly equivalent to 6 per cent to 8 per cent of the Gross Domestic Product (G.D.P.) of the United Kingdom.[3] Tax avoidance, on the other hand, is the lawful disposition of one's property in such a manner as to minimise the tax burden falling thereon.[4]

The trust is one of the main tools of such estate planning. Indeed, the modern law of trusts is largely concerned with the management and preservation of wealth. It is, of course, impossible to establish precisely either the number or the value of trusts in existence at any given time. Nonetheless, there is little doubt about the significance of trust property as a proportion of all private wealth. The Inland Revenue does not regularly compile statistics on the number of trusts in the United Kingdom or on the wealth held by them. In 1975 it estimated that there were some 400,000 trusts in existence. About 310,000 of these were trusts with interests in possession with assets worth £8.3 billion; some 90,000 were discretionary trusts holding assets worth £8.5 billion.

---

1 H & M, pp. 215–232; Thomas, *Taxation and Trusts* (1981); Whitehouse and Stuart-Buttle, *Revenue Law* (11th edn 1992); Linklaters & Paines' *Estate Planning*; Potter and Monroe, *Tax Planning with Precedents* (1995); White (ed), *Practical Tax Planning and Precedents* (1995). Specialised works include: Whiteman, *Income Tax* (3rd edn, 1988); *Capital Gains Tax* (4th edn, 1988); Dymond's *Capital Taxes* (1988); Ivory et al, *Inheritance Tax on Lifetime Gifts* (1987); *Foster's Inheritance Tax*: Butterworths *Wills, Probate and Administration Encyclopaedia; Simon's Taxes.* These works are updated by either supplement or loose-leaf pages; McCutcheon, *Inheritance Tax* (3rd edn, 1988). For a comprehensive intelligence service for practitioners engaged in trusts and estate planning (including taxation), see *Private Client Business* (published six times a year by Sweet & Maxwell). Statutes on income tax and capital gains tax are published annually in *Butterworths Yellow Tax Handbook*, and on inheritance tax in *Butterworths Orange Tax Handbook.* The taxes are also set out in The Taxes Acts, published annually by HMSO. See also *Butterworths UK Tax Guide*, published annually.
2 Dymond, p. *v.* The English equivalent seems to be the "shorn taxpayer": *Absalom v Talbot* [1943] 1 All ER 589 at 603, per DU PARCQ LJ.
3 The United Kingdom includes England, Wales, Scotland and Northern Ireland, but not the Channel Islands nor the Isle of Man. GDP for 1995 was £699,573 million.
4 The difference between evasion and avoidance is often defined as "the thickness of a prison wall", which underlines the fact that it is a legal distinction. In economic terms, the distinction is almost non-existent: the causes and consequences of evasion and avoidance are the same. And in view of the widespread practice of tax evasion, the moral distinction is blurred. Hence the birth of the mongrel term "tax avoision". For interesting views on the problem, see essays in the Institute of Economic Affairs' *Tax Avoision* (1979).

The total value of assets was thus around £16.8 billion or 6 per cent. of total personal wealth.[5]

Whatever the purpose for which a trust may be created, it is clear that taxation and investment are always prominent considerations. In this Part, we shall deal with the three major taxes, namely income tax, capital gains tax, and inheritance tax. Other taxes may also affect trusts—for instance, community charge and value added tax—but these are of comparatively subordinate importance. The emphasis is on inheritance tax, since this is the tax which usually concerns the trust lawyer most. At first sight, this might seem odd. The great bulk of the Government's tax revenue is derived from the taxation of income, not capital; and, despite some stringent anti-avoidance provisions, settlements can be used to minimise income tax. In reality, however, taxation is concerned not just with raising revenue but also with the redistribution of wealth within society. Such redistribution can only be achieved, it is said, by preventing aggregations of capital from passing unbroken from generation to generation. Despite the hopes of those who introduced it (in 1894), estate duty made little impact on the distribution of wealth, largely because it was so easy to avoid: it applied only on death (or within seven years of death) so lifetime gifts avoided it altogether; and discretionary trusts, in particular, were common vehicles for avoidance.[6] The replacement of estate duty by capital transfer tax[7] was intended to cure such defects. Nevertheless, judged by Colbert's standard, capital transfer tax proved rather disastrous: there was much hissing, and the yield of feathers was much reduced.[8] A series of concessions since 1975 rendered the tax anything but oppressive. For instance, the doubling in 1980 of the threshhold (i.e., the point at which tax becomes payable) from £25,000 to £50,000 immediately removed from charge two-thirds of the estates that would otherwise have been liable. Since then, the

---

5 Thomas, pp. 1–2. Over the years, the 1975 estimate has been extrapolated to allow for price changes, reaching a value of £28 billion in 1983 (Inland Revenue Statistics 1987, Table 7.2). By 1985/86 (when the most recent estimates were made), there were still some 55,500 discretionary (and accumulation and maintenance) trusts for which files were held in tax districts, a further 91,000 trusts administered by trustees such as clearing banks (and for which composite returns were made), a further 7,000 trusts dealt with by Claims Branch, Foreign Division, and some 112,000 trusts with interests in possession. However, during the first ten years of capital transfer tax, there seems to have been a substantial outflow of capital from discretionary trusts, either into interest in possession trusts or to individuals, or even offshore. An Inland Revenue estimate of wealth held in discretionary trusts at April, 1986, suggested a figure of £7.4 billion (£3.2 billion of which was attributable to discretionary trusts with income over £25,000 in 1985/86); and an estimate of £7–£8 billion therefore looked more reasonable than £28 billion. This would mean that the value of property in UK *discretionary trusts* as a proportion of the marketable wealth of all individuals and trusts had fallen from around 3.5% in 1975 to around 1% in 1985. See generally M.H. Robson and R.K. Timmins, *Discretionary Trusts – A Research Study* (Inland Revenue: August, 1988). See also p. 594, n. 19, post.

6 See *Inglewood (Lord) v IRC* [1983] 1 WLR 366 at 368–369, per Fox LJ, p. 659 post. In 1975, the Chancellor of the Exchequer (Mr. Healey) complained that estate duty, which was introduced "to prevent vast aggregations of inherited wealth being passed on undiminished from generation to generation", was largely avoided "by rich men who put their wealth into trusts": quoted in A.L. Chapman, *Capital Transfer Tax* (6th edn 1985), p. 2.

7 It was announced in March 1974, and introduced by FA 1975.

8 The yield is small in comparison with income tax. In 1994/95, capital transfer tax and inheritance tax together brought in £1,400 million out of a total revenue of £88,500 million, being less than 1.6 per cent of all Inland Revenue taxes. The comparable figure for death duties in 1895/96 was £14 million, or about 35 per cent: Dymond, p. 3. In 1994/95, income tax contributed £65,000 million, and capital gains £900 million. See Inland Revenue Statistics, published annually by HMSO.

threshhold has risen substantially—certainly by more than the rate of inflation would warrant—and now stands at £200,000.[9] Moreover, in 1986, capital transfer tax was abolished and replaced by inheritance tax. Although this was largely a cosmetic exercise, three important changes were made at the same time. First, the period over which a donor must account for and cumulate his chargeable transfers was reduced from ten to seven years. Second, a potentially exempt transfer became possible, whereby a transfer of value would not be chargeable at all, if the transferor survived it by at least seven years. Whereas these two changes were, and remain, of clear advantage to the taxpayer, a third change is not. A gift by a donor remains subject to charge, if he retains some benefit from, or interest in, the subject matter of the gift. These concepts are explained more fully below.

In the context of trusts, the accumulation and maintenance settlement was accorded favourable treatment from the very inception of capital transfer tax and this remains the case under inheritance tax; and the treatment of discretionary trusts (which was oppressive at first) was transformed in 1982 with the result that these can once again confer substantial tax advantages in the appropriate circumstances.[10] The advent of capital transfer tax and inheritance tax certainly made a profound impact on the modern law of trusts, but not necessarily in the manner intended by their originators.[11]

II. Tax Avoidance

Tax avoidance has become a "national habit"[12] usually graced with the description of "estate planning". It is also the foundation of a large industry of "tax planners" whose expertise and sophisticated techniques ensure that the live goose keeps as many of its feathers as it can.

Lord TOMLIN said in **IRC v Duke of Westminster** [1936] AC 1 at 19:[13]

"Every man is entitled if he can to arrange his affairs so that the tax attaching under the appropriate Acts is less than it otherwise would be. If he succeeds in ordering them so as to secure that result, then, however unappreciative the

---

9 IHTA 1984, Sch. 1; Inheritance Tax (Indexation) Order 1994 (SI 1994, No. 3011).
10 See pp. 581 et seq., post.
11 As introduced by a Labour Government the tax was intended to be the first stage in a wider tax on capital, by means of an annual wealth tax; White Paper on Capital Transfer Tax (1974) Cmnd 5705; Green Paper on Wealth Tax (1974) Cmnd 5704.
12 So described by Sir William Pile, Chairman of the Inland Revenue in 1975: *First Report from the Expenditure Committee of the House of Commons, Session 1975–76; Financing of Public Expenditure* (1976), vol. II, p. 182. In 1996 the Tax Law Review Committee of the Institute of Fiscal Studies turned its attentions to ways of curbing tax avoidance. Its members include Lords TEMPLEMAN and NOLAN, MILLETT LJ and CARNWATH J; its chairman is G. Aaronson QC.
13 The Duke, instead of paying his gardener £3 a week in wages, covenanted to pay him £1.18s a week for 7 years and the gardener was expected not to take the balance of £1.2s. It was held that the Duke was entitled to deduct the payment in computing his total income for surtax, the gardener being an annuitant under Schedule D and not an employee under Schedule E. Most covenants between individuals made after 14 March 1988 were rendered ineffective for the purposes by FA 1988, s. 36, inserting s. 347A into ICTA 1988.

Commissioners of Inland Revenue or his fellow taxpayers may be of his ingenuity, he cannot be compelled to pay an increased tax."[14]

The precise status of the *Westminster* principle is in doubt at present. In a series of cases beginning with *Ramsay v IRC* [1982] AC 300, [1981] 1 All ER 865[15] and reaching a high water mark with *Furniss v Dawson* [1984] AC 474, [1984] 1 All ER 530[16] the House of Lords, though paying lip service to the *Westminster* principle, held that where there is a pre-ordained series of transactions, or a single composite scheme, into which steps are inserted solely for the purpose of avoiding tax and which otherwise have no commercial or business purpose, the Court may disregard those steps and, instead of taxing the transactions or scheme as found, may tax what it identifies as the "relevant transaction". In other words, the *Ramsay/Furniss* principle is that the tax liability of a person involved in a scheme may be determined on the basis of a constructive transaction as opposed to the actual transaction to which he was a party. The classic statement of the new principle was put forward by Lord BRIGHTMAN in **Furniss v Dawson**[17] at 526, at 542:

"My Lords, in my opinion the rationale of the new approach is this. In a pre-planned tax-saving scheme, no distinction is to be drawn for fiscal purposes, because none exists in reality, between (i) a series of steps which are followed through by virtue of an arrangement which falls short of a binding contract, and (ii) a like series of steps which are followed through because the participants are contractually bound to take each step seriatim. In a contractual case the fiscal consequences will naturally fall to be assessed in the light of the contractually agreed results. For example, equitable interests may pass when the contract for sale is signed. In many cases equity will regard that

---

14 See also *Ayrshire Pullman Motor Services and D M Ritchie v IRC* (1929) 14 TC 754 at 763 where Lord CLYDE said: "No man in this country is under the smallest obligation, moral or other, so as arrange his legal relations to his business or to his property as to enable the Inland Revenue to put the largest possible shovel into his stores."

15 See now TCGA 1992, s. 30.

16 See now TCGA 1992, s. 137. See also *IRC v Burmah Oil Co Ltd* [1982] STC 30.

17 See *Craven v White* [1989] AC 398 at 478–479, [1988] 3 All ER 495, at 499–500 per Lord KEITH; at 497–498, at 513–516 per Lord OLIVER. Between *Ramsay* and *Craven v White*, several other cases, at first instance, also considered the doctrine: *Ewart v Taylor* [1983] STC 721; *Reed v Nova Securities Ltd* [1985] STC 124; *Young v Phillips* (1984) 58 TC 232; *Magnavox Electronics Co Ltd v Hall* [1985] STC 260; *Ingram v IRC* [1985] STC 835. For recent valid schemes which distinguish *Ramsay*, see *Ensign Tankers (Leasing) Ltd v Stokes* [1989] 1 WLR 1222; *Fitzwilliam v IRC* [1993] 3 All ER 184, [1993] STC 502, applied in *Hatton v IRC* [1992] STC 140; *Whittles v Uniholdings Ltd (No 3)* [1995] STC 185. Much has been written on the *Ramsay/Furniss* doctrine and associated problems. Among the more useful articles are the following: (1982) 98 LQR 201 (P.J. Millett); [1982] BTR 200 (H.H. Monroe); [1982] All ER Rev 285 (J. Tiley); [1983] Conv. 11 (G. Morse); [1983] BTR 221 (R.K. Ashton); (1985) *Recent Tax Problems* 1 (S. Oliver), 19 (J. Tiley); [1985] BTR 68 (D.A. Ward et al.); [1985] BTR 338 (R.T. Bartlett); [1986] BTR 327 (P.J. Millett); [1987] BTR 280 (G.R. Bretten and F. Stockton), [1987] BTR 180 and 220 (J. Tiley); [1988] BTR 63 and 108 (J. Tiley); [1988] BTR 209 (D.W.); [1988] BTR 482 (R.K. Ashton); [1991] BTR 283 (W.D. Popkin). See also the reported remarks of Lord TEMPLEMAN in *Fiscal Studies*, vol. 6, no, 3 (August, 1985), p. 51. One reported "unofficial estimate" stated that the decision in *Ramsay* alone would "yield the Exchequer in excess of £1,000 million in tax from pending cases alone": (1982) 98 LQR 201 at 209 (P.J. Millett).

as done which is contracted to be done. *Ramsay* says that the fiscal result is to be no different if the several steps are pre-ordained rather than pre-contracted ..."

The formulation by Lord Diplock in **IRC v Burmah Oil Co Ltd** [1982] STC 30 at 33 expresses the limitations of the *Ramsay* principle. "First, there must be a pre-ordained series of transactions; or, if one likes, one single composite transaction. This composite transaction may or may not include the achievement of a legitimate commercial (i.e. business) end ... Secondly, there must be steps inserted which have no commercial (business) *purpose* apart from the avoidance of a liability to tax—not 'no business *effect*.' If those two ingredients exist, the inserted steps are to be disregarded for fiscal purposes. The court must then look at the end result. Precisely how the end result will be taxed will depend on the terms of the taxing statute sought to be applied....

The formulation, therefore, involves two findings of fact, first, whether there was a pre-ordained series of transactions, i.e. a single composite transaction, secondly, whether that transaction contained steps which were inserted without any commercial or business purpose apart from a tax advantage. Those are facts to be found by the commissioners. They may be primary facts or, more probably, inferences to be drawn from the primary facts. If they are inferences, they are nevertheless facts to be found by the commissioners."

This far-reaching principle was severely restricted by the decision of the House of Lords in **Craven v White** and associated appeals [1989] AC 398, [1988] 3 All ER 495.[18] Lord OLIVER OF AYLMERTON (with whom Lord KEITH OF KINKEL and Lord JAUNCEY OF TULLICHETTLE expressly concurred) reviewed *Ramsay v IRC* and *Furniss v Dawson*, and identified the limits of the doctrine established in them. Lord OLIVER said at 514, at 527:

"As the law currently stands, the essentials emerging from *Furniss v Dawson* [1984] AC 474 appear to me to be four in number: (1) that the series of transactions was, at the time when the intermediate transaction was entered into, pre-ordained in order to produce a given result; (2) that that transaction had no other purpose than tax mitigation, (3) that there was at that time no practical likelihood that the pre-planned events would not take place in the order ordained, so that the intermediate transaction was not even contemplated practically as having an independent life, and (4) that the pre-ordained events did in fact take place. In these circumstances the court can be justified in linking the beginning with the end so as to make a single composite whole to which the fiscal results of the single composite whole are to be applied.

I do not, for my part, think that *Furniss v Dawson* goes further than that. The intellectual basis for the decision was *Ramsay* and the criteria for the

---

18 *Craven v White, IRC v Bowater Property Developments Ltd* and *Baylis v Gregory*. Lord TEMPLEMAN and Lord GOFF OF CHIEVELEY dissented in *Craven v White*, but not in the other two appeals.

application of the *Ramsay* doctrine were those enunciated by Lord Brightman. On those criteria, I see no escape from the conclusion reached in all the three appeals in the High Court and in the Court of Appeal that the appellants must fail. Nor do I readily see that the criteria are logically capable of expansion so as to apply to any similar case except one in which, when the intermediate transaction or transactions take place, the end result which in fact occurs is so certain of fulfilment that it is intellectually and practically possible to conclude that there has indeed taken place one single and indivisible process. To permit this it seems to me essential that the intermediate transaction bears the stamp of interdependence at the time when it takes place. A transaction does not change its nature because of an event, then uncertain, which subsequently occurs and *Ramsay* is concerned not with re-forming transactions but with ascertaining their reality. There is a real and not merely a metaphysical distinction between something that is done as a preparatory step towards a possible but uncertain contemplated future action and something which is done as an integral and interdependent part of a transaction already agreed and, effectively, pre-destined to take place. In the latter case, to link the end to the beginning involves no more than recognising the reality of what is effectively a single operation ab initio. In the former it involves quite a different process, viz. that of imputing to the parties, ex post facto, an obligation (either contractual or quasi contractual) which did not exist at the material time but which is to be attributed from the occurrence or juxtaposition of events which subsequently took place. That cannot be extracted from *Furniss v Dawson* as it stands nor can it be justified by any rational extension of the *Ramsay* approach. It involves the invocation of a different principle altogether, that is to say, the reconstruction of events into something that they were not, either in fact or in intention, not because they in fact constituted a single composite whole but because, and only because, one or more of them was motivated by a desire to avoid or minimise tax. That may be a very beneficial objective but it has to be recognised that the rational basis of *Ramsay* and *Furniss v Dawson* then becomes irrelevant and is replaced by a principle of nullifying a tax advantage derived from any 'associated operation.' The legislature has not gone this far and the question is should or can your Lordships?

My Lords, I do not think so. I am at one with those of your Lordships who find the complicated and stylised antics of the tax avoidance industry both unedifying and unattractive but I entirely dissent from the proposition that because there is present in each of the three appeals before this House the element of a desire to mitigate or postpone the respondents' tax burdens, this fact alone demands from your Lordships a predisposition to expand the scope of the doctrine of *Ramsay* and of *Furniss v Dawson* beyond its rational basis in order to strike down a transaction which would not otherwise realistically fall within it.

Nor do I consider that the *Ramsay* approach, which is no doubt applicable to a much wider variety of transactions than those embraced in the instant appeals, requires further exposition or clarification. Its basis is manifest and has been clearly explained by Lord Wilberforce. What the appellants urge upon your Lordships is a restatement of the approach in a formula based, as it seems to me, not upon a much wider, but at the moment undefined, general principle of judicial disapprobation of the lawful rearrangement of the subject's affairs designed to produce a result which is fiscally advantageous to him in relation to a transaction into which he anticipates entering. That is essentially a legislative exercise and one upon which, in my opinion, your Lordships should hesitate long before embarking.''

In **Hatton v IRC** [1992] STC 140, CHADWICK J said at 156, 157:
"It seems to me that when Lord Oliver refers in element (1) to a 'preordained series of transactions', he does not mean more than a series of transactions which have been pre-planned to take place in a specific order in circumstances in which there is, at the time when the first transaction is entered into, no practical likelihood that the remaining transactions will not take place in that order. In other words, he is using the phrase 'preordained' in element (1) in the sense explained in element (3). . . .
Essential element (2) reflects the further ingredient which is found in *Burmah*. Element (4) emphasises what is perhaps obvious, and which is expressed in the phrase 'not only conceived but carried out'; namely that the series of transactions which constituted the scheme as planned, did in fact take place in the manner and order intended. Elements (1) and (3) are a re-statement of what Lord Oliver had found to be established in *Ramsay*, namely the need for (i) a scheme involving a series of transactions plus (ii) an expectation it would be carried through from beginning to end, and (iii) no likelihood that it will not. In my view, having regard to the process of reasoning which led to his formulation of the four essentials, it is impossible to construe his reference in element (1) to a preordained series of transactions as requiring more than such a degree of certainty and control over the end result that it can properly be said that there is no practical likelihood that the transaction will not take place as planned.''

III. Statutory Construction

There is a long-standing general rule that references to Parliamentary material can not be referred to as an aid to statutory construction.[19] However, the rule was never absolute and has been gradually relaxed over the years. Thus, reports made by commissioners (including law commissioners) and on which legislation was based, and white papers, could be looked at for the purpose of ascertaining the mischief which a statute was intended to cure and also for drawing an inference as to Parliamentary intention (but not for the purpose of discovering the meaning of the words used by Parliament to effect such a cure[20]).

---

19 See, for example, *Davis v Johnson* [1979] AC 264, [1978] 1 All ER 1132, and *Hadmor Productions Ltd v Hamilton* [1983] 1 AC 191, [1982] 1 All ER 1042. On the construction of tax legislation, see [1994] BTR 126 (I.J. Ghosh) and [1994] BTR 42 and 147 (J. Ward).

20 *Pepper v Hart* [1993] AC 593, at 630–631, [1993] 1 All ER 42 at 60–61, per Lord BROWNE-WILKINSON, referring (inter alia) to *Eastman Photographic Materials Co Ltd v Comptroller-General of Patents, Designs and Trade Marks* [1898] AC 571, *Assam Railways and Trading Co Ltd v IRC* [1935] AC 445, and *R v Secretary of State for Transport, ex p Factortame Ltd* [1990] 2 AC 85, [1989] 2 All ER 692.

In **Pepper v Hart** [1993] AC 593, [1993] 1 All ER 42, the House of Lords[1] held that, subject to any question of Parliamentary privilege, the rule excluding reference to Parliamentary material as an aid to statutory construction should be relaxed. Lord Browne-Wilkinson[2] said, at 634, at 62:

"I have come to the conclusion that, as a matter of law, there are sound reasons for making a limited modification to the existing rule (subject to strict safeguards) unless there are constitutional or practical reasons which outweigh them. In my judgment, subject to the questions of the privileges of the House of Commons, reference to Parliamentary material should be permitted as an aid to the construction of legislation which is ambiguous or obscure or the literal meaning of which leads to an absurdity. Even in such cases references in court to Parliamentary material should only be permitted where such material clearly discloses the mischief aimed at or the legislative intention lying behind the ambiguous or obscure words. In the case of statements made in Parliament, as at present advised I cannot foresee that any statement other than the statement of the Minister or other promoter of the Bill is likely to meet these criteria."

---

1 Lord MACKAY OF CLASHFERN LC dissenting. The taxpayers were members of staff at Malvern College who, under a concessionary fees scheme, were allowed (at the College's absolute discretion) to have their sons educated at the College at one-fifth of the fees normally charged. The taxpayers were assessed to Schedule E income tax on the cash equivalent of the benefits they had received (which were treated as "emoluments" of their employment). The House of Lords, allowing the taxpayers' appeals, held that they were assessable only on the marginal cost to the employer and not on a rateable proportion of the overall expenditure incurred by the school in providing its facilities to all pupils.

2 With whose speech Lords BRIDGE, KEITH and ACKNER expressly agreed.

13. Income Tax

"Income tax, if I may be pardoned for saying so", said Lord MACNAGHTEN, "is a tax on income".[1] However, the fiscal legislation does not define income anywhere. Nor does it state that income tax is levied on a person's "income". Instead, there is an elaborate system of Schedules (which may be subdivided into Cases) enumerating *sources* of income as comprehensively as possible (for example, Schedule A charges profits or gains in respect of land in the United Kingdom; Schedule E charges emoluments from any office or employment). Section 1 of the Income and Corporation Taxes Act 1988 (ICTA 1988)[2] states that income tax shall be charged in respect of all property, profits or gains described or comprised in the Schedules. The first task then is to identify the source and the relevant Schedule, for it is in accordance with those rules applicable to that Schedule that it is to be assessed.[3]

I. Taxable Income

"Income", however, does not mean the same as "taxable income". In the case of an individual, certain reliefs and allowances may be deducted in calculating taxable income; for example, a person carrying on a trade may deduct certain expenses of the trade in computing profits to be taxed under Schedule D, Case I. Further sums may also be deducted from his income, the most common being personal reliefs (such as the married couple's allowance, or the individual's personal allowance),[4] which are fixed sums, and qualifying interest payments (such as mortgage interest relief, on a loan up to a maximum of £30,000[5]). Until recently, he would also have had to include the income of his wife, if they were living together.[6] This has now changed. For 1990–91 and

---

1 *London County Council v A-G* [1901] AC 26 at 35.
2 The Income and Corporation Taxes Act 1988 (ICTA 1988) consolidated all the substantive law of income tax and corporation tax (including such capital gains tax legislation as affects companies only) up to 9 February 1988. The Taxes Management Act 1970 consolidated the administrative provisions which regulate the administration of income tax, corporation tax and capital gains tax.
3 *Mitchell and Edon v Ross* [1962] AC 813 at 837, [1961] 3 All ER 49 at 54, per Lord RADCLIFFE.
     FA 1996 contains lengthy provisions (Chapter V, ss. 112–127 and Scheds 18–22) dealing with the new system of 'self-assessment'.
4 ICTA 1988, ss. 257–257F.
5 Ibid, ss. 369–379. The relief is equivalent to the 'appropriate percentage' of the loan interest payment (being 15 per cent. for 1995–96). Most residential mortgages fall under the MIRAS scheme.
6 This was the case ever since the introduction of income tax in 1799, although both spouses could elect (as from 1971–72) for the wife's earnings to be taxed separately.

subsequent years of assessment, the income of a married woman living with her husband will not be treated as his income for income tax purposes.[7] A husband and wife will each have his or her own basic rate income tax band and a full personal allowance, available against any kind of income.[8]

II. Rates of Tax

Income tax is a progressive tax. An individual's taxable income is taxed at the rates laid down annually in the Finance Act. At present (1996–97) the rates are as follows: (a) the lower rate of 20 per cent. which applies to the first £3,900 of taxable income, (b) the basic rate of 24 per cent. which applies to taxable income from £3,901 to £25,500, and (c) the higher rate of 40 per cent. on income above £25,500.[9]

III. Trusts

Where income arises from a trust, its taxation takes place at two different stages. The trustees are chargeable because they receive the income, and the beneficiaries are assessable on any income received from the trust, but their assessment will take account of any income tax already paid by the trustees.

A. Trustees

i. BASIC RATE

Income arising from trust assets (which is usually investment income) is treated as the income of the trustees: it is not deemed to be the settlor's income; nor are the trustees agents for the beneficiaries.[10] Trustees are chargeable to income tax simply because they are in receipt of the income.[11] It makes no difference that the beneficiaries may be entitled to it, not even if there is only one beneficiary and he is sui juris.[12]

---

7 FA 1988, s. 32. ICTA 1988, s. 279 is repealed: FA 1988, s. 148 and Sch. 14.
8 This change has necessitated further substantial alterations, e.g., those relating to personal reliefs, or to jointly held property. See FA 1988, ss. 32–35; ICTA 1988, ss. 282A, 282B.
9 FA 1996, s. 72(1), (2). Although the higher rate is expressed to apply where income exceeds £25,500 (for 1996–97), most taxpayers can claim personal (and probably other) allowances, so that, in practice, higher rates will apply only where total income exceeds £25,500 plus all allowances. The first ever Income Tax Act, introduced by William Pitt, became law on 9 January, 1799. Under it the rate was 2/- in the £ on any income over £200. Addington cancelled Pitt's income tax on 5 April 1802 and introduced his own on 11 August 1803 at half the former rate. Income tax ceased in 1816, but was revived by Peel in 1842 at 7d in the £. It remains an annual tax. Under the Labour Government the top rate of income tax on investment income in 1978–1979 was 98%. See Monroe, *Intolerable Inquisition*, chap. 1; [1967] BTR 177, 271 (W. Phillips). FA 1996 contains lengthy provisions (chapter V, ss. 121–136 and Scheds. 19 to 25) dealing with the new system of 'self-assessment'.
10 Cf. Taxes Management Act 1970, s. 72.
11 *Williams v Singer* [1921] 1 AC 65.
12 *IRC v Hamilton-Russell's Executors* [1943] 1 All ER 474.

Moreover, the taxation of trustees differs considerably from that of individuals. In general, the whole of the income of a trust is taxable. It makes no difference whether the income is absorbed by the expenses of administration, or paid to beneficiaries, or accumulated. The trustees' personal tax liability is ignored entirely, and the trust cannot therefore claim the benefit of the personal reliefs of the trustees. Neither can the trust claim any personal reliefs or allowances itself, because it is not an "individual". For the same reason, the higher rates of tax applicable to an individual's income do not apply to trust income: the basic rate applies even if such income were measured in £millions.[12a]

ii. THE ADDITIONAL RATE

There is an important exception in that an additional rate applies where there is no person currently entitled to the income of a trust, i.e. where income is accumulated or where it is payable at the discretion of the trustees (or of some other person), the additional rate of 10 per cent. is also levied[13] on the trustees. The basic disadvantage of a trust under which a beneficiary has an interest in possession (say, a life tenant) is that he is *entitled* to the trust income, if there is any. The trust income forms part of that beneficiary's total income, whether he actually receives it or not, and whether he wants it or not.[14] Consequently, if his marginal rate[15] rises over the years, the trust income may well be subject to a higher rate of income tax in his hands than it would have borne in the settlor's, had it not been settled.

A discretionary trust, on the other hand, provides considerable flexibility.[16] A discretionary beneficiary does not have an interest as such in the trust property and has no entitlement to income. He merely has a right to be considered as a potential beneficiary and a hope that the trustees will exercise their discretion in his favour. He will receive only what the trustees decide to give to him. It follows that a discretionary beneficiary cannot be liable to income tax unless and until the trustees exercise their discretion in his favour.[17] Consequently, the trustees can exercise their discretion to distribute income only to those beneficiaries who are liable to the lower tax rates or not liable at all. As circumstances change, payments can be reduced, increased or stopped, as appropriate. For this reason, discretionary trusts became (and still are) popular vehicles for the avoidance of income tax. The legislature's response was the imposition of the additional rate of 10 per cent., so that trustees of accumulation and discretionary trusts are thus subject to a rate of 35 per cent., not 24 per cent.[18]

12a See also FA 1996, s. 73 (application of lower rate to income from savings).
13 ICTA 1988, ss. 686, 687. See *IRC v Berrill* (1981) 58 TC 429; *Carver v Duncan* [1983] 1 WLR 494; *IRC v Regent Trust Co* (1979) 53 TC 54.
14 *IRC v Hamilton-Russell's Executors*, supra. The same applies if he is entitled to have income applied for his benefit, or to benefits in kind: *Lindus and Hortin v IRC* (1933) 17 TC 442.
15 Marginal rate means the rate of tax which will be charged on each extra pound earned by the taxpayer. For example, if a taxpayer has income (after reliefs and allowances) of £25,500 but then earns an extra £50, that £50 will be taxed at 40%, although his average rate of tax on the whole £25,500 will be lower.
16 Pp. 39–52, 71–95, ante.
17 *IRC v Hamilton-Russell's Executors*, [1943] 1 All ER 474; *Drummond v Collins* [1915] AC 1011; *IRC v Blackwell* [1924] 2 KB 351.
18 For accumulation and maintenance trusts, see pp. 597–606 post.

B. Beneficiaries

Income from the trust has thus already been taxed at the basic rate and, perhaps, at the additional rate too. Such payments to a beneficiary may be his sole income or, more probably, will form part of his total income.

The beneficiary will have to bring into account not just the net sum he is entitled to or has received from the trustees, but also the tax already paid thereon, i.e., the initial gross sum: for example, if he receives £760 and the trustees paid tax at 24 per cent., he must account for £1,000. Just like any other individual, he will then deduct all relevant allowances and reliefs to ascertain his total taxable income, which in turn determines his marginal rate of tax. Depending on that rate, one of three possible consequences will ensue:

a.   If his marginal rate is the same as the rate applied to the trustee (say 24 per cent.) the correct amount of tax has already been paid.

b.   If his marginal rate is higher (40 per cent.) than the trustees' rate (say 24 per cent.) he will be liable for the difference, for insufficient tax will have been paid on the sum in question; for example, £1,000 taxed at 40 per cent. = £400 tax; but only £240 has been paid by the trustees, so an additional liability for £160 remains.

c.   If his marginal rate is lower than the trustees' rate, or if he is not liable to tax at all (for example, because he has not exhausted all his allowances and reliefs), he will have been over-taxed on the sum in question and can claim a repayment, for example, if £1,000 is his sole income, he can reclaim from the Inland Revenue the £240 paid by the trustees.

C. Anti-Avoidance Provisions

Without more, the avoidance of income tax would clearly be a simple matter. Any taxpayer whose marginal rate of tax was 40 per cent. could simply create a trust, where the income would be taxed at only 24 per cent., and then derive some benefit from the settled property without incurring any further liability. If the settlor were a beneficiary, he would be taxed—as any other beneficiary— on income arising or received. However, any benefit might be indirect, for example, loans from the trust; distributions of capital from the trust; or income paid to his wife or children; and so forth. Various provisions have thus been enacted specifically to minimise the avoidance of income tax by means of settlements.

These anti-avoidance provisions are largely set out in Part XV of the Income and Corporation Taxes Act 1988 (ICTA 1988). However, most of the original provisions of Part XV have been repealed, wholly or partly, and replaced by new anti-avoidance provisions (inserted into Part XV) enacted in the Finance Act 1995.[19] Both the new and the retained sets of anti-avoidance provisions are complex and detailed and should be studied carefully. Only the briefest mention can be made of them here.

Of the unrepealed provisions, the main ones are those dealing with capital sums paid directly or indirectly in any year of assessment by the trustees of a

19 ICTA 1988, chapters I (ss. 660–662), II (ss. 663–670), III (in part: ss. 671–676, 679–681) and IV (ss. 683–685) were repealed by Finance Act 1995, Sch. 29, Part VIII (8), with effect from the year 1995–96; and replaced by Chapter IA (ss. 660A–660G), inserted by FA 1995, s. 74, Sch. 17, Part 1. Former Chapters III and IV of Part XV, in so far as unrepealed, are renumbered as Chapter IB and IC (FA 1995, Sch. 17, Part II, paras. 8, 12).

settlement to the settlor or to the settlor's spouse (either alone or jointly with another person).[20] In broad terms, their effect is that, where there is such a payment, it is treated for all income tax purposes as the income of the settlor for that year, to the extent that the amount of that payment falls within the amount of income available up to the end of that year.[1] There are also complex provisions to deal with capital sums paid to the settlor by a company connected with the settlement.[2]

The new anti-avoidance provisions are contained in sections 660A–660G (introduced by Schedule 17 to the Finance Act 1995). As from 6 April, 1995, they apply to all settlements, whenever created. Their main purpose and effect is to tidy up and rationalise the chaotic structure of earlier anti-avoidance provisions;[3] and they do not introduce a major change in underlying policy.

Section 660A (which alone replaces around 18 of the earlier 27 sections) contains the main provisions and deals with income arising under a settlement where the settlor has retained an interest. Section 660A (1) provides that income arising under a settlement during the life of the settlor shall be treated for all purposes of the Income Tax Acts as the income of the settlor and not as the income of any other person, unless the income arises from property in which the settlor has no interest. A settlor shall be regarded (subject to the provisions of the section)[4] as having an interest in property if that property, or any derived property, is or will or may become payable to or applicable for the benefit of the settlor or his spouse in any circumstances whatsoever.[5]

The section then elucidates certain key terms. A settlor's "spouse" does not include a person to whom the settlor is not for the time being married but may later marry, or a spouse from whom the settlor is separated (under a Court Order, or under a separation agreement, or in such circumstances that the separation is likely to be permanent) or the widow or widower of the settlor.[6] "Derived property", is defined in a convoluted manner and means, "in relation to any property, income from that property or any other property directly or indirectly representing the proceeds of, or of income from, that property or income therefrom."[7] The terms "settlor" and "settlement" are both widely defined (in section 660G (1) and (2)) as in the earlier provisions which they replace. A "settlement" includes "any disposition, trust, covenant,

---

20 S. 677 of ICTA 1988 (now in Chapter IB of Part XV).
1 S. 677 (1). The capital payment is allocated first against income of the trust in the year of the payment; and, if that is not sufficient, any excess of the capital payment is set against the next and subsequent years in turn (up to a maximum of ten such later years). There are elaborate provisions for determining the amount of income available (ss. (2)); there is a wide definition of "capital sum" (sub-s. (9) (*a*)); and there are extended provisions to catch payments by trustees to certain third parties (ss. (10) which reverses *Potts' Executors v IRC* [1951] AC 443, [1951] 1 All ER 76.
2 S. 678. See also [1981] BTR 140.
3 Anti-avoidance provisions were introduced piecemeal over several decades. Most were in place before the consolidation effected by the Income Tax Act 1952, although some additions and changes were made thereafter, before they were re-enacted in Part XV of ICTA 1988.
4 See, for example, the exceptions in ss. (4) and (5) which largely re-enact earlier provisions in s. 685 (2) of ICTA 1988. Note, however, that sub-s. (4) (*d*) refers to "*the death of a child of the settlor who had become beneficially entitled* ... *at an age not exceeding 25*", whereas section 685 (2) (*d*) of ICTA 1988 referred to "the death under the age of 25 or some lower age of *some person* who *would be* beneficially entitled ... on attaining that age".
5 S. 660A (2).
6 S. 660A (3). Sub-section (3) (*c*) expressly enacts what was decided in *Lord Vestey's Executors v IRC* [1949] 1 All ER 1108. See also s. 660A (8).
7 S. 660A (10).

agreement, arrangement or transfer of assets"; and a "settlor", in relation to a settlement, means "any person by whom the settlement was made". Moreover, a person shall be deemed, for these purposes, to have made a settlement if he has made or entered into the settlement directly or indirectly and, in particular, if he has provided or undertaken to provide funds directly or indirectly for the purpose of the settlement, or has made with another person a reciprocal arrangement for that other person to make or enter into the settlement.[8]

On the other hand, a settlement does not include an outright gift by one spouse to the other of property from which income arises, unless the gift does not carry a right to the whole of that income, or the property given is wholly or substantially a right to income; nor does it include an irrevocable allocation of pension rights by one spouse to the other.[9] Moreover, on the breakup of a marriage, one party can provide that the income of settled property is payable to the other, but that the settled property itself reverts to him or her, without becoming assessable in respect of that income.[10]

Under section 660B, a payment of income arising under a settlement to or for the benefit of a minor unmarried child of the settlor, during the settlor's life, is treated as the settlor's income (if not already so treated under section 660A).[11] Where income of the settlement has been accumulated or retained by the trustees, any payment of income or capital of the settlement to or for the benefit of a minor unmarried child of the settlor is treated as a payment of income (and taxable as the settlor's income) if or to the extent that there is available retained or accumulated income. For this purpose, retained or accumulated income shall be taken to be available at any time when the total amount of settlement income is more than the total of amounts treated as income of the settlor or a beneficiary, payments to other beneficiaries, or payments of expenses properly chargeable to income.[12] Stepchildren and illegitimate children are included;[13] [but payments to a child of £100 or less in a year of assessment are excepted.[14]

Thus, in broad terms, the new anti-avoidance provisions maintain the underlying policy and preserve the thrust of the earlier provisions which they replace, but in a clearer and simplified form. Most of the basic concepts and definitions at the core of the earlier provisions are retained, and it seems clear that the substantial body of caselaw dealing with those provisions will be equally relevant to the new ones.[15] Moreover, it is implicit in these new provisions, as with the old, that some element of bounty is necessary before there can be a settlement, so that bona fide commercial transactions are not within their scope.[16]

These provisions clearly reduce the settlor's scope for minimising his income tax liability. Not only is he himself prevented from deriving any direct

8 ICTA 1988, s. 660G (2).
9 Ibid, s. 660A (6) and (7), re-enacting earlier provisions in section 685 (4A)—(4C) of ICTA 1988 which were introduced as part of the new system for separate taxation of husband and wife.
10 Ibid, s. 660A (8).
11 This corresponds with s. 663 (1) of ICTA 1988.
12 ICTA 1988, s. 660B (2), (3). These provisions broadly correspond with s. 664 (2) and (3) of ICTA 1988.
13 Ibid, s. 660B (6), which corresponds with the definition in s. 670 of ICTA 1988.
14 Ibid, s. 660B (5), corresponding to s. 663 (4) of ICTA 1988.
15 See, for example, *Vandervell v IRC* [1967] 2 AC 291, [1967] 1 All ER 1, p. 54 ante.
16 *Chamberlain v IRC* (1943) 59 TLR 343; *IRC v Leiner* (1964) 41 TC 589; *Bulmer v IRC* [1967] Ch 145, [1966] 3 All ER 801; *IRC v Plummer* [1980] AC 896, [1979] 3 All ER 775.

benefit from the trust he has created, but also the "splitting" of income between him and his wife or children is largely curtailed. However, the trust is still not totally ineffective for the purpose of avoiding income tax. A settlor may still provide for his adult children (and married minor children), or for any of his relations (particularly grandchildren), or anyone else he cares to specify, without suffering any adverse income tax consequences, and may do much more besides.

14. Capital Gains Tax

Capital gains tax (CGT) was introduced by the Finance Act 1965. Its governing provisions were consolidated by the Capital Gains Tax Act 1979 (CGTA 1979) which was itself replaced by the Taxation of Chargeable Gains Act 1992 (TCGA 1992).

CGT is a tax chargeable on capital gains accruing to a person in a year of assessment during any part of which he is resident in the United Kingdom or during which he is ordinarily resident in the United Kingdom,[1] i.e., it is a tax on the difference in the value of a chargeable asset between the date of its acquisition and the date of its disposal. A major concession was made in 1988, when legislation[2] provided that, where a disposal is made on or after 5 April, 1988, of an asset held by the disponor on 31 March, 1982, his acquisition cost for the purposes of calculating the capital gain will be the asset's value on 31 March, 1982. In any event, there must be clearly a disposal and a chargeable gain.

I. Chargeable Assets

Chargeable assets include options, debts and incorporeal property generally; any currency other than sterling; and any form of property created by the person disposing of it (for example, paintings, copyright, patents), or otherwise coming to be owned without being acquired (for example, goodwill).[3] There are certain exemptions, such as, for example, a person's only or main private residence,[4] a private car,[5] a chattel which is disposed of for a consideration not exceeding £6,000,[6] gilt-edged securities and qualifying

---

1 TCGA 1992, s. 2 (1).
2 FA 1988, s. 96 (2). See now TCGA 1992, s. 35 (1), (2): but see the exceptions in s. 35 (3); (1988) 121 Tax 456 (M. Gunn).
3 TCGA 1992, s. 21 (1).
4 Ibid, ss. 222–223; including its garden or grounds up to an area (inclusive of the site of the house) of one acre. This may be larger if it is required for the reasonable enjoyment of the house as a residence. See also *Honour v Norris* [1992] STC 304; *Griffin v Craig-Harvey* [1994] STC 54; *Sansom v Peay* [1976] STC 494; [1993] BTR 24 (W. Norris); [1994] BTR 32 (W. Norris).
5 Ibid., s. 263.
6 Ibid., s. 262 (1). Where the consideration exceeds £6,000, the exemption is dealt with under s. 262 (2).

corporate bonds,[7] national savings certificates and other non-marketable government securities,[8] and life assurance policies.[9]

II. Chargeable Gains

A certain amount of capital gains made by an individual—which, as from 6 April, 1990, applied to each of a husband and wife—in any year of assessment is completely exempt. This exempt amount for 1996–97 is £5,800. This threshhold will rise automatically in line with inflation (unless Parliament otherwise determines), i.e., it will rise in proportion to the rise in the retail prices index (from December to December).[10] Above this limit, chargeable gains are added to the taxpayer's income and charged at what would then be his marginal rate (be it 24 per cent or 40 per cent).[11] Trustees generally are eligible for relief only up to half that available to individuals. If more than one trust is created by the same settlor the exemption is divided between them.[12]

In 1982, in order to counteract the effects of inflation, the Finance Act introduced an indexation allowance in respect of a disposal itself.[13] The gain is reduced to take account of the increase in the retail prices index between the month of acquisition and the month of disposal. (The allowance cannot, however, be used to turn a gain into a loss.)[14] In addition, as from 6 April, 1988, the base cost or acquisition value of an asset held by the disponor on 31 March, 1982, and disposed of by him after 5 April 1988, will be its value on 31 March, 1982.[15]

III. Disposal

The legislation does not define "disposal", but the view of the Inland Revenue is that "the disposal of an asset includes any occasion when the ownership of the asset is transferred, whether in whole or in part, from one person to another (except on death), for example, by sale, exchange or gift, or when the owner of the asset derives a capital sum from it."[16] The word is wide enough to include destruction of an asset, a part disposal,[17] or the receipt of a capital sum in return for the surrender or forfeiture of any rights.[18]

---

7 TCGA, 1992, s. 15.
8 Ibid., s. 121.
9 Ibid., s. 210.
10 Ibid., s. 3: CGT (Annual Exempt Amount) Order 1994, S.I. 1994 No. 3008.
11 TCGA 1992, ss. 4–6.
12 Ibid., s. 3 (8), Sch. 1, para. 2 (1)(2). Trustees for mentally disabled persons and persons receiving attendance allowance are eligible for the full £5,800 exemption.
13 Ibid., ss. 53–54.
14 See *Smith v Schofield* [1990] STC 602.
15 See now TCGA 1992, s. 35 (2) (replacing FA 1988, s. 96 (2)). There are exceptions; see TCGA, s. 35 (3), [1987] BTR 417 (D. Stopforth).
16 I.R. Pamphlet, CGT 8 (1980) p. 6, para. 9; see too TCGA 1992, s. 21 (2).
17 There are special provisions to deal with part disposals: see TCGA 1992, ss. 42, 56.
18 Ibid., s. 22. See also *Zim Properties Ltd v Procter* [1985] STC 90; Extra-Statutory Concession D33 (1994).

In the case of a gift, the asset is deemed to be disposed of and acquired at market value.[19] Similarly whenever there is a bargain which is not at arm's length, or where a transaction is made between "connected persons", such as husband and wife.[20]

IV. Death

There is no CGT liability on death. The person or persons upon whom the deceased's property devolves are deemed to acquire it at market value.[1] But there is no deemed disposal by the deceased, so although no CGT is payable on death, the acquisition cost (or base value) of the assets when disposed of in the future will conveniently have been uplifted to the market value at the time of death.

V. Alterations of Dispositions Taking Effect on Death

Where, within the period of two years after a person's death, any of the dispositions (whether effected by will, under the law relating to intestacy or otherwise) of the property of which he was competent to dispose are varied, or the benefit conferred by any of those dispositions is disclaimed, by an instrument in writing made by the persons or any of the persons who benefit or would benefit under the dispositions, the variation or disclaimer shall not constitute a disposal for the purposes of the TCGA 1992,[2] and the variation shall be treated as if it had been effected by the deceased or, as the case may be, as if the disclaimed benefit had never been confirmed.[3] This, together with its equivalent in the inheritance tax legislation,[4] is a much used provision, and enables the dispositions of a deceased's estate to be rearranged or redirected without adverse capital gains tax consequences.

VI. Settlements

There is no definition of "settlement" for CGT purposes. "Settled property" is defined as property held in trust other than property held by a person as nominee or as bare trustee.[5] Where the trustee holds property for one who is absolutely entitled as against the trustee, then, even though a trust exists, there is no settlement for CGT purposes: the acts of the trustee are treated as the acts

19 TCGA 1992, s. 17.
20 Ibid., ss. 18, 286; *Whitehouse v Ellam* [1995] STC 503n.
 1 Ibid., s. 62.
 2 But it may constitute a disposal for the purposes of capital gains tax provisions in other legislation: see *Marshall v Kerr* [1994] STC 638.
 3 TCGA 1992, s. 62 (6)–(10).
 4 IHTA 1984, s. 142; see p. 606 post.
 5 TCGA 1992, ss. 60 (1), 68.

of that person. Any capital gain arising, or loss incurred, on a disposal by the trustee is therefore a gain, or loss, of the "beneficiary".[6]

A. Disposal by Settlor

On the creation of a settlement inter vivos, there is a disposal by the settlor of the entire property thereby settled, whether the settlement is revocable or irrevocable, and whether or not the settlor retains any interest under the settlement.[7] Thereafter, all gains and losses are those of the trust. The settlor and the trustees are "connected persons": in fact, the trustees are "connected" not only with the settlor himself but also with any person connected with the settlor or any corporate body deemed to be connected with the settlor.[8] Accordingly, the disposal value is the market value of the property at the time the settlement is created.[9] "Hold-over relief" may be available in certain circumstances, with the result that a charge to CGT need not occur on the creation of a settlement, but can be postponed. This is explained more fully below.[10]

If the trustees of a United Kingdom-resident settlement realise chargeable gains and, at any time during that year of assessment, the settlor has an interest in the settlement, the trustees are not chargeable to tax on those gains: instead, they are treated as accruing to the settlor.[11] These provisions therefore negate the obvious advantage to a settlor (who may be chargeable to capital gains tax at the rate of 40%) in transferring property to trustees of a settlement under which he retains an interest (which trustees would, but for these provisions, be chargeable to capital gains tax at 24%). A settlor has an interest in the settlement for these purposes if any property which may at any time be comprised in the settlement or any income which may arise under the settlement is, or will or may become, applicable for the benefit of or payable to the settlor or the spouse of the settlor in any circumstances whatsoever, or the settlor or the spouse of the settlor enjoys a benefit deriving directly or indirectly from any such property or income.[12]

B. Disposal by Trustees

Once the settlement has been created, the trustees will be chargeable to CGT on gains accruing to them when they dispose of assets in the course of administration of the trust (usually when they switch the trust investments). There are no special rules here, other than the limits on exempt annual gains already mentioned.[13]

Apart from such actual disposals, the CGT legislation also makes provision for two deemed disposals by the trustees:

6 TCGA 1992, s. 60 (1).
7 Ibid., s. 70.
8 Ibid., s. 286 (3).
9 Ibid., ss. 17, 18.
10 Pp. 566–568, post.
11 TCGA 1992, s. 77 (1), (2).
12 Ibid., s. 77 (3). There are exceptions which broadly mirror the exceptions found in the income tax legislation: s. 77 (4)–(8).
13 P. 558, ante.

i. Termination of a Life Interest in Possession[14]

Prior to 6 April, 1982 the termination of a life interest in possession in settled property which did not then cease to be settled (unless on the death of the life tenant) was a chargeable occasion. This charge has now been abolished. However, if the life interest in possession terminates on the death of the person entitled to it, and the property in which it subsists does not then cease to be settled property, there is still a deemed disposal and reacquisition at market value, by the trustees of that property, but no chargeable gain accrues on that disposal,[15] i.e., there is an uplift in the base value of the property, but no charge to CGT on any gain.

ii. Beneficiary Becoming Absolutely Entitled

There is a deemed disposal when a beneficiary becomes absolutely entitled to the settled property (in whole or in part),[16] unless this occurs on the death of a previous beneficiary.[17] The trustees are deemed to have disposed of and immediately reacquired the property at market value at the date of the termination of the prior interest, and any gain may be chargeable to CGT. The trustees may well retain the property in their hands, but they will do so thereafter as bare trustees for the beneficiary now absolutely entitled.

This provision has been the subject of a great deal of litigation.[18] It has been held, for example, that a person is not "absolutely entitled" for the purposes of this provision unless and until he is both absolutely entitled in equity to the property in question and able to direct the trustees how to deal with it and to give the trustee a good receipt for that property. There need be no difficulty in this respect in the case of cash, unsecured loans, securities, and so forth. However, the position may be different where land is concerned.

In **Stephenson v Barclays Bank Trust Co Ltd** [1975] 1 WLR 882, [1975] 1 All ER 625, Walton J said, at 889, at 637:

"When the situation is that a single person who is sui juris has an absolutely vested beneficial interest in a share of the trust fund, his rights are not, I think, quite as extensive as those of the beneficial holders as a body. In general, he is entitled to have transferred to him ... an aliquot share of each and every asset of the trust fund which presents no difficulty so far as division is concerned. This will apply to such items as cash, money at the bank or an unsecured loan,

---

14 For "life interest", see TCGA 1992, s. 72 (4).
15 Ibid., ss. 72, 73.
16 *Pexton v Bell* [1975] 1 All ER 498; *Crowe v Appleby* [1975] 3 All ER 529, (both affirmed on appeal [1976] STC 301).
17 TCGA 1992, s. 71 (1).
18 See, for example, *Tomlinson v Glyns Executor and Trustee Co* [1970] Ch 112; *Kidson v Macdonald* [1974] Ch 339; *Stephenson v Barclays Bank Trust Co Ltd,* supra; *Pexton v Bell, Crowe v Appleby* [1976] 1 WLR 885, [1976] 2 All ER 914; *Hart v Briscoe* [1979] Ch 1, [1978] 1 All ER 791; *Hoare Trustees v Gardner* [1979] Ch 10, [1978] 1 All ER 791; *Harthan v Mason* [1980] STC 94; *Roome v Edwards* [1982] AC 279, [1981] 1 All ER 736; *Bond v Pickford* [1983] STC 517; *Swires v Renton* [1991] STC 490.

Stock Exchange Securities and the like. However, as regards land, certainly, in all cases, as regards shares in a private company in very special circumstances (see *Re Weiner* [1956] 1 WLR 579, [1956] 2 All ER 482) and possibly (although the logic of the addition in fact escapes me)[19] mortgage debts (see *Re Marshall* [1914] 1 Ch 192 per Cozens-Hardy MR) the situation is not so simple, and even a person with a vested interest in possession in an aliquot share of the trust fund may have to wait until the land is sold, and so forth, before being able to call on the trustees as of right to account to him for his share of the assets.''

Another source of difficulty is that, in this context, "absolutely entitled" does not mean "absolutely and beneficially entitled", so that an advancement or an appointment by trustees to new trustees on new trusts could give rise to a deemed disposal and a charge to CGT. The central point at issue is whether one settlement has ended and another has taken its place. This complex question ceased to be of such importance when an election for "hold-over relief" could be made, thus avoiding a charge to tax.[20] However, with the abolition of the general "holdover relief" in the Finance Act 1989, this question, and the associated caselaw, once again became important.[1]

In **Roome v Edwards** [1982] AC 279, [1981] 1 All ER 736, Lord WILBERFORCE said at 292, at 739:
"There are a number of obvious indicia which may help to show whether a settlement, or a settlement separate from another settlement, exists. One might expect to find separate and defined property; separate trusts; and separate trustees. One might also expect to find a separate disposition bringing the separate settlement into existence. These indicia may be helpful, but they are not decisive. For example, a single disposition, e.g., a will with a single set of trustees, may create what are clearly separate settlements, relating to different properties, in favour of different beneficiaries, and conversely separate trusts may arise in what is clearly a single settlement, e.g. when the settled property is divided into shares. There are so many possible combinations of fact that even where these indicia or some of them are present, the answer may be doubtful, and may depend upon an appreciation of them as a whole.
Since 'settlement' and 'trusts' are legal terms, which are also used by business men or laymen in a business or practical sense, I think that the question whether a particular set of facts amounts to a settlement should be approached by asking what a person, with knowledge of the legal context of the word under established doctrine and applying this knowledge in a practical and common-sense manner to the facts under examination, would conclude.

---

19 The logic of the addition of mortgages is that they include not only the debt but also the estate and powers of the mortgagee: *Crowe v Appleby* [1975] 3 All ER 529.
20 The question could arise still: e.g., where hold-over relief is not available because the first set of trustees are not resident in the United Kingdom; or where the relief is available but the beneficiary ceases to be resident in the United Kingdom within six years.
1 See infra.

To take two fairly typical cases. Many settlements contain powers to appoint a part or a proportion of the trust property to beneficiaries: some may also confer power to appoint separate trustees of the property so appointed, or such power may be conferred by law: see Trustee Act 1925, section 37. It is established doctrine that the trusts declared by a document exercising a special power of appointment are to be read into the original settlement: see *Muir (or Williams) v Muir* [1943] AC 468. If such a power is exercised, whether or not separate trustees are appointed, I do not think that it would be natural for such a person as I have presupposed to say that a separate settlement had been created: still less so if it were found that provisions of the original settlement continued to apply to the appointed fund, or that the appointed fund were liable, in certain events, to fall back into the rest of the settled property. On the other hand, there may be a power to appoint and appropriate a part or portion of the trust property to beneficiaries and to settle it for their benefit. If such a power is exercised, the natural conclusion might be that a separate settlement was created, all the more so if a complete new set of trusts were declared as to the appropriated property, and if it could be said that the trusts of the original settlement ceased to apply to it. There can be many variations on these cases each of which will have to be judged on its facts.''

In **Swires v Renton** [1991] STC 490, HOFFMANN J said at 499:
    "The decision of the House of Lords in *Roome v Edwards*, as expressed in the speech of Lord Wilberforce, shows that the question must be answered according to the view which would be taken of the transaction by a person with knowledge of trusts who uses language in a practical and commonsense way. Which description would be considered more appropriate: that new trusts had been grafted onto the old settlement or that a new settlement had been created?
    The more recent decision of the Court of Appeal in 1983 in *Bond v Pickford* [1983] STC 517 shows that a critical element in deciding how to describe the transaction may be the scope of the power which has been exercised. If that power allows the trustees to define or vary the beneficial interest but not remove the assets from the settlement or delegate their powers and discretions it is difficult to imagine any appointment within the scope of the power which could be construed as the creation of a new settlement. On the other hand, the power may be expressed in terms wide enough to permit the creation of a new settlement, and the question will then be whether this is what the trustees have chosen to do.
    The cases show there is no single litmus test for deciding that question. The paradigm case of the creation of a new settlement would involve the segregation of particular assets, the appointment of new trustees, the creation of fresh trusts which exhaust the beneficial interest in the assets and administrative powers which make further reference to the original settlement redundant (see *Hart v Briscoe* [1979] Ch 1, at 8, [1978] 1 All ER 791 at 807 per Brightman J). The absence of one or more of those features is not necessarily inconsistent with a resettlement. It seems to me that the question is one of construction of the settlement using the approach recommended by Lord Wilberforce and looking at the documents in the light of the surrounding circumstances. Putting the same thing another way, it is a matter of endeavouring to ascertain the intention of the parties.''

C. Disposal by Beneficiaries

In general, a disposal by a beneficiary of his interest under a settlement does not give rise to a chargeable gain.[2] However, there are two important exceptions to this rule. First, where a person acquired (or derives title from someone who acquired) the interest for a consideration in money or money's worth, a gain on the disposal of that interest by such person will be chargeable.[3] Second, the disposal of an interest in settled property is chargeable if, at the time of the disposal, the trustees are neither resident nor ordinarily resident in the United Kingdom.[4]

D. Attribution of Gains of Overseas Trusts to Beneficiaries

Special rules apply to a settlement for any year of assessment during which the trustees of which are not resident or ordinarily resident in the United Kingdom,[5] and which was created by a settlor who is at any time during that year, or was, at the time of making the settlement, domiciled and resident (or ordinarily resident) in the United Kingdom.[6] The broad effect of these rules is that gains realised by the trustees (called "trust gains") may be attributed to the beneficiaries. Trust gains are cumulated. Capital payments received by beneficiaries who are domiciled in the United Kingdom at some time during the year are then attributed to those trust gains and they become chargeable in the hands of those beneficiaries.[7] The gains are attributed to the beneficiaries in proportion to the capital payments received by them (but are not to exceed those payments).[8] For the purposes of these special rules, a "settlement" bears the wide income tax meaning, and not the narrower meaning attributed to it for general capital gains tax purposes.[9] A "capital payment" is also widely defined and means any payment which is not chargeable to income tax: it includes a transfer of an asset and the conferring of any other benefit; and a beneficiary is regarded as having received a capital payment from the trustees if he receives it from them directly or indirectly, or if it is applied by them (directly or indirectly) in the payment of any debt of his, or otherwise for his benefit, or if it is received by a third party at the beneficiary's direction.[10]

There are also provisions for the attribution of the gains of a non-resident (or dual resident) settlement to the settlor if (a) he is domiciled in the United Kingdom at some time in the year of assessment and is either resident in the

---

2 TCGA 1992, s. 76 (1).

3 Ibid., s. 76 (1).

4 Ibid., s. 85. This is intended to prevent avoidance: previously it was common for trusts to become non-resident and for beneficiaries to sell their interests to non-residents: see, for example, *Berry v Warnett* [1982] 2 All ER 630.

5 Trustees are treated as resident or ordinarily resident in the United Kingdom unless the majority of them are not so resident and the general administration of the trust is ordinarily carried on overseas: TCGA 1992, s. 69 (1). The rule is relaxed for professional trustees of a trust created by a person resident or domiciled outside the United Kingdom: ibid., s. 69 (2). See also SP 5/92, paras. 2 and 3; and *Roome v Edwards* [1982] AC 279, [1981] 1 All ER 736, p. 563 ante. There may also be a charge to capital gains tax on the migration of a trust: TCGA 1992, ss. 89, 90.

6 TCGA 1992, s. 87.

7 Ibid., s. 87 (8).

8 Ibid., s. 87 (5).

9 Ibid., s. 97 (7).

10 Ibid, s. 97 (2), (5). See also *Jones v Lincoln-Lewis* [1991] STC 307; *de Rothschild v Lawrenson* [1995] STC 623.

United Kingdom during any part of the year or ordinarily resident in the United Kingdom during the year, and (b) at any time during the year the settlor has an interest in the settlement.[11] A settlor has an interest in a settlement for these purposes if any relevant property (being property originating from the settlor) which is or may at any time be comprised in the settlement, or any relevant income (being income originating from the settlor) which arises or may arise under the settlement, is or will or may become applicable for the benefit of the settlor or a member of his immediate family (called a "defined person").[12]

VII. Hold-over Relief

Hold-over relief was originally enacted in 1965 as relief for *business* assets.[13] Although this form of relief remained in force, it was displaced in importance by a wider form of hold-over relief for gifts generally introduced in 1980.[14] Between 1980 and 1989 (when the general relief was abolished),[15] transfers of assets into and out of trust were effected entirely free of CGT, by claiming this general hold-over relief on the transfer. Relief was available in respect of a transfer of assets made after 5 April, 1980, other than by way of bargain at arm's length. Initially, the relief applied only to transfers between individuals, but in 1981 it was extended to disposals between an individual and the trustees of a settlement, and in 1982 to disposals made by trustees themselves.[16] The effect of these provisions was that when there was a disposal by the settlor or by the trustees,[17] any gain could be held over or postponed. The chargeable gain which would otherwise have accrued to the transferor was eliminated or reduced; but, at the same time, the consideration which the transferee would otherwise have been regarded as giving was reduced by a corresponding amount. The charge was thus postponed until the occurrence of a future chargeable disposal, when the base value of the property or asset would be lower than it would otherwise have been. Consequently, there need not be a charge to CGT on the creation of the settlement or when a beneficiary became absolutely entitled to the settled property (unless a charge was desired, or where the relief was not available, for example because the trustees were not resident in the United Kingdom).

This general hold-over relief was abolished in the Finance Act 1989,[18] which in effect restores the pre-1980 position. However, although the relief (now found in section 165 of TCGA 1992) is largely confined to business assets, as before, this is not exclusively the case. Certain gifts of non-business assets will also enjoy the relief, the main category being those which are immediately

11 TCGA 1992, ss. 86, 88, Sch. 5.
12 Ibid., Sch. 5, para. 2.
13 FA 1965, s. 34; reset in FA 1978, s. 46; consolidated in CGTA 1979, s. 126.
14 FA 1980, s. 79.
15 FA 1989, s. 124.
16 FA 1980, s. 79; FA 1981, s. 78; FA 1982, s. 82. See (1982) 110 Tax 299, 327 (K. Tingley).
17 On the creation of the settlement, the settlor alone claims the relief. If the trustees make a disposal, both the trustees and the transferee must claim the relief.
18 FA 1989, s. 124 and Sch. 14.

chargeable transfers for the purposes of Inheritance Tax.[19] There will therefore be a boost to the popularity of discretionary trusts—particularly the "nil-rate band" discretionary trusts[20]—transfers into which are chargeable.

Thus, the position with regard to hold-over relief is now broadly as follows. Shares qualify for relief if they are shares or securities of a trading company, or of the holding company of a trading group, and either (i) those shares are not quoted on a recognised stock exchange or (ii) the trading company or holding company is the transferor's personal company.[1] An asset qualifies for relief if it is (or is an interest in) an asset used for the purposes of a trade, profession or vocation carried on by the transferor, his family company, or a member of a trading group of which the holding company is his personal company.[2] The terms "personal company", "trading company" and "holding company" are defined,[3] the most important requirement being that, in the case of a "personal company", the donor must himself own at least 5 per cent. of the voting rights.[4]

The relief is available to trustees as well as individuals, again in a non-arm's length transaction, but it is more restrictive in that trustees must hold at least 25% of the voting rights in a family company, i.e., there is no alternative provision to cover the case where they and other trustees, or they and the beneficiaries, hold at least that much. The most common non-arm's length transaction with which trustees are concerned is that occurring when a beneficiary, or the trustees of another settlement, become absolutely entitled as against the trustees of the first settlement.[5] Of particular concern to trustees will be the possibility that the exercise of powers by them, in respect of non-qualifying shares or assets, will inadvertently make someone absolutely entitled, e.g., an appointment or advancement of trust assets to another settlement.[6] Such an occasion will not be a chargeable transfer of value for Inheritance Tax purposes,[7] and it seems as if the alternative head of relief will therefore not apply.

Trustees should also be wary of section 260 (2)(*d*) of TCGA 1992, which provides that hold-over relief will apply to a disposal which, by virtue of section 71(4) of the Inheritance Tax Act 1984, does not constitute an occasion on

---

19 TCGA 1992, s. 260. Other gifts of non-business assets qualifying for relief are those involving heritage property and gifts to political parties.

20 See p. 594, post. The creation of a "nil-rate band" discretionary trust constitutes a chargeable transfer for these purposes.

1 The concept of the "personal company" was introduced by FA 1993, Sch. 7, para. 1 (2) and inserted into section 165 of TCGA 1992 in place of the "family company", in relation to disposals after 15 March, 1993.

2 TCGA 1992, s. 165 (2). The relief also extends to agricultural property enjoying relief for inheritance tax purposes. There are restrictions where assets have been only partially used for business purposes, or where a company's assets include non-business assets; and also where the transferee is not resident or ordinarily resident in the United Kingdom. Payment of tax by instalments is permitted in certain circumstances.

3 Ibid., s. 165 (8), Sch. 6, para. 1; FA 1993, Sch. 7, para. 1 (2).

4 FA 1993, Sch. 7, para. 1 (2). For disposals before 16 March, 1993, the crucial expression was "family company", which was defined as a company the voting rights in which were exercisable as to not less than 25 per cent. by the individual, or as to more than 50 per cent. exercisable by the individual or a member of his family and, as to not less than 5 per cent. exercisable by the individual himself: TCGA 1992, Sch. 6, para. 1 (2).

5 TCGA 1992, s. 71. See p. 563, ante.

6 *Roome v Edwards* [1982] AC 279, [1981] 1 All ER 736, p. 563, ante; *Hoare Trustees v Gardner* [1979] Ch 10; *Hart v Briscoe* [1979] Ch 1, [1978] 1 All ER 791; *Bond v Pickford* [1983] STC 517.

7 IHTA 1984, s. 81.

which inheritance tax is chargeable under that section. The effect of this provision is that, if a beneficiary becomes absolutely entitled to capital held in an accumulation and maintenance trust on or before attaining a specified age (not exceeding 25), hold-over relief will be available on that occasion. However, if that beneficiary were to become entitled to income only (for example, because of the application of section 31 of the Trustee Act 1925, p. 762, post), and only subsequently became entitled to capital, hold-over relief would not be available.

15. Inheritance Tax

In **Inglewood (Lord) v IRC** [1983] 1 WLR 366, Fox LJ said at 368:
"From 1894 to 1975 the main instrument of capital taxation was estate duty. It has been described as a voluntary tax. That goes too far but certainly it contained loopholes which enabled its impact to be much reduced. First, it was a death tax only and while gifts of property or dispositions of life interests were, in effect, taxable on death though made inter vivos that, in general, only applied to gifts or dispositions made during the statutory period, which was latterly seven years before the death. Secondly, discretionary trusts were an effective means of avoiding estate duty. There was normally no charge to duty on the death of one of the discretionary objects leaving more than one other such object surviving him, since no property interest passed or determined by

reason of such death. This was so though the deceased had been receiving part, or even the whole, of the income during his lifetime. The position was altered to some extent by the Finance Act 1969 which imposed a charge for duty on the death of a discretionary object which was geared to the proportion of income which had actually been paid out to him during the statutory period. The Finance Act 1975 revolutionised the position. It abolished estate duty and created capital transfer tax which was a tax not merely in relation to death but also to other dispositions of capital. Thus a voluntary disposition of property inter vivos to an individual will attract capital transfer tax.''

I. Introduction

Inheritance Tax (IHT) was introduced in 1986, ostensibly as a replacement for Capital Transfer Tax, although the basic provisions of the two taxes are similar. IHT is governed by the Inheritance Tax Act 1984 (IHTA 1984)[1] and the FA 1986. It is a direct tax on the transfer (or the deemed transfer) of capital.[1a] It falls primarily on the estate passing on death, but it is also a tax on certain lifetime gifts. For IHT purposes, there are essentially five categories of transfers to consider: exempt transfers (on death or during lifetime); potentially exempt transfers (PETS); chargeable lifetime transfers; gifts with a reservation of benefit (GROBS);[2] and chargeable transfers on death.

II. Lifetime Transfers

Inheritance Tax (IHT) is charged on the value transferred by a chargeable transfer.[3] A chargeable transfer is any transfer of value made by an individual[4] after 26 March, 1974[5] other than an exempt transfer.[6] A transfer of value means any disposition made by a person ("the transferor") as a result of which the value of his estate immediately after the disposition is less than it would be but for the disposition; and the amount by which it is less is the value transferred by the transfer.[7]

A. Disposition

This is not defined, but it includes not only an act but also an omission[8] (for example, failure to exercise an option), and probably the destruction of an

---

1 Originally called Capital Transfer Act 1984, and renamed by Finance Act 1986, s. 100 (1) (*a*).
1a For alternative proposals, see [1988] BTR 473 (W. Goodhart).
2 PETS and GROBS, of their very nature, cannot be made on death.
3 IHTA 1984, s. 1.
4 Subject to specific provisions relating to close companies (see ibid., ss. 94–102), companies are generally not chargeable.
5 This was the date on which capital transfer tax was announced in the House of Commons.
6 IHTA 1984, s. 2.
7 Ibid, s. 3 (1).
8 Ibid., s. 3 (3).

asset (for example, the surrender of a lease). Clearly, where a settlor transfers property into settlement (under which neither he nor his wife has an interest in possession)[9] there has been a disposition, and it will be a chargeable transfer of value, unless it is a PET or otherwise exempt.[10]

B. Estate

A person's estate is the aggregate of all the property to which he is beneficially entitled, except that the estate of a person immediately before his death does not include "excluded property".[11] Property includes rights and interests of any description.[12] Moreover, a person who has a general power of appointment over property (other than settled property, which is dealt with separately) is treated as beneficially entitled to that property.[13] Similarly, someone who is beneficially entitled to an interest in possession (for example, a life interest) in settled property is treated as beneficially entitled to the property in which that interest subsists, so that such property will form part of his estate.[14]

"Excluded property" covers, for example, most reversionary interests, and property which is situated overseas and which belongs to someone domiciled outside the United Kingdom.[15]

C. Loss in Value of Estate

The value transferred is not the amount received by the transferee, nor the value of the property transferred, but the loss to the estate of the transferor: for example, if A owns 51% of the shares in X Ltd, and B owns 49%, and A transfers 3% of his shares to the trustees of a discretionary trust, then the trustees acquire little but A loses control of X Ltd.

It follows that, where full consideration is provided in return for the disposition, there is no diminution in the value of the transferor's estate and hence no transfer of value; and where less than full consideration is provided, the value transferred is the difference between the consideration and the loss to the transferor's estate.[16]

D. Grossing-up

IHT may be paid either by the transferor or by the transferee.

If the transferor pays the IHT the diminution in his estate will also include the amount of tax. Assume, for example, that A transfers £220,000 into a discretionary trust; the cumulative IHT on this transfer (at the lifetime rates)[17] is £4,000. If the trustees pay the tax, they are left with £216,000; and the loss to A's estate is simply £220,000.

---

9 As to the significance of this qualification, see pp. 582–591, post.
10 Pp. 572–575, post.
11 IHTA 1984, s. 5 (1).
12 Ibid., s. 272.
13 Ibid., s. 5 (2).
14 Ibid., s. 49 (1).
15 Ibid., ss. 6, 48, 155 (1).
16 There may still not be a transfer of value if the conditions in s. 10 (1) are satisfied.
17 IHTA 1984, Sch 1, substituted by the Inheritance Tax (Indexation) Order 1994, SI 1994, No 3011.

On the other hand, if A pays the IHT, the cost to him of making the transfer also includes that tax (£4,000): it is as if he were making two gifts, one to the trustees and one to the Inland Revenue. He thus has to pay tax on that tax. In other words, the loss to his estate is the sum which, when taxed at the appropriate rates, will leave the trustees with £220,000 (which is, in fact, £225,000). This process is known as "grossing-up"; and the sum of £225,000 is the "grossed-up equivalent" of £220,000.

E. Computation

The amount of tax payable on any chargeable transfer depends largely on two factors:

(*a*) The transferor's cumulative total of chargeable transfers. IHT is a cumulative tax.[18] The gross amount of each chargeable transfer is added to the last. Originally, as the total amount transferred increased, so did the rate of tax. What it means now, however, is that if the total value of chargeable transfers exceeds £200,000, any excess over that threshhold is subject to tax at 40% (on death) or 20% (during lifetime).[19] However, only those chargeable gifts made during the previous seven years are cumulated; those made more than seven years before the chargeable transfer in question will drop out of the cumulative total. The threshhold will be increased, unless Parliament otherwise determines, in proportion to the rise in the retail prices index (from December to December) and each new threshhold will be rounded up to the nearest £1,000.[20]

(*b*) The time of the transfer, in particular, whether it is during lifetime or on death (or within three years of death, when the death rates will apply)[1], or, in the case of PETS, whether death occurs within seven years.

F. Exempt Transfers[2]

The main exemptions are: all transfers between spouses;[3] lifetime gifts which represent normal expenditure out of the transferor's income;[4] lifetime gifts not exceeding £3,000[5] in a tax year; outright lifetime gifts to any one person in a tax year up to a total value of £250;[6] gifts in consideration of marriage (up to £5,000 if made by a parent to his or her child, up to £2,500 if made by a

---

18 There is only one table of rates, namely those applicable on death. Chargeable lifetime transfers are charged at one-half of those rates.

19 See n. 17, supra.

20 Unless the threshhold is raised expressly in the Finance Act (as in FA 1996, s. 183), it is increased by Statutory Instrument to keep up with inflation.

1 Some of the reliefs, e.g. in respect of business property or agricultural land are available only if ownership for specified periods can be established; hence timing is crucial in this context too.

2 These are dealt with in Part II of IHTA 1984.

3 IHTA 1984, s. 18 (1). In respect of transfers of value made after March 8, 1982, this is subject to a maximum limit of £55,000 where the transferor, but not the transferor's spouse, is domiciled in the United Kingdom immediately before the transfer: s. 18 (2).

4 Ibid., s. 21; *Bennett v IRC* [1995] STC 54.

5 Increased from £2,000 as from 6 April, 1981: FA 1981, s. 94 (1), (7).

6 Increased from £100 as from 6 April, 1980: FA 1980, s. 86 (3), (5).

grandparent, and up to £1,000 in any other case[7]); lifetime gifts for the maintenance of children and dependent relatives;[8] gifts and bequests to charities and political parties (subject in the case of the latter, to a limit of £100,000 if made on or within one year of death[9]); and gifts and bequests to certain bodies concerned with the preservation of the national heritage or of a public nature, such as the National Gallery, the British Museum, any university in the United Kingdom, and any local authority or Government department.[10]

There are also exemptions and reliefs in particular circumstances for particular types of property, notably business property,[11] agricultural land,[12] woodlands,[13] works of art and historic houses.[14]

G. Business Property and Agricultural Property Relief

Business property and agricultural property are accorded particularly favourable treatment for inheritance tax purposes. Relief at 100% is available for certain kinds of "relevant business property", such as property consisting of a business or interest in a business, or a controlling shareholding in an unquoted company; and 50% relief is available in certain other cases.[15] Moreover, the property in question must have been owned by the transferor throughout the two years immediately preceding the transfer.[16]

A similar generous relief is available in respect of "agricultural property".[17] 100% relief is available in some cases, e.g., where the interest of the transferor in the property immediately before the transfer carries the right to vacant possession. In other cases, relief is available at only 50%.[18] As in the case of business property, there is a minimum period of ownership: the relief is only available if the property was occupied by the transferor for the purposes of agriculture throughout the period of two years ending with the date of the transfer, or it was owned by him throughout the period of seven years ending with the date of transfer and was throughout that period occupied (by him or another) for the purpose of agriculture.[19] (Thus, short-term investment in agricultural land for tax avoidance is prevented). There are also special rules

---

7 IHTA 1984, s. 22.
8 Ibid., s. 11.
9 Ibid., ss. 23, 24.
10 Ibid., ss. 25, 26.
11 Ibid., ss. 103–114; *Finch v IRC* [1983] STC 157.
12 Ibid., ss. 115–124. See also *Finch v IRC*, supra; *Starke v IRC* [1995] STC 689.
13 Ibid., ss. 125–130.
14 Ibid., ss. 25–27.
15 Ibid, ss. 104 (1), (1A), 105 (1) (a)–(e); and F(No.2)A 1992, Sch. 14, paras. 1, 8 (in relation to transfers of value occurring after 9 March, 1992). A business or interest in a business, or shares in or securities of a company, do not qualify for relief if the business consists wholly or mainly of dealing in securities or shares, land or buildings, or making or holding investments: IHTA 1984, s. 105 (3). Note the exceptions in sub-s. (4), however. See also FA 1996, s. 184 (in relation to transfer of value occurring after the date specified in s. 184(5)).
16 Ibid., s. 106. There are provisions dealing with replacement property and cases where the transferor became entitled to the property on the death of another person: ibid., ss. 107, 108.
17 Ibid., ss. 115–124B. There is an extended definition of "agricultural property" in s. 115 (2); *Starke v IRC* [1995] STC 689.
18 Ibid., s. 116 (2)–(4), and F(No.2)A 1992, Sch. 14, paras. 4, 8 (in respect of transfers of value occurring after 9 March, 1992, subject to transitional provisions in Sch. 14, para. 9).
19 Ibid., s. 117.

dealing with replacement property, occupation by a company or partnership, and property acquired on the death of another.[20]

These two reliefs are obviously of considerable benefit and, provided the relevant conditions (which require close and careful study) are satisfied, a transferor may be able to transfer qualifying property entirely free of inheritance tax—the availability of 100% relief is essentially equivalent to a complete exemption from tax. Thus, agricultural or business property can be transferred out of the transferor's estate and into (say) a discretionary trust, entirely free of inheritance tax (or, at least, at 50% tax).

H. Potentially Exempt Transfers (PETS).

i. GENERAL

The key elements of a PET are that it must be a transfer of value made by way of gift by an individual, after 18 March, 1986; it must be to another individual or into an accumulation and maintenance trust, or into an interest in possession trust or disabled trust[1] (so that a transfer into a discretionary trust or to a close company cannot be a PET): and it must otherwise have been a chargeable transfer (so that a transfer by a husband to his wife cannot be a PET, for it is an immediate exempt transfer).

When a PET is made, it is assumed that it will become exempt in due course: there is no tax payable; there is not even a requirement that it be reported. A PET becomes actually exempt when the transferor has survived it by a period of seven years. If he fails to survive by seven years, IHT is chargeable on the value of the property transferred at the time of the PET (not at the date of death), although the rates of tax applicable are those in force at the time of death (not those at the time of the PET). It would be clearly unjust if the same amount of tax were payable irrespective of whether the transferor died one day after the transfer or one day before the expiry of the seven year period. There is, therefore, a "tapering relief"[2] whereby the rate of tax applicable to the PET (not the value of the property) diminishes as the length of time by which the transferor survives the PET increases.

Time of death	*Percentage of tax rate*
Not more than 3 years from PET	100%
More than 3, but not more than 4, years	80%
More than 4, but not more than 5, years	60%
More than 5, but not more than 6, years	40%
More than 6, but not more than 7, years	20%
More than 7 years from PET	nil (completely exempt)

20 IHTA 1984, ss. 118–121. See also FA 1996, s. 185, inserting new provisions in relation to the death after 1 September 1995 of certain agricultural tenants.

1 See pp. 597–606, post for the meaning of these terms. F (No 2) A 1987, s. 96.

2 IHTA 1984, ss. 3A, 7 (4). Although called a "relief", the position is in some ways worse under IHT than it was under Capital Transfer Tax: a chargeable lifetime transfer would then have been taxed at 50% of the death rates even where the transferor died within 5, but more than 3, years from death, whereas under IHT the rates are 80% and 60%.

Although the premature death of the transferor renders a PET retrospectively chargeable, the PET is not treated as forming part of his estate on death, so that the value transferred by a PET will not bear IHT rateably with the estate on death. Also, it is the donee of the PET who is primarily liable for the IHT payable on it.

ii. PETS AND TRUSTS

A transfer of value ranks as a PET not only where there is a direct transfer to an individual but also where the transferee is a trustee of an accumulation and maintenance trust, or of a disabled trust, or (since 17 March, 1987) of an interest in possession trust. Thus, if S creates a settlement for A (an individual) for life, this is a PET (unless A is S's spouse). If A's life interest terminates (or is treated as terminated) during A's lifetime—for example, by assignment, surrender or revocation—and the settled property vests in an individual, absolutely or for an interest in possession, or is held thereafter on accumulation and maintenance trusts, there is again a PET. On the other hand, if S were to create a discretionary trust, or if discretionary trusts were to arise on the termination of A's life interest, this would not be a PET: it would be an immediately chargeable transfer. Also, clearly there could be no PET if A's life interest were to terminate on death, irrespective of who then became entitled to the property or what kind of trust then arose.

One effect of these provisions is that the calculation of IHT in the event that a PET becomes chargeable retrospectively can be extremely complex.

iii. EFFECT ON CUMULATIVE TOTALS AND RECALCULATION

EXAMPLE

T dies on 1 March, 1998, having made the following transfers of value (TOVs):
  (1) 1 January, 1991: a gift of £50,000 to his private company (a close company).
  (2) 1 June, 1991: gift of £60,000 to his son.
  (3) 1 August, 1991: a gift of £150,000 into a discretionary trust.
  (4) 1 May, 1992: a gift of £25,000 to his daughter.
  (5) 1 March, 1998: T dies leaving an estate of £250,000.
Assume that any reliefs and exemptions available have been utilised (including the nil rate band), that the donee pays the tax, and that there is no gift with reservation of benefit (GROB).

First round
  (1) The 1 January, 1991, gift: this is not a PET and it is immediately chargeable at the appropriate lifetime rates (T's cumulative total becomes £50,000 above the threshold).
  (2) The 1 June, 1991, gift: this is a PET (a gift to an individual) and so gives rise to no immediate charge.
  (3) The 1 August, 1991, gift into discretionary trust: this is not a PET and so is immediately chargeable.
    (i) The rates of tax applicable are *half* those specified in the Table.
    (ii) What is the chargeable total?

(*a*) The latest TOV (i.e., that of 1 June, 1991) is not immediately aggregable, for it was a PET and therefore assumed not to be chargeable.

(*b*) The penultimate TOV (i.e., that of 1 January, 1991) is aggregable, for it was not a PET and occurred within the preceding seven years.

Thus, the chargeable TOV here is £150,000, forming the top slice of an aggregate total of £200,000.

(4) The 1 May, 1992, gift: this is also a PET and is therefore not immediately chargeable.

Second round.

On T's death on 1 March, 1998, the above TOVs have to be reopened and tax thereon recalculated.

(1) The 1 January, 1991, gift: this is not affected, because it occurred more than seven years before 1 March 1998.

(2) The 1 June, 1991, gift: this now becomes a chargeable TOV of £60,000.

What is the aggregate of chargeable TOVs? The previous gift (i.e., that of 1 January, 1991) comes into the aggregate total, because it occurred within seven years before 1 June, 1991.

Thus the chargeable gift is the top £60,000 of a total of £110,000.

At what rates?

The rates are those in force at the date of T's death. Since the gift in question occurred more than 6 years before T's death, IHT is charged at 20% of the full *rate* as determined in accordance with the Table at death.

(3) The gift of 1 August, 1991, into discretionary trust: although chargeable at the time it was made, this too has to be reopened now, for the aggregate of prior chargeable TOVs is different.

What is the aggregate?

Both the prior chargeable gifts (i.e., those of 1 January, 1991 and 1 June, 1991) must now be aggregated.

Thus the charge is on the top £150,000 of an aggregable total of £260,000.

At what rates?

Again, the transfer occurred more than 6 years before T's death, so IHT is chargeable at 20% of the full rate applicable according to the Table in force at T's death.

If the resulting amount of tax exceeds that which was actually paid in 1991, that excess is payable. If the resulting amount of tax is less than that actually paid, then there is no refund.

Exit charges?[3]

If there were any exit charges in respect of the discretionary trust in the period between creation and death, those exit charges must also be recalculated, taking into account the now aggregable gifts of 1 January, and 1 June, 1991.

(4) The gift of 1 May, 1992: this also becomes a chargeable TOV.

What is the aggregate?

All the previous gifts will have been or become chargeable and so must be brought into the cumulative total. This gift is thus of the top £25,000 of an aggregate of £285,000.

---

3 See pp. 592–594, post.

At what rates?
Since this gift was made more than 5 years but not more than 6 years before T's death, IHT is chargeable at 40% of the full rates in force at the time of death.

(5) On T's death, on 1 March 1988, the charge will be at full rates on an estate of £250,000 which will be transferred after prior chargeable TOVS amounting in total to £235,000, i.e., the transfer of 1 January, 1991 has dropped out of the cumulative total.

I. Gifts with Reservation of Benefit (GROBs).

Though introduced to the IHT regime late in the day, by section 81 of the FA 1986, the GROB provisions were, in fact, a familiar feature of the old Estate Duty, having been present in one form or another from at least as early as section 38 (2) of the Customs and Inland Revenue Act 1881[4]. It was of these provisions, almost identical to those now in force, that Lord RADCLIFFE said, in *St Aubyn v A-G.*[5]

"I think it regrettable that when, in 1940, opportunity was found to wipe out the old sections and to enact a new set of provisions, opportunity was not at the same time found to make those provisions more readily intelligible. I can appreciate that at any rate some of the transactions with which section 43 and section 56 appear to be concerned are deplorable from the point of view of those interested in revenue collection, but for all that, the taxpayer is entitled to be told with some reasonable certainty in what circumstances and under what conditions liability to tax is incurred or else to be told explicitly that the circumstances and conditions are just those which the Commissioners of Inland Revenue in their administrative discretion may consider appropriate."

Despite such pointed criticism, these old provisions have been reintroduced and the opportunity still has not been taken to make them more intelligible.

i. THE NEW PROVISIONS

Section 102 (3) of the Finance Act 1986 provides that if, immediately before the death of a donor, there is any property which, in relation to him, is "property subject to a reservation", then to the extent that the property would not, apart from this section, form part of the donor's estate immediately before his death, that property shall be treated for the purposes of Inheritance Tax as property to which he was beneficially entitled immediately before his death. An obvious example might be the case where a donor gives his house to a child

---

4 As amended by (inter alia) the Customs and Inland Revenue Act 1889, s. 11 (1) and FA 1940, s. 43 (2).
5 [1952] AC 15 at 44–45, [1951] 2 All ER 473 at 493.

but continues living in it; the house will be regarded as remaining comprised in his estate at his death (unless he has moved out before then).[6]

(a) Property Subject to a Reservation

"Property subject to a reservation" is defined as property disposed of by an individual by way of gift, on or after 18 March, 1986, and *either* (i) possession and enjoyment of the property is not bona fide assumed by the donee at or before the beginning of the relevant period, *or* (ii) at any time in the relevant period the property is not enjoyed to the entire exclusion, or virtually to the entire exclusion,[7] of the donor and of any benefit to him by contract or otherwise.[8] The "relevant period" for these purposes is defined as the period ending on the donor's death and beginning seven years before death or (if later) the date of the gift.[9]

The GROB provisions do not apply if, or to the extent that, the disposal of the property by way of gift is an exempt transfer of the kinds listed. The list includes all exempt transfers for IHT purposes[10] except the annual exemption (of £3,000) and normal expenditure out of income.

There is no definition of "gift" in the Act, so the general law applies for the purposes of determining whether there is an effective gift.[11]

(b) Possession and Enjoyment

Although section 81 (1) (*a*) provides that possession and enjoyment of the property must be bona fide assumed "by the donee", it is sufficient if the transfer is to the donee's agent or to a trustee for the donee, even where the donor is one of the trustees[12] or the sole trustee.[13] Thus, if the donor holds or deals with the gifted property in a purely fiduciary capacity, the GROB provisions need not apply, although it will be otherwise if the donor derives some benefit, e.g., if he is remunerated for acting as trustee.[14] "Bona fide" means that there must be a genuine and real assumption of possession and enjoyment, without any secret or covinous arrangement or reservation.[15]

---

6 There are further provisions to cover the case where the reserved benefit ceases before the donor's death, and also to prevent double charges to tax (as would be the case, e.g., if the property were taxed at the time the gift was made and again at the date when the reserved benefit ceased): see The Inheritance Tax (Double Charges Relief) Regulations 1987: SI 1987, No. 1130. Moreover, there are important exceptions in para. 6 of Schedule 19 to FA 1986, the main ones being actual occupation of land, or actual possession of a chattel, by the donor for full consideration in money's worth, and actual occupation of land by the donor as a result of a change in his circumstances since the time of the gift.

7 This is intended to cover a case such as that where the donor has given his house to a child but returns to visit the child, and stays in the house, periodically.

8 FA 1986, s. 102 (1), (2).

9 Ibid., s. 102 (1). The GROB provisions are thus rendered consistent with the seven year cumulation period: see p. 572, ante.

10 Ibid., s. 102 (5). See p. 572, ante.

11 See, for example: *Re Fitzwilliam's Agreement* [1950] Ch 448, [1950] 1 All ER 191; *Re Thornley* (1928) 7 ATC 178; *A-G v Worrall* [1895] 1 QB 99; *A-G v Johnson* [1903] 1 KB 617 at 624–625.

12 *Commissioner of Stamp Duties of New South Wales v Perpetual Trustee Co Ltd* [1943] AC 425.

13 *Oakes v Commissioner of Stamp Duties of NSW* [1954] AC 57, [1953] 2 All ER 1563.

14 *Oakes v Commissioner of Stamp Duties of NSW*, supra. This is of particular concern where a settlor wishes to settle shares in his family company but remain as one of the directors and draw director's fees. Whether the GROB provisions apply or not depends on whether his position and remuneration as a director remain unaffected by the gift of shares. For the Inland Revenue's practice, see *Foster's Inheritance Tax* X 6.36 and X 6.40.

15 *A-G v Duke of Richmond* [1907] 2 KB 923, at 937 per BRAY J; affd in *A-G v Duke of Richmond and Gordon* [1909] AC 466 at 472, 475.

Acquiring the legal right to possess under the terms of the gift is not possession.[16] And it is payment, not the obligation to pay, that confers enjoyment.[17]

(c) Exclusion of the Donor and Any Benefit to Him.

The condition in section 102 (1) (*b*) of FA 1986 comprises two limbs. The property which is the subject matter of the gift must be enjoyed to the entire exclusion (i) "of the donor" and (ii) "of any benefit to him by contract or otherwise".[18] Limb (i) raises the difficult question of what precisely was disposed of by the gift and from which the donor must be totally excluded. As Lord SIMONDS stated in *St Aubyn v A-G*:[19]

"The question is what he has given: it may be a life interest in part of the settled property; it may be a part of the income of settled funds and that part may be a fixed sum which is payable in priority or the residue after the prior payment of a fixed sum thereout . . . much of the confusion . . . [is] due to the failure to bear in mind that that of which enjoyment is to be assumed and retained and from which there is to be exclusion of the donor and any benefit to him by contract or otherwise is that which is truly given, a proposition which is obvious enough in the case of two separate estates but more difficult to follow and apply where trusts are declared of a single property which are not completely exhaustive in favour of a donee."

Thus, where the donor gives property away but thereafter enters into a partnership with the donee and the partnership uses the gifted property, the GROB provisions will apply and the property will be treated as remaining comprised in the donor's estate.[20] The same result will follow where a settlor is paid income from property settled by him;[1] or has a power of attorney to deal with gifted property.[2] In contrast, where the donor has reserved to himself, or carved out of the property, certain rights or interests prior to making the gift, the subject matter of the gift will be the property "shorn" of such rights or interests (of which the donee will assume possession and enjoyment) and the GROB provisions will not therefore apply;[3] for example, if S settles property on himself for life, with remainder to B, the subject matter of the gift is the interest in remainder given to B; or if S grants a lease to himself and his wife, and then gives the freehold reversion to a child, he has given away the reversion, from which he is excluded, and retained the pre-existing lease. A person cannot, however, grant a lease to himself; and a transfer of property to a nominee, coupled with a rent-free lease-back in favour of the transferor, has been held to be ineffective in law, because a nominee can not grant a lease to his principal.[4]

---

16 *HM Advocate v M'Taggart Stewart* (1906) 43 SLR 465 at 474.

17 *HM Advocate v Heywood-Lonsdale's Trustees* 1906 43 SLR 529, at 532. See also *Commissioner of Stamp Duties of NSW v Permanent Trustee Co of NSW* [1956] AC 512; and *HM Advocate v M'Taggart Stewart*, supra.

18 *Chick v Commissioner of Stamp Duties of NSW* [1958] AC 435, [1958] 2 All ER 623.

19 [1952] AC 15, at 22.

20 *Chick v Commissioner of Stamp Duties of NSW*, supra; *Commissioner of Stamp Duties of NSW v Owens* (1953) 88 CLR 67.

1 *Commissioner of Stamp Duties of NSW v Permanent Trustee Co of NSW* [1956] AC 512.

2 *O'Connor v Commissioner of Stamp Duties* (1932) 47 CLR 601.

3 *Munro v Commissioner of Stamp Duties of NSW* [1934] AC 61. But beware of *Nichols v IRC* [1975] 2 All ER 120.

4 *Ingram v IRC* [1995] STC 564; *Kildrummy (Jersey) Ltd v IRC* [1990] STC 657. See also *Rye v Rye* [1962] AC 496, [1962] 1 All ER 146.

However, where the nominee, on the principal's instructions, then transferred the property, subject to the intended lease, to trustees, it was held that the lease took effect, either in equity or by virtue of section 65 of the Law of Property Act 1925, from the very same moment as the trust first had the property subject to the equitable interest in favour of the transferor; and the gift to the trust was therefore not subject to a reservation.[5] If the donor is not excluded, it is not relevant to ask why this is so; and it is immaterial that the donee could make no better use of the property given to him than by not excluding the donor, even on terms advantageous to the donee.[6]

Limb (ii) raises difficulties of its own. It is unclear, for example, whether the phrase "by contract or otherwise" must be construed *ejusdem generis*, i.e., whether the possession and enjoyment or benefit from which the donor must be entirely excluded must be derived from some enforceable right (be it an understanding or arrangement) although if there be such a right it is immaterial that it lies against a third party and not the donee of the gift.[7]

The benefit concerned may be one issuing out of the property itself, or it may be entirely collateral in the sense that it may issue out of some other property altogether, or be a benefit given by a separate and independent contract. For instance, the donee may covenant to pay an annuity to the donor,[8] or to pay the donor's funeral and testamentary expenses.[9] Loans to the donor are caught, notwithstanding that they have to be repaid.[10] Similarly, section 81 will apply where the donor has a power to charge a capital sum on the property[11] or a right to remuneration as a trustee of it,[12] or he creates a discretionary trust of which he is an object.[13]

ii. THE CHARGE

The charge on a GROB bites at either of two points. If there is "property subject to a reservation of benefit" at the time of the donor's death, then he is treated as beneficially entitled to that property at his death.[14] If it ceases to be property subject to a reservation of benefit before the donor's death, the donor is treated as making a PET at that time. There are elaborate and complex provisions to prevent double charges to IHT which might otherwise arise if the donor were to make a chargeable lifetime transfer of property and that same property were to be chargeable at his death under the GROB provisions.[15] It is the donee of a GROB who is primarily liable for any tax

---

5 *Ingram v IRC*, supra; cf. *Nichols v IRC* [1975] 2 All ER 120.
6 *Lang v Webb* (1912) 13 CLR 503; the facts of this case are now covered by the exception in FA 1986, Sch. 19, para. 6 (1).
7 *A-G v Seccombe* [1911] 2 KB 688; *A-G v St Aubyn (No 2)* [1950] 2 KB 429, at 450; *A-G v Sandwich (Earl)* [1922] 2 KB 500 at 515. Cf. *R v Special Commissioners of Income Tax, ex p Shaftesbury Homes and Arethusa Training Ship* [1923] 1 KB 393 at 396, 400; *NALGO v Bolton Corpn* [1943] AC 166 at 186.
8 *A-G v Worrall* [1895] 1 QB 99; and see *Re Harmsworth* [1967] Ch 826, [1967] 2 All ER 249.
9 *Grey v A-G* [1900] AC 124.
10 *St Aubyn v A-G* [1952] AC 15 at 57–58.
11 *Re Clarke* (1906) 40 ILTR 117.
12 *Oakes v Commissioners of Stamp Duties of NSW* [1954] AC 57, [1953] 2 All ER 1563.
13 *A-G v Heywood* (1887) 19 QBD 326; *A-G v Farrell* [1931] 1 KB 81.
14 FA 1986, s. 81 (3).
15 The Inheritance Tax (Double Charges Relief) Regulations 1987 (SI 1987 No. 1130). There are also provisions to deal with replacement or substituted property.

payable in respect thereof, but only to the extent to which his estate was increased by the transfer.

III. Transfers on Death

On the death of any person after 12 March, 1975 (FA 1975 became effective on March 13) IHT is charged as if, immediately before his death, he had made a transfer of value and the value transferred by it had been equal to the value of his estate immediately before his death.[16]

Transfers on death differ from lifetime transfers in a number of ways. A few examples will suffice:

(*a*) There is no need to "gross up", for the transfer on death must of necessity be gross: the value transferred is the value of the estate which, after distribution, will have been completely exhausted.

(*b*) The rate of tax is higher for transfers on death than for lifetime transfers: in fact, it is double (40%) the lifetime rates (20%).[17]

(*c*) Some exemptions apply only to lifetime transfers; for example, the annual exemption for gifts not exceeding £3000.

(*d*) Death itself may affect the value of the estate; for example, the proceeds of a life assurance policy falling in, and these changes are treated as occurring before death.[18]

(*e*) Dispositions effected either by will or on intestacy can be varied by the beneficiaries (if of full age and *sui juris*, and provided the specified conditions are complied with) and the estate is then administered as if such variations were the deceased's own dispositions.[19]

(*f*) PETS and GROBS cannot be made on death, although both may become chargeable as a result of death.

IV. Settled Property

The term "settlement" is very widely defined for IHT purposes. It covers not only straightforward cases, such as those where property is held in trust for persons in succession, but also a state of affairs which in ordinary circumstances would not be thought of as a settlement at all, for example, a lease of property which is for life or lives, unless granted for full consideration in money or money's worth.[20] On the other hand, common examples of trusts are not settlements for IHT purposes, such as property held by joint tenants or tenants in common for themselves absolutely.

Whatever form the settlement may take, the principle underlying the IHT treatment of settled property is that the charge to tax should generally be

---

16 IHTA 1984, s. 4 (1); [1988] BTR 431 (B. McCutcheon).
17 See p. 572, ante.
18 IHTA 1984, s. 171.
19 Ibid., s. 142. This is a very important and much-used provision in IHT planning: see pp. 606–607, post.
20 Ibid., s. 43 (3).

neither greater nor smaller than the charge on property held absolutely (known as "the parity principle").

The IHT provisions differentiate between settled property in which someone is beneficially entitled to an interest in possession (e.g. a life interest) and settled property in which there is no interest in possession (e.g. a discretionary trust).

A. What is an Interest in Possession?

PEARSON v INLAND REVENUE COMMISSIONERS[1]

[1981] AC 753, [1980] 2 All ER 479 (HL, Viscount DILHORNE, LORDS SALMON, RUSSELL OF KILLOWEN, KEITH OF KINKEL and LANE).

VISCOUNT DILHORNE: My Lords, the only question to be decided in this appeal is whether Fiona Pilkington and her two sisters, Serena and Julia, were after they were 21 and before March 27, 1974, entitled to interests in possession in settled property. The respondents say that they were and the revenue says that they were not.

By a settlement made on November 30, 1964, the settlor, Sir William Pilkington, transferred to trustees 13,333 ordinary shares of £10 each in Pilkington Brothers Ltd. Clause 2 of the deed established a trust in relation to the capital and income of the trust fund under which the trustees had power to appoint capital and income for the benefit of all or any one or more of the "discretionary objects" of the trust. "Discretionary objects" was defined as meaning the principal beneficiaries, their children and remoter issue and the respective wives, husbands, widows and widowers of the principal beneficiaries and their children and remoter issue. The principal beneficiaries were all the children of the settlor.

Clause 3 provided, inter alia:

"In default of and until and subject to any appointment made under the last foregoing clause the trustees shall hold the capital and income of the trust fund upon the following trusts that is to say:—(a) During the trust period or the period of 21 years from the execution hereof (whichever shall be the shorter period) the trustees shall accumulate so much (if any) of the income of the trust fund as they shall think fit . . . (b) Subject thereto the trustees shall hold the capital and income of the trust fund upon trust for such of the principal beneficiaries as shall attain the age of 21 or marry under that age and if more than one in equal shares absolutely."

Clause 14 read as follows:

"The trustees shall in respect of any property subject to the trusts hereof have all the powers of management and exploitation of an absolute beneficial owner . . . "

Clause 21 was in the following terms:

"The trustees may at any time or times apply any income of the trust fund in or towards the payment or discharge of any duties taxes costs charges

1   For criticism of this majority decision reversing CA [1980] Ch 1, [1979] 3 All ER 7 (BUCKLEY, BRIDGE and TEMPLEMAN LJJ) which had affirmed Fox J [1980] Ch 1, [1979] 1 All ER 273, see Thomas, *Taxation and Trusts*, pp. 192–194, pp. 587–588, post; Chapman, *Inheritance Tax* (7th edn, 1987), pp. 174–182; Venables, Thornhill and Jepson, *Tax Planning Through Wills* (1981), pp. 20–27; [1982] BTR 105 (J.Jopling). See also [1976] BTR 49 (R. Walker), and (1975) 72 LSG 1259 (C. McCall and N.R.D. Powell).

fees or other outgoings which but for the provisions of this clause would be payable out of or charged upon the capital of the trust fund or any part thereof.''

Fiona and her sisters had all reached the age of 21 by the end of February 1974. The position then was that, subject to the trustees' power of appointment under clause 2 and their power to accumulate income under clause 3 (a) and the possibility of partial defeasance on the birth of further children to the settlor, the trust fund was held in trust for Fiona and her sisters in equal shares.

By a deed of appointment made on March 20, 1976, the trustees appointed that £16,000 should be held on trust to pay the income thereof to Fiona during her life or during the trust period whichever should be the shorter.

The Finance Act 1975 introduced the capital transfer tax under which tax is charged "on the value transferred by a chargeable transfer." Subject to certain exceptions, a transfer of value is any disposition made by a person as a result of which the value of his estate immediately after the disposition is less than it would be but for the disposition: and a chargeable transfer is any transfer of value made by an individual after March 26, 1974: see Finance Act 1975, section 20 (2) and (4).

Schedule 5 to the Act has effect with regard to settled property. This Schedule draws a distinction between what may be called fixed interest trusts and discretionary trusts. A person entitled to an interest in possession in settled property is in general treated as if he was beneficially entitled to the property in which his interest subsists. If during his life his interest in possession comes to an end, there is a charge to tax as if he had himself made a transfer of value and the value transferred had been equal to the value of the property in which his interest subsisted: Schedule 5, paragraph 4 (2). If he dies and is then entitled to an interest in possession, tax is charged as if immediately before his death he had made a transfer of value equal to the value of his estate (section 22) of which his interest in possession formed part. On the other hand, if he becomes absolutely entitled to the property in which he had an interest in possession, there is no charge to tax; nor is there if his interest in possession comes to an end but on the same occasion he becomes entitled to another interest in possession in the property: Schedule 5, paragraph 4 (3).

It follows that if Fiona had an interest in possession in the 13,333 shares settled by her father, she would not have become liable to capital transfer tax on the appointment to her of the £16,000. On the other hand, if ... Fiona became entitled to the £16,000 at a time when no interest in possession subsisted in that, a capital distribution of £16,000 has to be treated as having been made. Further every 10 years from the date of the relevant transfer occurring after April 1, 1980, tax is charged at the rate of 30 per cent. of the rate which would otherwise be chargeable on the value of the property in the settlement in which no interest in possession subsists: Schedule 5, paragraph 12. . . .

The meaning to be given to the words "interest in possession in settled property" is thus of vital importance in ascertaining liability to capital transfer tax. . . .

No attempt is made in the Finance Act 1975 to define "interest in possession" apart from the definition in paragraph 11 (10) and the definition for the purpose of applying the Schedule to Scotland. What then should be the approach to construing those words in the Act? In my view one should first seek to determine the ordinary and natural meaning of those words and then consider whether there is anything in the context in which they are used to lead to the conclusion that the proper interpretation of them involves a departure from the ordinary and natural meaning.

In *Preston; Treatise on Estates* (1820), p. 89 an estate in possession is stated to be one which gives "a present right of present enjoyment." This was contrasted with an estate in remainder which it was said gave "a right of future enjoyment." In *Fearne on Contingent Remainders*, 10th edn. (1844), vol. 1, p. 2 it was said that an estate is vested when there is an immediate fixed right of present or future enjoyment; that an estate is vested in possession when there exists a right of present enjoyment; that an estate is vested in interest when there is a present fixed right of future enjoyment; and that an estate is contingent when a right of enjoyment is to accrue on an event which is dubious and uncertain.

In the light of these statements, it appears that in the 19th century the words "an interest in possession" would have been interpreted as ordinarily meaning the possession of a right to the present enjoyment of something. The appellants in their case contend that:

" ... a beneficiary only has an interest in possession if his interest enables him to claim the whole or an ascertainable part of the net income, if any, of the property at the moment at which it is in the hands of the trustees."

The respondents in their case contend that "the phrase 'interest in possession' simply denotes an interest which is not in reversion—a present right of present enjoyment."

So the parties agree that for there to be an interest in possession, there must be a present right to the present enjoyment of something, the revenue contending that it must be to the enjoyment of the whole or part of the net income of the settled property. It is not the case—and in argument the respondents did not contend that it was—that if it is established that the interest is not in remainder or reversion or contingent, it must be concluded that it is in possession. In the present case Fox J [1980] Ch 1, 8ʜ, [1979] 1 All ER 273, 278 held that "There must be a present right of present enjoyment." This was endorsed by Buckley LJ and Templeman LJ in the Court of Appeal [1980] Ch 1 at 23ꜰ and 26ꜰ, [1979] 3 All ER 7 at 11 and 14. . . .

It suffices to say that I see nothing in the Act itself to suggest that the phrase should be given any other meaning than that of a present right of present enjoyment. In my opinion that is its meaning in the Finance Act 1975.

The difficulty lies in its application to the facts of the present case. It is said by both parties to be one of fundamental importance. Whether or not that is the case, all we have to decide is whether on reaching 21, Fiona and her sisters acquired interests in possession in settled property. In other words had they then a present right of present enjoyment of anything?

As to that, there are, it seems to me, two possible conclusions. The first is that the power of appointment under clause 2 not having been exercised, the three sisters on reaching that age acquired interests in possession defeasible should the trustees decide to exercise their power to accumulate income. They were then entitled absolutely to the capital and income of the trust fund in equal shares subject to the exercise of that power. The second is that they never secured an interest in possession for they never acquired on reaching that age the right to the enjoyment of anything. Their enjoyment of any income from the trust fund depended on the trustees' decision as to the accumulation of income. They would only have a right to any income from the trust fund if the trustees decided it should not be accumulated or if they failed to agree that it should be or if they delayed a decision on this matter for so long that a decision then to accumulate and withhold income from the sisters would have been unreasonable ...

In *Gartside v IRC* [1968] AC 553, [1968] 1 All ER 121, an estate duty case, Lord Reid said, at 607, at 128,

" 'In possession' must mean that your interest enables you to claim now whatever may be the subject of the interest. For instance, if it is the current income from a certain fund your claim may yield nothing if there is no income, but your claim is a valid claim, and if there is any income you are entitled to get it. But a right to require trustees to consider whether they will pay you something does not enable you to claim anything. If the trustees do decide to pay you something, you do not get it by reason of having the right to have your case considered; you get it only because the trustees have decided to give it to you."

That case concerned a discretionary trust where payment was made to the beneficiaries at the discretion of the trustees. Here the three sisters' entitlement to income was subject to the trustees' power to accumulate. On reaching 21 they had no valid claim to anything. If there was any income from the settled property, they were not entitled to it. Their right to anything depended on what the trustees did or did not do and the receipt of income by them appears to me to have been just as much at the discretion of the trustees as was the receipt of income by the beneficiaries in the *Gartside* case.

It was recognised by the respondents that if clause 3 had created a trust to accumulate subject to which the trust fund was to be held in trust for the three sisters absolutely on their attaining 21 they would not have secured an interest in possession on reaching that age. It makes all the difference, so it was said, that the trustees were not under a duty to accumulate but only had power to do so if they thought fit. I am not able to accept this for in neither case can it in my opinion be said that the sisters on attaining that age secured the right to the present enjoyment of anything.

Fox J [1980] Ch 1 at 14D, [1979] 1 All ER 273 at 282 in the course of his judgment distinguished the cases of *A-G v Power* [1906] 2 IR 272 and *Gartside v IRC* from the present case on the ground that in those cases "the beneficiaries got nothing unless the trustees decided to give it to them" whereas in the present case the sisters were "absolutely entitled to income unless the trustees decided to accumulate."

I do not think that is the case. I do not read the trust deed as providing that. Clause 3 (a) gives the trustees power to accumulate as they think fit and the sisters' entitlement depends on whether that power is exercised. If it were the case that the deed did so provide, then I would agree that the sisters had a defeasible interest in possession. Such an interest may be terminated by the exercise of a power of revocation or of an overriding power of appointment such as that contained in clause 2 in this case. The existence of such a power does not prevent the holding of an interest in possession prior to the exercise of the power and until it is exercised, the holder of the interest has a present right of present enjoyment.

A distinction has in my opinion to be drawn between the exercise of a power to terminate a present right of present enjoyment and the exercise of a power which prevents a present right of present enjoyment arising. If in this case the power of appointment under clause 2 had been exercised before the sisters became 21, it could not be said that they then got an interest in possession.

The revenue, while contending that it made no difference in this case that the sisters' entitlement was subject to a power to accumulate as distinct from being subject to a trust to do so, contended that a distinction was to be drawn between what may be called the administrative and the dispositive powers in a trust deed . . . and in my opinion there is a very real distinction. A life tenant has an interest in possession but his interest only extends to the net income of the property, that is to say, after deduction from the gross income of expenses etc. properly incurred in the management of the trust by the trustees in the exercise of their powers. A dispositive power is a power to dispose of the net income. Sometimes the line between an administrative and a dispositive power may be difficult to draw but that does not mean that there is not a valid distinction. In the present case the revenue contended that the power given by clause 21 to apply income towards the payment of duties, taxes etc. which but for the provisions of the clause would be payable out of or charged upon capital was a dispositive power and that this clause alone would prevent the sisters having an interest in possession on reaching 21. I do not think that this is so. I think this clause falls on the administrative side of the line and merely elucidates the meaning to be given to clause 14.

In my opinion the words "interest in possession" in Schedule 5 should be given their ordinary natural meaning which I take to be a present right of present enjoyment and as in my view the sisters on attaining 21 did not obtain that, this appeal should succeed and paragraphs 1 and 2 of the commissioners' determination should be upheld.

LORD RUSSELL OF KILLOWEN (dissenting): In my opinion the provisions of clause 3 clearly constitute (i) a mere *power* in the trustees to accumulate, and (ii) subject to (*a*) that power (*b*) the clause 3 power of appointment and (*c*) (until the death of the settlor which occurred in December 1976) the possibility of partial defeasance by further children being born to him, an absolute trust as to capital and income and any accumulations for the three daughters in equal shares on attaining the age of 21 years, which as stated all three had attained by the end of February 1974. It will be observed that this is not a case of a gift of income for the benefit of a discretionary class, as was the case in *Gartside v IRC* [1968] AC 553, [1968] 1 All ER 121. Ignoring, as for present purposes may admittedly be done, factors (*b*) and (*c*), the three daughters were absolutely entitled each to one third of the income of the trust subject only to a power in the trustees to divert all or part by deciding to accumulate (during a period permitted by law) some or all of the income as it accrued. In fact the trustees accumulated all income accruing: on the one hand the appellants' claim would have been exactly the same if none had been accumulated: on the other hand the respondents' case equally is that it makes no difference that all had been accumulated: it was therefore common ground that the answer to the question posed in this appeal in no way depended upon what the trustees did or did not do by way of exercise of their power of accumulation.

The only other clause in the settlement requiring notice was clause 21.

The appellants contended that, even without the clause 3 power of accumulation, this clause contained a power in effect to accumulate which, though not in fact operated, had the same result in terms of the liability for capital transfer tax asserted. . . .

The crucial question, in my opinion, lies in the well known distinction between a trust and a power, a distinction recognised by this House in *Re Baden's Deed Trusts* [1971] AC 424, [1970] 2 All ER 228, p. 71, ante, and there only regretted as a distinction which might lead in a given case to invalidity of the disposition. As I have already indicated this is clearly a case of a mere power to accumulate, as distinct from a trust to accumulate unless and to the extent to which the trustees exercised a power to pay allowances to the sisters or any of them. The sisters were able to say that as income accrued on the £16,000 they were then entitled to that income, subject to the possibility that the trustees might *subsequently divert* it from them by a decision to accumulate it. (Indeed but for the clause 2 power of appointment, and the possibility until the death of the settlor in December 1976 of the birth of further children, they were, notwithstanding the power of accumulation, entitled to claim transfer of the £16,000.) Similar considerations apply to the possibility of the exercise of the clause 21 application of the income for a capital purpose. The case is also distinguishable from the case of a discretionary trust of income among a class—as in *Gartside* [1968] AC 553, [1968] 1 All ER 121.

These considerations persuade me that at the time of the 1976 appointment it is not correct to say that no interest in possession subsisted in the three sisters in the £16,000.

Thomas, *Taxation and Trusts* (1981), pp. 192–194.

"There is no doubt that, whichever conclusion the House of Lords came to, anomalies and injustice would arise in a number of instances. Suppose, for example, that an interest in possession had been found to exist; also that the power of accumulation was used to the full. If the power was still subsisting at the life tenant's death, the entire settled property would form part of her estate and be subject to charge, even though she had never received any income from the trust. On the other hand, if there is no interest in possession there is presumably a charge to [IHT] when the power of accumulation terminates during F's lifetime (as it must do, being subject to the statutory limits) and a life interest in possession (F's) commences. However, an argument based on anomalies should only be called in aid when there is some ambiguity in the words of the statute. 'It cannot be right,' according to Lord Normand in *Dale v IRC* [1954] AC 11 at 30, [1953] 2 All ER 671 at 676, 'to decide an action on a balance of competing anomalies when anomalies must arise whatever construction be adopted.' This rule was, in fact, adhered to firmly in both the Court of Appeal and the House of Lords. One may well ask, however, how the judicial mind can hold that there is no ambiguity in a statutory provision when so many anomalies are thrown up by it, and when six out of nine judges disagree with the results and one may wonder whether the traditional rule of strict interpretation—which is supposed to give the taxpayer the benefit of any doubt—is now well and truly buried.

Ultimately, perhaps all we can and need say about *Pearson* is that it is a straightforward 'policy decision'. As we have seen, the policy behind the [IHT] treatment of settlements is that there should be no difference (for the purposes of the tax) between putting property into trust and holding it absolutely. Killing off, or at least immobilising, the discretionary trust was an essential part of that strategy. Had *Pearson* been decided differently, it might have opened the way for the rehabilitation of the discretionary trust in a new form and to other methods of tax avoidance. Trustees would have enjoyed not just the benefits of the interest in possession regime but also the flexibility of a discretionary trust as regards distribution of income. Moreover, accumulation of income would have been possible for beneficiaries over the age of 25 without endangering the 'interest in possession status' of the trust (which is only possible now for 'under 25s' under an accumulation and maintenance trust). Amending legislation would no doubt have followed. The majority of the House of Lords, however, simply refused to aid and abet in a decision which defeated legislative policy, despite the fact that the problem at issue had been manifest when CTT was introduced and that the Government had simply refused to do anything about it.

In truth, the 1975 Act attempted to force all settlements into (basically) two distinct categories, whereas the trust lawyer's world is more complicated than this. Hybrid trusts which partake of the nature of both types abound. Perhaps it is also an oversimplification to think in terms of either (i) 'an interest in possession' or (ii) 'no interest in possession' or (iii) 'reversionary interest'. It is evident from *Pearson* that it was not satisfactory to class F's interest under either (i) or (ii), but it could not have fallen under (iii) either (see s. 51 (1) for the definition of a reversionary interest), especially if the power of accumulation were never exercised. Though not in accord with the scheme of the 1975 Act, there can be said to be an innominate *tertium quid* of a transmissible interest which is neither an interest in possession nor a reversionary interest. In any event, *Pearson* provided the House of Lords with the opportunity to clarify the law in this area and to bring home to the draftsman of the 1975 Act that every possible contingency had not been foreseen and catered for. The application of the trust-power distinction—which is, after all, fundamental to the law of trusts in general, defining as it does the extent and nature of a trustee's obligations and of the beneficiary's rights and interests—would, it is submitted, have made for a more coherent and comprehensible conclusion. The majority in the House of Lords rejected this approach without any convincing legal argument. Though recognising the importance of the issue before them, they have done both the taxpayer and the legal profession a great disservice.''

Chapman: *Inheritance Tax* (8th edn, 1990) pp. 190–191

''It cannot be pretended that the law in this area is free from doubt but it is hoped that the following statements summarise the present position clearly:
  (*a*) a person entitled to an interest in possession has an interest in the net income of the property;
  (*b*) net income of the property is the gross amount less any expenses properly paid out of income in the exercise of an administrative power;
  (*c*) the existence of a dispositive power to divert that net income away from the beneficiary *after it has arisen* will cause the interest not to be an interest in possession;
  (*d*) a power of accumulation of income or a power to distribute income amongst a class is a dispositive power (usually exercisable in relation to income after it has arisen) whereas, for example, a power to apply income in the payment of premiums for the insurance of trust property is an administrative power;
  (*e*) the existence of a dispositive power which cannot affect net income after it has arisen will not cause the interest not to be an interest in

possession—it is for this reason that powers of appointment will rarely, by their mere existence, cause an interest not to be in possession; and

(*f*) there will be cases where, in construing a deed, the distinction between an administrative and a dispositive power is difficult; for example, the power contained in the Pilkington settlement to apply income towards the payment of taxes otherwise payable out of capital. It should be noted that the Inland Revenue are of the view that this is a dispositive power although Viscount Dilhorne said, obiter, that it was an administrative power.[2]

An example of a trust in which there is no 'interest in possession' is where the whole income is being validly accumulated for the benefit of persons with contingent interests[3] (e.g. contingent on a person attaining a specified age). Once an infant attains his majority however, he is, subject to the terms of the trust, entitled to the trust income as it arises by virtue of section 31 of the Trustee Act 1925 (as amended)[4] and his interest will then be in 'possession'.

Whether there is an interest in possession in property held in trust for a minor for any interest whatsoever, whether vested or contingent, appears to depend on whether the rules in section 31 (2) (or the terms of the trust if section 31 is excluded) will lead in any event to the accumulations being held for the minor absolutely. If there is an absolute entitlement to the accumulations it seems that there would be an interest in possession in view of the comments at the end of the penultimate paragraph of the Inland Revenue's statement [in (1976) 73 Guardian Gazette 29]. Consequently if property is held on trust for X, a minor, absolutely, X will have an interest in possession because under section 31 (2) any accumulations made will belong to the infant if he reaches 18 years or will fall into his estate if he does not. The terms of the trust instrument may provide for accumulations of income to fall into the estate of a minor who has a life interest in the event of his death during minority and in these circumstances also the minor would have an interest in possession.

The following are further examples of beneficiaries whose interests rank as 'interests in possession' in settled property for the purposes of inheritance tax.

(i) A life tenant in possession (but not a life tenant in remainder), for example, where property is settled on A for life, remainder to B for life with remainder to C absolutely: A enjoys an interest in possession but not B or C.

(ii) A tenant *pur autre vie*, for example, where property is settled on A for the life of X (the *cestui que vie*); such an interest determines on the death of X but not on the death of A: A enjoys an interest in possession.

(iii) A tenant in tail in possession, for example, where land is settled on A for life, B in tail with remainder to C absolutely, and A is dead: B enjoys an interest in possession.

(iv) An annuitant or other person entitled to a specified amount or proportion of the income from a trust fund (but not the purchaser

2 See also *Stenhouse's Trustees v Lord Advocate* [1984] STC 195 where the withholding by trustees of payment until receipt of an indemnity seems to have been treated as the exercise of an administrative power.

3 See, e.g. *A-G v Power* [1906] 2 IR 272, and see generally an article by V.J. Washtell in the September 1981 issue of *CTT News*.

4 P. 762, post.

of an annuity from, say, an insurance company or one secured by personal covenant only)."

B. Settled Property in Which Someone is Beneficially Entitled to an Interest in Possession

i. GENERAL

The relevant provisions here are set out in Sections 49 to 57 of IHTA 1984. Their effect is to treat the person beneficially entitled to the interest in possession as beneficially entitled to the settled property itself. Therefore, there should in principle be a charge to IHT on the full value of the settled property whenever the beneficial enjoyment of it ceases (for example, by surrender or on death) or changes hands (for example, on assignment). It follows, however, that there is no charge where the settled property is distributed to the person who then enjoys the interest in possession, since he is already deemed to own it. Similarly, a reversionary interest in that settled property is excluded from charge: ascribing value to such an interest would involve an element of double taxation.

ii. THE PET PROVISIONS

However, the PET provisions[5] must also be borne in mind here. Their effect is that each of the following events will rank as a PET and thus not be chargeable to IHT when made, and not at all unless there is a relevant death within seven years of its occurrence.

(1) The creation of an interest in possession trust by the settlor (unless the first interest in possession is that of the settlor himself or of his spouse).

(2) The termination of an interest in possession during the lifetime of the person beneficially entitled to it, whether by way of surrender, assignment, revocation or otherwise, provided that upon such termination another individual becomes absolutely entitled to the property in which the interest subsists, or entitled to an interest in possession in it, or the property is thereafter held on accumulation and maintenance trusts.[6]

On the other hand, the following do not rank as PETs:

(1) The termination of a beneficial interest in possession on the death of the person entitled to it.[7]

(2) An event upon the happening of which the spouse of the settlor (or of the person entitled to the preceding interest in possession) becomes entitled to the property or to a beneficial interest in possession in it.

(3) The termination of a beneficial interest in possession which is succeeded by discretionary trusts of the property in which it subsisted.

Clearly, where a settlor makes a PET, it is his death within seven years that renders the PET retrospectively chargeable. On the other hand, where the

---

5 See pp. 574–575, ante.
6 F (No. 2) A 1987, s. 96, amending IHTA 1984, ss. 3A, 49, 55. A transfer to a close company is not a PET.
7 Liability on death is apportioned between the trustees and the personal representatives according to the respective values of the trust property and the estate: IHTA 1984, s. 200.

termination of a beneficial interest in possession ranks as a PET, it is the death, within seven years of the termination, of the person entitled to that interest that triggers the charge to IHT, and it is his cumulative total that enters into the reckoning. As can be seen from the Example below,[8] the fact that a PET (such as the creation of an interest in possession trust, or the termination of an interest in possession) becomes retrospectively chargeable may have a knock-on effect on other chargeable transfers made by the relevant transferor, in that all past transfers of value may have to be reopened and the IHT liability thereon recalculated.

C. Settled Property in Which There is No Interest in Possession

The common cases are where property is held on trust to accumulate the income or to apply the income at the discretion of the trustees (with or without power to accumulate any surplus). The application of the parity principle where no one has an interest or right to enjoyment[9] is clearly difficult.[10] The only obvious occasion of charge is when property is distributed to a beneficiary, but that need not occur until the termination of the trust, after some 80 years or more. The original provisions, found in Schedule 5 to the Finance Act 1975, were both complex and punitive. These were repealed by the Finance Act 1982[11] and replaced with new provisions, still complex but far less punitive, which are now found in IHTA 1984, ss. 58–85.

The basic scheme of the new provisions is to divide property into (i) relevant property; and (ii) property held on favoured trusts, for example, qualifying accumulation and maintenance trusts.[12] "Relevant property" is defined as "settled property in which no qualifying interest in possession subsists", subject to specific exceptions, these being favoured trusts and excluded property.[13] A "qualifying interest in possession" is an interest in possession to which an individual is beneficially entitled (or one to which a company is entitled if its business is the acquisition of settled interests and certain circumstances exist).[14]

There are two types of charge on relevant property:

i. AN AUTOMATIC CHARGE EVERY TEN YEARS[15]

This is usually called the "ten-yearly charge" or the "periodic charge". It is levied ten years after the creation of the settlement, and at the end of each subsequent ten-year period during the life of the settlement.

The amount charged to tax at each ten-year anniversary is the value (after any reliefs) of any relevant property then comprised in the settlement. The

8 See pp. 575–577, ante.
9 See [1980] BTR 393 (W. Goodhart) for a simpler alternative approach to the problem.
10 See *Gartside v IRC* [1968] AC 553 at 607, [1968] 1 All ER 121 at 128, and p. 585 ante, per Lord REID. The principles enunciated in *Gartside* v IRC also apply to a discretionary trust where the income has to be distributed and there is only one living member of the class of beneficiaries: *Re Trafford's Settlement* [1985] Ch 32, [1984] 1 All ER 1108, applying *Re Weir's Settlement Trusts* [1971] Ch 145, [1970] 1 All ER 297. Nor do the objects of an exhaustive discretionary trust, as a class, have an interest in possession: *Sainsbury v IRC* [1970] Ch 712, [1969] 3 All ER 919.
11 FA 1982, s. 101, Sch. 22, Pt. VII.
12 P. 598, post. See also [1982] BTR 162 (R. Walker).
13 IHTA 1984, s. 58 (1).
14 Ibid., s. 59.
15 Ibid., s. 64.

rate of tax on this amount is found by a complex process (which is explained in greater detail below), but its essence is the same as for any transfer, namely that the rate of tax depends not only on the amount to be charged but also on the amount charged in the previous seven years. The rate of tax on a ten-yearly charge is 30 per cent of the effective rate which would be charged on a hypothetical chargeable transfer which follows a cumulative total of chargeable transfers made (or assumed to have been made) during the preceding seven years. Lifetime rates are always used.[16]

These rules are modified in the case of trusts set up before 27 March, 1974,[17] and also if there have been distributions from the trust before 9 March, 1982.

Moreover, special rules apply for determining the rate of tax if, after 8 March, 1982, the settlor adds property (or value) to his settlement.[18] And the rate of tax must be reduced on any part of the relevant property which has not been relevant property for the full ten years, for example, because an interest in possession subsisted in such part during a fraction of the period.[19]

ii. THE EXIT CHARGE

There are two alternative heads of the charge. The first and most important applies where property comprised in a settlement ceases to be relevant property.[20] The main examples here are: (*a*) when the settlement terminates; (*b*) when property is distributed to beneficiaries; (*c*) when an individual becomes beneficially entitled to an interest in possession in the settled property; (*d*) when the property is appointed on favoured trusts (for example, accumulation and maintenance trusts); and (*e*) when the property becomes excluded property.

The second head (which applies only where the first does not) imposes a charge when the trustees make a disposition (which includes an omission to exercise a right,[1]) which reduces the value of the relevant property comprised in the settlement,[2] for example, by granting a lease of trust property to a beneficiary at a peppercorn rent.

There are some exceptions to the exit charge. For example, tax is not charged on payments by trustees of costs and expenses which are fairly attributable to relevant property, nor on payments which are subject to income tax in the hands of the recipient;[3] nor if the event in question occurs within three months of the commencement of the settlement or of a tenth anniversary;[4] nor where property settled by a person domiciled outside the United Kingdom becomes excluded property and thereby ceases to be relevant property.[5] Moreover, under the second head, there is no charge if the trustees' disposition is such that, were they beneficially entitled to the settled property, it would not be a transfer of value by virtue of being a commercial transaction

---

16 IHTA 1984, s. 66.
17 Ibid, ss. 66 (6), 68 (6).
18 Ibid., s. 67.
19 Ibid., s. 66 (2).
20 Ibid., s. 65 (1) (*a*).
 1 Ibid., s. 65 (9).
 2 Ibid., s. 65 (1) (*b*).
 3 Ibid., s. 65 (5).
 4 Ibid., s. 65 (4).
 5 Ibid., s. 65 (7), (8).

made at arm's length (within s. 10 of the IHTA 1984),[6] or the grant for full consideration of an agricultural tenancy (within s. 16 of the IHTA 1984).[7]

(a) Amount

The amount on which the exit charge is imposed is the amount by which the value of the relevant property in the settlement is reduced by the event in question. However, if the IHT payable is paid out of relevant property remaining in the settlement, the loss must be grossed-up.[8]

(b) Rate

The rate of tax,[9] as a general rule, is the appropriate fraction of the rate which was charged at the last ten-year anniversary (the latter rate being, it will be recalled, 30 per cent of the effective lifetime rate of tax applicable to the hypothetical chargeable transfer then in question).

The "appropriate fraction" is easily found. Each ten-year period is divided into forty quarters. One ascertains the number of complete successive quarters in the period beginning with the most recent ten-year anniversary and ending with the day before the occasion of the charge. The "appropriate fraction" is simply the number of quarters thus found divided by forty. For example, at the last ten-year anniversary, IHT of £3,000 (i.e., 30% of £10,000) was charged on relevant property valued at £50,000. Five years (or 20 quarters) later, £30,000 is distributed to a beneficiary. IHT on this distribution (assuming no change in rates of tax over the five year period) is:

$$30,000 \times \frac{3,000}{50,000} \times \frac{20}{40} = £900$$

(c) Additions etc.

The rate has to be recalculated if, since the date of the last ten-year anniversary, (i) any property has been added to the settlement, or (ii) any property already in the settlement has become relevant property. That property is treated as if it had been relevant property in the settlement at the date of the last ten-year anniversary; and the rate of tax at that anniversary is then recalculated. In the case of (i), the property is brought in at the value it had immediately after it became comprised in the settlement; and in the case of (ii), it bears the value it had when it became (or last became) relevant property.[10]

(d) Rate before First Ten-year Anniversary[11]

Special rules apply where the exit charge falls before the first ten-year anniversary, although the process of calculation is basically the same. The object is to find the appropriate fraction of the effective rate at which tax would

---

6 P. 571, ante.
7 IHTA 1984, s. 65 (6). There is no exit charge either where property ceases to be relevant property on becoming held on employee trusts (s. 72), for a charity or other exempt body (s. 79), or on approved trusts for maintenance of heritage property (IHTA 1984, Sch 4, paras. 16–18).
8 Ibid., s. 65 (2).
9 Ibid., s. 66.
10 Ibid, s. 66 (2), (3).
11 Ibid., s. 68.

be charged on the value transferred by a chargeable transfer of the description specified in s. 68(4).[12] The basic process is this.

First, ascertain the value transferred by the hypothetical chargeable transfer. This is an amount equal to the aggregate of: (i) the value of the settled property at the commencement of the settlement; (ii) the value of property in any related settlement (i.e., one commencing on the same day and with a common settlor;[13]) and (iii) the value of any property added to the settlement after its commencement.[14] This transfer is deemed to be made *at the time of the charge* by a hypothetical transferor with an existing cumulative total of chargeable transfers made by him over the preceding seven years.

The second step, therefore, is to ascertain this cumulative total, which is in fact equal to the aggregate of any chargeable transfers made by the *settlor* during the seven years ending with the day on which the settlement commenced (but disregarding transfers made on that day).[15]

The third step is to find the tax chargeable on the hypothetical chargeable transfer (found at the first step), by applying the appropriate lifetime rates.[16]

Fourth, find the effective rate of tax, which is the rate found by expressing the tax chargeable as a percentage of the amount on which it is charged.

Fifth, ascertain what is the "appropriate fraction": this is three-tenths multiplied by so many fortieths as there are complete successive quarters in the period beginning with the day the settlement commenced and ending with the day before the occasion of charge.

Sixth, and finally, the actual rate of tax chargeable is the appropriate fraction of the effective rate.[17] The whole process is illustrated by way of example below.[18]

iii. TAX PLANNING

Thus, it will be seen that there is considerable scope for tax planning here although the number of discretionary trusts seems to be declining,[19]

---

12 IHTA 1984, s. 68 (1).
13 Ibid., s. 62 (1).
14 Ibid., s. 68 (5) (*c*).
15 Ibid., s. 68 (4) (*b*).
16 Ibid., s. 68 (4) (*c*).
17 Ibid., s. 68 (1), see also s. 68 (3).
18 Pp. 595–596.
19 The numbers of discretionary trusts whose tenth anniversaries fell in each year from 1984/85 to 1993/94, together with the estimated value of assets held in such trusts on those anniversaries, are set out in the Inland Revenue's statistics for 1995, and are as follows (the number of trusts being the actual number, and the amount of assets being expressed in £thousands):

Year	No.	Amount
1984/85	618	316,880
1985/86	482	180,334
1986/87	512	245,494
1987/88	600	305,784
1988/89	266	215,771
1989/90	352	333,000
1990/91	300	156,048
1991/92	336	198,842
1992/93	303	219,571
1993/94	237	129,927

particularly in the use of "nil rate band" discretionary trusts. Assets valued at under £200,000 (say, shares in a family company, or an insurance policy, or similar assets which are likely to appreciate in value in future years) can be transferred into settlement free of IHT. The new and more restricted CGT holdover relief might be available on such a transfer, where it might otherwise not be.[20] Provided the settlor has not created any related settlements, any distribution out of the discretionary trust before its first tenth anniversary will be free of IHT, for the value of the "relevant property" is pegged at the date the settlement was created (and will therefore be within the nil rate band) and the value which it might have attained by the date of distribution is immaterial. (In fact, the charge at the tenth anniversary, based on the value of the trust property at that time, is itself likely to be modest, so there may be no great incentive to distribute prematurely in any event.)

DISCRETIONARY TRUST EXAMPLES

1 June, 1994: S settles £100,000 on trustees. Of this, £75,000 is held on discretionary trusts for Objects A to F; and £25,000 is held in a separate settlement on trust for G for life, remainder on the same last-mentioned discretionary trusts.

S has already exhausted his nil rate band. He thus made a chargeable transfer of £75,000, all of which was charged at 20%; and a PET of £25,000.

Event 1: 6 July, 1997: the trustees appoint an interest in possession in £10,000 to A (who undertakes to pay any IHT due).

Event 2: 15 October, 2001: the trustees appoint £15,000 to B absolutely (B undertaking to pay any IHT due).

Event 3: 1 June, 2004: the trust's first tenth anniversary, at which time the trustees still hold £60,000 on discretionary trusts.

Event 4: 2 July, 2006: the trustees appoint a further £30,000 to D absolutely (D undertaking to pay any IHT due).

(a) CHARGE BEFORE FIRST TENTH ANNIVERSARY

Tax on Event 1:
What is the hypothetical chargeable transfer?—£100,000
(Note: the fact that £25,000 constituted a PET is irrelevant at this stage. There are no additions or related settlements.)
What is the cumulative total?—£250,000 (being the nil rate band (for 1994–1995) of £150,000 plus £100,000).
What is the IHT on transfers between £150,000 and £250,000, at current rates?—£20,000.
What is the effective rate of IHT on a chargeable transfer of £100,000? It is

$$\frac{20,000}{100,000} = 20\%$$

(This then becomes the effective rate of IHT on all exit charges before the first tenth anniversary.)
What is the tax payable?

(a) there are twelve complete quarters between 1 June, 1994, and 6 July, 1997

---

20 See pp. 566–568, ante.

(b) the appropriate fraction is $\frac{3}{10}$ x $\frac{12}{40}$ = $\frac{9}{100}$

(c) multiply $\frac{9}{100}$ x 20% = 1.8%

(d) tax payable = 1.8% of £10,000 = £180

(If the tax were not payable by A, but out of the retained trust property, grossing-up would be necessary.)

Tax on Event 2 is calculated in the same way.

(b) Tenth Anniversary Charge.

Tax on Event 3

What is the hypothetical chargeable transfer?

(a) £60,000 (value of relevant property on 1 June, 2004) plus

(b) £25,000 (value of property in which an interest in possession subsisted at 1 June, 1994)

[(c)no related settlements here] = £85,000

What is the hypothetical cumulative total?

(a) £150,000 (up to 1 June, 1994) plus

(b) £25,000 (exit charges of 6 July, 1997 and 15 October, 2001) = £175,000

What is the tax payable?

On a cumulative total of £260,000 = £22,000

Less IHT on £175,000 (i.e., less £5,000) = £17,000

What is the effective rate of IHT?

$$\frac{17,000}{85,000} = 20\%$$

30% of the effective rate = 6%

IHT payable on 1 June, 2004 = £60,000 @ 6% = £3,600

(c) Charge After Tenth Anniversary.

Event 4.

(a) Effective rate at tenth anniversary was 20%

(b) There are eight complete quarters between 1 June, 2004 and 2 July, 2006

(c) IHT payable = £30,000 x $\dfrac{3,600}{60,000}$ x $\dfrac{8}{40}$ = £360.

Note: In these examples, the IHT is payable out of the property which is subject to the charge; otherwise, grossing-up is necessary. Moreover, the calculations are more complicated where, for example, tax rates change, or property is added to the settlement, or changes character within the settlement, or where there is a pre-27 March, 1974, settlement, and so on.

iv. SETTLEMENTS CREATED BEFORE 27 MARCH, 1974 ("PRE-CTT SETTLEMENTS")

The provisions specifying the rate of tax outlined above are modified when they apply to pre-CTT settlements. The main difference relates to the calculation of the rate of the exit charge on an occasion preceding the first ten-year anniversary of the settlement. These modifications are too numerous and detailed to be covered here. Moreover, many (probably most) pre-CTT discretionary trusts have been broken up long ago under the favourable transitional provisions operative until 1 April, 1983. Reference should therefore be made to IHTA 1984, ss. 66 (6), 68 (6) and 70 (9).

v. INITIAL INTEREST OF SETTLOR OR SPOUSE

Special provision is made[1] where the settlor or his/her spouse (or his/her widow or widower) is beneficially entitled to an interest in possession in property and it becomes held on discretionary trusts. In such a case, if the property was settled after March 26, 1974, the rules governing the tax treatment of the discretionary trusts apply as though the property is in a separate settlement made by that one of them who ceased (or last ceased) to be beneficially entitled to an interest in possession in it. However, the settlement has the same ten-year anniversary dates as those of the original settlement.[2]

D. Favoured Trusts

i. THE TRUSTS

Property held on certain specified types of discretionary trusts does not rank as relevant property. These favoured trusts are thus not liable to the automatic ten-yearly charge or the proportionate charge, to which, of course, they would be subject (as trusts without a qualifying interest in possession) but for special treatment. Into this category fall trusts under which property is held for charitable purposes only;[3] or as part of a trade or professional compensation fund;[4] or for approved superannuation schemes;[5] or on discretionary trusts for the benefit of employees in a particular occupation or of a particular firm, or the relatives and dependants of such employees;[6] or on the discretionary trusts which arose under section 33 (1) (ii) of the Trustee Act 1925 (protective trusts) on the failure or determination before 12 April, 1978, of the principal beneficiary's interest;[7] or on discretionary trusts for disabled persons.[8]

---

1 IHTA 1984, s. 80.
2 Ibid., s. 61 (2).
3 Ibid., s. 58 (1) (*a*); see also s. 84; *Guild v IRC* [1992] 2 AC 310, [1992] 2 All ER 10. p. 423, ante.
4 Ibid., s. 58 (1) (*c*), (3).
5 Ibid., ss. 58 (1) (*d*), (2), 151.
6 Ibid., ss. 58 (1) (*b*), 86.
7 Ibid., ss. 58 (1) (*b*), 73. After 11 April, 1978, the principal beneficiary is treated as being beneficially entitled to an interest in possession notwithstanding the failure or determination of his interest; this change in the law was necessary to counteract tax avoidance by means of a deliberate forfeiture: IHTA 1984, s. 88. See also *Thomas v IRC* [1981] STC 382.
8 Ibid., ss. 58 (1) (*b*), 74, in relation to property settled before 10 March, 1981; and s. 89, in relation to trusts created after 9 March, 1981: in these trusts the disabled person is treated as having an interest in possession.

ii. ACCUMULATION AND MAINTENANCE TRUSTS

By far the most important for our immediate purposes, however, are accumulation and maintenance trusts.[9] These enjoy favourable treatment largely because it is regarded as undesirable to give a minor capital or a vested interest in income. Indeed, a minor cannot hold a legal estate in land,[10] although he can hold legal title to personalty. Moreover, a minor cannot give a valid receipt for capital, and only a married minor can give a valid receipt for income.[11] On the other hand, it may be unwise to tie up property completely, for even a minor may need money, for example, to pay for clothing and food. Trustees, therefore, usually have a power of maintenance which enables them to apply trust income for the routine recurring expenses of the minor beneficiary. Any income not so applied is accumulated, i.e., added to capital. Such a power may be conferred expressly by the trust instrument. Usually, however, it is derived from section 31 of the Trustee Act 1925.[12]

Being regarded as socially desirable, accumulation and maintenance trusts enjoy many advantages over other trusts. They are not subject to the ten-yearly charge. There is no exit charge when a beneficiary becomes entitled to the settled property itself or to an interest in possession therein (for example, on attaining the age of 18). If a beneficiary dies during the accumulation and maintenance period, IHT is not chargeable. Also, the creation of an accumulation and maintenance trust ranks as a PET (unless the property was previously subject to discretionary trusts).

In order to qualify for such favoured treatment, the trust must satisfy the stringent requirements specified.[13] Basically, these are that:

(i) there is no interest in possession in the settled property;
(ii) one or more persons will become beneficially entitled to the property, or to an interest in possession in it, by the age of 25;[14] and
(iii) in the meantime, any income which is not applied for the maintenance, education or benefit of a qualifying beneficiary is to be accumulated.

There is a further anti-avoidance provision specifying that, unless all the qualifying beneficiaries are grandchildren of a common grandparent (or the widows, widowers or children of such grandchildren who die before they become entitled as specified in (ii) above), there is a 25-year limit to this favoured treatment (running from the time the statutory conditions became satisfied).[15]

(a) Basis of charge

Subject to the exemptions from charge mentioned above, tax is charged when property ceases to be held on accumulation and maintenance trusts or when

---

9 IHTA 1984, s. 71, in relation to events after 8 March, 1982. This is broadly similar to the law before that date: FA 1975, Sch. 5, para. 15 (hence, such trusts were often called "paragraph 15 trusts").
10 LPA 1925, s. 1 (6).
11 Ibid., s. 21.
12 For TA 1925, s. 31, see p. 762, post.
13 IHTA 1984, s. 71 (1).
14 A trust to which TA 1925, s. 31 applies will satisfy this requirement even if the beneficiary's interest will not vest until *after* the age of 25, since the trustees must pay the income to him from the age of 18: TA 1925, s. 31 (1) (ii), p. 762, post.
15 IHTA 1984, s. 71 (2). There are transitional provisions for accumulation and maintenance trusts in existence at 15 April, 1976: ibid., s. 71 (6).

the trustees make a disposition which reduces the value of such property.[16] This charge, like the exit charge, falls on the amount by which the value of the settled property is reduced as a result of the chargeable event; and there is grossing up if the IHT is paid out of property remaining in the settlement.[17]

(b) Rate of charge

Tax is charged at a flat rate which tapers over time, depending on the period (measured in quarters) which has elapsed since the property on which the charge falls became (or last became) held on accumulation and maintenance trusts. The rate is the aggregate of the following percentages: 0.25 per cent. for each of the first complete forty quarters; 0.20 per cent. for each of the next forty; 0.15 per cent. for each of the next forty; 0.10 per cent. for each of the next forty; and 0.05 per cent. for each of the next forty (hence a maximum total rate of 30 per cent.). No period falling before 13 March, 1975, is counted.[18]

EXAMPLE

A is the sole beneficiary of an accumulation and maintenance trust created on 1 January, 1989. He is to take an interest in possession at the age of 25. On 1 January, 2001 (when the trust has existed for twelve years), at his eighteenth birthday, A assigns all his right and interest under the trust to B, aged 30. At the time, the settled property is valued at £170,000.

The charge to IHT is:

	%
0.25% per quarter for the first 40 quarters	10
0.20% per quarter for the next 8 quarters	1.6
	11.6

£170,000 x 11.6% = £19,720.

INGLEWOOD (LORD) v INLAND REVENUE COMMISSIONERS
[1983] 1 WLR 366 (CA, OLIVER, FOX and ROBERT GOFF LJJ).

FOX LJ: This case is concerned with the ambit of the relief from capital transfer tax granted in respect of certain accumulation and maintenance settlements by paragraph 15 of Schedule 5 to the Finance Act 1975.[19] The question, which we are told has attracted some debate in the profession, can be stated, shortly, as follows. Paragraph 15 (1) (*a*) of Schedule 5 limits the application of paragraph 15 to a settlement where, inter alia:

"one or more persons ... will, on or before attaining a specified age not exceeding 25, become entitled to, or to an interest in possession in, the settled property ... "

Suppose that property is held upon trust for A, a minor, absolutely upon attaining the age of 25 but subject to a power in the trustees to revoke that trust

---

16 IHTA 1984, s. 71 (3).
17 Ibid., s. 70 (3) to (8) and (10), as applied by s. 71 (5).
18 Ibid., ss. 70 (6) (7), 71 (5).
19 Para. 15 was to the same effect as IHTA 1984, s. 71.

and to appoint the property to other persons in such manner as the trustees determine. Can it be said, having regard to the power of revocation, that A "will" become entitled to the property on attaining 25? ...

It is evident that the provisions of paragraphs 6 and 12 of Schedule 5[20] might operate harshly in relation to property which is held on trust for a minor contingently upon attaining a specified age. Thus in the common case of a trust for a child upon attaining 21 there will normally be no interest in possession subsisting in the property at any rate while the child is under 18. In the meantime the statutory power of maintenance conferred by section 31 of the Trustee Act 1925 would normally apply and the income could at the discretion of the trustees be applied for the child's benefit and subject thereto would be accumulated. The consequences of there being no interest in possession would be twofold. First, the property would be subjected to the periodic charge. Secondly, when the child became entitled to an interest in possession there would be a charge under paragraph 6 (2). That imposes a heavy burden on maintenance and accumulation trusts. Paragraph 15 of Schedule 5 gives relief from that. Paragraph 15 (1) and (2) are in the following terms. ...

The power of revocation and reappointment contained in clause 5 [of the settlement], which authorised appointment among a wide class in such manner as the trustees, with the consent of Lord Barnard, thought fit, was released on March 29, 1976. Lord Barnard had four daughters, the eldest of whom was Carolyn; she attained 21 on May 5, 1975. The others were Elizabeth born in 1956, and two younger daughters born in 1962 and 1968 respectively. Lord Barnard has also a son, Harry, who was born in 1959. None of the children had married at any date relevant to these proceedings. Immediately after the execution of the 1976 release the trustees held the capital of the trust fund as to 1/19th for Carolyn absolutely, as to 1/19th for Elizabeth contingently, as to 15/19ths for Harry contingently and as to 1/19th each for the two youngest daughters contingently. The Crown claimed that a charge to capital transfer tax arose as to 1/19th of the capital of the fund when Carolyn attained 21 and as to 18/19ths of the capital on the execution of the 1976 deed of release. That claim is resisted by the trustees.

The Crown contended that until the execution of the 1976 release, the provisions of the appointment did not satisfy the requirements of paragraph 15 because, having regard to the power of revocation, it could not be postulated of any beneficiary that he or she "will" on or before attaining an age not exceeding 25 become entitled to or to an interest in possession in the trust fund. Vinelott J accepted that view and rejected the trustees' contention that the word "will" in paragraph 15 must be construed as meaning "will if no event happens to disentitle him or her"; i.e., that word must, in effect, be interpreted rebus sic stantibus.

In our opinion, Vinelott J's construction is, prima facie, correct. Paragraph 15 is prescribing conditions for the applicability of a relief from taxation. One of those conditions is that "one or more persons ... will on or before attaining a specified age not exceeding 25, become entitled to, or to an interest in possession in, the settled property or part of it." It seems to us that the ordinary

---

20 Although the harshness of the old (i.e. pre-1982) discretionary trust régime has now been ameliorated, the points at issue in the *Inglewood (Lord) v IRC* remain of considerable importance.

meaning of those words is that the condition will not be satisfied unless it can be said that, if the person or persons attain an age not exceeding 25 they will be bound to become entitled. We do not think that that involves stretching the meaning at all. And it does not involve reading in any words. The meaning is, to some extent, one of impression and we feel that as a matter of the ordinary use of English the word "will", in the context, imports a degree of certainty. It suggests rigidity rather than flexibility. And it seems to us to be pushing the ordinary usage of English altogether too far to say that a person "will" become entitled to property if he attains 21 or marries when his contingent interest can, at any time, be totally destroyed at the absolute discretion of the trustees and solely for the benefit of third parties. There is nothing in the language of paragraph 15 (1) (*a*) to suggest that possible future events may be disregarded. As a matter of language, therefore, our opinion of the meaning of paragraph 15 (1) coincides with that of Vinelott J. [His Lordship referred to *Green v Bowes-Lyon* [1963] AC 420, [1961] 3 All ER 843, and continued:]

The trustees contended that the Crown's construction cannot be made to fit sensibly into the legal structure with which paragraph 15 must necessarily be dealing and is really destructive of the paragraph altogether. If the Crown are right, it was said, how does one accommodate the provisions of paragraph 15 to the facts that (a) a beneficiary's interest may be lawfully disposed of by him after he attains 18 and before it vests in possession; (b) his interest may be taken away from him on bankruptcy; (c) his interest may be prevented from vesting in him by reason of an order made under the Variation of Trusts Act 1958 (p. 789 post), or under the statutory jurisdiction of the Family Division on divorce or an order made by the Court of Protection in the event of his incapacity to manage his affairs, or (d) he may die before attaining a vested interest. As to the last of those, it seems to us that the contingency is inherent in the provisions of paragraph 15 itself. The paragraph applies where a person will on or before attaining a specified age not exceeding 25 become entitled to an interest in possession in settled property. The paragraph is dealing with contingent interests. A trust cannot be excluded from the operation of the paragraph because of the possible happening of an event inherent in the contingency which brings the trust within the paragraph in the first place. In our view, therefore, there is no substance in this point. As to the other matters we think that the answer is this. Paragraph 15 (1) provides that "This paragraph applies to any settlement where ... " In our opinion "where" means "whereby". Accordingly, we think the paragraph is concerned only with provisions which are contained in the settlement itself. That would include not only the express provisions of the settlement but also any which are incorporated by statutory provision. None of the matters to which we have referred in (a), (b) and (c) can be so described. They are the consequences which cannot be avoided of the operation of the general law on property interests. They are extraneous to the settlement and are not provisions of the settlement itself.

The trustees, however, took a further and more substantial objection to the Crown's case. They pointed to the statutory power of advancement conferred by section 32 of the Trustee Act 1925 (p. 771 post). By section 69 (2) of that Act the settlor can exclude or vary the statutory power as he thinks fit. Accordingly where it is not excluded it must, we think, be regarded as simply a provision of the settlement. If property is held upon trust for a beneficiary contingently on his attaining a specified age, the statutory power enables one half of the capital to be applied for the benefit of the person contingently entitled to the property. The word "benefit" is very widely construed: see *Re Pilkington's Will Trusts* [1964] AC 612, [1962] 3 All ER 622, p. 772, post. It will thus be possible, by an exercise of the statutory power, to advance half the fund to the trustees of a new settlement under which the beneficiary's interest is postponed to an age later than 25 or, indeed, under which he took no interest at all: see *Re Hampden Settlement Trusts* [1977] TR 177. The sole criterion is the benefit of the beneficiary. If it is for his benefit, for example for fiscal or family reasons, to make such an advance as I have mentioned, there would be power to do so. . . It is in the highest degree unlikely that Parliament could have intended that a trust should to any extent fall outside the provisions of paragraph 15 merely because it incorporated the statutory power of advancement. That would exclude from paragraph 15 the statutory trusts arising on an intestacy. And it would exclude the majority of other trusts as well. Very few settlements provide that the statutory power is not to apply—though some extend the power or contain express advancement provisions more extended than the statutory power. The trustees contended that the statutory power is, as to one moiety of the settled property, no different from a special power of appointment which enables the trustees to revoke the primary trusts and to resettle upon trusts under which persons may take at ages in excess of 25. On the Crown's view it is said that paragraph 15 would be excluded as to one half, It is no doubt true that, for the purpose of the rule against perpetuities, the statutory power should be equated with a special power. But it is, in our opinion, quite unreal in relation to paragraph 15 to equate it to a power of revocation. A power of advancement is not given for the purposes of revoking the primary trust and resettling the trust property. Its purpose is auxiliary. It is given as an aid to enable the trust property to be used for the fullest benefit of the beneficiary and, as such, is a normal adjunct of any trust for a person contingently on attaining a specified age. . . To that extent it is similar to an administrative power. Its purpose, like an administrative power, is to aid the beneficial trusts and not to destroy them. Some administrative powers (for example, the power conferred by section 55 of the Settled Land Act 1925 to give away small parts of the trust land for public purposes or a power to trustees to apply income for capital purposes) do affect beneficial interests but they are not truly dispositive in nature: see *Pearson v IRC* [1981] AC 753 at 784, [1980] 2 All ER 479 at 494, p. 582, ante.

The result, in our opinion, is this. The word "will" in paragraph 15 does import a degree of certainty which is not satisfied if the trust can be revoked and the fund re-appointed to some other person at an age exceeding 25. But a power of advancement has been for so long such a normal provision in a settlement for a person contingently on attaining a specified age, and since its sole purpose is to enable the trust property to be applied for that person's benefit before he attains the specified age, it would be artificial to regard the trust as not satisfying the provisions of the paragraph. A trust for A if he attains 25 is within the paragraph. It is impossible to see any rational ground why a trust for A if he attains 25 and with a power of advancement should not satisfy it also—more particularly since the exclusion of a power of advancement in such a case must be rare indeed. . . .

Our conclusion regarding the power of advancement is that while the prima facie meaning of paragraph 15 (1) (*a*) is clear it must be interpreted in the context of the practical application of the law of trusts. The statutory power of advancement is so commonly incorporated in trusts that paragraph 15 (1) (*a*) must be read so as to accommodate that and not so as to withdraw the benefit of the paragraph from a trust containing such a power. We would not regard the much-used extension of the statutory power from a moiety to the whole as in any different position. . . .

We come then to consider the effects of the trustees' construction of paragraph 15. In our view, it displays in its operation two major weaknesses. First, it produces an illogical distinction between capital and income powers. Suppose a trust for such of the children of A as attain 21 in equal shares but with a power to the trustees to apply income for the benefit of the testator's widow during her lifetime. That does not satisfy the requirements of paragraph 15 (1) (*b*) because it cannot be said that income will be accumulated so far as not applied for the maintenance, education or benefit of the beneficiary. Now suppose a trust for such of the children of A as attain 21 in equal shares but with a power to the trustees to apply capital for the benefit of the testator's widow. It is the contention of the trustees in the present case that this trust is within paragraph 15. One simply looks, it is said, at the position as it stands at the moment though a large part, or the whole, of the capital might be applied for the widow's benefit to the destruction of the children's interests. That is a very remarkable result which is avoided on the Crown's construction. It cannot, we think, have been the intention of Parliament to produce so strange a disparity between the operation of sub-paragraphs (*a*) and (*b*). Secondly, the trustees' construction involves an illogical distinction between contingencies, of which account must be taken, and defeasance, the possibility of which is to be ignored. Thus the trustees would say that a trust for "A at 18 if X is alive," A and X both being living persons, is within paragraph 15 (1) (*a*) because you look at the position for the time being and assume it will continue. On the other hand, and for the same reasons, a trust for "A at 18 if X is then dead," A and X both being living persons, would be outside paragraph 15 (1) (*a*). Mr. Nugee said that because an interest can be an interest in possession notwithstanding the possibility of defeasance (see *Pearson v IRC* [1981] AC 753, [1980] 2 All ER 479), paragraph 15 trusts should similarly be unaffected by defeasibility. The two cases, in our opinion, are not comparable. If property is given to A for life but subject to a power of revocation, A is entitled to the income from the inception of the trust until it is revoked. That is an interest in possession. What we are concerned with here is something quite different. It is whether it can be said that somebody "will" become entitled to an interest if it is capable of revocation. . . .

Looking at the whole matter more widely it appears to us unlikely that Parliament can have intended that a trust should have the benefit of paragraph 15 if it was subject to a power of revocation which could be exercised for the benefit of other persons at ages exceeding 25. The Finance Act 1975 plainly continued and extended the policy of the Finance Act 1969 of reducing the fiscal advantages enjoyed by discretionary trusts. It did that by imposing the discretionary trust regime. That regime was burdensome on trusts for persons contingently upon attaining a specified age—which are necessarily very common because it is undesirable to give capital to persons absolutely at too early an age. Paragraph 15 was enacted accordingly. Existing trusts could be converted into paragraph 15 trusts at low rates of tax under the provisions of paragraph 14. Parliament, having decided on assistance for contingent trusts, would, it seems to us, in the context of this legislation, be likely to confine it within fairly strict boundaries. In particular, it seems to us, highly unlikely that the benefit of paragraph 15 was intended to be available to what were, in effect, discretionary trusts, by reason of the existence of wide powers of revocation and reappointment, merely by the device of a primary trust for a person at 25 which could be revoked at any time.

We summarise our view of the matter as follows: (1) Paragraph 15 (1) (*a*) leaves upon us the strong prima facie impression that its provisions are not satisfied by a trust subject to a power of revocation and reappointment under which the beneficiary's interest can be destroyed and reappointed to another person at the absolute discretion of the trustees. The word "will" involves a degree of certainty which is inconsistent with such a power. (2) We accept that the word "will" is capable of bearing such a meaning as that for which the trustees contended but it involves the addition of words which are not in the paragraph and we see no circumstances which compel us to adopt it. Thus: (a) none of the possible events in which a beneficiary might be prevented from attaining a vested interest (death, bankruptcy, etc.) seem to us to be of any weight at all in support of the trustees' construction except the power of advancement. That power is so wholly different in its nature from an unrestricted power of revocation that its acceptance by Parliament must for practical reasons be assumed. (b) Whilst the Crown's construction may involve some anomalies so does the trustees' construction. (3) The legislative framework and purpose of the statute seem to us to be more in accord with the Crown's construction. In the circumstances we think that the judge's decision was correct and that the appeal should be dismissed.

Thomas, *Taxation and Trusts* (1981), pp. 131–134.

"Accumulation and maintenance settlements are—and are likely to remain—popular vehicles for the transfer of assets from one generation to the next. The cost of creating such a settlement can be relatively low. Suppose, for instance, that two grandparents each transfer £3,000 a year (exempt) into such a trust, and another £1,000 a year as normal expenditure out of income (also exempt). Over 18 years, the total transferred is £126,000, which, with prudent management, should amount to considerably more. Add to this an exempt first transfer of £50,000 and the fund becomes quite large.[21] Even relatively low sums—say, £500 a year each—would produce £18,000 plus interest over 18 years, so there is considerable scope for tax planning to suit individual or family circumstances.

Such trusts are also excellent vehicles for holding certain types of property. For instance, shares in a newly formed company, whose value is now low but likely to increase, could be settled on the founder's children or grandchildren (with the benefit of a power to vary the beneficiaries' entitlement while they remain under 18). Insurance policies can be, and often are, written in favour of such trusts. Reversionary interests, too, as excluded property, can be settled free of IHT, and, provided the [s 71] conditions are satisfied, there need be no later charge either.

Once created, trust income can be capitalised free of higher rate tax and (provided all pitfalls are avoided) without being attributed to the parent. This

---

21 The raising of the nil-rate band limit to £200,000 also provides considerable scope for substantial tax-free transfers. Similarly, property which qualifies for business relief or agricultural property itself can be transferred with advantage: see pp. 573–574, ante.

is clearly of benefit to many, despite the imposition of the additional rate on accumulated income. . . .

It is clear from this that, if full advantage is to be extracted from the fiscal laws, the *form* of the accumulation and maintenance trust is crucial. Tax law, not trust law—and certainly not the settlor's desires—will dictate what ought or ought not to be done. A typical accumulation and maintenance trust will, therefore, take the following form.

1. Assets are to be held on trust (probably subject to an eighty-year perpetuity period) for a specified class of children (or grandchildren) of the settlor, now in existence and under 18 or hereafter to be born, *contingently* upon attaining the age of 25 (possibly in equal shares absolutely if more than one, or, as noted above, advantage may be derived from giving each beneficiary a life interest only).

A settlement in favour of grandchildren may well be more advantageous than one in favour of children. "Generation skipping" will avoid payment of tax on the death of (or on transfers by) children; and, in practice, a longer period for accumulating income will be available.

2. Section 31 of the TA 1925 can be incorporated, probably with some of the modifications mentioned on p. 110 above; or, alternatively, an express trust to accumulate income (usually for 21 years from the date of the settlement) coupled with a power to maintain can be used instead.

3. Clearly, the intermediate income must be carried.

4. The section 32 power of advancement can be included and, probably, modified to permit advancement of the entire fund.

5. A power of appointment may be incorporated to vary the shares of each beneficiary, and even to exclude some beneficiaries altogether. Clearly, such a power must be subject to the limitation that it is exercisable only in favour of a person under 25 who is a member of the class.

6. A wide overriding power of appointment in favour of, say, the beneficiaries' spouses and issue would also be useful—in order, perhaps, to prevent a beneficiary calling for the capital. Such a power must not be capable of being exercised, however, *until* a beneficiary has attained an interest in possession, as it would otherwise infringe [section 71] . The *exercise* of such a power would, of course, result in a charge to [IHT] under [section 52].[1] Also, unless the beneficiaries have a common grandparent, the 25-year limit alone is available.

7. Unless the class of beneficiaries closes when the first member attains the specified age, the birth of a subsequent beneficiary could result in the partial termination of the existing beneficiaries' interests and thus a charge to [IHT] would arise [section 52]. The trust deed should, therefore, ensure that the class closes at the right time. Alternatively, the deed could confer a power to apportion a part of the fund to the first beneficiary (and so on) which would then be unaffected by any subsequent birth.

8. If the twenty-five-year time limit applies, some members of the class of beneficiaries may not have attained full age and an interest in possession before the period expires (as they must all do). Clearly, power to make outright transfers of capital to the infant beneficiaries (and to accept receipts

---

1 These events would now rank as PETs and might therefore not be chargeable; pp. 574–575, ante.

from them or their parents) would suffice, but interests in possession may be more desirable. However, interests *accelerated* in this way would normally be caught by section 31. So the trust deed could, perhaps, not only empower such acceleration but also provide that if and when such an event occurred, section 31 should not apply thereafter. This power would only be exercised, in any event, after giving consideration to section [660B] of the ICTA [1988] and the likely effects on the parent's tax position.

9. All the pitfalls of Part [XV] of ICTA [1988] must be avoided assiduously.''[1a]

iii. PROTECTIVE TRUSTS

We have already described the protective trust in Chapter 5. It cuts across the categories into which trusts are divided for the purposes of IHT; there is an interest in possession during the currency of the interest of the principal beneficiary, but a discretionary trust after that interest has been forfeited. There is a charge to IHT upon the death of the principal beneficiary, but not on the termination by forfeiture of his life interest.

E. Trusts Within Two Years of Death

i. ALTERATION OF DISPOSITIONS TAKING EFFECT ON DEATH

Where, within two years of a person's death, any of the dispositions (whether effected by will, under the law relating to intestacy, or otherwise) of the property comprised in his estate immediately before his death are varied, or the benefit conferred by any of those dispositions is disclaimed, by an instrument in writing made by the persons, or any of the persons, who benefit or would benefit under the dispositions, then such variation or disclaimer shall not be a transfer of value and the IHT provisions apply as if the variation had been effected by the deceased or, as the case may be, the disclaimed benefit had never been conferred.[2]

This is a much used provision. Its effect, essentially, is that the dispositions of the deceased's estate can be rearranged or redirected without adverse IHT consequences. Whether a disclaimer or a variation is used depends on the circumstances. It is generally assumed that one cannot disclaim part of a gift,[3] for example. Moreover, although there are similar provisions in the CGT and stamp duty legislation,[4] there is no such special treatment for income tax purposes. A deed of variation may, in the appropriate circumstances, be a settlement for income tax purposes, whereas a disclaimer will not.

1a See pp. 554–557, ante.
2 IHTA 1984, s. 142; *Russell v IRC* [1988] STC 195; *Lake v Lake* [1989] STC 865. The Finance Bill 1989 contained provisions restricting the scope of s. 142—indeed, effectively rendering it ineffective. Under pressure, these provisions were withdrawn. The Government indicated, however, that some reform of s. 142 would take place in the future, after further consideration of the problem.
3 This is doubtful, however: see *Dewar v IRC* (1935) 19 TC 561 at 579. See also [1978] BTR 47 (J.L. Wosner).
4 TCGA 1992, s. 62 (6)–(8); *Marshall v Kerr* [1994] STC 638; FA 1985, s. 84.

ii. Two-Year Discretionary Trusts

Another valuable provision relates to the creation of "two-year discretionary trusts".[5] Basically, where property comprised in a person's estate immediately before his death is settled by his will and, within two years of his death and before an interest in possession has subsisted in the property, an event occurs which would otherwise be chargeable to IHT, then tax is not to be charged on that event and the IHT legislation applies as if the will itself had provided for the making of the distribution of capital, or creation of the interest in possession, or whatever. This enables a testator to leave his property on discretionary trusts which can be unscrambled within two years of his death, in the light of the then prevailing fiscal and family circumstances, without adverse IHT consequences. It also surmounts obstacles which would prevent the operation of s. 142 of the IHTA 1984, for example, because there are minor beneficiaries who cannot disclaim or consent to a variation.

QUESTIONS

1. "Trusts without Tax is Hamlet without the Prince." Do you agree?
2. Does the *Ramsay/Furniss* doctrine apply to trusts? If so, how?
3. Consider the scheme of Capital Gains Tax. Is there any point in retaining this tax on capital? Chap. 14; Inland Revenue Statistics (published annually by HMSO), paras. 1.2 (net receipts of Inland Revenue taxes); 12 (Inheritance tax); 14 (Capital gains tax); pp. 554, n. 8, 594, n. 19, ante; Hansard, HC Deb. 9 Mar. 1982, vol. 19, col. 755.
4. (*a*) "One of the less important but more convenient results of the decision in *Pearson v IRC* [1981] AC 753, [1980] 2 All ER 479 is that it is now possible, with a fair degree of accuracy, to refer to the two kinds of settled property as property held on fixed interest and discretionary trusts respectively": *IRC v Trustees of Sir John Aird's Settlement* [1982] 1 WLR 270 at 272, [1982] 2 All ER 929 at 936, per NOURSE J. Is it possible?
   (*b*) If you had been a Lord of Appeal in *Pearson v IRC* what would you have said?
   Pp. 582–590, ante, and articles in p. 582, n. 1.

---

5 IHTA 1984 s. 144. The discretionary trusts need not be limited to a two-year period. All that is required for s. 144 to apply is that the appointment or distribution occurs within two years of death. Section 144 was to be repealed by the FA 1989; but the Government dropped the relevant provision from the Finance Act.

Part Four. Trustees

16. General Principles Relating to Trustees[1]

I. Duties and Discretions[2]

A trustee's duties are imperative. Equity requires strict compliance. The standard required is that of *exacta diligentia*. Failure to comply may render a trustee liable for breach of trust; even though he thought that what he did was right, and even if it was done with the intention of benefiting the beneficiaries. However, onerous though the duties of a trustee are, a clause may be inserted in the trust instrument exempting a trustee from liability (the extent of its effectiveness is discussed below),[3] and section 61 of the Trustee Act 1925 gives the court a discretion to excuse a trustee who has acted honestly and reasonably and ought fairly to be excused.[4]

Powers are discretionary, and there can be no rule of strict compliance. This is also true where the discretion is coupled with a duty to exercise it; as with the selection of beneficiaries of a discretionary trust, and with the selection of investments in performance of the duty to invest in a particular type of

---

1 For a general commentary on the Trustee Act 1925, see Wolstenholme & Cherry, *Conveyancing Statutes* (13th edn, 1972) vol. 4. See also Sladen, *Practical Trust Administration* (3rd edn 1993).
2 H & M, pp. 469–476; P & M, pp. 388–391; Pettit, pp. 355–356; Riddall, pp. 278–279; Snell, pp. 212–213; Underhill, pp. 545–562.
3 P. 613, post.
4 P. 876, post.

investment. In exercising a power or discretion the rule is that a trustee must use the same due diligence and care as an ordinary, prudent man of business would use in the management of his own affairs.

In 1982 the Law Reform Committee recommended various changes in the law relating to the powers and duties of trustees,[5] and these recommendations are incorporated throughout Part III. The most important one is the repeal of the Trustee Investments Act 1961 and its replacement by a new statute giving wider powers of investment to trustees.[6]

A. Paid and Unpaid Trustees

In **Bartlett v Barclays Bank Trust Co Ltd (No 1)** [1980] Ch 515, [1980] 1 All ER 139,[7] BRIGHTMAN J said at 531, at 149:

"The cases establish that it is the duty of a trustee to conduct the business of the trust with the same care as an ordinary prudent man of business would extend towards his own affairs: *Re Speight* (1883) 22 ChD 727, per Sir George Jessel MR at 739 and Bowen LJ at 762; affirmed on appeal, *Speight v Gaunt* (1883) 9 App Cas 1, and see Lord Blackburn at 19. In applying this principle, Lindley LJ (who was the third member of the court in the *Speight* case) added in *Re Whiteley* (1886) 33 ChD 347 at 355:

'... care must be taken not to lose sight of the fact that the business of the trustee, and the business which the ordinary prudent man is supposed to be conducting for himself, is the business of investing money for the benefit of persons who are to enjoy it at some future time, and not for the sole benefit of the person entitled to the present income. The duty of a trustee is not to take such care only as a prudent man would take if he had only himself to consider; the duty rather is to take such care as an ordinary prudent man would take if he were minded to make an investment for the benefit of other people for whom he felt morally bound to provide. That is the kind of business the ordinary prudent man is supposed to be engaged in; and unless this is borne in mind the standard of a trustee's duty will be fixed too low; lower than it has ever yet been fixed, and lower certainly than the House of Lords or this Court endeavoured to fix it in *Speight v Gaunt*.'

See on appeal *Learoyd v Whiteley* (1887) 12 App Cas 727, where Lord Watson added, at 733:

'Business men of ordinary prudence may, and frequently do, select investments which are more or less of a speculative character, but it is the duty of a trustee to confine himself to the class of investments which are permitted by the trust, and likewise to avoid all investments of that class which are attended with hazard.'

That does not mean that the trustee is bound to avoid all risk and in effect act as an insurer of the trust fund: see Bacon V-C in *Re Godfrey* (1883) 23 ChD 483 at 493:

'No doubt it is the duty of a trustee, in administering the trusts of a will, to deal with property intrusted into his care exactly as any prudent man would deal with his own property. But the words in which the rule is

---

5 Law Reform Committee 23rd Report (The Powers and Duties of Trustees) 1982 Cmnd. 8733.
6 P. 708, post.
7 See p. 688, post.

expressed must not be strained beyond their meaning. Prudent businessmen in their dealings incur risk. That may and must happen in almost all human affairs.'

The distinction is between a prudent degree of risk on the one hand, and hazard on the other. Nor must the court be astute to fix liability upon a trustee who has committed no more than an error of judgment, from which no business man, however prudent, can expect to be immune: see Lopes LJ in *Re Chapman* [1896] 2 Ch 763 at 778:

'A trustee who is honest and reasonably competent is not to be held responsible for a mere error in judgment when the question which he has to consider is whether a security of a class authorised, but depreciated in value, should be retained or realized, provided he acts with reasonable care, prudence, and circumspection.'

So far, I have applied the test of the ordinary prudent man of business. Although I am not aware that the point has previously been considered, except briefly in *Re Waterman's Will Trusts* [1952] 2 All ER 1054,[8] I am of opinion that a higher duty of care is plainly due from someone like a trust corporation which carries on a specialised business of trust management. A trust corporation holds itself out in its advertising literature as being above ordinary mortals. With a specialist staff of trained trust officers and managers, with ready access to financial information and professional advice, dealing with and solving trust problems day after day, the trust corporation holds itself out, and rightly, as capable of providing an expertise which it would be unrealistic to expect and unjust to demand from the ordinary prudent man or woman who accepts, probably unpaid and sometimes reluctantly from a sense of family duty, the burdens of a trusteeship. Just as, under the law of contract, a professional person possessed of a particular skill is liable for breach of contract if he neglects to use the skill and experience which he professes, so I think that a professional corporate trustee is liable for breach of trust if loss is caused to the trust fund because it neglects to exercise the special care and skill which it professes to have.'[9]

B. Trustee Exemption Clauses[10]

Hansbury & Martin, *Modern Equity* (14th edn), pp. 473–474.

"A question on which there appears to be no modern English authority is whether and how far the settlor may effectively exempt a trustee from liability. Before considering express clauses, reference should be made to section 30 of the Trustee Act 1925, which provides that a trustee shall not be answerable for the defaults of co-trustees or other persons with whom trust money or securities are deposited unless the loss results from his own wilful default. The weight of opinion is that 'wilful default' in this context includes want of

---

8 "I do not forget that a paid trustee is expected to exercise a higher standard of diligence and knowledge than an unpaid trustee", per HARMAN J at 1055. See H & M, pp. 472–473.

9 In *Nestlé v National Westminster Bank plc* (29 June 1988, unreported), p. 719, post, HOFFMANN J said: "Trustees like the Bank act for reward and therefore owe duties of professional skill, but the engagement into which they enter is not one of insurance. They do not guarantee results."

10 For a discussion of the position in the United Kingdom and other jurisdictions, see [1989] Conv 42 (P. Matthews).

ordinary prudence, although there is authority that it covers only intentional wrongdoing or recklessness.[11]

It appears from pre-1926 English[12] and Scottish[13] authorities that exemption clauses, which are strictly construed against trustees, will not protect them in cases of bad faith, recklessness, gross negligence or deliberate breach of duty. To allow protection in such cases would be contrary to public policy.[14] This is also the position in the United States.[15] On this view, it would be possible to confer protection against liability for ordinary negligence.[16] Another view is that exemption clauses should not even be effective in the case of want of ordinary prudence,[17] bearing in mind the possibility of insurance. It has also been held that a provision that only the settlor or employers could sue the trustees of a pension fund was ineffective.[18]

Assuming that an exemption clause may be effective in cases of negligence, a question would then arise as to the application of the Unfair Contract Terms Act 1977 to professional trustees appointed by the settlor. Provided the appointment may be regarded as contractual, the validity of the clause would depend upon its reasonableness, under section 2(3) of the Act.[19]

Finally, there is a distinction between clauses which exempt from breach and those which prevent the duty from arising. Such a clause as the latter may be effective where there was no pre-existing fiduciary relationship between the parties, especially in the context of a commercial agreement between parties of equal status.''[20]

C. Pension Trustees

Under the Pensions Act 1995, exemption clauses are not available to pension trustees.

PENSIONS ACT 1995

33. Investment powers: duty of care—(1) Liability for breach of an obligation under any rule of law to take care or exercise skill in the performance of any investment functions, where the function is exercisable—

  (a) by a trustee of a trust scheme, or

  (b) by a person to whom the function has been delegated under section 34, cannot be excluded or restricted by any instrument or agreement.

  (2) In this section, references to excluding or restricting liability include—

  (a) making the liability or its enforcement subject to restrictive or onerous conditions,

---

11 Re *Vickery* [1931] 1 Ch 572; p. 748 post.
12 *Wilkins v Hogg* (1861) 31 LJ Ch 41; *Pass v Dundas* (1880) 43 LT 665. See also *Rehden v Wesley* (1861) 29 Beav 213.
13 *Knox v Mackinnon* (1888) 13 App Cas 753; *Rae v Meek* (1889) 14 App Cas 558.
14 See *Armitage v Nurse* [1995] NPC 110 (trustees accused of deliberate but honest breach exonerated by clause making them liable only for "own actual fraud".).
15 [1989] Conv 42 at p. 49.
16 See Law Commission Consultation Paper No. 124 (1992), Fiduciary Duties and Regulatory Rules, para. 3.3.13. which considers that the position as to gross negligence is in doubt.
17 Ontario Law Reform Committee, *Report on the Law of Trusts* (1984), Vol. 1, pp. 40–42.
18 *Jones v Shipping Federation of British Columbia* (1963) 37 DLR (2d) 273.
19 See [1980] Conv 333 (W. Goodhart).
20 Law Commission Consultation Paper No. 124, paras. 3.3.11, 3.3.12.

(b) excluding or restricting any right or remedy in respect of the liability, or subjecting a person to any prejudice in consequence of his pursuing any such right or remedy, or

(c) excluding or restricting rules of evidence or procedure.

II. Appointment[1]

A. Appointment by Donee of Power to Appoint

i. NUMBER OF TRUSTEES

TRUSTEE ACT 1925

34. Limitation of the number of trustees.[2]—(1) Where, at the commencement of this Act, there are more than four trustees of a settlement of land, or more than four trustees holding land on trust for sale, no new trustees shall (except where as a result of the appointment the number is reduced to four or less) be capable of being appointed until the number is reduced to less than four, and thereafter the number shall not be increased beyond four.

(2) In the case of settlements and dispositions on trust for sale of land made or coming into operation after the commencement of this Act—

(*a*) the number of trustees thereof shall not in any case exceed four, and where more than four persons are named as such trustees, the four first named (who are able and willing to act) shall alone be the trustees, and the other persons named shall not be trustees unless appointed on the occurrence of a vacancy;

(*b*) the number of the trustees shall not be increased beyond four.

(3) This section only applies to settlements and dispositions of land, and the restrictions imposed on the number of trustees do not apply—

(*a*) in the case of land vested in trustees for charitable, ecclesiastical, or public purposes; or

(*b*) where the net proceeds of the sale of the land are held for like purposes; or

(*c*) to the trustees of a term of years absolute limited by a settlement on trusts for raising money, or of a like term created under the statutory remedies relating to annual sums charged on land.

Law Reform Committee 23rd Report (The Powers and Duties of Trustees) 1982 Cmnd 8733, para. 9.1.II.1.

"1. Where the settlor makes no specific provision about the number of trustees, they should be limited to four regardless of the nature of the trust property, subject to the existing restrictions in the case of trusts for sale of land and settled land and to the exceptions presently contained in section 34 (3) (*a*) of the Trustee Act 1925. (paragraph 2.2)"

---

1 H & M, pp. 481–487; K & S, pp. 253–257; P & M, 356–377; Pettit, pp. 317–335; Riddall, pp. 234–251; Snell, pp. 199–208; Underhill, pp. 435–436, 729–752.
2 The restrictions affecting the number of persons entitled to hold land on trust for sale and the number of trustees of a settlement apply to registered land: LRA 1925, s. 95.

ii. APPOINTMENT OF NEW OR ADDITIONAL TRUSTEES

TRUSTEE ACT 1925

36. Power of appointing new or additional trustees.—(1) Where a trustee, either original or substituted, and whether appointed by a court or otherwise, is dead, or remains out of the United Kingdom for more than twelve months, or desires to be discharged from all or any of the trusts or powers reposed in or conferred on him, or refuses or is unfit to act therein, or is incapable of acting therein, or is an infant, then, subject to the restrictions imposed by this Act on the number of trustees,—

(*a*) the person or persons nominated for the purpose of appointing new trustees by the instrument, if any, creating the trust; or

(*b*) if there is no such person, or no such person able and willing to act, then the surviving or continuing trustees or trustee for the time being, or the personal representatives of the last surviving or continuing trustee,[3]

may, by writing, appoint one or more other persons (whether or not being the persons exercising the power) to be a trustee or trustees in the place of the trustee so deceased, remaining out of the United Kingdom, desiring to be discharged, refusing, or being unfit or being incapable, or being an infant, as aforesaid.

(2) Where a trustee has been removed under a power contained in the instrument creating the trust, a new trustee or new trustees may be appointed in the place of the trustee who is removed, as if he were dead, or, in the case of a corporation, as if the corporation desired to be discharged from the trust, and the provisions of this section shall apply accordingly, but subject to the restrictions imposed by this Act on the number of trustees.

(3) Where a corporation being a trustee is or has been dissolved, either before or after the commencement of this Act, then, for the purposes of this section and of any enactment replaced thereby, the corporation shall be deemed to be and to have been from the date of the dissolution incapable of acting in the trusts or powers reposed in or conferred on the corporation.

(4) The power of appointment given by subsection (1) of this section or any similar previous enactment to the personal representatives of a last surviving or continuing trustee shall be and shall be deemed always to have been exercisable by the executors for the time being (whether original or by representation) of such surviving or continuing trustee who have proved the will of their testator or by the administrators for the time being of such trustee without the concurrence of any executor who has renounced or has not proved.

(5) But a sole or last surviving executor intending to renounce, or all the executors where they all intend to renounce, shall have and shall be deemed always to have had power, at any time before renouncing probate, to exercise the power of appointment given by this section, or by any similar previous

---

3 Or the executor of a deceased sole trustee: *Re Shafto's Trusts* (1885) 29 ChD 247. A personal representative may exercise the power without having obtained probate: *Re Crowhurst Park* [1974] 1 WLR 583, [1974] 1 All ER 991; but a trustee so appointed will be unable to prove his title unless a grant is obtained. Apart from the circumstances covered by the sub-para., executors do not have power to appoint new trustees; see *Re King's Will Trusts* [1964] Ch 542, [1964] 1 All ER 833.

enactment, if willing to act for that purpose and without thereby accepting the office of executor.

(6) Where a sole trustee, other than a trust corporation, is or has been originally appointed to act in a trust, or where, in the case of any trust, there are not more than three trustees (none of them being a trust corporation) either original or substituted and whether appointed by the court or otherwise, then and in any such case—

(*a*) the person or persons nominated for the purpose of appointing new trustees by the instrument, if any, creating the trust; or

(*b*) if there is no such person, or no such person able and willing to act, then the trustee or trustees for the time being;

may, by writing, appoint another person or other persons[4] to be an additional trustee or additional trustees, but it shall not be obligatory to appoint any additional trustee, unless the instrument, if any, creating the trust, or any statutory enactment provides to the contrary, nor shall the number of trustees be increased beyond four by virtue of any such appointment.

(7) Every new trustee appointed under this section as well before as after all the trust property becomes by law, or by assurance, or otherwise, vested in him, shall have the same powers, authorities, and discretions, and may in all respects act as if he had been originally appointed a trustee by the instrument, if any, creating the trust.

(8) The provisions of this section relating to a trustee who is dead include the case of a person nominated trustee in a will but dying before the testator, and those relative to a continuing trustee include a refusing or retiring trustee, if willing to act in the execution of the provisions of this section.[5]

(9) Where a trustee is incapable, by reason of mental disorder within the meaning of the Mental Health Act, 1983, of exercising his functions as trustee and is also entitled in possession to some beneficial interest in the trust property, no appointment of a new trustee in his place shall be made by virtue of paragraph (*b*) of subsection (1) of this section unless leave to make the appointment has been given by the authority having jurisdiction under Part VII of the Mental Health Act 1983.[6]

Law Reform Committee 23rd Report (The Powers and Duties of Trustees) 1982 Cmnd. 8733, para. 9.1.II.2.

"2. Section 36(6) of the Trustee Act 1925 should be amended as follows:

(i) the restriction on the appointment of additional trustees where a trust corporation is the original sole trustee or is one of the existing trustees should be removed (paragraph 2.6) and

---

4 And not therefore himself: *Re Power's Settlement Trusts* [1951] Ch 1074, [1951] 2 All ER 513. Under sub-s. (1) the donee may appoint himself.

5 See Trustee Act 1925, s. 37 (1) (*c*) which provides that a trustee shall not be discharged unless there is a trust corporation or at least two individuals to act as trustees to perform the trust. There is an exception where only one trustee was appointed and a sole trustee will be able to give a receipt for capital money. In *Mettoy Pension Trustees Ltd v Evans* [1990] 1 WLR 1587 at 1607, [1991] 2 All ER 513 at 534, WARNER J doubted whether the express terms of the settlement can override these provisions.

6 As substituted by Mental Health Act 1959, Sch. 7 and Mental Health Act 1983, s. 148, Sch. 4, para. 4(*a*).

(ii) the person or persons who have the power to appoint additional trustees should also be enabled to appoint themselves as additional trustees. (paragraph 2.6)"

The Trusts of Land and Appointments of Trustees Bill 1995,[6a] requires trustees, whether of land or personalty, to serve a notice of their intention to appoint a new trustee on beneficiaries who are of full age and capacity (clause 19); empowers the beneficiaries to give a written direction to the trustees to appoint a particular person or persons (clause 20); covers cases where an existing trustee becomes mentally incapable and there are no other trustees capable and willing to make a new appointment. In such circumstances, the beneficiaries may direct certain persons acting for the incapable trustee to appoint a particular person or persons (clause 21).

iii. "INCAPABLE" OR "UNFIT"

In **Re Wheeler and De Rochow** [1896] 1 Ch 315,[7] a marriage settlement gave to the husband and wife, or the survivor of them, the power to appoint new trustees in certain specified circumstances, including that of a trustee becoming "incapable". One of the trustees became bankrupt. This rendered him "unfit" but not "incapable". The question was whether a new trustee should be appointed by the husband (as the survivor), under para. (*a*) of s. 36 (1), or by the continuing trustees under para. (*b*).[8] KEKEWICH J held that the husband and wife (or the survivor) were the "persons nominated for the purpose of appointing new trustees by the instrument" only in the circumstances specified in the settlement. No such circumstances had occurred, and the new trustee must therefore be appointed by the continuing trustees.

iv. "SURVIVING" OR "CONTINUING"

Section 36 (8) enables a retiring sole trustee or a retiring group of trustees to appoint their successors. It is usual for retiring trustees to participate in the appointment of new trustees. But it is not essential.

In **Re Coates to Parsons** (1886) 34 ChD 370, the title to a Methodist chapel at Thrapston, Northamptonshire, was vested in eleven trustees. One died, and another, W.R. Dearlove, remained out of the United Kingdom for twelve months. The nine remaining trustees purported to appoint T.M. Coleman a trustee, acting under the statutory power.[9]

A purchaser under a contract for sale of the land by the trustees objected to the title, one of the grounds being that W.R. Dearlove had not participated in

---

6a See Law Commission Report on Trusts of Land 1989 (Law Com No. 181), para. 9.1.
  7 Followed reluctantly in *Re Sichel's Settlements* [1916] 1 Ch 358.
  8 The section applicable was TA 1893, s. 10 (1), which was substantially the same as TA 1925, s. 36 (1).
  9 Given by Conveyancing Act 1881, s. 31 (1).

the appointment of new trustees. NORTH J upheld the appointment, saying at 377:

"I hold, therefore, that under the terms of the Act the nine trustees, who were clearly continuing trustees were competent to make the appointment, unless it was shewn that the person who had been absent for so long, and in whose place there was a clear right to substitute a new trustee, was willing and competent to act. This has not been shewn, and it seems to me, therefore, that the first objection, viz. that *W.R. Dearlove* ought to have concurred in making the appointment, is not established."

In **Re Stoneham's Settlement Trusts** [1953] Ch 59, [1952] 2 All ER 694, one trustee, Stoneham, who had absented himself from the United Kingdom for over twelve months, was willing to continue to act. His co-trustee, intending to retire, appointed two others in place of Stoneham and himself. Stoneham wished to continue. DANCKWERTS J held that the appointments were valid. The co-trustee could make them as a retiring trustee. Stoneham's participation was not necessary. "I come to the conclusion quite plainly that a trustee who is removed against his will is not a refusing or retiring trustee, not, at any rate, in the case of a trustee removed because of his absence outside the United Kingdom for consecutive periods of more than 12 months."

v. INFLUENCE OF BENEFICIARIES

In **Re Higginbottom** [1892] 3 Ch 132, Mary Jane Broadbent, an illiterate person of no means, and having no beneficial interest in the trust property, was sole executrix of the surviving trustee of a trust fund, and entitled to exercise the statutory power of appointing new trustees. A large majority of the beneficiaries desired the Court to appoint William Wood and Ralph Rupert Wood as trustees. Mary Jane wished to exercise the power herself. KEKEWICH J refused to make an appointment at the request of the majority of beneficiaries.

In **Re Brockbank** [1948] Ch 206, [1948] 1 All ER 287, the testator's residuary estate was held on trust for his widow for life and after her death for his children. Ward and Bates were the trustees. Ward wished to retire. The widow and all the children wished that Lloyds Bank Ltd. should be appointed trustee. Bates thought that this would impose an unnecessary charge upon the small estate. Ward, the widow and the children brought this summons, asking that Lloyds Bank Ltd. should be appointed sole trustee in the place of Ward and Bates. VAISEY J refused and said at 208, at 287:

"This case involves a question which is said to be novel. It is possible, I think, that the reason for the novelty is that the courage required for the raising of it has hitherto been lacking.

The two alternative grounds of relief claimed are sought to be justified by the following argument: It is said that where all the beneficiaries concur, they may force a trustee to retire, compel his removal and direct the trustees, having the power to nominate their successors, to appoint as such successors such persons or person or corporation as may be indicated by the beneficiaries, and it is suggested that the trustees have no option but to comply.

I do not follow this. The power of nominating a new trustee is a discretionary power, and, in my opinion is no longer exercisable and, indeed, can no longer exist if it has become one of which the exercise can be dictated by others. But then it is said that the beneficiaries could direct the trustees to transfer the trust property either to themselves absolutely, or to any other person or persons or corporation, upon trusts identical with or corresponding to the trusts of the testator's will. I agree, provided that the trustees are adequately protected against any possible claim for future death duties and are fully indemnified as regards their costs, charges and expenses....

It seems to me that the beneficiaries must choose between two alternatives. Either they must keep the trusts of the will on foot, in which case those trusts must continue to be executed by trustees duly appointed pursuant either to the original instrument or to the powers of s. 36 of the Trustee Act, 1925, and not by trustees arbitrarily selected by themselves; or they must, by mutual agreement, extinguish and put an end to the trusts....

The claim of the beneficiaries to control the exercise of the defendant's fiduciary power of making or compelling an appointment of the trustees is, in my judgment, untenable. The court itself regards such a power as deserving of the greatest respect and as one with which it will not interfere.''

vi. SELECTION OF TRUSTEES

The selection of the right trustees is a matter of the greatest importance. Modern settlements usually give many discretionary powers to the trustees. In selecting the original trustees, the settlor will select persons who can be relied on to exercise these powers in a manner of which he would himself approve. He cannot, however, control the trustees in the exercise of their powers and discretions. Nor, unless he retains the power to appoint new trustees, can he determine future appointments.

The question has been raised whether the statutory power enables a donee of the power to appoint a person outside the United Kingdom.[10]

In **Richard v The Hon A.B. Mackay** (14 March 1987, unreported) the English trustees of a settlement made in 1965 by Lord Tanlaw, on trusts governed by English law, sought a declaration that transfer of part of the trust fund (the fund was worth £7½m) to a new settlement to be established in Bermuda was valid. The beneficiaries under the proposed new settlement were the infant children of Lord Tanlaw, and, although the family had international connections, Lord Tanlaw was domiciled and resident in the United Kingdom. MILLETT J said:

"In *Re Whitehead's Will Trusts* [1971] 1 WLR 833, [1971] 2 All ER 1334 Sir John Pennycuick, the Vice-Chancellor, was asked to declare that an appointment of foreign trustees of an English trust was effective to discharge the English trustees.

---

10 Once made, however, such an appointment, whether made under an express or statutory power, is valid: *Meinertzhagen v Davis* (1844) 1 Coll 335; *Re Smith's Trusts* (1872) 26 LT 820; (1969) 85 LQR 15 (P.V.B.); (1976) 40 Conv (NS) 295 (T.G. Watkin).

At p. 837, at p. 1337, he said:

'. . . the law has been quite well established for upwards of a century that there is no absolute bar to the appointment of persons resident abroad as trustees of an English trust. I say "no absolute bar", in the sense that such an appointment would be prohibited by law and would consequently be invalid. On the other hand, apart from exceptional circumstances, it is not proper to make such an appointment, that is to say, the court would not, apart from exceptional circumstances, make such an appointment; nor would it be right for the donees of the power to make such an appointment out of court. If they did, presumably the court would be likely to interfere at the instance of the beneficiaries. There do, however, exist exceptional circumstances in which such an appointment can properly be made. The most obvious exceptional circumstances are those in which the beneficiaries have settled permanently in some country outside the United Kingdom and what is proposed to be done is to appoint new trustees in that country. In those exceptional circumstances it has, I believe, almost uniformly been accepted as the law that trustees in the country where the beneficiaries have settled can properly be appointed.'

At p. 838, at p. 1338, the learned Vice-Chancellor added:

'. . . It cannot, I think, make any difference whether the court is asked under the Variation of Trusts Act 1958 to transfer a fund to a new settlement in a foreign country or whether one is concerned merely with the appointment of new trustees of the existing settlement.'

This is not a case where the family concerned or the beneficiaries have become resident abroad. The settlor and his two children live in England. Nor is it a case where the proposed new settlement is to be formed in the country where the beneficiaries reside or may be expected to reside in the future. The possibility which is envisaged is that they may well wish to live in the Far East, whereas the seat of the proposed settlement is to be Bermuda.

But in my judgment the language of Sir John Pennycuick, which is narrowly drawn, is too restrictive for the circumstances of the present day if, at least, it is intended to lay down any rule of practice. Nor in my view is it accurate to equate the approach that the court adopts to exercise its own discretion with the approach it adopts when asked to authorise the trustees to exercise theirs.

Where the court is invited to exercise an original discretion of its own, whether by appointing trustees under the Trustee Act 1925 or by approving a scheme under the Variation of Trust Act 1958, or where the trustees surrender their discretion to the court, the court will require to be satisfied that the discretion should be exercised in the manner proposed. The applicants must make out a positive case for the exercise of the discretion, and the court is unlikely to assist them where the scheme is nothing more than a device to avoid tax and has no other advantages of any kind.

Where, however, the transaction is proposed to be carried out by the trustees in exercise of their own discretion, entirely out of court, the trustees retaining their discretion and merely seeking the authorisation of the court for their own protection, then in my judgment the question that the court asks itself is quite different. It is concerned to ensure that the proposed exercise of the trustees' power is lawful and within the power and that it does not infringe the trustees' duty to act as ordinary, reasonable and prudent trustees might act, but it requires only to be satisfied that the trustees can properly form the view that the proposed transaction is for the benefit of beneficiaries or the trust estate.

[His Lordship referred to *Re Kay MacKinnon v Stringer* [1927] VLR 66 and continued:]
Certainly in the conditions of today, when one can have an international family with international interests, and where they are as likely to make their home in one country as in another and as likely to choose one jurisdiction as another for the investment of their capital, I doubt that the language of Sir John Pennycuick is really in tune with the times. In my judgment, where the trustees retain their discretion, as they do in the present case, the court should need to be satisfied only that the proposed transaction is not so inappropriate that no reasonable trustee could entertain it.

I have evidence before me that the proposed trustee is the leading trustee corporation in Bermuda, that the trust law of Bermuda is similar to and based upon and derived from English law, and that there are no restrictions upon the free movement of capital. I think I can take judicial notice of the fact that Bermuda has a stable regime within the United States sphere of influence and that many wealthy families, acting in their own interests and in a businesslike way, have been in the habit in recent years of entrusting substantial portions of their fortunes to trustees in that jurisdiction.

There are obvious potential advantages in diversification. What is proposed is only the removal from the jurisdiction of 25 per cent of a very substantial fund. There is great force in the submission that what is proposed is positively a prudent step, and I have no doubt at all that it cannot possibly be stigmatised as imprudent or unreasonable.

So far as the appropriateness of what is proposed is concerned, as I have already indicated the family have a strong connection with the Far East; there is a considerable likelihood that the children, when they grow up, may wish to live or make the basis of their careers in the Far East; and to have some proportion at least of the trust funds out of the United Kingdom in an appropriate but stable area may properly be considered to be to their advantage.

Accordingly I consider that there is no reason why the trustees should not take the view that the proposed transaction is for the benefit of the principal beneficiaries, and I will give the direction sought."[11]

vii.   VESTING OF THE PROPERTY IN THE TRUSTEES

TRUSTEE ACT 1925

40. Vesting of trust property in new or continuing trustees.— (1) Where by a deed a new trustee is appointed to perform any trust, then—

(a) if the deed contains a declaration by the appointor to the effect that any estate or interest in any land subject to the trust, or in any chattel so subject, or the right to recover or receive any debt or other thing in action so subject, shall vest in the persons who by virtue of the deed

---

11 See also *Re Beatty* (28 February, 1991, unreported), (VINELOTT J); The Offshore Tax Planning Review (1990/1991), vol. 1, Issue, pp. 1–2 (R. Bramwell QC); (1992) Capital Taxes and Estate Planning Quarterly, pp. 81–85 (G. Clarke), pointing out that neither of these cases concerns the appointment of non-resident trustees of an English trust, with exclusively United Kingdom resident beneficiaries. But, in spite of the strong language of CA in *Re Weston's Settlements* [1969] 1 Ch 223, [1968] 3 All ER 338, pp. 807 post, it is now "highly likely that such an appointment would be upheld as proper."

become or are the trustees for performing the trust, the deed shall operate, without any conveyance or assignment, to vest in those persons as joint tenants and for the purposes of the trust the estate interest or right to which the declaration relates; and

(*b*) if the deed is made after the commencement of this Act and does not contain such a declaration, the deed shall, subject to any express provision to the contrary therein contained, operate as if it had contained such a declaration by the appointor extending to all the estates interests and rights with respect to which a declaration could have been made.

(2) Where by a deed a retiring trustee is discharged under the statutory power without a new trustee being appointed, then—

(*a*) if the deed contains such a declaration as aforesaid by the retiring and continuing trustees, and by the other person, if any, empowered to appoint trustees, the deed shall, without any conveyance or assignment, operate to vest in the continuing trustees alone, as joint tenants, and for the purposes of the trust, the estate, interest, or right to which the declaration relates; and

(*b*) if the deed is made after the commencement of this Act and does not contain such a declaration, the deed shall, subject to any express provision to the contrary therein contained, operate as if it had contained such a declaration by such persons as aforesaid extending to all the estates, interests and rights with respect to which a declaration could have been made.

(3) An express vesting declaration, whether made before or after the commencement of this Act, shall, notwithstanding that the estate, interest or right to be vested is not expressly referred to, and provided that the other statutory requirements were or are complied with, operate and be deemed always to have operated (but without prejudice to any express provision to the contrary contained in the deed of appointment or discharge) to vest in the persons respectively referred to in subsections (1) and (2) of this section, as the case may require, such estate, interests and rights as are capable of being and ought to be vested in those persons.

(4) This section does not extend—

(*a*) to land conveyed by way of mortgage for securing money subject to the trust, except land conveyed on trust for securing debentures or debenture stock;

(*b*) to land held under a lease which contains any covenant, condition or agreement against assignment or disposing of the land without licence or consent, unless, prior to the execution of the deed containing expressly or impliedly the vesting declaration, the requisite licence or consent has been obtained, or unless, by virtue of any statute or rule of law, the vesting declaration, express or implied, would not operate as a breach of covenant or give rise to a forfeiture;

(*c*) to any share, stock, annuity or property which is only transferable in books kept by a company or other body, or in a manner directed by or under an Act of Parliament.[12]

In this subsection "lease" includes an underlease and an agreement for a lease or underlease.

(5) For purposes of registration of the deed in any registry, the person or persons making the declaration expressly or impliedly, shall be deemed the

12 See (1992) 142 NLJ 541 (M. Russell).

conveying party or parties, and the conveyance shall be deemed to be made by him or them under a power conferred by this Act.

(6) This section applies to deeds of appointment or discharge executed on or after the first day of January, eighteen hundred and eighty-two.

LAND REGISTRATION ACT 1925

47. Voting instruments and dispositions in name of proprietors.[13]—(1) The registrar shall give effect on the register to any vesting order or vesting declaration (express or implied) made on the appointment or discharge of a trustee or otherwise, and to dispositions made in the name and on behalf of a proprietor by a person authorised to make the disposition; and the provisions of the Trustee Act, 1925, relating to the appointment and discharge of trustees and the vesting of trust property, shall apply to registered land subject to the proper entry being made on the register.

(2) The registrar shall also give effect on the register in the prescribed manner to any vesting instrument which may be made pursuant to any statutory power.

B. Appointment by the Court

i. THE POWER TO APPOINT

TRUSTEE ACT 1925

41. Power of court to appoint new trustees.—(1) The court may, whenever it is expedient to appoint a new trustee or new trustees, and it is found inexpedient difficult or impracticable so to do without the assistance of the court,[14] make an order appointing a new trustee or new trustees either in substitution for or in addition to any existing trustee or trustees, or although there is no existing trustee.

In particular and without prejudice to the generality of the foregoing provision, the court may make an order appointing a new trustee in substitution for a trustee who is incapable, by reason of mental disorder within the meaning of the Mental Health Act 1983, of exercising his functions as trustee or is a bankrupt, or is a corporation which is in liquidation or has been dissolved.[15]

(4) Nothing in this section gives power to appoint an executor or administrator.

43. Powers of new trustee appointed by the court.—Every trustee appointed by a court of competent jurisdiction shall, as well before as after the trust property becomes by law, or by assurance, or otherwise, vested in him, have the same powers, authorities, and discretions, and may in all respects act as if he had

---

13 See Registered Land Practice Notes (2nd edn 1986), NI, pp. 51–52.
14 If the power of appointment given by TA 1925, s. 36, can be exercised, the court should not be asked to make an appointment: *Re Gibbon's Trusts* (1882) 30 WR 287; see also *Re May's Will Trusts* [1941] Ch 109.
15 As amended by Mental Health Act 1959, s. 149 (1), Sch. 7, Part I and Mental Health Act 1983, s. 148, Sch. 4, para. 4 (*b*).

been originally appointed a trustee by the instrument, if any, creating the trust.

ii. SELECTION OF TRUSTEES

RE TEMPEST
(1866) 1 Ch App 485 (CA in Ch, TURNER and KNIGHT-BRUCE LJJ)

A family settlement was created by the will of Sir Charles Robert Tempest, Bart., appointing the Hon. T.E. Stoner and Mr. J. Fleming as trustees. Mr. Stoner predeceased the testator. The persons to whom the power of appointing new trustees was given were unable to agree upon a selection. A petition was presented, asking the court to appoint the Hon. Edward Petre. One beneficiary opposed, on the ground that Mr. Petre was connected with, and proposed by, a branch of the family with which the testator was not on friendly terms, and which he had excluded from participation in the management of his property. The Master of the Rolls appointed Mr. Petre and Lord Camoys "hoping to satisfy both parties".

Held. Mr. Petre was not a person whom the Court would appoint.

TURNER LJ: There are two questions raised by this appeal. First, whether the order of the Master of the Rolls ought to be reversed in so far as it appoints Mr. *Petre* to be a trustee of the testator's will; and secondly, whether assuming that the order ought to be reversed in this respect, Lord *Camoys* ought to be appointed the trustee. The first of these questions has not seemed to me to be altogether free from difficulty, and in my view of this case it is by no means an unimportant question. It involves, as I think, to no inconsiderable extent the principles on which this Court ought to act in the appointment of new trustees.

It was said in argument, and has been frequently said, that in making such appointments the Court acts upon and exercises its discretion; and this, no doubt, is generally true; but the discretion which the Court has and exercises in making such appointments, is not, as I conceive, a mere arbitrary discretion, but a discretion in the exercise of which the Court is, and ought to be, guided by some general rules and principles, and, in my opinion, the difficulty which the Court has to encounter in these cases lies not so much in ascertaining the rules and principles by which it ought to be guided, as in applying those rules and principles to the varying circumstances of each particular case. The following rules and principles may, I think, safely be laid down as applying to all cases of appointments by the Court of new trustees.

First, the Court will have regard to the wishes of the persons by whom the trust has been created, if expressed in the instrument creating the trust, or clearly to be collected from it. I think this rule may be safely laid down, because if the author of the trust has in terms declared that a particular person, or a person filling a particular character, should not be a trustee of the instrument, there cannot, as I apprehend, be the least doubt that the Court would not appoint to the office a person whose appointment was so prohibited, and I do not think that upon a question of this description any distinction can be drawn between express declarations and demonstrated intention. The analogy of the course which the Court pursues in the appointment of guardians affords, I think, some support to this rule. The Court in those cases attends to the wishes of the parents, however informally they may be expressed.

Another rule which may, I think, safely be laid down is this—that the Court will not appoint a person to be trustee with a view to the interest of some of the persons interested under the trust, in opposition either to the wishes of the testator or to the interests of others of the *cestuis que trusts.* I think so for this reason, that it is of the essence of the duty of every trustee to hold an even hand between the parties interested under the trust. Every trustee is in duty bound to look to the interests of all, and not of any particular member or class of members of his *cestuis que trusts.*

A third rule which, I think, may safely be laid down is,—that the Court in appointing a trustee will have regard to the question, whether his appointment will promote or impede the execution of the trust, for the very purpose of the appointment is that the trust may be better carried into execution.

These are the principles by which, in my judgment, we ought to be guided in determining whether Mr. *Petre* ought to be appointed to be a trustee of this will, and, in my opinion, there are substantial objections to his appointment on each of the three grounds to which I have referred. There is not, of course, and cannot be, any possible objection to Mr. *Petre* in point of character, position, or ability, and I desire most anxiously to be understood as not intending, in disapproving his appointment, to cast the slightest possible reflection upon him. I have not for one moment doubted that he is a gentleman of most unexceptionable character, and well qualified in every respect to fill the office of trustee; but I think that the principles to which I have referred are opposed to his appointment.

First, as to the wishes of this testator, it is impossible, I think, to read this will without being fully satisfied that the great object and purpose of the testator was to exclude Mr. *Charles Henry Tempest* not only from all interest in, but from all connection with his estate. A more complete exclusion of him, both from any interest in and from any power over the estate, could not, as it seems to me, have been devised. Is it then consistent with this purpose of the testator that a trustee should be appointed who, upon the evidence before us, I cannot doubt is the nominee of Mr. *Charles Henry Tempest,* and is proposed for the purpose of carrying into effect his wishes and intentions? The facts, I think, prove that this is the position of Mr. *Petre.* He is proposed by Mr. *Washington Hibbert,* the father-in-law of Mr. *C.H. Tempest,* and the very person the connection with whom led to the making of this will, by which he was excluded. He is supported, and I desire not to be understood as saying, in any other than a legal sense, improperly, by Mr. *A.C. Tempest* his brother, who it appears upon the evidence declined to attend the testator's funeral on account of the dispositions of the will; and one of the principal witnesses in support of his appointment, and the person most active in these proceedings is Mr. *Broadbent,* the solicitor of Sir *C.H. Tempest,* under whose advice we find that Mr. *Petre* adopted that most unfortunate and, I must say, ill-advised step of declining to meet his co-trustees. Looking to all these circumstances, and to the whole of the evidence before us, I have as little doubt as to what led to the proposal of Mr. *Petre* as I have as to the intentions of this testator, and upon this ground, therefore, I think that Mr. *Petre* ought not to be appointed to be a trustee of this will.

It was said for the respondents, that the testator's dispositions were captious and absurd, and ought not therefore to be regarded, but much as we may regret that such dispositions were made, we cannot disregard them.

Then, as to the second ground, the objection to the appointment of Mr. *Petre* seems to me to be still more decisive. The evidence, in my opinion, very plainly shews that Mr. *Petre* has been proposed as a trustee, and has accepted that office, with a view to his acting in the trust in the interests of some only of the objects of it, and in opposition to the wishes of the testator, and not with a view to his acting as an independent trustee for the benefit of all the objects of the trusts, and I do not hesitate to say that, in my opinion, this fact is alone sufficient to prevent us from confirming his appointment. It was objected on the part of the respondents, that the proof of this fact rests upon evidence of what has occurred since the order under appeal was pronounced, and ought not, therefore, to be attended to; but this is a rehearing of the Petition under which Mr. *Petre* has been appointed. The question before us, therefore, is, whether he ought now to be appointed or not—a question of his present fitness or unfitness—and I am aware of no rule which precludes us from receiving upon such a question evidence of what has occurred since the original hearing. Supposing, however, that there was any difficulty upon that point, I apprehend there can be no doubt that the evidence of what has so occurred ought to be looked at as shewing the purpose for which he was proposed, and that it was not proper that he should be appointed at the time when the order appointing him was made.

It was also argued on the part of the respondents, that their interests ought to be considered in the appointment to be made by the Court, and there would have been great force in this argument, if it could have been considered that Mr. *Petre* was proposed as an independent trustee to act on behalf of, and with a view to, the interests of all the *cestui que trusts*; but when the purpose for which he is proposed is seen, this argument loses all weight and cannot be attended to. It is the appointment of a trustee for the benefit of all, and not with a view to the interests of some, that the wishes of *cestui que trusts* are to be consulted, for the trustee to be appointed must represent and consult the interests of all, and not of some only of the *cestui que trusts*. It was indeed with this view, that in the course of the argument I suggested to the parties the expediency of their agreeing upon the appointment of an independent trustee.

The third and remaining ground of objection to the appointment of Mr. *Petre* is, I think, open to more difficulty. On the one hand, there cannot, I think, be any doubt that the Court ought not to appoint a trustee whose appointment will impede the due execution of the trust; but, on the other hand, if the continuing or surviving trustee refuses to act with a trustee who may be proposed to be appointed — and I make this observation with reference to what appears to have been said by Mr. *Fleming*, as to Mr. *Petre* having come forward in opposition to his wishes—I think it would be going too far to say that the Court ought, on that ground alone, to refuse to appoint the proposed trustee; for this would, as suggested in the argument, be to give the continuing or surviving trustee a veto upon the appointment of the new trustee. In such a case, I think it must be the duty of the Court to inquire and ascertain whether the objection of the surviving or continuing trustee is well founded or not, and to act or refuse to act upon it accordingly. If the surviving or continuing trustee has improperly refused to act with the proposed trustee, it might be a ground for removing him from the trust. Upon the facts of this case, however, it seems to me that the objections taken by Mr. *Fleming* to the appointment of Mr. *Petre* were and are well founded, and upon the whole case, therefore, my opinion is, that the order under appeal, so far as it appoints Mr. *Petre*, ought to be discharged. . . .

The order upon this appeal should, I think, be to discharge the order at the Rolls, to appoint Lord *Camoys* to be the trustee in the place of Mr. *Stonor*, and to vest the estate in him and Mr. *Fleming*.

iii. VESTING ORDERS

TRUSTEE ACT 1925

44. Vesting orders of land.—In any of the following cases, namely:—
  (i) Where the court appoints or has appointed a trustee, or where a trustee has been appointed out of court under any statutory or express power;
  (ii) Where a trustee entitled to or possessed of any land or interest therein, whether by way of mortgage or otherwise, or entitled to a contingent right therein, either solely or jointly with any other person—
    (*a*) is under disability; or
    (*b*) is out of the jurisdiction of the High Court; or
    (*c*) cannot be found, or being a corporation, has been dissolved;
  (iii) Where it is uncertain who was the survivor of two or more trustees jointly entitled to or possessed of any interest in land;
  (iv) Where it is uncertain whether the last trustee known to have been entitled to or possessed of any interest in land is living or dead;
  (v) Where there is no personal representative of a deceased trustee who was entitled to or possessed of any interest in land, or where it is uncertain who is the personal representative of a deceased trustee who was entitled to or possessed of any interest in land;
  (vi) Where a trustee jointly or solely entitled to or possessed of any interest in land, or entitled to a contingent right therein, has been required, by or on behalf of a person entitled to require a conveyance of the land or interest or a release of the right, to convey the land or interest or to release the right, and has wilfully[16] refused or neglected to convey the land or interest or release the right for twenty-eight days after the date of the requirement;
  (vii) Where land or any interest therein is vested in a trustee whether by way of mortgage or otherwise, and it appears to the court to be expedient;
the court may make an order (in this Act called a vesting order) vesting the land or interest therein in any such person in any such manner and for any such estate or interest as the court may direct, or releasing or disposing of the contingent right to such person as the court may direct:
  Provided that—
    (*a*) Where the order is consequential on the appointment of a trustee the land or interest therein shall be vested for such estate as the court may direct in the persons who on the appointment are the trustees; and
    (*b*) Where the order relates to a trustee entitled or formerly entitled jointly with another person, and such trustee is under disability or out of the jurisdiction of the High Court or cannot be found, or being a corporation has been dissolved, the land interest or right shall be vested

---

16 Law Reform Committee 23rd Report (The Powers and Duties of Trustees) 1982 Cmnd 8733, paras. 5–8, recommends the removal of the word "wilfully"; cf. TA 1925, s. 51 (1) (ii) (*d*).

in such other person who remains entitled, either alone or with any other person the court may appoint.[17]

III. Retirement[18]

TRUSTEE ACT 1925

39. Retirement of trustee without a new appointment.—(1) Where a trustee is desirous of being discharged from the trust, and after his discharge there will be either a trust corporation or at least two individuals[19] to act as trustees to perform the trust, then, if such trustee as aforesaid by deed declares that he is desirous of being discharged from the trust, and if his co-trustees and such other person, if any, as is empowered to appoint trustees, by deed consent to the discharge of the trustee, and to the vesting in the co-trustees alone of the trust property, the trustee desirous of being discharged shall be deemed to have retired from the trust, and shall, by the deed, be discharged therefrom under this Act, without any new trustee being appointed in his place.[20]

(2) Any assurance or thing requisite for vesting the trust property in the continuing trustees alone shall be executed or done.

A trustee who retires, whether by replacement under s. 36 or under this section should seek from the beneficiaries a formal discharge from liability. Even without this, he will incur no liability in respect of future breaches of trust, unless he resigned in order to facilitate a breach.[1]

The Law Reform Committee 23rd Report (The Powers and Duties of Trustees) 1982 Cmnd 8733, para. 9.1. VII.43, recommends, however, that
"43. Both executors and administrators should be able to retire:—
  (i) where the demands of the office are such as to impose unreasonable and unforeseen burdens; and
 (ii) where the personal representative is suffering from serious supervening ill health.
with, in each case, the leave of the court. (paragraphs 7.2–7.3)"

---

17 For further provisions relating to orders made by the court, see also ss. 45–56 and MHA 1959, s. 141 (1), Sch. 7, and MHA 1983, s. 148, Sch. 4, para. 4 (c), (d), replacing TA 1925, s. 54.
18 H & M, pp. 492–493; K & S, pp. 258–260; P & M, pp. 377–379; Pettit, pp. 341–345; Riddall, p. 257; Snell, pp. 211–213; Underhill, pp. 724–728.
19 A sole trustee other than a trust corporation does not suffice, even if he has power to give a valid receipt for capital money: (1986) 1 TL & P 16 (M. Jacobs). See also (1987) 2 TL & P 43 (J. Hayes); (1990) 106 LQR 87 at 94 (D. Hayton).
20 It is unlikely that these conditions can be avoided by the terms of the settlement: (1986) 1 TL & P 95 (M. Jacobs); *Mettoy Pension Trustees Ltd v Evans* [1990] 1 WLR 1587, [1991] 2 All ER 513.
1 *Head v Gould* [1898] 2 Ch 250 at 272, p. 875, post.

IV. Removal[2]

TRUSTEE ACT 1925

36. Power of appointing new or additional trustees: see p. 616, ante.
41. Power of court to appoint new trustees: see p. 624, ante.

In **Letterstedt v Broers** (1884) 9 App Cas 371, the Privy Council had to consider whether, independently of statute, it should remove the Board of Executors of Cape Town, the sole surviving executors and trustees of the will of Jacob Letterstedt, against whom the appellant, a beneficiary, made allegations of misconduct in the administration of the trust. The Board was removed; but the allegations were not substantiated, and no costs were awarded. Lord BLACKBURN described at 385 the principles upon which the court's discretion should be exercised:

"The whole case has been argued here, and, as far as their Lordships can perceive, in the Court below, as depending on the principles which should guide an English Court of Equity when called upon to remove old trustees and substitute new ones. It is not disputed that there is a jurisdiction 'in cases requiring such a remedy,' as is said in *Story's Equity Jurisprudence*, s. 1287, but there is very little to be found to guide us in saying what are the cases requiring such a remedy; so little that their Lordships are compelled to have recourse to general principles.

Story says, s. 1289, 'But in cases of positive misconduct, Courts of Equity have no difficulty in interposing to remove trustees who have abused their trust; it is not indeed every mistake or neglect of duty, or inaccuracy of conduct of trustees, which will induce Courts of Equity to adopt such a course. But the acts or omissions must be such as to endanger the trust property or to shew a want of honesty, or a want of proper capacity to execute the duties, or a want of reasonable fidelity.'

It seems to their Lordships that the jurisdiction which a Court of Equity has no difficulty in exercising under the circumstances indicated by Story is merely ancillary to its principal duty, to see that the trusts are properly executed. This duty is constantly being performed by the substitution of new trustees in the place of original trustees for a variety of reasons in non-contentious cases. And therefore, though it should appear that the charges of misconduct were either not made out, or were greatly exaggerated, so that the trustee was justified in resisting them, and the Court might consider that in awarding costs, yet if satisfied that the continuance of the trustee would prevent the trusts being properly executed, the trustee might be removed. It must always be borne in mind that trustees exist for the benefit of those to whom the creator of the trust has given the trust estate.

The reason why there is so little to be found in the books on this subject is probably that suggested by Mr. Davey in his argument. As soon as all questions

---

2 H & M, pp. 493–494; K & S, pp. 258–260; P & M, pp. 379–380; Pettit, pp. 344–345; Riddall, pp. 239–240; Snell, p. 212; Underhill, pp. 728–729. On removal of executors, see *Re Clore* [1982] Ch 456, [1982] 3 All ER 419. Under AJA 1985, s. 50, the High Court has power to appoint a substitute for, or to remove, a personal representative: *Practice Direction* [1948] WN 273 (evidence on removal of trustee under disability).

of character are as far settled as the nature of the case admits, if it appears clear that the continuance of the trustee would be detrimental to the execution of the trusts, even if for no other reason than that human infirmity would prevent those beneficially interested, or those who act for them, from working in harmony with the trustee, and if there is no reason to the contrary from the intentions of the framer of the trust to give this trustee a benefit or otherwise, the trustee is always advised by his own counsel to resign, and does so. If, without any reasonable ground, he refused to do so, it seems to their Lordships that the Court might think it proper to remove him; but cases involving the necessity of deciding this, if they ever arise, do so without getting reported. It is to be lamented that the case was not considered in this light by the parties in the Court below, for, as far as their Lordships can see, the Board would have little or no profit from continuing to be trustees, and as such coming into continual conflict with the appellant and her legal advisers, and would probably have been glad to resign, and get out of an onerous and disagreeable position. But the case was not so treated.

In exercising so delicate a jurisdiction as that of removing trustees, their Lordships do not venture to lay down any general rule beyond the very broad principle above enunciated, that their main guide must be the welfare of the beneficiaries. Probably it is not possible to lay down any more definite rule in a matter so essentially dependent on details often of great nicety. But they proceed to look carefully into the circumstances of the case ...

It is quite true that friction or hostility between trustees and the immediate possessor of the trust estate is not of itself a reason for the removal of the trustees. But where the hostility is grounded on the mode in which the trust has been administered, where it has been caused wholly or partially by substantial overcharges against the trust estate, it is certainly not to be disregarded.

Looking therefore at the whole circumstances of this very peculiar case, the complete change of position, the unfortunate hostility that has arisen, and the difficult and delicate duties that may yet have to be performed, their Lordships can come to no other conclusion than that it is necessary, for the welfare of the beneficiaries, that the Board should no longer be trustees.

Probably if it had been put in this way below they would have consented. But for the benefit of the trust they should cease to be trustees, whether they consent or not.

Their Lordships think therefore that the portion of the final judgment which is, 'That the prayer for removal of the executors be refused,' should be reversed, and that in lieu of it the Court below should be directed to remove the Board from the further execution of the trusts created by the will, and to take all necessary and proper proceedings for the appointment of other and proper persons to execute such trusts in future, and to transfer to them the trust property in so far as it remains vested in the Board. The rest of the judgment should stand.''[3]

---

3 See *Chellaram v Chellaram* [1985] Ch 409, [1985] 1 All ER 1043, where the court had jurisdiction to administer a foreign trust even where the trust funds were outside the jurisdiction, and had power to remove the trustees and appoint new trustees by orders in personam against the existing trustees requiring them to resign and to vest the trust funds in the new trustees; (1986) 102 LQR 28 (D. Evans); [1985] All ER Rev 62 (J.G. Collier). See Recognition of Trusts Act 1987, Sch. 1, art. 8, p. 50 ante.

In **Re Wrightson** [1908] 1 Ch 789, the trustees had been guilty of a breach of trust, in connection with an advance of a part of the trust funds upon mortgage. In an administration action, one question was whether the trustees should be removed. WARRINGTON J said at 800:

"The next question is, Ought I to make an order for the removal of the trustees upon the materials which were before the Court at the trial, which, in my judgment, are the only materials at which I can look? That raises a somewhat troublesome question. The trustees admitted that they were guilty of a breach of trust. The statement to which I have already referred, together with the proposals of the trustees, was remarked upon in strong language by the judge at the trial, and I desire to associate myself with the remarks which he made without further explanation that that statement is one which the trustees ought not to have made, and I think that the learned judge intended that an application for the removal of the trustees founded on that statement should prima facie be one which would at all events receive the favourable attention of the Court. But I have now before me not only the plaintiffs, but other beneficiaries representing somewhere about one-half of the estate. The plaintiffs' interest, if you are to count heads, predominates to some extent, but I have a very substantial proportion of the beneficiaries who object to the removal of the trustees, and who say there is no ground for it. Now, what are the grounds on which the Court removes trustees? The only case that I can find which helps one at all in this matter is the case of *Letterstedt v Broers* (1884) 9 App Cas 371, in the Privy Council. There some very valuable remarks were made by Lord Blackburn, who delivered the judgment of the Judicial Committee at 385. [His Lordship quoted from the extract on p. 630, ante, and continued:] And then [Lord Blackburn] thus sums up what he regards as expressing the general principle guiding the Court in these cases at 387: 'In exercising so delicate a jurisdiction as that of removing trustees, their Lordships do not venture to lay down any general rule beyond the very broad principle enunciated, that their main guide must be the welfare of the beneficiaries. Probably it is not possible to lay down any more definite rule in a matter so essentially dependent on details often of great nicety. But they proceed to look carefully into the circumstances of the case.' Is it necessary here, having regard to the welfare of the beneficiaries and for the protection of this trust, to remove the trustees? At the present moment nothing remains for the trustees to do except to wind up the estate; the testator's widow is dead; the whole of the estate is divisible amongst a number of persons who are sui juris. But the summons was taken out on February 27, 1906, two years ago, at a time when the widow was alive and the estate was not immediately divisible, and therefore I must, with a view at any rate of dealing with the costs, look at the state of things as they existed at the date when the summons was issued. Is it necessary for the welfare of the trust now to remove the trustees on the grounds alleged in the statement of claim? There is one contention on the part of the plaintiffs to which I think I ought to refer. Mr. Cave as one argument, or as one reason for the removal of the trustees, said, in effect, 'We do not like to have these persons who have been charged with a breach of trust and have admitted it, and who have made that statement which is set out in the pleadings, in custody of our trust estate.' That is not enough, especially when there are other cestuis que trust entitled. A somewhat similar question arose in the case of *Forster v Davies* (1861) 4 De G F & J 133 at 139, in which Turner LJ expressed the view, which I have just expressed, that disagreement between the cestuis que trust and the trustees, or the disinclination on the part of the cestuis que trust to have the trust property remain in the hands of a particular individual, is not a sufficient ground for the removal of the trustees. You must find something which induces the court to think either that the trust property will not be safe, or that the trust will not be properly executed in the interests of the beneficiaries. Is that so here, and is it for the welfare of the trust generally, and not merely of the plaintiffs, that these trustees should be removed? I think it is not. The trustees were undoubtedly guilty of a breach of trust, and they undoubtedly in the statement to which I have referred expressed views which have occasioned the blame which has been attached to the trustees both by Buckley J and myself, but, having regard to the fact that the Court has now the power of seeing that the trust is properly executed, to the fact that a large proportion of the beneficiaries do not require the trustees to be removed, and further (and this is of great importance), to the extra expense and loss to the trust estate which must be occasioned by the change of trustees, I think it would not be for the welfare of the cestuis que trust generally, or necessary for the protection of the trust estate, that these trustees should be removed. I must therefore refuse the application for their removal as well as the application for the further accounts and inquiries.''

In **Moore v M'Glynn** [1894] 1 IR 74, William M'Glynn appointed his brother Edward and his son Patrick as trustees of his estate for the benefit of his widow and children. After his death, Edward managed the testator's business of shopkeeper and local postmaster. Subsequently Edward was appointed postmaster, and later started his own business which was similar to that of the trust. CHATTERTON V-C held that Edward had committed no breach of trust; but that the conflict required that he should be discharged from his office as trustee.[4]

CHARITIES ACT 1993

18. Power to act for protection of Charities.—(2)(b)(i) p. 537, ante.

Report of the Charity Commissioners for England and Wales for the year 1976, paras. 25–29.

''*Sanctuary*
25. In paragraphs 90 to 96 of our report for 1971 we mentioned that, following an inquiry and report under section 6 of the Charities Act 1960, we had made an order removing Mr. Robert Jones and his sister from being trustees of the charity called Sanctuary, that Mr. Jones' appeal to the High Court against our order had been dismissed by Mr. Justice Ungoed-Thomas

---

4 *Re Edwards' Will Trusts* [1982] Ch 30, [1981] 2 All ER 941, where BUCKLEY LJ, in upholding removal of a trustee, said at 42, at 950: "such an order should only be made on cogent grounds, but the jurisdiction is undoubtedly discretionary"; *Clarke v Heathfield* [1985] ICR 203; *Clarke v Heathfield (No 2)* [1985] ICR 606, where, in an interlocutory application, an order was made to remove the three trustees of the National Union of Mineworkers "who were in flagrant breach of an order of the High Court" and to appoint a receiver.

and that Mr. Jones was appealing to the Court of Appeal. In 1973 the Court of Appeal resolved that the case should be remitted for a rehearing in the Court of first instance on the grounds that the Judge might have attributed too little weight to the appellant's affidavit evidence in which he sought to challenge some of the findings in the report of the inquiry. The Court of Appeal held that it was for an appellant who appeals against such an order to show that it had been wrongly made, but the report of the inquiry, to the extent that it was not challenged by him, should be treated as evidence in the appeal (*Jones v A-G* [1974] Ch 148, [1973] 3 All ER 518).

26. The rehearing took place before Mr. Justice Brightman, and Mr. Jones application was dismissed. In his Judgment dated the 9th November 1976 the Judge noted that out of a sum exceeding £10,000 collected from the public over a period of some three years not one penny was ever spent on any charitable purpose; that collecting boxes left in public places were frequently abandoned because it was uneconomic to collect them; that most of the personal collectors for the charity, but not Mr. Jones himself, received a percentage remuneration sometimes as high as 35 per cent, and probably even as high as 50 per cent; and that the administrative expenses of the charity were so high that between January 1970 and May 1971 only 11 pennies out of each pound remained available for charitable purposes.

27. The Judge commented on the fact that during the three years that Mr Jones ran the charity he was living on social security and had indicated that he would probably have tried to stay on social security for the rest of his life so as to carry on the charity. The Judge found it disturbing that a person could draw public funds for his maintenance while engaged in charitable activities selected by himself.

28. Another point which troubled Mr Justice Brightman was the legality of commissions charged by people who took round charity collecting boxes. A collecting box which named a charity as the recipient of a donation represented that money placed in the box went to the charity, and if the collector retained commission this was contrary to the representation on the collecting box and to the belief of most contributors. Furthermore, a person who solicited money for a charity was a trustee of the contribution and unless he made it known to the donor that he intended to retain a percentage of the contribution for himself it seemed to the Judge that he had no title to that percentage.

29. The Judge also referred to the use of deceptive labels and letter headings, failure to check the credentials of area organisers, an untruthful application for a licence under the House to House Collections Act, a failure to maintain proper books of account over part of the period, misuse of charity money, and lack of security in regard to the issue and sealing of collecting boxes. In his judgment there was overwhelming evidence to support the allegations of misconduct and mismanagement which had been made against Mr. Jones, and he found the allegations proved. In his judgment it was out of the question to set aside our order removing Mr. Jones from the trusteeship of Sanctuary."[5]

---

5 CA upheld the decision of BRIGHTMAN J as "wholly unassailable": Annual Report for 1977 paras. 31–33.

v. Particular Trustees[6]

A. Judicial Trustees

JUDICIAL TRUSTEES ACT 1896

1. Power of court on application to appoint judicial trustee.—(1) Where application is made to the court by or on behalf of the person creating or intending to create a trust, or by or on behalf of a trustee or beneficiary, the court may, in its discretion, appoint a person (in this Act called a judicial trustee) to be a trustee of that trust, either jointly with any other person or as sole trustee, and, if sufficient cause is shown, in place of all or any existing trustees.

(2) The administration of the property of a deceased person, whether a testator or intestate, shall be a trust, and the executor or administrator a trustee, within the meaning of this Act.

(3) Any fit and proper person nominated for the purpose in the application may be appointed a judicial trustee, and, in the absence of such nomination, or if the court is not satisfied of the fitness of a person so nominated, an official of the court may be appointed, and in any case a judicial trustee shall be subject to the control and supervision of the court as an officer thereof.

(4) The court may, either on request or without request, give to a judicial trustee any general or special directions in regard to the trust or the administration thereof.

(5) There may be paid to a judicial trustee out of the trust property such remuneration, not exceeding the prescribed limits, as the court may assign in each case, subject to any rules under this Act respecting the application of such remuneration where the judicial trustee is an official of the court, and the remuneration so assigned to any judicial trustee shall, save as the court may for special reasons otherwise order, cover all his work and personal outlay.

(6) In any case where the court shall so direct, an inquiry into the administration by a judicial trustee of any trust, or into any dealing or transaction of a judicial trustee, shall be made in the prescribed manner.[7]

(7) Where an application relating to the estate of a deceased person is made to the court under this section, the court may, if it thinks fit, proceed as if the application were, or included an application under section 50 of the Administration of Justice Act 1985 (power of High Court to appoint substitute for, or to remove, personal representative).[8]

---

6 H & M, pp. 208–210; K & S, pp. 66–76; P & M, pp. 361–363; Pettit, pp. 346–354; Riddall, p. 246; Snell, pp. 208–210; Underhill, pp. 762–780. See also Keeton, *Modern Developments of the Law of Trusts* (1971) pp. 16–27.

7 As amended by AJA 1982, s. 57 (1). On the auditing of accounts, see Judicial Trustees Act 1896, s. 4 (1), paras. 11 and 12, as added by AJA 1982, s. 57 (2) and Judicial Trustee Rules 1983 (S.I. 1983, No. 370).
   A new category of corporate trustee was created by r. 2, for whose accounts separate provision is made, and exemption granted from automatic audit by the court; r. 13. A corporate trustee "means the Official Solicitor, the Public Trustee, or a corporation either appointed by the Court in any particular case to be a trustee or entitled by rules made under section 4 (3) of the Public Trustee Act 1906 to act as custodian trustee." Cf the definition of a trust corporation, p. 646, post.

8 As added by AJA 1985, s. 50 (6).

In **Re Ridsdel** [1947] Ch 597, [1947] 2 All ER 312, the question arose whether r. 12 of the Judicial Trustee Rules 1897,[9] under which the judicial trustee may at any time request the court to give him directions as to the trust or its administration, by implication deprived him of the power of compromise under s. 15 of the Trustee Act 1925. JENKINS J held that it did not, and said at 605, at 316:

"I cannot think that that is the effect of this rule. After all, the object of the Judicial Trustees Act 1896, as I understand it, was to provide a middle course in cases where the administration of the estate by the ordinary trustees had broken down and it was not desired to put the estate to the expense of a full administration. In those circumstances, a solution was found in the appointment of a judicial trustee, who acts in close concert with the court and under conditions enabling the court to supervise his transactions. I cannot think that it was intended to complicate the matter by prohibiting such a trustee from exercising any discretion without first going to the court and asking for directions. That, as Mr. Stamp points out, involves this, that whenever the trustee wanted to exercise some discretion, such as the power of compromise under s. 15 of the Trustee Act 1925, he would perforce have to come to the court for directions; but (to give only one instance) the court would give no directions without summoning before it all persons interested in the exercise of the discretion in order that the matter might be argued and decided in the presence of all parties. One would thus reduce the administration of an estate by a judicial trustee to very much the same position as where an estate is being administered by the court and every step has to be taken in pursuance of the court's directions. It does not seem to me to be right or necessary to construe the Judicial Trustee Rules 1897, as having any such effect."

B. The Public Trustee

Public Trust Office Annual Report 1988–1989, paras. 1.1–1.3, 2.1–2.2.

"1.1 The Office of Public Trustee was created by the Public Trustee Act 1906. The functions were increased by the Public Trustee and Administration of Funds Act 1986 and by the appointment of the Public Trustee as Accountant General of the Supreme Court. The organisation was constituted in its present form on 2 January 1987 with the title of the 'Public Trust Office'.[10]
1.2. The main functions of the Office are:
(a) The administration of estates and trusts under the Public Trustee Act 1906; the aim is to provide the services of an experienced and reliable executor or trustee particularly in situations where a commerical or private trustee cannot be found to act.
(b) The protection of the property and affairs of mentally incapable persons under Part VII of the Mental Health Act 1983 (in this work there are close links with the Court of Protection).

---

9 See now Judicial Trustee Rules 1983, r. 8, S.I. 1983 No. 370.
10 The Public Trust Office is known as Stewart House in memory of the first Public Trustee, and is located at 24 Kingsway, London, W.C.2. For an outline of the history of the Public Trust Office from 1907 to 1986, see 78th Annual Report of the Public Trustee, Appendix.

(c) The management as Receiver of the property and affairs of mentally incapable persons for whom there is no other suitable Receiver.[11]

(d) The administration of Funds in Court as Accountant General; this includes administering awards of damages on behalf of minors pending their attainment of their majority and accounting for litigation monies paid into Court in satisfaction of a claim or by order of Court.

1.3 This work is carried out respectively in the Trust, Protection, and Receivership Divisions and in the Court Funds Office.[12] These casework areas have the support of an Investment Division and an Internal Services Sector which deals with common services.

2.1 The Trust Division aims to provide an efficient and cost effective executor and trustee service in cases where the testator or settlor seeks to invoke the provisions of the Public Trustee Act 1906 and the Public Trustee, in line with current policy, considers it appropriate that he should act.

2.2 The Public Trustee may act as an ordinary trustee alone or with others, as a custodian trustee, or as executor or administrator of an estate. He frequently acts as a trustee of last resort. The Public Trustee may not accept a trust which is exclusively charitable or for the benefit of creditors or a foreign trust or an insolvent estate. The Public Trustee may decline to accept a trust but not on the ground only of the small value of the trust property.''

PUBLIC TRUSTEE ACT 1906

1. Office of public trustee.—(1) There shall be established the office of public trustee.

(2) The public trustee shall be a corporation sole under that name, with perpetual succession and an official seal, and may sue and be sued under the above name like any other corporation sole, but any instruments sealed by him shall not, by reason of his using a seal, be rendered liable to a higher stamp duty than if he were an individual.

2. General powers and duties of public trustee.—(1) Subject to and in accordance with the provisions of this Act and rules made thereunder, the public trustee may, if he thinks fit—

(*a*) act in the administration of estates of small value;

(*b*) act as custodian trustee;

(*c*) act as an ordinary trustee;

(*d*) be appointed to be a judicial trustee; ...

(2) Subject to the provisions of this Act, and to the rules made thereunder, the public trustee may act either alone or jointly with any person or body of persons in any capacity to which he may be appointed in pursuance of this Act, and shall have all the same powers, duties, and liabilities, and be entitled to the same rights and immunities and be subject to the control and orders of the court, as a private trustee acting in the same capacity.

11 Practice Direction (Mental Health: Public Trustee) [1987] 1 WLR 63, [1987] 1 All ER 403.

12 In 1994–95 caseload under Mental Health Act 1983 was 30,100; references lodged under Enduring Powers of Attorney Act were 6,820; receivership caseload was 2,880; trusts and estates under administration were 2,374 (approximate value £500 million); and court funds lodgements 57,155 (approximate value £1.1 billion): Annual Report of Trust Office 1994–95, pp. 16–20.

(3) The public trustee may decline, either absolutely or except on the prescribed conditions, to accept any trust, but he shall not decline to accept any trust on the ground only of the small value of the trust property.

(4) The public trustee shall not accept any trust which involves the management or carrying on of any business, except in the cases in which he may be authorised to do so by rules made under this Act, nor any trust under a deed of arrangement for the benefit of creditors, nor the administration of any estate known or believed by him to be insolvent.

(5) The public trustee shall not accept any trust exclusively for religious or charitable purposes,[13] and nothing in this Act contained, or in the rules to be made under the powers in this Act contained, shall abridge or affect the powers or duties of the official trustee of charity lands or official trustees of charitable funds.[14]

(1) In the Administration of Small Estates

3. Administration of small estates.—(1) Any person who in the opinion of the public trustee would be entitled to apply to the court for an order for the administration by the court of an estate, the gross capital value whereof is proved to the satisfaction of the public trustee to be less than one thousand pounds, may apply to the public trustee to administer the estate, and, where any such application is made and it appears to the public trustee that the persons beneficially entitled are persons of small means, the public trustee shall administer the estate, unless he sees good reason for refusing to do so.

(2) On the public trustee undertaking, by declaration in writing signed and sealed by him, to administer the estate the trust property other than stock shall, by virtue of this Act, vest in him, and the right to transfer or call for the transfer of any stock forming part of the estate shall also vest in him, in like manner as if vesting orders had been made for the purpose by the High Court under the Trustee Act 1893,[15] and that Act shall apply accordingly. As from such vesting any trustee entitled under the trust to administer the estate shall be discharged from all liability attaching to the administration, except in respect of past acts:

. . .

(5) Where proceedings have been instituted in any court for the administration of an estate, and by reason of the small value of the estate it appears to the court that the estate can be more economically administered by the public trustee than by the court, or that for any other reason it is expedient that the estate should be administered by the public trustee instead of the court, the court may order that the estate shall be administered by the public trustee, and thereupon (subject to any directions by the court) this section shall apply as if the administration of the estate had been undertaken by the public trustee in pursuance of this section.

(2) As Custodian Trustee

4. Custodian trustee.—(1) Subject to rules[16] under this Act the public trustee may, if he consents to act as such, and whether or not the number of trustees

---

13 The Public Trustee accepted the trusts of the will of George Bernard Shaw under which he left the residue of his estate to be applied to the reform of the alphabet: *Re Shaw* [1957] 1 WLR 729, [1957] 1 All ER 745, p. 317, ante. HARMAN J held that the gift was not charitable.
14 Now the Official Custodian for Charities.
15 Now TA 1925.
16 Public Trustee Rules 1912, rr. 6–11 (r. 10 as amended by S.R.&O. 1916 No. 489).

has been reduced below the original number, be appointed to be custodian trustee of any trust—

(*a*) by order of the court made on the application of any person on whose application the court may order the appointment of a new trustee; or

(*b*) by the testator, settlor, or other creator of any trust; or

(*c*) by the person having power to appoint new trustees.

(2) Where the public trustee is appointed to be custodian trustee of any trust—

(*a*) The trust property shall be transferred to the custodian trustee as if he were sole trustee, and for that purpose vesting orders may, where necessary, be made under the Trustee Act 1893:[17]

(*b*) The management of the trust property and the exercise of any power or discretion exercisable by the trustees under the trust shall remain vested in the trustees other than the custodian trustee (which trustees are hereinafter referred to as the managing trustees):

(*c*) As between the custodian trustee and the managing trustees, and subject and without prejudice to the rights of any other persons, the custodian trustee shall have the custody of all securities and documents of title relating to the trust property, but the managing trustee shall have free access thereto and be entitled to take copies thereof or extracts therefrom:

(*d*) The custodian trustee shall concur in and perform all acts necessary to enable the managing trustees to exercise their powers of management or any other power or discretion vested in them (including the power to pay money or securities into court), unless the matter in which he is requested to concur is a breach of trust, or involves a personal liability upon him in respect of calls or otherwise, but, unless he so concurs, the custodian trustee shall not be liable for any act or default on the part of the managing trustees or any of them:

(*e*) All sums payable to or out of the income or capital of the trust property shall be paid to or by the custodian trustee: Provided that the custodian trustee may allow the dividends and other income derived from the trust property to be paid to the managing trustees or to such persons as they direct, or into such bank to the credit of such person as they may direct, and in such case shall be exonerated from seeing to the application thereof and shall not be answerable for any loss or misapplication thereof:

(*f*) The power of appointing new trustees, when exercisable by the trustees, shall be exercisable by the managing trustees alone, but the custodian trustee shall have the same power of applying to the court for the appointment of a new trustee as any other trustee:

(*g*) In determining the number of trustees for the purposes of the Trustee Act 1893,[18] the custodian trustee shall not be reckoned as a trustee.

(*h*) The custodian trustee, if he acts in good faith, shall not be liable for accepting as correct and acting upon the faith of any written statement by the managing trustees as to any birth, death, marriage, or other matter of pedigree or relationship, or other matter of fact, upon which the title to the trust property or any part thereof may depend, nor for

17 Now TA 1925.
18 Now TA 1925.

acting upon any legal advice obtained by the managing trustees independently of the custodian trustee:

(*i*) The court may, on the application of either the custodian trustee, or any of the managing trustees, or of any beneficiary, and on proof to their satisfaction that it is the general wish of the beneficiaries, or that on other grounds it is expedient, to terminate the custodian trusteeship, make an order for that purpose, and the court may thereupon make such vesting orders and give such directions as under the circumstances may seem to the court to be necessary or expedient.

(3) The provisions of this section shall apply in like manner as to the public trustee to any banking or insurance company or other body corporate entitled by rules made under this Act to act as custodian trustee,[19] with power for such company or body corporate to charge and retain or pay out of the trust property fees not exceeding the fees chargeable by the public trustee as custodian trustee.

(3) *As an Ordinary Trustee*

5. Appointment of public trustee to be trustee, executor, &c.—(1) The public trustee may by that name, or any other sufficient description, be appointed to be trustee of any will or settlement or other instrument creating a trust or to perform any trust or duty belonging to a class which he is authorised by the rules made under this Act to accept, and may be so appointed whether the will or settlement or instrument creating the trust or duty was made or came into operation before or after the passing of this Act, and either as an original or as a new trustee, or as an additional trustee, in the same cases, and in the same manner, and by the same persons or court, as if he were a private trustee, with this addition, that, though the trustees originally appointed were two or more, the public trustee may be appointed sole trustee.[20]

(2) Where the public trustee has been appointed a trustee of any trust, a co-trustee may retire from the trust under and in accordance with section eleven of the Trustee Act 1893,[21] notwithstanding that there are not more than two trustees, and without such consents as are required by that section.

(3) The public trustee shall not be appointed either as a new or additional trustee where the will, settlement, or other instrument creating the trust or duty contains a direction to the contrary, unless the court otherwise order.

7. Liability of Consolidated Fund.—(1) The Consolidated Fund of the United Kingdom shall be liable to make good all sums required to discharge any liability which the public trustee, if he were a private trustee, would be personally liable to discharge, except where the liability is one to which neither the public trustee nor any of his officers has in any way contributed, and which neither he nor any of his officers could by the exercise of reasonable diligence have averted, and in that case the public trustee shall not, nor shall the Consolidated Fund, be subject to any liability.

---

19 Section 14; Public Trustee Rules 1912, r. 30, as substituted by the Public Trustee (Custodian Trustee) Rules 1975, S.I. 1975, No. 1189, p. 641, post.

20 *Re Moxon* [1916] 2 Ch 595; *Re Duxbury's Settlement Trusts* [1995] 1 WLR 425, [1995] 3 All ER 145 (appointment as sole trustee of discretionary settlement valid, in spite of express clause prohibiting exercise of trustees' powers by fewer than two trustees).

21 Now TA 1925, s. 39, p. 629, ante.

9. Fees charged by public trustee.—(1) There shall be charged in respect of the duties of the public trustee such fees, whether by way of percentage or otherwise, as the Treasury with the sanction of the Lord Chancellor may fix, and such fees shall be collected and accounted for by such persons, and in such manner, and shall be paid to such account, as the Treasury direct.[1]

10. Appeal to the court.—(1) A person aggrieved by any act or omission or decision of the public trustee in relation to any trust may apply to the court, and the court may make such order in the matter as the court thinks just.

(2) Subject to rules of court, an application under this section to the High Court shall be made to a judge of the Chancery Division of the High Court in Chambers.

ADMINISTRATION OF ESTATES ACT 1925

9. Vesting of estate in Public Trustee where intestacy or lack of executors[2]— (1) Where a person dies intestate, his real and personal estate shall vest in the Public Trustee until the grant of administration.

(2) Where a testator dies and—
(a) at the time of his death there is no executor with power to obtain probate of the will, or
(b) at any time before probate of the will is granted there ceases to be any executor with power to obtain probate,
the real and personal estate of which he disposes by the will shall vest in the Public Trustee until the grant of representation.

(3) The vesting of real or personal estate in the Public Trustee by virtue of this section does not confer on him any beneficial interest in, or impose on him any duty, obligation or liability in respect of, the property.

C. Custodian Trustees[3]

PUBLIC TRUSTEE ACT 1906

4. Custodian Trustee, (2), (3): see p. 639, ante.

PUBLIC TRUSTEE RULES 1912[4]

30. Corporate Bodies as Custodian Trustees.—(1) The following corporations shall be entitled to act as custodian trustees:—
(*a*) the Treasury Solicitor;
(*b*) any corporation which:—
(i) is constituted under the law of the United Kingdom or of any part thereof, or under the law of any other Member State of the European Economic Community or of any part thereof;

---

1 See Public Trustee (Fees) Act 1957; Administration of Justice Act 1965, s. 2; Public Trustee (Fees) Order 1983, S.I. 1983 No. 443 as amended by Public Trustee (Fees) (Amendment) Order 1987, S.I. 1987 No. 403; 1988, S.I. 1988 No. 571; 1989, S.I. 1989 No. 437; 1990, S.I. 1990 No. 702; 1992 S.I. 1992, No. 724; 1994, S.I. No. 714; 1995, S.I. No. 1425.

2 As substituted by LP (Miscellaneous Provisions) Act 1994, s. 14 (1); Public Trustee (Notices affecting land) (Title on death) Regs 1995 (S.I. 1995 No. 1330). See Law Commission Report: Title on Death 1989 (Law Com No. 184), paras. 2.20–2.26.

3 See generally (1960) 24 Conv (NS) 196 (S.G. Maurice).

4 SR & O 1912, No. 348, as substituted by the Public Trustee (Custodian Trustee) Rules 1975 S.I. 1975, No. 1189, r. 2, and as added by S.I. 1976, No. 836, S.I. 1981, No. 358; S.I. 1984, No. 109; S.I. 1985, No. 132; S.I. 1987, No. 1891.

(ii)   is empowered by its constitution to undertake trust business (which for the purpose of this rule means the business of acting as trustee under wills and settlements and as executor and administrator) in England and Wales;[5]

(iii) has one or more places of business in the United Kingdom; and

(iv)   is—

a company incorporated by special Act of Parliament or Royal Charter, or

a company registered (with or without limited liability) in the United Kingdom under the Companies Act 1985 or under the Companies Act (Northern Ireland) 1960 or in another Member State of the European Economic Community and having a capital (in stock or shares) for the time being issued of not less than £250,000 (or its equivalent in the currency of the State where the company is registered), of which not less than £100,000 (or its equivalent) has been paid up in cash, or a company which is registered without limited liability in the United Kingdom under the Companies Act 1985 or the Companies Act (Northern Ireland) 1960 or in another member State of the European Economic Community and of which one of the members is a company within any of the classes defined in this sub-paragraph;

(v)   the Common Council of the City of London;

(c) any corporation which is incorporated by special Act or Royal Charter or under the Charitable Trustees Incorporation Act 1872 which is empowered by its constitution to act as a trustee for any charitable purposes, but only in relation to trusts in which its constitution empowers it to act;

(d) any corporation which is constituted under the law of the United Kingdom or of any part thereof and having its place of business there, and which is either:—

(i)   established for the purpose of undertaking trust business for the benefit of Her Majesty's Navy, Army, Air Force or Civil Service or of any unit, department, member or association of members thereof, and having among its directors or members any persons appointed or nominated by the Defence Council or any Department of State or any one or more of those Departments, or

(ii) authorised by the Lord Chancellor to act in relation to any charitable, ecclesiastical or public trusts as a trust corporation, but only in connection with any such trust as is so authorised;

(e) (i)   any Regional Health Authority, District Health Authority or special health authority, but only in relation to any trust which the authority is authorised to accept or hold by virtue of section 90 of the National Health Service Act 1977;

(ii) any preserved Board as defined by section 15 (6) of the National Health Service Reorganisation Act 1973, but only in relation to any trust which the Board is authorised to accept or hold by virtue of an order made under that section;[6]

(f) the British Gas Corporation or any subsidiary of the British Gas Corporation, but only in relation to a pension scheme or pension fund

---

5 *Re Bigger* [1977] Fam 203, [1977] 2 All ER 644 (Bank of Ireland).
6 As substituted by Public Trustee (Custodian Trustee) Rules 1984 (S.I. No. 109).

established or maintained by the Corporation by virtue of section 36 of the Gas Act 1972;[7]

(*g*) the London Transport Executive, but only in relation to a pension scheme or pension fund—

    (i) which is established or administered by the Executive by virtue of section 6 of the Transport (London) Act 1969, or

    (ii) in relation to which rights, liabilities and functions have been transferred to the Executive by an order under section 74 of the Transport Act 1962 as applied by section 18 of the Transport (London) Act 1969;

(*h*) any of the following, namely:—

    (i) the Greater London Council,[8]

    (ii) the corporation of any London borough (acting by the council),

    (iii) a county council, district council, parish council or community council,

    (iv) the Council of the Isles of Scilly,

but only in relation to charitable or public trusts (and not trusts for an ecclesiastical charity or for a charity for the relief of poverty) for the benefit of the inhabitants of the area of the local authority concerned and its neighbourhood, or any part of that area,

    (v) the Common Council of the City of London

(*i*) any of the following, namely:—

    (i) a metropolitan district council or a non-metropolitan district council,

    (ii) the corporation of any London borough (acting by the council),

    (iii) the Common Council of the City of London,

    (iv) the Council of the Isles of Scilly,

but only in relation to any trust under which property devolves for the sole benefit of a person who occupies residential accommodation provided under section 21 (1) (*a*) of the National Assistance Act 1948 by the local authority concerned or is in the care of that authority; and a corporation acting as a custodian trustee by virtue of this paragraph in relation to any trust shall be entitled to continue so to act in relation to that trust until a new custodian trustee is appointed, notwithstanding that the person concerned ceases to occupy such accommodation or to be in the care of that authority, as the case may be;[9]

(*j*) the British Coal Corporation or any subsidiary of the British Coal Corporation, but only in relation to a scheme or arrangements established under regulations made under section 37 of the Coal Industry Nationalisation Act 1946.[9a]

(*k*) any corporation acting as trustee of the trusts of any pension scheme or pension fund established or maintained by the British Broadcasting Corporation, but only in relation to those trusts.[10]

---

7 As added by Public Trustee (Custodian Trustee) Rules 1985 (S.I. No. 132).

8 The GLC ceased to exist on 1 April 1986; LGA 1985, s. 1.

9 As added by Public Trustee (Custodian Trustee) Rules 1976, S.I. 1976, No. 836.

9a As substituted by Coal Industry Act 1987, s. 1(3).

10 As added by Public Trustee (Custodian Trustee) Rules 1987, S.I. 1987, No. 1891.

(2) In this rule "subsidiary" has the same meaning as in section 736 of the Companies Act 1985.[11]

In **Re Brooke Bond & Co Ltd's Trust Deed** [1963] Ch 357, [1963] 1 All ER 454,[12] the Welfare Insurance Co Ltd were custodian trustee under a trust deed which secured the pension fund of the employees of Brooke Bond & Co Ltd. Its managing trustees had powers to take out a group insurance policy and they desired to take it out with Welfare Insurance Co Ltd, the custodian trustee. The question was whether, without leave of the court, the custodian trustee could enter into the policy with the managing trustees and retain for their own benefit any profit which they might make. CROSS J held that they could not and said at 363, at 457:

"It is apparent that the duties of a custodian trustee differ substantially from those of an ordinary trustee. If the trust instrument or the general law gives the trustee power to do this, that or the other, it is not for the custodian trustee to consider whether it should be done. The exercise of powers or discretions is a matter for the managing trustees with which the custodian trustee has no concern, and he is bound to deal with the trust property so as to give effect to the decisions and actions taken by the managing trustees unless what he is requested to do by them would be a breach of trust or would involve him in personal liability. On the other hand, it is plain that he is a trustee holding the trust property and its income on trust for the beneficiaries according to the terms of the trust instrument and he is prima facie liable to the beneficiaries for any dealing with capital or income which is a breach of trust. In practice this liability may be considerably qualified as regards income by the provisions of subsection (2) (e)[13] and as regards capital or income by the provisions of subsection (2) (h); but subject to the protection provided by those subsections the custodian trustee, as I understand the matter, is as liable as an ordinary trustee to be sued by a beneficiary for the misapplication of the trust property. His position is quite unlike that of a third party—a bailee of the trust property, for instance—who is in contractual relationship with the trustee but owes no duty to the beneficiaries.

It is, however, argued that the fact that a custodian trustee is not concerned with the management of the trust makes the rule that a trustee may not make a profit out of his trust inapplicable to him. If trustees have power to sell or lease the trust property or to invest it in some way, the custodian trustee is not concerned with the question whether the power should be exercised and is not concerned with any negotiations which take place between the managing trustees and the other contracting parties. All the custodian trustee is concerned to do is to be satisfied that the managing trustees have the power to enter into the transaction which they call on him to carry out.

That being the position, it is said how can there be any conflict between his interest and duty if he himself is the other contracting party? He must indeed

---

11 As added by Public Trustee (Custodian Trustee) Rules 1981, S.I. 1981, No. 358.
12 (1963) 79 LQR 177 (R.E.M.). See also *Forster v Williams Deacon's Bank Ltd* [1935] Ch 359 (bank may not be appointed both managing trustee and custodian trustee in order to allow it to charge fees as custodian trustee).
13 Public Trustee Act 1906, s. 4 (2), p. 639, ante.

satisfy himself that the proposed transaction is one which the managing trustees have power to enter into just as he would have to do if they had contracted with a third party, but once he is satisfied as to that, his duty in the matter is at an end and he can properly look only to his own interests in negotiating the terms of the contract in question with the managing trustees.

This argument is ingenious but in my judgment it is unsound. In the first place, it presupposes that a hard and fast line can always be drawn between the power to enter into a contract of a certain character and the terms of the contract. I do not think that this is always the case. For example, the managing trustees may have power to lease the trust property but only on the terms that they obtain the best rent reasonably obtainable. In such a case if the proposal was to grant a lease to a nominee of the custodian trustee, the custodian trustee would be under a duty to see that the best rent was obtained so that no breach of trust was committed, but it would be to his interest as the prospective lessee to have the rent fixed at as low a figure as possible. Again it is prima facie the duty of a trustee to place at the disposal of the beneficiaries any special knowledge he has of the value of the trust property or of any advantages or disadvantages of any contract which is in contemplation with regard to it. It may be that if the contract is being made by the managing trustees with a third party, a custodian trustee is under no positive duty to communicate any such knowledge which he may have to the managing trustees. I do not say whether that is so or not, but assuming it is so it does not follow by any means that if the custodian trustee was himself the other contracting party he could properly refrain from disclosing any such special knowledge to the managing trustees as a third party would be entitled to refrain from disclosing it. I appreciate that it may well be that the chances of there being a conflict between interest and duty are less in the case of transactions between a custodian trustee and managing trustees than they are in the case of transactions between an ordinary trustee and his co-trustees. But the possibility of conflict is still there and the rule, as Lord Herschell pointed out in *Bray v Ford* [1896] AC 44, is an inflexible one unless the trust instrument provides for a profit being made by the trustees or the court makes a special order in a particular case.

For the reasons I have tried to give, I can see no sound reason for saying that the rule does not apply to a custodian trustee as much as to an ordinary trustee."

D. Trustees of Charitable Trusts

TRUSTEE ACT 1925

34 (3). Limitation of the number of trustees: see p. 534, ante.

CHARITIES ACT 1993

16 (8). Concurrent jurisdiction with High Court for certain purposes: see p. 518, ante.
18. Power to act for protection of charities: see pp. 535, 536, ante.
83 (1). Transfer and evidence of title to property vested in trustees: see p. 535, ante.

E. Trust Corporation

TRUSTEE ACT 1925[14]

68 (18). Definitions.—(1) In this Act, unless the context otherwise requires, the following expressions have the meanings hereby assigned to them respectively, that is to say:—

(xxx) "Trust corporation" means the Public Trustee or a corporation either appointed by the court in any particular case to be a trustee or entitled by rules made under subsection (3) of section four of the Public Trustee Act 1906, to act as a custodian trustee . . .[15]

LAW OF PROPERTY (AMENDMENT) ACT 1926

3. **Meaning of "trust corporation".**—(1) For the purposes of the Law of Property Act, 1925, the Settled Land Act 1925, the Trustee Act 1925, the Administration of Estates Act 1925, and the Supreme Court Act 1981,[16] the expression "Trust Corporation" includes the Treasury Solicitor, the Official Solicitor and any person holding any other official position prescribed by the Lord Chancellor, and, in relation to the property of a bankrupt and property subject to a deed of arrangement, includes the trustee in bankruptcy and the trustee under the deed respectively, and, in relation to charitable ecclesiastical and public trusts, also includes any local or public authority so prescribed, and any other corporation constituted under the laws of the United Kingdom or any part thereof which satisfies the Lord Chancellor that it undertakes the administration of any such trusts without remuneration, or that by its constitution it is required to apply the whole of its net income after payment of outgoings for charitable, ecclesiastical or public purposes, and is prohibited from distributing, directly or indirectly, any part thereof by way of profits amongst any of its members, and is authorised by him to act in relation to such trusts as a trust corporation.

(2) For the purposes of this provision, the expression "Treasury Solicitor" means the solicitor for the affairs of His Majesty's Treasury, and includes the solicitor for the affairs of the Duchy of Lancaster.

VI. Control of Trustees[17]

Although the court will compel a trustee to carry out a specific duty, there are difficulties in determining what is the right course to take in respect of powers and discretions. Generally the court will not intervene, in the absence of mala fides, in the exercise of a power. But the trustee may, as in the case of a discretionary trust, be under an obligation to exercise a discretion. If he does not exercise it, the court may in appropriate circumstances, as has been seen,

---

14 See also SLA 1925, s. 117 (xxx); LPA 1925, s. 205 (1) (xxviii); AEA 1925, s. 55 (1) (xxvi); Supreme Court Act 1981, s. 128.
15 See p. 640, ante.
16 As substituted by Supreme Court Act 1981, s. 152 (1) Sch. 5.
17 H & M, pp. 494–498; P & M, pp. 389–391; Pettit, pp. 376–378; Riddall, p. 344; Snell, pp. 235–238.

exercise it for him.[18] But if he does exercise it within the terms of the power or discretion, how can the court interfere? The discretion is that of the trustee, not that of the court. The court can interfere in the case of fraud; or if the trustees show that they reached a conclusion for wrong reasons. But if they say nothing, there is little that the court can do. The problem is particularly acute if a complainant suspects fraud or mala fides on the part of the trustees; but cannot prove this unless the trustees disclose their deliberations.

TEMPEST v LORD CAMOYS

(1882) 21 ChD 571 (CA, JESSEL MR, BRETT and COTTON LJJ)

Under the will of Sir Charles Robert Tempest, Bart., Mr. James Fleming and Mr. Wilfred Tempest, the trustees, had power at their absolute discretion to sell land, to apply the purchase money in the purchase of other land, and to raise money by mortgage for the purpose.

Some of the family wished to purchase Bracewell Hall for £60,000, using £30,000 of available money, and raising the balance by mortgage. Tempest supported the suggestion, Fleming opposed. Tempest brought this petition, asking that the purchase might be ordered.

Held (affirming CHITTY J). The Court would not interfere with the *bona fide* exercise of his discretion by a trustee.

JESSEL MR: It is very important that the law of the Court on this subject should be understood. It is settled law that when a testator has given a pure discretion to trustees as to the exercise of a power, the Court does not enforce the exercise of the power against the wish of the trustees, but it does prevent them from exercising it improperly. The Court says that the power, if exercised at all, is to be properly exercised. This may be illustrated by the case of persons having a power of appointing new trustees. Even after a decree in a suit for administering the trusts has been made they may still exercise the power, but the Court will see that they do not appoint improper persons.

But in all cases where there is a trust or duty coupled with the power the Court will then compel the trustees to carry it out in a proper manner and within a reasonable time. In the present case there was a power which amounts to a trust to invest the fund in question in the purchase of land. The trustees would not be allowed by the Court to disregard that trust, and if Mr. *Fleming* had refused to invest the money in land at all the Court would have found no difficulty in interfering. But that is a very different thing from saying that the Court ought to take from the trustees their uncontrolled discretion as to the particular time for the investment and the particular property which should be purchased. In this particular case it appears to me that the testator in his will has carefully distinguished between what is to be at the discretion of his trustees and what is obligatory on them.

There is another difficulty in this case. The estate proposed to be purchased will cost £60,000, and only £30,000 is available for the purchase, and the trustees will have to borrow the remaining £30,000. There is power to raise money by mortgage at the absolute discretion of the trustees, and assuming that such a transaction as this is within the power, and that the trustees can mortgage the estate before they have actually bought it, there is no trust to mortgage, it is purely discretionary. The Court cannot force Mr. *Fleming* to take

18 *McPhail v Doulton* [1971] AC 424, [1970] 2 All ER 228, p. 71, ante; *Re Locker's Settlement* [1977] 1 WLR 1323, [1978] 1 All ER 216, p. 78, n. 10, ante.

the view that it is proper to mortgage the estate in this way; he may very well have a different opinion from the other trustee. Here again the Court cannot interfere with his discretion. The appeal must therefore be dismissed.

RE BELOVED WILKES' CHARITY
(1851) 3 Mac & G 440 (Lord Truro LC)

Trustees of a charitable trust were to select a boy to be educated at Oxford in preparation for him to become a Minister of the Church of England. Preference was to be given to boys from four named parishes if, in the judgment of the trustees, a fit and proper candidate therefrom could be found.

In 1848 the trustees selected Charles Joyce, who did not come from one of the four parishes. They gave no reasons for their choice, but stated that they had considered the candidates impartially. It appeared however that Joyce's brother was a Minister, who had sought the assistance of one of the trustees in favour of Charles. The court was asked to set aside the selection, and to select William Gale, whose father was a respectable farmer residing in one of the specified parishes.

Held. In the absence of evidence that the trustees had exercised their discretion unfairly or dishonestly, the Court would not interfere.

LORD TRURO LC: The question, therefore, is, whether it was the duty of the trustees to enter into particulars, or whether the law is not, that trustees who are appointed to execute a trust according to discretion, that discretion to be influenced by a variety of circumstances (as, in this instance, by those particular circumstances which should be connected with the fitness of a lad to be brought up as a minister of the Church of England), are not bound to go into a detail of the grounds upon which they come to their conclusion, their duty being satisfied by shewing that they have considered the circumstances of the case, and have come to their conclusion accordingly. Without occupying time by going into a lengthened examination of the decisions, the result of them appears to me so clear and reasonable, that it will be sufficient to state my conclusion in point of law to be, that in such cases as I have mentioned it is to the discretion of the trustees that the execution of the trust is confided, that discretion being exercised with an entire absence of indirect motive, with honesty of intention, and with a fair consideration of the subject. The duty of supervision on the part of this Court will thus be confined to the question of the honesty, integrity, and fairness with which the deliberation has been conducted, and will not be extended to the accuracy of the conclusion arrived at, except in particular cases. If, however, as stated by Lord Ellenborough in *The King v Archbishop of Canterbury* (1812) 15 East 117, trustees think fit to state a reason, and the reason is one which does not justify their conclusion, then the Court may say that they have acted by mistake and in error, and that it will correct their decision; but if, without entering into details, they simply state, as in many cases it would be most prudent and judicious for them to do, that they have met and considered and come to a conclusion, the Court has then no means of saying that they have failed in their duty, or to consider the accuracy of their conclusion.[19] It seems, therefore, to me, that having in the present case to look to the motives of the trustees as developed in the affidavits, no ground exists for imputing bad motives. The Petitioners, indeed, candidly state, on the

---

19 See *Re Londonderry's Settlement* [1965] Ch 918, [1964] 3 All ER 855, p. 732, post.

face of their petition, that they do not impute such motives, they merely charge the trustees with a miscarriage as regards the duty which they had to perform. I cannot, therefore, deal with the case as if the petition had contained a statement of a different kind, and if I could, still I should say, having read the affidavits, that I see nothing whatever which can lay the foundation for any judicial conclusion that the trustees intentionally and from bad motives failed in their duty, if they failed at all.

KLUG v KLUG
[1918] 2 Ch 67 (ChD, NEVILLE J)

Madame Moro (as Frida Klug) became entitled, on attaining the age of 21 in August, 1915, to a share in her father's estate. Legacy duty had to be paid, and it was agreed with the Inland Revenue that this should be paid by four equal instalments. Owing to the fall in income of the investments and the rise in the cost of living after the war, she was unable to make the payments out of income, and asked the trustees of her father's will to make an advancement to her out of the capital of her share, as they had power to do under the advancement clause of the will.

The trustees were the Public Trustee, and Mrs. Klug, the mother of Madame Moro. The Public Trustee wished to make an advancement; but Mrs. Klug refused, on the ground that Madame Moro had married without her approval.

Held. Payment out of the capital was ordered.

NEVILLE J: In this case Madame Moro is entitled to a life interest in one third of her father's residuary estate with remainder to her children, and has to pay a legacy duty of 10 per cent. because, according to English law, she is to be considered a stranger to her father. But that is not material, the real question here being when and how far the Court will interfere with the discretion given to trustees. I should be sorry by anything I may say to be thought to diminish the jurisdiction and control which the Court has over trustees in exercising their discretion, but on the other hand I should be loth to say that, where trustees have honestly exercised their discretion, the Court will interfere in the absence of special circumstances. Here the trustees are the Public Trustee and the testator's widow, and they have power to advance not more than a moiety of the capital of Madame Moro's settled share for her advancement and benefit, and the question is whether it will be for her benefit that the instalments of the legacy duty that have been paid and the two remaining instalments that are due should be paid out of the corpus instead of out of the income of her settled share. She is in difficulties owing to the times in which we are living. When the summons was previously before me I decided that the trustees could in the exercise of their discretion under the powers of advancement, if they thought fit, advance out of capital a sum sufficient to pay this legacy duty. The Public Trustee thinks that their discretion should be so exercised, but his co-trustee, the mother, declines to join him in so doing, not because she has considered whether nor not it would be for her daughter's welfare that the advance should be made, but because her daughter has married without her consent, and her letters show, in my opinion, that she has not exercised her discretion at all. What, then, ought the Court to do when one trustee very properly desires to exercise his discretion under a power for the benefit of a beneficiary and his co-trustee will not exercise her discretion? I think that in such circumstances it is the duty of the Court to interfere and, in the exercise of its control over the discretion given to the trustees, to direct a sum to be raised out of the capital sufficient to pay off the mortgage of 250*l.* and two remaining instalments of the legacy duty, and that is the order I now make.

Hanbury & Maudsley: *Modern Equity* (13th edn, 1989), p. 480.

"Some cases[20] in the nineteenth century reserve to the courts a jurisdiction to investigate the exercise of a discretion that has already been made and that, on external evidence only, appears to have been 'mischievously and ruinously exercised'. Lord Normand, in a Scottish appeal to the House of Lords, thought that 'The principles on which the courts must proceed are the same whether the trustees' reasons for their decision are disclosed or not,[1] but it is not clear whether all the propositions in this case are acceptable as part of the English law of trusts. A conclusion can only be drawn in the form that it will never be easy to persuade a court to review the exercise of a discretion by trustees in the absence of some clear facts from which it is not difficult to discern that the discretion has been irregularly exercised."[2]

VII. Power of Decision[3]

A settlor or testator sometimes gives to his trustees express power to make decisions concerning issues relating to the trust. The dividing line between what is permitted and what is not is very obscure. Certainly, "a testator cannot confide to another the right to make a will for him."[4] Nor can the jurisdiction of the court be excluded.

RE COXEN
[1948] Ch 747, [1948] 2 All ER 492 (ChD, JENKINS J)

The testator devised a dwelling-house to trustees upon trust to permit his wife to reside therein; and he declared that, "if in the opinion of my trustees she shall have ceased permanently to reside therein", the house was to fall into residue. The question was whether this proviso constituted a valid limitation upon the gift.

---

20 *Re Hodges* (1878) 7 ChD 754; *Re Roper's Trusts* (1879) 11 ChD 272; *Re Brittlebank* (1881) 30 WR 99. But the jurisdiction may be confined to the protection of trust assets. *cf. Re D'Epinoix's Settlement* [1914] 1 Ch 890.
1 *Dundee General Hospitals v Walker* [1952] 1 All ER 896 at 900; *Re Hastings-Bass* [1975] Ch 25, [1974] 2 All ER 193.
2 See (1990) 107 LQR 214 at pp. 219–220 (S. Gardner), suggesting that the appointment of new trustees is preferable to positive intervention, such as the judicial exercise of fiduciary discretions: *Mettoy Pension Trustees Ltd v Evans* [1990] 1 WLR 1587, [1991] 2 All ER 513.
3 H & M, pp. 497–498; K & S, p. 322; Petit, pp. 371–373; Riddall, pp. 31–32; Snell, pp. 235–236; Underhill, pp. 818–821.
4 Per Lord PENZANCE in *In Bonis Smith's Goods* (1869) LR 1 P & D 717; (1953) 69 LQR 334 (D.M. Gordon).

Held. The condition was not void for uncertainty. The decision of the trustees would be sufficient to determine the widow's interest.

JENKINS J: I have so far treated the condition as if it was simply in the terms "if she shall have ceased permanently to reside," whereas its actual terms are "if in the opinion of my trustees she shall have ceased permanently to reside." That I think makes a very material difference. The opinion of the trustees that the double event has happened, and not simply the happening of the double event, is what brings about the cesser of Lady Coxen's interest. If the testator had insufficiently defined the state of affairs on which the trustees were to form their opinion, he would not I think have saved the condition from invalidity on the ground of uncertainty merely by making their opinion the criterion, although the declaration by the trustees of this or that opinion would be an event about which in itself there could be no uncertainty. But as I have already indicated, I think the relevant double event is sufficiently defined to make it perfectly possible for the trustees (as the judges of fact for this purpose) to decide whether it has happened or not, and in my view the testator by making the trustees' opinion the criterion has removed the difficulties which might otherwise have ensued from a gift over in a double event the happening of which, though in itself sufficiently defined, may necessarily be a matter of inference involving nice questions of fact and degree.

In **Re Wynn** [1952] Ch 271, [1952] 1 All ER 341, the question was whether a clause in a will in the following terms was valid: "I authorise and empower my trustees to determine what articles pass under any specific bequest contained in this my will . . . and whether any moneys are to be considered as capital or income and how valuations are to be made and or value determined for any purpose in connexion with the trusts and provisions of this my will . . . and to apportion blended trust funds and to determine all questions and matters of doubt arising in the execution of the trusts of this my will . . . and I declare that every such determination whether made upon a question actually raised or only implied in the acts and proceedings of . . . my trustees shall be conclusive and binding upon all persons interested under this my will."

DANCKWERTS J held it void. He said at 279, at 346:

"No doubt it may be said that it is convenient to have matters regarding the apportionment of capital moneys and the application of moneys in the payment of expenses referred to some informal decision, and that in that way expense may be saved which would be necessarily incurred if the matters had to be referred to the court; but in my view a clause of this kind has no effect if it is attempted to use it so as to prevent the beneficiaries requiring the matter to be decided by the court. As long as the clause is not contested, it may be that the beneficiaries will be content to have the matters dealt with by the trustees in the course of their operations in the administration of the estate; and it may, of course, be that the trustees have applied their minds and carried out their duties in a perfectly proper manner in the way in which they deal with matters connected with the estate; but it seems to me that the result is that any beneficiary is entitled to go to the court to have his rights considered and, if necessary, upheld; and that a testator may not by the provisions of his will exclude the right of the court to decide the matters, even though the trustees have considered them and reached a certain decision."

In **Re Jones** [1953] Ch 125, [1953] 1 All ER 357, a testator directed his trustees to hold his residuary trust fund after the death of his wife upon trust to purchase an annuity for his daughter Doris Mabel, and he directed that "if at any time . . . my . . . daughter Doris . . . shall in the uncontrolled opinion of the company [the trustees] have social or other relationship with [a certain named person] . . . then in such case as from the occurrence of such event my said daughter . . . shall absolutely forfeit and lose one half of the annuity payments hereinbefore directed to be paid to her . . . "

On the question whether the forfeiture clause was valid, DANCKWERTS J held (a) that it was void for uncertainty and (b) that the reference to the opinion of the trustees did not prevent that invalidity. He said at 128, at 360:

"Unless [the difficulty] is cured by reference to the opinion of the trustees, it seems to me that this clause cannot be regarded as sufficiently certain to be upheld as a forfeiture clause or a condition subsequent. The words in the present case are 'shall in the uncontrolled opinion of the company have social or other relationship'. Mr. Albery has submitted that that surmounts the difficulty, because the guiding factor is not the existence of 'social or other relationship', but the existence of 'the uncontrolled opinion' on the part of the executor company, the bank.

He has referred me to a decision of the House of Lords, which certainly is of great interest in regard to the matter: *Dundee General Hospitals Board of Management v Walker* [1952] 1 All ER 896 at 898. In that case, in order that a named body should qualify for a legacy, the trustees had to be satisfied as regarded a certain hospital, the Dundee Royal Infirmary, that 'the said infirmary has not been taken over wholly or partly by or otherwise placed under the control of the State or of a local authority or of a body directly or indirectly responsible to the State and/or a local authority'. As Mr. Albery perfectly correctly said, after quoting a well-known observation of Bowen LJ that the state of a man's mind was as much a fact as the state of his digestion[5], it is the existence of an opinion or the non-existence of a particular opinion on the part of the company, the trustees, which is the test of forfeiture or otherwise in the present case.

In the present case, however, the opinion of the trustees is substituted for the opinion of the court, and it is the trustees who have to decide whether or not a certain obscure and difficult state of facts has occurred; the trustees might be unable to decide the question just as the court might be unable to decide it, and further the court might have to decide the matter or to attempt to decide the matter upon a reference to it by the trustees."

In **Re Tuck's Settlement Trusts** [1978] Ch 49, [1978] 1 All ER 1047,[6] the settlor provided an income for the holder for the time being of the family baronetcy if and when and so long as he should be of the Jewish faith and married and living with "an approved wife" or, if separated, being so separated through no fault of his. An "approved wife" was defined as a wife of Jewish blood by one or both of her parents, who had been brought up in the Jewish faith, had never departed from it, and, who, at the date of the marriage, continued to worship

---

5 *Edgington v Fitzmaurice* (1885) 29 ChD 459 at 483.
6 [1978] Conv 242 (F.R. Crane).

according to the Jewish faith. The Chief Rabbi in London of either the Portuguese or the Anglo-German community was designated to decide any question as to who was an approved wife, and whether any separation was or was not due to the fault of the baronet.

The question was whether the trusts were void for uncertainty; and whether the reference to the Chief Rabbi was effective, or void as an ouster of the jurisdiction of the court. The Court of Appeal held that the condition was sufficiently certain. On the question whether, if it had been void for uncertainty, the trust would have been saved by the provision making the Chief Rabbi's decision conclusive, Lord DENNING MR referred to *Dundee General Hospitals Board of Management v Walker* [1952] 1 All ER 896 as being a decision "of the highest persuasive value", and continued at 61, at 1053:

"I see no reason why a testator or settler should not provide that any dispute or doubt should be resolved by his executors or trustees, or even by a third person. To prove this, I will first state the law in regard to contracts. Here the general principle is that whenever persons agree together to refer a matter to a third person for decision, and further agree that his decision is to be final and binding upon them, then, so long as he arrives at his decision honestly and in good faith, the two parties are bound by it. . . .

If two contracting parties can by agreement leave a doubt or difficulty to be decided by a third person, I see no reason why a testator or settlor should not leave the decision to his trustees or to a third party. He does not thereby oust the jurisdiction of the court. If the appointed person should find difficulty in the actual wording of the will or settlement, the executors or trustees can always apply to the court for directions so as to assist in the interpretation of it. But if the appointed person is ready and willing to resolve the doubt or difficulty, I see no reason why he should not do so. So long as he does not misconduct himself or come to a decision which is wholly unreasonable, I think his decision should stand. After all, that was plainly the intention of the testator or settlor."[7]

VIII. Termination of Trust at the Instance of the Beneficiaries. Rule in *Saunders v Vautier*

Under the rule in *Saunders v Vautier*, an adult beneficiary, who is of sound mind and entitled to the whole beneficial interest under a trust, can direct the trustees to transfer the trust property to him, and thus put an end to the trust.[8]

---

7 *Re Tepper's Will Trusts* [1987] Ch 358, [1987] 1 All ER 970 (gift by a devout and practising Jewish testator to children provided that "they shall not marry outside the Jewish faith": SCOTT J was reluctant to find the condition subsequent void for uncertainty and adjourned the case for further evidence of the Jewish faith as practised by the testator and his family); [1987] All ER Rev 159 (P.J. Clarke), 260 (C.H. Sherrin).

8 (1841) 4 Beav 115; affd (1841) Cr & Ph 240; *IRC v Executors of Hamilton-Russell* [1943] 1 All ER 474; *Stephenson v Barclays Bank Trust Co Ltd* [1975] 1 WLR 882, [1975] 1 All ER 625, infra.
The rule applies even if the settlor purports to exclude it: *Stokes v Cheek* (1860) 28 Beav 620. It also applies in favour of a charity: *Wharton v Masterman* [1895] AC 186; cf. *Re Levy* [1960] Ch 346, [1960] 1 All ER 42; *Re Jefferies* [1936] 2 All ER 626; *Re Beesty's Will Trusts* [1966] Ch 223, [1964] 3 All ER 82.

The rule was extended during the nineteenth century to include cases where there are two or more beneficiaries,[9] and even where there are beneficiaries entitled in succession.[10] In both these cases all the beneficiaries must be of full age and of sound mind and together entitled to the whole beneficial interest, and must concur in the direction to the trustees.

SAUNDERS v VAUTIER
(1841) 4 Beav 115 (Lord LANGDALE MR)

A testator bequeathed £2,000 East India stock to trustees on trust to accumulate the dividends until Vautier should attain the age of 25, and then to transfer the capital and accumulated dividends to Vautier. Vautier, having attained the age of 21,[11] claimed that he was entitled to have the whole fund transferred to him: "he had a vested interest and as the accumulation and postponement of payment was for his benefit alone, he might waive it and call for an immediate transfer of the fund".

Held. The whole fund was to be transferred to Vautier.

LORD LANGALE MR: I think that principle has been repeatedly acted upon; and where a legacy is directed to accumulate for a certain period, or where the payment is postponed, the legatee, if he has an absolute indefeasible interest in the legacy, is not bound to wait until the expiration of that period, but may require payment the moment he is competent to give a valid discharge.

On a subsequent hearing before Lord COTTENHAM LC (1841) Cr & Ph 240, it was argued on behalf of the testator's residuary legatees that Vautier's interest was contingent on his attaining 25 and therefore this rule did not apply. The Lord Chancellor held that the interest was vested, but that the enjoyment of it was merely postponed.

In **Stephenson v Barclays Bank Trust Co Ltd** [1975] 1 WLR 882, [1975] 1 All ER 625, where, on the exercise of a deed of family arrangement, grand-children became "absolutely entitled as against the trustees" under Finance Act 1965, s. 22 (5)[12] to the assets of the residuary estate, and therefore on its disposal by the trustees to them, capital gains tax was chargeable, WALTON J said at 889, at 637:

"Now it is trite law that the persons who between them hold the entirety of the beneficial interests in any particular trust fund are as a body entitled to direct the trustees how that trust fund is to be dealt with, and this is obviously the legal territory from which that definition derives. However, in view of the arguments advanced to me by Mr. Lawton, and more particularly that advanced by him on the basis of the decision of Vaisey J in *Re Brockbank* [1948] Ch 206, [1948] 1 All ER 287, I think it may be desirable to state what I conceive to be certain elementary principles.

---

9 *Re Sandeman's Will Trusts* [1937] 1 All ER 368; *Re Smith* [1928] Ch 915, p. 37 ante.
10 *Brown v Pringle* (1845) 4 Hare 124; *Anson v Potter* (1879) 13 ChD 141; *Re White* [1901] 1 Ch 570.
11 The age of majority is now 18: Family Law Reform Act 1969, s. 1.
12 Now TCGA 1992, s. 60, p. 560, ante.

(1) In a case where the persons who between them hold the entirety of the beneficial interests in any particular trust fund are all sui juris and acting together, ("the beneficial interest holders"), they are entitled to direct the trustees how the trust fund may be dealt with. (2) This does not mean, however, that they can at one and the same time override the pre-existing trusts and keep them in existence. Thus, in *Re Brockbank* itself the beneficial interest holders were entitled to override the pre-existing trusts by, for example, directing the trustees to transfer the trust fund to X and Y, whether X and Y were the trustees of some other trust or not, but they were not entitled to direct the existing trustee to appoint their own nominee as a new trustee of the existing trust. By so doing they would be pursuing inconsistent rights. (3) Nor, I think, are the beneficial interest holders entitled to direct the trustees as to the particular investment they should make of the trust fund. I think this follows for the same reasons as the above. Moreover, it appears to me that once the beneficial interest holders have determined to end the trust they are not entitled, unless by agreement, to the further services of the trustees. Those trustees can of course be compelled to hand over the entire trust assets to any person or persons selected by the beneficiaries against a proper discharge, but they cannot be compelled, unless they are in fact willing to comply with the directions, to do anything else with the trust fund which they are not in fact willing to do. (4) Of course, the rights of the beneficial interest holders are always subject to the right of the trustees to be fully protected against such matters as duty, taxes, costs or other outgoings; for example, the rent under a lease which the trustees have properly accepted as part of the trust property."[13]

QUESTIONS

1. Consider the dilemma of a disappointed beneficiary, such as the plaintiff in *Re Beloved Wilkes' Charity* (1851) 3 Mac & G 440, p. 648, ante, who suspects that the trustees' discretion has been wrongly, or even fraudulently, exercised, but can only establish such fact if he can compel the trustees to give their reasons.

   Is this problem insoluble? Compare *Re Londonderry's Settlement* [1965] Ch 918, [1964] 3 All ER 855, p. 732, post.

2. Assume that you are:

   a) The owner of £100,000 more than you can ever need, and you decide to make a settlement. Whom would you choose as your trustees?

   b) The trustee of a family trust. You are old and doddery, and out of touch with finance and investment. But you are very conscientious and loyal, and in spite of the wish of the other trustees and all the beneficiaries that you resign, you insist on keeping your last promise to the deceased, made in 1939, that you will look after his affairs. What, if anything, can the other trustees or the beneficiaries do about you?

   c) The trustee of a family trust, whose value has quadrupled since 1985, The beneficiaries wish you to resign from the trust, so that some Jersey resident trustees can be appointed, and the trust managed in Jersey. The beneficiaries are all resident in England. What would you do?

---

13 *Lloyds Bank plc v Duker* [1987] 1 WLR 1324, [1987] 3 All ER 193 (Palace Hotel, Torquay); [1987] All ER Rev 262 (C.H. Sherrin). See p. 562 ante.

17. Duties of Trustees

I. Duty on Becoming Trustee[1]

Parker and Mellows: *Modern Law of Trusts* (6th edn, 1994), p. 383.

"When a person accepts a trusteeship, he should do four things, and if he fails to do any he may make himself liable for an action for breach of trust. These things are:

(*a*) acquaint himself with the terms of the trust;

---

1 H & M, pp. 499–502; K & S, pp. 272–275; P & M, pp. 383–385; Pettit, pp. 357–359; Riddall, pp. 234–236; Snell, pp. 213–215; Underhill, pp. 465–468; *Re Strahan* (1856) 8 De GM & G 291; *Harvey v Olliver* (1887) 57 LT 239; *Hallows v Lloyd* (1888) 39 ChD 686; *Re Chapman* (1894) 72 LT 66; *Re Lucking's Will Trusts* [1968] 1 WLR 866, [1967] 3 All ER 726, p. 751, post.

(b) inspect the trust instrument and any other trust deeds;

(c) procure that all the property subject to the trust is vested in the joint names of himself and his co-trustees, and that all title deeds are placed under their joint control; and

(d) in the case of an appointment as a new trustee of an existing trust, to investigate any suspicious circumstances which indicate a prior breach of trust, and to take action to recoup the trust fund if any breach has in fact taken place.''

RE BROGDEN[2]
(1888) 38 ChD 546 (ChD, NORTH J; CA, COTTON, FRY and LOPES LJJ)

By his will, John Brogden, a successful contractor in Manchester, left substantial legacies to members of his family, and provided that none of them should be payable until five years after his death, nor should money be paid out of the partnership between him and his sons for five years thereafter, unless his sons so required. He also covenanted to pay £10,000 to the trustees of his daughter's (Mrs. Billing's) marriage settlement, within five years of his death. This sum and the legacies were to carry interest meanwhile. John Brogden died on December 9, 1869.

Samuel Budgett was one of the trustees of Mrs. Billing's marriage settlement. He pressed the Brogden brothers on many occasions for payment, before and after the expiration of the five year period. On several occasions security for the payment was given, one of these being in response to an action started by Budgett for the administration of the estate.

The Brogden partnership became increasingly unprosperous. Budgett throughout was trying to avoid disturbance within the family, and any crisis which would upset the solvency of the firm. Eventually the firm became insolvent, and the securities were inadequate. The question was whether Budgett was liable to Mrs. Billing for breach of trust.

Held. Budgett was liable, as he had not taken all possible steps to obtain payment of the £10,000.

COTTON LJ: Now what was the duty of the trustee, Mr. *Budgett?* It was his duty, in my opinion, at the expiration of five years, to call for payment and to take reasonable means of enforcing payment if the executors did not pay the debt and the legacy. And there having been a postponed period during which no steps were to be taken against the partners or against the executors, it was the more his duty at the expiration of that period to assume that the executors had done what it was their duty to do by preparing for paying the debts and paying the legacies of the testator.... And, in my opinion, in the case here, it became the duty of Mr. *Budgett* to take active measures immediately after the expiration of the five years—that is immediately the legacy became payable and immediately the debt became payable.

We must therefore consider what he did. The five years expired in the beginning of December, 1874. I do not suggest that during the remaining of that month of December he should have taken any legal proceedings. That would hardly be expected, but what in my opinion he ought to have done, if not in December, 1874, early in the year 1875, was to have demanded payment, and if payment was not made, then he ought to have taken effectual proceedings in order to recover payment both of the legacy and of the debt. I

2 Cf. *Ward v Ward* (1843) 2 HL Cas 777n. See also *Harris v Black* (1983) 46 P & CR 366.

do not say it was his duty to recover them, because that assumes that he could have done so: but in my opinion it was his duty to demand payment of them, and to take effectual proceedings for the purpose of recovering them.

Now, what did he do? On the 12th of December, 1874, Mr. *Billing*, who was anxious, subject to what I shall hereafter mention, to recover payment of the sum settled on his wife and children, wrote to him urging him to see about getting payment of these sums of money. That was on the 12th of December, 1874, and he did nothing as far as one can see—nothing in the way of taking any proceedings at all, till some time in March, 1875. On the 18th of March, 1875, he had an interview with Mr. *Alexander Brogden*, who was the eldest son, and was the senior surviving partner in the firm, and who apparently had the command which his position gave him. Then there is a letter from Mr. *Holmes*. ... Mr. *Holmes* of Messrs. *Ingle, Cooper & Holmes*, writes a letter on the 18th of March, 1875, to Mr. *Alexander Brogden*, he says this:—[His Lordship read the letter and proceeded:] In my opinion this points to what was the great blot in the proceedings taken by Mr. *Budgett*. He did not say "you must pay". He was willing to enter into negotiations for the purpose of getting security. And what seems to have been proposed—we have not got very satisfactory evidence as to what took place at the interview—was that they should have a charge upon certain shares in order to secure the money. I gather from that letter that he did not direct Mr. *Holmes* to demand the payment: he did not say "do not make any doubt about it: have payment. If you cannot have payment, then let the partners see that I am determined, as being the only independent trustee, to do my duty, and to enforce payment from them by such means as are open to me".

Then we come to two other letters, which are the only other ones I shall read, namely, those from Mr. *Budgett* to Mrs. *Billing* of the 27th of May, 1875, and from Mr. *Budgett* to his solicitors of the 29th June, 1875:—[His Lordship read portions of these letters.] I do not at all say that I have any suspicion that Mr. *Budgett* acted from any self-interested motives, I think it was suggested that his wife had a legacy left to her, and her interests were looked after better than Mrs. *Billing's* interests. I have no such suspicion. What I think is this: it was natural that he should be unwilling to take any active proceedings against his brother-in-law; he trusted him in the belief that this firm, which then stood in good credit, was a perfectly solvent firm, and that the money was safe; and that being so he did not take those proceedings which he ought to have taken to make them understand that it was his duty to obtain payment, and that he must obtain payment from them. He did not take that course, and he takes the risk of whatever the consequences may be.

To proceed with the story. In October, 1875, proceedings were taken, but they were not taken by him. They were taken by his brother, who was a trustee for Mrs. *Budgett*. As I say, I do not at all suggest that that was done to get her any benefit rather than Mrs. *Billing*, but that left the control of the proceedings not in Mr. *Budgett's* hands, and when a settlement was made in March of the following year, it was a settlement only to give security for the legacy and the debt which was due to his brother, the trustee for his wife.

Then, again in May, 1876, he does take proceedings, and does not get any security which can excuse him for the loss of the money, because he took in September, 1876, the security of a leasehold colliery, and although it is possible that if he had at once realized that security in the then state of the market he might have got money enough to pay everything of which he was trustee, yet, it was a leasehold colliery; coals went down; there was a difficulty about the rent;

the landlord took proceedings; there had to be a large sum paid in order to get that colliery; and when it was realized it realized a sum insufficient to provide for the payment of these sums for which Mr. *Budgett* was trustee. That being so it is said that a trustee who is acting as he was, and not without consulting his solicitor, has never been held liable for what must be considered as an error of judgment.

In my opinion that is not the true way to state the case. If he had determined to get payment for this—if he had applied for payment in such a way as to shew that he meant to have it, and had consulted solicitors as to the best mode of proceedings, that might have been an error of judgement. But the conclusion to which I come, having regard to those letters, is this, that he did not do his duty in requiring payment—demanding it, and taking what he was advised were the best means of enforcing payment at least till the period of October, 1876—a late period, when we consider the state of the market as regards coal and iron. In regard to that the evidence is this; that in 1874 coal was in a very good state, collieries were very valuable property. But, although they were good in 1875, and not quite so good in 1876, both coal and iron then went rapidly down; and although in 1874 and 1875 there was a good state of coal and iron, unhappily at a later period that was not the case.

That decides the first question, with regard to which the rule is well laid down by Lord *Cottenham* in the case of *Clough v Bond* (1838) 3 My & Cr 490 at 496, that where a trustee does not do that which it is his duty to do, *prima facie* he is answerable for any loss occasioned thereby.

Then comes this question, if any loss is occasioned, on whom does it lie to shew whether any good would have resulted if the trustee had taken proceedings? Is that for the *cestuis que trust*, who are seeking to make Mr. *Budgett* liable, or is it for Mr. *Budgett* to shew that no good would have resulted? Is it for the *cestuis que trust* to shew that he could have got the money, or for Mr. *Budgett* to shew that he could not have got it if he had taken such proceedings as it was his duty to take?

In my opinion it is not for the *cestuis que trust* seeking to make the trustee liable, to shew that if he had done his duty he would have got the money for which they are seeking to make him answerable. It is the trustee who is seeking to excuse himself for the consequences of his breach of duty. It was his duty to take active proceedings if necessary earlier—to take active proceedings by way of action at law, if necessary; and if the trustee is to excuse himself, it is for him to shew that if he had taken proceedings no good would have resulted from it. Once shew that he has neglected his duty and *prima facie* he is answerable for all the consequences of that neglect; and in this case the result has been that only a very small sum could be recovered from the security which he took in the year 1876. That being so, has the trustee made out that if he had taken proceedings against the executors—against those who were carrying on the business, he would not have got any good from it? In my opinion he has not made that out, and my reason for thinking so is this—that at the time of the expiration of the five years, and certainly during the early part of the year 1875—probably up to the autumn of that year, the firm of *Brogden & Sons* was in very good credit. Immediately before the expiration of the five years, as I say, coal and iron had both been, as regards vendors, in a very satisfactory state. Coal was at an extraordinarily high price, and iron was good in the market....

I have therefore come to the conclusion that the decision of Mr. Justice *North* must be affirmed. It is an unfortunate position no doubt for Mr. *Budgett*, and I quite think that he believed that the firm were perfectly solvent, and that he was incurring no risk in letting the money remain with them. He ought not to have trusted them; as he did that and his expectations and those of the family have turned out to be wrong, and he has not shewn that no good would have resulted from his performing his duty by pressing for payment, and if necessary by taking proceedings to enforce payment, he must be held liable.

In **Buttle v Saunders** [1950] 2 All ER 193,[3] trustees for the sale of land had orally agreed to sell it to Mrs. Simpson for £6,142. One of the beneficiaries, Canon Buttle, wished to purchase it for a charity. After all the documents had been prepared for the sale to Mrs. Simpson, but before the contract was signed, Canon Buttle offered £6,500. The trustees felt that they had reached a stage in the negotiation with Mrs. Simpson from which they could not honourably withdraw. Canon Buttle brought this action to restrain the trustees from selling for any price below that which he offered. By a counterclaim, the trustees asked for the directions of the court. WYNN-PARRY J held that the trustees must accept Canon Buttle's offer. He said at 195:

"It has been argued on behalf of the trustees that they were justified in the circumstances in not pursuing the offer made by Canon Buttle and in deciding to go forward with the transaction with Mrs. Simpson. It is true that persons who are not in the position of trustees are entitled, if they so desire, to accept a lesser price than that which they might obtain on the sale of property, and not infrequently a vendor, who has gone some lengths in negotiating with a prospective purchaser, decides to close the deal with that purchaser, notwithstanding that he is presented with a higher offer. It redounds to the credit of a man who acts like that in such circumstances. Trustees, however, are not vested with such complete freedom. They have an overriding duty to obtain the best price which they can for their beneficiaries. It would, however, be an unfortunate simplification of the problem if one were to take the view that the mere production of an increased offer at any stage, however late in the negotiations, should throw on the trustees a duty to accept the higher offer and resile from the existing offer. For myself, I think that trustees have such a discretion in the matter as will allow them to act with proper prudence. I can see no reason why trustees should not pray in aid the common-sense rule underlying the old proverb: 'A bird in the hand is worth two in the bush.' I can imagine cases where trustees could properly refuse a higher offer and proceed with a lower offer. Each case must, of necessity, depend on its own facts. In regard to the case now before me, my view is that the trustees and their solicitors acted on an incorrect principle. The only consideration which was present to their minds was that they had gone so far in the negotiations with Mrs. Simpson that they could not properly, from the point of view of commercial morality, resile from those negotiations. That being so, they did not, to any extent, probe Canon Buttle's offer as, in my view, they should have done. It was urged on me that, by pausing to probe his offer, they ran the risk of losing the contract with Mrs. Simpson. On the view of the facts which I take,

---

3 (1950) 14 Conv (NS) 228 (E.H. Bodkin); (1975) 39 Conv (NS) 177 (A. Samuels). See *Cowan v Scargill* [1985] Ch 270 at 288, [1984] 2 All ER 750 at 761, p. 679, post; *Sargeant v National Westminster Bank* (1990) 61 P & CR 518.

As to whether trustees can sell at a valuation to be determined by a third party, see [1985] Conv 44 (G. Lightman). For the duty of charitable trustees when selling under Charities Act 1993, ss. 26, 36, p. 524 ante.

I do not consider that that was much of a risk. Mrs. Simpson had bought the leasehold term, which was nearing its end, and she was a very anxious purchaser. Equally, Canon Buttle had demonstrated beyond a peradventure that he was a very anxious buyer, and, as it seems to me, the least the trustees should have done would have been to have said to him: 'You have come on the scene at a late stage. You have made this offer well past the eleventh hour. We have advanced negotiations with Mrs. Simpson which can be concluded within a matter of hours. If you are really serious in your offer, you must submit in the circumstances to somewhat stringent terms, and you must be prepared to bind yourself at once to purchase the property for the sum of £6,500 on the terms, so far as applicable, of the draft contract which otherwise would be entered into with Mrs. Simpson.' I have not the slightest doubt but that in the circumstances Canon Buttle would have agreed to those stringent terms and that the matter would have been carried out. The trustees, however, perfectly *bona fide*, maintained their attitude ... ''[4]

QUESTION

What would you have done in Mr. Budgett's place in 1875–76? To what extent would his position have been eased if the Trustee Act 1925, s. 15 (or its predecessor) had been in operation at that time? See p. 741, post. *Re Greenwood* (1911) 105 LT 509; *Re Ezekiel's Settlement Trusts* [1942] Ch 230, [1942] 2 All ER 224.

II. Duty to Invest[5]

A. Introductory

Trustees are under a duty to invest the trust property in proper securities and so make it productive.[6] It is usual to give trustees a wide power of investment in the trust instrument setting up the trust. Otherwise their powers are limited to those which are given in the Trustee Investments Act 1961. This Act is now out of date; in 1982 the Law Reform Committee characterised it "as tiresome, cumbrous and expensive in operation with the result that its provisions are now seen to be inadequate."[7] It recommended that the Act should be repealed and replaced by a new statute more in keeping with present day investment practice. So far nothing substantial has been done.

However, in 1995 the Trust Law Committee under Sir John VINELOTT began to examine the power of investment in the aftermath of the new provisions for

---

4 The property was subsequently ordered to be sold to Mrs. Simpson for £6,600.
5 H & M, pp. 502–522; K & S, pp. 275–286; P & M, pp. 431–436; Pettit, pp. 379–403; Riddall, pp. 261–282; Snell, pp. 213–225; Underhill, pp. 563–609. See (1988) 85 LSG 22, p. 14 (R. Aldwinckle); p. 30(R. Reid), discussing how far the Financial Services Act 1986 applies to trustees and personal representatives.
6 *Re Wragg* [1919] 2 Ch 58 at 64, per P.O. Lawrence J.
7 The Powers and Duties of Trustees (1982) Cmnd. 8733, para. 3.20; p. 708 post; [1992] Conv 425 (R. Bartlett); [1993] Conv 317 (C.M. Jarman); (1995) 9 Trust Law Investment (LORD NICHOLLS OF BIRKENHEAD).

pension trustees under the Pensions Act 1995 (p. 706 post). And in November of that year H.M. Treasury announced that the proportion of a fund which could be invested in wider-range investments should be increased from 50 to 75 per cent.[8] It was also decided that the powers conferred by the Deregulation and Contracting Out Act 1994 could properly be used to remove restrictions on trustees' powers of investment.[8a]

B. Express Power of Investment

i. CONSTRUCTION

In **Re Harari's Settlement Trusts** [1949] 1 All ER 430[9], a settlement made by Sir Victor Harari, Pasha, gave power to the trustees to retain, or, with his daughter's consent, to sell and invest the proceeds and all other capital moneys subject to the trust "in or upon such investments as to them may seem fit". The existing investments were certain Egyptian bonds and securities; none was a trustee investment.

The question was whether the provision gave to the trustees power to invest outside the usual range of trustee investments; or whether the power authorised the trustees to exercise their discretion only within the authorised range. JENKINS J held that the trustees were authorised to invest in any investments which they honestly thought to be desirable. He said at 432:

"There is, however, a good deal of authority . . . to the effect that investment clauses should be strictly construed and should not be construed as authorising investments outside the trustee range unless they clearly and unambiguously indicate an intention to that effect." [He then referred to a number of cases and continued:] "That, I think, is a representative collection of the authorities bearing on this topic, and, having given them the best consideration I can, it seems to me that I am left free to construe this settlement according to what I consider to be the natural and proper meaning of the words used in their context, and, so construing the words 'in or upon such investments as to them may seem fit', I see no justification for implying any restriction. I think the trustees have power, under the plain meaning of those words, to invest in any investments which, to adopt Kekewich J's observation, they 'honestly think' are desirable investments for the investment of moneys subject to the trusts of the settlement. To hold otherwise would really be to read words into the settlement which are not there. The wide construction which the words themselves are, in my view, sufficient to bear, is, I think, to some extent, supported by the fact that the investments brought in, in the first place, are non-trustee investments, and also to some small extent by the reference in para. 2 to 'investment money or property representing' the trust fund. There is nothing in those words that one can say is really inconsistent with a limitation on the range of investment to trustee investments, but there is, perhaps, more likelihood of something which in common parlance would be described as 'property' rather than an 'investment' coming into the hands of the trustees in the course of exercising

---

8 Trustee Investments Act, s. 2(1), p. 664 post. For a similar relaxation in the rules for charitable trusts, see Charities (Trustee Investments Act 1961) Order 1995 (S.I. 1995 No 1092).

8a The Act provides a power by statutory instrument to remove or reduce statutory burdens on businesses or individuals so long as necessary protection is not reduced.

9 *Re Peczenik's Settlement Trusts* [1964] 1 WLR 720, [1964] 2 All ER 339.

their powers of investment if the range is the unrestricted one rather than the narrow one. The real ground, however, for my decision is the plain and ordinary meaning of the words 'in or upon such investments as to them may seem fit'. Having found nothing in the authorities to constrain me to construe those words otherwise than in accordance with their plain meaning, that is the meaning I propose to place on them''.

ii. PRECEDENT

Encyclopaedia of Forms and Precedents (4th edn) vol. 20, p. 678

"Any capital monies or other monies required to be invested under the trusts hereof may be invested in the names or under the control of the trustees in the purchase of or at interest upon the security of such stocks funds shares securities or other investments or property or interests (whether in possession or in remainder and whether vested or contingent) or in any property of whatsoever nature and wheresoever situate and whether or not involving liability and whether or not producing income (including the purchase of any chattels for use with any of the settled land) and also including the purchase of or (subject to the rules of law as to insurable interest) the effecting and (without prejudice to the powers contained in clause 4 hereof) the keeping up of any policy or policies of insurance (including an endowment policy or endowment policies) on the life of lives of any person or persons as the trustees shall from time to time in their absolute discretion think fit or may be placed and left on deposit with the National Savings Bank or with any bank or building society or other institution carrying on business in the United Kingdom whose business includes the receipt of money on deposit for such period or periods and on such terms as to interest and otherwise in all respects as the trustees shall in the like discretion from time to time think fit PROVIDED that where any such monies are invested in the purchase of any interest in any property which is contingent on any event the trustees may at the same time apply a further sufficient part of the capital monies in purchasing or effecting a policy or policies of insurance against such event for such amount as the trustees shall in their absolute discretion consider appropriate in all the circumstances.''[10]

C. Statutory Power: Trustee Investments Act 1961

i. AUTHORISED INVESTMENTS

TRUSTEE INVESTMENTS ACT 1961[11]

1. New powers of investment of trustees.—(1) A trustee may invest any property in his hands, whether at the time in a state of investment or not, in any

---

10 For alternative forms of investment clauses, see Forms 1:F:1 to 1:F:20.
11 See (1961) 25 Conv (NS) 372 (A. Samuels); and, for an American view, see (1954) CLP 139 (C. Latham); (1974) 23 ICLQ 748 (D. Grosh); Model Prudent Man Investment Act (1961), reproduced in (1974) 23 ICLQ at pp. 767–8; (1975) 39 Conv (NS) 327 (D. Paling); see also (1976) American Bar Foundation Research Journal 1 (J.H. Langbein and R.A. Posner).
  For the application of the Act to the investment of a superannuation fund's moneys under the Local Government Superannuation Regs 1986, see S.I. 1986 No. 24, Part P 3 as amended by Local Government Superannuation Regs 1990 (S.I. 1990 No. 2480); 1993 (S.I. 1993 No. 1848); 1994 (S.I. 1994 No. 1909).

manner specified in Part I or II of the First Schedule to this Act, or, subject to the next following section, in any manner specified in Part III of that Schedule, and may also from time to time vary any such investments.

(2) The supplemental provisions contained in Part IV of that Schedule shall have effect for the interpretation and for restricting the operation of the said Parts I to III.

(3) No provision relating to the powers of the trustee contained in any instrument (not being an enactment or an instrument made under an enactment) made before the passing of this Act shall limit the powers conferred by this section, but those powers are exercisable only in so far as a contrary intention is not expressed in any Act or instrument made under an enactment, whenever passed or made, and so relating or in any other instrument so relating which is made after the passing of this Act.

(4) In this Act "narrower-range investment" means an investment falling within Part I or II of the First Schedule to this Act and "wider-range investment" means an investment falling within Part III of that Schedule.

2. Restrictions on wider-range investment.—(1) A trustee shall not have power by virtue of the foregoing section to make or retain any wider-range investment unless the trust fund has been divided into two parts (hereinafter referred to as the narrower-range part and the wider-range part), the parts being, subject to the provisions of this Act, equal in value at the time of the division,[12] and where such a division has been made no subsequent division of the same fund shall be made for the purposes of this section, and no property shall be transferred from one part of the fund to the other unless either—

(a) the transfer is authorised or required by the following provisions of this Act, or

(b) a compensating transfer is made at the same time.

In this section "compensating transfer", in relation to any transferred property, means a transfer in the opposite direction of property of equal value.

(2) Property belonging to the narrower-range part of a trust fund shall not by virtue of the foregoing section be invested except in narrower-range investments, and any property invested in any other manner which is or becomes comprised in that part of the trust fund shall either be transferred to the wider-range part of the fund, with a compensating transfer, or be reinvested in narrower-range investments as soon as may be.

(3) Where any property accrues to a trust fund after the fund has been divided in pursuance of subsection (1) of this section, then—

(a) if the property accrues to the trustee as owner or former owner of property comprised in either part of the fund,[13] it shall be treated as belonging to that part of the fund;

(b) in any other case, the trustee shall secure, by appointment of the accruing property or the transfer of property from one part of the fund to the other, or both, that the value of the wider-range part of the fund is increased by an amount which bears the specified proportion to the

---

12 The proportion is now 75:25, see p. 622, ante; Charities (Trustee Investments Act 1961) Order 1995 (S.I. 1995 No. 1092), p. 522, n. 8 ante.

13 As a "bonus issue" of shares.

amount by which the value of the narrower-range part of the fund is increased.[14]

Where a trustee acquires property in consideration of a money payment the acquisition of the property shall be treated for the purposes of this section as investment and not as the accrual of property to the trust fund, notwithstanding that the amount of the consideration is less than the value of the property acquired;[15] and paragraph (*a*) of this subsection shall not include the case of a dividend or interest becoming part of a trust fund.

(4) Where in the exercise of any power or duty of a trustee property falls to be taken out of the trust fund, nothing in this section shall restrict his discretion as to the choice of property to be taken out.

Section 1

FIRST SCHEDULE

Manner of Investment

Part I

Narrower-Range Investments not Requiring Advice

1. In Defence Bonds, National Savings Certificates and Ulster Savings Certificates, Ulster Development Bonds,[16] National Development Bonds,[17] British Savings Bonds,[18] National Savings Income Bonds,[19] National Savings Deposit Bonds,[20] National Savings Indexed-Income Bonds,[1] National Savings Capital Bonds,[2] National Savings FIRST Option Bonds[3] and Pensions Guaranteed Income Bonds.[4]

2. In deposits in the National Savings Bank,[5] and deposits in a bank or department thereof certified under subsection (3) of section nine of the Finance Act 1956.

Part II

Narrower-Range Investments Requiring Advice

1. In securities issued by Her Majesty's Government in the United Kingdom, the Government of Northern Ireland or the Government of the Isle of Man, not being securities falling within Part I of this Schedule and being fixed-interest securities registered in the United Kingdom or the Isle of Man, Treasury Bills or Tax Reserve Certificates or any variable interest securities

---

14 As added by Charities (Trustee Investments Act 1961) Order 1995 (S.I. 1995 No. 1092).
15 As a "rights issue": which is thus added to the part of the fund which makes the purchase.
16 Trustee Investments (Additional Powers) (No. 2) Order 1962, S.I. 1962 No. 2611.
17 Trustee Investments (Additional Powers) Order 1964, S.I. 1964 No. 703.
18 Trustee Investments (Additional Powers) Order 1968, S.I. 1968 No. 470.
19 Trustee Investments (Additional Powers) Order 1982, S.I. 1982 No. 1086.
20 Trustee Investments (Additional Powers) (No. 2) Order 1983, S.I. 1983 No. 1525.
 1 Trustee Investments (Additional Powers) Order 1985, S.I. 1985, No. 1780.
 2 Trustee Investments (Additional Powers) Order 1988, S.I. 1988 No. 2254.
 3 Trustee Investment (Additional Powers) Order 1992, S.I. 1992, No. 1738.
 4 Trustee Investment (Additional Powers) Order 1994, S.I. 1994, No. 265.
 5 Post Office Act 1969, ss. 94, 114, Sch. 6, Part III.

issued by Her Majesty's Government in the United Kingdom and registered in the United Kingdom.[6]

2. In any securities the payment of interest on which is guaranteed by Her Majesty's Government in the United Kingdom or the Government of Northern Ireland.

3. In fixed-interest securities issued in the United Kingdom by any public authority or nationalised industry or undertaking in the United Kingdom.

4. In fixed-interest securities issued in the United Kingdom by the government of any overseas territory within the Commonwealth or by any public or local authority within such a territory, being securities registered in the United Kingdom.

References in this paragraph to an overseas territory or to the government of such a territory shall be construed as if they occurred in the Overseas Service Act, 1958.

4A. In securities issued in the United Kingdom by the government of an overseas territory within the Commonwealth or by any public or local authority within such a territory, being securities registered in the United Kingdom and in respect of which the rate of interest is variable by reference to one or more of the following:—

   (*a*) the Bank of England's minimum lending rate;[7]
   (*b*) the average rate of discount on allotment on 91-day Treasury bills;
   (*c*) a yield on 91-day Treasury bills;
   (*d*) a London sterling inter-bank offered rate;
   (*e*) a London sterling certificate of deposit rate.

References in this paragraph to an overseas territory or to the government of such a territory shall be construed as if they occurred in the Overseas Service Act 1958.[8]

5. In fixed-interest securities issued in the United Kingdom by the African Development Bank, the Asian Development Bank, the Caribbean Development Bank, the European Bank for Reconstruction and Development,[9] the International Finance Corporation, the International Monetary Fund or by[10] the International Bank for Reconstruction and Development, being securities registered in the United Kingdom, and in fixed-interest securities issued in the United Kingdom by the Inter-American Development Bank,[11] and in fixed-interest securities issued in the United Kingdom by the European Atomic Energy Community, the European Economic Community, the European Investment Bank, or by the European Coal and Steel Community,[12] being securities registered in the United Kingdom.

5A. In securities issued in the United Kingdom by
   (i)   the International Bank for Reconstruction and Development or by the European Investment Bank or by the European Coal and Steel

---

6 Trustee Investments (Additional Powers) Order 1977, S.I. 1977 No. 831.
7 This is no longer posted.
8 Trustee Investments (Additional Powers) (No. 2) Order 1977, S.I. 1977 No.1878.
9 Trustee Investments (Additional Powers) Order 1991, S.I. 1991 No. 999.
10 Trustee Investments (Additional Powers) Order 1983, S.I. 1983 No. 772.
11 Trustee Investments (Additional Powers) (No. 2) Order 1964, S.I. 1964 No. 1404.
12 Trustee Investments (Additional Powers) Order 1972, S.I. 1972 No. 1818.

Community, being securities registered in the United Kingdom
or
(ii) the Inter-American Development Bank
being securities in respect of which the rate of interest is variable by reference
to one or more of the following:—
(a) the Bank of England's minimum lending rate;
(b) the average rate of discount on allotment on 91-day Treasury bills;
(c) a yield on 91-day Treasury bills;
(d) a London sterling inter-bank offered rate;
(e) a London sterling certificate of deposit rate.[13]

5B. In securities issued in the United Kingdom by the African Development
Bank, the Asian Development Bank, the Caribbean Development Bank, the
European Atomic Energy Community, the European Bank for Reconstruction
and Development,[14] the European Economic Community, the International
Finance Corporation or by the International Monetary Fund, being securities
registered in the United Kingdom and in respect of which the rate of interest
is variable by reference to one or more of the following:—
(a) the average rate of discount on allotment on 91-day Treasury Bills;
(b) a yield on 91-day Treasury Bills;
(c) a London sterling inter-bank offered rate;
(d) a London sterling certificate of deposit rate.[15]

6. In debentures issued in the United Kingdom by a company incorporated
in the United Kingdom, being debentures registered in the United
Kingdom.

7. In stock of the Bank of Ireland and in Bank of Ireland 7 per cent. Loan
Stock 1986/91.[16]

9. In loans to any authority to which this paragraph applies charged on all or
any of the revenues of the authority or on a fund into which all or any of those
revenues are payable, in any fixed-interest securities issued in the United
Kingdom by any such authority for the purpose of borrowing money so
charged, and in deposits with any such authority by way of temporary loan
made on the giving of a receipt for the loan by the treasurer or other similar
officer of the authority and on the giving of an undertaking by the authority
that, if requested to charge the loan as aforesaid, it will either comply with the
request or repay the loan.

This paragraph applies to the following authorities, that is to say—
(a) any local authority in the United Kingdom;
(b) any authority all the members of which are appointed or elected by one
or more local authorities in the United Kingdom;
(c) any authority the majority of the members of which are appointed or
elected by one or more local authorities in the United Kingdom, being
an authority which by virtue of any enactment has power to issue a
precept to a local authority in England and Wales, or a requisition to a
local authority in Scotland, or to the expenses of which, by virtue of any
enactment, a local authority in the United Kingdom is or can be
required to contribute;

13 Trustee Investments (Additional Powers) (No. 2) Order 1977, S.I. 1977 No. 1878.
14 Trustee Investments (Additional Powers) Order 1991, S.I. 1991 No. 999.
15 Trustee Investments (Additional Powers) Order 1983, S.I. 1983 No. 772.
16 Trustee Investments (Additional Powers) Order 1966, S.I. 1966 No. 401.

(d) the Receiver for the Metropolitan Police District or a police authority established under section 3 of the Police Act 1964;[17]

(e) the Belfast City and District Water Commissioners;

(f) the Great Ouse Water Authority;[18]

(g) any district council in Northern Ireland;[19]

(i) any residuary body established by sections 57 of the Local Government Act 1985.[20]

9A. In any securities issued in the United Kingdom by any authority to which paragraph 9 applies for the purpose of borrowing money charged on all or any of the revenues of the authority or on a fund into which all or any of these revenues are payable and being securities in respect of which the rate of interest is variable by reference to one or more of the following:—

(a) the Bank of England's minimum lending rate;

(b) the average rate of discount on allotment on 91-day Treasury bills;

(c) a yield on 91-day Treasury bills;

(d) a London sterling inter-bank offered rate;

(e) a London sterling certificate of deposit rate;[1]

10. In debentures or in the guaranteed or preference stock of any incorporated company, being statutory water undertakers within the meaning of the Water Act 1945,[2] or any corresponding enactment in force in Northern Ireland, and having during each of the ten years immediately preceding the calender year in which the investment was made paid a dividend of not less than $3\frac{1}{2}$ per cent.[3] on its ordinary shares.[4]

10A. In any units of a gilt unit trust scheme.

References in this Schedule to a gilt unit trust scheme are references to a collective investment scheme—

(a) which is an authorised unit trust scheme within the meaning of the Financial Services Act 1986, a recognised scheme within the meaning of that Act or a UCITS; and

(b) whose objective is to invest not less than 90% of the property of the scheme in loan stock, bonds and other instruments creating or acknowledging indebtedness which are transferable and which are issued or guaranteed by—

(i) the government of the United Kingdom or of any other country or territory,[4a]

(ii) a local authority in the United Kingdom or in a relevant state, or

(iii) by an international organisation the members of which include the United Kingdom or a relevant state;

---

17 As amended by Police and Magistrates' Courts Act 1994, s. 43, Sch 4, Pt II, para. 47.

18 Trustee Investments (Additional Powers) Order 1962, S.I. 1962 No. 658. By the Water Resources Act 1963, s. 6 (6) and Sch. 4, para. 33, any river which, apart from that para., would not be included among the authorities to which para. 9 applies is, by virtue of that Act, included among those authorities.

19 Trustee Investments (Additional Powers) Order 1973, S.I. 1973 No. 1332.

20 Trustee Investments (Additional Powers) Order 1986, S.I. 1986 No. 601.

1 Trustee Investments (Additional Powers) (No. 2) Order 1977, S.I. 1977 No. 1878.

2 As amended by Water Act 1948, s. 1.

3 Replacing 5 per cent. from 1973; Trustee Investments (Water Companies) Order 1973, S.I. 1973 No. 1393.

4 Repealed, except insofar as it relates to the debentures or guaranteed or preference stock of a company which is a statutory water undertaker within the meaning of an enactment in Northern Ireland by the Water Act 1989, s. 190(1), Sch 25, para. 29.

4a Trustee Investments (Additional Powers) Order 1995, S.I. 1995 No 768.

and, in respect of the remainder of the property of the scheme, whose objective is to invest in any instrument falling with any of paragraphs 1 to 3, 5 or 6 of Schedule 1 to the Financial Services Act 1986.[5]

12. In deposits with a building society within the meaning of the Building Societies Act 1986.[6]

13. In mortgages of freehold property in England and Wales or Northern Ireland and of leasehold property in those countries of which the unexpired term at the time of investment is not less than sixty years, and in loans on heritable security in Scotland.

14. In perpetual rent-charges charged on land in England and Wales or Northern Ireland and fee-farm rents (not being rent-charges) issuing out of such land, and in feu-duties or ground annuals in Scotland.

15. In certificates of tax deposit.[7]

16. In fixed-interest or variable interest securities issued by the government of a relevant state.

17. In any securities the payment of interest on which is guaranteed by the government of a relevant state.

18. In fixed-interest securities issued in any relevant state by any public authority or nationalised industry or undertaking in that state.

19. In fixed-interest or variable interest securities issued in a relevant state by the government of any overseas territory with the Commonwealth or by any public or local authority within such a territory.

References in this paragraph to an overseas territory or to the government of such a territory shall be construed as if they occurred in the Overseas Development and Co-operation Act 1980.

20. In the fixed-interest or variable interest securities issued in a relevant state by—

(a) the African Development Bank;
(b) the Asian Development Bank;
(c) the Caribbean Development Bank;
(d) the International Finance Corporation;
(e) the International Monetary Fund;
(f) the International Bank for Reconstruction and Development;
(g) the Inter-American Development Bank;
(h) the European Atomic Energy Community;
(i) the European Bank for Reconstruction and Development;
(j) the European Economic Community;
(k) the European Investment Bank; or
(l) the European Coal and Steel Community.

21. In debentures issued in any relevant state by a company incorporated in that state.

22. In loans to any authority to which this paragraph applies secured on all or any of the revenues of the authority or on a fund into which all or any of those revenues are payable, in fixed-interest or variable interest securities issued in a relevant state by any such authority in that state for the purpose of borrowing money so secured, and in deposits with any authority to which this paragraph applies by way of temporary loan made on the giving of a receipt for

---

5 As substituted by Trustee Investments (Additional Powers) (No. 2) Order 1994 (S.I. 1994, No. 1908).
6 As substituted by Building Societies Act 1986, s. 120 (1), Sch. 18, Pt 1, para. 4.
7 Trustee Investments (Additional Powers) Order 1975, S.I. 1975 No. 1710.

the loan by the treasurer or other similar officer of the authority and on the giving of an undertaking by the authority that, if requested to charge the loan as aforesaid, it will either comply with the request or repay the loan.

This paragraph applies to the following authorities, that is to say—

(*a*) any local authority in a relevant state; or

(*b*) any local authority all the members of which are appointed or elected by one or more local authorities in any such state.

23. In deposits with a mutual investment society whose head office is located in a relevant state.

24. In loans secured on any interest in property in a relevant state which corresponds to an interest in property falling within paragraph 13 of this Part of this Schedule.[8]

Part III

Wider-Range Investments

1. In any securities issued in the United Kingdom by a company incorporated in the United Kingdom, being securities registered in the United Kingdom and not being securities falling within Part II of this Schedule.

2. In shares in a building society within the meaning of the Building Societies Act 1986.[8a]

3. In any units of an authorised unit trust scheme within the meaning of the Financial Services Act 1986.[9]

4. In any securities issued in any relevant state by a company incorporated in that state or by any unincorporated body constituted under the law of that state, not being (in either case) securities falling within Part II of this Schedule or paragraph 6 of this part of this schedule.

5. In shares in a mutual investment society whose head office is located in a relevant state.

6. In any units of a collective investment scheme which is—

(*a*) a recognised scheme within the meaning of the Financial Services Act 1986 which is constituted in a relevant state; or

(*b*) a UCITS;

and which does not fall within Part II of this Schedule.[10]

Part IV

Supplemental

1. The securities mentioned in Parts I to III of this Schedule do not include any securities where the holder can be required to accept repayment of the principal, or the payment of any interest, otherwise than in sterling, in the currency of a relevant state or in the European currency unit (as defined in article 1 of Council Regulation No. 3180/78/EEC).

2. The securities mentioned in paragraphs 1 to 8 of Part II, other than Treasury Bills or Tax Reserve Certificates, securities issued before the passing

---

8 Paras. 16–24 were added by Trustee Investments (Additional Powers) (No. 2) Order 1994 (S.I. 1994 No. 1908).

8a As substituted by Building Societies Act 1986, s. 120 (1), Sch. 18, Pt 1, para. 4.

9 As amended by Financial Services Act 1986, s. 212 (2), Sch. 16, para. 2 (*b*).

10 Paras 4–6 were added by Trustee Investments (Additional Powers) (No. 2) Order 1994 (S.I. 1994 No. 1908).

of this Act by the Government of the Isle of Man, securities falling within paragraph 4 of the said Part II issued before the passing of this Act or securities falling within paragraph 9 of that Part, and the securities mentioned in paragraph 1 of Part III of this Schedule, do not include—

(*a*) securities the price of which is not quoted on a recognised investment exchange within the meaning of the Financial Services Act 1986[11] or on an investment exchange which constitutes the principal or only market established in a relevant state on which securities admitted to official listing are dealt in or traded;

(*b*) shares or debenture stock not fully paid up (except shares or debenture stock which by the terms of issue are required to be fully paid up within nine months of the date of issue).

2A. The securities mentioned in paragraphs 16 to 21 of Part II of this Schedule, other than securities traded on a relevant money market or securities falling within paragraph 22 of Part II of this Schedule, and the securities mentioned in paragraph 4 of Part III of this Schedule do not include—

(*a*) securities the price for which is not quoted on a recognised investment exchange within the meaning of the Financial Services Act 1986 or on an investment exchange which constitutes the principal or only market established in a relevant state on which securities admitted to official listing are dealt in or traded;

(*b*) shares or debenture stock not fully paid up (except shares or debenture stock which by the terms of issue are required to be fully paid up within nine months of the date of issue or shares issued with no nominal value).[12]

3. The securities mentioned in paragraphs 6 and 21 of Part II and paragraph 1 or 4 of Part III of this Schedule do not include—

(*a*) shares or debentures of an incorporated company of which the total issued and paid up share capital is less than one million pounds;

(*ab*) shares or debentures of an incorporated company of which the total issued and paid up share capital at any time on the business day before the investment is made is less than the equivalent of one million pounds in the currency of a relevant state (at the exchange rate prevailing in the United Kingdom at the close of business on the day before the investment is made);[12]

(*b*) shares or debentures of an incorporated company which has not in each of the five years immediately preceding the calendar year in which the investment is made paid a dividend on all the shares issued by the company, excluding any shares issued after the dividend was declared and any shares which by their terms of issue did not rank for the dividend for that year.[12a]

For the purposes of sub-paragraph (*b*) of this paragraph a company formed—

(i) to take over the business of another company or other companies, or

---

11 As amended by Financial Services Act 1986, s. 212 (2), Sch. 16, para. 2 (*c*).
12 As added by Trustee Investments (Additional Powers) (No. 2) Order 1994 (S.I. 1994, No. 1908).
12a See Atomic Energy Authority Act 1995, s. 6, Sched 2, para 8 in relation to investment in successor companies.

(ii) to acquire the securities of, or control of, another company or other companies,

or for either of those purposes and for other purposes shall be deemed to have paid a dividend as mentioned in that sub-paragraph in any year in which such a dividend has been paid by the other company or all the other companies, as the case may be.[13]

For the purposes of sub-paragraph (*b*) of this paragraph in relation to investment in shares or debentures of a successor company within the meaning of the Electricity (Northern Ireland) Order 1992 the company shall be deemed to have paid a dividend as mentioned in that sub-paragraph—

(iii) in every year preceding the calendar year in which the transfer date within the meaning of Part III of that Order of 1992 falls ("the first investment year") which is included in the relevant five years; and

(iv) in the first investment year, if that year is included in the relevant five years and that company does not in fact pay such a dividend in that year; and

"the relevant five years" means the five years immediately preceding the year in which the investment in question is made or proposed to be made.[14]

4. In this Schedule, unless the context otherwise requires, the following expressions have the meanings hereby respectively assigned to them, that is to say—

"relevant state" means Austria, Finland, Iceland, Liechtenstein,[14a] Norway, Sweden or a member state other than the United Kingdom.

ii. SPECIAL RANGE

TRUSTEE INVESTMENTS ACT 1961

3. Relationship between Act and other powers of investment.—(1) The powers conferred by section one of this Act are in addition to and not in derogation from any power conferred otherwise than by this Act of investment or postponing conversion exercisable by a trustee (hereinafter referred to as a "special power").

(2) Any special power (however expressed) to invest property in any investment for the time being authorised by law for the investment of trust property, being a power conferred on a trustee before the passing of this Act or conferred on him under any enactment passed before the passing of this Act, shall have effect as a power to invest property in like manner and subject to the like provisions as under the foregoing provisions of this Act.

(3) In relation to property, including wider-range but not including narrower-range investments,—

(*a*) which a trustee is authorised to hold apart from—

(i) the provisions of section one of this Act or any of the provisions of Part I of the Trustee Act 1925 or any of the provisions of the Trusts (Scotland) Act 1921, or

(ii) any such power to invest in authorised investments as is mentioned in the foregoing subsection, or

---

13 For further details and definitions, see paras. 4–6.
14 As added by Electricity (Northern Ireland Consequential Amendments) Order 1992, S.I. 1992, No. 232, art 4.
14a As added by Trustee Investments (Additional Powers) Order 1995, S.I. 1995 No. 765.

(*b*) which became part of a trust fund in consequence of the exercise by the trustee, as owner of property falling within this subsection, of any power conferred by subsection (3) or (4) of section ten of the Trustee Act 1925, or paragraph (*o*) or (*p*) of subsection (1) of section four of the Trusts (Scotland) Act 1921,

the foregoing section shall have effect subject to the modifications set out in the Second Schedule to this Act.

Section 3

SECOND SCHEDULE

MODIFICATION OF S. 2 IN RELATION TO PROPERTY FALLING WITHIN S. 3 (3)

1. In this Schedule "special-range property" means property falling within subsection (3) of section three of this Act.

2.—(1) Where a trust fund includes special-range property, subsection (1) of section two of this Act shall have effect as if references to the trust fund were references to so much thereof as does not consist of special-range property, and the special-range property shall be carried to a separate part of the fund.

(2) Any property which—

(*a*) being property belonging to the narrower-range or wider-range part of a trust fund, is converted into special-range property, or

(*b*) being special-range property, accrues to a trust fund after the division of the fund or part thereof in pursuance of subsection (1) of section two of this Act or of that subsection as modified by sub-paragraph (1) of this paragraph,

shall be carried to such a separate part of the fund as aforesaid; and subsections (2) and (3) of the said section two shall have effect subject to this sub-paragraph.

(3) Where property carried to such a separate part as aforesaid is converted into property other than special-range property,—

(*a*) it shall be transferred to the narrower-range part of the fund or the wider-range part of the fund or apportioned between them, and

(*b*) any transfer of property from one of those parts to the other shall be made which is necessary to secure that the value of the wider-range part of the fund is increased by an amount which bears the specified proportion to the amount by which the value of the narrower-range part of the fund is increased.[15]

THIRD SCHEDULE

Section 3

PROVISIONS SUPPLEMENTARY TO S. 3 (4)

1. Where in a case falling within subsection (4) of section three of this Act, property belonging to the narrower-range part of a trust fund—

(*a*) is invested otherwise than in a narrower-range investment, or

---

15 As substituted by Charities (Trustee Investments Act 1961) Order 1995 (S.I. 1995 No. 1092).

(*b*) being so invested, is retained and not transferred or as soon as may be reinvested as mentioned in subsection (2) of section two of this Act, then, so long as the property continues so invested and comprised in the narrower-range part of the fund, section one of this Act shall not authorise the making or retention of any wider-range investment.

2. Section four of the Trustee Act 1925, or section thirty-three of the Trusts (Scotland) Act 1921 (which relieve a trustee from liability for retaining an investment which has ceased to be authorised), shall not apply where an investment ceases to be authorised in consequence of the foregoing paragraph.

iii. Valuation for Purposes of Sections 2–4

TRUSTEE INVESTMENTS ACT 1961

5. Certain valuations to be conclusive for purposes of division of trust fund.— (1) If for the purposes of section two or four of this Act or the Second Schedule thereto a trustee obtains, from a person reasonably believed by the trustee to be qualified to make it, a valuation in writing of any property, the valuation shall be conclusive in determining whether the division of the trust fund in pursuance of subsection (1) of the said section two, or any transfer or apportionment of property under that section or the said Second Schedule, has been duly made.

(2) The foregoing subsection applies to any such valuation notwithstanding that it is made by a person in the course of his employment as an officer or servant.

iv. Method of Selection

TRUSTEE INVESTMENTS ACT 1961

4. Interpretation of references to trust property and trust funds.—(1) In this Act "property" includes real or personal property of any description, including money and things in action:

Provided that it does not include an interest in expectancy, but the falling into possession of such an interest, or the receipt of proceeds of the sale thereof, shall be treated for the purposes of this Act as an accrual of property to the trust fund.

(2) So much of the property in the hands of a trustee shall for the purposes of this Act constitute one trust fund as is held on trusts which (as respects the beneficiaries or their respective interests or the purposes of the trust or as respects the powers of the trustee) are not identical with those on which any other property in his hands is held.

(3) Where property is taken out of a trust fund by way of appropriation so as to form a separate fund, and at the time of the appropriation the trust fund had (as to the whole or a part thereof) been divided in pursuance of subsection (1) of section two of this Act, or that subsection as modified by the Second Schedule to this Act, then if the separate fund is so divided the narrower-range and wider-range parts of the separate fund may be constituted so as to bear to

each other either the specified proportion or[16] the same proportion as the two corresponding parts of the fund out of which it was so appropriated (the values of those parts of those funds being ascertained as at the time of appropriation), or some intermediate proportion.

6. Duty of trustees in choosing investments.—(1) In the exercise of his powers of investment a trustee shall have regard—

(*a*) to the need for diversification of investments of the trust, in so far as is appropriate to the circumstances of the trust;

(*b*) to the suitability to the trust of investments of the description of investment proposed and of the investment proposed as an investment of that description.

(2) Before exercising any power conferred by section one of this Act to invest in a manner specified in Part II or III of the First Schedule to this Act, or before investing in any such manner in the exercise of a power falling within subsection (2) of section three of this Act, a trustee shall obtain and consider proper advice on the question whether the investment is satisfactory having regard to the matters mentioned in paragraphs (*a*) and (*b*) of the foregoing subsection.

(3) A trustee retaining any investment made in the exercise of such a power and in such a manner as aforesaid shall determine at what intervals the circumstances, and in particular the nature of the investment, make it desirable to obtain such advice as aforesaid, and shall obtain and consider such advice accordingly.

(4) For the purposes of the two foregoing subsections, proper advice is the advice of a person who is reasonably believed by the trustee to be qualified by his ability in and practical experience of financial matters; and such advice may be given by a person notwithstanding that he gives it in the course of his employment as an officer or servant.

(5) A trustee shall not be treated as having complied with subsection (2) or (3) of this section unless the advice was given or has been subsequently confirmed in writing.

(6) Subsections (2) and (3) of this section shall not apply to one of two or more trustees where he is the person giving the advice required by this section to his co-trustee or co-trustees, and shall not apply where powers of a trustee are lawfully exercised by an officer or servant competent under subsection (4) of this section to give proper advice.

(7) Without prejudice to section eight of the Trustee Act, 1925, or section thirty of the Trusts (Scotland) Act, 1921 (which relate to valuation, and the proportion of the value to be lent, where a trustee lends on the security of property) the advice required by this section shall not include, in the case of a loan on the security of freehold or leasehold property in England and Wales or Northern Ireland or on heritable security in Scotland, advice on the suitability of the particular loan.

15. Saving for powers of court.—The enlargement of the investment powers of trustees by this Act shall not lessen any power of a court to confer wider powers of investment on trustees, or affect the extent to which any such power is to be exercised.

---

16 As substituted by Charities (Trustee Investments Act 1961) Order 1995 (S.I. 1995 No. 1092).

D. Selecting Investments

i. GENERAL DUTY

NESTLE v NATIONAL WESTMINSTER BANK PLC[17]
[1993] 1 WLR 1260, [1994] 1 All ER 118 (CA, DILLON, STAUGHTON and LEGGATT LJJ)

Miss Nestle's grandfather, who died in 1922, appointed the National Provincial Bank Ltd (which later merged with the National Westminster Bank plc) as his executor and trustee. Under his will his widow had a life interest in Winterbourne, the family home, and an annuity. On her death their two sons each had an annuity from the ages of 21 to 25, and then a half-interest in the residue. When the sons died, their shares went to their children.

In 1986 Miss Nestle, who then became absolutely entitled to the capital, claimed that the trust fund which was then valued at £269,203 should have been worth well over £1 million. She brought an action against the trustee bank for default in the management of the fund.

Held. For the bank.

LEGGATT LJ: When trusts came into their own in Victorian times they were no doubt intended to preserve capital while assuring beneficiaries of a steady, if conservative, income. Little was demanded of a trustee beyond the safeguarding of the trust fund by refraining from improvident investment. This process was no doubt also intended to save beneficiaries from trouble and anxiety, or what is now called "hassle." But during the 64 years for which the trust set up by the plaintiff's grandfather endured, the contentment of his descendants declined. The plaintiff's uncle and father conducted with the respondent bank vigorous campaigns designed to improve their respective incomes, which, if the bank had not resisted them, would have worked to the ultimate detriment of the plaintiff, while the plaintiff herself is now locked in mortal financial combat with the bank.

George and John Nestle saw the bank, or said they saw the bank, as unfairly looking out for the plaintiff at their expense. In fact John turns out to have had a fortune of his own, which was invested in equities. So to the extent that he was successful in getting the bank to invest in gilts he was achieving a balance between his funds. The plaintiff, on the other hand, with whom her father was latterly at odds, has become obsessed with the idea that the bank over the years has failed to look after her interests. She claims that the sum of £269,203 which she inherited should have been larger than it was. It will not be of any consolation to her to reflect that, if since 1986 she had in that period done for the fund what she claims that the bank ought to have done for it previously, and it had grown at the same rate as the cost of living, it would probably now be worth over £400,000.

There is no dispute about the nature of the bank's duty. It was, as Lindley LJ has expressed it, a duty "to take such care as an ordinary prudent man would take if he were minded to make an investment for the benefit of other people for whom he felt morally bound to provide:" *Re Whiteley* (1886) 33 Ch D 347, 355. The trustee must have regard "not only to the interests of those who are entitled to the income, but to the interests of those who will take in future:" per Cotton LJ, at p. 350. "A trustee must not choose investments other than

---

17 (1992) 142 NLJ 1279 (J.E.Martin); [1993] Conv 61 (A. Kenny); Moffatt. *Trusts, Law: Text and Materials*, Chap 10; p. 718 post.

those which the terms of his trust permit:" *Speight v Gaunt* (1883) 9 App Cas 1, 19, per Lord Blackburn. So confined, the trustee must also "avoid all investments of that class which are attended with hazard:" *Learoyd v Whiteley* (1887) 12 App Cas 727, 733, per Lord Watson. The power of investment "must be exercised so as to yield the best return for the beneficiaries, judged in relation to the risks of the investments in question; and the prospects of the yield of income and capital appreciation both have to be considered in judging the return from the investment:" *Cowan v Scargill* [1985] Ch 270, 287, [1984] 2 All ER 750, 760, p. 679 post'.

Since the Trustee Investments Act 1961 came into force a trustee has been required by section 6(1) to have regard in the exercise of his powers of investment "to the need for diversification of investments of the trust, in so far as is appropriate to the circumstances of the trust." It is common ground that a trustee with a power of investment must undertake periodic reviews of the investments held by the trust. In relation to this trust, that would have meant a review carried out at least annually, and whenever else a reappraisal of the trust portfolio was requested or was otherwise requisite. It must also be borne in mind that, as expressed by the Report of the Scarman Committee on the Powers and Duties of Trustees (1982) (Law Reform Committee: 23rd Report Cmnd. 8733), at para. 2.15, "Professional trustees, such as banks, are under a special duty to display expertise in every aspect of their administration of the trust."

The plaintiff alleges that the bank is in breach of trust because over the years since her grandfather set up the trust the bank has supposed that its power of investment was more limited than it was; has failed to carry out periodic reviews of the portfolio, and to maintain a proper balance between equities and gilts, and to diversify the equity investments; and has unduly favoured the interests of her father and her uncle as life-tenants at the expense of her own interest as remainderman. She says that in consequence the trust fund was worth less in 1986 than it should have been.

The essence of the bank's duty was to take such steps as a prudent businessman would have taken to maintain and increase the value of the trust fund. Unless it failed to do so, it was not in breach of trust. A breach of duty will not be actionable, and therefore will be immaterial, if it does not cause loss. In this context I would endorse the concession of Mr Nugee for the bank that "loss" will be incurred by a trust fund when it makes a gain less than would have been made by a prudent businessman. A claimant will therefore fail who cannot prove a loss in this sense caused by breach of duty. So here in order to make a case for an inquiry, the plaintiff must show that loss was caused by breach of duty on the part of the bank.

On the plaintiff's behalf Mr Lyndon-Stanford seeks to rely on a presumption against a wrongdoing trustee. He invokes Brightman J's dictum in *Bartlett v Barclays Bank Trust Co Ltd (No 2)* [1980] Ch 515, 545, [1980] 2 All ER 92 at 96 that "The trustee's obligation is to restore to the trust estate the assets of which he has deprived it." But that presupposes deprivation.

The plaintiff alleges, and I am content to assume, that the bank was at all material times under a misapprehension about the meaning of the investment clause in the will, with the result that the bank believed that the scope of its powers of investment was more confined than it was. I also regard it as unlikely that the bank conducted any reviews of the portfolio between 1922 and 1959. If any were conducted, they were unplanned, sporadic and indecisive. Mr Lyndon-Stanford argues that it should be presumed that, had there been a better balance between gilts and equities and had the equity investment been more diversified, the fund would ultimately have been worth more than it was. The fallacy is that it does not follow from the fact that a wider power of investment was available to the bank than it realised either that it would have been exercised or that, if it had been, the exercise of it would have produced a result more beneficial to the bank than actually was produced. Loss cannot be presumed, if none would necessarily have resulted. Until it was proved that there was a loss, no attempt could be made to assess the amount of it.

[His Lordship referred to *Guerin v The Queen* (1984) 13 DLR (4th) 321, and continued:]

In my judgment either there was a loss in the present case or there was not. Unless there was a loss, there was no cause of action. It was for the plaintiff to prove on balance of probabilities that there was, or must have been, a loss. If proved, the court would then have had to assess the amount of it, and for the purpose of doing so might have had recourse to presumptions against the bank. In short, it if were shown that a loss was caused by breach of trust, such a presumption might avail the plaintiff in quantifying the loss. The plaintiff's difficulty is in reaching that stage.

The plaintiff therefore had to prove that a prudent trustee, knowing of the scope of the bank's investment power and conducting regular reviews, would so have invested the trust funds as to make it worth more than it was worth when the plaintiff inherited it. That was a matter for expert evidence. In the result there was evidence which the judge was entitled to accept and did accept that the bank did no less than expected of it up to the death of the testator's widow in 1960.

The proportion of the fund already invested in equities at the time when "Winterbourne" was sold makes it impossible in my judgment to impugn the decision to put the proceeds of sale into conversion stock.

After 1960 investment of the trust funds preponderantly in tax-exempt gilts for the benefit of life-tenants resident abroad is not shown to have produced a less satisfactory result for the remainderman than an investment in equities after taking into account savings in estate duty and capital transfer tax, because this policy had the effect of preserving the capital. By the time that John Nestle died the equities to replace the tax-exempt gilts would have had to be worth more than twice as much as the gilts in order to achieve the same benefit net of tax.

It is true that the calculations upon which the bank relied in making these comparisons were based on the assumptions that the whole fund was subject to estate duty, and that the bank did not contemplate that it might be able to take advantage of a late switch into gilts, especially in relation to Mrs. Elsie Nestle. But even if a less favourable assumption were made in relation to estate duty, the result would not have been so inferior as to demonstrate failure to look out for the remainderman amounting to a breach of trust. Similarly, although the fact that Mrs. Elsie Nestle returned to live in this country now indicates that it might have been advantageous if a switch into equities had been made after George's death, the bank cannot in my judgment be reproached for failing to anticipate that she would outlive her husband by 10 years, and that she would destroy the benefit of investment in tax-exempt gilts by resuming her domicile in England. Had she not done so, it would have been impossible for the bank to assess with any accuracy the timing of a switch back into gilts. In any event, without having pleaded any defect in the management of Mrs. Elsie Nestle's fund, the plaintiff cannot now rely on this argument.

No testator, in the light of this example, would choose this bank for the effective management of his investment. But the bank's engagement was as a trustee; and as such, it is to be judged not so much by success as by absence of proven default. The importance of preservation of a trust fund will always outweigh success in its advancement. Inevitably, a trustee in the bank's position wears a complacent air, because the virtue of safety will in practice put a premium on inactivity. Until the 1950s active management of the portfolio might have been seen as speculative, and even in these days such dealing would have to be notably successful before the expense would be justified. The very process of attempting to achieve a balance, or (if that be old-fashioned) fairness, as between the interests of life-tenants and those of a remainderman inevitably means that each can complain of being less well served than he or she ought to have been. But by the undemanding standard of prudence the bank is not shown to have committed any breach of trust resulting in loss.

I am therefore constrained to agree that the appeal must be dismissed.[18]

ii. Ethical Considerations

COWAN v SCARGILL[19]
[1985] Ch 270, [1984] 2 All ER 750 (Ch D, Sir Robert Megarry V-C)

A mineworkers' pension fund, with assets of some £3,000 million and very wide powers of investment, was managed by a committee of ten trustees, of whom five were appointed by the National Coal Board, and five, including the defendant, by the National Union of Mineworkers. They were assisted in their investment decisions by an advisory panel of experts. Prior to 1982 the plan for investment included overseas investment, and investment in oil and gas. In 1982 when a revised plan was considered, the five union trustees, on the basis of union policy determined at the annual conference, refused to accept the revised plan, unless it was amended so that there would be no increase in overseas investment; that overseas investment already made would be withdrawn at the most opportune time; and that there would be no investment in energies competing with coal. The five Board trustees applied to the court for directions.

Held. The five union trustees were in breach of their duties as members of the committee of management in refusing to concur in adopting the revised plan for investment.

Sir Robert Megarry V-C: The first defendant, Mr Arthur Scargill, appeared in person. He had, I think, dispensed with the services of a chancery silk and junior some days before the case began, but he had retained the services of a solicitor, who was able to sit with him in court and assist him. The other four defendants took no part in the argument, but Mr Scargill told me

---

18 See also *Martin v City of Edinburgh District Council* 1988 SLT 329 (declaration granted by Scottish Court that policy to oppose apartheid by disinvesting in companies with South Africa was a breach of duty, even though no loss occurred).

19 [1984] All ER Rev 306 (P.J. Clarke); (1984) 81 LSG 2291 (S.C. Butler); (1986) 102 LQR 32 (J.H. Farrar and J.K. Maxton). See also *Nestlé v National Westminster Bank plc* (29 June 1988, unreported), p. 676. As to charity trustees, see p. 521, ante.

that he was presenting his argument on behalf of them as well as on his own behalf. I should say at the outset that Mr Scargill argues his case throughout with both courtesy and competence. I wish to emphasise this, particularly in view of the number of occasions on which I found it necessary to interrupt his submissions, usually because he was going too fast for coherent note-taking, or because I wished to be sure that I had correctly understood his submission, or that he was not overlooking some point which tended against him.

The main issue (and I put it very shortly) is whether the defendants are in breach of their fiduciary duties in refusing approval of an investment plan for the scheme unless it is amended so as to prohibit any increase in overseas investment, to provide for the withdrawal of existing overseas investments at the most opportune time, and to prohibit investment in energies which are in direct competition with coal. . . .

I turn to the law. The starting point is the duty of the trustees to exercise their powers in the best interests of the present and future beneficiaries of the trust, holding the scales impartially between different classes of beneficiaries. This duty of the trustees towards their beneficiaries is paramount. They must, of course, obey the law; but subject to that, they must put the interests of their beneficiaries first. When the purpose of the trusts is to provide financial benefits for the beneficiaries, as is usually the case, the best interests of the beneficiaries are normally their best financial interests. In the case of a power of investment, as in the present case, the power must be exercised so as to yield the best return for the beneficiaries, judged in relation to the risks of the investments in question; and the prospects of the yield of income and capital appreciation both have to be considered in judging the return from the investment.

The legal memorandum that the union obtained from their solicitors is generally in accord with these views. In considering the possibility of investment for "socially beneficial reasons which may result in lower returns to the fund," the memorandum states that "the trustees' only concern is to ensure that the return is the maximum possible consistent with security"; and then it refers to the need for diversification. However, it continues by saying:

"Trustees cannot be criticised for failing to make a particular investment for social or political reasons, such as in South African stock for example, but may be held liable for investing in assets which yield a poor return or for disinvesting in stock at inappropriate times for non-financial criteria."

This last sentence must be considered in the light of subsequent passages in the memorandum which indicate that the sale of South African securities by trustees might be justified on the ground of doubts about political stability in South Africa and the long-term financial soundness of its economy, whereas trustees could not properly support motions at a company meeting dealing with pay levels in South Africa, work accidents, pollution control, employment conditions for minorities, military contracting and consumer protection. The assertion that trustees could not be criticised for failing to make a particular investment for social or political reasons is one that I would not accept in its full width. If the investment in fact made is equally beneficial to the beneficiaries, then criticism would be difficult to sustain in practice, whatever the position in theory. But if the investment in fact made is less beneficial, then both in theory and in practice the trustees would normally be open to criticism.

This leads me to the second point, which is a corollary of the first. In considering what investments to make trustees must put on one side their own personal interests and views. Trustees may have strongly held social or political views. They may be firmly opposed to any investment in South Africa or other countries, or they may object to any form of investment in companies concerned with alcohol, tobacco, armaments or many other things. In the conduct of their own affairs, of course, they are free to abstain from making any such investments. Yet under a trust, if investments of this type would be more beneficial to the beneficiaries than other investments, the trustees must not refrain from making the investments by reason of the views that they hold.

Trustees may even have to act dishonourably (though not illegally) if the interests of their beneficiaries require it. Thus where trustees for sale had struck a bargain for the sale of trust property but had not bound themselves by a legally enforceable contract, they were held to be under a duty to consider and explore a better offer that they received, and not to carry through the bargain to which they felt in honour bound: *Buttle v Saunders* [1950] 2 All ER 193, p. 660, ante. In other words, the duty of trustees to their beneficiaries may include a duty to "gazump", however honourable the trustees. As Wynn-Parry J said at p. 195, trustees "have an overriding duty to obtain the best price which they can for their beneficiaries". In applying this to an official receiver in *Re Wyvern Developments Ltd* [1974] 1 WLR 1097, 1106, [1974] 2 All ER 535, 544, Templeman J said that he "must do his best by his creditors and contributories. He is in a fiduciary capacity and cannot make moral gestures, nor can the court authorise him to do so." In the words of Sir James Wigram V-C in *Balls v Strutt* (1841) 1 Hare 146, 149:

"It is a principle in this court, that a trustee shall not be permitted to use the powers which the trust may confer upon him at law, except for the legitimate purposes of his trust; ... "

Powers must be exercised fairly and honestly for the purposes for which they are given and not so as to accomplish any ulterior purpose, whether for the benefit of the trustees or otherwise: see *Duke of Portland v Lady Topham* (1864) 11 HL Cas 32, a case on a power of appointment that must apply a fortiori to a power to trustees as such.

Thirdly, by way of caveat I should say that I am not asserting that the benefit of the beneficiaries which a trustee must make his paramount concern inevitably and solely means their financial benefit, even if the only object of the trust is to provide financial benefits. Thus if the only actual or potential beneficiaries of a trust are all adults with very strict views on moral and social matters, condemning all forms of alcohol, tobacco and popular entertainment, as well as armaments, I can well understand that it might not be for the "benefit" of such beneficiaries to know that they are obtaining rather larger financial returns under the trust by reason of investments in those activities than they would have received if the trustees had invested the trust funds in other investments. The beneficiaries might well consider that it was far better to receive less than to receive more money from what they consider to be evil and tainted sources. "Benefit" is a word with a very wide meaning, and there are circumstances in which arrangements which work to the financial disadvantage of a beneficiary may yet be for his benefit: see, for example, *Re T's Settlement Trusts* [1964] Ch 158, [1963] 3 All ER 759 and *Re CL* [1969] 1 Ch 587, [1968] 1 All ER 1104. But I would emphasise that such cases are likely to be very rare, and in any case I think that under a trust for the provision of financial benefits the burden would rest, and rest heavily, on him who asserts that it is for the benefit of the beneficiaries as a whole to receive less by reason of the exclusion of some of the possibly more profitable forms of investment. Plainly the present case is not one of this rare type of cases. Subject to such matters, under a trust for the provision of financial benefits, the paramount duty of the trustees is to provide the greatest financial benefits for the present and future beneficiaries.

Fourth, the standard required of a trustee in exercising his powers of investment is that he must

"take such care as an ordinary prudent man would take if he were minded to make an investment for the benefit of other people for whom he felt morally bound to provide:"

per Lindley LJ in *Re Whiteley* (1886) 33 Ch D 347, 355; see also at pp. 350, 358; and see *Learoyd v Whiteley* (1887) 12 App Cas 727. That duty includes the duty to seek advice on matters which the trustee does not understand, such as the making of investments, and on receiving that advice to act with the same degree of prudence. This requirement is not discharged merely by showing that the trustee has acted in good faith and with sincerity. Honesty and sincerity are not the same as prudence and reasonableness. Some of the most sincere people are the most unreasonable; and Mr Scargill told me that he had met quite a few of them. Accordingly, although a trustee who takes advice on investments is not bound to accept and act on that advice, he is not entitled to reject it merely because he sincerely disagrees with it, unless in addition to being sincere he is acting as an ordinary prudent man would act.

Fifth, trustees have a duty to consider the need for diversification of investments. By section 6 (1) of the Trustee Investments Act 1961, p. 675, ante:

[His Lordship read this subsection and continued:]

The reference to the "circumstances of the trust" plainly includes matters such as the size of the trust funds: the degree of diversification that is practicable and desirable for a large fund may plainly be impracticable or undesirable (or both) in the case of a small fund.

In the case before me, it is not in issue that there ought to be diversification of the investments held by the fund. The contention of the defendants, put very shortly, is that there can be a sufficient degree of diversification without any investment overseas or in oil, and that in any case there is no need to increase the level of overseas investments beyond the existing level. Other pension funds got on well enough without overseas investments, it was said, and in particular the N.U.M.'s own scheme had, in 1982, produced better results than the scheme here in question. This was not so, said Mr Jenkins, if you compared like with like, and excluded investments in property, which figure substantially in the mineworkers' scheme but not at all in the N.U.M. scheme: and in any case the latter scheme was much smaller, being of the order of £7 million.

I shall not pursue this matter. Even if other funds in one particular year, or in many years, had done better than the scheme which is before me, that does not begin to show that it is beneficial to this scheme to be shorn of the ability to invest overseas. The main difference between the 1980 and the 1982 plans, I may say, is that although the target for overseas investments remains at 15 per cent., the 1982 plan increases the percentage of the cash flow that can be invested in overseas realty from $7\frac{1}{2}$ to 10 per cent., and relaxes the overall limit of 15 per cent. in this respect. It should be added that, in addition, something like 10 per cent. of the assets of British companies in which the fund has invested consist of overseas holdings, so that there is this additional foreign element. As for oil, the 1982 plan made no real difference: the existing holdings of just under 12 per cent. could have been maintained if that plan had been implemented.

Sixth, there is the question whether the principles that I have been stating apply, with or without modification, to trusts of pension funds. Mr Stamler asserted that they applied without modification, and that it made no difference that some of the funds came from the members of the pension scheme, or that the funds were often of a very substantial size. Mr Scargill did not in terms assert the contrary. He merely said that this was one of the questions to be decided, and that pension funds may be subject to different rules. I was somewhat unsuccessful in my attempts to find out from him why this was so, and what the differences were. What it came down to, I think, was that the rules for trusts had been laid down for private and family trusts and wills a long time ago; that pension funds were very large and affected large numbers of people; that in the present case the well-being of all within the coal industry was affected; and that there was no authority on the point except *Evans v London Co-operative Society Ltd* (1976) Times, 6 July, and certain overseas cases.

I shall refer to the authorities in a moment, and consider the question of principle first. I can see no reason for holding that different principles apply to pension fund trusts from those which apply to other trusts. Of course, there are many provisions in pension schemes which are not to be found in private trusts, and to these the general law of trusts will be subordinated. But subject to that, I think that the trusts of pension funds are subject to the same rules as other trusts. The large size of pension funds emphasises the need for diversification, rather than lessening it, and the fact that much of the fund has been contributed by the members of the scheme seems to me to make even more important that the trustees should exercise their powers in the best interests of the beneficiaries. In a private trust, most, if not all, of the beneficiaries are the recipients of the bounty of the settlor, whereas under the trusts of a pension fund many (though not all) of the beneficiaries are those who, as members, contributed to the funds so that in due time they would receive pensions. It is thus all the more important that the interests of the beneficiaries should be paramount, so that they may receive the benefits which in part they have paid for. I can see no justification for holding that the benefits to them should run the risk of being lessened because the trustees were pursuing an investment policy intended to assist the industry that the pensioners have left, or their union.

[His Lordship referred to *Evans v London Co-operative Society Ltd* (1976) Times, 6 July; *Blankenship v Boyle* 329 F Supp 1089 (1971) in the US District Court for the District of Columbia; *Withers v Teachers' Retirement System of the City of New York* 444 F Supp 1248 (1978) and continued:]

I can see no escape from the conclusion that the N.U.M. trustees were attempting to impose the prohibitions in order to carry out union policy; and mere assertions that their sole considerations was the benefit of the beneficiaries do not alter that conclusion. If the N.U.M. trustees were thinking only of the benefit of the beneficiaries, why all the references to union policy instead of proper explanations of how and why the prohibitions would bring benefits to the beneficiaries? No doubt some trustees with strong feelings find it irksome to be forced to submerge those feelings and genuinely put the interests of the beneficiaries first. Indeed, there are some who are temperamentally unsuited to being trustees, and are more fitted for campaigning for changes in the law. This, of course, they are free to do; but if they choose to become trustees they must accept it that the rules of equity will bind them in all they do as trustees.

iii. CHARITABLE TRUSTEES

In **Harries v Church Commissioners for England**[20][1992] 1 WLR 1241, [1993] 2 All ER 300, the Bishop of Oxford and other clergy claimed that the Church Commissioners, whose purpose was to promote the Christian faith through the Church of England, should not select investments in a manner incompatible with that purpose, even if this involved a risk of significant financial detriment. Sir Donald NICHOLLS V-C in holding that ethical considerations could be taken into account only in so far as the profitability of investments was not jeopardised, said at 1243, at 301:

"The Church Commissioners for England administer vast estates and large funds. At the end of 1990 their holdings of land were valued at about £1.7bn., their mortgages and loans at about £165m., and their stock exchange investments at about £780m. In 1990 these items yielded altogether an investment income of £164m. The commissioners' income included also some £66m. derived principally from parish and diocesan contributions to clergy stipends. So the commissioners' total income last year was £230m.

The needs which the commissioners seek to satisfy out of this income are daunting. In 1990 they provided almost one half of the costs of the stipends of the Church of England serving clergy, much of their housing costs, and almost all their pension costs. These items absorbed over 85 per cent. of the commissioners' income: that is, a sum of almost £200m. Unfortunately, this does not mean that the clergy are well remunerated or that the retired clergy receive good pensions. Far from it. The commissioners' income has to be spread widely, and hence thinly, over 11,400 serving clergy and 10,100 clergy pensioners and widows. So, as is well known, the amount each receives is not generous. In 1990–1991 the national average stipend of incumbents was only £11,308. The full-service pension from April 1991 was £6,700 per year.

For some time there have been voices in the Church of England expressing disquiet at the investment policy of the commissioners. They do not question either the good faith or the investment expertise of the commissioners. Their concern is not that the commissioners have failed to get the best financial return from their property and investments. Their concern is that, in making investment decisions, the commissioners are guided too rigorously by purely financial considerations, and that the commissioners give insufficient weight to what are now called 'ethical' considerations. They contend, moreover, that the commissioners have fallen into legal error. The commissioners attach overriding importance to financial considerations, and that is a misapprehension of the approach they ought properly to adopt when making investment decisions. The commissioners ought to have in mind that the underlying purpose for which they hold their assets is the promotion of the Christian faith through the Church of England. The commissioners should

---

20 [1992] Conv 115 (R. Nobles); (1992) 55 MLR 587 (P. Luxton); (1992) 6 Trust Law International 119 at p. 123 (Lord BROWNE-WILKINSON); [1993] All ER Rev 258 (P.J. Clarke). On the investment powers of charitable trustees under the Charities Act 1993, ss. 24(7), 70 and 71, see p. 521 ante.

not exercise their investment functions in a manner which would be incompatible with that purpose even if that involves a risk of incurring significant financial detriment.

Before going further into the criticism made of the commissioners I will consider the general principles applicable to the exercise of powers of investment by charity trustees. It is axiomatic that charity trustees, in common with all other trustees, are concerned to further the purposes of the trust of which they have accepted the office of trustee. That is their duty. To enable them the better to discharge that duty, trustees have powers vested in them. Those powers must be exercised for the purpose for which they have been given: to further the purposes of the trust. That is the guiding principle applicable to the issues in these proceedings. Everything which follows is no more than the reasoned application of that principle in particular contexts.

Broadly speaking, property held by charity trustees falls into two categories. First, there is property held by trustees for what may be called functional purposes. The National Trust own historic houses and open spaces. The Salvation Army owns hostels for the destitute. And many charities need office accommodation in which to carry out essential administrative work. Second, there is property held by trustees for the purpose of generating money, whether from income or capital growth, with which to further the work of the trust. In other words, property held by trustees as an investment. Where property is so held, prima facie the purposes of the trust will be best served by the trustees seeking to obtain therefrom the maximum return, whether by way of income or capital growth, which is consistent with commercial prudence. That is the starting point for all charity trustees when considering the exercise of their investment powers. Most charities need money; and the more of it there is available, the more the trustees can seek to accomplish.

In most case this prima facie position will govern the trustees' conduct. In most cases the best interests of the charity require that the trustees' choice of investments should be made solely on the basis of well-established investment criteria, having taken expert advice where appropriate and having due regard to such matters as the need to diversify, the need to balance income against capital growth, and the need to balance risk against return.

In a minority of cases the position will not be so straightforward. There will be some cases, I suspect comparatively rare, when the objects of the charity are such that investments of a particular type would conflict with the aims of the charity. Much-cited examples are those of cancer research companies and tobacco shares, trustees of temperance charities and brewery and distillery shares, and trustees of charities of the Society of Friends and shares in companies engaged in production of armaments. If, as would be likely in those examples, trustees were satisfied that investing in a company engaged in a particular type of business would conflict with the very objects their charity is seeking to achieve, they should not so invest. Carried to its logical conclusion the trustees should take this course even if it would be likely to result in significant financial detriment to the charity. The logical conclusion, whilst sound as a matter of legal analysis, is unlikely to arise in practice. It is not easy to think of an instance where in practice the exclusion for this reason of one or more companies or sectors from the whole range of investments open to trustees would be likely to leave them without an adequately wide range of investments from which to choose a properly diversified portfolio.

There will also be some cases, again I suspect comparatively rare, when trustees' holdings of particular investments might hamper a charity's work either by making potential recipients of aid unwilling to be helped because of the source of the charity's money, or by alienating some of those who support the charity financially. In these cases, the trustees will need to balance the difficulties they would encounter, or likely financial loss they would sustain, if they were to hold the investments against the risk of financial detriment if those investments were excluded from their portfolio. The greater the risk of financial detriment, the more certain the trustees should be of countervailing disadvantages to the charity before they incur that risk. Another circumstance where trustees would be entitled, or even required, to take into account non-financial criteria would be where the trust deed so provides.

No doubt there will be other cases where trustees are justified in departing from what should always be their starting point. The instances I have given are not comprehensive. But I must emphasise that of their very nature, and by definition, investments are held by trustees to aid the work of the charity in a particular way: by generating money. That is the purpose for which they are held. That is their raison d'être. Trustees cannot properly use assets held as an investment for other, viz., non-investment, purposes. To the extent that they do they are not properly exercising their powers of investment. This is not to say that trustees who own land may not act as responsible landlords or those who own shares may not act as responsible shareholders. They may. The law is not so cynical as to require trustees to behave in a fashion which would bring them or their charity into disrepute (although their consciences must not be too tender: see *Buttle v Saunders* [1950] 2 All ER 193 p.660 ante.). On the other hand, trustees must act prudently. They must not use property held by them for investment purposes as a means for making moral statements at the expense of the charity of which they are trustees. Those who wish may do so with their own property, but that is not a proper function of trustees with trust assets held as an investment.

I should mention one other particular situation. There will be instances today when those who support or benefit from a charity take widely different views on a particular type of investment, some saying that on moral grounds it conflicts with the aims of the charity, others saying the opposite. One example is the holding of arms industry shares by a religious charity. There is a real difficulty here. To many questions raising moral issues there are no certain answers. On moral questions widely differing views are held by well-meaning, responsible people. This is not always so. But frequently, when questions of the morality of conduct are being canvassed, there is no identifiable yardstick which can be applied to a set of facts so as to yield one answer which can be seen to be 'right' and the other 'wrong.' If that situation confronts trustees of a charity, the law does not require them to find an answer to the unanswerable. Trustees may, if they wish, accommodate the views of those who consider that on moral grounds a particular investment would be in conflict with the objects of the charity, so long as the trustees are satisfied that course would not involve a risk of significant financial detriment. But when they are not so satisfied trustees should not make investment decisions on the basis of preferring one view of whether on moral grounds in investment conflicts with the objects of the charity over another. This is so even when one view is more widely supported than the other.

I have sought above to consider charity trustees' duties in relation to investment as a matter of basic principle. I was referred to no authority bearing directly on these matters. My attention was drawn to *Cowan v Scargill* [1985] Ch

270, [1984] 2 All ER 750, p. 679 ante., a case concerning a pension fund. I believe the views I have set out accord with those expressed by Sir Robert Megarry V-C in that case, bearing in mind that he was considering trusts for the provision of financial benefits for individuals. In this case I am concerned with trusts of charities, whose purposes are multifarious.

[His Lordship considered the Commissioners' objects and their investment policy, and continued:]

The statement of policy records that the commissioners do not invest in companies whose main business is in armaments, gambling, alcohol, tobacco or newspapers. Of these, newspapers fall into a category of their own. The commissioners' policy regarding newspapers is based on the fact that many newspapers are associated, to a greater or lesser extent, with a particular political party or political view. Leaving aside newspapers, the underlying rationale of the commissioners's policy on these items is that there is a body of members of the Church of England opposed to the businesses in question on religious or moral grounds. There are members who believe these business activities are morally wrong, and that they are in conflict with Christian teaching and its moral values. But this list has only to be read for it to be obvious that many committed members of the Church of England take the contrary view. To say that not all members of the Church of England eschew gambling, alcohol or tobacco would be an understatement. As to armaments, the morality of war, and the concepts of a 'just war,' are issues which have been debated for centuries. These are moral questions on which no single view can be shown to be 'right' and the others 'wrong.' As I understand the position, the commissioners have felt able to exclude these items from their investments despite the conflicting views on the morality of holding these items as investments because there has remained open to the commissioners an adequate width of alternative investments.

I have already indicated that at the heart of the plaintiffs' case is a contention that the commissioners' policy is erroneous in law in that the commissioners are only prepared to take non-financial considerations into account to the extent that such considerations do not significantly jeopardise or interfere with accepted investment principles. I think it is implicit, if not explicit, in the commissioners' evidence that they do regard themselves as constrained in this way. So far as I have been able to see, this is the only issue identifiable as an issue of law raised in these proceedings. In my view this self-constraint applied by the commissioners is not one which in practice has led to any error of law on their part, nor is it likely to do so. I have already indicated that the circumstances in which charity trustees are bound or entitled to make a financially disadvantageous investment decision for ethical reasons are extremely limited. I have noted that it is not easy to think of a practical example of such a circumstances. There is no evidence before me to suggest that any such circumstance exists here....

[His Lordship considered the relief claimed, and continued:]

I add only this. In bringing these proceedings the Bishop of Oxford and his colleagues are actuated by the highest moral concern. But, as I have sought to show, the approach they wish the commissioners to adopt to investment decisions would involve a departure by the commissioners from their legal obligations. Whether such a departure would nor would not be desirable is, of course, not an issue in these proceedings. That is a matter to be pursued, if at all, elsewhere than in this court.''

E.   Trustees Holding Controlling Interest in a Company

BARTLETT v BARCLAYS BANK TRUST CO LTD (No 1)[1]
[1980] Ch 515, [1980] 1 All ER 139 (Ch D, BRIGHTMAN J).

The bank was trustee of the Bartlett Trust, of which the sole asset was a holding of 99.8% of shares in a private property company. The beneficiaries were the settlor's family and issue. By 1960 no beneficiary or member of the settlor's family was on the board of the company, and none of the directors was a nominee of the bank. Money being required to pay estate duty, the bank and the board considered a public quotation of the company's shares. Merchant bankers advised the board that this would be more likely to succeed if the company invested in land development. The bank agreed to this so long as the beneficiaries were not left short of income.

Investment was made in two projects, without consulting the bank, one at Guildford, which was successful, and the other, opposite the Old Bailey, which was not. The profit from the former was used to finance the latter, which resulted in a substantial loss. The bank was content with information issued at annual general meetings; it was not aware of the hazardous nature of the projects and did not intervene to prevent them.

The beneficiaries sued the bank as trustee for breach of trust.

Held. The bank was liable for the loss. The profit on the one project could be set off against the loss on the other.

BRIGHTMAN J: I turn to the question, what was the duty of the bank as the holder of shares? I will first answer this question without regard to the position of the bank as a specialist trustee, to which I will advert later. The bank, as trustee, was bound to act in relation to the shares and to the controlling position which they conferred, in the same manner as a prudent man of business. The prudent man of business will act in such manner as is necessary to safeguard his investment. He will do this in two ways. If facts come to his knowledge which tell him that the company's affairs are not being conducted as they should be, or which put him on inquiry, he will take appropriate action. Appropriate action will no doubt consist in the first instance of inquiry of and consultation with the directors, and in the last but most unlikely resort, the convening of a general meeting to replace one or more directors. What the prudent man of business will *not* do is to content himself with the receipt of such information on the affairs of the company as a shareholder ordinarily receives at annual general meetings. Since he has the power to do so, he will go further and see that he has sufficient information to enable him to make a responsible decision from time to time either to let matters proceed as they are proceeding, or to intervene if he is dissatisfied. This topic was considered by Cross J in *Re Lucking's Will Trusts* [1968] 1 WLR 866, more fully reported in [1967] 3 All ER 726.[2] In that case nearly 70 per cent. of the shares in the company were held by two trustees, L and B, as part of the estate of a deceased; about 29 per cent. belonged to L in his own right, and 1 per cent. belonged to L's wife. The directors in 1954 were Mr and Mrs L and D, who was the manager of the business. In 1956 B was appointed trustee to act jointly with L. The company was engaged in the manufacture and sale of shoe accessories. It had

---

1   [1980] Conv 155 (G.A. Shindler); [1983] Conv 127 (R. Pearce and A. Samuels).
2   See p. 751, post on the question of the application of TA 1925, ss. 23 (1), 30 (1); [1979] Conv 345, 358 (J.E. Stannard).

a small factory employing about 20 people, and one or two travellers. It also had an agency in France. D wrongfully drew some £15,000 from the company's bank account in excess of his remuneration, and later became bankrupt. The money was lost. Cross J said, at 874, at 732:

"The conduct of the defendant trustees is, I think, to be judged by the standard applied in *Speight v Gaunt* (1883) 9 App. Cas. 1, namely, that a trustee is only bound to conduct the business of the trust in such a way as an ordinary prudent man would conduct a business of his own. Now what steps, if any, does a reasonably prudent man who finds himself a majority shareholder in a private company take with regard to the management of the company's affairs? He does not, I think, content himself with such information as to the management of the company's affairs as he is entitled to as shareholder, but ensures that he is represented on the board. He may be prepared to run the business himself as managing director or, at least, to become a non-executive director while having the business managed by someone else. Alternatively, he may find someone who will act as his nominee on the board and report to him from time to time as to the company's affairs. In the same way, as it seems to me, trustees holding a controlling interest ought to ensure so far as they can that they have such information as to the progress of the company's affairs as directors would have. If they sit back and allow the company to be run by the minority shareholder and receive no more information than shareholders are entitled to, they do so at their risk if things go wrong."

I do not understand Cross J to have been saying that in every case where trustees have a controlling interest in a company it is their duty to ensure that one of their number is a director or that they have a nominee on the board who will report from time to time on the affairs of the company. He was merely outlining convenient methods by which a prudent man of business (as also a trustee) with a controlling interest in a private company, can place himself in a position to make an informed decision whether any action is appropriate to be taken for the protection of his asset. Other methods may be equally satisfactory and convenient, depending upon the circumstances of the individual case. Alternatives which spring to mind are the receipt of copies of the agenda and minutes of board meetings if regularly held, the receipt of monthly management accounts in the case of a trading concern, or quarterly reports. Every case will depend on its own facts. The possibilities are endless. It would be useless, indeed misleading, to seek to lay down a general rule. The purpose to be achieved is not that of monitoring every move of the directors, but of making it reasonably probable, so far as circumstances permit, that the trustee or (as in the *Lucking* case) one of them will receive an adequate flow of information in time to enable the trustees to make use of their controlling interest should this be necessary for the protection of their trust asset, namely, the shareholding. The obtaining of information is not an end in itself, but merely a means of enabling the trustees to safeguard the interests of their beneficiaries.

The principle enunciated in the *Lucking* case appears to have been applied in *Re Miller's Deed Trusts* (21 March, 1978, unreported), a decision of Oliver J. No transcript of the judgment is available but the case is briefly noted in the Law Society's Gazette published on 3 May, 1978. There is also a number of American decisions proceeding upon the same lines, to which counsel has helpfully referred me....

It was not proper for the bank to confine itself to the receipt of the annual balance sheet and profit and loss account, detailed annual financial statements and the chairman's report and statement, and to attendance at the annual general meetings and the luncheons that followed, which were the limits of the bank's regular sources of information. Had the bank been in receipt of more frequent information it would have been able to step in and stop, and ought to have stopped, the board embarking on the Old Bailey project. That project was imprudent and hazardous and wholly unsuitable for a trust whether undertaken by the bank direct or through the medium of its wholly owned company. Even without the regular flow of information which the bank ought to have had, it knew enough to put it upon inquiry. There were enough obvious points at which the bank should have intervened and asked questions.

F. Enlargement of Investment Powers by the Court

In **Trustees of the British Museum v Attorney-General** [1984] 1 WLR 418, [1984] 1 All ER 337,[3] Sir Robert MEGARRY V-C, in approving a scheme to give the trustees wider powers of investment, said at 419, at 338:

"In this case the Trustees of the British Museum have issued an originating summons relating to charitable funds held by them.... The object of the summons is to obtain the approval of the court to a scheme that will give the trustees wider powers of investment than those that they have at present under a scheme approved by Pennycuick J on 18 July 1960.... The main point of importance is whether the court should continue to apply the principle that was laid down in cases such as *Re Kolb's Will Trusts* [1962] Ch 531, [1961] 3 All ER 811 (a case in which an appeal was compromised: see (1962) 106 SJ 669), *Re Cooper's Settlement* [1962] Ch 826, [1961] 3 All ER 636 and *Re Porritt's Will Trusts* (1961) 105 SJ 931, and was recognised in *Re Clarke's Will Trusts* [1961] 1 WLR 1471, [1961] 3 All ER 1133 and *Re University of London Charitable Trusts* [1964] Ch 282, [1963] 3 All ER 859.[4]

As is well known, the instrument establishing a trust may prescribe powers of investment which are either narrower or wider than those laid down by the general law: see Trustee Act 1925, s. 69(2); Trustee Investments Act 1961, s. 1(3), p. 664, ante. Subject to any such provision in the instrument, statute has prescribed the range of authorised investments for trustees. Under Part I of the Trustee Act 1925, and in particular s. 1, the range of authorised investments was in the main confined to what are generally called gilt-edged securities, and other securities which carried interest at fixed rates. It did not extend to industrial equities, no matter how large and prosperous the concerns. However suitable this was before the 1939–1945 war, with a stable pound, it had ceased to be satisfactory when the post-war inflation began to emerge; and in establishing new trusts it became increasingly common to insert investment clauses that were markedly wider than the statutory provisions. That, however, did not help pre-existing trusts, and in these cases a number of successful applications to the courts to widen the investment powers were made under

---

3 [1984] Conv 373 (H.E. Norman).
4 See also *Re Rank's Settlement Trusts* [1979] 1 WLR 1242, where an arrangement included a power of appointment in terms wide enough to permit the donee to give wider powers of investment to the trustees for the benefit of the appointees; *Motor and Cycle Trades Benevolent Fund v A-G:* Annual Report of the Charity Commissioners for 1982, p. 42.

the Trustee Act 1925, s. 57,[5] under the Variation of Trusts Act 1958, p. 789, post, and, in the case of charities, under the Charitable Trusts Acts 1853 to 1925, as was done in respect of the 1960 scheme in the present case.

In the end, the Trustee Investments Act 1961 was enacted. By this time, the purchasing power of the pound was about half what it had been in 1939. The Act laid down an elaborate code. Under this, a much wider range of investments was authorised if the trustees first divided the trust fund into two equal parts. One part was confined to 'narrower-range' investments, which very roughly corresponded to the investments which were authorised under the Trustee Act 1925. The other part extended to 'wider-range' investments. The most important constituents of these (and I put it very shortly) were fully paid up securities in United Kingdom companies with a paid-up capital of at least £1m which were quoted on a recognised United Kingdom stock exchange and each year for the previous five years had paid a dividend on all shares ranking for dividend. Equities in such companies thus became available for trustee investment; but as with all investments authorised by the Act, save only certain narrower-range investments, the trustees were required to obtain proper advice in accordance with the Act before making the investment.

The Act was passed on 3 August, 1961; and in October of that year the first three cases that I have cited, *Kolb, Cooper* and *Porritt,* all fell for decision. In each case an application had been made, doubtless before the Act was passed, for an extension of the powers of investment. Each case seems to have been decided without either of the others being cited; but in each the judge (Cross, Buckley and Pennycuick JJ respectively) reached the same conclusion. In the words of Cross J: 'The powers given by the Act must, I think, be taken to be prima facie sufficient and ought only to be extended if, on the particular facts, a special case for extending them can be made out': *Re Kolb* at 540, at 815. . . .

That was in 1961; and no doubt for some time that doctrine remained soundly based. However, in recent years the court, usually in chambers, has become ready to authorise extensions of the power of investment, often by an increased willingness to accept circumstances as being 'special'. Further, it has become increasingly common for draftsmen of wills and settlements to insert special investment powers which are far wider than those conferred by the Act of 1961. Then in October 1982 the Law Reform Committee made its 23rd Report (Cmnd. 8733), p. 708, post, this time on the subject of the powers and duties of trustees; and in this the Committee reached the conclusion that the Act of 1961 has proved to be 'tiresome, cumbrous and expensive in operation', and that 'the present statutory powers are out of date and ought to be revised': para. 3.17. The Committee's proposals for reform rejected any scheme for fixed proportions of the trust fund which could be invested in one type of investment or another, and instead proposed that investments should be divided into those which could be made without taking advice and those which could be made only upon taking advice. The former category would include all the narrower-range securities, with certain additions, and the latter would include all other investments quoted on the English Stock Exchange. Subject to taking advice when necessary, trustees should be free to invest in such proportions as they choose: para. 3.21, 22. That was the recommendation.

I cite the Report not as authority but as showing what the distinguished members of the Committee recognised to be the position some twenty years after the Act of 1961 was passed. In addition to that, I have before me detailed

5 P. 782, post; *Mason v Farbrother* [1983] 2 All ER 1078 at 1086.

evidence of changes in the investment market that have occurred since the 1960 scheme was approved. Before I consider that evidence, I must say something about that scheme.

[His Lordship reviewed the terms of the 1960 scheme and continued:]

The evidence before me establishes that over the last twenty years significant changes in investment practice have occurred, especially in the case of large trust funds. The main factors producing these changes may be summarised as follows. First, increased rates of inflation have encouraged a movement from fixed interest investments to equities and property. As I have mentioned, by 1960 the purchasing power of the pound had fallen to about half of what it had been in 1939; and in the next twenty years it lost some five-sixths of that reduced value. Second, differences in rates of inflation between one country and another have from time to time made it wise to replace investments in one country by those in another. Third, the exploitation of oil and other natural resources in certain countries has markedly affected the value of particular currencies. Fourth, in recent years the rate of economic growth has been greater in some countries (not least in Japan) than in the United Kingdom. Fifth, leading companies in the United Kingdom have found it difficult to grow faster than the economy as a whole, whereas some smaller companies with specialist markets have been able to grow faster. There have also been trends away from the manufacture of capital goods towards the service and energy industries, and away from manufacturing 'high volume' goods towards manufacturing which adds a high value to the goods. Sixth, the abolition of exchange controls in October 1979 has greatly facilitated overseas investment. Coupled with these factors has been an increased volatility in prices, with sharp changes taking place within three or four days, and sometimes a day. Seventh, unit trusts and certain forms of unsecured loans such as Eurobonds now offer valuable investment opportunities.

I feel no doubt that it is in the best interests of the trustees and the trusts that there should be relaxation of the terms of the 1960 scheme which will take account of these changes. At the same time, any scheme must have appropriate safeguards. The main features of the scheme put forward in this case, as it stands revised after discussion, may be stated as follows.

[His Lordship stated the main features of the scheme and continued:]

I am conscious that such a scheme gives extremely wide powers of investment to the trustees. At the same time I consider that it is proper and desirable that such powers should be given, and I have made an order accordingly. There are four factors that I should mention in particular. First, there is the eminence and responsibility of the trustees, the machinery for obtaining highly skilled advice, and the success that this machinery has achieved over the past twenty years. Second, there are the changed conditions of investment, conditions which require great liberty of choice if, upon skilled advice, advantage is to be taken of opportunities which often present themselves upon short notice and for short periods; and for this, the provision for delegation is plainly advantageous. Third, there is obvious advantage in there being freedom to invest in any part of the world. At the same time, there is due recognition of prudence of maintaining a solid core of relatively safe investments while setting free a substantial part for investment which, though less 'safe', offer greater opportunities for a substantial enhancement of value. Opinions may vary about the precise percentages; certainly my views have fluctuated. However, in the end I have reached the conclusion that the percentages put forward are reasonable. . . .

Fourth, I bear in mind the large size of the trust fund.[6] From the point of view of powers of investment, this carries the matter out of the realm of the ordinary private trust into the field of pension funds and large institutional investors; and for success in this field a wide flexibility of the powers of investment is plainly desirable, if not essential.

From what I have said it will be seen that much of what I say depends to a greater or lesser extent upon the special position of the trustees and the trust funds in the case before me. On the other hand, there is much that is of more general application, and it may be convenient if I attempt to summarise my views.

1. In my judgment, the principle laid down in the line of cases headed by *Re Kolb's Will Trusts* [1962] Ch 531, [1961] 3 All ER 811 is one that should no longer be followed, since conditions have changed so greatly in the last twenty years. Though authoritative, those cases were authorities only *rebus sic stantibus;* and in 1983 they bind no longer. However, if Parliament acts on the recommendation of the Law Reform Committee and replaces the Act of 1961 with revised powers of investment, the *Kolb* principle may well become applicable once more. Until then, the court should be ready to grant suitable applications for the extension of trustees' powers of investment, judging each application on its merits, and without being constrained by the provisions of the Act of 1961.

2. In determining what extended powers of investment should be conferred, there are many matters which will have to be considered. I shall refer to five, without in any way suggesting that this list is exhaustive, or that anything I say is intended to fetter the discretion that the court has to exercise in each case.

(i) The court is likely to give great weight to the width and efficacy of any provisions for advice and control. The wider the powers, the more important these provisions will be. An existing system of proven efficacy, as here, is likely to be especially cogent.

(ii) Where the powers are of great width, as in the present case, there is much to be said for some scheme of fractional division, confining part of the fund to relatively safe investments, and allowing the other part to be used for investments in which the greater risks will be offset by substantial prospects of a greater return. On the other hand, when the powers are appreciably less wide than they are in the present case, I would in general respectfully concur with the views expressed by the Law Reform Committee that no division of the fund into fractions should be required, and that the only division should be into investments which require advice and those which do not. Nevertheless, although a division of the fund into fractions should not be essential, there may well be cases where such a division may be of assistance in obtaining the approval of the court.

(iii) The width of the powers in the present scheme seems to me to be at or near the extreme limit for charitable funds. Without the fractional division of the fund and the assurance of effective control and advice I very much doubt whether such a scheme could have been approved. What the court has to judge is the combined effect of width, division, advice and control, which all interact, together with the standing of the trustees.

(iv) The size of the fund in question may be very material. A fund that is very large may well justify a latitude of investment that would be denied to a more

6 Between £5m and £6m.

modest fund; for the spread of investments possible for a larger fund may justify the greater risks that wider powers will permit to be taken.

(v) The object of the trust may be very material. In the present case, the desirability of having an increase of capital value which will make possible the purchase of desirable acquisitions for the museum despite soaring prices does something to justify the greater risks whereby capital appreciation may be obtained.

Since writing this judgment I have been referred to the very recent decision in *Mason v Farbrother* [1983] 2 All ER 1078, p. 783, post; and counsel on both sides sent me a helpful joint note on the subject. Much of the judgment is directed to questions of jurisdiction and the details of the revised investment clause there under consideration. Of these matters I need say nothing. However, in considering whether the jurisdiction to approve the revised clause ought to be exercised, Judge Blackett-Ord, the Vice-Chancellor of Lancaster, appears to have treated the *Kolb* line of cases as still being binding authorities, saying (as indeed is the case) that the rule was not absolute but applied in the absence of special circumstances. He then said at 1086 that 'the special circumstances in the present case are manifest: in a word, inflation since 1961'. He added that the trust in question was unusual in that it was not a private or family trust but a trust of a pension fund with perhaps something of a public element in it.

For my part, I would hesitate to describe inflation since 1961 as amounting to 'special circumstances'; it is, unhappily, a very general circumstance. With all respect, I can see little virtue (judicial comity and humility apart) in seeking to preserve the rule and yet establishing universal special circumstances that will engulf the rule. I do not, of course, know what arguments on this point were addressed to the court, but for the reasons that I have given I would prefer to say that the rule has gone, and with it any question of what circumstances are special. However, the ultimate result is much the same, and although the reasoning in the two cases differs, I am happy to think that there is this support for my conclusion in the present case.''

In **Steel v Wellcome Custodian Trustees Ltd** [1988] 1 WLR 167,[7] the entire share capital of the Wellcome Foundation Ltd was bequeathed to trustees for the purpose of funding medical research. The trustees were directed to retain the shares unsold and investment powers were limited to trustee securities and mortgages on land. In 1956, by an order of the court, these powers were extended to allow for investment in fixed interest stocks and equities. It was however provided that these extended powers would only be used for two-thirds of the fund (excluding the Wellcome Foundation shares). In 1985 the trustees were concerned at having nearly the whole fund invested in a single company, and, under a scheme approved by the Charity Commissioners, they

---

7 [1988] Conv 380 (B. Dale).

transferred the shares in the Wellcome Foundation to a quoted holding company, called Wellcome Plc. Pursuant to the order, the trustees sold about 25% of the shares to the public. "The sale realised about £200 million but the increase in the quoted price of Wellcome Plc. shares means that they presently represent over 90% of the value of a fund worth a total of £3,200 million."

In approving a scheme extending powers of investment to the acquisition of any property whatever as if the trustees were beneficial owners of the fund, and including a power to delegate to professional fund managers and advisers, HOFFMANN J said at 173:

"The most important difference between the scheme in this case and that approved in the *British Museum* case [1984] 1 WLR 418, [1984] 1 All ER 337, p. 690 ante, is that the latter scheme contained a requirement that part of the fund should be invested in narrower range securities and some restrictions upon the kind of securities authorised for the rest of the fund. The present scheme has no division of the fund and no restriction upon the nature of the investments. The report of the Law Reform Committee to which I have already referred recommended that there should be no divisions of the fund but that the only distinction should be between investments which could be made only after advice and those which could be made with advice. In the present case, no investments will be made without advice and that distinction therefore has no place.

Sir Robert Megarry V-C did however attach some importance to the division of the fund in the case before him, saying, at 425, at 342:

'Where the powers are of great width, as in the present case, there is much to be said for some scheme of fractional division, confining part of the fund to relatively safe investments and allowing the other part to be used for investments in which the greater risks will be offset by substantial prospects of a greater return.'

Earlier, at 424, at 342, he had spoken of the 'due recognition of the prudence of maintaining a solid core of relatively safe investments'. The advantages of division therefore depend on the proposition that gilt-edged investments are safer than investments in equities and other forms of property.

Taking a single investment with another, this is of course true. A gilt-edged stock will maintain its nominal value whereas shares in any given company may become valueless. But the proposition is less obviously true when one compares a fund invested in gilt-edged with a well diversified fund invested in equities and property. The chances of *all* those investments becoming valueless is extremely remote and the experience of the last half-century is that a fund of the latter kind will over almost any period have done better than gilt-edged. On the basis of the statistical evidence presented in this case, I accept the evidence of Sir Ian Fraser, the former chairman of Lazard Brothers & Co., that in the only sense relevant to a large diversified fund like this, gilt-edged has on past form been a less safe form of investment than equities and property. The trustees will be free to invest in gilt-edged if at any time they should think it expedient, but a mandatory requirement that a part of the fund should always be so invested seems to me contrary to the general principle of prudence. I therefore think that if I were to insist in this case on a specific provision which Sir Robert Megarry V-C in the *British Museum* case thought appropriate for a different fund in 1983, I would be failing to apply the general principle on which he acted, namely that the court should judge each application on its merits.

There is also a particular feature of this case which makes it desirable to avoid any restriction upon the discretion of the trustees. As I have mentioned, about 90% of the fund is invested in Wellcome Plc. and is likely to remain so invested for some time to come. The object of the sale and flotation of Wellcome stock was to enable the trustees to diversify some of their holding. It seems to me important that in dealing with the remaining 10 per cent, the trustees should have as much flexibility as possible. In respect of this part of the fund, the trustees should be left to apply the prudence principle at a fairly high level of abstraction, with the safeguards entrusted to the provisions for expert advice in accordance with the guidelines of the scheme rather than confining them to fixed categories of authorised investments.

Having regard therefore to the size of this fund, the eminence of the trustees, the provisions of the scheme for obtaining and acting on advice and the quality of advice available, as well as the special circumstances pertaining to the large holding in the shares of a single company, I am willing to approve the present scheme without any restriction on the kind of assets in which all or any of the fund may be invested.

I can deal relatively shortly with the power of delegation. In practice it is inevitable that the day to day investment decisions concerning a fund of this size would have to be delegated to advisers. Only two of the trustees are appointed on account of their experience of business and despite their undoubted eminence, it is inconceivable that they could apply their minds to every investment decision which has to be made. The proposed delegation, being terminable within a maximum of a year, is similar to that which the trustees could make by power of attorney under section 25 (1) of the Trustee Act 1925 (p. 747, post). The difference is that, under section 25 (2), the trustees would remain liable for the acts or defaults of their agents as if they were their own. The present scheme proposes to restrict the liability of the trustees in the manner in which I have described. It does not however confer that complete exemption from liability (bad faith apart) which the trustees would have enjoyed if the delegation had been within the more restricted terms of section 23 (1) of the Act of 1925.

The trustees are, under the terms of the will as amended by various orders of the court, paid for their services by annual salaries, presently at the rate of £20,000 a year. The courts have always been reluctant to relieve paid trustees of liability for breach of trust. But I do not think that it would be fair in a case like this, where delegation is a practical necessity, to insist that the trustees should be insurers of the acts of their investment advisers. To impose such strict liability might make it difficult to obtain the services of persons of high quality. On the other hand, I think that paid trustees should be willing to accept responsibility for a higher standard of conduct than mere abstinence from bad faith. The terms of the scheme, under which the trustees are to be liable for negligence in choosing their agents or fixing or enforcing the terms on which they are engaged or in failing to take reasonable steps to require action to remedy breaches of which the trustees have notice, are in my view a reasonable compromise between the strict liability of section 25 (2) of the Trustee Act 1925 and the complete exemption of section 23 (1).

For these reasons I approve the scheme.''

G. Mortgages of Land[8]

i. Authorised Investments

TRUSTEE INVESTMENTS ACT 1961

FIRST SCHEDULE
Part II, para. 13, see p. 669, ante.

Lewin on Trusts (16th edn, 1964) pp. 370–371

'Before August 3, 1961, the rule was that trustees should not invest on second, contributory or equitable mortgages, . . . but it is at least doubtful whether this rule has survived the commencement of the Trustee Investments Act 1961, on the above date. For investment 'in mortgages of freehold property . . . and of leasehold property' with sixty years to run is a narrower-range investment not requiring advice under that Act, and, unless the context otherwise requires, mortgage' has the same meaning as in the Trustee Act 1925,[9] in which it relates to 'every estate and interest regarded in equity as merely a security for money'.[10] There does not seem to be anything in the context of the Act of 1961 (whose object is plainly to increase trustees' powers) to require a more limited meaning to be put on 'mortgages' in the relevant provision, and it is submitted that the effect of the Act is to sweep away the old provisions on inferior types of mortgage.

But if the legislature intended this, it was a strong thing to do with a referential interpretation section, and in case the above submission is wrong as well as to cover pre-1961 mortgages the old rules are now discussed. . . ."

ii. Valuation

TRUSTEE ACT 1925

8. Loans and investments by trustees not chargeable as breaches of trust.—(1) A trustee lending money on the security of any property on which he can properly lend shall not be chargeable with breach of trust by reason only of the proportion borne by the amount of the loan to the value of the property at the time when the loan was made, if it appears to the court—

(*a*) that in making the loan the trustee was acting upon a report as to the value of the property made by a person whom he reasonably believed to be an able practical surveyor or valuer instructed and employed independently of any owner of the property, whether such surveyor or valuer carried on business in the locality where the property is situate or elsewhere; and

(*b*) that the amount of the loan does not exceed two third parts of the value of the property as stated in the report; and

(*c*) that the loan was made under the advice of the surveyor or valuer expressed in the report.

---

8 H & M, pp. 517–520; K & S, pp. 280–282; P & M, pp. 451–455; Pettit, pp. 394–396; Riddall, pp. 270–274; Snell, pp. 220–222; Underhill, pp. 603–608.
9 See Trustee Investments Act 1961, s. 17 (4).
10 See TA 1925, s. 68 (7).

(2) A trustee lending money on the security of any leasehold property shall not be chargeable with breach of trust only upon the ground that in making such loan he dispensed either wholly or partly with the production or investigation of the lessor's title.

10. Powers supplementary to powers of investment.—(1) Trustees lending money on the security of any property on which they can lawfully lend may contract that such money shall not be called in during any period not exceeding seven years from the time when the loan was made, provided interest be paid within a specified time not exceeding thirty days after every half-yearly or other day on which it becomes due, and provided there be no breach of any covenant by the mortgagor contained in the instrument of mortgage or charge for the maintenance and protection of the property.

(2) On a sale of land for an estate in fee simple or for a term having at least five hundred years to run by trustees or by a tenant for life or statutory owner, the trustees, or the tenant for life or statutory owner on behalf of the trustees of the settlement, may, where the proceeds are liable to be invested, contract that the payment of any part, not exceeding two-thirds, of the purchase money shall be secured by a charge by way of legal mortgage or a mortgage by demise or sub-demise for a term of at least five hundred years (less a nominal reversion when by sub-demise), of the land sold, with or without the security of any other property, such charge or mortgage, if any buildings are comprised in the mortgage, to contain a covenant by the mortgagor to keep them insured against loss or damage by fire to the full value thereof.

The trustees shall not be bound to obtain any report as to the value of the land or other property to be comprised in such charge or mortgage, or any advice as to the making of the loan, and shall not be liable for any loss which may be incurred by reason only of the security being insufficient at the date of the charge or mortgage; and the trustees of the settlement shall be bound to give effect to such contract made by the tenant for life or statutory owner.

iii. EXTENT OF LIABILITY

TRUSTEE ACT 1925

9. Liability for loss by reason of improper investment.—(1) Where a trustee improperly advances trust money on a mortgage security which would at the time of the investment be a proper investment in all respects for a smaller sum than is actually advanced thereon, the security shall be deemed an authorised investment for the smaller sum, and the trustee shall only be liable to make good the sum advanced in excess thereof with interest.

(2) This section applies to investments made before as well as after the commencement of this Act.

SHAW v CATES
[1909] 1 Ch 389 (ChD, PARKER J)

A valuation was made of land in Folkestone which contained two houses which were built and occupied, and two others in the course of construction. They were valued at £9,180 by one Barton, and recommended as suitable for a mortgage up to two-thirds of that sum. A schedule to the report gave the separate values of the four properties. After inspection the trustees, without further consulting the valuer, lent £4,400 on the security of the partially constructed houses, the sum being exactly two-thirds of the value as shown in the schedule.

Barton was also the rent-collector of the mortgagor. No covenant was given by the mortgagor to keep the premises in repair. The premises deteriorated, and, on the bankruptcy of the mortgagor, proved to be an inadequate security.

The beneficiaries sought to hold the trustees liable for the whole sum involved.

Held. The trustees were liable for the excess.

PARKER J: In this action the beneficiaries under the will of a Mrs Davis, who died in June, 1891, ask to have the defendant Cates, a trustee of the will, and the estate of Mildred Whiteley, deceased, a former trustee of the will, declared liable for breach of trust in respect of the investment on 22 October, 1897, of 4400*l.*, part of the trust moneys on the security of a legal mortgage of certain freehold houses in Shorncliffe Road, Folkestone. The beneficiaries contend (1) that this investment was altogether improper, because, having regard to the nature of the property, it was too hazardous to be accepted as a trust investment; and (2) that, even if otherwise proper to be accepted as a trust investment, it was not a proper investment for so large a sum as 4400*l.*

The defendants join issue on both these contentions, and, as to the second contention, further say that they are entitled to the protection of s. 8 of the Trustee Act 1893,[11] or at any rate that the defendant Cates and Mildred Whiteley, in making the investment in question, acted honestly and reasonably, taking all the precautions which a man of ordinary prudence might have been expected to take in the conduct of his own affairs, and relying, as they were entitled to rely, on expert advice as to values; and further, if those defences fail, they ask to be wholly relieved from liability for breach of trust under s. 3 of the Judicial Trustees Act 1896,[12] or to be partially relieved from such liability by virtue of s. 9 of the Trustee Act 1893.[13]

It is clear that the trustees had in the present case power to invest upon the security of freehold hereditaments. The onus, therefore, of proving that the investment in question was altogether too hazardous to be accepted as a trust investment lies upon the plaintiffs. In my opinion they have not discharged this onus. . . .

Section 4 of the Trustee Act 1888[14] somewhat modified the law as above stated. It provided as follows: "No trustee lending money upon the security of any property shall be chargeable with breach of trust by reason only of the proportion borne by the amount of the loan to the value of such property at the time when the loan was made, provided that it shall appear to the Court that in making such loan the trustee was acting upon a report as to the value of the property made by a person whom the trustee reasonably believed to be an able practical surveyor or valuer, instructed and employed independently of any owner of the property, whether such surveyor or valuer carried on business in the locality where the property is situate or elsewhere, and that the amount

---

11 TA 1925, s. 8, p. 697, ante.
12 Ibid, s. 61, p. 876, post.
13 Ibid, s. 9, p. 698, ante.
14 Ibid, s. 8, p. 697, ante.

of the loan does not exceed two equal third parts of the value of the property as stated in such report, and that the loan was made under the advice of such surveyor or valuer expressed in such report." Since the Act, therefore, a trustee has been, and is, justified in acting on expert advice, not only as to the value of the property, but also as to the amount he may properly advance thereon, provided the advice be given in such manner, and by such person, as is contemplated in the section, and that, whatever be the nature of the property, the amount advanced is not more than two thirds of its value. The principle involved seems to be that within the limits of what is often called the "two thirds" rule a prudent man may, as to the amount which can properly be advanced on any proposed security, whether the property be agricultural land or houses or buildings used for trade purposes, rely on expert advice obtained with certain precautions, it being of course assumed that in giving the advice the expert will consider all the circumstances of the case, including the nature of the property, and will not advise a larger advance than under all the circumstances can be prudently made. I dissent entirely from the position taken up by some of the defendants' expert witnesses, that when once they have ascertained the value of the property they are, whatever its nature and whatever method of valuation they have adopted, at least prima facie justified in advising an advance of two thirds of its value. Such a position in my opinion defeats the object of the section by making what the Legislature has recognised as the standard of the minimum protection which a prudent man will require into a standard of the normal risk which, whatever the nature of the property, a prudent man will be prepared to run; and it deprives the expert advice on which the trustee is to rely as to the margin of protection to be required of all its value. It is as true now as it was before the Act that the maximum sum which a prudent man can be advised to lend upon a mortgage depends on the nature of the property and upon all the circumstances of the case. If the property is liable to deteriorate or is specially subject to fluctuations in value, or depends for its value on circumstances the continual existence of which is precarious, a prudent man will now, as much as before the Act, require a larger margin for his protection than he would in the case of property attended by no such disadvantages, and an expert who does his duty will take this into consideration....

I have come to the conclusion that, under the circumstances which I have shortly stated, Mr Barton's report is not such a report as was contemplated by the Act. To advise an advance of two thirds of the value of four properties is not the same thing as advising an advance of two thirds of the value of any one or more of the properties apart from the others or other. This is more especially the case where one of the properties is not at the date of the report an income-bearing property. As I have already pointed out, the amount of income which a property is producing is material in considering what amount can properly be advanced thereon. In the present case the income of three of the four properties originally proposed to be mortgaged was sufficient to provide, with a considerable margin, for the payment of interest on the amount proposed to be advanced, although the other property was unlet. The importance of this point was fully recognised by Beckingsale & Co. when considering the propriety of an advance on the first three properties mentioned in the report only, the income of which was more than sufficient to provide for the interest. I cannot explain why they no longer thought it of consequence when they came to consider the propriety of an advance on the first two properties, the existing income from which did not amount to the interest on the proposed advance.

In my opinion the advance which was actually made was not the advance which Mr Barton advised, and his report, therefore, cannot be relied on as within s. 8 of the Trustee Act, 1893. Again, I do not think that Mr Barton was in fact instructed and employed independently of the mortgagor. He was suggested by the mortgagor, instructed by the mortgagor's solicitors, referred to the mortgagor both as to his fee and as to the properties he was to value, and was accompanied by the mortgagor when he made his survey. I am not suggesting that he was consciously influenced by the mortgagor or that he acted otherwise than honestly in the matter, but I do not think that he in fact fulfilled the conditions mentioned in the section as to his instructions and employment. If, according to the true meaning of the section, the belief of the trustees is the material point, I am unable to hold that the trustees did reasonably believe that Mr Barton was instructed and employed independently of the mortgagor. They left the instructions to be given by Beckingsale & Co., who were also the mortgagor's solicitors, and after ascertaining that Mr Barton was a competent person took no further trouble in the matter.

Lastly, it appears that one of the properties which Mr Barton in fact valued differed from that actually comprised in the mortgage, because Mr Barton valued a property with an easement of access across other land of the mortgagor, whereas the mortgage contained no such easement. I need not express an opinion whether this alone would, under the circumstances, have prevented the trustees from relying on the section. I mention it because the fact seems to me to illustrate the importance of the surveyor who makes the valuation being independently instructed and employed. In valuing for the mortgagor, and on information supplied by the mortgagor, it might have been immaterial to mention this suggested easement, the proposed dominant and proposed servient tenement being in the same hands. In valuing for a mortgage of the proposed dominant tenement it was a point of great importance, and yet there is no mention of it in Mr Barton's report, and because of this omission, coupled with the subsequent readiness of the solicitors to accept the mortgagor's statement of the property to be included in the mortgage, the mortgagees have got a property without an easement, whereas Mr Barton valued it with an easement. I very much doubt whether this could have happened if the surveyor who made the valuation had been instructed and employed independently of the mortgagor, and had not in talking matters over with the mortgagor been influenced by the mortgagor's view of how he could deal with his various properties to the best advantage, as opposed to the question what the mortgagee of one of these properties could make of it.

If, apart from s. 8 of the Trustee Act 1893, I ask myself whether in the matter of this mortgage the trustees acted reasonably and took all the precautions which a prudent man acting in his own affairs might be expected to have taken, I can only answer the question in the negative. In leaving Mr Barton to be instructed by their solicitors, whom they knew to be acting for the mortgagor, in taking no means to see that he was properly instructed or that he was instructed and employed independently of the mortgagor, in not themselves considering the surveyor's report when made, but leaving it to their solicitors to decide whether the report might be acted on, in making an advance not advised in the report to two thirds of the value of two only of the properties mentioned in the report, notwithstanding that one of the properties consisted of unfinished houses—in all this it seems to me that they failed to act as a prudent man might reasonably be expected to act in the management of his own affairs.

I am of opinion also that under the circumstances, however honestly they acted—and no one has suggested or could suggest that they did not act honestly—they cannot be said to have acted reasonably within the meaning of s. 3 of the Judicial Trustees Act 1896, if only because they neglected to do what a reasonable man would do in the prudent management of his own business.

It remains, therefore, to consider whether the three houses comprised in the mortgage were in fact of sufficient value to justify an advance of trust money to the amount of 4400*l.*, and, if not, for what amount they might properly have been accepted as security by the trustees; for having decided that there was nothing hazardous in advancing trust moneys thereon the trustees are, in my opinion, entitled to the benefit of s. 9 of the Trustee Act 1893.

For the purpose of considering these questions it seems to me that the Court ought to be guided by the same general considerations which would have guided it prior to the Trustee Act 1888. Section 8[15] of that Act merely protects trustees who within certain limits and under certain circumstances act on expert opinions as to the amount they may advance. It does not, as has been suggested, abrogate all distinction between agricultural land and houses or buildings used for trade in determining the margin of protection to be required by a prudent man, or indicate that a prudent man may, prima facie, be content in all cases with a margin of one third the value of the property. At most it suggests that the extra margin of protection beyond one third the value depends on the particular circumstances of each case, and assumes that whatever may be the nature of the property the expert employed will give the matter his bona fide consideration, advising with a view to the security of the trust money, and not only in such a way as to protect the trustees from liability for breach of trust. In cases not within the section it perhaps suggests that the rule which the Courts had laid down in the case of houses and buildings used for trade is less stringent than the two thirds rule laid down in the case of agricultural land, and this I believe to have been the case before the Act. As well since the Act as before it, it is therefore necessary to consider not only the value of the property proposed to be mortgaged, but also the margin of protection which a prudent man would require remembering that the margin of protection to be required must depend on the nature of the property and all the circumstances of the case. . . .

Considering all the facts of this case, I have come to the conclusion that the largest sum for which the property could be considered a good security in 1897 is 3400*l.* and therefore, under s. 9 of the Act, the trustees' liability is confined to making good the excess of the amount actually advanced over this amount and with interest.

Re Solomon [1912] 1 Ch 261 was another case in which a mortgage security, made on the advice of valuers, proved to be insufficient, and the beneficiaries

---

15 Presumably s. 4 of the 1888 Act was intended.

sought to make the trustees account. WARRINGTON J reviewed the facts in great detail and continued at 280:

"Now, do [the trustees] make out that they are within the second part of the sub-section?[16] The second part is, first, that in making the loan the trustee is acting upon a certain report. That the trustees in this case acted on the report of Messrs. Toplis & Harding is abundantly clear, and I need say no more about that. Then, that report must be a report as to the value of the property; and that of course it was, and it was to be made by a person whom the trustee reasonably believed to be an able practical surveyor. As to that there can be no question. Messrs. Toplis & Harding were surveyors and valuers of long standing and of good reputation. They had been employed by the trustees for years in making such valuations; they had been employed by the defendant Meyer himself in making valuations on his own behalf. It seems to me beyond question that the trustees in this case believed Mr Harding, who attended to the business, to be an able practical surveyor or valuer. Next, he must be, or be believed to be,— there is a question about that—instructed and employed independently of any owner of the property. Now, what is meant by 'instructed and employed independently of any owner of the property'? I think it means this: that the relation existing between employer and employed must exist as between the trustees and the valuer, and between them only—that the valuer must be entitled to look for his remuneration to the person who employs him, and, on the other hand, must be responsible to that person and to that person only for the due performance of his duty as valuer. When you have that, he is instructed and employed by the trustee, and he is instructed and employed by him independently of the owner.[17] I do not think it is incumbent on the trustee to inquire into all the previous business transactions of the valuer and to find out whether he has at any time recently or long before advised or acted for the mortgagor. He must in this matter be instructed and employed independently of the mortgagor, and, if that is made out, then I think the provisions of the sub-section are satisfied. Is that made out in the present case? The plaintiffs say it is not. I think it is. The trustees, through their solicitors, gave the instructions to the surveyor, and, but for the fact that certain particulars appended to those instructions had, as must necessarily be the case, been furnished by the mortgagor, the mortgagor had nothing whatever to do with the instructions given to Messrs. Toplis & Harding. Then, were they employed by, or partly by, the mortgagor? There again the mortgagor, it seems to me, had nothing to do with their employment. He was not responsible to them for their fee. The contract to value was made between the trustees and the valuers. The duty which the valuers owed they owed to the trustees, and to them alone, and it was the trustees alone who were responsible to them for their remuneration. I think it is abundantly made out that that was the true relation between the trustees and the valuers, and that therefore the trustees have, in this case, established that they have acted on a report of a valuer instructed and employed independently of the owner of the property.

---

16 TA 1893, s. 8 (1), now TA 1925, s. 8 (1), p. 697, ante.
17 In *Re Somerset* [1894] 1 Ch 231, KEKEWICH J held that the valuer must *in fact* be instructed and employed independently. It was not sufficient that the trustee believed him to have been so employed.

The next point is that the sub-section further requires the amount of the loan not to exceed two equal third parts of the value of the property as stated in the report. As to that, there is no question; there is no doubt that the amount advanced did not exceed two third parts of the value of the property as stated in the report.

Now, on that, I think it is desirable to add my opinion to that of other judges who have dealt with this question of valuers' reports made to trustees. It has, I think, undoubtedly become the practice of valuers, thinking that they are thereby complying with the requirements of the Act, to advise practically in every case that trustees may safely advance two-thirds of the value, and that practice appears to be based on the fact that, so far as the liabilities of the trustees are concerned, the Act makes no distinction between one kind of property and another; it only requires that they shall not advance more than two third parts of the value of the property. That, I think, is a mistake. It is the duty of the valuer to consider not only the value of the property, but the proportion which, in his opinion, as an expert and practical man, the trustees would, in each particular case, be justified in advancing. But the fact that the valuer has advised a loan of two-thirds of the value does not make the report a bad one. He has reported that the trustees may safely advance that amount, and that is sufficient for them. I think valuers should bear in mind that it is their duty, in advising trustees, to advise them not only as to what they consider the actual value, but what proportion of that value the trustees may safely advance upon the security quite independently of any supposed rule relating to the two-thirds; only, of course, if the valuers were so satisfied with the security as to advise the advance, say, of three-fourths, the trustees would not be justified in acting on that advice, because the Act confines them to two-thirds. The trustees, therefore, have not advanced more than two-thirds of the value of the property as stated in the report.

The next requirement of the sub-section is 'that the loan was made under the advice of the surveyor or valuer expressed in the report'. It is said that that condition has not been complied with because the surveyor and valuer in this case did not in so many words say 'I advise the trustees to advance so much money'. In my opinion, to so hold would be to cast away the substance for the shadow. The surveyors are told, in their instructions, that a certain security is offered to the trustees, and they are asked to survey that property and to report what, in their opinion, is the value of the security offered, and what amount can be advanced by trustees thereon; and in answer to those instructions they tell the trustees what they consider to be the value of the property, and that that property forms a sufficient security for the amount which they are told in the instructions the trustees are asking them to advise upon. What can that mean except that the surveyors are telling the trustees that they may, in their opinion, properly advance that sum—in other words that they are advising the trustees to make that advance? Could it possibly be contended by the surveyors that the trustees, acting on that report and making the advance, if there were circumstances of negligence or misconduct on the part of the surveyors, could not claim that they were misled by the report and induced to make the advance by it? Of course it could not. The surveyor making this report in answer to such instructions as those must be taken to have known that if his report was favourable the trustees would make the advance, and make the advance to the amount for which he advised the property was sufficient security.

I think, therefore, that the trustees in the present case have complied also with the final requirement of the sub-section, and sufficiently made it appear to the Court that the loan was made under the advice of the surveyor or valuer, and that the advice was expressed in the report.

That being the conclusion at which I have arrived, it follows that the trustees in the present case are not chargeable with the breach of trust which is alleged against them, and the result is that I must dismiss this action against all the defendants with costs.''

In **Re Walker** (1890) 62 LT 449, trustees made an improper investment of trust funds on a mortgage of land. The security proved insufficient. The trustees claimed to be protected under Trustee Act 1888, s. 5 (now Trustee Act 1925, s. 9). KEKEWICH J, having held that the investment was improper, said at 452:

"Then, as regards the 5th section of the Act, a different question arises. That is a beneficial section, the object of which is to provide that, when a trustee has advanced more money on mortgage of the property than was reasonably prudent, and the estate fails, then he is not to be chargeable with the whole, but only with so much as would have been a loss if you take the real value at the time of investment, not the value he put upon it. That is the substance of it. Supposing, for instance, a man invests 100*l* on property that would bear only 80*l*; he is not to lose the whole 100*l* because of that. That is a reasonable provision on behalf of trustees. But the whole section depends on this: 'When a trustee shall have improperly advanced trust money on a mortgage security which would, at the time of the investment, have been a proper investment in all respects for a less sum than was actually advanced thereon'. That I understood to mean that the impropriety consists in the amount invested. If the investment is otherwise improper—as, for instance, if a man invests on mortgage of trade buildings when he is only entitled to invest on mortgage of agricultural land—he cannot claim the benefit of the section, and say, 'I might take the value at two-thirds of the advance, although not the whole'. He must establish the propriety of the investment independently of value, and then he has the benefit of the section to save him from any loss greater than that which would have been incurred by advancing too large a sum on what otherwise would be a proper security.''

In **Re Stuart** [1897] 2 Ch 583, a trustee acted on a valuation which stated merely the amount for which the property was a good security, without stating the value of the property, and advanced more than two-thirds of the amount stated in the valuation. The valuer was employed by the solicitor who acted for the mortgagor. Liability was admitted and the question was whether the trustee should be relieved under the predecessor to Trustee Act 1925, s. 61, p. 876, post. In refusing relief, STIRLING J said at 591:

"As to the valuations, which have been produced, they do not satisfy the requirements of s. 4 of the Trustee Act 1888, which has now been replaced by s. 8 of the Trustee Act 1893. It was contended, and in my opinion rightly contended, that this was not necessarily a fatal obstacle to the application of the section. Still, I think that those requirements cannot be left out of consideration. The Legislature in 1888 dealt with the duties of trustees with regard to investments, and laid down certain rules for their guidance which in some respects relaxed those previously existing and are in themselves reasonable, and they appear to me to constitute a standard by which reasonable conduct is to be judged.''

In **Re Chapman** [1896] 2 Ch 763, the estate of the testator included several mortgages. Because of a general agricultural depression, the value of the properties had decreased and become insufficient to cover the mortgages. The trustees decided to hold the securities, and wait for a more favourable time for realisation. The question was whether the defendants were liable as executors because of their failure to call in the mortgage within twelve months of the testator's death, or as trustees for the subsequent retention. The Court of Appeal found for the defendants. LINDLEY LJ said at 776:

"There is no rule of law which compels the Court to hold that an honest trustee is liable to make good loss sustained by retaining an authorised security in a falling market, if he did so honestly and prudently, in the belief that it was the best course to take in the interest of all parties. Trustees acting honestly, with ordinary prudence and within the limits of their trust, are not liable for mere errors of judgment. Any loss sustained by the trust estate under such circumstances falls upon and must be borne by the owners of the property— i.e., the cestuis que trust—and cannot be thrown by them on their trustees, who have done no wrong, though the result may prove that they possibly might have done better. *Learoyd v Whiteley* (1887) 12 App Cas 727 is a clear authority to this effect; so are *Buxton v Buxton* (1835) 1 My & Cr 80 and *Marsden v Kent* (1877) 5 ChD 598.

The case is an important one not only to the trustees of this particular will, but to trustees of mortgages generally. Owing to the great fall in the value of agricultural land trustees of mortgage securities have been placed in a position of great difficulty. To throw on the trustees the loss sustained by the fall in value of securities authorised by the trust, wilful default, which includes want of ordinary prudence on the part of the trustees, must be proved; but it is not proved in this case. In my opinion, wilful default is disproved in all the important cases and is not proved in the doubtful ones.

The appeals must be allowed.''

H. Purchase of Land

Unless expressly authorised, trustees, other than tenants for life under the Settled Land Act 1925 and trustees for sale, are not permitted to invest in the purchase of land. Tenants for life are authorised by Settled Land Act 1925, s. 73, to apply capital money in the purchase of land in fee simple or of leasehold land with at least 60 years unexpired. And trustees for sale are by Law of Property Act 1925, s. 28, given the same powers as tenants for life of settled land.[18]

It is common to give to other trustees express powers to purchase land, enabling them, for example, to purchase a house for a widow.

---

18 See *Re Wakeman* [1945] Ch 177, [1945] 1 All ER 421; *Re Wellsted's Will Trusts* [1949] Ch 296, [1949] 1 All ER 577; Maudsley and Burn, *Land Law Cases and Materials* (6th edn) pp. 235–236.

I. Pension Trustees

PENSIONS ACT 1995

33. Investment powers: duty of care—(1) Liability for breach of an obligation under any rule of law to take care or exercise skill in the performance of any investment functions, where the function is exercisable—
(a) by a trustee of a trust scheme, or
(b) by a person to whom the function has been delegated under section 34,[18a] cannot be excluded or restricted by any instrument or agreement.

34. Power of investment and delegation—(1) The trustees of a trust scheme have, subject to any restriction imposed by the scheme, the same power to make an investment of any kind as if they were absolutely entitled to the assets of the scheme.

35. Investment principles—(1) The trustees of a trust scheme must secure that there is prepared, maintained and from time to time revised a written statement of the principles governing decisions about investments for the purposes of the scheme.
(2) The statement must cover, among other things—
(a) the trustees' policy for securing compliance with sections 36 and 56, and
(b) their policy about the following matters.
(3) Those matters are—
(a) the kinds of investments to be held,
(b) the balance between different kinds of investments,
(c) risk,
(d) the expected return on investments,
(e) the realisation of investments, and
(f) such other matters as may be prescribed.
(4) Neither the trust scheme nor the statement may impose restrictions (however expressed) on any power to make investments by reference to the consent of the employer.
(5) The trustees of a trust scheme must, before a statement under this section is prepared or revised—
(a) obtain and consider the written advice of a person who is reasonably believed by the trustees to be qualified by his ability in and practical experience of financial matters and to have the appropriate knowledge and experience of the management of the investments of such schemes, and
(b) consult the employer.
(6) If in the case of any trust scheme—
(a) a statement under this section has not been prepared or is not being maintained, or
(b) the trustees have not obtained and considered advice in accordance with subsection (5).
sections 3 and 10[19] apply to any trustee who has failed to take all such steps as are reasonable to secure compliance.

18aSee p. 760, post.
19 S. 3 (Prohibition orders); s. 10 (Civil penalties).

36. Choosing investments—(1) The trustees of a trust scheme must exercise their powers of investment in accordance with subsections (2) to (4) and any fund manager to whom any discretion has been delegated under section 34[20] must exercise the discretion in accordance with subsection (2).

(2) The trustees or fund manager must have regard—

(a) to the need for diversification of investments, in so far as appropriate to the circumstances of the scheme, and

(b) to the suitability to the scheme of investments of the description of investment proposed and of the investment proposed as an investment of that description.

(3) Before investing in any manner (other than in a manner mentioned in Part I of Schedule 1 to the Trustee Investments Act 1961) the trustees must obtain and consider proper advice on the question whether the investment is satisfactory having regard to the matters mentioned in subsection (2) and the principles contained in the statement under section 35.

(4) Trustees retaining any investment must—

(a) determine at what intervals the circumstances, and in particular the nature of the investment, make it desirable to obtain such advice as is mentioned in subsection (3), and

(b) obtain and consider such advice accordingly.

(5) The trustees, or the fund manager to whom any discretion has been delegated under section 34, must exercise their powers of investment with a view to giving effect to the principles contained in the statement under section 35, so far as reasonably practicable.

(6) For the purposes of this section "proper advice" means—

(a) where giving the advice constitutes carrying on investment business in the United Kingdom (within the meaning of the Financial Services Act 1986), advice—

  (i) given by a person authorised under Chapter III of Part I of that Act,

  (ii) given by a person exempted under Chapter IV of that Part who, in giving the advice, is acting in the course of the business in respect of which he is exempt,

  (iii) given by a person where, by virtue of paragraph 27 of Schedule 1 to that Act, paragraph 15 of that Schedule does not apply to giving the advice, or

  (iv) given by a person who, by virtue of regulation 5 of the Banking Coordination (Second Council Directive) Regulations 1992, may give the advice though not authorised as mentioned in sub-paragraph (i) above.

(b) in any other case, the advice of a person who is reasonably believed by the trustees to be qualified by his ability in and practical experience of financial matters and to have the appropriate knowledge and experience of the management of the investments of trust schemes.

(7) Trustees shall not be treated as having complied with subsection (3) or (4) unless the advice was given or has subsequently been confirmed in writing.

---

20 P. 760 post.

(8) If the trustees of a trust scheme do not obtain and consider advice in accordance with this section, sections 3 and 10 apply to any trustee who has failed to take all such steps as are reasonable to secure compliance.

J. Law Reform

Law Reform Committee 23rd Report (The Powers and Duties of Trustees) 1982 Cmnd 8733, paras. 9.1. II.6–10, 27 and 28.[21]

"(*a*) *Investment in Land* (paragraphs 3.1–3.14)

6. Trustees' powers to purchase freehold and leasehold land should be widened as follows:—
    (i) all trustees should have the power to buy freehold property as an investment, subject to their first obtaining favourable professional advice; (paragraph 3.2)
    (ii) all trustees should be empowered to invest in leasehold land, provided that appropriate advice is taken; (paragraph 3.3)
    (iii) the absolute prohibition on the purchase of leaseholds with less than sixty years to run should be removed; (paragraph 3.4)
    (iv) the decision in *Re Power* [1947] Ch 572, [1947] 2 All ER 282, should be reversed and a new statutory power introduced enabling trustees to purchase a residence for occupation by the person entitled to the income on the moneys laid out in the purchase or eligible to have it applied for his benefit; (paragraph 3.5)
7. Trustees should be empowered to make purchases under recommendation 6 (iv) above on mortgage. (paragraph 3.11)
8. Trustees' powers to invest in mortgages should be widened so as to permit them to invest in second mortgages. (paragraphs 3.12–3.13)
9. The 10 year limit on the exercise of options should be abolished and trustees should be empowered to stipulate that the purchase price may be calculated by reference to the market value of the property at the time of the exercise of the option. (paragraph 3.14)

(*b*) *The Trustee Investments Act 1961* (paragraphs 3.15– 3.25)

10. The statutory powers contained in the Trustee Investments Act 1961 are out of date and ought now to be revised.[1] We recommend that the 1961 Act be repealed and the following new powers be conferred upon trustees:—
    (i) investments should be divided into those which can be made without advice and those which can be made only with advice; (paragraph 3.21)
    (ii) the former category should comprise those investments presently known as narrower-range securities and listed in Parts I and II of the 1961 Act and also unit trusts and investment trusts, as defined in section

---

21 See Law Commission Thirtieth Annual Report 1995 (Law Com No. 239), para 5.16; HM Treasury Consultation Document: Investment Powers of Trustees (May 1996).
1 See *Trustees of the British Museum v A-G* [1984] 1 WLR 418 at 421, [1984] 1 All ER 337 at 339, p. 690, ante.

359 of the Income and Corporation Taxes Act 1970;[2] (paragraph 3.21)

(iii) the latter category should comprise any other investment quoted on the English Stock Exchange; (paragraph 3.21)

(iv) trustees should be free to invest in such proportions as they choose; (paragraph 3.21)

(v) the provisions on advice presently contained in section 6 of the 1961 Act should be retained; (paragraph 3.22)

(vi) express reference should be made in the new statutory provision to the duty of trustees to maintain a balance between income and capital so as to protect all those interested under the trust fund; (paragraph 3.22)

(vii) the requirement in section 6 (1) (*a*) of the 1961 Act which compels trustees to have regard to the need for diversification of investments in so far as is appropriate to the circumstances of the trust is sufficient and further restrictions on the trustees' discretion are not required; (paragraph 3.23)

(viii) investments in foreign securities should not be made unless expressly authorised by the trust instrument; (paragraph 3.24)

(ix) trustees should continue to be able to apply to the court under section 57 of the Trustee Act 1925 (p. 782, post) to make otherwise unauthorised investments; (paragraph 3.25)

(x) additionally, since section 57 is concerned only with the authorisation of specific dealings trustees should be entitled to make an application under the Variation of Trusts Act 1958 (p. 789, post) to ask the court to widen their investment powers generally. (paragraph 3.25)

27. We recommend that the existing restrictions on the use of nominees should be relaxed. Banks, trust corporations and stockbroking companies who are members of the Stock Exchange should be empowered by legislation to act as nominees for the purpose of trust investments. (paragraph 4.23)

28. The same institutions should also be empowered to act as marking names[3] for the purposes of trust investment, so long as they are recognised as such by the Stock Exchange. (paragraph 4.25)''

QUESTIONS

1. How should the duty and power of investment be reformed? How far should the provisions for pension funds under the Pensions Act 1995 be reflected in the general trust law on this topic? Law Reform Committee 23rd Report (The Powers and Duties of Trustees) 1982 Cmnd 8733, paras. 9.1.II. 6–10, p. 708 ante; Pensions Act 1995, ss. 34(1), 35 and 36, p. 706 ante.

2. You are trustee of a new trust and the investment clause provides for investment in securities authorised by law. The fund is worth £500,00, all in cash. What would you do? If you cannot answer this question, read the financial

---

2 Now ICTA 1988, s. 842.

3 This is a facility which has been developed for use in connection with North American securities held in the United Kingdom and dealt in on United Kingdom stockmarkets. A shareholder will hold North American investments in the form of certificates registered in the marking name and endorsed on the back with the name of the actual owner. The companies would pay dividends direct to the marking names, who would then pass them on to the actual shareholder. This practice minimises transfer costs when such securities are sold.

pages of a leading newspaper each day for a month, and then telephone a friendly stockbroker, and have a talk with him.

III. Duty to Distribute[4]

A beneficiary can compel a trustee to pay to him what he is entitled to under the trust. Usually this gives rise to no difficulties. But situations may arise where the trustees' duty is not clear; either because there is doubt as to the beneficiaries' entitlement, or because known beneficiaries cannot be found. In doubtful cases, a trustee may seek the directions of the court; and is of course safe in following them. There are various ways in which he may seek protection.

A. Release on Completion

Lewin on Trusts (16th edn, 1964), p. 189

"In practice, trustees frequently require a release under seal, which throws on the beneficiary a heavy burden of proving fraud, concealment, mistake or undue influences.[5] But strictly a trustee (in contradistinction to an executor) cannot, in the absence of special circumstances, insist upon a release under seal."[6]

B. Advertisement for Claimants

TRUSTEE ACT 1925

27. Protection by means of advertisements.—(1) With a view to the conveyance to or distribution among the persons entitled to any real or personal property, the trustees of a settlement or of a disposition on trust for sale or personal representatives, may give notice by advertisement in the Gazette, and in a newspaper[7] circulating in the district in which the land is situated, and such other like notices, including notices elsewhere than in England and Wales, as would, in any special case, have been directed by a court of competent jurisdiction in an action for administration, of their intention to make such conveyance or distribution as aforesaid, and requiring any person interested to send to the trustees or personal representatives within the time, not being less than two months, fixed in the notice or, where more than one

---

4 H & M, pp. 522–525; K & S, pp. 316–323; P & M, pp. 398–399; Pettit, pp. 363–374; Riddall, pp. 336–339; Snell, pp. 272–274; Underhill, pp. 610–617.
5 *Fowler v Wyatt* (1857) 24 Beav 232.
6 *Chadwick v Heatley* (1845) 2 Coll 137; *Re Wright's Trusts* (1857) 3 K & J 419; *Re Cater's Trusts (No 2)* (1858) 25 Beav 366; *Re Foligno's Mortgage* (1863) 32 Beav 131. See also *King v Mullins* (1852) 1 Drew 308 at 311.
7 As amended by LP (A) A 1926, Sched.

notice is given, in the last of the notices, particulars of his claim in respect of the property or any part thereof to which the notice relates.

(2) At the expiration of the time fixed by the notice the trustees or personal representatives may convey or distribute the property or any part thereof to which the notice relates, to or among the persons entitled thereto, having regard only to the claims, whether formal or not, of which the trustees or personal representatives then had notice and shall not, as respects the property so conveyed or distributed, be liable to any person of whose claim the trustees or personal representatives have not had notice at the time of conveyance or distribution; but nothing in this section—

(*a*) prejudices the right of any person to follow the property, or any property representing the same, into the hands of any person, other than a purchaser, who may have received it; or

(*b*) frees the trustees or personal representatives from any obligation to make searches or obtain official certificates of search similar to those which an intending purchaser would be advised to make or obtain.

(3) This section applies notwithstanding anything to the contrary in the will or other instrument, if any, creating the trust.

———————

Law Reform Committee 23rd Report (The Powers and Duties of Trustees) 1982 Cmnd 8733, para. 5.1.

"Adverse Claims

5.1 We have considered the suggestion that trustees should be protected from liability from claims arising after a distribution if they have obtained counsel's opinion that a distribution should be made which has been sent to the beneficiaries. However, difficulties could arise where trustees have notice of a possible claim by creditors. The trustees could not safely distribute in such circumstances and they should be able to set some sort of time limit for positive action failing which distribution can proceed. We recommend that a provision be introduced to the effect that trustees should be empowered to write to any potential creditors, enclosing a copy of counsel's opinion, informing them that they should make their claim within three months of receiving the opinion and if no claim is made within that time they will proceed with the distribution. Then if no claim is made, they should be free to make the distribution proposed without incurring liability to the creditor concerned, but without prejudice to the latter's right to follow the trust assets."

C. Setting Aside a Fund to Meet Claims in Respect of Rents and Covenants

TRUSTEE ACT 1925

26. Protection against liability in respect of rents and covenants.—(1) Where a personal representative or trustee liable as such for—

(*a*) any rent, covenant, or agreement reserved by or contained in any lease; or

(*b*) any rent, covenant or agreement payable under or contained in any grant made in consideration of a rent charge; or

(*c*) any indemnity given in respect of any rent, covenant or agreement referred to in either of the foregoing paragraphs;

satisfies all liabilities under the lease or grant which may have accrued and been claimed,[8] up to the date of the conveyance hereinafter mentioned, and, where necessary, sets apart a sufficient fund to answer any future claim that may be made in respect of any fixed and ascertained sum which the lessee or grantee agreed to lay out on the property demised or granted, although the period for laying out the same may not have arrived, then and in any such case the personal representative or trustee may convey the property demised or granted to a purchaser, legatee, devisee, or other person entitled to call for a conveyance thereof and thereafter—

   (i) he may distribute the residuary real and personal estate of the deceased testator or intestate, or, as the case may be, the trust estate (other than the fund, if any, set apart as aforesaid) to or amongst the persons entitled thereto, without appropriating any part, or any further part, as the case may be, of the estate of the deceased or of the trust estate to meet any future liability under the said lease or grant;

   (ii) notwithstanding such distribution, he shall not be personally liable in respect of any subsequent claim under the said lease or grant.

(2) This section operates without prejudice to the right of the lessor or grantor, or the persons deriving title under the lessor or grantor, to follow the assets of the deceased or the trust property into the hands of the persons amongst whom the same may have been respectively distributed, and applies notwithstanding anything to the contrary in the will or other instrument, if any, creating the trust.

(3) In this section "lease" includes an underlease and an agreement for a lease or underlease and any instrument giving any such indemnity as aforesaid or varying the liabilities under the lease; "grant" applies to a grant whether the rent is created by limitation, grant, reservation, or otherwise, and includes an agreement for a grant and any instrument giving any such indemnity as aforesaid or varying the liabilities under the grant; "lessee" and "grantee" include persons respectively deriving title under them.

D. Benjamin Order

In **Re Benjamin** [1902] 1 Ch 723, Philip Benjamin was entitled, if he was living on June 25, 1893, the date of his father's death, to a share (about £30,000) in his father's estate. He had disappeared in September 1892, and searching enquiries failed to produce any news of him. JOYCE J said at 725:

"I think in this case that Philip David Benjamin must be presumed to be dead . . . The question is as to when he died. If he is to be presumed to be dead, I think the case of *Re Walker* (1871) 7 Ch App 120 distinctly applies, and the onus of proof is on his administrator. He has failed to adduce any evidence to shew that P.D. Benjamin survived the testator. I myself consider it highly probable that he died on September 1, 1892, or at all events shortly after. I am clearly of opinion that the onus is on those claiming under him to prove that he survived the testator. In my opinion, therefore, the trustees are at liberty to distribute. I am anxious, however, not to do anything which would prevent his representative from making any claim if evidence of his death at any other time

---

8 As amended by LP (A) A 1926, Sched.

should be subsequently forthcoming. I shall not, therefore, declare that he is dead, but I will make an order in the following form:—

In the absence of any evidence that the said P.D. Benjamin survived the testator, let the trustees of the testator's will be at liberty to divide the share of the testator's estate devised and bequeathed in favour of the said P.D. Benjamin, his wife and children, upon the footing that P.D. Benjamin was unmarried and did not survive the testator."[9]

E. Personal Indemnity

Lewin on Trusts (16th edn, 1964) p. 258

"Sometimes where there is only a shadow of a doubt as to the parties interested and the chance of an adverse claim being made is extremely remote, a trustee may be willing to distribute in reliance on an indemnity, but it should be realised that an indemnity (especially from an individual) is an unsatisfactory safeguard. For, when the danger arises, the person giving the indemnity may be insolvent or his assets may have been distributed. Sometimes an insurance company will issue an indemnity policy; in fixing the amount of the policy the impact of [inheritance tax] and of any rise in the value of investments which may have to be replaced should be borne in mind."

F. Payments by Personal Representatives to Infants

ADMINISTRATION OF ESTATES ACT 1925

42. Power to appoint trustees of infants' property.—(1) Where an infant is absolutely entitled under the will or on the intestacy of a person dying before or after the commencement of this Act (in this subsection called "the deceased") to a devise or legacy, or to the residue of the estate of the deceased, or any share therein, and such devise, legacy, residue or share is not under the will, if any, of the deceased, devised or bequeathed to trustees for the infant, the personal representatives of the deceased may appoint a trust corporation or two or more individuals not exceeding four (whether or not including the personal representatives or one or more of the personal representatives), to be the trustee or trustees of such devise, legacy, residue or share for the infant, and to be trustees of any land devised or any land being or forming part of such residue or share for the purposes of the Settled Land Act, 1925, and of the statutory provisions relating to the management of land during a minority, and may execute or do any assurance or thing requisite for vesting such devise, legacy, residue or share in the trustee or trustees so appointed.

On such appointment the personal representatives, as such, shall be discharged from all further liability in respect of such devise, legacy, residue, or share, and the same may be retained in its existing condition or state of investment, or may be converted into money, and such money may be invested in any authorised investment.

---

9 See RSC 1965 Ord. 85, r. 2 (2), p. 714, post; and Ord. 92, r. 5 (17); *Ministry of Health v Simpson* [1951] AC 251, [1950] 2 All ER 1137; *Re Lowe's Will Trusts* [1973] 1 WLR 882 at 887, [1973] 2 All ER 1136 at 1140; *Re Green's Will Trusts* [1985] 3 All ER 455; [1986] Conv 138 (P. Luxton).

G. Application to the Court

RULES OF THE SUPREME COURT 1965
ORDER 85

ADMINISTRATION AND SIMILAR ACTIONS

Interpretation
1. In this Order "administration action" means an action for the administration under the direction of the Court of the estate of a deceased person or for the execution under the direction of the Court of a trust.

Determination of questions, etc., without administration
2.—(1) An action may be brought for the determination of any question or for any relief which could be determined or granted, as the case may be, in an administration action and a claim need not be made in the action for the administration or execution under the direction of the Court of the estate or trust in connection with which the question arises or the relief is sought.

(2) Without prejudice to the generality of paragraph (1), an action may be brought for the determination of any of the following questions:—

(*a*) any question arising in the administration of the estate of a deceased person or in the execution of a trust;

(*b*) any question as to the composition of any class of persons having a claim against the estate of a deceased person or a beneficial interest in the estate of such a person or in any property subject to a trust;

(*c*) any question as to the rights or interests of a person claiming to be a creditor of the estate of a deceased person or to be entitled under a will or on the intestacy of a deceased person or to be beneficially entitled under a trust.

(3) Without prejudice to the generality of paragraph (1), an action may be brought for any of the following reliefs:—

(*a*) an order requiring an executor, administrator or trustee to furnish and, if necessary, verify accounts;

(*b*) an order requiring the payment into court of money held by a person in his capacity as executor, administrator or trustee;

(*c*) an order directing a person to do or abstain from doing a particular act in his capacity as executor, administrator or trustee;

(*d*) an order approving any sale, purchase, compromise or other transaction by a person in his capacity as executor, administrator or trustee;

(*e*) an order directing any act to be done in the administration of the estate of a deceased person or in the execution of a trust which the Court could order to be done if the estate or trust were being administered or executed, as the case may be, under the direction of the Court.

Parties
3.—(1) All the executors or administrators of the estate or trustees of the trust, as the case may be, to which an administration action or such an action as is referred to in rule 2 relates must be parties to the action, and where the action is brought by executors, administrators or trustees, any of them who does not consent to being joined as a plaintiff must be made a defendant.

(2) Notwithstanding anything in Order 15, rule 4 (2), and without prejudice to the powers of the Court under that Order, all the persons having a beneficial

interest in or claim against the estate or having a beneficial interest under the trust, as the case may be, to which such an action as is mentioned in paragraph (1) relates need not be parties to the action; but the plaintiff may make such of those persons, whether all or any one or more of them, parties as, having regard to the nature of the relief or remedy claimed in the action, he thinks fit.

(1966) 82 LQR 306 (R. E. M.)

"The facts in *Re Allen-Meyrick's Will Trusts* [1966] 1 WLR 499, [1966] 1 All ER 740 were simple and elegant. A testatrix gave her residue to trustees in trust to apply the income thereof 'in their absolute discretion for the maintenance of my ... husband', and subject to the exercise of this discretion, she gave the residue in trust for her two godchildren equally. The trustees had made certain payments for the benefit of the husband, who was bankrupt, but had been unable to agree whether any further income should be so applied. In these circumstances, the trustees sought to surrender their discretion to the court, and also sought to have it determined whether their discretion still existed in relation to past accumulations of income.

It is well settled that trustees confronted by a particular problem may surrender their discretion to the court, and so be relieved both of the agony of decision and the responsibility for the result.[10] But it is another matter where it is sought to surrender discretion which is not merely present and confined but prospective and indefinite. The Court of Chancery had a long history of administrative jurisdiction; but it exercised this jurisdiction not on its own investigations but on facts duly put before it in evidence by those concerned. It is not surprising, therefore, that Buckley J refused to accept the proffered general surrender of discretion. Whenever a specific problem arose upon specific facts, the aid of the court could be sought; but that was all. As regards past accumulations of income, the position was simple. The whole of the property, capital and income, belonged to the two godchildren except in so far as the trustees had effectually exercised their discretionary power to apply income to the husband. Trustees must, of course, be unanimous in exercising any powers vested in them, and so if within a reasonable time of receiving any income they had failed to exercise their discretion in favour of the husband, it ceased to be exercisable, and the godchildren became entitled to it.[11] The principles are old, the facts new, and the result satisfactory".

Law Reform Committee 23rd Report (The Powers and Duties of Trustees) 1982 Cmnd 8733, para. 9.1.V.36
"36. Where it appears that the cost of taking out a summons is out of all proportion to the amount at stake, trustees should be empowered to take the advice of counsel (in the case of trusts having adult beneficiaries only) or Queen's Counsel practising in the Chancery Division of the High Court or

10 *Marley v Mutual Security Merchant Bank and Trust Co Ltd* [1991] 3 All ER 198.
11 Cf. *Re Locker's Settlement Trusts* [1977] 1 WLR 1323, [1978] 1 All ER 216, where the trustees' discretion was not extinguished on the lapse of a reasonable time for distribution under an exhaustive discretionary trust.

conveyancing counsel of the court (where there are infant beneficiaries) and to distribute on the basis of that advice if no adult beneficiary starts proceedings within 3 months of being sent a copy of the relevant opinion. (paragraph 5.4)''[12]

H. Payment into Court

TRUSTEE ACT 1925

63. Payment into court by trustees.—(1) Trustees, or the majority of trustees, having in their hands or under their control money or securities belonging to a trust, may pay the same into court.[13]

(2) The receipt or certificate of the proper officer shall be a sufficient discharge to trustees for the money or securities so paid into court.

(3) Where money or securities are vested in any persons as trustees, and the majority are desirous of paying the same into court, but the concurrence of the other or others cannot be obtained, the court may order the payment into court to be made by the majority without the concurrence of the other or others.

(4) Where any such money or securities are deposited with any banker, broker, or other depositary, the court may order payment or delivery of the money or securities to the majority of the trustees for the purpose of payment into court.

(5) Every transfer payment and delivery made in pursuance of any such order shall be valid and take effect as if the same had been made on the authority or by the act of all the persons entitled to the money and securities so transferred, paid, or delivered.

(1968) 84 LQR 65 (A.J. Hawkins)

"Payment into court, no matter how unjustified, was always effective, to give the trustees a good discharge. As Kindersley V-C said in *Re Lloyd's Trust*,[14] 'The intention of the Trustee Act was for the present relief of trustees'. Relief might prove expensive, but it appears to have been effective to the extent that trustees were relieved of the burden of future administration. The sanction against unjustifiable payment into court was a disallowance of the costs incurred in paying in. Trustees were later condemned in the costs incurred in the payment out to the beneficiaries. In the early cases they were not entitled to costs of the payment in if their actions had been vexatious.[15] Later, they had to justify their actions by showing doubt as to the identity of the beneficiaries,

---

12 Cf. a similar use of counsel's advice recommended to deal with possible adverse claims by creditors, p. 711, ante. See AJA 1985, s. 48 (power of High Court to authorise action to be taken in reliance on counsel's opinion where any question has arisen out of the terms of a will or a trust).

13 As amended by AJA 1965, s. 36 (4) and Sch. 3.

14 (1854) 2 WR 371.

15 *Re Lane's Trust* (1854) 3 WR 134.

the extent of their interest or their inability to give receipts.[16] 'The legislature did not intend that where the trust was clear, a trustee should pay the fund into court. A trustee cannot pay money into court merely to get rid of a trust he has undertaken to perform, and the Act would lead to greater oppression if it were otherwise.[17] Furthermore the trustees' doubts should be bona fide. This appears to have meant such doubts as would assail and disturb a practical lawyer, rather than ruffle the academic conscience of eminent conveyancers.[18] What is the effect of payment in? Clearly, payment into court does operate as a discharge of trustees. In other words, by paying in the trustees retire from the trust.[19] They will, of course, still be liable for any breaches of trust in the past[20] and responsible for any money that should come into their hands in the future.[1] Apparently, they also remain trustees for the purposes of receiving notices relating to dealings with the trust funds.[2] Subject to these two matters, however, new trustees can be appointed, either by the persons nominated as appointors in the trust instrument,[3] or by the Court.'[4]

IV.   Duty to Act Impartially Between Life Tenant and Remainderman[5]

It is the duty of a trustee to act in the interests of all the beneficiaries. Where there are beneficiaries whose interests conflict, as in the case of life tenant and remainderman, the trustee, acting in the general interests of all, must act impartially between them.[6]

Nowhere is this duty of greater significance than in the selection of investments. Even within the range of authorised investments, there are available fixed interest gilt-edged stocks giving a return of about 6 per cent., which will delight the life tenant; and a choice of "growth stocks" returning a mere 1 per cent., but with a prospect of substantial future capital growth, will be attractive to the remainderman. If we move outside the range of investments authorised by the general law, an even greater contrast can be seen. A copyright or an oil well may produce a handsome income, but for a limited time; while National Savings Certificates produce a capital increase

---

16 *Re Knight's Trusts* (1859) 27 Beav 45.
17 *Re Knight's Trusts* supra, at 49, per ROMILLY MR.
18 In *Re Knight's Trusts* supra, the fact that trustees acted on counsel's opinion was regretted but made no difference to their liability. In *Re Cull's Trusts* (1875) LR 20 Eq 561 the particular trustees were protected having taken counsel's opinion, but JESSEL MR added "the next set of trustees who come before me having so acted must pay costs".
19 *Re Williams' Settlement* (1858) 4 K & J 87.
20 *Barker v Peile* (1865) 2 Drew & Sm 340.
1 *Re Nettlefold's Trusts* (1888) 59 LT 315.
2 *Thompson v Tomkins* (1862) 2 Drew & Sm 8, and see also *Warburton v Hill* (1854) Kay 470.
3 *Re Bailey's Trust* (1854) 3 WR 31.
4 13 & 14 Vict. c. 60, ss. 32 and 33, replaced with significant changes by ss. 25 and 37 of the Trustee Act 1893. See now ss. 41 and 43 of the Trustee Act 1925.
5 H & M, pp. 526–539; K & S, pp. 258–316; P & M, pp. 461–481; Pettit, pp. 360–373; Riddall, pp. 283–295; Snell, pp. 226–231; Underhill, pp. 500–534. See also Lewin, p. 86.
6 On the general duty to act impartially, see *Lloyds Bank plc v Duker* [1987] 1 WLR 1324, [1987] 3 All ER 193; *Nestlé v National Westminster Bank plc* 29 June 1988 (unreported: HOFFMANN J), p. 719 post.

only and no income, and a new and developing business is likely to do the same.

A. General Duty

In the Court of Appeal in **Nestlé v National Westminster Bank plc** [1993] 1 WLR 1260, [1994] 1 All ER 118, p. 676 ante.

STAUGHTON LJ said at 1279, at 136:
"The obligation of a trustee is to administer the trust fund impartially, or fairly (I can see no significant difference), having regard to the different interests of beneficiaries. Wilberforce J said in *Re Pauling's Settlement Trusts (No 2)* [1963] Ch 576, 586, [1963] 1 All ER 857, 862:
    'The new trustees would be under the normal duty of preserving an equitable balance, and if at any time it was shown they were inclining one way or the other, it would not be a difficult matter to bring them to account.'
At times it will not be easy to decide what is an equitable balance. A life tenant may be anxious to receive the highest possible income, whilst the remainderman will wish the real value of the trust fund to be preserved. If the life tenant is living in penury and the remainderman already has ample wealth, common sense suggests that a trustee should be able to take that into account, not necessarily by seeking the highest possible income at the expense of capital but by inclining in that direction. However, before adopting that course a trustee should, I think, require some verification of the facts. In this case the trustees did not, so far as I am aware, have any reliable information as to the relative wealth of the life tenants and the plaintiff. They did send an official to interview Mr John Nestle in Cyprus on one occasion; but the information which they obtained was conflicting and (as it turned out) incomplete.
Similarly I would not regard it as a breach of trust for the trustees to pay some regard to the relationship between Mr George Nestle and the plaintiff. He was merely her uncle, and she would have received nothing from his share of the fund if he had fathered a child who survived him. The trustees would be entitled, in my view, to incline towards income during his life tenancy and that of his widow, on that ground. Again common sense suggests to me that such a course might be appropriate, and I do not think that it would be a breach of the duty to act fairly, or impartially.
The dominant consideration for the trustees, however, was that George's fund from 1960, and John's from 1969, would not be subject to United Kingdom income tax in so far as it was invested in exempt gilts. That was a factor which the trustees were entitled—and I would say bound—to take into account. A beneficiary who has been left a life interest in a trust fund has an arguable case for saying that he should not be compelled to bear tax on the income if he is not lawfully obliged to do so.
It was no more than a factor for the trustees to bear in mind, and would rarely justify more than a modest degree of preference for income paid gross over capital growth.
A trustee should also bear in mind, as the trustees did, that estate duty or capital transfer tax is likely to be reduced in such a case if part of the fund is invested in tax-exempt gilts. That may provide a compensating benefit for the remainderman. Of course it is by no means certain that the benefit will materialise; the life tenant may return to this country, as happened in the case

of Mrs Elsie Nestle. It has been said that nothing in this world is certain except death and taxes. But even the tax benefit was imponderable, since it could not be forecast what rate of tax would be applicable on the death of a life tenant.''

At first instance in **Nestlé v National Westminster Bank plc** (29 June 1988, unreported), HOFFMANN J said:

"There was no dispute over the general principles to be applied. First, there is the prudence principle. The classic statement is that of LINDLEY LJ (*Re Whiteley* (1886) 33 Ch D 347 at 355):

'The duty of a trustee is not to take such care only as a prudent man would take if he had only himself to consider, the duty rather is to take such care as the ordinary prudent man would take if he were minded to make an investment for the benefit of other people for whom he felt morally bound to provide.'

This is an extremely flexible standard capable of adaptation to current economic conditions and contemporary understanding of markets and investments, for example, investments which were imprudent in the days of the gold standard may be sound and sensible in times of high inflation. Modern trustees acting within their investment powers are entitled to be judged by the standards of current portfolio theory, which emphasises the risk level of the entire portfolio rather than the risk attaching to each investment taken in isolation. (This is not to say that losses on investments made in breach of trust can be set off against gains in the rest of the portfolio but only that an investment which in isolation is too risky and therefore in breach of trust may be justified when held in conjunction with other investments. See Jeffrey N Gordon, The Puzzling Persistence of the Constrained Prudent Man Rule (j1987) 62 NY Univ LR 52). But in reviewing the conduct of trustees over a period of more than 60 years, one must be careful not to endow the prudent trustee with prophetic vision or expect him to have ignored the received wisdom of his time.

Mr Gerard Wright, who appeared for Miss Nestlé, referred me to another passage in *Re Whiteley* at p 350 in which COTTON LJ said:

'Trustees are bound to preserve the money for those entitled to the corpus in remainder, and they are bound to invest it in such a way as will produce a reasonable income for those enjoying the income for the present.'

In 1886 what COTTON LJ had in mind was the safety of the capital in purely monetary terms. But Mr Wright submitted that in the conditions which prevail a century later, the trustees were under an overriding duty to preserve the real value of the capital. In my judgment this cannot be right. The preservation of the monetary value of the capital requires no skill or luck. The trustees can discharge their duties, as they often did until 1961, by investing the whole fund in gilt-edged securities. Preservation of real values can be no more than an aspiration which some trustees may have the good fortune to achieve. Plainly they must have regard to the interests of those entitled in the future to capital and such regard will require them to take into consideration the potential effects of inflation, but a rule that real capital values must be maintained would be unfair to both income beneficiaries and trustees.

This brings me to the second principle on which there was general agreement, namely that the trustee must act fairly in making investment decisions which may have different consequences for different classes of beneficiaries. There are two reasons why I prefer this formulation to the traditional image of holding the scales equally between tenant for life and remainderman. The first is that the image of the scales suggests a weighing of known quantities whereas investment decisions are concerned with predictions of the future. Investments will carry current expectations of their future income yield and capital appreciation and these expectations will be reflected in their current market price, but there is always a greater or lesser risk that the outcome will deviate from those expectations. A judgment on the fairness of the choices made by the trustees must have regard to these imponderables. The second reason is that the image of the scales suggests a more mechanistic process than I believe the law requires. The trustees have in my judgment a wide discretion. They are for example entitled to take into account the income needs of the tenant for life or the fact that the tenant for life was a person known to the settlor or a stranger. Of course these cannot be allowed to become the overriding considerations but the concept of fairness between classes of beneficiaries does not require them to be excluded. It would be an inhuman law which required trustees to adhere to some mechanical rule for preserving the real value of the capital when the tenant for life was the testator's widow who had fallen upon hard times and the remainderman was young and well off.''

[His Lordship then rejected "the theory of index ipse loquitur''].

(1943) 7 Conv (NS) 128 (S.J. Bailey)

"In ordinary circumstances, when property has been settled upon trust for A for life, and thereafter for B absolutely, the whole of the net income derived from the property until A dies is payable to him. Such is his right, neither more nor less. Though this income be abnormally high, nothing of it is held back for the benefit of B. Though it be abnormally low or non-existent, neither A nor his executors after him has any right to claim a compensation out of the capital value of the property or out of any enhanced income it may yield after he dies. So long as the trust comprises property which produces an abnormally low or high income, any incidental hardship to A or B must be borne. But if the trustees have the power to dispose of that particular property and reinvest in something which will produce a more fair and steady income, this inequitable state of affairs will cease if and when they choose to do so.[7] It is perhaps surprising that equity has not cast upon trustees, in every such case, a duty to convert the trust property as soon as practicable into something more likely to produce an equitable result. One might have expected further, perhaps, that in every such case equity would require the trustees to make some financial adjustment, as between the beneficiaries, to cover the intervening period during which the desired conversion is delayed. In fact, however, equity does

---

7 The so-called equitable duty of trustees "to hold the scales evenly between the beneficiaries'' does not ordinarily appear to compel them to realise and reinvest in such a case: see *Re Courtier* (1886) 34 ChD 136; *Re Searle* [1900] 2 Ch 829 at 834 ("if the estate produces nothing, the tenant for life can get nothing''), per KEKEWICH J. On the other hand, when trustees do exercise a power to invest they must not allow themselves to be persuaded into an investment prejudicial to one beneficiary, in order to benefit another of their beneficiaries; *Raby v Ridehalgh* (1855) 7 De GM & G 104.

not ordinarily intervene in these cases; but to this there are three celebrated exceptions. The three exceptions have much in common: they apply only where the trust is created by will, and only in so far as the property comprised in the trust is the residuary personal estate of the testator; and they are said to rest upon his presumed intention to deal evenly with the beneficiaries under the trust. This is no doubt the reason why they are often grouped together, and described as the rule in *Howe v Lord Dartmouth*.[8] In origin, however, they are three distinct rules: (i) the rule in *Gibson v Bott*,[9] (ii) the rule in *Howe v Lord Dartmouth*; and (iii) the rule in *Re Chesterfield's Trusts*.[10] Of these, rules (i) and (ii) operate chiefly to prevent a life tenant from obtaining an unjust advantage to the detriment of the remainderman,[11] whilst rule (iii) operates in the reverse direction in order to prevent an injustice to the tenant for life.''

B. The Rule in *Howe v Lord Dartmouth*[12]

i. DUTY TO CONVERT

A duty to convert may be imposed by statute;[13] or by the trust instrument, or by the Rule in *Howe v Lord Dartmouth*.

Lewin on Trusts (16th edn, 1964) p. 228

"The first branch of the Rule in *Howe v Lord Dartmouth* may be stated in outline as follows:

If a testator gives his residuary personal estate in trust for, or directly to, persons in succession without imposing a trust for sale and it comprises wasting assets or unauthorised investments then, unless the tenant for life can show that the testator meant him to enjoy the income of those assets or investments in specie, they must be sold and the proceeds invested in authorised securities.''

ii. DUTY OF APPORTIONMENT PENDING CONVERSION

Lewin on Trusts (16th edn, 1964), pp. 235–238

"The rule in *Howe v Lord Dartmouth* has a second branch which applies in the absence of a contrary intention where for any reason (be it a trust for sale

---

8 (1802) 7 Ves 137. See, e.g., *Macdonald v Irvine* (1878) 8 ChD 101 at 112, per BAGGALLAY LJ.

9 (1802) 7 Ves 89.

10 (1883) 24 ChD 643. Note that the judgment of SIMONDS J in *Re Woodhouse* [1941] Ch 332, [1941] 2 All ER 265, which finally decided that this rule has no application to trusts of real estate, was based in part on the fact that the other two rules do not apply to real estate. And the learned Judge, throughout his judgment, treated the three rules as distinct from one another. "This is an equitable rule established by this Court in order to deal fairly in the administration of estates between persons having successive interests in a residuary estate. It is a rule of administration which, in my judgment, is to be regarded as complementary to other rules of administration established also to do justice as between persons entitled to successive interests, as, for example, the rule in *Howe v Earl of Dartmouth*": *Re Woodhouse* [1941] Ch 332 at 334–335, [1941] 2 All ER 265 at 267.

11 It has recently been made clear, in *Re Fawcett* [1940] Ch 402, that these two rules may also operate to prevent injustice to the life tenant.

12 (1802) 7 Ves 137. See (1943) 7 Conv (NS) 128, 191 (S.J. Bailey); (1952) 16 Conv (NS) 349 (L.A. Sheridan); (1981) 59 CBR 687 (J. Smith).

13 AEA 1925, s. 33.

expressed in the trust instrument or imposed by statute or implied by the first branch of the Rule) pure personal property which is held on trust for persons in succession ought to have been sold. When the second branch of the Rule applies then, as between tenant for life and remainderman, the settled property must be treated as if it had been sold and the proceeds reinvested in the proper investments; the life tenant is entitled to the fair equivalent of the income he would have received if that had been done, but no more. . . .

Calculation of the 'fair equivalent'
Where the second branch of the Rule applies the tenant for life is entitled before conversion to the fair equivalent of the income he would have enjoyed if conversion had taken place, that is, he is given interest on the value of the unconverted property.

In the days when the court always directed investment in consols the rate of interest was that which consols would have yielded,[14] but when the range of authorised investments was extended[15] the rate of interest allowed was standardised at 4 per cent.[16], later reduced to 3 per cent.,[17] but then increased again to 4 per cent.,[18] at which rate it is generally assumed now to stand.[19] There seems to be no reported case in which the rate was reduced on account of the fall in interest rates generally after 1945 and if the 4 per cent. rate were to be changed it would be necessary to show that the yield of authorised investments when the trust was established was generally above or below 4 per cent.[20]

The interest is to be calculated on the value of the assets on the first anniversary of the testator's death[1] unless they are sold within that year, when the interest is calculated on the amount they fetched,[2] or unless there is a power to postpone sale, when for want of any better date the assets are to be valued at the date of death.[3]

Whenever the interest is calculated it runs from the testator's death to the date on which the asset is sold."[4]

In **Re Fawcett**[5] [1940] Ch 402, a testatrix bequeathed her residuary estate, which contained unauthorized investments, upon trust to pay the income to her nieces and nephews in equal shares for their lives, and after their death to divide the capital money among their children on attaining the age of 21. In

14 *Howe v Earl of Dartmouth* (1802) Ves 137.
15 See *Re Fawcett* [1940] Ch 402 at 407, per FARWELL J.
16 *Meyer v Simonsen* (1852) 5 De G & Sm 723.
17 *Re Owen* [1912] 1 Ch 519.
18 *Re Beech* [1920] 1 Ch 40.
19 *Re Fawcett* [1940] Ch 402; *Re Parry* [1947] Ch 23, [1946] 2 All ER 412.
20 *Re Parry* [1947] Ch 23, especially at 46–47, [1946] 2 All ER 412 at 423, per ROMER J.
 1 *Re Fawcett* [1940] Ch 402, especially at 407 and 409, para. (a).
 2 *Re Fawcett* [1940] Ch 402, especially at 409, para. (b).
 3 *Re Parry* [1947] Ch 23, [1946] 2 All ER 412, and cases there cited.
 4 *Re Fawcett* [1940] Ch 402; *Re Parry* [1947] Ch 23, [1946] 2 All ER 412. The rate of 4 per cent. is now so far out of line with the current return from gilt-edged investments that it is difficult to see how it could still be supported. Trustees may be well advised to take instructions from the court. Cf. *Wallersteiner v Moir (No 2)* [1975] QB 373, [1975] 1 All ER 849, p. 872, post; *Bartlett v Barclays Bank Trust Co Ltd (No 2)* [1980] Ch 515, [1980] 2 All ER 92, p. 874, post, and see generally *Tehno-Impex v Gebr Van Weelde Scheepvaartkantoor BV* [1981] QB 648 at 665–666, [1981] 2 All ER 669 at 677–678, per Lord DENNING MR.
 5 For details of calculation and accounting, see Josling, *Apportionments for Executors and Trustees* (4th edn, 1976) pp. 34–39.

holding that the rule in *Howe v Lord Dartmouth* applied, FARWELL J made an order as follows:

"In answer to question 2 of the summons I will make a declaration that (*a*) in the case of unauthorized investments which were still retained unsold at the end of one year from the death of the testatrix the life tenants were and are entitled to interest at the rate of 4 per cent. per annum on the value of such investments taken at the end of such year but commencing from the date of the death and running on until the realization of such investments respectively; (*b*) in the case of unauthorized investments realised during the first year after the death of the testatrix the life tenants are entitled to interest at the rate aforesaid on the net proceeds of such realization respectively from the date of the death down to the respective dates of completions of such realizations; (*c*) the unauthorized investments for the time being unsold ought to be taken en bloc as one aggregate for the purposes of the rule in *Howe v Lord Dartmouth* (1802) 7 Ves 137; (*d*) in applying that rule the Apportionment Act, 1870, ought not to be applied in the income accounts at the death of the testatrix or at the beginning or end of any accounting period with reference to the income of unauthorized investments; (*e*) any excess of income from unauthorized investments beyond the interest payable in respect of such investments to the life tenants ought to be invested in authorized investments as part of the capital with the other authorized investments, and accordingly the whole of the actual subsequent income of such invested excess income is payable as income; (*f*) the interest so payable in respect of unauthorized investments was and is payable out of moneys being income from unauthorized investments or, so far as such income is insufficient, being proceeds of realization of such investments, and any interest so payable for the time being in arrears is payable (but calculated as simple interest only) out of subsequent income from unauthorized investments which are for the time being retained and out of the proceeds of sale of such investments as and when realized, but neither any excess income from unauthorized investments, which at the end of any accounting period is available under head (*e*) for investment in authorized investments, nor any proceeds of realization of unauthorized investments not required at the date of realization to pay interest payable as aforesaid for the time being in arrears and accordingly available to be invested in authorized investments, were or are applicable towards payment of subsequently accruing interest as aforesaid in respect of unauthorized investments then still retained."

iii. EXCLUSION

The duty to convert or to apportion may be excluded by appropriate language in the will. The exclusion of the duty to convert necessarily excludes the duty to apportion. But the testator may desire the property to be converted, but may allow the life tenant the whole income pending conversion. There has been much litigation to determine these questions.[6] It is usual now to provide expressly for the exclusion of both duties.

Key & Elphinstone, *Precedents in Conveyancing* (15th edn, 1953), vol. 2, p. 926

---

6 H & M, pp. 531–532; Petit, pp. 408–409; Underhill, pp. 520–522.

"CONVERSION AND INVESTMENT

1. UPON trust that my trustees shall sell, call in, collect and convert into money the said real and personal property at such time or times, and in such manner as they shall think fit (but as to reversionary property not until it falls into possession, unless it shall appear to my trustees that an earlier sale would be beneficial), with power to postpone the sale, calling in or conversion of the whole or any part or parts of the said property [including leaseholds or other property of a terminable hazardous or wasting nature] during such period as they shall think proper, and to retain the same or any part thereof in its actual form of investment, without being responsible for loss. And I direct that the income of such of the same premises as for the time being shall remain unsold shall as well during the first year after my death as afterwards be applied as if the same were income arising from investments hereinafter directed to be made of the proceeds of sale thereof, and that no reversionary or other property not actually producing income shall be treated as producing income for the purposes of this my will."[7]

iv. THE RULE TODAY

Hanbury & Martin: *Modern Equity* (14th edn, 1993), p. 534

"The rules relating to conversion and apportionment demonstrate basic principles of equity.[8] But they should be understood in their proper perspective.

(a) *Exclusion of Duty to Apportion.* The duty to apportion is in practice nearly always excluded, both in respect of income from unauthorised securities and in respect of reversionary interests. The duty to convert, where it exists, thus appears in the context of a duty to change the investments.

(b) *Trustee Investments Act* 1961. Authorised securities now mean those investments which are authorised by the Trustee Investments Act 1961. It should be noted that wider-range securities and narrower-range requiring advice are only authorised when advice to retain them has been received. Presumably, therefore, 'If the trustees follow advice to sell and reinvest such property it would seem the rule [in *Howe v Earl of Dartmouth*] applies until such sale.'[9]

(c) *Paradoxical Effect of Current Investment Situation.* In the investment context of the present day, the rules of conversion and apportionment are in some way misplaced. The problem still exists of speculative and wasting securities. But the rule requires unauthorised investments, in the form of equities (other than those authorised by the Trustee Investments Act 1961) to be sold in order to protect the capital for the benefit of the remainderman; and it deprives the life tenant of the high income which is supposedly earned by them. 'At a time when investment in equities may be the only way in which the capital value of the fund can in fact be maintained the traditional theory that re-investment is necessary to protect those interested in the capital no longer holds good. Conversely, the yield on fixed interest investments is now such as to provide the tenant for life with an income which is as high and may be higher than the

---

7 Footnotes omitted.
8 (1952) 16 Conv (NS) 349 (L.A. Sheridan).
9 Hayton & Marshall, *Cases and Commentary on the Law of Trusts* (9th edn) p. 669.

average yield on authorised equities'.[10] The positions are therefore reversed. The life tenant now wants fixed interest investments in order to provide a high income; the remainderman wants unauthorised securities for the preservation of the real value of the capital. It is the life tenant who will be pressing the trustees to convert urgently into gilt-edged securities; for they bring an income three or four times the mere 4 per cent. allowed to the life tenant by the rule of apportionment."

C. Reversionary Interests

The problem discussed related to wasting and hazardous securities which may be expected to produce too high an income for the life tenant, and to leave unprotected the remainderman's interest in the capital. The converse problem is that of a reversionary interest; that is to say one which is not yet an interest in possession.

Assume that a fund of £500,000 is held on trust for A for life, remainder to B absolutely. A is entitled to the income, and B, on A's death, to the capital. B dies before A, leaving his estate to Mrs. B for life with remainder to his children. The capital of B's testamentary trust is a valuable reversionary interest, its value depending, of course, on A's age and state of health, and also upon the total value of other transfers of capital made by A inter vivos or upon his death.

However that may be, the corpus of the testamentary trust is a valuable reversionary interest which is producing no income. It could of course be sold, and the proceeds of sale invested. But it is obvious, because of all the uncertainties involved, that it is difficult for the trustees to obtain a satisfactory price; usually it is uneconomical to sell a reversionary interest. If Mrs. B needs the income, something will have to be done, whether by selling, or by borrowing against the security of the fund, or by some other method.

Unless the reversionary interest is immediately sold and the proceeds re-invested the problem arises of apportioning the value of the reversionary interest. The solution is to take the value of the reversionary interest when it falls in (or when it is sold), and then calculate backwards to see what sum, if available at B's death, and if used to pay a reasonable income to Mrs. B until the date when the reversionary interest actually becomes available, would have produced the capital sum now available. That sum is notionally the capital of the fund. The children are entitled to that. Mrs. B, who has had no income in the meantime, is entitled to the balance.

In **Re Earl of Chesterfield's Trusts** (1883) 24 ChD 643, CHITTY J ordered the apportionment of a reversionary interest between life tenant and remainderman as follows:

"Upon the petition &c, this Court is of opinion that the [reversionary] moneys are apportionable between principal and income by ascertaining the respective sums which, put out at 4 per cent. per annum on the [date of death of the testator] and accumulating at compound interest calculated at that rate with yearly rests, and deducting income tax, would, with the accumulations of interest, have produced, at the respective dates of receipt, the amounts actually

10 Law Reform Committee, 23rd Report, para. 3.31.

received; and that the aggregate of the sums so ascertained ought to be treated as principal and be applied accordingly, and the residue should be treated as income.''

The calculations are not as difficult as is sometimes supposed.

J.F. Josling: *Apportionments for Executors and Trustees* (4th edn, 1976),[11] p. 39.

''[A reversionary interest under the will of a testator dying on 1st January 1976] is allowed to remain for some time unrealised, and on realisation (or falling in) the sum of £15,000 is obtained. This sum is to be regarded as capital and income on that capital for the period of retention.

This item was realised on 2nd April, 1978, and the sum obtained therefore represents $2\frac{1}{4}$ years of £x accruing at 4 per cent. compound interest, less tax at 35 per cent.[12]

Invested on 2nd April, 1977, £100 at 4 per cent., less tax, would become £102.60. In order to discover the sum which would become £15,000 the formula is therefore:—

$$\frac{100}{102.6} \times £15,000$$

This process is repeated for the previous year

$$\frac{100}{102.6} \times \frac{100}{102.6} \times £15,000$$

and in respect of the quarter from the date of death to 2nd April, 1976, the fraction is

$$\frac{100}{100.65}$$

The amount attributable to capital in respect of this interest is thus

$$\frac{100}{100.65} \times \frac{100}{102.6} \times \frac{100}{102.6} \times £15,000 = £14,157.37$$

and the balance amounting to £842.63 is apportionable to income.

These respective amounts should be credited to the capital account and to the income account under a heading to indicate the apportionment under this rule.''

D. The Rule in *Allhusen v Whittell*[13]

Where the testator leaves debts which are not paid immediately out of his estate, the tenant for life receives interest on capital in fact required for the payment of those debts. In a calculation often involving minute amounts of money, that part of his income so required has to be deducted. The rule may

---

11 See Chandler's *Trust Accounts* (6th edn, 1936) pp. 117–118; Bailey, *Law of Wills* (7th edn, 1973) pp. 131–134; P & M, pp. 466–468; Rowland's *Trust Accounts* (3rd edn, 1964).
12 For current rates of income tax, see p. 552 ante.
13 (1867) LR 4 Eq 295.

be excluded by contrary intention, or when its application would in the circumstances be inappropriate.[14]

In **Corbett v Inland Revenue Commissioners** [1938] 1 KB 567, [1937] 4 All ER 700, ROMER LJ said at 584, at 709:

"For the purpose of adjusting rights as between the tenant for life and the remainderman of a residuary estate, debts, legacies, estate duties, probate duties and so forth are to be deemed to have been paid out of such capital of the testator's estate as will be sufficient for that purpose, when to that capital is added interest on that capital from the date of the testator's death to the date of the payment of the legacy or debt, or whatever it may have been, interest being calculated at the average rate of interest[15] earned by the testator's estate during the relevant period."[16]

E. Leaseholds

The rule in *Howe v Lord Dartmouth* applied to leaseholds before 1926. Since 1925, however, leaseholds with sixty years or more unexpired are authorised trustee investments for settled land and for trustees of land held upon trust for sale.

It seems also that Law of Property Act 1925, s. 28 (2) excludes a duty to apportion the income of leaseholds. There may still be a duty to convert. In the absence of a duty to apportion, however, the duty to convert is of no significance in this context. As Pettit says at 413: "The practical importance lies chiefly in whether the leasehold will be settled land . . . or land held on trust for sale."

In **Re Trollope's Will Trusts** [1927] 1 Ch 596, TOMLIN J held that the rule in *Howe v Lord Dartmouth* applied after 1925 to unauthorised investments of residuary personalty which were retained under a power to postpone conversion. In discussing the application of the rule to leaseholds, he said at 601:

"The question is whether under the recent property statutes a change has been effected by the law in this respect. The material statutes are the Law of Property Act 1925, and the Administration of Estates Act 1925. The Law of Property Act 1925, s. 28, sub-s. 2, contains a provision relating to trustees for sale of land in these terms: 'Subject to any direction to the contrary in the disposition on trust for sale or in the settlement of the proceeds of sale, the net

---

14 *Re McEuen* [1913] 2 Ch 704; *Re Darby* [1939] Ch 905, [1939] 3 All ER 6.
15 *Re Wills* [1915] 1 Ch 769; *Re Oldham* (1927) 71 SJ 491.
16 Assuming a debt of £50, an average rate of income of 10 per cent., income tax at 25 per cent., and payment of the debt one year from the death, the apportionment will be:

$$\text{From Capital: 46.51 (being } \frac{100}{107.5} \times 50)$$

$$\text{From Income: 3.49 (being } \frac{7.5}{107.5} \times 50)$$

See H & M, p. 537 n. 79

rents and profits of the land until sale, after keeping down costs of repairs and insurance and other outgoings shall be paid or applied, except so far as any part thereof may be liable to be set aside as capital money under the Settled Land Act 1925, in like manner as the income of investments representing the purchase money would be payable or applicable if the sale had been made and proceeds had been duly invested.'[17]

The effect of that sub-section is that in regard to the property which is the subject-matter of the section, the rule in *Howe v Lord Dartmouth* no longer applies, because, subject to provision being made for outgoings, the income is to be applied as if it were income of proper investments of the proceeds of sale. Lawrence J in *Re Brooker* [1926] WN 93 in fact held with regard to leaseholds which are included in the definition of 'land' in the Law of Property Act 1925, s. 205, sub-s. 1 (ix), that 'the principle laid down in *Howe v Lord Dartmouth* hitherto applied by Courts of equity during the period of the postponement of the sale of leaseholds held on trust for sale, was no longer applicable to a case like the present.'

Therefore, so far as leaseholds held in trust for sale are concerned, the rule of *Howe v Lord Dartmouth* is gone.''

In **Re Brooker** [1926] WN 93, the testator's estate, which included leasehold properties, was held upon an express trust for sale and conversion, with power to postpone. Each of his three daughters was tenant for life of one-fifth share of the estate. Since the testator's death in 1903, the trustees had paid to the three daughters interest at the rate of $3\frac{1}{2}$ per cent. per annum on the probate value of the leasehold properties.

One question which arose in the administration of the estate was whether each daughter was entitled, as from January 1, 1926 to one-fifth of the net rents and profits of the leaseholds. LAWRENCE J held that they were.

F. Law Reform

Law Reform Committee 23rd Report (The Powers and Duties of Trustees) 1982 Cmnd 8733, paras. 3.31, 36, 37.

"3.31 Our experience, confirmed by the evidence we received, is that in practice the rules of apportionment [in *Howe v Earl of Dartmouth*, *Re Earl of Chesterfield's Trusts*, and *Allhusen v Whittell*] are in well drawn settlements almost always excluded. It is quite clear that in present day investment conditions the rules both of conversion and apportionment pending conversion have little if any relevance. When they do apply they require, in effect, the sale of equities, other than those authorised by the Trustee Investments Act 1961, and reinvestment in gilt-edged securities. At a time when investment in equities may be the only way in which the capital value of the fund can in fact be maintained the traditional theory that reinvestment is necessary to protect those interested in the capital no longer holds good. Conversely, the yield on fixed interest investments is now such as to provide the tenant for life with an income which is as high and may be higher than the average yield on unauthorised equities. The second reason why the equitable rules are frequently excluded in practice is that the calculations they require are so

17 See p. 739, post.

complex that the costs and administrative difficulties involved are quite out of proportion to any advantage that they might, in very exceptional cases, confer. Nearly all our witnesses took particular exception to the rule in *Allhusen v Whittell,* which was described as complex, fiddlesome and resulting in a disproportionate amount of work and expense. It was suggested that where not excluded it was often simply ignored.

3.36 After careful consideration, we agree that the best solution would be for the rules both as to conversion and apportionment in *Howe v Earl of Dartmouth, Re Chesterfield* and *Allhusen v Whittell* to be subsumed in a new statutory duty to hold a fair balance between the beneficiaries, in particular those entitled to capital and those entitled to income. Coupled with such a general duty should be an express power for such purposes to convert income into capital and vice-versa. In compliance with such a general duty to act impartially and to protect the various interests in the trust, the trustees could, if they thought fit, continue to convert investments and to apportion pending conversion. But in deciding whether or not this was necessary, trustees would be able to have regard to the whole investment policy of the trust. Where they decided that apportionment was desirable or where it was required by virtue of an express duty to convert, the existing rules would not have to be rigidly applied although, where their application was the best way of achieving justice between the beneficiaries, they would continue to be used. To provide for conversion and apportionment in this way within the context of a statutory duty to hold an even hand would, we think, make it clear to trustees that they must consider whether or not apportionment is necessary whilst at the same time allowing them a sufficient degree of flexibility.

3.37 Clearly it should be open to the beneficiaries to ensure that this general duty is fulfilled and we therefore recommend that any beneficiary should be entitled to apply to the court for an order directing the trustees either to make or to adjust an apportionment. The onus would, however, be upon the beneficiary seeking such an order to show that the trustees' exercise of their discretion had substantially prejudiced his interests. This would mean, for example, that trustees would not be bound to apportion in accordance with the existing equitable rules if satisfied that a fair result could be achieved in some other way. But on the application of a beneficiary, the court would be empowered to order the application of the existing rules if it were shown that this would make a substantial difference to the result. What is 'substantial' would clearly depend upon the size of the trust. On such an application, the court would have to examine the overall administration of the trust fund and, bearing in mind the vast choice of investments available to trustees, in practice it would be exceptional for it to conclude that they had not held an even balance. The practical importance of the existing apportionment rules would be diminished although, in as much as they are an attempt by equity to do exact mathematical justice, they might continue to be applied in exceptional cases. Should the court order an adjustment of the division between the beneficiaries, trustees should not, we think, be open to an action for breach of trust, provided that they acted in good faith throughout.''

QUESTIONS

1.   Consider the various contexts (in addition to those here discussed) in which it is necessary to make a distinction between income and capital. For example:

a) For the payment of income tax in respect of dividends earned partly before and partly after the death of the life tenant. Apportionment Act 1870, s. 2; Josling: *Apportionments for Executors and Trustees* (4th edn, 1976), pp. 4–10.

b) For the treatment of distributions by companies as capital distributions or as dividends: *Bouch v Sproule* (1887) 12 App Cas 385; (1975) 39 Conv (NS) 355 (W.H. Goodhart); *Re Sechiari* [1950] 1 All ER 417; *Re Kleinwort's Settlements* [1951] Ch 860, [1951] 2 All ER 328; *Re Rudd's Will Trusts* [1952] 1 All ER 254; (1953) 17 Conv (NS) 22 (A.J. Bland); *Re Malam* [1894] 3 Ch 578; *Re Lee* [1993] 3 All ER 926; [1993] All ER Rev 417 (C.H. Sherrin).

c) For the allocation to income or capital dividends when sold and purchased by trustees cum dividend: *Scholefield v Redfern* (1863) 2 Drew & Sm 173; *Freman v Whitbread* (1865) LR 1 Eq 266; *Bulkeley v Stephens* [1896] 2 Ch 241; *Re Henderson* [1940] Ch 368, [1940] 1 All ER 623; *Re Maclaren's Settlement Trusts* [1951] 2 All ER 414 at 420; *Re Ellerman's Settlement Trusts* [1984] LS Gaz R 430; (1986) 1 TL & P 62 (I. Pittaway); Underhill, pp. 510–511.

d) For the allocation of the proceeds of sale of mortgaged property where the monies are insufficient to repay in full: *Re Atkinson* [1904] 2 Ch 160.

e) For the allocation of interest awarded for non-receipt from a trustee of money that ought to have been received: *Bartlett v Barclays Bank Trust Co Ltd (No 2)* [1980] Ch 515, [1980] 2 All ER 92, p. 871, post.

2. Observe that trustees may, by choosing among authorised investments and therefore consistently with the rule in *Howe v Lord Dartmouth*, produce an income of about 8 per cent. by investing in undated gilts (thereby favouring the life tenant); or an income of about 2 per cent. by choosing short-dated gilts and growth equities (thereby favouring the remainderman). Would not the rule of apportionment be more usefully applied if it provided a rule to deal with that problem, rather than assuming (wrongly at the present time) that investment in gilts preserves the capital?

V. Duty in Respect of Accounts and Audit[18]

A trustee must keep accounts of the trust and disclose them to the beneficiaries as requested.[19] Commonly, copies are given to the beneficiaries, but strictly a beneficiary is only entitled to a copy if he pays for it.

TRUSTEE ACT 1925

22. Reversionary interests, valuations, and audit.—(4) Trustees may, in their absolute discretion, from time to time, but not more than once in every three

---

18 H & M, pp. 539–540; K & S, pp. 286–287; P & M, pp. 391–393; Pettit, p. 364; Riddall, pp. 327–328; Snell, pp. 232–233; Underhill, pp. 657–663. For the duty of charitable trustees to account, see pp. 529, ante.

19 *Pearse v Green* (1819) 1 Jac & W 135 at 140, per PLUMER MR.

years unless the nature of the trust or any special dealings with the trust property make a more frequent exercise of the right reasonable, cause the accounts of the trust property to be examined or audited by an independent accountant, and shall, for that purpose, produce such vouchers and give such information to him as he may require; and the costs of such examination or audit, including the fee of the auditor, shall be paid out of the capital or income of the trust property, or partly in one way and partly in the other, as the trustees, in their absolute discretion, think fit, but, in default of any direction by the trustees to the contrary in any special case, costs attributable to capital shall be borne by capital and those attributable to income by income.

PUBLIC TRUSTEE ACT 1906

13. Investigation and audit of trust accounts.[20]—(1) Subject to rules under this Act and unless the court otherwise orders, the condition and accounts of any trust shall, on an application being made and notice thereof given in the prescribed manner by any trustee or beneficiary, be investigated and audited by such solicitor or public accountant as may be agreed on by the applicant and the trustees or, in default of agreement, by the public trustee or some person appointed by him:

Provided that (except with the leave of the court) such an investigation or audit shall not be required within twelve months after any such previous investigation or audit, and that a trustee or beneficiary shall not be appointed under this section to make an investigation or audit.

(2) The person making the investigation or audit (hereinafter called the auditor) shall have a right of access to the books, accounts, and vouchers of the trustees, and to any securities and documents of title held by them on account of the trust, and may require from them such information and explanation as may be necessary for the performance of his duties, and upon the completion of the investigation and audit shall forward to the applicant and to every trustee a copy of the accounts, together with a report thereon, and a certificate signed by him to the effect that the accounts exhibit a true view of the state of the affairs of the trust and that he has had the securities of the trust fund investments produced to and verified by him or (as the case may be) that such accounts are deficient in such respects as may be specified in such certificate.

(3) Every beneficiary under the trust shall, subject to rules under this Act, be entitled at all reasonable times to inspect and take copies of the accounts, report, and certificate, and, at his own expense, to be furnished with copies thereto or extracts therefrom.

JUDICIAL TRUSTEES ACT 1896

1. Power of court on application to appoint judicial trustee.[21]—(6): see p. 635, ante.

---

20 See Public Trustee Rules 1912, rr. 31–37. Law Reform Committee 23rd Report (The Powers and Duties of Trustees) 1982 Cmnd 8733, para. 9.48 recommends the abolition of s. 13. It is only occasionally used and contains no powers to enforce the findings of the Public Trustee.
21 See Judicial Trustee Rules 1983, S.I. 1983 No. 370, rr. 9, 10, 12–14.

VI. Duty to Provide Information. Trust Documents[1]

A trustee must provide information to the beneficiaries concerning the state of the trust[2]. For this purpose, it is convenient to keep a Minute Book and a Trust Diary, in which day to day events are recorded.

Documents connected with the trust are the property of the beneficiaries; and the beneficiaries are therefore entitled to them. However, we have seen that, where trustees exercise discretionary powers, they cannot be required to disclose their reasons; but where reasons are disclosed, they may be challenged, and, if unjustifiable, may be the subject of a suit by the beneficiaries[3]. A nice question thus arises: What are the rights of the beneficiaries where the reasons for the exercise by trustees of discretionary powers are contained in documents connected with the trust?

RE LONDONDERRY'S SETTLEMENT[4]
[1965] Ch 918, [1964] 3 All ER 855 (CA, Harman, Danckwerts and Salmon LJJ)

The trustees of a family settlement created by the Seventh Marquess of Londonderry decided, in accordance with the provisions of the settlement, to distribute the capital among the beneficiaries, and to bring the settlement to an end.

The defendant, a daughter of the settlor, was dissatisfied with the provision which the trustees decided to make for her and her children. She asked to see the minutes of the trustees' meetings, agendas and other documents prepared for their meetings, and the correspondence between the trustees, the settlor (then deceased), the trustees' solicitor, and other persons concerned with the administration of the trust. The trustees took the view that it was not in the interests of the family as a whole to disclose all these documents, and they supplied the complainant only with copies of the intended appointments of capital, and copies of the accounts of the trust. The question was whether she was entitled to inspect the other documents.

Held (reversing Plowman J). The Trustees were not under a duty to supply the documents or to disclose the reasons for their decisions.

Harman LJ: I have found this a difficult case. It raises what in my judgment is a novel question on which there is no authority exactly in point although several cases have been cited to us somewhere near it. The court is really required here to resolve two principles that come into conflict, or at least apparent conflict. The first is that, as the defendant beneficiary admits, trustees exercising a discretionary power are not bound to disclose to their beneficiaries the reasons actuating them in coming to a decision. This is a long-standing principle and rests largely I think on the view that nobody could be called upon to accept a trusteeship involving

---

1 H & M, pp. 540–542; K & S, pp. 364–367; P & M, pp. 391–393; Pettit, pp. 360–363; Riddall, p. 344; Snell, pp. 231–232; Underhill, pp. 659–663.
2 But this does not put the trustees "under any duty to proffer information to their beneficiary, or to see that he has proper advice merely because they are trustees for him and know that he is entering into a transaction with his beneficial interest with some person or body connected in some way with the trustees, such as a company in which the trustees own some shares beneficially.": *Tito v Waddell (No 2)* [1977] Ch 106 at 243, [1977] 3 All ER 129 at 242, per Megarry V-C; questioned at (1977) 41 Conv (NS) 438 (F.R. Crane).
3 See pp. 646, 649, ante.
4 (1965) 81 LQR 192 (R.E.M.). See *Chaine-Nickson v Bank of Ireland* [1976] IR 393.

the exercise of a discretion unless, in the absence of bad faith, he were not liable to have his motives or his reasons called in question either by the beneficiaries or by the court. To this there is added a rider, namely, that if trustees do give reasons, their soundness can be considered by the court. Compare the observations of James LJ in *Re Gresham Life Assurance Society, ex p Penney* (1872) 8 Ch App 446 at 449, 450 on the analogous position of directors.

It would seem on the face of it that there is no reason why this principle should be confined to decisions orally arrived at and should not extend to a case, like the present, where owing to the complexity of the trust and the large sums involved, the trustees, who act subject to the consent of another body called the appointors, have brought into existence various written documents, including, in particular, agenda for and minutes of their meetings from time to time held in order to consider distributions made of the fund and its income. It is here that the conflicting principle is said to emerge. All these documents, it is argued, came into existence for the purposes of the trust and are in the possession of the trustees as such and are, therefore, trust documents, the property of the beneficiaries, and as such open to them to inspect. . . .

The defendant relied on certain observations in *O'Rourke v Darbishire* [1920] AC 581. The decision was that the plaintiff was not entitled to the production of what were called the "trust documents", and I find Lord Parmoor making this observation at 619. "A cestui que trust, in an action against his trustees, is generally entitled to the production for inspection of all documents relating to the affairs of the trust. It is not material for the present purpose whether this right is to be regarded as a paramount proprietary right in the cestui que trust, or as a right to be enforced under the law of discovery." Lord Wrenbury says at 626. "If the plaintiff is right in saying that he is a beneficiary, and if the documents are documents belonging to the executors as executors, he has a right to access to the documents which he desires to inspect upon what has been called in the judgments in this case a proprietary right. The beneficiary is entitled to see all the trust documents because they are trust documents and because he is a beneficiary. They are in a sense his own. Action or no action, he is entitled to access to them. This has nothing to do with discovery. The right to discovery is a right to see someone else's documents. A proprietary right is a right to access to documents which are your own. No question of professional privilege arises in such a case. Documents containing professional advice taken by the executors as trustees contain advice taken by trustees for their cestuis que trust, and the beneficiaries are entitled to see them because they are beneficiaries."

General observations of this sort give very little guidance, for first they beg the question what are trust documents, and secondly their lordships were not considering the point here that papers are asked for which bear on the question of the exercise of the trustees' discretion. In my judgment category (a) mentioned in the notice of appeal, viz., the minutes of the meetings of the trustees of the settlement; and part of (b), viz., agenda prepared for trustees' meetings, are, in the absence of an action impugning the trustees' good faith, documents which a beneficiary cannot claim the right to inspect. If the defendant is allowed to examine these, she will know at once the very matters which the trustees are not bound to disclose to her, namely, their motives and reasons. Trustees who wish to preserve their rights in this respect must either commit nothing to paper or destroy everything from meeting to meeting. Indeed, if the defendant be right, I doubt if the last course is open, for she must succeed, if at all, on the ground that the papers belong to her, and if so, the trustees have no right to destroy them.

I would hold that even if documents of this type ought properly to be described as trust documents, they are protected for the special reason which protects the trustees' deliberations on a discretionary matter from disclosure. If necessary, I hold that this principle overrides the ordinary rule. This is, in my judgment, no less in the true interest of the beneficiary than of the trustees. Again, if one of the trustees commits to paper his suggestions and circulates them among his co-trustees; or if inquiries are made in writing as to the circumstances of a member of the class; I decline to hold that such documents are trust documents the property of the beneficiaries. In my opinion such documents are not trust documents in the proper sense at all. On the other hand, if the solicitor advising the trustees commits to paper an aide-mémoire summarising the state of the fund or of the family and reminding the trustees of past distributions and future possibilities I think that must be a document which any beneficiary must be at liberty to inspect. It seems to me, therefore, that category (b) in the notice of appeal embraces documents on both sides of the line.

As to (c), which is: "Correspondence relating to the administration of the trust property or otherwise to the execution of the trusts of the said settlement and passing between (i) the individuals for the time being holding office as trustees of or appointors under the said settlement, (ii) the said trustees and appointors or any of them on the one hand and the solicitors to the trustees on the other hand; (iii) the said trustees and appointors or any of them on the one hand and the beneficiaries under the said settlement on the other hand"; I cannot think that communications passing between individual trustees and appointors are documents in which beneficiaries have a proprietary right. On the other hand, as to category (ii), in general the letters of the trustees' solicitors to the trustees do seem to me to be trust documents in which the beneficiaries have a property. As to category (iii), I do not think letters to or from an individual beneficiary ought to be open to inspection by another beneficiary. Thus I think the judge's order went too far, but it is very difficult to frame a declaration which will not cut down the rights of the beneficiaries too much. I would propose that we should discuss this matter after my brethren have given their opinions on the matter.

SALMON LJ: There is another possible approach to the present case. The category of trust documents has never been comprehensively defined. Nor could it be—certainly not by me. Trust documents do, however, have these characteristics in common: (1) they are documents in the possession of the trustees as trustees; (2) they contain information about the trust which the beneficiaries are entitled to know; (3) the beneficiaries have a proprietary interest in the documents and, accordingly, are entitled to see them. If any parts of a document contain information which the beneficiaries are not entitled to know, I doubt whether such parts can truly be said to be integral parts of a trust document. Accordingly, any part of a document that lacked the second characteristic to which I have referred would automatically be excluded from the document in its character as a trust document.

I agree with my Lords that the appeal should be allowed.

(1965) 81 LQR 196 (R.E.M.)

"It seems safe to say that the last of *Re Londonderry's Settlement* has not been heard. Perhaps the most obvious point which may arise is whether a beneficiary who is determined to discover all he can about the grounds upon which a discretion has been exercised may not achieve this by instituting litigation alleging that the trustees have exercised their discretion in some improper way, and then obtaining discovery of documents in those proceedings, as in *Talbot v Marshfield* (1865) 2 Drew & Sm 549. Will the courts permit the bonds of secrecy to be invaded by the simple process of commencing hostile litigation against the trustees? It is not easy to see how the courts can prevent this. True, questions of relevance may obviously arise; but on discovery the test of relevance is wide. The classical statement is that of Brett LJ: an applicant is entitled to discovery of any document 'which may fairly lead him to a train of inquiry' that may 'either directly or indirectly enable the party requiring the affidavit either to advance his own case or to damage the case of his adversary' (*Compagnie Financière et Commerciale du Pacifique v Peruvian Guano Co* (1882) 11 QBD 55 at 63). Indeed, the formal order of the court, . . . seems to recognise this possibility.

The other main point which plainly needs further exploration is the ambit of the term 'trust documents'. The negative proposition is now plain: not all documents held by trustees as such are 'trust documents'.[5] But even after a detailed examination of the judgments it is difficult to frame any positive proposition with any degree of confidence. Nor does the formal order of the court (see at 938, at 863) lessen the difficulty; indeed, it contributes its own quota of problems. The order states that without prejudice to any right of the defendant to discovery in any subsequent proceedings against the trustees, and subject to any order of the court in any particular circumstances, there are four categories of documents which the trustees are not bound to disclose to the defendant. The first of these categories is 'The agenda of the meetings of the trustees of the settlement'; the second and third categories consist of correspondence of the trustees *inter se* and with the beneficiaries; and the fourth category consists of minutes of the meetings of the trustees and other documents disclosing their deliberations as to the manner in which they should exercise their discretion or disclosing their reasons for any particular exercise of their discretion, or the materials therefor. It is thus only the minutes and the other documents in the fourth category which appear to be qualified by words relating to disclosure of the trustees' reasons for exercising their discretion in a particular way; the freedom from disclosure seems to apply to all agenda and correspondence, whether or not they would reveal any such reasons or the material on which they were based. Nor does the order make it plain how it applies to documents in the fourth category which not only disclose confidential matters but also deal with other points as well; the inclusion of any confidential matter seems to confer exemption upon the entire document, and not merely upon the confidential matter. The order did, however, declare that the trustees were bound to disclose to the defendant any written advice from their solicitors or counsel as to the manner in which the trustees were in law entitled to exercise their discretion.

Putting all the material together, it seems at present to be difficult to say more than that all documents held by trustees *qua* trustees are prima facie trust documents, but that there is a class of exceptions from this rule which is ill defined but includes confidential documents which the beneficiaries ought not to see. For greater precision than that we must await further decisions by the courts. The Court of Appeal has taken a firm step in the right direction; but that is all.'[6]

---

5 Per DANCKWERTS LJ at 935–936, at 861–862.

6 In *Wilson v Law Debenture Trust Corpn plc* [1995] 2 All ER 337 it was held that the *Re Londonderry* principle applied to pension fund trustees. Cf. (1992) 6 Trust International 119 at p. 125 (Lord BROWNE-WILKINSON).

18. Powers of Trustees[1]

I. General

Trustees have such powers as are given to them by statute or by the trust instrument. It is necessary therefore to read all the statutory provisions which give them their powers. Only the main provisions can be reproduced here.

TRUSTEE ACT 1925

69. Application of Act.—(2) The powers conferred by this Act on trustees are in addition to the powers conferred by the instrument, if any, creating the trust, but those powers,[2] unless otherwise stated, apply if and so far only as a contrary intention is not expressed in the instrument,[2a] if any, creating the trust, and have effect subject to the terms of that instrument.

Ockelton, *Trusts for Accountants*, p. 107

"So if we want to know the powers of the trustees in relation to a particular trust, we should always look at the trust instrument first, for the powers

---

1 H & M, pp. 543–574; K & S, pp. 263–271, 287–288, 323–339; P & M, pp. 364, 374, 395–396, 492–519; Pettit, pp. 440–459; Riddall, pp. 254–256, 296–312; Snell, pp. 260–282; Underhill, pp. 665–709.

2 I.e. the powers conferred by the Act.

2a *Re Delamere's Settlement Trust, Kenny v Cunningham-Reid* [1984] 1 WLR 813, [1984] 1 All ER 584 ('equal shares absolutely' in trustees' deed of appointment held to mean 'indefeasibly', thus giving rise to a contrary intention); [1985] Conv 153 (R. Griffith). See p. 763, post.

conferred by the Act may be modified or excluded by it. It is for the settlor to decide what powers he gives to his trustee: the Act merely gives him a model, which he can accept (by saying nothing) or reject as he pleases. It is true, however, that s 69 (2) does include the words 'unless otherwise stated'. The powers given to trustees despite anything in the trust instrument are those under s 14 (power of trustees to give receipts), s 16 (power to raise money by sale, mortgage, etc) and s 27 (protection by means of advertisements). In the case of all other powers of trustees, the settlor's wishes expressed in the trust instrument take precedence over the Act.''

II. Power of Sale[3]

TRUSTEE ACT 1925

12. Power of trustees for sale to sell by auction, &c.—(1) Where a trust for sale or a power of sale of property is vested in a trustee, he may sell or concur with any other person in selling all or any part of the property, either subject to prior charges or not, and either together or in lots, by public auction or by private contract, subject to any such conditions respecting title or evidence of title or other matter as the trustee thinks fit, with power to vary any contract for sale, and to buy in at any auction, or to rescind any contract for sale and to resell, without being answerable for any loss.

(2) A trust or power to sell or dispose of land includes a trust or power to sell or dispose of part thereof, whether the division is horizontal, vertical, or made in any other way.

(3) This section does not enable an express power to sell settled land to be exercised where the power is not vested in the tenant for life or statutory owner.

16. Power to raise money by sale, mortgage, &c.—(1) Where trustees are authorised by the instrument, if any, creating the trust or by law to pay or apply capital money subject to the trust for any purpose or in any manner, they shall have and shall be deemed always to have had power to raise the money required by sale, conversion, calling in, or mortgage of all or any part of the trust property for the time being in possession.[4]

(2) This section applies notwithstanding anything to the contrary contained in the instrument, if any, creating the trust, but does not apply to trustees of property held for charitable purposes, or to trustees of a settlement for the purposes of the Settled Land Act, 1925, not being also the statutory owners.

SETTLED LAND ACT 1925

38. Powers of sale and exchange[5]—A tenant for life—

    (i) May sell the settled land, or any part thereof, or any easement, right or privilege of any kind over or in relation to the land; and

---

3 H & M, pp. 544–546; K & S, pp. 287–288; P & M, p. 396; Pettit, pp. 440–443; Riddall, pp. 340–341; Snell, pp. 260–263; Underhill, pp. 676–682.

4 But this does not authorise trustees to raise money by charging existing investments in order to purchase others: *Re Suenson-Taylor's Settlement Trusts* [1974] 1 WLR 1280, [1974] 3 All ER 397.

5 See also ss. 39, 40, 72.

(ii) ... [6]

(iii) May make an exchange of the settled land, or any part thereof, or of any easement, right, or privilege of any kind, whether or not newly created, over or in relation to the settled land, or any part thereof, for other land, or for any easement, right or privilege of any kind, whether or not newly created, over or in relation to other land, including an exchange in consideration of money paid for equality of exchange.

LAW OF PROPERTY ACT 1925

28. Powers of management, &c. conferred on trustees for sale.—(1) Trustees for sale shall, in relation to land or to manorial incidents and to the proceeds of sale, have all the powers of a tenant for life and the trustees of a settlement under the Settled Land Act, 1925, including in relation to the land the powers of management conferred by that Act during a minority and where by statute settled land is or becomes vested in the trustees of the settlement upon the statutory trusts, such trustees and their successors in office shall also have all the additional or larger powers (if any) conferred by the settlement on the tenant for life, statutory owner, or trustees of the settlement;[7] and (subject to any express trust to the contrary) all capital money arising under the said powers shall, unless paid or applied for any purpose authorised by the Settled Land Act, 1925, be applicable in the same manner as if the money represented proceeds of sale arising under the trust for sale.

All land acquired under this subsection shall be conveyed to the trustees on trust for sale.

The powers conferred by this subsection shall be exercised with such consents (if any) as would have been required on a sale under the trust for sale, and when exercised shall operate to overreach any equitable interests or powers which are by virtue of this Act or otherwise made to attach to the net proceeds of sale as if created by a trust affecting those proceeds.[8]

SETTLED LAND ACT 1925

67. Sale and purchase of heirlooms under order of court.—(1) Where personal chattels are settled so as to devolve with settled land, or to devolve therewith as nearly as may be in accordance with the law or practice in force at the date of the settlement, or are settled together with land, or upon trusts declared by reference to the trusts affecting land, a tenant for life of the land may sell the chattels or any of them.

(2) The money arising by the sale shall be capital money arising under this Act, and shall be paid, invested, or applied and otherwise dealt with in like manner in all respects as by this Act directed with respect to other capital money arising under this Act, or may be invested in the purchase of other chattels of the same or any other nature, which, when purchased, shall be settled and held on the same trusts, and shall devolve in the same manner as the chattels sold.

6 Para. (ii) was repealed by Statute Law (Repeals) Act 1969, s. 1, Schedule, Part III.
7 As amended by LP(A)A 1926, Schedule.
8 The Trusts of Land and Appointment of Trustees Bill 1995 provides for the abolition of the present dual system of trusts for sale and strict settlements and for its replacement by a new single system of trusts of land. Under clause 4 (which replaces s. 28) trustees of land have, in relation to the land subject to the trust, all the powers of an absolute owner. The Bill is based on the Law Commission Report on Trusts of Land 1989 (Law Com No. 181).

(3) A sale or purchase of chattels under this section shall not be made without an order of the court.

In **Re Hope** [1899] 2 Ch 679, the Court of Appeal refused to approve the sale by the tenant for life of the "Hope" diamond. His financial troubles, they said, had been brought about by his own extravagance. An account of the jewel and of its history is given on pp. 694, 695 of the report.

LAW OF PROPERTY ACT 1925

130. Creation of entailed interests in real and personal property.—(5) Where personal chattels are settled without reference to settled land on trusts creating entailed interests therein, the trustees, with the consent of the usufructuary for the time being if of full age, may sell the chattels or any of them, and the net proceeds of any such sale shall be held in trust for and shall go to the same persons successively, in the same manner and for the same interests, as the chattels sold would have been held and gone if they had not been sold, and the income of investments representing such proceeds of sale shall be applied accordingly.[8a]

TRUSTEE ACT 1925

57. Power of court to authorise dealings with trust property.—(1) Where in the management or administration of any property vested in trustees, any sale, lease, mortgage, surrender, release, or other disposition, or any purchase, investment, acquisition, expenditure, or other transaction, is in the opinion of the court expedient, but the same cannot be effected by reason of the absence of any power for that purpose vested in the trustees by the trust instrument, if any, or by law, the court may by order confer upon the trustees, either generally or in any particular instance, the necessary power for the purpose, on such terms, and subject to such provisions and conditions, if any, as the court may think fit and may direct in what manner any money authorised to be expended, and the costs of any transaction, are to be paid or borne as between capital and income.

(2) The court may, from time to time, rescind or vary any order made under this section, or may make any new or further order.

(3) An application to the court under this section may be made by the trustees, or by any of them, or by any person beneficially interested under the trust.

(4) This section does not apply to trustees of a settlement for the purposes of the Settled Land Act, 1925.

In **Re Hope's Will Trust** [1929] 2 Ch 136, the Court approved under s. 57 (1) the sale of family portraits which were held upon trusts which should, as nearly

---

8a The Trusts of Land and Appointment of Trustees Bill 1995 provides that no new entailed interests can be created in any property (clause 2, Sched 1, para. 5); Law Commission Report on Trusts of Land 1989 (Law Com No. 181), para. 16.1.

as the rules of law and equity would permit, correspond with the limitations of real estate in tail. Eve J said at 140:

"Having come to the clear conclusion that the sale is one which will be beneficial to all parties interested, and indeed is almost unavoidable, I find no difficulty in authorizing the trustees to carry it out under s. 57."

III. Power to Give Receipts[9]

TRUSTEE ACT 1925

14. Power of trustees to give receipts.—(1) The receipt in writing of a trustee for any money, securities, or other personal property or effects payable, transferable, or deliverable to him under any trust or power shall be a sufficient discharge to the person paying, transferring, or delivering the same and shall effectually exonerate him from seeing to the application or being answerable for any loss or misapplication thereof.

(2) This section does not, except where the trustee is a trust corporation, enable a sole trustee to give a valid receipt for—

(*a*) the proceeds of sale or other capital money arising under a ... trust for sale of land,[10]

(*b*) capital money arising under the Settled Land Act, 1925.

(3) This section applies notwithstanding anything to the contrary in the instrument, if any, creating the trust.

IV. Power to Compound Liabilities and to Settle Claims[11]

TRUSTEE ACT 1925

15. Power to compound liabilities.—A personal representative, or two or more trustees acting together, or, subject to the restrictions imposed in regard to receipts by a sole trustee not being a trust corporation, a sole acting trustee whereby the instrument, if any, creating the trust, or by statute, a sole trustee is authorised to execute the trusts and powers reposed in him, may if and as he or they think fit—

(*a*) accept any property, real or personal, before the time at which it is made transferable or payable; or

(*b*) sever and apportion any blended trust funds or property; or

(*c*) pay or allow any debt or claim on any evidence that he or they think sufficient; or

(*d*) accept any composition or any security, real or personal, for any debt or for any property, real or personal, claimed; or

9 H & M, p. 546; K & S, p. 274; P & M, pp. 364, 374; Pettit, p. 443; Riddall, p. 365; Snell, p. 263; Underhill, pp. 685–686.
10 As amendcd by LP(A)A 1926, Schedule.
11 H & M, pp. 547–548; K & S, p. 274; P & M, pp. 395–396; Pettit, pp. 445–446; Snell, pp. 270–271; Underhill, pp. 685–686.

(*e*) allow any time of payment of any debt; or

(*f*) compromise, compound, abandon, submit to arbitration, or otherwise settle any debt, account, claim, or thing whatever relating to the testator's or intestate's estate or to the trust;[12]

and for any of those purposes may enter into, give, execute, and do such agreements, instruments of composition or arrangement, releases, and other things as to him or them seem expedient, without being responsible for any loss occasioned by any act or thing so done by him or them in good faith.[13]

v. Power to Insure[14]

TRUSTEE ACT 1925

19. Power to insure.—(1) A trustee may insure against loss or damage by fire any building or other insurable property to any amount, including the amount of any insurance already on foot, not exceeding three fourth parts of the full value of the building or property, and pay the premiums for such insurance out of the income thereof or out of the income of any other property subject to the same trusts without obtaining the consent of any person who may be entitled wholly or partly to such income.

(2) This section does not apply to any building or property which a trustee is bound forthwith to convey absolutely to any beneficiary upon being requested to do so.

20. Application of insurance money where policy kept up under any trust, power or obligation.—(1) Money receivable by trustees or any beneficiary under a policy of insurance against the loss or damage of any property subject to a trust or to a settlement within the meaning of the Settled Land Act, 1925, whether by fire or otherwise, shall, where the policy has been kept up under any trust in that behalf or under any power statutory or otherwise, or in performance of any covenant or of any obligation statutory or otherwise, or by a tenant for life impeachable for waste, be capital money for the purposes of the trust or settlement, as the case may be.

(3) Any such money—

(*a*) if it was receivable in respect of settled land within the meaning of the Settled Land Act, 1925, or any building or works thereon, shall be deemed to be capital money arising under that Act from the settled land, and shall be invested or applied by the trustees, or, if in court, under the direction of the court, accordingly;

---

12 *Re Earl of Strafford* [1980] Ch 28, [1979] 1 All ER 513 (surrender of beneficial interest as part of compromise of dispute as to ownership of chattels between trust and beneficiaries).

13 *Re Greenwood* (1911) 105 LT 509 (inaction by a trustee provides no defence). There was no such statutory power before the Conveyancing Act 1881 came into effect. It was not therefore available to the trustees in *Re Brogden* (1888) 38 ChD 546, p. 657, ante where the incidents occurred before that time. See also *Alsop Wilkinson v Neary* (1994) Times, 4 November, where a trustee, against whom hostile litigation had been brought challenging the validity of a settlement, had no duty to defend the trust but must remain neutral leaving it to the rival claimants to the beneficial interest to fight their own battles.

14 H & M, pp. 546–547; K & S, p. 287; P & M, p. 395; Pettit, pp. 443–445; Snell, pp. 264–265; Underhill, pp. 556–557.

(*b*) if it was receivable in respect of personal chattels settled as heirlooms within the meaning of the Settled Land Act, 1925, shall be deemed to be capital money arising under that Act, and shall be applicable by the trustees, or, if in court, under the direction of the court, in like manner as provided by that Act with respect to money arising by a sale of chattels settled as heirlooms as aforesaid;

(*c*) if it was receivable in respect of property held upon trust for sale, shall be held upon the trusts and subject to the powers and provisions applicable to money arising by a sale under such trust;

(*d*) in any other case, shall be held upon trusts corresponding as nearly as may be with the trusts affecting the property in respect of which it was payable.

(4) Such money, or any part thereof, may also be applied by the trustees, or, if in court, under the direction of the court, in rebuilding, reinstating, replacing, or repairing the property lost or damaged, but any such application by the trustees shall be subject to the consent of any person whose consent is required by the instrument, if any, creating the trust to the investment of money subject to the trust, and, in the case of money which is deemed to be capital money arising under the Settled Land Act, 1925, be subject to the provisions of that Act with respect to the application of capital money by the trustees of the settlement.

Law Reform Committee 23rd Report (The Powers and Duties of Trustees) 1982 Cmnd 8733, para. 9.1.IV.29, 30, 31

"*Insurance* (paragraphs 4.29–4.36)

29. We recommend that trustees be placed under a *duty* to insure against any risk in all the circumstances in which an ordinary prudent man of business would so insure, but that this should not be imposed on existing trusts. (paragraph 4.33)

30. All trustees should have the power to insure the trust property up to its full replacement value in all cases in which it would be sensible to do that, and in other cases up to its market value. (paragraph 4.31)

31. Trustees should be empowered to pay insurance premiums out of capital as well as income but should make the payments in such a way as to maintain the balance between the interests of the life tenant and the interests of the remainderman. (paragraph 4.36)".[15]

VI. Power in Connection with Reversionary Interests[16]

TRUSTEE ACT 1925

22. Reversionary interests, valuations and audit.—(1) Where trust property includes any share or interest in property not vested in the trustees, or the

----

15 See also (1982) 79 LSG 755 (A. and P. Kenny).

16 H & M, p. 548; K & S, p. 272; Pettit, pp. 446–447; Snell, pp. 271–272; Underhill, pp. 686–687.

proceeds of the sale of any such property, or any other thing in action, the trustees on the same falling into possession, or becoming payable or transferable may—

(a) agree or ascertain the amount or value thereof or any part thereof in such manner as they may think fit;

(b) accept in or towards satisfaction thereof, at the market or current value, or upon any valuation or estimate of value which they may think fit, any authorised investments;

(c) allow any deductions for duties, costs, charges and expenses which they may think proper or reasonable;

(d) execute any release in respect of the premises so as effectually to discharge all accountable parties from all liability in respect of any matters coming within the scope of such release;

without being responsible in any such case for any loss occasioned by any act or thing so done by them in good faith.

(2) The trustees shall not be under any obligation and shall not be chargeable with any breach of trust by reason of any omission—

(a) to place any distringas notice or apply for any stop or other like order upon any securities or other property out of or on which such share or interest or other thing in action as aforesaid is derived, payable or charged; or

(b) to take any proceedings on account of any act, default, or neglect on the part of the persons in whom such securities or other property or any of them or any part thereof are for the time being, or had at any time been, vested;

unless and until required in writing so to do by some person, or the guardian of some person, beneficially interested under the trust, and unless also due provision is made to their satisfaction for payment of the costs of any proceedings required to be taken:

Provided that nothing in this subsection shall relieve the trustees of the obligation to get in and obtain payment or transfer of such share or interest or other thing in action on the same falling into possession.

(3) Trustees may, for the purpose of giving effect to the trust, or any of the provisions of the instrument, if any, creating the trust or of any statute, from time to time (by duly qualified agents) ascertain and fix the value of any trust property in such manner as they think proper, and any valuation so made in good faith shall be binding upon all persons interested under the trust.

VII. Power to Delegate[17]

A. Trustee Act 1925

Originally a trustee was expected, in theory, to perform all his duties personally. *Delegatus non potest delegare.* Whether or not this was ever a practical proposition, it early became impracticable because of the increasing complications of business life.

---

17 H & M, pp. 549–559; K & S, pp. 263–271; P & M, pp. 400–406; Pettit, pp. 428–439; Riddall, pp. 255–256; Snell, pp. 265–270; Underhill, pp. 618–633; (1931) 47 LQR 330 (H.P.), 463 (W.S.H.); (1959) 22 MLR 381 (G.H. Jones).

By 1925, it could be said that a trustee could delegate certain functions; not, of course, his discretionary powers. He had to show that the appointment of some person to perform them was reasonably necessary in the circumstances, or was in accordance with ordinary business practice.[18] The trustee must exercise proper care in the selection of the agent, must employ him in his proper field, and must exercise general supervision.[19] Further, an exculpatory clause, limiting the trustee's liability to wilful default, was strictly construed; it was said in 1889 that such a clause merely had the effect of changing the onus of proof and of placing it on "those who seek to charge a . . . trustee with a loss arising from the default of an agent, when the propriety of employing the agent has been established".[20]

It is clear that the power of a trustee to delegate is widened by the Trustee Act 1925. The effect of ss. 23 and 30 has been the subject of differences of opinion, among which the reader must judge.[1] Sir William Holdsworth[2] said that s. 23 required no more of a trustee than subjective good faith in selecting an agent, that *Re Vickery*[3] was correctly decided, but "it shows that the Legislature has gone too far in whittling away the liabilities of trustees, with the result that, in some respects, the *cestui que trust* is insufficiently protected". Parker and Mellows "have little doubt that the decision in *Re Vickery* was technically incorrect on the legal principles previously established." They also believe that the result of the case is desirable. "Surely Maugham J, while admittedly changing the law, introduced a measure of equity where little existed before. A trustee is still plainly liable if he is consciously negligent or reckless: why should he be liable for more?"[4] Gareth Jones took the view that although *Re Vickery* might, in the result, be correctly decided, the reasoning is fallacious, and that the 1925 legislation, properly understood, while widening the permitted scope for delegation, retains the old principles of liability.[5]

TRUSTEE ACT 1925

23. Power to employ agents.—(1) Trustees or personal representatives may, instead of acting personally, employ and pay an agent, whether a solicitor, banker, stockbroker, or other person, to transact any business or do any act required to be transacted or done in the execution of the trust, or the administration of the testator's or intestate's estate, including the receipt and payment of money, and shall be entitled to be allowed and paid all charges and expenses so incurred, and shall not be responsible for the default of any such agent if employed in good faith.[6]

(2) Trustees or personal representatives may appoint any person to act as their agent or attorney for the purpose of selling, converting, collecting, getting in, and executing and perfecting insurances[7] of, or managing or

18 *Re Parsons, ex p Belchier* (1754) Amb 218; *Speight v Gaunt* (1883) 9 App Cas 1.
19 *Speight v Gaunt*, supra; *Learoyd v Whiteley* (1887) 12 App Cas 727; *Fry v Tapson* (1884) 28 ChD 268.
20 *Re Brier* (1884) 26 ChD 238 at 243 per Lord SELBORNE.
1 See also TA 1925, ss. 8, 21, 22 and 25 (as amended by Powers of Attorney Act 1971).
2 (1931) 47 LQR 463.
3 [1931] 1 Ch 572; p. 748, post.
4 P & M, p. 405.
5 (1959) 22 MLR 381, p. 752, post. For the comments and recommendations of the Law Reform Committee's 23rd Report (1982 Cmnd 8733), paras. 4.1–4.28, see p. 757, post.
6 On the delegation of investment powers by trustees, see (1989) 3 TL & P 110 (C. Francis); (1990) 106 LQR 87 (D. Hayton).
7 "Obviously a misprint for 'assurances' "; *Green v Whitehead* [1930] 1 Ch 38 at 40, per EVE J.

cultivating, or otherwise administering any property, real or personal, moveable or immoveable, subject to the trust or forming part of the testator's or intestate's estate, in any place outside the United Kingdom or executing or exercising any discretion or trust or power vested in them in relation to any such property, with such ancillary powers, and with and subject to such provisions and restrictions as they may think fit, including a power to appoint substitutes, and shall not, by reason only of their having made such appointment, be responsible for any loss arising thereby.

(3) Without prejudice to such general power of appointing agents as aforesaid—

(*a*) A trustee may appoint a solicitor to be his agent to receive and give a discharge for any money or valuable consideration or property receivable by the trustee under the trust, by permitting the solicitor to have the custody of, and to produce, a deed having in the body thereof or endorsed thereon a receipt for such money or valuable consideration or property, the deed being executed, or the endorsed receipt being signed, by the person entitled to give a receipt for that consideration;

(*b*) A trustee shall not be chargeable with breach of trust by reason only of his having made or concurred in making any such appointment; and the production of any such deed by the solicitor shall have the same statutory validity and effect as if the person appointing the solicitor had not been a trustee;

(*c*) A trustee may appoint a banker or solicitor to be his agent to receive and give a discharge for any money payable to the trustee under or by virtue of a policy of insurance, by permitting the banker or solicitor to have the custody of and to produce the policy of insurance with a receipt signed by the trustee, and a trustee shall not be chargeable with a breach of trust by reason only of his having made or concurred in making any such appointment.

Provided that nothing in this subsection shall exempt a trustee from any liability which he would have incurred if this Act and any enactment replaced by this Act had not been passed, in case he permits any such money, valuable consideration, or property to remain in the hands or under the control of the banker or solicitor for a period longer than is reasonably necessary to enable the banker or solicitor, as the case may be, to pay or transfer the same to the trustee.

This subsection applies whether the money or valuable consideration or property was or is received before or after the commencement of this Act.

25. Power to delegate trusts during absence abroad.[8]—(1) Notwithstanding any rule of law or equity to the contrary, a trustee may, by power of attorney,

---

8 As amended by Powers of Attorney Act 1971, s. 9, which, by sub-s. (4), "applies whenever the trusts, powers or discretions in question arose but does not invalidate anything done by virtue of the said section 25 as in force at the commencement of this Act." The exercise of the power no longer depends on absence abroad; the marginal note was not amended and is therefore inaccurate.

A power of attorney under s. 25 cannot be an enduring power: Enduring Powers of Attorney Act 1985, s. 2 (8). See *Walia v Michael Naughton Ltd* [1985] 1 WLR 1115, [1985] 3 All ER 673; Enduring Powers of Attorney Act, s. 3 (3). Law Commission Report: Delegation by Individual Trustees 1994 (Law Com. No. 220), paras. 4.1, and 4.15, p. 760 post.

delegate for a period not exceeding twelve months the execution or exercise of all or any of the trusts, powers and discretions vested in him as trustee either alone or jointly with any other person or persons.

(2) The persons who may be donees of a power of attorney under this section include a trust corporation but not (unless a trust corporation) the only other co-trustee of the donor of the power.

(3) An instrument creating a power of attorney under this section shall be attested by at least one witness.

(4) Before or within seven days after giving a power of attorney under this section the donor shall give written notice thereof (specifying the date on which the power comes into operation and its duration, the donee of the power, the reason why the power is given and, where some only are delegated, the trusts, powers and discretions delegated) to—

(*a*) each person (other than himself), if any, who under any instrument creating the trust power has power (whether alone or jointly) to appoint a new trustee; and

(*b*) each of the other trustees, if any;

but failure to comply with this subsection shall not, in favour of a person dealing with the donee of the power, invalidate any act done or instrument executed by the donee.

(5) The donor of a power of attorney given under this section shall be liable for the acts or defaults of the donee in the same manner as if they were the acts or defaults of the donor.

(6) For the purpose of executing or exercising the trusts or powers delegated to him, the donee may exercise any of the powers conferred on the donor as trustee by statute or by the instrument creating the trust, including power, for the purpose of the transfer of any inscribed stock, himself to delegate to an attorney power to transfer but not including the power of delegation conferred by this section.

(7) The fact that it appears from any power of attorney given under this section, or from any evidence required for the purposes of any such power of attorney or otherwise, that in dealing with any stock the donee of the power is acting in the execution of a trust shall not be deemed for any purpose to affect any person in whose books the stock is inscribed or registered with any notice of the trust.

(8) This section applies to a personal representative, tenant for life and statutory owner as it applies to a trustee except that subsection (4) shall apply as if it required the notice there mentioned to be given—

(*a*) in the case of a personal representative, to each of the other personal representatives, if any, except any executor who has renounced probate;

(*b*) in the case of a tenant for life, to the trustees of the settlement and to each person, if any, who together with the person giving the notice constitutes the tenant for life;

(*c*) in the case of a statutory owner, to each of the persons, if any, who together with the person giving the notice constitute the statutory owner and, in the case of a statutory owner by virtue of section 23 (1) (*a*) of the Settled Land Act, 1925, to the trustees of the settlement.

30. Implied indemnity of trustees.—(1) A trustee shall be chargeable only for money and securities actually received by him notwithstanding his signing any receipt for the sake of conformity, and shall be answerable and accountable only for his own acts, receipts, neglects, or defaults, and not for those of any other trustee, nor for any banker, broker, or other person with whom any trust money or securities may be deposited, nor for the insufficiency or deficiency of any securities, nor for any other loss, unless the same happens through his own wilful default.

RE VICKERY
[1931] 1 Ch 572 (ChD, MAUGHAM J)

The defendant, Mr. Stephens, was a missionary, ignorant of business affairs. He was the sole executor of Mrs. Vickery who died in December, 1926, leaving an estate worth about £300. Stephens employed a solicitor named Jennens, who, unknown to him, had at one time been suspended from practice.

The plaintiffs, sons of Mrs. Vickery, objected to the appointment, pressed the defendant to expedite the administration of the estate, and in September, 1927 told the defendant of the past improprieties of Jennens, and asked the defendant to instruct a different solicitor. Jennens repeatedly assured the defendant that the matter would be quickly completed. Another solicitor was instructed in December, 1927. Proceedings were taken against Jennens, who absconded without payment.

The plaintiffs asked for a declaration that the defendant was guilty of a breach of trust in permitting sums of £214 14s. 5d. in the Post Office Savings Bank and £62 4s. 0d. in Savings Certificates to be received and retained by Jennens.

Held. The defendant was not liable.

MAUGHAM J: The question that arises is whether in the circumstances, and in view of my findings as to the facts, the defendant is liable to make good these sums with interest by reason of his negligence either in employing Jennens to receive the sums, or in permitting those sums to remain in his hands, in the circumstances of the case, for a longer period than was necessary.

In considering this question the Court has to bear in mind in particular two sections of the Trustee Act, 1925. Section 23, sub-s. 1, is as follows: [His Lordship read the sub-section, and continued:] This sub-section is new and, in my opinion, authorized the defendant in signing the authorities to Jennens & Jennens to collect the two sums in question; for I do not think it can be doubted that the defendant acted in good faith in employing Jennens for the purpose. It will be observed that the sub-section has no proviso or qualification to it such as we find in relation to s. 23, sub-s. 3. It is hardly too much to say that it revolutionizes the position of a trustee or an executor so far as regards the employment of agents. He is no longer required to do any actual work himself, but he may employ a solicitor or other agent to do it, whether there is any real necessity for the employment or not. No doubt he should use his discretion in selecting an agent, and should employ him only to do acts within the scope of the usual business of the agent; but, as will be seen, a question arises whether even in these respects he is personally liable for a loss due to the employment of the agent unless he has been guilty of wilful default.

Section 23, sub-s. 3, is in the following terms: [His Lordship read the sub-section and continued:] This sub-section is a reproduction with amendments of s. 17 of the Trustee Act, 1893, which replaced s. 2 of the Trustee Act, 1888. It will be observed that para. (*a*) of the sub-section relates to the production of a deed having endorsed thereon a receipt for money or other property, and that para. (*c*) refers to the receipt of money payable to the trustee under a policy of insurance. In these cases, no doubt, there is no reason why the banker or the solicitor should do anything more than receive the money and pay the same to the trustee or as he shall direct. The proviso must, I think, be limited to these two cases; and, of course, it is not intended to preclude a trustee from keeping trust funds at his bank pending investment or other proper use of them; and it has nothing to do, in my opinion, with the case I have to decide, in which the powers given by paras. (*a*) and (*c*) were not utilized by the defendant. There was no doubt a good reason for not making the proviso extend to sub-s. 1 of s. 23, since in many cases where, for example, a banker or other agent is employed by a trustee to receive money, the money cannot at once be conveniently paid to the trustee, but has to be employed by the banker or other agent in a number of ways.

I have now to consider s. 30, sub-s. 1, of the Trustee Act, 1925, a section which replaces s. 24 of the Trustee Act, 1893, which in its turn re-enacted Lord Cranworth's Act, s. 31. It is in the following terms: [His Lordship read the sub-section, and continued:] Reliance has been placed on the words concluding the sub-section "nor for any other loss, unless the same happens through his own wilful default." To avoid misconception I wish to say that, having regard to the numerous decisions since the enactment of Lord Cranworth's Act in relation to the liability of trustees for innocent breaches of trust, it is impossible now to hold that the words "for any other loss" are quite general, with the result that no trustee is ever liable for breach of trust unless the breach is occasioned by his own wilful default. In my opinion the words are confined to losses for which it is sought to make the trustee liable occasioned by his signing receipts for the sake of conformity or by reason of the wrongful acts or defaults of another trustee or of an agent with whom trust money or securities have been deposited, or for the insufficiency or deficiency of securities or some other analogous loss. It may be noted that if the phrase is not so limited it is difficult to see how there could have been any need for s. 3 of the Judicial Trustees Act 1896, now re-enacted as s. 61 of the Trustee Act 1925, or for s. 29 of that Act; nor would it be possible to explain the numerous cases before 1896 where trustees were made liable for honest mistakes either of construction or fact: see, for example, *Learoyd v Whiteley* (1887) 12 App Cas 727, *National Trustees Co of Australasia v General Finance Co of Australasia* [1905] AC 373, and cases there cited.

On the other hand, since s. 30, sub-s. 1, expressly refers to the defaults of bankers, brokers, or other persons with whom any trust money or other securities may be deposited, I am unable—dealing here with the more limited case—to escape the conclusion that the trustee cannot be made liable for the default of such a person unless the loss happens through the "wilful default" of the trustee. Before considering the meaning of the words "wilful default" in this connection, I would observe that in the case of *Re Brier* (1884) 26 ChD 238 the Court of Appeal, consisting of Lord Selborne LC, and Cotton and Fry LJJ, gave effect to Lord Cranworth's Act, s. 31, and held the trustees and executors not liable inasmuch as it had not been established that the loss occasioned by the agent's insolvency (in a case where, as the law then required, it was shown that the employment of the agent was a proper one) was due to the wilful default of the trustees and executors.

Now the meaning of the phrase "wilful default" has been expounded by the Court of Appeal in the case of *Re Trusts of Leeds City Brewery Ltd's Deed* [1925] Ch

532n, and in the case of *Re City Equitable Fire Insurance Co* [1925] Ch 407. It should be noted that in both those cases the indemnity, given to the trustees in the first case and to the directors and officers of the company in the second case, was worded in a general form so that it could not be contended that they were liable for any matter or thing done or omitted unless it could be shown that the loss so occasioned arose from their own wilful default. This, as I have said, is not true of an ordinary executor or trustee; but the exposition of the phrase "wilful default" is not the less valuable. The Court of Appeal held, following in the case of *Re City Equitable Fire Insurance Co* the decision of Romer J, that a person is not guilty of wilful neglect or default unless he is conscious that, in doing the act which is complained of or in omitting to do the act which it is said he ought to have done, he is committing a breach of his duty, or is recklessly careless whether it is a breach of his duty or not. I accept with respect what Warrington LJ said [1925] Ch at 524—namely, that in the case of trustees there are definite and precise rules of law as to what a trustee may or may not do in the execution of his trust, and that a trustee in general is not excused in relation to a loss occasioned by a breach of trust merely because he honestly believed that he was justified in doing the act in question. But for the reasons which I have given I think that, where an executor employs a solicitor or other agent to receive money belonging to the estate in reliance on s. 23, sub-s. 1, of the Trustee Act, 1925, he will not be liable for a loss of the money occasioned by the misconduct of the agent unless the loss happens through the wilful default of the executor, using those words as implying, as the Court of Appeal have decided, either a consciousness of negligence or breach of duty, or a recklessness in the performance of a duty.

Returning to the facts of the present case, it should be noted that, having taken the step of employing a solicitor not merely to obtain probate and to wind up the estate, but also to collect the War Bonds, the sums in the Post Office Savings Bank, and the sums in Savings Certificates, the position was different from that of a trustee who has simply employed a solicitor or other agent to collect money; for the only practical way of compelling the solicitor to account in the circumstances under consideration was to require him by the usual process to deliver a bill of costs and cash account. This procedure, I may observe, is not a very effective one in the case of a fraudulent solicitor, since it lends itself in dishonest hands, as it did in the present case, to serious delay.

It is essential in this case to guard oneself against judging the conduct of the defendant in the light of subsequent events. To have employed a new solicitor as soon as the defendant became aware that H.H. Jennens was a person with a tarnished reputation for honesty would certainly have meant further costs. It might have proved quite unnecessary even on the supposition that Jennens was a rogue. Even a man of the world might have thought that the sum involved— the sum of 300*l*. or thereabouts—was far too small to make it probable that the solicitor would be likely—unless, indeed, in the case of stern necessity—for such a sum to expose himself to the orders of the Court and to the action of the Law Society. Nor must it be forgotten that upon the facts as I find them it was not till the month of September, 1927, that the defendant had any real reason for suspecting that Jennens was unworthy of confidence; and it seems that after that date he kept on pressing for an immediate settlement and kept on being assured that a settlement would immediately take place. On the whole I have come to the conclusion that the defendant was on any view of the facts guilty only of an error of judgment, and this, in the case of a loss occasioned by the defalcations of a solicitor, does not amount to wilful default on the part of the executor. The action accordingly in my judgment fails and must be dismissed.

In **Re Lucking's Will Trusts** [1968] 1 WLR 866, [1967] 3 All ER 726, the trust fund consisted of a majority holding in Stephen Lucking Ltd. Philip Charles Lucking, a shareholder and also a beneficiary, was sole trustee.

Peter Dewar, an old friend of Lucking, was appointed managing director of the company. Considerable sums of money were applied by Dewar for his own purposes, the money being drawn by cheques which Lucking signed in blank and Dewar counter-signed. Some £15,000 was irrecoverable in Dewar's subsequent bankruptcy.

Lucking was held liable for the breach of trust.[9] On the question of the application of Trustee Act 1925, ss. 23 (1) and 30 (1), CROSS J said at 874, at 732:

"In support of the proposition that a trustee who is carrying on an unincorporated business is only liable for negligence in his supervision of a manager employed by him if the negligence amounts to 'wilful default', counsel relied on the decision of Maugham J in *Re Vickery* [1931] 1 Ch 572. In that case an executor employed a solicitor to obtain payment of sums of money due to the estate and furnished him with documents for the purpose. The solicitor made away with the money and it was said that having regard to what the executor had learnt of the reputation of the solicitor in question he ought to have cancelled the authority given him before the money got into his hands. Maugham J held that section 23 of the Trustee Act 1925 empowered the executor to employ the solicitor for the purpose in question in the first instance and that as section 30 of the Act provides, inter alia, that a trustee shall not be liable for the defaults of any person with whom any trust money or securities may be distributed unless the resulting loss happens through his own wilful default. The executor in the case before him would only be liable if he was guilty of wilful default. I see no reason whatever to think that Maugham J would have considered that a person employed by a trustee to manage a business owned by the trust was a person with whom trust money or securities were deposited within the meaning of section 30. In support of the proposition that directors are only liable for 'wilful default' counsel referred to the *City Equitable* case [1925] Ch 407, but there one of the company's articles provided that directors should only be liable for 'wilful default'. Romer J made it clear in his judgment that but for that article he would have held some of the directors liable in some matters for negligence falling short of 'wilful default'. In my view, 'wilful default' does not enter into the picture in this case at all. The conduct of the defendant trustees is, I think, to be judged by the standard applied in *Speight v Gaunt* (1883) 9 App Cas 1, namely, that a trustee is only bound to conduct the business of the trust in such a way as an ordinary prudent man would conduct a business of his own."

(1959) 22 MLR 388 (G.H. Jones)

"*Re Vickery—a criticism*

It is the present writer's submission that, although in the result *Re Vickery* might be correctly decided, the reasons given by Maugham J for the decision cannot

---

9 See *Bartlett v Barclays Bank Trust Co Ltd (No 1)* [1980] Ch 515 at 532–534, [1980] 1 All ER 139 at 151–152, p. 688; ante, where BRIGHTMAN J discusses *Re Lucking's Will Trusts*.

be supported, and that it is consequently not safe or desirable for a trustee to rely on this decision as authority for the proposition that, 'I am safe if I act honestly but foolishly in appointing my agents.'[10] His Lordship's interpretation of section 23 (1) must inevitably lead to a conflict between that section and the remaining delegation sections of the Act. Indeed, some of the sections would seem to be otiose if Maugham J is correct.

(i) The interpretation of Maugham J of section 23 (1) has rendered section 23 (3) of the Trustee Act 'meaningless and unnecessary.'[11] This subsection allows a banker or solicitor to give a discharge for any monies which have been paid to them, and allows the trustee to give to such agents custody of a deed or receipt signed by the trustee. The trustee is made liable if the trust monies are permitted to remain in the hands of the banker or solicitor for a 'period longer than is reasonably necessary to enable the banker or solicitor, as the case may be, to pay or transfer the same to the trustee'.[12] The learned judge held that section 23 (3) was irrelevant in *Re Vickery* since the trustee had not purported to act thereunder. Foolish indeed will be the trustee who will so act; if the banker or solicitor is appointed 'in good faith' within section 23 (1), then the trustee is protected even if the agent subsequently defaults. Harmony between the two subsections cannot be achieved by limiting section 23 (1) to agents other than bankers or solicitors, for the section is quite general in terms. The most obvious reconciliation of section 23 (1) and section 23 (3) is, of course, to construe the words 'in good faith' in section 23 (1) so that they limit only the *act* of employment. In fact, the trustee will not be liable for his agent's defaults by reason only of an appointment, which was not legally or morally necessary, provided the appointment was in good faith.[13] Such an interpretation, which gives meaning to the words 'without prejudice to such general power of appointing agents as aforesaid,' which introduce and limit section 23 (3), was not acceptable to the learned judge.[14]

(ii) If *Re Vickery* is correct it is difficult to see what is the precise scope of sections 23 (2) and 25. Both sections deal with situations where either the trustee or the trust property is outside the United Kingdom. It will be remembered that Eve J in *Green v Whitehead*[15] had considered section 23 (2) to be of much wider application than section 23 (1) and, certainly, there is a significant difference of wording. Whereas section 23 (1) speaks of the employment of an agent 'to transact any business' in the execution of the trust,

---

10 Lewin (15th edn) p. 185, and Underhill (10th edn) p. 351, accept cautiously the decision. Hanbury (7th edn) pp. 228–229 also accepts the case but subject to important limitations, namely, that a trustee advancing money on a mortgage should not employ the solicitor or valuer of the mortgagor, that a trustee must pay an agent only reasonable remuneration and that the *ejusdem generis* rule of interpretation will be applied to the words "or other person" within s. 23 (1). Keeton, in the latest edition of his *Law of Trusts* (8th edn) p. 257, is of the opinion that the reasoning of MAUGHAM J is erroneous.

11 (1931) 47 LQR 330 (H. Potter).

12 The learned judge's reasons for the absence of this proviso in s. 23 (1) are, with respect, unconvincing: "in many cases where, for example, a banker or other agent is employed by a trustee to receive money, the money cannot at once be conveniently paid to the trustee, but has to be employed by the banker or other agent in a number of ways" (at p. 581).

13 Cf the words of s. 23 (2) which concludes that trustees "shall not, by reason only of their having made such appointment, be responsible for any loss arising thereby."

14 For he had held that s. 23 (1) protected a trustee even for his agent's defaults after appointment.

15 [1930] 1 Ch 38.

section 23 (2) enables the trustee to delegate in addition his 'discretion'; similarly, section 25 permits a trustee to delegate his 'discretions'. It is clear that section 23 (1) is limited to ministerial acts but it is difficult to see what extra powers are delegable under sections 23 (2) and 25. It is submitted that under neither section can the trustee rid himself of his trusteeship. The draftsman, in all probability, envisaged that under sections 23 (2) and 25 the trustee would be able to delegate certain particular discretions, such as the discretion to choose between various tenders, or the discretion to pay agents a reasonable sum in remuneration, or even the discretion to appoint an agent. Only if a trustee desires his agent to have such discretion should he purport to act under these sections, otherwise, the trustee should act under section 23 (1). The reason for this is a simple one—*Speight v Gaunt*.[16] Section 25 enacts specifically that the trustee shall be liable for the acts or defaults of his agent[17] and while it is true that section 23 (2) does not contain such a provision, it is significant that this subsection does say that the trustee shall not be liable for any loss by reason only of making the *appointment*. Consequently, even under section 23 (2) it is most probable that the norm of the reasonable man of business will determine the liability of the trustee for the acts or defaults of his agent once appointed. Thus, the wise trustee, if *Re Vickery* represents the law, will act in all cases under section 23 (1) and be protected by the umbrella of an honest appointment—even though the trustee be out of the United Kingdom for more than a month and even though the trust property is outside the United Kingdom.

(iii) His Lordship in *Re Vickery* did not directly address his mind to the problem of reconciling section 30 (1) of the Trustee Act 1925 with section 23 (1).[18] Maugham J limited section 30 (1) to 'bankers and brokers' and the words 'any other loss'[19] to cases where the loss had arisen through the signing of receipts for the sake of conformity, or where the wrongful acts of another trustee or the agent with whom the trust money had been deposited had resulted in the loss, or where the loss is due to the deficiency or insufficiency of securities or other analogous loss.[20] This limitation does not solve, unfortunately, the conundrum of how a trustee can be free of liability if he appoints in good faith and yet later be liable for the acts or defaults of these particular agents if he, the trustee, has been guilty of a wilful default. Further, the learned judge's definition of 'wilful default' as a conscious or reckless breach of duty on the part of the trustee cannot be supported; the words should have been construed, in their pre-1926 sense, so as to include want of reasonable care. His Lordship purported to follow the judgment of Romer J in the *Re City Equitable* case. In that decision, Romer J was called upon, inter alia, to construe a set of articles of association, and in particular, a clause which was in terms similar to the indemnity clause (s. 24) of the Trustee Act 1893. It was

---

16 (1883) 9 App Cas 1.

17 Section 25 (2).

18 Semble, MAUGHAM J was of opinion that if the trustee was guilty of wilful default then he would have been liable. But he did not discuss the effect of this view on s. 23 (1).

19 Section 30 (1) states that the trustee shall not be responsible for " ... the insufficiency or deficiency of any securities, nor for *any other loss*, unless the same happens through his own wilful default." (Italics supplied).

20 At 582.

inevitable, therefore, that counsel should rely[1] on the *Re Brier*[2] line of cases, which had impliedly interpreted 'wilful default' to include lack of reasonable care, as well as a conscious act of commission or recklessness on the part of the trustee. Romer J rejected this argument. He pointed out that these cases did not involve a consideration of these precise words and that, in the *Re Brier* line of cases, the court was concerned with the 'law as to the employment of agents by trustees.'[3] Directors and auditors were not trustees in the strict sense of the word and there is little resemblance between their duties and the 'duties of a trustee of a will or a marriage settlement.' His Lordship preferred to follow a number of company law decisions, which were authority for a *Derry v Peek*[4] definition of 'wilful default.'

> 'An act, or an omission to do an act, is wilful where the person of whom we are speaking knows what he is doing and intends to do what he is doing. But if that act or omission amounts to a breach of his duty, and therefore to negligence, is the person guilty of wilful negligence? In my opinion that question must be answered in the negative unless he knows that he is committing, and intends to commit, a breach of this duty, or is recklessly careless in the sense of not caring whether his act or omission is or is not a breach of duty.'[5]

This definition was later accepted by Astbury J in *Re Munton*,[6] a decision which was concerned with the liability of a trustee for the acts or defaults of his agent. The learned judge held that a retiring trustee was not guilty of a breach of trust in executing a power of attorney authorising a broker to sell stock and receive the purchase price, the broker having, without authority, handed over the proceeds of sale to a co-trustee who had misappropriated them. The reasoning of the learned judge is, with respect, a little difficult to follow. The following passage is significant:

> 'The indemnity clauses, containing the exception of wilful default, in the Trustee Acts, may or may not have added anything to the previous law, but in *Re City Equitable Fire Insurance Co Ltd* the whole question of wilful default as regards a fiduciary agent is dealt with at great length. Warrington LJ says: "Romer J was quite right in arriving at the conclusion that a person is not guilty of 'wilful neglect or default' unless he is conscious that in doing the act which is complained of, or in omitting to do the act which it is said he ought to have done, he is committing a breach of his duty, and also, as he said, recklessly careless whether it is a breach of the duty or not...."
>
> The plaintiff's counsel say that the *City Equitable* case has made no change in the law as regards an ordinary trustee's liability. I do not propose to discuss that. I have read the passage representing the general result of the decision and it seems to me to apply to the present case'.[7]

The question was not raised in the Court of Appeal and their Lordships did not comment on these observations of Astbury J.

It is submitted, with respect, that the translation of the definition of 'wilful default' in *Re City Equitable* to section 30 (1) of the Trustee Act 1925, was

---

1 *Re City Equitable Fire Insurance Co Ltd* [1925] Ch 407 at 424.
2 (1884) 26 ChD 238.
3 At 439. MAUGHAM J in *Re Vickery* recognised this distinction but found the exposition of ROMER J of "wilful default" none the less valuable (at 583).
4 (1889) 14 App Cas 337.
5 At 434.
6 [1927] 1 Ch 262.
7 At 274.

completely unjustified. Romer J was construing a particular set of articles of association and the decision on the facts of *Re City Equitable* was to have no application to the case of trustees, *stricto sensu*. This, indeed, was the view of Warrington LJ, in the Court of Appeal, in that case, and his approval of Romer J's definition, quoted by Astbury J in the above passage, was a strictly limited approval. The following extract from the learned Lord Justice's judgment is relevant.[8]

'With all respect to counsel who cited those trustee cases to us, I think there is great danger of being misled if we attempt to apply decisions as to the duties of trustees to a case as to the conduct of persons in the position of auditors in this case. In the case of trustees there are certain definite and precise rules of law as to what a trustee may or may not do in the execution of his trust, and it is no answer for a trustee to say, if, for example, he invests the trust property in his hands, in a security which the law regards as an unauthorised security: 'I honestly believed that I was justified in doing that.' No honest belief will justify him in committing that which is a breach of such a rule of law, and therefore the question which we have to determine in expressing a view on the construction of such words in a contract like the present is not solved by seeing how the question has been determined in a case relating to the duties of a trustee.'

In effect, neither Romer J nor the Court of Appeal in *Re City Equitable* intended to derogate from the pre-1926 decisions, which, impliedly if not expressly, interpreted the words 'wilful default', within section 24 of the 1893 Act, so as to include lack of reasonable care. Section 30 (1) is a mere re-enactment of section 24 of the Trustee Act 1893, and like that section should, it is submitted, render the trustee liable if he failed to act with reasonable care.[9]

The delegation sections—a suggested interpretation

It must be remembered in construing the Trustee Act 1925, that primarily it 'is a Consolidation Act' and that it is 'therefore extremely unlikely, to say the least of it, that it effected any substantial change in the pre-existing law'.[10] If a literal interpretation of the delegation sections leads to conflict between these sections, then the sections should be narrowly construed in accordance with the pre-1926 law, and, in particular, the principles laid down in *Speight v Gaunt*.

For reasons just set out, it is suggested that section 30 (1) should be regarded as a re-enactment of section 24 of the 1893 Act and interpreted accordingly. Sections 23 (2) and 25 present no great difficulty. They were enacted to meet the case of the trustee being absent from the United Kingdom or where the trust property was abroad, and for these special reasons the trustee is permitted to delegate his discretions. Sections 23 (2) and 25 do not, however, allow the trustee to rid himself of his trusteeship; he should still exercise, as far as is reasonably possible, an anxious surveillance over the trust interests, and his liability for his agent's defaults should be judged by the norm of the reasonable

---

8 *Re City Equitable Fire Insurance Co Ltd* [1925] Ch 407 at 523–524.
9 See [1979] Conv 345 (J.E. Stannard) for a detailed review of "wilful default", showing that it is used in two senses: (*a*) at common law as "intentional misconduct" in contract cases or other similar instances (*b*) in equity as "failure to do what is reasonable" in the construction of a trustee indemnity clause and in cases involving a liability to account on the basis of wilful default. See also *Re Tebbs* [1976] 1 WLR 924, [1976] 2 All ER 858; [1989] Conv 42 at pp. 44–46 (P. Matthews).
10 ROMER J in *Re Turner's Will Trusts* [1937] Ch 15 at 24.

business man, the same standard as is imposed on bankers and solicitors by the proviso to section 23 (3). But what of section 23 (1)? If the *Re Vickery* interpretation is unacceptable, what is the scope of section 23 (1)? The words of the section are sweeping and it is probable that the section does at least remove the limitation imposed on the trustee's power to delegate by the decision in *ex p Belchier*[11]—a trustee can now delegate even though there is no legal or moral necessity so to do. In our submission the subsection does no more. A trustee should not, by means of an honest appointment, be able to ignore with complacency the activities of his agent; his liability for that agent's acts or defaults should still be determined by the rule in *Speight v Gaunt* and the norm of the reasonable man of business. Such an interpretation would afford meaning to section 23 (1) and would reconcile the section with the remaining delegation sections of the Trustee Act 1925, and, in particular, section 30 (1).

It must be admitted, however, that section 23 (1) is open to an alternative construction, namely, that the words 'in good faith' qualify not only the *act* of employment but the defaults of the agent once appointed. The section, in fact, concludes with the words, that the trustee 'shall not be responsible for the default of any such agent if employed in good faith'. If this interpretation is given to the section, then section 23 (1) can be reconciled with the other delegation sections only by interpreting 'in good faith' restrictively, so as to mean in good-faith and without negligence. Eve J in *Re Greenwood*[12] was required to consider section 21 (2) of the Trustee Act 1893, and adopted a similar construction. This section, which was concerned with the composition of debts, laid down that the trustee was not responsible 'for any loss occasioned by any act or thing so done by him or them in good faith.' His Lordship commented upon these words as follows:[13]

> 'The question whether that section applies turns mainly on the proper meaning to be attributed to the concluding words of the subsection I have read. They seem to involve the doing of some act, or at least the exercise of some active discretion on the part of the trustee, not the mere passive attitude of leaving matters alone. Inaction ... cannot be the same thing as 'an act or thing done in good faith ...' In determining, therefore, whether the conduct of the trustees has or has not been *bona fide* in any particular case, the court is bound to have regard to all the circumstances, and if these lead to the conclusion that the loss has arisen from the neglect or carelessness or supineness of the trustee, and not from a mistaken but bona fide exercise by him of the statutory powers vested in him, then, in my opinion, the case is outside the subsection altogether, and in respect of which no relief is thereby afforded to the trustee.'

The Court of Appeal has recently adopted a similar approach in a decision, involving consideration of section 72 of the National Health Service Act 1946.[14] Such an interpretation is not as radical, therefore, as it may seem at first.

In conclusion, it is to be noted that section 23 (1) speaks simply of the liability of the trustee for the acts of his *agent*, and the section concludes that the trustee shall 'not be responsible for the default of any such agent if employed in good faith.' The section does not deal with responsibility, which

---

11 (1754) Amb 218. It is suggested that the *Belchier* principle does not limit ss. 23 (2) and 25.
12 (1911) 105 LT 509.
13 At 514.
14 In *Bullard v Croydon Hospital Group Management Committee* [1953] 1 QB 511, [1953] 1 All ER 596.

the *trustee* himself assumed when he undertook the trust. Thus, in *Re Vickery* Maugham J was concerned with liability of the trustee for the act of the solicitor, and not with the question whether the trustee was in breach of his own *primary* duty as trustee to supervise the trust, and, in particular, his agents. What norm is to determine if the trustee has properly supervised the acts of his agents? The reasonable business man of *Speight v Gaunt?* If this be the standard, and it is suggested that it is, then the decision in *Re Vickery* is effectively circumscribed. The judgment of the trustee must be constantly exercised. To exercise this judgment, as a reasonable trustee should, will demand that the trustee appoints an agent to do work which he is qualified to do, to appoint a solicitor as a solicitor, a broker as a broker,[15] and, after the appointment of such agents, to supervise their acts. A trustee cannot give an agent a carte blanche. This 'primary' liability of the trustee is independent of his vicarious liability for the acts or defaults of his agent, and it is with this latter head of liability that section 23 (1) is concerned.[16] It is suggested, therefore, that it is open for the courts to hold that the trustee has a primary duty, imposed on him by equity, to supervise at all times the trust and the trust funds; and it is further submitted that the norm of the reasonable man of business will determine whether in fact he has discharged that duty.''

B. Law Reform

Law Reform Committee 23rd Report (The Powers and Duties of Trustees) 1982 Cmnd 8733, paras. 4.6–8, 10, 11, 19.[17]

"4.6 We think that section 23 (1) should be qualified in such a way that a trustee can only charge the trust fund for the services of a delegate when those charges have been reasonably incurred. To this end we suggest that the subsection be rephrased, with the words 'and pay . . . ' being omitted, so that it reads as follows:

'Trustees or personal representatives may, instead of acting personally, employ [and pay] an agent, whether a solicitor, banker, stockbroker, or other person to transact any business or do any act required to be transacted or done in the execution of the trust, or the administration of the testator's or intestate's estate, including the receipt and payment of money . . . '

The sub-section should continue to the effect that the trustee or personal representative should nevertheless only be entitled to be allowed and paid all such charges and expenses of delegation as are reasonably incurred, taking

---

15 But see MAUGHAM J in *Re Vickery*, at 581.
16 Cf. the words of s. 30 (1), which gives the trustee an indemnity, unless "the same happens through his own wilful default". The master and servant cases in tort are, of course, an obvious parallel: see *Gold v Essex County Council* [1942] 2 KB 293, [1942] 2 All ER 237; *Carmarthenshire County Council v Lewis* [1955] AC 549, [1955] 1 All ER 565; *Staveley Iron and Chemical Co Ltd v Jones* [1956] AC 627, [1956] 1 All ER 403. The analogy is only a limited one.
17 See (1983) 133 NLJ 1095 (C.T. Emery); Law Commission Thirtieth Annual Report 1996 (Law Com No. 239), para. 5.18.

into account the trustee's knowledge, qualifications and experience and the level of remuneration received by him.

4.7   The effect of the statutory powers of delegation contained in the Trustee Act 1925 on the overall responsibilities of trustees, and in particular the extent of their liability for acts done by their agents, is a matter of some dispute. The question turns on the construction of section 23 (1) and section 30 (1) ...

4.8   *Re Vickery* has been the subject of considerable academic criticism and some writers have suggested that the judge was wrong in adopting that particular definition of wilful default. It has often been pointed out that the exemption from liability in the concluding phrase of section 23 (1) applies only to trustees' vicarious liability and not to their primary duties of managing the affairs of the trust, taking decisions and supervising the work of agents to whom proper delegation has been made. This view is not inconsistent with anything that Maugham J actually said in *Re Vickery* and is, if anything, supported by the decision of Cross J in *Re Lucking's Will Trusts*, where it was held that in the employment of agents, trustees must act as ordinary prudent men of business and that part of that duty is the adequate supervision of their agents' activities. ...

4.10   Section 23 (1) is concerned with the trustee's vicarious liability for the misfeasances of his agent, where that agent has not been employed in good faith. Section 30 (1), on the other hand, is concerned with the primary liability of the trustee where loss has been caused to the trust fund by the acts of other persons and, had it not been for the trustee's own wilful default, the loss could have been prevented. We are satisfied that the 'wilful default' test is the correct one to apply in this situation. A trustee should be liable for loss caused by the actions of another person where the trustee has connived at those actions in some way: in other words, where his default has been wilful.

4.11   We think that the standard of care presently found in section 23 (1) is not stringent enough. At the moment a trustee is not held responsible for the default of his agent where the agent has been employed in good faith. We consider that a trustee who has delegated some of his responsibilities should be expected to keep a check on the actions of his agent. To this end, we have considered whether the same kind of test should be used in relation to a trustee's liability for his agent as is provided in section 2 (4) (*b*) of the Occupiers' Liability Act 1957 in relation to an occupier's liability for his contractor. We think that this provision forms a suitable model and that the final phrase of section 23 (1), which provides that a trustee 'shall not be responsible for the default of any such agent if employed in good faith' should be replaced by a provision to the effect that a trustee shall escape responsibility for the default of his agent only where it was reasonable for him to employ an agent, where he has taken reasonable steps to ensure that the agent employed is competent and where he has taken reasonable steps to ensure that the agent's work has been done competently.

4.19   We understand that some doubt exists about the question whether a delegate under section 25 can properly be paid for his services. We take the view that there is a strong case for removing any doubt about this matter and we therefore recommend that section 25 be amended so that trustees are entitled to be allowed any expenses reasonably incurred in remunerating a delegate employed under the provisions of the section."

C. Enduring Powers of Attorney Act 1985[18]

ENDURING POWERS OF ATTORNEY ACT 1985

2. Characteristics of an enduring power.—

(8) A power of attorney under section 25 of the Trustee Act 1925 (power to delegate trusts etc. by power of attorney) cannot be an enduring power.

3. Scope of authority etc of attorney under enduring power.—

(3) Subject to any conditions or restrictions contained in the instrument, an attorney under an enduring power, whether general or limited, may (without obtaining any consent) execute or exercise all or any of the trusts, powers or discretions vested in the donor as trustee and may (without the concurrence of any other person) give a valid receipt for capital or other money paid.

Hansbury & Martin, *Modern Equity* (14th edn, 1993), pp. 558–559

"Until recently there was no possibility of a power of attorney which would continue in force after the donor had become mentally incapable, as such incapacity automatically revoked the power. Now the Enduring Powers of Attorney Act 1985 permits the creation of a power of attorney which will survive the donor's subsequent incapacity.

This Act is relevant to trustees in two respects. First, [section 2 (8)] provides that a power of attorney under section 25 of the Trustee Act 1925 cannot be an enduring power. The reasoning here is that mental incapacity is a ground for replacing a trustee.[19] Secondly, and inconsistently with the latter point, section 3 (3) of the 1985 Act provides that the donee of an enduring power of attorney may 'execute or exercise all or any of the trusts, powers or discretions vested in the donor as trustee' and may give a valid receipt for capital money. Thus a trustee cannot create an enduring power under section 25 of the 1925 Act, but such a power may be created under the 1985 Act.

The purpose of section 3 (3) was to enable a trustee of a house under a co-ownership trust for sale to delegate the power to execute a conveyance of the house to his co-trustee in such a way that the subsequent incapacity of the delegating trustee would not terminate the power.[20] The subsection, however, is not limited to this situation,[1] and appears to permit a trustee to delegate all his functions indefinitely.[2] The execution of an enduring power of attorney will have this effect whether or not the trustee has considered the matter. Unlike section 25, delegation to the only other co-trustee is permitted, there is no time limit, and no requirement of notice to co-trustees. The rule requiring

---

18 See generally Cretney, *Enduring Powers of Attorney* (3rd edn, 1991).

19 See Law Commission Report: *The Incapacitated Principal* 1983 (Law Com. No. 122), para 4.2. The 12 month limit under s. 25 would in any event have made the concept of an enduring power under s. 25 of little use. See also LPA 1925, s. 22 (2) (mentally incapacitated trustee for sale to be discharged).

20 This overcomes difficulties illustrated by *Walia v Michael Naughton Ltd* [1985] 1 WLR 1115, [1985] 3 All ER 673.

1 For the view that it is impliedly so limited, see (1990) 106 LQR 87 at 89 (D. Hayton).

2 See (1986) 130 SJ 23 (R.T. Oerton); (1986) 1 *Trust Law and Practice* 54. The provision was added by the Lord Chancellor's Department after the *Walia* decision, and was not considered by the Law Commission.

payment of capital money to two trustees is also ousted. If this is correct, section 3 (3) is a 'legislative blunder.'[3] If a trustee wants to delegate for more than 12 months and may become incompetent, he should retire. The matter is presently under review by the Law Commission.[4]"

In 1994 the Law Commission Report on Delegation by Individual Trustees (Law Com No. 220) recommended that

(a) section 3 (3) should be repealed.[5]

"In general trustee cases (i.e. where trustees hold the property only for third parties) we should revert to the position that individual trustees who wish to delegate their functions should be governed by section 25, which offers greater safeguards for the trust beneficiaries" (para 4.1.)

(b) it should be made clear that the statutory rules which require two trustees to receive trust money, and related provisions,[6] should not be satisfied by one person alone (other than a trust corporation). But a trustee and an attorney for another trustee, or joint attorneys for more than one trustee, should suffice" (para. 4.15).

D. Pensions Funds

PENSIONS ACT 1995

34. Power of investment and delegation—

(2) Any discretion of the trustees of a trust scheme to make any decision about investments—

(a) may be delegated by or on behalf of the trustees to a fund manager to whom subsection (3) applies to be exercised in accordance with section 36,[7] but

(b) may not otherwise be delegated except under section 25 of the Trustee Act 1925 (delegation of trusts during absence abroad) or subsection (5) below.

(3) This subsection applies to a fund manager who, in relation to the decisions in question, falls, or is treated as falling, within any of paragraphs (a) to (c) of section 191 (2) of the Financial Services Act 1986 (occupational pension schemes: exemptions where decisions taken by authorised and other persons).

(4) The trustees are not responsible for the act or default of any fund manager in the exercise of any discretion delegated to him under subsection (2) (a) if they have taken all such steps as are reasonable to satisfy themselves or the person who made the delegation on their behalf has taken all such steps as are reasonable to satisfy himself—

(a) that the fund manager has the appropriate knowledge and experience for managing the investments of the scheme, and

---

3 (1986) 130 SJ 23 at 25; (1988) 85 LS Gaz. No. 19, p. 4.
4 Law Commission Consultation Paper, *The Law of Trusts: Delegation by Individual Trustees* 1991 (Law Com. No. 118).
5 See also Law Commission Report on Mental Incapacity 1995 (Law Com. No. 231), para. 7.2.
6 SLA 1925, ss. 18 (1) (*c*) (capital money); TA 1925, s. 14 (2) (receipts); LPA 1925 ss. 2 (1) (ii) (overreaching); 27 (2) (payment of proceeds of sale).
7 P. 707, ante.

(b) that he is carrying out his work competently and complying with section 36.[7]

(5) Subject to any restriction imposed by a trust scheme—

(a) the trustees may authorise two or more of their number to exercise on their behalf any discretion to make any decision about investments, and

(b) any such discretion may, where giving effect to the decision would not constitute carrying on investment business in the United Kingdom (within the meaning of the Financial Services Act 1986), be delegated by or on behalf of the trustees to a fund manager to whom subsection (3) does not apply to be exercised in accordance with section 36;

but in either case the trustees are liable for any acts or defaults in the exercise of the discretion if they would be so liable if they were the acts or defaults of the trustees as a whole.

(6) Section 33[7a] does not prevent the exclusion or restriction of any liability of the trustees of a trust scheme for the acts or defaults of a fund manager in the exercise of a discretion delegated to him under subsection (5) (b) where the trustees have taken all such steps as are reasonable to satisfy themselves, or the person who made the delegation on their behalf has taken all such steps as are reasonable to satisfy himself—

(a) that the fund manager has the appropriate knowledge and experience for managing the investments of the scheme, and

(b) that he is carrying out his work competently and complying with section 36

and subsection (2) of section 33 applies for the purposes of this subsection as it applies for the purposes of that section.

(7) The provisions of this section override any restriction inconsistent with the provisions imposed by any rule of law or by or under any enactment, other than an enactment contained in, or made under, this Part or the Pension Schemes Act 1993.

QUESTION

How should the power of delegation be reformed? How far should the provisions for pension funds under the Pensions Act 1995 be reflected in the general trust law on this topic?
Law Reform Committee 23rd Report (The Powers and Duties of Trustees) Cmnd 8733 paras. 4.6–8, 10, 11, 19; p. 757 ante; Pensions Act 1995, s. 34, p. 760, supra.

VIII. Power of Maintenance[8]

The statutory power of maintenance gives to trustees a power to apply income for the benefit of beneficiaries who are minors, or who are not yet entitled to the income. Minors and persons contingently entitled would otherwise be

---

7a P. 760, ante.
8 H & M, pp. 559–566; K & S, pp. 323–330; P & M, pp. 490–501; Pettit, pp. 447–453; Riddall, pp. 301–312; Snell, pp. 274–282; Underhill, pp. 689–698. See generally (1953) 17 Conv (NS) 273 (B.S. Ker).

unable to benefit from the income. The policy is to allow the gift to "carry the intermediate income" unless the income is otherwise disposed of, or there are good reasons to the contrary. Thus, the trustees may apply the income for the maintenance, education and benefit of minor beneficiaries; and are required to pay the income to adult persons who are contingently entitled to the capital on the happening of some future event.

A. The Statutory Power
TRUSTEE ACT 1925

31. Power to apply income for maintenance and to accumulate surplus income during a minority.—(1) Where any property is held by trustees in trust for any person for any interest whatsoever, whether vested or contingent, then, subject to any prior interests or charges affecting that property—
  (i) during the infancy of any such person, if his interest so long continues, the trustees may, at their sole discretion, pay to his parent or guardian, if any, or otherwise apply for or towards his maintenance, education, or benefit, the whole or such part, if any, of the income of that property as may, in all the circumstances, be reasonable, whether or not there is—
  (*a*) any other fund applicable to the same purpose; or
  (*b*) any person bound by law to provide for his maintenance or education; and
  (ii) if such person on attaining the age of eighteen years has not a vested interest in such income, the trustees shall thenceforth pay the income of that property and of any accretion thereto under subsection (2) of this section to him, until he either attains a vested interest therein or dies, or until failure of his interest:
Provided that, in deciding whether the whole or any part of the income of the property is during a minority to be paid or applied for the purposes aforesaid, the trustees shall have regard to the age of the infant and his requirements and generally to the circumstances of the case, and in particular to what other income, if any, is applicable for the same purposes; and where trustees have notice that the income of more than one fund is applicable for those purposes, then, so far as practicable, unless the entire income of the funds is paid or applied as aforesaid or the court otherwise directs, a proportionate part only of the income of each fund shall be so paid or applied.
  (2) During the infancy of any such person, if his interest so long continues, the trustees shall accumulate all the residue of that income in the way of compound interest by investing the same and the resulting income thereof from time to time in authorised investments, and shall hold those accumulations as follows:—
  (i) If any such person—
  (*a*) attains the age of eighteen[9] years, or marries under that age, and his interest in such income during his infancy or until his marriage is a vested interest; or

---

9 Reduced from 21 by Family Law Reform Act 1969 in the case of instruments made (not only those coming into effect) on or after January 1, 1970. A will made before that date is not to be treated as made on or after that date by reason only that the will is confirmed by a codicil executed on or after that date; s. 1, and Sch. 3, para. 5. See *Begg-McBrearty v Stilwell* (1996) Times, 15 March.

(*b*) on attaining the age of eighteen[9] years or on marriage under that
age becomes entitled to the property from which such income
arose in fee simple, absolute or determinable[10] or absolutely, or for
an entailed interest;

the trustees shall hold the accumulations in trust for such person
absolutely, but without prejudice to any provision with respect thereto
contained in any settlement by him made under any statutory powers
during his infancy, and so that the receipt of such person after
marriage, and though still an infant, shall be a good discharge; and

(ii) In any other case the trustees shall, notwithstanding that such person
had a vested interest in such income, hold the accumulations as an
accretion to the capital of the property from which such accumulations
arose, and as one fund with such capital for all purposes, and so that, if
such property is settled land, such accumulations shall be held upon the
same trusts as if the same were capital money arising therefrom;

but the trustees may, at any time during the infancy of such person if his
interest so long continues, apply those accumulations, or any part thereof, as if
they were income arising in the then current year.

(3) This section applies in the case of a contingent interest only if the
limitation or trust carries the intermediate income of the property, but it
applies to a future or contingent legacy by the parent of, or a person standing
in loco parentis to, the legatee, if and for such period as, under the general law,
the legacy carries interest for the maintenance of the legatee, and in any such
case as last aforesaid the rate of interest shall (if the income available is
sufficient, and subject to any rules of court to the contrary) be five pounds per
centum per annum.

(4) This section applies to a vested annuity in like manner as if the annuity
were the income of property held by trustees in trust to pay the income thereof
to the annuitant for the same period for which the annuity is payable, save that
in any case accumulations made during the infancy of the annuitant shall be
held in trust for the annuitant or his personal representatives absolutely.

(5) This section does not apply where the instrument, if any, under which the
interest arises came into operation before the commencement of this Act.

B. Contrary Intention

TRUSTEE ACT 1925

69. Application of Act.—(2) p. 762 ante.

In **Re Turner's Will Trust** [1937] Ch 15, [1936] 2 All ER 1435, Robert Turner,
the testator, gave a share of his residuary estate in trust for such of the children
of his late son Charles as should attain the age of 28 years. The will contained
an express power of maintenance and a power to pay the income to such of
them as shall have attained the age of 21 years, and instructed the trustees to
accumulate the surplus.

Two of the testator's grandchildren had attained the age of 28 years at the
testator's death. The third grandchild, Geoffrey, was then aged 21, and died

---

10 *Re Sharp's Settlement Trusts* [1973] Ch 331, [1972] 3 All ER 151; (1974) 34 Conv (NS) 436 (D.J.
Hayton).

three years later. His share of the income had all been accumulated. The question was whether he had been entitled to such income under Trustee Act 1925, s. 31. If so, the fund would pass on his death for estate duty purposes.

The Court of Appeal, reversing BENNETT J, held that Geoffrey had not been entitled to the income. The imperative terms of s. 31 must be read subject to s. 69 (2), so that the contrary intention prevailed. ROMER LJ said at 27, at 1447:

"The fact that s. 31 contains provisions that are directory is immaterial. Powers of maintenance, in the comprehensive meaning of that term, usually do. Nothing is more common, for instance, than a direction to trustees to accumulate during the minority income not applied in maintenance. Such a direction is merely ancillary to the power of maintenance strictly so called, and may well be regarded as a part of the power of maintenance in its comprehensive sense. Such a direction is indeed contained in sub-s. 2 of s. 31 of the Trustee Act, 1925, and is an essential part of the statutory power of maintenance conferred upon trustees by the section. In the same way the direction contained in cl. (ii) of sub-s. 1 can be regarded as being merely an essential part of the new statutory power. This statutory power of maintenance, that is to say, the totality of the provisions to be found in s. 31 of the Act, is, in our opinion, one of the 'powers conferred by this Act' within the meaning of s. 69, sub-s. 2, and therefore only applies if and so far as a contrary intention is not expressed in the instrument creating the trust and has effect subject to the terms of that instrument. For these reasons we are of opinion that the accumulations of the income of the presumptive share of Geoffrey Heap Turner made by the trustees did not form part of his estate, but accrued by way of addition to the shares of the defendants Robert Heap Turner and Doris Heap Lyons in the residuary estate of the testator."[11]

C. Intermediate Income[12]

(1953) 17 Conv (NS) pp. 275–276 (B.S. Ker)

"The question now arises as to when a 'limitation or trust' carries the intermediate income of the property. The rules are as follows:

1. A contingent gift by will of *residuary* personalty carries with it all the income it earns from the testator's death, for the simple reason that there is no one besides the residuary legatee to whom it could go. North J said in *Re Adams* [1893] 1 Ch 329, at 334, 'Here no child has [a vested interest in the residue]. How does the matter stand as to the income? It is said that they take an interest in that also. I think it is fallacious to say that they take an interest in the income, *qua* income of the capital they take an interest in. *But it is undisposed-of income, and as such becomes part of the residue*; but, being part of the residue, the income belongs contingently to the children, in the same way as the capital belongs contingently to them.' If this income is accumulated until the contingency vesting the money in the beneficiaries happens the rules in sections 164–166 of

---

11 Followed in *Re Erskine's Settlement Trusts* [1971] 1 WLR 162, [1971] 1 All ER 572.
12 For a tabular presentation, see (1976) 95 Law Notes 110 (M.J. Wells).

the Law of Property Act, 1925, must be observed. (See *Bective v Hodgson* (1864) 10 HL Cas 656.)

2. The rule as to contingent *specific* gifts of personalty and contingent specific or residuary gifts of realty is contained in section 175 of the Law of Property Act, 1925: 'A contingent or future specific devise or bequest of property, whether real or personal, and a contingent residuary devise of freehold land, and a specific or residuary devise of freehold land to trustees upon trust for persons whose interests are contingent or executory shall, subject to the statutory provisions relating to accumulations, carry the intermediate income of that property from the death of the testator, except so far as such income, or any part thereof, may be otherwise expressly disposed of.' This section applies only to *wills* coming into operation after 1925, but it has been held in *Re Raine* [1929] 1 Ch 716, not to apply to a pecuniary legacy. Further, it draws a distinction between 'land' and 'freehold' land. This is because leaseholds rank as personal property and therefore the ordinary rules (supra and infra) as to the income of contingent gifts of personalty apply: see *Guthrie v Walrond* (1883) 22 ChD 573, and *Re Woodin* [1895] 2 Ch 309, per Lindley LJ and Kay LJ.

Pecuniary Legacies

3. In view of the decision on *Re Raine* (supra) the rules of the general law as to when contingent pecuniary legacies bear interest require examination. The broad rule is that no interest is payable on a contingent pecuniary legacy from the testator's death while the gift is in suspense (see per Kay LJ, in *Re George* (1877) 5 ChD 837). There are, however, the following exceptions in which the legacy, subject to any contrary intention in the will, carries interest from the testator's death ...

Summarising, then: the three cases in which, apart from statute, contingent legacies carry interest from the date of death are—

(*a*) where the testator was the father of, or *in loco parentis* to, the legatee,

(*b*) where, without being either of the foregoing, the testator shows an intention to maintain (*Re Churchill* [1909] 2 Ch 431), or

(*c*) where the testator has segregated the legacy for the legatee (*Re Medlock* (1886) 55 LJ Ch 738).

It will be noticed that section 31 (3) of the Trustee Act, 1925, expressly mentions the rule in (*a*) only—the golden rule. Does it impliedly exclude the rules in (*b*) and (*c*), or does it merely single out that in (*a*) for the purpose of fixing interest at 5 per cent. per annum? If it excludes (*b*) and (*c*) then section 31 will not apply at all to cases of the *Re Churchill* and *Re Medlock* kinds and this would need to be borne in mind when considering, in particular, subsection (1) (ii) and (2). The arguments both ways have already been set out (p. 275, ante). It is submitted that the correct view is that subsection (3) does embrace the *Re Churchill* and *Re Medlock* types of case and that the specific mention of the rule in (*a*) above is only for the purpose of establishing a suitable rate of interest. The learned author of Williams on Wills (p. 803) seems to take this view.

Before leaving subsection (3) it may be worth noticing that while the rule— (*a*) above—of the general law is that the donor of the legacy must be the *father* of the legatee, the statute, in adopting the rule has used the word 'parent' instead of father. At common law, of course, it is the father's duty to maintain his child—not the mother's unless she has deliberately taken upon herself a father's duty. Section 31 (3) may thus have enlarged the law here to cover a legacy by a mother not *in loco parentis*. However, the term 'parent' would probably be held to mean 'parent responsible in law for the children's maintenance' and thus refer only to the legatee's father, unless the mother had assumed the duty of maintenance."

In **Re McGeorge** [1963] Ch 544, [1963] 1 All ER 519,[13] the testator devised land to his daughter and provided that the devise "shall not take effect until after the death of my ... wife should she survive me". If the daughter should die before the wife, leaving issue, the issue, on attaining the age of 21, were to take by substitution the devise to the daughter. CROSS J held that the devise to the daughter carried the intermediate income; that the income must be accumulated, to be paid to whoever became entitled to it—that is, the daughter or her issue, depending on whether the daughter survived the widow. CROSS J said at 550, at 522:

"The devise ... is, it is said, a future specific devise within the meaning of the section [LPA 1925, s. 175]; the testator has not made any express disposition of the income accruing from it between his death and the death of his widow, therefore that income is carried by the gift. At first sight it is hard to see how Parliament could have enacted a section which produces such a result. If a testator gives property to A after the death of B, then whether or not he disposes of the income accruing during B's life he is at all events showing clearly that A is not to have it. Yet if the future gift to A is absolute and the intermediate income is carried with it by force of this section, A can claim to have the property transferred to him at once, since no one else can be interested in it. The section, that is to say, will have converted a gift in remainder into a gift in possession in defiance of the testator's wishes. The explanation for the section taking the form it does is, I think, probably as follows. It has long been established that a gift of residuary personalty to a legatee in being on a contingency or to an unborn person at birth, carries the intermediate income so far as the law will allow it to be accumulated, but that rule had been held for reasons depending on the old land law not to apply to gifts of real property, and it was apparently never applied to specific dispositions of personalty. Section 175 of the Law of Property Act was plainly intended to extend the rule to residuary devises and to specific gifts whether of realty or of personalty. It is now, however, established at all events in courts of first instance that the old rule does not apply to residuary bequests whether vested or contingent which are expressly deferred to a future date which must come sooner or later. (See *Re Oliver* [1947] 2 All ER 162, *Re Gillett's Will Trusts* [1950] Ch 102, [1949] 2 All ER 893, and *Re Geering* [1964] Ch 136, [1962] 3 All ER 1043). There is a good reason for this distinction. If a testator gives property to X contingently on his attaining the age of 30 it is reasonable to assume, in the absence of a direction to the contrary, that he would wish X if he attains 30 to have the income produced by the property between his death and the happening of the contingency. If, on the other hand, he gives property to X for any sort of interest after the death of A, it is reasonable to assume that he does not wish X to have the income accruing during A's lifetime unless he directs that he is to have it. But this distinction between an immediate gift on a contingency and a gift which is expressly deferred was not drawn until after the

Law of Property Act, 1925, was passed. There were statements in textbooks and even in judgments to the effect that the rule applied to deferred as well as to contingent gifts of residuary personalty. (See Jarman, 7th edn (1930) p. 1006).

The legislature, when it extended this rule to residuary devises and specific gifts, must, I think, have adopted this erroneous view of the law. I would have liked, if I could, to construe the reference to 'future specific devises' and 'executory interest' in the section in such a way as to make it consistent with the recent cases on the scope of the old rule applicable to residuary bequests. But to do that would be to rectify the Act, not to construe it, and I see no escape from the conclusion that whereas before 1926 a specific gift or a residuary devise which was not vested in possession did not prima facie carry intermediate income at all, now such a gift may carry intermediate income in circumstances in which a residuary bequest would not carry it.

It was argued in this case that the fact that the will contained a residuary gift constituted an express disposition of the income of the land in question which prevented the section from applying. I am afraid that I cannot accept this submission. I have little doubt that the testator expected the income of the land to form part of the income of residue during his widow's lifetime, but he has made no express disposition of it. I agree with what was said in this connection by Eve J in *Re Raine* [1929] 1 Ch 716 at 719.

As the devise is not vested indefeasibly in the daughter but is subject to defeasance during the mother's lifetime the intermediate income which the gift carries by virtue of section 175 ought prima facie to be accumulated to see who eventually becomes entitled to it. It was, however, submitted by counsel for the daughter that she could claim payment of it under section 31 (1) of the Trustee Act 1925. So far as material, that subsection provides that where any property is held by trustees in trust for any person for any interest whatsoever, whether vested or contingent, then, subject to any prior interests or charges affecting that property, if such person on attaining the age of 21 years has not a vested interest in such income, the trustees shall thenceforth pay the income of that property and of any accretion of such income made during his infancy to him until he either attains a vested interest therein or dies or until failure of his interest. There are, as I see it, two answers to the daughter's claim. The first—and narrower—answer is that her interest in the income of the devised land is in a vested interest. It is a future interest liable to be divested but it is not contingent. Therefore, section 31 (1) (ii) does not apply to it. The second—and wider—answer is that the whole framework of section 31 shows that it is inapplicable to a future gift of this sort and that a will containing such a gift expresses a contrary intention within section 69 (2) which prevents the section from applying. By deferring the enjoyment of the devise until after the widow's death the testator has expressed the intention that the daughter shall not have the immediate income. It is true that as he has not expressly disposed of it in any other way, section 175 of the Law of Property Act, 1925, defeats that intention to the extent of making the future devise carry the income so that the daughter will get it eventually if she survives her mother or dies before her leaving no children to take by substitution. But even if the words of section 31 fitted the case, there would be no warrant for defeating the testator's intention still further by reading it into the will and thus giving the daughter an interest in possession in the income during her mother's lifetime. In the result, in my judgment the income of the fund must be accumulated for 21 years if the widow so long lives.''

D. Tax Considerations

i. INCOME TAX

(a) Maintenance payments

Sums applied for the maintenance, education or benefit of a minor beneficiary form part of his total income.[14] Such sums are accordingly grossed up at the basic and additional rates in force during the appropriate year, which is the year when the money is applied and not the year in which it arose.

Where the minor beneficiary is an unmarried child of the settlor, any income paid to or applied for his benefit is treated for basic and higher rate purposes as the income of the settlor.[15]

There are further provisions dealing with cases where income is retained or accumulated, the broad effect of which is that any payment whatsoever made thereafter to or for the benefit of an unmarried minor child of the settlor is treated as income of the settlor if, or to the extent that, there is then available retained or accumulated income.[16]

(b) Accumulated income

Generally, where trust income is accumulated, the trustees are liable to the additional rate of 10% as well as to the basic rate of tax.[17] However, the treatment of undistributed income depends upon whether a minor beneficiary has a vested or contingent interest in the capital. For instance, income to which a child is indefeasibly entitled, albeit accumulated pending the attainment of his majority, forms part of his total income year by year as it arises.[18] The test is simply whether the income would be his income now but for the fact that, because of minority, he cannot give a good receipt for it.[19]

If the child has a vested interest in income only, for example, if he is a life tenant, the effect of section 31 (2) of the Trustee Act 1925 (unless amended by the trust instrument)[1] is to place him, for all practical purposes, in precisely the same position as if his interest in surplus income were contingent. If his interest in capital is contingent, his interest in the trust income during minority must also be contingent. The trustees are then liable for the additional rate as well as for the basic rate. On attaining his majority, he may become entitled to the trust capital, in which case accumulated income will pass to him as capital not income.[2] If he does not then obtain a vested interest

---

14 *IRC v Blackwell* [1926] 1 KB 389; *Hood-Barrs v IRC* [1946] 2 All ER 768; *Arthur d'Abreu v IRC* [1978] STC 538; *Drummond v Collins* [1915] AC 1011.

15 ICTA 1988, ss. 660 B, p. 556, ante. Both income settlements (i.e. transfers under deed of covenant) and capital settlements are caught. There is a de minimis exception where the child's income does not exceed £100 per annum: s. 660 B (5). "Child" includes a step-child and an illegitimate child: s. 660 B (6). "Settlement" is defined to include any disposition, trust, covenant, agreement, arrangement or transfer of assets: s. 660 G (1).

16 Ibid., s. 660 B (2), (3).

17 Ibid., s. 686.

18 Ibid., s. 686 (2) (*b*); *Stanley v IRC* [1944] KB 255 at 259 per Lord GREENE MR; *IRC v Blackwell*, supra; *IRC v Countess of Longford* [1927] 1 KB 594.

19 Another formulation to the same effect is whether, in the event of the child's death while still a minor, his estate would receive the accumulated income.

1 TA 1925, s. 69 (2).

2 TA 1925, s. 31 (1) (i), (ii).

in the capital, the trust income must be paid to him as of right, until he attains a vested interest or dies or his interest fails, and his income will form part of his total income.

STANLEY v INLAND REVENUE COMMISSIONERS
[1944] KB 255, [1944] 1 All ER 230 (CA, Lord GREENE MR, MacKINNON and GODDARD LJJ)

The appellant had a vested interest as life tenant of a trust fund, the income of which, apart from certain payments for maintenance, accumulated in the hands of the trustees during the four years of his minority. On his attaining majority, the trustees paid the accumulated income to him. The Inland Revenue claimed sur-tax in respect of each year of the minority.
Held. No sur-tax payable on the accumulated income. By virtue of section 31 (2) of the Trustee Act 1925, the income was not the income of the appellant during the four years of his minority.
LORD GREENE MR: If the Crown is right in its claim, it can only be for the reason that assessments could lawfully have been made year by year during the minority of the appellant in respect of the surplus income of the estate and the circumstance that, in the event, he in fact attained his majority is entirely irrelevant. In order that a person may be charged with sur-tax, the income in respect of which he is assessed must be his income. Apart from any special provision in the instrument under which an infant derives his interest and apart from statutory provisions, an infant who has a vested interest in possession is the person entitled to the income. It is his income although he cannot give a good receipt for it. On his death under twenty-one income which has accumulated during his minority goes to his legal personal representatives. In such a case there can be no doubt that the income accruing during minority is the income of the infant. He is, accordingly, chargeable with sur-tax in respect of it. A creditor who has lawfully obtained judgment against the infant, for example in an action of tort, can levy the appropriate form of execution against it. If, on the other hand, the infant is only entitled contingently on his attaining twenty-one he has no title to any income until that event takes place. If the event does take place, he becomes entitled to future income and (in appropriate circumstances) to accumulations of past income, but that past income was not his income in the years in which it accrued, and no one suggests that he could be assessed to sur-tax in respect of it.
[His Lordship quoted Conveyancing Act 1881, s. 42 and Trustee Act 1925, s. 31 (2) which "has effected a radical change in the law", and continued:] Some highly technical arguments were addressed to us on the question what precise interest in surplus income an infant having a vested interest enjoys during his infancy in view of these provisions. This, no doubt, is a relevant question, but the fundamental question remains, namely, is that interest such as to make the surplus income income of the infant for the purposes of sur-tax? It was said on behalf of the Crown that the infant has a vested interest in the surplus income as it accrues and that there is nothing in the section that deprives him of that interest during infancy—all that the section does is to divest him of his title to the accumulations of surplus income if he dies before attaining his majority. In other words, it was said, he has a vested interest in the accumulations which is defeasible in the event of his dying under twenty-one

and, therefore, the surplus income is, during minority, income of the infant and as such is assessable year by year. It is necessary at this point to call attention to a distinction which apparently was not appreciated by the Special Commissioners. The expression "defeasible interest in income" may be used in two senses. In the case of an adult he receives and enjoys the income until the defeasance takes place. Until that event occurs the income is his income and he is assessable accordingly, but the same expression (if it be the correct one to use in reference to surplus income in such a case as the present) means, in the case of an infant in the situation of the appellant, something quite different. The infant does not during infancy enjoy the surplus income. It is not his in any real sense. The title to it is held in suspense to await the event, and if he dies under twenty-one his interest in it (whether or not it be truly described as a vested interest) is destroyed. He is, in fact, for all practical purposes in precisely the same position as if his interest in surplus income were contingent. If he attains twenty-one he takes the accumulations, if he dies under twenty-one he does not, but, as a matter of fact, the section itself does use words of contingency, since the trust of the accumulations is expressed to be for the infant "if he attains the age of twenty-one years or marries under that age". We are disposed to think that the effect of the section is better described, not as leaving the interest of the infant as a vested interest subject to defeasance, but as engrafting on the vested interest originally conferred on the infant by the settlement or other disposition a qualifying trust of a special nature which confers on the infant a title to the accumulations if and only if he attains twenty-one or marries. The words in sub-s. (2) (i) (*a*), "If his interest during infancy or until his marriage is a vested interest"; and the corresponding words in sub-s. 2 (ii), "notwithstanding that 'such person had a vested interest in such income,' appear to us to refer to the nature of the interest conferred upon the infant by the settlement or other disposition and not to affirm that the interest of the infant in the surplus income remains a vested interest notwithstanding the alteration in his rights effected by the section. If this view is right, the interest of the appellant in the surplus income during his minority was a contingent interest only and he was not assessable.

ii. Inheritance Tax

Accumulation and maintenance settlements [3] have been given, as has been seen, a privileged position under the inheritance tax legislation. Although there is no interest in possession pending the vesting of the beneficiary's interest, the settlement is not subjected to the 10-year periodic charge to IHT; nor is there a proportionate charge where the beneficiary becomes entitled to the settled property itself or to an interest in possession therein. Further there is no charge on the death of a beneficiary during the accumulation and maintenance period, or when payments of capital are made to him.[4] For IHT purposes, the property is treated, in effect, as if it was beneficially owned by the minor. Tax will be payable of course on the creation of an accumulation and maintenance settlement, and also if a beneficiary, having attained a vested

---

3 Defined in IHTA 1984, s. 71 (1), (2), p. 598, ante.
4 IHTA 1984, s. 71 (4).

interest determines or assigns that interest[5] or having received the property gives it away.

IX. Power of Advancement[6]

The statutory power of advancement relates to the payment of capital for special purposes. Those purposes related, and until recent times were limited, to specific occasions in the establishment in life of a beneficiary.[7] In modern cases however, a wide construction is given to the phrase "advancement or benefit", and this was used to permit blocks of capital to be paid to contingent remaindermen in order to avoid estate duty liability in respect of that property on the death of a life tenant. The fiscal advantages, which used to be less significant under capital transfer tax, have become more important with its replacement by inheritance tax. When the life tenant's interest determines in his lifetime and the remainderman becomes absolutely entitled, the PET provisions apply, and, accordingly, there is no charge to inheritance tax, unless the life tenant dies within seven years of the termination.[8] Where, however, the property is held on trust for a minor contingently on obtaining a specified age not in excess of 25, and there is no prior interest in possession, there is no charge to tax upon the minor's attainment of that specified age, nor upon payments of capital being made to him.[9]

A. The Statutory Power

TRUSTEE ACT 1925

32. Power of advancement.—(1) Trustees may at any time or times pay or apply any capital money subject to a trust, for the advancement or benefit, in such manner as they may, in their absolute discretion, think fit, of any person entitled to the capital of the trust property or of any share thereof, whether absolutely or contingently on his attaining any specified age or on the occurrence of any other event, or subject to a gift over on his death under any specified age or on the occurrence of any other event, and whether in possession or in remainder or reversion, and such payment or application may be made notwithstanding that the interest of such person is liable to be defeated by the exercise of a power of appointment or revocation, or to be diminished by the increase of the class to which he belongs:

Provided that—

(*a*) the money so paid or applied for the advancement or benefit of any person shall not exceed altogether in amount one-half of the

---

5 Unless in return for another commensurate interest under the trust.
6 H & M, pp. 566–574; K & S, pp. 698–707; P & M, pp. 503–519; Pettit, pp. 454–459; Riddall pp. 296–301; Snell, pp. 279–281; Underhill, pp. 616–625; (1958) 22 Conv (NS) 413; (1959) 23 Conv (NS) 27, 423 (D.W.M. Waters).
7 See *Pilkington v IRC* [1964] AC 612, [1962] 3 All ER 622, p. 772, post.
8 FA (No 2) 1987, s. 96 p. 575, ante.
9 IHTA 1984, s. 71, p. 597, ante. If the specified age exceeds 18, he will, of course, acquire an interest in possession in the trust property on attaining the age of majority, by virtue of TA 1925, s. 31 (1) (ii) (unless amended by the trust instrument), but there is no charge to IHT on this occasion either.

presumptive or vested share or interest of that person in the trust property;[10] and

(*b*) if that person is or becomes absolutely and indefeasibly entitled to a share in the trust property the money so paid or applied shall be brought into account as part of such share; and

(*c*) no such payment or application shall be made so as to prejudice any person entitled to any prior life or other interest, whether vested or contingent, in the money paid or applied unless such person is in existence and of full age and consents in writing to such payment or application.[11]

(2) This section applies only where the trust property consists of money or securities or of property held upon trust for sale calling in and conversion, and such money or securities, or the proceeds, of such sale calling in and conversion are not by statute or in equity considered as land, or applicable as capital money for the purposes of the Settled Land Act, 1925.

(3) This section does not apply to trusts constituted or created before the commencement of this Act.[12]

B. Advancement or Benefit

PILKINGTON v INLAND REVENUE COMMISSIONERS [13]
[1964] AC 612, [1962] 3 All ER 622 (HL, Lord REID, Viscount RADCLIFFE, Lords JENKINS, HODSON and DEVLIN)

William Norman Pilkington, by his will dated December 14, 1934, gave the income of his residuary estate upon trusts for his nephews and nieces (the beneficiaries) in equal shares. Each share was settled on protective trusts, and the will provided that the consent of a beneficiary to the exercise by the trustees of their statutory power of advancement should not cause a forfeiture. The capital was to be held upon trust for the children of each beneficiary in such shares as the beneficiary should appoint, and in default of appointment in equal shares.

---

10 *Re Marquess of Abergavenny's Estate Act Trusts* [1981] 1 WLR 843, [1981] 2 All ER 643 (where trustees had express power to raise and pay to the life tenant "any part or parts not exceeding in all one half in value of the settled fund", GOULDING J held that an advance of one half exhausted the exercise of the power, so that it could not be exercised in the future, even though the retained assets in the fund later increased in value). Cf *Re Richardson* [1896] 1 Ch 512; *Re Gollin's Declaration of Trust* [1969] 1 WLR 1858, [1969] 3 All ER 1591. See [1982] Conv 158 (J.W. Price).

11 *Henley v Wardell* (1988) Times, 29 January (consent of prior beneficiary necessary, even though the statutory power was expressly enlarged so as to give to the trustees "an absolute and uncontrolled discretion" to advance capital for the benefit of a beneficiary).

12 The application of s. 32 is subject to the expression of a contrary intention: *Re Evans' Settlement* [1967] 1 WLR 1294, [1967] 3 All ER 343. But "very few settlements provide that the statutory power is not to apply—though some extend the power or contain express advancement provisions more extended than the statutory power": *Inglewood (Lord) v IRC* [1983] 1 WLR 366 at 373, per Fox LJ.

13 (1963) 27 Conv (NS) 65 (F.R. Crane); *Re Wills' Will Trusts* [1959] Ch 1, [1958] 2 All ER 472 (advancement upon new trusts); *Re Clore's Settlement Trusts* [1966] 1 WLR 955, [1966] 2 All ER 272 (payment to charity held to be for the benefit of rich minor who felt himself under moral obligation to make the gift); *Re Pauling's Settlement Trusts* [1964] Ch 303, [1963] 3 All ER 1 (advancement nominally to children was really made to benefit parents); p. 887; post; *Inglewood (Lord) v IRC*, supra, at 372, p. 599, ante.

Richard Godfrey Pilkington was one of the beneficiaries. He was married and had three children, one of whom was Penelope, a child two years old and born after the death of the testator. The trustees decided, with Richard's consent, to advance one half of Penelope's expectant share in the trust, and to pay it to the trustees of a new trust which was being set up for Penelope's benefit. The main object of the trustees was to save the estate duty which would be payable upon that part of the fund in the event of Richard's death. The new trusts were that until Penelope attained the age of 21 the income should be applied for her maintenance, education and benefit, and the surplus accumulated; and that on her attaining the age of 21 the income should be paid to her; and that the capital should be paid to her on attaining the age of 30.

The question was whether the trustees could properly so exercise the power of advancement.

Held. (i) Such an exercise was within the statutory power as being for Penelope's benefit, although her interest under the trust would vest later than under the will; (ii) But the particular exercise was void for perpetuity.[14]

VISCOUNT RADCLIFFE: The word "advancement" itself meant in this context the establishment in life of the beneficiary who was the object of the power or at any rate some step that would contribute to the furtherance of his establishment. Thus it was found in such phrases as "preferment or advancement" (*Lowther v Bentinck* (1874) LR 19 Eq 166), "business, profession, or employment or … advancement or preferment in the world" (*Roper-Curzon v Roper-Curzon* (1871) LR 11 Eq 452) and "placing out or advancement in life" (*Re Breeds' Will* (1875) 1 ChD 226). Typical instances of expenditure for such purposes under the social conditions of the nineteenth century were an apprenticeship or the purchase of a commission in the army or of an interest in business. In the case of a girl there could be advancement on marriage (*Lloyd v Cocker* (1860) 27 Beav 645). Advancement had, however, to some extent a limited range of meaning, since it was thought to convey the idea of some step in life of permanent significance, and accordingly, to prevent uncertainties about the permitted range of objects for which moneys could be raised and made available, such words as "or otherwise for his or her benefit" were often added to the word "advancement". It was always recognised that these added words were "large words" (see Jessel MR in *Re Breeds' Will* (1875) 1 ChD 226 at 228) and indeed in another case (*Lowther v Bentinck* (1874) LR 19 Eq 166 at 169) the same judge spoke of preferment and advancement as being "both large words" but of "benefit" as being the "largest of all". So, too, Kay J in *Re Brittlebank* (1881) 30 WR 99 at 100. Recent judges have spoken in the same terms—see Farwell J in *Re Halsted's Will Trusts* [1937] 2 All ER 570 at 571 and Danckwerts J in *Re Moxon's Will Trusts* [1958] 1 WLR 165 at 168, [1958] 1 All ER 386 at 387. This wide construction of the range of the power, which evidently did not stand upon niceties of distinction provided that the proposed application could fairly be regarded as for the benefit of the beneficiary who was the object of the power, must have been carried into the statutory power created by section 32, since it adopts without qualification the accustomed wording "for the advancement or benefit in such manner as they may in their absolute discretion think fit".

14 *Re Abraham's Will Trusts* [1969] 1 Ch 463, [1967] 2 All ER 1175; *Re Hastings-Bass* [1975] Ch 25, [1974] 2 All ER 193; *Mettoy Pension Trustees Ltd v Evans* [1990] 1 WLR 1587, [1991] 2 All ER 513; *Stannard v Fisons Pension Trust Ltd* [1992] I RLR 27.

So much for "advancement", which I now use for brevity to cover the combined phrase "advancement or benefit". It means any use of the money which will improve the material situation of the beneficiary. It is important, however, not to confuse the idea of "advancement" with the idea of advancing the money out of the beneficiary's expectant interest. The two things have only a casual connection with each other. The one refers to the operation of finding money by way of anticipation of an interest not yet absolutely vested in possession or, if so vested, belonging to an infant: the other refers to the status of the beneficiary and the improvement of his situation. The power to carry out the operation of anticipating an interest is not conferred by the word "advancement" but by those other words of the section which expressly authorise the payment or application of capital money for the benefit of a person entitled "whether absolutely or contingently on his attaining any specified age or on the occurrence of any other event, or subject to a gift over on his death under any specified age or on the occurrence of any other event, and whether in possession or in remainder or reversion," etc.

I think, with all respect to the commissioners, a good deal of their argument is infected with some of this confusion. To say, for instance, that there cannot be a valid exercise of a power of advancement that results in a deferment of the vesting of the beneficiary's absolute title (Miss Penelope, it will be remembered, is to take at 30 under the proposed settlement instead of at 21 under the will) is in my opinion to play upon words. The element of anticipation consists in the raising of money for her now before she has any right to receive anything under the existing trusts: the advancement consists in the application of that money to form a trust fund, the provisions of which are thought to be for her benefit. I have not forgotten, of course, the references to powers of advancement which are found in such cases as *Re Joicey* [1915] 2 Ch 115, *Re May's Settlement* [1926] Ch 135 and *Re Mewburn's Settlement* [1934] Ch 112, to which our attention was called, or the answer supplied by Cotton LJ in *Re Aldridge*[15] to his own question "What is advancement?"; but I think that it will be apparent from what I have already said that the description that he gives (it cannot be a definition) is confined entirely to the aspect of anticipation or acceleration which renders the money available and not to any description or limitation of the purposes for which it can then be applied.

I have not been able to find in the words of section 32, to which I have now referred, anything which in terms or by implication restricts the width of the manner or purpose of advancement. It is true that, if this settlement is made, Miss Penelope's children, who are not objects of the power, are given a possible interest in the event of her dying under 30 leaving surviving issue. But if the disposition itself, by which I mean the whole provision made, is for her benefit, it is no objection to the exercise of the power that other persons benefit incidentally as a result of the exercise. Thus a man's creditors may in certain cases get the most immediate advantage from an advancement made for the purpose of paying them off, as in *Lowther v Bentinck* (1874) LR 19 Eq 166, and a power to raise money for the advancement of a wife may cover a payment made direct to her husband in order to set him up in business: *Re Kershaw's*

---

15   (1886) 55 LT 554 at 556: "It is a payment to persons who are presumably entitled to, or have a vested or contingent interest in, an estate or a legacy, before the time fixed by the will for their obtaining the absolute interest in a portion or the whole of that to which they would be entitled."

Trusts (1868) LR 6 Eq 322. The exercise will not be bad therefore on this ground.

Nor in my opinion will it be bad merely because the moneys are to be tied up in the proposed settlement. If it could be said that the payment or application permitted by section 32 cannot take the form of a settlement in any form but must somehow pass direct into or through the hands of the object of the power, I could appreciate the principle upon which the commissioners' objection was founded. But can that principle be asserted? Anyone can see, I think, that there can be circumstances in which, while it is very desirable that some money should be raised at once for the benefit of an owner of an expectant or contingent interest, it would be very undesirable that the money should not be secured to him under some arrangement that will prevent him having the absolute disposition of it. I find it very difficult to think that there is something at the back of section 32 which makes an advancement impossible. Certainly neither Danckwerts J nor the members of the Court of Appeal in this case took that view. Both Lord Evershed MR and Upjohn LJ [1961] Ch 466 at 481, 486, [1961] 2 All ER 330 at 335, 338 explicitly accept the possibility of a settlement being made in exercise of a power of advancement. Farwell J authorised one in *Re Halsted's Will Trusts* [1937] 2 All ER 570 at 572, a case in which the trustees had left their discretion to the court. The trustees should raise the money and "have" it "settled", he said. So too, Harman J in *Re Ropner's Settlement Trusts* [1956] 1 WLR 902 at 906, [1956] 3 All ER 332 n. at 333, authorised the settlement of an advance provided for an infant, saying that the child could not "consent or request the trustees to make the advance, but the transfer of a part of his contingent share to the trustees of the settlement for him must advance his interest and thus be for his benefit ... " All this must be wrong in principle if a power of advancement cannot cover an application of the moneys by way of settlement.

The truth is, I think, that the propriety of requiring a settlement of moneys found for advancement was recognised as long ago as 1871 in *Roper-Curzon v Roper-Curzon* (1871) LR 11 Eq 452 and, so far as I know, it has not been impugned since. Lord Romilly MR's decision passed into the text-books and it must have formed the basis of a good deal of subsequent practice. True enough, as counsel for the commissioners has reminded us, the beneficiary in that case was an adult who was offering to execute the post-nuptial settlement required: but I find it impossible to read Lord Romilly's words as amounting to anything less than a decision that he would permit an advancement under the power only on the terms that the money was to be secured by settlement. That was what the case was about. If, then, it is a proper exercise of a power of advancement for trustees to stipulate that the money shall be settled, I cannot see any difference between having it settled that way and having it settled by themselves paying it to trustees of a settlement which is in the desired form.[16]

It is not as if anyone were contending for a principle that a power of advancement cannot be exercised "over the head" of a beneficiary, that is, unless he actually asks for the money to be raised and consents to its application. From some points of view that might be a satisfactory limitation, and no doubt it is the way in which an advancement takes place in the great majority of cases. But, if application and consent were necessary requisites of

16 Cf. *Hart v Briscoe* [1979] Ch 1, [1978] 1 All ER 791, 803; *Hoare Trustees v Gardner* [1979] Ch 10, [1978] 1 All ER 791, p. 562, ante (capital gains tax).

advancement, that would cut out the possibility of making any advancement for the benefit of a person under age, at any rate without the institution of court proceedings and formal representation of the infant: and it would mean, moreover, that the trustees of an adult could not in any circumstances insist on raising money to pay his debts, however much the operation might be to his benefit, unless he agreed to that course. Counsel for the commissioners did not contend before us that the power of advancement was inherently limited in this way: and I do not think that such a limitation would accord with the general understanding. Indeed its "paternal" nature is well shown by the fact that it is often treated as being peculiarly for the assistance of an infant.

The commissioners' objections seem to be concentrated upon such propositions as that the proposed transaction is "nothing less than a resettlement" and that a power of advancement cannot be used so as to alter or vary the trusts created by the settlement from which it is derived. Such a transaction, they say, amounts to using the power of advancement as a way of appointing or declaring new trusts different from those of the settlement. The reason why I do not find that these propositions have any compulsive effect upon my mind is that they seem to me merely vivid ways of describing the substantial effect of that which is proposed to be done and they do not in themselves amount to convincing arguments against doing it. Of course, whenever money is raised for advancement on terms that it is to be settled on the beneficiary, the money only passes from one settlement to be caught up in the other. It is therefore the same thing as a resettlement. But, unless one is to say that such moneys can never be applied by way of settlement, an argument which, as I have shown, has few supporters and is contrary to authority, it merely describes the inevitable effect of such an advancement to say that it is nothing less than a resettlement. Similarly, if it is part of the trusts and powers created by one settlement that the trustees of it should have power to raise money and make it available for a beneficiary upon new trusts approved by them, then they are in substance given power to free the money from one trust and to subject it to another. So be it: but, unless they cannot require a settlement of it at all, the transaction they carry out is the same thing in effect as an appointment of new trusts.

In the same way I am unconvinced by the argument that the trustees would be improperly delegating their trust by allowing the money raised to pass over to new trustees under a settlement conferring new powers on the latter. In fact I think that the whole issue of delegation is here beside the mark. The law is not that trustees cannot delegate: it is that trustees cannot delegate unless they have authority to do so. If the power of advancement which they possess is so read as to allow them to raise money for the purpose of having it settled, then they do have the necessary authority to let the money pass out of the old settlement into the new trusts. No question of delegation of their powers or trusts arises. If, on the other hand, their power of advancement is read so as to exclude settled advances, cadit quaestio.[17]

I ought to note for the record (1) that the transaction envisaged does not actually involve the raising of money, since the trustees propose to appropriate a block of shares in the family's private limited company as the trust investment, and (2) there will not be any actual transfer, since the trustees of the proposed settlement and the will trustees are the same persons. As I have

17 See *Re Hay's Settlement Trusts* [1982] 1 WLR 202, [1981] 3 All ER 786, p. 39, ante.

already said, I do not attach any importance to these factors nor, I think, do the commissioners. To transfer or appropriate outright is only to do by short cut what could be done in a more roundabout way by selling the shares to a consenting party, paying the money over to the new settlement with appropriate instructions and arranging for it to be used in buying back the shares as the trust investment. It cannot make any difference to follow the course taken in *Re Collard's Will Trusts* [1961] Ch 293, [1961] 1 All ER 821 and deal with the property direct. On the other point, so long as there are separate trusts, the property effectually passes out of the old settlement into the new one, and it is of no relevance that, at any rate for the time being, the persons administering the new trust are the same individuals.

I have not yet referred to the ground which was taken by the Court of Appeal as their reason for saying that the proposed settlement was not permissible. To put it shortly, they held that the statutory power of advancement could not be exercised unless the benefit to be conferred was "personal to the person concerned, in the sense of being related to his or her own real or personal needs" [1961] Ch 466 at 481, [1961] 2 All ER 330 at 336. Or, to use other words of the learned Master of the Rolls at 484, at 337, the exercise of the power "must be an exercise done to meet the circumstances as they present themselves in regard to a person within the scope of the section, whose circumstances call for that to be done which the trustees think fit to do." Upjohn LJ at 487, at 340 expressed himself in virtually the same terms.

My Lords, I differ with reluctance from the views of judges so learned and experienced in matters of this sort: but I do not find it possible to import such restrictions into the words of the statutory power which itself does not contain them. First, the suggested qualification, that the considerations or circumstances must be "personal" to the beneficiary, seems to me uncontrollably vague as a guide to general administration. What distinguishes a personal need from any other need to which the trustees in their discretion think it right to attend in the beneficiary's interest? And, if the advantage of preserving the funds of a beneficiary from the incidence of death duty is not an advantage personal to that beneficiary, I do not see what is. Death duty is a present risk that attaches to the settled property in which Miss Penelope has her expectant interest, and even accepting the validity of the supposed limitation, I would not have supposed that there was anything either impersonal or unduly remote in the advantage to be conferred upon her of some exemption from that risk. I do not think, therefore, that I can support the interpretation of the power of advancement that has commended itself to the Court of Appeal, and, with great respect, I think that the judgments really amount to little more than a decision that in the opinion of the members of that court this was not a case in which there was any occasion to exercise the power. That would be a proper answer from a court to which trustees had referred their discretion with a request for its directions; but it does not really solve any question where, as here, they retain their discretion and merely ask whether it is impossible for them to exercise it.

To conclude, therefore, on this issue, I am of opinion that there is no maintainable reason for introducing into the statutory power of advancement a qualification that would exclude the exercise in the case now before us. It would not be candid to omit to say that, though I think that that is what the law requires, I am uneasy at some of the possible applications of this liberty, when advancements are made for the purposes of settlement or on terms that there is to be a settlement. It is quite true, as the commissioners have pointed out, that you might have really extravagant cases of resettlements being forced on beneficiaries in the name of advancement, even a few months before an absolute vesting in possession would have destroyed the power. I have tried to give due weight to such possibilities, but when all is said I do not think that they ought to compel us to introduce a limitation of which no one, with all respect, can produce a satisfactory definition. First, I do not believe that it is wise to try to cut down an admittedly wide and discretionary power, enacted for general use, through fear of its being abused in certain hypothetical instances. And moreover, as regards this fear, I think that it must be remembered that we are speaking of a power intended to be in the hands of trustees chosen by a settlor because of his confidence in their discretion and good sense and subject to the external check that no exercise can take place without the consent of a prior life-tenant; and that there does remain at all times a residual power in the court to restrain or correct any purported exercise that can be shown to be merely wanton or capricious and not to be attributable to a genuine discretion. I think, therefore, that, although extravagant possibilities exist, they may be more menacing in argument than in real life.

The other issue on which this case depends, that relating to the application of the rule against perpetuities, does not seem to me to present much difficulty. It is not in dispute that, if the limitations of the proposed settlement are to be treated as if they had been made by the testator's will and as coming into operation at the date of his death, there are trusts in it which would be void ab initio as violating the perpetuity rule. They postpone final vesting by too long a date. It is also a familiar rule of law in this field that, whereas appointments made under a general power of appointment conferred by will or deed are held as taking effect from the date of the exercise of the power, trusts declared by a special power of appointment, the distinguishing feature of which is that it can allocate property among a limited class of persons only, are treated as coming into operation at the date of the instrument that creates the power. The question therefore resolves itself into asking whether the exercise of a power of advancement which takes the form of a settlement should be looked upon as more closely analogous to a general or to a special power of appointment.

On this issue I am in full agreement with the views of Upjohn LJ in the Court of Appeal [1961] Ch 466 at 488, [1961] 2 All ER 330 at 340. Indeed, much of the reasoning that has led me to my conclusion on the first issue that I have been considering leads me to think that for this purpose there is an effective analogy between powers of advancement and special powers of appointment. When one asks what person can be regarded as the settlor of Miss Penelope's proposed settlement, I do not see how it is possible to say that she is herself or that the trustees are. She is the passive recipient of the benefit extracted for her from the original trusts; the trustees are merely exercising a fiduciary power in arranging for the desired limitations. It is not their property that constitutes the funds of Miss Penelope's settlement; it is the property subjected to trusts by the will of the testator and passed over into the new settlement through the instrumentality of a power which by statute is made appendant to those trusts. I do not think, therefore, that it is important to this issue that money raised under a power of advancement passes entirely out of the reach of the existing trusts and makes, as it were, a new start under fresh limitations, the kind of thing that happened under the old form of family resettlement when the tenant in tail in remainder barred the entail with the consent of the protector of the settlement. I think that the important point for the purpose of the rule against perpetuities is that the new settlement is only effected by the operation of a fiduciary power which itself "belongs" to the old settlement.

In the conclusion, therefore, there are legal objections to the proposed settlement which the trustees have placed before the court. Again I agree with Upjohn LJ that these objections go to the root of what is proposed and I do not think that it would be satisfactory that the court should try to frame a qualified answer to the question that they have propounded, which would express the general view that the power to advance by way of a settlement of this sort does exist and the special view that the power to make this particular settlement does not. Nor, I think, is such a course desired either by the appellants or the trustees. They will, I hope, know where they stand for the future, and so will the commissioners, and that is enough.

C. Application of the Money

In **Re Pauling's Settlement Trusts** [1964] Ch 303, [1963] 3 All ER 1,[18] one question was whether trustees, in making an advancement, were under an obligation to ensure that the money advanced was in fact applied for the purposes for which it was advanced. WILLMER LJ said at 334, at 8:

"Furthermore, it is clear that the power under the first limb [of the express power of appointment, giving the trustees power to advance up to one half of a child's expectant, presumptive or vested share and to pay the same to him for his absolute use or for his advancement or otherwise for his benefit in such manner as the trustees should think fit] may be exercised, if the circumstances warrant it, either by making an out-and-out payment to the person to be advanced, or for a particular purpose specified by the trustees. Thus in argument an example was given that when George [one of the beneficiaries] was called to the Bar the trustees might have quite properly advanced to him a sum of capital quite generally for his living expenses to support him while starting to practice, provided they thought that this was a reasonable thing to do, and that he was a type of person who could reasonably be trusted to make proper use of the money. On the other hand, if the trustees make the advance for a particular purpose which they state, they can quite properly pay it over to the advancee if they reasonably think they can trust him or her to carry out the prescribed purpose. What they cannot do is to prescribe a particular purpose, and then raise and pay the money over to the advancee leaving him or her entirely free, legally and morally, to apply it for that purpose or to spend it in any way he or she chooses, without any responsibility on the trustees even to inquire as to its application."

D. Effect of Inflation

Law Reform Committee 23rd Report (The Powers and Duties of Trustees) 1982 Cmnd 8733, paras. 4.43, 44, 47

"4.43   One of our witnesses discussed at some length the effects of inflation on the cash sum (or its equivalent) received by way of advancement by a beneficiary entitled to an undivided share in a trust fund. The position is that the beneficiary retains his interest in the relevant share but has to bring into

---

18 See p. 887, post.

account the cash sum when the final division takes place. This means that the amount advanced is accounted for at its value at the time of the advancement and not at the value prevailing at the time of the division. In times of stable values this produces no injustice, but can lead to capricious results in times of inflation. In such times the value of the advanced property (if it has not been spent altogether) will have appreciated as well as the value of the remaining part of the trust fund. The result might well be that the beneficiary who has received part of his share by way of advancement will in fact, in the long run, receive a larger proportion of the whole fund than would be expected given the value of his initial, undivided, share.

4.44   In order to deal with this problem it is suggested that it would be fairer to treat advances and appropriations as fractional distributions of entitlement rather than as cash sums to be brought into hotchpot. Each advance would have to be assessed as a fraction of the relevant beneficiary's entitlement and this would involve a valuation not only of the property advanced but also of the remainder of the fund. Such a process would be unduly laborious where only a small advance is being made but in such circumstances the trustees should be allowed to use the cash method at their discretion, rather than the fractional method, which should be used in all other cases.

4.47   We have considerable reservations about the mixing of the fractional and the cash bases of accounting. If there are mixed cash and fractional sums to add back together it would be necessary to do so in reverse order so that the correct hotchpot is arrived at. This might involve complicated calculations. We are agreed, however, that some form of indexation is needed to arrive at a just result. We are of the opinion that trustees should no longer use the cash basis when bringing advances into account. Any such sums should in future be accounted for at the time of the final division at their value at the time of the advance multiplied by any increase in the retail price index. At their discretion, the trustees should be able to use the exact fractional method which would be more appropriate in cases where, for example, the trust fund largely consisted of land. If both cash sums and fractions have to be brought into hotchpot in order to achieve proper equality, these sums should be added back in the reverse order to arrive at the correct figure.''

19. Variation of Trusts[1]

I. Introduction

A trustee must administer the trust in accordance with its terms; otherwise he commits a breach of trust. Sometimes, however, the observance of the terms is harmful to the beneficiaries. This has been seen in the context of the limited investment powers available to trustees before 1961.[2] It appears in many other contexts; and most especially in that of tax planning. In short, the old-fashioned settlement containing a succession of limited interests can be disadvantageous in terms of the liability to taxation on death. How can such a settlement, once established, be changed?

There is no difficulty if all the beneficiaries are of full age, under no disability, and all agree.[3] They can terminate the trust and share out; or agree to resettle upon other trusts. But it is usual in a family settlement that there should be some beneficiaries of later generations who are minor or unborn, and who could not therefore join in a termination or reconstruction of the settlement. Could the court approve a reconstruction on behalf of minors or unborn beneficiaries when it was for their benefit? The House of Lords decided that it could not.[4] As Lord MORTON OF HENRYTON said in *Chapman v Chapman*:[5] "If the court had power to approve, and did approve schemes such as the present scheme, the way would be open for a most undignified game of chess between the Chancery Division and the legislature". If, of course, there was a dispute between the beneficiaries, which the beneficiaries were prepared

---

1 H & M, pp. 599–617; K & S, pp. 408–434; P & M, pp. 541–555; Pettit, pp. 465–481; Riddall, pp. 313–326; Snell, pp. 235–245; Underhill, pp. 468–500; Harris, *Variation of Trusts* (1975).
2 See p. 661, ante.
3 *Saunders v Vautier* (1841) 4 Beav 115, p. 653, ante; affd (1841) Cr & Ph 240; *Re Chardon* [1928] Ch 464; *Re Smith* [1928] Ch 915, p. 37, ante.
4 *Chapman v Chapman* [1954] AC 429, [1954] 1 All ER 798.
5 At 468, at 818.

to compromise, the Court could sanction the compromise.[6] It must be a real dispute; but it is hardly necessary to add that greater ingenuity was needed to find a dispute in some cases than was necessary to find a tax-saving compromise.

Various statutory provisions relate to variation of trusts, and these will be mentioned.[7] The court also has inherent power to authorise certain acts by trustees which are beyond their powers. The inherent jurisdiction is narrow and is generally restricted to emergency and salvage operations.[8] Towering above them in significance is the Variation of Trusts Act 1958, under which most variations are now effected.

II. Trustee Act 1925, s. 57

TRUSTEE ACT 1925

57. Power of court to authorise dealings with trust property: see p. 740, ante.

Pettit: *Equity and the Law of Trusts* (7th edn, 1993), pp. 470–471.

"Of primary importance is the interpretation of the words 'management' and 'administration', which are largely, though very possibly not entirely, synonymous. The subject-matter of both words in section 57 is trust property which is vested in trustees, and 'trust property' cannot by any legitimate stretch of the language include the equitable interests which a settlor has created in that property. The application of both words is confined to the managerial supervision and control of trust property on behalf of beneficiaries, and the section accordingly does not permit the remoulding of the beneficial interests. The object of section 57, it was said,[9] is

'to secure that trust property should be managed as advantageously as possible in the interests of the beneficiaries, and, with that object in view, to authorise specific dealings with the property which the court might have felt itself unable to sanction under the inherent jurisdiction, either because no actual "emergency" had arisen or because of inability to show that the position which called for intervention was one which the creator of the trust could not reasonably have foreseen, but it was no part of the legislative aim to disturb the rule that the court will not rewrite a trust or to add to such exceptions to that rule as had already found their way into the inherent jurisdiction'.

Later in the judgment the majority adopted the statement of Farwell J in *Re Mair*,[10] that 'if and when the court sanctions an arrangement or transaction

---

6 See *Allen v Distillers Co (Biochemicals) Ltd* [1974] QB 384, [1974] 2 All ER 365; *Re Barbour's Settlement* [1974] 1 WLR 1198, [1974] 1 All ER 1188; *Re Earl of Strafford* [1980] Ch 28, [1979] 1 All ER 513, p. 742, n. 12, ante; *Mason v Farbrother* [1983] 2 All ER 1078, p. 783, post.

7 See pp. 782–789, post; (1954) 17 MLR 420 (O.R. Marshall).

8 *Re New* [1901] 2 Ch 534; *Re Tollemache* [1903] 1 Ch 955.

9 Per EVERSHED MR and ROMER LJ in *Re Downshire Settled Estates* [1953] Ch 218 at 248, 264, 268, [1953] 1 All ER 103 at 119, 129, 132. And see *Municipal and General Securities Co Ltd v Lloyds Bank Ltd* [1950] Ch 212, [1949] 2 All ER 937.

10 [1935] Ch 562 at 565.

under section 57, it must be taken to have done it as though the power which is being put into operation had been inserted in the trust instrument as an overriding power'. Perhaps Farwell J put it even more clearly later in his judgment where he said[11] 'the effect of the court permitting the exercise by trustees of some power which is not in the trust document itself, and, therefore, something which the trustees could not do except by the direction of the court, is the same as though that power had been inserted as an overriding power in the trust document'.

Applications under section 57 are almost invariably heard and disposed of in chambers and accordingly not reported. There are, however, a few reported cases which show that in the exercise of its jurisdiction under this section the court has authorised the sale of settled chattels,[12] a partition of land[13] and a sale of land where the necessary consent could not be obtained.[14] It has authorised two residuary estates left on identical charitable trusts to be blended into one fund.[15] It has, apparently commonly, authorised capital money to be expended on paying off the tenant for life's debts, on having its replacement secured by a policy of insurance so that the beneficial interests remain unaltered,[16] but although it has in exceptional circumstances sanctioned a similar expenditure of capital to purchase the life tenant's interest,[17] it is doubtful whether it would do so in an ordinary case, as it would come 'at least very near to altering the beneficial interests of the tenant for life'.[18] The court has also authorised the sale of a reversionary interest which under the trust instrument was not to be sold until it should fall into possession.[19] Finally ... the section may be used to extend trustees' powers of investment.''[20]

In **Mason v Farbrother** [1983] 2 All ER 1078, the trustees of the Co-operative Wholesale Society's Pension and Death Fund Scheme sought a variation of the trust deed by the insertion of a wider investment clause. In sanctioning the variation under section 57, Judge Blackett-Ord V-C said at 1086:

"That power was exercised by Danckwerts J in a charity case, *Re Shipwrecked Fishermen and Mariners' Royal Benevolent Society* [1959] Ch 220, [1958] 3 All ER 465, so as to extend the investment powers of the trustees.

Shortly afterwards, in *Re Coates' Will Trusts* [1959] 1 WLR 375, [1959] 2 All ER 47n, the view was put forward by Harman J that the proper way to proceed where trustees wished to obtain extended investment powers was by way of an

11 Supra, at 566.
12 *Re Hope's Will Trust* [1929] 2 Ch 136.
13 *Re Thomas* [1930] 1 Ch 194.
14 *Re Beale's Settlement Trusts* [1932] 2 Ch 15.
15 *Re Harvey* [1941] 3 All ER 284. The contrary decision in *Re Royal Society's Charitable Trusts* [1956] Ch 87, [1955] 3 All ER 14, where *Re Harvey* does not appear to have been cited, would seem to be wrong in the light of *Re Shipwrecked Fishermen and Mariners' Royal Benevolent Society* [1959] Ch 220, [1958] 3 All ER 465.
16 *Re Salting* [1932] 2 Ch 57; *Re Mair* [1935] Ch 562. These cases must be read in the light of the observations of the majority of the Court of Appeal in *Re Downshire Settled Estates* [1953] Ch 218 at 249–251, [1953] 1 All ER 103 at 119–121; and see *Re Forster's Settlement* [1954] 3 All ER 714.
17 *Re Forster's Settlement*, supra.
18 *Re Forster's Settlement*, supra, per HARMAN J at 720.
19 *Re Cockerell's Settlement Trusts* [1956] Ch 372, [1956] 2 All ER 172.
20 *Mason v Farbrother* [1983] 2 All ER 1078, infra.

application under the Variation of Trusts Act 1958,[1] and that advice, in my experience, was acted on and many applications were made under that Act; but the law as laid down by Danckwerts J in *Re Shipwrecked Fishermen and Mariners' Royal Benevolent Society* has not been overruled, and I am satisfied that where in the management or administration of trust property it is in the opinion of the court expedient, I have the power to authorise the substitution for cll 5 and 6 of the 1929 deed of the sort of investment clause which is being put forward here.

The next question to be considered is whether there is any reason why this should not be done, based on the Trustee Investments Act 1961.[2] I have indicated that after 1959 a great many applications were made by trustees of trusts under the Variation of Trusts Act 1958 to obtain wider investment powers, but Parliament then passed the 1961 Act extending investment powers of trustees and in two later cases, namely *Re Cooper's Settlement* [1962] Ch 826, [1961] 3 All ER 636, and *Re Kolb's Will Trusts* [1962] Ch 531, [1961] 3 All ER 811, Buckley J and Cross J respectively expressed the view that in the light of such a recent expression of the views of Parliament, it would not be right for the courts to continue to extend investment clauses with the enthusiasm with which they had done up to date; and for many years few applications, if any, were made.

But the rule was not an absolute one; it was said to apply in the absence of special circumstances, and the special circumstances in the present case are manifest: in a word, inflation since 1961. And also of course the fact that the trust is an unusual one in that it is not a private or family trust but a pension fund with perhaps something of a public element in it.

In my judgment, therefore, there is no reason why in a proper case an application such as the present one should not be acceded to under s. 57 of the Trustee Act 1925. And it seems to me on the evidence that it is (in the words of the section) 'expedient' that the application should succeed. Therefore, the way that I think it is proper to deal with the application is by making an order under s. 57 of the 1925 Act, and this I will do.''[3]

III. Settled Land Act 1925, s. 64

SETTLED LAND ACT 1925

64. General power for the tenant for life to effect any transaction under an order of the court.—(1) Any transaction affecting or concerning the settled land, or any part thereof, or any other land (not being a transaction otherwise authorised by this Act, or by the settlement) which in the opinion of the court

---

1 An application under Variation of Trusts Act 1958, s. 1, p. 789, post, was not pursued. It was also held that the court could not vary the deed under its inherent jurisdiction to sanction a compromise. "There is something to compromise, but the court cannot sweep the old away and substitute the new." See *Re Powell-Cotton's Re-Settlement* [1956] 1 WLR 23 at 27, [1956] 1 All ER 60 at 62, per EVERSHED MR.

2 P. 663, ante.

3 [1984] Conv 373 (H.E. Norman); [1984] All ER Rev 308 (P.J. Clarke). See *Trustees of the British Museum v A-G* [1984] 1 WLR, [1984] 1 All ER 337, especially the comments by MEGARRY V-C on *Mason v Farbrother* at 425, 343, 418, p. 694, ante.

would be for the benefit of the settled land, or any part thereof, or the persons interested under the settlement, may, under an order of the court, be effected by a tenant for life, if it is one which could have been validly effected by an absolute owner.

(2) In this section "transaction" includes any sale, exchange, assurance, grant, lease, surrender, reconveyance, release, reservation, or other disposition, and any purchase or other acquisition, and any covenant, contract, or option, and any application of capital money and any compromise or other dealing, or arrangement; and "effected" has the meaning appropriate to the particular transaction; and the references to land include references to restrictions and burdens affecting land.[4]

Harris: *Variation of Trusts* (1975), p. 19 [5]

"The jurisdiction was extended by section 1 of the Settled Land and Trustee Acts (Court's General Powers) Act 1943 (as amended by section 9 of the Emergency Laws (Miscellaneous Provisions) Act 1953); which empowers the court to authorise any expense of an action taken or proposed in or for the management of settled land to be treated as a capital outgoing, if the expenditure cannot otherwise be met and the action is for the benefit of those interested under the settlement.

The jurisdiction conferred by section 64 of the Settled Land Act enables the court to add to the powers conferred upon a tenant for life of settled land by the Act and by the settlement. As section 28 (1) of the Law of Property Act 1925 confers upon the trustees of land held upon trust for sale all the powers which the Settled Land Act confers upon a tenant for life of settled land, it has been held that the jurisdiction conferred by section 64 extends to land held on trust for sale: *Re Simmons* [1956] Ch 125, [1955] 3 All ER 818.

For a transaction to come within the jurisdiction, it must affect land. Acts performed in the management or administration of trusts of other kinds of property will normally come within the jurisdiction of section 57 of the Trustee Act. However, because of the wording of subsection 4 of section 57, neither section will apply '... in the case of a settlement the trustees of which are trustees for the purposes of the Settled Land Act, but which no longer comprises any unsold land': *Re Downshire's Settled Estates* [1953] Ch 218 at 254, [1953] 1 All ER 103 at 123 per Evershed MR. The Law Reform Committee recommended that section 64 should be amended to plug this gap: (1957 Cmnd 310, para 25). This recommendation has not been put into effect; and, in view of the breadth of the jurisdiction conferred by the variation of Trusts Act 1958, the practical consequences of doing so would be small.

---

4 As amended by Settled Land and Trustee Acts (Courts' General Powers) Act 1943, s. 2, and Statute Law (Repeals) Act 1969, Schedule, Part III.
5 See Maudsley and Burn, *Land Law Cases and Materials* (6th edn), pp. 233–234, for further cases in which s. 64 has been applied; *Raikes v Lygon* [1988] 1 WLR 281, [1988] 1 All ER 884 (creation of maintenance fund for Madresfield Court "a Tudor mansion house of outstanding beauty and of considerable architectural and historical interest"); *Hambro v Duke of Marlborough* [1994] Ch 158, [1994] 3 All ER 332 (court held to have jurisdiction to authorise tenant for life to vary beneficial interest of ascertained beneficiary of full age and capacity, even if that beneficiary did not consent).

The major difference between section 64 of the Settled Land Act and section 57 of the Trustee Act, which was brought to light in *Downshire*, is that the former section enables the court to authorise alterations in the beneficial interests under a settlement as well as alterations in its administrative provisions.

In *Downshire*, the court was asked to approve an arrangement under which the tenant for life of settled land would surrender a protected life interest, and provision would be made by means of insurance for any possible future beneficiaries under the protective trusts which would have arisen upon a forfeiture of the protected life interest. The corpus of the settlement comprised land worth £400,000 and capital money worth £700,000. Roxburgh J, at first instance, held that the word 'transaction' was limited to acts of administration: *Re D's Settled Estates* [1952] 2 All ER 603 at 606. But the Court of Appeal took the view that it was a ' ... word of the widest import as is emphasised, in our judgment, by the terms of the second subsection which make the meaning of the word comprehend (*inter alia*) any application of capital money and any compromise or other dealing or arrangement': [1953] Ch 218 at 252, [1953] 1 All ER 103 at 122, per Evershed MR.

The result was, so the court held, that section 64 enabled the court to authorise the tenant for life to make an arrangement with the trustees and with other adult beneficiaries under the settlement which completely remodelled the beneficial interests under the settlement. The court could do this, provided only that the 'transaction' benefited the settled land or any part thereof ' ... or the persons interested under the settlement ... '

Thus, in the case of settlements whose trust corpus includes settled land, there was already before 1958 a wide jurisdiction to approve tax-avoiding rearrangements of the beneficial interests. The jurisdiction might be applicable today in circumstances in which the Variation of Trusts Act jurisdiction is not."

IV. Trustee Act 1925, s. 53[6]

TRUSTEE ACT 1925

53. Vesting orders in relation to infant's beneficial interests.—Where an infant is beneficially entitled to any property the court may, with a view to the application of the capital or income thereof for the maintenance, education, or benefit of the infant, make an order—

(*a*) appointing a person to convey such property; or

(*b*) in the case of stock, or a thing in action, vesting in any person the right to transfer or call for a transfer of such stock, or to receive the dividends or income thereof, or to sue for and recover such thing in action, upon such terms as the court may think fit.

---

6 See (1957) 21 Conv (NS) 448 (O.R. Marshall).

Pettit: *Equity and the Law of Trusts* (7th edn), p. 469

"Under this section it was held in *Re Gower's Settlement*[7] that where there was an infant tenant in tail in remainder of Blackacre with divers remainders over, the court could effectually authorise a mortgage of Blackacre (subject to the interests having priority over the infant's tenancy in tail) framed so as to vest in the mortgagee a security which would be as effective a bar against the infant's issue taking under the entail and the subsequent remaindermen as if the infant were of full age and had executed the conveyance in accordance with the Fines and Recoveries Act 1833.

It was expressly assumed in *Re Gower's Settlement* that the requirement of the section that the mortgage should be made 'with a view to the application of the capital or income thereof for the maintenance, education or benefit of the infant' was satisfied. It was held that there was no such 'application' in *Re Heyworth's Settlements*[8] where it was proposed to put an end to the trusts created by the settlement by selling the infant's contingent reversionary interest to the life tenant for an outright cash payment. This decision was distinguished in *Re Meux's Will Trusts*[9] where the proceeds of sale were to be settled. It was held that the sale and settlement of the proceeds of sale were to be regarded as a single transaction, which did constitute an 'application' for the purposes of the section.[10] And in *Re Bristol's Settled Estates*[11] a person was appointed to execute a disentailing assurance to bar the infant's entail with a view to a settlement to be made with the assistance of the court under the Variation of Trusts Act 1958."

v. Matrimonial Causes Act 1973, s. 24

MATRIMONIAL CAUSES ACT 1973

24. Property adjustment orders in connection with divorce proceedings, etc.[12]—(1) On granting a decree of divorce, a decree of nullity of marriage or a decree of judicial separation or at any time thereafter (whether, in the case of a decree of divorce or of nullity of marriage, before or after the decree is made absolute), the court may make any one or more of the following orders that is to say—

  (*a*) an order that a party to the marriage shall transfer to the other party, to any child of the family or to such person as may be specified in the order for the benefit of such a child such property as may be so specified, being property to which the first-mentioned party is entitled either in possession or reversion;

---

7 [1934] Ch 365; *Re Lansdowne's Will Trusts* [1967] Ch 603, [1967] 1 All ER 888.
8 [1956] Ch 364, [1956] 2 All ER 21.
9 [1958] Ch 154, [1957] 2 All ER 630; *Re Lansdowne's Will Trusts*, supra.
10 Cf. *Re Ropner's Settlement Trusts* [1956] 1 WLR 902, [1956] 3 All ER 332n—a decision on similar words in TA 1925, s. 32, p. 771, ante.
11 [1965] 1 WLR 469, [1964] 3 All ER 939.
12 For the factors to be taken into account in making an order under this section, see ss. 25, 25A, as substituted by Matrimonial and Family Proceedings Act 1984, s. 3. See also Bromley *Family Law* (8th edn) pp. 738–742; Cretney and Masson, *Principles of Family Law* (5th edn) pp. 370–381. Cf. the power to vary ante- and post-nuptial settlements under Inheritance (Provision for Family and Dependants) Act 1975, s. 2 (1) (*f*).

(*b*) an order that a settlement[13] of such property as may be so specified, being property to which a party to the marriage is so entitled, be made to the satisfaction of the court for the benefit of the other party to the marriage and of the children of the family or either or any of them;

(*c*) an order varying for the benefit of the parties to the marriage and of the children of the family or either or any of them any ante-nuptial or post-nuptial settlement (including such a settlement made by will or codicil) made on the parties to the marriage;

(*d*) an order extinguishing or reducing the interest of either of the parties to the marriage under any such settlement;

subject, however, in the case of an order under paragraph (*a*) above, to the restrictions imposed by section 29 (1) and (3) below on the making of orders for a transfer of property in favour of children who have attained the age of eighteen.

24A. Orders for sale of property.—(1) Where the court makes under section 23 or 24 of this Act a secured periodical payments order, an order for the payment of a lump sum or a property adjustment order, then, on making that order or at any time thereafter, the court may make a further order for the sale of such property as may be specified in the order, being property in which or in the proceeds of sale of which either or both of the parties to the marriage has or have a beneficial interest, either in possession or reversion.[14]

31. Variation, discharge, etc., of certain orders for financial relief.—(1) Where the court has made an order to which this section applies, then, subject to the provisions of this section, the court shall have power to vary or discharge the order or to suspend any provision thereof temporarily and to revive the operation of any provision so suspended.

(2) This section applies to the following orders, that is to say— ...

(*e*) any order for a settlement of property under section 24 (1) (*b*) or for a variation of settlement under section 24 (1) (*c*) or (*d*) above, being an order made on or after the grant of a decree of judicial separation ...

(*f*) any order made under section 24A (1) above for sale of the property.[15]

(3) The powers exercisable by the court under this section in relation to an order shall be exercisable also in relation to any instrument executed in pursuance of the order.

(4) The court shall not exercise the powers conferred by this section in relation to an order for a settlement under section 24 (1) (*b*) or for a variation of settlement under section 24 (1) (*c*) or (*d*) above except on an application made in proceedings—

---

13 A wide meaning has been given to the word "settlement". It includes any provision (other than an absolute gift) made for the benefit of the parties to the marriage. See *Ulrich v Ulrich* [1968] 1 WLR 180, [1968] 1 All ER 67 (purchase of house intended to be matrimonial home held to be settlement); *Brooks v Brooks* [1995] 3 WLR 141, [1995] 3 All ER 257 (pension fund scheme providing for employee on retirement to surrender part of his entitlement for benefit of spouse held to be settlement).

14 Added by Matrimonial Homes and Property Act 1981, s. 7.

15 Ibid. s. 8.

(*a*) for the rescission of the decree of judicial separation by reference to which the order was made, or

(*b*) for the dissolution of the marriage in question.[16]

VI. Mental Health Act 1983, s. 96

Section 96 gives to the Court of Protection wide powers of making settlements of the property of mental patients, including variation.

96. Powers of the judge as to patient's property and affairs.—(3) Where under this section a settlement has been made of any property of a patient, and the Lord Chancellor or a nominated judge is satisfied, at any time before the death of the patient, that any material fact was not disclosed when the settlement was made, or that there has been any substantial change in circumstances, he may by order vary the settlement in such manner as he thinks fit, and give any consequential directions.[17]

VII. Variation of Trusts Act 1958[18]

A. Section 1

1. Jurisdiction of courts to vary trusts.—(1) Where property, whether real or personal, is held on trusts arising, whether before or after the passing of this Act, under any will, settlement or other disposition, the court may if it thinks fit by order approve on behalf of—

(*a*) any person having, directly or indirectly, an interest, whether vested or contingent, under the trusts who by reason of infancy or other incapacity is incapable of assenting, or

(*b*) any person (whether ascertained or not) who may become entitled, directly or indirectly, to an interest under the trusts as being at a future date or on the happening of a future event a person of any specified description or a member of any specified class of persons, so however that this paragraph shall not include any person who would be of that description, or a member of that class, as the case may be, if the said date had fallen or the said event had happened at the date of the application to the court, or

---

16 *Norman v Norman* [1983] 1 WLR 295, [1983] 1 All ER 486; *Carson v Carson* [1983] 1 WLR 285, [1983] 1 All ER 478; *Whitfield v Whitfield* [1986] 1 FLR 99; *Morley-Clarke v Jones* [1986] Ch 311, [1985] 3 All ER 193; *Thompson v Thompson* [1986] Fam 38, [1985] 2 All ER 243.

17 *Re CWHT* [1978] Ch 67, [1978] 1 All ER 210. A settlement made by a settlor before becoming a mental patient may be varied under Variation of Trusts Act 1958: *Re CL* [1969] 1 Ch 587, [1968] 1 All ER 1104.

18 H & M, pp. 599–617; K & S, pp. 412–425; P & M, pp. 546–558; Pettit, pp. 473–481; Riddall, pp. 316–326; Snell, pp. 241–245; Underhill, pp. 474–492; Harris, *Variation of Trusts* (1975) chap. 3 et seq. The Act was based on the recommendation of Law Reform Committee Sixth Report (Court's Power to Sanction Variation of Trusts) (1957) Cmnd. 310. See generally (1958) 22 Conv (NS) 373 (M.J. Mowbray); (1963) 27 Conv (NS) 6 (D.M. Evans); (1965) 43 CBR 181 (A.J. Maclean); (1969) 33 Conv (NS) 113, 183 (J.W. Harris).

(*c*) any person unborn, or

(*d*) any person in respect of any discretionary interest of his under protective trusts where the interest of the principal beneficiary has not failed or determined,[19]

any arrangement (by whomsoever proposed, and whether or not there is any other person beneficially interested who is capable of assenting thereto) varying or revoking all or any of the trusts, or enlarging the powers of the trustees of managing or administering any of the property subject to the trusts:

Provided that except by virtue of paragraph (*d*) of this subsection the court shall not approve an arrangement on behalf of any person unless the carrying out thereof would be for the benefit of that person.

(2) In the foregoing subsection "protective trusts" means the trusts specified in paragraphs (i) and (ii) of subsection (1) of section thirty-three of the Trustee Act, 1925, or any like trusts, "the principal beneficiary" has the same meaning as in the said subsection (1) and "discretionary interest" means an interest arising under the trust specified in paragraph (ii) of the said subsection (1) or any like trust.

(3) The jurisdiction conferred by subsection (1) of this section shall be exercisable by the High Court, except that the question whether the carrying out of any arrangement would be for the benefit of a person falling within paragraph (*a*) of the said subsection (1) shall be determined by order of the authority having jurisdiction under Part VII of the Mental Health Act 1983, if that person is a patient within the meaning of the said Part VII.[20]

(6) Nothing in this section shall be taken to limit the powers conferred by section sixty-four of the Settled Land Act 1925,[1] section fifty-seven of the Trustee Act 1925,[2] or the powers of the authority having jurisdiction under Part VII of the Mental Health Act 1983.[3]

B. Persons on Whose Behalf Approval May be Given

PRACTICE DIRECTION
(VARIATION OF TRUSTS: COUNSEL'S OPINION)
[No.2 of 1976]
[1976] 1 WLR 884, [1976] 3 All ER 160

1. Where any infants or unborn beneficiaries will be affected by an arrangement under the Variation of Trusts Act 1958, evidence must normally be before the court which shows that their guardians ad litem or the trustees support the arrangement as being in the interests of the infants or unborn beneficiaries, and exhibits a case to counsel and counsel's written opinion to this effect. In nearly every case such a written opinion is helpful, and in complicated cases it is usually essential to the understanding of the guardian

---

19 *Gibbon v Mitchell* [1990] 1 WLR 1304, [1990] 3 All ER 338.
20 As amended by County Courts Act 1959, s. 204, Sch. 3; Mental Health Act 1959, s. 149, Sch. 7 and Mental Health Act 1983, s. 148, Sch. 4, para 14 (*a*).
1 See p. 784, ante; *Hambro v Duke of Marlborough* [1994] Ch 158, [1994] 3 All ER 332.
2 See p. 789, ante.
3 As amended by Mental Health Act 1959, s. 149, Sch. 7, and Mental Health Act 1983, Sch. 4, para 14 (*b*). On stamp duty, see Practice Direction (ChD) (Stamp Duty on Orders under the Variation of Trusts Act 1958) (No 3/89).

ad litem and the trustees, and to the consideration by the court of the merits and the fiscal consequences of the arrangement.

2. Where the interests of two or more infants, or two or more of the infants and unborn beneficiaries, are similar, a single written case to counsel and opinion will suffice; and no case to counsel or written opinion is required in respect of those who fall within the proviso to section 1 (1) of the Act (discretionary interests under protective trusts). Further, in proper cases the requirement of a case to counsel and a written opinion may at any stage be dispensed with by the master or the judge.

3. The effect of this practice direction is to extend to variations of trusts the long-established practice in the Chancery Division of requiring a case to counsel and counsel's opinion when proceedings in which an infant is interested are compromised: see *The Supreme Court Practice* (1976) vol 2, para. 2073.

By the direction of the Vice-Chancellor,
R.E. BALL,
Chief Master.

July 27, 1976.

(i) APPROVAL GIVEN

In **Re Suffert's Settlement** [1961] Ch 1, [1960] 3 All ER 561, the income of a family trust fund was held on protective trusts for Miss Suffert, a spinster aged 61, and after her death, upon trusts, as to capital and income, in favour of her issue; and in default of such issue, and subject to a general testamentary power of appointment, in trust for those persons who would be her statutory next-of-kin if she died a spinster.

Miss Suffert sought a variation of the settlement under which a fund of £500 would be held on trusts in favour of persons interested in the original trust, and the remainder of the fund, amounting to some £8,300, should be held on trust for herself absolutely.

At the date of the application to the court, her nearest relatives were three adult first cousins. One of them was made a party and consented to the variation. The other two were not made parties. The court was asked to approve on behalf of those two, and on behalf of unborn and unascertained persons who might become interested. BUCKLEY J held that he could approve the variation on behalf of the unborn and unascertained persons; but not on behalf of the two cousins. They were within the exception contained in para (*b*) of s. 1 (1) of the Act. The two cousins should themselves decide whether to consent or refuse.

In **Re Moncrieff's Settlement Trusts** [1962] 1 WLR 1344, [1962] 3 All ER 838n, approval was requested on behalf of the statutory next-of-kin of Mrs. Joan Parkin. Her next-of-kin at the date of the application was an infant adopted son, Alan James Parkin, the first respondent. If she survived him, her next-of-kin would be the four infant grandchildren of her maternal aunt. They were made respondents to the summons, as were the trustees.

BUCKLEY J approved the arrangement. He could do so on behalf of the first respondent under para (*a*) of s. 1 (1) on the grounds of infancy, and in respect of the four infant grandchildren under para (*b*). It was not necessary therefore that the infant grandchildren should be made parties. BUCKLEY J said at 1346, at 839:

"Section 1 (1) (*b*) of the Variation of Trusts Act, 1958, enables me to approve the arrangement on behalf of 'any person (whether ascertained or not) who may become entitled, directly or indirectly, to an interest under the trusts as being at a future date or on the happening of a future event a person of any specified description or a member of any specified class of persons ... ' The first respondent would fall within that description, but the section goes on: 'so however that this paragraph shall not include any person who would be of that description, or a member of that class, as the case may be, if the said date had fallen or the said event had happened at the date of the application to the court ... ' The first respondent is excluded, therefore, from the persons on whose behalf I can sanction the arrangement under section 1 (1) (*b*), but none of the other persons who might become entitled to participate in the estate of the settlor were she to survive the first respondent and then die intestate is excluded because none of them would be within the class of next-of-kin if she died today. Therefore, I am in a position to approve the arrangement on behalf of all persons whether ascertained or not who might become interested in the settlor's estate at a future date with the exception of the first respondent.

At the time the summons was drafted, the effect of that was not appreciated and certain persons were joined who would, in certain events, be the persons who would be the settlor's next-of-kin. In my view, it was unnecessary for those persons to be joined. Their interests can be looked after by the trustees, and they are persons who may never fall within the class of beneficiaries because they may predecease the settlor or the first respondent may survive the settlor. The summons could have been framed with the settlor as applicant and the first respondent and the trustees as respondents. I am not criticising counsel for the way in which the summons was framed because at the time it was settled it was not realised that it was not necessary to join all possible future next-of-kin."

[His Lordship then considered the scheme and approved it on behalf of the infant respondents and all other persons who might thereafter become entitled to an interest in the trust fund.]

(ii) APPROVAL REFUSED

In **Knocker v Youle** [1986] 1 WLR 934, [1986] 2 All ER 914,[4] income from a share of a trust fund was held on trust for the settlor's daughter for life, with remainder to appointees under her will. In default of appointment there was a gift over to the settlor's son or, if he were dead, to the settlor's four married sisters living at the son's death, or, if they were then dead, to their issue who should attain 21. In 1984, the settlor's wife and four sisters having died, the settlor's son and daughter sought a variation of the trusts of the settlement, but none of the very numerous issue of the four sisters was made a party since it was not practicable to obtain their consent. In holding that the court had no jurisdiction to approve the variation on their behalf, WARNER J said at 937, at 916:

_____

4 (1986) 136 NLJ 1057 (P. Luxton); [1987] Conv 144 (J.G. Riddall).

"There are two difficulties. First, it is not strictly accurate to describe the cousins as persons 'who may become entitled ... to an interest under the trusts.' There is no doubt of course that they are members of a 'specified class.' Each of them is, however, entitled now to an interest under the trusts, albeit a contingent one (in the case of those who are under 21, a doubly contingent one) and albeit also that it is an interest that is defeasible on the exercise of the general testamentary powers of appointment vested in Mrs. Youle and Mr. Knocker. Nonetheless, it is properly described in legal language as an interest, and it seems to me plain that in this Act the word 'interest' is used in its technical, legal sense. Otherwise, the words 'whether vested or contingent' in section 1 (1) (*a*) would be out of place.

What counsel invited me to do was in effect to interpret the word 'interest' in section 1 (1) loosely, as a layman might, so as not to include an interest that was remote. I was referred to two authorities: *Re Moncrieff's Settlement Trusts (Practice Note)* [1962] 1 WLR 1344, [1962] 3 All ER 838n, p. 791, ante and the earlier case, *Re Suffert's Settlement* [1961] Ch 1, [1960] 3 All ER 561, p. 791, ante. In both those cases, however, the class in question was a class of prospective next of kin, and of course it is trite law that the prospective or presumptive next of kin of a living person do not have an interest. They have only a spes successionis, a hope of succeeding, and quite certainly they are the typical category of persons who fall within section 1 (1) (*b*). Another familiar example of a person falling within that provision is a potential future spouse. It seems to me, however, that a person who has an actual interest directly conferred upon him or her by a settlement, albeit a remote interest, cannot properly be described as one who 'may become' entitled to an interest.

The second difficulty (if one could think of a way of overcoming the first) is that there are, as I indicated earlier, 17 cousins who, if the failure or determination of the earlier trusts declared by the settlement had occurred at the date of the application to the court, would have been members of the specified class, in that they were then living and over 21. Therefore, they are prima facie excluded from section 1 (1) (*b*) by what has been conveniently called the proviso to it, that is to say the part beginning 'so however that this paragraph shall not include ... ' They are in the same boat, if I may express it in that way, as the first cousins in *Re Suffert's Settlement* and the adopted son in *Re Moncrieff's Settlement Trusts (Practice Note)*. The court cannot approve the arrangement on their behalf; only they themselves can do so.

Mr. Argles suggested that I could distinguish *Re Suffert's Settlement* and *Re Moncrieff's Settlement Trusts (Practice Note)* in that respect for two reasons. First, he suggested, that the proviso applied only if there was a single event on the happening of which one could ascertain the class. Here, he said, both Mr. Knocker and Mrs. Youle must die without exercising their general testamentary powers of appointment to the full before any of the cousins could take anything. But it seems to me that what the proviso is referring to is the event on which the class becomes ascertainable, and that that is a single event. It is, in this case, the death of the survivor of Mrs. Youle and Mr. Knocker, neither of them having exercised the power to the full; in the words of clause 7 of the settlement, it is 'the failure or determination of the trusts herein-before declared concerning the trust fund.'

The second reason suggested by Mr. Argles why I should distinguish the earlier authorities was that the event hypothesised in the proviso was the death of the survivor of Mr. Knocker and Mrs. Youle on the date when the originating summonses were issued, that is to say on 6 January 1984. There is evidence that on that day there were in existence wills of both of them exercising their testamentary powers to the full. The difficulty about that is that the proviso does not say 'so however that this paragraph shall not include any person who would have become entitled if the said event had happened at the date of the application to the court.' It says 'so however that this paragraph shall not include any person who would be of that description, or a member of that class, as the case may be, if the said date had fallen or the said event had happened at the date of the application to the court.' So the proviso is designed to identify the presumptive members of the class at the date of the application to the court and does not advert to the question whether at that date they would or would not have become entitled.

I was reminded by counsel of the principle that one must construe Acts of Parliament having regard to their purpose, and it was suggested that the purpose here was to exclude the need to join as parties to applications under the Variation of Trusts Act 1958 people whose interests were remote. In my view, however, that principle does not enable me to take the sort of liberty with the language of this statute that I was invited to take. It is noteworthy that remoteness does not seem to be the test if one thinks in terms of presumptive statutory next of kin. The healthy issue of an elderly widow who is on her death bed, and who has not made a will, have an expectation of succeeding to her estate; that could hardly be described as remote. Yet they are a category of persons on whose behalf the court could, subject of course to the proviso, approve an arrangement under this Act. On the other hand, people in the position of the cousins in this case have an interest that is extremely remote. Nonetheless, it is an interest, and the distinction between an expectation and an interest is one which I do not think that I am entitled to blur. So, with regret, having regard to the particular circumstances of this case, I have to say that I do not think that I have jurisdiction to approve these arrangements on behalf of the cousins.''

In **Re Christie-Miller's Settlement Trusts** [1961] 1 WLR 462, [1961] 1 All ER 855n, the question was whether persons who were possible objects of a power of appointment should be made parties to an application. The appointor was a party, and counsel agreed that the order should recite that he released the power. WILBERFORCE J held that it was not necessary to join as parties the possible objects of the power. Their possibility of ever becoming interested had been extinguished by the release.

C. How a Variation Takes Effect

i. THE EFFECT OF APPROVAL OF THE COURT

RE HOLT'S SETTLEMENT [5]
[1969] 1 Ch 100, [1968] 1 All ER 470 (ChD, MEGARRY J)

In 1959 the settlor settled £15,000 on trust for his daughter Mrs. Wilson for life, and after her death on trust for such of her children as should attain the age of 21.

---

5 (1968) 84 LQR 162 (P.V.B.).

The fund was invested in a private company, and it increased in value to some £320,000. Mrs. Wilson wished to surrender her life interest in one half of the fund in favour of her children, and to vary the trusts in such a way that the children would become entitled at the age of 30; and that one half of the income of each child's share should be accumulated until the child attained the age of 25, or until the earlier expiration of 21 years from the date of the court's order.

In the application to MEGARRY J for approval, various questions arose: (i) whether, on a variation after 1964, the periods of perpetuity permitted by the Perpetuities and Accumulations Act 1964 could be utilised; (ii) whether the application was properly a variation of existing trusts or whether it was a revocation and resettlement; (iii) whether a variation under the Variation of Trusts Act 1958 took effect upon the court's order alone or upon some other basis.

Held. The application was approved. It took effect by virtue of the order of the court, and the new periods of perpetuity could be included.

MEGARRY J: Two main questions have been debated before me. I propose to consider these now, and to deal separately with certain details of the proposed arrangement. These questions are: first, does an order under the Act of 1958 ipso facto vary the terms of the trust without the execution of the arrangement or any other document by or on behalf of any beneficiary, apart from those on whose behalf section 1 (1) of the Act empowers the court to approve the arrangement? Secondly, if after the commencement of the Perpetuities and Accumulations Act 1964, a variation is made in trusts constituted before the commencement of that Act, can that variation take advantage of the changes in the rules against perpetuities and accumulations which that Act has made?

Under the first head, the basic issue is whether an order under the Act of 1958 by itself varies the terms of the trust. Put rather differently, the question is whether the Act does no more than empower the court to supply on behalf of the infants, unborn persons and others mentioned in section 1 (1) that binding approval which they cannot give, leaving the other beneficiaries to provide their own approvals in some other document which will bind them. In the present case the arrangement was drafted on the assumption that the order of the court will ipso facto vary the terms of the trusts; for the "operative date" is defined as being the date of the order approving this arrangement, and the perpetuity period and the accumulation period (which are made use of in the terms of the trusts) each commences on the operative date.

The only authority directly on the point which has been cited to me is the decision in *Re Hambleden's Will Trusts* [1960] 1 WLR 82, [1960] 1 All ER 353. I do not think I need read the provisions of the trusts in that case. It was a summons under the Act of 1958, and the judgment of Wynn-Parry J as reported is very short. The report does, however, include certain interlocutory observations. Wynn-Parry J made it clear that his view was that the order of the court ipso facto varied the trusts. He had had cited to him the decision of Vaisey J in *Re Joseph's Will Trusts* [1959] 1 WLR 1019, [1959] 3 All ER 474 where that learned judge had inserted words in the order of the court which authorised and directed the trustees to carry the arrangement into effect. Wynn-Parry J said:

"I do not agree with that decision. I take the view that I have no jurisdiction to make an order including words directing the trustees to carry the arrangement into effect, and those words should be deleted from the draft minutes. Nothing is required except the approval of the court to the arrangement. If that approval is given the trusts are ipso facto altered, and the trustees are bound thereafter to give effect to the arrangement."

Later in the course of the argument he said [1960] 1 WLR 82 at 85, [1960] 1 All ER 353 at 355: "If I approve an arrangement, I alter the trusts. Res ipsa loquitur". Again, a little later, he said: "If I approve an arrangement, I vary the trusts." His judgment I will recite in its entirety:

"Very well. I hold that the effect of my approval is effective for all purposes to vary the trusts. Thereafter, the trusts are the trusts as varied. I approve the minutes of order, with the slight alterations which have been referred to, and the arrangement in the schedule."

If that were a decision of the Court of Appeal I could venerate and obey, even without fully comprehending. But the decision is at first instance, and so is of persuasive and not binding authority. It is my misfortune not to be persuaded by such assertions, even though fourfold, when made without explanation. . . .

Where the arrangement is put into effect there is a disposition of an equitable interest, so that unless there is some document signed by the adult beneficiaries, or by some agent authorised by them in writing, the requirements of section 53 (1) (*c*) [of the Law of Property Act 1925] are not satisfied. This contention is supported by a reference to the decision by the House of Lords in *Grey v IRC* [1960] AC 1, [1959] 3 All ER 603, p. 54, ante, that an oral direction by a beneficiary to his trustees to hold property on certain trusts is a disposition, and that "disposition" must be given its ordinary wide meaning. It is further said that as there is here a transaction under which a moiety of a life interest will pass from Mrs. Wilson to her children, this is a fortiori a "disposition". I may add that there is the minor point that the common form of order under the Act does not normally recite that all the adults have consented to the transaction, though where the insertion of such a recital is required by the parties, the registrars insert it.

Let me say at once that there would seem to be no great difficulty in averting the consequences of this argument for the future. The adults could either execute the arrangement or, perhaps more conveniently, give written authority to their solicitors or counsel to execute it on their behalf. The latter course would usually be the more convenient, because not infrequently changes (often minor) have to be made to the arrangement put before the court. It is, however, a fact that many thousands of orders must have been made in the past on the footing of *Re Hambleden's Will Trusts* [1960] 1 WLR 82, [1960] 1 All ER 353. If the argument is right, there is the very real difficulty that those orders will, perhaps in most cases, perhaps only in some, have effected no variation of the trusts. This is a consideration which is particularly awkward in that a question of jurisdiction is involved; for if the court has no jurisdiction to make an order which itself varies the trusts, and orders have been made on the footing that the orders do ipso facto vary the trusts, then it seems at least arguable that such orders were made without jurisdiction. It has also been pointed out that the Inland Revenue has for some while acted upon the decision, and that orders of the court have been stamped on the footing that they ipso facto vary the terms of the trusts. Yet again, it is plain that present practice is convenient. It avoids the burden which usually, perhaps, would not be very great, but in individual cases might be substantial, of getting the necessary signatures of the adults either to the document itself or to written authorities. I bear all those considerations in mind; nevertheless, it seems to me that there is very considerable force in the argument that has been advanced. The decision in *Re Hambleden's Will Trusts* provides authority to the contrary but no explanation of the grounds for the decision. Accordingly, a substantial part of the argument in this case has been directed to the discovery of some basis upon which the convenient practice of *Re Hambleden's Will Trusts* can be rested.

In attempting to summarise Mr. Godfrey's argument for the settlor, I am sure I shall fail to do it justice. As I understood it, he submitted that the decision in *Re Hambleden's Will Trusts* was quite wrong but that in effect this did not matter. All that the court has to do, he said, is to approve the arrangement (i.e., the proposal made), and there was no question of the court approving anything which in law amounted to a disposition. The arrangement was not a disposition but merely a bargain or proposal, which was not within the ambit of section 53 (1) (*c*) of the Law of Property Act, 1925. The court, he urged, was not concerned to see that the adults consented and certainly not that they executed any disposition. There might thus be no disposition at all; but the persons specified by section 1 (1) of the Act of 1958 would be bound by the order of the court approving the arrangement, and the other beneficiaries could not in practice go back on what their counsel had assented to, at any rate so far as it had been acted upon. The result would be that, although there would be no new equitable interests actually created under the arrangement, all the beneficiaries would by a species of estopped be treated as if they had those interests. I hope that Mr. Godfrey will forgive me if I say that I find this argument somewhat unattractive.[6] In particular, I find it very hard to believe that Parliament intended the court to approve on behalf of infants arrangements which depended for their efficacy upon the uncertainties of estoppel. I bear in mind, too, the wide meaning which *Grey v IRC* [1960] AC 1, [1959] 3 All ER 603 gave to the word "disposition" in section 53 (1) (*c*).

Mr. Brookes, for the trustees, boldly asserted that, when correctly read, the Act of 1958 indirectly did what *Re Hambleden's Will Trusts* said it did. He went back to the words of section 1 (1), and emphasised that the power of the court was a power exercisable "by order" and that that power was a power to approve an arrangement "varying or revoking" all or any of the trusts. In emphasising those phrases, he said that the right way to read the section was to say that the power of the court was merely a power to make an order approving an arrangement which in fact varied or revoked the trusts, and not an arrangement which failed to do any such thing. When the adults by their counsel assented to the arrangement, and the court on behalf of the infants by order approved the arrangement, then there was an arrangement which varied or revoked the trusts. So the order of the court both conferred jurisdiction and exercised it. His escape from section 53 (1) (*c*) had a similar dexterity about it: by conferring an express power on the court to do something by order, Parliament in the Act of 1958 had provided by necessary implication an exception from section 53 (1) (*c*). He buttressed his contention by a reference to *Re Joseph's Will Trusts* [1959] 1 WLR 1019, [1959] 3 All ER 474. Vaisey J there accepted that the order which he made, directing the trustees to carry the order of the court into effect, was neither contemplated by the Act nor expressly authorised by it. Rather than read into the Act words that are not there, said Mr. Brookes, one should construe the Act as authorising an order which is efficacious to achieve its avowed object. He pointed to the long title of

6 See *Spens v IRC* [1970] 1 WLR 1173 at 1183–1185, [1970] 3 All ER 295 at 300–302.

the Act which reads: "An Act to extend the jurisdiction of courts of law to vary trusts in the interests of beneficiaries and sanction dealings with trust property."

I hope that Mr. Brookes, too, will pardon me if I say that I did not find his argument compelling. Indeed, at times I think it tended to circularity. But I find it tempting; and I yield. It is not a construction which I think the most natural. But it is not an impossible construction; it accords with the long title; it accords with the practice which has been relied upon for many years in some thousands of cases; and it accords with considerations of convenience. The point is technical, and I do not think that I am doing more than straining a little at the wording in the interests of legislative efficacy.

However that is not all. Mr. Millett, for Mrs. Wilson, the tenant for life, provided another means of escape from section 53 (1) (*c*) in his helpful reply. Where, as here, the arrangement consists of an agreement made for valuable consideration, and that agreement is specifically enforceable, then the beneficial interests pass to the respective purchasers on the making of the agreement. Those interests pass by virtue of the species of constructive trust made familiar by contracts for the sale of land, where under the vendor becomes a constructive trustee for the purchaser as soon as the contract is made, albeit the constructive trust has special features about it.[7] Section 53 (2), he continued, provides that "This section does not affect the creation or operation of resulting, implied or constructive trusts." Accordingly, because the trust was constructive, section 53 (1) (*c*) was excluded. He supported this contention by the House of Lords decision in *Oughtred v IRC* [1960] AC 206, [1959] 3 All ER 623. He relied in particular upon passages in the speeches (at 227, 231, at 625, 628) of Lord Radcliffe and Lord Cohen, albeit that they were dissenting on the main point for decision. He pointed out that although Lord Jenkins (with whom Lord Keith concurred) had not decided the point, he had assumed for the purposes of his speech that it was correct (at 239, at 633), and that the rejection of the contention by Lord Denning (at 233, at 629) was in a very brief passage. Mr. Millett accepts that if there were to be some subsequent deed of family arrangement which would carry out the bargain, then this deed might well be caught by section 53 (1) (*c*); but that, he said, cannot affect the "arrangement", and the parties might well be willing to let matters rest on that. It seems to me that there is considerable force in this argument in cases where the agreement is specifically enforceable, and in its essentials I accept it. At all events it supports the conclusion that in such cases the practice established by *Re Hambleden's Will Trusts* [1960] 1 WLR 82, [1960] 1 All ER 353 is right. For this and the other reasons that I have given, though with some hesitation, I accordingly hold this to be the case.

Finally, before turning to the second main point, I should mention that in this case the arrangement carries out its purpose by revoking all the existing trusts and establishing a new set of trusts. That being so, it is said that some difficulty arises on the wording of section 1 (1) of the Act of 1958. This merely empowers the court to approve an arrangement "varying or revoking all or any of the trusts", and so, it is said, the court cannot approve an arrangement which, instead of merely "revoking" or merely "varying", proceeds to revoke and then to set up new trusts, thereby producing an effect equivalent to the process of settlement and resettlement. The section, it is argued, says nothing of establishing new trusts for old. As a matter of principle, however, I do not

7 See p. 287, ante.

really think that there is anything in this point, at all events in this case. Here the new trusts are in many respects similar to the old. In my judgment, the old trusts may fairly be said to have been varied by the arrangement whether the variation is effected directly, by leaving some of the old words standing and altering others, or indirectly, by revoking all the old words and then setting up new trusts partly, though not wholly, in the likeness of the old. One must not confuse machinery with substance; and it is the substance that matters. Comparing the position before and after the arrangement takes effect, I am satisfied that the result is a variation of the old trusts, even though effected by the machinery of revocation and resettlement.

[His Lordship considered *Re T's Settlement Trusts* [1964] Ch 158, [1963] 3 All ER 759, and continued:] A line may, perhaps, one day emerge from a sufficiently ample series of reported decisions; but for the present all that is necessary for me to say is whether the particular case before me is on the right side or the wrong side of any reasonable line that could be drawn. In this case I am satisfied that the arrangement proposed falls on the side of the line which bears the device "variation".[7a]

I can now turn to the second main point, namely, that under the Perpetuities and Accumulations Act 1964. The settlement in this case was made prior to the commencement of that Act, and any variation will be made after that commencement. Section 15 (5) provides that "The foregoing sections of this Act shall apply ... " (and there is then an exception with which I am not concerned) " ... only in relation to instruments taking effect after the commencement of this Act.... " There follows a reference to instruments made in the exercise of a special power of appointment. The Act received the Royal Assent on July 16, 1964, so that this is the date of its commencement.

The kind of question that arises is this. Suppose an instrument taking effect in 1959, as the original trusts did in this case, and a variation made under the Act of 1958 which merely alters a few words: will such a variation allow the Act of 1964 to apply to the trusts in their revised form? Again, suppose that, as here, there is a revocation of the old trusts and a declaration of new trusts, so that in form there is a new start, although in substance merely a variation: does this alter the position? Could something be done by the second method which cannot be done by a method which in form as well as in substance is a mere variation? Is it possible to have a variation under the Act of 1958 once every generation, and then with each variation start afresh with a relaxed perpetuity rule and a new accumulation period bounteously provided by the Act of 1964?

Mr. Millett boldly answered "Yes" to this last question, and harked back to those spacious days when strict settlements of land were common, and once a generation there was a process of settlement and resettlement, with all the old entails securely barred and new entails established. He pointed out that on each resettlement the settlors in effect changed, and that often there would be a similar result on a variation under the Act of 1958. When the settlement was first made the original settlor was the settlor; but when the first variation came to be made, then if there was any alteration in the beneficial interests (as distinct from the mere conferring of additional administrative powers quoad those beneficial interests) the beneficiaries concerned would be the settlors, transferring their interests to be held on new trusts. Thus in effect there would

---

7a Megarry J considered the point more fully in *Re Ball's Settlement Trusts* [1968] 1 WLR 899, [1968] 2 All ER 438, p. 801, post.

be a new start each time. Mr. Millett drew my attention to the decision of Plowman J in *Re Lloyd's Settlement* [1967] 2 WLR 1078, [1967] 2 All ER 314, where, he said, this in effect was done. In that case a settlement inter vivos was made on March 21, 1958 (March 21, 1959, in the headnote and March 31, 1958, in the statement of facts seem to be erroneous). The settlement directed an accumulation, and in the result the only appropriate accumulation period was that of the settlor's life. The effect was to expose the trust property to estate duty risks in respect of an interest which would pass on the settlor's death, and accordingly in 1966 a variation of the trusts was sought under the Act of 1958. By then the Act of 1964 had come into effect. Under the trusts as varied by the arrangement, accumulation was directed for a period of 21 years from the date of the settlement; and this period is one which was made available for the first time by the Act of 1964. Accordingly, under the Act of 1958 a settlement made prior to the Act of 1964 was varied after that Act in a way which took advantage of the provisions of that Act. The case is shortly reported, setting out the facts at some length, the cases cited in the argument, and the order made; but unfortunately there is no statement of the reasons of the learned judge. Nevertheless it seems to me that the variation in fact there made supports Mr. Millett's contention.

Mr. Millett also referred me to Lewin on Trusts, 16th edn (1964), at p. 741, where an argument which is in accord with Mr. Millett's submission is advanced by the learned editor (the passage cannot have been the work of the late Mr. Lewin). I would only observe that there appears on page 742 to have been a slip in the statement of *Pilkington v IRC* [1964] AC 612, [1962] 3 All ER 622, for the reference in the text should, it seems, be to a power of advancement rather than to a power of appointment, and the citation of the case is also erroneous. For myself, I find any analogy with powers of appointment and powers of advancement unsatisfactory. The mischief attacked by the rule against perpetuities in the case of powers of appointment, and now, since *Pilkington v IRC,* in the case of powers of advancement as well, is that the property is tied up ab initio. The power is conferred by the settlement, and that person exercising the power can do so only within pre-ordained limits. The power indeed "belongs" to the old settlement, if I may respectfully adopt the language of Lord Radcliffe in the *Pilkington* case at 642, at 632. Under the Act of 1958, there are no such limits. The property, as it seems to me, is freely disposable. Under an arrangement approved by the court the trusts may be brought wholly to an end. On the other hand, they may be varied; and there is no limit, other than the discretion of the court and the agreement of the parties, to the variation which may be made. Any variation owes its authority not to anything in the initial settlement but to the statute and the consent of the adults coming, as it were, ab extra. This certainly seems to be so in any case not within the Act where a variation or resettlement is made under the doctrine of *Saunders v Vautier* (1841) 4 Beav 115 by all the adults joining together; and I cannot see any real difference in principle in a case where the court exercises its jurisdiction on behalf of the infants under the Act of 1958. It seems to me that the arrangement, coupled with the order of the court, constitute an "instrument", or, since the singular includes the plural, "instruments", which take effect after July 15, 1964. Whether the documents are regarded as separate instruments or as together constituting one composite instrument, the effect is produced by the complex of documents; and what takes effect after July 15, 1964, is the result of this complex of documents. In my judgment, therefore, it is permissible to insert provisions deriving their validity from the Act of 1964 into an arrangement approved under the Act of 1958.

That, I think, suffices to dispose of the two substantial points; and I should perhaps say that I have been astute to do so without resort to the Fourth ([1956] Cmnd 18) and Sixth ([1957] Cmnd 310) Reports of the Law Reform Committee or the discussions which led to those reports, despite their relationship to the Acts of 1964 and 1958 respectively. I propose now to consider the merits of the arrangement put forward.

I can deal with the merits of this application quite shortly.

[His Lordship approved the arrangement as being for the benefit of each of the beneficiaries categorised by s. 1 (1) of the Act.]

In **Inland Revenue Commissioners v Holmden** [1968] AC 685, [1968] 1 All ER 148, Lord REID said at 701, at 151:

"Each beneficiary is bound because he has consented to the variation. If he was not of full age when the arrangement was made he is bound because the court was authorised by the Act to approve it on his behalf and did so by making an order . . . So the arrangement must be regarded as an arrangement made by the beneficiaries themselves. The court merely acted on behalf of or as representing those beneficiaries who were not in a position to give their own consent and approval."

And Lord HODSON at 705, at 153: "In my opinion, the effect of the arrangement varying the settlement was, as Harman LJ pointed out, to rewrite the settlement from the date of the order in the terms proposed and approved by the court."

ii. VARIATION OR RESETTLEMENT

In **Re Ball's Settlement Trusts**[8] [1968] 1 WLR 899, [1968] 2 All ER 438, MEGARRY J, approving an arrangement "revoking the trusts of the . . . settlement and resettling the subject-matter of the . . . settlement", said at 903, at 441:

"What section 1 (1) of the Act authorises the court to approve is 'any arrangement . . . varying or revoking all or any of the trusts, or enlarging the powers of the trustees of managing or administering any of the property subject to the trusts.'

The word 'resettling' or its equivalent nowhere appears. Accordingly, while there is plainly jurisdiction to approve the arrangement in so far as it revokes the trusts, in my view there is equally plainly no jurisdiction to approve the arrangement as regards 'resettling' the property, at any rate eo nomine. In this connection, I bear in mind the words of Wilberforce J in *Re T's Settlement Trusts* [1964] Ch 158, [1963] 3 All ER 759. He there said at 162, at 762:

'I have no desire to cut down the very useful jurisdiction which this Act has conferred upon the court. But I am satisfied that the proposal as originally made to me falls outside it. Though presented as "a variation" it is in truth a complete new resettlement. The former trust funds were to be got in

---

8 (1968) 84 LQR 459 (P.V.B.); *Allen v Distillers Co (Biochemical) Ltd* [1974] QB 384, [1974] 2 All ER 365; [1974] ASCL 524 (J. Hackney).

from the former trustees and held upon wholly new trusts such as might be made by an absolute owner of the funds. I do not think that the court can approve this.'

It seems to me that the originating summons correctly describes what is sought to be done in this case, and as so described there is clearly no jurisdiction for the court to approve the arrangement. But it does not follow that merely because an arrangement can correctly be described as effecting a revocation and resettlement, it cannot also be correctly described as effecting a variation of the trusts. The question then is whether the arrangement in this case can be so described. In the course of argument I indicated that it seemed desirable for the summons to be amended by substituting the words 'varying' for the word 'revoking' and deleting the reference to 'resettling', and that I would give leave for this amendment to be made. On the summons as so amended the question is thus whether the arrangement can fairly be said to be covered by the word 'varying' so that the court has power to approve it.

There was some discussion of the ambit of this word in *Re Holt's Settlement* [1969] 1 Ch 100, [1968] 1 All ER 470. It was there held that if in substance the new trusts were recognisable as the former trusts, though with variations, the change was comprehended within the word 'varying', even if it had been achieved by a process of revocation and new declaration. In that case, the new trusts were plainly recognisable as the old trusts with variations. In the present case, the new trusts are very different from the old. The settlor's life interest vanishes; so does the power of appointment, though that will now be released. In place of the provision in default of appointment for absolute interests for the two sons if they survive the settlor, and if not, for their issue stirpitally, there is now a life interest for each son, and vested absolute interests for the children of the sons born before October 1, 1977. There is a clean sweep of the somewhat exiguous administrative provisions and an equally exiguous new set in their place. The arrangement also makes altogether new provisions for insurance policies, both those which provide for death duties and are to be added to the trust fund and those which provide for the excluded persons and are to be held on separate trusts; but these portions of the arrangement, I should say, are not made part of the settlement as revised, but are to operate independently and outside its terms. All that remains of the old trusts are what I may call the general drift or purport, namely, that a moiety of the trust fund is to be held on certain trusts for each son and certain of his issue. Is the word 'varying' wide enough to embrace so categorical a change?

[His Lordship referred to *Re Dyer* [1935] VLR 273, and continued:] If an arrangement changes the whole substratum of the trust, then it may well be that it cannot be regarded merely as varying that trust. But if an arrangement, while leaving the substratum, effectuates the purpose of the original trust by other means, it may still be possible to regard that arrangement as merely varying the original trusts, even though the means employed are wholly different and even though the form is completely changed.

I am, of course, well aware that this view carries me a good deal farther than I went in *Re Holt's Settlement* [1969] 1 Ch 100, [1968] 1 All ER 470, p. 794, ante. I have felt some hesitation in the matter, but on the whole I consider that this is a proper step to take. The jurisdiction of the Act is beneficial and, in my judgment, the court should construe it widely and not be astute to confine its beneficent operation. I must remember that in essence the court is merely contributing on behalf of infants and unborn and unascertained persons the binding assents to the arrangement which they, unlike an adult beneficiary, cannot give. So far as is proper, the power of the court to give that assent should be assimilated to the wide powers which the ascertained adults have.

In this case, it seems to me that the substratum of the original trusts remains. True, the settlor's life interest disappears; but the remaining trusts are still in essence trusts of half of the fund for each of the two named sons and their families, with defined interests for the sons and their children in place of the former provisions for a power of appointment among the sons and their children and grandchildren and for the sons to take absolutely in default of appointment. In the events which are likely to occur, the differences between the old provision and the new may, I think, fairly be said to lie in detail rather than in substance. Accordingly, in my judgment, the arrangement here proposed, with the various revisions to it made in the course of argument, can properly be described as varying the trusts of the settlement. Subject to the summons being duly amended, I therefore approve the revised arrangement."

D. Fraud on a Power

Parker and Mellows: *Modern Law of Trusts* (6th edn) p. 554

"It is a statement of the obvious that if a variation is fraudulent or contrary to public policy it will not be sanctioned. A case of some interest on this point is *Re Robertson's Will Trusts*[9], where the applicant had exercised a special power of appointment in favour of his children as a preliminary to the proposed arrangement. His purpose and intention in making the appointment was to benefit his children and not himself. Later he was advised that his financial position would in fact be improved if the appointment were made and the scheme approved. But Russell J held that to suppose his original purpose and intention had been changed or added to was unjustified. It followed that there was no fraud on the power, though, if there had been, the court would not have been able to approve the scheme.

However, subsequent case-law appears to indicate a certain conflict as to the precise principles to be applied. In *Re Wallace's Settlement*[10] Megarry J said that the fact that protected life tenants had executed appointments in favour of their children in itself raised a case for inquiry because the life tenants benefited by the arrangement; but on the evidence he was satisfied that there was no fraud on the power because the benefit to the life tenants was not substantial and they had intended to make the appointment before the arrangement was approved. However, in *Re Brook's Settlement*[11] Stamp J adopted a rather different approach. He held that the exercise of a special power of appointment amounted to a fraud on the power and he was unable to approve the variation. Here one of the purposes of the appointment (by a protected life tenant in favour of his children from which he would also benefit from a division of the capital) was to enable the life tenant to obtain what he could not otherwise get, namely capital rather than income. This was enough to invalidate the appointment.

The important feature of *Re Brook* is that the judge emphasised that the question is whether the *purpose* of the appointment amounted to a fraud, not,

---

9 [1960] 1 WLR 1050, [1960] 3 All ER 146n.
10 [1968] 1 WLR 711, [1968] 2 All ER 209.
11 [1968] 1 WLR 1661, [1968] 3 All ER 416.

as was apparently suggested in *Re Wallace*, the *effect* of the appointment on the financial position of the appointor. It is thought that *Re Brook* applies the correct principle.

Release. The difficulties that may thus arise as a result of a fraud on the power, however inadvertent, may in some circumstances be avoided by releasing the power. For no question of a fraud on a power can arise on a mere release. And it has been held that, provided that the power in question can be released,[12] the court will approve an arrangement varying a settlement even though the objects of the power are ignored.[13] There appears to be some doubt whether the release should be effected by deed, or whether it can be inferred from the facts. The latter would seem sufficient.[14]

Even if the power cannot be released (e.g. if it was given to the donee *qua* trustee) it still seems possible to apply to the court for an arrangement extinguishing the power because this amounts to varying or revoking a trust within section 1 of the 1958 Act. But because the power is not of itself releasable the court is likely to impose conditions on the release. Thus Stamp J in *Re Drewe's Settlement*,[15] in approving an arrangement, insisted that it could only be effected by deed and with the consent of the trustees.''

E. Principles Applicable to the Exercise of the Discretion

i. OBSERVING THE SETTLOR'S INTENTION

RE STEED'S WILL TRUSTS[16]
[1960] Ch 407, [1960] 1 All ER 487 (CA, Lord EVERSHED MR, WILLMER and UPJOHN LJJ)

The testator gave property which included Loft Farm to trustees "upon protective trusts as defined by section 33 of the Trustee Act, 1925" for his housekeeper Gladys Sandford for her life, and after her death for such persons as she may by deed or will appoint; and in default of appointment upon trust for her next of kin.

The will declared (clause 9) that it was the testator's "wish that she shall have the use and enjoyment of the capital value thereof if she needs it during her life. And ... that if and when such property shall be sold my trustees may apply capital moneys from such sale to or for her benefit ... provided that they shall consider the necessity for retaining sufficient capital to prevent her from being without adequate means at any time during her life ..."

Gladys exercised the power of appointment in her own favour.

The farm was let to Gladys's brother. There was some doubt whether he paid any rent, or was able to do so. The trustees decided that the farm should be sold, and they received a good offer. Gladys asked the court to restrain the sale,

---

12 See *Re Wills' Trust Deeds* [1964] Ch 219, [1963] 1 All ER 390; (1968) 84 LQR 64 (A.J. Hawkins).

13 *Re Christie-Miller's Settlement Trusts* [1961] 1 WLR 462, [1961] 1 All ER 855n; *Re Courtauld's Settlement* [1965] 1 WLR 1385, [1965] 2 All ER 544n; *Re Ball's Settlement* [1968] 1 WLR 899, [1968] 2 All ER 438.

14 In *Re Ball* MEGARRY J insisted on a formal release, but in *Re Christie-Miller* and *Re Courtauld* an inferred release was regarded as sufficient.

15 [1966] 1 WLR 1518, [1966] 2 All ER 844n.

16 See also *Re Michelham's Will Trusts* [1964] Ch 550, [1963] 2 All ER 188; *Re Remnant's Settlement Trusts* [1970] Ch 560 at 567, [1970] 2 All ER 554 at 559, p. 811, post.

and brought a summons under the Variation of Trusts Act 1958, asking the court to approve an arrangement under which the trustee should hold the property on trust for herself absolutely.

Held. The court refused its approval.

LORD EVERSHED MR: This is in more ways than one, including matters of procedure, a somewhat unusual case, as Mr. Newsom observed. It is also in many respects an unhappy case, and I cannot refrain from expressing my own sympathy for the plaintiff on the one side, and for the three defendant trustees on the other.

I propose in this judgment to forbear from entering, except where absolutely necessary, into matters of fact which might only serve to rub salt into existing wounds. Suffice it to say that the plaintiff was one who served loyally and most skilfully for a long period of time the testator and the testator's wife. In consideration for those services the testator included in his will provisions for her benefit ...

It is, I think, quite plain on the evidence that the testator, while anxious to show his gratitude to the plaintiff, was no less anxious she should be well provided for and not exposed to the temptation, which he thought was real, of being, to use a common phrase, sponged upon by one of her brothers. I fully realise that the plaintiff's natural affection for that brother is not a matter which one can in any sense condemn. Blood is, after all, thicker than water, and the happiness of the plaintiff, according to her own view at any rate, is very much linked up with the association with that brother and the brother's daughter and wife.

[His Lordship decided that the court ought not to interfere with the exercise by the trustees of their discretion; and continued]: I now come to what has caused me greater difficulty, namely, the effect of the Variation of Trusts Act 1958 ...

In the present case, the proposed variation (that is, the "arrangement") which the plaintiff puts forward may be most briefly and accurately stated as involving this: in clause 9 of the will the words: "upon protective trusts as defined by section 33 of the Trustee Act 1925", should be omitted, and similarly in the next clause the words "protective" should be omitted. If those words were omitted, the result would be that the plaintiff would become absolutely entitled to the property, because she would then be the life tenant, having appointed by irrevocable deed to herself the reversion; and that is what she seeks.

The trustees have taken the view that it is not an arrangement which, having regard to their conception of their duties and the wishes of their testator, they should approve. For my part, I do not think that approval on behalf of the trustees is the court's function in this case, though the court in exercising its general discretion will certainly pay regard to what thy trustees say and the grounds for their saying it. Nor can I see, if this was the judge's view, that the court is called upon by the language of this section to approve the arrangement or proposal on behalf of the proposer; that is to say, whether they think she was wise or unwise to put her idea forward.

The duty of the court, as I read the section on the facts of this case, is that they must approve it on behalf of the only person or persons who might have an interest under the discretionary trusts and whose presence under the trusts now prevents the plaintiff saying that she can put an end to the settlement.

Having regard to the plaintiff's age, no doubt it is true to say that she will not and cannot now have children, but she might marry, and marry more than once. She says, with some reason, that having lived for 53 years unmarried she does not feel in the least likely to marry now. That may well be right, though many have said that before and subsequent events have proved them wrong. That, however, is neither here nor there. There does exist a discretionary trust, and a future husband of the plaintiff's is a person interested under those trusts, on whose behalf the court must now approve the proposal.

Having regard to what has happened between the plaintiff and her brother, it is possible that, strictly speaking, there has been a forfeiture, and if so, the future husband or husbands would be within paragraph (*b*) of the subsection, but if not, he would be within paragraph (*d*). Again, I think that does not, for present purposes, matter.

I repeat that the duty of the court is now to consider whether in the exercise of its discretion, which is framed in the widest possible language, it should approve the arrangement on behalf of what has been described in argument as the spectral spouse of the plaintiff. In doing that, what must the court consider? Not, I conceive, merely the material benefit or detriment of such spouse. Certainly not if he is to be regarded as being a person, under paragraph (*d*), though if he is to be regarded as falling under paragraph (*b*) it is expressly enjoined that the court shall not approve the arrangement unless it is for his benefit.

As I have said, I do not so read this Act as to mean that the court's duty in the exercise of this very wide and, indeed, revolutionary discretion is confined to saying: "Would it really much harm this spectral spouse if we approve the proposal?" Bearing in mind, of course, the admitted possibility that the spouse might cease to be spectral and become a reality, I think what the court is bound to do is to see whether, looked at on behalf of the person indicated, it approves the arrangement. It is the arrangement which has to be approved, not just the limited interest of the person on whose behalf the court's duty is to consider it.

If that is right, it then follows that the court must regard the proposal as a whole, and so regarding it, then ask itself whether in the exercise of its jurisdiction it should approve that proposal on behalf of the person who cannot give a consent, because he is not in a position to do so. If that is a right premise, then it follows that the court is bound to look at the scheme as a whole, and when it does so, to consider, as surely it must, what really was the intention of the benefactor. That such is a proper approach is at least supported by the provisions of RSC Ord. 55, r. 14A (3A),[17] which provides that in the case of an application under this Act, where there is a living settlor the living settlor is to be a party before the court. That rule seems to me to reinforce what I conceive to underly this provision, namely, that the court must, albeit that it is performing its duty on behalf of some person who cannot consent on his or her own part, regard the proposal in the light of the purpose of the trust as shown by the evidence of the will or settlement itself, and of any other relevant evidence available.

Having so formulated the duty, I have, for my part, come to the conclusion that it would not be right for the court in the exercise of its discretion to approve this variation or arrangement. I am not uninfluenced in coming to that conclusion by any means by the circumstance that the judge obviously did

17 Now Ord. 93, r. 6 (2).

not think it was a proposal which should be approved, though it is quite true that for reasons which I have indicated it may be said he was looking at it and basing his jurisdiction upon an interpretation of the section which I have not been altogether able to share, namely, it was his duty to approve it on behalf of the proposer, the plaintiff, and also that the scheme must be regarded as intended to be in some sense inter partes and, therefore, that he had to approve it on behalf of the trustees.

Disagreeing, if that is a fair view of his judgment, with that premise, nevertheless it is quite clear, I think, that the judge was by no means unsympathetic to the feelings and views of the plaintiff, but, on the other hand, was no less clear in his mind that the arrangement was one which so cut at the root of the testator's wishes and intentions that it was not one which the court should approve.

After all, if the court is asked to approve this proposal on behalf of a spectral spouse (if I may revert to that phrase), it must ask, I take it, why is the spectral spouse there at all under the trust? If one asks that question, nearly everything else, as it seems to me, follows. There is no doubt why the spectral spouse is there. It was part of the testator's scheme, made as I think manifest by the language which I have read from the clauses in the will, that it was the intention and the desire of the testator that this trust should be available for the plaintiff so that she would have proper provision made for her throughout her life, and would not be exposed to the risk that she might, if she had been handed the money, part with it in favour of another individual about whom the testator felt apprehension, which apprehension is plainly shared by the trustees.

For those reasons, therefore, I also conclude adversely to the plaintiff that we should not exercise jurisdiction under the Act of 1958 to approve the arrangement which has been put forward, and which I have tried to define. That is the end of the case. I only repeat the sympathy I have felt in a distressing matter of this kind, both with the plaintiff and with the trustees, whose difficulties in discharging their duty are obvious. I should like to express the hope that perhaps time, the healer, will do much to put an end to these troubles.

ii. BENEFIT: FISCAL, SOCIAL AND MORAL

RE WESTON'S SETTLEMENTS[18]
[1969] 1 Ch 223, [1968] 3 All ER 338 (CA, Lord DENNING MR, HARMAN and DANCKWERTS LJJ)

In 1964 Mr. Stanley Weston made two settlements, one in consideration of the marriage of his elder son Robert, who was born in 1942, and the other a voluntary settlement in favour of his younger son Alan, born in 1949. Under each settlement, the son in question received a life interest with a general power of appointment over part of the fund and subject thereto on trust for such of his children as he shall appoint and in default of appointment on trust

---

18 (1969) 85 LQR 15 (P.V.B.); (1968) 32 Conv (NS) 431 (F.R. Crane); (1976) 40 Conv (NS) 295 (T.G. Watkin).

for his children absolutely. The investments of both settlements were in the Stanley Weston Group Ltd.

These settlements were subject to fiscal disadvantages, namely to capital gains tax on disposal (introduced by the Finance Act 1965) and to estate duty upon the deaths of each of the sons. These problems were explained by STAMP J in the lower court [1969] 1 Ch 223 at 231–232, [1968] 1 All ER 720 at 723–724.

The settlor and the two sons (and the family of the elder son) moved their homes to Jersey, and claimed to be resident and domiciled there. The settlor asked the court to appoint (under Trustee Act 1925, s. 41, p. 624 ante) two persons of good repute, resident in Jersey, in the place of the existing English trustees; and asked the court to approve an arrangement under the Variation of Trusts Act 1958 which inserted in the trusts a power in the new trustees to discharge the property from the trusts of the English settlements and to subject it to identical trusts of a Jersey settlement.

Held (affirming STAMP J). The court refused.

LORD DENNING MR: If the court gives its approval to the proposed scheme, the result will be that the new trustees will be able to sell the shares in the Stanley Weston Group and buy other shares, without being accountable for capital gains. There will be also considerable savings of estate duty on the deaths of the two sons Robert and Alan. In short, there will be a tremendous tax advantage to the sons and grandchildren of Mr. Stanley Weston. The question is whether the court ought to sanction the scheme.

There is one reported case in which a scheme on these lines was approved. It was *Re Seale's Marriage Settlement* [1961] Ch 574, [1961] 3 All ER 136. In that case husband and wife married in 1931. They were both domiciled and resident in England: and a marriage settlement was made in an English trust in the ordinary form. They had three children who appear to have been born in England. But when the children were quite small the family emigrated to Canada. The children were brought up as Canadians and were likely to continue to live in Canada. The husband and wife intended to continue to live there. It was obviously advantageous for the settlement to be turned from an English settlement into a Canadian settlement—quite irrespective of tax advantages—and Buckley J made orders enabling Canadian trustees to be appointed and a Canadian settlement to be drawn up substantially in the same terms as the English settlement.

Those advising Mr. Weston ask the court to approve a similar scheme here. The judge refused. He said that this was a "cheap exercise in tax avoidance" which he ought not to sanction: but he hoped that the case would be taken to the Court of Appeal so as to have the views of this court.

Before the Variation of Trusts Act 1958, there was much discussion as to the power of the court to sanction the variation of trusts. If the beneficiaries were all sui juris, they could agree between themselves to revoke or vary the trusts. If there were infant beneficiaries or unborn persons, it needed the consent of the court. But the jurisdiction of the court so to consent was very limited. The court could not sanction it except in case of a compromise of disputed rights: see *Chapman v Chapman* [1954] AC 429, [1954] 1 All ER 798. By the Variation of Trusts Act 1958, this limitation was removed. The court has power to approve a variation or revocation of the trust, if it thinks fit, on behalf of infants or unborn persons. The statute gives no guide as to the way in which this discretion should be exercised. It says: "The court may *if it thinks fit* by order approve ... ". Likewise with the appointment of new trustees, the Trustee Act,

1925, gives no guide. It simply says the court may appoint new trustees "whenever it is expedient". There being no guidance in the statutes, it remains for the court to do the best it can.

Two propositions are clear: (i) In exercising its discretion, the function of the court is to protect those who cannot protect themselves. It must do what is truly for their benefit. (ii) It can give its consent to a scheme to avoid death duties or other taxes. Nearly every variation that has come before the court has tax avoidance for its principal object: and no one has ever suggested that this is undesirable or contrary to public policy.

But I think it necessary to add this third proposition: (iii) The court should not consider merely the financial benefit[19] to the infants or unborn children, but also their educational and social benefit. There are many things in life more worthwhile than money. One of these things is to be brought up in this our England, which is still "the envy of less happier lands". I do not believe it is for the benefit of children to be uprooted from England and transported to another country simply to avoid tax. It was very different with the children of the Seale family, which Buckley J considered. That family had emigrated to Canada many years before, with no thought of tax avoidance, and had brought up the children there as Canadians. It was very proper that the trust should be transferred to Canada. But here the family had only been in Jersey three months when they presented this scheme to the court. The inference is irresistible: the underlying purpose was to go there in order to avoid tax. I do not think that this will be all to the good for the children. I should imagine that, even if they had stayed in this country, they would have had a very considerable fortune at their disposal, even after paying tax. The only thing that Jersey can do for them is to give them an even greater fortune. Many a child has been ruined by being given too much.[20] The avoidance of tax may be lawful, but it is not yet a virtue. The Court of Chancery should not encourage or support it—it should not give its approval to it—if by so doing it would imperil the true welfare of the children, already born or yet to be born.

There is one thing more. I cannot help wondering how long these young people will stay in Jersey. It may be to their financial interest at present to make their home there permanently. But will they remain there once the capital gains are safely in hand, clear of tax? They may well change their minds and come back to enjoy their untaxed gains. Is such a prospect really for the benefit of the children? Are they to be wanderers over the face of the earth, moving from this country to that, according to where they can best avoid tax? I cannot believe that to be right. Children are like trees: they grow stronger with firm roots.

The long and short of it is, as the judge said, that the exodus of this family to Jersey is done to avoid British taxation. Having made great wealth here, they want to quit without paying the taxes and duties which are imposed on those who stay. So be it. If it really be for the benefit of the children, let it be done. Let them go, taking their money with them. But, if it be not truly for their benefit, the court should not countenance it. It should not give the scheme its

---

19 "The word 'benefit' is, I think, plainly not confined to financial benefit, but may extend to moral or social benefit": *Re Holt's Settlement* [1969] 1 Ch 100 at 121, [1968] 1 All ER 470 at 479, per MEGARRY J. See also *Re T's Settlement Trusts* [1964] Ch 158, [1963] 3 All ER 759; *Re CL* [1969] 1 Ch 587, [1968] 1 All ER 1104; *Re Remnant's Settlement Trusts* [1970] Ch 560, [1970] 2 All ER 554.

20 Each settlement was worth some £400,000.

blessing. The judge refused his approval. So would I. I would dismiss this appeal.[1]

HARMAN LJ: This is an essay in tax avoidance naked and unashamed, and none the worse for that, says the applicant. Indeed the judge agreed that this court is not the watch-dog of the Inland Revenue, and it is well known that much and perhaps the main use which has been made of the Act has been to produce schemes of variation of English trusts which will have the effect of reducing liabilities either on the capital of the trusts or the income of the beneficiaries. . . .

Now, the linchpin of the scheme is not to be carried out under the Variation of Trusts Act at all. It is essential that the court should exercise its powers under the Trustee Act 1925, either by appointing new trustees out of the jurisdiction or giving leave to the existing trustees to make the appointment. It is not suggested that the present trustees are unsuitable or that any difficulty has arisen in the administration of the trusts. The scheme is entirely conditioned by the wish to avoid the incidence of capital gains tax. For this purpose it is essential that the affairs of the trust should be administered from outside the United Kingdom and that this should be done by appointing two persons so resident as trustees. It is proposed that these trustees should then be empowered while still trustees of the English settlements to revoke the whole of the trusts of those instruments and to transfer the assets to themselves as trustees of the two settlements framed, it is said, so as to conform with the Jersey law.

Now, this law has never had any experience of trusts and so far as appears, the courts of Jersey have never made an order executing the trusts of a settlement. There is not, it appears, any Trustee Act in Jersey at all, and the effect of this last transaction must, so far as I can see, have nothing to recommend it from a trust point of view[2].

In the circumstances the judge was entitled to consider whether the court "should think fit" to accede to the scheme. The judge professed himself unsatisfied, and I think he was entitled to take that view. It is true that he expressed some dislike of tax avoidance of this sort, and in that he may have been mistaken, but he was in my opinion well justified in not being satisfied that a transfer of the whole trust to Jersey is expedient. The two young men who alone may be considered cannot be said to have proved that they truly intend to make Jersey their home. Indeed the younger of them has expressed no views on the subject at all. It seems to me most unlikely that two wealthy young men of this sort will be content at the threshold of their lives to settle down in the island and will not within a short time seek wider opportunities for

1 Cf. *Re Windeatt's Will Trusts* [1969] 1 WLR 692, [1969] 2 All ER 324, (variation approved by PENNYCUICK J where the "family had been in Jersey for 19 years and had made a genuine and permanent home there. The children were born there".); *Re Whitehead's Will Trusts* [1971] 1 WLR 833, [1971] 2 All ER 1334, p. 620, ante (where PENNYCUICK J approved appointment of trustees resident overseas approved by the court where beneficiaries were resident and domiciled in Jersey). See also *Re Chamberlain* (unreported) discussed in (1976) 126 NLJ 1034 (J.B. Morcom) (transfer of funds from trust governed by English law to trust governed by law of Guernsey where primary beneficiaries were resident and domiciled in France and remaindermen in Indonesia); *Richard v The Hon AB Mackay* (14 March 1987, unreported) p. 620, ante.

2 See Trusts (Jersey) Law 1984, and, generally, Matthews and Sowden, *Jersey Law of Trusts* (1988); Solly, *Jersey, A Low-Tax Area* (1982); Trusts (Guernsey) Law 1989; (1991) 5 Trust Law International 19 (R.A.R. Evans).

their talents and wealth than that island affords. It follows, as it seems to me, that on the facts of this case no case has been made out for the removal of the trusts to Jersey rather than any other part of the world. These are English settlements and they should I think remain so unless some good reason connected with the trusts themselves can be put forward. I am of opinion, therefore, that the judge was entitled in the exercise of his discretion to say that to use the powers of the Trustee Act in this way was not justified and I would dismiss the appeal.

iii. FAMILY HARMONY

In **Re Remnant's Settlement Trusts** [1970] Ch 560, [1970] 2 All ER 554, a trust fund in favour of the children of two sisters Mrs. Hooper ("Dawn") and Mrs. Crosthwaite ("Merrial") was subject to forfeiture in respect of any of their children who practised Roman Catholicism or was married to a Roman Catholic, with an accruer provision in favour of the children of the other. The children of Dawn were Protestant, those of Merrial were Roman Catholic. PENNYCUICK J was asked to approve an arrangement which deleted the forfeiture provision and accelerated the interest of the children of each sister in a sum of £10,000, part of the trust fund.

The deletion of the forfeiture clause was clearly not for the financial benefit of Dawn's Children; for they stood a very good chance of benefiting from it under the accruer provision. Nevertheless, PENNYCUICK J approved the arrangement. He said at 566, at 559:

"The three considerations set out by Mrs. Crosthwaite, and elaborated by counsel, are these: first, that the forfeiture provisions represent a deterrent to each of the Hooper children from adopting the Roman Catholic faith should she be minded to do so; secondly, that they operate as a deterrent to each of the Hooper children in the selection of a husband when the time comes; and thirdly, that the forfeiture provisions represent a source of possible family dissension. I am not sure that there is very much weight in the first of those considerations because there is no reason to suppose that any of these children has any particular concern with the Roman Catholic faith. On the other hand, I do think there is very real weight in the second and in the third considerations. Obviously a forfeiture provision of this kind might well cause very serious dissension between the families of the two sisters. On the best consideration I can give it I think that the deletion of the forfeiture provisions on the terms contained in the arrangement, including the provision for acceleration in £10,000, should be regarded as for the benefit of the three Hooper children.

I have not found this an easy point, but I think I am entitled to take a broad view of what is meant by 'benefit', and so taking it, I think this arrangement can fairly be said to be for their benefit . . .

I conclude then that the carrying out of this arrangement will be for the benefit of all the persons born and unborn on whose behalf I am concerned to approve the arrangement.

It remains to consider whether the arrangement is a fair and proper one. As far as I can see, there is no reason for saying otherwise, except that the arrangement defeats this testator's intention. That is a serious but by no means conclusive consideration. I have reached the clear conclusion that these forfeiture provisions are undesirable in themselves in the circumstances of this case and that an arrangement involving their deletion is a fair and proper one.

I propose accordingly to approve the arrangement with one or two modifications which are not material to this judgment.

I would only like to add this word of caution. The effect of any particular forfeiture provision must depend on the nature of the provision itself and upon the circumstances in which it is likely to operate. A forfeiture provision is by no means always intrinsically undesirable. Again, you may have the position that a forfeiture provision benefits exclusively one or the other party concerned, and in that case it might be very difficult to say that the deletion of the provision was for the benefit of that party, unless there was the fullest financial compensation. However, I am not concerned to go further into those matters. It is sufficient for me to say that on the facts of this particular case the deletion of the forfeiture provisions, upon the terms of the arrangement, is for the benefit of everyone concerned and that the arrangement is a fair and proper one.''

(1971) 34 MLR 98 (R.B.M. Cotterrell)
"Even more difficult problems arise in cases such as *Re Remnant* and *Re Weston* where it becomes necessary to weigh the relative importance of countervailing financial and non-financial considerations. Thus the court may find itself forced to evaluate such considerations as the benefit to an English child in being brought up in England,[3] or the benefit to a mental patient in releasing a trust interest which she would probably have wished to release if sane.[4] In such circumstances it is hard to avoid the conclusion that benefit and the measure of it is simply what the court says it is.

Since each case in this area of the law must be largely a matter of decision on the facts, comparison of the reported cases is difficult. Nevertheless they offer some guidance in an area where there is little else to guide the court and it is unfortunate that no cases other than *Re Weston* were discussed in *Re Remnant*. In the case of *Re Tinker's Settlement*,[5] Russell J refused to approve a variation on behalf of unborn children under which they would lose a contingent interest under the trust on the ground that the variation would not be for their benefit even though it might prevent dissatisfaction and conflict in the family. While the remarks in *Re Tinker's Settlement*[6] which suggest that financial benefit must be present to satisfy the requirement of 'benefit' now seem unacceptable, the actual decision in the case has not been challenged and was approved by Cross in *Re CL*.[7] The position in *Re Tinker* was strikingly similar to that in *Re Remnant* and, while grounds of distinction could have been found, it would have been more satisfactory to have some consideration of the relevant pre-*Weston* cases. In view of the awesome width of the court's present discretion, it will be regrettable if judges underestimate the importance of precedent, wisely used, as an aid to uniformity of treatment and coherence in trust variation law. Where such a heavy burden of decision is placed on the court these qualities seem particularly important and desirable.''

---

3 *Re Weston's Settlements* [1969] 1 Ch 223, [1968] 3 All ER 338, p. 807, ante.
4 *Re CL* [1969] 1 Ch 587, [1968] 1 All ER 1104.
5 [1960] 1 WLR 1011, [1960] 3 All ER 85n. The part of the proposed variation which conferred a purely financial benefit on the unborn children was approved.
6 The case was not cited in *Re Weston's Settlements* or *Re Remnant's Settlement Trusts*, but see CROSS J in *Re CL*, supra at 599, at 1109.
7 [1969] 1 Ch 587, [1968] 1 All ER 1104.

iv. TAKING A CHANCE

The question arises whether the court should approve on behalf of a beneficiary who will in almost every conceivable set of circumstances be benefited, but might be prejudiced in one possible foreseeable situation. To what extent should the court take the chance of his receiving a benefit?

In **Re Holt's Settlement** [1969] 1 Ch 100, [1968] 1 All ER 470 [8], MEGARRY J said at 121, at 479:

"The point that at one stage troubled me concerns the unborn issue. Mr. Brookes, as in duty bound, put before me a contention that it was possible to conceive of an unborn infant who would be so circumstanced that a proposed rearrangement would be entirely to his disadvantage. He postulated the case of a child born to Mrs. Wilson next year, and of Mrs. Wilson dying in childbirth, or shortly after the child's birth. In such a case, he said, the benefit of the acceleration of interest resulting from Mrs. Wilson surrendering the moiety of her life interest would be minimal, and there would be no saving of estate duty. All that would happen in regard to such an infant would be that the vesting of his interest would be postponed from age 21 to age 30; and the only possible advantage in that would be the non-financial moral or social advantage to which I have just referred. In support of this contention he referred me to the decision of Stamp J in *Re Cohen's Settlement Trusts* [1965] 1 WLR 1229, [1965] 3 All ER 139. There, the scheme originally proposed was not approved by the court because there was a possibility of there being a beneficiary who would get no advantage whatsoever from the proposed arrangement; it would merely be to his detriment.

Mr. Millett, however, points out that there is an essential distinction between that case and this; for there, whatever the surrounding circumstances, the unborn person contemplated could not benefit from the arrangement. In the present case, he says, all that Mr. Brookes has done is to put forward the case of an infant who might be born next year; and it would be a result of the surrounding circumstances, and not of the time of birth or the characteristics of the infant, that that infant might derive no benefit from the arrangement proposed. Mr. Millet referred me to *Re Cohen's Will Trusts* [1959] 1 WLR 865, [1959] 3 All ER 523 [9] where Danckwerts J held that in exercising the jurisdiction under the Act of 1958 the court must, on behalf of those persons for whom it was approving the arrangement, take the sort of risk which an adult would be prepared to take. Accordingly, says Mr. Millett, Mr. Brookes' special infant to be born next year was in the position that although there was the chance that its mother would die immediately afterwards, there was also the alternative chance that its mother would survive its birth for a substantial period of time. In the latter event, which was the more probable, the advantages of the arrangement would accrue to the infant. In short, he distinguishes the decision of Stamp J in *Re Cohen's Settlement Trusts* [1965] 1 WLR 1229, [1965] 3 All ER 139 on the footing that that was the case of an unborn person whose prospects were hopeless, whatever the events, whereas in the present case the hypothetical unborn person has the normal prospects of

---

8 For the facts see p. 794, ante. See also *Re Robinson's Settlement Trusts* [1976] 1 WLR 806, [1976] 3 All ER 61.
9 See (1960) 76 LQR 22 (R.E.M.).

events occurring which will either improve or not improve his position. Such an unborn person falls, he says, into the category of unborn persons on whose behalf the court should be prepared to take a risk if the arrangement appears on the whole to be for their benefit.

It seems to me that this is a proper distinction to make, and I accept it. Accordingly, I hold that the arrangement is for the benefit of the classes of persons specified in section 1 (1) of the Act, and I approve it.''

QUESTIONS

1. Which of the theories concerning the operation of the Variation of Trusts Act 1958 do you think is convincing? Should writing be required to effect a change in the beneficial interests of assenting adults? *Grey v IRC* [1960] AC 1, [1959] 3 All ER 603, p. 54, ante; *Oughtred v IRC* [1960] AC 206, [1959] 3 All ER 623, p. 57, ante; *Re Holt's Settlement* [1969] 1 Ch 100, [1968] 1 All ER 470, p. 794, ante.

2. Do you think that the Variation of Trusts Act 1958 provides too generous fiscal advantages for those lucky enough to have interests under settlements? Do you think it right that minors should suffer from the disadvantage that they are unable to make fiscally advantageous changes in their interests under settlements when adults in their situation could do so freely? L.R.C. Seventh Report, Cmnd. 310; (1965) 43 CBR 181 (A.J. Maclean).

3. Read again Part III on Trusts and Taxes, and consider in what circumstances you would advise a variation today.

4. Observe the differences in the meaning given to the word "benefit" in

   a) Variation of Trusts Act 1958; (1969) 33 Conv (NS) pp. 122–131.
   b) Trustee Act 1925, s. 31 (1) (power to apply income for maintenance education or benefit), p. 762, ante.
   c) Trustee Act 1925, s. 32 (1) (power to apply capital of a settlement for the advancement or benefit of beneficiaries), p. 762, ante.

20. Fiduciary Position of Trustees[1]

I. General[1a]

The principle of equity is that a trustee must not benefit from his position as trustee. He must not put himself in a position in which his duty to the trust may conflict with his personal interest.[1a] This, as will be seen, is manifested in various ways. A trustee must not trade in the trust estate, nor take profits or commissions. The rules have been laid down in the strongest terms; but the cases will show how difficult are the border-lines of its application. On the other hand, he has always been entitled to reimbursement of out-of-pocket expenses properly incurred[2]. And there is no objection to a provision in the trust instrument that trustees shall be remunerated. Indeed the complications of the administration of trusts at the present day necessitate the appointment of professionals.

---

1 H & M, pp. 575–598; K & S, pp. 228–235, 341–357; P & M, pp. 221–251, 397, 527–540; Pettit, pp. 418–424, 459–464; Riddall, pp. 328–336, 388–390; Snell, pp. 245–257; Underhill, pp. 345–369, 646–656, 787–803; Oakley, *Constructive Trusts* (2nd edn), chap. 3; Finn, *Fiduciary Obligations* (1977); Shepherd, *Law of Fiduciaries* (1981); (1989) 9 OJLS 285 (R. Flannigan); Bean, *Fiduciary Obligations and Joint Ventures* (1995); McKendrick, ed. *Commercial Aspects of Trusts and Fiduciary Obligations* (1992); Law Commission Report on Fiduciary Duties and Regulatory Rules 1995 (Law Com. No. 236).

1aSee *Sargeant v National Westminster Bank plc* (1990) 61 P & CR 518 (settlor placed trustees in such a position).

2 TA 1925, s. 30 (2), *infra*; *Stott v Milne* (1884) 25 ChD 710; *Re Chapman* (1894) 72 LT 66 (expenses unreasonable); *Turner v Hancock* (1882) 20 ChD 303 at 305 per JESSEL MR ("all their proper costs incident to the execution of the trusts").

    On costs of litigation, see *Holding and Management Ltd v Property Holding and Investment Trust plc* [1989] 1 WLR 1313, [1990] 1 All ER 938; *McDonald v Horn* [1995] 1 All ER 961 (power of court to order costs to be paid out of pension fund).

II. Payments to a Trustee[3]

A. Reimbursement of Expenses

TRUSTEE ACT 1925

30. Implied indemnity of trustees.—(2) A trustee may reimburse himself or pay or discharge out of the trust premises all expenses incurred in or about the execution of the trusts or powers.[4]

In **Hardoon v Belilios** [1901] AC 118, the plaintiff was employed by a firm of share brokers. In order to assist a syndicate speculating in shares, fifty £10 shares in the Bank of China, Japan and the Straits Ltd. were placed in his name. The defendant was the absolute beneficial owner of the shares.

On the liquidation of the Bank, the liquidator made calls upon the plaintiff for over £400. The Privy Council held that the defendant was personally liable to reimburse him. Lord LINDLEY said at 124:

"Where the only cestui que trust is a person sui juris, the right of the trustee to indemnity by him against liabilities incurred by the trustee by his retention of the trust property has never been limited to the trust property; it extends further, and imposes upon the cestui que trust a personal obligation enforceable in equity to indemnify his trustee. This is no new principle, but is as old as trusts themselves."[5]

B. Remuneration[6]

A professional trustee will always insist upon provision being made for the payment of proper fees for his work.

Encyclopedia of Forms and Precedents (4th edn) vol. 20, p. 635

"Any trustee for the time being hereof (other than the settlor or any wife of the settlor) being a solicitor or other person engaged in any profession or business

---

3 H & M, pp. 575–578; K & S, pp. 352–355; P & M, pp. 397, 521–540; Pettit, pp. 418–424, 459–464; Riddall, pp. 328–336; Snell, pp. 253–257; Underhill, pp. 787–803.
4 *Stott v Milne* (1884) 25 ChD 710; *Re Chapman* (1894) 72 LT 66; *Holding and Management Ltd v Property Holding and Investment Trust plc* [1989] 1 WLR 1313, [1990] 1 All ER 938.
5 See *JW Broomhead (Vic) Pty Ltd v JW Broomhead Pty Ltd* [1985] VR 891; (1990) 64 ALJ 567 (R.A. Hughes).
6 See also Public Trustee Act 1906, ss. 4, 9, pp. 638, 641, ante; Public Trustee (Fees) Act 1957; Administration of Justice Act 1965, s. 2; Public Trustee (Fees) Order 1983, SI 1983 No. 443; as amended, p. 635, n.1, ante; Judicial Trustees Act 1896, s. 1, p. 635, ante (under which a corporation appointed to act as custodian trustee, the Public Trustee and a judicial trustee are authorised to charge fees); (1952) 16 Conv (NS) 13 (G. Boughen Graham).
  On the remuneration of charity trustees, see Annual Report for 1989, paras. 87–95, Appx C; CC Leaflet 11 (Remuneration of Charity Trustees); [1994] 2 Ch Com Rep, pp. 14–15.
  See *Re Orwell's Will Trusts* [1982] 1 WLR 1337, [1982] 3 All ER 177, where a similar professional charging clause was held to entitle the literary executor of the widow of George Orwell to charge remuneration; *Space Investments Ltd v Canadian Imperial Bank of Commerce Trust Co (Bahamas) Ltd* [1986] 1 WLR 1072, [1986] 3 All ER 75.

shall be entitled to charge and be paid all usual professional or other charges for business done by him or his firm in relation to the trusts hereof and also his reasonable charges in addition to disbursements for all other work and business done and all time spent by him or his firm in connection with matters arising in the premises including matters which might or should have been attended to in person by a trustee not being a solicitor or other person so engaged but which such a trustee might reasonably require to be done by a solicitor or other person so engaged."[7]

C. Authorisation by the Court in Special Cases

The court may in appropriate cases authorise remuneration in favour of trustees or other persons acting in a fiduciary capacity.

In **Brown v Litton** (1711) 1 P Wms 140, the plaintiff's testator was captain of a ship, and had $800 with him on a voyage. He died. The defendant, the mate, became captain, took the dollars and traded successfully with them. On his return to England, the question was whether the defendant's obligation was to return the money with interest, or whether he was liable to account for the profits. Lord Keeper HARCOURT held that he must account for the profits; but that he should be given a proper reward for his work.

In **Re Jarvis** [1958] 1 WLR 815, [1958] 2 All ER 336, two sisters, Rosetta and Sheila, became entitled to half shares in their deceased father's shop. The shop was largely destroyed by enemy bombing in 1940. Sheila had it repaired and built up the business. UPJOHN J held that Sheila was accountable as constructive trustee as to half for Rosetta "subject to all just allowances for her time, energy and skill, for the assets she has contributed and the debts of the testator which she has paid."

In **Re Masters** [1953] 1 WLR 81, [1953] 1 All ER 19, on the death of Leslie Ninian Masters, a grant of administration was made to Coutts and Co., a trust corporation, and to the widow. No provision was made for remuneration. The estate was worth £95,000 gross. DANCKWERTS J held that Trustee Act 1925, s. 42 (which permits the court to authorise remuneration for a corporation appointed by it as trustee) applied to this case. The court also had inherent jurisdiction to authorise remuneration.

In **Boardman v Phipps** [1967] 2 AC 46, [1966] 3 All ER 721, p. 844, post, the defendant, Boardman, acted as solicitor to the Phipps family trust. Most of the funds were invested in a family firm, which was badly managed and

---

7 In the case of marriage settlements, it is desirable, in order to preserve IHT exemptions conferred in consideration of marriage, to add: "Provided that no such charges shall be of greater amount than is reasonable according to the nature of the work and business."

unprofitable. Acting in good faith throughout, Boardman purchased shares which enabled him to take control of the company. He made it highly profitable, and brought about a great increase in the value of the shares owned by the Phipps trust and those which he owned himself. The House of Lords held that he was accountable to the Phipps trust for the profits he had made, on the ground that the opportunity to make them arose from his fiduciary position; but that he was entitled to payment on a liberal scale in respect of his work and skill.[8]

In **O'Sullivan v Management Agency and Music Ltd** [1985] QB 428, [1985] 3 All ER 351,[9] a contract between a manager and his young and unknown composer and performer of popular music, whose retail sale of records realised a gross figure of some £14.5 million between 1970 and 1978, was set aside for undue influence. The Court of Appeal held that the defendants must account for the profits, but also should be entitled to a reasonable remuneration including a small profit element in respect of their skill and labour in promoting the plaintiff. Fox LJ said at 468, at 373:

"Once it is accepted that the court can make an appropriate allowance to a fiduciary for his skill and labour I do not see why, in principle, it should not be able to give him some part of the profit of the venture if it was thought that justice as between the parties demanded that. To give the fiduciary any allowance for his skill and labour involves some reduction of the profits otherwise payable to the beneficiary. And the business reality may be that the profits could never have been earned at all, as between fully independent persons, except on a profit sharing basis. But be that as it may, it would be one thing to permit a substantial sharing of profits in a case such as *Boardman v Phipps* where the conduct of the fiduciaries could not be criticised and quite another to permit it in a case such as the present where, though fraud was not alleged, there was an abuse of personal trust and confidence. I am not satisfied that it would be proper to exclude Mr. Mills and the M.A.M. companies from all reward for their efforts. I find it impossible to believe that they did not make a significant contribution to Mr. O'Sullivan's success. It would be unjust to deny them a recompense for that. I would, therefore, be prepared as was done in *Boardman v Phipps* to authorise the payment (over and above out of pocket expenses) of an allowance for the skill and labour of the first five defendants in promoting the compositions and performances and managing the business affairs of Mr. O'Sullivan, and that an inquiry (the terms of which would need to be considered with counsel) should be ordered for that purpose. Such an allowance could include a profit in the way that solicitors' costs do."

In **Guinness plc v Saunders** [1990] 2 AC 663, [1990] 1 All ER 652, p. 840, post, the House of Lords refused remuneration to a company director, who was assumed to have acted bona fide but in circumstances which involved a clear conflict of interest and duty. Lord GOFF OF CHIEVELEY said at 701, at 667:

"It will be observed that the decision [in *Boardman v Phipps* [1967] 2 AC 46, [1966] 3 All ER 721, supra] to make the allowance was founded upon the

8 See also *Re Barbour's Settlement* [1974] 1 WLR 1198, [1974] 1 All ER 1188; cf. *Re Codd's Will Trusts* [1975] 1 WLR 1139, [1975] 2 All ER 1051n.
9 (1986) 49 MLR 118 (W. Bishop and D.D. Prentice).

simple proposition that it would be inequitable now for the beneficiaries to step in and take the profit without paying for the skill and labour which has produced it. Ex hypothesi, such an allowance was not in the circumstances authorised by the terms of the trust deed; furthermore it was held that there had not been full and proper disclosure by the two defendants to the successful plaintiff beneficiary. The inequity was found in the simple proposition that the beneficiaries were taking the profit although, if Mr. Boardman (the solicitor) had not done the work, they would have had to employ an expert to do the work for them in order to earn that profit.

The decision has to be reconciled with the fundamental principle that a trustee is not entitled to remuneration for services rendered by him to the trust except as expressly provided in the trust deed. Strictly speaking, it is irreconcilable with the rule as so stated. It seems to me therefore that it can only be reconciled with it to the extent that the exercise of the equitable jurisdiction does not conflict with the policy underlying the rule. And, as I see it, such a conflict will only be avoided if the exercise of the jurisdiction is restricted to those cases where it cannot have the effect of encouraging trustees in any way to put themselves in a position where their interests conflict with their duties as trustees.

Not only was the equity underlying Mr. Boardman's claim in *Boardman v Phipps* clear and, indeed, overwhelming; but the exercise of the jurisdiction to award an allowance in the unusual circumstances of that case could not provide any encouragement to trustees to put themselves in a position where their duties as trustees conflicted with their interests. The present case is, however, very different. Whether any such an allowance might ever be granted by a court of equity in the case of a director of a company, as opposed to a trustee, is a point which has yet to be decided; and I must reserve the question whether the jurisdiction could be exercised in such a case, which may be said to involve interference by the court in the administration of a company's affairs when the company is not being wound up. In any event, however, like my noble and learned friend, Lord Templeman, I cannot see any possibility of such jurisdiction being exercised in the present case. I proceed, of course, on the basis that Mr. Ward acted throughout in complete good faith. But the simple fact remains that, by agreeing to provide his services in return for a substantial fee the size of which was dependent upon the amount of a successful bid by Guinness, Mr. Ward was most plainly putting himself in a position in which his interests were in stark conflict with his duty as a director. Furthermore, for such services as he rendered, it is still open to the board of Guinness (if it thinks fit, having had a full opportunity to investigate the circumstances of the case) to award Mr. Ward appropriate remuneration. In all the circumstances of the case, I cannot think that this is a case in which a court of equity (assuming that it has jurisdiction to do so in the case of a director of a company) would order the repayment of the £5.2m. by Mr. Ward to Guinness subject to a condition that an equitable allowance be made to Mr. Ward for his services."[10]

In **Foster v Spencer** [1996] 2 All ER 672, Judge Paul Baker QC awarded remuneration to the trustees of a cricket club for their past, but not future,

10 No reference was made to *O'Sullivan v Management Agency and Music Ltd* [1985] QB 428, [1985] 3 All ER 351, supra.

services. They were also entitled to past expenses but not to any interest thereon. "Where, as in this case, there were no funds out of which to pay remuneration at the time of their appointment, nor was a true appreciation of the extent of the task possible, a prospective application would be impracticable, if not impossible. The refusal of remuneration . . . would result in the beneficiaries being unjustly enriched at the expense of the trustees."

In **Re Duke of Norfolk's Settlement Trusts** [1982] Ch 61, [1981] 3 All ER 220,[11] a trustee company was entitled under a settlement made in 1958 to remuneration in accordance with its usual scale of fees then in force. In 1966 further property was added to the settlement, involving the trustee company in exceptionally burdensome work in connection with the development of Arundel Court in the Strand; this was entirely outside anything which could reasonably have been foreseen when the trustee company accepted office. The introduction of capital transfer tax in 1975 also involved further work. The trustee company sought extra remuneration for this extra work done, and also a general review of its fees for the future.

At first instance [1979] Ch 37, [1978] 3 All ER 907, WALTON J awarded the company additional remuneration in respect of the development, but not in respect of capital transfer tax. He further held that the court had no inherent jurisdiction to authorise any general increase in fees for the future. The Court of Appeal reversed the latter part of WALTON J's decision. BRIGHTMAN LJ said at 80, at 231:

"In this appeal we are concerned with the power of the High Court to authorise a trust corporation, which has been in office for some 20 years, to charge fees for its future services in excess of those laid down in the trust instrument. In his admirable submissions in the unwelcome role of *advocatus diaboli* which this court imposed upon him, Mr. Romer confined himself to that narrow issue. He did not dispute that the High Court can, in the exercise of its inherent jurisdiction, authorise a trustee to retain remuneration where none is provided by the terms of the trust. What the court has no jurisdiction to do, he submitted, was to authorise an increase in the general level of remuneration of a paid trustee by way of addition to the remuneration which is allowed by the trust, once the trust has been unconditionally accepted.

Where the court appoints a trust corporation to be a trustee, it has a statutory power to authorise it to charge remuneration: Trustee Act 1925, section 42. The inherent power of the court to authorise a prospective trustee to charge remuneration is exemplified by such cases as *Re Freeman's Settlement Trusts* (1887) 37 ChD 148. The inherent power to authorise an unpaid trustee to charge remuneration, notwithstanding prior acceptance of the unpaid office, was regarded by Lord Langdale MR in *Bainbrigge v Blair* (1845) 8 Beav 588 as undoubted.

If the court has an inherent power to authorise a prospective trustee to take remuneration for future services, and has a similar power in relation to an unpaid trustee who has already accepted office and embarked upon his fiduciary duties on a voluntary basis, I have some difficulty in appreciating the

---

11 (1981) 98 LQR 181 (P.V.B.); [1981] CLJ 243 (C.M.G. Ockleton); [1982] Conv 231 (K. Hodkinson); (1982) 45 MLR 211 (B. Green). See *Re Keeler's Settlement Trusts* [1981] Ch 156, [1981] 1 All ER 888, p. 834, post. On the powers of the court to reduce trustees' remuneration, see (1984) 128 SJ 41 (A.M. Kenny).

logic of the principle that the court has no power to increase or otherwise vary the future remuneration of a trustee who has already accepted office. It would mean that, if the remuneration specified in the trust instrument were lower than was acceptable to the incumbent trustee or any substitute who could be found, the court would have jurisdiction to authorise a substitute to charge an acceptable level of remuneration, but would have no jurisdiction to authorise the incumbent to charge precisely the same level of remuneration. Such a result appears to me bizarre, and to call in question the validity of the principle upon which it is supposedly based.

Two foundations for the principle are suggested. One is that the right to remuneration is based upon contract, and the court has no power to vary the terms of a contract. The contractual conception suffers from the difficulties explained in the judgment of Fox LJ. It also seems to me, in the context of the present debate, to give little weight to the fact that a trustee, whether paid or unpaid, is under no obligation, contractual or otherwise, to provide future services to the trust. He can at any time express his desire to be discharged from the trust and in that case a new trustee will in due course be appointed under section 36 or section 41 of the Trustee Act 1925 (pp. 616, 624, ante). The practical effect therefore of increasing the remuneration of the trustee (if the contractual conception is correct) will merely be to amend for the future, in favour of a trustee, the terms of a contract which the trustee has a unilateral right to determine. The interference of the court in such circumstances can hardly be said, in any real sense, to derogate from the contractual rights of the settlor or the beneficiaries if he or they are to be regarded as entitled to the benefit of the contract.

The other foundation suggested for the supposed principle is that the remuneration allowed to a trustee under the terms of the trust is a beneficial interest, and the court has no inherent jurisdiction to vary that beneficial interest save in special circumstances not here material: see *Chapman v Chapman* [1954] AC 429, [1954] 1 All ER 798, p. 781, ante. I agree that the remuneration given to a trustee by a will is an interest within the meaning of section 15 of the Wills Act 1837; that it is a gift upon a condition for the purposes of the legislation which formerly charged legacy duty upon testamentary gifts; and that an executor or trustee remunerated by the will cannot retain such remuneration against creditors if the estate turns out to be insolvent. There are obvious arguments why a testator should not be able to circumvent the provisions of the Wills Act, or avoid legacy duty, or defeat his creditors, by the award of remuneration to his executors or trustees. It does not follow that a remunerated trustee is to be considered as a cestui que trust for the purposes of the principles laid down in the *Chapman* case. If he were it is difficult, as Fox LJ says, to see what right the court would have to authorise remuneration to be charged by a prospective trustee, since such authority will have the inevitable effect of adding a new beneficiary to the trust at the expense of the existing beneficiaries.

I would allow the appeal.''

[The matter was remitted to the Chancery Division to enable the trustees to make such application and upon such further evidence as they thought fit.][12]

---

12 See also *Re Berkeley Applegate (Investment Consultants)* [1989] Ch 32, [1988] 3 All ER 71 (liquidators remunerated out of assets held on trust by company for investors).

D. Remuneration for Litigation Work by Solicitor-Trustees

There is an exception to the rule that a solicitor-trustee cannot, in the absence of an enabling clause, charge profit costs, which is known as the rule in *Cradock v Piper*.[13] Under the rule a solicitor-trustee may charge costs if he has acted for a co-trustee as well as himself in respect of business done in an action or matter in court, except in so far as the costs have been increased by his being one of the parties.

E. Law Reform

Law Reform Committee 23rd Report (The Powers and Duties of Trustees) 1982 Cmnd. 8. 733, para. 9.1, II. 18–20.

"Remuneration (paragraph 3.42–3.55)

18. All such expenses as are properly incurred in the administration of an estate and have been authorised by the testator should be given the priority which has always been given to administration expenses. (paragraph 3.45)

19. A beneficiary under a trust should be entitled to obtain a remuneration certificate from the Law Society in order to establish that the charges made by a solicitor-trustee under a charging clause are reasonable. (paragraph 3.50)

20. A presumption should be introduced to the effect that a trustee who is allowed to charge for his professional services should also be presumed to be able to charge for all work that could reasonably be done by a person of his expertise, even though it could also be done by a layman, if an ordinary prudent man of business would expect a trustee to do this work. (paragraph 3.52)"[14]

III. Purchase of Trust Property[15]

During the administration of a trust a trustee may wish to purchase either the trust property itself or a beneficiary's interest under the trust. Equity has evolved two rules to resolve the conflict which may arise between the duty of the trustee to the beneficiaries and his personal interest.[16] The first rule, which is called the self-dealing rule, provides that a trustee may not sell to himself, and renders the transaction voidable at the option of the beneficiaries. Under the second rule, the fair-dealing rule, if a trustee purchases a beneficiary's

---

13 (1850) 1 Mac & G 664.
14 [1984] Conv 275 (N.D.M. Parry).
15 H & M, pp. 579–581; K & S, pp. 228–233; P & M, pp. 235–239; Pettit, pp. 424–428; Riddall, pp. 334–336; Snell, pp. 249–251; Underhill, pp. 646–647; (1936) 49 HLR 521 (A.W. Scott); (1955) 8 CLP 91 (O.R. Marshall); Goff & Jones, *The Law of Restitution* (4th edn, 1993) chap. 33; (1968) 84 LQR 472 (G.H. Jones).
16 Cf. where it is the settlor who has placed the trustees in a position of conflict: *Sargeant v National Westminster Bank plc* (1990) 61 P & CR 518.

interest, the transaction is not voidable as of right by the beneficiary, but only if the trustee has behaved unfairly.

A. Self-dealing and Fair-dealing Rules

In **Tito v Waddell (No 2)** [1977] Ch 106, [1977] 3 All ER 129, MEGARRY V-C said at 240, at 241:

"(2) *Lease by a fiduciary to itself.* I turn to the other way that Mr. Mowbray put the point, based on the 1931 lease being a lease by a fiduciary to itself. The lease, of course, is in terms a lease by the resident commissioner to the British Phosphate Commissioners, and as such is literally far from being a lease by a person to himself. But of course equity looks beneath the surface, and applies its doctrines to cases where, although in form a trustee has not sold to himself, in substance he has. Again one must regard the realities. If the question is asked: 'Will a sale of trust property by the trustee to his wife be set aside?', nobody can answer it without being told more; for the question is asked in a conceptual form, and manifestly there are wives and wives. In one case the trustee may have sold privately to his wife with whom he was living in perfect amity; in another the property may have been knocked down at auction to the trustee's wife from whom he has been living separate and in enmity for a dozen years. So here one must look at the realities; and for my part I do not see how the British Phosphate Commissioners can in any way be sufficiently identified with the resident commissioner, duly exercising his statutory powers, so as to bring the equitable doctrine into play. Nor, for the reasons that I have given, do I see how the British Phosphate Commissioners can be said to be in any way the alter ego of the government of the colony, or the Crown in right of the colony.

(3) *Self-dealing and fair-dealing.* Let me revert briefly to the subject of the rules about self-dealing and fair-dealing, though on the view I take I doubt if much turns on this. As I have indicated, Mr. Vinelott took what I may call the orthodox view, namely, that there were two separate rules. The self-dealing rule is (to put it very shortly) that if a trustee sells the trust property to himself, the sale is voidable by any beneficiary ex debito justitiae, however fair the transaction. The fair-dealing rule is (again putting it very shortly) that if a trustee purchases the beneficial interest of any of his beneficiaries, the transaction is not voidable ex debito justitiae, but can be set aside by the beneficiary unless the trustee can show that he has taken no advantage of his position and has made full disclosure to the beneficiary, and that the transaction is fair and honest.

On the other hand, Mr. Mowbray strenuously contended that there was only one rule, though with two limbs, and he formulated an elaborate statement to that effect which I do not think I need set out. I can well see that both rules, or both limbs, have a common origin in that equity is astute to prevent a trustee from abusing his position or profiting from his trust: the shepherd must not become a wolf. But subject to that, it seems to me that for all practical purposes there are two rules: the consequences are different, and the property and the transactions which invoke the rules are different. I see no merit in attempting a forced union which has to be expressed in terms of disunity. I shall accordingly treat the rules as being in essence two distinct though allied rules."

B. Purchase of Trust Property. Self-dealing

HOLDER v HOLDER
[1968] Ch 353, [1968] 1 All ER 665 (CA, HARMAN, DANCKWERTS and SACHS LJJ)

The testator was the owner of two farms in Gloucestershire. His third son Victor, the defendant, was tenant with one Denley of part of one farm; and, as his father became advanced in years, Victor undertook responsibility for the farming of the remainder of the land, making annual payments to his father.

The testator died in 1959, having appointed his widow, a daughter and Victor his executors, and provided by his will that the estate should be divided equally between the widow and all the children. The executors took the preliminary steps towards the administration of the estate, which Victor later conceded were sufficient to prevent him from renouncing, as he attempted to do.

The farms were valued on the basis that Victor was tenant with Denley of part of one farm as previously stated, and also tenant of the remainder of the land. The eldest son Frank, the plaintiff, disputed this.

Victor purported to renounce the executorship, and subsequently purchased the farms at a fair price at an auction. The plaintiff received a cheque in respect of his share of the proceeds of sale. He later changed his solicitors and the new solicitor took, for the first time, the point that Victor, having begun to administer the estate, could not renounce, and could not therefore be a purchaser.

Held (reversing CROSS J). (i) In the special circumstances of the case, Victor, although an executor, was not precluded from purchasing; (ii) Frank had, by receiving his share of the purchase money, precluded himself from relief.

HARMAN LJ: The cross-appeal raises far more difficult questions and they are broadly three. First, whether the actions of Victor before probate made his renunciation ineffective. Secondly, whether on that footing he was disentitled from bidding at the sale. Thirdly, whether the plaintiff is disentitled from taking this point because of his acquiescence.

It was admitted at the bar in the court below that the acts of Victor were enough to constitute intermeddling with the estate and that his renunciation was ineffective. On this footing he remained a personal representative, even after probate had been granted to his co-executors, and could have been obliged by a creditor or a beneficiary to re-assume the duties of an executor. The judge decided in favour of the plaintiff on this point because Victor at the time of the sale was himself still in a fiduciary position and like any other trustee could not purchase the trust property. I feel the force of this argument, but doubt its validity in the very special circumstances of this case. The reason for the rule is that a man may not be both vendor and purchaser; but Victor was never in that position here. He took no part in instructing the valuer who fixed the reserves or in the preparations for the auction. Everyone in the family knew that he was not a seller but a buyer. In this case Victor never assumed the duties of an executor. It is true that he concurred in signing a few cheques for trivial sums and endorsing a few insurance policies, but he never, so far as appears, interfered in any way with the administration of the estate. It is true he managed the farms, but he did that as tenant and not as executor. He acquired no special knowledge as executor. What he knew he knew as tenant of the farms.

Another reason lying behind the rule is that there must never be a conflict of duty and interest, but in fact there was none here in the case of Victor, who made no secret throughout that he intended to buy. There is of course ample authority that a trustee cannot purchase. The leading cases are decisions of Lord Eldon—*Ex p Lacey* (1802) 6 Ves 625 and *Ex p James* (1803) 8 Ves 337 at 344. In the former case the Lord Chancellor expressed himself thus at 626:

> "The rule I take to be this; not, that a trustee cannot buy from his cestuy que trust, but, that he shall not buy from himself. If a trustee will so deal with his cestuy que trust, that the amount of the transaction shakes off the obligation, that attaches upon him as trustee, then he may buy. If that case[17] is rightly understood, it cannot lead to much mistake. The true interpretation of what is there reported does not break in upon the law as to trustees. The rule is this. A trustee, who is entrusted to sell and manage for others, undertakes in the same moment, in which he becomes a trustee, not to manage for the benefit and advantage of himself."

In *Ex p James* the same Lord Chancellor said at 344:

> "This doctrine as to purchases by trustees, assignees, and persons having a confidential character, stands much more upon general principle than upon the circumstances of any individual case. It rests upon this; that the purchase is not permitted in any case, however honest the circumstances; the general interests of justice requiring it to be destroyed in every instance."

These are no doubt strong words, but it is to be observed that Lord Eldon was dealing with cases where the purchaser was at the time of sale acting for the vendors. In this case Victor was not so acting: his interference with the administration of the estate was of a minimal character and the last cheque he signed was in August before he executed the deed of renunciation. He took no part in the instructions for probate, nor in the valuations or fixing of the reserves. Everyone concerned knew of the renunciation and of the reason for it, namely, that he wished to be a purchaser. Equally, everyone, including the three firms of solicitors engaged, assumed that the renunciation was effective and entitled Victor to bid. I feel great doubt whether the admission made at the bar was correct, as did the judge, but assuming it was right, the acts were only technically acts of intermeddling and I find no case where the circumstances are parallel. Of course, I feel the force of the judge's reasoning that if Victor remained an executor he is within the rule, but in a case where the reasons behind the rule do not exist I do not feel bound to apply it. My reasons are that the beneficiaries never looked to Victor to protect their interests. They all knew he was in the market as purchaser; that the price paid was a good one and probably higher than anyone not a sitting tenant would give. Further, the first two defendants alone acted as executors and sellers; they alone could convey: they were not influenced by Victor in connection with the sales.

I hold, therefore, that the rule does not apply in order to disentitle Victor to bid at the auction, as he did. If I be wrong on this point and the rule applies so as to disentitle Victor to purchase, there arises a further defence, namely, that of acquiescence ...

On the whole I am of opinion that in the circumstances of this case it would not be right to allow the plaintiff to assert his right (assuming he has one) because with full knowledge of the facts he affirmed the sale. He has had

17 *Whichcote v Lawrence* (1798) 3 Ves 740 at 749.

£2,000 as a result. He has caused [Victor] to embark on liabilities which he cannot recoup. There can in fact be no restitutio in integrum, which is a necessary element in rescission ...

DANCKWERTS LJ: ... The principle that a trustee cannot purchase part of the trust estate goes back to the statement of it by Lord Eldon in 1802 in *Ex p Lacey* (1802) 6 Ves 625 ...

It is said that it makes no difference, even though the sale may be fair and honest and may be made at a public auction: see Snell's Equity, 26th Edn, 1966 p. 260. But the court may sanction such a purchase, and if the court can do that (see Snell's Equity, p. 219), there can be no more than a practice that the court should not allow a trustee to bid. In my view it is a matter for the discretion of the judge.

———————

In **Re Thompson's Settlement** [1986] Ch 99, [1985] 2 All ER 720,[18] estates in Norfolk, Lincolnshire and Perthshire were held under a settlement on trust for grandchildren and their issue. The estates were leased to companies of which the directors were the settlor and the trustees. The leases were later informally assigned, one to a new company and the other to a partnership. One of the trustees of the settlement was the managing director of the company, in which he and his family held a majority shareholding. The partnership was formed by another trustee of the settlement and his family.

The trustees of the settlement sought a declaration whether the leases were voidable at the option of the beneficiaries.

In holding that the leases were voidable under the self-dealing rule, VINELOTT J said at 106, at 723:

"The application raises a question of some general importance concerning the ambit of the rule (which has been called the self-dealing rule) that a dealing such as a sale between a trustee and himself can be set aside by a beneficiary ex debito justitiae and without proof that the transaction was in any way unfair ...

Mr. Price's other and more radical submission founded upon *Holder v Holder* [1968] Ch 353, [1968] 1 All ER 665, p. 824, ante, was that the self-dealing rule only applies to a sale by trustees to one of their number, alone or jointly with others, or to a purchase by trustees from one of their number, alone or jointly with others, and to analogous dealings with trust property or trust moneys such as the grant of a lease by or to trustees. He founded that submission upon the statement by Harman LJ, at p. 391, that 'The reason for the rule is that a man may not be both vendor and purchaser ... ' He submitted that in the instant case the only dealings analogous to the sale of property were the assignments or purported assignments of the leases which were never themselves trust property. He submitted that in such a case the fair-dealing rule applies (because it is founded on the principle that a man must not put himself in a position where his duty and interest conflict and because in relation to the trustees it was their duty to consider whether to consent to the assignments) but not the self-dealing rule which only applies if there is a sale or purchase by

———————

18 (1986) 1 TL&P 66 (C.H. Sherrin); *Movitex Ltd v Bulfield* [1988] BCLC 104. A mortgagee cannot sell to himself when exercising his power of sale, but he can sell to a company in which he has an interest if he acts in good faith and obtains the best price reasonably obtainable: *Tse Kwong Lam v Wong Chit Sen* [1983] 1 WLR 1349, [1983] 3 All ER 54; Maudsley & Burn, *Land Law: Cases and Materials* (6th edn), pp. 776–778.

trustees or something analogous to it. I do not think that the self-dealing rule can be so confined. It is clear that the self-dealing rule is an application of the wider principle that a man must not put himself in a position where duty and interest conflict or where his duty to one conflicts with his duty to another: see in particular the opinion of Lord Dunedin in *Wright v Morgan* [1926] AC 788 which I have cited. The principle is applied stringently in cases where a trustee concurs in a transaction which cannot be carried into effect without his concurrence and who also has an interest in or owes a fiduciary duty to another in relation to the same transaction. The transaction cannot stand if challenged by a beneficiary because in the absence of an express provision in the trust instrument the beneficiaries are entitled to require that the trustees act unanimously and that each brings to bear a mind unclouded by any contrary interest or duty in deciding whether it is in the interest of the beneficiaries that the trustees concur in it.

The same principle also applies, but less stringently, in a case within the fair-dealing rule, such as the purchase by a trustee of a beneficiary's beneficial interest. There, there are genuinely two parties to the transaction and it will be allowed to stand if freely entered into and if the trustee took no advantage from his position or from any knowledge acquired from it.

In the instant case the concurrence of the trustees of the grandchildren's settlement was required if the leases were to be assigned to or new tenancies created in favour of the new company and the partnership. The beneficiaries were entitled to ask that the trustees should give unprejudiced consideration to the question whether they should refuse to concur in the assignments in the expectation that a surrender of the leases might be negotiated from the old company and the estates sold or let on the open market.

The decision of the Court of Appeal in *Holder v Holder* does not in my judgment assist Mr. Price. The reason why, in the words of Harman LJ, the rule did not apply was that Victor, though he might technically have been made an executor notwithstanding the purported renunciation, had never acted as executor in a way which could be taken to amount to acceptance of a duty to act in the interests of the beneficiaries under his father's will.

Mr. Parker submitted that whenever a trustee, alone or as a partner or as a director of a company takes an assignment of a lease of trust property he holds the lease as a constructive trustee. He submitted that in such a case it is the duty of the trustee as trustee to consider whether the trustees should negotiate a surrender of the lease by the tenant (who in such a case must be taken to wish to dispose of the lease) and that the trustees cannot be permitted to negotiate on his own behalf or on behalf of others for an assignment. He relied by analogy on the well-known case of *Keech v Sandford* (1726) Sel Cas Ch 61, p. 829, post. The principle established in *Keech v Sandford* has been held to apply to the purchase of a reversion by a trustee if the lease is renewable by contract or custom; but it has been held not to apply where there is no custom or right of renewal: see *Bevan v Webb* [1905] 1 Ch 620 and the cases there cited. Mr. Parker's submission seems to me to face considerable difficulty but I do not need to decide whether there are circumstances in which the principle in *Keech v Sandford* would apply by analogy to the purchase of a lease of trust property by a trustee of the reversion and I express no opinion on the question. It is sufficient for the purposes of the present case that the leases could not be vested in the new company or the partnership, whether by assignment or surrender and regrant, without the concurrence of the trustees of the grandchildren's trust, and that they were no more capable of binding the trust by so concurring than of binding the trust estates by a sale of the land to the new company or the partnership.''

C. Purchase from Beneficiary. Fair-dealing

In **Coles v Trecothick** (1804) 9 Ves 234, Lord ELDON LC said at 247:

"Upon the question as to a purchase by a trustee from the *cestui que trust* I agree, the *cestui que trust* may deal with his trustee, so that the trustee may become the purchaser of the estate. But, though permitted, it is a transaction of great delicacy, and which the Court will watch with the utmost diligence: so much, that it is very hazardous for a trustee to engage in such a transaction. . . .

As to the objection to a purchase by the trustee, the answer is, that a trustee may buy from the *cestui que trust*, provided there is a distinct and clear contract, ascertained to be such after a jealous and scrupulous examination of all the circumstances, proving, that the *cestui que trust* intended, the trustee should buy; and there is no fraud, no concealment, no advantage taken, by the trustee of information, acquired by him in the character of trustee. I admit, it is a difficult case to make out, wherever it is contended, that the exception prevails. The principle was clearly recognised in *Fox v Mackreth* (1788) 2 BroCC 400; and was established long before.''

In **Thomson v Eastwood** (1877) 2 App Cas 215, Lord CAIRNS LC said at 236:

"They were cases of this kind—cases where a trustee has entered into dealings with his *cestui que trust*—dealings which may be legitimate, but which, on the other hand, are open to examination when they are complained of. A trustee, for example, buys from his *cestui que trust* the trust property; there is no rule of law which says that a trustee shall not buy trust property from a *cestui que trust*, but it is a well-known doctrine of Equity that if a transaction of that kind is challenged in proper time, a Court of Equity will examine into it, will ascertain the value that was paid by the trustee, and will throw upon the trustee the *onus* of proving that he gave full value, and that all information was laid before the *cestui que trust* when it was sold.''[19]

D. Law Reform

Law Reform Committee 23rd Report (The Powers and Duties of Trustees) 1982 Cmnd. 8733, para. 3.59.

"3.59　We appreciate that there are circumstances, such as in the case of family trusts, where transfers between trusts with common trustees are envisaged which are not possible as the law stands at present without the sanction of the court.[20] If a change is to be made, we think it is necessary for there to be some sort of safeguard on this kind of transaction. One possibility is to provide that such a

---

19　*Hill v Langley* (1988) Times, 28 January.
20　SLA 1925, s. 68 caters for the position where a tenant for life wants to deal with the settled land for his own benefit, even where he is one of the trustees.

transaction can be made without the sanction of the court provided that there are at least two independent trustees on each side and the common trustee or trustees take no part in the transaction. Alternatively, there could be a requirement of a supporting valuation by a genuinely independent valuer rather than a requirement that the common trustee plays no part in the transaction. Our conclusion is that, so long as the common trustees are not beneficiaries under either of the trusts concerned, the trustees should be able to do business with one another with the common trustees playing such part as it is thought fit, provided that the market value of any property dealt with has been certified by a truly independent valuer as being the proper market price for that property.''

IV. Incidental Profits[21]

A. Trustees

i. THE RULE IN *KEECH v SANDFORD*

(a) Renewal of a Lease[1]

KEECH v SANDFORD
(1726) Sel Cas Ch 61 (KING LC)

The lessee of the profits of Romford market devised his estate to a trustee on trust for an infant. Prior to the expiration of the lease, the trustee applied to the lessor for a renewal of the lease for the benefit of the infant. The lessor refused, on the ground that, because the lease was of the profits only and not of the land, his remedy for recovery of rent was not by distress, but upon the covenant only, by which an infant would not be bound. The trustee then took a lease for himself.

The infant sought to have the lease assigned to him.

Held. The lease should be assigned to the infant, with an account of the profits received by the trustee.

KING LC: I must consider this as a trust for the infant; for I very well see, if a trustee, on the refusal to renew, might have a lease to himself, few trust estates would be renewed to *cestui que use*; though I do not say there is a fraud in this case, yet he should rather have let it run out, than to have had the lease to himself. This may seem hard, that the trustee is the only person of all mankind who might not have the lease; but it is very proper that rule should be strictly pursued, and not in the least relaxed; for it is very obvious what would be the

---

21 H & M, pp. 581–598; K & S, pp. 244–248, 341–352; P & M, pp. 239–251; Pettit, pp. 157–166; Riddall, pp. 330–333, 389–390; Snell, pp. 245–247, 251–253; Underhill, pp. 345–369; (1968) 84 LQR 472 (G.H. Jones). See generally [1967] CLJ 83 (L.S. Sealy); (1981) 97 LQR 51 (J.C. Shepherd); (1983) 46 MLR 289 (W. Bishop and D.D. Prentice); Goff and Jones, *Law of Restitution* (4th edn), chap. 33; *Hospital Products Ltd v US Surgical Corpn* (1984) 156 CLR 41; (1986) OJLS 444 (R.P. Austin).

 1 White and Tudor's *Leading Cases in Equity* (9th edn, 1928), pp. 648 et seq; *Re Knowles' Will Trusts* [1948] 1 All ER 866; *Re Jarvis* [1958] 1 WLR 815, [1958] 2 All ER 336; *Re Edwards' Will Trusts* [1982] Ch 30, [1981] 2 All ER 941; *Chan v Zacharia* (1983) 154 CLR 178.
    See too (1969) 33 Conv (NS) 161 (S.M. Cretney) on the historical reasons for the rule; (1984) 58 ALJ 660 (J. Starke).

consequences of letting trustees have the lease, on refusal to renew to *cestui que use.*

————————

In **Re Biss** [1903] 2 Ch 40, John Biss had carried on a profitable business of a common lodging-house keeper on premises leased to him under a seven-year lease. On its expiration he continued as a yearly tenant. He died, leaving a widow and three children, one of whom was an infant. The widow, who was his administratrix, and an adult son continued the business, and they applied for a renewal of the lease. This was refused, but a new three-year lease was then granted to the adult son. The question was whether he should be compelled, under the rule in *Keech v Sandford,* to hold the lease upon trust. The Court of Appeal decided that he could hold it beneficially. The son, in obtaining the lease, was not in breach of any fiduciary duty. COLLINS MR said at 57:

"In the present case the appellant is simply one of the next of kin of the former tenant, and had, as such, a possible interest in the term. He was not, as such, a trustee for the others interested, nor was he in possession. The administratrix represented the estate and alone had the right to renew incident thereto, and she unquestionably could renew only for the benefit of the estate. But is the appellant in the same category? Or is he entitled to go into the facts to shew that he has not, in point of fact, abused his position, or in any sense intercepted an advantage coming by way of accretion to the estate? He did not take under a will or a settlement with interests coming after his own, but simply got a possible share upon an intestacy in case there was a surplus of assets over debts. It seems to me that his obligation cannot be put higher than that of any other tenant in common against whom it would have to be established, not as a presumption of law but as an inference of fact, that he had abused his position. If he is not under a personal incapacity to take a benefit, he is entitled to shew that the renewal was not in fact an accretion to the original term, and that it was not until there had been an absolute refusal on the part of the lessor, and after full opportunity to the administratrix to procure it for the estate if she could, that he accepted a proposal of renewal made to him by the lessor. These questions cannot be considered or discussed when the party is by his position debarred from keeping a personal advantage derived directly or indirectly out of his fiduciary or quasi-fiduciary position; but when he is not so debarred I think it becomes a question of fact whether that which he has received was in his hands an accretion to the interest of the deceased, or whether the connection between the estate and the renewal had not been wholly severed by the action of the lessor before the appellant accepted a new lease. This consideration seems to get rid of any difficulty that one of the next of kin was an infant. The right or hope of renewal incident to the estate was determined before the plaintiff intervened."[2]

————————

2 *Brenner v Rose* [1973] 1 WLR 443, [1973] 2 All ER 535. See also *Harris v Black* (1983) 46 P & CR 366, where CA held that the court had jurisdiction at the suit of one trustee to compel his co-trustee to apply for the renewal of a lease under Part II Landlord and Tenant Act 1954. The matter was one for discretion and CA refused to exercise it.

(b) Purchase of the Reversion

In **Thompson's Trustee in Bankruptcy v Heaton** [1974] 1 WLR 605, [1974] 1 All ER 1239,[3] PENNYCUICK V-C said at 606, at 1241:

"The action is concerned with a property known as Lissington Manor Farm in Lincolnshire, to which I shall refer as 'Lissington'. Summarily Mr. Thompson and Mr. Heaton acquired a leasehold interest in Lissington as partners in 1948. The partnership was dissolved in 1952 under some arrangement between them. Mr. Heaton and, subsequently, the company [William T. Heaton Ltd, a private company whose shares were owned by Mr. and Mrs. Heaton] remained in sole occupation of Lissington. Mr. Heaton died in 1966. Then in 1967 his executors acquired the freehold reversion in Lissington on behalf of the company. Since the commencement of the action the company has sold Lissington at a very substantial profit. [Mr. Thompson having become bankrupt] the plaintiff trustee in bankruptcy now contends that he is entitled in effect to half of that profit [on the ground that the farm was an undistributed asset of the partnership].

It remains to consider whether the defendants are accountable to the plaintiff in respect of the freehold reversion and the proceeds of sale of the freehold. It is well established that where someone holding a leasehold interest in a fiduciary capacity acquires a renewal of the leasehold interest he must hold the renewed interest as part of the trust estate. This principle is known as the rule in *Keech v Sandford* (1726) Sel Cas Ch 61: *Snell's Principles of Equity*, 27th edn (1973), p. 236. It is also, I think, well established that where someone holding a leasehold interest in a fiduciary capacity acquires the freehold reversion, he must hold that reversion as part of the trust estate: see *Protheroe v Protheroe* [1968] 1 WLR 519, [1968] 1 All ER 1111, where Lord Denning MR says at 521, at 1112:

'The short answer to the husband's contention is this: although the house was in the husband's name, he was a trustee of it for both. It was a family asset which the husband and wife owned in equal shares. Being a trustee, he had an especial advantage in getting the freehold. There is a long established rule of equity from *Keech v Sandford* (1726) Sel Cas Ch 61 downwards that if a trustee, who owns the leasehold, gets in the freehold, that freehold belongs to the trust and he cannot take the property for himself.'

That decision is cited, with some implied criticism, in *Snell's Principles of Equity*, p. 238. It seems to me, however, that, apart from the fact that it binds me, this decision, like the rule in *Keech v Sandford* is really in modern terms an application of the broad principle that a trustee must not make a profit out of the trust estate. This principle applies to all kinds of collateral advantages, for instance directors' remuneration received by a trustee acting as a director for a company controlled through the shares of the trust. In *Phillips v Phillips* (1885) 29 ChD 673 the Court of Appeal applied the principle to the purchase of a reversion by a tenant for life. I ought to make one observation in this connection. Obviously the beneficiary under the trust in such circumstances cannot be compelled to accept and pay for the reversion. If he refuses to do so, either before or after the acquisition by the trustee, no doubt the latter is entitled to acquire and retain the reversion for his own use, but if the beneficiary does require that the reversion be brought into the trust estate,

---

3 (1974) 38 Conv (NS) 288 (F.R. Crane); (1975) 38 MLR 226 (P. Jackson).

then the trustee must deal with it accordingly, subject of course to recoupment out of the trust estate.

There can, I think, be no doubt that so long as a partnership subsists each partner is under a corresponding obligation to his co-partners. See as to this point section 29 of the Partnership Act 1890 and *Lindley on Partnership* 13th edn (1971), p. 337....

The fiduciary relation here arises not from a trust of property but from the duty of good faith which each partner owes to the other. It is immaterial for this purpose in which partner the legal estate in the leasehold interest concerned is vested.''

ii. TRUSTEES AS COMPANY DIRECTORS

RE MACADAM[4]
[1946] Ch 73, [1945] 2 All ER 664 (ChD, COHEN J)

The articles of a company provided that the trustees of the testator's will may ''so long as they shall hold shares in the company as such trustees, appoint two persons ... to be directors of the company.'' The trustees appointed themselves.

The question was whether the trustees could retain, as their own, the directors' fees.

Held. They were accountable.

COHEN J: The question has been raised whether the plaintiffs are entitled to retain the directors' fees received by them from the company or whether they are accountable to the trust estate for the sums received by them as remuneration in respect of the office of director. I desire to say at once that nobody suggested any impropriety on their part in regard to this remuneration. The question was asked purely as one of law whether, having regard to all the provisions of the material documents, on general principles of law, they are accountable or not. My attention was called to a number of cases bearing on this matter, but I think that Mr. Gray and Mr. Timins were right in saying that they are all applications of the same general principle, though the consequence of applying that principle has resulted in some cases in the person concerned being allowed to retain the remuneration, and in others in his being held accountable. The principle, I think, is well stated in a passage from the speech of Lord Herschell in *Bray v Ford* [1896] AC 44 at 51 which was cited by Russell J in *Williams v Barton* [1927] 2 Ch 9 at 11. The citation is as follows: ''It is an inflexible rule of a court of equity that a person in a fiduciary position ... is not, unless otherwise expressly provided, entitled to make a profit; he is not allowed to put himself in a position where his interest and duty conflict.''

---

4 *Re Gee* [1948] Ch 284, [1948] 1 All ER 498 (trustees appointed independently of the voters of the trust shares); *Re Francis* (1905) 74 LJ Ch 198; *Re Lewis* (1910) 103 LT 495 (independent appointment); *Re Llewellin's Will Trusts* [1949] Ch 225, [1949] 1 All ER 487 (appointment authorised by trust instrument); *Re Keeler's Settlement Trusts* [1981] Ch 156, [1981] 1 All ER 888, p. 834, post (appointment authorised by trust instrument); *Re Orwell's Will Trusts* [1982] 1 WLR 1337, [1982] 3 All ER 177.

The first of the cases to which my attention was called was *Re Francis* (1905) 92 LT 77. [His Lordship referred also to *Re Dover Coalfield Extension Ltd* [1907] 2 Ch 76; affd [1908] 1 Ch 65, and to *Re Lewis* (1910) 103 LT 495, of which case he said:] It seems to me that the distinction between that case and this is that there he secured the appointment as salesman not by virtue of the exercise of any discretion in him as trustee, but by virtue of a bargain with his co-partners; whereas in the present case the plaintiffs got their appointment, by the exercise of a power which is vested in them—not, it is true, by the testator's will, but by the articles of the company approved by the court, but none the less vested in them as trustees.

The last, and perhaps the nearest, case to the present—although it is a much stronger case than the one I have to decide — is *Williams v Barton* [1927] 2 Ch 9 decided by Russell J from which I have already cited a short passage. In that case the headnote says: "The defendant, one of two trustees of a will, was employed as a clerk by a firm of stockbrokers on the terms that his salary should consist of half the commission earned by the firm on business introduced by him. At the recommendation of the defendant, the firm was employed to value his testator's securities. The firm's charges were paid out of the testator's estate and, in accordance with their contract with the defendant, they paid to him half the fees so earned. The defendant took no part in making the valuations or in fixing the fees to be charged. In an action by his co-trustee claiming that the defendant was bound to treat the fees so paid to him as part of the testator's estate:—*Held*, that it was the defendant's duty as a trustee to give the estate the benefit of his unfettered advice in choosing stockbrokers to act for the estate, but, as the recipient of half the fees earned by the firm on business introduced by him, it was to his interest to choose his firm to act. The services rendered to the firm by the defendant remained unchanged but his remuneration for them was increased, and increased by virtue of his trusteeship. That increase was a profit which the defendant would not have made but for his position as trustee and he was therefore bound to treat it as part of the estate of his testator." After citing the passage which I have read from the speech of Lord Herschell in *Bray v Ford* [1896] AC 44, Russell J continued—and I think his remarks apply to this case too — "The point is not an easy one and there is little, if any, authority to assist in its determination ... it seems to me evident that the case falls within the mischief which is sought to be prevented by the rule. The case is clearly one where his duty as trustee and his interest in an increased remuneration are in direct conflict. As a trustee it is his duty to give the estate the benefit of his unfettered advice in choosing the stockbrokers to act for the estate; as the recipient of half the fees to be earned by George Burnand & Co on work introduced by him his obvious interest is to choose or recommend them for the job." Pausing there, it seems to me that, with a certain substitution, that last sentence applies to this case. As trustees it is the duty of the plaintiffs to give the estate the benefit of their unfettered advice in choosing the persons to act as directors of the company, as, if appointed, they will receive such remuneration as may be voted to them; as recipients of the remuneration of directors their obvious interest is to choose themselves for the job. Then the learned judge goes on: "In the event that has happened they have been chosen, and chosen because the defendant was a trustee, with the result that half of what the estate pays must necessarily pass through them to the defendant as part of his remuneration for other services rendered, but as an addition to the remuneration which he would otherwise have received for those self-same services. The services rendered remain unchanged but the remuneration for them has been increased. He has increased his remuneration by virtue of his trusteeship. In my opinion this increase of remuneration is a profit made by the defendant out of and by reason of his trusteeship, which he would not have made but for his position as trustee." Then he goes on to deal with *Re Dover Coalfield Extension Ltd* [1907] 2 Ch 76, [1908] 1 Ch 65, 70, and says: "But that case seems to me very different. At the request of the Dover company Mr. Cousins had entered into a contract with the Kent company to serve them as a director, the Kent company paying him remuneration for his services. The necessary qualification shares were provided by the Dover company and in respect of those shares he became a trustee for the Dover company. He had not, however, used his position as a trustee for the purpose of acquiring his directorship. He had, in fact, been appointed a director before he became a trustee of the shares. The profit which he gained was not procured by him by the use of his position as trustee but was a profit earned by reason of work which he did for the Kent company and which would not have been earned by him had he not been willing to do the work for which it was the remuneration. It was not (as in the present case) a profit acquired solely by reason of his use of his position as trustee and a profit in respect of which no extra services were rendered."

That case is, as Mr. Christie rightly says, much stronger than the present case, because, first, the profit in a sense came directly out of the estate, and, secondly, because it was a profit earned in a sense without any work done by him. I think that the root of the matter really is: Did he acquire the position in respect of which he drew the remuneration by virtue of his position as trustee? In the present case there can be no doubt that the only way in which the plaintiffs became directors was by exercise of the powers vested in the trustees of the will under art. 68 of the articles of association of the company. The principle is one which has always been regarded as of the greatest importance in these courts, and I do not think I ought to do anything to weaken it. As I have said, although the remuneration was remuneration for services as director of the company, the opportunity to receive that remuneration was gained as a result of the exercise of a discretion vested in the trustees, and they had put themselves in a position where their interest and duty conflicted. In those circumstances, I do not think this court can allow them to make a profit out of doing so, and I do not think the liability to account for a profit can be confined to cases where the profit is derived directly from the trust estate. I leave over the matter of the exact wording of the order, because I do not want to do anything to prejudice the question whether, in the circumstances, I ought not to allow the plaintiffs to retain the whole or a part of the remuneration. If I can be satisfied (and that is the point I have not considered) that they were the best persons to be directors, I do not think it would be right for me to expect them to do the extra work for nothing.

In **Re Keeler's Settlement Trusts** [1981] Ch 156, [1981] 1 All ER 888, a settlement of shares in two companies authorised the trustees to be appointed directors of the companies. There was a professional charging clause, but no power authorising trustees to retain remuneration earned in their directorships. Trustee directors had been appointed. One question was whether they could retain past remuneration received as directors.[5] GOULDING J, in directing accounts and inquiries, said at 160, at 892:

"In *Re Macadam* [1946] Ch 73, [1945] 2 All ER 664, Cohen J held that certain trustees were in the circumstances of the case accountable for directors' fees received by them and, at 82, at 672 (quoted supra), left over the question whether they might be allowed to retain them, in whole or in part, presumably under the inherent jurisdiction of the court ...

In *Re Masters* [1953] 1 WLR 81 at 83, [1953] 1 All ER 19 at 20 Danckwerts J commented on *Re Macadam* in which he had been junior counsel for the trustees, and said that to his knowledge the course suggested by Cohen J was adopted and the remuneration was in fact authorised. He said so in delivering a judgment which authorised a trust corporation to charge for acting as administrator and trustee of an intestate's estate.

I observe in passing that the reports of *Re Macadam* (1945) 62 TLR 48 at 52 and 115 LJ Ch 14 at 21 suggest that the question reserved by Cohen J was in fact ultimately disposed of by compromise.

In *Re Duke of Norfolk's Settlement Trusts* [1979] Ch 37, [1978] 3 All ER 907, Walton J carefully reviewed the earlier authorities on the whole subject of the court's inherent jurisdiction to allow remuneration to trustees.... The test I have taken from the judgment of Walton J in the *Norfolk* case is whether any exceptional effort or skill was shown in acquiring the remuneration. That was his formulation at 54, at 921 of the report. He paraphrased it at 59, at 925:

'those cases where the trustees are held to be accountable for profits which they have made out of the trust, but are in general allowed to keep that proportion of the profits so made—doubtless, in many cases, the whole— which results from their own exertions above and beyond those expected of a trustee ...'

I do not think that any and every effort or skill applied by a trustee in executing the office of a company director is to be regarded as exceptional or unexpected for this purpose, certainly not in the present case, where it is made perfectly clear by clause 4 of the settlement that a trustee may be proposed for appointment as a director of any company in which the trustees have an interest. The director trustee, in my judgment, may in a proper case be allowed to retain reasonable remuneration for effort and skill applied by him in performing the duties of the directorship over and above the effort and skill ordinarily required of a director appointed to represent the interests of a substantial shareholder. The latter is something that a prudent man of business would in general undertake in the management of his own investments, and so in my view is in general an exertion reasonably expected of a trustee. Compare the observation of Upjohn J in *Re Worthington* [1954] 1 WLR 526 at 529, [1954] 1 All ER 677 at 679, cited in the *Norfolk* case [1979] Ch 37 at 55, [1978] 3 All ER 907 at 922".

iii. OTHER PROFITS BY TRUSTEES

There are other situations in which trustees are accountable for incidental profits. "Whenever it can be shewn that the trustee has so arranged matters as

---

5 A claim in respect of future remuneration was refused, following WALTON J in *Re Duke of Norfolk's Settlement Trusts* [1979] Ch 37, [1978] 3 All ER 907. This is no longer authoritative in view of the Court of Appeal's reversal of WALTON J on this point [1982] Ch 61, [1981] 3 All ER 220, p. 820, ante.

to obtain an advantage, whether in money or money's worth, to himself personally through the execution of his trust, he will not be permitted to retain it, but be compelled to make it over to his constituent".[6]

In **Williams v Barton** [1927] 2 Ch 9, a trustee of a will was employed as a clerk by stockbrokers on the terms that his salary should be half the commission earned by the firm on business introduced by him. He persuaded his co-trustee to employ his firm to value the testator's securities. In holding that the trustee was accountable for the half commission received by him, RUSSELL J said at 12:

"The case is clearly one where his duty as trustee and his interest in an increased remuneration are in direct conflict. As a trustee it is his duty to give the estate the benefit of his unfettered advice in choosing the stockbrokers to act for the estate; as the recipient of half the fees to be earned by George Burnand & Co. on work introduced by him his obvious interest is to choose or recommend them for the job. . . . He has increased his remuneration by virtue of his trusteeship. In my opinion this increase of remuneration is a profit made by the defendant out of and by reason of his trusteeship, which he would not have made but for his position as trustee."

B. Other Fiduciaries

Similar principles apply to profits made by other persons who are in breach of a fiduciary relationship, for example, agents,[7] solicitors,[8] company directors,[9]

---

6 *Huntington Copper and Sulphur Co Ltd v Henderson* (1877) 4 R 294 at 308, per Lord YOUNG; *Sugden v Crossland* (1856) 3 Sm & G 192 (payment of £75 to trustee in consideration of his retiring and appointing the payer as new trustee); *Re Smith* [1896] 1 Ch 71 (payment of £300 commission on investing trust funds in debentures of a particular company); *Brown v IRC* [1965] AC 244, [1964] 3 All ER 119 (interest earned by Scottish solicitor on deposits of clients' moneys); (1964) 80 LQR 480; Solicitors Act 1974, s. 33; Solicitors' Accounts (Deposit Interest) Rules 1988.

    Re Thomson [1930] 1 Ch 203 (injunction granted to restrain executor from carrying on testator's business as yacht broker in competition with the trust); Partnership Act 1890, s. 30; *Moore v M'Glynn* [1894] 1 IR 74.

7 *De Bussche v Alt* (1878) 8 ChD 286; *New Zealand Netherlands Society "Oranje" Inc v Kuys* [1973] 1 WLR 1126 at 1129, [1973] 2 All ER 1222 at 1225, per Lord WILBERFORCE; *English v Dedham Vale Properties Ltd* [1978] 1 WLR 93, [1978] 1 All ER 382, p. 844, n. 2, post ("self-appointed agent"); *Boardman v Phipps* [1967] 2 AC 46, [1966] 3 All ER 721, p. 844 post; cf. *Royal Products Ltd v Midland Bank Ltd* [1981] 2 Lloyd's Rep 194; *Alimand Computers Systems v Radcliffes & Co* (1991) Times, 6 November (solicitors trustees of funds paid to them as stakeholders by clients); *Kelly v Cooper* [1993] AC 205.

8 *Brown v IRC* [1965] AC 244, [1964] 3 All ER 119; (1964) 80 LQR 470; *Oswald Hickson, Collier & Co v Carter-Ruck* [1984] AC 720, [1984] 2 All ER 15; *Islamic Republic of Iran Shipping Lines v Denby* [1987] 1 Lloyd's Rep 367 (accountable for bribe). See also *Hanson v Lorenz* [1987] 1 FTLR 23 (no liability to account to client for his profits from a joint venture where client had understood the agreement). As to whether a head of chambers is in a fiduciary position to the members, see *Appleby v Cowley* (1982) Times, April 14; Maudsley & Burn, *Land Law: Cases and Materials*, (6th edn), pp. 604–605.

9 *Infra.*

company promoters,[10] partners,[11] confidential employees,[12] certain bailees[13] and non-commissioned officers in the Army.[14] It is not always easy to determine when a fiduciary relationship exists, but the category is not closed.[15]

Finn, *Fiduciary Law and the Modern Commercial World* (1992), pp. 8–10 in McKendrick, *Commercial Aspects of Trusts and Fiduciary Obligations*:

"A Fiduciary—A Fiduciary Relationship?

The answer to this, the most fundamental question, continues to elude us.[16] The question itself presupposes that we have a developed conception of the purpose and burden of fiduciary law. Yet these are matters on which there is widespread disagreement throughout the common law world. The present Chief Justice of the High Court of Australia has justly observed that 'the fiduciary relationship is a concept in search of a principle'.[17] Confusion here has had a number of causes: the use of the 'fiduciary' to fill hiatuses in available doctrines—hence, for example, the modern propensity to manufacture a fiduciary relationship between the directors of a marginally solvent company and corporate creditors;[18] the dilution of fiduciary obligations to exact what is in essence a duty of good faith and fair dealing;[19] the colourable findings of fiduciary relationships to gain access to equitable, but particularly profit-based,

---

10 *Erlanger v New Sombrero Phosphate Co* (1878) 3 App Cas 1218; *Gluckstein v Barnes* [1900] AC 240; *Jubilee Cotton Mills Ltd v Lewis* [1924] AC 958.

11 *Featherstonhaugh v Fenwick* (1810) 17 Ves 298; *Clegg v Fishwick* (1849) 1 Mac & G 294.

12 *Triplex Safety Glass Co v Scorah* [1938] Ch 211, [1937] 4 All ER 693; *British Celanese Ltd v Moncrieff* [1948] Ch 564, [1948] 2 All ER 44; *British Syphon Co v Homewood* [1956] 1 WLR 1190; [1956] 2 All ER 897; *A-G v Guardian Newspapers Ltd (No 2)* [1990] 1 AC 109, [1988] 3 All ER 545 (the "Spycatcher" case).

13 *Aluminium Industrie Vaassen BV v Romalpa Aluminium Ltd* [1976] 1 WLR 676, [1976] 2 All ER 552; *Re Andrabell Ltd* [1984] 3 All ER 407.

14 *Reading v A-G* [1951] AC 507, [1951] 1 All ER 617 (bribes received by sergeant while on duty in Cairo); *A-G v Goddard* (1929) 98 LJKB 743. (sergeant in the Metropolitan Police); *A-G for Hong Kong v Reid* [1994] 1 AC 324, [1994] 1 All ER, 1 p. 854, post (acting director of public prosecutions).

15 Finn, *Fiduciary Obligations* (1977); Finn, *Fiduciary Law and the Modern Commercial World* in McKendrick, *Commercial Aspects of Trusts and Fiduciary Obligations* (1992); Law Commission Consultation Paper No 124; Fiduciary Duties and Regulatory Rules (1992), para. 2.4.
   In the context of equitable tracing, see *Chase Manhattan Bank NA v Israel-British Bank (London) Ltd* [1981] Ch 105, [1979] 3 All ER 1025, where one bank mistakenly made a double payment to another: cf. *Swain v The Law Society* [1983] 1 AC 598, [1982] 2 All ER 827 (Law Society held not accountable for commercial policy for compulsory insurance scheme negotiated on behalf of all solicitors). For the refusal of the court to impose fiduciary obligations where commercial relationships were entered into at arm's length and on an equal footing, see *Polly Peck International v Nadir (No 2)* [1992] 4 All ER 769; *Kelly v Cooper* [1993] AC 205; *Re Goldcorp Exchange Ltd* [1994] 3 WLR 199 at 216, [1994] 2 All ER 806 at 822, per Lord MUSTILL; P & M, pp. 223–225; (1994) 110 LQR 238 (Sir Anthony MASON).

16 See generally Finn, 'The Fiduciary Principle', in Youdan (ed.), Equity, Fiduciaries and Trusts (1989); see also R. Flannigan, 'Fiduciary Obligation in the Supreme Court' (1990) 54 Sask. LR 45.

17 Sir Anthony Mason, 'Themes and Prospects', in P.D. Finn (ed.), *Essays in Equity*, (1985), 246.

18 The subject of Ch. 4.

19 A prevalent phenomenon in Canadian, New Zealand, and United States jurisprudence in particular: see Finn, 'The Fiduciary Principle', supra. n. 3; see also *Pacific Industrial Corpn SA v Bank of New Zealand* [1991] 1 NZLR 368; *Plaza Fibreglass Manufacturing Ltd v Cardinal Insurance Co* (1990) 68 DLR (4th) 586.

remedies;[20] uncertainty as to what precisely are fiduciary duties and whether they encompass in some measure the law of undue influence,[1] breach of confidence,[2] and, in relation to professional advisers, a negligence-like duty of care,[3] etc. When this has been acknowledged, it should equally be said that, for somewhat different reasons, the laws of Britain and Australia hold most closely to the old orthodoxies.[4]

For reasons of space, but also because the matter has been dealt with elsewhere,[5] I will simply note without elaboration my own understanding of (i) when, in our respective systems, a person can properly be said to be a fiduciary; and (ii) what is the obligation imposed in consequence of a fiduciary finding.

At best, all one can give is a description of a fiduciary—and one which, if it expresses the fiduciary idea, is no more precise than a description of the tort of negligence. It is as follows:

> A person will be a fiduciary in his relationship with another when and in so far as[6] that other is entitled to expect[7] that he will act in that other's interests or (as in a partnership) in their joint interests, to the exclusion of his own several interest.

Put crudely, the central idea is service of another's interests. And the consequential obligation a fiduciary finding attracts is itself one designed essentially to procure loyalty in service. It can be cast compendiously in the following terms:

> A fiduciary
>
> (*a*) cannot misuse his position, or knowledge or opportunity resulting from it, to his own or to a third party's possible advantage; or
>
> (*b*) cannot, in any matter falling within the scope of his service, have a personal interest or an inconsistent engagement with a third party— unless this is freely and informedly consented to by the beneficiary or is authorised by law.[8]

Two themes, it should be noted, are embodied in this: one, concerned with misuse of position, aims to preclude the fiduciary from using his position to advantage interests other than his beneficiary's; the second, concerned with

20 An excellent UK example is *English v Dedham Vale Properties Ltd* [1978] 1 WLR 93, [1978] 1 All ER 382; cf. the judgment of DEANE J in *Hospital Products Ltd v US Surgical Corpn* (1984) 55 ALR 417.

1 See e.g. *National Westminster Bank plc v Morgan* [1985] AC 686, [1985] 1 All ER 821; and cf. the treatment of *Tate v Williamson* (1866) 2 Ch App 55 in *Bank of Credit and Commerce International SA v Aboody* [1990] 1 QB 923, [1992] 4 All ER 955.

2 Cf *LAC Minerals Ltd v International Corona Resources Ltd* (1989) 61 DLR (4th) 14.

3 The subject of some controversy in Canadian and New Zealand law in relation to the liability of particularly solicitors for non-disclosure: but for the Canadian reaction, see the comments of SOUTHIN J in *Giradet v Crease & Co* (1987) 11 BCLR 2d 361, at 362; and see Finn, 'The Fiduciary Principle', 25–6, 28–30.

4 In Australia, though the traditional line was held by the High Court in *Hospital Products Ltd v US Surgical Corpn* (1984) 55 ALR 417, the pressure for more 'creative' uses was blunted both by the evolution of unconscionability-based doctrines and by the scope for invention given Australian courts by the Trade Practices Act, 1974, s. 52.

5 See Finn, 'The Fiduciary Principle', supra.

6 Relationships commonly are fiduciary in part, non-fiduciary in part.

7 That entitlement may arise from what one party undertakes or appears to undertake—cf. *Croce v Kurnit* 565 F Supp 884 (1982)—for the other; from what actually is agreed between the parties; or, for reasons of public policy, from legal prescription.

8 The above is an adaptation of the formulation of DEANE J in *Chan v Zacharia* (1983) 53 ALR 417 at 435—the most comprehensive formulation to be found in modern Anglo-Australian law.

conflicts of interest or of duty, aims to preclude the fiduciary from being swayed in his service by considerations of personal or third-party interest.

The one general comment I would make both of the description given and of the rather severe obligation that fiduciary law imposes, is that our preparedness to discriminate amongst the host of 'service relationships' to be found in contemporary society and to designate some only as fiduciary (for example, solicitor or financial adviser and client) is informed in some measure by considerations of public policy aimed at preserving the integrity and utility of these relationships, given the expectation that the community is considered to have of behaviour in them, and given the purposes they serve in society. This, as will later be seen, is likely to have quite some bearing on how the courts are prepared to apply fiduciary duties to multi-function business enterprises and large professional partnerships.''

i. COMPANY DIRECTORS

(a) As Fiduciaries

Hanbury & Martin, *Modern Equity* (14th edn), pp. 587–591

"Company directors are treated as fiduciaries[9] in so far as they are prohibited from making a profit out of their office.[1] The leading case is the House of Lords decision in *Regal (Hastings) Ltd v Gulliver.*[2]

In that case R. Ltd set up a subsidiary, A. Ltd, to acquire the leases of two cinemas. A. Ltd had an authorised share capital of 5,000, £1 ordinary shares. The owner of the cinemas was only willing to lease them if the share capital of A. Ltd was completely subscribed for. However, R. Ltd had resources to subscribe for only 2,000 of the 5,000 shares and it was therefore agreed that the directors of R. Ltd should subscribe for the remaining 3,000. When the business of R. Ltd was transferred to new controllers the directors made a profit from their holdings in A. Ltd. The new controllers of R. Ltd caused the company to sue the ex-directors of R. Ltd for an account of the profit. The directors were held liable. They had made the profit out of their position as directors and, in the absence of shareholder approval,[3] they were obliged to account.

There a number of features of *Regal* which need to be emphasised: First, the directors were found by the court to have acted bona fide, but the liability of a

---

9 The duty is traditionally regarded as owed to the company, not to the shareholders; *Percival v Wright* [1902] 2 Ch 421. But see (1975) 28 CLP 83 (D. Prentice).

1 The office of director should not, however, be equated with that of trustee. The assets of the company, unlike trust property, are not vested in the director but in the company which is a separate legal entity and, more importantly, directors 'are ... commercial men managing a trading concern for the benefit of themselves and of all other shareholders in it ...' per JESSEL MR in *Re Forest of Dean Coal Mining Co Ltd* (1878) 10 Ch D 450 at 451–452. See also *Re Faure Electric Accumulator Co* (1888) 40 Ch D 141 at 150–152.

2 [1967] 2 AC 134n. This case was first reported in [1942] 2 All ER 378, but only found its way into the official reports after it had been cited extensively by the House of Lords in *Boardman v Phipps* [1967] 2 AC 46, [1966] 3 All ER 721.

3 Lord RUSSELL OF KILLOWEN considered that the shareholders could have ratified the directors' breach of duty: [1967] 2 AC 134n at 150, [1942] 1 All ER 378 at 389. On this controversial aspect of the case, see (1958) 16 CLJ 93 at 102–106; (K.W. Wedderburn); *Prudential Assurance Co Ltd v Newman Industries Ltd (No 2)* [1981] Ch 257, [1980] 2 All ER 841; (1981) 44 MLR 202.

fiduciary to account for a profit made from his office 'in no way depends on fraud, or absence of bona fides.'[4] Secondly, the new controllers obtained what was in effect a windfall. Having paid an agreed amount for the R. Ltd shares they were able, for all intents and purposes, to recoup part of their expenditure by compelling the directors to account.[5] Thirdly, it was arguable that the directors by purchasing the shares in A. Ltd had enabled R. Ltd to enter into a transaction which it was otherwise commercially impossible for the company to enter into. While there is some truth in this, the decision that R. Ltd did not have the necessary financial resources to enter into the transaction was made by the directors who were the very persons who benefited from this decision. Because of this a compelling argument can be made that a 'reasonable man looking at the relevant facts and circumstances of the particular case would think that there was a real sensible possibility of conflict.'[6]

A clear case of conflict of interest and duty arose in *Guinness plc v Saunders,*[7] where a director (Ward) agreed to provide his services in connection with a proposed take-over of another company (Distillers), on terms that he would be paid a fee the size of which depended on the amount of the take-over bid if successful. The bid was successful, and the fee paid to Ward was £5.2 million. The claim by Guinness for summary judgment for the repayment of this sum was upheld in the House of Lords. Ward's interest in obtaining a fee calculated on the above basis conflicted with his duty as director, which was to give impartial advice concerning the take-over. The agreement for the fee, made with two other directors, but not the board of directors, was void for want of authority. Ward had no arguable defence to Guinness's claim that he had received the money, paid under a void contract, as a constructive trustee.

The courts have imposed liability on directors to account where the directors have made the profit out of an economic opportunity, or information, even though they acquired it in a personal capacity, if it was information which could have been exploited by their company.[8]

In *Industrial Development Consultants Ltd v Cooley,*[9] the defendant was a director and general manager of the plaintiffs, who provided construction consultancy services for industrial enterprises. He attempted to interest a public Gas Board in a project, but was unsuccessful because the Gas Board's policy was not to employ development companies. The defendant was a distinguished architect who had worked in the gas industry for many years. For this reason the Gas Board decided to offer the contract to him personally, which he accepted, obtaining a release from the plaintiffs by falsely

---

4 [1967] 2 AC 134n at 144, [1942] 1 All ER 378 at 386.
5 See (1979) 42 MLR 215 (D. Prentice).
6 *Boardman v Phipps* [1967] 2 AC 46 at 124, [1966] 3 All ER 721 at 757, per Lord UPJOHN. Although Lord UPJOHN dissented, Lord SCARMAN in *Queensland Mines Ltd v Hudson* (1978) 18 ALR 1 at p. 3 adopted his reasoning on the grounds that Lord UPJOHN had dissented on the facts, but not on the law.
7 [1990] 2 AC 663, [1990] 1 All ER 652; (1990) 106 LQR 365 (J. Beatson and D. Prentice); [1990] CLJ 220 (J. Hopkins); [1990] Conv 296 (S. Goulding).
8 In most of the cases the company had developed an interest in the particular business opportunity, but the reasoning of the courts could also extend to situations where the opportunity falls within the general line of the company's business. See *Canadian Aero Service Ltd v O'Malley* (1973) 40 DLR (3d) 371 (SCC).
9 [1972] 1 WLR 443, [1972] 2 All ER 162 (the reports on the case are not identical); (1973) 89 LQR 187 (A. Yoran); (1972A) 30 CLJ 222 (J.G. Collier); (1972) 35 MLR 655 (H. Rajak); (1972) 50 CBR 623 (D. Prentice).

representing that he was ill. He was held to be liable to account to the plaintiffs for the profits from the contract.

The significance of the case is twofold. In the first place the court rejected Cooley's first line of defence, that the information concerning the Gas Board's contract came to him in his private capacity, and not as director of the plaintiffs; this 'is the first case in which it was decided that the prohibition on exploiting a corporate opportunity applies also to an opportunity which was presented to the director personally and not in his capacity with the company'.[10] Secondly, the decision whether or not the contract went to the company lay, not with the fiduciary, Cooley, but with a third party, the Gas Board.[11] In *Cooley*'s case there were special circumstances; this was exactly the type of opportunity which the company relied on Cooley to obtain; furthermore, the absence of bona fides was clear. Also, the imposition of liability will provide directors with an incentive to channel relevant economic opportunities to their companies and not exploit them for their personal advantage.

But there are other decisions which suggest that the courts are evincing a more benign attitude towards directors.

In *Queensland Mines Ltd v Hudson*[12] the plaintiff company had been interested in developing a mining operation and the defendant, the managing director, was successful in obtaining for the company the licences necessary to enable it to do so. However, because of severe liquidity problems it could not proceed. Hudson resigned his position as managing director and, with the knowledge of the plaintiff company's board, successfully developed the mines. The Privy Council held that Hudson was not liable to account, for either of two reasons: (*a*) the rejection of the opportunity by the plaintiff company because of cash difficulties took the venture outside the scope of Hudson's fiduciary duties or (*b*) because Hudson had acted with the full knowledge of the plaintiff company's board, they should be taken to have consented to his activities.[13]

This decision causes some difficulties.[14] First, to argue that a board's rejection of the opportunity for commercial reasons immunises a director against liability is difficult to reconcile with *Regal (Hastings) Ltd v Gulliver*. Although in the case Lord Reid deliberately left open the question of the effect of board rejection,[15] it is difficult to see how there would still not be a serious conflict of interest if directors were permitted to acquire for themselves opportunities which they had rejected on behalf of the company. To argue that the board could condone Hudson's breach is also difficult to accept unquestioningly as the appropriate organ of the company is the shareholders'

---

10 (1973) 89 LQR 187 at p. 189.
11 Roskill J found that there was only a 10 per cent chance that the Gas Board would have awarded the contract to the plaintiff company. Thus the case involved the paradoxical situation that the plaintiff company only benefited because Cooley had breached his duty.
12 (1978) 18 ALR 1; [1980] Conv 200 (W. Braithwaite). See also *Island Export Finance Ltd v Umunna* [1986] BCLC 460 (defendant not liable for developing a business opportunity after resigning as managing director because company was not actively pursuing the venture when he resigned, and his resignation was influenced not by any wish to acquire the business opportunity but by dissatisfaction with the company).
13 (1978) 18 ALR 1 at p. 10.
14 (1979) 42 MLR 711 (G.R. Sullivan).
15 [1967] 2 AC 134n. at 152–153, [1942] 1 All ER 378 at 391. In *Peso-Silver Mines Ltd v Cropper* (1966) 58 DLR (2d) 1 (SCC), it was held that board rejection did immunise a director against any action to account. But this decision has not gone uncriticised; (1967) 30 MLR 450 (D. Prentice); (1971) 49 CBR 80 (S.M. Beck).

meeting.[16] If the line of reasoning in *Queensland Mines Ltd v Hudson* were to be expanded, it would lead to the development of a line of defences, (such as bona fides,[17] illegality,[18] inability, or lack of desire on the part of the company to exploit the opportunity[19]) available to directors charged with breach of duty, a development which the law hitherto has not countenanced. Such a development would also have significant implications for fiduciary duties in general.''

(b) Insider Dealing[20]

Department of Trade: The Conduct of Company Directors, para. 22 (1977 Cmnd. 7037)

''22. Insider dealing is understood broadly to cover situations where a person buys or sells securities when he, but not the other party to the transaction, is in possession of confidential information which affects the value to be placed on those securities. Furthermore the confidential information in question will generally be in his possession because of some connection which he has with the company whose securities are to be dealt in (e.g. he may be a director, employee or professional adviser of that company) or because someone in such a position has provided him, directly or indirectly, with the information. Public confidence in directors and others closely associated with companies requires that such people should not use inside information to further their own interests. Furthermore, if they were to do so, they would frequently be in breach of their obligations to the companies, and could be held to be taking an unfair advantage of the people with whom they were dealing.''

In 1980 insider dealing was made a criminal offence. The law is consolidated in Part V of the Criminal Justice Act 1993.

CRIMINAL JUSTICE ACT 1993

52. The offence—(1) An individual who has information as an insider is guilty of insider dealing if, in the circumstances mentioned in subsection (3), he deals in securities that are price-affected securities in relation to the information.

---

16 (1979) 42 MLR at pp. 712–713 (G.R. Sullivan).
17 I.e. the directors acted bona fide. This was rejected in *Regal (Hastings) Ltd v Gulliver* [1967] 2 AC 134n, [1942] 1 All ER 378.
18 I.e. it would be illegal for the company to enter into the transaction. This is implicitly rejected by *Parker v McKenna* (1874) 10 Ch App 96, *Reading v A-G* [1951] AC 507.
19 The inability would arise because the third party would not deal with the company or it lacked the necessary resources. These, of course, were the issues dealt with in *Regal (Hastings) Ltd v Gulliver* [1967] 2 AC 134n, [1942] 1 All ER 378 and *Industrial Development Consultants Ltd v Cooley* [1972] 1 WLR 443, [1972] 2 All ER 162. Cf. *Island Export Finance v Umunna* [1986] BCLC 460, p. 842, n. 12, ante.
20 See Review of Investor Protection Report (Gower Committee) 1984 (Cmnd 9125), Part I, pp. 151–153, 157. On insider dealing generally, see P & M, pp. 459–460; Gore Brown, *Company Law*, chap. 12; Palmer's *Company Law*, paras, 11.101– 11.131. Hanigan, *Insider Dealing* (2nd edn 1994); Ashe and Counsell, *Insider Trading* (2nd edn 1993); (1994) 57 MLR 419 (K. Wotherspoon).

(2) An individual who has information as an insider is also guilty of insider dealing if—
  (a) he encourages another person to deal in securities that are (whether or not that other knows it) price-affected securities in relation to the information knowing or having reasonable cause to believe that the dealing would take place in the circumstances mentioned in sub-section (3); or
  (b) he discloses the information, otherwise than in the proper performance of the functions of his employment, office or profession, to another person.

(3) The circumstances referred to above are that the acquisition or disposal in question occurs on a regulated market, or that the person dealing relies on a professional intermediary or is himself acting as a professional intermediary.

(4) This section has effect subject to section 53.

Section 53 provides that there is no offence for dealing in three particular circumstances.[1]

House of Commons Standing Committee B, Col 175, June 10, 1993.

"The new section provides that there is no offence for dealing in three particular circumstances. The first is that the person dealing did not expect to make a profit attributable to the fact that he possessed information that was price sensitive to the securities in question. That defence might apply when, for example, someone sold shares while in possession of information [that] he expected to receive a favourable reaction from the market.

The second defence applies when someone believed on reasonable grounds that the information had been disclosed widely enough to ensure that none of those taking part in the dealing would be prejudiced by not having the information. That defence can come into play when the parties to a transaction are in contact with each other and they both possess information that can or cannot yet be made public. That is of particular importance in ensuring that the legislation does not impinge on properly conducted corporate finance transaction such as underwriting offers of listed securities and such like. The third defence applies when someone can show that he would have done what he did even if he had not had the information; for example, it allows a trustee who possesses insider information to deal in price-affected securities on the basis of independent investment advice. Analogous defences are also provided for the encouraging offence.

The position for disclosure is slightly different because the offence itself excludes disclosure in the proper performance of someone's employment and because the second defence applicable to dealing and encouraging is not applicable, as the defence itself requires both parties to possess the same information. Accordingly, the disclosure defences are provided when no dealing was expected or the dealing was not expected to lead to someone making a profit attributable to the fact that the securities involved were price affected in relation to the information in question."

---

1 For special defences, see Sched 1.

ii. EXTENT OF FIDUCIARY PRINCIPLE

BOARDMAN v PHIPPS[2]
[1967] 2 AC 46, [1966] 3 All ER 721 (HL, Viscount DILHORNE, Lords COHEN, HODSON, GUEST and UPJOHN)

Charles William Phipps left his residuary estate, which included 8,000 shares (approximately 27 per cent.) in Lester and Harris Ltd, upon trust for his widow for life and after her death for his four children. The trustees in 1955 were his widow (the life tenant), Mrs Noble (his daughter) and William Fox (a professional trustee and an accountant).

John Phipps, the plaintiff and respondent, was a son of the testator, and one of the beneficiaries. The defendants, now the appellants, were his brother Tom, also a beneficiary, and Thomas Gray Boardman, who acted as solicitor to the trust and to the Phipps family.

In 1956, the appellants were dissatisfied with the way in which the business of Lester and Harris Ltd was conducted. They made enquiries and took various steps, recorded in more detail below, which culminated in the purchase by the appellants of all the shares in the company other than those owned by the trust. They then effected sales of the company's premises in Australia and in Coventry, and distributed the proceeds of sale as capital profits; and reorganised the part of the business which remained. The transactions were highly profitable both for the trust and for the appellants.

The steps by which this was effected were grouped by the court into three phases. In Phase I, lasting from December 1955 to April 1957, the appellants, acting on behalf of the trustees, obtained valuable information about the company. They made an unsuccessful bid in their own names for the remainder of the shares of the company at £3 per share. Fox and Mrs Noble were informed, and approved. Mrs Phipps, the testator's widow, aged and in failing health, was not consulted.

In Phase 2, April 1957 to August 1958, Boardman, again acting on behalf of the trustees, was attempting to reach a solution by effecting a sharing of the assets between the Harris family, and the directors and the Phipps family. The plan failed, but, again during this phase, Boardman obtained further information about the company and the potential value of its shares.

In Phase 3, from 1958 to 1961, an agreement was reached in March 1959 under which Boardman and Tom Phipps should buy the directors' holdings for £4 10s. per share and would make a bid for the remainder of the shares on the same terms. The life tenant had died in 1958. Boardman wrote to the

2 (1967) 31 Conv (NS) 63 (F.R. Crane); (1968) 84 LQR 472 (G.H.Jones), p. 851, post; [1978] Conv 114 (B.A.K. Rider); *New Zealand Netherlands Society "Oranje" Inc v Kuys* [1973] 1 WLR 1126, [1973] 2 All ER 1222; (1973) 37 Conv (NS) 362 (F.R. Crane); (1975) 28 CLP 39 (J.D. Stephens); *English v Dedham Vale Properties Ltd* [1978] 1 WLR 93, [1978] 1 All ER 382 (duty to account imposed upon "self-appointed agent", where purchaser, without disclosure to vendor, applied for planning permission in vendor's name prior to contract and obtained it prior to completion); (1978) 94 LQR 347 (G. Samuel); 41 MLR 474 (A. Nicol). Cf. *Swain v Law Society* [1983] 1 AC 598, [1982] 2 All ER 827 (Law Society held not accountable to premium-paying solicitors for commission received as a result of indemnity insurance scheme); [1982] Conv 447 (A.M. Kenny).

For the view that "the liability of a fiduciary for the negligent transaction of his duties is not a separate head of liability but the paradigm of the general duty to act with care imposed by law on those who take it upon themselves to act for or advise others", see *Henderson v Merrett Syndicates Ltd* [1994] 3 WLR 761 at 799, per Lord BROWNE-WILKINSON; (1995) 111 LQR 1 (J.D. Heydon).

remaindermen, including the respondent, asking their approval to his taking a personal interest in the negotiation. Throughout the negotiations, Boardman acted with unquestioned bona fides, and thought that he had the approval of the trustees while the trust lasted, and of the remaindermen after the life tenant's death. This was not so; he never obtained the approval of old Mrs Phipps; and WILBERFORCE J found that the respondents had not been given complete information.

The agreements were carried out, and the profits distributed. The respondent then called upon the appellants to account for their profits on the ground that they held the shares as constructive trustees for the Phipps family.

Held (Viscount DILHORNE and Lord UPJOHN dissenting; and affirming WILBERFORCE J [1964] 1 WLR 993, [1964] 2 All ER 187, and the Court of Appeal [1965] Ch 992, [1965] 1 All ER 849): (i) The appellants, being persons who were enabled to make a profit by reason of a fiduciary relation, were liable to account for it; but (ii) having acted bona fide throughout, were entitled to payment on a liberal scale for their work and skill.

LORD COHEN: In the case before your Lordships it seems to me clear that the appellants throughout were obtaining information from the company for the purpose stated by Wilberforce J but it does not necessarily follow that the appellants were thereby debarred from acquiring shares in the company for themselves. They were bound to give the information to the trustees but they could not exclude it from their own minds. As Wilberforce J said [1964] 1 WLR 993 at 1011, [1964] 2 All ER 187 at 202, the mere use of any knowledge or opportunity which comes to the trustee or agent in the course of his trusteeship or agency does not necessarily make him liable to account. In the present case had the company been a public company and had the appellants bought the shares on the market, they would not, I think, have been accountable. But the company is a private company and not only the information but the opportunity to purchase these shares came to them through the introduction which Mr Fox gave them to the board of the company and in the second phase when the discussions related to the proposed split-up of the company's undertaking it was solely on behalf of the trustees that Mr Boardman was purporting to negotiate with the board of the company. The question is this: when in the third phase the negotiations turned to the purchase of the shares at £4 10s. a share, were the appellants debarred by their fiduciary position from purchasing on their own behalf the 21,986 shares in the company without the informed consent of the trustees and the beneficiaries?

Wilberforce J and, in the Court of Appeal, both Lord Denning MR and Pearson LJ based their decision in favour of the respondent on the decision of your Lordships' House in *Regal (Hastings) Ltd v Gulliver* [1967] 2 AC 134n, [1942] 1 All ER 378, p. 839, ante. I turn, therefore, to consider that case. Mr Walton relied upon a number of passages in the judgments of the learned Lords who heard the appeal: in particular on (1) a passage in the speech of Lord Russell of Killowen where he says at 144G–145A, at 386:

"The rule of equity which insists on those, who by use of a fiduciary position make a profit, being liable to account for that profit, in no way depends on fraud, or absence of bona fides; or upon such questions or considerations as whether the profit would or should otherwise have gone to the plaintiff, or whether the profiteer was under a duty to obtain the source of the profit for the plaintiff, or whether he took a risk or acted as he did for the benefit of the plaintiff, or whether the plaintiff has in fact been damaged or benefited by his action. The liability arises from the mere fact of a profit having, in the stated circumstances, been made."

(2) a passage in the speech of Lord Wright, where he says at 154B–C, at 392:

"That question can be briefly stated to be whether an agent, a director, a trustee or other person in an analogous fiduciary position, when a demand is made upon him by the person to whom he stands in the fiduciary relationship to account for profits acquired by him by reason of his fiduciary position, and by reason of the opportunity and the knowledge, or either, resulting from it, is entitled to defeat the claim upon any ground save that he made profits with the knowledge and assent of the other person. The most usual and typical case of this nature is that of principal and agent. The rule in such cases is compendiously expressed to be that an agent must account for net profits secretly (that is, without the knowledge of his principal) acquired by him in the course of his agency. The authorities show how manifold and various are the applications of the rule. It does not depend on fraud or corruption."

These paragraphs undoubtedly help the respondent but they must be considered in relation to the facts of that case. In that case the profit arose through the application by four of the directors of Regal for shares in a subsidiary company which it had been the original intention of the board should be subscribed for by Regal. Regal had not the requisite money available but there was no question of it being ultra vires Regal to subscribe for the shares. In the circumstances Lord Russell of Killowen said at 146G–147A, at 387:

"I have no hesitation in coming to the conclusion, upon the facts of this case, that these shares, when acquired by the directors, were acquired by reason, and only by reason of the fact that they were directors of Regal, and in the course of their execution of that office."

He goes on to consider whether the four directors were in a fiduciary relationship to Regal and concludes that they were. Accordingly, they were held accountable. Mr Bagnall argued that the present case is distinguishable. He puts his argument thus. The question you ask is whether the information could have been used by the principal for the purpose for which it was used by his agents? If the answer to that question is no, the information was not used in the course of their duty as agents. In the present case the information could never have been used by the trustees for the purpose of purchasing shares in the company; therefore purchase of shares was outside the scope of the appellant's agency and they are not accountable.

This is an attractive argument, but it does not seem to me to give due weight to the fact that the appellants obtained both the information which satisfied them that the purchase of the shares would be a good investment and the opportunity of acquiring them as a result of acting for certain purposes on behalf of the trustees. Information is, of course, not property in the strict sense of that word and, as I have already stated, it does not necessarily follow that because an agent acquired information and opportunity while acting in a fiduciary capacity he is accountable to his principals for any profit that comes his way as the result of the use he makes of that information and opportunity. His liability to account must depend on the facts of the case. In the present case much of the information came the appellants' way when Mr Boardman was acting on behalf of the trustees on the instructions of Mr Fox and the opportunity of bidding for the shares came because he purported for all purposes except for making the bid to be acting on behalf of the owners of the 8,000 shares in the company. In these circumstances it seems to me that the principle of the *Regal* case [1967] 2 AC 134n, [1942] 1 All ER 378 applies and that the courts below came to the right conclusion.

That is enough to dispose of the case but I would add that an agent is, in my opinion, liable to account for profits he makes out of trust property if there is a possibility of conflict between his interest and his duty to his principal. Mr Boardman and Tom Phipps were not general agents of the trustees but they were their agents for certain limited purposes. The information they had obtained and the opportunity to purchase the 21,986 shares afforded them by their relations with the directors of the company—an opportunity they got as the result of their introduction to the directors by Mr Fox—were not property in the strict sense but that information and that opportunity they owed to their representing themselves as agents for the holders of the 8,000 shares held by the trustees. In these circumstances they could not, I think, use that information and that opportunity to purchase the shares for themselves if there was any possibility that the trustees might wish to acquire them for the trust. Mr Boardman was the solicitor whom the trustees were in the habit of consulting if they wanted legal advice. Granted that he would not be bound to advise on any point unless he is consulted, he would still be the person they would consult if they wanted advice. He would clearly have advised them that they had no power to invest in shares of the company without the sanction of the court. In the first phase he would also have had to advise on the evidence then available that the court would be unlikely to give such sanction: but the appellants learnt much more during the second phase. It may well be that even in the third phase the answer of the court would have been the same but, in my opinion, Mr Boardman would not have been able to give unprejudiced advice if he had been consulted by the trustees and was at the same time negotiating for the purchase of the shares on behalf of himself and Tom Phipps. In other words, there was, in my opinion, at the crucial date (March, 1959), a possibility of a conflict between his interest and his duty.

In making these observations I have referred to the fact that Mr Boardman was the solicitor to the trust. Tom Phipps was only a beneficiary and was not as such debarred from bidding for the shares, but no attempt was made on the courts below to differentiate between them. Had such an attempt been made it would very likely have failed as Tom Phipps left the negotiations largely to Mr Boardman and it might well be held that if Mr Boardman was disqualified from bidding Tom Phipps could not be in a better position. Be that as it may, Mr Bagnall rightly did not seek at this stage to distinguish between the two. He did, it is true, say that Tom Phipps as a beneficiary would be entitled to any information the trustees obtained. This may be so, but nonetheless I find myself unable to distinguish between the two appellants. They were, I think, in March, 1959, in a fiduciary position vis-à-vis the trust. That fiduciary position was of such a nature that (as the trust fund was distributable) the appellants could not purchase the shares on their own behalf without the informed consent of the beneficiaries; it is now admitted that they did not obtain that consent. They are therefore, in my opinion, accountable to the respondent for his share of the net profits they derived from the transaction.

I desire to repeat that the integrity of the appellants is not in doubt. They acted with complete honesty throughout and the respondent is a fortunate man in that the rigour of equity enables him to participate in the profits which have accrued as the result of the action taken by the appellants in March, 1959, in purchasing the shares at their own risk. As the last paragraph of his judgment clearly shows, the trial judge evidently shared this view. He directed an inquiry as to what sum is proper to be allowed to the appellants or either of them in respect of his work and skill in obtaining the said shares and the profits in respect thereof. The trial judge concluded by expressing the opinion that payment should be on a liberal scale. With that observation I respectfully agree.

In the result I agree in substance with the judgments of Wilberforce J and of Lord Denning MR and Pearson LJ in the Court of Appeal, and I would dismiss the appeal.

LORD UPJOHN (dissenting): It is of cardinal importance, and, in my view fundamental to the decision of this case, to appreciate that at this stage there was no question whatever of the trustees contemplating the possibility of a purchase of further shares in the company. Mr Fox (whose evidence was accepted by the judge) made it abundantly plain that he would not consider any such proposition. The reasons for this attitude are worth setting out in full: (*a*) The acquisition of further shares in the company would have been a breach of trust, for they were not shares authorised by the investment clause in the will; (*b*) although not developed in evidence it must have been obvious to those concerned that no court would sanction the purchase of further shares in a small company which the trustees considered to be badly managed. It would have been throwing good money after bad. It would also have been necessary to bring in proposals for installing a new management. Mr Fox was a busy practising chartered accountant who obviously would not have considered it; no one from start to finish ever suggested that Tom, who was running the family concern of Phipps & Son Ltd, would be willing to undertake this arduous task on behalf of the trustees; (*c*) the trustees had no money available for the purchase of further shares ...

In these circumstances the respondent rather surprisingly seeks to hold the appellants accountable to him for his 5/18ths share of the 21,986 shares so purchased, on the footing that the appellants are constructive trustees of these shares for and on behalf of the trust. So I turn to the relevant law upon which this claim is based, but start by stating what is not in dispute, that the conduct of the appellants and each of them has never been anything except utterly honest and above board in every way. If they or either of them are accountable it is because of the operation of some harsh doctrine of equity upon consciences completely innocent in every way.

Rules of equity have to be applied to such a great diversity of circumstances that they can be stated only in the most general terms and applied with particular attention to the exact circumstances of each case. The relevant rule for the decision of this case is the fundamental rule of equity that a person in a fiduciary capacity must not make a profit out of his trust which is part of the wider rule that a trustee must not place himself in a position where his duty and his interest may conflict. I believe the rule is best stated in *Bray v Ford* [1896] AC 44 at 51 by Lord Herschell, who plainly recognised its limitations:

"It is an inflexible rule of a Court of Equity that a person in a fiduciary position, such as the respondent's, is not, unless otherwise expressly provided, entitled to make a profit; he is not allowed to put himself in a position where his interest and duty conflict. It does not appear to me that this rule is, as has been said, founded upon principles of morality. I regard it rather as based on the consideration that, human nature being what it is, there is danger, in such circumstances, of the person holding a fiduciary position being swayed by interest rather than by duty, and thus prejudicing those whom he was bound to protect. It has, therefore, been deemed expedient to lay down this positive rule. But I am satisfied that it might be departed from in many cases, without any breach of morality, without any wrong being inflicted, and without any consciousness of wrong-doing. Indeed, it is obvious that it might sometimes be to the advantage of the beneficiaries that their trustee should act for them professionally rather than a stranger, even though the trustee were paid for his services.''[3]

[His Lordship referred to *Aberdeen Rly Co v Blaikie Bros* (1854) 1 Macq 461; *Regal (Hastings) Ltd v Gulliver* [1967] 2 AC 134n, [1942] 1 All ER 378; *Keech v Sandford* (1726) Sel Cas Ch 61, and continued:] Secondly, as to the position of Mr Boardman himself. There is no doubt that from time to time he acted as solicitor to the trust and to the family and he was therefore throughout in a fiduciary capacity at least to the trustees. Whether he was ever in a fiduciary capacity to the respondent was not debated before your Lordships and I do not think it matters. I think, again, that some of the trouble that has arisen in this case, it being assumed rightly that throughout he was in such a capacity, is that it has been assumed that it has necessarily followed that any profit made by him renders him accountable to the trustees. This is not so. A solicitor who acts for a client from time to time is no doubt rightly described throughout as being in a fiduciary capacity to him but that means fundamentally no more than this, that if he has dealings with his clients, e.g., accepts a present from him or buys property from him, there is a presumption of undue influence and the onus is on the solicitor to justify the present or purchase (see, for example, *McMaster v Byrne* [1952] 1 All ER 1362 at 1368). That principle has no relevance to the present case. There is no such thing as an office of being solicitor to a trust (*Saffron Walden Second Benefit Building Society v Rayner* (1880) 14 ChD 406 at 409, per James LJ). Though these remarks of James LJ were admittedly obiter they represent the law. It is perfectly clear that a solicitor can if he so desires act against his clients in any matter in which he has not been retained by them provided, of course, that in acting for them generally he has not learnt information or placed himself in a position which would make it improper for him to act against them. This is an obvious application of the rule that he must not place himself in a position where his duty and his interest conflict. So in general a solicitor can deal in shares in a company in which the client is a shareholder, subject always to the general rule that the solicitor must never place himself in a position where his interest and his duty conflict; and in this connection it may be pointed out that the interest and duty may refer (and frequently do) to a conflict of interest and duty on behalf of different clients and have nothing to do with any conflict between the personal interest and duty of the solicitor, beyond his interest in earning his fees.

[His Lordship then referred to Wilberforce J and the Court of Appeal, and continued:] Before applying these principles to the facts, however, I shall refer to the judgment of Russell LJ, which proceeded on a rather different basis. He said [1965] Ch 992 at 1031, [1965] 1 All ER 849 at 864:

"The substantial trust shareholding was an asset of which one aspect was its potential use as a means of acquiring knowledge of the company's affairs, or

---

3 See *Re Drexel Burnham Lambert UK Pension Plan* [1995] 1 WLR 32 (pension fund trustees also beneficiaries under scheme; court held to have jurisdiction to give directions as to exercise of trustees' discretion).

of negotiating allocations of the company's assets, or of inducing other shareholders to part with their shares. That aspect was part of the trust assets."

My Lords, I regard that proposition as untenable.

In general, information is not property at all. It is normally open to all who have eyes to read and ears to hear. The true test is to determine in what circumstances the information has been acquired. If it has been acquired in such circumstances that it would be a breach of confidence to disclose it to another then courts of equity will restrain the recipient from communicating it to another. In such cases such confidential information is often and for many years has been described as the property of the donor, the books of authority are full of such references; knowledge of secret processes, "know-how", confidential information as to the prospects of a company or of someone's intention or the expected results of some horse race based on stable or other confidential information. But in the end the real truth is that it is not property in any normal sense but equity will restrain its transmission to another if in breach of some confidential relationship.

With all respect to the views of Russell LJ, I protest at the idea that information acquired by trustees in the course of their duties as such is necessarily part of the assets of the trust which cannot be used by the trustees except for benefit of the trust. Russell LJ referred at 1031, at 864 to the fact that two out of three of the trustees could have no authority to turn over this aspect of trust property to the appellants except for the benefit of the trust; this I do not understand, for if such information is trust property not all the trustees acting together could do it for they cannot give away trust property.

We heard much argument upon the impact of the fact that the testator's widow was at all material times incapable of acting in the trust owing to disability. Of course trustees must act all of them and unanimously in matters affecting trust affairs, but in this case they never performed any relevant act on behalf of the trust at all; I quoted Mr Fox's answer earlier for this reason. At no time after going to the meeting in December, 1956, did Mr Boardman or Tom rely on any express or implied authority or consent of the trustees in relation to trust property. They understood rightly that there was no question of the trustees acquiring any further trust property by purchasing further shares in the company, and it was only in the purchase of other shares that they were interested.

There is, in my view, and I know of no authority to the contrary, no general rule that information learnt by a trustee during the course of his duties is property of the trust and cannot be used by him. If that were to be the rule it would put the Public Trustee and other corporate trustees out of business and make it difffficult for private trustees to be trustees of more than one trust. This would be the greatest possible pity for corporate trustees and others may have much information which they may initially acquire in connection with some particular trust but without prejudice to that trust can make it readily available to other trusts to the great advantage of those other trusts.

The real rule is, in my view, that knowledge learnt by a trustee in the course of his duties as such is not in the least property of the trust and in general may be used by him for his own benefit or for the benefit of other trusts unless it is confidential information which is given to him (1) in circumstances which, regardless of his position as a trustee, would make it a breach of confidence for him to communicate to anyone for it has been given to him expressly or impliedly as confidential, or (2) in a fiduciary capacity, and its use would place him in a position where his duty and his interest might possibly conflict. Let me give one or two simple examples. A, as trustee of two settlements X and Y holding shares in the same small company, learns facts as trustee of X about the company which are encouraging. In the absence of special circumstances (such, for example, that X wants to buy more shares) I can see nothing whatever which would make it improper for him to tell his co-trustees of Y who feel inclined to sell that he has information that this would be a bad thing to do. Another example: A as trustee of X learns facts that make him and his co-trustees want to sell. Clearly he could not communicate this knowledge to his co-trustees of Y until at all events the holdings of X have been sold for there would be a plain conflict, reflected in the prices that might or might possibly be obtained . . .

As a result of the information they acquired, admittedly by reason of the trust holding, they found it worth while to offer a good deal more for the shares than in [the period January–April 1957]. I cannot see that in offering to purchase non-trust shares at a higher price they were in breach of any fiduciary relationship in using the information they had acquired for this purpose . . .

I have dealt with the problems that arise in this case at considerable length but it could, in my opinion, be dealt with quite shortly.

In *Barnes v Addy* (1874) 9 Ch App 244 at 251, Lord Selborne LC said:

"It is equally important to maintain the doctrine of trusts which is established in this court, and not to strain it by unreasonable construction beyond its due and proper limits. There would be no better mode of undermining the sound doctrines of equity than to make unreasonable and inequitable applications of them."

That, in my judgment, is applicable to this case.

The trustees were not willing to buy more shares in the company. The active trustees were very willing that the appellants should do so themselves for the benefit of their large minority holding. The trustees, so to speak, lent their name to the appellants in the course of prolonged and difficult negotiations and, of course, the appellants thereby learnt much which would have otherwise been denied to them. The negotiations were in the end brilliantly successful.

And how successful Tom was in his reorganisation of the company is apparent to all. They ought to be very grateful.

In the long run the appellants have bought for themselves at entirely their own risk with their own money shares which the trustees never contemplated buying and they did so in circumstances fully known and approved of by the trustees.

To extend the doctrines of equity to make the appellants accountable in such circumstances is, in my judgment, to make unreasonable and inequitable applications of such doctrines.

I would allow the appeal and dismiss the action.

(1968) 84 LQR 472 at p. 483 (G.H. Jones)[4]

"Lord Hodson and Lord Guest were of the opinion that confidential information could properly be regarded as 'the property of the trust', and for this reason alone Phipps and Boardman must account for the fruit of that

---

4 See also *Seager v Copydex Ltd* [1967] 1 WLR 923, [1967] 2 All ER 415; (1970) 86 LQR 463 (G.H. Jones).

property.[5] Lord Hodson went on to say that because the appellants had acted as agents and had 'obtained knowledge by reason of their fiduciary position . . . they cannot escape liability by saying that they were acting for themselves and not as agents of the trustees.'[6] And Lord Guest based his final conclusion on the ground that 'Boardman and Tom Phipps . . . [had] placed themselves in a special position which was of a fiduciary character in relation to the negotiations with the directors. . . . Out of such special position and in the course of such negotiations they obtained the opportunity to make a profit out of the shares and knowledge that the profit was there to be made.'[7] . . .

To say that the fiduciaries' profit was made solely through the use of property (the information) received *qua* fiduciaries, when the trust could not have utilised it and when the negotiations would have failed but for Boardman's business acumen and Boardman and Phipps' financial intervention, offends legal as well as common sense.[8] To categorise confidential information as 'property' or 'equitable property' cannot solve the essential questions whether Boardman and Phipps were unjustly enriched, and whether policy demands that they should disgorge their enrichment even though they were not unjustly enriched.[9]

The main ground of the decision was that there was a conflict between Boardman and Phipps' self-interest and their fiduciary duty; they had made a profit out of their special position of trust. It is difficult to accept, however, that any reasonable person could conclude on these facts that there was any real (as distinct from a hypothetical) conflict of interest. In our view the reasoning of the dissenting law lords is convincing. Lord Upjohn's realistic, commonsense approach is that of Justice Clark in the *Becker* case.[10] Both judges refused to apply blindly a rule of equity. In neither *Becker's* case nor *Phipps v Boardman* had the profit been made at the expense of the fiduciary's principal. In both cases the fiduciary's actions had benefited the principal: the purchase of the debentures in the *Becker* case encouraged public confidence in a company which was in a parlous financial position; in *Phipps v Boardman* the long negotiations conducted with considerable skill by Boardman, and the

---

5 In *Phipps v Boardman* the plaintiff in his writ had claimed that Boardman and Tom Phipps held 5/18ths of the shareholding as constructive trustees for the plaintiff (5/18ths being the extent of the plaintiff's beneficial interest in the trust fund); an account of profits made by Boardman and Phipps from the holdings, and an order that they should transfer the shares held as constructive trustees to the plaintiff, and pay him 5/18ths of the profit: see [1965] Ch 992 at 1006.

   At first instance [1964] 1 WLR 993 at 1018, [1964] 2 All ER 187 at 208, WILBERFORCE J had declared that the defendants were accountable and directed an account and an inquiry as to the allowances to which they were entitled. The order went on to say that "further consideration [would be given] of order to transfer the shares held by the defendants and payment of any profit found on the taking of the account adjourned".

6 [1967] 2 AC 46 at 111, [1966] 3 All ER 721 at 748.

7 At 118, at 752.

8 In the Court of Appeal, Lord DENNING MR suggested that the appellants should have told the trustees that the shares were a good buy, that they ought to purchase them and that they should apply to the court for power to do so: see [1965] Ch 992 at 1020, [1965] 1 All ER 849 at 857. No other judge in the Court of Appeal or House of Lords took up this point. Lord UPJOHN considered that it was a "difficult point", but was able to avoid it by saying that it was neither pleaded nor relied upon in argument: see [1967] 2 AC 46 at 131, [1966] 3 All ER 721 at 761. In any event, is it realistic to assume that parties would contemplate an application to the court during the course of confidential and protracted negotiations?

9 See Goff and Jones, *The Law of Restitution* pp. 38–40; and cf. Austin W. Scott, "Constructive Trusts" (1955) 71 LQR 39.

10 *Manufacturers Trust Co v Becker* 338 US 304, 70 Sup Ct 127 (1949).

purchase of the outstanding shares by Boardman and Tom Phipps, had resulted in great financial benefit to the trust. Neither the *Becker* directors nor *Boardman* was a Sergeant Reading. They had not unjustly enriched themselves at their principal's expense.

Conclusion

'Rules of equity have to be applied to such a great diversity of circumstances that they can be stated only in the most general terms and applied with particular attention to the exact circumstances of each case.'[11] The rule that a fiduciary must not profit from his trust is used to recover the fiduciary's unjust enrichment *and* to ensure that the conduct of all fiduciaries is maintained 'at a level higher than that trodden by the crowd.'[12]

In many cases these objects do not conflict. The dishonest fiduciary who is punished as a warning to others has been unjustly enriched. It is irrelevant that his gain has not been made at his principal's expense, in the sense that something has been taken 'from [the] plaintiff and added to the treasury of [the] defendant.'[13] For he has abused his position of trust, and 'in equity and good conscience [he] should not be permitted to retain that by which [he] has been enriched'. In other cases, however, the fiduciary's enrichment has not been unjustly gained. There is then a variance between the two objects which underlie equity's inflexible rule. Some but not all courts and judges have been aware of this clash of principle. A conscious appreciation and consideration of the qualifications of the large generalisation of unjust enrichment[14]—the inherent fairness of the transaction, the fiduciary's honesty and concern to protect his principal's interests, and the fact that the principal has suffered no real loss (the 'complex equation' of loss and gain)—has helped them to decide that there was, on the particular facts, no real sensible possibility of conflict between duty and self-interest.

The boundaries between just and unjust enrichment do not inevitably compose the limits of equity's 'inflexible rule'. There may be cases where it is absolutely necessary to punish the fiduciary whose enrichment cannot be said to be unjustly gained. That wise public policy which desires to remove all temptation and to extinguish all possibility of profit may insist that a fiduciary whose integrity is beyond doubt and who has materially benefited his principal should be deprived of profit. But this decision should be taken only after due and careful regard has been paid to the relevant policy considerations, to the nature of the responsibilities which the particular fiduciary owes his principal and to the question whether it is necessary to make an example of the innocent and conscientious that others may learn from their fate.

Finally, there is the question of the extent and degree of the fiduciary's liability. In our view the principal should be allowed a proprietary claim only if the court considers it appropriate that he should be granted the additional benefits which naturally flow from such a grant. The honest fiduciary who is deemed to have breached his duty of loyalty but who has not been unjustly enriched and whose principal has suffered no loss should only be liable to

---

11 *Boardman v Phipps* [1967] 2 AC 46 at 123, [1966] 3 All ER 721 at 756, per Lord UPJOHN.
12 *Meinherd v Salmon* 249 NY 456 at 464, 164 NE 545 at 546 (1928), per Chief Judge CARDOZO.
13 *Federal Sugar Refining Co v US Sugar Equalization Board Inc* 268 F 575 at 582 (1920), per Judge MAYER.
14 *Fibrosa Spolka Akcyjna v Fairbairn Lawson Combe Barbour Ltd* [1943] AC 32 at 62–63, [1942] 2 All ER 122 at 136, per Lord WRIGHT.

account for his profits. On the other hand a fiduciary who is dishonest or who has otherwise manifestly disregarded his principal's interest should be held to be a constructive trustee of the benefits obtained at his principal's expense. If, as a matter of policy, the court imposes on him a further and penal liability for profits made by third parties, his liability should only be a personal one, to account to his principal for those profits."

iii. BRIBES AND THE FIDUCIARY

Until the Privy Council decision in *A-G for Hong Kong v Reid* [1994] 1 AC 324, [1994] 1 All ER 1, the liability of a fiduciary who received a secret profit depended on whether the profit was in the form of a bribe or of some other type. The first gave rise only to a personal relationship of debtor and creditor between the fiduciary and his principal,[15] the second to a proprietary relationship. In the case of the bribe the principal could sue the fiduciary or the briber[16] for the amount of the bribe; in the other case the fiduciary became a constructive trustee for the principal,[17]as a result of which he had the proprietary remedy of tracing, and, where the fiduciary was bankrupt, a claim ahead of his general creditors.

This "glaring inconsistency" has been the subject of much criticism.[18] The Privy Council has now removed it and held that in both cases a constructive trust arises in favour of the principal.

ATTORNEY-GENERAL FOR HONG KONG v REID
[1994] 1 AC 324, [1994] 1 All ER 1 (PC, Lords TEMPLEMAN, GOFF OF CHIEVELEY, LOWRY, LLOYD OF BERWICK and Sir Thomas EICHELBAUM)

Mr Reid, a New Zealander, was Acting Director of Public Prosecutions in Hong Kong. In breach of his fiduciary duty to the Crown, he accepted bribes of NZ $2.5m as an inducement to him to exploit his official position by obstructing the prosecution of certain criminals. He was convicted, sentenced to eight years imprisonment and ordered to pay the Crown HK $12.4m, the equivalent of NZ $2.5m. Mr Reid used the bribes to purchase three freehold properties in New Zealand, two for himself and his wife, and one for his solicitor. Neither his wife nor his solicitor could establish that they were bona fide purchasers for value without notice.

The Attorney-General for Hong Kong lodged a caveat against the titles to the properties, in order to prevent any dealing with them pending a full hearing. Mr Reid argued that the Crown was entitled only to a personal claim for the value of the initial bribe and had no equitable interest in the properties. The Court of Appeal of New Zealand, following *Lister & Co v Stubbs* (1890) 45 ChD 1, found for Mr Reid.

---

15 *Lister & Co v Stubbs* (1890) 45 Ch D 1.
16 *Mahesan v Malaysia Government Officers' Co-operative Housing Society Ltd* [1979] AC 374 at 383, [1978] 2 All ER 405 at 411.
17 *Boardman v Phipps* [1967] 2 AC 46, [1966] 3 All ER 721, p. 844 ante.
18 P & M, pp. 230–231; Birks, *An Introduction to the Law of Restitution* (1985), p. 388; Goode (1987) 103 LQR 433, 442–445; Goff and Jones, *Law of Restitution* (3rd edn), pp. 656, 657; Finn, *Fiduciary Obligations* (1977), para. 513; Sir Anthony MASON, *Essays in Equity* (1985), p. 246; Sir Peter MILLETT [1993] RLR 7; Birks, ed. *The Frontiers of Liability* (1994), vol 1, Part II, Bribes and Secret Commissions (papers by Sir Peter MILLETT, P. Birks and WR Cornish); [1994] Conv 156 (A. Jones); [1994] CLJ 31 (A.J. Oakley); (1994) 110 LQR 178 (P. Watts); [1994] RLR 57 (D. Crilley); [1994] All ER Rev 252 (P.J. Clarke).

Held (reversing the Court of Appeal) for the Crown. It had an equitable interest under a constructive trust.

LORD TEMPLEMAN: A bribe is a gift accepted by a fiduciary as an inducement to him to betray his trust. A secret benefit, which may or may not constitute a bribe, is a benefit which the fiduciary derives from the trust property or obtains from knowledge which he acquires in the course of acting as a fiduciary. A fiduciary is not always accountable for a secret benefit but he is undoubtedly accountable for a secret benefit which consists of a bribe. In addition a person who provides the bribe and the fiduciary who accepts the bribe may each be guilty of a criminal offence. In the present case the first respondent was clearly guilty of a criminal offence.

Bribery is an evil practice which threatens the foundations of any civilised society. In particular bribery of policemen and prosecutors brings the administration of justice into disrepute. Where bribes are accepted by a trustee, servant, agent or other fiduciary, loss and damage are caused to the beneficiaries, master or principal whose interests have been betrayed. The amount of loss or damage resulting from the acceptance of a bribe may or may not be quantifiable. In the present case the amount of harm caused to the administration of justice in Hong Kong by the first respondent in return for bribes cannot be quantified.

When a bribe is offered and accepted in money or in kind, the money or property constituting the bribe belongs in law to the recipient. Money paid to the false fiduciary belongs to him. The legal estate in freehold property conveyed to the false fiduciary by way of bribe vests in him. Equity, however, which acts in personam, insists that it is unconscionable for a fiduciary to obtain and retain a benefit in breach of duty. The provider of a bribe cannot recover it because he committed a criminal offence when he paid the bribe. The false fiduciary who received the bribe in breach of duty must pay and account for the bribe to the person to whom that duty was owed. In the present case, as soon as the first respondent received a bribe in breach of the duties he owed to the Government of Hong Kong, he became a debtor in equity to the Crown for the amount of that bribe. So much is admitted. But if the bribe consists of property which increases in value or if a cash bribe is invested advantageously, the false fiduciary will receive a benefit from his breach of duty unless he is accountable not only for the original amount or value of the bribe but also for the increased value of the property representing the bribe. As soon as the bribe was received it should have been paid or transferred instanter to the person who suffered from the breach of duty. Equity considers as done that which ought to have been done. As soon as the bribe was received, whether in cash or in kind, the false fiduciary held the bribe on a constructive trust for the person injured. Two objections have been raised to this analysis. First it is said that if the fiduciary is in equity a debtor to the person injured, he cannot also be a trustee of the bribe. But there is no reason why equity should not provide two remedies, so long as they do not result in double recovery. If the property representing the bribe exceeds the original bribe in value, the fiduciary cannot retain the benefit of the increase in the value which he obtained solely as a result of his breach of duty. Secondly, it is said that if the false fiduciary holds property representing the bribe in trust for the person injured, and if the false fiduciary is or becomes insolvent, the unsecured creditors of the false fiduciary will be deprived of their right to share in the proceeds of that property. But the unsecured creditors cannot be in a better position than their debtor. The authorities show that property acquired by a trustee innocently but in breach of trust and the property from time to time representing the same belong in equity to the cestui que trust and not to the trustee personally whether he is solvent or insolvent. Property acquired by a trustee as a result of a criminal breach of trust and the property from time to time representing the same must also belong in equity to his cestui que trust and not to the trustee whether he is solvent or insolvent.

When a bribe is accepted by a fiduciary in breach of his duty then he holds that bribe in trust for the person to whom the duty was owed. If the property representing the bribe decreases in value the fiduciary must pay the difference between the value and the initial amount of the bribe because he should not have accepted the bribe or incurred the risk of loss. If the property increases in value, the fiduciary is not entitled to any surplus in excess of the initial value of the bribe because he is not allowed by any means to make a profit out of a breach of duty.

The courts of New Zealand were constrained by a number of precedents of the New Zealand, English and other common law courts which established a settled principle of law inconsistent with the foregoing analysis. That settled principle is open to review by the Board in the light of the foregoing analysis of the consequences in equity of the receipt of a bribe by a fiduciary. In *Keech v Sandford* (1726) Sel Cas Ch 61 a landlord refused to renew a lease to a trustee for the benefit of an infant. The trustee then took a new lease for his own benefit. The new lease had not formed part of the original trust property, the infant could not have acquired the new lease from the landlord and the trustee acted innocently, believing that he committed no breach of trust and that the new lease did not belong in equity to his cestui que trust. Lord King LC held nevertheless, at p. 62, that "the trustee is the only person of all mankind who might not have the lease;" the trustee was obliged to assign the new lease to the infant and account for the profits he had received. The rule must be that property which a trustee obtains by use of knowledge acquired as trustee becomes trust property. The rule must, a fortiori, apply to a bribe accepted by a trustee for a guilty criminal purpose which injuries the cestui que trust. The trustee is only one example of a fiduciary and the same rule applies to all other fiduciaries who accept bribes.

[His Lordship referred to *Fawcett v Whitehouse* (1829) 1 Russ & M 132 and *Sugden v Crossland* (1856) 3 Sm & G 192, and continued:]

This case is of importance because it disposes succinctly of the argument which appears in later cases and which was put forward by counsel in the present case that there is a distinction between a profit which a trustee takes out of a trust and a profit such as a bribe which a trustee receives from a third party. If in law a trustee, who in breach of trust invests trust moneys in his own name, holds the investment as trust property, it is difficult to see why a trustee who in breach of trust receives and invests a bribe in his own name does not hold those investments also as trust property.

[His Lordship referred to *Tyrrell v Bank of London* (1862) 10 HL Cas 26; *Re Canadian Oil Works Corpn (Hay's Case)* (1875) 10 Ch App 593; *Re Morvah Consols Tin Mining Co, McKay's Case* (1875) 2 ChD 1; *Re Caerphilly Colliery Co, Pearson's Case* (1877) 5 ChD 336; *Metropolitan Bank v Heiron* (1880) 5 Ex D 319, and continued:]

It has always been assumed and asserted that the law on the subject of bribes was definitively settled by the decision of the Court of Appeal in *Lister & Co v Stubbs* (1890) 45 ChD 1.

In that case the plaintiffs, Lister & Co, employed the defendant, Stubbs, as their servant to purchase goods for the firm. Stubbs, on behalf of the firm, bought goods from Varley & Co and received from Varley & Co bribes amounting to £5,541. The bribes were invested by Stubbs in freehold properties and investments. His masters, the firm Lister & Co, sought and failed to obtain an interlocutory injunction restraining Stubbs from disposing of these assets pending the trial of the action in which they sought, inter alia, £5,541 and damages. In the Court of Appeal the first judgment was given by Cotton LJ who had been party to the decision in *Metropolitan Bank v Heiron* (1880) 5 ExD 319. He was powerfully supported by the judgment of Lindley LJ and by the equally powerful concurrence of Bowen LJ. Cotton LJ said, at p. 12, that the bribe could not be said to be the money of the plaintiffs. He seemed to be reluctant to grant an interlocutory judgment which would provide security for a debt before that debt had been established. Lindley LJ said, at p. 15, that the relationship between the plaintiffs, Lister & Co, as masters and the defendant, Stubbs, as servant who had betrayed his trust and received a bribe:

> "is that of debtor and creditor; it is not that of trustee and cestui que trust. We are asked to hold that it is—which would involve consequences which, I confess, startle me. One consequence, of course, would be that, if Stubbs were to become bankrupt, this property acquired by him with the money paid to him by Messrs. Varley would be withdrawn from the mass of his creditors and be handed over bodily to Lister & Co. Can that be right? Another consequence would be that, if the appellants are right, Lister & Co could compel Stubbs to account to them, not only for the money with interest, but for all the profits which he might have made by embarking in trade with it. Can that be right?"

For the reasons which have already been advanced their Lordships would respectfully answer both these questions in the affirmative. If a trustee mistakenly invests money which he ought to pay over to his cestui que trust and then becomes bankrupt, the moneys together with any profit which has accrued from the investment are withdrawn from the unsecured creditors as soon as the mistake is discovered. A fortiori if a trustee commits a crime by accepting a bribe which he ought to pay over to his cestui que trust, the bribe and any profit made therefrom should be withdrawn from the unsecured creditors as soon as the crime is discovered.

The decision in *Lister & Co v Stubbs* is not consistent with the principles that a fiduciary must not be allowed to benefit from his own breach of duty, that the fiduciary should account for the bribe as soon as he receives it and that equity regards as done that which ought to be done. From these principles it would appear to follow that the bribe and the property from time to time representing the bribe are held on a constructive trust for the person injured. A fiduciary remains personally liable for the amount of the bribe if, in the event, the value of the property then recovered by the injured person proved to be less than that amount.

[His Lordship referred to *Powell and Thomas v Evans Jones & Co* [1905] 1 KB 11; *A-G v Goddard* (1929) 98 LJKB 743; *Regal (Hastings) Ltd v Gulliver* [1967] 2 AC 134n, [1942] 1 All ER 378; *Reading v A-G* [1951] AC 507; and *Islamic Republic of Iran Shipping Lines v Denby* [1987] 1 Lloyd's Rep 367, and continued:]

The authorities which followed *Lister & Co v Stubbs* do not cast any new light on that decision. Their Lordships are more impressed with the decision of Lai Kew Chai J in *Sumitomo Bank Ltd v Kartika Ratna Thahir* [1993] 1 SLR 735...

After considering in detail all the relevant authorities Lai Kew Chai J determined robustly, at p. 810, that *Lister & Co v Stubbs* (1890) 45 ChD 1, was wrong and that its "undesirable and unjust consequences should not be imported and perpetuated as part of" the law of Singapore. Their Lordships are also much indebted for the fruits of research and the careful discussion of the present topic in the address entitled "Bribes and Secret Commissions" [1993] RLR 7 delivered by Sir Peter Millett to a meeting of the Society of Public Teachers of Law at Oxford in 1993. The following passage, at p. 20, elegantly sums up the views of Sir Peter Millett:

"[The fiduciary] must not place himself in a position where his interest may conflict with his duty. If he has done so, equity insists on treating him as having acted in accordance with his duty; he will not be allowed to say that he preferred his own interest to that of his principal. He must not obtain a profit for himself out of his fiduciary position. If he has done so, equity insists on treating him as having obtained it for his principal; he will not be allowed to say that he obtained it for himself. He must not accept a bribe. If he has done so, equity insists on treating it as a legitimate payment intended for the benefit of the principal: he will not be allowed to say that it was a bribe."

The conclusions reached by Lai Kew Chai J in *Sumitomo Bank Ltd v Kartika Ratna Thahir* and the views expressed by Sir Peter Millett were influenced by the decision of the House of Lords in *Boardman v Phipps* [1967] 2 AC 46, [1966] 3 All ER 721 which demonstrates the strictness with which equity regards the conduct of a fiduciary and the extent to which equity is willing to impose a constructive trust on property obtained by a fiduciary by virtue of his office. In that case a solicitor acting for trustees rescued the interests of the trust in a private company by negotiating for a takeover bid in which he himself took an interest. He acted in good faith throughout and the information which the solicitor obtained about the company in the takeover bid could never have been used by the trustees. Nevertheless the solicitor was held to be a constructive trustee by a majority in the House of Lords because the solicitor obtained the information which satisfied him that the purchase of the shares in the takeover company would be a good investment and the opportunity of acquiring the shares as a result of acting for certain purposes on behalf of the trustees: see per Lord Cohen, at p. 103. If a fiduciary acting honestly and in good faith and making a profit which his principal could not make for himself becomes a constructive trustee of that profit then it seems to their Lordships that a fiduciary acting dishonestly and criminally who accepts a bribe and thereby causes loss and damage to his principal must also be a constructive trustee and must not be allowed by any means to make any profit from his wrongdoing. For the reasons indicated their Lordships consider that the three properties so far as they represent bribes accepted by the first respondent are held in trust for the Crown.

C. Services to Charities

Annual Report of the Charity Commissioners for England and Wales for the year 1970, paras. 92–93

"*Trustees supplying goods or services to a charity*

92. We considered during the year an interesting and specialised point relating to the fiduciary nature of trusteeship. It is a well established rule of law that, unless specifically authorised in the trust instrument, a charity trustee

shall not derive any personal profit from his trust or be placed in a position where his duty as a trustee conflicts with his interests as a private individual. It has been our practice for a long time to include in our schemes a clause providing that no trustee shall take or hold any interest in property belonging to the charity otherwise than as a trustee and that no trustee shall receive remuneration or be interested in the supply of goods or services at the cost of the charity. Representations were, however, made to us objecting to such a strict provision and claiming that charities often suffer as a result, since persons who are in a position to supply a charity with goods or services are frequently also suitable persons to be trustees and in small villages, in particular, might be the only persons suitable for appointment. Such persons are often willing to supply goods and services at reduced or cost price to the benefit of the charity, and in country districts they may be the only persons living locally who can supply such work or goods, but because of the restrictions imposed by the scheme they are faced with the choice of accepting trusteeship and dissociating themselves from supplying work or goods to the charity, or of declining trusteeship.

93. We came to the conclusion that while our common-form clause would still be appropriate in a large proportion of cases, and would continue to be used, it was too restrictive in the circumstances indicated above. We therefore adopted an alternative form of clause which, while providing reasonable safeguards, will permit the appointment of suitable persons as trustees without preventing them from supplying work or goods to a charity. The new clause will provide that a trustee shall absent himself from any meeting of the trustees at which they are discussing any transaction in which he is interested in the supply of services, work or goods at the cost of the charity and, further, that the other trustees must be satisfied that any transaction arising out of their deliberations is advantageous to the charity.''

QUESTIONS

1. In determining the borderline of a fiduciary liability, how relevant is it that:
   (*a*) the plaintiff suffered no loss;
   (*b*) the plaintiff benefited in addition to the fiduciary;
   (*c*) the fiduciary was bona fide;
   (*d*) the profit came through a decision of a third party (the Gas Board in *Industrial Development Consultants Ltd v Cooley* [1972] 1 WLR 443, [1972] 2 All ER 162, p. 840, ante);
   (*e*) the fiduciary is a trustee, solicitor, director;
   (*f*) the defendant is a friend of the fiduciary (the tippee)?
2. Do you think that fiduciary obligations should be imposed where there is also
   (*a*) a breach of duty of care in tort: Law Commission Consultation Paper: Fiduciary Duties and Regulatory Rules 1992 (Law Com No 124), para. 2.4.6.; p. 837, n. 15, ante; *Henderson v Merrett Syndicates Ltd* [1994] 3 WLR 761 at 799, [1994] 3 All ER 506 at 543, per Lord BROWNE-WILKINSON; (1995) 111 LQR 1 (J.D. Hayden), p. 844, n. 2, ante.
   (*b*) a breach of contract: P & M, pp. 223–225; *Polly Peck International plc v Nadir (No 2)* [1992] 4 All ER 769; *Kelly v Cooper* [1993] AC 205; *Re Goldcorp Exchange Ltd* [1995] 1 AC 74, [1994] 2 All ER 806; *United*

Dominions Corpn v Brian Pty Ltd (1985) 157 CLR 1; (1994) 101 LQR 238 at pp. 245–248 (Sir Anthony MASON).

3. The directors of a corporation purchased debentures at a discount, at prices varying from 3% to 14% of their face value. At the time of the purchase, the corporation was a going concern, but the market value of its property was insufficient to pay its outstanding debts. The purchase was made without failure to disclose any material facts to the sellers. On the liquidation of the corporation the directors stood to make a profit if their claims as debenture holders were allowed. The trustee for the debenture holders objected on the ground that the directors could not make a profit from the purchase of claims against an insolvent corporation.

What result? *Manufacturers Trust Co v Becker* 338 US 304, 70 Sup Ct 127 (1949); (1968) 84 LQR at pp. 479 et seq. See also *Boardman v Phipps* [1967] 2 AC 46 at 90, [1966] 3 All ER 721 at 735, where Viscount DILHORNE quoted LINDLEY LJ in *Aas v Benham* [1891] 2 Ch 244 at 255–256: "to hold that a partner can never derive any personal benefit from information which he obtains from a partner would be manifestly absurd"; H & M, p. 595.

4. If you had been a Lord of Appeal in *Boardman v Phipps*, what would you have said?

5. Was *Boardman v Phipps* a case concerning constructive trusts, or personal accountability? H & M, pp. 597–598; (1968) 84 LQR 502; *A-G for Hong Kong v Reid* [1994] 1 AC 324, p. 854 ante.

21. Breach of Trust[1]

I. Personal Liability to the Beneficiaries[2]

A trustee is personally liable to compensate the beneficiaries for the loss which a breach of trust causes to the trust property, either directly or indirectly, and the burden of proof is on the plaintiff to prove a causal connection between the breach and the loss.

The liability is joint and several. It is personal, not vicarious. A trustee is not vicariously liable for the acts of his co-trustees. But, and this is of great significance, trustees are required to act jointly. One trustee cannot escape liability by leaving his co-trustees to do all the work.

---

1 H & M, pp. 618–671; K & S, pp. 435–450; P & M, pp. 577–632; Pettit, pp. 482–578; Riddall, pp. 350–379; Snell, pp. 283–305; Underhill, pp. 825–935. See the definitions of breach of trust discussed by MEGARRY J in *Tito v Waddell (No 2)* [1977] Ch 106 at 247, [1977] 3 All ER 129 at 246.
  For criminal liability, see Theft Act 1968; *R v Barrick* (1985) 81 Cr App Rep 78 (guidelines on sentencing); *A-G's Reference (No 1 of 1985)* [1986] QB 491, [1986] 2 All ER 219 (making of secret profit for which a fiduciary was personally accountable held not to be theft within s. 5 (1), (3)); Debtors Act 1869, s. 4; (1975) 39 Conv (NS) 29 (R. Brazier); Underhill, pp. 875–880. As to whether this decision has been undermined by *A-G for Hong Kong v Reid* [1994] 1 AC 324, [1994] 1 All ER 1, see Law Commission Report: Conspiracy to Defraud 1994 (Law Com No 228), paras. 4.20–4.24; (1994) 110 LQR 180 (J.C. Smith).
2 H & M, pp. 619–640; K & S, pp. 435–448, 473–480; P & M, pp. 577–601; Pettit, pp. 482–504; Riddall, pp. 363–379; Snell, pp. 284–297; Underhill, pp. 731–751, 772–807.

A trustee's liability may be reduced by a provision in the trust instrument; and, as has been seen, it is limited by statute.[3] It is common also for professional trustees to protect themselves by insurance.[4]

A. Measure of Liability[5]

i. General Principles

TARGET HOLDINGS LTD v REDFERNS[6]

[1995] 3 WLR 352, [1995] 3 All ER 785 (HL, Lords Keith of Kinkel, Ackner, Jauncey of Tullichettle, Browne-Wilkinson and Lloyd of Berwick)

Mirage Properties Ltd, who were the owners of commercial property in Birmingham, made a contract to sell it to Crowngate Developments Ltd for £775,000. Target Holdings Ltd agreed to lend £1,525,000 on the security of the property. Redferns, who were acting as solicitors for both Crowngate and Target, held the mortgage advance on a bare trust for Target with authority to release the money to Crowngate only on receipt of the executed conveyances and mortgage of the property. However they released it before the documents were executed. It was admitted that this was a breach of trust. The property was in due course found to be worth only £500,000, through no fault on the part of Redferns.

Redferns argued that the breach of trust was technical and that Target had suffered no loss arising from the breach, because in due course it received the documents, and the same loss would have occurred even if there had been no breach. Target argued that the duty of a trustee who misapplied trust funds was to restore them, subject to giving credit for any money received on the sale of the mortgaged property.

Held (reversing the Court of Appeal [1994] 1 WLR 1089, [1994] 2 All ER 337) For Redferns.

Lord Browne-Wilkinson. My Lords, this appeal raises a novel point on the liability of a trustee who commits a breach of trust to compensate beneficiaries for such breach. Is the trustee liable to compensate the beneficiary not only for losses caused by the breach but also for losses which the beneficiary would, in any event, have suffered even if there had been no such breach? ...

Before considering the technical issues of law which arise, it is appropriate to look at the case more generally. Target alleged, and it is probably the case, that they were defrauded by third parties (Mr. Kohli and Mr. Musafir and possibly their associates) to advance money on the security of the property. If there had been no breach by Redferns of their instructions and the transaction had gone through, Target would have suffered a loss in round figures of £1.2m. (i.e. £1.7m. advanced less £500,000 recovered on the realisation of the security). Such loss would have been wholly caused by the fraud of the third parties. The breach of trust committed by Redferns left Target in exactly the same position as it would have been if there had been no such breach: Target advanced the same amount of money, obtained the same security and received the same

---

3 TA 1925, s. 30, p. 748, ante; *Re Brier* (1884) 26 ChD 238.
4 See (1994) 2 Ch Comm Rep 24–27.
5 H & M, pp. 620–625; K & S, pp. 435–439; P & M, pp. 580–589; Pettit, pp. 483–487; Snell, pp. 284–289; Underhill, pp. 825–847.
6 (1995) 139 SJ 894 (N.J. Patten QC counsel for the respondents).

amount on the realisation of that security. In any ordinary use of words, the breach of trust by Redferns cannot be said to have caused the actual loss ultimately suffered by Target unless it can be shown that, but for the breach of trust, the transaction would not have gone through, e.g. if Panther could not have obtained a conveyance from Mirage otherwise than by paying the purchase money to Mirage out of the moneys paid out, in breach of trust, by Redferns to Panther on 29 June. If that fact can be demonstrated, it can be said that Redferns' breach of trust was a cause of Target's loss: if the transaction had not gone through, Target would not have advanced the money at all and therefore Target would not have suffered any loss. But the Court of Appeal decided (see Ralph Gibson LJ, at 1100, at 347; Peter Gibson LJ at 1104, at 351) and it is common ground before your Lordships that there is a triable issue as to whether, had it not been for the breach of trust, the transaction would have gone through. Therefore the decision of the Court of Appeal in this case can only be maintained on the basis that, even if there is no causal link between the breach of trust and the actual loss eventually suffered by Target (i.e. the sum advanced less the sum recovered) the trustee in breach is liable to bear (at least in part) the loss suffered by Target.

The transaction in the present case is redolent of fraud and negligence. But, in considering the principles involved, suspicions of such wrongdoing must be put on one side. If the law as stated by the Court of Appeal is correct, it applies to cases where the breach of trust involves no suspicion of fraud or negligence. For example, say an advance is made by a lender to an honest borrower in reliance on an entirely honest and accurate valuation. The sum to be advanced is paid into the client account of the lender's solicitors. Due to an honest and non-negligent error (e.g. an unforeseeable failure in the solicitors' computer) the moneys in client account are transferred by the solicitors to the borrower one day before the mortgage is executed. That is a breach of trust. Then the property market collapses and when the lender realises his security by sale he recovers only half the sum advanced. As I understand the Court of Appeal decision, the solicitors would bear the loss flowing from the collapse in the market value: subject to the court's discretionary power to relieve a trustee from liability under section 61 of the Trustee Act 1925 (p. 876 post), the solicitors would be bound to repay the total amount wrongly paid out of the client account in breach of trust receiving credit only for the sum received on the sale of the security.

To my mind in the case of an unimpeachable transaction this would be an unjust and surprising conclusion. At common law there are two principles fundamental to the award of damages. First, that the defendant's wrongful act must cause the damage complained of. Second, that the plaintiff is to be put "in the same position as he would have been in if he had not sustained the wrong for which he is now getting his compensation or reparation:" *Livingstone v Rawyards Coal Co* (1880) 5 App Cas 25, 39, per Lord Blackburn. Although, as will appear, in many ways equity approaches liability for making good a breach of trust from a different starting point, in my judgment those two principles are applicable as much in equity as at common law. Under both systems liability is fault-based: the defendant is only liable for the consequences of the legal wrong he has done to the plaintiff and to make good the damage caused by such wrong. He is not responsible for damage not caused by his wrong or to pay by way of compensation more than the loss suffered from such wrong. The detailed rules of equity as to causation and the quantification of loss differ, at least ostensibly, from those applicable at common law. But the principles underlying both systems are the same. On the assumptions that had to be made in the present case until the factual issues are resolved (i.e. that the transaction would have gone through even if there had been no breach of trust), the result reached by the Court of Appeal does not accord with those principles. Redferns as trustees have been held liable to compensate Target for a loss caused otherwise than by the breach of trust. I approach the consideration of the relevant rules of equity with a strong predisposition against such a conclusion.

The considerations urged before your Lordships, although presented as a single argument leading to the conclusion that the views of the majority in the Court of Appeal are correct, on analysis comprise two separate lines of reasoning, viz.: (A) an argument developed by Mr. Patten (but not reflected in the reasons of the Court of Appeal) that Target is now (i.e. at the date of judgment) entitled to have the "trust fund" restored by an order that Redferns reconstitute the trust fund by paying back into client account the moneys paid away in breach of trust. Once the trust fund is so reconstituted, Redferns as bare trustee for Target will have no answer to a claim by Target for the payment over of the moneys in the reconstituted "trust fund". Therefore, Mr. Patten says, it is proper now to order payment direct to Target of the whole sum improperly paid away, less the sum which Target has received on the sale of property; and (B) the argument accepted by the majority of the Court of Appeal that, because immediately after the moneys were paid away by Redferns in breach of trust there was an immediate right to have the "trust fund" reconstituted, there was then an immediate loss to the trust fund for which loss Redferns are now liable to compensate Target direct.

The critical distinction between the two arguments is that argument (A) depends upon Target being entitled now to an order for restitution to the trust fund whereas argument (B) quantifies the compensation payable to Target as beneficiary by reference to a right to restitution to the trust fund at an earlier date and is not dependent upon Target having any right to have the client account reconstituted now.

Before dealing with these two lines of argument, it is desirable to say something about the approach to the principles under discussion. The argument both before the Court of Appeal and your Lordships concentrated on the equitable rules establishing the extent and quantification of the compensation payable by a trustee who is in breach of trust. In my judgment this approach is liable to lead to the wrong conclusions in the present case because it ignores an earlier and crucial question, viz., is the trustee who has committed a breach under any liability at all to the beneficiary complaining of the breach? There can be cases where, although there is an undoubted breach of trust, the trustee is under no liability at all to a beneficiary. For example, if a trustee commits a breach of trust with the acquiescence of one beneficiary, that beneficiary has no right to complain and an action for breach of trust brought by him would fail completely. Again there may be cases where the breach gives rise to no right to compensation. Say, as often occurs, a trustee commits a judicious breach of trust by investing in an unauthorised investment which proves to be very profitable to the trust. A carping beneficiary could insist that the unauthorised investment be sold and the proceeds invested in authorised investments: but the trustee would be under no liability to pay compensation either to the trust fund or to the beneficiary because the breach has caused no loss to the trust fund. Therefore, in each case the first question is to ask what are the rights of the beneficiary: only if some relevant right has been infringed so as to give rise to a loss is it necessary to consider the extent of the trustee's liability to compensate for such loss.

The basic right of a beneficiary is to have the trust duly administered in accordance with the provisions of the trust instrument, if any, and the general law. Thus, in relation to a traditional trust where the fund is held in trust for a number of beneficiaries having different, usually successive, equitable interests, (e.g. A for life with remainder to B), the right of each beneficiary is to have the whole fund vested in the trustees so as to be available to satisfy his equitable interest when, and if, it falls into possession. Accordingly, in the case of a breach of such a trust involving the wrongful paying away of trust assets, the liability of the trustee is to restore to the trust fund, often called "the trust estate", what ought to have been there.

The equitable rules of compensation for breach of trust have been largely developed in relation to such traditional trusts, where the only way in which all the beneficiaries rights can be protected is to restore to the trust fund what ought to be there. In such a case the basic rule is that a trustee in breach of trust must restore or pay to the trust estate either the assets which have been lost to the estate by reason of the breach or compensation for such loss. Courts of Equity did not award damages but, acting in personam, ordered the defaulting trustee to restore the trust estate: see *Nocton v Ashburton (Lord)* [1914] AC 932, 952, 958, per Viscount Haldane LC. If specific restitution of the trust property is not possible, then the liability of the trustee is to pay sufficient compensation to the trust estate to put it back to what it would have been had the breach not been committed: *Caffrey v Darby* (1801) 6 Ves 488; *Clough v Bond* (1838) 3 M & C 490. Even if the immediate cause of the loss is the dishonesty or failure of a third party, the trustee is liable to make good that loss to the trust estate if, but for the breach, such loss would not have occurred: see Underhill and Hayton, *Law of Trusts & Trustees* 14th edn (1987), pp. 734–736; *Re Dawson* [1966] 2 NSWR 211; *Bartlett v Barclays Bank Trust Co Ltd (Nos 1 and 2)* [1980] Ch 515, [1980] 2 All ER 92. Thus the common law rules of remoteness of damage and causation do not apply. However there does have to be some causal connection between the breach of trust and the loss to the trust estate for which compensation is recoverable, viz. the fact that the loss would not have occurred but for the breach: see also *Re Miller's Deed Trusts* (1978) 75 LSG 454; *Nestle v National Westminster Bank Plc* [1993] 1 WLR 1260, [1994] 1 All ER 118.

Hitherto I have been considering the rights of beneficiaries under traditional trusts where the trusts are still subsisting and therefore the right of each beneficiary, and his only right, is to have the trust fund reconstituted as it should be. But what if at the time of the action claiming compensation for breach of trust those trusts have come to an end? Take as an example again the trust for A for life with remainder to B. During A's lifetime B's only right is to have the trust duly administered and, in the event of a breach, to have the trust fund restored. After A's death, B becomes absolutely entitled. He of course has the right to have the trust assets retained by the trustees until they have fully accounted for them to him. But if the trustees commit a breach of trust, there is no reason for compensating the breach of trust by way of an order for restitution and compensation to the trust fund as opposed to the beneficiary himself. The beneficiary's right is no longer simply to have the trust duly administered: he is, in equity, the sole owner of the trust estate. Nor, for the same reason, is restitution to the trust fund necessary to protect other beneficiaries. Therefore, although I do not wholly rule out the possibility that even in those circumstances an order to reconstitute the fund may be appropriate, in the ordinary case where a beneficiary becomes absolutely entitled to the trust fund the court orders, not restitution to the trust estate, but the payment of compensation directly to the beneficiary. The measure of such compensation is the same, i.e. the difference between what the beneficiary has in fact received and the amount he would have received but for the breach of trust.

Thus in *Bartlett v Barclays Bank Trust Co Ltd (No 2)* [1980] Ch 515, [1980] 2 All ER 92 by the date of judgment some of the shares settled by the trust deed had become absolutely vested in possession: see at p. 543A, at p. 95. The compensation for breach of trust, though quantified by reference to what the fund would have been but for the breach of trust, was payable directly to the persons who were absolutely entitled to their shares of the trust fund: see at p. 544, at p. 96. Accordingly, in traditional trusts for persons by way of succession, in my judgment once those trusts have been exhausted and the fund has become absolutely vested in possession, the beneficiary is not normally entitled to have the exhausted trust reconstituted. His right is to be compensated for the loss he has suffered by reason of the breach.

I turn then to the two arguments urged before your Lordships.

Argument (A)

As I have said, the critical step in this argument is that Target is now entitled to an order for reconstitution of the trust fund by the repayment into client account of the moneys wrongly paid away, so that Target can now demand immediate repayment of the whole of such moneys without regard to the real loss it has suffered by reason of the breach.

Even if the equitable rules developed in relation to traditional trusts were directly applicable to such a case as this, as I have sought to show a beneficiary becoming absolutely entitled to a trust fund has no automatic right to have the fund reconstituted in all circumstances. Thus, even applying the strict rules so developed in relation to traditional trusts, it seems to me very doubtful whether Target is now entitled to have the trust fund reconstituted. But in my judgment it is in any event wrong to lift wholesale the detailed rules developed in the context of traditional trusts and then seek to apply them to trusts of quite a different kind. In the modern world the trust has become a valuable device in commercial and financial dealings. The fundamental principles of equity apply as much to such trusts as they do to the traditional trusts in relation to which those principles were originally formulated. But in my judgment it is important, if the trust is not to be rendered commercially useless, to distinguish between the basic principles of trust law and those specialist rules developed in relation to traditional trusts which are applicable only to such trusts and the rationale of which has no application to trusts of quite a different kind.

This case is concerned with a trust which has at all times been a bare trust. Bare trusts arise in a number of different contexts: e.g. by the ultimate vesting of the property under a traditional trust, nominee shareholdings and, as in the present case, as but one incident of a wider commercial transaction involving agency. In the case of moneys paid to a solicitor by a client as part of a conveyancing transaction, the purpose of that transaction is to achieve the commercial objective of the client, be it the acquisition of property or the lending of money on security. The depositing of money with the solicitor is but one aspect of the arrangements between the parties, such arrangements being for the most part contractual. Thus, the circumstances under which the solicitor can part with money from client account are regulated by the instructions given by the client: they are not part of the trusts on which the property is held. I do not intend to cast any doubt on the fact that moneys held by solicitors on client account are trust moneys or that the basic equitable principles apply to any breach of such trust by solicitors. But the basic equitable principle applicable to breach of trust is that the beneficiary is entitled to be compensated for any loss he would not have suffered but for the breach. I have no doubt that, until the underlying commercial transaction has been completed, the solicitor can be required to restore to client account moneys wrongly paid away. But to import into such trust an obligation to restore the trust fund once the transaction has been completed would be entirely artificial. The obligation to reconstitute the trust fund applicable in the case of traditional trusts reflects the fact that no one beneficiary is entitled to the trust property and the need to compensate all beneficiaries for the breach. That rationale has no application to a case such as the present. To impose such an obligation in order to enable the beneficiary solely entitled (i.e. the client) to recover from the solicitor more than the client has in fact lost flies in the face of common sense and is in direct conflict with the basic principles of equitable compensation. In my judgment, once a conveyancing transaction has been completed the client has no right to have the solicitor's client account reconstituted as a "trust fund."

Argument (B)

I have already summarised the reasons of the majority in the Court of Appeal for holding that Redferns were liable to pay to Target, by way of compensation, the whole sum paid away in breach of trust, less the sum recovered by Target. Mr. Patten supported this argument before your Lordships.

The key point in the reasoning of the Court of Appeal is that where moneys are paid away to a stranger in breach of trust, an immediate loss is suffered by the trust estate: as a result, subsequent events reducing that loss are irrelevant. They drew a distinction between the case in which the breach of trust consisted of some failure in the administration of the trust and the case where a trustee has actually paid away trust moneys to a stranger. There is no doubt that in the former case, one waits to see what loss is in fact suffered by reason of the breach, i.e. the restitution or compensation payable is assessed at the date of trial, not of breach. However, the Court of Appeal considered that where the breach consisted of paying away the trust moneys to a stranger it made no sense to wait: it seemed to Peter Gibson LJ [1994] 1 WLR 1089, 1103G–H [1994] 2 All ER 337, 351 obvious that in such a case "there is an immediate loss placing the trustee under an immediate duty to restore the moneys to the trust fund". The majority of the Court of Appeal therefore considered that subsequent events which diminished the loss in fact suffered were irrelevant, save for imposing on the compensated beneficiary an obligation to give credit for any benefit he subsequently received. In effect, in the view of the Court of Appeal one "stops the clock" at the date the moneys are paid away: events which occur between the date of breach and the date of trial are irrelevant in assessing the loss suffered by reason of the breach.

A trustee who wrongly pays away trust money, like a trustee who makes an unauthorised investment, commits a breach of trust and comes under an immediate duty to remedy such breach. If immediate proceedings are brought, the court will make an immediate order requiring restoration to the trust fund of the assets wrongly distributed or, in the case of an unauthorised investment, will order the sale of the unauthorised investment and the payment of compensation for any loss suffered. But the fact that there is an accrued cause of action as soon as the breach is committed does not in my judgment mean that the quantum of the compensation payable is ultimately fixed as at the date when the breach occurred. The quantum is fixed at the date of judgment at which date, according to the circumstances then pertaining, the compensation is assessed at the figure then necessary to put the trust estate or the beneficiary back into the position it would have been in had there been no breach. I can see no justification for "stopping the clock" immediately in some cases but not in others: to do so may, as in this case, lead to compensating the trust estate or the beneficiary for a loss which, on the facts known at trial, it has never suffered.

[His Lordship referred to *Re Dawson* [1966] 2 NSWR 211; *Canson Enterprises Ltd v Boughton & Co* (1991) 85 DLR (4th) 129; *Alliance & Leicester Building Society v Edgestop Ltd* (18 January 1991, unreported); *Bishopsgate Investment Management Ltd v Maxwell (No 2)* [1994] 1 All ER 261; *Nant-y-glo and Blaina Ironworks Co v Grave* (1878) 12 ChD 738; *Jaffray v Marshall* [1993] 1 WLR 1285, [1994] 1 All ER 143 and continued:]

For these reasons I reach the conclusion that, on the facts which must currently be assumed, Target has not demonstrated that it is entitled to any compensation for breach of trust. Assuming that moneys would have been forthcoming from some other source to complete the purchase from Mirage if the moneys had not been wrongly provided by Redferns in breach of trust, Target obtained exactly what it would have obtained had no breach occurred, i.e. a valid security for the sum advanced. Therefore, on the assumption made, Target has suffered no compensatable loss. Redferns are entitled to leave to defend the breach of trust claim.

However, I find it very difficult to make that assumption of fact. There must be a high probability that, at trial, it will emerge that the use of Target's money to pay for the purchase from Mirage and the other intermediate transactions was a vital feature of the transaction. The circumstances of the present case are clouded by suspicion, which suspicion is not dissipated by Mr. Bundy's untruthful letter dated 30 June informing Target that the purchase of the property and the charges to Target had been completed. If the moneys made available by Redferns' breach of trust were essential to enable the transaction to go through, but for Redferns' breach of trust Target would not have advanced any money. In that case the loss suffered by Target by reason of the breach of trust will be the total sum advanced to Crowngate less the proceeds of the security. It is not surprising that Mr. Sumption was rather muted in his submission that Redferns should have had unconditional leave to defend and that the order for payment into court of £1m. should be set aside. In my judgment such an order was fully justified.

I would therefore allow the appeal, set aside the order of the Court of Appeal and restore the order of Warner J.

ii. Purchase of Unauthorised Investments

In **Knott v Cottee** (1852) 16 Beav 77, the testator, who died in 1844, bequeathed his personal estate to trustees upon trust to invest in "the public or Government Stocks or Funds of Great Britain, or upon real security in England or Wales".

The executor invested in foreign stocks and in Exchequer bills. In a suit by the beneficiaries, he was required to deposit the Exchequer bills in court, and on November 18, 1846 they were sold, under an order of the court, at a loss. The court made a decree in 1848 declaring the investments to be unauthorised. By that time, the price of the bills had risen; if they had been sold then, there would have been a profit.

The question was whether the executor should be charged with the original sum due for investment plus 5 per cent., or with the sum which would have been produced if invested in Consols; and whether he should be credited with the proceeds of the Exchequer bills as sold in 1846, or with their (increased) value in 1848 when they were declared to be unauthorised. ROMILLY MR held that the executors should be charged with the amount improperly invested, and credited with the proceeds actually received on their sale. He said at 81:

"As to the mode of charging the executor in respect of the Exchequer bills, I treat the laying out in Exchequer bills in this way: The persons interested were entitled to ear-mark them, as being bought with the testator's assets, in the same manner as if the executor had bought a house with the trust funds; and though they do not recognize the investment, they had a right to make it available for what was due; and though part of the property of the executor, it was specifically applicable to the payment. When the Exchequer bills were sold and produced £3,955, the Court must consider the produce as a sum of money refunded by the executor to the testator's estate on that day; and on taking the account, the Master must give credit for this amount as on the day on which the Exchequer bills were sold."

iii. IMPROPER RETENTION OF UNAUTHORISED INVESTMENTS[7]

In **Fry v Fry** (1859) 27 Beav 144, a testator, who died in 1834, provided by his will that the Langford Inn should be sold "as soon as convenient after his decease . . . either by auction or private sale, and for the most money that could be reasonably obtained for the same".

The trustees had difficulty in selling. In 1836 they advertised and offered to sell for £1,000. They refused an offer of £900. In 1843 the Bristol and Exeter Railway was opened, and deprived the Inn of most of its coaching traffic. It was again advertised in 1854, but no offer was received. It remained unsold.

ROMILLY MR held the trustees liable in consequence of their negligence for so many years in not selling the property. The estates of the trustees (who had died) would be liable for the difference between the amount eventually received and £900.

iv. IMPROPER SALE OF AUTHORISED INVESTMENTS

In **Re Massingberd's Settlement** (1890) 63 LT 296,[8] the trustees of a settlement had power to invest in Government or real securities. In 1875 they sold Consols and reinvested in certain unauthorised mortgages. The mortgages were called in and the whole of the money invested was recovered.

Proceedings began in 1887, at which time Consols stood higher than they had done in 1875. The trustees argued that their obligation was only to

---

7 TA 1925, s. 4; Trustee Investments Act 1961, ss. 3 (4), 6 (2), p. 675, ante.
8 *Phillipson v Gatty* (1848) 7 Hare 516.

produce the capital sum; but the Court of Appeal held that they must produce the stock sold or its present money equivalent.

The date of valuation is as at the date of judgment, or, exceptionally, at the date when the asset sold in breach of trust would have been properly sold at a later date (*Re Bell's Indenture* [1980] 1 WLR 1217 at 1233, [1980] 3 All ER 425 at 438–439). It is not the date of the writ as was assumed without argument in *Re Massingberd's Settlement*, where "having regard to the stability of price of Consols over short periods in the 19th century the difference in price between the date of the writ and the date of the judgment of Kay J was insignificant" (per VINELOTT J in *Re Bell's Indenture*).

v. A PROFIT IN ONE TRANSACTION CANNOT BE SET OFF AGAINST A LOSS IN ANOTHER

DIMES v SCOTT
(1828) 4 Russ 195 (LC, Lord LYNDHURST)

By his will the testator, who died in 1802, left his estate upon trust for his widow for her life, and after her death upon trust for the plaintiff. The estate included an investment in an East India Company 10 per cent. loan whose retention was not authorised by the will.

Instead of selling this unauthorised investment within a year of the testator's death, the trustees retained it, and paid the whole income to the widow.

In 1813 the loan was repaid, and the proceeds were invested in 3 per cent. Consols. The price of Consols was lower than it was a year from the testator's death, and the trustees were able to purchase more Consols than they would have been able to purchase if they had made the switch a year from the testator's death.

The question was whether the trustees had committed a breach of trust by paying the whole income to the widow; and, if they had, whether they could set off, against that liability, the extra Consols which the delay had enabled them to purchase.

Held. The payments to the tenant for life were excessive; and the trustees could claim no credit in respect of the extra Consols.

LORD LYNDHURST: This testator left his property to trustees, who were directed to convert it into money, and to invest the proceeds in government or real securities; and he gave the interest of the money so to be invested to his widow for life, with remainder to the lady who is one of the present Plaintiffs. Part of his property consisted of a sum which he had subscribed to what is called the decennial loan. The trustees did not convert his share of this loan into money; but, suffering it to remain as they found it, paid the interest, which was £10 per cent., to the tenant for life. Was that a proper performance of their duty?

The directions of the will were most distinct; and, according to the case of *Howe v Lord Dartmouth* (1802) 7 Ves 137, and the principles of this Court, it was the duty of the trustees to have sold the property within the usual period after the testator's death. If they neglected to sell it, still, so far as regarded the tenant for life, the property was to be considered as if it had been duly converted. Had the conversion taken place, and the proceeds been invested in that which is considered in this Court as the fit and proper security, namely, £3 per cent. stock, the tenant for life would not have been entitled to more than the interest which would have resulted from such stock. The executor is therefore chargeable with the difference between the interest which the fund, if so converted, would have yielded, and the £10 per cent. which was actually produced by the fund, and was paid over by him to the tenant for life.

It is said, that, if the subscription to the decennial loan had been sold, and the produce invested in stock at the end of a year from the testator's death, the sale would have been much less advantageous to the estate than the course which has been actually followed; and that, if the executor is to be charged for not having made the conversion at the proper time, he ought on the other hand, to have the benefit of the advantage which has accrued from his course of conduct. The answer is this: With respect to the principal sum, at whatever period the subscription to the decennial loan was sold, the estate must have the whole amount of the stock that was bought; and if it was sold at a later period than the rules of the Court require, the executor is not entitled to any accidental advantage thence arising. As to the payments to the tenant for life, the executors are entitled to have credit only for sums I have adverted to, namely, the dividends on so much £3 per cent. stock as would have been purchased with the proceeds of the subscription to the decennial loan, if the conversion had taken place at the proper time. On the other hand, he is chargeable with the whole of the difference between the amount of those dividends and the amount of the sums which have been received in respect of interest on the money which was continued in the decennial loan. I think, therefore, that the judgment of the *Master of the Rolls* [Lord GIFFORD] must be affirmed.

Hanbury & Martin: *Modern Equity*, 14th edn (1993), p. 624.

"The rule is harsh though logical. It has not been applied where the court finds that the gain and loss were part of the same transaction. There is often difficulty in determining whether the question should or should not be regarded as a single transaction.

In *Fletcher v Green*[9] trust money was lent on mortgage to a firm of which one trustee was a partner. The trustees reclaimed the money; the security was sold at a loss and the proceeds paid into court and invested in Consols. The question was whether the trustees' accounts should credit them with the amount of the proceeds of sale or with the value of the Consols, which had risen in price. They were held entitled to take advantage of the rise. No reasons were given. The case is usually explained on the ground that the whole matter was treated as one transaction. If that is so, they should logically have been at risk in relation to a possible fall in the price of Consols; the trustees can hardly be allowed to take advantage of a rise but not the burden of a fall; but it would be hard on the trustees if they have to run the risk of loss on an investment made by the court."

In **Bartlett v Barclays Bank Trust Co Ltd (No 1)** [1980] Ch 515, [1980] 1 All ER 139, p. 708 ante, BRIGHTMAN J said at 538, at 155:

"The general rule as stated in all the textbooks, with some reservations, is that where a trustee is liable in respect of distinct breaches of trust, one of

---

9 (1864) 33 Beav 426.

which has resulted in a loss and the other in a gain, he is not entitled to set off the gain against the loss, unless they arise in the same transaction. The relevant cases are, however, not altogether easy to reconcile. All are centenarians and none is quite like the present. The Guildford development stemmed from exactly the same policy and (to a lesser degree because it proceeded less far) exemplified the same folly as the Old Bailey project. Part of the profit was in fact used to finance the Old Bailey disaster. By sheer luck the gamble paid off handsomely, on capital account. I think it would be unjust to deprive the bank of this element of salvage in the course of assessing the cost of the shipwreck. My order will therefore reflect the bank's right to an appropriate set-off.''

vi. INTEREST

A fiduciary may be liable, not only to replace trust capital which has been misapplied, but also to pay interest on that sum from the date of misapplication. In some cases interest is compounded. The nineteenth century cases laid down 4 per cent. as the normal rate of interest, with 5 per cent. in cases of fraud, active misconduct and the like. A rate of 1 per cent. over the minimum lending rate[10] was charged in **Wallersteiner v Moir (No 2)** [1975] QB 373, [1975] 1 All ER 849,[11] where the defendant, a company director and international financier, was shown to have improperly used company funds for his own benefit. SCARMAN LJ said at 406, at 870:

"I agree that we have power under the equitable jurisdiction of the court to include interest in the judgment entered against Dr. Wallersteiner. This judgment we have already said is to be for £234,773 and interest, but at the time we had not heard argument as to the propriety of including interest. The principle on which equitable interest is awarded was stated by Lord Hatherley LC in *Burdick v Garrick* (1870) 5 Ch App 233 at 241, and has been frequently applied to situations in which there was a fiduciary relationship at the time when the money was appropriated. In *Atwool v Merryweather* (1867) LR 5 Eq 464n, interest was awarded to a company upon money recovered for it in a minority shareholder's action.

There is, therefore, ample authority to support the claim made by Mr. Moir on behalf of the companies to interest from the date on which the companies made their loan to I.F.T.—a loan which in default of defence this court has accepted was instigated by Dr. Wallersteiner in breach of his duty as a director.

The question whether the interest to be awarded should be simple or compound depends upon evidence as to what the accounting party has, or is to be presumed to have done with the money. As Lord Hatherley LC said in *Burdick v Garrick* (1870) 5 Ch App 233 at 241:

'the court does not proceed against an accounting party by way of punishing him for making use of the plaintiff's money by directing rests, or payment of compound interest, but proceeds upon this principle, either that he has made, or has put himself into such a position as that he is to be presumed to have made, 5 per cent., or compound interest, as the case may be.'

10 The Bank of England's minimum lending rate is no longer posted. For a new formula, see p. 874, post.
11 (1975) 39 Conv (NS) 309 (J.T. Farrand); (1985) 101 LQR 30 (F.A. Mann).

Dr. Wallersteiner was at all material times engaged in the business of finance. Through a complex structure of companies he conducted financial operations with a view to profit. The quarter million pounds assistance which he obtained from the two companies in order to finance the acquisition of the shares meant that he was in a position to employ the money or its capital equivalent in those operations. Though the truth is unlikely ever to be fully known, shrouded as it is by the elaborate corporate structure within which Dr. Wallersteiner chose to operate, one may safely presume that the use of the money (or the capital it enabled him to acquire) was worth to him the equivalent of compound interest at commercial rates with yearly rests, if not more. I, therefore, agree that he should be ordered to pay compound interest at the rates, and with the rests, proposed by Lord Denning MR and Buckley LJ. This being a case for equitable interest, no question arises as to interest under section 3 of the Law Reform (Miscellaneous Provisions) Act 1934; I therefore express no opinion as to the true construction of subsection (1) of that section.''

In **O'Sullivan v Management Agency and Music Ltd** [1985] QB 428, [1985] 3 All ER 351 p. 818 ante, WALLER LJ said at 473, at 377:

"Should the interest be compound? When the question of compound interest was raised the judge referred only to *Wallersteiner v Moir (No 2)* [1975] QB 373. This was a case of very special facts and quite different from the present case. It was also a case decided at a time of low, steady rates of interest. The reason for awarding compound interest was that the interest which had not been paid must be taken to have been used by the defaulting party to make a profit for himself. We have not been referred to any other modern case where compound interest has been involved. In this case there is a joint venture and the effect of the joint venture would mean that in part at any rate the interest was being used to further the joint venture. Furthermore whilst compound interest is payable in equity matters it must be borne in mind that at common law it has been made unlawful and this indicates the nature of the circumstances required to justify it. I am of opinion therefore that this being a joint venture with one reservation I would not award compound interest. The reservation is with regard to the foreign royalties under the publishing agreement. In that case there were secret deductions which were not used in the joint interests of the plaintiff and the companies. As Dunn LJ has explained in his judgment a substantial proportion of these royalties were diverted to foreign subsidiaries of the defendants without the knowledge of the plaintiff. Accordingly it is to be inferred that the defendants had the use of the money for commercial purposes and Mr. Miller has conceded that compound interest should be charged. In so far as it has been shown clearly that it was not used for commercial purposes then only simple interest should be charged: see *A-G v Alford* (1855) 4 De GM & G 843. It is clear from this that the basis for ordering compound interest is that the defendant has actually used the money in trade. The principle therefore is that he must disgorge the profits which he has made. On this basis the adjustment which will have to be made to the rate of interest is to deduct the equivalent of corporation tax which would have had to be paid on those profits. Since this is a hypothetical calculation the rate to be calculated by way of compound interest will be the same throughout the whole period, ignoring the question of whether or not tax would be reclaimable by the defendants. The rate should be at 48 per cent. of market rate, taking corporation tax as 52 per cent. for this purpose.''

In **Bartlett v Barclays Bank Trust Co Ltd (No 2)** [1980] Ch 515, [1980] 2 All ER 92, BRIGHTMAN LJ said at 547, at 98:
"In my judgment, a proper rate of interest to be awarded, in the absence of special circumstances, to compensate beneficiaries and trust funds for non-receipt from a trustee of money that ought to have been received is that allowed from time to time on the courts' short-term investment account, established under section 6 (1) of the Administration of Justice Act 1965.[12] To some extent the high interest rates payable on money lent reflect and compensate for the continual erosion in the value of money by reason of galloping inflation. It seems to me arguable, therefore, that if a high rate of interest is payable in such circumstances, a proportion of that interest should be added to capital in order to help maintain the value of the corpus of the trust estate. It may be, therefore, that there will have to be some adjustment as between life tenant and remaindermen. I do not decide this point and I express no view upon it."

B. Liability Inter Se[13]

i. CONTRIBUTION

Before 1979 the equitable rules provided that the loss was to be shared equally between co-trustees, even where one of them was more to blame than another. The effect of the rules was strikingly illustrated in **Bahin v Hughes** (1886) 31 ChD 390, where the testator gave a legacy of £2,000 to his three daughters, Miss Hughes, Mrs. Edwards and Mrs. Burden, upon trust to pay the income to Mrs. Bahin, the plaintiff, for her life, and after her death to her children.

Miss Hughes managed the whole business of the trust. The money was placed in the name of Miss Hughes and Mrs. Burden's husband, and they effected an unauthorised investment in leasehold house property. Mrs. Edwards was informed by letter. When the security proved insufficient, Mrs. Bahin and her children sought to hold all the trustees liable. Mrs. Edwards having died, her husband served a notice on Miss Hughes, claiming an indemnity from her. The Court of Appeal held that the trustees were jointly and severally liable and that Mr. Edwards was not entitled to an indemnity. COTTON LJ said at 396: "It would be laying down a wrong rule to hold that where one trustee acts honestly, though erroneously, the other trustee is to be held entitled to indemnity who by doing nothing neglects his duty more than the acting trustee".

---

12 See also (1981) 78 LSG 1029 for an opinion by L.H. Hoffmann QC, in favour of "the prevailing London clearing banks' base rate"; [1982] Conv 93; *Guardian Ocean Cargoes Ltd v Banco do Brasil (No. 3)* [1992] 2 Lloyd's Rep 193 (1 per cent above New York prime rate).
13 H & M, pp. 625–627; K & S, pp. 445–448; P & M, pp. 589–592; Pettit, pp. 489–491; Riddall, pp. 366–367; Snell, pp. 296–297; Underhill, pp. 903–908.

These rules were superseded by:

CIVIL LIABILITY (CONTRIBUTION) ACT 1978[14]

1. Entitlement to contribution.—(1) Subject to the following provisions of this section, any person liable in respect of any damage suffered by another person may recover contribution from any other person liable in respect of the same damage[14a] (whether jointly with him or otherwise).[15]

2. Assessment of contribution.—(1) Subject to subsection (3) below,[16] in any proceedings for contribution under section 1 above the amount of the contribution recoverable from any person shall be such as may be found by the court to be just and equitable having regard to the extent of that person's responsibility for the damage in question.

(2) Subject to subsection (3) below, the court shall have power in any such proceedings to exempt any person from liability to make contribution, or to direct that the contribution to be recovered from any person shall amount to a complete indemnity.

6. Interpretation.—(1) A person is liable in respect of any damage for the purposes of this Act if the person who suffered it (or anyone representing his estate or dependants) is entitled to recover compensation from him in respect of that damage (whatever the legal basis of his liability, whether tort, breach of contract, breach of trust or otherwise).

ii. INDEMNITY

In **Re Partington** (1887) 57 LT 654, the trustees of a fund were Mr. Allen, a solicitor, and Mrs. Partington, the widow of the testator. A breach of trust was committed. Mr. Allen undertook the whole administration of the trust. STIRLING J held that he had not communicated sufficiently to Mrs. Partington concerning the affairs of the trust to enable her to exercise a judgment upon the unauthorised investment. "The trustee, Mrs. Partington, appears to me to have been misled by her co-trustee by reason of his not giving her full information as to the nature of the investments which he was asking her to advance the money upon, and I think he has been guilty of negligence also in his duty as a solicitor." Mrs. Partington was entitled to an indemnity.

In **Head v Gould** [1898] 2 Ch 250, an attempt to obtain an indemnity against a solicitor trustee failed. KEKEWICH J said at 265:
"True it is that the defendant Gould is a solicitor, and that he was appointed trustee for that very reason. True no doubt, also, that the legal business was managed by him, and I do not propose to absolve him from any responsibility

---

14 The Act was based on the Law Commission Report on Contribution, 1977 (Law Com. No. 79). See para. 28. It came into force on 1 January 1979. For special time limits for claiming contribution, see Limitation Act 1980, s. 10.
14a *Birse Construction Ltd v Haiste Ltd* (1995) Times, 12 December (two parties liable in respect of same damages suffered by a third party).
15 The Act applies to restitutionary claims: *Friends' Provident Life Office v Hillier Parker May & Rowden* [1996] 2 WLR 123, [1995] 4 All ER 260.
16 Sub-section (3) limits liability to make a contribution where there has been prior agreement for an upper limit or statutory reduction of damages.

attaching to him on that ground; but I do not myself think that Byrne J,[17] or any other judge ever intended to hold that a man is bound to indemnify his co-trustee against loss merely because he was a solicitor, when that co-trustee was an active participator in the breach of trust complained of, and is not proved to have participated merely in consequence of the advice and control of the solicitor . . . ''

In **Chillingworth v Chambers** [1896] 1 Ch 685, the plaintiff and defendant were trustees of a testamentary trust. The plaintiff, Chillingworth, was married to one of the beneficiaries, and, on her death, became himself a beneficiary.

The trustees made an unauthorised investment in mortgages of leasehold property, some being made before Mrs. Chillingworth's death, and some after. The mortgages proved insufficient. The deficiency of £1,580 was made good out of Mr. Chillingworth's interest.

He brought this action claiming contribution from Chambers, and failed. Kay LJ said at 707:

"On the whole, I think that the weight of authority is in favour of holding that a trustee who, being also cestui que trust, has received, as between himself and his co-trustee, an exclusive benefit by the breach of trust, must indemnify his co-trustee to the extent of his interest in the trust fund, and not merely to the extent of the benefit which he has received. I think that the plaintiff must be treated as having received such an exclusive benefit."

C. Protection of Trustees[18]

i. RELIEF BY THE COURT[19]

TRUSTEE ACT 1925

61. Power to relieve trustee from personal liability.—If it appears to the court that a trustee, whether appointed by the court or otherwise, is or may be personally liable for any breach of trust, whether the transaction alleged to be a breach of trust occurred before or after the commencement of this Act, but has acted honestly and reasonably, and ought fairly to be excused for the breach of trust and for omitting to obtain the directions of the court in the matter in which he committed such breach, then the court may relieve him either wholly or partly from personal liability for the same.

It is not possible to lay down with precision the occasions on which the section will be applied. The question has usually arisen in connection with the making of unauthorised investments,[20] and the payment of money to the wrong beneficiaries.

17 In *Re Turner* [1897] 1 Ch 536. See also *Lockhart v Reilly* (1856) 25 LJ Ch 697.
18 H & M, pp. 628–640; K & S, pp. 473–480; P & M, pp. 592–601; Pettit, pp. 491–503; Riddall, pp. 370–379; Snell, pp. 290–295; Underhill, pp. 881–900.
19 H & M, pp. 633–635; K & S, pp. 473–475; P & M, pp. 596–598; Pettit, pp. 500–502; Riddall, pp. 370–372; Snell, pp. 290–291; Underhill, pp. 881–887. See generally (1955) 19 Conv (NS) 420 (L.A. Sheridan).
20 *Bartlett v Barclays Bank Trust Co Ltd (No 1)* [1980] Ch 515, [1980] 1 All ER 139, p. 612, ante (trustees held not to have acted honestly).

Where a trustee is in doubt, he should always take legal advice. Having done so, an amateur trustee will nearly always be covered; but relief is not automatic. A solicitor should likewise take counsel's opinion. Professional trustees are within the section, but the court is less willing to apply its provisions in their favour.[21]

The best general explanation of the section—or rather its predecessor, Judicial Trustees Act 1896, s. 3—is found in *Perrins v Bellamy* [1898] 2 Ch 521, per KEKEWICH J and in *Re Stuart* [1897] 2 Ch 583, per STIRLING J. In each case trustees were guilty of a breach of trust. In the former they were excused; but not in the latter.[1]

In **Perrins v Bellamy** [1898] 2 Ch 521, KEKEWICH J said at 527:

"Broadly speaking, these trustees have committed a breach of trust, and they are responsible for it. But then the statute comes in, and the very foundation for the application of the statute is that the trustee whose conduct is in question 'is or may be personally liable for any breach of trust'. I am bound to look at the rest of the section by the light of those words, and with the view that, in cases falling within the section, the breach of trust is not of itself to render the trustee personally liable. Leaving out the intervening words, which merely make the section retrospective, I find when in general the trustee is to be relieved from personal liability. He is not to be held personally liable if he 'has acted honestly and reasonably, and ought fairly to be excused for the breach of trust'. In this case, as in the large majority of cases of breach of trust which come before the Court, the word 'honestly' may be left out of consideration. Cases do unfortunately occur from time to time in which trustees, and even solicitors in whom confidence has been reposed, run away with the money of their cestuis que trust, and where such flagrant dishonesty occurs breach of trust becomes a minor consideration. In the present case there is no imputation or ground for imputation of any dishonesty whatever. The Legislature has made the absence of all dishonesty a condition precedent to the relief of the trustee from liability. But that is not the grit of the section. The grit is in the words 'reasonably, and ought fairly to be excused for the breach of trust'. How much the latter words add to the force of the word 'reasonably' I am not at present prepared to say. I suppose, however, that in the view of the Legislature there might be cases in which a trustee, though he had acted reasonably, ought not fairly to be excused for the breach of trust. Indeed, I am not sure that some of the evidence adduced in this case was not addressed to a view of that kind, as, for instance, the evidence by which it was attempted to shew that these trustees, though they acted reasonably in selling the property, ought not fairly to be excused because the plaintiff Mrs. Perrins objected to their selling, and her objection was brought to their notice. In the section the copulative 'and' is used, and it may well be argued that in order to bring a case within the section it must be shewn not merely that the trustee has acted

---

21 *National Trustees Co of Australasia Ltd v General Finance Co of Australasia Ltd* [1905] AC 373; *Re Pauling's Settlement Trusts* [1964] Ch 303, [1963] 3 All ER 1, p. 887, post; *Re Rosenthal* [1972] 1 WLR 1273, [1972] 3 All ER 552; Law Reform Committee 23rd Report (The Powers and Duties of Trustees) 1982 Cmnd 8733, para. 2.16.

1 For initial criticism of the relief, see *Maitland's Equity* (2nd edn, 1926), pp. 99–100; (1898) 14 LQR 159 (H.F. Maugham).

'reasonably', but also that he ought 'fairly' to be excused for the breach of trust. I venture, however, to think that, in general and in the absence of special circumstances, a trustee who has acted 'reasonably' ought to be relieved, and that it is not incumbent on the Court to consider whether he ought 'fairly' to be excused, unless there is evidence of a special character shewing that the provisions of the section ought not to be applied in his favour. I need not pursue that subject further, because in the present case I find no ground whatever for saying that these trustees, if they acted reasonably, ought not to be excused. The question, and the only question, is whether they acted reasonably. In saying that, I am not unmindful of the words of the section which follow, and which require that it should be shewn that the trustee ought 'fairly' to be excused, not only 'for the breach of trust', but also 'for omitting to obtain the directions of the Court in the matter in which he committed such breach of trust'. I find it difficult to follow that. I do not see how the trustee can be excused for the breach of trust without being also excused for the omission referred to, or how he can be excused for the omission without also being excused for the breach of trust. If I am at liberty to guess, I should suppose that these words were added by way of amendment, and crept into the statute without due regard being had to the meaning of the context. The fact that a trustee has omitted to obtain the directions of the Court has never been held to be a ground for holding him personally liable, though it may be a reason guiding the Court in the matter of costs, or in deciding whether he has acted reasonably or otherwise, and especially so in these days when questions of difficulty, even as regards the legal estate, can be decided economically and expeditiously on originating summons. But if the Court comes to the conclusion that a trustee has acted reasonably, I cannot see how it can usefully proceed to consider, as an independent matter, the question whether he has or has not omitted to obtain the directions of the Court.''

In **Re Stuart** [1897] 2 Ch 583, STIRLING J said at 590:

"The effect of s. 3 of the Judicial Trustees Act, 1896, appears to me to be this. The law as it stood at the passing of the Act is not altered, but a jurisdiction is given to the Court under special circumstances, the Court being satisfied as to the several matters mentioned in the section, to relieve the trustee of the consequences of a breach of trust as regards his personal liability. But the Court must first be satisfied that the trustee has acted honestly and reasonably. As to the honesty of the trustee in this case there is no question; but that is not the only condition to be satisfied, and the question arises whether the other conditions are satisfied. I quite agree that this section applies to a trustee making an improper investment of the trust funds as well as to any other breach of trust. This matter has been considered by Byrne J in *Re Turner* [1897] 1 Ch 536 at 542, where he says this: 'I think that the section relied on is meant to be acted upon freely and fairly in the exercise of judicial discretion, but I think that the Court ought to be satisfied, before exercising the very large powers conferred upon it, by sufficient evidence, that the trustee acted reasonably. I do not think that I have sufficient evidence in this case that he so acted; in fact, it does not appear from the letters that Mr. Turner acted in respect of this mortgage as he would probably have acted had it been a transaction of his own. I think that if he was—and he well may have been—a businesslike man, he would not, before lending his money, have been satisfied without some further inquiry as to the means of the mortgagor and as to the nature and value of the property upon which he was about to advance his money.' That has since been approved by the Court of Appeal; and I willingly adopt what is there laid down as a guide to me in this matter. In my opinion the burden lies on the trustee who asks the Court to exercise the jurisdiction conferred by this section to shew that he has acted reasonably; and, certainly, it is fair in dealing with such a question to consider whether Mr. Box would have acted with reference to these investments as he did if he had been lending money of his own''.

ii. IMPOUNDING A BENEFICIARY'S INTEREST[2]

TRUSTEE ACT 1925

62. Power to make beneficiary indemnify for breach of trust.—(1) Where a trustee commits a breach of trust at the instigation or request or with the consent in writing of a beneficiary, the court may, if it thinks fit, make such order as to the court seems just, for impounding all or any part of the interest of the beneficiary in the trust estate by way of indemnity to the trustee or persons claiming through him.[3]

(2) This section applies to breaches of trust committed as well before as after the commencement of this Act.

In **Re Somerset** [1894] 1 Ch 231, the trustees of a marriage settlement lent an excessive sum upon mortgage. They lent the money at the instigation, request and consent in writing of the tenant for life, Vere Somerset. When the security proved to be inadequate, Vere Somerset and his infant children sued the trustees for breach of trust. Liability to the children was admitted, but the defendant trustees claimed, inter alia, that they were entitled to impound the life interest of Vere Somerset for the purposes of meeting the claim.

The Court of Appeal refused. Vere Somerset, though approving the investment, had not intended to be a party to a breach of trust, and in effect left the trustees to determine whether the investment was a proper one for the sum advanced. LINDLEY MR said at 265:

"Did the trustees commit the breach of trust for which they have been made liable at the instigation or request, or with the consent in writing of the Appellant? The section is intended to protect trustees, and ought to be construed so as to carry out that intention. But the section ought not, in my opinion, to be construed as if the word 'investment' had been inserted instead of 'breach of trust'. An enactment to that effect would produce great injustice in many cases. In order to bring a case within this section the *cestui que trust* must instigate, or request, or consent in writing to some act or omission which is itself a breach of trust, and not to some act or omission which only becomes a breach of trust by reason of want of care on the part of the trustees. If a *cestui que trust* instigates, requests, or consents in writing to an investment not in terms authorized by the power of investment, he clearly falls within the section;

---

2 H & M, pp. 631–632; K & S, p. 476; P & M, pp. 600–601; Pettit, pp. 494–495; Riddall, pp. 373–374; Snell, pp. 289–290; Underhill, pp. 909–910.
3 As amended by Married Women (Restraint upon Anticipation) Act 1949, s. 1 (4) and Sch. 2.

and in such a case his ignorance or forgetfulness of the terms of the power would not, I think, protect him—at all events, not unless he could give some good reason why it should, e.g., that it was caused by the trustee. But if all that a *cestui que trust* does is to instigate, request, or consent in writing to an investment which is authorized by the terms of the power, the case is, I think, very different. He has a right to expect that the trustees will act with proper care in making the investment, and if they do not they cannot throw the consequences on him unless they can shew that he instigated, requested, or consented in writing to their non-performance of their duty in this respect.

This is, in my opinion, the true construction of this section."

In **Re Pauling's Settlement Trusts (No 2)** [1963] Ch 576, [1963] 1 All ER 857, Coutts and Co, the trustees of a family trust, were held liable for breach of trust in respect of a number of advances of capital to the children of the life tenant, Mrs. Younghusband. At first instance, WILBERFORCE J made his order without prejudice to any right which the defendant bank might have to impound the interests of any beneficiary during the lives of the wife and any surviving husband of hers. The bank claimed to be entitled to impound the life interest of Mrs. Younghusband. The plaintiffs sought the appointment of two new trustees in the place of the bank, who opposed this on the ground that such an appointment might negate their right to impound.

WILBERFORCE J appointed new trustees, holding that such an appointment would not imperil the defendants' right to impound. After dealing with a number of other matters, he said at 583, at 860:

"Next I come to a separate series of objections which raise some difficult questions of law. The defendants, as I have already mentioned, have a claim to impound the life interest of Mrs. Younghusband now vested in the Guardian Assurance Co. Ltd. in order to recoup themselves against any money which they may be ordered to repay. What is said by the defendants is that that right to impound would be prejudiced if new trustees were appointed now and the trust fund handed over to them. That involves a consideration as to what is the nature of the right to impound which exists in favour of a trustee who has committed a breach of trust at the instigation of a beneficiary. I have to consider both the ordinary right which exists in equity apart from statute and also the further statutory right which has been conferred by section 62 of the Trustee Act, 1925, both of which are invoked by the defendants as plaintiffs in the Chancery action now pending. It seems to me that it is not possible to maintain, as is the defendants' contention here, that a trustee, having committed a breach of trust, is entitled to remain as a trustee until it has exercised its right to impound the income of the beneficiary in order to recoup itself. That seems to me an impossible proposition. It is quite true that, in the reported authorities, there is no case where the right to impound has been exercised by a former trustee as distinct from an existing trustee, but it seems to me in principle that it is impossible to contend that the right to impound is limited to the case where the trustee seeking the right is an actual trustee. The nature of the right to impound seems to me to turn on two things: first, that the money paid back to capital is in its origin the money of the trustee, and that when it comes to considering who should get the income of it, the trustee who has provided the money has a better right to it than the tenant for life who has instigated the breach of trust. The alternative way of putting the matter is that the trustee in breach of trust is in some way subrogated to the rights of the beneficiary. He stands in his position in order that he may be indemnified. That seems to me the way in which it was put by the Lords Justices in *Raby v Ridehalgh* (1855) 7 De GM & G 104. It does not seem to me that there is any support in authority or in principle for saying that the right depends upon the actual possession of the trust fund, and it appears to me that the analogy which has been sought to be drawn with the executor's right to retain is a false one and does not apply to this case. So much for the equitable right to impound as opposed to the statutory right.

As regards the statutory right, that depends on the language of section 62 of the Trustee Act, 1925, and at first sight it might look as if that right only exists in favour of a person who is actually a trustee. But, on consideration, that seems to me to be a misconstruction of the section. In the first place, the same objection against limiting the right in that way applies to the statutory jurisdiction. It seems to me an absurdity that it is required as a condition of exercising the right to obtain an impounding order, that the trustee who, ex hypothesi, is in breach of trust, must remain the trustee in order to acquire a right of indemnity. Further, it seems to me on the authorities, and, indeed, on the very terms of the section, that the section is giving an additional right, among other things, to deal with the case of a married woman beneficiary; that the statutory right is extending the equitable right and not limiting it, and that it is not right to read the section so as to apply only to a person who was formerly a trustee. The section begins with the words: 'Where a trustee commits a breach of trust', thereby indicating that at the time the breach of trust is committed the person in question must be a trustee. Then further down in the section there is a reference to a trustee and that appears to me to be merely a reference back to the same person as the person who committed the breach of trust and not as an indication that the person in question must be a trustee at the date of the order. I would add to that, that here the writ which has been issued in the Chancery Division was issued at a time when the defendants were trustees, and, therefore, at the date of the writ the requirement of being a trustee was fulfilled. So that, although I entirely appreciate that the defendants may be anxious not to lose their right to impound the income of the tenant for life, that right could not, in my view, be prejudiced by appointing new trustees at this stage.''

iii. Limitation Act and Laches[4]

(a) Time Limits

LIMITATION ACT 1980

21. Time limit for actions in respect of trust property.—(1) No period of limitation prescribed by this Act shall apply to an action by a beneficiary under a trust, being an action—

---

4 H & M, pp. 636–640; K & S, pp. 477–480; P & M, pp. 592–595; Pettit, pp. 495–500; Riddall, pp. 374–375; Snell, pp. 292–295; Underhill, pp. 887–894. See Cheshire and Burn, *Modern Law of Real Property* (15th edn, 1994), chap. 26; Preston and Newsom, *Limitation of Actions* (3rd edn, 1953), chap. 5; (4th edn, 1989), chap. 7; Franks, *Limitation of Actions* (1959), pp. 62–80; McGee, *Limitation Periods* (2nd edn 1994); Prime and Scanlan, *Modern Law of Limitation* (1993); [1989] CLJ 472 (H. McLean); *Tito v Waddell (No 2)* [1977] Ch 106 at 244–252, [1977] 3 All ER 129 at 244–253; Law Reform Committee 21st Report (Final Report on Limitation of Actions) (1977) Cmnd 6923, pp. 53–54.

(*a*) in respect of any fraud or fraudulent breach of trust to which the trustee was a party or privy;[5] or

(*b*) to recover from the trustee trust property or the proceeds of trust property in the possession of the trustee, or previously received by the trustee and converted to his use.[6]

(2)[7] Where a trustee who is also a beneficiary under the trust receives or retains trust property or its proceeds as his share on a distribution of trust property under the trust, his liability in any action brought by virtue of subsection (1) (*b*) above to recover that property or its proceeds after the expiration of the period of limitation prescribed by this Act for bringing an action to recover trust property shall be limited to the excess over his proper share.

This subsection only applies if the trustee acted honestly and reasonably in making the distribution.

(3) Subject to the preceding provisions of this section, an action by a beneficiary to recover trust property or in respect of any breach of trust,[8] not being an action for which a period of limitation is prescribed by any other provision of this Act, shall not be brought after the expiration of six years from the date on which the right of action accrued.

For the purposes of this subsection, the right of action shall not be treated as having accrued to any beneficiary entitled to a future interest in the trust property until the interest fell into possession.[9]

(4) No beneficiary as against whom there would be a good defence under this Act shall derive any greater or other benefit from a judgment or order obtained by any other beneficiary than he could have obtained if he had brought the action and this Act had been pleaded in defence.

22. Time limit for actions claiming personal estate of a deceased person.—
Subject to section 21 (1) and (2) of this Act—

(*a*) no action in respect of any claim to the personal estate of a deceased person or to any share or interest in any such estate (whether under a will or on intestacy) shall be brought after the expiration of twelve years from the date on which the right to receive the share or interest accrued; and

---

5 *North American Land and Timber Co Ltd v Watkins* [1904] 1 Ch 242; *Thorne v Heard* [1894] 1 Ch 599; on appeal, [1895] AC 495; *Armitage v Nurse* [1995] NPC 110 (deliberate but honest breach by trustees not fraud).

6 *Re Sharp* [1906] 1 Ch 793; *Re Howlett* [1949] Ch 767, [1949] 2 All ER 490; *Wassell v Leggatt* [1896] 1 Ch 554; *Re Eyre-Williams* [1923] 2 Ch 533; *Re Clark* (1920) 150 LT Jo 94. See also *Re Landi* [1939] Ch 828, [1939] 3 All ER 569; *Re Milking Pail Farm Trusts* [1940] Ch 996, [1940] 4 All ER 54; (1941) 57 LQR 26 (R.E.M.); (1971) 35 Conv (NS) 6 (G. Battersby).

7 S. 21 (2) was added by Limitation Amendment Act 1980, s. 5 (1).

8 In *Tito v Waddell (No 2)* [1977] Ch 106 at 249, [1977] 3 All ER 129 at 248, MEGARRY J concluded that this provision did not apply to situations governed by the self-dealing and fair-dealing rules applicable to trustees. Those cases are covered by the doctrine of laches.

9 *Re Somerset* [1894] 1 Ch 231; *Re Pauling's Settlement Trusts* [1964] Ch 303, [1963] 3 All ER 1, p. 887, post; *A-G v Cocke* [1988] Ch 414, [1988] 2 All ER 391 (s. 21 (3) does not apply to an action by the A-G to enforce a charitable trust for the benefit of the public at large; nor where there is no claim for any recovery of trust property or allegation of breach of trust); [1988] Conv 292 (J. Warburton); [1988] All ER Rev 183 (P.J. Clarke); *Armitage v Nurse* [1995] NPC 110 (beneficiary under discretionary trust held not to have interest in possession for purposes of s. 21(3)).

(*b*) no action to recover arrears of interest in respect of any legacy, or damages in respect of such arrears, shall be brought after the expiration of six years from the date on which the interest became due.

23. Time limit in respect of actions for an account.—An action for an account shall not be brought after the expiration of any time limit under this Act which is applicable to the claim which is the basis of the duty to account.

In **Nelson v Rye** [1996] 2 All ER 186 Mr Nelson, the plaintiff musician (who had been a member of a group called 'Be Pop Deluxe' and of another group known as 'Bill Nelson's Red Noise'), brought an action for an account against Mr Rye, his manager, for moneys received on his behalf. Mr Rye pleaded limitation and laches. Mr Rye was in breach of fiduciary duty to Mr Nelson to account annually and that duty gave rise to a constructive trust of the moneys for Mr Nelson. In holding that no limitation period applied,[9a] LADDIE J said at 197:

"Historically, actions by beneficiaries against trustees for misappropriation of trust property have been excluded from the imposition of such arbitrary time limits. The courts and the legislature have treated trustees as bearing a special responsibility to the trust property and the beneficiary's interest in it. The beneficiary's right to complain of breach of trust has been treated as persisting indefinitely unless, of course, in all the circumstances it would be inequitable to allow him to enforce his rights. There is nothing to which my attention has been drawn which suggests that the 1980 Act effected a significant change in this area.

In my view s. 23 of the 1980 Act simply confirms that the limitation period which applies to a particular cause of action applies equally to the relief by way of account which flows from it. For example, in this case certain claims for copyright infringement arise. Section 96(2) of the Copyright, Designs and Patents Act 1988 entitles a copyright owner to seek relief by way of an account where infringement is proved. The effect of s. 21 of the 1980 Act is that the limitation period for the account is the same as that for the claim for infringement. I do not accept that s. 21 has the effect of circumventing and rendering nugatory the provisions of s. 23. The former is concerned with whether or not there is a limitation period for actions for breach of trust, whereas the latter is only concerned with the limitation period to be applied to a form of relief which may be ordered in favour of a successful plaintiff.

Since that is so, what limitation period, if any, applies to the cause of action in this case? As I have indicated above, where a limitation period exists and can be invoked in relation to one cause of action, it is nihil ad rem that no, or a different, limitation period applies to an alternative cause of action which has been or could have been pleaded by the plaintiff. If the cause of action here is one for breach of fiduciary duty or breach of trust, it does not avail Mr Rye to argue that the relationship arose out of a contract and that the relationship

---

9a The defence of laches succeeded; p. 886, post.

between him and Mr Nelson can be treated as one between debtor and creditor. If Mr Nelson had chosen to sue for breach of contract alone, then the limitation period for contractual claims would have applied. He has not done so. . . .

I accept Mr Anderson's basic premise that the 1980 Act only imposes limitation periods on those actions it specifically identifies. A cause of action for which the 1980 Act, or other legislation, makes no limitation provision is not subject to a limitation period. Actions for breach of fiduciary duty are not expressly covered. It follows that prima facie no limitation applies to them. However, if this was all, s. 21 would serve little purpose. As far as I can see, in all cases of breach of trust covered by the section it would be possible to say that there had been a breach of fiduciary duty. Although, as I have held, no limitation period applies to actions for breach of fiduciary duty simpliciter and s. 21(1) provides that no limitation period applies in respect of many actions for breach of trust, some actions for breach of trust are the subject of limitation periods – see s. 21(3). If those are treated as actions for breach of fiduciary duty, the limitation would be sidestepped.

The fallacy, it appears to me, is to treat breach of fiduciary duty and breach of trust as different causes of action. In a case where, because of the existence of a fiduciary duty, a constructive trust comes into existence, breach of trust and breach of fiduciary duty are the same cause of action. Similarly, where an express trust has been created, breach of that trust and breach of fiduciary duty are also the same cause of action. It is therefore not possible to sidestep the limitation provisions of s. 21(3) by referring to the action as one for breach of fiduciary duty.

Since I accept Mr Oppenheim's argument that not all breaches of fiduciary duty give rise to constructive trusts, the following propositions appear to follow: (1) An action for breach of fiduciary duty simpliciter is outside the provisions of the Limitation Act 1980 and therefore is not subject to a period of limitation. (See *A-G v Cocke* [1988] Ch 414), [1988] 2 All ER 391, (2). Where a breach of fiduciary duty gives rise to a constructive trust, the provisions of s. 21 of the 1980 Act determine whether there is a limitation period, and its duration. (3) An action for breach of an express trust is, in like manner, subject to the limitation provisions of s. 21. (4) In neither case (2) or (3) is it possible to avoid any limitation period imposed by the 1980 Act by treating the case as one of breach of fiduciary duty.

There is no dispute between the parties that Mr Rye owed Mr Nelson a fiduciary duty. He was obliged to account to Mr Nelson annually. He did not. There has been a breach of that duty and, prima facie, no limitation period applies. Mr Oppenheim's arguments to the effect that the cause of action did not fall within the ambit of s. 21(1)(b) would only help Mr Rye if he had also succeeded in persuading me that the action should be treated as one for breach of contract rather than breach of fiduciary duty. Since he has failed to persuade me of that, no limitation period applies, either because the cause of action is outwith the 1980 Act or because it falls within s. 21(1)(b) (it was not suggested that the action came within s. 21(3)). In the circumstances it is not necessary to determine under which head this action falls. Nevertheless, it is clear to me that this case does fall within s. 21(1)(b). Although not all fiduciary relationships give rise to constructive trusts, this one did.''

For the definition of a trustee, see Limitation Act 1980, s. 3 (1); TA 1925, s. 68 (17). It includes personal representatives, certain fiduciary agents: *Burdick v Garrick* (1870) 5 Ch App 233, company directors: *Re Lands Allotment Co* [1894] 1 Ch 616; *Belmont Finance Corpn v Williams Furniture Ltd (No 2)* [1980] 1 All ER 393; a mortgagee in respect of the proceeds of sale: *Thorne v Heard* [1895] AC 495, but not a trustee in bankruptcy: *Re Cornish* [1896] 1 QB 99, nor the liquidator of a company in voluntary liquidation: *Re Windsor Steam Coal Co (1901) Ltd* [1928] Ch 609; on appeal [1929] 1 Ch 151.

(b) Extension and Postponement of Time Limits

LIMITATION ACT 1980

28. Extension of limitation period in case of disability.—(1) Subject to the following provisions of this section, if on the date when any right of action accrued for which a period of limitation is prescribed by this Act, the person to whom it accrued was under a disability, the action may be brought at any time before the expiration of six years from the date when he ceased to be under a disability or died (whichever first occurred) notwithstanding that the period of limitation has expired.

(2) This section shall not affect any case where the right of action first accrued to some person (not under a disability) through whom the person under a disability claims.

(3) When a right of action which has accrued to a person under a disability accrues, on the death of that person while still under a disability, to another person under a disability, no further extension of time shall be allowed by reason of the disability of the second person.

(4) No action to recover land or money charged on land shall be brought by virtue of this section by any person after the expiration of thirty years from the date on which the right of action accrued to that person or some person through whom he claims.

32. Postponement of limitation period in case of fraud, concealment or mistake.[10]—(1) Subject to subsection (3) below, where in the case of any action for which a period of limitation is prescribed by this Act, either—

(*a*) the action is based upon the fraud of the defendant; or

(*b*) any fact relevant to the plaintiff's right of action has been deliberately concealed from him by the defendant;[11] or

(*c*) the action is for relief from the consequences of a mistake;

the period of limitation shall not begin to run until the plaintiff has discovered the fraud, concealment or mistake (as the case may be) or could with reasonable diligence have discovered it.[12]

References in this subsection to the defendant include references to the defendant's agent and to any person through whom the defendant claims and his agent.

---

10 See Cheshire and Burn, *Modern Law of Real Property* (15th edn), pp. 910–911.

11 In *Bartlett v Barclays Bank Trust Co Ltd* [1980] Ch 515 at 537, [1980] 1 All ER 139 at 154, the trustee unsuccessfully pleaded the forerunner of para. (*b*) (Limitation Act 1939, s. 26 (*b*)). "There was no cover-up by the bank. The bank had no inkling that it was acting in breach of trust", per BRIGHTMAN J.

12 See *Peco Arts Inc v Hazlitt Gallery Ltd* [1983] 3 All ER 193 (drawing "Études Pour le Bain", by Ingres).

(2) For the purposes of subsection (1) above, deliberate commission of a breach of duty in circumstances in which it is unlikely to be discovered for some time amounts to deliberate concealment of the facts involved in that breach of duty.

(3) Nothing in this section shall enable any action—

(*a*) to recover, or recover the value of, any property, or

(*b*) to enforce any charge against, or set aside any transaction affecting, any property;

to be brought against the purchaser of the property or any person claiming through him in any case where the property has been purchased for valuable consideration by an innocent third party since the fraud or concealment or (as the case may be) the transaction in which the mistake was made took place.

(4) A purchaser is an innocent third party for the purposes of this section—

(*a*) in the case of fraud or concealment of any fact relevant to the plaintiff's right of action, if he was not a party to the fraud or (as the case may be) to the concealment of that fact and did not at the time of the purchase know or have reason to believe that the fraud or concealment had taken place; and

(*b*) in the case of mistake, if he did not at the time of the purchase know or have reason to believe that the mistake had been made.

An assignee, with notice, from a trustee is in the same position as the trustee was. In **Eddis v Chichester Constable** [1969] 2 Ch 345, [1969] 2 All ER 912,[13] a tenant for life of a painting attributed to Caravaggio sold it in 1951, through the agency of one Mrs. Blois, to an art consortium who resold it in 1952 to the William Rockhill Nelson Gallery of Art, Kansas City, Missouri, U.S.A. In 1963 the tenant for life died and the trustees for the first time became aware of the absence of the painting. In 1966 they sued the representative of the tenant for life for breach of trust and the art consortium for conversion. The Limitation Act 1939 was pleaded.

The main question was whether, assuming that the trustees' right of action was concealed by the fraud of the tenant for life, s. 26[14] prevented time from running against the trustees in favour of the art consortium. The Court of Appeal, affirming GOFF J, held that time did not run against the trustees until the fraud was discovered.

(c) Laches and Acquiescence

LIMITATION ACT 1980

36. Acquiescence.—(2) Nothing in this Act shall affect any equitable jurisdiction to refuse relief on the ground of acquiescence or otherwise.[15]

In **Nelson v Rye** [1996] 2 All ER 186, p. 883 ante, LADDIE J said at 200:

---

13 *Re Dixon* [1900] 2 Ch 561; *Re Eyre-Williams* [1923] 2 Ch 533; *GL Baker Ltd v Medway Building and Supplies Ltd* [1958] 1 WLR 1216, [1958] 3 All ER 540.

14 Now Limitation Act 1980, s. 32.

15 Thus preserving the doctrine of laches. See Cheshire and Burn, *Modern Law of Real Property* (15th edn), pp. 903–905; Brunyate, *Limitation of Actions in Equity*, (1932), chap. 7.

"It can be misleading to approach the equitable defences of laches and acquiescence as if they consisted of a series of precisely defined hurdles over each of which a litigant must struggle before the defence is made out.

[His Lordship cited *Lindsay Petroleum Co v Hurd* (1874) LR 5 PC 221 at 239, 240, and *Erlanger v New Sombrero Phosphate Co* (1878) 3 App Cas 1218 at 1279–1280, per Lord Blackburn, and continued:]

'So here, these defences are not technical or arbitrary. The courts have indicated over the years some of the factors which must be taken into consideration in deciding whether the defence runs. Those factors include the period of the delay, the extent to which the defendant's position has been prejudiced by the delay, and the extent to which that prejudice was caused by the actions of the plaintiff. I accept that mere delay alone will almost never suffice, but the court has to look at all the circumstances, including in particular those factors set out above, and then decide whether the balance of justice or injustice is in favour of granting the remedy or withholding it. If substantial prejudice will be suffered by the defendant, it is not necessary for the defendant to prove that it was caused by the delay. On the other hand, the plaintiff's knowledge that the delay will cause such prejudice is a factor to be taken into account. With these considerations in mind, I turn to the facts.'

[His Lordship held that the defences succeeded largely due to the plaintiff's wilful refusal to involve himself in his financial affairs.]

iv. SUMMARY

The various forms of protection of trustees were before the Court of Appeal in **Re Pauling's Settlement Trusts** [1964] Ch 303, [1963] 3 All ER 1. Commander and Mrs. Younghusband were married in 1919; their marriage settlement contained in clause 11 a power of advancement for the trustees, Coutts & Co., to raise, with the written consent of Mrs. Younghusband, any part not exceeding one half of the expectant or presumptive or vested share of any child of the wife and to pay to him for his own absolute use, or advancement or benefit in such manner as the trustees should think fit. Between 1948 and 1954 the trustees made a number of advancements to the children (Francis, George, Ann and Anthony) who, on some though not every occasion, received independent legal advice as to their rights under the settlement. The mother's consent was obtained in every case.

In 1954, as a result of a scheme of George's for avoiding estate duty on his mother's death, the children first became aware that the advancements might have been in breach of trust. In 1958 they brought an action against the trustees claiming £29,160, on the ground that this sum had been improperly paid out by way of advancement to beneficiaries who were presumed to be subject to undue influence and who were not emancipated from parental control.

WILLMER LJ said at 338, at 11:

"The bank also rely for relief from the consequences of any breach of trust upon section 61 of the Trustee Act, 1925. At this stage all we propose to say is that it would be a misconstruction of the section to say it does not apply to professional trustees, but, as was pointed out in the Judicial Committee of the Privy Council in *National Trustees Company of Australasia Ltd v General Finance Company of Australasia Ltd* [1905] AC 373 at 381 ' ... without saying that the remedial provisions of the section should never be applied to a trustee in the position of the appellants, their Lordships think it is a circumstance to be taken into account ... ' Where a banker undertakes to act as a paid trustee of a settlement created by a customer, and so deliberately places itself in a position where its duty as trustee conflicts with its interest as a banker, we think that the court should be very slow to relieve such a trustee under the provisions of the section.

We propose to deal with the bank's plea of the Limitation Act 1939 and the pleas of laches, acquiescence and delay when we have considered the detailed transactions. It only remains to state that the question of law on which this case was reported in the court below, *Re Pauling's Settlement Trusts* [1962] 1 WLR 86, [1961] 3 All ER 713, has not been argued before us, and many of the cases there cited have not been cited to us. Mr. Bagnall, however, accepts as accurate the proposition that 'The result of these authorities appears to me [Wilberforce J] to be that the court has to consider all the circumstances in which the concurrence of the cestui que trust was given with a view to seeing whether it is fair and equitable that, having given his concurrence, he should afterwards turn round and sue the trustees: that, subject to this, it is not necessary that he should know that what he is concurring in is a breach of trust, provided that he fully understands what he is concurring in, and that it is not necessary that he should himself have directly benefited by the breach of trust [1962] 1 WLR 86 at 108, [1961] 3 All ER 713 at 730'. We express no opinion on it.

[His Lordship then dealt with the impugned transactions *seriatim.* UPJOHN LJ continued the reading of the judgment of the court, and, on the question of undue influence, said at 347, at 16:] At the time of this advance the son George was twenty-three years old. He had done his military service, and was up at Cambridge. The judge thought him an exceptionally able young man, well acquainted with his rights, and able to take care of himself. He had no separate advice about this £2,000 advance, but he had been advised about the Hodson loan transaction, and in the course of receiving the explanations then offered he must have realised what the power was which the trustees were purporting to exercise. Indeed, the fatal opinion of counsel advising on the possibility of using clause 11 to purchase a house in the Isle of Man was, on the evidence, familiar not only to George, but to Ann. The judge held that he was emancipated from parental control, and well enough acquainted with his position to make his consent to this advance binding upon him, and this court cannot reverse that finding, depending, as it does, so much upon the demeanour of the witness.

The case of the other son, Francis, is quite different. He was at this time 28 years old, and was apparently living for the most part with his grandmother, so that he was removed from immediate parental control. On the other hand, we now know that he was a schizophrenic. This diagnosis had been made in 1940 when he found one day of life in the Royal Air Force altogether too much for him, and was repeated by a doctor who saw him in 1951. He was not called by either side, it being agreed that his memory was not at all to be trusted. Consent to this, as to other transactions in which he was involved, was written out and sent to him by his father. There is no letter from him anywhere in the correspondence. No representative of the bank ever saw him. He was obviously left purposely in the background. On the other hand, he was capable of teaching in a boys school, which he did for two years towards the end of the war, and was accepted for entry to Edinburgh University after the war, where also he continued for two years as a student. Further, when he went with his brother to be advised over the Hodson loan, the partner in Farrer & Co who saw him thought him capable of understanding the transaction. Moreover, it has never been alleged that he was at any material time incapacitated from contracting or conducting business affairs by reason of his mental health, though we cannot think that if the bank had known of his history of ill-health they would have acted on the consents he returned signed to his father. But the bank did not know the facts. We have considered anxiously whether, before making an advance, they should have made some inquiry into his circumstances. It is alleged in the particulars of the statement of claim (paragraph 10) that the law presumes undue influence to exist between a person suffering from mental ill-health and the person with whom he resides; but in the end Mr. Bagnall rightly abandoned this plea, for there is no such presumption though actual undue influence may not be difficult to prove. The presumption exists only as to the medical adviser. On the whole, we do not feel able to say that the presumption of undue influence must be held to exist between Francis and his parents having regard to his age and his absence from home, and we conclude that the bank were not bound to make inquiries as to his state of mind or fitness as an object of the power they were affecting to exercise. Accordingly, though this was the plainest breach of trust, we agree with the judge that the bank have a good defence, for they obtained consents from the two children concerned, and they were emancipated ...

The bank pleads the Limitation Act 1939, and as to this we wholly agree with what the judge said and need not repeat it. So, too, as to the defence of laches.[16] As to acquiescence, we think that this must be looked at rather broadly. We were, of course, pressed with the leading case of *Allcard v Skinner* (1887) 36 ChD 145, but in that case the plaintiff had her rights fully explained to her by a brother, who was a barrister, and by her solicitor, and yet she took no steps until five or six years later. Even that gave rise to a difference of opinion in a very strong Court of Appeal. In this case it would be wrong, we feel, to place any disability upon the beneficiaries because it so happened that George was a member of the bar, and had been in well-known chambers. He had not been in Chancery chambers where it may be said that these things are better understood; but the real truth of the matter is that a party cannot be held to have acquiesced unless he knew, or ought to have known, what his rights were. On the facts of this case we cannot criticise any of the plaintiffs for failing to appreciate their rights until another junior counsel, whom they consulted on a far-fetched and futile scheme of George's for avoiding estate duty on his mother's death, advised that the advances might be improper. That was in 1954, and thereupon the family, headed, of course, by George, took immediate steps to explore this matter. This is a most complicated action, and many matters had to be explored before an action for breach of trust could properly

---

16 [1962] 1 WLR 86 at 115, [1961] 3 All ER 713 at 735, per WILBERFORCE J: "I must now deal with certain special defences. (1) The Limitation Act 1939. The relevant provision is section 19 (2), and the whole question is whether the plaintiffs' rights are preserved by the proviso. In my judgment, they are. Undoubtedly they had 'a future interest' and, in my judgment, that interest did not fall into possession when the trustees by an (ex hypothesi) invalid advance raised a sum of money out of the capital. Mrs. Younghusband's consent to the advance was not, in my view, equivalent to a release of her life interest, and the only way (without a release) in which a capital sum could fall into possession would be by means of a valid advance. This defence, in my judgment fails.

(2) Laches. There being an express statutory provision, providing a period of limitation for the plaintiffs' claims, there is no room for the equitable doctrine of laches."

be mounted. The writ was issued in 1958, and we do not think it right to hold that the plaintiffs were debarred by acquiescence from bringing an action which otherwise, to the extent we have indicated, is justified.

We have already dealt with the impact of section 61 in general and in detail as we have gone through the various impugned transactions, and on that we need say nothing further.''

The Court of Appeal differed on the application of s. 61 to one of the advances. WILBERFORCE J described it at 310:

"On September 13, 1948, the bank, as trustees, had also advanced to Francis and George a sum of £2,600 (Advance No. 5) which was applied in discharging a loan, which the bank, as trustee of a settlement of another customer of the bank, a Mrs. Hodson, had made to their mother and which had been charged as a mortgage on their mother's life interest under her uncle's will. This loan (known as the Hodson loan) was also secured by four life insurance policies on the mother's life of a total nominal value of £3,000, whose surrender value was then about £650. On this transaction the sons did have separate advice. Charles Russell & Co advised that it would be a proper exercise of the power of advancement provided that Francis and George received an adequate quid pro quo in the shape of the assignment to them of the four policies, coupled with covenants by the mother to maintain the premiums and to pay interest on the money advanced. However, the assignment of the life policies, as executed, contained no such covenants by the mother. Burrell of Farrer & Co approved the draft assignment on behalf of the sons without ever consulting them. The sons retained the life policies till 1953 when they gave them back to their mother, on joining with their mother in executing a mortgage dated March 18, 1953, by the mother to the bank of her life interest under her uncle's will for the sum of £2,000. Apparently this was for the purpose of enabling the commander to raise further sums by charging them again.''

The Court of Appeal held that the payment of the £2,000 was a clear breach of trust. UPJOHN LJ, with whom HARMAN LJ concurred, said at 358, at 24:

"In my judgment, therefore, the only question that arises is whether the bank should be relieved from the consequences of their breach of trust under section 61 of the Trustee Act 1925, to any, and if so, what extent. This, I think, is a very difficult question. The judgment of the court has already pointed out that the bank were personally innocent, but they were ill-advised by their own solicitors; but the bank must accept responsibility for such negligence, and section 61 cannot possibly be invoked to relieve them from its consequences without more. The circumstance that seems to me to make the application of the section possible is that the bank received the letter quoted in the judgment of the court written by Burrell on behalf of Francis and George saying that the matter was in a satisfactory state. Thereafter it would have been quite unreasonable for the bank to take any further step to assure themselves that the transaction had been properly carried out, and they were lulled into a false sense of security. Section 61 is purely discretionary, and its application necessarily depends on the particular facts of each case. I think, in the circumstances of this case, that I am prepared to hold that the bank acted honestly (that is not in dispute) and reasonably and ought fairly to be excused to the extent of the surrender value of the policies transferred to the boys at the date of the transaction, about £650, but no doubt the exact figure can be ascertained. I do not see how the bank can properly be relieved to any greater extent. The fact that the mother paid the premiums for a few years, so enhancing the value of the policies, is (so far as the bank is concerned) as irrelevant as the fact that, as was to be expected, in due course the boys gave the policies back to their mother, and so, of course, to the commander, thereby losing all benefit from them."

QUESTIONS

1. "The obligation of a defaulting trustee is essentially that of effecting restitution to the trust estate." *Target Holdings Ltd v Redferns* [1995] 3 WLR 352, [1995] 3 All ER 785, p. 862, ante. *Bartlett v Barclays Bank Trust Co Ltd (No 2)* [1980] Ch 515 at 543; [1980] 2 All ER 92 at 95, per BRIGHTMAN LJ; *Re Dawson* [1966] 2 NSWR 211, per STREET J (quoted Underhill, p. 829); *Re Bell's Indenture* [1980] 1 WLR 1217 at 1236–1237, [1980] 3 All ER 425 at 442; H & M, pp. 620–621; (1982) 126 SJ 631 (A.M. Kenny).

   In what ways is the obligation of a defaulting trustee different from that of a contractual or tortious wrongdoer?

2. In assessing compensation payable to beneficiaries for breach of trust, should the tax liability of individuals be taken into account, so as to reduce the amount payable? *Bartlett v Barclays Bank Ltd (No 2); Re Bell's Indenture*, [1980] Conv 449 (G.A. Shindler); Pettit, p. 485.

II. Proprietary Remedies[17]

A proprietary remedy is one in which the plaintiff can claim that property in the hands of the defendant is to be treated as that of the plaintiff. It is not the same as a "real" remedy, which entitles the plaintiff to specific recovery. A proprietary remedy entitles the plaintiff to treat any property—usually, of course, money—in the hands of the defendant as being the plaintiff's to the extent that he can claim repayment in full regardless of the defendant's insolvency.

A. Tracing at Common Law[18]

If A lends his car to B and B becomes insolvent, then A's car does not go into B's bankruptcy. A steps in and claims it ahead of B's creditors. If B's trustee in bankruptcy refuses to return it, A has an action in conversion; and, whether or not A succeeds in obtaining an order for specific recovery under the Common Law Procedure Act 1852,[19] A will at least obtain judgment for the full value of

---

17 H & M, pp. 640–671; K & S, pp. 454–472; P & M, pp. 607–632; Pettit, pp. 505–518; Riddall, pp. 351–362; Snell, pp. 297–305; Underhill, pp. 850–871, 916–935; Goff and Jones, *Law of Restitution* (4th edn), chap. 2; Birks, *An Introduction to the Law of Restitution*, pp. 358 et seq; *American Restatement of Restitution*, paras. 160–162, 202–215; (1959) 75 LQR 234 (R.H. Maudsley); (1971) 34 MLR 12 (F.O.B. Babafemi); (1975) 28 CLP 64 (A.J. Oakley); (1976) 40 Conv (NS) 277 (R.A. Pearce); (1976) 92 LQR 360 at p. 367 (R.M. Goode); (1979) 95 LQR 78 (S. Khurshid and P. Matthews); (1981) 34 CLP 159 (P. Matthews).

18 (1986) WALR 463 (M. Scott).

19 Detinue was abolished by Torts (Interference with Goods) Act 1977, s. 2; the discretionary power of the court to order specific recovery is retained by s. 3.

the car. However, if A had lent B £500, A's claim for repayment would be reduced to a personal claim and he would have to compete in the bankruptcy with the other creditors.

Sometimes, and within very narrow limits, there is a proprietary remedy at common law. What should be A's right if he lent the car to B, and B wrongfully sold it to C for £500 and then went bankrupt, still holding the £500? Can A claim that the £500 is his, just as the car was? Or does it now turn into a money claim and abate with the other creditors? Or if a factor has received notes payable to A, and the notes have not been paid at the time of the factor's bankruptcy, should A be entitled to claim the money or merely a dividend in the factor's bankruptcy? In *Scott v Surman* (1742) Willes 400, WILLES LCJ said at 405:

"The assignees [in bankruptcy] having received this money which belongs to the plaintiffs and ought not to be applied to pay the bankrupt's debts, and they ought to have paid it to the plaintiffs, and not having done so, this action will lie against them for so much money had and received to the use of the plaintiffs." That is an example of the common law action for money had and received being used as a proprietary remedy, and entitling the plaintiff to claim the full amount due from the assignee in bankruptcy.

In **Taylor v Plumer** (1815) 3 M & S 562,[19a] Sir Thomas Plumer had given money to Walsh, a stockbroker, for investment. Walsh improperly purchased American investments and bullion and hurried to Falmouth to take a packet for Lisbon and so to North America. He was apprehended while waiting for the packet to put to sea, and the investments and bullion were seized. His assignees in bankruptcy claimed in this action to recover them from Sir Thomas. They failed. In other words Sir Thomas had a right to claim against Walsh the full value of the property into which money given to Walsh had been converted, and not merely a dividend in the bankruptcy.

The limits of such a claim were laid down by Lord ELLENBOROUGH at 575:

"It makes no difference in reason or law into what other form, different from the original, the change may have been made, whether it be into that of promissory notes for the security of the money which was produced by the sale of the goods of the principal, as in *Scott v Surman* (1742) Willes 400, or into other merchandise, as in *Whitecomb v Jacob* (1710) 1 Salk 160, for the product of or substitute for the original thing still follows the nature of the thing itself, as long as it can be ascertained to be such, and the right only ceases when the means of ascertainment fail, which is the case when the subject is turned into money, and mixed and confounded in a general mass of the same description. The difficulty which arises in such a case is a difficulty of fact and not of law, and the dictum that money has no ear-mark must be understood in the same way; i.e., as predicated only of an undivided and undistinguishable mass of current money. But money in a bag, or otherwise kept apart from other money, guineas, or other coin marked (if the fact were so) for the purpose of being distinguished, are so far ear-marked as to fall within the rule on this subject,

---

19a [1995] Lloyd's Maritime and Commercial Law Quarterly 240 (L.D. Smith).

which applies to every other description of personal property whilst it remains, (as the property in question did), in the hands of the factor, or his general legal representatives. That trust property in the possession of a factor empowered to dispose of it for his principal does not pass to his assignees under the stat. Jac. 1, upon his becoming a bankrupt, was established in the case of *L'Apostre v Le Plaistrier* (1708) 2 Eq Abr 113, first tried before Lord *Holt* at Nisi Prius in 1708, and afterwards so adjudged upon a case made for the opinion of the Court of King's Bench. The same point was held by Lord *Cowper* in *Copeman v Gallant* (1716) 1 P Wms 314 at 320. And in *Whitecomb v Jacob* in Chancery (1710) Trin 9 Ann (1 Salk 160), the doctrine was carried further, and to an extent which fully comprehends the present case. There, a factor entrusted with the disposal of merchandise for his principal, sold it, received the money, and, instead of paying the money to his principal, vested the produce in other goods, and died indebted in debts of a higher nature. There it was held that those goods should be taken as the merchant's estate, and not the factor's; and though that was not the case of a factor becoming a *bankrupt*, yet it makes no difference whether the person claiming to represent the factor was his executor or administrator, or his *assignee*, except only as far as the case might be affected by the stat. *Jac.* 1, and which it cannot be, if the factor bankrupt had the order and disposition of the property entrusted to him in the character of factor only, and not as owner: for that point the above-cited cases of *L'Apostre v Le Plaistrier* and *Copeman v Gallant* are authorities.''[20]

Agip (Africa) Ltd v Jackson [1990] Ch 265, [1992] 4 All ER 385[1] illustrates a fraudulent scheme for the international laundering of money on a substantial scale.

The plaintiff carried on oil exploration operations in Tunisia in the 1970s and early 1980s and they held an account with the Banque du Sud in Tunis to pay overseas suppliers. The plaintiff discovered that they had been defrauded of large sums of money by Z, its chief accountant. Z was not a director or an authorised signatory of the company but it was his task to put the completed payment orders before the authorised signatory and obtain his signature. Afterwards Z was responsible for taking the payment orders to the bank for payment.

Z affected the frauds by altering the names of the payees on the payment orders after obtaining the authorised signature. It was estimated that in a two-year period some $10.5 million had been diverted away from the proper payees of the plaintiff in this way.

This action though was concerned with only one payment of $518,822 which was made to Baker Oil Services Ltd. (Baker Oil) a company registered in the Isle of Man which held a dollar account at a branch of Lloyds Bank in London. This was a shell company which immediately before the transfer of the money to it had nothing standing in its credits in the account. Shortly after receiving

---

20 See also *Banque Belge Pour L'Etranger v Hambrouck* [1921] 1 KB 321.
  1 (1989) 105 LQR 528 (P. Birks); (1991) 107 LQR 71 (Sir Peter MILLETT); [1990] CLJ 217 (C. Harpum). On appeal (1991) 50 CLJ 409 (C. Harpum); (1992) Conv 367 (S. Goulding), from which the statement of the facts is taken.

the money the whole balance was transferred to the account of Jackson & Co., an accountancy firm the partners of which were the first and second defendants. They were also the directors and shareholders of Baker Oil. The third defendant was an employee of the partnership. The money was only held in the partnership account for the benefit of the partnership clients. From there it was then transferred to another company which held an account at the same branch of Lloyds Bank before being transferred overseas to the ultimate recipients and organisers of the frauds.

On discovering the frauds the plaintiff brought an unsuccessful action in Tunisia against the Banque du Sud for recovery of the money which had been debited to its account. It also obtained a judgment against Baker Oil but of course this was unsatisfied and was certain to remain so as Baker Oil was now in liquidation.

The plaintiff brought a number of claims against the defendants. It failed in its attempt to trace at common law, but succeeded in claims to trace in equity (p. 896 post) and for assistance in breach of trust (p. 251 ante). On the first, MILLETT J (whose decision on all three claims was upheld by the Court of Appeal: [1991] Ch 547, [1992] 4 All ER 451)[2] said at 285, at 398:

"The next question is whether the plaintiffs can follow the payment into the hands of Jackson & Co; for the fact that it was the plaintiffs' money which left the Banque du Sud does not mean that it was the plaintiffs' money which reached Baker Oil or Jackson & Co. Tracing at common law, unlike its counterpart in equity, is neither a cause of action nor a remedy but serves an evidential purpose. The cause of action is for money had and received. Tracing at common law enables the defendant to be identified as the recipient of the plaintiff's money and the measure of his liability to be determined by the amount of the plaintiff's money he is shown to have received.

The common law has always been able to follow a physical asset from one recipient to another. Its ability to follow an asset in the same hands into a changed form was established in *Taylor v Plumer* (1815) 3 M & S 562. In following the plaintiff's money into an asset purchased exclusively with it, no distinction is drawn between a chose in action such as the debt of a bank to its customer and any other asset: *Re Diplock* [1948] Ch 465, 519, [1948] 2 All ER 318, 416. But it can only follow a physical asset, such as a cheque or its proceeds, from one person to another. It can follow money but not a chose in action. Money can be followed at common law into and out of a bank account and into the hands of a subsequent transferee, provided that it does not cease to be identifiable by being mixed with other money in the bank account derived from some other source: *Banque Belge pour l'Etranger v Hambrouck* [1921] 1 KB 321. Applying these principles, the plaintiffs claim to follow their money through Baker Oil's account where it was not mixed with any other money and into Jackson & Co.'s account at Lloyds Bank.

The defendants deny this. They contend that tracing is not possible at common law because the money was mixed, first when it was handled in New York, and secondly in Jackson & Co.'s own account at Lloyds Bank.

The latter objection is easily disposed of. The cause of action for money had and received is complete when the plaintiff's money is received by the

---

2 See Fox LJ at 563, at 466.

defendant. It does not depend on the continued retention of the money by the defendant. Save in strictly limited circumstances it is no defence that he has parted with it. A fortiori it can be no defence for him to show that he has so mixed it with his own money that he cannot tell whether he still has it or not. Mixing by the defendant himself must, therefore, be distinguished from mixing by a prior recipient. The former is irrelevant, but the latter will destroy the claim, for it will prevent proof that the money received by the defendant was the money paid by the plaintiff.

In my judgment, however, the former objection is insuperable. The money cannot be followed by treating it as the proceeds of a cheque presented by the collecting bank in exchange for payment by the paying bank. The money was transmitted by telegraphic transfer. There was no cheque or any equivalent. The payment order was not a cheque or its equivalent. It remained throughout in the possession of the Banque du Sud. No copy was sent to Lloyds Bank or Baker Oil or presented to the Banque du Sud in exchange for the money. It was normally the plaintiffs' practice to forward a copy of the payment order to the supplier when paying an invoice but this was for information only. It did not authorise or enable the supplier to obtain payment. There is no evidence that this practice was followed in the case of forged payment orders and it is exceedingly unlikely that it was.

Nothing passed between Tunisia and London but a stream of electrons. It is not possible to treat the money received by Lloyds Bank in London or its correspondent bank in New York as representing the proceeds of the payment order or of any other physical asset previously in its hands and delivered by it in exchange for the money. The Banque du Sud merely telexed a request to Lloyd's Bank to make a payment to Baker Oil against its own undertaking to reimburse Lloyds Bank in New York. Lloyds Bank complied with the request by paying Baker Oil with its own money. It thereby took a delivery risk. In due course it was no doubt reimbursed, but it is not possible to identify the source of the money with which it was reimbursed without attempting to follow the money through the New York clearing system. Unless Lloyds Bank's correspondent bank in New York was also Citibank, this involves tracing the money through the accounts of Citibank and Lloyds Bank's correspondent bank with the Federal Reserve Bank, where it must have been mixed with other money. The money with which Lloyds Bank was reimbursed cannot therefore, without recourse to equity, be identified as being that of the Banque du Sud. There is no evidence that Lloyds Bank's correspondent bank in New York was Citibank, and accordingly the plaintiff's attempt to trace the money at common law must fail.

In **Lipkin Gorman v Karpnale Ltd** [1991] 2 AC 548, [1992] 4 All ER 512, p. 268, ante, one of the partners of the appellant firm, a compulsive gambler named Norman Cass, drew cheques on the firm's client account without authority and paid the proceeds to the Playboy Club, which was owned by the respondent. The Club being solvent, the appellant brought the common law personal action for money had and received against it. In order to succeed in that action the appellant had to establish, by the common law tracing rules, that the Club had received its property. (A common law tracing claim against the Club would have failed because the Club had mixed the money with its own). Lord GOFF OF CHIEVELEY said at 572, at 527:

"So, in the present case, the solicitors seek to show that the money in question was their property at common law. But their claim in the present case for money had and received is nevertheless a personal claim; it is not a proprietary claim, advanced on the basis that money remaining in the hands of the respondents is their property. Of course there is no doubt that, even if legal title to the money did vest in Cass immediately on receipt, nevertheless he would have held it on trust for his partners, who would accordingly have been entitled to trace it in equity into the hands of the respondents. However, your Lordships are not concerned with an equitable tracing claim in the present case, since no such case is advanced by the solicitors, who have been content to proceed at common law by a personal action, viz. an action for money had and received. I should add that in the present case, we are not concerned with the fact that money drawn by Cass from the solicitors' client account at the bank may have become mixed by Cass with his own money before he gambled it away at the club. For the respondents have conceded that, if the solicitors can establish legal title to the money in the hands of Cass, that title was not defeated by mixing of the money with other money of Cass while in his hands. On this aspect of the case, therefore, the only question is whether the solicitors can establish legal title to the money when received by Cass from the bank by drawing cheques on the client account without authority. . . . "
[His Lordship held that they could: p. 268 ante].

B. Tracing in Equity

The wider doctrine of tracing in equity is usually applicable where the property is in the hands of trustees or other fiduciaries, and often where the fiduciary is bankrupt. But the doctrine also applies in a commercial context; as where a seller, in order to protect himself in a customer's bankruptcy, provides expressly in the contract that property shall not pass in goods supplied until payment, nor in the proceeds of sale by a customer on a sub-sale. A seller may also provide in an "all-monies clause" that the property shall not pass until all the buyer's obligations to him have been satisfied, and not merely as to the particular consignment.[3] The seller's right to the proceeds will give him a priority over the general creditors in the event of the customer's bankruptcy.[4]

---

3 The Review Committee on Insolvency Law and Practice 1982 (Cmnd. 8558), para. 1645 proposed that such clauses should be regarded as creating charges and therefore be registrable. For the effect of such a clause in Scotland, see *Armour v Thyssen Edelstahlwerke AG* [1991] 2 AC 339; (1991) 141 NLJ 537 (B. Avery); (1991) 54 MLR 726 (R. Bradgate); *Re Highway Foods International Ltd* [1995] 1 BCLC 209.

4 H & M, pp. 657–662; Goode, *Proprietary Rights and Insolvency in Sales Transactions* (2nd edn 1989); McCormack, *Reservation of Title* (2nd edn); Wheeler, *Reservation of Title Clauses* (1992). *Aluminium Industrie Vaassen BV v Romalpa Aluminium Ltd* [1976] 1 WLR 676, [1976] 2 All ER 552 (unpaid seller of aluminium foil, who had reserved ownership of it, held able to trace into proceeds of sub-sale of such foil, over which the customer had an implied power of sale as agent for the seller); *Hendy Lennox (Industrial Engines) Ltd v Grahame Puttick Ltd* [1984] 1 WLR 485, [1984] 2 All ER 152; *Clough Mill Ltd v Martin* [1985] 1 WLR 111, [1984] 3 All ER 982; [1985] CLJ 33 (J.W.A. Thornely); [1985] 82 LSG 1075, 1128 (C. Whitehouse); (1985) 129 SJ 3, 26 (I. Davies); (1985) 20 Ir Jur (NS) 264 (R.A. Pearce); (1986) 60 ALJ 545 (D. Chalmers); (1986) 49 MLR 96 (W. Goodhart); [1987] Conv 434 (J.R. Bradgate); [1987] All ER Rev 31 (N.E. Palmer); (1986) 130 SJ 402 (A.R. Hicks); [1989] Conv 92 (G. McCormack).

i. THE DOCTRINE

In **Boscawen v Bajwa** [1996] 1 WLR 328,[5] MILLETT LJ said at 334:
"Equity lawyers habitually use the expressions 'the tracing claim' and 'the tracing remedy' to describe the proprietary claim and the proprietary remedy which equity makes available to the beneficial owner who seeks to recover his property in specie from those into whose hands it has come. Tracing properly so-called, however, is neither a claim nor a remedy but a process. Moreover, it is not confined to the case where the plaintiff seeks a proprietary remedy; it is equally necessary where he seeks a personal remedy against the knowing recipient or knowing assistant. It is the process by which the plaintiff traces what has happened to his property, identifies the persons who have handled or received it, and justifies his claim that the money which they handled or received (and, if necessary, which they still retain) can properly be regarded as representing his property. He needs to do this because his claim is based on the retention by him of a beneficial interest in the property which the defendant handled or received. Unless he can prove this he cannot (in the traditional language of equity) raise an equity against the defendant or (in the modern language of restitution) show that the defendant's unjust enrichment was at his expense.

In such a case the defendant will either challenge the plaintiff's claim that the property in question represents his property (i.e., he will challenge the validity of the tracing exercise) or he will raise a priority dispute (e.g., by claiming to be a bona fide purchaser without notice). If all else fails he will raise the defence of innocent change of position. This was not a defence which was recognised in England before 1991 but it was widely accepted throughout the common law world. In *Lipkin Gorman v Karpnale Ltd* [1991] 2 AC 548, [1992] 4 All ER 512, p. 268, ante the House of Lords acknowledged it to be part of English law also. The

See the limits placed on the doctrine by the requirement of registration of any equitable interest reserved under Companies Act 1985, ss. 395, 396, and by the difficulty of finding a fiduciary relationship precedent to tracing; *Re Bond Worth Ltd* [1980] Ch 228, [1979] 3 All ER 919; *Borden (UK) Ltd v Scottish Timber Products Ltd* [1981] Ch 25, [1979] 3 All ER 961; *Re Arthur Saunders Ltd* (1981) 17 BLR 125; *Re Peachdart Ltd* [1984] Ch 131, [1983] 3 All ER 204; (1984) 100 LQR 35 (S. Whittaker); [1984] CLJ 35 (J.W.A. Thornely); [1984] Conv 139 (D. Milman); [1983] All ER Rev 48 (N.E. Palmer); *Re Andrabell Ltd* [1984] 3 All ER 407; *Four Point Garage Ltd v Carter* [1985] 3 All ER 12; *Sauter Automation v Goodman (Mechanical Services)* (1986) 34 BLR 81; *E. Pfeiffer Weinkellerei-Weineinkauf Gmbh & Co v Arbuthnot Factors Ltd* [1988] 1 WLR 150; *Specialist Plant Services Ltd v Braithwaite Ltd* [1987] BCLC 1; *John Snow & Co v Woodcroft & Co Ltd* [1985] BCLC 54; (1989) 133 SJ 1052 (G. McCormack); *Compaq Computer Ltd v Abercorn Group Ltd* [1991] BCC 484; [1992] CLJ 19 (L. Sealy); *Re Weldtech Equipment Ltd* [1991] BCC 16; (1991) 54 MLR 736 (J. De Lacy); *Stroud Architectural Systems v John Laing Construction* [1994] BCC 18; [1994] Conv 242 (J. De Lacy); *Ian Chisholm Textiles v Griffiths* [1994] BCC 96; [1995] CLJ 43 (S. Cowen, A. Clarke and G. Goldberg).

Insolvency Act 1986, s. 15 (s. 251 contains a definition of a "retention of title agreement"); (1976) 92 LQR 360, 528 (R.M. Goode); (1976) 39 MLR 585 (R. Prior); (1977) 93 LQR 324 (D.T. Donaldson) and 487 (R.M. Goode); [1977] CLJ 27 (J.H. Farrow and N.E. Furey); [1978] Conv 37 (O.P. Wylie); (1979) 98 Law Notes 72 (N. Henderson); [1980] CLJ 48 (J.W.A. Thornely); (1980) 43 MLR 489 (W. Goodhart and G. Jones); (1980) 96 LQR 90 (D.W. McLauchlan). On reform generally, see Review Committee on Insolvency Law and Practice (1982) Cmnd 8558, paras. 1584–1681; (1986) 83 LS Gaz (C. Whitehouse); Department of Trade and Industry, *Security Interests in Property Other than Land* (1986).

On reservation of title clauses in Australia, see *Puma Australia Ltd v Sportsman's Australia Ltd* (1990) unreported; [1993] Conv 375 (J. De Lacy); in Ireland, *Re WJ Hickey Ltd* [1988] IR 126; [1990] Conv 128 (J. De Lacy); in New Zealand, (1986) 6 OJLS 456 (P. Watts); [1992] LS 195 (G. McCormack), and in Scotland, *Armour v Edelstahlwerke AG* supra.

5 (1995) 9 Trust Law International 124 (P. Birks).

introduction of this defence not only provides the court with a means of doing justice in future, but allows a re-examination of many decisions of the past in which the absence of the defence may have led judges to distort basic principles in order to avoid injustice to the defendant.

If the plaintiff succeeds in tracing his property, whether in its original or in some changed form, into the hands of the defendant, and overcomes any defences which are put forward on the defendant's behalf, he is entitled to a remedy. The remedy will be fashioned to the circumstances. The plaintiff will generally be entitled to a personal remedy; if he seeks a proprietary remedy he must usually prove that the property to which he lays claim is still in the ownership of the defendant. If he succeeds in doing this the court will treat the defendant as holding the property on a constructive trust for the plaintiff and will order the defendant to transfer it in specie to the plaintiff. But this is only one of the proprietary remedies which are available to a court of equity. If the plaintiff's money has been applied by the defendant, for example, not in the acquisition of a landed property but in its improvement, then the court may treat the land as charged with the payment to the plaintiff of a sum representing the amount by which the value of the defendant's land has been enhanced by the use of the plaintiff's money. And if the plaintiff's money has been used to discharge a mortgage on the defendant's land, then the court may achieve a similar result by treating the land as subject to a charge by way of subrogation in favour of the plaintiff.

Subrogation, therefore, is a remedy, not a cause of action; see *Goff & Jones, Law of Restitution*, 4th ed. (1993), pp. 589 et seq,[6] *Orakpo v Manson Investments Ltd.* [1978] AC 95, 104, per Lord Diplock and *Re T.H. Knitwear (Wholesale) Ltd* [1988] Ch 275, 284. It is available in a wide variety of different factual situations in which it is required in order to reverse the defendant's unjust enrichment. Equity lawyers speak of a right of subrogation, or of an equity of subrogation, but this merely reflects the fact that it is not a remedy which the court has a general discretion to impose whenever it thinks it just to do so. The equity arises from the conduct of the parties on well settled principles and in defined circumstances which make it unconscionable for the defendant to deny the proprietary interest claimed by the plaintiff. A constructive trust arises in the same way. Once the equity is established the court satisfies it by declaring that the property in question is subject to a charge by the way of subrogation in the one case or a constructive trust in the other.''

ii. Unmixed Funds

Where property is taken by a person in a fiduciary relation to the plaintiff, the plaintiff may claim that property from the fiduciary, or, if it has been sold, may claim the proceeds of sale; or may follow the property into the hands of a third party, but not if it comes into the hands of a bona fide purchaser for value.[7]

iii. Mixed Funds

In **Banque Belge Pour L'Etranger v Hambrouck** [1921] 1 KB 321, Atkin LJ said at p. 335:

---

6 See also Mitchell, *Law of Subrogation* (1994).
7 *Thorndike v Hunt* (1859) 3 De GF & J 563; *Taylor v Blakelock* (1886) 32 ChD 560; *Thomson v Clydesdale Bank Ltd* [1893] AC 282; *Coleman v Bucks and Oxon Union Bank* [1897] 2 Ch 243.

"The question always was, Had the means of ascertainment failed? But if in 1815 the common law halted outside the bankers' door, by 1879 equity had had the courage to lift the latch, walk in and examine the books: *Re Hallett's Estate* (1880) 13 ChD 696. I see no reason why the means of ascertainment should not now be available both for common law and equity proceedings."[8]

(a) Traceable Property

RE HALLETT'S ESTATE
(1880) 13 ChD 696 (CA, Sir George JESSEL MR, BAGGALLAY and THESIGER LJJ)

Henry Hughes Hallett was a solicitor. He was trustee of his own marriage settlement, and had paid some moneys from that trust into his own bank account.

He was solicitor to Mrs. Cotterill, and had been entrusted by her with money for investment. Part of this money was also paid into Hallett's bank account.

Hallett made various payments from, and into, the account, and also incurred further debts. At the date of his death, the account held sufficient funds to meet the claims of the trustees of the marriage settlement and of Mrs. Cotterill, but not the personal debts as well.

In an action for the administration of Hallett's estate, the main question was whether the trust and Mrs. Cotterill could claim in priority to the creditors.

Held. (i) Both the trust and Mrs. Cotterill were entitled to a charge upon the moneys in the bank account in priority to the general creditors; (ii) (THESIGER LJ dissenting) the various payments by Hallett out of the account must be treated as payments of his own money and not that of the trust or of Mrs. Cotterill.

JESSEL MR: There is no doubt, therefore, that Mr. *Hallett* stood in a fiduciary position towards Mrs. *Cotterill*. Mr. *Hallett*, before his death, I regret to say, improperly sold the bonds and put the money to his general account at his bankers. It is not disputed that the money remained at his bankers mixed with his own money at the time of his death; that is, he had not drawn out that money from his bankers. In that position of matters Mrs. *Cotterill* claimed to be entitled to receive the proceeds, or the amount of the proceeds, of the bonds out of money in the hands of Mr. *Hallett's* bankers at the time of his death, and that claim was allowed by the learned Judge of the Court below, and I think was properly so allowed. Indeed, as I understand the doctrines of Equity, it would have been too clear a case for argument, except for another decision of that learned Judge himself, *Ex p Dale & Co* (1879) 11 ChD 772. The modern doctrine of Equity as regards property disposed of by persons in a fiduciary position is a very clear and well-established doctrine. You can, if the sale was rightful, take the proceeds of the sale, if you can identify them. If the sale was wrongful, you can still take the proceeds of the sale, in a sense adopting the sale for the purpose of taking the proceeds, if you can identify them. There is no distinction, therefore, between a rightful and a wrongful disposition of the property, so far as regards the right of the beneficial owner to follow the proceeds. But it very often happens that you cannot identify the proceeds. The proceeds may have been invested together with money belonging to the person in a fiduciary position, in a purchase. He may have bought land with it,

---

8 *Chief Constable of Kent v V* [1983] QB 34 at 41, [1982] 3 All ER 36 at 39, per Lord DENNING MR.

for instance, or he may have bought chattels with it. Now, what is the position of the beneficial owner as regards such purchases? I will, first of all, take his position when the purchase is clearly made with what I will call, for shortness, the trust money, although it is not confined, as I will shew presently, to express trusts. In that case, according to the now well-established doctrine of Equity, the beneficial owner has a right to elect either to take the property purchased, or to hold it as a security for the amount of the trust money laid out in the purchase; or, as we generally express it, he is entitled at his election either to take the property, or to have a charge on the property for the amount of the trust money. But in the second case, where a trustee has mixed the money with his own, there is the distinction, that the *cestui que trust*, or beneficial owner, can no longer elect to take the property, because it is no longer bought with the trust-money simply and purely, but with a mixed fund. He is, however, still entitled to a charge on the property purchased, for the amount of the trust-money laid out in the purchase; and that charge is quite independent of the fact of the amount laid out by the trustee. The moment you get a substantial portion of it furnished by the trustee, using the word "trustee" in the sense I have mentioned, as including all persons in a fiduciary relation, the right to the charge follows. That is the modern doctrine of Equity. Has it ever been suggested, until very recently, that there is any distinction between an express trustee, or an agent, or a bailee, or a collector of rents, or anybody else in a fiduciary position? I have never heard, until quite recently, such a distinction suggested. It cannot, as far as I am aware (and since this Court sat last to hear this case, I have taken the trouble to look for authority), be found in any reported case even suggested, except in the recent decision of Mr. Justice *Fry*, to which I shall draw attention presently. It can have no foundation in principle, because the beneficial ownership is the same, wherever the legal ownership may be. If you have goods bargained and sold to a man upon trust to sell and hand over the net proceeds to another, that other is the beneficial owner; but if instead of being bargained and sold, so as to vest the legal ownership in the trustee, they are deposited with him to sell as agent, so that the legal ownership remains in the beneficial owner, can it be supposed, in a Court of Equity, that the rights of the beneficial owner are different, he being entire beneficial owner in both cases? I say on principle it is impossible to imagine there can be any difference. In practice we know there is no difference, because the moment you get into a Court of Equity, where a principal can sue an agent as well as a *cestui que trust* can sue a trustee, no such distinction was ever suggested, as far as I am aware. Therefore, the moment you establish the fiduciary relation, the modern rules of Equity, as regards following trust money, apply. I intentionally say modern rules, because it must not be forgotten that the rules of Courts of Equity are not, like the rules of the Common Law, supposed to have been established from time immemorial. It is perfectly well known that they have been established from time to time— altered, improved, and refined from time to time. In many cases we know the names of the Chancellors who invented them. No doubt they were invented for the purpose of securing the better administration of justice, but still they were invented. Take such things as these: the separate use of a married woman, the restraint on alienation, the modern rule against perpetuities, and the rules of equitable waste. We can name the Chancellors who first invented them, and state the date when they were first introduced into Equity jurisprudence; and, therefore in cases of this kind, the older precedents in Equity are of very little value. The doctrines are progressive, refined, and improved; and if we want to know what the rules of Equity are, we must look, of course, rather to the more modern than the more ancient cases.

Now that being the established doctrine of Equity on this point, I will take the case of the pure bailee. If the bailee sells the goods bailed, the bailor can in Equity follow the proceeds, and can follow the proceeds wherever they can be distinguished, either being actually kept separate, or being mixed up with other moneys. I have only to advert to one other point, and that is this—supposing, instead of being invested in the purchase of land or goods, the moneys were simply mixed with other moneys of the trustee, using the term again in its full sense as including every person in a fiduciary relation, does it make any difference according to the modern doctrine of Equity? I say none. It would be very remarkable if it were to do so. Supposing the trust money was 1,000 sovereigns, and the trustee put them into a bag, and by mistake, or accident, or otherwise, dropped a sovereign of his own into the bag. Could anybody suppose that a Judge in Equity would find any difficulty is saying that the *cestui que trust* had a right to take 1,000 sovereigns out of that bag? I do not like to call it a charge of 1,000 sovereigns on the 1,001 sovereigns, but that is the effect of it. I have no doubt of it. It would make no difference if, instead of one sovereign, it was another 1,000 sovereigns. . . .

[His Lordship referred to various authorities, including *Taylor v Plumer* (1815) 3 M & S 562 from which he quoted Lord ELLENBOROUGH:]"and the right only ceases when the means of ascertainment fail". That is correct. Now there comes a point which is not correct, but which I am afraid only ceases to be correct because Lord *Ellenborough*'s knowledge of the rules of Equity was not quite commensurate with his knowledge of the rules of Common Law, "which is the case when the subject is turned into money, and mixed and confounded in a general mass of the same description". He was not aware of the rule of Equity which gave you a charge—that if you lent £1,000 of your own and £1,000 trust money on a bond for £2,000, or on a mortgage for £2,000, or on a promissory note for £2,000, Equity could follow it, and create a charge; but he gives that, not as law—the law is that it only fails when the means of ascertainment fail—he gives it as a case in which the means of ascertainment fail, not being aware of this refinement of Equity by which the means of ascertainment still remain. With the exception of that one fact, which is rather a fact than a statement of law, the rest of the judgment is in my opinion admirable. It goes on: "The difficulty which arises in such a case is a difficulty of fact, and not of law, and the *dictum* that money has no ear-mark must be understood in the same way, *i.e.*, as predicated only of an undivided and undistinguishable mass of current money." There, again, as I say, he did not know that Equity would have followed the money, even if put into a bag or into an undistinguishable mass, by taking out the same quantity . . .

I think after those authorities it must now be considered settled that there is no distinction, and never was a distinction, between a person occupying one fiduciary position or another fiduciary position as to the right of the beneficial owner to follow the trust fund, and that those cases which have been cited at Law so far from establishing a distinction, establish the contrary; and that the mere error of supposing that Equity could not follow or distinguish money in the cases supposed, if error it was, and perhaps it was not so originally (I am not sure that the doctrine of equity had got so far at the first start, but it was certainly an error at a later period), is attributable really to the fact that the Judges who followed the earlier cases were not aware of what I may call the gradual refinement of the doctrine of equity. Therefore, looking at the authorities to find out the principle, you do not find out any such distinction established as that suggested by Mr. Justice *Fry*, or anything of the kind even mentioned in them; and I do not know of anything more mischievous than for a Judge to say, "The cases before me establish no principle, but they quite establish something else which I will now enunciate, and therefore hold myself bound by those cases to establish another principle which was never suggested or thought of by the Judges who decided the original cases." It is only out of my great respect and esteem for the learned Judge from whom this appeal comes that I have thought it right to go so fully into the cases to shew that there is no foundation whatever for the suggested distinction, and therefore his decision in this case rests on no trivial or slight distinction between this case and the case of *Ex p Dale & Co* (1879) 11 ChD 772, but is grounded on the well-ascertained doctrines of equity.

[On the question whether the Rule in *Clayton's* case (1816) 1 Mer 572 applied as between the claims of the beneficiaries and Hallett's estate,[9] his Lordship continued:] I will first of all consider the case on principle, and then I will consider how far we are bound by authority to come to a decision opposed to principle. It may well be, and sometimes does so happen, that we are bound to come to a decision opposed to principle. Now, first upon principle, nothing can be better settled, either in our own law, or, I suppose, the law of all civilised countries, than this, that where a man does an act which may be rightfully performed, he cannot say that that act was intentionally and in fact done wrongly. A man who has a right of entry cannot say he committed a trespass in entering. A man who sells the goods of another as agent for the owner cannot prevent the owner adopting the sale, and deny that he acted as agent for the owner. It runs throughout our law, and we are familiar with numerous instances in the law of real property. A man who grants a lease believing he has sufficient estate to grant it, although it turns out that he has not, but has a power which enables him to grant it, is not allowed to say he did not grant it under the power. Wherever it can be done rightfully, he is not allowed to say, against the person entitled to the property or the right, that he has done it wrongfully. That is the universal law.

When we come to apply that principle to the case of a trustee who has blended trust moneys with his own, it seems to me perfectly plain that he cannot be heard to say that he took away the trust money when he had a right to take away his own money. The simplest case put is the mingling of trust moneys in a bag with money of the trustee's own. Suppose he has a hundred sovereigns in a bag, and he adds to them another hundred sovereigns of his own, so that they are commingled in such a way that they cannot be distinguished, and the next day he draws out for his own purposes £100, is it tolerable for anybody to allege that what he drew out was the first £100, the trust money, and that he misappropriated it, and left his own £100 in the bag? It is obvious he must have taken away that which he had a right to take away, his own £100. What difference does it make if, instead of being in a bag, he deposits it with his banker, and then pays in other money of his own, and draws out some money for his own purpose? Could he say that he had actually drawn

9 As there were sufficient moneys to satisfy both those prior claims, no question of competition between the marriage settlement trustees and Mrs. Cotterill arose. FRY J had held, below, that as between two *cestuis que trust* whose money had been paid by a trustee into his account, the rule in *Clayton's* case applied. See *Re Diplock* [1948] Ch 465 at 554, [1948] 2 All ER 318 at 364. On the rule generally, see p. 921, post.

out anything but his own money? His money was there, and he had a right to draw it out, and why should the natural act of simply drawing out the money be attributed to anything except to his ownership of money which was at the bankers.

It is said, no doubt, that according to the modern theory of banking, the deposit banker is a debtor for the money. So he is, and not a trustee in the strict sense of the word. At the same time one must recollect that the position of a deposit banker is different from that of an ordinary debtor. Still he is for some purposes a debtor, and it is said if a debt of this kind is paid by a banker, although the total balance is the amount owing by the banker, yet considering the repayments and the sums paid in by the depositor, you attribute the first sum drawn out to the first sum paid in. That was rule first established by Sir *William Grant* in *Clayton's Case* (1816) 1 Mer 572,[10] a very convenient rule, and I have nothing to say against it unless there is evidence either of agreement to the contrary or of circumstances from which a contrary intention must be presumed, and then of course that which is a mere presumption of law gives way to those other considerations. Therefore, it does appear to me there is nothing in the world laid down by Sir *William Grant* in *Clayton's Case*, or in the numerous cases which follow it, which in the slightest degree affects the principle, which I consider to be clearly established.

[His Lordship then held that he was not bound by *Pennell v Deffell* (1853) 4 De GM & G 372 and concluded:] Therefore in my opinion, the appeal must be allowed.[11]

In **Roscoe v Winder** [1915] 1 Ch 62, an agreement for the sale of the goodwill of a business provided that the purchaser, one Wigham, should collect certain of the book debts and pay that money over to the vendor. Wigham collected the debts and paid part of the money, £455 18s. 11d., into his private account. A few days later the balance in the account was reduced to £25 18s. At the date of Wigham's death, the balance has risen to £358 5s. 5d. The question was the extent to which the plaintiffs could claim a charge under the rules in *Hallett's* case.

SARGANT J held that Wigham had held the money as trustee; but that the charge was limited to £25 18s., the lowest intermediate balance subsequent to the appropriation. He said at 67:

"But there is a further circumstance in the present case which seems to me to be conclusive in favour of the defendant as regards the greater part of the balance of 358*l.* 5*s.* 5*d.* It appears that after the payment in by the debtor of a portion of the book debts which he had received the balance at the bank on May 19, 1913, was reduced by his drawings to a sum of 25*l.* 18*s.* only on May 21. So that, although the ultimate balance at the debtor's death was about 358*l.*, there had been an intermediate balance of only 25*l.* 18*s.* The result of that seems to me to be that the trust moneys cannot possibly be traced into this common fund, which was standing to the debtor's credit at his death, to an extent of more than 25*l.* 18*s.*, because, although prima facie under the second rule in *Re Hallett's Estate* (1880) 13 ChD 696 any drawings out by the debtor

10 See p. 921 post.
11 See also *Re Oatway* [1903] 2 Ch 356, explained in *Re Tilley's Will Trusts* [1967] Ch 1179, [1967] 2 All ER 303, p. 914, post.

ought to be attributed to the private moneys which he had at the bank and not to the trust moneys, yet, when the drawings out had reached such an amount that the whole of his private money part had been exhausted, it necessarily followed that the rest of the drawings must have been against trust moneys. There being on May 21, 1913, only 25*l*. 18*s*., in all, standing to the credit of the debtor's account, it is quite clear that on that day he must have denuded his account of all the trust moneys there—the whole 455*l*. 18*s*. 11*d*.—except to the extent of 25*l*. 18*s*.

Practically, what Mr. Martelli and Mr. Hansell have been asking me to do—although I think Mr. Hansell in particular rather disguised the claim by the phraseology he used—is to say that the debtor, by paying further moneys after May 21 into this common account, was impressing upon those further moneys so paid in the like trust or obligation, or charge of the nature of a trust, which had formerly been impressed upon the previous balances to the credit of that account. No doubt, Mr. Hansell did say 'No. I am only asking you to treat the account as a whole, and to consider the balance from time to time standing to the credit of that account as subject to one continual charge or trust.' But I think that really is using words which are not appropriate to the facts. You must, for the purpose of tracing, which was the process adopted in *Re Hallett's Estate*, put your finger on some definite fund which either remains in its original state or can be found in another shape. That is tracing, and tracing, by the very facts of this case, seems to be absolutely excluded except as to the 25*l*. 18*s*.

Then, apart from tracing, it seems to me possible to establish this claim against the ultimate balance of 358*l*. 5*s*. 5*d*. only by saying that something was done, with regard to the additional moneys which are needed to make up that balance, by the person to whom those moneys belonged, the debtor, to substitute those moneys for the purpose of, or to impose upon those moneys a trust equivalent to, the trust which rested on the previous balance. Of course, if there was anything like a separate trust account, the payment of the further moneys into that account would, in itself, have been quite a sufficient indication of the intention of the debtor to substitute those additional moneys for the original trust moneys, and accordingly to impose, by way of substitution, the old trusts upon those additional moneys. But, in a case where the account into which the moneys are paid is the general trading account of the debtor on which he has been accustomed to draw both in the ordinary course and in breach of trust when there were trust funds standing to the credit of that account which were convenient for that purpose, I think it is impossible to attribute to him that by the mere payment into the account of further moneys, which to a large extent he subsequently used for purposes of his own, he intended to clothe those moneys with a trust in favour of the plaintiffs.

Certainly, after having heard *Re Hallett's Estate* (1880) 13 ChD 696 stated over and over again, I should have thought that the general view of that decision was that it only applied to such an amount of the balance ultimately standing to the credit of the trustee as did not exceed the lowest balance of the account during the intervening period.'[12]

---

12 See also *Re Goldcorp Exchange Ltd* [1995] 1 AC 74, [1994] 2 All ER 806; *Bishopsgate Management Investment Ltd v Homan* [1995] Ch 211, [1995] 1 All ER 347 (held no tracing through overdrawn bank account whether overdrawn at time when money was paid in or subsequently); *cf. Space Investments Ltd v Canadian Imperial Bank of Commerce Trust Co (Bahamas) Ltd* [1986] 1 WLR 1072, [1986] 3 All ER 75.

(b) Fiduciary Relationship. Proprietary Interest

RE DIPLOCK
[1948] Ch 465, [1948] 2 All ER 318 (CA, Lord GREENE MR, WROTTESLEY and EVERSHED LJJ)[13]

By his will, Caleb Diplock directed his executors to apply his residuary estate "for such charitable institutions or other charitable or benevolent object or objects in England" as they should "in their . . . absolute discretion select".

It was assumed that the will created a valid charitable trust; and the executors distributed some £203,000 among 139 different charities before its validity was challenged by the next of kin.The House of Lords held the bequest void in *Chichester Diocesan Fund and Board of Finance Inc v Simpson* [1944] AC 341, [1944] 2 All ER 60, p. 459, ante.

The next of kin of the testator, having exhausted their remedy against the executors, made claims to recover the money from the charities. These claims against the different charities varied in details; but not on principle.

Held. The next of kin could succeed; both in respect of (i) a claim *in personam*. An unpaid or under-paid legatee was entitled to a personal claim in equity against an overpaid or wrongly paid legatee. This aspect of the case was later affirmed on appeal to the House of Lords in *Ministry of Health v Simpson* [1951] AC 251, [1950] 2 All ER 1137; and (ii) a claim *in rem*. The right to trace into a mixed fund was not restricted to cases where the defendant was the person who had mixed the moneys, or where the fiduciary relationship, necessary for a proprietary claim in equity, existed between the parties to the action.

The claim *in rem* only is discussed in this extract.

LORD GREENE MR: The first question which appears to us to fall for decision on this part of the present appeals may, we think, be thus formulated: Did the power of equity to treat Diplock "money" as recoverable from the charity, which undoubtedly existed down to the moment when the cheque was paid by the bank on which it was drawn, cease the moment that the "money" by the process of "mixture" came to be represented by an accretion to or an enlargement of the chose in action consisting of a debt already owing to the charity by its own bankers? Wynn-Parry J, in effect, decided that it did. His reason for taking this view, shortly stated, was as follows: The principle applicable was to be extracted from the decision in *Hallett's* case (1880) 13 ChD 696 and that principle was in no way extended by the decision in *Sinclair v Brougham* [1914] AC 398. The principle can operate only in cases where the mixing takes place in breach of a trust, actual or constructive, or in breach of some other fiduciary relationship and in proceedings against the trustee or fiduciary agent: here the mixing was not of this character, since it was effected by an innocent volunteer: there is no ground on which, according to principle, the conscience of such a volunteer can be held in equity to be precluded from setting up a title adverse to the claim: in every case, therefore, where a "mixture" has been carried out by the charity, the claim whether it be against

---

13 See (1987) 103 LQR 433 (R.M. Goode); Goff and Jones, *Law of Restitution* (4th edn) pp. 93–94, arguing that the requirements of a fiduciary relationship can produce unjust and anomalous results.

For Antipodean responses to *Re Diplock*, see [1981] OJLS 414 (W.A. Lee); and, for an historical perspective, see (1983) 4 Journal of Legal History 3 (S.J. Whittaker).

a mixed monetary fund or against investments made by means of such a mixed fund, must fail in limine.

Now we may say at once that this view of the inability of equity to deal with the case of the volunteer appears to us, with all respect to Wynn-Parry J, to be in conflict with the principles expounded, particularly by Lord Parker, in *Sinclair v Brougham.* If Lord Parker means what we think he meant, and if what he said is to be accepted as a correct statement of the law, Mr. Pennycuick, who argued this part of the case on behalf of the charities, admittedly felt great difficulty in supporting this part of the reasoning of the learned judge. We shall deal further with Lord Parker's observations on this topic when we come to them in our examination of *Sinclair v Brougham.* But here we may conveniently summarize what we consider to be the effect of them as follows: Where an innocent volunteer (as distinct from a purchaser for value without notice) mixes "money" of his own with "money" which in equity belongs to another person, or is found in possession of such a mixture, although that other person cannot claim a charge on the mass superior to the claim of the volunteer he is entitled, nevertheless, to a charge ranking pari passu with the claim of the volunteer. And Lord Parker's reasons for taking this view appear to have been on the following lines: Equity regards the rights of the equitable owner as being "in effect rights of property" though not recognized as such by the common law. Just as a volunteer is not allowed by equity in the case, e.g., of a conveyance of the legal estate in land, to set up his legal title adversely to the claim of a person having an equitable interest in the land, so in the case of a mixed fund of money the volunteer must give such recognition as equity considers him in conscience (as a volunteer) bound to give to the interest of the equitable owner of the money which has been mixed with the volunteer's own. But this burden on the conscience of the volunteer is not such as to compel him to treat the claim of the equitable owner as paramount. That would be to treat the volunteer as strictly as if he himself stood in a fiduciary relationship to the equitable owner which ex hypothesi he does not. The volunteer is under no greater duty of conscience to recognize the interest of the equitable owner than that which lies upon a person having an equitable interest in one of two trust funds of "money" which have become mixed towards the equitable owner of the other. Such a person is not in conscience bound to give precedence to the equitable owner of the other of the two funds.[14]

We may enlarge upon the implications which appear to us to be contained in Lord Parker's reasoning. First of all, it appears to us to be wrong to treat the principle which underlies *Hallett's* case as coming into operation only where the person who does the mixing is not only in a fiduciary position but is also a *party to the tracing action.* If he is a party to the action he is, of course, precluded from setting up a case inconsistent with the obligations of his fiduciary position. But supposing that he is not a party? The result cannot surely depend on what equity would or would not have allowed him to say if he had been a party. Suppose that the sole trustee of (say) five separate trusts draws 100*l.* out of each of the trust banking accounts, pays the resulting 500*l.* into an account which he opens in his own name, draws a cheque for 500*l.* on that account and gives it as a present to his son. A claim by the five sets of beneficiaries to follow the money of their respective trusts would be a claim against the son. He would stand in no fiduciary relationship to any of them. We recoil from the conclusion that all five beneficiaries would be dismissed empty handed by a

14 Cf. *Boscawen v Bajwa* [1996] 1 WLR 328.

court of equity and the son left to enjoy what in equity was originally their money. Yet that is the conclusion to which the reasoning of the learned judge would lead us. Lord Parker's reasoning, on the other hand, seems to us to lead to the conclusion that each set of beneficiaries could set up its equitable interest which would prevail against the bare legal title of the son as a volunteer and that they would be entitled to share pari passu in so much of the fund or its proceeds as remained identifiable.

An even more striking example was admitted by Mr. Pennycuick to be the result of his argument, and he vigorously maintained that it followed inevitably from the principles of equity involved. If a fiduciary agent takes cash belonging to his principal and gives it to his son, who takes it innocently, then so long as the son keeps it unmixed with other cash in one trouser pocket, the principal can follow it and claim it back. Once, however, the son, being under no fiduciary duty to the principal, transfers it to his other trouser pocket in which there are reposing a coin or two of his own of the same denomination, the son, by a sort of process of accretion, acquires an indefeasible title to what the moment before the transfer he could not have claimed as his own. This result appears to us to stultify the beneficent powers of equity to protect and enforce what it recognizes as equitable rights of property which subsist until they are destroyed by the operation of a purchase for value without notice.

The error into which, we respectfully suggest, the learned judge has fallen is in thinking that what, in *Hallett's* case was only the method (there appropriate) of bringing a much wider-based principle of equity into operation—viz., the method by which a fiduciary agent, who has himself wrongfully mixed the funds, is prohibited from asserting a breach of his duty—is an element which must necessarily be present before equity can afford protection to the equitable rights which it has brought into existence. We are not prepared to see the arm of equity thus shortened.

It is now time to examine in some detail the case of *Sinclair v Brougham.* Before us it was argued, on behalf of the respondents, that the principle on which it was decided was not that applied in *Hallett's* case but a different one altogether, invented with a view to solving a particular problem. We do not agree. The principle, in our view, was clearly the same; but in its application to new facts fresh light was thrown upon it, and it was shown to have a much wider scope than a narrow reading of *Hallett's* case itself would suggest.

We have examined with care not only the opinions themselves but the printed cases and the arguments of counsel as well as the judgments of the majority and of Fletcher Moulton LJ in the Court of Appeal. It is in the context of this material that the speeches must be interpreted.

The contest in *Sinclair v Brougham* was between shareholders and depositors in respect of a miscellaneous mass of assets distributable by the liquidator in the winding up of a building society. The deposits had been made, and the assets were used, in connexion with a banking business carried on in the name of the society but beyond its powers. Each of the two classes claimed priority over the other. Until the case reached the House of Lords the possibility that they might rank pari passu does not appear to have been considered. The majority of the Court of Appeal, affirming Neville J, gave the shareholders priority over the depositors. Fletcher Moulton LJ would have given the depositors priority over the shareholders. The House of Lords held that both views were wrong and that on the principle on which *Hallett's* case was founded, the two classes shared rateably. In one respect, no doubt, this application of the principle is an extension of it since, although the right of individuals to trace their own money (if they could) was preserved in the order of the House, the order provided for tracing the aggregate contributions of the two classes as classes. *Hallett*'s case was, of course, based on the right of an individual to follow what he could in equity identify as his own money. The extension of the principle in *Sinclair v Brougham* was the obvious and, indeed, on the facts, the only practical method of securing a just distribution of the assets. The importance of the point must not, however, be overlooked in considering the arguments and the speeches.

Apparently it had not occurred to any of the judges in the lower courts or to any of the eminent counsel who signed the cases or argued in the House of Lords that *Hallett*'s case had anything to do with such a case as *Sinclair v Brougham*. There is not a mention of it in any of the judgments below or in either of the printed cases or in argument in the House of Lords until Lord Haldane LC [1914] AC 398 at 404, 406, 407 suggested that the principle of *Hallett*'s case might apply. The point thus offered was accepted by counsel, who proceeded to base arguments upon it. Mr. Cave and Mr. Tomlin (as they then were), submitted on behalf of the depositors that *Hallett*'s case was really based, "not upon trusteeship in the narrow sense, but upon ownership" and argued that if the property of B is found in the hands of A, prima facie, A "is in a wide sense in a fiduciary relationship towards B because equity affects his conscience with regard to that particular property". This proposition, as stated, was not accepted by the House. From it counsel deduced the consequence that the depositors were entitled to priority in respect of the moneys which they had deposited. This argument was, of course, quite different from the other two arguments adduced on behalf of the depositors, viz., that based on money had and received and that based on the principles enunciated by Fletcher Moulton LJ in his dissenting judgment.

Mr. Upjohn and Mr. Younger (as he then was) for the shareholders agreed that (subject to a qualification not material on the facts) "money paid under an ultra vires contract does not become the property of the society but remains the property of the payer, and so long as he can identify it he may trace it through any number of changes and claim it on the footing that it is and always has been his property". But a claim based on property was, they said (and this relates to the point mentioned above) impossible in that case because no tracing order could be made without identification and the doctrine of tracing could not be applied to the collective claims of the depositors as a class. They also said that *Hallett*'s case was confined to fiduciary relationship in a strict sense.

Now it is to be remembered that the arguments of counsel on either side were directed to claiming priority for their respective clients and much of the reasoning in the speeches is directed to negativing these claims to priority. The House held that although the equity underlying *Hallett*'s case was applicable, the result of its proper application was that the conclusion sought by both arguments was wrong and that the fund was divisible rateably between the two classes of claimants. We may call attention in passing to the manner in which the House dealt with the argument of counsel for the shareholders that there could be no tracing save in favour of an individual who could follow and (in equity) identify his own property and that in consequence there could not be what would be in substance a tracing order in favour of a class. This argument does appear to raise a technical difficulty. But the House brushed it aside. Lord Sumner's speech contains the clearest exposition of the reasons for dealing with it in the manner approved by the House. He said [1914] AC 398 at 459:

"My Lords, I agree, without recapitulating reasons, that the principle on which *Hallett's* case is founded justifies an order allowing the appellants to follow the assets, not merely to the verge of actual identification, but even somewhat further in a case like the present, where after a process of exclusion only two classes or groups of persons, having equal claims, are left in and all superior claims have been eliminated. Tracing in a sense it is not, for we know that the money coming from A went into one security and that coming from B into another, and that the two securities did not probably depreciate exactly in the same percentage, and we know further that no one will ever know any more. Still I think this well within the 'tracing' equity, and that among persons making up these two groups the principle of rateable division of the assets is sound." This does at least show that in applying the equitable principle equity is entitled to adopt that method of application which in the circumstances of the case will lead to an equitable result.

We now proceed to consider some of the salient facts in *Sinclair v Brougham*.

The case is complicated by the fact that the claims of the depositors came to be considered at a time when the society was in liquidation, with the result that the shareholders came into the picture as competing claimants against the assets. But a problem precisely similar in all essentials would, as it appears to us, have arisen if the depositors had claimed to trace their money while the society was still a going concern. In that case the shareholders would not have appeared as claimants at all; the competition would have been between the depositors and the society. In the actual case the shareholders were the claimants but all that they could claim was such money as the society itself could have claimed as between itself and the depositors. We shall not be thought disrespectful if we call attention, perhaps rather more emphatically than was sometimes thought necessary in the opinions as delivered, to certain distinctions which must be borne clearly in mind. The first is the distinction between the directors and the society which could not be bound in any way or for any purpose, directly or indirectly, by the ultra vires acts of the directors. The second is the distinction between the society and the shareholders who were only entitled to such equitable rights in the assets as the society itself could have claimed, for that was all that the liquidators had the right to give them.

The third distinction is of no less importance, that between the ultra vires business (which was not in law the society's business) and the assets requiring distribution which were in the society's name and of which the society was the legal owner. So far as we have been able to discover, all the assets in question stood, as we would have expected them to stand, in the name of the society—they were, as Lord Dunedin said, "in the society's strong box"—and it was thus that they came into the hands of the liquidator. None of them was in the name of the directors who were, therefore, not necessary parties to the proceedings. In view of the argument addressed to us and of the judgment of Wynn-Parry J on the point, this is important and for the following reason. The starting point of the claim of the depositors was the existence of a fiduciary relationship as between themselves and the directors: that relationship arose from the fact that the depositors had entrusted their money to the directors for the purpose of a business which could not lawfully be carried on, so that the directors must be treated as holding the money on behalf of the depositors. If the directors had paid the money of a depositor into their own banking account he would have had an action against them exactly similar to the action in *Hallett's* case and it would have been correctly said that the directors could not be heard to set up a title of their own to the money standing in the account adverse to the claim of the depositor. But nothing of the sort could be said if the directors paid the money into the account of the society at its bankers. Neither the conscience of the society nor of its liquidator (if it went into liquidation) could ever come into the picture on the basis of a fiduciary relationship since the only parties to that relationship were the directors and the depositors. The society could not have been a party to it, since it had no power to accept the depositor's money. If, therefore, in such a case, the depositor could claim a charge on the society's account with its bankers the claim must have been based on some wider principle.

What can that principle be? In our judgment it must be the principle clearly indicated by Lord Parker, that equity may operate on the conscience not merely of those who acquire a legal title in breach of some trust, express or constructive, or of some other fiduciary obligation, but of volunteers provided that as a result of what has gone before some equitable proprietary interest has been created and attached to the property in the hands of the volunteer.[15]

In **Chase Manhattan Bank NA v Israel-British Bank (London) Ltd** [1981] Ch 105, [1979] 3 All ER 1025,[16] the plaintiff bank paid some two million dollars to another New York Bank, the Mellon Bank International, for the account of the defendant bank which carried on business in London. Later the same day the plaintiff bank made a book-keeping error and paid the same amount again.[17] A month later the defendant bank became insolvent and then went into compulsory liquidation.

The question arose whether the plaintiff bank was entitled in equity to trace the mistaken payment into the defendant bank's assets in priority to the general creditors. GOULDING J held that the mistaken payment gave rise to a constructive trust which entitled the plaintiff to trace the money, and said at 115, at 1029:

"The plaintiff's claim, viewed in the first place without reference to *any* system of positive law, raises problems to which the answers, if not always difficult, are at any rate not obvious. If one party P pays money to another party D by reason of a factual mistake, either common to both parties or made by P alone, few conscientious persons would doubt that D ought to return it. But suppose that D is, or becomes, insolvent before repayment is made, so that P comes into competition with D's general creditors, what then? If the money can still be traced, either in its original form or through successive conversions,

---

15 See also *Re J Leslie Engineers Co Ltd* [1976] 1 WLR 292, [1976] 2 All ER 85.

16 [1980] CLJ 272 (A. Tettenborn); 275 (G. Jones); (1980) 43 MLR 489, 500 (W. Goodhart and G. Jones). *Cf. Royal Products Ltd v Midland Bank Ltd* [1981] 2 Lloyd's Rep 194 ("there was no relevant factual mistake" at 210, per WEBSTER J). See also *Bankers Trust Co v Shapira* [1980] 1 WLR 1274, [1980] 3 All ER 353, where CA ordered discovery of documents in interlocutory proceedings against a bank, in order to assist in establishing a tracing claim; *A v C* [1981] QB 956n, [1980] 2 All ER 347; *Westdeutsche Landesbank Girozentrale v Islington Borough Council* [1994] 1 WLR 938, [1994] 4 All ER 890, p. 194, ante (£2.5m paid to local authority by bank under an ultra vires interest rate swap agreement held on resulting trust for the bank on receipt by the local authority); [1993] Conv 370 (J. Martin); [1994] Conv 395 (S. Evans).

17 See Law Commission Consultation Paper No 120 (1991) *Recovery of Payments made by Mistake of Law; Woolwich Equitable Building Society v IRC* [1993] AC 70; cf. *Morgan Guaranty Trust Co of New York v Lothian Regional Council* (1995) SLT 299 (under Scots law money paid under error of law is recoverable); [1995] CLJ 246 (N. Andrews).

and is found among D's remaining assets, ought not P to be able to claim it, or what represents it, as his own? If he ought, and if in a particular case the money has been blended with other assets and is represented by a mixed fund, no longer as valuable as the sum total of its original constituents, what priorities or equalities should govern the distribution of the mixed fund? If the money can no longer be traced, either separate or in mixture, should P have any priority over ordinary creditors of D? In any of these cases, does it make any difference whether the mistake was inevitable, or was caused by P's carelessness, or was contributed to by some fault, short of dishonesty, on the part of D?

At this stage I am asked to take only one step forward, and to answer the initial question of principle, whether the plaintiff is entitled in equity to trace the mistaken payment and to recover what now properly represents the money. The subsequent history of the payment and the rules for ascertaining what now represents it have not been proved or debated before me. They will have to be established in further proceedings if the plaintiff can clear the first hurdle today.

This initial question in the action appears not to be the subject of reported judicial decision in England. Let me read a few lines from *Goff and Jones, The Law of Restitution*, 2nd edn (1978), p. 89. The authors say:

'Whether a person who has paid money under a mistake of fact should be granted a restitutionary proprietary claim can arise in a number of contexts. It will be most important when the payee is insolvent and the payer seeks to gain priority over the payee's general creditors. The English courts have never had to consider this question. But in the United States it has arisen on a few occasions. A leading case is *Re Berry* 147 F 208 (1906).'...

The effect of the American case law, developed in a number of different states, as well as in the federal jurisdiction, is summarised as follows in the important book of Professor A.W. Scott, *The Law of Trusts*, 3rd edn (1967), vol. 5, p. 3428:

'Similarly where chattels are conveyed or money is paid by mistake, so that the person making the conveyance or payment is entitled to restitution, the transferee or payee holds the chattels or money upon a constructive trust. In such a case, it is true, the remedy at law for the value of the chattels or for the amount of money paid may be an adequate remedy, in which case a court of equity will not ordinarily give specific restitution. If the chattels are of a unique character, however, or if the person to whom the chattels are conveyed or to whom the money is paid is insolvent, the remedy at law is not adequate and a court of equity will enforce the constructive trust by decreeing specific restitution. The beneficial interest remains in the person who conveyed the chattel or who paid the money, since the conveyance or payment was made under a mistake.'

In my opinion, on the evidence that I have heard, to which I shall have to return later, the foregoing passages correctly represent the law of the State of New York. I believe they are also in accord with the general principles of equity as applied in England, and in the absence of direct English authority I should wish to follow them. Mr. Stubbs for the defendant contends that I am not at liberty to do so, because of the judgment of the Court of Appeal in *Re Diplock* [1948] Ch 465, [1948] 2 All ER 318, p. 904, ante, explaining and developing the earlier decision of the House of Lords in *Sinclair v Brougham* [1914] AC 398. *Re Diplock* itself went to the House of Lords, sub nom. *Ministry of Health v Simpson* [1951] AC 251, [1950] 2 All ER 1137, but the appeal did not relate to the question which is material in the present litigation. Mr.Stubbs says that, as stated in *Snell's Principles of Equity* 27th edn (1973), p. 289, there is no equitable right to trace property unless some initial fiduciary relationship exists, the right being founded on the existence of a beneficial owner with an equitable proprietary interest in property in the hands of a trustee or other fiduciary agent. Mr. Stubbs says further that the essential fiduciary relationship must initially arise from some consensual arrangement.

The facts and decisions in *Sinclair v Brougham* and in *Re Diplock* are well known and I shall not take time to recite them. I summarise my view of the *Diplock* judgment as follows: (1) The Court of Appeal's interpretation of *Sinclair v Brougham* was an essential part of their decision and is binding on me. (2) The court thought that the majority of the House of Lords in *Sinclair v Brougham* had not accepted Lord Dunedin's opinion in that case, and themselves rejected it. (3) The Court (as stated in *Snell,* loc. cit.) held that an initial fiduciary relationship is a necessary foundation of the equitable right of tracing. (4) They also held that the relationship between the building society directors and depositors in *Sinclair v Brougham* was a sufficient fiduciary relationship for the purpose: [1948] Ch 465 at 529, 540, [1948] 2 All ER 318 at 351, 357. The latter passage reads, at 540, at 357: 'A sufficient fiduciary relationship was found to exist between the depositors and the directors by reason of the fact that the purposes for which the depositors had handed their money to the directors were by law incapable of fulfilment.' It is founded, I think, on the observations of Lord Parker of Waddington at [1914] AC 398, 441.

This fourth point shows that the fund to be traced need not (as was the case in *Re Diplock* itself) have been the subject of fiduciary obligations before it got into the wrong hands. It is enough that, as in *Sinclair v Brougham*, the payment into wrong hands itself gave rise to a fiduciary relationship. The same point also throws considerable doubt on Mr. Stubbs's submission that the necessary fiduciary relationship must originate in a consensual transaction. It was not the intention of the depositors or of the directors in *Sinclair v Brougham* to create any relationship at all between the depositors and the directors as principals. Their object, which unfortunately disregarded the statutory limitations of the building society's powers, was to establish contractual relationships between the depositors and the society. In the circumstances, however, the depositors retained an equitable property in the funds they parted with, and fiduciary relationships arose between them and the directors. In the same way, I would suppose, a person who pays money to another under a factual mistake retains an equitable property in it and the conscience of that other is subjected to a fiduciary duty to respect his proprietary right. I am fortified in my opinion by the speech of Viscount Haldane LC in *Sinclair v Brougham* [1914] AC 398 at 419, 420, who, unlike Lord Dunedin, was not suspected of heresy in *Re Diplock.* Lord Haldane (who spoke for Lord Atkinson as well as himself) includes money paid under mistake of fact among the cases where money could be followed at common law, and he proceeds, at 421, to the auxiliary tracing remedy, available (as he said) wherever money was held to belong in equity to the plaintiff, without making any relevant exception. Thus my problem over *Re Diplock* [1948] Ch 465, [1948] 2 All ER 318 is in the end this: Can I adopt into English equity the passage I have quoted from Professor Scott without making the forbidden transition to the opinion of Lord Dunedin? I have carefully considered the passages, at 541 to 543, at 357 to 359, in *Re Diplock* where that opinion is criticised. In the end I believe that the whole subject of the Court of Appeal's condemnation was the suggestion that the tracing remedy could be applied wherever the defendant could be shown to have got an unjust enrichment, a superfluity as Lord Dunedin called it. The court insisted on the more precise test of a continuing right of property recognised in equity or of what I think to be its concomitant, 'a fiduciary or quasi-fiduciary relationship': at 520, at 346. At the same time they recognised that exactly what relationships were sufficient for the purpose had not yet been precisely laid down: see p. 540, p. 357.

Thus, in the belief that the point is not expressly covered by English authority and that *Re Diplock* does not conclude it by necessary implication, I hold that the equitable remedy of tracing is in principle available, on the ground of continuing proprietary interest, to a party who has paid money under a mistake of fact. On that prime question, I see no relevant difference between the law of England and the law of New York and there is no conflict of laws to be resolved.

It is important, however, to make clear the limits of what I have just said. I do not say, and I do not imply, that on the facts and figures of any particular case the courts of England and of New York, when tracing in equity a sum paid by mistake, will necessarily apply the same tracing rules or arrive at the same final result. For example, in *Re Berry* 147 F 208 (1906), an extract from which I have read, the American court applied the rule in *Re Hallett's Estate* (1880) 13 ChD 696, for the purpose of identifying the claimant's money in the bankrupt's bank account. Mr. Stubbs, when discussing *Re Berry* before me, has argued that if, contrary to his contention, an English court allowed tracing at all on the facts of that case, it would apply a different rule. I decline to answer any question of that sort until actually raised on ascertained facts.''

In **Agip (Africa) Ltd v Jackson** [1990] Ch 265 [1992], 4 All ER 385, MILLETT J said at 289, at 402:[18]
"There is no difficulty in tracing the plaintiffs' property in equity which can follow the money as it passed through the accounts of the correspondent banks in New York or, more realistically, follow the chose in action through its transmutation as a direct result of forged instructions from a debt owed by the Banque de Sud to the plaintiffs in Tunis into a debt owed by Lloyds Bank to Baker Oil in London.

The only restriction on the ability of equity to follow assets is the requirement that there must be some fiduciary relationship which permits the assistance of equity to be invoked. The requirement has been widely condemned and depends on authority rather than principle, but the law was settled by *Re Diplock* [1948] Ch 465, [1948] 2 All ER 318, p. 904, ante.[19] It may need to be reconsidered but not, I venture to think, at first instance. The requirement may be circumvented since it is not necessary that the fund to be traced should have been the subject of fiduciary obligations before it got into the wrong hands; it is sufficient that the payment to the defendant itself gives rise to a fiduciary relationship: *Chase Manhattan Bank NA v Israel-British Bank (London) Ltd* [1981] Ch 105, [1979] 3 All ER 1025, p. 910, ante. In that case,

---

18 Affirmed [1991] Ch 547, [1992] 4 All ER 451; see Fox LJ at 566, at 466.
19 For further judicial criticism of a fiduciary relationship as the basis of equitable tracing, see *Elders Pastoral Ltd v Bank of New Zealand* [1989] 2 NZLR 180; (1990) 106 LQR 552 (P. Watts); (1987) 103 LQR 433 (R.M. Goode); *Re Goldcorp Exchange Ltd* [1995] 1 AC 74 at 98, [1994] 2 All ER 806 at 821, per Lord MUSTILL; *El Ajou v Dollar Land Holdings* [1993] BCLC 735 at 753, per MILLETT J.

however, equity's assistance was not needed in order to trace the plaintiff's money into the hands of the defendant; it was needed in order to ascertain whether it had any of the plaintiff's money left. The case cannot, therefore, be used to circumvent the requirement that there should be an initial fiduciary relationship in order to start the tracing process in equity.

The requirement is, however, readily satisfied in most cases of commercial fraud, since the embezzlement of a company's funds almost inevitably involves a breach of fiduciary duty on the part of one of the company's employees or agents. That was so in present case. There was clearly a fiduciary relationship between Mr. Zdiri and the plaintiffs. Mr. Zdiri was not a director nor a signatory on the plaintiffs' bank account, but he was a senior and responsible officer. As such he was entrusted with possession of the signed payment orders to have them taken to the bank and implemented. He took advantage of his possession of them to divert the money and cause the separation between its legal ownership which passed to the payees and its beneficial ownership which remained in the plaintiffs. There is clear authority that there is a receipt of trust property when a company's funds are misapplied by a director and, in my judgment, this is equally the case when a company's funds are misapplied by any person whose fiduciary position gave him control of them or enabled him to misapply them.

The tracing claim in equity gives rise to a proprietary remedy which depends on the continued existence of the trust property in the hands of the defendant. Unless he is a bona fide purchaser for value without notice, he must restore the trust property to its rightful owner if he still has it. But even a volunteer who has received trust property cannot be made subject to a personal liability to account for it as a constructive trustee if he has parted with it without having previously acquired some knowledge of the existence of the trust: *Re Montagu's Settlement Trusts* [1987] Ch 264, [1992] 4 All ER 308, p. 261, *ante*.

The plaintiffs are entitled to the money in court which rightfully belongs to them. To recover the money which the defendants have paid away the plaintiffs must subject them to a personal liability to account as constructive trustees and prove the requisite degree of knowledge to establish the liability.''

(c) Entitlement to Increase in Value

In **Re Tilley's Will Trusts** [1967] Ch 1179, [1967] 2 All ER 303,[20] the testator, Henry Tilley, appointed his widow as an executrix and gave her a life interest in his estate with remainder to his children, Charles and Mabel. Mrs. Tilley, with the help of a bank overdraft, embarked on a highly successful career as a dealer in property. By 1952, having dealt with some properties, she had accumulated £2,237 trust capital, and over the years had thoroughly confused this trust money with her own private funds. She had overdraft facilities for over £22,000 in 1939, and by 1945 the overdraft was £23,536. She died in 1959, leaving an estate valued at some £94,000. The plaintiff, as executor of Mabel's estate, brought an action for an account of what was due to Mabel's estate.

The question was whether the property should be treated as Mrs. Tilley's, or whether all or part of it should be treated as belonging to the trusts of the testator's estate, and if so, in what proportions.

UNGOED-THOMAS J held that it was all her own free estate, on the ground that trust moneys had not been used for the property purchases. He said at

---

20 [1968] CLJ 28 (G.H. Jones). See also *Scott v Scott* (1963) 109 CLR 649; *Restatement of Restitution*, § 142.

1193, at 313, that "the trust moneys were not invested in properties at all but merely went in reduction of Mrs. Tilley's overdraft which was in reality the source of the purchase-moneys." If, however, trust moneys had been applied in the purchase of the properties, these properties would have been owned partly by Mrs. Tilley and partly by the trust, in proportions in which moneys from those sources had been used to make the purchases.

UNGOED-THOMAS J said at 1182, at 305:

"The plaintiff claims that Mabel's estate should, in virtue of Mabel's half-interest in the estate, subject to Mrs. Tilley's life interest, have half of the proportion of the profits of the purchases made by Mrs. Tilley to the extent to which the defendants, as her legal personal representatives, cannot show that those properties were purchased out of Mrs. Tilley's personal moneys. The defendants, on the other hand, say that the plaintiff is entitled only to a charge on the defendants' bank account for half the trust moneys paid into that bank account with interest, i.e., half the sum of £2,237, which is shown to have been paid into that bank account, and the interest on that amount.

I come first to the law. The plaintiff relied on the statement of the law in Lewin on Trusts, 16th edn (1964) at p. 223, and some of the cases cited in support of it. That statement reads:

'Wherever the trust property is placed, if a trustee amalgamates it with his own, his beneficiary will be entitled to every portion of the blended property which the trustee cannot prove to be his own.' ...

So the proposition in Lewin on Trusts, which I have read, is limited to cases where the amalgam of mixed assets is such that they cannot be sufficiently distinguished and treated separately; it is based on the lack of evidence to do so being attributable to the trustee's fault.

The defendants relied on *Re Hallett's Estate* (1880) 13 ChD 696, with a view to establishing that the trustee must be presumed to have drawn out his own moneys from the bank account of mixed moneys in priority to trust moneys, with the result that property bought by such prior drawings must be the trustee's exclusive personal property. In that case the claim was against a bank balance of mixed fiduciary and personal funds, and it is in the context of such a claim that it was held that the person in a fiduciary character drawing out money from the bank account must be taken to have drawn out his own money in preference to the trust money, so that the claim of the beneficiaries prevailed against the balance of the account. *Re Oatway* [1903] 2 Ch 356 was the converse of the decision in *Re Hallett's Estate*. In that case the claim was not against the balance left in the bank of such mixed moneys, but against the proceeds of sale of shares which the trustee had purchased with moneys which, as in *Re Hallett's Estate*, he had drawn from the bank account. But, unlike the situation in *Re Hallett's Estate*, his later drawings had exhausted the account, so that it was useless to proceed against the account. It was held that the beneficiary was entitled to the proceeds of sale of the shares, which were more than their purchase price but less than the trust moneys paid into the account. The law is reviewed and the principles stated by Joyce J who said [1903] 2 Ch 356 at 359–361:

'Trust money may be followed into land or any other property in which it has been invested; and when a trustee has, in making any purchase or investment, applied trust money together with his own, the cestuis que trust are entitled to a charge on the property purchased for the amount of the trust money laid out in the purchase or investment. Similarly, if money held by any person in a fiduciary capacity be paid into his own banking account, it may be followed by the equitable owner, who, as against the trustee, will have a charge for what belongs to him upon the balance to the credit of the account. If, then, the trustee pays in further sums, and from time to time draws out money by cheques, but leaves a balance to the credit of the account, it is settled that he is not entitled to have the rule in *Clayton's* case (1816) 1 Mer 572 applied so as to maintain that the sums which have been drawn out and paid away so as to be incapable of being recovered represented pro tanto the trust money, and that the balance remaining is not trust money, but represents only his own moneys paid into the account. *Brown v Adams* (1869) 4 Ch App 764 to the contrary ought not to be followed since the decision in *Re Hallett's Estate*. It is, in my opinion, equally clear that when any of the money drawn out has been invested, and the investment remains in the name or under the control of the trustee, the rest of the balance having been afterwards dissipated by him, he cannot maintain that the investment which remains represents his own money alone, and that what has been spent and can no longer be traced and recovered was the money belonging to the trust. In other words, when the private money of the trustee and that which he held in a fiduciary capacity have been mixed in the same banking account, from which various payments have from time to time been made, then, in order to determine to whom any remaining balance or any investment that may have been paid for out of the account ought to be deemed to belong, the trustee must be debited with all the sums that have been withdrawn and applied to his own use so as to be no longer recoverable, and the trust money in like manner be debited with any sums taken out and duly invested in the names of the proper trustees. The order of priority in which the various withdrawals and investments may have been respectively made is wholly immaterial. I have been referring, of course, to cases where there is only one fiduciary owner or set of cestuis que trust claiming whatever may be left as against the trustee. In the present case there is no balance left. The only investment or property remaining which represents any part of the mixed moneys paid into the banking account is the Oceana shares purchased for £2,137. Upon these, therefore, the trust had a charge for the £3,000 trust money paid into the account. That is to say, those shares and the proceeds thereof belong to the trust. It was objected that the investment in the Oceana shares was made at a time when Oatway's own share of the balance to the credit of the account (if the whole had been then justly distributed) would have exceeded £2,137, the price of the shares; that he was therefore entitled to withdraw that sum, and might rightly apply it for his own purposes; and that consequently the shares should be held to belong to his estate. To this I answer that he never was entitled to withdraw the £2,137 from the account, or, at all events, that he could not be entitled to take the sum from the account and hold it or the investment made therewith, freed from the charge in favour of the trust, unless or until the trust money paid into the account had been first restored, and the trust fund reinstated by due investment of the money in the joint names of the proper trustees, which never was done. The investment by Oatway, in his own name, of the £2,137 in Oceana shares no more got rid of the claim or charge of the trust upon the money so invested, than would have been the case if he had drawn a cheque for £2,137 and simply placed and retained the amount in a drawer without further disposing of the money in any way. The proceeds of the Oceana shares must be held to belong to the trust funds under the will of which Oatway and Maxwell Skipper were the trustees.'

So, contrary to the defendants' contention, it is not a presumption that a trustee's drawings from the mixed fund must necessarily be treated as drawings of the trustee's own money where the beneficiary's claim is against the property bought by such drawings. Further, *Re Oatway* [1903] 2 Ch 356 did not raise the question whether a beneficiary is entitled to any profit made out of the purchase of property by a trustee out of a fund consisting of his personal moneys which he mixed with the trust moneys, and so the judgment was not directed to, and did not deal with, that question.

I return now to the judgments in *Re Hallett's Estate* (1880) 13 ChD 696....

[His Lordship quoted extensively from the parts of the judgment which are extracted at p. 898, ante, and continued:]

Sinclair v Brougham [1914] AC 398 considered *Re Hallett's Estate*. Lord Parker said at 442:

'The principle on which, and the extent to which, trust money can be followed in equity is discussed at length in *Re Hallett's Estate* by Sir George Jessel. He gives two instances. First, he supposes the case of property being purchased by means of the trust money alone. In such a case the beneficiary may either take the property itself or claim a lien on it for the amount of the money expended in the purchase. Secondly, he supposes the case of the purchase having been made partly with the trust money and partly with money of the trustee ... '

The next sentence I shall come back to later.

'In such a case the beneficiary can only claim a charge on the property for the amount of the trust money expended in the purchase. The trustee is precluded by his own misconduct from asserting any interest in the property until such amount has been refunded. By the actual decision in the case, this principle was held applicable when the trust money had been paid into the trustee's banking account. I will add two further illustrations which have some bearing on the present case. Suppose the property is acquired by means of money, part of which belongs to one owner and part to another, the purchaser being in a fiduciary relationship to both. Clearly each owner has an equal equity. Each is entitled to a charge on the property for his own money, and neither can claim priority over the other. It follows that their charges must rank pari passu according to their respective amounts ... '

—again, I emphasise this—

'Further, I think that as against the fiduciary agent they could by agreement claim to take the property itself, in which case they would become tenants in common in shares proportioned to amounts for which either could claim a charge.'

It seems to me that when Lord Parker says in the sentence, to which I first called particular attention [1914] AC 398 at 442, that 'In such a case the beneficiary can only claim a charge on the property for the amount of the trust money expended in the purchase' he is merely contrasting the charge with the right to take the whole property which is the matter he had just been dealing with; Lord Parker is not, as I see it, addressing his mind to the question of whether the beneficiary could claim a proportion of the property corresponding to his own contribution to its purchase. This interpretation of the passage seems to me to be the only interpretation which in principle is consistent with Lord Parker's view expressed at the end of the passage which I quoted, and to which I drew particular attention, where the purchase is made by the trustee wholly out of moneys of two different beneficiaries. In that case he says that they are not limited to charges for their respective amounts, but are together entitled to the whole property. But if each of two beneficiaries can, in co-operation with the other, take the whole property which has resulted in profit from the trustee's action in buying it with their money, why can they not do so if the trustee himself has also paid some part of the purchase price? And if the two beneficiaries can do so, why not one? Indeed, it was conceded in argument that the passage should be so interpreted as suggested.

In Snell's Principles of Equity, 26th edn (1966), the law is thus stated at page 315:

'Where the trustee mixes trust money with his own, the equities are clearly unequal. Accordingly the beneficiaries are entitled to a first charge on the mixed fund, or on any land, securities or other assets purchased with it. Thus if the trustee purchases shares with part of the mixed fund, leaving enough of it to repay the trust moneys, and then dissipates the balance, the beneficiaries' charge binds the shares; for although under the rule in *Re Hallett's Estate* (1880) 13 ChD 696 the trustee is presumed to have bought the shares out of his own money, the charge attached to the entire fund, and could be discharged only by restoring the trust moneys. Where the property purchased has increased in value, the charge will be not merely for the amount of the trust moneys but for a proportionate part of the increased value. Thus if the trustee purchases land with £500 of his own money and £1,000 of trust moneys, and the land doubles in value, he would be profiting from his breach of trust if he were entitled to all except £1,000; the beneficiaries are accordingly entitled to a charge on the land for £2,000.'

For the defendants it has been rightly admitted that if a trustee wrongly uses trust money to pay the whole of the purchase price in respect of the purchase of an asset a beneficiary can elect either to treat the purchased asset as trust property or to treat the purchased asset as security for the recouping of the trust money. It was further conceded that this right of election by a beneficiary also applies where the asset is purchased by a trustee in part of his own money and in part out of the trust moneys, so that he may, if he wishes, require the asset to be treated as trust property with regard to that proportion of it which the trust moneys contributed to its purchase.

Does this case fall within that principle? ...

It seems to me that if, having regard to all the circumstances of the case objectively considered, it appears that the trustee has in fact, whatever his intention, laid out trust moneys in or towards a purchase, then the beneficiaries are entitled to the property purchased and any profits which it produces to the extent to which it has been paid for out of the trust moneys. But, even by this objective test, it appears to me that the trust moneys were not in this case so laid out. It seems to me, on a proper appraisal of all the facts of this particular case, that Mrs. Tilley's breach halted at the mixing of the funds in her bank account. Although properties bought out of those funds would, like the bank account itself, at any rate if the moneys in the bank account were inadequate, be charged with repayment of the trust moneys which then would stand in the same position as the bank account, yet the trust moneys were not invested in properties at all but merely went in reduction of Mrs. Tilley's overdraft which was in reality the source of the purchase-moneys.

The plaintiff's claim therefore fails and he is entitled to no more than repayment of the half of the £2,237 ... ''

(d) Loss of the Right to Trace

Goff and Jones: *The Law of Restitution* (4th edn 1993), pp. 90–93

"As the law now stands, the right to trace property in equity is lost, either in whole or in part, in the following circumstances:
  (a) if the property reaches the hands of a bona fide purchaser;
  (b) if it would be inequitable to allow the plaintiff to trace. This limitation on the right to trace was recognised in *Re Diplock*. The Court of Appeal instanced two cases where it would be inequitable to allow the plaintiff to trace in equity.[21] In the last edition of this book we described them as an emasculated application of the defence of change of position. Now that the House of Lords has recognised the defence as a general defence to all restitutionary claims,[22] the two examples, which we shall now discuss, should be seen as two possible illustrations of change of position.

In the view of the Court of Appeal, the equitable proprietary claim will fail if an innocent volunteer improves his land: the land may not have necessarily increased in value, the property to which a lien could attach may be uncertain, and it would be inequitable to require the sale of the property subject to the charge. These may be persuasive reasons on the facts of *Re Diplock*; there the innocent volunteers were hospitals, one of which had used the Diplock money to build a new ward. But on other facts it may not be inequitable to impose a lien. For example, the innocent volunteer may be a rich banker who has used the money wisely to increase the value of his country house; and he has, furthermore, ample liquid assets to discharge any lien imposed over it.

The second illustration given by the Court of Appeal was of the innocent volunteer who used the Diplock money to pay off his debts. The creditor who grants the discharge is, of course, a bona fide purchaser.[23] But if he was a secured creditor, should the plaintiff be allowed to step into his shoes and enjoy the priority which he once enjoyed? The Court of Appeal thought not.[1] But, on other facts, this may be an unattractive conclusion since it may give the general creditors of an insolvent volunteer a windfall at the expense of the plaintiff who did not take the risk of the innocent volunteer's insolvency.[2]

The defence of change of position should not be narrowly defined, and should be allowed to grow in a flexible and pragmatic fashion. In each case it is a question of fact whether it is inequitable, given the change of position, to reject the particular restitutionary claim.[3] It should not necessarily be a defence that the defendant is an innocent volunteer who has improved land or paid off a secured debt;

---

21 [1948] Ch 465, 546–547, [1948] 2 All ER 318 at 360–361.
22 *Lipkin Gorman v Karpnale Ltd* [1991] 2 AC 548, [1992] 4 All ER 512.
23 Unless he knew, an unlikely event, of the executor's mistake.
 1 [1991] 2 AC 548 at p. 549, [1992] 4 All ER 512 at p. 515.
 2 Cf. *Space Investments Ltd v Canadian Imperial Bank of Commerce Trust Co (Bahamas) Ltd* [1986] 1 WLR 1072, [1986] 3 All ER 75; see below, p. 98.
 3 *Lipkin Gorman v Karpnale Ltd* supra. at 579–580; [1986] 3 All ER 75 at 533–534, per Lord GOFF OF CHIEVELEY: see above, Chap. 40.

(c) if the claimant's property disappears, as will be the case if the defendant buys wine with the trust money and drinks it.[4] The right to trace is also lost if the claimant's property is mixed by the defendant with his own property of a different kind, thereby forming a new product.[5](We shall argue that, even though the plaintiff's money can no longer be identified, in accordance with equity's traditional rules, it may be just, *in some circumstances*, to impose a lien over the defendant's unsecured assets if, for example, it is necessary to ensure his priority over the defendant's general creditors[6]);

(d) if, in claims arising from the administration of an estate, the claimants have already recovered in an action against the executors for *devastavit* In *Re Diplock*[7] the Court of Appeal held that before the next-of-kin could bring a personal action against the charities they must first sue the executors, who had mistakenly paid the money; and any sums recovered from the executors should be credited rateably among the charities. The Court added that, 'prima facie and subject to discussion,'[8] the next-of-kin's proprietary claim should be similarly reduced. The limitation may be peculiar to claims arising from the administration of an estate, but it may also be applicable to claims arising under *inter vivos* trusts.[9] If it is accepted, the amount which a wrongly paid volunteer must disgorge is directly dependent on how much money can be extracted from the executors. In our view the next-of-kin's proprietary claim against volunteers should not be reduced or destroyed by the sums recoverable from the executors. If they are able to identify their property in the hands of a volunteer they should be able to recover that property and it should be no defence to the volunteer that the next-of-kin have recovered *in personam* against the executors. The executors should then be subrogated, as is an insurer in comparable circumstances, to that part of the next-of-kin's fund which represents the difference between the total of the sums recovered from the executors and the volunteer and the loss suffered by the next-of-kin.[10] But the most practical and sensible rule, which has been adopted by statute in New Zealand and Western Australia,[11] is to require the claimant to sue the volunteer before suing the executors who should be liable only for any amount which the claimant has failed to recover from the volunteer. The volunteer would enjoy the usual defences.

Equity's rules and presumptions enable the beneficiaries of the trust to identify their property in the hands of the trustee or an innocent volunteer. But when does the beneficial title to an asset vest in them when there are multiple transactions? For example, there is a mixed fund, consisting of £3,000 of trust money and £3,000 of the trustee's own money. The trustee withdraws £3,000 and uses the money to buy a painting from D, who knows of the breach

4 *Re Diplock* supra, at 521, at 347.
5 *Borden (UK) Ltd v Scottish Timber Products Ltd* [1981] Ch 25, [1979] 3 All ER 961.
6 See below, pp. 98–99.
7 [1948] Ch 465, [1948] 2 All ER 318; see below, for a further criticism of this principle.
8 Supra at 556, at 365. See also *John v Dodwell & Co* [1918] AC 563, 575.
9 See below, pp. 585–587.
10 Cf. below, p. 601; and cf. *Lord Napier and Ettrick v RF Kershaw Ltd* [1993] AC 713, [1993] 1 All ER 385.
11 New Zealand Administration Act 1952, s. 30B(5), added in 1960; Western Australia Trustee Act 1962, s. 65(7).

of trust. At the date of the purchase the painting is worth £6,000; it is now worth £8,000. The beneficiaries can proceed either against the trustee or D; they have an election to look to D, who is a constructive trustee, to make restitution of £3,000 or to claim the painting in the trustee's hands. Seemingly, they cannot recover both the painting and the £3,000. On these facts they will take the painting; their election would be very different if the painting is now worth only £2,000. The beneficial interest in the painting will probably vest in them at the date of their election, and not before. But there is slender authority to support this conclusion;[12] although there is also the analogy of the case law which holds that the right to have a deed set aside on account of fraud or undue influence is a 'mere equity.' "[13]

(e) The Rule in Clayton's Case

Goff and Jones: *The Law of Restitution* (4th edn 1993), pp. 88–90.

"If the mixed fund is in an active, unbroken banking account, such as a current (but not a deposit) account at a bank, then any withdrawals from the mixed fund will be borne between the two main trusts in accordance with the rule in *Clayton's* case,[14] namely first in, first out.[15] For example a trustee pays £500 from trust fund A into his bank account, which contains no other money, on January 1; two days later he pays £500 from trust fund B into the same account. On February 1, he withdraws £500. In accordance with the rule in *Clayton's* case the loss is wholly borne by trust fund A. The result is capricious and arbitrary. As Judge Learned Hand once said: 'when the law attempts a fiction, it is, or at least it should be, for some purpose of justice. To adopt [the fiction of first in, first out] . . . is to apportion a common misfortune through a test which has no relation whatever to the justice of the case.'[16]

If the mixed fund is not in an active, unbroken banking account, any loss is borne *pari passu* so that the parties recover proportionately in relation to their contributions. In the example just given, both trust funds would then bear the loss equally.

The scope of the rule in *Clayton's* case was recently considered by the Court of Appeal in *Barlow Clowes International Ltd v Vaughan*.[17] The authority of *Pennell v Deffell* and *Re Diplock* compelled the Court to conclude that the rule prima facie governed the competing claims of beneficiaries of different trusts and those of beneficiaries of a trust and innocent volunteers, whose moneys have been wrongfully mixed in a single current account. The Court also concluded that, on the particular facts, the 'North American' solution (namely, that

---

12 *Cf. Re J Leslie Engineering Co Ltd* [1976] 1 WLR 292, [1976] 2 All ER 85; *Lipkin Gorman v Karpnale Ltd* [1991] 2 AC 548, 573, [1992] 4 All ER 512, 528, per Lord GOFF OF CHIEVELEY.

13 Megarry and Wade, *The Law of Real Property* (5th edn), pp. 145–147, who discuss the relevant authorities.

14 (1817) 1 Mer. 572.

15 *Pennell v Deffell* (1853) 4 De GM & G. 372; *Re Hallett's Estate* (1880) 13 Ch D 696, 700, per FRY J (the point did not arise in the Court of Appeal); *Hancock v Smith* (1889) 41 Ch D 456, 461, per Lord HALSBURY LC; *Re Stenning* [1895] 2 Ch 433; *Mutton v Peat* [1899] 2 Ch 556; *Re Diplock* [1948] Ch 465, [1948] 2 All ER 318.

16 *Re Walter J Schmidt & Co* 298 F 314, 316 (1923). But precedent compelled the judge to apply the rule to the facts. See (1950) 36 Cornell LQ 170 at p. 176 (Z. Chaffee). The fiction of *Clayton's* case has now been rejected by the New Zealand Court of Appeal in *Re Registered Securities Ltd* [1991] 1 NZLR 545.

17 [1992] 4 All ER 22.

'credits to a bank account made at different times and from different sources [are treated] as a blend or cocktail with the result that when a withdrawal is made from the account it is treated as a withdrawal in the same proportions as the different interests in the account (here of the investors) bear to each other at the moment before the withdrawal is made'[18] was, on the particular facts, impracticable, although 'manifestly fairer'. However, the rule in *Clayton's* case should not be applied if it would be impracticable or result in injustice between the parties, such as investors whose moneys are to be paid into a common pool. It is a 'mere rule of evidence, and not an invariable rule of law . . . '[19] If there was a 'shared misfortune, the investors will be presumed to have intended the rule not to apply.'[20] The fund should then be shared rateably in proportion to the amount due to the different parties who had contributed to the mixed fund. There is, however, one significant *caveat* to that rule. It is this: the investor's claim is to the lowest intermediate balance in the fund. Consequently, if it can be shown that his money was deposited in a fund which had been exhausted, he has manifestly no claim to sums subsequently deposited by other investors.

The decision in *Barlow Clowes* is a welcome relaxation of the rule in *Clayton's* case. Both Woolf and Leggatt LJJ regretted that *Clayton's* case was binding on the Court of Appeal. The 'fairness of rateable division is obvious.' Dillon LJ was less sure that it was unfair to adopt the 'first in, first out' rule, later investors might well be aggrieved if their claims were to rank *pari passu* with those of earlier investors.[1]'

C. Law Reform

Law Commission Sixth Programme of Law Reform 1995 (Law Com No. 234), p. 33.

''*Remedies*
The remedies available for the recovery of trust property transferred in breach of trust or fiduciary duty have assumed a major significance in commercial dealings and have been the subject of much litigation. Although a wide range of remedies exist, none of them is wholly satisfactory and their interrelationship is uncertain. In addition, there are procedural and evidential shortcomings which can impede recovery, and in some cases no personal action is available so that the claimant is obliged to pursue the more expensive tracing remedy. We have begun an examination of personal remedies and hope to publish a consultation paper in 1996. We shall then commence work on a consultation paper on proprietary remedies.''

QUESTIONS

1. What is the purpose of a tracing claim? What is the relationship between a tracing claim and the imposition of a constructive trust? *Agip (Africa) Ltd v Jackson* [1990] Ch 265, [1992] 4 All ER 385; affd. [1991] Ch 547, [1992] 4 All ER 451, p. 913, ante.

---

18 At p. 35, per WOOLF LJ.
19 *Re British Red Cross Balkan Fund* [1914] 2 Ch 419, 421, per ASTBURY J.
20 At p. 42, per WOOLF LJ.
1 Cf LEGGATT LJ (at p. 44) and DILLON LJ (at p. 32).

2. Should a tracing claim lead inexorably to a proprietary remedy? Or should tracing simply be regarded as a series of rules which facilitate the identification of property?

3. Is a fiduciary relationship necessary in order to trace? Ought it to be? H & M, p. 648; Goff and Jones: *Law of Restitution* (4th edn) pp. 93–94, supra; *Chase Manhattan Bank NA v Israel-British Bank (London) Ltd* [1981] Ch 105, [1979] 3 All ER 1025, p. 919, ante; *Re Berry* 147 F 208 (1906), p. 911, ante; *Agip (Africa) Ltd v Jackson*, supra; especially cases at p. 913, n. 19.

4. What is the liability of an innocent volunteer, if he
   (a) still has the property,
   (b) has mixed the property with his own,
   (c) no longer has the property?
   Re Diplock [1948] Ch 465, [1948] 2 All ER 318, p. 904, ante; [1983] Conv 135 (K. Hodkinson).